DOCUMENTS IN INTERNATIONAL

Documents in International Economic Law

Trade, Investment, and Finance

Edited by

CHRISTIAN J. TAMS AND CHRISTIAN TIETJE

OXFORD

UNIVERSITY PRESS

OXFORD

UNIVERSITY PRESS

Great Clarendon Street, Oxford, OX2 6DP,
United Kingdom

Oxford University Press is a department of the University of Oxford.
It furthers the University's objective of excellence in research, scholarship,
and education by publishing worldwide. Oxford is a registered trade mark of
Oxford University Press in the UK and in certain other countries

© In editorial matter, Christian J. Tams and Christian Tietje, 2012

The moral rights of the authors have been asserted

First Edition published in 2012
Impression: 1

British Library Cataloguing in Publication Data
Data available

Library of Congress Cataloging in Publication Data
Data available

ISBN 978-0-19-965804-6 (Hbk.)
ISBN 978-0-19-965805-3 (Pbk.)

Printed and bound by
CPI Group (UK) Ltd, Croydon, CR0 4YY

Preface

The last few decades have seen International Economic Law rise to prominence. Once a matter for closely-knit groups of specialists only, the area is now of concern to many: practitioners and policy-makers, undergraduate and graduate students and their teachers, but also general international lawyers recognizing the practical and theoretical importance of economic law beyond the state.

The present collection brings together key documents on International Economic Law. As the subtitle of the book indicates, it covers the three main subjects, or 'pillars', of the discipline: trade, investment, and finance. Documents from these fields are preceded by a short introductory part comprising texts of general relevance. All documents are presented in their official version, but have been lightly edited to correct obvious typographical errors. For reasons of space, we have decided to excerpt them where necessary.

No selection is neutral. Our decisions about the shape and focus of this collection have been informed by two general considerations in particular.

First, by covering trade, investment, and finance in one volume, we seek to emphasize that all three subjects form part of one overarching discipline of International Economic Law, and ought to be seen in that perspective. Of course, trade, investment, and finance are subject to separate regimes: they have risen to prominence independently, and at different times. And yet, while often providing for different answers, the three subjects face common challenges: fundamentally, all three regulate transnational economic activity; all three are required to strike a balance between regulation and economic freedom and between institutionalization and interstate coordination; and all three seek to enable economic activity while ensuring that it is carried out in a sustainable way. On that basis, we are convinced that contemporary International Economic Law ought to transcend the boundaries traditionally separating trade, investment, and finance.

Second, by including essential texts of general relevance, we intend to emphasize the link between International Economic Law and the broader framework of general international law. International Economic Law of course requires special rules, and it often deliberately 'contracts out' of the general framework. Yet, international economic lawyers—whether primarily working within trade, investment, or finance—increasingly stress that 'their' subject cannot be seen in 'clinical isolation', but is part of a broader framework of international law. And indeed, as recently noted by the UN International Law Commission in its Fragmentation Report, 'no [special] regime is self-contained' in any strict sense (UN Doc A/CN.4/L.682, para 192). 'Contracting out' is a matter of degree, and even specialists are well advised to retain at least a basic knowledge of general international law.

The present collection is the result of these considerations. Its aim is to present International Economic Law as a broad discipline comprising three main pillars and embedded in a framework of general international law. To meet this aim within the space of an affordable single-volume collection, we have had to be strict in our selection of documents.

The collection's General Part (Part 1) thus necessarily focuses on essentials. We have included two categories of documents: those laying down 'meta-rules' of the international legal system and those setting out visions of the international economic order. The former category comprises the legal regime of treaty law (as laid down in the 1969 Vienna Convention), general rules governing claims and responsibility (notably the ILC's 2001 Articles on State Responsibility and its 2006 Draft Articles on Diplomatic Protection), and relevant aspects of the United Nations Charter. As regards visions of the international economic order, we have reproduced General Assembly resolutions formulating standards of international economic relations; while these are a product of their time, they remain instructive.

Part 2 brings together key texts on the regulation of trade. To a large extent, world trade law today is the law of the World Trade Organization (WTO). WTO law covers most regulatory aspects of the international trading regime from a public international law perspective. Thus, the most important documents of the three substantial pillars of WTO law—trade in goods, trade in services, trade-related aspects of intellectual property—are reproduced in this book. As World Trade Law not only deals with substantial aspects of trade, but also has an institutional side, the Agreement Establishing the World Trade Organization and the Understanding on Rules and Procedures Governing the Settlement of Disputes have also been included. Because of its economic importance, reproduced also is the Agreement on Government Procurement, which is not part of the multilateral trade agreements binding upon all 155 WTO members (as of May 2012), but has been accepted only by 41 of them (including the EU and all 27 EU member states). While including most of the standard WTO agreements (as well as important interpretative texts), we have decided not to include agreements addressing very special areas of international trade (eg customs law) and highly specialized instruments that have their roots outside WTO law such as the International Convention on the Simplification and Harmonization of Customs Procedure (Kyoto Convention) of the World Customs Organization. Finally, even though Preferential Trade Agreements (PTAs)—Free Trade Agreements and Custom Unions—are increasingly important in world trade, they have not been included; this seemed justified as PTAs largely follow the regulatory approach of WTO law and, even where they differ from WTO law with respect to the intensity of trade liberalization, their legal structure is similar to that of WTO law.

Compared to World Trade Law, the international regimes governing Investment and Finance are more fragmented. This is reflected in the remaining parts of the present collection.

Part 3 is intended to cover the different aspects of the contemporary investment law regime. Given the international community's failure to agree on a comprehensive multilateral treaty framework, it draws on documents of very diverse pedigree. International investment agreements are of obvious importance; taken together, they make up the core of substantive investment law and, at least in their contemporary variant, provide access to attractive dispute settlement frameworks. The collection covers a handful of bilateral investment treaties and investment-related provisions of multilateral agreements, both regional and sectoral. While the sample is small, in fact a mere fraction of the more than 3,000 treaties said to be in force, we believe it to be representative and reflective of the different generations of investment agreements. Alongside investment agreements, readers will find key texts on investment arbitration under the two main frameworks, ICSID and UNCITRAL, as well as the New York Convention on the Recognition and Enforcement of Foreign Arbitral Awards. Given the crucial role of arbitration as an instrument of dispute resolution as well as legal development, these texts are of primary relevance. By contrast, the international community has had considerable difficulty in agreeing on standards governing investments abroad. In the absence of a binding multilateral treaty, the collection includes two of the more influential non-binding codes, namely the OECD Guidelines for Multinational Enterprises and the ILO Tripartite Declaration of Principles concerning Multinational Enterprises and Social Policy. Finally, to convey a sense of the evolutionary character of investment law, we have thought it important to include a number of 'foundational' documents; comparison with these 'antecedents' (and with General Assembly resolutions included in Part 1) will allow readers to gauge developments in the international community's attempts to lay down binding standards for investment protection.

The last part of the collection (Part 4) covers international monetary and financial law. Unlike the legal regimes governing world trade and international investment, this area of law is dominated by soft law instruments laying down (non-binding) international standards. The focus on international standardization means that regulatory instruments are usually highly complex and detailed. For the purposes of teaching and studying in particular, comprehensive 'knowledge' of these detailed standards is not required, and we have thus refrained from including more than a handful of the more relevant texts. Instead, Part 4 provides international agreements and instruments that constitute the legal framework of international monetary and financial law. This includes, first, the institutional pillars of international financial governance, ie the IMF, the World Bank, the Bank for International Settlement, the Financial Stability Board, and some other institutions. Second, a limited number of documents on substantial regulatory standards concerning the international financial system are reproduced. These standards concern the most important regulatory areas of the international monetary and financial system, namely the integrity of the financial markets, governmental budgetary policy, corporate governance banking supervision, and securities regulation. Taken together, we believe that the documents selected will permit readers to appreciate the essentials of international monetary and financial law.

In preparing this collection, we have been fortunate to have the support of a team of dedicated research assistants, including Dr Karsten Nowrot and Dr Jasper Finke at Halle and James Devaney, formerly at Glasgow, now at EUI Florence. At the Press, Merel Alstein and John Louth have enthusiastically supported this project from the start and, together with Jodi Roberts, Catherine Cragg, and Philip Moore, have seen it through with experience and commitment. To all of these we are very grateful. Of course, the responsibility for all errors remains with the editors.

We hope that this collection will prove a useful and accessible roadmap through, and guide to, what is often perceived as a maze of International Economic Law. Comments, critical remarks, suggestions for improvement, etc are welcome and should be sent to christian.tietje@jura .uni-halle.de or christian.tams@cantab.net.

CHRISTIAN TAMS   CHRISTIAN TIETJE

Glasgow and Halle
May 2012

Contents

Part 3: International Investment Law

Part 4: International Monetary and Financial Law

PART I

Documents of General Relevance

I-1

Charter of the United Nations

Date   26 June 1945
In force   24 October 1945
Source   United Nations Conference on International Organization Documents, Vol XV (1945), 335
Link   <http://www.un.org/en/documents/charter/index.shtml>

PREAMBLE

WE THE PEOPLES OF THE UNITED NATIONS DETERMINED

to save succeeding generations from the scourge of war, which twice in our lifetime has brought untold sorrow to mankind, and

to reaffirm faith in fundamental human rights, in the dignity and worth of the human person, in the equal rights of men and women and of nations large and small, and

to establish conditions under which justice and respect for the obligations arising from treaties and other sources of international law can be maintained, and

to promote social progress and better standards of life in larger freedom,

AND FOR THESE ENDS

to practice tolerance and live together in peace with one another as good neighbours, and

to unite our strength to maintain international peace and security, and

to ensure, by the acceptance of principles and the institution of methods, that armed force shall not be used, save in the common interest, and

to employ international machinery for the promotion of the economic and social advancement of all peoples,

HAVE RESOLVED TO COMBINE OUR EFFORTS TO ACCOMPLISH THESE AIMS

Accordingly, our respective Governments, through representatives assembled in the city of San Francisco, who have exhibited their full powers found to be in good and due form, have agreed to the present Charter of the United Nations and do hereby establish an international organization to be known as the United Nations.

CHAPTER I   PURPOSES AND PRINCIPLES

Article 1
The Purposes of the United Nations are:

1. To maintain international peace and security, and to that end: to take effective collective measures for the prevention and removal of threats to the peace, and for the suppression of acts of aggression or other breaches of the peace, and to bring about by peaceful means, and in conformity with the principles of justice and international law, adjustment or settlement of international disputes or situations which might lead to a breach of the peace;

2. To develop friendly relations among nations based on respect for the principle of equal rights and self-determination of peoples, and to take other appropriate measures to strengthen universal peace;

3. To achieve international cooperation in solving international problems of an economic, social, cultural, or humanitarian character, and in promoting and encouraging respect for human rights and for fundamental freedoms for all without distinction as to race, sex, language, or religion; and

4. To be a centre for harmonizing the actions of nations in the attainment of these common ends.

Article 2

The Organization and its Members, in pursuit of the Purposes stated in Article 1, shall act in accordance with the following Principles.

1. The Organization is based on the principle of the sovereign equality of all its Members.

2. All Members, in order to ensure to all of them the rights and benefits resulting from membership, shall fulfill in good faith the obligations assumed by them in accordance with the present Charter.

3. All Members shall settle their international disputes by peaceful means in such a manner that international peace and security, and justice, are not endangered.

4. All Members shall refrain in their international relations from the threat or use of force against the territorial integrity or political independence of any state, or in any other manner inconsistent with the Purposes of the United Nations.

5. All Members shall give the United Nations every assistance in any action it takes in accordance with the present Charter, and shall refrain from giving assistance to any state against which the United Nations is taking preventive or enforcement action.

6. The Organization shall ensure that states which are not Members of the United Nations act in accordance with these Principles so far as may be necessary for the maintenance of international peace and security.

7. Nothing contained in the present Charter shall authorize the United Nations to intervene in matters which are essentially within the domestic jurisdiction of any state or shall require the Members to submit such matters to settlement under the present Charter; but this principle shall not prejudice the application of enforcement measures under Chapter VII.

CHAPTER II MEMBERSHIP

Article 3

The original Members of the United Nations shall be the states which, having participated in the United Nations Conference on International Organization at San Francisco, or having previously signed the Declaration by United Nations of 1 January 1942, sign the present Charter and ratify it in accordance with Article 110.

Article 4

1. Membership in the United Nations is open to all other peace-loving states which accept the obligations contained in the present Charter and, in the judgment of the Organization, are able and willing to carry out these obligations.

2. The admission of any such state to membership in the United Nations will be effected by a decision of the General Assembly upon the recommendation of the Security Council.

Article 5

A Member of the United Nations against which preventive or enforcement action has been taken by the Security Council may be suspended from the exercise of the rights and privileges of membership by the General Assembly upon the recommendation of the Security Council. The exercise of these rights and privileges may be restored by the Security Council.

Article 6

A Member of the United Nations which has persistently violated the Principles contained in the present Charter may be expelled from the Organization by the General Assembly upon the recommendation of the Security Council.

CHAPTER III ORGANS

Article 7

1. There are established as principal organs of the United Nations: a General Assembly, a Security Council, an Economic and Social Council, a Trusteeship Council, an International Court of Justice and a Secretariat.

2. Such subsidiary organs as may be found necessary may be established in accordance with the present Charter.

Article 8

The United Nations shall place no restrictions on the eligibility of men and women to participate in any capacity and under conditions of equality in its principal and subsidiary organs.

CHAPTER IV THE GENERAL ASSEMBLY

Composition

Article 9

1. The General Assembly shall consist of all the Members of the United Nations.

2. Each Member shall have not more than five representatives in the General Assembly.

Functions and Powers

Article 10

The General Assembly may discuss any questions or any matters within the scope of the present Charter or relating to the powers and functions of any organs provided for in the present Charter, and, except as provided in Article 12, may make recommendations to the Members of the United Nations or to the Security Council or to both on any such questions or matters.

Article 11

1. The General Assembly may consider the general principles of cooperation in the maintenance of international peace and security, including the principles governing disarmament and the regulation of armaments, and may make recommendations with regard to such principles to the Members or to the Security Council or to both.

2. The General Assembly may discuss any questions relating to the maintenance of international peace and security brought before it by any Member of the United Nations, or by the Security Council, or by a state which is not a Member of the United Nations in accordance with Article 35, paragraph 2, and, except as provided in Article 12, may make recommendations with regard to any such questions to the state or states concerned or to the Security Council or to both. Any such question on which action is necessary shall be referred to the Security Council by the General Assembly either before or after discussion.

3. The General Assembly may call the attention of the Security Council to situations which are likely to endanger international peace and security.

4. The powers of the General Assembly set forth in this Article shall not limit the general scope of Article 10.

Article 12

1. While the Security Council is exercising in respect of any dispute or situation the functions assigned to it in the present Charter, the General Assembly shall not make any recommendation with regard to that dispute or situation unless the Security Council so requests.

2. The Secretary-General, with the consent of the Security Council, shall notify the General Assembly at each session of any matters relative to the maintenance of international peace and security which are being dealt with by the Security Council and shall similarly notify the General Assembly, or the Members of the United Nations if the General Assembly is not in session, immediately the Security Council ceases to deal with such matters.

Article 13

1. The General Assembly shall initiate studies and make recommendations for the purpose of: a. promoting international cooperation in the political field and encouraging the progressive development of international law and its codification; b. promoting international cooperation in the economic, social, cultural, educational, and health fields, and assisting in the realization of human rights and fundamental freedoms for all without distinction as to race, sex, language, or religion.

2. The further responsibilities, functions and powers of the General Assembly with respect to matters mentioned in paragraph 1(b) above are set forth in Chapters IX and X.

Article 14

Subject to the provisions of Article 12, the General Assembly may recommend measures for the peaceful adjustment of any situation, regardless of origin, which it deems likely to impair the general welfare or friendly relations among nations, including situations resulting from a violation of the provisions of the present Charter setting forth the Purposes and Principles of the United Nations.

Article 15

1. The General Assembly shall receive and consider annual and special reports from the Security Council; these reports shall include an account of the measures that the Security Council has decided upon or taken to maintain international peace and security.

2. The General Assembly shall receive and consider reports from the other organs of the United Nations.

Article 16

The General Assembly shall perform such functions with respect to the international trusteeship system as are assigned to it under Chapters XII and XIII, including the approval of the trusteeship agreements for areas not designated as strategic.

Article 17

1. The General Assembly shall consider and approve the budget of the Organization.

2. The expenses of the Organization shall be borne by the Members as apportioned by the General Assembly.

3. The General Assembly shall consider and approve any financial and budgetary arrangements with specialized agencies referred to in Article 57 and shall examine the administrative budgets of such specialized agencies with a view to making recommendations to the agencies concerned.

Voting

Article 18

1. Each member of the General Assembly shall have one vote.

2. Decisions of the General Assembly on important questions shall be made by a two-thirds majority of the members present and voting. These questions shall include: recommendations with respect to the maintenance of international peace and security, the election of the non-permanent members of the Security Council, the election of the members of the Economic and Social Council, the election of members of the Trusteeship Council in accordance with paragraph 1(c) of Article 86, the admission of new Members to the United Nations, the

suspension of the rights and privileges of membership, the expulsion of Members, questions relating to the operation of the trusteeship system, and budgetary questions.

3. Decisions on other questions, including the determination of additional categories of questions to be decided by a two-thirds majority, shall be made by a majority of the members present and voting.

Article 19

A Member of the United Nations which is in arrears in the payment of its financial contributions to the Organization shall have no vote in the General Assembly if the amount of its arrears equals or exceeds the amount of the contributions due from it for the preceding two full years. The General Assembly may, nevertheless, permit such a Member to vote if it is satisfied that the failure to pay is due to conditions beyond the control of the Member.

Procedure

Article 20

The General Assembly shall meet in regular annual sessions and in such special sessions as occasion may require. Special sessions shall be convoked by the Secretary-General at the request of the Security Council or of a majority of the Members of the United Nations.

Article 21

The General Assembly shall adopt its own rules of procedure. It shall elect its President for each session.

Article 22

The General Assembly may establish such subsidiary organs as it deems necessary for the performance of its functions.

CHAPTER V   THE SECURITY COUNCIL

Composition

Article 23

1. The Security Council shall consist of fifteen Members of the United Nations. The Republic of China, France, the Union of Soviet Socialist Republics, the United Kingdom of Great Britain and Northern Ireland, and the United States of America shall be permanent members of the Security Council. The General Assembly shall elect ten other Members of the United Nations to be non-permanent members of the Security Council, due regard being specially paid, in the first instance to the contribution of Members of the United Nations to the maintenance of international peace and security and to the other purposes of the Organization, and also to equitable geographical distribution.

2. The non-permanent members of the Security Council shall be elected for a term of two years. In the first election of the non-permanent members after the increase of the membership of the Security Council from eleven to fifteen, two of the four additional members shall be chosen for a term of one year. A retiring member shall not be eligible for immediate re-election.

3. Each member of the Security Council shall have one representative.

Functions and Powers

Article 24

1. In order to ensure prompt and effective action by the United Nations, its Members confer on the Security Council primary responsibility for the maintenance of international peace and security, and agree that in carrying out its duties under this responsibility the Security Council acts on their behalf.

2. In discharging these duties the Security Council shall act in accordance with the Purposes and Principles of the United Nations. The specific powers granted to the Security Council for the discharge of these duties are laid down in Chapters VI, VII, VIII, and XII.

3. The Security Council shall submit annual and, when necessary, special reports to the General Assembly for its consideration.

Article 25

The Members of the United Nations agree to accept and carry out the decisions of the Security Council in accordance with the present Charter.

Article 26

In order to promote the establishment and maintenance of international peace and security with the least diversion for armaments of the world's human and economic resources, the Security Council shall be responsible for formulating, with the assistance of the Military Staff Committee referred to in Article 47, plans to be submitted to the Members of the United Nations for the establishment of a system for the regulation of armaments.

Voting

Article 27

1. Each member of the Security Council shall have one vote.

2. Decisions of the Security Council on procedural matters shall be made by an affirmative vote of nine members.

3. Decisions of the Security Council on all other matters shall be made by an affirmative vote of nine members including the concurring votes of the permanent members; provided that, in decisions under Chapter VI, and under paragraph 3 of Article 52, a party to a dispute shall abstain from voting.

Procedure

Article 28

1. The Security Council shall be so organized as to be able to function continuously. Each member of the Security Council shall for this purpose be represented at all times at the seat of the Organization.

2. The Security Council shall hold periodic meetings at which each of its members may, if it so desires, be represented by a member of the government or by some other specially designated representative.

3. The Security Council may hold meetings at such places other than the seat of the Organization as in its judgment will best facilitate its work.

Article 29

The Security Council may establish such subsidiary organs as it deems necessary for the performance of its functions.

Article 30

The Security Council shall adopt its own rules of procedure, including the method of selecting its President.

Article 31

Any Member of the United Nations which is not a member of the Security Council may participate, without vote, in the discussion of any question brought before the Security Council whenever the latter considers that the interests of that Member are specially affected.

Article 32

Any Member of the United Nations which is not a member of the Security Council or any state which is not a Member of the United Nations, if it is a party to a dispute under consideration by the Security Council, shall be invited to participate, without vote, in the discussion relating to the dispute. The Security Council shall lay down such conditions as it deems just for the participation of a state which is not a Member of the United Nations.

CHAPTER VI PACIFIC SETTLEMENT OF DISPUTES

Article 33

1. The parties to any dispute, the continuance of which is likely to endanger the maintenance of international peace and security, shall, first of all, seek a solution by negotiation, enquiry, mediation, conciliation, arbitration, judicial settlement, resort to regional agencies or arrangements, or other peaceful means of their own choice.

2. The Security Council shall, when it deems necessary, call upon the parties to settle their dispute by such means.

. . .

CHAPTER VII ACTION WITH RESPECT TO THREATS TO THE PEACE, BREACHES OF THE PEACE, AND ACTS OF AGGRESSION

Article 39

The Security Council shall determine the existence of any threat to the peace, breach of the peace, or act of aggression and shall make recommendations, or decide what measures shall be taken in accordance with Articles 41 and 42, to maintain or restore international peace and security.

Article 40

In order to prevent an aggravation of the situation, the Security Council may, before making the recommendations or deciding upon the measures provided for in Article 39, call upon the parties concerned to comply with such provisional measures as it deems necessary or desirable. Such provisional measures shall be without prejudice to the rights, claims, or position of the parties concerned. The Security Council shall duly take account of failure to comply with such provisional measures.

Article 41

The Security Council may decide what measures not involving the use of armed force are to be employed to give effect to its decisions, and it may call upon the Members of the United Nations to apply such measures. These may include complete or partial interruption of economic relations and of rail, sea, air, postal, telegraphic, radio, and other means of communication, and the severance of diplomatic relations.

. . .

CHAPTER IX INTERNATIONAL ECONOMIC AND SOCIAL COOPERATION

Article 55

With a view to the creation of conditions of stability and well-being which are necessary for peaceful and friendly relations among nations based on respect for the principle of equal rights and self-determination of peoples, the United Nations shall promote:

a. higher standards of living, full employment, and conditions of economic and social progress and development;

b. solutions of international economic, social, health, and related problems; and international cultural and educational cooperation; and

c. universal respect for, and observance of, human rights and fundamental freedoms for all without distinction as to race, sex, language, or religion.

Article 56

All Members pledge themselves to take joint and separate action in cooperation with the Organization for the achievement of the purposes set forth in Article 55.

Article 57

1. The various specialized agencies, established by intergovernmental agreement and having wide international responsibilities, as defined in their basic instruments, in economic, social, cultural, educational, health, and related fields, shall be brought into relationship with the United Nations in accordance with the provisions of Article 63.

2. Such agencies thus brought into relationship with the United Nations are hereinafter referred to as specialized agencies.

Article 58

The Organization shall make recommendations for the coordination of the policies and activities of the specialized agencies.

Article 59

The Organization shall, where appropriate, initiate negotiations among the states concerned for the creation of any new specialized agencies required for the accomplishment of the purposes set forth in Article 55.

Article 60

Responsibility for the discharge of the functions of the Organization set forth in this Chapter shall be vested in the General Assembly and, under the authority of the General Assembly, in the Economic and Social Council, which shall have for this purpose the powers set forth in Chapter X.

CHAPTER X   THE ECONOMIC AND SOCIAL COUNCIL

Composition

Article 61

1. The Economic and Social Council shall consist of fifty-four Members of the United Nations elected by the General Assembly.

2. Subject to the provisions of paragraph 3, eighteen members of the Economic and Social Council shall be elected each year for a term of three years. A retiring member shall be eligible for immediate re-election.

3. At the first election after the increase in the membership of the Economic and Social Council from twenty-seven to fifty-four members, in addition to the members elected in place of the nine members whose term of office expires at the end of that year, twenty-seven additional members shall be elected. Of these twenty-seven additional members, the term of office of nine members so elected shall expire at the end of one year, and of nine other members at the end of two years, in accordance with arrangements made by the General Assembly.

4. Each member of the Economic and Social Council shall have one representative.

Functions and Powers

Article 62

1. The Economic and Social Council may make or initiate studies and reports with respect to international economic, social, cultural, educational, health, and related matters and may make recommendations with respect to any such matters to the General Assembly to the Members of the United Nations, and to the specialized agencies concerned.

2. It may make recommendations for the purpose of promoting respect for, and observance of, human rights and fundamental freedoms for all.

3. It may prepare draft conventions for submission to the General Assembly, with respect to matters falling within its competence.

4. It may call, in accordance with the rules prescribed by the United Nations, international conferences on matters falling within its competence.

Article 63

1. The Economic and Social Council may enter into agreements with any of the agencies referred to in Article 57, defining the terms on which the agency concerned shall be brought into relationship with the United Nations. Such agreements shall be subject to approval by the General Assembly.

2. It may coordinate the activities of the specialized agencies through consultation with and recommendations to such agencies and through recommendations to the General Assembly and to the Members of the United Nations.

Article 64

1. The Economic and Social Council may take appropriate steps to obtain regular reports from the specialized agencies. It may make arrangements with the Members of the United Nations and with the specialized agencies to obtain reports on the steps taken to give effect to its own recommendations and to recommendations on matters falling within its competence made by the General Assembly.

2. It may communicate its observations on these reports to the General Assembly.

Article 65

The Economic and Social Council may furnish information to the Security Council and shall assist the Security Council upon its request.

Article 66

1. The Economic and Social Council shall perform such functions as fall within its competence in connection with the carrying out of the recommendations of the General Assembly.

2. It may, with the approval of the General Assembly, perform services at the request of Members of the United Nations and at the request of specialized agencies.

3. It shall perform such other functions as are specified elsewhere in the present Charter or as may be assigned to it by the General Assembly.

Voting

Article 67

1. Each member of the Economic and Social Council shall have one vote.

2. Decisions of the Economic and Social Council shall be made by a majority of the members present and voting.

Procedure

Article 68

The Economic and Social Council shall set up commissions in economic and social fields and for the promotion of human rights, and such other commissions as may be required for the performance of its functions.

Article 69

The Economic and Social Council shall invite any Member of the United Nations to participate, without vote, in its deliberations on any matter of particular concern to that Member.

Article 70

The Economic and Social Council may make arrangements for representatives of the specialized agencies to participate, without vote, in its deliberations and in those of the commissions established by it, and for its representatives to participate in the deliberations of the specialized agencies.

Article 71

The Economic and Social Council may make suitable arrangements for consultation with non-governmental organizations which are concerned with matters within its competence. Such arrangements may be made with international organizations and, where appropriate, with national organizations after consultation with the Member of the United Nations concerned.

Article 72

1. The Economic and Social Council shall adopt its own rules of procedure, including the method of selecting its President.

2. The Economic and Social Council shall meet as required in accordance with its rules, which shall include provision for the convening of meetings on the request of a majority of its members.

. . .

I-2

Vienna Convention on the Law of Treaties

Date   23 May 1969
In force 27 January 1980
Source 1155 UNTS 331
Link   <http://untreaty.un.org/ilc/texts/instruments/english/conventions/1_1_1969.pdf>

The States Parties to the present Convention,

Considering the fundamental role of treaties in the history of international relations,

Recognizing the ever-increasing importance of treaties as a source of international law and as a means of developing peaceful cooperation among nations, whatever their constitutional and social systems,

Noting that the principles of free consent and of good faith and the *pacta sunt servanda* rule are universally recognized,

Affirming that disputes concerning treaties, like other international disputes, should be settled by peaceful means and in conformity with the principles of justice and international law,

Recalling the determination of the peoples of the United Nations to establish conditions under which justice and respect for the obligations arising from treaties can be maintained,

Having in mind the principles of international law embodied in the Charter of the United Nations, such as the principles of the equal rights and self-determination of peoples, of the sovereign equality and independence of all States, of non-interference in the domestic affairs of States, of the prohibition of the threat or use of force and of universal respect for, and observance of, human rights and fundamental freedoms for all,

Believing that the codification and progressive development of the law of treaties achieved in the present Convention will promote the purposes of the United Nations set forth in the Charter, namely, the maintenance of international peace and security, the development of friendly relations and the achievement of cooperation among nations,

Affirming that the rules of customary international law will continue to govern questions not regulated by the provisions of the present Convention,

Have agreed as follows:

PART I   INTRODUCTION

Article 1 Scope of the present Convention
The present Convention applies to treaties between States.

Article 2 Use of terms
1. For the purposes of the present Convention:
    (*a*) "treaty" means an international agreement concluded between States in written form and governed by international law, whether embodied in a single instrument or in two or more related instruments and whatever its particular designation;
    (*b*) "ratification", "acceptance", "approval" and "accession" mean in each case the international act so named whereby a State establishes on the international plane its consent to be bound by a treaty;
    (*c*) "full powers" means a document emanating from the competent authority of a State designating a person or persons to represent the State for negotiating, adopting or

authenticating the text of a treaty, for expressing the consent of the State to be bound by a treaty, or for accomplishing any other act with respect to a treaty;

(*d*) "reservation" means a unilateral statement, however phrased or named, made by a State, when signing, ratifying, accepting, approving or acceding to a treaty, whereby it purports to exclude or to modify the legal effect of certain provisions of the treaty in their application to that State;

(*e*) "negotiating State" means a State which took part in the drawing up and adoption of the text of the treaty;

(*f*) "contracting State" means a State which has consented to be bound by the treaty, whether or not the treaty has entered into force;

(*g*) "party" means a State which has consented to be bound by the treaty and for which the treaty is in force;

(*h*) "third State" means a State not a party to the treaty;

(*i*) "international organization" means an intergovernmental organization.

2. The provisions of paragraph 1 regarding the use of terms in the present Convention are without prejudice to the use of those terms or to the meanings which may be given to them in the internal law of any State.

Article 3   International agreements not within the scope of the present Convention

The fact that the present Convention does not apply to international agreements concluded between States and other subjects of international law or between such other subjects of international law, or to international agreements not in written form, shall not affect:

(*a*) the legal force of such agreements;

(*b*) the application to them of any of the rules set forth in the present Convention to which they would be subject under international law independently of the Convention;

(*c*) the application of the Convention to the relations of States as between themselves under international agreements to which other subjects of international law are also parties.

Article 4   Non-retroactivity of the present Convention

Without prejudice to the application of any rules set forth in the present Convention to which treaties would be subject under international law independently of the Convention, the Convention applies only to treaties which are concluded by States after the entry into force of the present Convention with regard to such States.

Article 5   Treaties constituting international organizations and treaties adopted within an international organization

The present Convention applies to any treaty which is the constituent instrument of an international organization and to any treaty adopted within an international organization without prejudice to any relevant rules of the organization.

PART II   CONCLUSION AND ENTRY INTO FORCE OF TREATIES

SECTION 1   CONCLUSION OF TREATIES

Article 6   Capacity of States to conclude treaties

Every State possesses capacity to conclude treaties.

Article 7   Full powers

1. A person is considered as representing a State for the purpose of adopting or authenticating the text of a treaty or for the purpose of expressing the consent of the State to be bound by a treaty if:

(*a*) he produces appropriate full powers; or

(b) it appears from the practice of the States concerned or from other circumstances that their intention was to consider that person as representing the State for such purposes and to dispense with full powers.

2. In virtue of their functions and without having to produce full powers, the following are considered as representing their State:

   (a) Heads of State, Heads of Government and Ministers for Foreign Affairs, for the purpose of performing all acts relating to the conclusion of a treaty;

   (b) heads of diplomatic missions, for the purpose of adopting the text of a treaty between the accrediting State and the State to which they are accredited;

   (c) representatives accredited by States to an international conference or to an international organization or one of its organs, for the purpose of adopting the text of a treaty in that conference, organization or organ.

Article 8 Subsequent confirmation of an act performed without authorization

An act relating to the conclusion of a treaty performed by a person who cannot be considered under article 7 as authorized to represent a State for that purpose is without legal effect unless afterwards confirmed by that State.

Article 9 Adoption of the text

1. The adoption of the text of a treaty takes place by the consent of all the States participating in its drawing up except as provided in paragraph 2.

2. The adoption of the text of a treaty at an international conference takes place by the vote of two thirds of the States present and voting, unless by the same majority they shall decide to apply a different rule.

Article 10 Authentication of the text

The text of a treaty is established as authentic and definitive:

(a) by such procedure as may be provided for in the text or agreed upon by the States participating in its drawing up; or

(b) failing such procedure, by the signature, signature ad referendum or initialling by the representatives of those States of the text of the treaty or of the Final Act of a conference incorporating the text.

Article 11 Means of expressing consent to be bound by a treaty

The consent of a State to be bound by a treaty may be expressed by signature, exchange of instruments constituting a treaty, ratification, acceptance, approval or accession, or by any other means if so agreed.

Article 12 Consent to be bound by a treaty expressed by signature

1. The consent of a State to be bound by a treaty is expressed by the signature of its representative when:

   (a) the treaty provides that signature shall have that effect;

   (b) it is otherwise established that the negotiating States were agreed that signature should have that effect; or

   (c) the intention of the State to give that effect to the signature appears from the full powers of its representative or was expressed during the negotiation.

2. For the purposes of paragraph 1:

   (a) the initialling of a text constitutes a signature of the treaty when it is established that the negotiating States so agreed;

   (b) the signature ad referendum of a treaty by a representative, if confirmed by his State, constitutes a full signature of the treaty.

Article 13 Consent to be bound by a treaty expressed by an exchange of instruments constituting a treaty

The consent of States to be bound by a treaty constituted by instruments exchanged between them is expressed by that exchange when:

(*a*) the instruments provide that their exchange shall have that effect; or

(*b*) it is otherwise established that those States were agreed that the exchange of instruments should have that effect.

Article 14 Consent to be bound by a treaty expressed by ratification, acceptance or approval

1. The consent of a State to be bound by a treaty is expressed by ratification when:

 (*a*) the treaty provides for such consent to be expressed by means of ratification;

 (*b*) it is otherwise established that the negotiating States were agreed that ratification should be required;

 (*c*) the representative of the State has signed the treaty subject to ratification; or

 (*d*) the intention of the State to sign the treaty subject to ratification appears from the full powers of its representative or was expressed during the negotiation.

2. The consent of a State to be bound by a treaty is expressed by acceptance or approval under conditions similar to those which apply to ratification.

Article 15 Consent to be bound by a treaty expressed by accession

The consent of a State to be bound by a treaty is expressed by accession when:

(*a*) the treaty provides that such consent may be expressed by that State by means of accession;

(*b*) it is otherwise established that the negotiating States were agreed that such consent may be expressed by that State by means of accession; or

(*c*) all the parties have subsequently agreed that such consent may be expressed by that State by means of accession.

Article 16 Exchange or deposit of instruments of ratification, acceptance, approval or accession

Unless the treaty otherwise provides, instruments of ratification, acceptance, approval or accession establish the consent of a State to be bound by a treaty upon:

(*a*) their exchange between the contracting States;

(*b*) their deposit with the depositary; or

(*c*) their notification to the contracting States or to the depositary, if so agreed.

Article 17 Consent to be bound by part of a treaty and choice of differing provisions

1. Without prejudice to articles 19 to 23, the consent of a State to be bound by part of a treaty is effective only if the treaty so permits or the other contracting States so agree.

2. The consent of a State to be bound by a treaty which permits a choice between differing provisions is effective only if it is made clear to which of the provisions the consent relates.

Article 18 Obligation not to defeat the object and purpose of a treaty prior to its entry into force

A State is obliged to refrain from acts which would defeat the object and purpose of a treaty when:

(*a*) it has signed the treaty or has exchanged instruments constituting the treaty subject to ratification, acceptance or approval, until it shall have made its intention clear not to become a party to the treaty; or

(*b*) it has expressed its consent to be bound by the treaty, pending the entry into force of the treaty and provided that such entry into force is not unduly delayed.

SECTION 2   RESERVATIONS

. . .

SECTION 3   ENTRY INTO FORCE AND PROVISIONAL APPLICATION OF TREATIES

Article 24   Entry into force
1. A treaty enters into force in such manner and upon such date as it may provide or as the negotiating States may agree.
2. Failing any such provision or agreement, a treaty enters into force as soon as consent to be bound by the treaty has been established for all the negotiating States.
3. When the consent of a State to be bound by a treaty is established on a date after the treaty has come into force, the treaty enters into force for that State on that date, unless the treaty otherwise provides.
4. The provisions of a treaty regulating the authentication of its text, the establishment of the consent of States to be bound by the treaty, the manner or date of its entry into force, reservations, the functions of the depositary and other matters arising necessarily before the entry into force of the treaty apply from the time of the adoption of its text.

Article 25   Provisional application
1. A treaty or a part of a treaty is applied provisionally pending its entry into force if:
   (a) the treaty itself so provides; or
   (b) the negotiating States have in some other manner so agreed.
2. Unless the treaty otherwise provides or the negotiating States have otherwise agreed, the provisional application of a treaty or a part of a treaty with respect to a State shall be terminated if that State notifies the other States between which the treaty is being applied provisionally of its intention not to become a party to the treaty.

PART III   OBSERVANCE, APPLICATION AND INTERPRETATION OF TREATIES

SECTION 1   OBSERVANCE OF TREATIES

Article 26   "Pacta sunt servanda"
Every treaty in force is binding upon the parties to it and must be performed by them in good faith.

Article 27   Internal law and observance of treaties
A party may not invoke the provisions of its internal law as justification for its failure to perform a treaty. This rule is without prejudice to article 46.

SECTION 2   APPLICATION OF TREATIES

Article 28   Non-retroactivity of treaties
Unless a different intention appears from the treaty or is otherwise established, its provisions do not bind a party in relation to any act or fact which took place or any situation which ceased to exist before the date of the entry into force of the treaty with respect to that party.

Article 29   Territorial scope of treaties
Unless a different intention appears from the treaty or is otherwise established, a treaty is binding upon each party in respect of its entire territory.

Article 30   Application of successive treaties relating to the same subject matter

1. Subject to Article 103 of the Charter of the United Nations, the rights and obligations of States Parties to successive treaties relating to the same subject matter shall be determined in accordance with the following paragraphs.

2. When a treaty specifies that it is subject to, or that it is not to be considered as incompatible with, an earlier or later treaty, the provisions of that other treaty prevail.

3. When all the parties to the earlier treaty are parties also to the later treaty but the earlier treaty is not terminated or suspended in operation under article 59, the earlier treaty applies only to the extent that its provisions are compatible with those of the later treaty.

4. When the parties to the later treaty do not include all the parties to the earlier one:
    (*a*) as between States Parties to both treaties the same rule applies as in paragraph 3;
    (*b*) as between a State party to both treaties and a State party to only one of the treaties, the treaty to which both States are parties governs their mutual rights and obligations.

5. Paragraph 4 is without prejudice to article 41, or to any question of the termination or suspension of the operation of a treaty under article 60 or to any question of responsibility which may arise for a State from the conclusion or application of a treaty the provisions of which are incompatible with its obligations towards another State under another treaty.

SECTION 3   INTERPRETATION OF TREATIES

Article 31   General rule of interpretation

1. A treaty shall be interpreted in good faith in accordance with the ordinary meaning to be given to the terms of the treaty in their context and in the light of its object and purpose.

2. The context for the purpose of the interpretation of a treaty shall comprise, in addition to the text, including its preamble and annexes:
    (*a*) any agreement relating to the treaty which was made between all the parties in connection with the conclusion of the treaty;
    (*b*) any instrument which was made by one or more parties in connection with the conclusion of the treaty and accepted by the other parties as an instrument related to the treaty.

3. There shall be taken into account, together with the context:
    (*a*) any subsequent agreement between the parties regarding the interpretation of the treaty or the application of its provisions;
    (*b*) any subsequent practice in the application of the treaty which establishes the agreement of the parties regarding its interpretation;
    (*c*) any relevant rules of international law applicable in the relations between the parties.

4. A special meaning shall be given to a term if it is established that the parties so intended.

Article 32   Supplementary means of interpretation

Recourse may be had to supplementary means of interpretation, including the preparatory work of the treaty and the circumstances of its conclusion, in order to confirm the meaning resulting from the application of article 31, or to determine the meaning when the interpretation according to article 31:

(*a*) leaves the meaning ambiguous or obscure; or

(*b*) leads to a result which is manifestly absurd or unreasonable.

Article 33   Interpretation of treaties authenticated in two or more languages

1. When a treaty has been authenticated in two or more languages, the text is equally authoritative in each language, unless the treaty provides or the parties agree that, in case of divergence, a particular text shall prevail.

2. A version of the treaty in a language other than one of those in which the text was authenticated shall be considered an authentic text only if the treaty so provides or the parties so agree.

3. The terms of the treaty are presumed to have the same meaning in each authentic text.

4. Except where a particular text prevails in accordance with paragraph 1, when a comparison of the authentic texts discloses a difference of meaning which the application of articles 31 and 32 does not remove, the meaning which best reconciles the texts, having regard to the object and purpose of the treaty, shall be adopted.

SECTION 4   TREATIES AND THIRD STATES

Article 34   General rule regarding third States
A treaty does not create either obligations or rights for a third State without its consent.

Article 35   Treaties providing for obligations for third States
An obligation arises for a third State from a provision of a treaty if the parties to the treaty intend the provision to be the means of establishing the obligation and the third State expressly accepts that obligation in writing.

Article 36   Treaties providing for rights for third States
1. A right arises for a third State from a provision of a treaty if the parties to the treaty intend the provision to accord that right either to the third State, or to a group of States to which it belongs, or to all States, and the third State assents thereto. Its assent shall be presumed so long as the contrary is not indicated, unless the treaty otherwise provides.

2. A State exercising a right in accordance with paragraph 1 shall comply with the conditions for its exercise provided for in the treaty or established in conformity with the treaty.

Article 37   Revocation or modification of obligations or rights of third States
1. When an obligation has arisen for a third State in conformity with article 35, the obligation may be revoked or modified only with the consent of the parties to the treaty and of the third State, unless it is established that they had otherwise agreed.

2. When a right has arisen for a third State in conformity with article 36, the right may not be revoked or modified by the parties if it is established that the right was intended not to be revocable or subject to modification without the consent of the third State.

Article 38   Rules in a treaty becoming binding on third States through international custom
Nothing in articles 34 to 37 precludes a rule set forth in a treaty from becoming binding upon a third State as a customary rule of international law, recognized as such.

PART IV   AMENDMENT AND MODIFICATION OF TREATIES

Article 39   General rule regarding the amendment of treaties
A treaty may be amended by agreement between the parties. The rules laid down in Part II apply to such an agreement except insofar as the treaty may otherwise provide.

Article 40   Amendment of multilateral treaties
1. Unless the treaty otherwise provides, the amendment of multilateral treaties shall be governed by the following paragraphs.

2. Any proposal to amend a multilateral treaty as between all the parties must be notified to all the contracting States, each one of which shall have the right to take part in:
   (*a*) the decision as to the action to be taken in regard to such proposal;
   (*b*) the negotiation and conclusion of any agreement for the amendment of the treaty.

3. Every State entitled to become a party to the treaty shall also be entitled to become a party to the treaty as amended.

4. The amending agreement does not bind any State already a party to the treaty which does not become a party to the amending agreement; article 30, paragraph 4 (*b*), applies in relation to such State.

5. Any State which becomes a party to the treaty after the entry into force of the amending agreement shall, failing an expression of a different intention by that State:
   (*a*) be considered as a party to the treaty as amended; and
   (*b*) be considered as a party to the unamended treaty in relation to any party to the treaty not bound by the amending agreement.

Article 41   Agreements to modify multilateral treaties between certain of the parties only

1. Two or more of the parties to a multilateral treaty may conclude an agreement to modify the treaty as between themselves alone if:
   (*a*) the possibility of such a modification is provided for by the treaty; or
   (*b*) the modification in question is not prohibited by the treaty and:
      (i) does not affect the enjoyment by the other parties of their rights under the treaty or the performance of their obligations;
      (ii) does not relate to a provision, derogation from which is incompatible with the effective execution of the object and purpose of the treaty as a whole.

2. Unless in a case falling under paragraph 1 (*a*) the treaty otherwise provides, the parties in question shall notify the other parties of their intention to conclude the agreement and of the modification to the treaty for which it provides.

PART V   INVALIDITY, TERMINATION AND SUSPENSION OF THE OPERATION OF TREATIES

SECTION 1   GENERAL PROVISIONS

Article 42   Validity and continuance in force of treaties

1. The validity of a treaty or of the consent of a State to be bound by a treaty may be impeached only through the application of the present Convention.

2. The termination of a treaty, its denunciation or the withdrawal of a party, may take place only as a result of the application of the provisions of the treaty or of the present Convention. The same rule applies to suspension of the operation of a treaty.

Article 43   Obligations imposed by international law independently of a treaty

The invalidity, termination or denunciation of a treaty, the withdrawal of a party from it, or the suspension of its operation, as a result of the application of the present Convention or of the provisions of the treaty, shall not in any way impair the duty of any State to fulfil any obligation embodied in the treaty to which it would be subject under international law independently of the treaty.

Article 44   Separability of treaty provisions

1. A right of a party, provided for in a treaty or arising under article 56, to denounce, withdraw from or suspend the operation of the treaty may be exercised only with respect to the whole treaty unless the treaty otherwise provides or the parties otherwise agree.

2. A ground for invalidating, terminating, withdrawing from or suspending the operation of a treaty recognized in the present Convention may be invoked only with respect to the whole treaty except as provided in the following paragraphs or in article 60.

3. If the ground relates solely to particular clauses, it may be invoked only with respect to those clauses where:

(a) the said clauses are separable from the remainder of the treaty with regard to their application;

(b) it appears from the treaty or is otherwise established that acceptance of those clauses was not an essential basis of the consent of the other party or parties to be bound by the treaty as a whole; and

(c) continued performance of the remainder of the treaty would not be unjust.

4. In cases falling under articles 49 and 50, the State entitled to invoke the fraud or corruption may do so with respect either to the whole treaty or, subject to paragraph 3, to the particular clauses alone.

5. In cases falling under articles 51, 52 and 53, no separation of the provisions of the treaty is permitted.

Article 45   Loss of a right to invoke a ground for invalidating, terminating, withdrawing from or suspending the operation of a treaty

A State may no longer invoke a ground for invalidating, terminating, withdrawing from or suspending the operation of a treaty under articles 46 to 50 or articles 60 and 62 if, after becoming aware of the facts:

(a) it shall have expressly agreed that the treaty is valid or remains in force or continues in operation, as the case may be; or

(b) it must by reason of its conduct be considered as having acquiesced in the validity of the treaty or in its maintenance in force or in operation, as the case may be.

SECTION 2   INVALIDITY OF TREATIES

Article 46   Provisions of internal law regarding competence to conclude treaties

1. A State may not invoke the fact that its consent to be bound by a treaty has been expressed in violation of a provision of its internal law regarding competence to conclude treaties as invalidating its consent unless that violation was manifest and concerned a rule of its internal law of fundamental importance.

2. A violation is manifest if it would be objectively evident to any State conducting itself in the matter in accordance with normal practice and in good faith.

Article 47   Specific restrictions on authority to express the consent of a State

If the authority of a representative to express the consent of a State to be bound by a particular treaty has been made subject to a specific restriction, his omission to observe that restriction may not be invoked as invalidating the consent expressed by him unless the restriction was notified to the other negotiating States prior to his expressing such consent.

Article 48   Error

1. A State may invoke an error in a treaty as invalidating its consent to be bound by the treaty if the error relates to a fact or situation which was assumed by that State to exist at the time when the treaty was concluded and formed an essential basis of its consent to be bound by the treaty.

2. Paragraph 1 shall not apply if the State in question contributed by its own conduct to the error or if the circumstances were such as to put that State on notice of a possible error.

3. An error relating only to the wording of the text of a treaty does not affect its validity; article 79 then applies.

Article 49   Fraud

If a State has been induced to conclude a treaty by the fraudulent conduct of another negotiating State, the State may invoke the fraud as invalidating its consent to be bound by the treaty.

Article 50   Corruption of a representative of a State

If the expression of a State's consent to be bound by a treaty has been procured through the corruption of its representative directly or indirectly by another negotiating State, the State may invoke such corruption as invalidating its consent to be bound by the treaty.

Article 51   Coercion of a representative of a State

The expression of a State's consent to be bound by a treaty which has been procured by the coercion of its representative through acts or threats directed against him shall be without any legal effect.

Article 52   Coercion of a State by the threat or use of force

A treaty is void if its conclusion has been procured by the threat or use of force in violation of the principles of international law embodied in the Charter of the United Nations.

Article 53   Treaties conflicting with a peremptory norm of general international law ("jus cogens")

A treaty is void if, at the time of its conclusion, it conflicts with a peremptory norm of general international law. For the purposes of the present Convention, a peremptory norm of general international law is a norm accepted and recognized by the international community of States as a whole as a norm from which no derogation is permitted and which can be modified only by a subsequent norm of general international law having the same character.

SECTION 3   TERMINATION AND SUSPENSION OF THE OPERATION OF TREATIES

Article 54   Termination of or withdrawal from a treaty under its provisions or by consent of the parties

The termination of a treaty or the withdrawal of a party may take place:

(*a*) in conformity with the provisions of the treaty; or

(*b*) at any time by consent of all the parties after consultation with the other contracting States.

Article 55   Reduction of the parties to a multilateral treaty below the number necessary for its entry into force

Unless the treaty otherwise provides, a multilateral treaty does not terminate by reason only of the fact that the number of the parties falls below the number necessary for its entry into force.

Article 56   Denunciation of or withdrawal from a treaty containing no provision regarding termination, denunciation or withdrawal

1. A treaty which contains no provision regarding its termination and which does not provide for denunciation or withdrawal is not subject to denunciation or withdrawal unless:
   (*a*) it is established that the parties intended to admit the possibility of denunciation or withdrawal; or
   (*b*) a right of denunciation or withdrawal may be implied by the nature of the treaty.
2. A party shall give not less than twelve months' notice of its intention to denounce or withdraw from a treaty under paragraph 1.

Article 57   Suspension of the operation of a treaty under its provisions or by consent of the parties

The operation of a treaty in regard to all the parties or to a particular party may be suspended:

(*a*) in conformity with the provisions of the treaty; or

(*b*) at any time by consent of all the parties after consultation with the other contracting States.

Article 58   Suspension of the operation of a multilateral treaty by agreement between certain of the parties only

1. Two or more parties to a multilateral treaty may conclude an agreement to suspend the operation of provisions of the treaty, temporarily and as between themselves alone, if:
    (a) the possibility of such a suspension is provided for by the treaty; or
    (b) the suspension in question is not prohibited by the treaty and:
        (i) does not affect the enjoyment by the other parties of their rights under the treaty or the performance of their obligations;
        (ii) is not incompatible with the object and purpose of the treaty.
2. Unless in a case falling under paragraph 1 (a) the treaty otherwise provides, the parties in question shall notify the other parties of their intention to conclude the agreement and of those provisions of the treaty the operation of which they intend to suspend.

Article 59   Termination or suspension of the operation of a treaty implied by conclusion of a later treaty

1. A treaty shall be considered as terminated if all the parties to it conclude a later treaty relating to the same subject matter and:
    (a) it appears from the later treaty or is otherwise established that the parties intended that the matter should be governed by that treaty; or
    (b) the provisions of the later treaty are so far incompatible with those of the earlier one that the two treaties are not capable of being applied at the same time.
2. The earlier treaty shall be considered as only suspended in operation if it appears from the later treaty or is otherwise established that such was the intention of the parties.

Article 60 Termination or suspension of the operation of a treaty as a consequence of its breach

1. A material breach of a bilateral treaty by one of the parties entitles the other to invoke the breach as a ground for terminating the treaty or suspending its operation in whole or in part.
2. A material breach of a multilateral treaty by one of the parties entitles:
    (a) the other parties by unanimous agreement to suspend the operation of the treaty in whole or in part or to terminate it either:
        (i) in the relations between themselves and the defaulting State; or
        (ii) as between all the parties;
    (b) a party specially affected by the breach to invoke it as a ground for suspending the operation of the treaty in whole or in part in the relations between itself and the defaulting State;
    (c) any party other than the defaulting State to invoke the breach as a ground for suspending the operation of the treaty in whole or in part with respect to itself if the treaty is of such a character that a material breach of its provisions by one party radically changes the position of every party with respect to the further performance of its obligations under the treaty.
3. A material breach of a treaty, for the purposes of this article, consists in:
    (a) a repudiation of the treaty not sanctioned by the present Convention; or
    (b) the violation of a provision essential to the accomplishment of the object or purpose of the treaty.
4. The foregoing paragraphs are without prejudice to any provision in the treaty applicable in the event of a breach.
5. Paragraphs 1 to 3 do not apply to provisions relating to the protection of the human person contained in treaties of a humanitarian character, in particular to provisions prohibiting any form of reprisals against persons protected by such treaties.

Article 61   Supervening impossibility of performance

1. A party may invoke the impossibility of performing a treaty as a ground for terminating or withdrawing from it if the impossibility results from the permanent disappearance or destruction of an object indispensable for the execution of the treaty. If the impossibility is temporary, it may be invoked only as a ground for suspending the operation of the treaty.

2. Impossibility of performance may not be invoked by a party as a ground for terminating, withdrawing from or suspending the operation of a treaty if the impossibility is the result of a breach by that party either of an obligation under the treaty or of any other international obligation owed to any other party to the treaty.

Article 62   Fundamental change of circumstances

1. A fundamental change of circumstances which has occurred with regard to those existing at the time of the conclusion of a treaty, and which was not foreseen by the parties, may not be invoked as a ground for terminating or withdrawing from the treaty unless:

   (*a*) the existence of those circumstances constituted an essential basis of the consent of the parties to be bound by the treaty; and

   (*b*) the effect of the change is radically to transform the extent of obligations still to be performed under the treaty.

2. A fundamental change of circumstances may not be invoked as a ground for terminating or withdrawing from a treaty:

   (*a*) if the treaty establishes a boundary; or

   (*b*) if the fundamental change is the result of a breach by the party invoking it either of an obligation under the treaty or of any other international obligation owed to any other party to the treaty.

3. If, under the foregoing paragraphs, a party may invoke a fundamental change of circumstances as a ground for terminating or withdrawing from a treaty it may also invoke the change as a ground for suspending the operation of the treaty.

   . . .

ILC Articles on Responsibility of States for Internationally Wrongful Acts

Date 12 December 2001
Source Annex to GA Res 56/83, corrected by Doc A/56/49(Vol. I)/Corr.4
Link <http://untreaty.un.org/ilc/texts/instruments/english/draft%20articles/9_6_2001.pdf>

PART ONE   THE INTERNATIONALLY WRONGFUL ACT OF A STATE

CHAPTER I   GENERAL PRINCIPLES

Article 1   Responsibility of a State for its internationally wrongful acts
Every internationally wrongful act of a State entails the international responsibility of that State.

Article 2   Elements of an internationally wrongful act of a State
There is an internationally wrongful act of a State when conduct consisting of an action or omission:

(*a*) is attributable to the State under international law; and

(*b*) constitutes a breach of an international obligation of the State.

Article 3   Characterization of an act of a State as internationally wrongful
The characterization of an act of a State as internationally wrongful is governed by international law. Such characterization is not affected by the characterization of the same act as lawful by internal law.

CHAPTER II   ATTRIBUTION OF CONDUCT TO A STATE

Article 4   Conduct of organs of a State
1. The conduct of any State organ shall be considered an act of that State under international law, whether the organ exercises legislative, executive, judicial or any other functions, what-ever position it holds in the organization of the State, and whatever its character as an organ of the central government or of a territorial unit of the State.

2. An organ includes any person or entity which has that status in accordance with the internal law of the State.

Article 5   Conduct of persons or entities exercising elements of governmental authority
The conduct of a person or entity which is not an organ of the State under article 4 but which is empowered by the law of that State to exercise elements of the governmental authority shall be considered an act of the State under international law, provided the person or entity is acting in that capacity in the particular instance.

Article 6   Conduct of organs placed at the disposal of a State by another State
The conduct of an organ placed at the disposal of a State by another State shall be considered an act of the former State under international law if the organ is acting in the exercise of elements of the governmental authority of the State at whose disposal it is placed.

Article 7   Excess of authority or contravention of instructions
The conduct of an organ of a State or of a person or entity empowered to exercise elements of the governmental authority shall be considered an act of the State under international law if the

organ, person or entity acts in that capacity, even if it exceeds its authority or contravenes instructions.

Article 8   Conduct directed or controlled by a State

The conduct of a person or group of persons shall be considered an act of a State under international law if the person or group of persons is in fact acting on the instructions of, or under the direction or control of, that State in carrying out the conduct.

Article 9   Conduct carried out in the absence or default of the official authorities

The conduct of a person or group of persons shall be considered an act of a State under international law if the person or group of persons is in fact exercising elements of the governmental authority in the absence or default of the official authorities and in circumstances such as to call for the exercise of those elements of authority.

Article 10   Conduct of an insurrectional or other movement

1. The conduct of an insurrectional movement which becomes the new government of a State shall be considered an act of that State under international law.

2. The conduct of a movement, insurrectional or other, which succeeds in establishing a new State in part of the territory of a pre-existing State or in a territory under its administration shall be considered an act of the new State under international law.

3. This article is without prejudice to the attribution to a State of any conduct, however related to that of the movement concerned, which is to be considered an act of that State by virtue of articles 4 to 9.

Article 11   Conduct acknowledged and adopted by a State as its own

Conduct which is not attributable to a State under the preceding articles shall nevertheless be considered an act of that State under international law if and to the extent that the State acknowledges and adopts the conduct in question as its own.

CHAPTER III   BREACH OF AN INTERNATIONAL OBLIGATION

Article 12   Existence of a breach of an international obligation

There is a breach of an international obligation by a State when an act of that State is not in conformity with what is required of it by that obligation, regardless of its origin or character.

Article 13   International obligation in force for a State

An act of a State does not constitute a breach of an international obligation unless the State is bound by the obligation in question at the time the act occurs.

Article 14   Extension in time of the breach of an international obligation

1. The breach of an international obligation by an act of a State not having a continuing character occurs at the moment when the act is performed, even if its effects continue.

2. The breach of an international obligation by an act of a State having a continuing character extends over the entire period during which the act continues and remains not in conformity with the international obligation.

3. The breach of an international obligation requiring a State to prevent a given event occurs when the event occurs and extends over the entire period during which the event continues and remains not in conformity with that obligation.

Article 15   Breach consisting of a composite act

1. The breach of an international obligation by a State through a series of actions or omissions defined in aggregate as wrongful, occurs when the action or omission occurs which, taken with the other actions or omissions, is sufficient to constitute the wrongful act.

2. In such a case, the breach extends over the entire period starting with the first of the actions or omissions of the series and lasts for as long as these actions or omissions are repeated and remain not in conformity with the international obligation.

CHAPTER IV   RESPONSIBILITY OF A STATE IN CONNECTION WITH THE ACT OF ANOTHER STATE

Article 16   Aid or assistance in the commission of an internationally wrongful act
A State which aids or assists another State in the commission of an internationally wrongful act by the latter is internationally responsible for doing so if:

(*a*) that State does so with knowledge of the circumstances of the internationally wrongful act; and

(*b*) the act would be internationally wrongful if committed by that State.

Article 17   Direction and control exercised over the commission of an internationally wrongful act
A State which directs and controls another State in the commission of an internationally wrongful act by the latter is internationally responsible for that act if:

(*a*) that State does so with knowledge of the circumstances of the internationally wrongful act; and

(*b*) the act would be internationally wrongful if committed by that State.

Article 18   Coercion of another State
A State which coerces another State to commit an act is internationally responsible for that act if:

(*a*) the act would, but for the coercion, be an internationally wrongful act of the coerced State; and

(*b*) the coercing State does so with knowledge of the circumstances of the act.

Article 19   Effect of this chapter
This chapter is without prejudice to the international responsibility, under other provisions of these articles, of the State which commits the act in question, or of any other State.

CHAPTER V   CIRCUMSTANCES PRECLUDING WRONGFULNESS

Article 20   Consent
Valid consent by a State to the commission of a given act by another State precludes the wrongfulness of that act in relation to the former State to the extent that the act remains within the limits of that consent.

Article 21   Self-defence
The wrongfulness of an act of a State is precluded if the act constitutes a lawful measure of self-defence taken in conformity with the Charter of the United Nations.

Article 22   Countermeasures in respect of an internationally wrongful act
The wrongfulness of an act of a State not in conformity with an international obligation towards another State is precluded if and to the extent that the act constitutes a countermeasure taken against the latter State in accordance with chapter II of part three.

Article 23   Force majeure
1. The wrongfulness of an act of a State not in conformity with an international obligation of that State is precluded if the act is due to force majeure, that is the occurrence of an irresistible force or of an unforeseen event, beyond the control of the State, making it materially impossible in the circumstances to perform the obligation.

2. Paragraph 1 does not apply if:
    (a) the situation of force majeure is due, either alone or in combination with other factors, to the conduct of the State invoking it; or
    (b) the State has assumed the risk of that situation occurring.

Article 24   Distress

1. The wrongfulness of an act of a State not in conformity with an international obligation of that
   State is precluded if the author of the act in question has no other reasonable way, in a situation
   of distress, of saving the author's life or the lives of other persons entrusted to the author's care.

2. Paragraph 1 does not apply if:
   (*a*) the situation of distress is due, either alone or in combination with other factors, to the
         conduct of the State invoking it; or
   (*b*) the act in question is likely to create a comparable or greater peril.

Article 25   Necessity

1. Necessity may not be invoked by a State as a ground for precluding the wrongfulness of an act
   not in conformity with an international obligation of that State unless the act:
   (*a*) is the only way for the State to safeguard an essential interest against a grave and
         imminent peril; and
   (*b*) does not seriously impair an essential interest of the State or States towards which the
         obligation exists, or of the international community as a whole.

2. In any case, necessity may not be invoked by a State as a ground for precluding wrongfulness if:
   (*a*) the international obligation in question excludes the possibility of invoking necessity; or
   (*b*) the State has contributed to the situation of necessity.

Article 26   Compliance with peremptory norms

Nothing in this chapter precludes the wrongfulness of any act of a State which is not in
conformity with an obligation arising under a peremptory norm of general international law.

Article 27   Consequences of invoking a circumstance precluding wrongfulness

The invocation of a circumstance precluding wrongfulness in accordance with this chapter is
without prejudice to:

(*a*) compliance with the obligation in question, if and to the extent that the circumstance
      precluding wrongfulness no longer exists;

(*b*) the question of compensation for any material loss caused by the act in question.

PART TWO   CONTENT OF THE INTERNATIONAL RESPONSIBILITY OF A STATE

CHAPTER I   GENERAL PRINCIPLES

Article 28   Legal consequences of an internationally wrongful act

The international responsibility of a State which is entailed by an internationally wrongful act in
accordance with the provisions of part one involves legal consequences as set out in this part.

Article 29   Continued duty of performance

The legal consequences of an internationally wrongful act under this part do not affect the
continued duty of the responsible State to perform the obligation breached.

Article 30   Cessation and non-repetition

The State responsible for the internationally wrongful act is under an obligation:

(*a*) to cease that act, if it is continuing;

(*b*) to offer appropriate assurances and guarantees of non-repetition, if circumstances so require.

Article 31   Reparation

1. The responsible State is under an obligation to make full reparation for the injury caused by
   the internationally wrongful act.

2. Injury includes any damage, whether material or moral, caused by the internationally wrongful act of a State.

Article 32   Irrelevance of internal law

The responsible State may not rely on the provisions of its internal law as justification for failure to comply with its obligations under this part.

Article 33   Scope of international obligations set out in this part

1. The obligations of the responsible State set out in this part may be owed to another State, to several States, or to the international community as a whole, depending in particular on the character and content of the international obligation and on the circumstances of the breach.

2. This part is without prejudice to any right, arising from the international responsibility of a State, which may accrue directly to any person or entity other than a State.

CHAPTER II   REPARATION FOR INJURY

Article 34   Forms of reparation

Full reparation for the injury caused by the internationally wrongful act shall take the form of restitution, compensation and satisfaction, either singly or in combination, in accordance with the provisions of this chapter.

Article 35   Restitution

A State responsible for an internationally wrongful act is under an obligation to make restitution, that is, to re-establish the situation which existed before the wrongful act was committed, provided and to the extent that restitution:

(a) is not materially impossible;

(b) does not involve a burden out of all proportion to the benefit deriving from restitution instead of compensation.

Article 36   Compensation

1. The State responsible for an internationally wrongful act is under an obligation to compensate for the damage caused thereby, insofar as such damage is not made good by restitution.

2. The compensation shall cover any financially assessable damage including loss of profits insofar as it is established.

Article 37   Satisfaction

1. The State responsible for an internationally wrongful act is under an obligation to give satisfaction for the injury caused by that act insofar as it cannot be made good by restitution or compensation.

2. Satisfaction may consist in an acknowledgement of the breach, an expression of regret, a formal apology or another appropriate modality.

3. Satisfaction shall not be out of proportion to the injury and may not take a form humiliating to the responsible State.

Article 38   Interest

1. Interest on any principal sum due under this chapter shall be payable when necessary in order to ensure full reparation. The interest rate and mode of calculation shall be set so as to achieve that result.

2. Interest runs from the date when the principal sum should have been paid until the date the obligation to pay is fulfilled.

Article 39   Contribution to the injury

In the determination of reparation, account shall be taken of the contribution to the injury by wilful or negligent action or omission of the injured State or any person or entity in relation to whom reparation is sought.

CHAPTER III SERIOUS BREACHES OF OBLIGATIONS UNDER PEREMPTORY NORMS OF GENERAL INTERNATIONAL LAW

Article 40 Application of this chapter

1. This chapter applies to the international responsibility which is entailed by a serious breach by a State of an obligation arising under a peremptory norm of general international law.

2. A breach of such an obligation is serious if it involves a gross or systematic failure by the responsible State to fulfil the obligation.

Article 41 Particular consequences of a serious breach of an obligation under this chapter

1. States shall cooperate to bring to an end through lawful means any serious breach within the meaning of article 40.

2. No State shall recognize as lawful a situation created by a serious breach within the meaning of article 40, nor render aid or assistance in maintaining that situation.

3. This article is without prejudice to the other consequences referred to in this part and to such further consequences that a breach to which this chapter applies may entail under international law.

PART THREE THE IMPLEMENTATION OF THE INTERNATIONAL RESPONSIBILITY OF A STATE

CHAPTER I INVOCATION OF THE RESPONSIBILITY OF A STATE

Article 42 Invocation of responsibility by an injured State

A State is entitled as an injured State to invoke the responsibility of another State if the obligation breached is owed to:

(*a*) that State individually; or

(*b*) a group of States including that State, or the international community as a whole, and the breach of the obligation:
  (i) specially affects that State; or
  (ii) is of such a character as radically to change the position of all the other States to which the obligation is owed with respect to the further performance of the obligation.

Article 43 Notice of claim by an injured State

1. An injured State which invokes the responsibility of another State shall give notice of its claim to that State.

2. The injured State may specify in particular:
  (*a*) the conduct that the responsible State should take in order to cease the wrongful act, if it is continuing;
  (*b*) what form reparation should take in accordance with the provisions of part two.

Article 44 Admissibility of claims

The responsibility of a State may not be invoked if:

(*a*) the claim is not brought in accordance with any applicable rule relating to the nationality of claims;

(*b*) the claim is one to which the rule of exhaustion of local remedies applies and any available and effective local remedy has not been exhausted.

Article 45 Loss of the right to invoke responsibility

The responsibility of a State may not be invoked if:

(*a*) the injured State has validly waived the claim;

(*b*) the injured State is to be considered as having, by reason of its conduct, validly acquiesced in the lapse of the claim.

Article 46   Plurality of injured States

Where several States are injured by the same internationally wrongful act, each injured State may separately invoke the responsibility of the State which has committed the internationally wrongful act.

Article 47   Plurality of responsible States

1. Where several States are responsible for the same internationally wrongful act, the responsibility of each State may be invoked in relation to that act.

2. Paragraph 1:
   (*a*) does not permit any injured State to recover, by way of compensation, more than the damage it has suffered;
   (*b*) is without prejudice to any right of recourse against the other responsible States.

Article 48   Invocation of responsibility by a State other than an injured State

1. Any State other than an injured State is entitled to invoke the responsibility of another State in accordance with paragraph 2 if:
   (*a*) the obligation breached is owed to a group of States including that State, and is established for the protection of a collective interest of the group; or
   (*b*) the obligation breached is owed to the international community as a whole.

2. Any State entitled to invoke responsibility under paragraph 1 may claim from the responsible State:
   (*a*) cessation of the internationally wrongful act, and assurances and guarantees of non-repetition in accordance with article 30; and
   (*b*) performance of the obligation of reparation in accordance with the preceding articles, in the interest of the injured State or of the beneficiaries of the obligation breached.

3. The requirements for the invocation of responsibility by an injured State under articles 43, 44 and 45 apply to an invocation of responsibility by a State entitled to do so under paragraph 1.

CHAPTER II   COUNTERMEASURES

Article 49   Object and limits of countermeasures

1. An injured State may only take countermeasures against a State which is responsible for an internationally wrongful act in order to induce that State to comply with its obligations under part two.

2. Countermeasures are limited to the non-performance for the time being of international obligations of the State taking the measures towards the responsible State.

3. Countermeasures shall, as far as possible, be taken in such a way as to permit the resumption of performance of the obligations in question.

Article 50   Obligations not affected by countermeasures

1. Countermeasures shall not affect:
   (*a*) the obligation to refrain from the threat or use of force as embodied in the Charter of the United Nations;
   (*b*) obligations for the protection of fundamental human rights;
   (*c*) obligations of a humanitarian character prohibiting reprisals;
   (*d*) other obligations under peremptory norms of general international law.

2. A State taking countermeasures is not relieved from fulfilling its obligations:
   (*a*) under any dispute settlement procedure applicable between it and the responsible State;
   (*b*) to respect the inviolability of diplomatic or consular agents, premises, archives and documents.

Article 51   Proportionality

Countermeasures must be commensurate with the injury suffered, taking into account the gravity of the internationally wrongful act and the rights in question.

Article 52   Conditions relating to resort to countermeasures

1. Before taking countermeasures, an injured State shall:
   (*a*) call on the responsible State, in accordance with article 43, to fulfil its obligations under part two;
   (*b*) notify the responsible State of any decision to take countermeasures and offer to negotiate with that State.
2. Notwithstanding paragraph 1 (*b*), the injured State may take such urgent countermeasures as are necessary to preserve its rights.
3. Countermeasures may not be taken, and if already taken must be suspended without undue delay if:
   (*a*) the internationally wrongful act has ceased; and
   (*b*) the dispute is pending before a court or tribunal which has the authority to make decisions binding on the parties.
4. Paragraph 3 does not apply if the responsible State fails to implement the dispute settlement procedures in good faith.

Article 53   Termination of countermeasures

Countermeasures shall be terminated as soon as the responsible State has complied with its obligations under part two in relation to the internationally wrongful act.

Article 54   Measures taken by States other than an injured State

This chapter does not prejudice the right of any State, entitled under article 48, paragraph 1 to invoke the responsibility of another State, to take lawful measures against that State to ensure cessation of the breach and reparation in the interest of the injured State or of the beneficiaries of the obligation breached.

PART FOUR   GENERAL PROVISIONS

Article 55   Lex specialis

These articles do not apply where and to the extent that the conditions for the existence of an internationally wrongful act or the content or implementation of the international responsibility of a State are governed by special rules of international law.

Article 56   Questions of State responsibility not regulated by these articles

The applicable rules of international law continue to govern questions concerning the responsibility of a State for an internationally wrongful act to the extent that they are not regulated by these articles.

Article 57   Responsibility of an international organization

These articles are without prejudice to any question of the responsibility under international law of an international organization, or of any State for the conduct of an international organization.

Article 58   Individual responsibility

These articles are without prejudice to any question of the individual responsibility under international law of any person acting on behalf of a State.

Article 59   Charter of the United Nations

These articles are without prejudice to the Charter of the United Nations.

I-4

ILC Draft Articles on Diplomatic Protection

Date   8 August 2006
Source Official Records of the General Assembly, Sixty-first Session, Supplement No 10 (A/61/10)
Link   <http://untreaty.un.org/ilc/texts/instruments/english/draft%20articles/9_8_2006.pdf>

PART ONE   GENERAL PROVISIONS

Article 1   Definition and scope

For the purposes of the present draft articles, diplomatic protection consists of the invocation by a State, through diplomatic action or other means of peaceful settlement, of the responsibility of another State for an injury caused by an internationally wrongful act of that State to a natural or legal person that is a national of the former State with a view to the implementation of such responsibility.

Article 2   Right to exercise diplomatic protection

A State has the right to exercise diplomatic protection in accordance with the present draft articles.

PART TWO   NATIONALITY

CHAPTER I   GENERAL PRINCIPLES

Article 3   Protection by the State of nationality

1. The State entitled to exercise diplomatic protection is the State of nationality.

2. Notwithstanding paragraph 1, diplomatic protection may be exercised by a State in respect of a person that is not its national in accordance with draft article 8.

CHAPTER II   NATURAL PERSONS

Article 4   State of nationality of a natural person

For the purposes of the diplomatic protection of a natural person, a State of nationality means a State whose nationality that person has acquired, in accordance with the law of that State, by birth, descent, naturalization, succession of States or in any other manner, not inconsistent with international law.

Article 5   Continuous nationality of a natural person

1. A State is entitled to exercise diplomatic protection in respect of a person who was a national of that State continuously from the date of injury to the date of the official presentation of the claim. Continuity is presumed if that nationality existed at both these dates.

2. Notwithstanding paragraph 1, a State may exercise diplomatic protection in respect of a person who is its national at the date of the official presentation of the claim but was not a national at the date of injury, provided that the person had the nationality of a predecessor State or lost his or her previous nationality and acquired, for a reason unrelated to the bringing

of the claim, the nationality of the former State in a manner not inconsistent with international law.

3. Diplomatic protection shall not be exercised by the present State of nationality in respect of a person against a former State of nationality of that person for an injury caused when that person was a national of the former State of nationality and not of the present State of nationality.

4. A State is no longer entitled to exercise diplomatic protection in respect of a person who acquires the nationality of the State against which the claim is brought after the date of the official presentation of the claim.

Article 6   Multiple nationality and claim against a third State

1. Any State of which a dual or multiple national is a national may exercise diplomatic protection in respect of that national against a State of which that person is not a national.

2. Two or more States of nationality may jointly exercise diplomatic protection in respect of a dual or multiple national.

Article 7   Multiple nationality and claim against a State of nationality

A State of nationality may not exercise diplomatic protection in respect of a person against a State of which that person is also a national unless the nationality of the former State is predominant, both at the date of injury and at the date of the official presentation of the claim.

Article 8   Stateless persons and refugees

1. A State may exercise diplomatic protection in respect of a stateless person who, at the date of injury and at the date of the official presentation of the claim, is lawfully and habitually resident in that State.

2. A State may exercise diplomatic protection in respect of a person who is recognized as a refugee by that State, in accordance with internationally accepted standards, when that person, at the date of injury and at the date of the official presentation of the claim, is lawfully and habitually resident in that State.

3. Paragraph 2 does not apply in respect of an injury caused by an internationally wrongful act of the State of nationality of the refugee.

CHAPTER III   LEGAL PERSONS

Article 9   State of nationality of a corporation

For the purposes of the diplomatic protection of a corporation, the State of nationality means the State under whose law the corporation was incorporated. However, when the corporation is controlled by nationals of another State or States and has no substantial business activities in the State of incorporation, and the seat of management and the financial control of the corporation are both located in another State, that State shall be regarded as the State of nationality.

Article 10   Continuous nationality of a corporation

1. A State is entitled to exercise diplomatic protection in respect of a corporation that was a national of that State, or its predecessor State, continuously from the date of injury to the date of the official presentation of the claim. Continuity is presumed if that nationality existed at both these dates.

2. A State is no longer entitled to exercise diplomatic protection in respect of a corporation that acquires the nationality of the State against which the claim is brought after the presentation of the claim.

3. Notwithstanding paragraph 1, a State continues to be entitled to exercise diplomatic protection in respect of a corporation which was its national at the date of injury and which, as the result of the injury, has ceased to exist according to the law of the State of incorporation.

Article 11   Protection of shareholders

A State of nationality of shareholders in a corporation shall not be entitled to exercise diplomatic protection in respect of such shareholders in the case of an injury to the corporation unless:

(*a*) The corporation has ceased to exist according to the law of the State of incorporation for a reason unrelated to the injury; or

(*b*) The corporation had, at the date of injury, the nationality of the State alleged to be responsible for causing the injury, and incorporation in that State was required by it as a precondition for doing business there.

Article 12   Direct injury to shareholders

To the extent that an internationally wrongful act of a State causes direct injury to the rights of shareholders as such, as distinct from those of the corporation itself, the State of nationality of any such shareholders is entitled to exercise diplomatic protection in respect of its nationals.

Article 13   Other legal persons

The principles contained in this chapter shall be applicable, as appropriate, to the diplomatic protection of legal persons other than corporations.

PART THREE   LOCAL REMEDIES

Article 14   Exhaustion of local remedies

1. A State may not present an international claim in respect of an injury to a national or other person referred to in draft article 8 before the injured person has, subject to draft article 15, exhausted all local remedies.

2. "Local remedies" means legal remedies which are open to an injured person before the judicial or administrative courts or bodies, whether ordinary or special, of the State alleged to be responsible for causing the injury.

3. Local remedies shall be exhausted where an international claim, or request for a declaratory judgement related to the claim, is brought preponderantly on the basis of an injury to a national or other person referred to in draft article 8.

Article 15   Exceptions to the local remedies rule

Local remedies do not need to be exhausted where:

(*a*) There are no reasonably available local remedies to provide effective redress, or the local remedies provide no reasonable possibility of such redress;

(*b*) There is undue delay in the remedial process which is attributable to the State alleged to be responsible;

(*c*) There was no relevant connection between the injured person and the State alleged to be responsible at the date of injury;

(*d*) The injured person is manifestly precluded from pursuing local remedies; or

(*e*) The State alleged to be responsible has waived the requirement that local remedies be exhausted.

PART FOUR   MISCELLANEOUS PROVISIONS

Article 16   Actions or procedures other than diplomatic protection

The rights of States, natural persons, legal persons or other entities to resort under international law to actions or procedures other than diplomatic protection to secure redress for injury suffered as a result of an internationally wrongful act, are not affected by the present draft articles.

Article 17   Special rules of international law

The present draft articles do not apply to the extent that they are inconsistent with special rules of international law, such as treaty provisions for the protection of investments.

Article 18   Protection of ships' crews

The right of the State of nationality of the members of the crew of a ship to exercise diplomatic protection is not affected by the right of the State of nationality of a ship to seek redress on behalf of such crew members, irrespective of their nationality, when they have been injured in connection with an injury to the vessel resulting from an internationally wrongful act.

Article 19   Recommended practice

A State entitled to exercise diplomatic protection according to the present draft articles, should:

(*a*) Give due consideration to the possibility of exercising diplomatic protection, especially when a significant injury has occurred;

(*b*) Take into account, wherever feasible, the views of injured persons with regard to resort to diplomatic protection and the reparation to be sought; and

(*c*) Transfer to the injured person any compensation obtained for the injury from the responsible State subject to any reasonable deductions.

GA Res. 1803: Permanent Sovereignty over Natural Resources

Date 14 December 1962
Source UN Doc A/RES/1803(XVII)
Link <http://daccess-dds-ny.un.org/doc/RESOLUTION/GEN/NR0/193/11/PDF/NR019311.pdf>

The General Assembly,

Recalling its resolutions 523 (VI) of 12 January 1952 and 626 (VII) of 21 December 1952,

Bearing in mind its resolution 1314 (XIII) of 12 December 1958, by which it established the Commission on Permanent Sovereignty over Natural Resources and instructed it to conduct a full survey of the status of permanent sovereignty over natural wealth and resources as a basic constituent of the right to self-determination, with recommendations, where necessary, for its strengthening, and decided further that, in the conduct of the full survey of the status of the permanent sovereignty of peoples and nations over their natural wealth and resources, due regard should be paid to the rights and duties of States under international law and to the importance of encouraging international co-operation in the economic development of developing countries,

Bearing in mind its resolution 1515 (XV) of 15 December 1960, in which it recommended that the sovereign right of every State to dispose of its wealth and its natural resources should be respected,

Considering that any measure in this respect must be based on the recognition of the inalienable right of all States freely to dispose of their natural wealth and resources in accordance with their national interests, and on respect for the economic independence of States,

Considering that nothing in paragraph 4 below in any way prejudices the position of any Member State on any aspect of the question of the rights and obligations of successor States and Governments in respect of property acquired before the accession to complete sovereignty of countries formerly under colonial rule,

Noting that the subject of succession of States and Governments is being examined as a matter of priority by the International Law Commission,

Considering that it is desirable to promote international co-operation for the economic development of developing countries, and that economic and financial agreements between the developed and the developing countries must be based on the principles of equality and of the right of peoples and nations to self-determination,

Considering that the provision of economic and technical assistance, loans and increased foreign investment must not be subject to conditions which conflict with the interests of the recipient State,

Considering the benefits to be derived from exchanges of technical and scientific information likely to promote the development and use of such resources and wealth, and the important part which the United Nations and other international organizations are called upon to play in that connexion,

Attaching particular importance to the question of promoting the economic development of developing countries and securing their economic independence,

Noting that the creation and strengthening of the inalienable sovereignty of States over their natural wealth and resources reinforces their economic independence,

Desiring that there should be further consideration by the United Nations of the subject of permanent sovereignty over natural resources in the spirit of international co-operation in the field of economic development, particularly that of the developing countries,

Declares that:

1. The right of peoples and nations to permanent sovereignty over their natural wealth and resources must be exercised in the interest of their national development and of the well-being of the people of the State concerned.

2. The exploration, development and disposition of such resources, as well as the import of the foreign capital required for these purposes, should be in conformity with the rules and conditions which the peoples and nations freely consider to be necessary or desirable with regard to the authorization, restriction or prohibition of such activities.

3. In cases where authorization is granted, the capital imported and the earnings on that capital shall be governed by the terms thereof, by the national legislation in force, and by international law. The profits derived must be shared in the proportions freely agreed upon, in each case, between the investors and the recipient State, due care being taken to ensure that there is no impairment, for any reason, of that State's sovereignty over its natural wealth and resources.

4. Nationalization, expropriation or requisitioning shall be based on grounds or reasons of public utility, security or the national interest which are recognized as overriding purely individual or private interests, both domestic and foreign. In such cases the owner shall be paid appropriate compensation, in accordance with the rules in force in the State taking such measures in the exercise of its sovereignty and in accordance with international law. In any case where the question of compensation gives rise to a controversy, the national jurisdiction of the State taking such measures shall be exhausted. However, upon agreement by sovereign States and other parties concerned, settlement of the dispute should be made through arbitration or international adjudication.

5. The free and beneficial exercise of the sovereignty of peoples and nations over their natural resources must be furthered by the mutual respect of States based on their sovereign equality.

6. International co-operation for the economic development of developing countries, whether in the form of public or private capital investments, exchange of goods and services, technical assistance, or exchange of scientific information, shall be such as to further their independent national development and shall be based upon respect for their sovereignty over their natural wealth and resources.

7. Violation of the rights of peoples and nations to sovereignty over their natural wealth and resources is contrary to the spirit and principles of the Charter of the United Nations and hinders the development of international co-operation and the maintenance of peace.

8. Foreign investment agreements freely entered into by or between sovereign States shall be observed in good faith; States and international organizations shall strictly and conscientiously respect the sovereignty of peoples and nations over their natural wealth and resources in accordance with the Charter and the principles set forth in the present resolution.

I-6

GA Res. 3201: Declaration on the Establishment of a New International Economic Order

Date 1 May 1974
Source UN Doc A/RES/3201(S-VI)
Link <http://daccess-dds-ny.un.org/doc/RESOLUTION/GEN/NR0/071/94/IMG/NR007194.pdf>

The General Assembly

Adopts the following Declaration:

DECLARATION ON THE ESTABLISHMENT OF A NEW INTERNATIONAL ECONOMIC ORDER

We, the Members of the United Nations,

Having convened a special session of the General Assembly to study for the first time the problems of raw materials and development, devoted to the consideration of the most important economic problems facing the world community,

Bearing in mind the spirit, purposes and principles of the Charter of the United Nations to promote the economic advancement and social progress of all peoples,

Solemnly proclaim our united determination to work urgently for the Establishment of a New International Economic Order based on equity, sovereign equality, interdependence, common interest and co-operation among all States, irrespective of their economic and social systems which shall correct inequalities and redress existing injustices, make it possible to eliminate the widening gap between the developed and the developing countries and ensure steadily accelerating economic and social development and peace and justice for present and future generations, and, to that end, declare:

1. The greatest and most significant achievement during the last decades has been the independence from colonial and alien domination of a large number of peoples and nations which has enabled them to become members of the community of free peoples. Technological progress has also been made in all spheres of economic activities in the last three decades, thus providing a solid potential for improving the well-being of all peoples. However, the remaining vestiges of alien and colonial domination, foreign occupation, racial discrimination, apartheid and neo-colonialism in all its forms continue to be among the greatest obstacles to the full emancipation and progress of the developing countries and all the peoples involved. The benefits of technological progress are not shared equitably by all members of the international community. The developing countries, which constitute 70 per cent of the world's population, account for only 30 per cent of the world's income. It has proved impossible to achieve an even and balanced development of the international community under the existing international economic order. The gap between the developed and the developing countries continues to widen in a system which was established at a time when most of the developing countries did not even exist as independent States and which perpetuates inequality.

2. The present international economic order is in direct conflict with current developments in international political and economic relations. Since 1970 the world economy has experienced

a series of grave crises which have had severe repercussions, especially on the developing countries because of their generally greater vulnerability to external economic impulses. The developing world has become a powerful factor that makes its influence felt in all fields of international activity. These irreversible changes in the relationship of forces in the world necessitate the active, full and equal participation of the developing countries in the formulation and application of all decisions that concern the international community.

3. All these changes have thrust into prominence the reality of interdependence of all the members of the world community. Current events have brought into sharp focus the realization that the interests of the developed countries and those of the developing countries can no longer be isolated from each other, that there is a close interrelationship between the prosperity of the developed countries and the growth and development of the developing countries, and that the prosperity of the international community as a whole depends upon the prosperity of its constituent parts. International co-operation for development is the shared goal and common duty of all countries. Thus the political, economic and social well-being of present and future generations depends more than ever on co-operation between all the members of the international community on the basis of sovereign equality and the removal of the disequilibrium that exists between them.

4. The new international economic order should be founded on full respect for the following principles:

(a) Sovereign equality of States, self-determination of all peoples, inadmissibility of the acquisition of territories by force, territorial integrity and non-interference in the internal affairs of other States;

(b) The broadest co-operation of all the States members of the international community, based on equity, whereby the prevailing disparities in the world may be banished and prosperity secured for all;

(c) Full and effective participation on the basis of equality of all countries in the solving of world economic problems in the common interest of all countries, bearing in mind the necessity to ensure the accelerated development of all the developing countries, while devoting particular attention to the adoption of special measures in favour of the least developed land-locked and island developing countries as well as those developing countries most seriously affected by economic crises and natural calamities, without losing sight of the interests of other developing countries;

(d) The right of every country to adopt the economic and social system that it deems the most appropriate for its own development and not to be subjected to discrimination of any kind as a result;

(e) Full permanent sovereignty of every State over its natural resources and all economic activities. In order to safeguard these resources, each State is entitled to exercise effective control over them and their exploitation with means suitable to its own situation, including the right to nationalization or transfer of ownership to its nationals, this right being an expression of the full permanent sovereignty of the State. No State may be subjected to economic, political or any other type of coercion to prevent the free and full exercise of this inalienable right;

(f) The right of all States, territories and peoples under foreign occupation, alien and colonial domination or *apartheid* to restitution and full compensation for the exploitation and depletion of, and damages to, the natural resources and all other resources of those States, territories and peoples;

(g) Regulation and supervision of the activities of transnational corporations by taking measures in the interest of the national economies of the countries where such transnational corporations operate on the basis of the full sovereignty of those countries;

(*h*) The right of the developing countries and the peoples of territories under colonial and racial domination and foreign occupation to achieve their liberation and to regain effective control over their natural resources and economic activities;

(*i*) The extending of assistance to developing countries, peoples and territories which are under colonial and alien domination, foreign occupation, racial discrimination or *apartheid* or are subjected to economic, political or any other type of coercive measures to obtain from them the subordination of the exercise of their sovereign rights and to secure from them advantages of any kind, and to neo-colonialism in all its forms, and which have established or are endeavouring to establish effective control over their natural resources and economic activities that have been or are still under foreign control;

(*j*) Just and equitable relationship between the prices of raw materials, primary commodities, manufactured and semi-manufactured goods exported by developing countries and the prices of raw materials, primary commodities, manufactures, capital goods and equipment imported by them with the aim of bringing about sustained improvement in their unsatisfactory terms of trade and the expansion of the world economy;

(*k*) Extension of active assistance to developing countries by the whole international community, free of any political or military conditions;

(*l*) Ensuring that one of the main aims of the reformed international monetary system shall be the promotion of the development of the developing countries and the adequate flow of real resources to them;

(*m*) Improving the competitiveness of natural materials facing competition from synthetic substitutes;

(*n*) Preferential and non-reciprocal treatment for developing countries, wherever feasible, in all fields of international economic co-operation whenever possible;

(*o*) Securing favourable conditions for the transfer of financial resources to developing countries.

(*p*) Giving to the developing countries access to the achievements of modern science and technology, and promoting the transfer of technology and the creation of indigenous technology for the benefit of the developing countries in forms and in accordance with procedures which are suited to their economies;

(*q*) The need for all States to put an end to the waste of natural resources, including food products;

(*r*) The need for developing countries to concentrate all their resources for the cause of development;

(*s*) The strengthening, through individual and collective actions, of mutual economic, trade, financial and technical co-operation among the developing countries, mainly on a preferential basis;

(*t*) Facilitating the role which producers' associations may play within the framework of international co-operation and, in pursuance of their aims, *inter alia* assisting in the promotion of sustained growth of the world economy and accelerating the development of developing countries.

5. The unanimous adoption of the International Development Strategy for the Second United Nations Development Decade (Resolution 2626 (XXV)) was an important step in the promotion of international economic co-operation on a just and equitable basis. The accelerated implementation of obligations and commitments assumed by the international community within the framework of the Strategy, particularly those concerning imperative development needs of developing countries, would contribute significantly to the fulfilment of the aims and objectives of the present Declaration.

6. The United Nations as a universal organization should be capable of dealing with problems of international economic co-operation in a comprehensive manner and ensuring equally the

interests of all countries. It must have an even greater role in the establishment of a new international economic order. The Charter of Economic Rights and Duties of States, for the preparation of which the present Declaration will provide an additional source of inspiration, will constitute a significant contribution in this respect. All the States Members of the United Nations are therefore called upon to exert maximum efforts with a view to securing the implementation of the present Declaration, which is one of the principal guarantees for the creation of better conditions for all peoples to reach a life worthy of human dignity.

7. The present Declaration on the Establishment of a New International Economic Order shall be one of the most important bases of economic relations between all peoples and all nations.

GA Res. 3281: Charter of Economic Rights and Duties of States (1974)

Date   12 December 1974
Source   UN Doc A/RES/3281(XXIX)
Link   <http://daccess-dds-ny.un.org/doc/RESOLUTION/GEN/NR0/738/83/IMG/NR073883.pdf>

The General Assembly,

Recalling that the United Nations Conference on Trade and Development, in its resolution 45 (III) of 18 May 1972, stressed the urgency to establish generally accepted norms to govern international economic relations systematically and recognized that it is not feasible to establish a just order and a stable world as long as a charter to protect the rights of all countries, and in particular the developing States, is not formulated,

Recalling further that in the same resolution it was decided to establish a Working Group of governmental representatives to draw up a draft Charter of Economic Rights and Duties of States, which the General Assembly, in its resolution 3037 (XXVII) of 19 December 1972, decided should be composed of forty Member States,

Noting that, in its resolution 3082 (XXVIII) of 6 December 1973, it reaffirmed its conviction of the urgent need to establish or improve norms of universal application for the development of international economic relations on a just and equitable basis and urged the Working Group on the Charter of Economic Rights and Duties of States to complete, as the first step in the codification and development of the matter, the elaboration of a final draft Charter of Economic Rights and Duties of States, to be considered and approved by the General Assembly at its twenty-ninth session,

Bearing in mind the spirit and terms of its resolutions 3201 (S-VI) and 3202 (S-VI) of 1 May 1974, containing, respectively, the Declaration and the Programme of Action on the Establishment of a New International Economic Order, which underlined the vital importance of the Charter to be adopted by the General Assembly at its twenty-ninth session and stressed the fact that the Charter shall constitute an effective instrument towards the establishment of a new system of international economic relations based on equity, sovereign equality and interdependence of the interests of developed and developing countries,

Having examined the report of the Working Group on the Charter of Economic Rights and Duties of States on its fourth session, transmitted to the Generally Assembly by the Trade and Development Board at its fourteenth session,

Expressing its appreciation to the Working Group on the Charter of Economic Rights and Duties of States which, as a result of the task performed in its four sessions held between February 1973 and June 1974, assembled the elements required for the completion and adoption of the Charter of Economic Rights and Duties at the twenty-ninth session of the General Assembly, as previously recommended,

Adopts and solemnly proclaims the following Charter:

CHARTER OF ECONOMIC RIGHTS AND DUTIES OF STATES

PREAMBLE

The General Assembly,

Reaffirming the fundamental purposes of the United Nations, in particular the maintenance of international peace and security, the development of friendly relations among nations and the achievement of international co-operation in solving international problems in the economic and social fields,

Affirming the need for strengthening international co-operation for development,

Reaffirming further the need for strengthening international co-operation for development,

Declaring that it is a fundamental purpose of the present Charter to promote the establishment of the new international economic order, based on equality, sovereign equality, interdependence, common interest and co-operation among all States, irrespective of their economic and social systems,

Desirous of contributing to the criterion of conditions for:

(*a*) The attainment of wider prosperity among all countries and of higher standards of living for all peoples,

(*b*) The promotion by the entire international community of the economic and social progress of all countries, especially developing countries,

(*c*) The encouragement of co-operation, on the basis of mutual advantage and equitable benefits for all peace-loving States which are willing to carry out the provisions of the present Charter, in the economic, trade, scientific and technical fields, regardless of political, economic or social systems,

(*d*) The overcoming of main obstacles in the way of economic development of the developing countries,

(*e*) The acceleration of the economic growth of developing countries with a view to bridging the economic gap between developing and developed countries,

(*f*) The protection, preservation and enhancement of the environment,

Mindful of the need to establish and maintain a just and equitable economic and social order through:

(*a*) The achievement of more rational and equitable international economic relations and the encouragement of structural changes in the world economy,

(*b*) The creation of conditions which permit the further expansion of trade and intensification of economic co-operation among all nations,

(*c*) The strengthening of the economic independence of developing countries,

(*d*) The establishment and promotion of international economic relations, taking into account the agreed differences in development of the developing countries and their specific needs,

Determined to promote collective economic security for development, in particular of the developing countries, with strict respect for the sovereign equality of each State and through the co-operation of the entire international community,

Considering that genuine co-operation among States, based on joint consideration of and concerted action regarding international economic problems, is essential for fulfilling the international community's common desire to achieve a just and rational development of all parts of the world,

Stressing the importance of ensuring appropriate conditions for the conduct of normal economic relations among all States, irrespective of differences in social and economic systems, and for the full respect of the rights of all peoples, as well as strengthening instruments of international economic co-operation as a means for the consolidation of peace for the benefit of all,

Convinced of the need to develop a system of international economic relations on the basis of sovereign equality, mutual and equitable benefit and the close interrelationship of the interests of all States,

Reiterating that the responsibility for the development of every country rests primarily upon itself but that concomitant and effective international co-operation is an essential factor for the full achievement of its own development goals,

Firmly convinced of the urgent need to evolve a substantially improved system of international economic relations,

Solemnly adopts the present Charter of Economic Rights and Duties of States.

CHAPTER I   FUNDAMENTALS OF INTERNATIONAL ECONOMIC RELATIONS

Economic as well as political and other relations among States shall be governed, *inter alia*, by the following principles:

(*a*) Sovereignty, territorial integrity and political independence of States;

(*b*) Sovereign equality of all States;

(*c*) Non-aggression;

(*d*) Non-intervention;

(*e*) Mutual and equitable benefit;

(*f*) Peaceful coexistence;

(*g*) Equal rights and self-determination of peoples;

(*h*) Peaceful settlement of disputes;

(*i*) Remedying of injustices which have been brought about by force and which deprive a nation of the natural means necessary for its normal development;

(*j*) Fulfilment in good faith of international obligations;

(*k*) Respect for human rights and international obligations;

(*l*) No attempt to seek hegemony and spheres of influence;

(*m*) Promotion of international social justice;

(*n*) International co-operation for development;

(*o*) Free access to and from the sea by land-locked countries within the framework of the above principles.

CHAPTER II   ECONOMIC RIGHTS AND DUTIES OF STATES

Article 1

Every State has the sovereign and inalienable right to choose its economic system as well as its political, social and cultural systems in accordance with the will of its people, without outside interference, coercion or threat in any form whatsoever.

Article 2

1. Every State has and shall freely exercise full permanent sovereignty, including possession, use and disposal, over all its wealth, natural resources and economic activities.

2. Each State has the right:

    (*a*) To regulate and exercise authority over foreign investment within its national jurisdiction in accordance with its laws and regulations and in conformity with its national objectives and priorities. No State shall be compelled to grant preferential treatment to foreign investment;

(*b*) To regulate and supervise the activities of transnational corporations within its national jurisdiction and take measures to ensure that such activities comply with its laws, rules and regulations and conform with its economic and social policies. Transnational corporations shall not intervene in the internal affairs of a host State. Every State should, with full regard for its sovereign rights, co-operate with other States in the exercise of the right set forth in this subparagraph;

(*c*) To nationalize, expropriate or transfer ownership of foreign property, in which case appropriate compensation should be paid by the State adopting such measures, taking into account its relevant laws and regulations and all circumstances that the State considers pertinent. In any case where the question of compensation gives rise to a controversy, it shall be settled under the domestic law of the nationalizing State and by its tribunals, unless it is freely and mutually agreed by all States concerned that other peaceful means be sought on the basis of the sovereign equality of States and in accordance with the principle of free choice of means.

Article 3

In the exploitation of natural resources shared by two or more countries, each State must co-operate on the basis of a system of information and prior consultations in order to achieve optimum use of such resources without causing damage to the legitimate interest of others.

Article 4

Every State has the right to engage in international trade and other forms of economic co-operation irrespective of any differences in political, economic and social systems. No State shall be subjected to discrimination of any kind based solely on such differences. In the pursuit of international trade and other forms of economic co-operation, every State is free to choose the forms of organization of its foreign economic relations and to enter into bilateral and multilateral arrangements consistent with its international obligations and with the needs of international economic co-operation.

Article 5

All States have the right to associate in organizations of primary commodity producers in order to develop their national economies, to achieve stable financing for their development and, in pursuance of their aims, to assist in the promotion of sustained growth of the world economy. In particular accelerating the development of developing countries. Correspondingly, all States have the duty to respect that right by refraining from applying economic and political measures that would limit it.

Article 6

It is the duty of States to contribute to the development of international trade of goods, particularly by means of arrangements and by the conclusion of long-term multilateral commodity agreements, where appropriate, and taking into account the interest of producers and consumers. All States share the responsibility to promote the regular flow and access of all commercial goods traded at stable, remunerative and equitable prices, thus contributing to the equitable development of the world economy, taking into account, in particular, the interests of developing countries.

Article 7

Every State has the primary responsibility to promote the economic, social and cultural development of its people. To this end, each State has the right and the responsibility to choose its means and goals of development, fully to mobilize and use its resources, to implement progressive economic and social reforms and to ensure the full participation of its people in the process and benefits of development. All States have the duty, individually and collectively, to co-operate in eliminating obstacles that hinder such mobilization and use.

Article 8

States should co-operate in facilitating more rational and equitable international economic relations and in encouraging structural changes in the context of a balanced world economy in harmony with the needs and interests of all countries, especially developing countries, and should take appropriate measures to this end.

Article 9

All States have the responsibility to co-operate in the economic, social, cultural, scientific and technological fields for the promotion of economic and social progress throughout the world, especially that of the developing countries.

Article 10

All States are juridically equal and, as equal members of the international community, have the right to participate fully and effectively in the international decision-making process in the solution of world economic, financial and monetary problems, *inter alia*, through the appropriate international organizations in accordance with their existing and evolving rules, and to share in the benefits resulting therefrom.

Article 11

All States should co-operate to strengthen and continuously improve the efficiency of international organizations in implementing measures to stimulate the general economic progress of all countries, particularly of developing countries, and therefore should co-operate to adapt them, when appropriate, to the changing needs of international economic co-operation.

Article 12

1. States have the right, in agreement with the parties concerned, to participate in subregional, regional and interregional co-operation in the pursuit of their economic and social development. All States engaged in such co-operation have the duty to ensure that the policies of those groupings to which they belong correspond to the provisions of the present Charter and are outward-looking, consistent with their international obligations and with the needs of international economic co-operation, and have full regard for the legitimate interests of third countries, especially developing countries.

2. In the case of groupings to which the States concerned have transferred or may transfer certain competences as regards matters that come within the scope of the present Charter, its provisions shall also apply to those groupings in regard to such matters, consistent with the responsibilities of such States as members of such groupings. Those States shall co-operate in the observance by the groupings of the provisions of this Charter.

Article 13

1. Every State has the right to benefit from the advances and development in science and technology for the acceleration of its economic and social development.

2. All States should promote international scientific and technological co-operation and the transfer of technology, with proper regard for all legitimate interests including, *inter alia*, the rights and duties of holders, suppliers and recipients of technology. In particular, all States should facilitate the access of developing countries to the achievements of modern science and technology, the transfer of technology and the creation of indigenous technology for the benefit of the developing countries in forms and in accordance with procedures which are suited to their economies and their needs.

3. Accordingly, developed countries should co-operate with the developing countries in the establishment, strengthening and development of their scientific and technological infrastructures and their scientific research and technological activities so as to help to expand and transform the economies of developing countries.

4. All Sates should co-operate in research with a view to evolving further internationally accepted guidelines or regulations for the transfer of technology, taking fully into account the interest of developing countries.

Article 14

Every State has the duty to co-operate in promoting a steady and increasing expansion and liberalization of world trade and an improvement in the welfare and living standards of all peoples, in particular those of developing countries. Accordingly, all States should co-operate, *inter alia*, towards the progressive dismantling of obstacles to trade and the improvement of the international framework for the conduct of world trade and, to these ends, co-ordinated efforts shall be made to solve in an equitable way the trade problems of all countries, taking into account the specific trade problems of the developing countries. In this connexion, States shall take measures aimed at securing additional benefits for the international trade of developing countries so as to achieve a substantial increase in their foreign exchange earnings, the diversification of their exports, the acceleration of the rate of growth of their trade, taking into account their development needs, an improvement in the possibilities for these countries to participate in the expansion of world trade and a balance more favourable to developing countries in the sharing of the advantages resulting from this expansion, through, in the largest possible measure, a substantial improvement in the conditions of access for the products of interest to the developing countries and, wherever appropriate, measures designed to attain stable, equitable and remunerative prices for primary products.

Article 15

All States have the duty to promote the achievement of general and complete disarmament under effective international control and to utilize the resources released by effective disarmament measures for the economic and social development of countries, allocating a substantial portion of such resources as additional means for the development needs of developing countries.

Article 16

1. It is the right and duty of all States, individually and collectively, to eliminate colonialism, *apartheid*, racial discrimination, neo-colonialism and all forms of foreign aggression, occupation and domination, and the economic and social consequences thereof, as a prerequisite for development. States which practise such coercive policies are economically responsible to the countries, territories and peoples affected for the restitution and full compensation for the exploitation and depletion of, and damages to, the natural and all other resources of those countries, territories and peoples. It is the duty of all States to extend assistance to them.

2. No State has the right to promote or encourage investments that may constitute an obstacle to the liberation of a territory occupied by force.

Article 17

International co-operation for development is the shared goal and common duty of all States. Every State should co-operate with the efforts of developing countries to accelerate their economic and social development by providing favourable external conditions and by extending active assistance to them, consistent with their development needs and objectives, with strict respect for the sovereign equality of States and free of any conditions derogating from their sovereignty.

Article 18

Developed countries should extend, improve and enlarge the system of generalized non-reciprocal and non-discriminatory tariff preferences to the developing countries consistent with the relevant agreed conclusions and relevant decisions as adopted on this subject, in the framework of the competent international organizations. Developed countries should also give serious consideration to the adoption of other differential measures, in areas where this is feasible and appropriate and in ways which will provide special and more favourable treatment, in order to meet the trade and development needs of the developing countries. In the conduct of inter-national economic relations the developed countries should endeavour to avoid measures having a negative effect on the development of the national economies of the developing countries, as promoted by generalized tariff preferences and other generally agreed differential measures in their favour.

Article 19

With a view to accelerating the economic growth of developing countries and bridging the economic gap between developed and developing countries, developed countries should grant generalized preferential, non-reciprocal and non-discriminatory treatment to developing coun-tries in those fields of international economic co-operation where it may be feasible.

Article 20

Developing countries should, in their efforts to increase their over-all trade, give due attention to the possibility of expanding their trade with socialist countries, by granting to these countries conditions for trade not inferior to those granted normally to the developed market economy countries.

Article 21

Developing countries should endeavour to promote the expansion of their mutual trade and to this end may, in accordance with the existing and evolving provisions and procedures of international agreements where applicable, grant trade preferences to other developing coun-tries without being obliged to extend such preferences to developed countries, provided these arrangements do not constitute an impediment to general trade liberalization and expansion.

Article 22

1. All States should respond to the generally recognized or mutually agreed development needs and objectives of developing countries by promoting increased net flows of real resources to the developing countries from all sources, taking into account any obligations and commit-ments undertaken by the States concerned, in order to reinforce the efforts of developing countries to accelerate their economic and social development.

2. In this context, consistent with the aims and objectives mentioned above and taking into account any obligations and commitments undertaken in this regard, it should be their endeavour to increase the net amount of financial flows from official sources to developing countries and to improve the terms and conditions thereof.

3. The flow of development assistance resources should include economic and technical assist-ance.

Article 23

To enhance the effective mobilization of their own resources, the developing countries should strengthen their economic co-operation and expand their mutual trade so as to accelerate their economic and social development. All countries, especially developed countries, individually as well as through the competent international organizations of which they are members, should provide appropriate and effective support and co-operation.

Article 24

All States have the duty to conduct their mutual economic relations in a manner which takes into account the interest of other countries. In particular, all States should avoid prejudicing the interests of developing countries.

Article 25

In furtherance of world economic development, the international community, especially its developed members, shall pay special attention to the particular needs and problems of the least developed among the developing countries, of land-locked developing countries and also island developing countries, with a view to helping them to overcome their particular difficulties and thus contribute to their economic and social development.

Article 26

All States have the duty to coexist in tolerance and live together in peace, irrespective of differences in political, economic, social and cultural systems, and to facilitate trade between States having different economic and social systems. International trade should be conducted without prejudice to generalized non-discriminatory and non-reciprocal preferences in favour of developing countries, on the basis of mutual advantage, equitable benefits and the exchange of most-favoured-nation treatment.

Article 27

1. Every State has the right to enjoy fully the benefits of world invisible trade and to engage in the expansion of such trade.

2. World invisible trade, based on efficiency and mutual and equitable benefit, furthering the expansion of the world economy, is the common goal of all States. The role of developing countries in world invisible trade should be enhanced and strengthened consistent with the above objectives, particular attention being paid to the special needs of developing countries.

3. All States should co-operate with developing countries in their endeavours to increase their capacity to earn foreign exchange from invisible transactions, in accordance with the potential and needs of each developing country and consistent with the objectives mentioned above.

Article 28

All States have the duty to co-operate in achieving adjustments in the prices of exports of developing countries in relation to prices of their imports so as to promote just and equitable terms of trade for them, in a manner which is remunerative for producers and equitable for producers and consumers.

CHAPTER III   COMMON RESPONSIBILITIES TOWARDS THE INTERNATIONAL COMMUNITY

Article 29

The sea-bed and ocean floor and the subsoil thereof, beyond the limits of national jurisdiction, as well as the resources of the area, are the common heritage of mankind. On the basis of the principles adopted by the General Assembly in resolution 2749 (XXV) of 17 December 1970, all States shall ensure that the exploration of the area and exploitation of its resources are carried out exclusively for peaceful purposes and that the benefits derived therefore are shared equitably by all States, taking into account the particular interest and needs of developing countries; an international régime applying to the area and its resources and including appropriate international machinery to give effect to its provisions shall be established by an international treaty of a universal character, generally agreed upon.

Article 30

The protection, preservation and enhancement of the environment for the present and future generations is the responsibility of all States. All States shall endeavour to establish their own environment and development policies in conformity with such responsibility. The environmental policies of all States should enhance and not adversely affect the present and future development potential of developing countries. All States have the responsibility to ensure that activities within their jurisdiction or control do not cause damage to the environment of other States or of areas beyond the limits of national jurisdiction. All States should co-operate in evolving international norms and regulations in the field of the environment.

CHAPTER IV   FINAL PROVISIONS

Article 31

All States have the duty to contribute to the balanced expansion of the world economy, taking duly into account the close interrelationship between the well-being of the developed countries and the growth and development of the developing countries, and the fact that the prosperity of the international community as a whole depends upon the prosperity of its constituent parts.

Article 32

No State may use or encourage the use of economic, political or any other type of measures to coerce another State in order to obtain from it the subordination of the exercise of its sovereign rights.

Article 33

1. Nothing in the present Charter shall be construed as impairing or derogating from the provisions of the Charter of the United Nations or actions taken into pursuance thereof.

2. In their interpretation and application, the provisions of the present Charter are interrelated and each provision should be construed in the context of the other provisions.

Article 34

An item on the Charter of Economic Rights and Duties of Sates shall be included in the agenda of the General Assembly at its thirtieth session, and thereafter on the agenda of every fifth session, In this way a systematic and comprehensive consideration of the implementation of the Charter, covering both progress achieved and any improvement and additions which might become necessary, would be carried out and appropriate measures recommended. Such consideration should take into account the evolution of all the economic, social, legal and other factors related to the principles upon which the present Charter is based and on its purpose.

PART 2

World Trade Law

General

II-1

Agreement Establishing the World Trade Organization (with Annexes)*

Date   15 April 1994
In force 1 January 1995
Source   1867 UNTS I-31874
Link   <http://www.wto.org/english/docs_e/legal_e/legal_e.htm>

The *Parties* to this Agreement,

Recognizing that their relations in the field of trade and economic endeavour should be conducted with a view to raising standards of living, ensuring full employment and a large and steadily growing volume of real income and effective demand, and expanding the production of and trade in goods and services, while allowing for the optimal use of the world's resources in accordance with the objective of sustainable development, seeking both to protect and preserve the environment and to enhance the means for doing so in a manner consistent with their respective needs and concerns at different levels of economic development,

Recognizing further that there is need for positive efforts designed to ensure that developing countries, and especially the least developed among them, secure a share in the growth in international trade commensurate with the needs of their economic development,

Being desirous of contributing to these objectives by entering into reciprocal and mutually advantageous arrangements directed to the substantial reduction of tariffs and other barriers to trade and to the elimination of discriminatory treatment in international trade relations,

Resolved, therefore, to develop an integrated, more viable and durable multilateral trading system encompassing the General Agreement on Tariffs and Trade, the results of past trade liberalization efforts, and all of the results of the Uruguay Round of Multilateral Trade Negotiations,

Determined to preserve the basic principles and to further the objectives underlying this multilateral trading system,

Agree as follows:

Article I   Establishment of the Organization
The World Trade Organization (hereinafter referred to as "the WTO") is hereby established.

Article II   Scope of the WTO
1. The WTO shall provide the common institutional framework for the conduct of trade relations among its Members in matters related to the agreements and associated legal instruments included in the Annexes to this Agreement.

---

* Note by the Editors: The Annexes reproduced in the following form part of the Agreement Establishing the World Trade Organization; unless otherwise indicated, they entered into force together with it and are published in the same volume of the United Nations Treaty Series.

2. The agreements and associated legal instruments included in Annexes 1, 2 and 3 (hereinafter referred to as "Multilateral Trade Agreements") are integral parts of this Agreement, binding on all Members.

3. The agreements and associated legal instruments included in Annex 4 (hereinafter referred to as "Plurilateral Trade Agreements") are also part of this Agreement for those Members that have accepted them, and are binding on those Members. The Plurilateral Trade Agreements do not create either obligations or rights for Members that have not accepted them.

4. The General Agreement on Tariffs and Trade 1994 as specified in Annex 1A (hereinafter referred to as "GATT 1994") is legally distinct from the General Agreement on Tariffs and Trade, dated 30 October 1947, annexed to the Final Act Adopted at the Conclusion of the Second Session of the Preparatory Committee of the United Nations Conference on Trade and Employment, as subsequently rectified, amended or modified (hereinafter referred to as "GATT 1947").

Article III   Functions of the WTO

1. The WTO shall facilitate the implementation, administration and operation, and further the objectives, of this Agreement and of the Multilateral Trade Agreements, and shall also provide the framework for the implementation, administration and operation of the Plurilateral Trade Agreements.

2. The WTO shall provide the forum for negotiations among its Members concerning their multilateral trade relations in matters dealt with under the agreements in the Annexes to this Agreement. The WTO may also provide a forum for further negotiations among its Members concerning their multilateral trade relations, and a framework for the implementation of the results of such negotiations, as may be decided by the Ministerial Conference.

3. The WTO shall administer the Understanding on Rules and Procedures Governing the Settlement of Disputes (hereinafter referred to as the "Dispute Settlement Understanding" or "DSU") in Annex 2 to this Agreement.

4. The WTO shall administer the Trade Policy Review Mechanism (hereinafter referred to as the "TPRM") provided for in Annex 3 to this Agreement.

5. With a view to achieving greater coherence in global economic policy-making, the WTO shall cooperate, as appropriate, with the International Monetary Fund and with the International Bank for Reconstruction and Development and its affiliated agencies.

Article IV   Structure of the WTO

1. There shall be a Ministerial Conference composed of representatives of all the Members, which shall meet at least once every two years. The Ministerial Conference shall carry out the functions of the WTO and take actions necessary to this effect. The Ministerial Conference shall have the authority to take decisions on all matters under any of the Multilateral Trade Agreements, if so requested by a Member, in accordance with the specific requirements for decision-making in this Agreement and in the relevant Multilateral Trade Agreement.

2. There shall be a General Council composed of representatives of all the Members, which shall meet as appropriate. In the intervals between meetings of the Ministerial Conference, its functions shall be conducted by the General Council. The General Council shall also carry out the functions assigned to it by this Agreement. The General Council shall establish its rules of procedure and approve the rules of procedure for the Committees provided for in paragraph 7.

3. The General Council shall convene as appropriate to discharge the responsibilities of the Dispute Settlement Body provided for in the Dispute Settlement Understanding. The Dispute Settlement Body may have its own chairman and shall establish such rules of procedure as it deems necessary for the fulfilment of those responsibilities.

4. The General Council shall convene as appropriate to discharge the responsibilities of the Trade Policy Review Body provided for in the TPRM. The Trade Policy Review Body may have its own chairman and shall establish such rules of procedure as it deems necessary for the fulfilment of those responsibilities.

5. There shall be a Council for Trade in Goods, a Council for Trade in Services and a Council for Trade-Related Aspects of Intellectual Property Rights (hereinafter referred to as the "Council for TRIPS"), which shall operate under the general guidance of the General Council. The Council for Trade in Goods shall oversee the functioning of the Multilateral Trade Agreements in Annex 1A. The Council for Trade in Services shall oversee the functioning of the General Agreement on Trade in Services (hereinafter referred to as "GATS"). The Council for TRIPS shall oversee the functioning of the Agreement on Trade-Related Aspects of Intellectual Property Rights (hereinafter referred to as the "Agreement on TRIPS"). These Councils shall carry out the functions assigned to them by their respective agreements and by the General Council. They shall establish their respective rules of procedure subject to the approval of the General Council. Membership in these Councils shall be open to representatives of all Members. These Councils shall meet as necessary to carry out their functions.

6. The Council for Trade in Goods, the Council for Trade in Services and the Council for TRIPS shall establish subsidiary bodies as required. These subsidiary bodies shall establish their respective rules of procedure subject to the approval of their respective Councils.

7. The Ministerial Conference shall establish a Committee on Trade and Development, a Committee on Balance-of-Payments Restrictions and a Committee on Budget, Finance and Administration, which shall carry out the functions assigned to them by this Agreement and by the Multilateral Trade Agreements, and any additional functions assigned to them by the General Council, and may establish such additional Committees with such functions as it may deem appropriate. As part of its functions, the Committee on Trade and Development shall periodically review the special provisions in the Multilateral Trade Agreements in favour of the least-developed country Members and report to the General Council for appropriate action. Membership in these Committees shall be open to representatives of all Members.

8. The bodies provided for under the Plurilateral Trade Agreements shall carry out the functions assigned to them under those Agreements and shall operate within the institutional framework of the WTO. These bodies shall keep the General Council informed of their activities on a regular basis.

Article V   Relations with Other Organizations

1. The General Council shall make appropriate arrangements for effective cooperation with other intergovernmental organizations that have responsibilities related to those of the WTO.

2. The General Council may make appropriate arrangements for consultation and cooperation with non-governmental organizations concerned with matters related to those of the WTO.

Article VI   The Secretariat

1. There shall be a Secretariat of the WTO (hereinafter referred to as "the Secretariat") headed by a Director-General.

2. The Ministerial Conference shall appoint the Director-General and adopt regulations setting out the powers, duties, conditions of service and term of office of the Director-General.

3. The Director-General shall appoint the members of the staff of the Secretariat and determine their duties and conditions of service in accordance with regulations adopted by the Ministerial Conference.

4. The responsibilities of the Director-General and of the staff of the Secretariat shall be exclusively international in character. In the discharge of their duties, the Director-General and the staff of the Secretariat shall not seek or accept instructions from any government or

any other authority external to the WTO. They shall refrain from any action which might adversely reflect on their position as international officials. The Members of the WTO shall respect the international character of the responsibilities of the Director-General and of the staff of the Secretariat and shall not seek to influence them in the discharge of their duties.

Article VII   Budget and Contributions

1. The Director-General shall present to the Committee on Budget, Finance and Administration the annual budget estimate and financial statement of the WTO. The Committee on Budget, Finance and Administration shall review the annual budget estimate and the financial statement presented by the Director-General and make recommendations thereon to the General Council. The annual budget estimate shall be subject to approval by the General Council.

2. The Committee on Budget, Finance and Administration shall propose to the General Council financial regulations which shall include provisions setting out:
   (a) the scale of contributions apportioning the expenses of the WTO among its Members; and
   (b) the measures to be taken in respect of Members in arrears.

   The financial regulations shall be based, as far as practicable, on the regulations and practices of GATT 1947.

3. The General Council shall adopt the financial regulations and the annual budget estimate by a two-thirds majority comprising more than half of the Members of the WTO.

4. Each Member shall promptly contribute to the WTO its share in the expenses of the WTO in accordance with the financial regulations adopted by the General Council.

Article VIII   Status of the WTO

1. The WTO shall have legal personality, and shall be accorded by each of its Members such legal capacity as may be necessary for the exercise of its functions.

2. The WTO shall be accorded by each of its Members such privileges and immunities as are necessary for the exercise of its functions.

3. The officials of the WTO and the representatives of the Members shall similarly be accorded by each of its Members such privileges and immunities as are necessary for the independent exercise of their functions in connection with the WTO.

4. The privileges and immunities to be accorded by a Member to the WTO, its officials, and the representatives of its Members shall be similar to the privileges and immunities stipulated in the Convention on the Privileges and Immunities of the Specialized Agencies, approved by the General Assembly of the United Nations on 21 November 1947.

5. The WTO may conclude a headquarters agreement.

Article IX   Decision-Making

1. The WTO shall continue the practice of decision-making by consensus followed under GATT 1947.[1] Except as otherwise provided, where a decision cannot be arrived at by consensus, the matter at issue shall be decided by voting. At meetings of the Ministerial Conference and the General Council, each Member of the WTO shall have one vote. Where the European Communities exercise their right to vote, they shall have a number of votes equal to the number of their member States[2] which are Members of the WTO. Decisions of the Ministerial Conference and the General Council shall be taken by a majority of the votes

---

1 The body concerned shall be deemed to have decided by consensus on a matter submitted for its consideration, if no Member, present at the meeting when the decision is taken, formally objects to the proposed decision.
2 The number of votes of the European Communities and their member States shall in no case exceed the number of the member States of the European Communities.

cast, unless otherwise provided in this Agreement or in the relevant Multilateral Trade Agreement.[3]

2. The Ministerial Conference and the General Council shall have the exclusive authority to adopt interpretations of this Agreement and of the Multilateral Trade Agreements. In the case of an interpretation of a Multilateral Trade Agreement in Annex 1, they shall exercise their authority on the basis of a recommendation by the Council overseeing the functioning of that Agreement. The decision to adopt an interpretation shall be taken by a three-fourths majority of the Members. This paragraph shall not be used in a manner that would undermine the amendment provisions in Article X.

3. In exceptional circumstances, the Ministerial Conference may decide to waive an obligation imposed on a Member by this Agreement or any of the Multilateral Trade Agreements, provided that any such decision shall be taken by three fourths[4] of the Members unless otherwise provided for in this paragraph.

   (a) A request for a waiver concerning this Agreement shall be submitted to the Ministerial Conference for consideration pursuant to the practice of decision-making by consensus. The Ministerial Conference shall establish a time-period, which shall not exceed 90 days, to consider the request. If consensus is not reached during the time-period, any decision to grant a waiver shall be taken by three fourths[4] of the Members.

   (b) A request for a waiver concerning the Multilateral Trade Agreements in Annexes 1A or 1B or 1C and their annexes shall be submitted initially to the Council for Trade in Goods, the Council for Trade in Services or the Council for TRIPS, respectively, for consideration during a time-period which shall not exceed 90 days. At the end of the time-period, the relevant Council shall submit a report to the Ministerial Conference.

4. A decision by the Ministerial Conference granting a waiver shall state the exceptional circumstances justifying the decision, the terms and conditions governing the application of the waiver, and the date on which the waiver shall terminate. Any waiver granted for a period of more than one year shall be reviewed by the Ministerial Conference not later than one year after it is granted, and thereafter annually until the waiver terminates. In each review, the Ministerial Conference shall examine whether the exceptional circumstances justifying the waiver still exist and whether the terms and conditions attached to the waiver have been met. The Ministerial Conference, on the basis of the annual review, may extend, modify or terminate the waiver.

5. Decisions under a Plurilateral Trade Agreement, including any decisions on interpretations and waivers, shall be governed by the provisions of that Agreement.

Article X   Amendments

1. Any Member of the WTO may initiate a proposal to amend the provisions of this Agreement or the Multilateral Trade Agreements in Annex 1 by submitting such proposal to the Ministerial Conference. The Councils listed in paragraph 5 of Article IV may also submit to the Ministerial Conference proposals to amend the provisions of the corresponding Multilateral Trade Agreements in Annex 1 the functioning of which they oversee. Unless the Ministerial Conference decides on a longer period, for a period of 90 days after the proposal has been tabled formally at the Ministerial Conference any decision by the Ministerial Conference to submit the proposed amendment to the Members for acceptance shall be taken by consensus. Unless the provisions of paragraphs 2, 5 or 6 apply, that decision shall specify whether the provisions of paragraphs 3 or 4 shall apply. If consensus is reached, the Ministerial Conference shall forthwith submit the proposed amendment to the Members for acceptance. If consensus is not reached at a meeting

---

3 Decisions by the General Council when convened as the Dispute Settlement Body shall be taken only in accordance with the provisions of paragraph 4 of Article 2 of the Dispute Settlement Understanding.

4 A decision to grant a waiver in respect of any obligation subject to a transition period or a period for staged implementation that the requesting Member has not performed by the end of the relevant period shall be taken only by consensus.

of the Ministerial Conference within the established period, the Ministerial Conference shall decide by a two-thirds majority of the Members whether to submit the proposed amendment to the Members for acceptance. Except as provided in paragraphs 2, 5 and 6, the provisions of paragraph 3 shall apply to the proposed amendment, unless the Ministerial Conference decides by a three-fourths majority of the Members that the provisions of paragraph 4 shall apply.

2. Amendments to the provisions of this Article and to the provisions of the following Articles shall take effect only upon acceptance by all Members:
   Article IX of this Agreement;
   Articles I and II of GATT 1994;
   Article II:1 of GATS;
   Article 4 of the Agreement on TRIPS.

3. Amendments to provisions of this Agreement, or of the Multilateral Trade Agreements in Annexes 1A and 1C, other than those listed in paragraphs 2 and 6, of a nature that would alter the rights and obligations of the Members, shall take effect for the Members that have accepted them upon acceptance by two thirds of the Members and thereafter for each other Member upon acceptance by it. The Ministerial Conference may decide by a three-fourths majority of the Members that any amendment made effective under this paragraph is of such a nature that any Member which has not accepted it within a period specified by the Ministerial Conference in each case shall be free to withdraw from the WTO or to remain a Member with the consent of the Ministerial Conference.

4. Amendments to provisions of this Agreement or of the Multilateral Trade Agreements in Annexes 1A and 1C, other than those listed in paragraphs 2 and 6, of a nature that would not alter the rights and obligations of the Members, shall take effect for all Members upon acceptance by two thirds of the Members.

5. Except as provided in paragraph 2 above, amendments to Parts I, II and III of GATS and the respective annexes shall take effect for the Members that have accepted them upon acceptance by two thirds of the Members and thereafter for each Member upon acceptance by it. The Ministerial Conference may decide by a three-fourths majority of the Members that any amendment made effective under the preceding provision is of such a nature that any Member which has not accepted it within a period specified by the Ministerial Conference in each case shall be free to withdraw from the WTO or to remain a Member with the consent of the Ministerial Conference. Amendments to Parts IV, V and VI of GATS and the respective annexes shall take effect for all Members upon acceptance by two thirds of the Members.

6. Notwithstanding the other provisions of this Article, amendments to the Agreement on TRIPS meeting the requirements of paragraph 2 of Article 71 thereof may be adopted by the Ministerial Conference without further formal acceptance process.

7. Any Member accepting an amendment to this Agreement or to a Multilateral Trade Agreement in Annex 1 shall deposit an instrument of acceptance with the Director-General of the WTO within the period of acceptance specified by the Ministerial Conference.

8. Any Member of the WTO may initiate a proposal to amend the provisions of the Multilateral Trade Agreements in Annexes 2 and 3 by submitting such proposal to the Ministerial Conference. The decision to approve amendments to the Multilateral Trade Agreement in Annex 2 shall be made by consensus and these amendments shall take effect for all Members upon approval by the Ministerial Conference. Decisions to approve amendments to the Multilateral Trade Agreement in Annex 3 shall take effect for all Members upon approval by the Ministerial Conference.

9. The Ministerial Conference, upon the request of the Members parties to a trade agreement, may decide exclusively by consensus to add that agreement to Annex 4. The Ministerial

Conference, upon the request of the Members parties to a Plurilateral Trade Agreement, may decide to delete that Agreement from Annex 4.

10. Amendments to a Plurilateral Trade Agreement shall be governed by the provisions of that Agreement.

Article XI   Original Membership

1. The contracting parties to GATT 1947 as of the date of entry into force of this Agreement, and the European Communities, which accept this Agreement and the Multilateral Trade Agreements and for which Schedules of Concessions and Commitments are annexed to GATT 1994 and for which Schedules of Specific Commitments are annexed to GATS shall become original Members of the WTO.

2. The least-developed countries recognized as such by the United Nations will only be required to undertake commitments and concessions to the extent consistent with their individual development, financial and trade needs or their administrative and institutional capabilities.

Article XII   Accession

1. Any State or separate customs territory possessing full autonomy in the conduct of its external commercial relations and of the other matters provided for in this Agreement and the Multilateral Trade Agreements may accede to this Agreement, on terms to be agreed between it and the WTO. Such accession shall apply to this Agreement and the Multilateral Trade Agreements annexed thereto.

2. Decisions on accession shall be taken by the Ministerial Conference. The Ministerial Conference shall approve the agreement on the terms of accession by a two-thirds majority of the Members of the WTO.

3. Accession to a Plurilateral Trade Agreement shall be governed by the provisions of that Agreement.

Article XIII   Non-Application of Multilateral Trade Agreements between Particular Members

1. This Agreement and the Multilateral Trade Agreements in Annexes 1 and 2 shall not apply as between any Member and any other Member if either of the Members, at the time either becomes a Member, does not consent to such application.

2. Paragraph 1 may be invoked between original Members of the WTO which were contracting parties to GATT 1947 only where Article XXXV of that Agreement had been invoked earlier and was effective as between those contracting parties at the time of entry into force for them of this Agreement.

3. Paragraph 1 shall apply between a Member and another Member which has acceded under Article XII only if the Member not consenting to the application has so notified the Ministerial Conference before the approval of the agreement on the terms of accession by the Ministerial Conference.

4. The Ministerial Conference may review the operation of this Article in particular cases at the request of any Member and make appropriate recommendations.

5. Non-application of a Plurilateral Trade Agreement between parties to that Agreement shall be governed by the provisions of that Agreement.

Article XIV   Acceptance, Entry into force and Deposit

1. This Agreement shall be open for acceptance, by signature or otherwise, by contracting parties to GATT 1947, and the European Communities, which are eligible to become original Members of the WTO in accordance with Article XI of this Agreement. Such acceptance shall apply to this Agreement and the Multilateral Trade Agreements annexed hereto. This Agreement and the Multilateral Trade Agreements annexed hereto shall enter into force on the date determined by Ministers in accordance with paragraph 3 of the Final Act Embodying the Results of the Uruguay Round of Multilateral Trade Negotiations and shall remain open

for acceptance for a period of two years following that date unless the Ministers decide otherwise. An acceptance following the entry into force of this Agreement shall enter into force on the 30th day following the date of such acceptance.

2. A Member which accepts this Agreement after its entry into force shall implement those concessions and obligations in the Multilateral Trade Agreements that are to be implemented over a period of time starting with the entry into force of this Agreement as if it had accepted this Agreement on the date of its entry into force.

3. Until the entry into force of this Agreement, the text of this Agreement and the Multilateral Trade Agreements shall be deposited with the Director-General to the CONTRACTING PARTIES to GATT 1947. The Director-General shall promptly furnish a certified true copy of this Agreement and the Multilateral Trade Agreements, and a notification of each acceptance thereof, to each government and the European Communities having accepted this Agreement. This Agreement and the Multilateral Trade Agreements, and any amendments thereto, shall, upon the entry into force of this Agreement, be deposited with the Director-General of the WTO.

4. The acceptance and entry into force of a Plurilateral Trade Agreement shall be governed by the provisions of that Agreement. Such Agreements shall be deposited with the Director-General to the CONTRACTING PARTIES to GATT 1947. Upon the entry into force of this Agreement, such Agreements shall be deposited with the Director-General of the WTO.

Article XV   Withdrawal

1. Any Member may withdraw from this Agreement. Such withdrawal shall apply both to this Agreement and the Multilateral Trade Agreements and shall take effect upon the expiration of six months from the date on which written notice of withdrawal is received by the Director-General of the WTO.

2. Withdrawal from a Plurilateral Trade Agreement shall be governed by the provisions of that Agreement.

Article XVI   Miscellaneous Provisions

1. Except as otherwise provided under this Agreement or the Multilateral Trade Agreements, the WTO shall be guided by the decisions, procedures and customary practices followed by the CONTRACTING PARTIES to GATT 1947 and the bodies established in the framework of GATT 1947.

2. To the extent practicable, the Secretariat of GATT 1947 shall become the Secretariat of the WTO, and the Director-General to the CONTRACTING PARTIES to GATT 1947, until such time as the Ministerial Conference has appointed a Director-General in accordance with paragraph 2 of Article VI of this Agreement, shall serve as Director-General of the WTO.

3. In the event of a conflict between a provision of this Agreement and a provision of any of the Multilateral Trade Agreements, the provision of this Agreement shall prevail to the extent of the conflict.

4. Each Member shall ensure the conformity of its laws, regulations and administrative procedures with its obligations as provided in the annexed Agreements.

5. No reservations may be made in respect of any provision of this Agreement. Reservations in respect of any of the provisions of the Multilateral Trade Agreements may only be made to the extent provided for in those Agreements. Reservations in respect of a provision of a Plurilateral Trade Agreement shall be governed by the provisions of that Agreement.

6. This Agreement shall be registered in accordance with the provisions of Article 102 of the Charter of the United Nations.

DONE at Marrakesh this fifteenth day of April one thousand nine hundred and ninety-four, in a single copy, in the English, French and Spanish languages, each text being authentic.

Explanatory Notes

The terms "country" or "countries" as used in this Agreement and the Multilateral Trade Agreements are to be understood to include any separate customs territory Member of the WTO.

In the case of a separate customs territory Member of the WTO, where an expression in this Agreement and the Multilateral Trade Agreements is qualified by the term "national", such expression shall be read as pertaining to that customs territory, unless otherwise specified.

II-2
List of Annexes[*]

ANNEX 1

Annex 1A   Multilateral Agreements on Trade in Goods

General Agreement on Tariffs and Trade 1994

Agreement on Agriculture

Agreement on the Application of Sanitary and Phytosanitary Measures

Agreement on Textiles and Clothing[*]

Agreement on Technical Barriers to Trade

Agreement on Trade-Related Investment Measures

Agreement on Implementation of Article VI of the General Agreement on
   Tariffs and Trade 1994

Agreement on Implementation of Article VII of the General Agreement on
   Tariffs and Trade 1994

Agreement on Preshipment Inspection[*]

Agreement on Rules of Origin[*]

Agreement on Import Licensing Procedures[*]

Agreement on Subsidies and Countervailing Measures

Agreement on Safeguards

Annex 1B   General Agreement on Trade in Services and Annexes

Annex 1C   Agreement on Trade-Related Aspects of Intellectual Property Rights

**ANNEX 2   UNDERSTANDING ON RULES AND PROCEDURES
            GOVERNING THE SETTLEMENT OF DISPUTES**

ANNEX 3   TRADE POLICY REVIEW MECHANISM[*]

ANNEX 4   PLURILATERAL TRADE AGREEMENTS

Agreement on Trade in Civil Aircraft

Agreement on Government Procurement[*]

International Dairy Agreement[*]

International Bovine Meat Agreement[*]

---

[*] Note by the Editors: Agreements marked with an asterisk (*) are not reproduced in this volume.

II-3

General Interpretative Note to Annex 1A (Multilateral Agreements on Trade in Goods)

In the event of conflict between a provision of the General Agreement on Tariffs and Trade 1994 and a provision of another agreement in Annex 1A to the Agreement Establishing the World Trade Organization (referred to in the agreements in Annex 1A as the "WTO Agreement"), the provision of the other agreement shall prevail to the extent of the conflict.

II-4

General Agreement on Tariffs and Trade 1994

1. The General Agreement on Tariffs and Trade 1994 ("GATT 1994") shall consist of:
   (a) the provisions in the General Agreement on Tariffs and Trade, dated 30 October 1947, annexed to the Final Act Adopted at the Conclusion of the Second Session of the Preparatory Committee of the United Nations Conference on Trade and Employment (excluding the Protocol of Provisional Application), as rectified, amended or modified by the terms of legal instruments which have entered into force before the date of entry into force of the WTO Agreement;
   (b) the provisions of the legal instruments set forth below that have entered into force under the GATT 1947 before the date of entry into force of the WTO Agreement:
      (i) protocols and certifications relating to tariff concessions;
      (ii) protocols of accession (excluding the provisions (a) concerning provisional application and withdrawal of provisional application and (b) providing that Part II of GATT 1947 shall be applied provisionally to the fullest extent not inconsistent with legislation existing on the date of the Protocol);
      (iii) decisions on waivers granted under Article XXV of GATT 1947 and still in force on the date of entry into force of the WTO Agreement[1];
      (iv) other decisions of the CONTRACTING PARTIES to GATT 1947;
   (c) the Understandings set forth below:
      (i) Understanding on the Interpretation of Article II:1(b) of the General Agreement on Tariffs and Trade 1994;
      (ii) Understanding on the Interpretation of Article XVII of the General Agreement on Tariffs and Trade 1994;
      (iii) Understanding on Balance-of-Payments Provisions of the General Agreement on Tariffs and Trade 1994;
      (iv) Understanding on the Interpretation of Article XXIV of the General Agreement on Tariffs and Trade 1994;
      (v) Understanding in Respect of Waivers of Obligations under the General Agreement on Tariffs and Trade 1994;
      (vi) Understanding on the Interpretation of Article XXVIII of the General Agreement on Tariffs and Trade 1994; and
   (d) the Marrakesh Protocol to GATT 1994.
2. Explanatory Notes
   (a) The references to "contracting party" in the provisions of GATT 1994 shall be deemed to read "Member". The references to "less-developed contracting party" and "developed contracting party" shall be deemed to read "developing country Member" and "developed country Member". The references to "Executive Secretary" shall be deemed to read "Director-General of the WTO".

---

1 The waivers covered by this provision are listed in footnote 7 on pages 11 and 12 in Part II of document MTN/FA of 15 December 1993 and in MTN/FA/Corr.6 of 21 March 1994. The Ministerial Conference shall establish at its first session a revised list of waivers covered by this provision that adds any waivers granted under GATT 1947 after 15 December 1993 and before the date of entry into force of the WTO Agreement, and deletes the waivers which will have expired by that time.

(b) The references to the CONTRACTING PARTIES acting jointly in Articles XV:1, XV:2, XV:8, XXXVIII and the Notes *Ad* Article XII and XVIII; and in the provisions on special exchange agreements in Articles XV:2, XV:3, XV:6, XV:7 and XV:9 of GATT 1994 shall be deemed to be references to the WTO. The other functions that the provisions of GATT 1994 assign to the CONTRACTING PARTIES acting jointly shall be allocated by the Ministerial Conference.

(c) (i) The text of GATT 1994 shall be authentic in English, French and Spanish.

   (ii) The text of GATT 1994 in the French language shall be subject to the rectifications of terms indicated in Annex A to document MTN.TNC/41.

  (iii) The authentic text of GATT 1994 in the Spanish language shall be the text in Volume IV of the Basic Instruments and Selected Documents series, subject to the rectifications of terms indicated in Annex B to document MTN.TNC/41.

3. (a) The provisions of Part II of GATT 1994 shall not apply to measures taken by a Member under specific mandatory legislation, enacted by that Member before it became a contracting party to GATT 1947, that prohibits the use, sale or lease of foreign-built or foreign-reconstructed vessels in commercial applications between points in national waters or the waters of an exclusive economic zone. This exemption applies to: (*a*) the continuation or prompt renewal of a non-conforming provision of such legislation; and (*b*) the amendment to a non-conforming provision of such legislation to the extent that the amendment does not decrease the conformity of the provision with Part II of GATT 1947. This exemption is limited to measures taken under legislation described above that is notified and specified prior to the date of entry into force of the WTO Agreement. If such legislation is subsequently modified to decrease its conformity with Part II of GATT 1994, it will no longer qualify for coverage under this paragraph.

(b) The Ministerial Conference shall review this exemption not later than five years after the date of entry into force of the WTO Agreement and thereafter every two years for as long as the exemption is in force for the purpose of examining whether the conditions which created the need for the exemption still prevail.

(c) A Member whose measures are covered by this exemption shall annually submit a detailed statistical notification consisting of a five-year moving average of actual and expected deliveries of relevant vessels as well as additional information on the use, sale, lease or repair of relevant vessels covered by this exemption.

(d) A Member that considers that this exemption operates in such a manner as to justify a reciprocal and proportionate limitation on the use, sale, lease or repair of vessels constructed in the territory of the Member invoking the exemption shall be free to introduce such a limitation subject to prior notification to the Ministerial Conference.

(e) This exemption is without prejudice to solutions concerning specific aspects of the legislation covered by this exemption negotiated in sectoral agreements or in other fora.

II-5

The General Agreement on Tariffs and Trade (GATT 1947)

The Governments of the Commonwealth of Australia, the Kingdom of Belgium, the United States of Brazil, Burma, Canada, Ceylon, the Republic of Chile, the Republic of China, the Republic of Cuba, the Czechoslovak Republic, the French Republic, India, Lebanon, the Grand-Duchy of Luxemburg, the Kingdom of the Netherlands, New Zealand, the Kingdom of Norway, Pakistan, Southern Rhodesia, Syria, the Union of South Africa, the United Kingdom of Great Britain and Northern Ireland, and the United States of America:

Recognizing that their relations in the field of trade and economic endeavour should be conducted with a view to raising standards of living, ensuring full employment and a large and steadily growing volume of real income and effective demand, developing the full use of the resources of the world and expanding the production and exchange of goods,

Being desirous of contributing to these objectives by entering into reciprocal and mutually advantageous arrangements directed to the substantial reduction of tariffs and other barriers to trade and to the elimination of discriminatory treatment in international commerce,

Have through their Representatives agreed as follows:

PART I

Article I   General Most-Favoured-Nation Treatment

1. With respect to customs duties and charges of any kind imposed on or in connection with importation or exportation or imposed on the international transfer of payments for imports or exports, and with respect to the method of levying such duties and charges, and with respect to all rules and formalities in connection with importation and exportation, and with respect to all matters referred to in paragraphs 2 and 4 of Article III,* any advantage, favour, privilege or immunity granted by any contracting party to any product originating in or destined for any other country shall be accorded immediately and unconditionally to the like product originating in or destined for the territories of all other contracting parties.

2. The provisions of paragraph 1 of this Article shall not require the elimination of any preferences in respect of import duties or charges which do not exceed the levels provided for in paragraph 4 of this Article and which fall within the following descriptions:
   (*a*) Preferences in force exclusively between two or more of the territories listed in Annex A, subject to the conditions set forth therein;
   (*b*) Preferences in force exclusively between two or more territories which on July 1, 1939, were connected by common sovereignty or relations of protection or suzerainty and which are listed in Annexes B, C and D, subject to the conditions set forth therein;
   (*c*) Preferences in force exclusively between the United States of America and the Republic of Cuba;
   (*d*) Preferences in force exclusively between neighbouring countries listed in Annexes E and F.

3. The provisions of paragraph 1 shall not apply to preferences between the countries formerly a part of the Ottoman Empire and detached from it on July 24, 1923, provided such preferences

---

* Note by the Editors: In the Preface to the Agreement it states 'asterisks mark the portions of the text which should be read in conjunction with notes and supplementary provisions in Annex I to the Agreement'.

are approved under paragraph 5[1], of Article XXV which shall be applied in this respect in the light of paragraph 1 of Article XXIX.

4. The margin of preference* on any product in respect of which a preference is permitted under paragraph 2 of this Article but is not specifically set forth as a maximum margin of preference in the appropriate Schedule annexed to this Agreement shall not exceed:

   (a) in respect of duties or charges on any product described in such Schedule, the difference between the most-favoured-nation and preferential rates provided for therein; if no preferential rate is provided for, the preferential rate shall for the purposes of this paragraph be taken to be that in force on April 10, 1947, and, if no most-favoured-nation rate is provided for, the margin shall not exceed the difference between the most-favoured-nation and preferential rates existing on April 10, 1947;

   (b) in respect of duties or charges on any product not described in the appropriate Schedule, the difference between the most-favoured-nation and preferential rates existing on April 10, 1947.

   In the case of the contracting parties named in Annex G, the date of April 10, 1947, referred to in sub-paragraph (a) and (b) of this paragraph shall be replaced by the respective dates set forth in that Annex.

Article II   Schedules of Concessions

1. (a) Each contracting party shall accord to the commerce of the other contracting parties treatment no less favourable than that provided for in the appropriate Part of the appropriate Schedule annexed to this Agreement.

   (b) The products described in Part I of the Schedule relating to any contracting party, which are the products of territories of other contracting parties, shall, on their importation into the territory to which the Schedule relates, and subject to the terms, conditions or qualifications set forth in that Schedule, be exempt from ordinary customs duties in excess of those set forth and provided therein. Such products shall also be exempt from all other duties or charges of any kind imposed on or in connection with the importation in excess of those imposed on the date of this Agreement or those directly and mandatorily required to be imposed thereafter by legislation in force in the importing territory on that date.

   (c) The products described in Part II of the Schedule relating to any contracting party which are the products of territories entitled under Article I to receive preferential treatment upon importation into the territory to which the Schedule relates shall, on their importation into such territory, and subject to the terms, conditions or qualifications set forth in that Schedule, be exempt from ordinary customs duties in excess of those set forth and provided for in Part II of that Schedule. Such products shall also be exempt from all other duties or charges of any kind imposed on or in connection with importation in excess of those imposed on the date of this Agreement or those directly or mandatorily required to be imposed thereafter by legislation in force in the importing territory on that date. Nothing in this Article shall prevent any contracting party from maintaining its requirements existing on the date of this Agreement as to the eligibility of goods for entry at preferential rates of duty.

2. Nothing in this Article shall prevent any contracting party from imposing at any time on the importation of any product:

   (a) a charge equivalent to an internal tax imposed consistently with the provisions of paragraph 2 of Article III* in respect of the like domestic product or in respect of an article from which the imported product has been manufactured or produced in whole or in part;

---

1 The authentic text erroneously reads "sub-paragraph 5 (a)".

(*b*) any anti-dumping or countervailing duty applied consistently with the provisions of Article VI;*

(*c*) fees or other charges commensurate with the cost of services rendered.

3. No contracting party shall alter its method of determining dutiable value or of converting currencies so as to impair the value of any of the concessions provided for in the appropriate Schedule annexed to this Agreement.

4. If any contracting party establishes, maintains or authorizes, formally or in effect, a monopoly of the importation of any product described in the appropriate Schedule annexed to this Agreement, such monopoly shall not, except as provided for in that Schedule or as otherwise agreed between the parties which initially negotiated the concession, operate so as to afford protection on the average in excess of the amount of protection provided for in that Schedule. The provisions of this paragraph shall not limit the use by contracting parties of any form of assistance to domestic producers permitted by other provisions of this Agreement.*

5. If any contracting party considers that a product is not receiving from another contracting party the treatment which the first contracting party believes to have been contemplated by a concession provided for in the appropriate Schedule annexed to this Agreement, it shall bring the matter directly to the attention of the other contracting party. If the latter agrees that the treatment contemplated was that claimed by the first contracting party, but declares that such treatment cannot be accorded because a court or other proper authority has ruled to the effect that the product involved cannot be classified under the tariff laws of such contracting party so as to permit the treatment contemplated in this Agreement, the two contracting parties, together with any other contracting parties substantially interested, shall enter promptly into further negotiations with a view to a compensatory adjustment of the matter.

6. (*a*) The specific duties and charges included in the Schedules relating to contracting parties members of the International Monetary Fund, and margins of preference in specific duties and charges maintained by such contracting parties, are expressed in the appropriate currency at the par value accepted or provisionally recognized by the Fund at the date of this Agreement. Accordingly, in case this par value is reduced consistently with the Articles of Agreement of the International Monetary Fund by more than twenty per centum, such specific duties and charges and margins of preference may be adjusted to take account of such reduction; *provided* that the CONTRACTING PARTIES (*i.e.*, the contracting parties acting jointly as provided for in Article XXV) concur that such adjustments will not impair the value of the concessions provided for in the appropriate Schedule or elsewhere in this Agreement, due account being taken of all factors which may influence the need for, or urgency of, such adjustments.

(*b*) Similar provisions shall apply to any contracting party not a member of the Fund, as from the date on which such contracting party becomes a member of the Fund or enters into a special exchange agreement in pursuance of Article XV.

7. The Schedules annexed to this Agreement are hereby made an integral part of Part I of this Agreement.

PART II

Article III*   National Treatment on Internal Taxation and Regulation

1. The contracting parties recognize that internal taxes and other internal charges, and laws, regulations and requirements affecting the internal sale, offering for sale, purchase, transportation, distribution or use of products, and internal quantitative regulations requiring the mixture, processing or use of products in specified amounts or proportions, should not be applied to imported or domestic products so as to afford protection to domestic production.*

2. The products of the territory of any contracting party imported into the territory of any other contracting party shall not be subject, directly or indirectly, to internal taxes or other internal charges of any kind in excess of those applied, directly or indirectly, to like domestic products. Moreover, no contracting party shall otherwise apply internal taxes or other internal charges to imported or domestic products in a manner contrary to the principles set forth in paragraph 1.*

3. With respect to any existing internal tax which is inconsistent with the provisions of paragraph 2, but which is specifically authorized under a trade agreement, in force on April 10, 1947, in which the import duty on the taxed product is bound against increase, the contracting party imposing the tax shall be free to postpone the application of the provisions of paragraph 2 to such tax until such time as it can obtain release from the obligations of such trade agreement in order to permit the increase of such duty to the extent necessary to compensate for the elimination of the protective element of the tax.

4. The products of the territory of any contracting party imported into the territory of any other contracting party shall be accorded treatment no less favourable than that accorded to like products of national origin in respect of all laws, regulations and requirements affecting their internal sale, offering for sale, purchase, transportation, distribution or use. The provisions of this paragraph shall not prevent the application of differential internal transportation charges which are based exclusively on the economic operation of the means of transport and not on the nationality of the product.

5. No contracting party shall establish or maintain any internal quantitative regulation relating to the mixture, processing or use of products in specified amounts or proportions which requires, directly or indirectly, that any specified amount or proportion of any product which is the subject of the regulation must be supplied from domestic sources. Moreover, no contracting party shall otherwise apply internal quantitative regulations in a manner contrary to the principles set forth in paragraph 1.*

6. The provisions of paragraph 5 shall not apply to any internal quantitative regulation in force in the territory of any contracting party on July 1, 1939, April 10, 1947, or March 24, 1948, at the option of that contracting party; *Provided* that any such regulation which is contrary to the provisions of paragraph 5 shall not be modified to the detriment of imports and shall be treated as a customs duty for the purpose of negotiation.

7. No internal quantitative regulation relating to the mixture, processing or use of products in specified amounts or proportions shall be applied in such a manner as to allocate any such amount or proportion among external sources of supply.

8. (*a*) The provisions of this Article shall not apply to laws, regulations or requirements governing the procurement by governmental agencies of products purchased for governmental purposes and not with a view to commercial resale or with a view to use in the production of goods for commercial sale.

   (*b*) The provisions of this Article shall not prevent the payment of subsidies exclusively to domestic producers, including payments to domestic producers derived from the proceeds of internal taxes or charges applied consistently with the provisions of this Article and subsidies effected through governmental purchases of domestic products.

9. The contracting parties recognize that internal maximum price control measures, even though conforming to the other provisions of this Article, can have effects prejudicial to the interests of contracting parties supplying imported products. Accordingly, contracting parties applying such measures shall take account of the interests of exporting contracting parties with a view to avoiding to the fullest practicable extent such prejudicial effects.

10. The provisions of this Article shall not prevent any contracting party from establishing or maintaining internal quantitative regulations relating to exposed cinematograph films and meeting the requirements of Article IV.

Article IV   Special Provisions relating to Cinematograph Films

If any contracting party establishes or maintains internal quantitative regulations relating to exposed cinematograph films, such regulations shall take the form of screen quotas which shall conform to the following requirements:

(a) Screen quotas may require the exhibition of cinematograph films of national origin during a specified minimum proportion of the total screen time actually utilized, over a specified period of not less than one year, in the commercial exhibition of all films of whatever origin, and shall be computed on the basis of screen time per theatre per year or the equivalent thereof;

(b) With the exception of screen time reserved for films of national origin under a screen quota, screen time including that released by administrative action from screen time reserved for films of national origin, shall not be allocated formally or in effect among sources of supply;

(c) Notwithstanding the provisions of sub-paragraph (b) of this Article, any contracting party may maintain screen quotas conforming to the requirements of sub-paragraph (a) of this Article which reserve a minimum proportion of screen time for films of a specified origin other than that of the contracting party imposing such screen quotas; *Provided* that no such minimum proportion of screen time shall be increased above the level in effect on April 10, 1947;

(d) Screen quotas shall be subject to negotiation for their limitation, liberalization or elimination.

Article V   Freedom of Transit

1. Goods (including baggage), and also vessels and other means of transport, shall be deemed to be in transit across the territory of a contracting party when the passage across such territory, with or without trans-shipment, warehousing, breaking bulk, or change in the mode of transport, is only a portion of a complete journey beginning and terminating beyond the frontier of the contracting party across whose territory the traffic passes. Traffic of this nature is termed in this article "traffic in transit".

2. There shall be freedom of transit through the territory of each contracting party, via the routes most convenient for international transit, for traffic in transit to or from the territory of other contracting parties. No distinction shall be made which is based on the flag of vessels, the place of origin, departure, entry, exit or destination, or on any circumstances relating to the ownership of goods, of vessels or of other means of transport.

3. Any contracting party may require that traffic in transit through its territory be entered at the proper custom house, but, except in cases of failure to comply with applicable customs laws and regulations, such traffic coming from or going to the territory of other contracting parties shall not be subject to any unnecessary delays or restrictions and shall be exempt from customs duties and from all transit duties or other charges imposed in respect of transit, except charges for transportation or those commensurate with administrative expenses entailed by transit or with the cost of services rendered.

4. All charges and regulations imposed by contracting parties on traffic in transit to or from the territories of other contracting parties shall be reasonable, having regard to the conditions of the traffic.

5. With respect to all charges, regulations and formalities in connection with transit, each contracting party shall accord to traffic in transit to or from the territory of any other contracting party treatment no less favourable than the treatment accorded to traffic in transit to or from any third country.*

6. Each contracting party shall accord to products which have been in transit through the territory of any other contracting party treatment no less favourable than that which would have been accorded to such products had they been transported from their place of origin to

their destination without going through the territory of such other contracting party. Any contracting party shall, however, be free to maintain its requirements of direct consignment existing on the date of this Agreement, in respect of any goods in regard to which such direct consignment is a requisite condition of eligibility for entry of the goods at preferential rates of duty or has relation to the contracting party's prescribed method of valuation for duty purposes.

7. The provisions of this Article shall not apply to the operation of aircraft in transit, but shall apply to air transit of goods (including baggage).

Article VI   Anti-dumping and Countervailing Duties

1. The contracting parties recognize that dumping, by which products of one country are introduced into the commerce of another country at less than the normal value of the products, is to be condemned if it causes or threatens material injury to an established industry in the territory of a contracting party or materially retards the establishment of a domestic industry. For the purposes of this Article, a product is to be considered as being introduced into the commerce of an importing country at less than its normal value, if the price of the product exported from one country to another

   (a) is less than the comparable price, in the ordinary course of trade, for the like product when destined for consumption in the exporting country, or,

   (b) in the absence of such domestic price, is less than either

      (i) the highest comparable price for the like product for export to any third country in the ordinary course of trade, or

      (ii) the cost of production of the product in the country of origin plus a reasonable addition for selling cost and profit.

   Due allowance shall be made in each case for differences in conditions and terms of sale, for differences in taxation, and for other differences affecting price comparability.*

2. In order to offset or prevent dumping, a contracting party may levy on any dumped product an anti-dumping duty not greater in amount than the margin of dumping in respect of such product. For the purposes of this Article, the margin of dumping is the price difference determined in accordance with the provisions of paragraph 1.*

3. No countervailing duty shall be levied on any product of the territory of any contracting party imported into the territory of another contracting party in excess of an amount equal to the estimated bounty or subsidy determined to have been granted, directly or indirectly, on the manufacture, production or export of such product in the country of origin or exportation, including any special subsidy to the transportation of a particular product. The term "countervailing duty" shall be understood to mean a special duty levied for the purpose of offsetting any bounty or subsidy bestowed, directly, or indirectly, upon the manufacture, production or export of any merchandise.*

4. No product of the territory of any contracting party imported into the territory of any other contracting party shall be subject to anti-dumping or countervailing duty by reason of the exemption of such product from duties or taxes borne by the like product when destined for consumption in the country of origin or exportation, or by reason of the refund of such duties or taxes.

5. No product of the territory of any contracting party imported into the territory of any other contracting party shall be subject to both anti-dumping and countervailing duties to compensate for the same situation of dumping or export subsidization.

6. (a) No contracting party shall levy any anti-dumping or countervailing duty on the importation of any product of the territory of another contracting party unless it determines that the effect of the dumping or subsidization, as the case may be, is such as to cause or

threaten material injury to an established domestic industry, or is such as to retard materially the establishment of a domestic industry.

(*b*) The CONTRACTING PARTIES may waive the requirement of sub-paragraph (*a*) of this paragraph so as to permit a contracting party to levy an anti-dumping or counter-vailing duty on the importation of any product for the purpose of offsetting dumping or subsidization which causes or threatens material injury to an industry in the territory of another contracting party exporting the product concerned to the territory of the importing contracting party. The CONTRACTING PARTIES shall waive the require-ments of sub-paragraph (*a*) of this paragraph, so as to permit the levying of a counter-vailing duty, in cases in which they find that a subsidy is causing or threatening material injury to an industry in the territory of another contracting party exporting the product concerned to the territory of the importing contracting party.*

(*c*) In exceptional circumstances, however, where delay might cause damage which would be difficult to repair, a contracting party may levy a countervailing duty for the purpose referred to in sub-paragraph (*b*) of this paragraph without the prior approval of the CONTRACTING PARTIES; *Provided* that such action shall be reported immediately to the CONTRACTING PARTIES and that the countervailing duty shall be withdrawn promptly if the CONTRACTING PARTIES disapprove.

7. A system for the stabilization of the domestic price or of the return to domestic producers of a primary commodity, independently of the movements of export prices, which results at times in the sale of the commodity for export at a price lower than the comparable price charged for the like commodity to buyers in the domestic market, shall be presumed not to result in material injury within the meaning of paragraph 6 if it is determined by consultation among the contracting parties substantially interested in the commodity concerned that:

(*a*) the system has also resulted in the sale of the commodity for export at a price higher than the comparable price charged for the like commodity to buyers in the domestic market, and

(*b*) the system is so operated, either because of the effective regulation of production, or otherwise, as not to stimulate exports unduly or otherwise seriously prejudice the interests of other contracting parties.

Article VII   Valuation for Customs Purposes

1. The contracting parties recognize the validity of the general principles of valuation set forth in the following paragraphs of this Article, and they undertake to give effect to such principles, in respect of all products subject to duties or other charges* or restrictions on importation and exportation based upon or regulated in any manner by value. Moreover, they shall, upon a request by another contracting party review the operation of any of their laws or regulations relating to value for customs purposes in the light of these principles. The CONTRACTING PARTIES may request from contracting parties reports on steps taken by them in pursuance of the provisions of this Article.

2. (*a*) The value for customs purposes of imported merchandise should be based on the actual value of the imported merchandise on which duty is assessed, or of like merchandise, and should not be based on the value of merchandise of national origin or on arbitrary or fictitious values.*

(*b*) "Actual value" should be the price at which, at a time and place determined by the legislation of the country of importation, such or like merchandise is sold or offered for sale in the ordinary course of trade under fully competitive conditions. To the extent to which the price of such or like merchandise is governed by the quantity in a particular transaction, the price to be considered should uniformly be related to either (i) compar-able quantities, or (ii) quantities not less favourable to importers than those in which the greater volume of the merchandise is sold in the trade between the countries of export-ation and importation.*

(c) When the actual value is not ascertainable in accordance with sub-paragraph (b) of this paragraph, the value for customs purposes should be based on the nearest ascertainable equivalent of such value.*

3. The value for customs purposes of any imported product should not include the amount of any internal tax, applicable within the country of origin or export, from which the imported product has been exempted or has been or will be relieved by means of refund.

4. (a) Except as otherwise provided for in this paragraph, where it is necessary for the purposes of paragraph 2 of this Article for a contracting party to convert into its own currency a price expressed in the currency of another country, the conversion rate of exchange to be used shall be based, for each currency involved, on the par value as established pursuant to the Articles of Agreement of the International Monetary Fund or on the rate of exchange recognized by the Fund, or on the par value established in accordance with a special exchange agreement entered into pursuant to Article XV of this Agreement.

(b) Where no such established par value and no such recognized rate of exchange exist, the conversion rate shall reflect effectively the current value of such currency in commercial transactions.

(c) The CONTRACTING PARTIES, in agreement with the International Monetary Fund, shall formulate rules governing the conversion by contracting parties of any foreign currency in respect of which multiple rates of exchange are maintained consistently with the Articles of Agreement of the International Monetary Fund. Any contracting party may apply such rules in respect of such foreign currencies for the purposes of paragraph 2 of this Article as an alternative to the use of par values. Until such rules are adopted by the CONTRACTING PARTIES, any contracting party may employ, in respect of any such foreign currency, rules of conversion for the purposes of paragraph 2 of this Article which are designed to reflect effectively the value of such foreign currency in commercial transactions.

(d) Nothing in this paragraph shall be construed to require any contracting party to alter the method of converting currencies for customs purposes which is applicable in its territory on the date of this Agreement, if such alteration would have the effect of increasing generally the amounts of duty payable.

5. The bases and methods for determining the value of products subject to duties or other charges or restrictions based upon or regulated in any manner by value should be stable and should be given sufficient publicity to enable traders to estimate, with a reasonable degree of certainty, the value for customs purposes.

Article VIII Fees and Formalities connected with Importation and Exportation*

1. (a) All fees and charges of whatever character (other than import and export duties and other than taxes within the purview of Article III) imposed by contracting parties on or in connection with importation or exportation shall be limited in amount to the approximate cost of services rendered and shall not represent an indirect protection to domestic products or a taxation of imports or exports for fiscal purposes.

(b) The contracting parties recognize the need for reducing the number and diversity of fees and charges referred to in sub-paragraph (a).

(c) The contracting parties also recognize the need for minimizing the incidence and complexity of import and export formalities and for decreasing and simplifying import and export documentation requirements.*

2. A contracting party shall, upon request by another contracting party or by the CONTRACTING PARTIES, review the operation of its laws and regulations in the light of the provisions of this Article.

3. No contracting party shall impose substantial penalties for minor breaches of customs regulations or procedural requirements. In particular, no penalty in respect of any omission or mistake in customs documentation which is easily rectifiable and obviously made without fraudulent intent or gross negligence shall be greater than necessary to serve merely as a warning.

4. The provisions of this Article shall extend to fees, charges, formalities and requirements imposed by governmental authorities in connection with importation and exportation, including those relating to:
   (*a*) consular transactions, such as consular invoices and certificates;
   (*b*) quantitative restrictions;
   (*c*) licensing;
   (*d*) exchange control;
   (*e*) statistical services;
   (*f*) documents, documentation and certification;
   (*g*) analysis and inspection; and
   (*h*) quarantine, sanitation and fumigation.

Article IX   Marks of Origin

1. Each contracting party shall accord to the products of the territories of other contracting parties treatment with regard to marking requirements no less favourable than the treatment accorded to like products of any third country.

2. The contracting parties recognize that, in adopting and enforcing laws and regulations relating to marks of origin, the difficulties and inconveniences which such measures may cause to the commerce and industry of exporting countries should be reduced to a minimum, due regard being had to the necessity of protecting consumers against fraudulent or misleading indications.

3. Whenever it is administratively practicable to do so, contracting parties should permit required marks of origin to be affixed at the time of importation.

4. The laws and regulations of contracting parties relating to the marking of imported products shall be such as to permit compliance without seriously damaging the products, or materially reducing their value, or unreasonably increasing their cost.

5. As a general rule, no special duty or penalty should be imposed by any contracting party for failure to comply with marking requirements prior to importation unless corrective marking is unreasonably delayed or deceptive marks have been affixed or the required marking has been intentionally omitted.

6. The contracting parties shall co-operate with each other with a view to preventing the use of trade names in such manner as to misrepresent the true origin of a product, to the detriment of such distinctive regional or geographical names of products of the territory of a contracting party as are protected by its legislation. Each contracting party shall accord full and sympathetic consideration to such requests or representations as may be made by any other contracting party regarding the application of the undertaking set forth in the preceding sentence to names of products which have been communicated to it by the other contracting party.

Article X   Publication and Administration of Trade Regulations

1. Laws, regulations, judicial decisions and administrative rulings of general application, made effective by any contracting party, pertaining to the classification or the valuation of products for customs purposes, or to rates of duty, taxes or other charges, or to requirements, restrictions or prohibitions on imports or exports or on the transfer of payments therefor, or affecting their sale, distribution, transportation, insurance, warehousing inspection, exhibition, processing, mixing or other use, shall be published promptly in such a manner as to

enable governments and traders to become acquainted with them. Agreements affecting international trade policy which are in force between the government or a governmental agency of any contracting party and the government or governmental agency of any other contracting party shall also be published. The provisions of this paragraph shall not require any contracting party to disclose confidential information which would impede law enforcement or otherwise be contrary to the public interest or would prejudice the legitimate commercial interests of particular enterprises, public or private.

2. No measure of general application taken by any contracting party effecting an advance in a rate of duty or other charge on imports under an established and uniform practice, or imposing a new or more burdensome requirement, restriction or prohibition on imports, or on the transfer of payments therefor, shall be enforced before such measure has been officially published.

3. (*a*) Each contracting party shall administer in a uniform, impartial and reasonable manner all its laws, regulations, decisions and rulings of the kind described in paragraph 1 of this Article.

   (*b*) Each contracting party shall maintain, or institute as soon as practicable, judicial, arbitral or administrative tribunals or procedures for the purpose, *inter alia*, of the prompt review and correction of administrative action relating to customs matters. Such tribunals or procedures shall be independent of the agencies entrusted with administrative enforcement and their decisions shall be implemented by, and shall govern the practice of, such agencies unless an appeal is lodged with a court or tribunal of superior jurisdiction within the time prescribed for appeals to be lodged by importers; *Provided* that the central administration of such agency may take steps to obtain a review of the matter in another proceeding if there is good cause to believe that the decision is inconsistent with established principles of law or the actual facts.

   (*c*) The provisions of sub-paragraph (*b*) of this paragraph shall not require the elimination or substitution of procedures in force in the territory of a contracting party on the date of this Agreement which in fact provide for an objective and impartial review of administrative action even though such procedures are not fully or formally independent of the agencies entrusted with administrative enforcement. Any contracting party employing such procedures shall, upon request, furnish the CONTRACTING PARTIES with full information thereon in order that they may determine whether such procedures conform to the requirements of this sub-paragraph.

Article XI*   General Elimination of Quantitative Restrictions

1. No prohibitions or restrictions other than duties, taxes or other charges, whether made effective through quotas, import or export licences or other measures, shall be instituted or maintained by any contracting party on the importation of any product of the territory of any other contracting party or on the exportation or sale for export of any product destined for the territory of any other contracting party.

2. The provisions of paragraph 1 of this Article shall not extend to the following:

   (*a*) Export prohibitions or restrictions temporarily applied to prevent or relieve critical shortages of foodstuffs or other products essential to the exporting contracting party;

   (*b*) Import and export prohibitions or restrictions necessary to the application of standards or regulations for the classification, grading or marketing of commodities in international trade;

   (*c*) Import restrictions on any agricultural or fisheries product, imported in any form,* necessary to the enforcement of governmental measures which operate:

       (i) to restrict the quantities of the like domestic product permitted to be marketed or produced, or, if there is no substantial domestic production of the like product, of a domestic product for which the imported product can be directly substituted; or

(ii) to remove a temporary surplus of the like domestic product, or, if there is no substantial domestic production of the like product, of a domestic product for which the imported product can be directly substituted, by making the surplus available to certain groups of domestic consumers free of charge or at prices below the current market level; or

(iii) to restrict the quantities permitted to be produced of any animal product the production of which is directly dependent, wholly or mainly, on the imported commodity, if the domestic production of that commodity is relatively negligible.

Any contracting party applying restrictions on the importation of any product pursuant to sub-paragraph (c) of this paragraph shall give public notice of the total quantity or value of the product permitted to be imported during a specified future period and of any change in such quantity or value. Moreover, any restrictions applied under (i) above shall not be such as will reduce the total of imports relative to the total of domestic production, as compared with the proportion which might reasonably be expected to rule between the two in the absence of restrictions. In determining this proportion, the contracting party shall pay due regard to the proportion prevailing during a previous representative period and to any special factors* which may have affected or may be affecting the trade in the product concerned.

Article XII*   Restrictions to Safeguard the Balance of Payments

1. Notwithstanding the provisions of paragraph 1 of Article XI, any contracting party, in order to safeguard its external financial position and its balance of payments, may restrict the quantity or value of merchandise permitted to be imported, subject to the provisions of the following paragraphs of this Article.

2. (a) Import restrictions instituted, maintained or intensified by a contracting party under this Article shall not exceed those necessary:

(i) to forestall the imminent threat of, or to stop, a serious decline in its monetary reserves; or

(ii) in the case of a contracting party with very low monetary reserves, to achieve a reasonable rate of increase in its reserves.

Due regard shall be paid in either case to any special factors which may be affecting the reserves of such contracting party or its need for reserves, including, where special external credits or other resources are available to it, the need to provide for the appropriate use of such credits or resources.

(b) Contracting parties applying restrictions under sub-paragraph (a) of this paragraph shall progressively relax them as such conditions improve, maintaining them only to the extent that the conditions specified in that sub-paragraph still justify their application. They shall eliminate the restrictions when conditions would no longer justify their institution or maintenance under that sub-paragraph.

3. (a) Contracting parties undertake, in carrying out their domestic policies, to pay due regard to the need for maintaining or restoring equilibrium in their balance of payments on a sound and lasting basis and to the desirability of avoiding an uneconomic employment of productive resources. They recognize that, in order to achieve these ends, it is desirable so far as possible to adopt measures which expand rather than contract international trade.

(b) Contracting parties applying restrictions under this Article may determine the incidence of the restrictions on imports of different products or classes of products in such a way as to give priority to the importation of those products which are more essential.

(c) Contracting parties applying restrictions under this Article undertake:

(i) to avoid unnecessary damage to the commercial or economic interests of any other contracting party;*

(ii) not to apply restrictions so as to prevent unreasonably the importation of any description of goods in minimum commercial quantities the exclusion of which would impair regular channels of trade; and

(iii) not to apply restrictions which would prevent the importations of commercial samples or prevent compliance with patent, trade mark, copyright, or similar procedures.

(d) The contracting parties recognize that, as a result of domestic policies directed towards the achievement and maintenance of full and productive employment or towards the development of economic resources, a contracting party may experience a high level of demand for imports involving a threat to its monetary reserves of the sort referred to in paragraph 2 (a) of this Article. Accordingly, a contracting party otherwise complying with the provisions of this Article shall not be required to withdraw or modify restrictions on the ground that a change in those policies would render unnecessary restrictions which it is applying under this Article.

4. (a) Any contracting party applying new restrictions or raising the general level of its existing restrictions by a substantial intensification of the measures applied under this Article shall immediately after instituting or intensifying such restrictions (or, in circumstances in which prior consultation is practicable, before doing so) consult with the CONTRACTING PARTIES as to the nature of its balance of payments difficulties, alternative corrective measures which may be available, and the possible effect of the restrictions on the economies of other contracting parties.

(b) On a date to be determined by them,* the CONTRACTING PARTIES shall review all restrictions still applied under this Article on that date. Beginning one year after that date, contracting parties applying import restrictions under this Article shall enter into consultations of the type provided for in sub-paragraph (a) of this paragraph with the CONTRACTING PARTIES annually.

(c) (i) If, in the course of consultations with a contracting party under sub-paragraph (a) or (b) above, the CONTRACTING PARTIES find that the restrictions are not consistent with provisions of this Article or with those of Article XIII (subject to the provisions of Article XIV), they shall indicate the nature of the inconsistency and may advise that the restrictions be suitably modified.

(ii) If, however, as a result of the consultations, the CONTRACTING PARTIES determine that the restrictions are being applied in a manner involving an inconsistency of a serious nature with the provisions of this Article or with those of Article XIII (subject to the provisions of Article XIV) and that damage to the trade of any contracting party is caused or threatened thereby, they shall so inform the contracting party applying the restrictions and shall make appropriate recommendations for securing conformity with such provisions within the specified period of time. If such contracting party does not comply with these recommendations within the specified period, the CONTRACTING PARTIES may release any contracting party the trade of which is adversely affected by the restrictions from such obligations under this Agreement towards the contracting party applying the restrictions as they determine to be appropriate in the circumstances.

(d) The CONTRACTING PARTIES shall invite any contracting party which is applying restrictions under this Article to enter into consultations with them at the request of any contracting party which can establish a *prima facie* case that the restrictions are inconsistent with the provisions of this Article or with those of Article XIII (subject to the provisions of Article XIV) and that its trade is adversely affected thereby. However, no such invitation shall be issued unless the CONTRACTING PARTIES have ascertained that direct discussions between the contracting parties concerned have not been successful. If, as a result of the consultations with the CONTRACTING PARTIES, no agreement is reached and they determine that the restrictions are being applied inconsistently with such provisions, and that damage to the trade of the contracting party initiating the procedure is caused or threatened thereby, they shall recommend the withdrawal or modification of the restrictions. If the restrictions are not withdrawn or modified within such time as the CONTRACTING PARTIES may prescribe, they may release the contracting party initiating the procedure from such obligations under this Agreement towards the contracting party applying the restrictions as they determine to be appropriate in the circumstances.

(e) In proceeding under this paragraph, the CONTRACTING PARTIES shall have due regard to any special external factors adversely affecting the export trade of the contracting party applying the restrictions.*

(f) Determinations under this paragraph shall be rendered expeditiously and, if possible, within sixty days of the initiation of the consultations.

5. If there is a persistent and widespread application of import restrictions under this Article, indicating the existence of a general disequilibrium which is restricting international trade, the CONTRACTING PARTIES shall initiate discussions to consider whether other measures might be taken, either by those contracting parties the balance of payments of which are under pressure or by those the balance of payments of which are tending to be exceptionally favourable, or by any appropriate intergovernmental organization, to remove the underlying causes of the disequilibrium. On the invitation of the CONTRACTING PARTIES, contracting parties shall participate in such discussions.

Article XIII*   Non-discriminatory Administration of Quantitative Restrictions

1. No prohibition or restriction shall be applied by any contracting party on the importation of any product of the territory of any other contracting party or on the exportation of any product destined for the territory of any other contracting party, unless the importation of the like product of all third countries or the exportation of the like product to all third countries is similarly prohibited or restricted.

2. In applying import restrictions to any product, contracting parties shall aim at a distribution of trade in such product approaching as closely as possible the shares which the various contracting parties might be expected to obtain in the absence of such restrictions and to this end shall observe the following provisions:

(a) Wherever practicable, quotas representing the total amount of permitted imports (whether allocated among supplying countries or not) shall be fixed, and notice given of their amount in accordance with paragraph 3 (b) of this Article;

(b) In cases in which quotas are not practicable, the restrictions may be applied by means of import licences or permits without a quota;

(c) Contracting parties shall not, except for purposes of operating quotas allocated in accordance with sub-paragraph (d) of this paragraph, require that import licences or permits be utilized for the importation of the product concerned from a particular country or source;

(d) In cases in which a quota is allocated among supplying countries the contracting party applying the restrictions may seek agreement with respect to the allocation of shares in the quota with all other contracting parties having a substantial interest in supplying the product concerned. In cases in which this method is not reasonably practicable, the contracting party concerned shall allot to contracting parties having a substantial interest in supplying the product shares based upon the proportions, supplied by such contracting parties during a previous representative period, of the total quantity or value of imports of the product, due account being taken of any special factors which may have affected or may be affecting the trade in the product. No conditions or formalities shall be imposed which would prevent any contracting party from utilizing fully the share of any such total quantity or value which has been allotted to it, subject to importation being made within any prescribed period to which the quota may relate.*

3. (a) In cases in which import licences are issued in connection with import restrictions, the contracting party applying the restrictions shall provide, upon the request of any contracting party having an interest in the trade in the product concerned, all relevant information concerning the administration of the restrictions, the import licences granted over a recent period and the distribution of such licences among supplying countries; *Provided* that there shall be no obligation to supply information as to the names of importing or supplying enterprises.

(b) In the case of import restrictions involving the fixing of quotas, the contracting party applying the restrictions shall give public notice of the total quantity or value of the product or products which will be permitted to be imported during a specified future period and of any change in such quantity or value. Any supplies of the product in question which were *en route* at the time at which public notice was given shall not be excluded from entry; *Provided* that they may be counted so far as practicable, against the quantity permitted to be imported in the period in question, and also, where necessary, against the quantities permitted to be imported in the next following period or periods; and *Provided* further that if any contracting party customarily exempts from such restrictions products entered for consumption or withdrawn from warehouse for consumption during a period of thirty days after the day of such public notice, such practice shall be considered full compliance with this sub-paragraph.

(c) In the case of quotas allocated among supplying countries, the contracting party applying the restrictions shall promptly inform all other contracting parties having an interest in supplying the product concerned of the shares in the quota currently allocated, by quantity or value, to the various supplying countries and shall give public notice thereof.

4. With regard to restrictions applied in accordance with paragraph 2 (*d*) of this Article or under paragraph 2 (*c*) of Article XI, the selection of a representative period for any product and the appraisal of any special factors* affecting the trade in the product shall be made initially by the contracting party applying the restriction; *Provided* that such contracting party shall, upon the request of any other contracting party having a substantial interest in supplying that product or upon the request of the CONTRACTING PARTIES, consult promptly with the other contracting party or the CONTRACTING PARTIES regarding the need for an adjustment of the proportion determined or of the base period selected, or for the reappraisal of the special factors involved, or for the elimination of conditions, formalities or any other provisions established unilaterally relating to the allocation of an adequate quota or its unrestricted utilization.

5. The provisions of this Article shall apply to any tariff quota instituted or maintained by any contracting party, and, in so far as applicable, the principles of this Article shall also extend to export restrictions.

Article XIV* Exceptions to the Rule of Non-discrimination ✓

1. A contracting party which applies restrictions under Article XII or under Section B of Article XVIII may, in the application of such restrictions, deviate from the provisions of Article XIII in a manner having equivalent effect to restrictions on payments and transfers for current international transactions which that contracting party may at that time apply under Article VIII or XIV of the Articles of Agreement of the International Monetary Fund, or under analogous provisions of a special exchange agreement entered into pursuant to paragraph 6 of Article XV.*

2. A contracting party which is applying import restrictions under Article XII or under Section B of Article XVIII may, with the consent of the CONTRACTING PARTIES, temporarily deviate from the provisions of Article XIII in respect of a small part of its external trade where

the benefits to the contracting party or contracting parties concerned substantially outweigh any injury which may result to the trade of other contracting parties.*

3. The provisions of Article XIII shall not preclude a group of territories having a common quota in the International Monetary Fund from applying against imports from other countries, but not among themselves, restrictions in accordance with the provisions of Article XII or of Section B of Article XVIII on condition that such restrictions are in all other respects consistent with the provisions of Article XIII.

4. A contracting party applying import restrictions under Article XII or under Section B of Article XVIII shall not be precluded by Articles XI to XV or Section B of Article XVIII of this Agreement from applying measures to direct its exports in such a manner as to increase its earnings of currencies which it can use without deviation from the provisions of Article XIII.

5. A contracting party shall not be precluded by Articles XI to XV, inclusive, or by Section B of Article XVIII, of this Agreement from applying quantitative restrictions:
   (a) having equivalent effect to exchange restrictions authorized under Section 3 (b) of Article VII of the Articles of Agreement of the International Monetary Fund, or
   (b) under the preferential arrangements provided for in Annex A of this Agreement, pending the outcome of the negotiations referred to therein.

Article XV   Exchange Arrangements

1. The CONTRACTING PARTIES shall seek co-operation with the International Monetary Fund to the end that the CONTRACTING PARTIES and the Fund may pursue a co-ordinated policy with regard to exchange questions within the jurisdiction of the Fund and questions of quantitative restrictions and other trade measures within the jurisdiction of the CONTRACTING PARTIES.

2. In all cases in which the CONTRACTING PARTIES are called upon to consider or deal with problems concerning monetary reserves, balances of payments or foreign exchange arrangements, they shall consult fully with the International Monetary Fund. In such consultations, the CONTRACTING PARTIES shall accept all findings of statistical and other facts presented by the Fund relating to foreign exchange, monetary reserves and balances of payments, and shall accept the determination of the Fund as to whether action by a contracting party in exchange matters is in accordance with the Articles of Agreement of the International Monetary Fund, or with the terms of a special exchange agreement between that contracting party and the CONTRACTING PARTIES. The CONTRACTING PARTIES in reaching their final decision in cases involving the criteria set forth in paragraph 2 (a) of Article XII or in paragraph 9 of Article XVIII, shall accept the determination of the Fund as to what constitutes a serious decline in the contracting party's monetary reserves, a very low level of its monetary reserves or a reasonable rate of increase in its monetary reserves, and as to the financial aspects of other matters covered in consultation in such cases.

3. The CONTRACTING PARTIES shall seek agreement with the Fund regarding procedures for consultation under paragraph 2 of this Article.

4. Contracting parties shall not, by exchange action, frustrate* the intent of the provisions of this Agreement, nor, by trade action, the intent of the provisions of the Articles of Agreement of the International Monetary Fund.

5. If the CONTRACTING PARTIES consider, at any time, that exchange restrictions on payments and transfers in connection with imports are being applied by a contracting party in a manner inconsistent with the exceptions provided for in this Agreement for quantitative restrictions, they shall report thereon to the Fund.

6. Any contracting party which is not a member of the Fund shall, within a time to be determined by the CONTRACTING PARTIES after consultation with the Fund, become a member of the Fund, or, failing that, enter into a special exchange agreement with the

CONTRACTING PARTIES. A contracting party which ceases to be a member of the Fund shall forthwith enter into a special exchange agreement with the CONTRACTING PARTIES. Any special exchange agreement entered into by a contracting party under this paragraph shall thereupon become part of its obligations under this Agreement.

7. (a) A special exchange agreement between a contracting party and the CONTRACTING PARTIES under paragraph 6 of this Article shall provide to the satisfaction of the CONTRACTING PARTIES that the objectives of this Agreement will not be frustrated as a result of action in exchange matters by the contracting party in question.

(b) The terms of any such agreement shall not impose obligations on the contracting party in exchange matters generally more restrictive than those imposed by the Articles of Agreement of the International Monetary Fund on members of the Fund.

8. A contracting party which is not a member of the Fund shall furnish such information within the general scope of section 5 of Article VIII of the Articles of Agreement of the International Monetary Fund as the CONTRACTING PARTIES may require in order to carry out their functions under this Agreement.

9. Nothing in this Agreement shall preclude:

(a) the use by a contracting party of exchange controls or exchange restrictions in accordance with the Articles of Agreement of the International Monetary Fund or with that contracting party's special exchange agreement with the CONTRACTING PARTIES, or

(b) the use by a contracting party of restrictions or controls in imports or exports, the sole effect of which, additional to the effects permitted under Articles XI, XII, XIII and XIV, is to make effective such exchange controls or exchange restrictions.

Article XVI*   Subsidies

Section A—Subsidies in General

1. If any contracting party grants or maintains any subsidy, including any form of income or price support, which operates directly or indirectly to increase exports of any product from, or to reduce imports of any product into, its territory, it shall notify the CONTRACTING PARTIES in writing of the extent and nature of the subsidization, of the estimated effect of the subsidization on the quantity of the affected product or products imported into or exported from its territory and of the circumstances making the subsidization necessary. In any case in which it is determined that serious prejudice to the interests of any other contracting party is caused or threatened by any such subsidization, the contracting party granting the subsidy shall, upon request, discuss with the other contracting party or parties concerned, or with the CONTRACTING PARTIES, the possibility of limiting the subsidization.

Section B—Additional Provisions on Export Subsidies*

2. The contracting parties recognize that the granting by a contracting party of a subsidy on the export of any product may have harmful effects for other contracting parties, both importing and exporting, may cause undue disturbance to their normal commercial interests, and may hinder the achievement of the objectives of this Agreement.

3. Accordingly, contracting parties should seek to avoid the use of subsidies on the export of primary products. If, however, a contracting party grants directly or indirectly any form of subsidy which operates to increase the export of any primary product from its territory, such subsidy shall not be applied in a manner which results in that contracting party having more than an equitable share of world export trade in that product, account being taken of the shares of the contracting parties in such trade in the product during a previous representative period, and any special factors which may have affected or may be affecting such trade in the product.*

4. Further, as from 1 January 1958 or the earliest practicable date thereafter, contracting parties shall cease to grant either directly or indirectly any form of subsidy on the export of any product other than a primary product which subsidy results in the sale of such product for export at a price lower than the comparable price charged for the like product to buyers in the domestic market. Until 31 December 1957 no contracting party shall extend the scope of any such subsidization beyond that existing on 1 January 1955 by the introduction of new, or the extension of existing, subsidies.*

5. The CONTRACTING PARTIES shall review the operation of the provisions of this Article from time to time with a view to examining its effectiveness, in the light of actual experience, in promoting the objectives of this Agreement and avoiding subsidization seriously prejudicial to the trade or interests of contracting parties.

Article XVII   State Trading Enterprises

1.* (a) Each contracting party undertakes that if it establishes or maintains a State enterprise, wherever located, or grants to any enterprise, formally or in effect, exclusive or special privileges,* such enterprise shall, in its purchases or sales involving either imports or exports, act in a manner consistent with the general principles of non-discriminatory treatment prescribed in this Agreement for governmental measures affecting imports or exports by private traders.

(b) The provisions of sub-paragraph (a) of this paragraph shall be understood to require that such enterprises shall, having due regard to the other provisions of this Agreement, make any such purchases or sales solely in accordance with commercial considerations,* including price, quality, availability, marketability, transportation and other conditions of purchase or sale, and shall afford the enterprises of the other contracting parties adequate opportunity, in accordance with customary business practice, to compete for participation in such purchases or sales.

(c) No contracting party shall prevent any enterprise (whether or not an enterprise described in sub-paragraph (a) of this paragraph) under its jurisdiction from acting in accordance with the principles of sub-paragraphs (a) and (b) of this paragraph.

2. The provisions of paragraph 1 of this Article shall not apply to imports of products for immediate or ultimate consumption in governmental use and not otherwise for resale or use in the production of goods* for sale. With respect to such imports, each contracting party shall accord to the trade of the other contracting parties fair and equitable treatment.

3. The contracting parties recognize that enterprises of the kind described in paragraph 1 (a) of this Article might be operated so as to create serious obstacles to trade; thus negotiations on a reciprocal and mutually advantageous basis designed to limit or reduce such obstacles are of importance to the expansion of international trade.*

4. (a) Contracting parties shall notify the CONTRACTING PARTIES of the products which are imported into or exported from their territories by enterprises of the kind described in paragraph 1 (a) of this Article.

(b) A contracting party establishing, maintaining or authorizing an import monopoly of a product, which is not the subject of a concession under Article II, shall, on the request of another contracting party having a substantial trade in the product concerned, inform the CONTRACTING PARTIES of the import mark-up* on the product during a recent representative period, or, when it is not possible to do so, of the price charged on the resale of the product.

(c) The CONTRACTING PARTIES may, at the request of a contracting party which has reason to believe that its interest[s] under this Agreement are being adversely affected by the operations of an enterprise of the kind described in paragraph 1 (a), request the contracting party establishing, maintaining or authorizing such enterprise to supply information about its operations related to the carrying out of the provisions of this Agreement.

(d) The provisions of this paragraph shall not require any contracting party to disclose confidential information which would impede law enforcement or otherwise be contrary to the public interest or would prejudice the legitimate commercial interests of particular enterprises.

Article XVIII*   Governmental Assistance to Economic Development

1. The contracting parties recognize that the attainment of the objectives of this Agreement will be facilitated by the progressive development of their economies, particularly of those contracting parties the economies of which can only support low standards of living* and are in the early stages of development.*

2. The contracting parties recognize further that it may be necessary for those contracting parties, in order to implement programmes and policies of economic development designed to raise the general standard of living of their people, to take protective or other measures affecting imports, and that such measures are justified in so far as they facilitate the attainment of the objectives of this Agreement. They agree, therefore, that those contracting parties should enjoy additional facilities to enable them (a) to maintain sufficient flexibility in their tariff structure to be able to grant the tariff protection required for the establishment of a particular industry* and (b) to apply quantitative restrictions for balance of payments purposes in a manner which takes full account of the continued high level of demand for imports likely to be generated by their programmes of economic development.

3. The contracting parties recognize finally that, with those additional facilities which are provided for in Sections A and B of this Article, the provisions of this Agreement would normally be sufficient to enable contracting parties to meet the requirements of their economic development. They agree, however, that there may be circumstances where no measure consistent with those provisions is practicable to permit a contracting party in the process of economic development to grant the governmental assistance required to promote the establishment of particular industries* with a view to raising the general standard of living of its people. Special procedures are laid down in Sections C and D of this Article to deal with those cases.

4. (a) Consequently, a contracting party, the economy of which can only support low standards of living* and is in the early stages of development,* shall be free to deviate temporarily from the provisions of the other Articles of this Agreement, as provided in Sections A, B and C of this Article.

   (b) A contracting party, the economy of which is in the process of development, but which does not come within the scope of sub-paragraph (a) above, may submit applications to the CONTRACTING PARTIES under Section D of this Article.

5. The contracting parties recognize that the export earnings of contracting parties, the economies of which are of the type described in paragraph 4 (a) and (b) above and which depend on exports of a small number of primary commodities, may be seriously reduced by a decline in the sale of such commodities. Accordingly, when the exports of primary commodities by such a contracting party are seriously affected by measures taken by another contracting party, it may have resort to the consultation provisions of Article XXII of this Agreement.

6. The CONTRACTING PARTIES shall review annually all measures applied pursuant to the provisions of Sections C and D of this Article.

Section A

7. (a) If a contracting party coming within the scope of paragraph 4 (a) of this Article considers it desirable, in order to promote the establishment of a particular industry* with a view to raising the general standard of living of its people, to modify or withdraw a concession included in the appropriate Schedule annexed to this Agreement, it shall notify the CONTRACTING PARTIES to this effect and enter into negotiations with any con-

tracting party with which such concession was initially negotiated, and with any other contracting party determined by the CONTRACTING PARTIES to have a substantial interest therein. If agreement is reached between such contracting parties concerned, they shall be free to modify or withdraw concessions under the appropriate Schedules to this Agreement in order to give effect to such agreement, including any compensatory adjustments involved.

(b) If agreement is not reached within sixty days after the notification provided for in sub-paragraph (a) above, the contracting party which proposes to modify or withdraw the concession may refer the matter to the CONTRACTING PARTIES which shall promptly examine it. If they find that the contracting party which proposes to modify or withdraw the concession has made every effort to reach an agreement and that the compensatory adjustment offered by it is adequate, that contracting party shall be free to modify or withdraw the concession if, at the same time, it gives effect to the compensatory adjustment. If the CONTRACTING PARTIES do not find that the compensation offered by a contracting party proposing to modify or withdraw the concession is adequate, but find that it has made every reasonable effort to offer adequate compensation, that contracting party shall be free to proceed with such modification or withdrawal. If such action is taken, any other contracting party referred to in sub-paragraph (a) above shall be free to modify or withdraw substantially equivalent concessions initially negotiated with the contracting party which has taken the action.*

Section B

8. The contracting parties recognize that contracting parties coming within the scope of paragraph 4 (a) of this Article tend, when they are in rapid process of development, to experience balance of payments difficulties arising mainly from efforts to expand their internal markets as well as from the instability in their terms of trade.

9. In order to safeguard its external financial position and to ensure a level of reserves adequate for the implementation of its programme of economic development, a contracting party coming within the scope of paragraph 4 (a) of this Article may, subject to the provisions of paragraphs 10 to 12, control the general level of its imports by restricting the quantity or value of merchandise permitted to be imported; *Provided* that the import restrictions instituted, maintained or intensified shall not exceed those necessary:
   (a) to forestall the threat of, or to stop, a serious decline in its monetary reserves, or
   (b) in the case of a contracting party with inadequate monetary reserves, to achieve a reasonable rate of increase in its reserves.

   Due regard shall be paid in either case to any special factors which may be affecting the reserves of the contracting party or its need for reserves, including, where special external credits or other resources are available to it, the need to provide for the appropriate use of such credits or resources.

10. In applying these restrictions, the contracting party may determine their incidence on imports of different products or classes of products in such a way as to give priority to the importation of those products which are more essential in the light of its policy of economic development; *Provided* that the restrictions are so applied as to avoid unnecessary damage to the commercial or economic interests of any other contracting party and not to prevent unreasonably the importation of any description of goods in minimum commercial quantities the exclusion of which would impair regular channels of trade; and *Provided* further that the restrictions are not so applied as to prevent the importation of commercial samples or to prevent compliance with patent, trade mark, copyright or similar procedures.

11. In carrying out its domestic policies, the contracting party concerned shall pay due regard to the need for restoring equilibrium in its balance of payments on a sound and lasting basis and to the desirability of assuring an economic employment of productive resources. It shall

progressively relax any restrictions applied under this Section as conditions improve, maintaining them only to the extent necessary under the terms of paragraph 9 of this Article and shall eliminate them when conditions no longer justify such maintenance; *Provided* that no contracting party shall be required to withdraw or modify restrictions on the ground that a change in its development policy would render unnecessary the restrictions which it is applying under this Section.*

12. (a) Any contracting party applying new restrictions or raising the general level of its existing restrictions by a substantial intensification of the measures applied under this Section, shall immediately after instituting or intensifying such restrictions (or, in circumstances in which prior consultation is practicable, before doing so) consult with the CONTRACTING PARTIES as to the nature of its balance of payments difficulties, alternative corrective measures which may be available, and the possible effect of the restrictions on the economies of other contracting parties.

(b) On a date to be determined by them* the CONTRACTING PARTIES shall review all restrictions still applied under this Section on that date. Beginning two years after that date, contracting parties applying restrictions under this Section shall enter into consultations of the type provided for in sub-paragraph (a) above with the CONTRACTING PARTIES at intervals of approximately, but not less than, two years according to a programme to be drawn up each year by the CONTRACTING PARTIES; *Provided* that no consultation under this sub-paragraph shall take place within two years after the conclusion of a consultation of a general nature under any other provision of this paragraph.

(c) (i) If, in the course of consultations with a contracting party under sub-paragraph (a) or (b) of this paragraph, the CONTRACTING PARTIES find that the restrictions are not consistent with the provisions of this Section or with those of Article XIII (subject to the provisions of Article XIV), they shall indicate the nature of the inconsistency and may advise that the restrictions be suitably modified.

(ii) If, however, as a result of the consultations, the CONTRACTING PARTIES determine that the restrictions are being applied in a manner involving an inconsistency of a serious nature with the provisions of this Section or with those of Article XIII (subject to the provisions of Article XIV) and that damage to the trade of any contracting party is caused or threatened thereby, they shall so inform the contracting party applying the restrictions and shall make appropriate recommendations for securing conformity with such provisions within a specified period. If such contracting party does not comply with these recommendations within the specified period, the CONTRACTING PARTIES may release any contracting party the trade of which is adversely affected by the restrictions from such obligations under this Agreement towards the contracting party applying the restrictions as they determine to be appropriate in the circumstances.

(d) The CONTRACTING PARTIES shall invite any contracting party which is applying restrictions under this Section to enter into consultations with them at the request of any contracting party which can establish a *prima facie* case that the restrictions are inconsistent with the provisions of this Section or with those of Article XIII (subject to the provisions of Article XIV) and that its trade is adversely affected thereby. However, no such invitation shall be issued unless the CONTRACTING PARTIES have ascertained that direct discussions between the contracting parties concerned have not been successful. If, as a result of the consultations with the CONTRACTING PARTIES no agreement is reached and they determine that the restrictions are being applied inconsistently with such provisions, and that damage to the trade of the contracting party initiating the procedure is caused or threatened thereby, they shall recommend the withdrawal or modification of the restrictions. If the restrictions are not withdrawn or modified within such time as the CONTRACTING PARTIES may prescribe, they may release the contracting party initiating the procedure from such obligations under this Agreement towards the contracting party applying the restrictions as they determine to be appropriate in the circumstances.

(e) If a contracting party against which action has been taken in accordance with the last sentence of sub-paragraph (c) (ii) or (d) of this paragraph, finds that the release of obligations authorized by the CONTRACTING PARTIES adversely affects the operation of its programme and policy of economic development, it shall be free, not later than sixty days after such action is taken, to give written notice to the Executive Secretary[2] to the Contracting Parties of its intention to withdraw from this Agreement and such withdrawal shall take effect on the sixtieth day following the day on which the notice is received by him.

(f) In proceeding under this paragraph, the CONTRACTING PARTIES shall have due regard to the factors referred to in paragraph 2 of this Article. Determinations under this paragraph shall be rendered expeditiously and, if possible, within sixty days of the initiation of the consultations.

Section C

13. If a contracting party coming within the scope of paragraph 4 (a) of this Article finds that governmental assistance is required to promote the establishment of a particular industry* with a view to raising the general standard of living of its people, but that no measure consistent with the other provisions of this Agreement is practicable to achieve that objective, it may have recourse to the provisions and procedures set out in this Section.*

14. The contracting party concerned shall notify the CONTRACTING PARTIES of the special difficulties which it meets in the achievement of the objective outlined in paragraph 13 of this Article and shall indicate the specific measure affecting imports which it proposes to introduce in order to remedy these difficulties. It shall not introduce that measure before the expiration of the time-limit laid down in paragraph 15 or 17, as the case may be, or if the measure affects imports of a product which is the subject of a concession included in the appropriate Schedule annexed to this Agreement, unless it has secured the concurrence of the CONTRACTING PARTIES in accordance with provisions of paragraph 18; *Provided* that, if the industry receiving assistance has already started production, the contracting party may, after informing the CONTRACTING PARTIES, take such measures as may be necessary to prevent, during that period, imports of the product or products concerned from increasing substantially above a normal level.*

15. If, within thirty days of the notification of the measure, the CONTRACTING PARTIES do not request the contracting party concerned to consult with them,* that contracting party shall be free to deviate from the relevant provisions of the other Articles of this Agreement to the extent necessary to apply the proposed measure.

16. If it is requested by the CONTRACTING PARTIES to do so, *the contracting party concerned shall consult with them as to the purpose of the proposed measure, as to alternative measures which may be available under this Agreement, and as to the possible effect of the measure proposed on the commercial and economic interests of other contracting parties. If, as a result of such consultation, the CONTRACTING PARTIES agree that there is no measure consistent with the other provisions of this Agreement which is practicable in order to achieve the objective outlined in paragraph 13 of this Article, and concur* in the proposed measure, the contracting party concerned shall be released from its

---

2 By the Decision of 23 March 1965, the CONTRACTING PARTIES changed the title of the head of the GATT secretariat from "Executive Secretary" to "Director-General".

obligations under the relevant provisions of the other Articles of this Agreement to the extent necessary to apply that measure.

17. If, within ninety days after the date of the notification of the proposed measure under paragraph 14 of this Article, the CONTRACTING PARTIES have not concurred in such measure, the contracting party concerned may introduce the measure proposed after informing the CONTRACTING PARTIES.

18. If the proposed measure affects a product which is the subject of a concession included in the appropriate Schedule annexed to this Agreement, the contracting party concerned shall enter into consultations with any other contracting party with which the concession was initially negotiated, and with any other contracting party determined by the CONTRACTING PARTIES to have a substantial interest therein. The CONTRACTING PARTIES shall concur* in the measure if they agree that there is no measure consistent with the other provisions of this Agreement which is practicable in order to achieve the objective set forth in paragraph 13 of this Article, and if they are satisfied:
    (a) that agreement has been reached with such other contracting parties as a result of the consultations referred to above, or
    (b) if no such agreement has been reached within sixty days after the notification provided for in paragraph 14 has been received by the CONTRACTING PARTIES, that the contracting party having recourse to this Section has made all reasonable efforts to reach an agreement and that the interests of other contracting parties are adequately safeguarded.*
    The contracting party having recourse to this Section shall thereupon be released from its obligations under the relevant provisions of the other Articles of this Agreement to the extent necessary to permit it to apply the measure.

19. If a proposed measure of the type described in paragraph 13 of this Article concerns an industry the establishment of which has in the initial period been facilitated by incidental protection afforded by restrictions imposed by the contracting party concerned for balance of payments purposes under the relevant provisions of this Agreement, that contracting party may resort to the provisions and procedures of this Section; *Provided* that it shall not apply the proposed measure without the concurrence* of the CONTRACTING PARTIES.*

20. Nothing in the preceding paragraphs of this Section shall authorize any deviation from the provisions of Articles I, II and XIII of this Agreement. The provisos to paragraph 10 of this Article shall also be applicable to any restriction under this Section.

21. At any time while a measure is being applied under paragraph 17 of this Article any contracting party substantially affected by it may suspend the application to the trade of the contracting party having recourse to this Section of such substantially equivalent concessions or other obligations under this Agreement the suspension of which the CONTRACTING PARTIES do not disapprove;* *Provided* that sixty days' notice of such suspension is given to the CONTRACTING PARTIES not later than six months after the measure has been introduced or changed substantially to the detriment of the contracting party affected. Any such contracting party shall afford adequate opportunity for consultation in accordance with the provisions of Article XXII of this Agreement.

Section D

22. A contracting party coming within the scope of sub-paragraph 4 (b) of this Article desiring, in the interest of the development of its economy, to introduce a measure of the type described in paragraph 13 of this Article in respect of the establishment of a particular industry* may apply to the CONTRACTING PARTIES for approval of such measure. The CONTRACTING PARTIES shall promptly consult with such contracting party and shall, in making their decision, be guided by the considerations set out in paragraph 16. If the CONTRACTING PARTIES concur* in the proposed measure the contracting party

concerned shall be released from its obligations under the relevant provisions of the other Articles of this Agreement to the extent necessary to permit it to apply the measure. If the proposed measure affects a product which is the subject of a concession included in the appropriate Schedule annexed to this Agreement, the provisions of paragraph 18 shall apply.*

23. Any measure applied under this Section shall comply with the provisions of paragraph 20 of this Article.

Article XIX   Emergency Action on Imports of Particular Products

1. (*a*) If, as a result of unforeseen developments and of the effect of the obligations incurred by a contracting party under this Agreement, including tariff concessions, any product is being imported into the territory of that contracting party in such increased quantities and under such conditions as to cause or threaten serious injury to domestic producers in that territory of like or directly competitive products, the contracting party shall be free, in respect of such product, and to the extent and for such time as may be necessary to prevent or remedy such injury, to suspend the obligation in whole or in part or to withdraw or modify the concession.

   (*b*) If any product, which is the subject of a concession with respect to a preference, is being imported into the territory of a contracting party in the circumstances set forth in sub-paragraph (*a*) of this paragraph, so as to cause or threaten serious injury to domestic producers of like or directly competitive products in the territory of a contracting party which receives or received such preference, the importing contracting party shall be free, if that other contracting party so requests, to suspend the relevant obligation in whole or in part or to withdraw or modify the concession in respect of the product, to the extent and for such time as may be necessary to prevent or remedy such injury.

2. Before any contracting party shall take action pursuant to the provisions of paragraph 1 of this Article, it shall give notice in writing to the CONTRACTING PARTIES as far in advance as may be practicable and shall afford the CONTRACTING PARTIES and those contracting parties having a substantial interest as exporters of the product concerned an opportunity to consult with it in respect of the proposed action. When such notice is given in relation to a concession with respect to a preference, the notice shall name the contracting party which has requested the action. In critical circumstances, where delay would cause damage which it would be difficult to repair, action under paragraph 1 of this Article may be taken provisionally without prior consultation, on the condition that consultation shall be effected immediately after taking such action.

3. (*a*) If agreement among the interested contracting parties with respect to the action is not reached, the contracting party which proposes to take or continue the action shall, nevertheless, be free to do so, and if such action is taken or continued, the affected contracting parties shall then be free, not later than ninety days after such action is taken, to suspend, upon the expiration of thirty days from the day on which written notice of such suspension is received by the CONTRACTING PARTIES, the application to the trade of the contracting party taking such action, or, in the case envisaged in paragraph 1 (*b*) of this Article, to the trade of the contracting party requesting such action, of such substantially equivalent concessions or other obligations under this Agreement the suspension of which the CONTRACTING PARTIES do not disapprove.

   (*b*) Notwithstanding the provisions of sub-paragraph (*a*) of this paragraph, where action is taken under paragraph 2 of this Article without prior consultation and causes or threatens serious injury in the territory of a contracting party to the domestic producers of products affected by the action, that contracting party shall, where delay would cause damage difficult to repair, be free to suspend, upon the taking of the action and throughout the period of consultation, such concessions or other obligations as may be necessary to prevent or remedy the injury.

Article XX   General Exceptions

Subject to the requirement that such measures are not applied in a manner which would constitute a means of arbitrary or unjustifiable discrimination between countries where the same conditions prevail, or a disguised restriction on international trade, nothing in this Agreement shall be construed to prevent the adoption or enforcement by any contracting party of measures:

(*a*) necessary to protect public morals;

(*b*) necessary to protect human, animal or plant life or health;

(*c*) relating to the importations or exportations of gold or silver;

(*d*) necessary to secure compliance with laws or regulations which are not inconsistent with the provisions of this Agreement, including those relating to customs enforcement, the enforcement of monopolies operated under paragraph 4 of Article II and Article XVII, the protection of patents, trade marks and copyrights, and the prevention of deceptive practices;

(*e*) relating to the products of prison labour;

(*f*) imposed for the protection of national treasures of artistic, historic or archaeological value;

(*g*) relating to the conservation of exhaustible natural resources if such measures are made effective in conjunction with restrictions on domestic production or consumption;

(*h*) undertaken in pursuance of obligations under any intergovernmental commodity agreement which conforms to criteria submitted to the CONTRACTING PARTIES and not disapproved by them or which is itself so submitted and not so disapproved;*

(*i*) involving restrictions on exports of domestic materials necessary to ensure essential quantities of such materials to a domestic processing industry during periods when the domestic price of such materials is held below the world price as part of a governmental stabilization plan; *Provided* that such restrictions shall not operate to increase the exports of or the protection afforded to such domestic industry, and shall not depart from the provisions of this Agreement relating to non-discrimination;

(*j*) essential to the acquisition or distribution of products in general or local short supply; *Provided* that any such measures shall be consistent with the principle that all contracting parties are entitled to an equitable share of the international supply of such products, and that any such measures, which are inconsistent with the other provisions of the Agreement shall be discontinued as soon as the conditions giving rise to them have ceased to exist. The CONTRACTING PARTIES shall review the need for this sub-paragraph not later than 30 June 1960.

Article XXI   Security Exceptions

Nothing in this Agreement shall be construed

(*a*) to require any contracting party to furnish any information the disclosure of which it considers contrary to its essential security interests; or

(*b*) to prevent any contracting party from taking any action which it considers necessary for the protection of its essential security interests
  (i) relating to fissionable materials or the materials from which they are derived;
  (ii) relating to the traffic in arms, ammunition and implements of war and to such traffic in other goods and materials as is carried on directly or indirectly for the purpose of supplying a military establishment;
  (iii) taken in time of war or other emergency in international relations; or

(*c*) to prevent any contracting party from taking any action in pursuance of its obligations under the United Nations Charter for the maintenance of international peace and security.

Article XXII   Consultation

1. Each contracting party shall accord sympathetic consideration to, and shall afford adequate opportunity for consultation regarding, such representations as may be made by another contracting party with respect to any matter affecting the operation of this Agreement.

2. The CONTRACTING PARTIES may, at the request of a contracting party, consult with any contracting party or parties in respect of any matter for which it has not been possible to find a satisfactory solution through consultation under paragraph 1.

Article XXIII   Nullification or Impairment

1. If any contracting party should consider that any benefit accruing to it directly or indirectly under this Agreement is being nullified or impaired or that the attainment of any objective of the Agreement is being impeded as the result of

   (*a*) the failure of another contracting party to carry out its obligations under this Agreement, or

   (*b*) the application by another contracting party of any measure, whether or not it conflicts with the provisions of this Agreement, or

   (*c*) the existence of any other situation,

   the contracting party may, with a view to the satisfactory adjustment of the matter, make written representations or proposals to the other contracting party or parties which it considers to be concerned. Any contracting party thus approached shall give sympathetic consideration to the representations or proposals made to it.

2. If no satisfactory adjustment is effected between the contracting parties concerned within a reasonable time, or if the difficulty is of the type described in paragraph 1 (*c*) of this Article, the matter may be referred to the CONTRACTING PARTIES. The CONTRACTING PARTIES shall promptly investigate any matter so referred to them and shall make appropriate recommendations to the contracting parties which they consider to be concerned, or give a ruling on the matter, as appropriate. The CONTRACTING PARTIES may consult with contracting parties, with the Economic and Social Council of the United Nations and with any appropriate inter-governmental organization in cases where they consider such consultation necessary. If the CONTRACTING PARTIES consider that the circumstances are serious enough to justify such action, they may authorize a contracting party or parties to suspend the application to any other contracting party or parties of such concessions or other obligations under this Agreement as they determine to be appropriate in the circumstances. If the application to any contracting party of any concession or other obligation is in fact suspended, that contracting party shall then be free, not later than sixty days after such action is taken, to give written notice to the Executive Secretary[3] to the Contracting Parties of its intention to withdraw from this Agreement and such withdrawal shall take effect upon the sixtieth day following the day on which such notice is received by him.

PART III

Article XXIV   Territorial Application—Frontier Traffic—Customs Unions and Free-trade Areas

1. The provisions of this Agreement shall apply to the metropolitan customs territories of the contracting parties and to any other customs territories in respect of which this Agreement has been accepted under Article XXVI or is being applied under Article XXXIII or pursuant to the Protocol of Provisional Application. Each such customs territory shall, exclusively for the purposes of the territorial application of this Agreement, be treated as though it were a contracting party; *Provided* that the provisions of this paragraph shall not be construed to

---

3 By the Decision of 23 March 1965, the CONTRACTING PARTIES changed the title of the head of the GATT secretariat from "Executive Secretary" to "Director-General".

create any rights or obligations as between two or more customs territories in respect of which this Agreement has been accepted under Article XXVI or is being applied under Article XXXIII or pursuant to the Protocol of Provisional Application by a single contracting party.

2. For the purposes of this Agreement a customs territory shall be understood to mean any territory with respect to which separate tariffs or other regulations of commerce are maintained for a substantial part of the trade of such territory with other territories.

3. The provisions of this Agreement shall not be construed to prevent:
    (a) Advantages accorded by any contracting party to adjacent countries in order to facilitate frontier traffic;
    (b) Advantages accorded to the trade with the Free Territory of Trieste by countries contiguous to that territory, provided that such advantages are not in conflict with the Treaties of Peace arising out of the Second World War.

4. The contracting parties recognize the desirability of increasing freedom of trade by the development, through voluntary agreements, of closer integration between the economies of the countries parties to such agreements. They also recognize that the purpose of a customs union or of a free-trade area should be to facilitate trade between the constituent territories and not to raise barriers to the trade of other contracting parties with such territories.

5. Accordingly, the provisions of this Agreement shall not prevent, as between the territories of contracting parties, the formation of a customs union or of a free-trade area or the adoption of an interim agreement necessary for the formation of a customs union or of a free-trade area; *Provided* that:
    (a) with respect to a customs union, or an interim agreement leading to a formation of a customs union, the duties and other regulations of commerce imposed at the institution of any such union or interim agreement in respect of trade with contracting parties not parties to such union or agreement shall not on the whole be higher or more restrictive than the general incidence of the duties and regulations of commerce applicable in the constituent territories prior to the formation of such union or the adoption of such interim agreement, as the case may be;
    (b) with respect to a free-trade area, or an interim agreement leading to the formation of a free-trade area, the duties and other regulations of commerce maintained in each of the constituent territories and applicable at the formation of such free-trade area or the adoption of such interim agreement to the trade of contracting parties not included in such area or not parties to such agreement shall not be higher or more restrictive than the corresponding duties and other regulations of commerce existing in the same constituent territories prior to the formation of the free-trade area, or interim agreement as the case may be; and
    (c) any interim agreement referred to in sub-paragraphs (a) and (b) shall include a plan and schedule for the formation of such a customs union or of such a free-trade area within a reasonable length of time.

6. If, in fulfilling the requirements of sub-paragraph 5 (a), a contracting party proposes to increase any rate of duty inconsistently with the provisions of Article II, the procedure set forth in Article XXVIII shall apply. In providing for compensatory adjustment, due account shall be taken of the compensation already afforded by the reduction brought about in the corresponding duty of the other constituents of the union.

7. (a) Any contracting party deciding to enter into a customs union or free-trade area, or an interim agreement leading to the formation of such a union or area, shall promptly notify the CONTRACTING PARTIES and shall make available to them such information regarding the proposed union or area as will enable them to make such reports and recommendations to contracting parties as they may deem appropriate.

(b) If, after having studied the plan and schedule included in an interim agreement referred to in paragraph 5 in consultation with the parties to that agreement and taking due account of the information made available in accordance with the provisions of sub-paragraph (a), the CONTRACTING PARTIES find that such agreement is not likely to result in the formation of a customs union or of a free-trade area within the period contemplated by the parties to the agreement or that such period is not a reasonable one, the CONTRACT-ING PARTIES shall make recommendations to the parties to the agreement. The parties shall not maintain or put into force, as the case may be, such agreement if they are not prepared to modify it in accordance with these recommendations.

(c) Any substantial change in the plan or schedule referred to in paragraph 5 (c) shall be communicated to the CONTRACTING PARTIES, which may request the contracting parties concerned to consult with them if the change seems likely to jeopardize or delay unduly the formation of the customs union or of the free-trade area.

8. For the purposes of this Agreement:

(a) A customs union shall be understood to mean the substitution of a single customs territory for two or more customs territories, so that

(i) duties and other restrictive regulations of commerce (except, where necessary, those permitted under Articles XI, XII, XIII, XIV, XV and XX) are eliminated with respect to substantially all the trade between the constituent territories of the union or at least with respect to substantially all the trade in products originating in such territories, and,

(ii) subject to the provisions of paragraph 9, substantially the same duties and other regulations of commerce are applied by each of the members of the union to the trade of territories not included in the union;

(b) A free-trade area shall be understood to mean a group of two or more customs territories in which the duties and other restrictive regulations of commerce (except, where necessary, those permitted under Articles XI, XII, XIII, XIV, XV and XX) are elimin-ated on substantially all the trade between the constituent territories in products originating in such territories.

9. The preferences referred to in paragraph 2 of Article I shall not be affected by the formation of a customs union or of a free-trade area but may be eliminated or adjusted by means of negotiations with contracting parties affected.* This procedure of negotiations with affected contracting parties shall, in particular, apply to the elimination of preferences required to conform with the provisions of paragraph 8 (a)(i) and paragraph 8 (b).

10. The CONTRACTING PARTIES may by a two-thirds majority approve proposals which do not fully comply with the requirements of paragraphs 5 to 9 inclusive, provided that such proposals lead to the formation of a customs union or a free-trade area in the sense of this Article.

11. Taking into account the exceptional circumstances arising out of the establishment of India and Pakistan as independent States and recognizing the fact that they have long constituted an economic unit, the contracting parties agree that the provisions of this Agreement shall not prevent the two countries from entering into special arrangements with respect to the trade between them, pending the establishment of their mutual trade relations on a definitive basis.*

12. Each contracting party shall take such reasonable measures as may be available to it to ensure observance of the provisions of this Agreement by the regional and local governments and authorities within its territories.

Article XXV   Joint Action by the Contracting Parties

1. Representatives of the contracting parties shall meet from time to time for the purpose of giving effect to those provisions of this Agreement which involve joint action and, generally, with a view to facilitating the operation and furthering the objectives of this Agreement.

Wherever reference is made in this Agreement to the contracting parties acting jointly they are designated as the CONTRACTING PARTIES.

2. The Secretary-General of the United Nations is requested to convene the first meeting of the CONTRACTING PARTIES, which shall take place not later than March 1, 1948.

3. Each contracting party shall be entitled to have one vote at all meetings of the CONTRACTING PARTIES.

4. Except as otherwise provided for in this Agreement, decisions of the CONTRACTING PARTIES shall be taken by a majority of the votes cast.

5. In exceptional circumstances not elsewhere provided for in this Agreement, the CONTRACTING PARTIES may waive an obligation imposed upon a contracting party by this Agreement; *Provided* that any such decision shall be approved by a two-thirds majority of the votes cast and that such majority shall comprise more than half of the contracting parties. The CONTRACTING PARTIES may also by such a vote
   (i) define certain categories of exceptional circumstances to which other voting requirements shall apply for the waiver of obligations, and
   (ii) prescribe such criteria as may be necessary for the application of this paragraph.[4]

Article XXVI   Acceptance, Entry into Force and Registration

1. The date of this Agreement shall be 30 October 1947.

2. This Agreement shall be open for acceptance by any contracting party which, on 1 March 1955, was a contracting party or was negotiating with a view to accession to this Agreement.

3. This Agreement, done in a single English original and a single French original, both texts authentic, shall be deposited with the Secretary-General of the United Nations, who shall furnish certified copies thereof to all interested governments.

4. Each government accepting this Agreement shall deposit an instrument of acceptance with the Executive Secretary[5] to the Contracting Parties, who will inform all interested governments of the date of deposit of each instrument of acceptance and of the day on which this Agreement enters into force under paragraph 6 of this Article.

5. (a) Each government accepting this Agreement does so in respect of its metropolitan territory and of the other territories for which it has international responsibility, except such separate customs territories as it shall notify to the Executive Secretary[5] to the CONTRACTING PARTIES at the time of its own acceptance.
   (b) Any government, which has so notified the Executive Secretary[5] under the exceptions in sub-paragraph (a) of this paragraph, may at any time give notice to the Executive Secretary[5] that its acceptance shall be effective in respect of any separate customs territory or territories so excepted and such notice shall take effect on the thirtieth day following the day on which it is received by the Executive Secretary.[5]
   (c) If any of the customs territories, in respect of which a contracting party has accepted this Agreement, possesses or acquires full autonomy in the conduct of its external commercial relations and of the other matters provided for in this Agreement, such territory shall, upon sponsorship through a declaration by the responsible contracting party establishing the above-mentioned fact, be deemed to be a contracting party.

6. This Agreement shall enter into force, as among the governments which have accepted it, on the thirtieth day following the day on which instruments of acceptance have been deposited with Executive Secretary[6] to the Contracting Parties on behalf of governments named in

---

4 The authentic text erroneously reads "sub-paragraph".
5 By the Decision of 23 March 1965, the CONTRACTING PARTIES changed the title of the head of the GATT secretariat from "Executive Secretary" to "Director-General".
6 By the Decision of 23 March 1965, the CONTRACTING PARTIES changed the title of the head of the GATT secretariat from "Executive Secretary" to "Director-General".

Annex H, the territories of which account for 85 per centum of the total external trade of the territories of such governments, computed in accordance with the applicable column of percentages set forth therein. The instrument of acceptance of each other government shall take effect on the thirtieth day following the day on which such instrument has been deposited.

7. The United Nations is authorized to effect registration of this Agreement as soon as it enters into force.

Article XXVII   Withholding or Withdrawal of Concessions

Any contracting party shall at any time be free to withhold or to withdraw in whole or in part any concession, provided for in the appropriate Schedule annexed to this Agreement, in respect of which such contracting party determines that it was initially negotiated with a government which has not become, or has ceased to be, a contracting party. A contracting party taking such action shall notify the CONTRACTING PARTIES and, upon request, consult with contracting parties which have a substantial interest in the product concerned.

Article XXVIII*   Modification of Schedules

1. On the first day of each three-year period, the first period beginning on 1 January 1958 (or on the first day of any other period* that may be specified by the CONTRACTING PARTIES by two-thirds of the votes cast) a contracting party (hereafter in this Article referred to as the "applicant contracting party") may, by negotiation and agreement with any contracting party with which such concession was initially negotiated and with any other contracting party determined by the CONTRACTING PARTIES to have a principal supplying interest* (which two preceding categories of contracting parties, together with the applicant contracting party, are in this Article hereinafter referred to as the "contracting parties primarily concerned"), and subject to consultation with any other contracting party determined by the CONTRACTING PARTIES to have a substantial interest* in such concession, modify or withdraw a concession* included in the appropriate schedule annexed to this Agreement.

2. In such negotiations and agreement, which may include provision for compensatory adjustment with respect to other products, the contracting parties concerned shall endeavour to maintain a general level of reciprocal and mutually advantageous concessions not less favourable to trade than that provided for in this Agreement prior to such negotiations.

3. (a) If agreement between the contracting parties primarily concerned cannot be reached before 1 January 1958 or before the expiration of a period envisaged in paragraph 1 of this Article, the contracting party which proposes to modify or withdraw the concession shall, nevertheless, be free to do so and if such action is taken any contracting party with which such concession was initially negotiated, any contracting party determined under paragraph 1 to have a principal supplying interest and any contracting party determined under paragraph 1 to have a substantial interest shall then be free not later than six months after such action is taken, to withdraw, upon the expiration of thirty days from the day on which written notice of such withdrawal is received by the CONTRACTING PARTIES, substantially equivalent concessions initially negotiated with the applicant contracting party.

   (b) If agreement between the contracting parties primarily concerned is reached but any other contracting party determined under paragraph 1 of this Article to have a substantial interest is not satisfied, such other contracting party shall be free, not later than six months after action under such agreement is taken, to withdraw, upon the expiration of thirty days from the day on which written notice of such withdrawal is received by the CONTRACTING PARTIES, substantially equivalent concessions initially negotiated with the applicant contracting party.

4. The CONTRACTING PARTIES may, at any time, in special circumstances, authorize* a contracting party to enter into negotiations for modification or withdrawal of a concession included in the appropriate Schedule annexed to this Agreement subject to the following procedures and conditions:

   (*a*) Such negotiations* and any related consultations shall be conducted in accordance with the provisions of paragraph 1 and 2 of this Article.

   (*b*) If agreement between the contracting parties primarily concerned is reached in the negotiations, the provisions of paragraph 3 (*b*) of this Article shall apply.

   (*c*) If agreement between the contracting parties primarily concerned is not reached within a period of sixty days* after negotiations have been authorized, or within such longer period as the CONTRACTING PARTIES may have prescribed, the applicant contracting party may refer the matter to the CONTRACTING PARTIES.

   (*d*) Upon such reference, the CONTRACTING PARTIES shall promptly examine the matter and submit their views to the contracting parties primarily concerned with the aim of achieving a settlement. If a settlement is reached, the provisions of paragraph 3 (*b*) shall apply as if agreement between the contracting parties primarily concerned had been reached. If no settlement is reached between the contracting parties primarily concerned, the applicant contracting party shall be free to modify or withdraw the concession, unless the CONTRACTING PARTIES determine that the applicant contracting party has unreasonably failed to offer adequate compensation.* If such action is taken, any contracting party with which the concession was initially negotiated, any contracting party determined under paragraph 4 (*a*) to have a principal supplying interest and any contracting party determined under paragraph 4 (*a*) to have a substantial interest, shall be free, not later than six months after such action is taken, to modify or withdraw, upon the expiration of thirty days from the day on which written notice of such withdrawal is received by the CONTRACTING PARTIES, substantially equivalent concessions initially negotiated with [the] applicant contracting party.

5. Before 1 January 1958 and before the end of any period envisaged in paragraph 1 a contracting party may elect by notifying the CONTRACTING PARTIES to reserve the right, for the duration of the next period, to modify the appropriate Schedule in accordance with the procedures of paragraph 1 to 3. If a contracting party so elects, other contracting parties shall have the right, during the same period, to modify or withdraw, in accordance with the same procedures, concessions initially negotiated with that contracting party.

Article XXVIII bis   Tariff Negotiations

1. The contracting parties recognize that customs duties often constitute serious obstacles to trade; thus negotiations on a reciprocal and mutually advantageous basis, directed to the substantial reduction of the general level of tariffs and other charges on imports and exports and in particular to the reduction of such high tariffs as discourage the importation even of minimum quantities, and conducted with due regard to the objectives of this Agreement and the varying needs of individual contracting parties, are of great importance to the expansion of international trade. The CONTRACTING PARTIES may therefore sponsor such negotiations from time to time.

2. (*a*) Negotiations under this Article may be carried out on a selective product-by-product basis or by the application of such multilateral procedures as may be accepted by the contracting parties concerned. Such negotiations may be directed towards the reduction of duties, the binding of duties at then existing levels or undertakings that individual duties or the average duties on specified categories of products shall not exceed specified levels. The binding against increase of low duties or of duty-free treatment shall, in principle, be recognized as a concession equivalent in value to the reduction of high duties.

(*b*) The contracting parties recognize that in general the success of multilateral negotiations would depend on the participation of all contracting parties which conduct a substantial proportion of their external trade with one another.

3. Negotiations shall be conducted on a basis which affords adequate opportunity to take into account:

(*a*) the needs of individual contracting parties and individual industries;

(*b*) the needs of less-developed countries for a more flexible use of tariff protection to assist their economic development and the special needs of these countries to maintain tariffs for revenue purposes; and

(*c*) all other relevant circumstances, including the fiscal,* developmental, strategic and other needs of the contracting parties concerned.

Article XXIX   The Relation of this Agreement to the Havana Charter

1. The contracting parties undertake to observe to the fullest extent of their executive authority the general principles of Chapters I to VI inclusive and of Chapter IX of the Havana Charter pending their acceptance of it in accordance with their constitutional procedures.*

2. Part II of this Agreement shall be suspended on the day on which the Havana Charter enters into force.

3. If by September 30, 1949, the Havana Charter has not entered into force, the contracting parties shall meet before December 31, 1949, to agree whether this Agreement shall be amended, supplemented or maintained.

4. If at any time the Havana Charter should cease to be in force, the CONTRACTING PARTIES shall meet as soon as practicable thereafter to agree whether this Agreement shall be supplemented, amended or maintained. Pending such agreement, Part II of this Agreement shall again enter into force; *Provided* that the provisions of Part II other than Article XXIII shall be replaced, *mutatis mutandis*, in the form in which they then appeared in the Havana Charter; and *Provided* further that no contracting party shall be bound by any provisions which did not bind it at the time when the Havana Charter ceased to be in force.

5. If any contracting party has not accepted the Havana Charter by the date upon which it enters into force, the CONTRACTING PARTIES shall confer to agree whether, and if so in what way, this Agreement in so far as it affects relations between such contracting party and other contracting parties, shall be supplemented or amended. Pending such agreement the provisions of Part II of this Agreement shall, notwithstanding the provisions of paragraph 2 of this Article, continue to apply as between such contracting party and other contracting parties.

6. Contracting parties which are Members of the International Trade Organization shall not invoke the provisions of this Agreement so as to prevent the operation of any provision of the Havana Charter. The application of the principle underlying this paragraph to any contracting party which is not a Member of the International Trade Organization shall be the subject of an agreement pursuant to paragraph 5 of this Article.

Article XXX   Amendments

1. Except where provision for modification is made elsewhere in this Agreement, amendments to the provisions of Part I of this Agreement or the provisions of Article XXIX or of this Article shall become effective upon acceptance by all the contracting parties, and other amendments to this Agreement shall become effective, in respect of those contracting parties which accept them, upon acceptance by two-thirds of the contracting parties and thereafter for each other contracting party upon acceptance by it.

2. Any contracting party accepting an amendment to this Agreement shall deposit an instrument of acceptance with the Secretary-General of the United Nations within such period as the CONTRACTING PARTIES may specify. The CONTRACTING PARTIES may decide that any amendment made effective under this Article is of such a nature that any contracting

party which has not accepted it within a period specified by the CONTRACTING PARTIES shall be free to withdraw from this Agreement, or to remain a contracting party with the consent of the CONTRACTING PARTIES.

Article XXXI   Withdrawal

Without prejudice to the provisions of paragraph 12 of Article XVIII, of Article XXIII or of paragraph 2 of Article XXX, any contracting party may withdraw from this Agreement, or may separately withdraw on behalf of any of the separate customs territories for which it has international responsibility and which at the time possesses full autonomy in the conduct of its external commercial relations and of the other matters provided for in this Agreement. The withdrawal shall take effect upon the expiration of six months from the day on which written notice of withdrawal is received by the Secretary-General of the United Nations.

Article XXXII   Contracting Parties

1. The contracting parties to this Agreement shall be understood to mean those governments which are applying the provisions of this Agreement under Articles XXVI or XXXIII or pursuant to the Protocol of Provisional Application.

2. At any time after the entry into force of this Agreement pursuant to paragraph 6 of Article XXVI, those contracting parties which have accepted this Agreement pursuant to paragraph 4 of Article XXVI may decide that any contracting party which has not so accepted it shall cease to be a contracting party.

Article XXXIII   Accession

A government not party to this Agreement, or a government acting on behalf of a separate customs territory possessing full autonomy in the conduct of its external commercial relations and of the other matters provided for in this Agreement, may accede to this Agreement, on its own behalf or on behalf of that territory, on terms to be agreed between such government and the CONTRACTING PARTIES. Decisions of the CONTRACTING PARTIES under this paragraph shall be taken by a two-thirds majority.

Article XXXIV   Annexes

The annexes to this Agreement are hereby made an integral part of this Agreement.

Article XXXV   Non-application of the Agreement between Particular Contracting Parties

1. This Agreement, or alternatively Article II of this Agreement, shall not apply as between any contracting party and any other contracting party if:
    (a) the two contracting parties have not entered into tariff negotiations with each other, and
    (b) either of the contracting parties, at the time either becomes a contracting party, does not consent to such application.

2. The CONTRACTING PARTIES may review the operation of this Article in particular cases at the request of any contracting party and make appropriate recommendations.

PART IV*   TRADE AND DEVELOPMENT

Article XXXVI   Principles and Objectives

1.* The contracting parties,
    (a) recalling that the basic objectives of this Agreement include the raising of standards of living and the progressive development of the economies of all contracting parties, and considering that the attainment of these objectives is particularly urgent for less-developed contracting parties;
    (b) considering that export earnings of the less-developed contracting parties can play a vital part in their economic development and that the extent of this contribution depends on the prices paid by the less-developed contracting parties for essential imports, the volume of their exports, and the prices received for these exports;

(c) noting, that there is a wide gap between standards of living in less-developed countries and in other countries;

(d) recognizing that individual and joint action is essential to further the development of the economies of less-developed contracting parties and to bring about a rapid advance in the standards of living in these countries;

(e) recognizing that international trade as a means of achieving economic and social advancement should be governed by such rules and procedures—and measures in conformity with such rules and procedures—as are consistent with the objectives set forth in this Article;

(f) noting that the CONTRACTING PARTIES may enable less-developed contracting parties to use special measures to promote their trade and development;

agree as follows.

2. There is need for a rapid and sustained expansion of the export earnings of the less-developed contracting parties.

3. There is need for positive efforts designed to ensure that less-developed contracting parties secure a share in the growth in international trade commensurate with the needs of their economic development.

4. Given the continued dependence of many less-developed contracting parties on the exportation of a limited range of primary products,* there is need to provide in the largest possible measure more favourable and acceptable conditions of access to world markets for these products, and wherever appropriate to devise measures designed to stabilize and improve conditions of world markets in these products, including in particular measures designed to attain stable, equitable and remunerative prices, thus permitting an expansion of world trade and demand and a dynamic and steady growth of the real export earnings of these countries so as to provide them with expanding resources for their economic development.

5. The rapid expansion of the economies of the less-developed contracting parties will be facilitated by a diversification* of the structure of their economies and the avoidance of an excessive dependence on the export of primary products. There is, therefore, need for increased access in the largest possible measure to markets under favourable conditions for processed and manufactured products currently or potentially of particular export interest to less-developed contracting parties.

6. Because of the chronic deficiency in the export proceeds and other foreign exchange earnings of less-developed contracting parties, there are important inter-relationships between trade and financial assistance to development. There is, therefore, need for close and continuing collaboration between the CONTRACTING PARTIES and the international lending agencies so that they can contribute most effectively to alleviating the burdens these less-developed contracting parties assume in the interest of their economic development.

7. There is need for appropriate collaboration between the CONTRACTING PARTIES, other intergovernmental bodies and the organs and agencies of the United Nations system, whose activities relate to the trade and economic development of less-developed countries.

8. The developed contracting parties do not expect reciprocity for commitments made by them in trade negotiations to reduce or remove tariffs and other barriers to the trade of less-developed contracting parties.*

9. The adoption of measures to give effect to these principles and objectives shall be a matter of conscious and purposeful effort on the part of the contracting parties both individually and jointly.

Article XXXVII Commitments

1. The developed contracting parties shall to the fullest extent possible—that is, except when compelling reasons, which may include legal reasons, make it impossible—give effect to the following provisions:

   (*a*) accord high priority to the reduction and elimination of barriers to products currently or potentially of particular export interest to less-developed contracting parties, including customs duties and other restrictions which differentiate unreasonably between such products in their primary and in their processed forms;*

   (*b*) refrain from introducing, or increasing the incidence of, customs duties or non-tariff import barriers on products currently or potentially of particular export interest to less-developed contracting parties; and

   (*c*)   (i) refrain from imposing new fiscal measures, and

       (ii) in any adjustments of fiscal policy accord high priority to the reduction and elimination of fiscal measures, which would hamper, or which hamper, significantly the growth of consumption of primary products, in raw or processed form, wholly or mainly produced in the territories of less-developed contracting parties, and which are applied specifically to those products.

2. (*a*) Whenever it is considered that effect is not being given to any of the provisions of sub-paragraph (*a*), (*b*) or (*c*) of paragraph 1, the matter shall be reported to the CONTRACT-ING PARTIES either by the contracting party not so giving effect to the relevant provisions or by any other interested contracting party.

   (*b*)   (i) The CONTRACTING PARTIES shall, if requested so to do by any interested contracting party, and without prejudice to any bilateral consultations that may be undertaken, consult with the contracting party concerned and all interested contracting parties with respect to the matter with a view to reaching solutions satisfactory to all contracting parties concerned in order to further the objectives set forth in Article XXXVI. In the course of these consultations, the reasons given in cases where effect was not being given to the provisions of sub-paragraph (*a*), (*b*) or (*c*) of paragraph 1 shall be examined.

      (ii) As the implementation of the provisions of sub-paragraph (*a*), (*b*) or (*c*) of paragraph 1 by individual contracting parties may in some cases be more readily achieved where action is taken jointly with other developed contracting parties, such consultation might, where appropriate, be directed towards this end.

     (iii) The consultations by the CONTRACTING PARTIES might also, in appropriate cases, be directed towards agreement on joint action designed to further the objectives of this Agreement as envisaged in paragraph 1 of Article XXV.

3. The developed contracting parties shall:

   (*a*) make every effort, in cases where a government directly or indirectly determines the resale price of products wholly or mainly produced in the territories of less-developed contracting parties, to maintain trade margins at equitable levels;

   (*b*) give active consideration to the adoption of other measures* designed to provide greater scope for the development of imports from less-developed contracting parties and collaborate in appropriate international action to this end;

   (*c*) have special regard to the trade interests of less-developed contracting parties when considering the application of other measures permitted under this Agreement to meet particular problems and explore all possibilities of constructive remedies before applying such measures where they would affect essential interests of those contracting parties.

4. Less-developed contracting parties agree to take appropriate action in implementation of the provisions of Part IV for the benefit of the trade of other less-developed contracting parties, in so far as such action is consistent with their individual present and future development, financial and trade needs taking into account past trade developments as well as the trade interests of less-developed contracting parties as a whole.

5. In the implementation of the commitments set forth in paragraph 1 to 4 each contracting party shall afford to any other interested contracting party or contracting parties full and prompt opportunity for consultations under the normal procedures of this Agreement with respect to any matter or difficulty which may arise.

Article XXXVIII   Joint Action

1. The contracting parties shall collaborate jointly, with the framework of this Agreement and elsewhere, as appropriate, to further the objectives set forth in Article XXXVI.

2. In particular, the CONTRACTING PARTIES shall:

   (*a*) where appropriate, take action, including action through international arrangements, to provide improved and acceptable conditions of access to world markets for primary products of particular interest to less-developed contracting parties and to devise measures designed to stabilize and improve conditions of world markets in these products including measures designed to attain stable, equitable and remunerative prices for exports of such products;

   (*b*) seek appropriate collaboration in matters of trade and development policy with the United Nations and its organs and agencies, including any institutions that may be created on the basis of recommendations by the United Nations Conference on Trade and Development;

   (*c*) collaborate in analysing the development plans and policies of individual less-developed contracting parties and in examining trade and aid relationships with a view to devising concrete measures to promote the development of export potential and to facilitate access to export markets for the products of the industries thus developed and, in this connection, seek appropriate collaboration with governments and international organizations, and in particular with organizations having competence in relation to financial assistance for economic development, in systematic studies of trade and aid relationships in individual less-developed contracting parties aimed at obtaining a clear analysis of export potential, market prospects and any further action that may be required;

   (*d*) keep under continuous review the development of world trade with special reference to the rate of growth of the trade of less-developed contracting parties and make such recommendations to contracting parties as may, in the circumstances, be deemed appropriate;

   (*e*) collaborate in seeking feasible methods to expand trade for the purpose of economic development, through international harmonization and adjustment of national policies and regulations, through technical and commercial standards affecting production, transportation and marketing, and through export promotion by the establishment of facilities for the increased flow of trade information and the development of market research; and

   (*f*) establish such institutional arrangements as may be necessary to further the objectives set forth in Article XXXVI and to give effect to the provision of this Part.

ANNEX A   LIST OF TERRITORIES REFERRED TO IN PARAGRAPH 2 (A) OF ARTICLE I

United Kingdom of Great Britain and Northern Ireland
Dependent territories of the United Kingdom of Great Britain and Northern Ireland
Canada
Commonwealth of Australia
Dependent territories of the Commonwealth of Australia
New Zealand
Dependent territories of New Zealand
Union of South Africa including South West Africa
Ireland
India (as on April 10, 1947)
Newfoundland
Southern Rhodesia
Burma
Ceylon

Certain of the territories listed above have two or more preferential rates in force for certain products. Any such territory may, by agreement with the other contracting parties which are principal suppliers of such products at the most-favoured-nation rate, substitute for such preferential rates a single preferential rate which shall not on the whole be less favourable to suppliers at the most-favoured-nation rate than the preferences in force prior to such substitution.

The imposition of an equivalent margin of tariff preference to replace a margin of preference in an internal tax existing on April 10, 1947 exclusively between two or more of the territories listed in this Annex or to replace the preferential quantitative arrangements described in the following paragraph, shall not be deemed to constitute an increase in a margin of tariff preference.

The preferential arrangements referred to in paragraph 5 (*b*) of Article XIV are those existing in the United Kingdom on 10 April 1947, under contractual agreements with the Governments of Canada, Australia and New Zealand, in respect of chilled and frozen beef and veal, frozen mutton and lamb, chilled and frozen pork and bacon. It is the intention, without prejudice to any action taken under sub-paragraph (*h*)[7] of Article XX, that these arrangements shall be eliminated or replaced by tariff preferences, and that negotiations to this end shall take place as soon as practicable among the countries substantially concerned or involved.

The film hire tax in force in New Zealand on 10 April 1947, shall, for the purposes of this Agreement, be treated as a customs duty under Article I. The renters' film quota in force in New Zealand on April 10, 1947, shall, for the purposes of this Agreement, be treated as a screen quota under Article IV.

The Dominions of India and Pakistan have not been mentioned separately in the above list since they had not come into existence as such on the base date of April 10, 1947.

ANNEX B   LIST OF TERRITORIES OF THE FRENCH UNION REFERRED TO IN PARAGRAPH 2 (*b*) OF ARTICLE I

France
French Equatorial Africa (Treaty Basin of the Congo[8] and other territories)
French West Africa
Cameroons under French Trusteeship[8]
French Somali Coast and Dependencies
French Establishments in Oceania
French Establishments in the Condominium of the New Hebrides[8]
Indo-China
Madagascar and Dependencies
Morocco (French zone)[8]
New Caledonia and Dependencies
Saint-Pierre and Miquelon
Togo under French Trusteeship[8]
Tunisia

ANNEX C   LIST OF TERRITORIES REFERRED TO IN PARAGRAPH 2 (*b*) OF ARTICLE I AS RESPECTS THE CUSTOMS UNION OF BELGIUM, LUXEMBURG AND THE NETHERLANDS

The Economic Union of Belgium and Luxemburg
Belgian Congo
Ruanda Urundi
Netherlands

---

7 The authentic text erroneously reads "part I (*h*)".
8 For imports into Metropolitan France and Territories of the French Union.

New Guinea
Surinam
Netherlands Antilles
Republic of Indonesia

For imports into the territories constituting the Customs Union only.

ANNEX D   LIST OF TERRITORIES REFERRED TO IN PARAGRAPH 2 (*b*) OF ARTICLE I AS RESPECTS THE UNITED STATES OF AMERICA

United States of America (customs territory)
Dependent territories of the United States of America
Republic of the Philippines

The imposition of an equivalent margin of tariff preference to replace a margin of preference in an internal tax existing on 10 April, 1947, exclusively between two or more of the territories listed in this Annex shall not be deemed to constitute an increase in a margin of tariff preference.

ANNEX E   LIST OF TERRITORIES COVERED BY PREFERENTIAL ARRANGEMENTS BETWEEN CHILE AND NEIGHBOURING COUNTRIES REFERRED TO IN PARAGRAPH 2 (*d*) OF ARTICLE I

Preferences in force exclusively between Chile on the one hand, and

1. Argentina
2. Bolivia
3. Peru

on the other hand.

ANNEX F   LIST OF TERRITORIES COVERED BY PREFERENTIAL ARRANGEMENTS BETWEEN LEBANON AND SYRIA AND NEIGHBOURING COUNTRIES REFERRED TO IN PARAGRAPH 2 (*d*) OF ARTICLE I

Preferences in force exclusively between the Lebano-Syrian Customs Union, on the one hand, and

1. Palestine
2. Transjordan

on the other hand.

ANNEX G   DATES ESTABLISHING MAXIMUM MARGINS OF PREFERENCE REFERRED TO IN PARAGRAPH 4[9] OF ARTICLE I

Australia	October 15, 1946
Canada	July 1, 1939
France	January 1, 1939
Lebano-Syrian Customs Union	November 30, 1938
Union of South Africa	July 1, 1938
Southern Rhodesia	May 1, 1941

---

9 The authentic text erroneously reads "Paragraph 3".

ANNEX H PERCENTAGE SHARES OF TOTAL EXTERNAL TRADE TO BE USED FOR THE PURPOSE OF MAKING THE DETERMINATION REFERRED TO IN ARTICLE XXVI

(based on the average of 1949–1953)

If, prior to the accession of the Government of Japan to the General Agreement, the present Agreement has been accepted by contracting parties the external trade of which under Column I accounts for the percentage of such trade specified in paragraph 6 of Article XXVI, Column I shall be applicable for the purposes of that paragraph. If the present Agreement has not been so accepted prior to the accession of the Government of Japan, Column II shall be applicable for the purposes of that paragraph.

	Column I	Column II
	(Contracting parties on 1 March 1955)	(Contracting parties on 1 March 1955 and Japan)
Australia	3.1	3.0
Austria	0.9	0.8
Belgium-Luxemburg	4.3	4.2
Brazil	2.5	2.4
Burma	0.3	0.3
Canada	6.7	6.5
Ceylon	0.5	0.5
Chile	0.6	0.6
Cuba	1.1	1.1
Czechoslovakia	1.4	1.4
Denmark	1.4	1.4
Dominican Republic	0.1	0.1
Finland	1.0	1.0
France	8.7	8.5
Germany, Federal Republic of	5.3	5.2
Greece	0.4	0.4
Haiti	0.1	0.1
India	2.4	2.4
Indonesia	1.3	1.3
Italy	2.9	2.8
Netherlands, Kingdom of the	4.7	4.6
New Zealand	1.0	1.0
Nicaragua	0.1	0.1
Norway	1.1	1.1
Pakistan	0.9	0.8
Peru	0.4	0.4
Rhodesia and Nyasaland	0.6	0.6
Sweden	2.5	2.4
Turkey	0.6	0.6
Union of South Africa	1.8	1.8
United Kingdom	20.3	19.8
United States of America	20.6	20.1
Uruguay	0.4	0.4
Japan	–	2.3
	100.0	100.0

Note: These percentages have been computed taking into account the trade of all territories in respect of which the General Agreement on Tariffs and Trade is applied.

ANNEX I   NOTES AND SUPPLEMENTARY PROVISIONS

AD *ARTICLE I*

Paragraph 1

The obligations incorporated in paragraph 1 of Article I by reference to paragraphs 2 and 4 of Article III and those incorporated in paragraph 2 (*b*) of Article II by reference to Article VI shall be considered as falling within Part II for the purposes of the Protocol of Provisional Application.

The cross-references, in the paragraph immediately above and in paragraph 1 of Article I, to paragraphs 2 and 4 of Article III shall only apply after Article III has been modified by the entry into force of the amendment provided for in the Protocol Modifying Part II and Article XXVI of the General Agreement on Tariffs and Trade, dated September 14, 1948.[10]

Paragraph 4

The term "margin of preference" means the absolute difference between the most-favoured-nation rate of duty and the preferential rate of duty for the like product, and not the proportionate relation between those rates. As examples:

(1) If the most-favoured-nation rate were 36 per cent *ad valorem* and the preferential rate were 24 per cent *ad valorem*, the margin of preference would be 12 per cent *ad valorem*, and not one-third of the most-favoured-nation rate;

(2) If the most-favoured-nation rate were 36 per cent *ad valorem* and the preferential rate were expressed as two-thirds of the most-favoured-nation rate, the margin of preference would be 12 per cent *ad valorem*;

(3) If the most-favoured-nation rate were 2 francs per kilogramme and the preferential rate were 1.50 francs per kilogramme, the margin of preference would be 0.50 franc per kilogramme.

The following kinds of customs action, taken in accordance with established uniform procedures, would not be contrary to a general binding of margins of preference:

(i) The re-application to an imported product of a tariff classification or rate of duty, properly applicable to such product, in cases in which the application of such classification or rate to such product was temporarily suspended or inoperative on April 10, 1947; and

(ii) The classification of a particular product under a tariff item other than that under which importations of that product were classified on April 10, 1947, in cases in which the tariff law clearly contemplates that such product may be classified under more than one tariff item.

AD *ARTICLE II*

Paragraph 2 (a)

The cross-reference, in paragraph 2 (*a*) of Article II, to paragraph 2 of Article III shall only apply after Article III has been modified by the entry into force of the amendment provided for in the Protocol Modifying Part II and Article XXVI of the General Agreement on Tariffs and Trade, dated September 14, 1948.[11]

Paragraph 2 (b)

See the note relating to paragraph 1 of Article I.

Paragraph 4

Except where otherwise specifically agreed between the contracting parties which initially negotiated the concession, the provisions of this paragraph will be applied in the light of the provisions of Article 31 of the Havana Charter.

---

10 This Protocol entered into force on 14 December 1948.
11 This Protocol entered into force on 14 December 1948.

AD *ARTICLE III*

Any internal tax or other internal charge, or any law, regulation or requirement of the kind referred to in paragraph 1 which applies to an imported product and to the like domestic product and is collected or enforced in the case of the imported product at the time or point of importation, is nevertheless to be regarded as an internal tax or other internal charge, or a law, regulation or requirement of the kind referred to in paragraph 1, and is accordingly subject to the provisions of Article III.

Paragraph 1

The application of paragraph 1 to internal taxes imposed by local governments and authorities with the territory of a contracting party is subject to the provisions of the final paragraph of Article XXIV. The term "reasonable measures" in the last-mentioned paragraph would not require, for example, the repeal of existing national legislation authorizing local governments to impose internal taxes which, although technically inconsistent with the letter of Article III, are not in fact inconsistent with its spirit, if such repeal would result in a serious financial hardship for the local governments or authorities concerned. With regard to taxation by local governments or authorities which is inconsistent with both the letter and spirit of Article III, the term "reasonable measures" would permit a contracting party to eliminate the inconsistent taxation gradually over a transition period, if abrupt action would create serious administrative and financial difficulties.

Paragraph 2

A tax conforming to the requirements of the first sentence of paragraph 2 would be considered to be inconsistent with the provisions of the second sentence only in cases where competition was involved between, on the one hand, the taxed product and, on the other hand, a directly competitive or substitutable product which was not similarly taxed.

Paragraph 5

Regulations consistent with the provisions of the first sentence of paragraph 5 shall not be considered to be contrary to the provisions of the second sentence in any case in which all of the products subject to the regulations are produced domestically in substantial quantities. A regulation cannot be justified as being consistent with the provisions of the second sentence on the ground that the proportion or amount allocated to each of the products which are the subject of the regulation constitutes an equitable relationship between imported and domestic products.

AD *ARTICLE V*

Paragraph 5

With regard to transportation charges, the principle laid down in paragraph 5 refers to like products being transported on the same route under like conditions.

AD *ARTICLE VI*

Paragraph 1

1. Hidden dumping by associated houses (that is, the sale by an importer at a price below that corresponding to the price invoiced by an exporter with whom the importer is associated, and also below the price in the exporting country) constitutes a form of price dumping with respect to which the margin of dumping may be calculated on the basis of the price at which the goods are resold by the importer.

2. It is recognized that, in the case of imports from a country which has a complete or substantially complete monopoly of its trade and where all domestic prices are fixed by the

State, special difficulties may exist in determining price comparability for the purposes of paragraph 1, and in such cases importing contracting parties may find it necessary to take into account the possibility that a strict comparison with domestic prices in such a country may not always be appropriate.

Paragraphs 2 and 3

1. As in many other cases in customs administration, a contracting party may require reasonable security (bond or cash deposit) for the payment of anti-dumping or countervailing duty pending final determination of the facts in any case of suspected dumping or subsidization.

2. Multiple currency practices can in certain circumstances constitute a subsidy to exports which may be met by countervailing duties under paragraph 3 or can constitute a form of dumping by means of a partial depreciation of a country's currency which may be met by action under paragraph 2. By "multiple currency practices" is meant practices by governments or sanctioned by governments.

Paragraph 6 (b)

Waivers under the provisions of this sub-paragraph shall be granted only on application by the contracting party proposing to levy an anti-dumping or countervailing duty, as the case may be.

AD ARTICLE VII

Paragraph 1

The expression "or other charges" is not to be regarded as including internal taxes or equivalent charges imposed on or in connection with imported products.

Paragraph 2

1. It would be in conformity with Article VII to presume that "actual value" may be represented by the invoice price, plus any non-included charges for legitimate costs which are proper elements of "actual value" and plus any abnormal discount or other reduction from the ordinary competitive price.

2. It would be in conformity with Article VII, paragraph 2 (b), for a contracting party to construe the phrase "in the ordinary course of trade ... under fully competitive conditions", as excluding any transaction wherein the buyer and seller are not independent of each other and price is not the sole consideration.

3. The standard of "fully competitive conditions" permits a contracting party to exclude from consideration prices involving special discounts limited to exclusive agents.

4. The wording of sub-paragraphs (a) and (b) permits a contracting party to determine the value for customs purposes uniformly either (1) on the basis of a particular exporter's prices of the imported merchandise, or (2) on the basis of the general price level of like merchandise.

AD ARTICLE VIII

1. While Article VIII does not cover the use of multiple rates of exchange as such, paragraphs 1 and 4 condemn the use of exchange taxes or fees as a device for implementing multiple currency practices; if, however, a contracting party is using multiple currency exchange fees for balance of payments reasons with the approval of the International Monetary Fund, the provisions of paragraph 9 (a) of Article XV fully safeguard its position.

2. It would be consistent with paragraph 1 if, on the importation of products from the territory of a contracting party into the territory of another contracting party, the production of certificates of origin should only be required to the extent that is strictly indispensable.

AD *ARTICLES XI, XII, XIII, XIV AND XVIII*

Throughout Articles XI, XII, XIII, XIV and XVIII, the terms "import restrictions" or "export restrictions" include restrictions made effective through state-trading operations.

AD *ARTICLE XI*

Paragraph 2 (c)

The term "in any form" in this paragraph covers the same products when in an early stage of processing and still perishable, which compete directly with the fresh product and if freely imported would tend to make the restriction on the fresh product ineffective.

Paragraph 2, last sub-paragraph

The term "special factors" includes changes in relative productive efficiency as between domestic and foreign producers, or as between different foreign producers, but not changes artificially brought about by means not permitted under the Agreement.

AD *ARTICLE XII*

The CONTRACTING PARTIES shall make provision for the utmost secrecy in the conduct of any consultation under the provisions of this Article.

Paragraph 3 (c)(i)

Contracting parties applying restrictions shall endeavour to avoid causing serious prejudice to exports of a commodity on which the economy of a contracting party is largely dependent.

Paragraph 4 (b)

It is agreed that the date shall be within ninety days after the entry into force of the amendments of this Article effected by the Protocol Amending the Preamble and Parts II and III of this Agreement. However, should the CONTRACTING PARTIES find that conditions were not suitable for the application of the provisions of this sub-paragraph at the time envisaged, they may determine a later date; *Provided* that such date is not more than thirty days after such time as the obligations of Article VIII, Sections 2, 3 and 4, of the Articles of Agreement of the International Monetary Fund become applicable to contracting parties, members of the Fund, the combined foreign trade of which constitutes at least fifty per centum of the aggregate foreign trade of all contracting parties.

Paragraph 4 (e)

It is agreed that paragraph 4 (e) does not add any new criteria for the imposition or maintenance of quantitative restrictions for balance of payments reasons. It is solely intended to ensure that all external factors such as changes in the terms of trade, quantitative restrictions, excessive tariffs and subsidies, which may be contributing to the balance of payments difficulties of the contracting party applying restrictions, will be fully taken into account.

AD *ARTICLE XIII*

Paragraph 2 (d)

No mention was made of "commercial considerations" as a rule for the allocation of quotas because it was considered that its application by governmental authorities might not always be practicable. Moreover, in cases where it is practicable, a contracting party could apply these considerations in the process of seeking agreement, consistently with the general rule laid down in the opening sentence of paragraph 2.

Paragraph 4

See note relating to "special factors" in connection with the last sub-paragraph of paragraph 2 of Article XI.

AD *ARTICLE XIV*

Paragraph 1

The provisions of this paragraph shall not be so construed as to preclude full consideration by the CONTRACTING PARTIES, in the consultations provided for in paragraph 4 of Article XII and in paragraph 12 of Article XVIII, of the nature, effects and reasons for discrimination in the field of import restrictions.

Paragraph 2

One of the situations contemplated in paragraph 2 is that of a contracting party holding balances acquired as a result of current transactions which it finds itself unable to use without a measure of discrimination.

AD *ARTICLE XV*

Paragraph 4

The word "frustrate" is intended to indicate, for example, that infringements of the letter of any Article of this Agreement by exchange action shall not be regarded as a violation of that Article if, in practice, there is no appreciable departure from the intent of the Article. Thus, a contracting party which, as part of its exchange control operated in accordance with the Articles of Agreement of the International Monetary Fund, requires payment to be received for its exports in its own currency or in the currency of one or more members of the International Monetary Fund will not thereby be deemed to contravene Article XI or Article XIII. Another example would be that of a contracting party which specifies on an import licence the country from which the goods may be imported, for the purpose not of introducing any additional element of discrimination in its import licensing system but of enforcing permissible exchange controls.

AD *ARTICLE XVI*

The exemption of an exported product from duties or taxes borne by the like product when destined for domestic consumption, or the remission of such duties or taxes in amounts not in excess of those which have accrued, shall not be deemed to be a subsidy.

Section B

1. Nothing in Section B shall preclude the use by a contracting party of multiple rates of exchange in accordance with the Articles of Agreement of the International Monetary Fund.
2. For the purposes of Section B, a "primary product" is understood to be any product of farm, forest or fishery, or any mineral, in its natural form or which has undergone such processing as is customarily required to prepare it for marketing in substantial volume in international trade.

Paragraph 3

1. The fact that a contracting party has not exported the product in question during the previous representative period would not in itself preclude that contracting party from establishing its right to obtain a share of the trade in the product concerned.

2. A system for the stabilization of the domestic price or of the return to domestic producers of a primary product independently of the movements of export prices, which results at times in the sale of the product for export at a price lower than the comparable price charged for the like product to buyers in the domestic market, shall be considered not to involve a subsidy on exports within the meaning of paragraph 3 if the CONTRACTING PARTIES determine that:

   (*a*) the system has also resulted, or is so designed as to result, in the sale of the product for export at a price higher than the comparable price charged for the like product to buyers in the domestic market; and

   (*b*) the system is so operated, or is designed so to operate, either because of the effective regulation of production or otherwise, as not to stimulate exports unduly or otherwise seriously to prejudice the interests of other contracting parties.

Notwithstanding such determination by the CONTRACTING PARTIES, operations under such a system shall be subject to the provisions of paragraph 3 where they are wholly or partly financed out of government funds in addition to the funds collected from producers in respect of the product concerned.

Paragraph 4

The intention of paragraph 4 is that the contracting parties should seek before the end of 1957 to reach agreement to abolish all remaining subsidies as from 1 January 1958; or, failing this, to reach agreement to extend the application of the standstill until the earliest date thereafter by which they can expect to reach such agreement.

AD *ARTICLE XVII*

Paragraph 1

The operations of Marketing Boards, which are established by contracting parties and are engaged in purchasing or selling, are subject to the provisions of sub-paragraphs (*a*) and (*b*).

The activities of Marketing Boards which are established by contracting parties and which do not purchase or sell but lay down regulations covering private trade are governed by the relevant Articles of this Agreement.

The charging by a state enterprise of different prices for its sales of a product in different markets is not precluded by the provisions of this Article, provided that such different prices are charged for commercial reasons, to meet conditions of supply and demand in export markets.

Paragraph 1 (*a*)

Governmental measures imposed to insure standards of quality and efficiency in the operation of external trade, or privileges granted for the exploitation of national natural resources but which do not empower the government to exercise control over the trading activities of the enterprise in question, do not constitute "exclusive or special privileges".

Paragraph 1 (*b*)

A country receiving a "tied loan" is free to take this loan into account as a "commercial consideration" when purchasing requirements abroad.

Paragraph 2

The term "goods" is limited to products as understood in commercial practice, and is not intended to include the purchase or sale of services.

Paragraph 3

Negotiations which contracting parties agree to conduct under this paragraph may be directed towards the reduction of duties and other charges on imports and exports or towards the conclusion of any other mutually satisfactory arrangement consistent with the provisions of this Agreement. (See paragraph 4 of Article II and the note to that paragraph.)

Paragraph 4 (*b*)

The term "import mark-up" in this paragraph shall represent the margin by which the price charged by the import monopoly for the imported product (exclusive of internal taxes within the purview of Article III, transportation, distribution, and other expenses incident to the purchase, sale or further processing, and a reasonable margin of profit) exceeds the landed cost.

AD *ARTICLE XVIII*

The CONTRACTING PARTIES and the contracting parties concerned shall preserve the utmost secrecy in respect of matters arising under this Article.

Paragraphs 1 and 4

1. When they consider whether the economy of a contracting party "can only support low standards of living", the CONTRACTING PARTIES shall take into consideration the normal position of that economy and shall not base their determination on exceptional circumstances such as those which may result from the temporary existence of exceptionally favourable conditions for the staple export product or products of such contracting party.

2. The phrase "in the early stages of development" is not meant to apply only to contracting parties which have just started their economic development, but also to contracting parties the economies of which are undergoing a process of industrialization to correct an excessive dependence on primary production.

Paragraphs 2, 3, 7, 13 and 22

The reference to the establishment of particular industries shall apply not only to the establishment of a new industry, but also to the establishment of a new branch of production in an existing industry and to the substantial transformation of an existing industry, and to the substantial expansion of an existing industry supplying a relatively small proportion of the domestic demand. It shall also cover the reconstruction of an industry destroyed or substantially damaged as a result of hostilities or natural disasters.

Paragraph 7 (*b*)

A modification or withdrawal, pursuant to paragraph 7 (*b*), by a contracting party, other than the applicant contracting party, referred to in paragraph 7 (*a*), shall be made within six months of the day on which the action is taken by the applicant contracting party, and shall become effective on the thirtieth day following the day on which such modification or withdrawal has been notified to the CONTRACTING PARTIES.

Paragraph 11

The second sentence in paragraph 11 shall not be interpreted to mean that a contracting party is required to relax or remove restrictions if such relaxation or removal would thereupon produce conditions justifying the intensification or institution, respectively, of restrictions under paragraph 9 of Article XVIII.

Paragraph 12 (*b*)

The date referred to in paragraph 12 (*b*) shall be the date determined by the CONTRACTING PARTIES in accordance with the provisions of paragraph 4 (*b*) of Article XII of this Agreement.

Paragraphs 13 and 14

It is recognized that, before deciding on the introduction of a measure and notifying the CONTRACTING PARTIES in accordance with paragraph 14, a contracting party may need a reasonable period of time to assess the competitive position of the industry concerned.

Paragraphs 15 and 16

It is understood that the CONTRACTING PARTIES shall invite a contracting party proposing to apply a measure under Section C to consult with them pursuant to paragraph 16 if they are requested to do so by a contracting party the trade of which would be appreciably affected by the measure in question.

Paragraphs 16, 18, 19 and 22

1. It is understood that the CONTRACTING PARTIES may concur in a proposed measure subject to specific conditions or limitations. If the measure as applied does not conform to the terms of the concurrence it will to that extent be deemed a measure in which the CONTRACTING PARTIES have not concurred. In cases in which the CONTRACTING PARTIES have concurred in a measure for a specified period, the contracting party concerned, if it finds that the maintenance of the measure for a further period of time is required to achieve the objective for which the measure was originally taken, may apply to the CONTRACTING PARTIES for an extension of that period in accordance with the provisions and procedures of Section C or D, as the case may be.

2. It is expected that the CONTRACTING PARTIES will, as a rule, refrain from concurring in a measure which is likely to cause serious prejudice to exports of a commodity on which the economy of a contracting party is largely dependent.

Paragraph 18 and 22

The phrase "that the interests of other contracting parties are adequately safeguarded" is meant to provide latitude sufficient to permit consideration in each case of the most appropriate method of safeguarding those interests. The appropriate method may, for instance, take the form of an additional concession to be applied by the contracting party having recourse to Section C or D during such time as the deviation from the other Articles of the Agreement would remain in force or of the temporary suspension by any other contracting party referred to in paragraph 18 of a concession substantially equivalent to the impairment due to the introduction of the measure in question. Such contracting party would have the right to safeguard its interests through such a temporary suspension of a concession; *Provided* that this right will not be exercised when, in the case of a measure imposed by a contracting party coming within the scope of paragraph 4 (*a*), the CONTRACTING PARTIES have determined that the extent of the compensatory concession proposed was adequate.

Paragraph 19

The provisions of paragraph 19 are intended to cover the cases where an industry has been in existence beyond the "reasonable period of time" referred to in the note to paragraphs 13 and 14, and should not be so construed as to deprive a contracting party coming within the scope of paragraph 4 (*a*) of Article XVIII, of its right to resort to the other provisions of Section C, including paragraph 17, with regard to a newly established industry even though it has benefited from incidental protection afforded by balance of payments import restrictions.

Paragraph 21

Any measure taken pursuant to the provisions of paragraph 21 shall be withdrawn forthwith if the action taken in accordance with paragraph 17 is withdrawn or if the CONTRACTING PARTIES concur in the measure proposed after the expiration of the ninety-day time limit specified in paragraph 17.

AD *ARTICLE XX*

Sub-paragraph (*h*)

The exception provided for in this sub-paragraph extends to any commodity agreement which conforms to the principles approved by the Economic and Social Council in its resolution 30 (IV) of 28 March 1947.

114 WORLD TRADE LAW

AD *ARTICLE XXIV*

Paragraph 9

It is understood that the provisions of Article I would require that, when a product which has been imported into the territory of a member of a customs union or free-trade area at a preferential rate of duty is re-exported to the territory of another member of such union or area, the latter member should collect a duty equal to the difference between the duty already paid and any higher duty that would be payable if the product were being imported directly into its territory.

Paragraph 11

Measures adopted by India and Pakistan in order to carry out definitive trade arrangements between them, once they have been agreed upon, might depart from particular provisions of this Agreement, but these measures would in general be consistent with the objectives of the Agreement.

AD *ARTICLE XXVIII*

The CONTRACTING PARTIES and each contracting party concerned should arrange to conduct the negotiations and consultations with the greatest possible secrecy in order to avoid premature disclosure of details of prospective tariff changes. The CONTRACTING PARTIES shall be informed immediately of all changes in national tariffs resulting from recourse to this Article.

Paragraph 1

1. If the CONTRACTING PARTIES specify a period other than a three-year period, a contracting party may act pursuant to paragraph 1 or paragraph 3 of Article XXVIII on the first day following the expiration of such other period and, unless the CONTRACTING PARTIES have again specified another period, subsequent periods will be three-year periods following the expiration of such specified period.

2. The provision that on 1 January 1958, and on other days determined pursuant to paragraph 1, a contracting party "may . . . modify or withdraw a concession" means that on such day, and on the first day after the end of each period, the legal obligation of such contracting party under Article II is altered; it does not mean that the changes in its customs tariff should necessarily be made effective on that day. If a tariff change resulting from negotiations undertaken pursuant to this Article is delayed, the entry into force of any compensatory concessions may be similarly delayed.

3. Not earlier than six months, nor later than three months, prior to 1 January 1958, or to the termination date of any subsequent period, a contracting party wishing to modify or withdraw any concession embodied in the appropriate Schedule, should notify the CONTRACTING PARTIES to this effect. The CONTRACTING PARTIES shall then determine the contracting party or contracting parties with which the negotiations or consultations referred to in paragraph 1 shall take place. Any contracting party so determined shall participate in such negotiations or consultations with the applicant contracting party with the aim of reaching agreement before the end of the period. Any extension of the assured life of the Schedules shall relate to the Schedules as modified after such negotiations, in accordance with paragraphs 1, 2, and 3 of Article XXVIII. If the CONTRACTING PARTIES are arranging for multilateral tariff negotiations to take place within the period of six months before 1 January 1958, or before any other day determined pursuant to paragraph 1, they shall include in the arrangements for such negotiations suitable procedures for carrying out the negotiations referred to in this paragraph.

4. The object of providing for the participation in the negotiation of any contracting party with a principle supplying interest, in addition to any contracting party with which the concession was originally negotiated, is to ensure that a contracting party with a larger share in the trade affected by the concession than a contracting party with which the concession was originally negotiated shall have an effective opportunity to protect the contractual right which it enjoys under this Agreement. On the other hand, it is not intended that the scope of the negotiations should be such as to make negotiations and agreement under Article XXVIII unduly difficult nor to create complications in the application of this Article in the future to concessions which result from negotiations thereunder. Accordingly, the CONTRACTING PARTIES should only determine that a contracting party has a principal supplying interest if that contracting party has had, over a reasonable period of time prior to the negotiations, a larger share in the market of the applicant contracting party than a contracting party with which the concession was initially negotiated or would, in the judgement of the CONTRACTING PARTIES, have had such a share in the absence of discriminatory quantitative restrictions maintained by the applicant contracting party. It would therefore not be appropriate for the CONTRACTING PARTIES to determine that more than one contracting party, or in those exceptional cases where there is near equality more than two contracting parties, had a principal supplying interest.

5. Notwithstanding the definition of a principal supplying interest in note 4 to paragraph 1, the CONTRACTING PARTIES may exceptionally determine that a contracting party has a principal supplying interest if the concession in question affects trade which constitutes a major part of the total exports of such contracting party.

6. It is not intended that provision for participation in the negotiations of any contracting party with a principal supplying interest, and for consultation with any contracting party having a substantial interest in the concession which the applicant contracting party is seeking to modify or withdraw, should have the effect that it should have to pay compensation or suffer retaliation greater than the withdrawal or modification sought, judged in the light of the conditions of trade at the time of the proposed withdrawal or modification, making allowance for any discriminatory quantitative restrictions maintained by the applicant contracting party.

7. The expression "substantial interest" is not capable of a precise definition and accordingly may present difficulties for the CONTRACTING PARTIES. It is, however, intended to be construed to cover only those contracting parties which have, or in the absence of discriminatory quantitative restrictions affecting their exports could reasonably be expected to have, a significant share in the market of the contracting party seeking to modify or withdraw the concession.

Paragraph 4

1. Any request for authorization to enter into negotiations shall be accompanied by all relevant statistical and other data. A decision on such request shall be made within thirty days of its submission.

2. It is recognized that to permit certain contracting parties, depending in large measure on a relatively small number of primary commodities and relying on the tariff as an important aid for furthering diversification of their economies or as an important source of revenue, normally to negotiate for the modification or withdrawal of concessions only under paragraph 1 of Article XXVIII, might cause them at such time to make modifications or withdrawals which in the long run would prove unnecessary. To avoid such a situation the CONTRACTING PARTIES shall authorize any such contracting party, under paragraph 4, to enter into negotiations unless they consider this would result in, or contribute substantially towards, such an increase in tariff levels as to threaten the stability of the Schedules to this Agreement or lead to undue disturbance of international trade.

3. It is expected that negotiations authorized under paragraph 4 for modification or withdrawal of a single item, or a very small group of items, could normally be brought to a conclusion in sixty days. It is recognized, however, that such a period will be inadequate for cases involving negotiations for the modification or withdrawal of a larger number of items and in such cases, therefore, it would be appropriate for the CONTRACTING PARTIES to prescribe a longer period.

4. The determination referred to in paragraph 4 (*d*) shall be made by the CONTRACTING PARTIES within thirty days of the submission of the matter to them unless the applicant contracting party agrees to a longer period.

5. In determining under paragraph 4 (*d*) whether an applicant contracting party has unreasonably failed to offer adequate compensation, it is understood that the CONTRACTING PARTIES will take due account of the special position of a contracting party which has bound a high proportion of its tariffs at very low rates of duty and to this extent has less scope than other contracting parties to make compensatory adjustment.

AD *ARTICLE XXVIII* BIS

Paragraph 3
It is understood that the reference to fiscal needs would include the revenues aspect of duties and particularly duties imposed primarily for revenue purpose, or duties imposed on products which can be substituted for products subject to revenue duties to prevent the avoidance of such duties.

AD *ARTICLE XXIX*

Paragraph 1
Chapters VII and VIII of the Havana Charter have been excluded from paragraph 1 because they generally deal with the organization, functions and procedures of the International Trade Organization.

AD *PART IV*

The words "developed contracting parties" and the words "less-developed contracting parties" as used in Part IV are to be understood to refer to developed and less-developed countries which are parties to the General Agreement on Tariffs and Trade.

AD *ARTICLE XXXVI*

Paragraph 1
This Article is based upon the objectives set forth in Article I as it will be amended by Section A of paragraph 1 of the Protocol Amending Part I and Articles XXIX and XXX when that Protocol enters into force.[12]

Paragraph 4
The term "primary products" includes agricultural products, *vide* paragraph 2 of the note *ad* Article XVI, Section B.

Paragraph 5
A diversification programme would generally include the intensification of activities for the processing of primary products and the development of manufacturing industries, taking into

---

12 This Protocol was abandoned on 1 January 1968.

account the situation of the particular contracting party and the world outlook for production and consumption of different commodities.

Paragraph 8
It is understood that the phrase "do not expect reciprocity" means, in accordance with the objectives set forth in this Article, that the less-developed contracting parties should not be expected, in the course of trade negotiations, to make contributions which are inconsistent with their individual development, financial and trade needs, taking into consideration past trade developments.

   This paragraph would apply in the event of action under Section A of Article XVIII, Article XXVIII, Article XXVIII *bis* (Article XXIX after the amendment set forth in Section A of paragraph 1 of the Protocol Amending Part I and Articles XXIX and XXX shall have become effective[13]), Article XXXIII, or any other procedure under this Agreement.

AD *ARTICLE XXXVII*

Paragraph 1 (*a*)
This paragraph would apply in the event of negotiations for reduction or elimination of tariffs or other restrictive regulations of commerce under Articles XXVIII, XXVIII *bis* (XXIX after the amendment set forth in Section A of paragraph 1 of the Protocol Amending Part I and Articles XXIX and XXX shall have become effective[13]), and Article XXXIII, as well as in connection with other action to effect such reduction or elimination which contracting parties may be able to undertake.

Paragraph 3 (*b*)
The other measures referred to in this paragraph might include steps to promote domestic structural changes, to encourage the consumption of particular products, or to introduce measures of trade promotion.

---

13 This Protocol was abandoned on 1 January 1968.

Differential and More Favourable Treatment, Reciprocity and Fuller Participation of Developing Countries (The 'Enabling Clause')

Text GATT Doc L/4903, BISD 26S/203
Date 28 November 1979
Link <http://www.wto.org/english/docs_e/legal_e/tokyo_enabling_e.pdf>

Following negotiations within the framework of the Multilateral Trade Negotiations, the CONTRACTING PARTIES *decide* as follows:

1. Notwithstanding the provisions of Article I of the General Agreement, contracting parties may accord differential and more favourable treatment to developing countries[1], without according such treatment to other contracting parties.

2. The provisions of paragraph 1 apply to the following:[2]
   (*a*) Preferential tariff treatment accorded by developed contracting parties to products originating in developing countries in accordance with the Generalized System of Preferences,[3]
   (*b*) Differential and more favourable treatment with respect to the provisions of the General Agreement concerning non-tariff measures governed by the provisions of instruments multilaterally negotiated under the auspices of the GATT;
   (*c*) Regional or global arrangements entered into amongst less developed contracting parties for the mutual reduction or elimination of tariffs and, in accordance with criteria or conditions which may be prescribed by the CONTRACTING PARTIES, for the mutual reduction or elimination of non-tariff measures, on products imported from one another;
   (*d*) Special treatment on the least developed among the developing countries in the context of any general or specific measures in favour of developing countries.

3. Any differential and more favourable treatment provided under this clause:
   (*a*) shall be designed to facilitate and promote the trade of developing countries and not to raise barriers to or create undue difficulties for the trade of any other contracting parties;
   (*b*) shall not constitute an impediment to the reduction or elimination of tariffs and other restrictions to trade on a most-favoured-nation basis;
   (*c*) shall in the case of such treatment accorded by developed contracting parties to developing countries be designed and, if necessary, modified, to respond positively to the development, financial and trade needs of developing countries.

---

1 The words "developing countries" as used in this text are to be understood to refer also to developing territories.

2 It would remain open for the CONTRACTING PARTIES to consider on an *ad hoc* basis under the GATT provisions for joint action any proposals for differential and more favourable treatment not falling within the scope of this paragraph.

3 As described in the Decision of the CONTRACTING PARTIES of 25 June 1971, relating to the establishment of "generalized, non-reciprocal and non discriminatory preferences beneficial to the developing countries" (BISD 18S/24).

4. Any contracting party taking action to introduce an arrangement pursuant to paragraphs 1, 2 and 3 above or subsequently taking action to introduce modification or withdrawal of the differential and more favourable treatment so provided shall:[1]

   (*a*) notify the CONTRACTING PARTIES and furnish them with all the information they may deem appropriate relating to such action;

   (*b*) afford adequate opportunity for prompt consultations at the request of any interested contracting party with respect to any difficulty or matter that may arise. The CONTRACTING PARTIES shall, if requested to do so by such contracting party, consult with all contracting parties concerned with respect to the matter with a view to reaching solutions satisfactory to all such contracting parties.

5. The developed countries do not expect reciprocity for commitments made by them in trade negotiations to reduce or remove tariffs and other barriers to the trade of developing countries, i.e., the developed countries do not expect the developing countries, in the course of trade negotiations, to make contributions which are inconsistent with their individual development, financial and trade needs. Developed contracting parties shall therefore not seek, neither shall less-developed contracting parties be required to make, concessions that are inconsistent with the latter's development, financial and trade needs.

6. Having regard to the special economic difficulties and the particular development, financial and trade needs of the least developed countries, the developed countries shall exercise the utmost restraint in seeking any concessions or contributions for commitments made by them to reduce or remove tariffs and other barriers to the trade of such countries, and the least-developed countries shall not be expected to make concessions or contributions that are inconsistent with the recognition of their particular situation and problems.

7. The concessions and contributions made and the obligations assumed by developed and less-developed contracting parties under the provisions of the General Agreement should promote the basic objectives of the Agreement, including those embodied in the Preamble and in Article XXXVI. Less-developed contracting parties expect that their capacity to make contributions or negotiated concessions or take other mutually agreed action under the provisions and procedures of the General Agreement would improve with the progressive development of their economies and improvement in their trade situation and they would accordingly expect to participate more fully in the framework of rights and obligations under the General Agreement.

8. Particular account shall be taken of the serious difficulty of the least-developed countries in making concessions and contributions in view of their special economic situation and their development, financial and trade needs.

9. The contracting parties will collaborate in arrangements for review of the operation of these provisions, bearing in mind the need for individual and joint efforts by contracting parties to meet the development needs of developing countries and the objectives of the General Agreement.

---

1 Nothing in these provisions shall affect the rights of contracting parties under the General Agreement.

Understanding on the Interpretation of Article XXIV of the General Agreement on Tariffs and Trade 1994

Members,

Having regard to the provisions of Article XXIV of GATT 1994;

Recognizing that customs unions and free trade areas have greatly increased in number and importance since the establishment of GATT 1947 and today cover a significant proportion of world trade;

Recognizing the contribution to the expansion of world trade that may be made by closer integration between the economies of the parties to such agreements;

Recognizing also that such contribution is increased if the elimination between the constituent territories of duties and other restrictive regulations of commerce extends to all trade, and diminished if any major sector of trade is excluded;

Reaffirming that the purpose of such agreements should be to facilitate trade between the constituent territories and not to raise barriers to the trade of other Members with such territories; and that in their formation or enlargement the parties to them should to the greatest possible extent avoid creating adverse effects on the trade of other Members;

Convinced also of the need to reinforce the effectiveness of the role of the Council for Trade in Goods in reviewing agreements notified under Article XXIV, by clarifying the criteria and procedures for the assessment of new or enlarged agreements, and improving the transparency of all Article XXIV agreements;

Recognizing the need for a common understanding of the obligations of Members under paragraph 12 of Article XXIV;

Hereby *agree* as follows:

1. Customs unions, free-trade areas, and interim agreements leading to the formation of a customs union or free-trade area, to be consistent with Article XXIV, must satisfy, *inter alia*, the provisions of paragraphs 5, 6, 7 and 8 of that Article.

Article XXIV:5

2. The evaluation under paragraph 5(a) of Article XXIV of the general incidence of the duties and other regulations of commerce applicable before and after the formation of a customs union shall in respect of duties and charges be based upon an overall assessment of weighted average tariff rates and of customs duties collected. This assessment shall be based on import statistics for a previous representative period to be supplied by the customs union, on a tariff-line basis and in values and quantities, broken down by WTO country of origin. The Secretariat shall compute the weighted average tariff rates and customs duties collected in accordance with the methodology used in the assessment of tariff offers in the Uruguay Round of Multilateral Trade Negotiations. For this purpose, the duties and charges to be taken into consideration shall be the applied rates of duty. It is recognized that for the purpose of the overall assessment of the incidence of other regulations of commerce for which quantification and aggregation are difficult, the examination of individual measures, regulations, products covered and trade flows affected may be required.

3. The "reasonable length of time" referred to in paragraph 5(c) of Article XXIV should exceed 10 years only in exceptional cases. In cases where Members parties to an interim agreement believe that 10 years would be insufficient they shall provide a full explanation to the Council for Trade in Goods of the need for a longer period.

Article   XXIV:6

4. Paragraph 6 of Article XXIV establishes the procedure to be followed when a Member forming a customs union proposes to increase a bound rate of duty. In this regard Members reaffirm that the procedure set forth in Article XXVIII, as elaborated in the guidelines adopted on 10 November 1980 (BISD 27S/26–28) and in the Understanding on the Interpretation of Article XXVIII of GATT 1994, must be commenced before tariff concessions are modified or withdrawn upon the formation of a customs union or an interim agreement leading to the formation of a customs union.

5. These negotiations will be entered into in good faith with a view to achieving mutually satisfactory compensatory adjustment. In such negotiations, as required by paragraph 6 of Article XXIV, due account shall be taken of reductions of duties on the same tariff line made by other constituents of the customs union upon its formation. Should such reductions not be sufficient to provide the necessary compensatory adjustment, the customs union would offer compensation, which may take the form of reductions of duties on other tariff lines. Such an offer shall be taken into consideration by the Members having negotiating rights in the binding being modified or withdrawn. Should the compensatory adjustment remain unacceptable, negotiations should be continued. Where, despite such efforts, agreement in negotiations on compensatory adjustment under Article XXVIII as elaborated by the Understanding on the Interpretation of Article XXVIII of GATT 1994 cannot be reached within a reasonable period from the initiation of negotiations, the customs union shall, nevertheless, be free to modify or withdraw the concessions; affected Members shall then be free to withdraw substantially equivalent concessions in accordance with Article XXVIII.

6. GATT 1994 imposes no obligation on Members benefiting from a reduction of duties consequent upon the formation of a customs union, or an interim agreement leading to the formation of a customs union, to provide compensatory adjustment to its constituents.

Review of Customs Unions and Free-Trade Areas

7. All notifications made under paragraph 7(a) of Article XXIV shall be examined by a working party in the light of the relevant provisions of GATT 1994 and of paragraph 1 of this Understanding. The working party shall submit a report to the Council for Trade in Goods on its findings in this regard. The Council for Trade in Goods may make such recommendations to Members as it deems appropriate.

8. In regard to interim agreements, the working party may in its report make appropriate recommendations on the proposed time-frame and on measures required to complete the formation of the customs union or free-trade area. It may if necessary provide for further review of the agreement.

9. Members parties to an interim agreement shall notify substantial changes in the plan and schedule included in that agreement to the Council for Trade in Goods and, if so requested, the Council shall examine the changes.

10. Should an interim agreement notified under paragraph 7(a) of Article XXIV not include a plan and schedule, contrary to paragraph 5(c) of Article XXIV, the working party shall in its report recommend such a plan and schedule. The parties shall not maintain or put into force, as the case may be, such agreement if they are not prepared to modify it in accordance with these recommendations. Provision shall be made for subsequent review of the implementation of the recommendations.

11. Customs unions and constituents of free-trade areas shall report periodically to the Council for Trade in Goods, as envisaged by the CONTRACTING PARTIES to GATT 1947 in their instruction to the GATT 1947 Council concerning reports on regional agreements (BISD 18S/38), on the operation of the relevant agreement. Any significant changes and/or developments in the agreements should be reported as they occur.

Dispute Settlement

12. The provisions of Articles XXII and XXIII of GATT 1994 as elaborated and applied by the Dispute Settlement Understanding may be invoked with respect to any matters arising from the application of those provisions of Article XXIV relating to customs unions, free-trade areas or interim agreements leading to the formation of a customs union or free-trade area.

Article XXIV:12

13. Each Member is fully responsible under GATT 1994 for the observance of all provisions of GATT 1994, and shall take such reasonable measures as may be available to it to ensure such observance by regional and local governments and authorities within its territory.

14. The provisions of Articles XXII and XXIII of GATT 1994 as elaborated and applied by the Dispute Settlement Understanding may be invoked in respect of measures affecting its observance taken by regional or local governments or authorities within the territory of a Member. When the Dispute Settlement Body has ruled that a provision of GATT 1994 has not been observed, the responsible Member shall take such reasonable measures as may be available to it to ensure its observance. The provisions relating to compensation and suspension of concessions or other obligations apply in cases where it has not been possible to secure such observance.

15. Each Member undertakes to accord sympathetic consideration to and afford adequate opportunity for consultation regarding any representations made by another Member concerning measures affecting the operation of GATT 1994 taken within the territory of the former.

Marrakesh Protocol to the General Agreement on Tariffs and Trade 1994

Members,

Having carried out negotiations within the framework of GATT 1947, pursuant to the Ministerial Declaration on the Uruguay Round,

Hereby *agree* as follows:

1. The schedule annexed to this Protocol relating to a Member shall become a Schedule to GATT 1994 relating to that Member on the day on which the WTO Agreement enters into force for that Member. Any schedule submitted in accordance with the Ministerial Decision on measures in favour of least-developed countries shall be deemed to be annexed to this Protocol.

2. The tariff reductions agreed upon by each Member shall be implemented in five equal rate reductions, except as may be otherwise specified in a Member's Schedule. The first such reduction shall be made effective on the date of entry into force of the WTO Agreement, each successive reduction shall be made effective on 1 January of each of the following years, and the final rate shall become effective no later than the date four years after the date of entry into force of the WTO Agreement, except as may be otherwise specified in that Member's Schedule. Unless otherwise specified in its Schedule, a Member that accepts the WTO Agreement after its entry into force shall, on the date that Agreement enters into force for it, make effective all rate reductions that have already taken place together with the reductions which it would under the preceding sentence have been obligated to make effective on 1 January of the year following, and shall make effective all remaining rate reductions on the schedule specified in the previous sentence. The reduced rate should in each stage be rounded off to the first decimal. For agricultural products, as defined in Article 2 of the Agreement on Agriculture, the staging of reductions shall be implemented as specified in the relevant parts of the schedules.

3. The implementation of the concessions and commitments contained in the schedules annexed to this Protocol shall, upon request, be subject to multilateral examination by the Members. This would be without prejudice to the rights and obligations of Members under Agreements in Annex 1A of the WTO Agreement.

4. After the schedule annexed to this Protocol relating to a Member has become a Schedule to GATT 1994 pursuant to the provisions of paragraph 1, such Member shall be free at any time to withhold or to withdraw in whole or in part the concession in such Schedule with respect to any product for which the principal supplier is any other Uruguay Round participant the schedule of which has not yet become a Schedule to GATT 1994. Such action can, however, only be taken after written notice of any such withholding or withdrawal of a concession has been given to the Council for Trade in Goods and after consultations have been held, upon request, with any Member, the relevant schedule relating to which has become a Schedule to GATT 1994 and which has a substantial interest in the product involved. Any concessions so withheld or withdrawn shall be applied on and after the day on which the schedule of the Member which has the principal supplying interest becomes a Schedule to GATT 1994.

5. (a) Without prejudice to the provisions of paragraph 2 of Article 4 of the Agreement on Agriculture, for the purpose of the reference in paragraphs 1:(b) and 1(c) of Article II of GATT 1994 to the date of that Agreement, the applicable date in respect of each product

which is the subject of a concession provided for in a schedule of concessions annexed to this Protocol shall be the date of this Protocol.

(b) For the purpose of the reference in paragraph 6(a) of Article II of GATT 1994 to the date of that Agreement, the applicable date in respect of a schedule of concessions annexed to this Protocol shall be the date of this Protocol.

6. In cases of modification or withdrawal of concessions relating to non-tariff measures as contained in Part III of the schedules, the provisions of Article XXVIII of GATT 1994 and the "Procedures for Negotiations under Article XXVIII" adopted on 10 November 1980 (BISD 27S/26–28) shall apply. This would be without prejudice to the rights and obligations of Members under GATT 1994.

7. In each case in which a schedule annexed to this Protocol results for any product in treatment less favourable than was provided for such product in the Schedules of GATT 1947 prior to the entry into force of the WTO Agreement, the Member to whom the schedule relates shall be deemed to have taken appropriate action as would have been otherwise necessary under the relevant provisions of Article XXVIII of GATT 1947 or 1994. The provisions of this paragraph shall apply only to Egypt, Peru, South Africa and Uruguay.

8. The Schedules annexed hereto are authentic in the English, French or Spanish language as specified in each Schedule.

9. The date of this Protocol is 15 April 1994.

[The agreed schedules of participants will be annexed to the Marrakesh Protocol in the treaty copy of the WTO Agreement.]

II-9

Agreement on Agriculture

Members,

Having decided to establish a basis for initiating a process of reform of trade in agriculture in line with the objectives of the negotiations as set out in the Punta del Este Declaration;

Recalling that their long-term objective as agreed at the Mid-Term Review of the Uruguay Round "is to establish a fair and market-oriented agricultural trading system and that a reform process should be initiated through the negotiation of commitments on support and protection and through the establishment of strengthened and more operationally effective GATT rules and disciplines";

Recalling further that "the above-mentioned long-term objective is to provide for substantial progressive reductions in agricultural support and protection sustained over an agreed period of time, resulting in correcting and preventing restrictions and distortions in world agricultural markets";

Committed to achieving specific binding commitments in each of the following areas: market access; domestic support; export competition; and to reaching an agreement on sanitary and phytosanitary issues;

Having agreed that in implementing their commitments on market access, developed country Members would take fully into account the particular needs and conditions of developing country Members by providing for a greater improvement of opportunities and terms of access for agricultural products of particular interest to these Members, including the fullest liberalization of trade in tropical agricultural products as agreed at the Mid-Term Review, and for products of particular importance to the diversification of production from the growing of illicit narcotic crops;

Noting that commitments under the reform programme should be made in an equitable way among all Members, having regard to non-trade concerns, including food security and the need to protect the environment; having regard to the agreement that special and differential treatment for developing countries is an integral element of the negotiations, and taking into account the possible negative effects of the implementation of the reform programme on least-developed and net food-importing developing countries;

Hereby *agree* as follows:

PART I

Article 1   Definition of Terms

In this Agreement, unless the context otherwise requires:

(a) "Aggregate Measurement of Support" and "AMS" mean the annual level of support, expressed in monetary terms, provided for an agricultural product in favour of the producers of the basic agricultural product or non-product-specific support provided in favour of agricultural producers in general, other than support provided under programmes that qualify as exempt from reduction under Annex 2 to this Agreement, which is:

  (i) with respect to support provided during the base period, specified in the relevant tables of supporting material incorporated by reference in Part IV of a Member's Schedule; and

  (ii) with respect to support provided during any year of the implementation period and thereafter, calculated in accordance with the provisions of Annex 3 of this Agreement and taking into account the constituent data and methodology used in the tables of supporting material incorporated by reference in Part IV of the Member's Schedule;

(b) "basic agricultural product" in relation to domestic support commitments is defined as the product as close as practicable to the point of first sale as specified in a Member's Schedule and in the related supporting material;

(c) "budgetary outlays" or "outlays" includes revenue foregone;

(d) "Equivalent Measurement of Support" means the annual level of support, expressed in monetary terms, provided to producers of a basic agricultural product through the application of one or more measures, the calculation of which in accordance with the AMS methodology is impracticable, other than support provided under programmes that qualify as exempt from reduction under Annex 2 to this Agreement, and which is:

   (i) with respect to support provided during the base period, specified in the relevant tables of supporting material incorporated by reference in Part IV of a Member's Schedule; and

   (ii) with respect to support provided during any year of the implementation period and thereafter, calculated in accordance with the provisions of Annex 4 of this Agreement and taking into account the constituent data and methodology used in the tables of supporting material incorporated by reference in Part IV of the Member's Schedule;

(e) "export subsidies" refers to subsidies contingent upon export performance, including the export subsidies listed in Article 9 of this Agreement;

(f) "implementation period" means the six-year period commencing in the year 1995, except that, for the purposes of Article 13, it means the nine-year period commencing in 1995;

(g) "market access concessions" includes all market access commitments undertaken pursuant to this Agreement;

(h) "Total Aggregate Measurement of Support" and "Total AMS" mean the sum of all domestic support provided in favour of agricultural producers, calculated as the sum of all aggregate measurements of support for basic agricultural products, all non-product-specific aggregate measurements of support and all equivalent measurements of support for agricultural products, and which is:

   (i) with respect to support provided during the base period (i.e. the "Base Total AMS") and the maximum support permitted to be provided during any year of the implementation period or thereafter (i.e. the "Annual and Final Bound Commitment Levels"), as specified in Part IV of a Member's Schedule; and

   (ii) with respect to the level of support actually provided during any year of the implementation period and thereafter (i.e. the "Current Total AMS"), calculated in accordance with the provisions of this Agreement, including Article 6, and with the constituent data and methodology used in the tables of supporting material incorporated by reference in Part IV of the Member's Schedule;

(i) "year" in paragraph (f) above and in relation to the specific commitments of a Member refers to the calendar, financial or marketing year specified in the Schedule relating to that Member.

Article 2   Product Coverage

This Agreement applies to the products listed in Annex 1 to this Agreement, hereinafter referred to as agricultural products.

PART II

Article 3   Incorporation of Concessions and Commitments

1. The domestic support and export subsidy commitments in Part IV of each Member's Schedule constitute commitments limiting subsidization and are hereby made an integral part of GATT 1994.

2. Subject to the provisions of Article 6, a Member shall not provide support in favour of domestic producers in excess of the commitment levels specified in Section I of Part IV of its Schedule.

3. Subject to the provisions of paragraphs 2(b) and 4 of Article 9, a Member shall not provide export subsidies listed in paragraph 1 of Article 9 in respect of the agricultural products or groups of products specified in Section II of Part IV of its Schedule in excess of the budgetary outlay and quantity commitment levels specified therein and shall not provide such subsidies in respect of any agricultural product not specified in that Section of its Schedule.

PART III

Article 4   Market Access

1. Market access concessions contained in Schedules relate to bindings and reductions of tariffs, and to other market access commitments as specified therein.

2. Members shall not maintain, resort to, or revert to any measures of the kind which have been required to be converted into ordinary customs duties[1], except as otherwise provided for in Article 5 and Annex 5.

Article 5   Special Safeguard Provisions

1. Notwithstanding the provisions of paragraph 1(b) of Article II of GATT 1994, any Member may take recourse to the provisions of paragraphs 4 and 5 below in connection with the importation of an agricultural product, in respect of which measures referred to in paragraph 2 of Article 4 of this Agreement have been converted into an ordinary customs duty and which is designated in its Schedule with the symbol "SSG" as being the subject of a concession in respect of which the provisions of this Article may be invoked, if:

    (a) the volume of imports of that product entering the customs territory of the Member granting the concession during any year exceeds a trigger level which relates to the existing market access opportunity as set out in paragraph 4; or, but not concurrently:

    (b) the price at which imports of that product may enter the customs territory of the Member granting the concession, as determined on the basis of the c.i.f. import price of the shipment concerned expressed in terms of its domestic currency, falls below a trigger price equal to the average 1986 to 1988 reference price[2] for the product concerned.

2. Imports under current and minimum access commitments established as part of a concession referred to in paragraph 1 above shall be counted for the purpose of determining the volume of imports required for invoking the provisions of subparagraph 1(a) and paragraph 4, but imports under such commitments shall not be affected by any additional duty imposed under either subparagraph 1(a) and paragraph 4 or subparagraph 1(b) and paragraph 5 below.

3. Any supplies of the product in question which were *en route* on the basis of a contract settled before the additional duty is imposed under subparagraph 1(a) and paragraph 4 shall be exempted from any such additional duty, provided that they may be counted in the volume of imports of the product in question during the following year for the purposes of triggering the provisions of subparagraph 1(a) in that year.

---

1 These measures include quantitative import restrictions, variable import levies, minimum import prices, discretionary import licensing, non-tariff measures maintained through state-trading enterprises, voluntary export restraints, and similar border measures other than ordinary customs duties, whether or not the measures are maintained under country-specific derogations from the provisions of GATT 1947, but not measures maintained under balance-of-payments provisions or under other general, non-agriculture-specific provisions of GATT 1994 or of the other Multilateral Trade Agreements in Annex 1A to the WTO Agreement.

2 The reference price used to invoke the provisions of this subparagraph shall, in general, be the average c.i.f. unit value of the product concerned, or otherwise shall be an appropriate price in terms of the quality of the product and its stage of processing. It shall, following its initial use, be publicly specified and available to the extent necessary to allow other Members to assess the additional duty that may be levied.

4. Any additional duty imposed under subparagraph 1(a) shall only be maintained until the end of the year in which it has been imposed, and may only be levied at a level which shall not exceed one third of the level of the ordinary customs duty in effect in the year in which the action is taken. The trigger level shall be set according to the following schedule based on market access opportunities defined as imports as a percentage of the corresponding domestic consumption[3] during the three preceding years for which data are available:

(a) where such market access opportunities for a product are less than or equal to 10 per cent, the base trigger level shall equal 125 per cent;

(b) where such market access opportunities for a product are greater than 10 per cent but less than or equal to 30 per cent, the base trigger level shall equal 110 per cent;

(c) where such market access opportunities for a product are greater than 30 per cent, the base trigger level shall equal 105 per cent.

In all cases the additional duty may be imposed in any year where the absolute volume of imports of the product concerned entering the customs territory of the Member granting the concession exceeds the sum of (x) the base trigger level set out above multiplied by the average quantity of imports during the three preceding years for which data are available and (y) the absolute volume change in domestic consumption of the product concerned in the most recent year for which data are available compared to the preceding year, provided that the trigger level shall not be less than 105 per cent of the average quantity of imports in (x) above.

5. The additional duty imposed under subparagraph 1(b) shall be set according to the following schedule:

(a) if the difference between the c.i.f. import price of the shipment expressed in terms of the domestic currency (hereinafter referred to as the "import price") and the trigger price as defined under that subparagraph is less than or equal to 10 per cent of the trigger price, no additional duty shall be imposed;

(b) if the difference between the import price and the trigger price (hereinafter referred to as the "difference") is greater than 10 per cent but less than or equal to 40 per cent of the trigger price, the additional duty shall equal 30 per cent of the amount by which the difference exceeds 10 per cent;

(c) if the difference is greater than 40 per cent but less than or equal to 60 per cent of the trigger price, the additional duty shall equal 50 per cent of the amount by which the difference exceeds 40 per cent, plus the additional duty allowed under (b);

(d) if the difference is greater than 60 per cent but less than or equal to 75 per cent, the additional duty shall equal 70 per cent of the amount by which the difference exceeds 60 per cent of the trigger price, plus the additional duties allowed under (b) and (c);

(e) if the difference is greater than 75 per cent of the trigger price, the additional duty shall equal 90 per cent of the amount by which the difference exceeds 75 per cent, plus the additional duties allowed under (b), (c) and (d).

6. For perishable and seasonal products, the conditions set out above shall be applied in such a manner as to take account of the specific characteristics of such products. In particular, shorter time periods under subparagraph 1(a) and paragraph 4 may be used in reference to the corresponding periods in the base period and different reference prices for different periods may be used under subparagraph 1(b).

7. The operation of the special safeguard shall be carried out in a transparent manner. Any Member taking action under subparagraph 1(a) above shall give notice in writing, including relevant data, to the Committee on Agriculture as far in advance as may be practicable and in any event within 10 days of the implementation of such action. In cases where changes in

---

3 Where domestic consumption is not taken into account, the base trigger level under subparagraph 4(a) shall apply.

consumption volumes must be allocated to individual tariff lines subject to action under paragraph 4, relevant data shall include the information and methods used to allocate these changes. A Member taking action under paragraph 4 shall afford any interested Members the opportunity to consult with it in respect of the conditions of application of such action. Any Member taking action under subparagraph 1(b) above shall give notice in writing, including relevant data, to the Committee on Agriculture within 10 days of the implementation of the first such action or, for perishable and seasonal products, the first action in any period. Members undertake, as far as practicable, not to take recourse to the provisions of subparagraph 1(b) where the volume of imports of the products concerned are declining. In either case a Member taking such action shall afford any interested Members the opportunity to consult with it in respect of the conditions of application of such action.

8. Where measures are taken in conformity with paragraphs 1 through 7 above, Members undertake not to have recourse, in respect of such measures, to the provisions of paragraphs 1(a) and 3 of Article XIX of GATT 1994 or paragraph 2 of Article 8 of the Agreement on Safeguards.

9. The provisions of this Article shall remain in force for the duration of the reform process as determined under Article 20.

PART IV

Article 6   Domestic Support Commitments

1. The domestic support reduction commitments of each Member contained in Part IV of its Schedule shall apply to all of its domestic support measures in favour of agricultural producers with the exception of domestic measures which are not subject to reduction in terms of the criteria set out in this Article and in Annex 2 to this Agreement. The commitments are expressed in terms of Total Aggregate Measurement of Support and "Annual and Final Bound Commitment Levels".

2. In accordance with the Mid-Term Review Agreement that government measures of assistance, whether direct or indirect, to encourage agricultural and rural development are an integral part of the development programmes of developing countries, investment subsidies which are generally available to agriculture in developing country Members and agricultural input subsidies generally available to low-income or resource-poor producers in developing country Members shall be exempt from domestic support reduction commitments that would otherwise be applicable to such measures, as shall domestic support to producers in developing country Members to encourage diversification from growing illicit narcotic crops. Domestic support meeting the criteria of this paragraph shall not be required to be included in a Member's calculation of its Current Total AMS.

3. A Member shall be considered to be in compliance with its domestic support reduction commitments in any year in which its domestic support in favour of agricultural producers expressed in terms of Current Total AMS does not exceed the corresponding annual or final bound commitment level specified in Part IV of the Member's Schedule.

4. (a) A Member shall not be required to include in the calculation of its Current Total AMS and shall not be required to reduce:
     (i) product-specific domestic support which would otherwise be required to be included in a Member's calculation of its Current AMS where such support does not exceed 5 per cent of that Member's total value of production of a basic agricultural product during the relevant year; and
     (ii) non-product-specific domestic support which would otherwise be required to be included in a Member's calculation of its Current AMS where such support does not exceed 5 per cent of the value of that Member's total agricultural production.

(b) For developing country Members, the *de minimis* percentage under this paragraph shall be 10 per cent.

5. (a) Direct payments under production-limiting programmes shall not be subject to the commitment to reduce domestic support if:

    (i) such payments are based on fixed area and yields; or
    (ii) such payments are made on 85 per cent or less of the base level of production; or
    (iii) livestock payments are made on a fixed number of head.

   (b) The exemption from the reduction commitment for direct payments meeting the above criteria shall be reflected by the exclusion of the value of those direct payments in a Member's calculation of its Current Total AMS.

Article 7   General Disciplines on Domestic Support

1. Each Member shall ensure that any domestic support measures in favour of agricultural producers which are not subject to reduction commitments because they qualify under the criteria set out in Annex 2 to this Agreement are maintained in conformity therewith.

2. (a) Any domestic support measure in favour of agricultural producers, including any modification to such measure, and any measure that is subsequently introduced that cannot be shown to satisfy the criteria in Annex 2 to this Agreement or to be exempt from reduction by reason of any other provision of this Agreement shall be included in the Member's calculation of its Current Total AMS.

   (b) Where no Total AMS commitment exists in Part IV of a Member's Schedule, the Member shall not provide support to agricultural producers in excess of the relevant *de minimis* level set out in paragraph 4 of Article 6.

PART V

Article 8   Export Competition Commitments

Each Member undertakes not to provide export subsidies otherwise than in conformity with this Agreement and with the commitments as specified in that Member's Schedule.

Article 9   Export Subsidy Commitments

1. The following export subsidies are subject to reduction commitments under this Agreement:

   (a) the provision by governments or their agencies of direct subsidies, including payments-in-kind, to a firm, to an industry, to producers of an agricultural product, to a cooperative or other association of such producers, or to a marketing board, contingent on export performance;

   (b) the sale or disposal for export by governments or their agencies of non-commercial stocks of agricultural products at a price lower than the comparable price charged for the like product to buyers in the domestic market;

   (c) payments on the export of an agricultural product that are financed by virtue of governmental action, whether or not a charge on the public account is involved, including payments that are financed from the proceeds of a levy imposed on the agricultural product concerned or on an agricultural product from which the exported product is derived;

   (d) the provision of subsidies to reduce the costs of marketing exports of agricultural products (other than widely available export promotion and advisory services) including handling, upgrading and other processing costs, and the costs of international transport and freight;

   (e) internal transport and freight charges on export shipments, provided or mandated by governments, on terms more favourable than for domestic shipments;

   (f) subsidies on agricultural products contingent on their incorporation in exported products.

2. (a) Except as provided in subparagraph (b), the export subsidy commitment levels for each year of the implementation period, as specified in a Member's Schedule, represent with respect to the export subsidies listed in paragraph 1 of this Article:

   (i) in the case of budgetary outlay reduction commitments, the maximum level of expenditure for such subsidies that may be allocated or incurred in that year in respect of the agricultural product, or group of products, concerned; and

   (ii) in the case of export quantity reduction commitments, the maximum quantity of an agricultural product, or group of products, in respect of which such export subsidies may be granted in that year.

   (b) In any of the second through fifth years of the implementation period, a Member may provide export subsidies listed in paragraph 1 above in a given year in excess of the corresponding annual commitment levels in respect of the products or groups of products specified in Part IV of the Member's Schedule, provided that:

   (i) the cumulative amounts of budgetary outlays for such subsidies, from the beginning of the implementation period through the year in question, does not exceed the cumulative amounts that would have resulted from full compliance with the relevant annual outlay commitment levels specified in the Member's Schedule by more than 3 per cent of the base period level of such budgetary outlays;

   (ii) the cumulative quantities exported with the benefit of such export subsidies, from the beginning of the implementation period through the year in question, does not exceed the cumulative quantities that would have resulted from full compliance with the relevant annual quantity commitment levels specified in the Member's Schedule by more than 1.75 per cent of the base period quantities;

   (iii) the total cumulative amounts of budgetary outlays for such export subsidies and the quantities benefiting from such export subsidies over the entire implementation period are no greater than the totals that would have resulted from full compliance with the relevant annual commitment levels specified in the Member's Schedule; and

   (iv) the Member's budgetary outlays for export subsidies and the quantities benefiting from such subsidies, at the conclusion of the implementation period, are no greater than 64 per cent and 79 per cent of the 1986–1990 base period levels, respectively. For developing country Members these percentages shall be 76 and 86 per cent, respectively.

3. Commitments relating to limitations on the extension of the scope of export subsidization are as specified in Schedules.

4. During the implementation period, developing country Members shall not be required to undertake commitments in respect of the export subsidies listed in subparagraphs (d) and (e) of paragraph 1 above, provided that these are not applied in a manner that would circumvent reduction commitments.

Article 10   Prevention of Circumvention of Export Subsidy Commitments

1. Export subsidies not listed in paragraph 1 of Article 9 shall not be applied in a manner which results in, or which threatens to lead to, circumvention of export subsidy commitments; nor shall non-commercial transactions be used to circumvent such commitments.

2. Members undertake to work toward the development of internationally agreed disciplines to govern the provision of export credits, export credit guarantees or insurance programmes and, after agreement on such disciplines, to provide export credits, export credit guarantees or insurance programmes only in conformity therewith.

3. Any Member which claims that any quantity exported in excess of a reduction commitment level is not subsidized must establish that no export subsidy, whether listed in Article 9 or not, has been granted in respect of the quantity of exports in question.

4. Members donors of international food aid shall ensure:
  (a) that the provision of international food aid is not tied directly or indirectly to commercial exports of agricultural products to recipient countries;
  (b) that international food aid transactions, including bilateral food aid which is monetized, shall be carried out in accordance with the FAO "Principles of Surplus Disposal and Consultative Obligations", including, where appropriate, the system of Usual Marketing Requirements (UMRs); and
  (c) that such aid shall be provided to the extent possible in fully grant form or on terms no less concessional than those provided for in Article IV of the Food Aid Convention 1986.

Article 11   Incorporated Products
In no case may the per-unit subsidy paid on an incorporated agricultural primary product exceed the per-unit export subsidy that would be payable on exports of the primary product as such.

PART VI

Article 12   Disciplines on Export Prohibitions and Restrictions
1. Where any Member institutes any new export prohibition or restriction on foodstuffs in accordance with paragraph 2(a) of Article XI of GATT 1994, the Member shall observe the following provisions:
  (a) the Member instituting the export prohibition or restriction shall give due consideration to the effects of such prohibition or restriction on importing Members' food security;
  (b) before any Member institutes an export prohibition or restriction, it shall give notice in writing, as far in advance as practicable, to the Committee on Agriculture comprising such information as the nature and the duration of such measure, and shall consult, upon request, with any other Member having a substantial interest as an importer with respect to any matter related to the measure in question. The Member instituting such export prohibition or restriction shall provide, upon request, such a Member with necessary information.
2. The provisions of this Article shall not apply to any developing country Member, unless the measure is taken by a developing country Member which is a net-food exporter of the specific foodstuff concerned.

PART VII

Article 13   Due Restraint
During the implementation period, notwithstanding the provisions of GATT 1994 and the Agreement on Subsidies and Countervailing Measures (referred to in this Article as the "Subsidies Agreement"):

(a) domestic support measures that conform fully to the provisions of Annex 2 to this Agreement shall be:
  (i) non-actionable subsidies for purposes of countervailing duties[4];
  (ii) exempt from actions based on Article XVI of GATT 1994 and Part III of the Subsidies Agreement; and
  (iii) exempt from actions based on non-violation nullification or impairment of the benefits of tariff concessions accruing to another Member under Article II of GATT 1994, in the sense of paragraph 1(b) of Article XXIII of GATT 1994;

---

4 "Countervailing duties" where referred to in this Article are those covered by Article VI of GATT 1994 and Part V of the Agreement on Subsidies and Countervailing Measures.

(b) domestic support measures that conform fully to the provisions of Article 6 of this Agreement including direct payments that conform to the requirements of paragraph 5 thereof, as reflected in each Member's Schedule, as well as domestic support within *de minimis* levels and in conformity with paragraph 2 of Article 6, shall be:

   (i) exempt from the imposition of countervailing duties unless a determination of injury or threat thereof is made in accordance with Article VI of GATT 1994 and Part V of the Subsidies Agreement, and due restraint shall be shown in initiating any countervailing duty investigations;

   (ii) exempt from actions based on paragraph 1 of Article XVI of GATT 1994 or Articles 5 and 6 of the Subsidies Agreement, provided that such measures do not grant support to a specific commodity in excess of that decided during the 1992 marketing year; and

   (iii) exempt from actions based on non-violation nullification or impairment of the benefits of tariff concessions accruing to another Member under Article II of GATT 1994, in the sense of paragraph 1(b) of Article XXIII of GATT 1994, provided that such measures do not grant support to a specific commodity in excess of that decided during the 1992 marketing year;

(c) export subsidies that conform fully to the provisions of Part V of this Agreement, as reflected in each Member's Schedule, shall be:

   (i) subject to countervailing duties only upon a determination of injury or threat thereof based on volume, effect on prices, or consequent impact in accordance with Article VI of GATT 1994 and Part V of the Subsidies Agreement, and due restraint shall be shown in initiating any countervailing duty investigations; and

   (ii) exempt from actions based on Article XVI of GATT 1994 or Articles 3, 5 and 6 of the Subsidies Agreement.

PART VIII

Article 14   Sanitary and Phytosanitary Measures

Members agree to give effect to the Agreement on the Application of Sanitary and Phytosanitary Measures.

PART IX

Article 15   Special and Differential Treatment

1. In keeping with the recognition that differential and more favourable treatment for developing country Members is an integral part of the negotiation, special and differential treatment in respect of commitments shall be provided as set out in the relevant provisions of this Agreement and embodied in the Schedules of concessions and commitments.

2. Developing country Members shall have the flexibility to implement reduction commitments over a period of up to 10 years. Least-developed country Members shall not be required to undertake reduction commitments.

PART X

Article 16   Least-Developed and Net Food-Importing Developing Countries

1. Developed country Members shall take such action as is provided for within the framework of the Decision on Measures Concerning the Possible Negative Effects of the Reform Programme on Least-Developed and Net Food-Importing Developing Countries.

2. The Committee on Agriculture shall monitor, as appropriate, the follow-up to this Decision.

PART XI

Article 17   Committee on Agriculture
A Committee on Agriculture is hereby established.

Article 18   Review of the Implementation of Commitments
1. Progress in the implementation of commitments negotiated under the Uruguay Round reform programme shall be reviewed by the Committee on Agriculture.
2. The review process shall be undertaken on the basis of notifications submitted by Members in relation to such matters and at such intervals as shall be determined, as well as on the basis of such documentation as the Secretariat may be requested to prepare in order to facilitate the review process.
3. In addition to the notifications to be submitted under paragraph 2, any new domestic support measure, or modification of an existing measure, for which exemption from reduction is claimed shall be notified promptly. This notification shall contain details of the new or modified measure and its conformity with the agreed criteria as set out either in Article 6 or in Annex 2.
4. In the review process Members shall give due consideration to the influence of excessive rates of inflation on the ability of any Member to abide by its domestic support commitments.
5. Members agree to consult annually in the Committee on Agriculture with respect to their participation in the normal growth of world trade in agricultural products within the framework of the commitments on export subsidies under this Agreement.
6. The review process shall provide an opportunity for Members to raise any matter relevant to the implementation of commitments under the reform programme as set out in this Agreement.
7. Any Member may bring to the attention of the Committee on Agriculture any measure which it considers ought to have been notified by another Member.

Article 19   Consultation and Dispute Settlement
The provisions of Articles XXII and XXIII of GATT 1994, as elaborated and applied by the Dispute Settlement Understanding, shall apply to consultations and the settlement of disputes under this Agreement.

PART XII

Article 20   Continuation of the Reform Process
Recognizing that the long-term objective of substantial progressive reductions in support and protection resulting in fundamental reform is an ongoing process, Members agree that negotiations for continuing the process will be initiated one year before the end of the implementation period, taking into account:
(a) the experience to that date from implementing the reduction commitments;
(b) the effects of the reduction commitments on world trade in agriculture;
(c) non-trade concerns, special and differential treatment to developing country Members, and the objective to establish a fair and market-oriented agricultural trading system, and the other objectives and concerns mentioned in the preamble to this Agreement; and
(d) what further commitments are necessary to achieve the above mentioned long-term objectives.

PART XIII

Article 21   Final Provisions
1. The provisions of GATT 1994 and of other Multilateral Trade Agreements in Annex 1A to the WTO Agreement shall apply subject to the provisions of this Agreement.
2. The Annexes to this Agreement are hereby made an integral part of this Agreement.

ANNEX 1 PRODUCT COVERAGE

1. This Agreement shall cover the following products:

(i)	HS Chapters 1 to 24 less fish and fish products, plus*		
(ii)	HS Code	2905.43	(mannitol)
	HS Code	2905.44	(sorbitol)
	HS Heading	33.01	(essential oils)
	HS Headings	35.01 to 35.05	(albuminoidal substances, modified starches, glues)
	HS Code	3809.10	(finishing agents)
	HS Code	3823.60	(sorbitol n.e.p.)
	HS Headings	41.01 to 41.03	(hides and skins)
	HS Heading	43.01	(raw furskins)
	HS Headings	50.01 to 50.03	(raw silk and silk waste)
	HS Headings	51.01 to 51.03	(wool and animal hair)
	HS Headings	52.01 to 52.03	(raw cotton, waste and cotton carded or combed)
	HS Heading	53.01	(raw flax)
	HS Heading	53.02	(raw hemp)

2. The foregoing shall not limit the product coverage of the Agreement on the Application of Sanitary and Phytosanitary Measures.

ANNEX 2 DOMESTIC SUPPORT: THE BASIS FOR EXEMPTION FROM THE REDUCTION COMMITMENTS

1. Domestic support measures for which exemption from the reduction commitments is claimed shall meet the fundamental requirement that they have no, or at most minimal, trade-distorting effects or effects on production. Accordingly, all measures for which exemption is claimed shall conform to the following basic criteria:
   (a) the support in question shall be provided through a publicly-funded government programme (including government revenue foregone) not involving transfers from consumers; and,
   (b) the support in question shall not have the effect of providing price support to producers; plus policy-specific criteria and conditions as set out below.

Government Service Programmes

2. General services
   Policies in this category involve expenditures (or revenue foregone) in relation to programmes which provide services or benefits to agriculture or the rural community. They shall not involve direct payments to producers or processors. Such programmes, which include but are not restricted to the following list, shall meet the general criteria in paragraph 1 above and policy-specific conditions where set out below:
   (a) research, including general research, research in connection with environmental programmes, and research programmes relating to particular products;
   (b) pest and disease control, including general and product-specific pest and disease control measures, such as early-warning systems, quarantine and eradication;
   (c) training services, including both general and specialist training facilities;

---

* The product descriptions in round brackets are not necessarily exhaustive.

(d) extension and advisory services, including the provision of means to facilitate the transfer of information and the results of research to producers and consumers;

(e) inspection services, including general inspection services and the inspection of particular products for health, safety, grading or standardization purposes;

(f) marketing and promotion services, including market information, advice and promotion relating to particular products but excluding expenditure for unspecified purposes that could be used by sellers to reduce their selling price or confer a direct economic benefit to purchasers; and

(g) infrastructural services, including: electricity reticulation, roads and other means of transport, market and port facilities, water supply facilities, dams and drainage schemes, and infrastructural works associated with environmental programmes. In all cases the expenditure shall be directed to the provision or construction of capital works only, and shall exclude the subsidized provision of on-farm facilities other than for the reticulation of generally available public utilities. It shall not include subsidies to inputs or operating costs, or preferential user charges.

3. Public stockholding for food security purposes[5]

Expenditures (or revenue foregone) in relation to the accumulation and holding of stocks of products which form an integral part of a food security programme identified in national legislation. This may include government aid to private storage of products as part of such a programme.

The volume and accumulation of such stocks shall correspond to predetermined targets related solely to food security. The process of stock accumulation and disposal shall be financially transparent. Food purchases by the government shall be made at current market prices and sales from food security stocks shall be made at no less than the current domestic market price for the product and quality in question.

4. Domestic food aid[6]

Expenditures (or revenue foregone) in relation to the provision of domestic food aid to sections of the population in need.

Eligibility to receive the food aid shall be subject to clearly-defined criteria related to nutritional objectives. Such aid shall be in the form of direct provision of food to those concerned or the provision of means to allow eligible recipients to buy food either at market or at subsidized prices. Food purchases by the government shall be made at current market prices and the financing and administration of the aid shall be transparent.

5. Direct payments to producers

Support provided through direct payments (or revenue foregone, including payments in kind) to producers for which exemption from reduction commitments is claimed shall meet the basic criteria set out in paragraph 1 above, plus specific criteria applying to individual types of direct payment as set out in paragraphs 6 through 13 below. Where exemption from reduction is claimed for any existing or new type of direct payment other than those specified in paragraphs 6 through 13, it shall conform to criteria (b) through (e) in paragraph 6, in addition to the general criteria set out in paragraph 1.

---

5 For the purposes of paragraph 3 of this Annex, governmental stockholding programmes for food security purposes in developing countries whose operation is transparent and conducted in accordance with officially published objective criteria or guidelines shall be considered to be in conformity with the provisions of this paragraph, including programmes under which stocks of foodstuffs for food security purposes are acquired and released at administered prices, provided that the difference between the acquisition price and the external reference price is accounted for in the AMS.

6 For the purposes of paragraphs 3 and 4 of this Annex, the provision of foodstuffs at subsidized prices with the objective of meeting food requirements of urban and rural poor in developing countries on a regular basis at reasonable prices shall be considered to be in conformity with the provisions of this paragraph.

6. Decoupled income support
    (a) Eligibility for such payments shall be determined by clearly-defined criteria such as income, status as a producer or landowner, factor use or production level in a defined and fixed base period.
    (b) The amount of such payments in any given year shall not be related to, or based on, the type or volume of production (including livestock units) undertaken by the producer in any year after the base period.
    (c) The amount of such payments in any given year shall not be related to, or based on, the prices, domestic or international, applying to any production undertaken in any year after the base period.
    (d) The amount of such payments in any given year shall not be related to, or based on, the factors of production employed in any year after the base period.
    (e) No production shall be required in order to receive such payments.

7. Government financial participation in income insurance and income safety-net programmes
    (a) Eligibility for such payments shall be determined by an income loss, taking into account only income derived from agriculture, which exceeds 30 per cent of average gross income or the equivalent in net income terms (excluding any payments from the same or similar schemes) in the preceding three-year period or a three-year average based on the preceding five-year period, excluding the highest and the lowest entry. Any producer meeting this condition shall be eligible to receive the payments.
    (b) The amount of such payments shall compensate for less than 70 per cent of the producer's income loss in the year the producer becomes eligible to receive this assistance.
    (c) The amount of any such payments shall relate solely to income; it shall not relate to the type or volume of production (including livestock units) undertaken by the producer; or to the prices, domestic or international, applying to such production; or to the factors of production employed.
    (d) Where a producer receives in the same year payments under this paragraph and under paragraph 8 (relief from natural disasters), the total of such payments shall be less than 100 per cent of the producer's total loss.

8. Payments (made either directly or by way of government financial participation in crop insurance schemes) for relief from natural disasters
    (a) Eligibility for such payments shall arise only following a formal recognition by government authorities that a natural or like disaster (including disease outbreaks, pest infestations, nuclear accidents, and war on the territory of the Member concerned) has occurred or is occurring; and shall be determined by a production loss which exceeds 30 per cent of the average of production in the preceding three-year period or a three-year average based on the preceding five-year period, excluding the highest and the lowest entry.
    (b) Payments made following a disaster shall be applied only in respect of losses of income, livestock (including payments in connection with the veterinary treatment of animals), land or other production factors due to the natural disaster in question.
    (c) Payments shall compensate for not more than the total cost of replacing such losses and shall not require or specify the type or quantity of future production.
    (d) Payments made during a disaster shall not exceed the level required to prevent or alleviate further loss as defined in criterion (b) above.
    (e) Where a producer receives in the same year payments under this paragraph and under paragraph 7 (income insurance and income safety-net programmes), the total of such payments shall be less than 100 per cent of the producer's total loss.

9. Structural adjustment assistance provided through producer retirement programmes
   (a) Eligibility for such payments shall be determined by reference to clearly defined criteria in programmes designed to facilitate the retirement of persons engaged in marketable agricultural production, or their movement to non-agricultural activities.
   (b) Payments shall be conditional upon the total and permanent retirement of the recipients from marketable agricultural production.

10. Structural adjustment assistance provided through resource retirement programmes
    (a) Eligibility for such payments shall be determined by reference to clearly defined criteria in programmes designed to remove land or other resources, including livestock, from marketable agricultural production.
    (b) Payments shall be conditional upon the retirement of land from marketable agricultural production for a minimum of three years, and in the case of livestock on its slaughter or definitive permanent disposal.
    (c) Payments shall not require or specify any alternative use for such land or other resources which involves the production of marketable agricultural products.
    (d) Payments shall not be related to either the type or quantity of production or to the prices, domestic or international, applying to production undertaken using the land or other resources remaining in production.

11. Structural adjustment assistance provided through investment aids
    (a) Eligibility for such payments shall be determined by reference to clearly-defined criteria in government programmes designed to assist the financial or physical restructuring of a producer's operations in response to objectively demonstrated structural disadvantages. Eligibility for such programmes may also be based on a clearly-defined government programme for the reprivatization of agricultural land.
    (b) The amount of such payments in any given year shall not be related to, or based on, the type or volume of production (including livestock units) undertaken by the producer in any year after the base period other than as provided for under criterion (e) below.
    (c) The amount of such payments in any given year shall not be related to, or based on, the prices, domestic or international, applying to any production undertaken in any year after the base period.
    (d) The payments shall be given only for the period of time necessary for the realization of the investment in respect of which they are provided.
    (e) The payments shall not mandate or in any way designate the agricultural products to be produced by the recipients except to require them not to produce a particular product.
    (f) The payments shall be limited to the amount required to compensate for the structural disadvantage.

12. Payments under environmental programmes
    (a) Eligibility for such payments shall be determined as part of a clearly-defined government environmental or conservation programme and be dependent on the fulfilment of specific conditions under the government programme, including conditions related to production methods or inputs.
    (b) The amount of payment shall be limited to the extra costs or loss of income involved in complying with the government programme.

13. Payments under regional assistance programmes
    (a) Eligibility for such payments shall be limited to producers in disadvantaged regions. Each such region must be a clearly designated contiguous geographical area with a definable economic and administrative identity, considered as disadvantaged on the basis of neutral and objective criteria clearly spelt out in law or regulation and indicating that the region's difficulties arise out of more than temporary circumstances.

(b) The amount of such payments in any given year shall not be related to, or based on, the type or volume of production (including livestock units) undertaken by the producer in any year after the base period other than to reduce that production.

(c) The amount of such payments in any given year shall not be related to, or based on, the prices, domestic or international, applying to any production undertaken in any year after the base period.

(d) Payments shall be available only to producers in eligible regions, but generally available to all producers within such regions.

(e) Where related to production factors, payments shall be made at a degressive rate above a threshold level of the factor concerned.

(f) The payments shall be limited to the extra costs or loss of income involved in undertaking agricultural production in the prescribed area.

ANNEX 3   DOMESTIC SUPPORT: CALCULATION OF AGGREGATE MEASUREMENT OF SUPPORT

1. Subject to the provisions of Article 6, an Aggregate Measurement of Support (AMS) shall be calculated on a product-specific basis for each basic agricultural product receiving market price support, non-exempt direct payments, or any other subsidy not exempted from the reduction commitment ("other non-exempt policies"). Support which is non-product specific shall be totalled into one non-product-specific AMS in total monetary terms.

2. Subsidies under paragraph 1 shall include both budgetary outlays and revenue foregone by governments or their agents.

3. Support at both the national and sub-national level shall be included.

4. Specific agricultural levies or fees paid by producers shall be deducted from the AMS.

5. The AMS calculated as outlined below for the base period shall constitute the base level for the implementation of the reduction commitment on domestic support.

6. For each basic agricultural product, a specific AMS shall be established, expressed in total monetary value terms.

7. The AMS shall be calculated as close as practicable to the point of first sale of the basic agricultural product concerned. Measures directed at agricultural processors shall be included to the extent that such measures benefit the producers of the basic agricultural products.

8. Market price support: market price support shall be calculated using the gap between a fixed external reference price and the applied administered price multiplied by the quantity of production eligible to receive the applied administered price. Budgetary payments made to maintain this gap, such as buying-in or storage costs, shall not be included in the AMS.

9. The fixed external reference price shall be based on the years 1986 to 1988 and shall generally be the average f.o.b. unit value for the basic agricultural product concerned in a net exporting country and the average c.i.f. unit value for the basic agricultural product concerned in a net importing country in the base period. The fixed reference price may be adjusted for quality differences as necessary.

10. Non-exempt direct payments: non-exempt direct payments which are dependent on a price gap shall be calculated either using the gap between the fixed reference price and the applied administered price multiplied by the quantity of production eligible to receive the administered price, or using budgetary outlays.

11. The fixed reference price shall be based on the years 1986 to 1988 and shall generally be the actual price used for determining payment rates.

12. Non-exempt direct payments which are based on factors other than price shall be measured using budgetary outlays.

13. Other non-exempt measures, including input subsidies and other measures such as marketing-cost reduction measures: the value of such measures shall be measured using government budgetary outlays or, where the use of budgetary outlays does not reflect the full extent of the subsidy concerned, the basis for calculating the subsidy shall be the gap between the price of the subsidized good or service and a representative market price for a similar good or service multiplied by the quantity of the good or service.

ANNEX 4   DOMESTIC SUPPORT: CALCULATION OF EQUIVALENT MEASUREMENT OF SUPPORT

1. Subject to the provisions of Article 6, equivalent measurements of support shall be calculated in respect of all basic agricultural products where market price support as defined in Annex 3 exists but for which calculation of this component of the AMS is not practicable. For such products the base level for implementation of the domestic support reduction commitments shall consist of a market price support component expressed in terms of equivalent measurements of support under paragraph 2 below, as well as any non-exempt direct payments and other non-exempt support, which shall be evaluated as provided for under paragraph 3 below. Support at both national and sub-national level shall be included.

2. The equivalent measurements of support provided for in paragraph 1 shall be calculated on a product-specific basis for all basic agricultural products as close as practicable to the point of first sale receiving market price support and for which the calculation of the market price support component of the AMS is not practicable. For those basic agricultural products, equivalent measurements of market price support shall be made using the applied administered price and the quantity of production eligible to receive that price or, where this is not practicable, on budgetary outlays used to maintain the producer price.

3. Where basic agricultural products falling under paragraph 1 are the subject of non-exempt direct payments or any other product-specific subsidy not exempted from the reduction commitment, the basis for equivalent measurements of support concerning these measures shall be calculations as for the corresponding AMS components (specified in paragraphs 10 through 13 of Annex 3).

4. Equivalent measurements of support shall be calculated on the amount of subsidy as close as practicable to the point of first sale of the basic agricultural product concerned. Measures directed at agricultural processors shall be included to the extent that such measures benefit the producers of the basic agricultural products. Specific agricultural levies or fees paid by producers shall reduce the equivalent measurements of support by a corresponding amount.

ANNEX 5   SPECIAL TREATMENT WITH RESPECT TO PARAGRAPH 2 OF ARTICLE 4

Section A

1. The provisions of paragraph 2 of Article 4 shall not apply with effect from the entry into force of the WTO Agreement to any primary agricultural product and its worked and/or prepared products ("designated products") in respect of which the following conditions are complied with (hereinafter referred to as "special treatment"):

   (a) imports of the designated products comprised less than 3 per cent of corresponding domestic consumption in the base period 1986–1988 ("the base period");

   (b) no export subsidies have been provided since the beginning of the base period for the designated products;

(c) effective production-restricting measures are applied to the primary agricultural product;

(d) such products are designated with the symbol "ST-Annex 5" in Section I-B of Part I of a Member's Schedule annexed to the Marrakesh Protocol, as being subject to special treatment reflecting factors of non-trade concerns, such as food security and environmental protection; and

(e) minimum access opportunities in respect of the designated products correspond, as specified in Section I-B of Part I of the Schedule of the Member concerned, to 4 per cent of base period domestic consumption of the designated products from the beginning of the first year of the implementation period and, thereafter, are increased by 0.8 per cent of corresponding domestic consumption in the base period per year for the remainder of the implementation period.

2. At the beginning of any year of the implementation period a Member may cease to apply special treatment in respect of the designated products by complying with the provisions of paragraph 6. In such a case, the Member concerned shall maintain the minimum access opportunities already in effect at such time and increase the minimum access opportunities by 0.4 per cent of corresponding domestic consumption in the base period per year for the remainder of the implementation period. Thereafter, the level of minimum access opportunities resulting from this formula in the final year of the implementation period shall be maintained in the Schedule of the Member concerned.

3. Any negotiation on the question of whether there can be a continuation of the special treatment as set out in paragraph 1 after the end of the implementation period shall be completed within the time-frame of the implementation period itself as a part of the negotiations set out in Article 20 of this Agreement, taking into account the factors of non-trade concerns.

4. If it is agreed as a result of the negotiation referred to in paragraph 3 that a Member may continue to apply the special treatment, such Member shall confer additional and acceptable concessions as determined in that negotiation.

5. Where the special treatment is not to be continued at the end of the implementation period, the Member concerned shall implement the provisions of paragraph 6. In such a case, after the end of the implementation period the minimum access opportunities for the designated products shall be maintained at the level of 8 per cent of corresponding domestic consumption in the base period in the Schedule of the Member concerned.

6. Border measures other than ordinary customs duties maintained in respect of the designated products shall become subject to the provisions of paragraph 2 of Article 4 with effect from the beginning of the year in which the special treatment ceases to apply. Such products shall be subject to ordinary customs duties, which shall be bound in the Schedule of the Member concerned and applied, from the beginning of the year in which special treatment ceases and thereafter, at such rates as would have been applicable had a reduction of at least 15 per cent been implemented over the implementation period in equal annual instalments. These duties shall be established on the basis of tariff equivalents to be calculated in accordance with the guidelines prescribed in the attachment hereto.

Section B

7. The provisions of paragraph 2 of Article 4 shall also not apply with effect from the entry into force of the WTO Agreement to a primary agricultural product that is the predominant staple in the traditional diet of a developing country Member and in respect of which the following conditions, in addition to those specified in paragraph 1(a) through 1(d), as they apply to the products concerned, are complied with:

(a) minimum access opportunities in respect of the products concerned, as specified in Section I-B of Part I of the Schedule of the developing country Member concerned, correspond to 1 per cent of base period domestic consumption of the products concerned from the beginning of the first year of the implementation period and are increased in equal annual instalments to 2 per cent of corresponding domestic consumption in the base period at the beginning of the fifth year of the implementation period. From the beginning of the sixth year of the implementation period, minimum access opportunities in respect of the products concerned correspond to 2 per cent of corresponding domestic consumption in the base period and are increased in equal annual instalments to 4 per cent of corresponding domestic consumption in the base period until the beginning of the 10th year. Thereafter, the level of minimum access opportunities resulting from this formula in the 10th year shall be maintained in the Schedule of the developing country Member concerned;

(b) appropriate market access opportunities have been provided for in other products under this Agreement.

8. Any negotiation on the question of whether there can be a continuation of the special treatment as set out in paragraph 7 after the end of the 10th year following the beginning of the implementation period shall be initiated and completed within the time-frame of the 10th year itself following the beginning of the implementation period.

9. If it is agreed as a result of the negotiation referred to in paragraph 8 that a Member may continue to apply the special treatment, such Member shall confer additional and acceptable concessions as determined in that negotiation.

10. In the event that special treatment under paragraph 7 is not to be continued beyond the 10th year following the beginning of the implementation period, the products concerned shall be subject to ordinary customs duties, established on the basis of a tariff equivalent to be calculated in accordance with the guidelines prescribed in the attachment hereto, which shall be bound in the Schedule of the Member concerned. In other respects, the provisions of paragraph 6 shall apply as modified by the relevant special and differential treatment accorded to developing country Members under this Agreement.

Attachment to Annex 5   Guidelines for the Calculation of Tariff Equivalents for the Specific Purpose Specified in Paragraphs 6 and 10 of this Annex

1. The calculation of the tariff equivalents, whether expressed as *ad valorem* or specific rates, shall be made using the actual difference between internal and external prices in a transparent manner. Data used shall be for the years 1986 to 1988. Tariff equivalents:
   (a) shall primarily be established at the four-digit level of the HS;
   (b) shall be established at the six-digit or a more detailed level of the HS wherever appropriate;
   (c) shall generally be established for worked and/or prepared products by multiplying the specific tariff equivalent(s) for the primary agricultural product(s) by the proportion(s) in value terms or in physical terms as appropriate of the primary agricultural product(s) in the worked and/or prepared products, and take account, where necessary, of any additional elements currently providing protection to industry.

2. External prices shall be, in general, actual average c.i.f. unit values for the importing country. Where average c.i.f. unit values are not available or appropriate, external prices shall be either:
   (a) appropriate average c.i.f. unit values of a near country; or
   (b) estimated from average f.o.b. unit values of (an) appropriate major exporter(s) adjusted by adding an estimate of insurance, freight and other relevant costs to the importing country.

3. The external prices shall generally be converted to domestic currencies using the annual average market exchange rate for the same period as the price data.

4. The internal price shall generally be a representative wholesale price ruling in the domestic market or an estimate of that price where adequate data is not available.

5. The initial tariff equivalents may be adjusted, where necessary, to take account of differences in quality or variety using an appropriate coefficient.

6. Where a tariff equivalent resulting from these guidelines is negative or lower than the current bound rate, the initial tariff equivalent may be established at the current bound rate or on the basis of national offers for that product.

7. Where an adjustment is made to the level of a tariff equivalent which would have resulted from the above guidelines, the Member concerned shall afford, on request, full opportunities for consultation with a view to negotiating appropriate solutions.

Agreement on the Application of Sanitary and Phytosanitary Measures

Members,

Reaffirming that no Member should be prevented from adopting or enforcing measures necessary to protect human, animal or plant life or health, subject to the requirement that these measures are not applied in a manner which would constitute a means of arbitrary or unjustifiable discrimination between Members where the same conditions prevail or a disguised restriction on international trade;

Desiring to improve the human health, animal health and phytosanitary situation in all Members;

Noting that sanitary and phytosanitary measures are often applied on the basis of bilateral agreements or protocols;

Desiring the establishment of a multilateral framework of rules and disciplines to guide the development, adoption and enforcement of sanitary and phytosanitary measures in order to minimize their negative effects on trade;

Recognizing the important contribution that international standards, guidelines and recommendations can make in this regard;

Desiring to further the use of harmonized sanitary and phytosanitary measures between Members, on the basis of international standards, guidelines and recommendations developed by the relevant international organizations, including the Codex Alimentarius Commission, the International Office of Epizootics, and the relevant international and regional organizations operating within the framework of the International Plant Protection Convention, without requiring Members to change their appropriate level of protection of human, animal or plant life or health;

Recognizing that developing country Members may encounter special difficulties in complying with the sanitary or phytosanitary measures of importing Members, and as a consequence in access to markets, and also in the formulation and application of sanitary or phytosanitary measures in their own territories, and desiring to assist them in their endeavours in this regard;

Desiring therefore to elaborate rules for the application of the provisions of GATT 1994 which relate to the use of sanitary or phytosanitary measures, in particular the provisions of Article XX (b)[1];

Hereby *agree* as follows:

Article 1   General Provisions

1. This Agreement applies to all sanitary and phytosanitary measures which may, directly or indirectly, affect international trade. Such measures shall be developed and applied in accordance with the provisions of this Agreement.

2. For the purposes of this Agreement, the definitions provided in Annex A shall apply.

3. The annexes are an integral part of this Agreement.

4. Nothing in this Agreement shall affect the rights of Members under the Agreement on Technical Barriers to Trade with respect to measures not within the scope of this Agreement.

---

1 In this Agreement, reference to Article XX(b) includes also the chapeau of that Article.

Article 2   Basic Rights and Obligations

1. Members have the right to take sanitary and phytosanitary measures necessary for the protection of human, animal or plant life or health, provided that such measures are not inconsistent with the provisions of this Agreement.

2. Members shall ensure that any sanitary or phytosanitary measure is applied only to the extent necessary to protect human, animal or plant life or health, is based on scientific principles and is not maintained without sufficient scientific evidence, except as provided for in paragraph 7 of Article 5.

3. Members shall ensure that their sanitary and phytosanitary measures do not arbitrarily or unjustifiably discriminate between Members where identical or similar conditions prevail, including between their own territory and that of other Members. Sanitary and phytosanitary measures shall not be applied in a manner which would constitute a disguised restriction on international trade.

4. Sanitary or phytosanitary measures which conform to the relevant provisions of this Agreement shall be presumed to be in accordance with the obligations of the Members under the provisions of GATT 1994 which relate to the use of sanitary or phytosanitary measures, in particular the provisions of Article XX(b).

Article 3   Harmonization

1. To harmonize sanitary and phytosanitary measures on as wide a basis as possible, Members shall base their sanitary or phytosanitary measures on international standards, guidelines or recommendations, where they exist, except as otherwise provided for in this Agreement, and in particular in paragraph 3.

2. Sanitary or phytosanitary measures which conform to international standards, guidelines or recommendations shall be deemed to be necessary to protect human, animal or plant life or health, and presumed to be consistent with the relevant provisions of this Agreement and of GATT 1994.

3. Members may introduce or maintain sanitary or phytosanitary measures which result in a higher level of sanitary or phytosanitary protection than would be achieved by measures based on the relevant international standards, guidelines or recommendations, if there is a scientific justification, or as a consequence of the level of sanitary or phytosanitary protection a Member determines to be appropriate in accordance with the relevant provisions of paragraphs 1 through 8 of Article 5.[2] Notwithstanding the above, all measures which result in a level of sanitary or phytosanitary protection different from that which would be achieved by measures based on international standards, guidelines or recommendations shall not be inconsistent with any other provision of this Agreement.

4. Members shall play a full part, within the limits of their resources, in the relevant international organizations and their subsidiary bodies, in particular the Codex Alimentarius Commission, the International Office of Epizootics, and the international and regional organizations operating within the framework of the International Plant Protection Convention, to promote within these organizations the development and periodic review of standards, guidelines and recommendations with respect to all aspects of sanitary and phytosanitary measures.

5. The Committee on Sanitary and Phytosanitary Measures provided for in paragraphs 1 and 4 of Article 12 (referred to in this Agreement as the "Committee") shall develop a procedure to

---

2 For the purposes of paragraph 3 of Article 3, there is a scientific justification if, on the basis of an examination and evaluation of available scientific information in conformity with the relevant provisions of this Agreement, a Member determines that the relevant international standards, guidelines or recommendations are not sufficient to achieve its appropriate level of sanitary or phytosanitary protection.

monitor the process of international harmonization and coordinate efforts in this regard with the relevant international organizations.

Article 4   Equivalence

1. Members shall accept the sanitary or phytosanitary measures of other Members as equivalent, even if these measures differ from their own or from those used by other Members trading in the same product, if the exporting Member objectively demonstrates to the importing Member that its measures achieve the importing Member's appropriate level of sanitary or phytosanitary protection. For this purpose, reasonable access shall be given, upon request, to the importing Member for inspection, testing and other relevant procedures.

2. Members shall, upon request, enter into consultations with the aim of achieving bilateral and multilateral agreements on recognition of the equivalence of specified sanitary or phytosanitary measures.

Article 5   Assessment of Risk and Determination of the Appropriate Level of Sanitary or Phytosanitary Protection

1. Members shall ensure that their sanitary or phytosanitary measures are based on an assessment, as appropriate to the circumstances, of the risks to human, animal or plant life or health, taking into account risk assessment techniques developed by the relevant international organizations.

2. In the assessment of risks, Members shall take into account available scientific evidence; relevant processes and production methods; relevant inspection, sampling and testing methods; prevalence of specific diseases or pests; existence of pest- or disease-free areas; relevant ecological and environmental conditions; and quarantine or other treatment.

3. In assessing the risk to animal or plant life or health and determining the measure to be applied for achieving the appropriate level of sanitary or phytosanitary protection from such risk, Members shall take into account as relevant economic factors: the potential damage in terms of loss of production or sales in the event of the entry, establishment or spread of a pest or disease; the costs of control or eradication in the territory of the importing Member; and the relative cost-effectiveness of alternative approaches to limiting risks.

4. Members should, when determining the appropriate level of sanitary or phytosanitary protection, take into account the objective of minimizing negative trade effects.

5. With the objective of achieving consistency in the application of the concept of appropriate level of sanitary or phytosanitary protection against risks to human life or health, or to animal and plant life or health, each Member shall avoid arbitrary or unjustifiable distinctions in the levels it considers to be appropriate in different situations, if such distinctions result in discrimination or a disguised restriction on international trade. Members shall cooperate in the Committee, in accordance with paragraphs 1, 2 and 3 of Article 12, to develop guidelines to further the practical implementation of this provision. In developing the guidelines, the Committee shall take into account all relevant factors, including the exceptional character of human health risks to which people voluntarily expose themselves.

6. Without prejudice to paragraph 2 of Article 3, when establishing or maintaining sanitary or phytosanitary measures to achieve the appropriate level of sanitary or phytosanitary protection, Members shall ensure that such measures are not more trade-restrictive than required to achieve their appropriate level of sanitary or phytosanitary protection, taking into account technical and economic feasibility.[3]

---

3 For purposes of paragraph 6 of Article 5, a measure is not more trade-restrictive than required unless there is another measure, reasonably available taking into account technical and economic feasibility, that achieves the appropriate level of sanitary or phytosanitary protection and is significantly less restrictive to trade.

7. In cases where relevant scientific evidence is insufficient, a Member may provisionally adopt sanitary or phytosanitary measures on the basis of available pertinent information, including that from the relevant international organizations as well as from sanitary or phytosanitary measures applied by other Members. In such circumstances, Members shall seek to obtain the additional information necessary for a more objective assessment of risk and review the sanitary or phytosanitary measure accordingly within a reasonable period of time.

8. When a Member has reason to believe that a specific sanitary or phytosanitary measure introduced or maintained by another Member is constraining, or has the potential to constrain, its exports and the measure is not based on the relevant international standards, guidelines or recommendations, or such standards, guidelines or recommendations do not exist, an explanation of the reasons for such sanitary or phytosanitary measure may be requested and shall be provided by the Member maintaining the measure.

Article 6   Adaptation to Regional Conditions, Including Pest- or Disease-Free Areas and Areas of Low Pest or Disease Prevalence

1. Members shall ensure that their sanitary or phytosanitary measures are adapted to the sanitary or phytosanitary characteristics of the area—whether all of a country, part of a country, or all or parts of several countries—from which the product originated and to which the product is destined. In assessing the sanitary or phytosanitary characteristics of a region, Members shall take into account, *inter alia*, the level of prevalence of specific diseases or pests, the existence of eradication or control programmes, and appropriate criteria or guidelines which may be developed by the relevant international organizations.

2. Members shall, in particular, recognize the concepts of pest- or disease-free areas and areas of low pest or disease prevalence. Determination of such areas shall be based on factors such as geography, ecosystems, epidemiological surveillance, and the effectiveness of sanitary or phytosanitary controls.

3. Exporting Members claiming that areas within their territories are pest- or disease-free areas or areas of low pest or disease prevalence shall provide the necessary evidence thereof in order to objectively demonstrate to the importing Member that such areas are, and are likely to remain, pest- or disease-free areas or areas of low pest or disease prevalence, respectively. For this purpose, reasonable access shall be given, upon request, to the importing Member for inspection, testing and other relevant procedures.

Article 7   Transparency

Members shall notify changes in their sanitary or phytosanitary measures and shall provide information on their sanitary or phytosanitary measures in accordance with the provisions of Annex B.

Article 8   Control, Inspection and Approval Procedures

Members shall observe the provisions of Annex C in the operation of control, inspection and approval procedures, including national systems for approving the use of additives or for establishing tolerances for contaminants in foods, beverages or feedstuffs, and otherwise ensure that their procedures are not inconsistent with the provisions of this Agreement.

Article 9   Technical Assistance

1. Members agree to facilitate the provision of technical assistance to other Members, especially developing country Members, either bilaterally or through the appropriate international organizations. Such assistance may be, *inter alia*, in the areas of processing technologies, research and infrastructure, including in the establishment of national regulatory bodies, and may take the form of advice, credits, donations and grants, including for the purpose of seeking technical expertise, training and equipment to allow such countries to adjust to, and comply with, sanitary or phytosanitary measures necessary to achieve the appropriate level of sanitary or phytosanitary protection in their export markets.

2. Where substantial investments are required in order for an exporting developing country Member to fulfil the sanitary or phytosanitary requirements of an importing Member, the latter shall consider providing such technical assistance as will permit the developing country Member to maintain and expand its market access opportunities for the product involved.

Article 10   Special and Differential Treatment

1. In the preparation and application of sanitary or phytosanitary measures, Members shall take account of the special needs of developing country Members, and in particular of the least-developed country Members.

2. Where the appropriate level of sanitary or phytosanitary protection allows scope for the phased introduction of new sanitary or phytosanitary measures, longer time-frames for compliance should be accorded on products of interest to developing country Members so as to maintain opportunities for their exports.

3. With a view to ensuring that developing country Members are able to comply with the provisions of this Agreement, the Committee is enabled to grant to such countries, upon request, specified, time-limited exceptions in whole or in part from obligations under this Agreement, taking into account their financial, trade and development needs.

4. Members should encourage and facilitate the active participation of developing country Members in the relevant international organizations.

Article 11   Consultations and Dispute Settlement

1. The provisions of Articles XXII and XXIII of GATT 1994 as elaborated and applied by the Dispute Settlement Understanding shall apply to consultations and the settlement of disputes under this Agreement, except as otherwise specifically provided herein.

2. In a dispute under this Agreement involving scientific or technical issues, a panel should seek advice from experts chosen by the panel in consultation with the parties to the dispute. To this end, the panel may, when it deems it appropriate, establish an advisory technical experts group, or consult the relevant international organizations, at the request of either party to the dispute or on its own initiative.

3. Nothing in this Agreement shall impair the rights of Members under other international agreements, including the right to resort to the good offices or dispute settlement mechanisms of other international organizations or established under any international agreement.

Article 12   Administration

1. A Committee on Sanitary and Phytosanitary Measures is hereby established to provide a regular forum for consultations. It shall carry out the functions necessary to implement the provisions of this Agreement and the furtherance of its objectives, in particular with respect to harmonization. The Committee shall reach its decisions by consensus.

2. The Committee shall encourage and facilitate ad hoc consultations or negotiations among Members on specific sanitary or phytosanitary issues. The Committee shall encourage the use of international standards, guidelines or recommendations by all Members and, in this regard, shall sponsor technical consultation and study with the objective of increasing coordination and integration between international and national systems and approaches for approving the use of food additives or for establishing tolerances for contaminants in foods, beverages or feedstuffs.

3. The Committee shall maintain close contact with the relevant international organizations in the field of sanitary and phytosanitary protection, especially with the Codex Alimentarius Commission, the International Office of Epizootics, and the Secretariat of the International Plant Protection Convention, with the objective of securing the best available scientific and technical advice for the administration of this Agreement and in order to ensure that unnecessary duplication of effort is avoided.

4. The Committee shall develop a procedure to monitor the process of international harmonization and the use of international standards, guidelines or recommendations. For this purpose, the Committee should, in conjunction with the relevant international organizations, establish a list of international standards, guidelines or recommendations relating to sanitary or phytosanitary measures which the Committee determines to have a major trade impact. The list should include an indication by Members of those international standards, guidelines or recommendations which they apply as conditions for import or on the basis of which imported products conforming to these standards can enjoy access to their markets. For those cases in which a Member does not apply an international standard, guideline or recommendation as a condition for import, the Member should provide an indication of the reason therefor, and, in particular, whether it considers that the standard is not stringent enough to provide the appropriate level of sanitary or phytosanitary protection. If a Member revises its position, following its indication of the use of a standard, guideline or recommendation as a condition for import, it should provide an explanation for its change and so inform the Secretariat as well as the relevant international organizations, unless such notification and explanation is given according to the procedures of Annex B.

5. In order to avoid unnecessary duplication, the Committee may decide, as appropriate, to use the information generated by the procedures, particularly for notification, which are in operation in the relevant international organizations.

6. The Committee may, on the basis of an initiative from one of the Members, through appropriate channels invite the relevant international organizations or their subsidiary bodies to examine specific matters with respect to a particular standard, guideline or recommendation, including the basis of explanations for non-use given according to paragraph 4.

7. The Committee shall review the operation and implementation of this Agreement three years after the date of entry into force of the WTO Agreement, and thereafter as the need arises. Where appropriate, the Committee may submit to the Council for Trade in Goods proposals to amend the text of this Agreement having regard, *inter alia*, to the experience gained in its implementation.

Article 13   Implementation

Members are fully responsible under this Agreement for the observance of all obligations set forth herein. Members shall formulate and implement positive measures and mechanisms in support of the observance of the provisions of this Agreement by other than central government bodies. Members shall take such reasonable measures as may be available to them to ensure that non-governmental entities within their territories, as well as regional bodies in which relevant entities within their territories are members, comply with the relevant provisions of this Agreement. In addition, Members shall not take measures which have the effect of, directly or indirectly, requiring or encouraging such regional or non-governmental entities, or local governmental bodies, to act in a manner inconsistent with the provisions of this Agreement. Members shall ensure that they rely on the services of non-governmental entities for implementing sanitary or phytosanitary measures only if these entities comply with the provisions of this Agreement.

Article 14   Final Provisions

The least-developed country Members may delay application of the provisions of this Agreement for a period of five years following the date of entry into force of the WTO Agreement with respect to their sanitary or phytosanitary measures affecting importation or imported products. Other developing country Members may delay application of the provisions of this Agreement, other than paragraph 8 of Article 5 and Article 7, for two years following the date of entry into force of the WTO Agreement with respect to their existing sanitary or phytosanitary measures affecting importation or imported products, where such application is prevented by a lack of technical expertise, technical infrastructure or resources.

ANNEX A   DEFINITIONS[4]

1. *Sanitary or phytosanitary measure*—Any measure applied:
   (a) to protect animal or plant life or health within the territory of the Member from risks arising from the entry, establishment or spread of pests, diseases, disease-carrying organisms or disease-causing organisms;
   (b) to protect human or animal life or health within the territory of the Member from risks arising from additives, contaminants, toxins or disease-causing organisms in foods, beverages or feedstuffs;
   (c) to protect human life or health within the territory of the Member from risks arising from diseases carried by animals, plants or products thereof, or from the entry, establishment or spread of pests; or
   (d) to prevent or limit other damage within the territory of the Member from the entry, establishment or spread of pests.

   Sanitary or phytosanitary measures include all relevant laws, decrees, regulations, requirements and procedures including, *inter alia*, end product criteria; processes and production methods; testing, inspection, certification and approval procedures; quarantine treatments including relevant requirements associated with the transport of animals or plants, or with the materials necessary for their survival during transport; provisions on relevant statistical methods, sampling procedures and methods of risk assessment; and packaging and labelling requirements directly related to food safety.

2. *Harmonization*—The establishment, recognition and application of common sanitary and phytosanitary measures by different Members.

3. *International standards, guidelines and recommendations*
   (a) for food safety, the standards, guidelines and recommendations established by the Codex Alimentarius Commission relating to food additives, veterinary drug and pesticide residues, contaminants, methods of analysis and sampling, and codes and guidelines of hygienic practice;
   (b) for animal health and zoonoses, the standards, guidelines and recommendations developed under the auspices of the International Office of Epizootics;
   (c) for plant health, the international standards, guidelines and recommendations developed under the auspices of the Secretariat of the International Plant Protection Convention in cooperation with regional organizations operating within the framework of the International Plant Protection Convention; and
   (d) for matters not covered by the above organizations, appropriate standards, guidelines and recommendations promulgated by other relevant international organizations open for membership to all Members, as identified by the Committee.

4. *Risk assessment*—The evaluation of the likelihood of entry, establishment or spread of a pest or disease within the territory of an importing Member according to the sanitary or phytosanitary measures which might be applied, and of the associated potential biological and economic consequences; or the evaluation of the potential for adverse effects on human or animal health arising from the presence of additives, contaminants, toxins or disease-causing organisms in food, beverages or feedstuffs.

---

4 For the purpose of these definitions, "animal" includes fish and wild fauna; "plant" includes forests and wild flora; "pests" include weeds; and "contaminants" include pesticide and veterinary drug residues and extraneous matter.

5. *Appropriate level of sanitary or phytosanitary protection*—The level of protection deemed appropriate by the Member establishing a sanitary or phytosanitary measure to protect human, animal or plant life or health within its territory.

NOTE: Many Members otherwise refer to this concept as the "acceptable level of risk".

6. *Pest- or disease-free area*—An area, whether all of a country, part of a country, or all or parts of several countries, as identified by the competent authorities, in which a specific pest or disease does not occur.

NOTE: A pest- or disease-free area may surround, be surrounded by, or be adjacent to an area—whether within part of a country or in a geographic region which includes parts of or all of several countries—in which a specific pest or disease is known to occur but is subject to regional control measures such as the establishment of protection, surveillance and buffer zones which will confine or eradicate the pest or disease in question.

7. *Area of low pest or disease prevalence*—An area, whether all of a country, part of a country, or all or parts of several countries, as identified by the competent authorities, in which a specific pest or disease occurs at low levels and which is subject to effective surveillance, control or eradication measures.

ANNEX B TRANSPARENCY OF SANITARY AND PHYTOSANITARY REGULATIONS

Publication of regulations

1. Members shall ensure that all sanitary and phytosanitary regulations[5] which have been adopted are published promptly in such a manner as to enable interested Members to become acquainted with them.

2. Except in urgent circumstances, Members shall allow a reasonable interval between the publication of a sanitary or phytosanitary regulation and its entry into force in order to allow time for producers in exporting Members, and particularly in developing country Members, to adapt their products and methods of production to the requirements of the importing Member.

Enquiry points

3. Each Member shall ensure that one enquiry point exists which is responsible for the provision of answers to all reasonable questions from interested Members as well as for the provision of relevant documents regarding:

   (a) any sanitary or phytosanitary regulations adopted or proposed within its territory;
   (b) any control and inspection procedures, production and quarantine treatment, pesticide tolerance and food additive approval procedures, which are operated within its territory;
   (c) risk assessment procedures, factors taken into consideration, as well as the determination of the appropriate level of sanitary or phytosanitary protection;
   (d) the membership and participation of the Member, or of relevant bodies within its territory, in international and regional sanitary and phytosanitary organizations and systems, as well as in bilateral and multilateral agreements and arrangements within the scope of this Agreement, and the texts of such agreements and arrangements.

4. Members shall ensure that where copies of documents are requested by interested Members, they are supplied at the same price (if any), apart from the cost of delivery, as to the nationals[6] of the Member concerned.

---

5 Sanitary and phytosanitary measures such as laws, decrees or ordinances which are applicable generally.

6 When "nationals" are referred to in this Agreement, the term shall be deemed, in the case of a separate customs territory Member of the WTO, to mean persons, natural or legal, who are domiciled or who have a real and effective industrial or commercial establishment in that customs territory.

Notification procedures

5. Whenever an international standard, guideline or recommendation does not exist or the content of a proposed sanitary or phytosanitary regulation is not substantially the same as the content of an international standard, guideline or recommendation, and if the regulation may have a significant effect on trade of other Members, Members shall:

(a) publish a notice at an early stage in such a manner as to enable interested Members to become acquainted with the proposal to introduce a particular regulation;

(b) notify other Members, through the Secretariat, of the products to be covered by the regulation together with a brief indication of the objective and rationale of the proposed regulation. Such notifications shall take place at an early stage, when amendments can still be introduced and comments taken into account;

(c) provide upon request to other Members copies of the proposed regulation and, whenever possible, identify the parts which in substance deviate from international standards, guidelines or recommendations;

(d) without discrimination, allow reasonable time for other Members to make comments in writing, discuss these comments upon request, and take the comments and the results of the discussions into account.

6. However, where urgent problems of health protection arise or threaten to arise for a Member, that Member may omit such of the steps enumerated in paragraph 5 of this Annex as it finds necessary, provided that the Member:

(a) immediately notifies other Members, through the Secretariat, of the particular regulation and the products covered, with a brief indication of the objective and the rationale of the regulation, including the nature of the urgent problem(s);

(b) provides, upon request, copies of the regulation to other Members;

(c) allows other Members to make comments in writing, discusses these comments upon request, and takes the comments and the results of the discussions into account.

7. Notifications to the Secretariat shall be in English, French or Spanish.

8. Developed country Members shall, if requested by other Members, provide copies of the documents or, in case of voluminous documents, summaries of the documents covered by a specific notification in English, French or Spanish.

9. The Secretariat shall promptly circulate copies of the notification to all Members and interested international organizations and draw the attention of developing country Members to any notifications relating to products of particular interest to them.

10. Members shall designate a single central government authority as responsible for the implementation, on the national level, of the provisions concerning notification procedures according to paragraphs 5, 6, 7 and 8 of this Annex.

General reservations

11. Nothing in this Agreement shall be construed as requiring:

(a) the provision of particulars or copies of drafts or the publication of texts other than in the language of the Member except as stated in paragraph 8 of this Annex; or

(b) Members to disclose confidential information which would impede enforcement of sanitary or phytosanitary legislation or which would prejudice the legitimate commercial interests of particular enterprises.

ANNEX C   CONTROL, INSPECTION AND APPROVAL PROCEDURES[7]

1. Members shall ensure, with respect to any procedure to check and ensure the fulfilment of sanitary or phytosanitary measures, that:

---

7 Control, inspection and approval procedures include, *inter alia*, procedures for sampling, testing and certification.

(a) such procedures are undertaken and completed without undue delay and in no less favourable manner for imported products than for like domestic products;

(b) the standard processing period of each procedure is published or that the anticipated processing period is communicated to the applicant upon request; when receiving an application, the competent body promptly examines the completeness of the documentation and informs the applicant in a precise and complete manner of all deficiencies; the competent body transmits as soon as possible the results of the procedure in a precise and complete manner to the applicant so that corrective action may be taken if necessary; even when the application has deficiencies, the competent body proceeds as far as practicable with the procedure if the applicant so requests; and that upon request, the applicant is informed of the stage of the procedure, with any delay being explained;

(c) information requirements are limited to what is necessary for appropriate control, inspection and approval procedures, including for approval of the use of additives or for the establishment of tolerances for contaminants in food, beverages or feedstuffs;

(d) the confidentiality of information about imported products arising from or supplied in connection with control, inspection and approval is respected in a way no less favourable than for domestic products and in such a manner that legitimate commercial interests are protected;

(e) any requirements for control, inspection and approval of individual specimens of a product are limited to what is reasonable and necessary;

(f) any fees imposed for the procedures on imported products are equitable in relation to any fees charged on like domestic products or products originating in any other Member and should be no higher than the actual cost of the service;

(g) the same criteria should be used in the siting of facilities used in the procedures and the selection of samples of imported products as for domestic products so as to minimize the inconvenience to applicants, importers, exporters or their agents;

(h) whenever specifications of a product are changed subsequent to its control and inspection in light of the applicable regulations, the procedure for the modified product is limited to what is necessary to determine whether adequate confidence exists that the product still meets the regulations concerned; and

(i) a procedure exists to review complaints concerning the operation of such procedures and to take corrective action when a complaint is justified.

Where an importing Member operates a system for the approval of the use of food additives or for the establishment of tolerances for contaminants in food, beverages or feedstuffs which prohibits or restricts access to its domestic markets for products based on the absence of an approval, the importing Member shall consider the use of a relevant international standard as the basis for access until a final determination is made.

2. Where a sanitary or phytosanitary measure specifies control at the level of production, the Member in whose territory the production takes place shall provide the necessary assistance to facilitate such control and the work of the controlling authorities.

3. Nothing in this Agreement shall prevent Members from carrying out reasonable inspection within their own territories.

II-11
Agreement on Technical Barriers to Trade

Members,

Having regard to the Uruguay Round of Multilateral Trade Negotiations;

Desiring to further the objectives of GATT 1994;

Recognizing the important contribution that international standards and conformity assessment systems can make in this regard by improving efficiency of production and facilitating the conduct of international trade;

Desiring therefore to encourage the development of such international standards and conformity assessment systems;

Desiring however to ensure that technical regulations and standards, including packaging, marking and labelling requirements, and procedures for assessment of conformity with technical regulations and standards do not create unnecessary obstacles to international trade;

Recognizing that no country should be prevented from taking measures necessary to ensure the quality of its exports, or for the protection of human, animal or plant life or health, of the environment, or for the prevention of deceptive practices, at the levels it considers appropriate, subject to the requirement that they are not applied in a manner which would constitute a means of arbitrary or unjustifiable discrimination between countries where the same conditions prevail or a disguised restriction on international trade, and are otherwise in accordance with the provisions of this Agreement;

Recognizing that no country should be prevented from taking measures necessary for the protection of its essential security interest;

Recognizing the contribution which international standardization can make to the transfer of technology from developed to developing countries;

Recognizing that developing countries may encounter special difficulties in the formulation and application of technical regulations and standards and procedures for assessment of conformity with technical regulations and standards, and desiring to assist them in their endeavours in this regard;

Hereby *agree* as follows:

Article 1   General Provisions

1.1 General terms for standardization and procedures for assessment of conformity shall normally have the meaning given to them by definitions adopted within the United Nations system and by international standardizing bodies taking into account their context and in the light of the object and purpose of this Agreement.

1.2 However, for the purposes of this Agreement the meaning of the terms given in Annex 1 applies.

1.3 All products, including industrial and agricultural products, shall be subject to the provisions of this Agreement.

1.4 Purchasing specifications prepared by governmental bodies for production or consumption requirements of governmental bodies are not subject to the provisions of this Agreement but are addressed in the Agreement on Government Procurement, according to its coverage.

1.5 The provisions of this Agreement do not apply to sanitary and phytosanitary measures as defined in Annex A of the Agreement on the Application of Sanitary and Phytosanitary Measures.

1.6 All references in this Agreement to technical regulations, standards and conformity assessment procedures shall be construed to include any amendments thereto and any additions to the rules or the product coverage thereof, except amendments and additions of an insignificant nature.

TECHNICAL REGULATIONS AND STANDARDS

Article 2   Preparation, Adoption and Application of Technical Regulations by Central Government Bodies

With respect to their central government bodies:

2.1 Members shall ensure that in respect of technical regulations, products imported from the territory of any Member shall be accorded treatment no less favourable than that accorded to like products of national origin and to like products originating in any other country.

2.2 Members shall ensure that technical regulations are not prepared, adopted or applied with a view to or with the effect of creating unnecessary obstacles to international trade. For this purpose, technical regulations shall not be more trade-restrictive than necessary to fulfil a legitimate objective, taking account of the risks non-fulfilment would create. Such legitimate objectives are, *inter alia*: national security requirements; the prevention of deceptive practices; protection of human health or safety, animal or plant life or health, or the environment. In assessing such risks, relevant elements of consideration are, *inter alia*: available scientific and technical information, related processing technology or intended end-uses of products.

2.3 Technical regulations shall not be maintained if the circumstances or objectives giving rise to their adoption no longer exist or if the changed circumstances or objectives can be addressed in a less trade-restrictive manner.

2.4 Where technical regulations are required and relevant international standards exist or their completion is imminent, Members shall use them, or the relevant parts of them, as a basis for their technical regulations except when such international standards or relevant parts would be an ineffective or inappropriate means for the fulfilment of the legitimate objectives pursued, for instance because of fundamental climatic or geographical factors or fundamental technological problems.

2.5 A Member preparing, adopting or applying a technical regulation which may have a significant effect on trade of other Members shall, upon the request of another Member, explain the justification for that technical regulation in terms of the provisions of paragraphs 2 to 4. Whenever a technical regulation is prepared, adopted or applied for one of the legitimate objectives explicitly mentioned in paragraph 2, and is in accordance with relevant international standards, it shall be rebuttably presumed not to create an unnecessary obstacle to international trade.

2.6 With a view to harmonizing technical regulations on as wide a basis as possible, Members shall play a full part, within the limits of their resources, in the preparation by appropriate international standardizing bodies of international standards for products for which they either have adopted, or expect to adopt, technical regulations.

2.7 Members shall give positive consideration to accepting as equivalent technical regulations of other Members, even if these regulations differ from their own, provided they are satisfied that these regulations adequately fulfil the objectives of their own regulations.

2.8 Wherever appropriate, Members shall specify technical regulations based on product requirements in terms of performance rather than design or descriptive characteristics.

2.9 Whenever a relevant international standard does not exist or the technical content of a proposed technical regulation is not in accordance with the technical content of relevant international standards, and if the technical regulation may have a significant effect on trade of other Members, Members shall:

2.9.1 publish a notice in a publication at an early appropriate stage, in such a manner as to enable interested parties in other Members to become acquainted with it, that they propose to introduce a particular technical regulation;

2.9.2 notify other Members through the Secretariat of the products to be covered by the proposed technical regulation, together with a brief indication of its objective and rationale. Such notifications shall take place at an early appropriate stage, when amendments can still be introduced and comments taken into account;

2.9.3 upon request, provide to other Members particulars or copies of the proposed technical regulation and, whenever possible, identify the parts which in substance deviate from relevant international standards;

2.9.4 without discrimination, allow reasonable time for other Members to make comments in writing, discuss these comments upon request, and take these written comments and the results of these discussions into account.

2.10 Subject to the provisions in the lead-in to paragraph 9, where urgent problems of safety, health, environmental protection or national security arise or threaten to arise for a Member, that Member may omit such of the steps enumerated in paragraph 9 as it finds necessary, provided that the Member, upon adoption of a technical regulation, shall:

2.10.1 notify immediately other Members through the Secretariat of the particular technical regulation and the products covered, with a brief indication of the objective and the rationale of the technical regulation, including the nature of the urgent problems;

2.10.2 upon request, provide other Members with copies of the technical regulation;

2.10.3 without discrimination, allow other Members to present their comments in writing, discuss these comments upon request, and take these written comments and the results of these discussions into account.

2.11 Members shall ensure that all technical regulations which have been adopted are published promptly or otherwise made available in such a manner as to enable interested parties in other Members to become acquainted with them.

2.12 Except in those urgent circumstances referred to in paragraph 10, Members shall allow a reasonable interval between the publication of technical regulations and their entry into force in order to allow time for producers in exporting Members, and particularly in developing country Members, to adapt their products or methods of production to the requirements of the importing Member.

Article 3 Preparation, Adoption and Application of Technical Regulations by Local Government Bodies and Non-Governmental Bodies

With respect to their local government and non-governmental bodies within their territories:

3.1 Members shall take such reasonable measures as may be available to them to ensure compliance by such bodies with the provisions of Article 2, with the exception of the obligation to notify as referred to in paragraphs 9.2 and 10.1 of Article 2.

3.2 Members shall ensure that the technical regulations of local governments on the level directly below that of the central government in Members are notified in accordance with the provisions of paragraphs 9.2 and 10.1 of Article 2, noting that notification shall not be required for technical regulations the technical content of which is substantially the same as that of previously notified technical regulations of central government bodies of the Member concerned.

3.3 Members may require contact with other Members, including the notifications, provision of information, comments and discussions referred to in paragraphs 9 and 10 of Article 2, to take place through the central government.

3.4 Members shall not take measures which require or encourage local government bodies or non-governmental bodies within their territories to act in a manner inconsistent with the provisions of Article 2.

3.5 Members are fully responsible under this Agreement for the observance of all provisions of Article 2. Members shall formulate and implement positive measures and mechanisms in support of the observance of the provisions of Article 2 by other than central government bodies.

Article 4   Preparation, Adoption and Application of Standards

4.1 Members shall ensure that their central government standardizing bodies accept and comply with the Code of Good Practice for the Preparation, Adoption and Application of Standards in Annex 3 to this Agreement (referred to in this Agreement as the "Code of Good Practice"). They shall take such reasonable measures as may be available to them to ensure that local government and non-governmental standardizing bodies within their territories, as well as regional standardizing bodies of which they or one or more bodies within their territories are members, accept and comply with this Code of Good Practice. In addition, Members shall not take measures which have the effect of, directly or indirectly, requiring or encouraging such standardizing bodies to act in a manner inconsistent with the Code of Good Practice. The obligations of Members with respect to compliance of standardizing bodies with the provisions of the Code of Good Practice shall apply irrespective of whether or not a standardizing body has accepted the Code of Good Practice.

4.2 Standardizing bodies that have accepted and are complying with the Code of Good Practice shall be acknowledged by the Members as complying with the principles of this Agreement.

CONFORMITY WITH TECHNICAL REGULATIONS AND STANDARDS

Article 5   Procedures for Assessment of Conformity by Central Government Bodies

5.1 Members shall ensure that, in cases where a positive assurance of conformity with technical regulations or standards is required, their central government bodies apply the following provisions to products originating in the territories of other Members:

5.1.1 conformity assessment procedures are prepared, adopted and applied so as to grant access for suppliers of like products originating in the territories of other Members under conditions no less favourable than those accorded to suppliers of like products of national origin or originating in any other country, in a comparable situation; access entails suppliers' right to an assessment of conformity under the rules of the procedure, including, when foreseen by this procedure, the possibility to have conformity assessment activities undertaken at the site of facilities and to receive the mark of the system;

5.1.2 conformity assessment procedures are not prepared, adopted or applied with a view to or with the effect of creating unnecessary obstacles to international trade. This means, *inter alia*, that conformity assessment procedures shall not be more strict or be applied more strictly than is necessary to give the importing Member adequate confidence that products conform with the applicable technical regulations or standards, taking account of the risks non-conformity would create.

5.2 When implementing the provisions of paragraph 1, Members shall ensure that:

5.2.1 conformity assessment procedures are undertaken and completed as expeditiously as possible and in a no less favourable order for products originating in the territories of other Members than for like domestic products;

5.2.2 the standard processing period of each conformity assessment procedure is published or that the anticipated processing period is communicated to the applicant upon request; when receiving an application, the competent body promptly examines the completeness of the documentation and informs the applicant in a precise and complete manner of all deficiencies; the competent body transmits as soon as possible the results of the assessment in a precise and complete manner to the applicant so that corrective action may be taken if necessary; even when the application has deficiencies, the competent body proceeds as far as practicable with the conformity assessment if the applicant so requests; and that, upon request, the applicant is informed of the stage of the procedure, with any delay being explained;

5.2.3 information requirements are limited to what is necessary to assess conformity and determine fees;

5.2.4 the confidentiality of information about products originating in the territories of other Members arising from or supplied in connection with such conformity assessment procedures is respected in the same way as for domestic products and in such a manner that legitimate commercial interests are protected;

5.2.5 any fees imposed for assessing the conformity of products originating in the territories of other Members are equitable in relation to any fees chargeable for assessing the conformity of like products of national origin or originating in any other country, taking into account communication, transportation and other costs arising from differences between location of facilities of the applicant and the conformity assessment body;

5.2.6 the siting of facilities used in conformity assessment procedures and the selection of samples are not such as to cause unnecessary inconvenience to applicants or their agents;

5.2.7 whenever specifications of a product are changed subsequent to the determination of its conformity to the applicable technical regulations or standards, the conformity assessment procedure for the modified product is limited to what is necessary to determine whether adequate confidence exists that the product still meets the technical regulations or standards concerned;

5.2.8 a procedure exists to review complaints concerning the operation of a conformity assessment procedure and to take corrective action when a complaint is justified.

5.3 Nothing in paragraphs 1 and 2 shall prevent Members from carrying out reasonable spot checks within their territories.

5.4 In cases where a positive assurance is required that products conform with technical regulations or standards, and relevant guides or recommendations issued by international standardizing bodies exist or their completion is imminent, Members shall ensure that central government bodies use them, or the relevant parts of them, as a basis for their conformity assessment procedures, except where, as duly explained upon request, such guides or recommendations or relevant parts are inappropriate for the Members concerned, for, *inter alia*, such reasons as: national security requirements; the prevention of deceptive practices; protection of human health or safety, animal or plant life or health, or the environment; fundamental climatic or other geographical factors; fundamental technological or infrastructural problems.

5.5 With a view to harmonizing conformity assessment procedures on as wide a basis as possible, Members shall play a full part, within the limits of their resources, in the preparation by appropriate international standardizing bodies of guides and recommendations for conformity assessment procedures.

5.6 Whenever a relevant guide or recommendation issued by an international standardizing body does not exist or the technical content of a proposed conformity assessment procedure is not in accordance with relevant guides and recommendations issued by international standardizing bodies, and if the conformity assessment procedure may have a significant effect on trade of other Members, Members shall:

5.6.1 publish a notice in a publication at an early appropriate stage, in such a manner as to enable interested parties in other Members to become acquainted with it, that they propose to introduce a particular conformity assessment procedure;

5.6.2 notify other Members through the Secretariat of the products to be covered by the proposed conformity assessment procedure, together with a brief indication of its objective and rationale. Such notifications shall take place at an early appropriate stage, when amendments can still be introduced and comments taken into account;

5.6.3 upon request, provide to other Members particulars or copies of the proposed procedure and, whenever possible, identify the parts which in substance deviate from relevant guides or recommendations issued by international standardizing bodies;

5.6.4 without discrimination, allow reasonable time for other Members to make comments in writing, discuss these comments upon request, and take these written comments and the results of these discussions into account.

5.7 Subject to the provisions in the lead-in to paragraph 6, where urgent problems of safety, health, environmental protection or national security arise or threaten to arise for a Member, that Member may omit such of the steps enumerated in paragraph 6 as it finds necessary, provided that the Member, upon adoption of the procedure, shall:

5.7.1 notify immediately other Members through the Secretariat of the particular procedure and the products covered, with a brief indication of the objective and the rationale of the procedure, including the nature of the urgent problems;

5.7.2 upon request, provide other Members with copies of the rules of the procedure;

5.7.3 without discrimination, allow other Members to present their comments in writing, discuss these comments upon request, and take these written comments and the results of these discussions into account.

5.8 Members shall ensure that all conformity assessment procedures which have been adopted are published promptly or otherwise made available in such a manner as to enable interested parties in other Members to become acquainted with them.

5.9 Except in those urgent circumstances referred to in paragraph 7, Members shall allow a reasonable interval between the publication of requirements concerning conformity assessment procedures and their entry into force in order to allow time for producers in exporting Members, and particularly in developing country Members, to adapt their products or methods of production to the requirements of the importing Member.

Article 6   Recognition of Conformity Assessment by Central Government Bodies

With respect to their central government bodies:

6.1 Without prejudice to the provisions of paragraphs 3 and 4, Members shall ensure, whenever possible, that results of conformity assessment procedures in other Members are accepted, even when those procedures differ from their own, provided they are satisfied that those procedures offer an assurance of conformity with applicable technical regulations or standards equivalent to their own procedures. It is recognized that prior consultations may be necessary in order to arrive at a mutually satisfactory understanding regarding, in particular:

6.1.1 adequate and enduring technical competence of the relevant conformity assessment bodies in the exporting Member, so that confidence in the continued reliability of their conformity assessment results can exist; in this regard, verified compliance, for instance through accreditation, with relevant guides or recommendations issued by international standardizing bodies shall be taken into account as an indication of adequate technical competence;

6.1.2 limitation of the acceptance of conformity assessment results to those produced by designated bodies in the exporting Member.

6.2 Members shall ensure that their conformity assessment procedures permit, as far as practicable, the implementation of the provisions in paragraph 1.

6.3 Members are encouraged, at the request of other Members, to be willing to enter into negotiations for the conclusion of agreements for the mutual recognition of results of each other's conformity assessment procedures. Members may require that such agreements fulfil the criteria of paragraph 1 and give mutual satisfaction regarding their potential for facilitating trade in the products concerned.

6.4 Members are encouraged to permit participation of conformity assessment bodies located in the territories of other Members in their conformity assessment procedures under conditions no less favourable than those accorded to bodies located within their territory or the territory of any other country.

Article 7   Procedures for Assessment of Conformity by Local Government Bodies
With respect to their local government bodies within their territories:

7.1 Members shall take such reasonable measures as may be available to them to ensure compliance by such bodies with the provisions of Articles 5 and 6, with the exception of the obligation to notify as referred to in paragraphs 6.2 and 7.1 of Article 5.

7.2 Members shall ensure that the conformity assessment procedures of local governments on the level directly below that of the central government in Members are notified in accordance with the provisions of paragraphs 6.2 and 7.1 of Article 5, noting that notifications shall not be required for conformity assessment procedures the technical content of which is substantially the same as that of previously notified conformity assessment procedures of central government bodies of the Members concerned.

7.3 Members may require contact with other Members, including the notifications, provision of information, comments and discussions referred to in paragraphs 6 and 7 of Article 5, to take place through the central government.

7.4 Members shall not take measures which require or encourage local government bodies within their territories to act in a manner inconsistent with the provisions of Articles 5 and 6.

7.5 Members are fully responsible under this Agreement for the observance of all provisions of Articles 5 and 6. Members shall formulate and implement positive measures and mechanisms in support of the observance of the provisions of Articles 5 and 6 by other than central government bodies.

Article 8   Procedures for Assessment of Conformity by Non-Governmental Bodies
8.1 Members shall take such reasonable measures as may be available to them to ensure that non-governmental bodies within their territories which operate conformity assessment procedures comply with the provisions of Articles 5 and 6, with the exception of the obligation to notify proposed conformity assessment procedures. In addition, Members shall not take measures which have the effect of, directly or indirectly, requiring or encouraging such bodies to act in a manner inconsistent with the provisions of Articles 5 and 6.

8.2 Members shall ensure that their central government bodies rely on conformity assessment procedures operated by non-governmental bodies only if these latter bodies comply with the provisions of Articles 5 and 6, with the exception of the obligation to notify proposed conformity assessment procedures.

Article 9   International and Regional Systems
9.1 Where a positive assurance of conformity with a technical regulation or standard is required, Members shall, wherever practicable, formulate and adopt international systems for conformity assessment and become members thereof or participate therein.

9.2 Members shall take such reasonable measures as may be available to them to ensure that international and regional systems for conformity assessment in which relevant bodies within their territories are members or participants comply with the provisions of Articles 5 and 6. In addition, Members shall not take any measures which have the effect of, directly or indirectly, requiring or encouraging such systems to act in a manner inconsistent with any of the provisions of Articles 5 and 6.

9.3 Members shall ensure that their central government bodies rely on international or regional conformity assessment systems only to the extent that these systems comply with the provisions of Articles 5 and 6, as applicable.

INFORMATION AND ASSISTANCE

Article 10   Information About Technical Regulations, Standards and Conformity Assessment Procedures

10.1 Each Member shall ensure that an enquiry point exists which is able to answer all reasonable enquiries from other Members and interested parties in other Members as well as to provide the relevant documents regarding:

10.1.1 any technical regulations adopted or proposed within its territory by central or local government bodies, by non-governmental bodies which have legal power to enforce a technical regulation, or by regional standardizing bodies of which such bodies are members or participants;

10.1.2 any standards adopted or proposed within its territory by central or local government bodies, or by regional standardizing bodies of which such bodies are members or participants;

10.1.3 any conformity assessment procedures, or proposed conformity assessment procedures, which are operated within its territory by central or local government bodies, or by non-governmental bodies which have legal power to enforce a technical regulation, or by regional bodies of which such bodies are members or participants;

10.1.4 the membership and participation of the Member, or of relevant central or local government bodies within its territory, in international and regional standardizing bodies and conformity assessment systems, as well as in bilateral and multilateral arrangements within the scope of this Agreement; it shall also be able to provide reasonable information on the provisions of such systems and arrangements;

10.1.5 the location of notices published pursuant to this Agreement, or the provision of information as to where such information can be obtained; and

10.1.6 the location of the enquiry points mentioned in paragraph 3.

10.2 If, however, for legal or administrative reasons more than one enquiry point is established by a Member, that Member shall provide to the other Members complete and unambiguous information on the scope of responsibility of each of these enquiry points. In addition, that Member shall ensure that any enquiries addressed to an incorrect enquiry point shall promptly be conveyed to the correct enquiry point.

10.3 Each Member shall take such reasonable measures as may be available to it to ensure that one or more enquiry points exist which are able to answer all reasonable enquiries from other Members and interested parties in other Members as well as to provide the relevant documents or information as to where they can be obtained regarding:

10.3.1 any standards adopted or proposed within its territory by non-governmental standardizing bodies, or by regional standardizing bodies of which such bodies are members or participants; and

10.3.2 any conformity assessment procedures, or proposed conformity assessment procedures, which are operated within its territory by non-governmental bodies, or by regional bodies of which such bodies are members or participants;

10.3.3 the membership and participation of relevant non-governmental bodies within its territory in international and regional standardizing bodies and conformity assessment systems, as well as in bilateral and multilateral arrangements within the scope of this Agreement; they shall also be able to provide reasonable information on the provisions of such systems and arrangements.

10.4 Members shall take such reasonable measures as may be available to them to ensure that where copies of documents are requested by other Members or by interested parties in other Members, in accordance with the provisions of this Agreement, they are supplied at an equitable price (if any) which shall, apart from the real cost of delivery, be the same for the nationals[1] of the Member concerned or of any other Member.

10.5 Developed country Members shall, if requested by other Members, provide, in English, French or Spanish, translations of the documents covered by a specific notification or, in case of voluminous documents, of summaries of such documents.

10.6 The Secretariat shall, when it receives notifications in accordance with the provisions of this Agreement, circulate copies of the notifications to all Members and interested international standardizing and conformity assessment bodies, and draw the attention of developing country Members to any notifications relating to products of particular interest to them.

10.7 Whenever a Member has reached an agreement with any other country or countries on issues related to technical regulations, standards or conformity assessment procedures which may have a significant effect on trade, at least one Member party to the agreement shall notify other Members through the Secretariat of the products to be covered by the agreement and include a brief description of the agreement. Members concerned are encouraged to enter, upon request, into consultations with other Members for the purposes of concluding similar agreements or of arranging for their participation in such agreements.

10.8 Nothing in this Agreement shall be construed as requiring:

10.8.1 the publication of texts other than in the language of the Member;

10.8.2 the provision of particulars or copies of drafts other than in the language of the Member except as stated in paragraph 5; or

10.8.3 Members to furnish any information, the disclosure of which they consider contrary to their essential security interests.

10.9 Notifications to the Secretariat shall be in English, French or Spanish.

10.10 Members shall designate a single central government authority that is responsible for the implementation on the national level of the provisions concerning notification procedures under this Agreement except those included in Annex 3.

10.11 If, however, for legal or administrative reasons the responsibility for notification procedures is divided among two or more central government authorities, the Member concerned shall provide to the other Members complete and unambiguous information on the scope of responsibility of each of these authorities.

Article 11   Technical Assistance to Other Members

11.1 Members shall, if requested, advise other Members, especially the developing country Members, on the preparation of technical regulations.

---

1 "Nationals" here shall be deemed, in the case of a separate customs territory Member of the WTO, to mean persons, natural or legal, who are domiciled or who have a real and effective industrial or commercial establishment in that customs territory.

11.2 Members shall, if requested, advise other Members, especially the developing country Members, and shall grant them technical assistance on mutually agreed terms and conditions regarding the establishment of national standardizing bodies, and participation in the international standardizing bodies, and shall encourage their national standardizing bodies to do likewise.

11.3 Members shall, if requested, take such reasonable measures as may be available to them to arrange for the regulatory bodies within their territories to advise other Members, especially the developing country Members, and shall grant them technical assistance on mutually agreed terms and conditions regarding:

11.3.1 the establishment of regulatory bodies, or bodies for the assessment of conformity with technical regulations; and

11.3.2 the methods by which their technical regulations can best be met.

11.4 Members shall, if requested, take such reasonable measures as may be available to them to arrange for advice to be given to other Members, especially the developing country Members, and shall grant them technical assistance on mutually agreed terms and conditions regarding the establishment of bodies for the assessment of conformity with standards adopted within the territory of the requesting Member.

11.5 Members shall, if requested, advise other Members, especially the developing country Members, and shall grant them technical assistance on mutually agreed terms and conditions regarding the steps that should be taken by their producers if they wish to have access to systems for conformity assessment operated by governmental or non-governmental bodies within the territory of the Member receiving the request.

11.6 Members which are members or participants of international or regional systems for conformity assessment shall, if requested, advise other Members, especially the developing country Members, and shall grant them technical assistance on mutually agreed terms and conditions regarding the establishment of the institutions and legal framework which would enable them to fulfil the obligations of membership or participation in such systems.

11.7 Members shall, if so requested, encourage bodies within their territories which are members or participants of international or regional systems for conformity assessment to advise other Members, especially the developing country Members, and should consider requests for technical assistance from them regarding the establishment of the institutions which would enable the relevant bodies within their territories to fulfil the obligations of membership or participation.

11.8 In providing advice and technical assistance to other Members in terms of paragraphs 1 to 7, Members shall give priority to the needs of the least-developed country Members.

Article 12   Special and Differential Treatment of Developing Country Members

12.1 Members shall provide differential and more favourable treatment to developing country Members to this Agreement, through the following provisions as well as through the relevant provisions of other Articles of this Agreement.

12.2 Members shall give particular attention to the provisions of this Agreement concerning developing country Members' rights and obligations and shall take into account the special development, financial and trade needs of developing country Members in the implementation of this Agreement, both nationally and in the operation of this Agreement's institutional arrangements.

12.3 Members shall, in the preparation and application of technical regulations, standards and conformity assessment procedures, take account of the special development, financial and trade needs of developing country Members, with a view to ensuring that such technical regulations, standards and conformity assessment procedures do not create unnecessary obstacles to exports from developing country Members.

12.4 Members recognize that, although international standards, guides or recommendations may exist, in their particular technological and socio-economic conditions, developing country Members adopt certain technical regulations, standards or conformity assessment procedures aimed at preserving indigenous technology and production methods and processes compatible with their development needs. Members therefore recognize that developing country Members should not be expected to use international standards as a basis for their technical regulations or standards, including test methods, which are not appropriate to their development, financial and trade needs.

12.5 Members shall take such reasonable measures as may be available to them to ensure that international standardizing bodies and international systems for conformity assessment are organized and operated in a way which facilitates active and representative participation of relevant bodies in all Members, taking into account the special problems of developing country Members.

12.6 Members shall take such reasonable measures as may be available to them to ensure that international standardizing bodies, upon request of developing country Members, examine the possibility of, and, if practicable, prepare international standards concerning products of special interest to developing country Members.

12.7 Members shall, in accordance with the provisions of Article 11, provide technical assistance to developing country Members to ensure that the preparation and application of technical regulations, standards and conformity assessment procedures do not create unnecessary obstacles to the expansion and diversification of exports from developing country Members. In determining the terms and conditions of the technical assistance, account shall be taken of the stage of development of the requesting Members and in particular of the least-developed country Members.

12.8 It is recognized that developing country Members may face special problems, including institutional and infrastructural problems, in the field of preparation and application of technical regulations, standards and conformity assessment procedures. It is further recognized that the special development and trade needs of developing country Members, as well as their stage of technological development, may hinder their ability to discharge fully their obligations under this Agreement. Members, therefore, shall take this fact fully into account. Accordingly, with a view to ensuring that developing country Members are able to comply with this Agreement, the Committee on Technical Barriers to Trade provided for in Article 13 (referred to in this Agreement as the "Committee") is enabled to grant, upon request, specified, time-limited exceptions in whole or in part from obligations under this Agreement. When considering such requests the Committee shall take into account the special problems, in the field of preparation and application of technical regulations, standards and conformity assessment procedures, and the special development and trade needs of the developing country Member, as well as its stage of technological development, which may hinder its ability to discharge fully its obligations under this Agreement. The Committee shall, in particular, take into account the special problems of the least-developed country Members.

12.9 During consultations, developed country Members shall bear in mind the special difficulties experienced by developing country Members in formulating and implementing standards and technical regulations and conformity assessment procedures, and in their desire to assist developing country Members with their efforts in this direction, developed country Members shall take account of the special needs of the former in regard to financing, trade and development.

12.10 The Committee shall examine periodically the special and differential treatment, as laid down in this Agreement, granted to developing country Members on national and international levels.

INSTITUTIONS, CONSULTATION AND DISPUTE SETTLEMENT

Article 13   The Committee on Technical Barriers to Trade

13.1 A Committee on Technical Barriers to Trade is hereby established, and shall be composed of representatives from each of the Members. The Committee shall elect its own Chairman and shall meet as necessary, but no less than once a year, for the purpose of affording Members the opportunity of consulting on any matters relating to the operation of this Agreement or the furtherance of its objectives, and shall carry out such responsibilities as assigned to it under this Agreement or by the Members.

13.2 The Committee shall establish working parties or other bodies as may be appropriate, which shall carry out such responsibilities as may be assigned to them by the Committee in accordance with the relevant provisions of this Agreement.

13.3 It is understood that unnecessary duplication should be avoided between the work under this Agreement and that of governments in other technical bodies. The Committee shall examine this problem with a view to minimizing such duplication.

Article 14   Consultation and Dispute Settlement

14.1 Consultations and the settlement of disputes with respect to any matter affecting the operation of this Agreement shall take place under the auspices of the Dispute Settlement Body and shall follow, *mutatis mutandis*, the provisions of Articles XXII and XXIII of GATT 1994, as elaborated and applied by the Dispute Settlement Understanding.

14.2 At the request of a party to a dispute, or at its own initiative, a panel may establish a technical expert group to assist in questions of a technical nature, requiring detailed consideration by experts.

14.3 Technical expert groups shall be governed by the procedures of Annex 2.

14.4 The dispute settlement provisions set out above can be invoked in cases where a Member considers that another Member has not achieved satisfactory results under Articles 3, 4, 7, 8 and 9 and its trade interests are significantly affected. In this respect, such results shall be equivalent to those as if the body in question were a Member.

FINAL PROVISIONS

Article 15   Final Provisions

Reservations

15.1 Reservations may not be entered in respect of any of the provisions of this Agreement without the consent of the other Members.

Review

15.2 Each Member shall, promptly after the date on which the WTO Agreement enters into force for it, inform the Committee of measures in existence or taken to ensure the implementation and administration of this Agreement. Any changes of such measures thereafter shall also be notified to the Committee.

15.3 The Committee shall review annually the implementation and operation of this Agreement taking into account the objectives thereof.

15.4 Not later than the end of the third year from the date of entry into force of the WTO Agreement and at the end of each three-year period thereafter, the Committee shall review the operation and implementation of this Agreement, including the provisions relating to transparency, with a view to recommending an adjustment of the rights and obligations of this Agreement where necessary to ensure mutual economic advantage and balance of rights and obligations, without prejudice to the provisions of Article 12. Having regard, *inter alia*, to the experience gained in the implementation of the Agreement, the Committee shall, where appropriate, submit proposals for amendments to the text of this Agreement to the Council for Trade in Goods.

Annexes

15.5 The annexes to this Agreement constitute an integral part thereof.

ANNEX 1   TERMS AND THEIR DEFINITIONS FOR THE PURPOSE OF THIS AGREEMENT

The terms presented in the sixth edition of the ISO/IEC Guide 2: 1991, General Terms and Their Definitions Concerning Standardization and Related Activities, shall, when used in this Agreement, have the same meaning as given in the definitions in the said Guide taking into account that services are excluded from the coverage of this Agreement.

For the purpose of this Agreement, however, the following definitions shall apply:

1. *Technical regulation*

    Document which lays down product characteristics or their related processes and production methods, including the applicable administrative provisions, with which compliance is mandatory. It may also include or deal exclusively with terminology, symbols, packaging, marking or labelling requirements as they apply to a product, process or production method.
    Explanatory note
    The definition in ISO/IEC Guide 2 is not self-contained, but based on the so-called "building block" system.

2. *Standard*

    Document approved by a recognized body, that provides, for common and repeated use, rules, guidelines or characteristics for products or related processes and production methods, with which compliance is not mandatory. It may also include or deal exclusively with terminology, symbols, packaging, marking or labelling requirements as they apply to a product, process or production method.
    Explanatory note
    The terms as defined in ISO/IEC Guide 2 cover products, processes and services. This Agreement deals only with technical regulations, standards and conformity assessment procedures related to products or processes and production methods. Standards as defined by ISO/IEC Guide 2 may be mandatory or voluntary. For the purpose of this Agreement standards are defined as voluntary and technical regulations as mandatory documents. Standards prepared by the international standardization community are based on consensus. This Agreement covers also documents that are not based on consensus.

3. *Conformity assessment procedures*

    Any procedure used, directly or indirectly, to determine that relevant requirements in technical regulations or standards are fulfilled.
    Explanatory note
    Conformity assessment procedures include, *inter alia*, procedures for sampling, testing and inspection; evaluation, verification and assurance of conformity; registration, accreditation and approval as well as their combinations.

4. *International body or system*

    Body or system whose membership is open to the relevant bodies of at least all Members.

5. *Regional body or system*

    Body or system whose membership is open to the relevant bodies of only some of the Members.

6. *Central government body*

   Central government, its ministries and departments or any body subject to the control of the central government in respect of the activity in question.

   Explanatory note:

   In the case of the European Communities the provisions governing central government bodies apply. However, regional bodies or conformity assessment systems may be established within the European Communities, and in such cases would be subject to the provisions of this Agreement on regional bodies or conformity assessment systems.

7. *Local government body*

   Government other than a central government (e.g. states, provinces, Länder, cantons, municipalities, etc.), its ministries or departments or any body subject to the control of such a government in respect of the activity in question.

8. *Non-governmental body*

   Body other than a central government body or a local government body, including a non-governmental body which has legal power to enforce a technical regulation.

ANNEX 2   TECHNICAL EXPERT GROUPS

The following procedures shall apply to technical expert groups established in accordance with the provisions of Article 14.

1. Technical expert groups are under the panel's authority. Their terms of reference and detailed working procedures shall be decided by the panel, and they shall report to the panel.

2. Participation in technical expert groups shall be restricted to persons of professional standing and experience in the field in question.

3. Citizens of parties to the dispute shall not serve on a technical expert group without the joint agreement of the parties to the dispute, except in exceptional circumstances when the panel considers that the need for specialized scientific expertise cannot be fulfilled otherwise. Government officials of parties to the dispute shall not serve on a technical expert group. Members of technical expert groups shall serve in their individual capacities and not as government representatives, nor as representatives of any organization. Governments or organizations shall therefore not give them instructions with regard to matters before a technical expert group.

4. Technical expert groups may consult and seek information and technical advice from any source they deem appropriate. Before a technical expert group seeks such information or advice from a source within the jurisdiction of a Member, it shall inform the government of that Member. Any Member shall respond promptly and fully to any request by a technical expert group for such information as the technical expert group considers necessary and appropriate.

5. The parties to a dispute shall have access to all relevant information provided to a technical expert group, unless it is of a confidential nature. Confidential information provided to the technical expert group shall not be released without formal authorization from the government, organization or person providing the information. Where such information is requested from the technical expert group but release of such information by the technical expert group is not authorized, a non-confidential summary of the information will be provided by the government, organization or person supplying the information.

6. The technical expert group shall submit a draft report to the Members concerned with a view to obtaining their comments, and taking them into account, as appropriate, in the final report, which shall also be circulated to the Members concerned when it is submitted to the panel.

ANNEX 3   CODE OF GOOD PRACTICE FOR THE PREPARATION, ADOPTION AND APPLICATION OF STANDARDS

General Provisions

A. For the purposes of this Code the definitions in Annex 1 of this Agreement shall apply.

B. This Code is open to acceptance by any standardizing body within the territory of a Member of the WTO, whether a central government body, a local government body, or a non-governmental body; to any governmental regional standardizing body one or more members of which are Members of the WTO; and to any non-governmental regional standardizing body one or more members of which are situated within the territory of a Member of the WTO (referred to in this Code collectively as "standardizing bodies" and individually as "the standardizing body").

C. Standardizing bodies that have accepted or withdrawn from this Code shall notify this fact to the ISO/IEC Information Centre in Geneva. The notification shall include the name and address of the body concerned and the scope of its current and expected standardization activities. The notification may be sent either directly to the ISO/IEC Information Centre, or through the national member body of ISO/IEC or, preferably, through the relevant national member or international affiliate of ISONET, as appropriate.

SUBSTANTIVE PROVISIONS

D. In respect of standards, the standardizing body shall accord treatment to products originating in the territory of any other Member of the WTO no less favourable than that accorded to like products of national origin and to like products originating in any other country.

E. The standardizing body shall ensure that standards are not prepared, adopted or applied with a view to, or with the effect of, creating unnecessary obstacles to international trade.

F. Where international standards exist or their completion is imminent, the standardizing body shall use them, or the relevant parts of them, as a basis for the standards it develops, except where such international standards or relevant parts would be ineffective or inappropriate, for instance, because of an insufficient level of protection or fundamental climatic or geographical factors or fundamental technological problems.

G. With a view to harmonizing standards on as wide a basis as possible, the standardizing body shall, in an appropriate way, play a full part, within the limits of its resources, in the preparation by relevant international standardizing bodies of international standards regarding subject matter for which it either has adopted, or expects to adopt, standards. For standardizing bodies within the territory of a Member, participation in a particular international standardization activity shall, whenever possible, take place through one delegation representing all standardizing bodies in the territory that have adopted, or expect to adopt, standards for the subject matter to which the international standardization activity relates.

H. The standardizing body within the territory of a Member shall make every effort to avoid duplication of, or overlap with, the work of other standardizing bodies in the national territory or with the work of relevant international or regional standardizing bodies. They shall also make every effort to achieve a national consensus on the standards they develop. Likewise the regional standardizing body shall make every effort to avoid duplication of, or overlap with, the work of relevant international standardizing bodies.

I. Wherever appropriate, the standardizing body shall specify standards based on product requirements in terms of performance rather than design or descriptive characteristics.

J. At least once every six months, the standardizing body shall publish a work programme containing its name and address, the standards it is currently preparing and the standards which it has adopted in the preceding period. A standard is under preparation from the moment a decision has been taken to develop a standard until that standard has been adopted. The titles of specific draft standards shall, upon request, be provided in English, French or Spanish. A notice of the existence of the work programme shall be published in a national or, as the case may be, regional publication of standardization activities.

The work programme shall for each standard indicate, in accordance with any ISONET rules, the classification relevant to the subject matter, the stage attained in the standard's development, and the references of any international standards taken as a basis. No later than at the time of publication of its work programme, the standardizing body shall notify the existence thereof to the ISO/IEC Information Centre in Geneva.

The notification shall contain the name and address of the standardizing body, the name and issue of the publication in which the work programme is published, the period to which the work programme applies, its price (if any), and how and where it can be obtained. The notification may be sent directly to the ISO/IEC Information Centre, or, preferably, through the relevant national member or international affiliate of ISONET, as appropriate.

K. The national member of ISO/IEC shall make every effort to become a member of ISONET or to appoint another body to become a member as well as to acquire the most advanced membership type possible for the ISONET member. Other standardizing bodies shall make every effort to associate themselves with the ISONET member.

L. Before adopting a standard, the standardizing body shall allow a period of at least 60 days for the submission of comments on the draft standard by interested parties within the territory of a Member of the WTO. This period may, however, be shortened in cases where urgent problems of safety, health or environment arise or threaten to arise. No later than at the start of the comment period, the standardizing body shall publish a notice announcing the period for commenting in the publication referred to in paragraph J. Such notification shall include, as far as practicable, whether the draft standard deviates from relevant international standards.

M. On the request of any interested party within the territory of a Member of the WTO, the standardizing body shall promptly provide, or arrange to provide, a copy of a draft standard which it has submitted for comments. Any fees charged for this service shall, apart from the real cost of delivery, be the same for foreign and domestic parties.

N. The standardizing body shall take into account, in the further processing of the standard, the comments received during the period for commenting. Comments received through standardizing bodies that have accepted this Code of Good Practice shall, if so requested, be replied to as promptly as possible. The reply shall include an explanation why a deviation from relevant international standards is necessary.

O. Once the standard has been adopted, it shall be promptly published.

P. On the request of any interested party within the territory of a Member of the WTO, the standardizing body shall promptly provide, or arrange to provide, a copy of its most recent work programme or of a standard which it produced. Any fees charged for this service shall, apart from the real cost of delivery, be the same for foreign and domestic parties.

Q. The standardizing body shall afford sympathetic consideration to, and adequate opportunity for, consultation regarding representations with respect to the operation of this Code presented by standardizing bodies that have accepted this Code of Good Practice. It shall make an objective effort to solve any complaints.

II-12

Agreement on Trade-Related Investment Measures

Members,

Considering that Ministers agreed in the Punta del Este Declaration that "Following an examination of the operation of GATT Articles related to the trade restrictive and distorting effects of investment measures, negotiations should elaborate, as appropriate, further provisions that may be necessary to avoid such adverse effects on trade";

Desiring to promote the expansion and progressive liberalisation of world trade and to facilitate investment across international frontiers so as to increase the economic growth of all trading partners, particularly developing country Members, while ensuring free competition;

Taking into account the particular trade, development and financial needs of developing country Members, particularly those of the least-developed country Members;

Recognizing that certain investment measures can cause trade-restrictive and distorting effects; Hereby *agree* as follows:

Article 1   Coverage
This Agreement applies to investment measures related to trade in goods only (referred to in this Agreement as "TRIMs").

Article 2   National Treatment and Quantitative Restrictions
1. Without prejudice to other rights and obligations under GATT 1994, no Member shall apply any TRIM that is inconsistent with the provisions of Article III or Article XI of GATT 1994.

2. An illustrative list of TRIMs that are inconsistent with the obligation of national treatment provided for in paragraph 4 of Article III of GATT 1994 and the obligation of general elimination of quantitative restrictions provided for in paragraph 1 of Article XI of GATT 1994 is contained in the Annex to this Agreement.

Article 3   Exceptions
All exceptions under GATT 1994 shall apply, as appropriate, to the provisions of this Agreement.

Article 4   Developing Country Members
A developing country Member shall be free to deviate temporarily from the provisions of Article 2 to the extent and in such a manner as Article XVIII of GATT 1994, the Understanding on the Balance-of-Payments Provisions of GATT 1994, and the Declaration on Trade Measures Taken for Balance-of-Payments Purposes adopted on 28 November 1979 (BISD 26S/205–209) permit the Member to deviate from the provisions of Articles III and XI of GATT 1994.

Article 5   Notification and Transitional Arrangements
1. Members, within 90 days of the date of entry into force of the WTO Agreement, shall notify the Council for Trade in Goods of all TRIMs they are applying that are not in conformity with the provisions of this Agreement. Such TRIMs of general or specific application shall be notified, along with their principal features.[1]

2. Each Member shall eliminate all TRIMs which are notified under paragraph 1 within two years of the date of entry into force of the WTO Agreement in the case of a developed country

---

[1] In the case of TRIMs applied under discretionary authority, each specific application shall be notified. Information that would prejudice the legitimate commercial interests of particular enterprises need not be disclosed.

Member, within five years in the case of a developing country Member, and within seven years in the case of a least-developed country Member.

3. On request, the Council for Trade in Goods may extend the transition period for the elimination of TRIMs notified under paragraph 1 for a developing country Member, including a least-developed country Member, which demonstrates particular difficulties in implementing the provisions of this Agreement. In considering such a request, the Council for Trade in Goods shall take into account the individual development, financial and trade needs of the Member in question.

4. During the transition period, a Member shall not modify the terms of any TRIM which it notifies under paragraph 1 from those prevailing at the date of entry into force of the WTO Agreement so as to increase the degree of inconsistency with the provisions of Article 2. TRIMs introduced less than 180 days before the date of entry into force of the WTO Agreement shall not benefit from the transitional arrangements provided in paragraph 2.

5. Notwithstanding the provisions of Article 2, a Member, in order not to disadvantage established enterprises which are subject to a TRIM notified under paragraph 1, may apply during the transition period the same TRIM to a new investment (*i*) where the products of such investment are like products to those of the established enterprises, and (*ii*) where necessary to avoid distorting the conditions of competition between the new investment and the established enterprises. Any TRIM so applied to a new investment shall be notified to the Council for Trade in Goods. The terms of such a TRIM shall be equivalent in their competitive effect to those applicable to the established enterprises, and it shall be terminated at the same time.

Article 6   Transparency

1. Members reaffirm, with respect to TRIMs, their commitment to obligations on transparency and notification in Article X of GATT 1994, in the undertaking on "Notification" contained in the Understanding Regarding Notification, Consultation, Dispute Settlement and Surveillance adopted on 28 November 1979 and in the Ministerial Decision on Notification Procedures adopted on 15 April 1994.

2. Each Member shall notify the Secretariat of the publications in which TRIMs may be found, including those applied by regional and local governments and authorities within their territories.

3. Each Member shall accord sympathetic consideration to requests for information, and afford adequate opportunity for consultation, on any matter arising from this Agreement raised by another Member. In conformity with Article X of GATT 1994 no Member is required to disclose information the disclosure of which would impede law enforcement or otherwise be contrary to the public interest or would prejudice the legitimate commercial interests of particular enterprises, public or private.

Article 7   Committee on Trade-Related Investment Measures

1. A Committee on Trade-Related Investment Measures (referred to in this Agreement as the "Committee") is hereby established, and shall be open to all Members. The Committee shall elect its own Chairman and Vice-Chairman, and shall meet not less than once a year and otherwise at the request of any Member.

2. The Committee shall carry out responsibilities assigned to it by the Council for Trade in Goods and shall afford Members the opportunity to consult on any matters relating to the operation and implementation of this Agreement.

3. The Committee shall monitor the operation and implementation of this Agreement and shall report thereon annually to the Council for Trade in Goods.

Article 8   Consultation and Dispute Settlement

The provisions of Articles XXII and XXIII of GATT 1994, as elaborated and applied by the Dispute Settlement Understanding, shall apply to consultations and the settlement of disputes under this Agreement.

Article 9   Review by the Council for Trade in Goods

Not later than five years after the date of entry into force of the WTO Agreement, the Council for Trade in Goods shall review the operation of this Agreement and, as appropriate, propose to the Ministerial Conference amendments to its text. In the course of this review, the Council for Trade in Goods shall consider whether the Agreement should be complemented with provisions on investment policy and competition policy.

ANNEX   ILLUSTRATIVE LIST

1. TRIMs that are inconsistent with the obligation of national treatment provided for in paragraph 4 of Article III of GATT 1994 include those which are mandatory or enforceable under domestic law or under administrative rulings, or compliance with which is necessary to obtain an advantage, and which require:
   (a) the purchase or use by an enterprise of products of domestic origin or from any domestic source, whether specified in terms of particular products, in terms of volume or value of products, or in terms of a proportion of volume or value of its local production; or
   (b) that an enterprise's purchases or use of imported products be limited to an amount related to the volume or value of local products that it exports.

2. TRIMs that are inconsistent with the obligation of general elimination of quantitative restrictions provided for in paragraph 1 of Article XI of GATT 1994 include those which are mandatory or enforceable under domestic law or under administrative rulings, or compliance with which is necessary to obtain an advantage, and which restrict:
   (a) the importation by an enterprise of products used in or related to its local production, generally or to an amount related to the volume or value of local production that it exports;
   (b) the importation by an enterprise of products used in or related to its local production by restricting its access to foreign exchange to an amount related to the foreign exchange inflows attributable to the enterprise; or
   (c) the exportation or sale for export by an enterprise of products, whether specified in terms of particular products, in terms of volume or value of products, or in terms of a proportion of volume or value of its local production.

Agreement on Implementation of Article VI of the General Agreement on Tariffs and Trade 1994

Members hereby *agree* as follows:

PART I

Article 1 Principles

An anti-dumping measure shall be applied only under the circumstances provided for in Article VI of GATT 1994 and pursuant to investigations initiated[1] and conducted in accordance with the provisions of this Agreement. The following provisions govern the application of Article VI of GATT 1994 in so far as action is taken under anti-dumping legislation or regulations.

Article 2 Determination of Dumping

2.1 For the purpose of this Agreement, a product is to be considered as being dumped, i.e. introduced into the commerce of another country at less than its normal value, if the export price of the product exported from one country to another is less than the comparable price, in the ordinary course of trade, for the like product when destined for consumption in the exporting country.

2.2 When there are no sales of the like product in the ordinary course of trade in the domestic market of the exporting country or when, because of the particular market situation or the low volume of the sales in the domestic market of the exporting country[2], such sales do not permit a proper comparison, the margin of dumping shall be determined by comparison with a comparable price of the like product when exported to an appropriate third country, provided that this price is representative, or with the cost of production in the country of origin plus a reasonable amount for administrative, selling and general costs and for profits.

2.2.1 Sales of the like product in the domestic market of the exporting country or sales to a third country at prices below per unit (fixed and variable) costs of production plus administrative, selling and general costs may be treated as not being in the ordinary course of trade by reason of price and may be disregarded in determining normal value only if the authorities[3] determine that such sales are made within an extended period of time[4] in substantial quantities[5] and are at prices which do not provide for the recovery of all costs within a reasonable period of time. If prices which are below per unit costs at the time of sale are above weighted average per unit costs for the period of

---

1 The term "initiated" as used in this Agreement means the procedural action by which a Member formally commences an investigation as provided in Article 5.

2 Sales of the like product destined for consumption in the domestic market of the exporting country shall normally be considered a sufficient quantity for the determination of the normal value if such sales constitute 5 per cent or more of the sales of the product under consideration to the importing Member, provided that a lower ratio should be acceptable where the evidence demonstrates that domestic sales at such lower ratio are nonetheless of sufficient magnitude to provide for a proper comparison.

3 When in this Agreement the term "authorities" is used, it shall be interpreted as meaning authorities at an appropriate senior level.

4 The extended period of time should normally be one year but shall in no case be less than six months.

5 Sales below per unit costs are made in substantial quantities when the authorities establish that the weighted average selling price of the transactions under consideration for the determination of the normal value is below the weighted average per unit costs, or that the volume of sales below per unit costs represents not less than 20 per cent of the volume sold in transactions under consideration for the determination of the normal value.

investigation, such prices shall be considered to provide for recovery of costs within a reasonable period of time.

2.2.1.1 For the purpose of paragraph 2, costs shall normally be calculated on the basis of records kept by the exporter or producer under investigation, provided that such records are in accordance with the generally accepted accounting principles of the exporting country and reasonably reflect the costs associated with the production and sale of the product under consideration. Authorities shall consider all available evidence on the proper allocation of costs, including that which is made available by the exporter or producer in the course of the investigation provided that such allocations have been historically utilized by the exporter or producer, in particular in relation to establishing appropriate amortization and depreciation periods and allowances for capital expenditures and other development costs. Unless already reflected in the cost allocations under this sub-paragraph, costs shall be adjusted appropriately for those non-recurring items of cost which benefit future and/or current production, or for circumstances in which costs during the period of investigation are affected by start-up operations.[6]

2.2.2 For the purpose of paragraph 2, the amounts for administrative, selling and general costs and for profits shall be based on actual data pertaining to production and sales in the ordinary course of trade of the like product by the exporter or producer under investigation. When such amounts cannot be determined on this basis, the amounts may be determined on the basis of:

(i) the actual amounts incurred and realized by the exporter or producer in question in respect of production and sales in the domestic market of the country of origin of the same general category of products;

(ii) the weighted average of the actual amounts incurred and realized by other exporters or producers subject to investigation in respect of production and sales of the like product in the domestic market of the country of origin;

(iii) any other reasonable method, provided that the amount for profit so established shall not exceed the profit normally realized by other exporters or producers on sales of products of the same general category in the domestic market of the country of origin.

2.3 In cases where there is no export price or where it appears to the authorities concerned that the export price is unreliable because of association or a compensatory arrangement between the exporter and the importer or a third party, the export price may be constructed on the basis of the price at which the imported products are first resold to an independent buyer, or if the products are not resold to an independent buyer, or not resold in the condition as imported, on such reasonable basis as the authorities may determine.

2.4 A fair comparison shall be made between the export price and the normal value. This comparison shall be made at the same level of trade, normally at the ex-factory level, and in respect of sales made at as nearly as possible the same time. Due allowance shall be made in each case, on its merits, for differences which affect price comparability, including differences in conditions and terms of sale, taxation, levels of trade, quantities, physical characteristics, and any other differences which are also demonstrated to affect price comparability.[7] In the cases referred to in paragraph 3, allowances for costs, including duties and taxes, incurred between importation and resale, and for profits accruing, should also be

---

6 The adjustment made for start-up operations shall reflect the costs at the end of the start-up period or, if that period extends beyond the period of investigation, the most recent costs which can reasonably be taken into account by the authorities during the investigation.

7 It is understood that some of the above factors may overlap, and authorities shall ensure that they do not duplicate adjustments that have been already made under this provision.

made. If in these cases price comparability has been affected, the authorities shall establish the normal value at a level of trade equivalent to the level of trade of the constructed export price, or shall make due allowance as warranted under this paragraph. The authorities shall indicate to the parties in question what information is necessary to ensure a fair comparison and shall not impose an unreasonable burden of proof on those parties.

    2.4.1 When the comparison under paragraph 4 requires a conversion of currencies, such conversion should be made using the rate of exchange on the date of sale[8], provided that when a sale of foreign currency on forward markets is directly linked to the export sale involved, the rate of exchange in the forward sale shall be used. Fluctuations in exchange rates shall be ignored and in an investigation the authorities shall allow exporters at least 60 days to have adjusted their export prices to reflect sustained movements in exchange rates during the period of investigation.

    2.4.2 Subject to the provisions governing fair comparison in paragraph 4, the existence of margins of dumping during the investigation phase shall normally be established on the basis of a comparison of a weighted average normal value with a weighted average of prices of all comparable export transactions or by a comparison of normal value and export prices on a transaction-to-transaction basis. A normal value established on a weighted average basis may be compared to prices of individual export transactions if the authorities find a pattern of export prices which differ significantly among different purchasers, regions or time periods, and if an explanation is provided as to why such differences cannot be taken into account appropriately by the use of a weighted average-to-weighted average or transaction-to-transaction comparison.

2.5 In the case where products are not imported directly from the country of origin but are exported to the importing Member from an intermediate country, the price at which the products are sold from the country of export to the importing Member shall normally be compared with the comparable price in the country of export. However, comparison may be made with the price in the country of origin, if, for example, the products are merely transshipped through the country of export, or such products are not produced in the country of export, or there is no comparable price for them in the country of export.

2.6 Throughout this Agreement the term "like product" ("produit similaire") shall be interpreted to mean a product which is identical, i.e. alike in all respects to the product under consideration, or in the absence of such a product, another product which, although not alike in all respects, has characteristics closely resembling those of the product under consideration.

2.7 This Article is without prejudice to the second Supplementary Provision to paragraph 1 of Article VI in Annex I to GATT 1994.

Article 3   Determination of Injury[9]

3.1 A determination of injury for purposes of Article VI of GATT 1994 shall be based on positive evidence and involve an objective examination of both *(a)* the volume of the dumped imports and the effect of the dumped imports on prices in the domestic market for like products, and *(b)* the consequent impact of these imports on domestic producers of such products.

3.2 With regard to the volume of the dumped imports, the investigating authorities shall consider whether there has been a significant increase in dumped imports, either in absolute terms or relative to production or consumption in the importing Member. With regard to the effect of the dumped imports on prices, the investigating authorities shall consider

---

8 Normally, the date of sale would be the date of contract, purchase order, order confirmation, or invoice, whichever establishes the material terms of sale.

9 Under this Agreement the term "injury" shall, unless otherwise specified, be taken to mean material injury to a domestic industry, threat of material injury to a domestic industry or material retardation of the establishment of such an industry and shall be interpreted in accordance with the provisions of this Article.

whether there has been a significant price undercutting by the dumped imports as compared with the price of a like product of the importing Member, or whether the effect of such imports is otherwise to depress prices to a significant degree or prevent price increases, which otherwise would have occurred, to a significant degree. No one or several of these factors can necessarily give decisive guidance.

3.3 Where imports of a product from more than one country are simultaneously subject to anti-dumping investigations, the investigating authorities may cumulatively assess the effects of such imports only if they determine that *(a)* the margin of dumping established in relation to the imports from each country is more than *de minimis* as defined in paragraph 8 of Article 5 and the volume of imports from each country is not negligible and *(b)* a cumulative assessment of the effects of the imports is appropriate in light of the conditions of competition between the imported products and the conditions of competition between the imported products and the like domestic product.

3.4 The examination of the impact of the dumped imports on the domestic industry concerned shall include an evaluation of all relevant economic factors and indices having a bearing on the state of the industry, including actual and potential decline in sales, profits, output, market share, productivity, return on investments, or utilization of capacity; factors affecting domestic prices; the magnitude of the margin of dumping; actual and potential negative effects on cash flow, inventories, employment, wages, growth, ability to raise capital or investments. This list is not exhaustive, nor can one or several of these factors necessarily give decisive guidance.

3.5 It must be demonstrated that the dumped imports are, through the effects of dumping, as set forth in paragraphs 2 and 4, causing injury within the meaning of this Agreement. The demonstration of a causal relationship between the dumped imports and the injury to the domestic industry shall be based on an examination of all relevant evidence before the authorities. The authorities shall also examine any known factors other than the dumped imports which at the same time are injuring the domestic industry, and the injuries caused by these other factors must not be attributed to the dumped imports. Factors which may be relevant in this respect include, *inter alia*, the volume and prices of imports not sold at dumping prices, contraction in demand or changes in the patterns of consumption, trade restrictive practices of and competition between the foreign and domestic producers, developments in technology and the export performance and productivity of the domestic industry.

3.6 The effect of the dumped imports shall be assessed in relation to the domestic production of the like product when available data permit the separate identification of that production on the basis of such criteria as the production process, producers' sales and profits. If such separate identification of that production is not possible, the effects of the dumped imports shall be assessed by the examination of the production of the narrowest group or range of products, which includes the like product, for which the necessary information can be provided.

3.7 A determination of a threat of material injury shall be based on facts and not merely on allegation, conjecture or remote possibility. The change in circumstances which would create a situation in which the dumping would cause injury must be clearly foreseen and imminent.[10] In making a determination regarding the existence of a threat of material injury, the authorities should consider, *inter alia*, such factors as:

(i) a significant rate of increase of dumped imports into the domestic market indicating the likelihood of substantially increased importation;

---

10 One example, though not an exclusive one, is that there is convincing reason to believe that there will be, in the near future, substantially increased importation of the product at dumped prices.

    (ii) sufficient freely disposable, or an imminent, substantial increase in, capacity of the exporter indicating the likelihood of substantially increased dumped exports to the importing Member's market, taking into account the availability of other export markets to absorb any additional exports;

    (iii) whether imports are entering at prices that will have a significant depressing or suppressing effect on domestic prices, and would likely increase demand for further imports; and

    (iv) inventories of the product being investigated.

No one of these factors by itself can necessarily give decisive guidance but the totality of the factors considered must lead to the conclusion that further dumped exports are imminent and that, unless protective action is taken, material injury would occur.

3.8 With respect to cases where injury is threatened by dumped imports, the application of anti-dumping measures shall be considered and decided with special care.

Article 4 Definition of Domestic Industry

4.1 For the purposes of this Agreement, the term "domestic industry" shall be interpreted as referring to the domestic producers as a whole of the like products or to those of them whose collective output of the products constitutes a major proportion of the total domestic production of those products, except that:

    (i) when producers are related[11] to the exporters or importers or are themselves importers of the allegedly dumped product, the term "domestic industry" may be interpreted as referring to the rest of the producers;

    (ii) in exceptional circumstances the territory of a Member may, for the production in question, be divided into two or more competitive markets and the producers within each market may be regarded as a separate industry if *(a)* the producers within such market sell all or almost all of their production of the product in question in that market, and *(b)* the demand in that market is not to any substantial degree supplied by producers of the product in question located elsewhere in the territory. In such circumstances, injury may be found to exist even where a major portion of the total domestic industry is not injured, provided there is a concentration of dumped imports into such an isolated market and provided further that the dumped imports are causing injury to the producers of all or almost all of the production within such market.

4.2 When the domestic industry has been interpreted as referring to the producers in a certain area, i.e. a market as defined in paragraph 1(ii), anti-dumping duties shall be levied[12] only on the products in question consigned for final consumption to that area. When the constitutional law of the importing Member does not permit the levying of anti-dumping duties on such a basis, the importing Member may levy the anti-dumping duties without limitation only if *(a)* the exporters shall have been given an opportunity to cease exporting at dumped prices to the area concerned or otherwise give assurances pursuant to Article 8 and adequate assurances in this regard have not been promptly given, and *(b)* such duties cannot be levied only on products of specific producers which supply the area in question.

4.3 Where two or more countries have reached under the provisions of paragraph 8(a) of Article XXIV of GATT 1994 such a level of integration that they have the characteristics of a single, unified market, the industry in the entire area of integration shall be taken to be the domestic industry referred to in paragraph 1.

---

11 For the purpose of this paragraph, producers shall be deemed to be related to exporters or importers only if *(a)* one of them directly or indirectly controls the other; or *(b)* both of them are directly or indirectly controlled by a third person; or *(c)* together they directly or indirectly control a third person, provided that there are grounds for believing or suspecting that the effect of the relationship is such as to cause the producer concerned to behave differently from non-related producers. For the purpose of this paragraph, one shall be deemed to control another when the former is legally or operationally in a position to exercise restraint or direction over the latter.

12 As used in this Agreement "levy" shall mean the definitive or final legal assessment or collection of a duty or tax.

4.4 The provisions of paragraph 6 of Article 3 shall be applicable to this Article.

Article 5   Initiation and Subsequent Investigation

5.1 Except as provided for in paragraph 6, an investigation to determine the existence, degree and effect of any alleged dumping shall be initiated upon a written application by or on behalf of the domestic industry.

5.2 An application under paragraph 1 shall include evidence of *(a)* dumping, *(b)* injury within the meaning of Article VI of GATT 1994 as interpreted by this Agreement and *(c)* a causal link between the dumped imports and the alleged injury. Simple assertion, unsubstantiated by relevant evidence, cannot be considered sufficient to meet the requirements of this paragraph. The application shall contain such information as is reasonably available to the applicant on the following:

  (i)   the identity of the applicant and a description of the volume and value of the domestic production of the like product by the applicant. Where a written application is made on behalf of the domestic industry, the application shall identify the industry on behalf of which the application is made by a list of all known domestic producers of the like product (or associations of domestic producers of the like product) and, to the extent possible, a description of the volume and value of domestic production of the like product accounted for by such producers;

  (ii) a complete description of the allegedly dumped product, the names of the country or countries of origin or export in question, the identity of each known exporter or foreign producer and a list of known persons importing the product in question;

  (iii) information on prices at which the product in question is sold when destined for consumption in the domestic markets of the country or countries of origin or export (or, where appropriate, information on the prices at which the product is sold from the country or countries of origin or export to a third country or countries, or on the constructed value of the product) and information on export prices or, where appropriate, on the prices at which the product is first resold to an independent buyer in the territory of the importing Member;

  (iv) information on the evolution of the volume of the allegedly dumped imports, the effect of these imports on prices of the like product in the domestic market and the consequent impact of the imports on the domestic industry, as demonstrated by relevant factors and indices having a bearing on the state of the domestic industry, such as those listed in paragraphs 2 and 4 of Article 3.

5.3 The authorities shall examine the accuracy and adequacy of the evidence provided in the application to determine whether there is sufficient evidence to justify the initiation of an investigation.

5.4 An investigation shall not be initiated pursuant to paragraph 1 unless the authorities have determined, on the basis of an examination of the degree of support for, or opposition to, the application expressed[13] by domestic producers of the like product, that the application has been made by or on behalf of the domestic industry.[14] The application shall be considered to have been made "by or on behalf of the domestic industry" if it is supported by those domestic producers whose collective output constitutes more than 50 per cent of the total production of the like product produced by that portion of the domestic industry expressing either support for or opposition to the application. However, no investigation shall be initiated when domestic producers expressly supporting the application account for less than 25 per cent of total production of the like product produced by the domestic industry.

---

13 In the case of fragmented industries involving an exceptionally large number of producers, authorities may determine support and opposition by using statistically valid sampling techniques.

14 Members are aware that in the territory of certain Members employees of domestic producers of the like product or representatives of those employees may make or support an application for an investigation under paragraph 1.

5.5 The authorities shall avoid, unless a decision has been made to initiate an investigation, any publicizing of the application for the initiation of an investigation. However, after receipt of a properly documented application and before proceeding to initiate an investigation, the authorities shall notify the government of the exporting Member concerned.

5.6 If, in special circumstances, the authorities concerned decide to initiate an investigation without having received a written application by or on behalf of a domestic industry for the initiation of such investigation, they shall proceed only if they have sufficient evidence of dumping, injury and a causal link, as described in paragraph 2, to justify the initiation of an investigation.

5.7 The evidence of both dumping and injury shall be considered simultaneously *(a)* in the decision whether or not to initiate an investigation, and *(b)* thereafter, during the course of the investigation, starting on a date not later than the earliest date on which in accordance with the provisions of this Agreement provisional measures may be applied.

5.8 An application under paragraph 1 shall be rejected and an investigation shall be terminated promptly as soon as the authorities concerned are satisfied that there is not sufficient evidence of either dumping or of injury to justify proceeding with the case. There shall be immediate termination in cases where the authorities determine that the margin of dumping is *de minimis,* or that the volume of dumped imports, actual or potential, or the injury, is negligible. The margin of dumping shall be considered to be *de minimis* if this margin is less than 2 per cent, expressed as a percentage of the export price. The volume of dumped imports shall normally be regarded as negligible if the volume of dumped imports from a particular country is found to account for less than 3 per cent of imports of the like product in the importing Member, unless countries which individually account for less than 3 per cent of the imports of the like product in the importing Member collectively account for more than 7 per cent of imports of the like product in the importing Member.

5.9 An anti-dumping proceeding shall not hinder the procedures of customs clearance.

5.10 Investigations shall, except in special circumstances, be concluded within one year, and in no case more than 18 months, after their initiation.

Article 6   Evidence

6.1 All interested parties in an anti-dumping investigation shall be given notice of the information which the authorities require and ample opportunity to present in writing all evidence which they consider relevant in respect of the investigation in question.

6.1.1 Exporters or foreign producers receiving questionnaires used in an anti-dumping investigation shall be given at least 30 days for reply.[15] Due consideration should be given to any request for an extension of the 30-day period and, upon cause shown, such an extension should be granted whenever practicable.

6.1.2 Subject to the requirement to protect confidential information, evidence presented in writing by one interested party shall be made available promptly to other interested parties participating in the investigation.

6.1.3 As soon as an investigation has been initiated, the authorities shall provide the full text of the written application received under paragraph 1 of Article 5 to the known exporters[16] and to the authorities of the exporting Member and shall make it available, upon request, to other interested parties involved. Due regard shall be paid to the requirement for the protection of confidential information, as provided for in paragraph 5.

---

15 As a general rule, the time-limit for exporters shall be counted from the date of receipt of the questionnaire, which for this purpose shall be deemed to have been received one week from the date on which it was sent to the respondent or transmitted to the appropriate diplomatic representative of the exporting Member or, in the case of a separate customs territory Member of the WTO, an official representative of the exporting territory.

16 It being understood that, where the number of exporters involved is particularly high, the full text of the written application should instead be provided only to the authorities of the exporting Member or to the relevant trade association.

6.2 Throughout the anti-dumping investigation all interested parties shall have a full opportunity for the defence of their interests. To this end, the authorities shall, on request, provide opportunities for all interested parties to meet those parties with adverse interests, so that opposing views may be presented and rebuttal arguments offered. Provision of such opportunities must take account of the need to preserve confidentiality and of the convenience to the parties. There shall be no obligation on any party to attend a meeting, and failure to do so shall not be prejudicial to that party's case. Interested parties shall also have the right, on justification, to present other information orally.

6.3 Oral information provided under paragraph 2 shall be taken into account by the authorities only in so far as it is subsequently reproduced in writing and made available to other interested parties, as provided for in subparagraph 1.2.

6.4 The authorities shall whenever practicable provide timely opportunities for all interested parties to see all information that is relevant to the presentation of their cases, that is not confidential as defined in paragraph 5, and that is used by the authorities in an anti-dumping investigation, and to prepare presentations on the basis of this information.

6.5 Any information which is by nature confidential (for example, because its disclosure would be of significant competitive advantage to a competitor or because its disclosure would have a significantly adverse effect upon a person supplying the information or upon a person from whom that person acquired the information), or which is provided on a confidential basis by parties to an investigation shall, upon good cause shown, be treated as such by the authorities. Such information shall not be disclosed without specific permission of the party submitting it.[17]

    6.5.1 The authorities shall require interested parties providing confidential information to furnish non-confidential summaries thereof. These summaries shall be in sufficient detail to permit a reasonable understanding of the substance of the information submitted in confidence. In exceptional circumstances, such parties may indicate that such information is not susceptible of summary. In such exceptional circumstances, a statement of the reasons why summarization is not possible must be provided.

    6.5.2 If the authorities find that a request for confidentiality is not warranted and if the supplier of the information is either unwilling to make the information public or to authorize its disclosure in generalized or summary form, the authorities may disregard such information unless it can be demonstrated to their satisfaction from appropriate sources that the information is correct.[18]

6.6 Except in circumstances provided for in paragraph 8, the authorities shall during the course of an investigation satisfy themselves as to the accuracy of the information supplied by interested parties upon which their findings are based.

6.7 In order to verify information provided or to obtain further details, the authorities may carry out investigations in the territory of other Members as required, provided they obtain the agreement of the firms concerned and notify the representatives of the government of the Member in question, and unless that Member objects to the investigation. The procedures described in Annex I shall apply to investigations carried out in the territory of other Members. Subject to the requirement to protect confidential information, the authorities shall make the results of any such investigations available, or shall provide disclosure thereof pursuant to paragraph 9, to the firms to which they pertain and may make such results available to the applicants.

---

17 Members are aware that in the territory of certain Members disclosure pursuant to a narrowly-drawn protective order may be required.
18 Members agree that requests for confidentiality should not be arbitrarily rejected.

6.8 In cases in which any interested party refuses access to, or otherwise does not provide, necessary information within a reasonable period or significantly impedes the investigation, preliminary and final determinations, affirmative or negative, may be made on the basis of the facts available. The provisions of Annex II shall be observed in the application of this paragraph.

6.9 The authorities shall, before a final determination is made, inform all interested parties of the essential facts under consideration which form the basis for the decision whether to apply definitive measures. Such disclosure should take place in sufficient time for the parties to defend their interests.

6.10 The authorities shall, as a rule, determine an individual margin of dumping for each known exporter or producer concerned of the product under investigation. In cases where the number of exporters, producers, importers or types of products involved is so large as to make such a determination impracticable, the authorities may limit their examination either to a reasonable number of interested parties or products by using samples which are statistically valid on the basis of information available to the authorities at the time of the selection, or to the largest percentage of the volume of the exports from the country in question which can reasonably be investigated.

    6.10.1 Any selection of exporters, producers, importers or types of products made under this paragraph shall preferably be chosen in consultation with and with the consent of the exporters, producers or importers concerned.

    6.10.2 In cases where the authorities have limited their examination, as provided for in this paragraph, they shall nevertheless determine an individual margin of dumping for any exporter or producer not initially selected who submits the necessary information in time for that information to be considered during the course of the investigation, except where the number of exporters or producers is so large that individual examinations would be unduly burdensome to the authorities and prevent the timely completion of the investigation. Voluntary responses shall not be discouraged.

6.11 For the purposes of this Agreement, "interested parties" shall include:

    (i) an exporter or foreign producer or the importer of a product subject to investigation, or a trade or business association a majority of the members of which are producers, exporters or importers of such product;

    (ii) the government of the exporting Member; and

    (iii) a producer of the like product in the importing Member or a trade and business association a majority of the members of which produce the like product in the territory of the importing Member.

This list shall not preclude Members from allowing domestic or foreign parties other than those mentioned above to be included as interested parties.

6.12 The authorities shall provide opportunities for industrial users of the product under investigation, and for representative consumer organizations in cases where the product is commonly sold at the retail level, to provide information which is relevant to the investigation regarding dumping, injury and causality.

6.13 The authorities shall take due account of any difficulties experienced by interested parties, in particular small companies, in supplying information requested, and shall provide any assistance practicable.

6.14 The procedures set out above are not intended to prevent the authorities of a Member from proceeding expeditiously with regard to initiating an investigation, reaching preliminary or final determinations, whether affirmative or negative, or from applying provisional or final measures, in accordance with relevant provisions of this Agreement.

Article 7   Provisional Measures

7.1 Provisional measures may be applied only if:

    (i) an investigation has been initiated in accordance with the provisions of Article 5, a public notice has been given to that effect and interested parties have been given adequate opportunities to submit information and make comments;

    (ii) a preliminary affirmative determination has been made of dumping and consequent injury to a domestic industry; and

    (iii) the authorities concerned judge such measures necessary to prevent injury being caused during the investigation.

7.2 Provisional measures may take the form of a provisional duty or, preferably, a security—by cash deposit or bond—equal to the amount of the anti-dumping duty provisionally estimated, being not greater than the provisionally estimated margin of dumping. With-holding of appraisement is an appropriate provisional measure, provided that the normal duty and the estimated amount of the anti-dumping duty be indicated and as long as the withholding of appraisement is subject to the same conditions as other provisional measures.

7.3 Provisional measures shall not be applied sooner than 60 days from the date of initiation of the investigation.

7.4 The application of provisional measures shall be limited to as short a period as possible, not exceeding four months or, on decision of the authorities concerned, upon request by exporters representing a significant percentage of the trade involved, to a period not exceeding six months. When authorities, in the course of an investigation, examine whether a duty lower than the margin of dumping would be sufficient to remove injury, these periods may be six and nine months, respectively.

7.5 The relevant provisions of Article 9 shall be followed in the application of provisional measures.

Article 8   Price Undertakings

8.1 Proceedings may[19] be suspended or terminated without the imposition of provisional measures or anti-dumping duties upon receipt of satisfactory voluntary undertakings from any exporter to revise its prices or to cease exports to the area in question at dumped prices so that the authorities are satisfied that the injurious effect of the dumping is eliminated. Price increases under such undertakings shall not be higher than necessary to eliminate the margin of dumping. It is desirable that the price increases be less than the margin of dumping if such increases would be adequate to remove the injury to the domestic industry.

8.2 Price undertakings shall not be sought or accepted from exporters unless the authorities of the importing Member have made a preliminary affirmative determination of dumping and injury caused by such dumping.

8.3 Undertakings offered need not be accepted if the authorities consider their acceptance impractical, for example, if the number of actual or potential exporters is too great, or for other reasons, including reasons of general policy. Should the case arise and where practic-able, the authorities shall provide to the exporter the reasons which have led them to consider acceptance of an undertaking as inappropriate, and shall, to the extent possible, give the exporter an opportunity to make comments thereon.

8.4 If an undertaking is accepted, the investigation of dumping and injury shall nevertheless be completed if the exporter so desires or the authorities so decide. In such a case, if a negative determination of dumping or injury is made, the undertaking shall automatically lapse, except in cases where such a determination is due in large part to the existence of a price

---

19 The word "may" shall not be interpreted to allow the simultaneous continuation of proceedings with the implementation of price undertakings except as provided in paragraph 4.

undertaking. In such cases, the authorities may require that an undertaking be maintained for a reasonable period consistent with the provisions of this Agreement. In the event that an affirmative determination of dumping and injury is made, the undertaking shall continue consistent with its terms and the provisions of this Agreement.

8.5 Price undertakings may be suggested by the authorities of the importing Member, but no exporter shall be forced to enter into such undertakings. The fact that exporters do not offer such undertakings, or do not accept an invitation to do so, shall in no way prejudice the consideration of the case. However, the authorities are free to determine that a threat of injury is more likely to be realized if the dumped imports continue.

8.6 Authorities of an importing Member may require any exporter from whom an undertaking has been accepted to provide periodically information relevant to the fulfilment of such an undertaking and to permit verification of pertinent data. In case of violation of an under-taking, the authorities of the importing Member may take, under this Agreement in conformity with its provisions, expeditious actions which may constitute immediate appli-cation of provisional measures using the best information available. In such cases, definitive duties may be levied in accordance with this Agreement on products entered for consump-tion not more than 90 days before the application of such provisional measures, except that any such retroactive assessment shall not apply to imports entered before the violation of the undertaking.

Article 9   Imposition and Collection of Anti-Dumping Duties

9.1 The decision whether or not to impose an anti-dumping duty in cases where all requirements for the imposition have been fulfilled, and the decision whether the amount of the anti-dumping duty to be imposed shall be the full margin of dumping or less, are decisions to be made by the authorities of the importing Member. It is desirable that the imposition be permissive in the territory of all Members, and that the duty be less than the margin if such lesser duty would be adequate to remove the injury to the domestic industry.

9.2 When an anti-dumping duty is imposed in respect of any product, such anti-dumping duty shall be collected in the appropriate amounts in each case, on a non-discriminatory basis on imports of such product from all sources found to be dumped and causing injury, except as to imports from those sources from which price undertakings under the terms of this Agreement have been accepted. The authorities shall name the supplier or suppliers of the product concerned. If, however, several suppliers from the same country are involved, and it is impracticable to name all these suppliers, the authorities may name the supplying country concerned. If several suppliers from more than one country are involved, the authorities may name either all the suppliers involved, or, if this is impracticable, all the supplying countries involved.

9.3 The amount of the anti-dumping duty shall not exceed the margin of dumping as established under Article 2.

9.3.1 When the amount of the anti-dumping duty is assessed on a retrospective basis, the determination of the final liability for payment of anti-dumping duties shall take place as soon as possible, normally within 12 months, and in no case more than 18 months, after the date on which a request for a final assessment of the amount of the anti-dumping duty has been made.[20] Any refund shall be made promptly and normally in not more than 90 days following the determination of final liability made pursuant to this sub-paragraph. In any case, where a refund is not made within 90 days, the authorities shall provide an explanation if so requested.

---

20 It is understood that the observance of the time-limits mentioned in this subparagraph and in subparagraph 3.2 may not be possible where the product in question is subject to judicial review proceedings.

9.3.2 When the amount of the anti-dumping duty is assessed on a prospective basis, provision shall be made for a prompt refund, upon request, of any duty paid in excess of the margin of dumping. A refund of any such duty paid in excess of the actual margin of dumping shall normally take place within 12 months, and in no case more than 18 months, after the date on which a request for a refund, duly supported by evidence, has been made by an importer of the product subject to the anti-dumping duty. The refund authorized should normally be made within 90 days of the above-noted decision.

9.3.3 In determining whether and to what extent a reimbursement should be made when the export price is constructed in accordance with paragraph 3 of Article 2, authorities should take account of any change in normal value, any change in costs incurred between importation and resale, and any movement in the resale price which is duly reflected in subsequent selling prices, and should calculate the export price with no deduction for the amount of anti-dumping duties paid when conclusive evidence of the above is provided.

9.4 When the authorities have limited their examination in accordance with the second sentence of paragraph 10 of Article 6, any anti-dumping duty applied to imports from exporters or producers not included in the examination shall not exceed:

(i) the weighted average margin of dumping established with respect to the selected exporters or producers or,

(ii) where the liability for payment of anti-dumping duties is calculated on the basis of a prospective normal value, the difference between the weighted average normal value of the selected exporters or producers and the export prices of exporters or producers not individually examined,

provided that the authorities shall disregard for the purpose of this paragraph any zero and *de minimis* margins and margins established under the circumstances referred to in paragraph 8 of Article 6. The authorities shall apply individual duties or normal values to imports from any exporter or producer not included in the examination who has provided the necessary information during the course of the investigation, as provided for in subparagraph 10.2 of Article 6.

9.5 If a product is subject to anti-dumping duties in an importing Member, the authorities shall promptly carry out a review for the purpose of determining individual margins of dumping for any exporters or producers in the exporting country in question who have not exported the product to the importing Member during the period of investigation, provided that these exporters or producers can show that they are not related to any of the exporters or producers in the exporting country who are subject to the anti-dumping duties on the product. Such a review shall be initiated and carried out on an accelerated basis, compared to normal duty assessment and review proceedings in the importing Member. No anti-dumping duties shall be levied on imports from such exporters or producers while the review is being carried out. The authorities may, however, withhold appraisement and/or request guarantees to ensure that, should such a review result in a determination of dumping in respect of such producers or exporters, anti-dumping duties can be levied retroactively to the date of the initiation of the review.

Article 10   Retroactivity

10.1 Provisional measures and anti-dumping duties shall only be applied to products which enter for consumption after the time when the decision taken under paragraph 1 of Article 7 and paragraph 1 of Article 9, respectively, enters into force, subject to the exceptions set out in this Article.

10.2 Where a final determination of injury (but not of a threat thereof or of a material retardation of the establishment of an industry) is made or, in the case of a final determination of a threat of injury, where the effect of the dumped imports would, in the absence of the provisional measures, have led to a determination of injury, anti-dumping duties may be levied retroactively for the period for which provisional measures, if any, have been applied.

10.3 If the definitive anti-dumping duty is higher than the provisional duty paid or payable, or the amount estimated for the purpose of the security, the difference shall not be collected. If the definitive duty is lower than the provisional duty paid or payable, or the amount estimated for the purpose of the security, the difference shall be reimbursed or the duty recalculated, as the case may be.

10.4 Except as provided in paragraph 2, where a determination of threat of injury or material retardation is made (but no injury has yet occurred) a definitive anti-dumping duty may be imposed only from the date of the determination of threat of injury or material retardation, and any cash deposit made during the period of the application of provisional measures shall be refunded and any bonds released in an expeditious manner.

10.5 Where a final determination is negative, any cash deposit made during the period of the application of provisional measures shall be refunded and any bonds released in an expeditious manner.

10.6 A definitive anti-dumping duty may be levied on products which were entered for consumption not more than 90 days prior to the date of application of provisional measures, when the authorities determine for the dumped product in question that:

(i) there is a history of dumping which caused injury or that the importer was, or should have been, aware that the exporter practises dumping and that such dumping would cause injury, and

(ii) the injury is caused by massive dumped imports of a product in a relatively short time which in light of the timing and the volume of the dumped imports and other circumstances (such as a rapid build-up of inventories of the imported product) is likely to seriously undermine the remedial effect of the definitive anti-dumping duty to be applied, provided that the importers concerned have been given an opportunity to comment.

10.7 The authorities may, after initiating an investigation, take such measures as the withholding of appraisement or assessment as may be necessary to collect anti-dumping duties retroactively, as provided for in paragraph 6, once they have sufficient evidence that the conditions set forth in that paragraph are satisfied.

10.8 No duties shall be levied retroactively pursuant to paragraph 6 on products entered for consumption prior to the date of initiation of the investigation.

Article 11   Duration and Review of Anti-Dumping Duties and Price Undertakings

11.1 An anti-dumping duty shall remain in force only as long as and to the extent necessary to counteract dumping which is causing injury.

11.2 The authorities shall review the need for the continued imposition of the duty, where warranted, on their own initiative or, provided that a reasonable period of time has elapsed since the imposition of the definitive anti-dumping duty, upon request by any interested party which submits positive information substantiating the need for a review.[21] Interested parties shall have the right to request the authorities to examine whether the continued imposition of the duty is necessary to offset dumping, whether the injury would be likely to continue or recur if the duty were removed or varied, or both. If, as a result of the review

---

21 A determination of final liability for payment of anti-dumping duties, as provided for in paragraph 3 of Article 9, does not by itself constitute a review within the meaning of this Article.

under this paragraph, the authorities determine that the anti-dumping duty is no longer warranted, it shall be terminated immediately.

11.3 Notwithstanding the provisions of paragraphs 1 and 2, any definitive anti-dumping duty shall be terminated on a date not later than five years from its imposition (or from the date of the most recent review under paragraph 2 if that review has covered both dumping and injury, or under this paragraph), unless the authorities determine, in a review initiated before that date on their own initiative or upon a duly substantiated request made by or on behalf of the domestic industry within a reasonable period of time prior to that date, that the expiry of the duty would be likely to lead to continuation or recurrence of dumping and injury.[22] The duty may remain in force pending the outcome of such a review.

11.4 The provisions of Article 6 regarding evidence and procedure shall apply to any review carried out under this Article. Any such review shall be carried out expeditiously and shall normally be concluded within 12 months of the date of initiation of the review.

11.5 The provisions of this Article shall apply *mutatis mutandis* to price undertakings accepted under Article 8.

Article 12   Public Notice and Explanation of Determinations

12.1 When the authorities are satisfied that there is sufficient evidence to justify the initiation of an anti-dumping investigation pursuant to Article 5, the Member or Members the products of which are subject to such investigation and other interested parties known to the investigating authorities to have an interest therein shall be notified and a public notice shall be given.

12.1.1 A public notice of the initiation of an investigation shall contain, or otherwise make available through a separate report[23], adequate information on the following:

  (i) the name of the exporting country or countries and the product involved;

  (ii) the date of initiation of the investigation;

  (iii) the basis on which dumping is alleged in the application;

  (iv) a summary of the factors on which the allegation of injury is based;

  (v) the address to which representations by interested parties should be directed;

  (vi) the time-limits allowed to interested parties for making their views known.

12.2 Public notice shall be given of any preliminary or final determination, whether affirmative or negative, of any decision to accept an undertaking pursuant to Article 8, of the termination of such an undertaking, and of the termination of a definitive anti-dumping duty. Each such notice shall set forth, or otherwise make available through a separate report, in sufficient detail the findings and conclusions reached on all issues of fact and law considered material by the investigating authorities. All such notices and reports shall be forwarded to the Member or Members the products of which are subject to such determination or undertaking and to other interested parties known to have an interest therein.

12.2.1 A public notice of the imposition of provisional measures shall set forth, or otherwise make available through a separate report, sufficiently detailed explanations for the preliminary determinations on dumping and injury and shall refer to the matters of fact and law which have led to arguments being accepted or rejected. Such a notice or report shall, due regard being paid to the requirement for the protection of confidential information, contain in particular:

  (i) the names of the suppliers, or when this is impracticable, the supplying countries involved;

---

22 When the amount of the anti-dumping duty is assessed on a retrospective basis, a finding in the most recent assessment proceeding under subparagraph 3.1 of Article 9 that no duty is to be levied shall not by itself require the authorities to terminate the definitive duty.

23 Where authorities provide information and explanations under the provisions of this Article in a separate report, they shall ensure that such report is readily available to the public.

     (ii) a description of the product which is sufficient for customs purposes;

    (iii) the margins of dumping established and a full explanation of the reasons for the methodology used in the establishment and comparison of the export price and the normal value under Article 2;

    (iv) considerations relevant to the injury determination as set out in Article 3;

    (v) the main reasons leading to the determination.

12.2.2 A public notice of conclusion or suspension of an investigation in the case of an affirmative determination providing for the imposition of a definitive duty or the acceptance of a price undertaking shall contain, or otherwise make available through a separate report, all relevant information on the matters of fact and law and reasons which have led to the imposition of final measures or the acceptance of a price undertaking, due regard being paid to the requirement for the protection of confidential information. In particular, the notice or report shall contain the information described in subparagraph 2.1, as well as the reasons for the acceptance or rejection of relevant arguments or claims made by the exporters and importers, and the basis for any decision made under subparagraph 10.2 of Article 6.

12.2.3 A public notice of the termination or suspension of an investigation following the acceptance of an undertaking pursuant to Article 8 shall include, or otherwise make available through a separate report, the non-confidential part of this undertaking.

12.3 The provisions of this Article shall apply *mutatis mutandis* to the initiation and completion of reviews pursuant to Article 11 and to decisions under Article 10 to apply duties retroactively.

Article 13 Judicial Review

Each Member whose national legislation contains provisions on anti-dumping measures shall maintain judicial, arbitral or administrative tribunals or procedures for the purpose, *inter alia*, of the prompt review of administrative actions relating to final determinations and reviews of determinations within the meaning of Article 11. Such tribunals or procedures shall be independent of the authorities responsible for the determination or review in question.

Article 14 Anti-Dumping Action on Behalf of a Third Country

14.1 An application for anti-dumping action on behalf of a third country shall be made by the authorities of the third country requesting action.

14.2 Such an application shall be supported by price information to show that the imports are being dumped and by detailed information to show that the alleged dumping is causing injury to the domestic industry concerned in the third country. The government of the third country shall afford all assistance to the authorities of the importing country to obtain any further information which the latter may require.

14.3 In considering such an application, the authorities of the importing country shall consider the effects of the alleged dumping on the industry concerned as a whole in the third country; that is to say, the injury shall not be assessed in relation only to the effect of the alleged dumping on the industry's exports to the importing country or even on the industry's total exports.

14.4 The decision whether or not to proceed with a case shall rest with the importing country. If the importing country decides that it is prepared to take action, the initiation of the approach to the Council for Trade in Goods seeking its approval for such action shall rest with the importing country.

Article 15 Developing Country Members

It is recognized that special regard must be given by developed country Members to the special situation of developing country Members when considering the application of anti-dumping measures under this Agreement. Possibilities of constructive remedies provided for by this

Agreement shall be explored before applying anti-dumping duties where they would affect the essential interests of developing country Members.

PART II

Article 16   Committee on Anti-Dumping Practices

16.1 There is hereby established a Committee on Anti-Dumping Practices (referred to in this Agreement as the "Committee") composed of representatives from each of the Members. The Committee shall elect its own Chairman and shall meet not less than twice a year and otherwise as envisaged by relevant provisions of this Agreement at the request of any Member. The Committee shall carry out responsibilities as assigned to it under this Agreement or by the Members and it shall afford Members the opportunity of consulting on any matters relating to the operation of the Agreement or the furtherance of its objectives. The WTO Secretariat shall act as the secretariat to the Committee.

16.2 The Committee may set up subsidiary bodies as appropriate.

16.3 In carrying out their functions, the Committee and any subsidiary bodies may consult with and seek information from any source they deem appropriate. However, before the Committee or a subsidiary body seeks such information from a source within the jurisdiction of a Member, it shall inform the Member involved. It shall obtain the consent of the Member and any firm to be consulted.

16.4 Members shall report without delay to the Committee all preliminary or final anti-dumping actions taken. Such reports shall be available in the Secretariat for inspection by other Members. Members shall also submit, on a semi-annual basis, reports of any anti-dumping actions taken within the preceding six months. The semi-annual reports shall be submitted on an agreed standard form.

16.5 Each Member shall notify the Committee (a) which of its authorities are competent to initiate and conduct investigations referred to in Article 5 and (b) its domestic procedures governing the initiation and conduct of such investigations.

Article 17   Consultation and Dispute Settlement

17.1 Except as otherwise provided herein, the Dispute Settlement Understanding is applicable to consultations and the settlement of disputes under this Agreement.

17.2 Each Member shall afford sympathetic consideration to, and shall afford adequate opportunity for consultation regarding, representations made by another Member with respect to any matter affecting the operation of this Agreement.

17.3 If any Member considers that any benefit accruing to it, directly or indirectly, under this Agreement is being nullified or impaired, or that the achievement of any objective is being impeded, by another Member or Members, it may, with a view to reaching a mutually satisfactory resolution of the matter, request in writing consultations with the Member or Members in question. Each Member shall afford sympathetic consideration to any request from another Member for consultation.

17.4 If the Member that requested consultations considers that the consultations pursuant to paragraph 3 have failed to achieve a mutually agreed solution, and if final action has been taken by the administering authorities of the importing Member to levy definitive anti-dumping duties or to accept price undertakings, it may refer the matter to the Dispute Settlement Body ("DSB"). When a provisional measure has a significant impact and the Member that requested consultations considers that the measure was taken contrary to the provisions of paragraph 1 of Article 7, that Member may also refer such matter to the DSB.

17.5 The DSB shall, at the request of the complaining party, establish a panel to examine the matter based upon:

(i) a written statement of the Member making the request indicating how a benefit accruing to it, directly or indirectly, under this Agreement has been nullified or impaired, or that the achieving of the objectives of the Agreement is being impeded, and

(ii) the facts made available in conformity with appropriate domestic procedures to the authorities of the importing Member.

17.6 In examining the matter referred to in paragraph 5:

(i) in its assessment of the facts of the matter, the panel shall determine whether the authorities' establishment of the facts was proper and whether their evaluation of those facts was unbiased and objective. If the establishment of the facts was proper and the evaluation was unbiased and objective, even though the panel might have reached a different conclusion, the evaluation shall not be overturned;

(ii) the panel shall interpret the relevant provisions of the Agreement in accordance with customary rules of interpretation of public international law. Where the panel finds that a relevant provision of the Agreement admits of more than one permissible interpretation, the panel shall find the authorities' measure to be in conformity with the Agreement if it rests upon one of those permissible interpretations.

17.7 Confidential information provided to the panel shall not be disclosed without formal authorization from the person, body or authority providing such information. Where such information is requested from the panel but release of such information by the panel is not authorized, a non-confidential summary of the information, authorized by the person, body or authority providing the information, shall be provided.

PART III

Article 18   Final Provisions

18.1 No specific action against dumping of exports from another Member can be taken except in accordance with the provisions of GATT 1994, as interpreted by this Agreement.[24]

18.2 Reservations may not be entered in respect of any of the provisions of this Agreement without the consent of the other Members.

18.3 Subject to subparagraphs 3.1 and 3.2, the provisions of this Agreement shall apply to investigations, and reviews of existing measures, initiated pursuant to applications which have been made on or after the date of entry into force for a Member of the WTO Agreement.

18.3.1 With respect to the calculation of margins of dumping in refund procedures under paragraph 3 of Article 9, the rules used in the most recent determination or review of dumping shall apply.

18.3.2 For the purposes of paragraph 3 of Article 11, existing anti-dumping measures shall be deemed to be imposed on a date not later than the date of entry into force for a Member of the WTO Agreement, except in cases in which the domestic legislation of a Member in force on that date already included a clause of the type provided for in that paragraph.

18.4 Each Member shall take all necessary steps, of a general or particular character, to ensure, not later than the date of entry into force of the WTO Agreement for it, the conformity of its laws, regulations and administrative procedures with the provisions of this Agreement as they may apply for the Member in question.

---

24 This is not intended to preclude action under other relevant provisions of GATT 1994, as appropriate.

18.5 Each Member shall inform the Committee of any changes in its laws and regulations relevant to this Agreement and in the administration of such laws and regulations.

18.6 The Committee shall review annually the implementation and operation of this Agreement taking into account the objectives thereof. The Committee shall inform annually the Council for Trade in Goods of developments during the period covered by such reviews.

18.7 The Annexes to this Agreement constitute an integral part thereof.

ANNEX I PROCEDURES FOR ON-THE-SPOT INVESTIGATIONS PURSUANT TO PARAGRAPH 7 OF ARTICLE 6

1. Upon initiation of an investigation, the authorities of the exporting Member and the firms known to be concerned should be informed of the intention to carry out on-the-spot investigations.

2. If in exceptional circumstances it is intended to include non-governmental experts in the investigating team, the firms and the authorities of the exporting Member should be so informed. Such non-governmental experts should be subject to effective sanctions for breach of confidentiality requirements.

3. It should be standard practice to obtain explicit agreement of the firms concerned in the exporting Member before the visit is finally scheduled.

4. As soon as the agreement of the firms concerned has been obtained, the investigating authorities should notify the authorities of the exporting Member of the names and addresses of the firms to be visited and the dates agreed.

5. Sufficient advance notice should be given to the firms in question before the visit is made.

6. Visits to explain the questionnaire should only be made at the request of an exporting firm. Such a visit may only be made if *(a)* the authorities of the importing Member notify the representatives of the Member in question and *(b)* the latter do not object to the visit.

7. As the main purpose of the on-the-spot investigation is to verify information provided or to obtain further details, it should be carried out after the response to the questionnaire has been received unless the firm agrees to the contrary and the government of the exporting Member is informed by the investigating authorities of the anticipated visit and does not object to it; further, it should be standard practice prior to the visit to advise the firms concerned of the general nature of the information to be verified and of any further information which needs to be provided, though this should not preclude requests to be made on the spot for further details to be provided in the light of information obtained.

8. Enquiries or questions put by the authorities or firms of the exporting Members and essential to a successful on-the-spot investigation should, whenever possible, be answered before the visit is made.

ANNEX II BEST INFORMATION AVAILABLE IN TERMS OF PARAGRAPH 8 OF ARTICLE 6

1. As soon as possible after the initiation of the investigation, the investigating authorities should specify in detail the information required from any interested party, and the manner in which that information should be structured by the interested party in its response. The authorities should also ensure that the party is aware that if information is not supplied within a reasonable time, the authorities will be free to make determinations on the basis of the facts available, including those contained in the application for the initiation of the investigation by the domestic industry.

2. The authorities may also request that an interested party provide its response in a particular medium (e.g. computer tape) or computer language. Where such a request is made, the authorities should consider the reasonable ability of the interested party to respond in the preferred medium or computer language, and should not request the party to use for its response a computer system other than that used by the party. The authority should not maintain a request for a computerized response if the interested party does not maintain computerized accounts and if presenting the response as requested would result in an unreasonable extra burden on the interested party, e.g. it would entail unreasonable additional cost and trouble. The authorities should not maintain a request for a response in a particular medium or computer language if the interested party does not maintain its computerized accounts in such medium or computer language and if presenting the response as requested would result in an unreasonable extra burden on the interested party, e.g. it would entail unreasonable additional cost and trouble.

3. All information which is verifiable, which is appropriately submitted so that it can be used in the investigation without undue difficulties, which is supplied in a timely fashion, and, where applicable, which is supplied in a medium or computer language requested by the authorities, should be taken into account when determinations are made. If a party does not respond in the preferred medium or computer language but the authorities find that the circumstances set out in paragraph 2 have been satisfied, the failure to respond in the preferred medium or computer language should not be considered to significantly impede the investigation.

4. Where the authorities do not have the ability to process information if provided in a particular medium (e.g. computer tape), the information should be supplied in the form of written material or any other form acceptable to the authorities.

5. Even though the information provided may not be ideal in all respects, this should not justify the authorities from disregarding it, provided the interested party has acted to the best of its ability.

6. If evidence or information is not accepted, the supplying party should be informed forthwith of the reasons therefor, and should have an opportunity to provide further explanations within a reasonable period, due account being taken of the time-limits of the investigation. If the explanations are considered by the authorities as not being satisfactory, the reasons for the rejection of such evidence or information should be given in any published determinations.

7. If the authorities have to base their findings, including those with respect to normal value, on information from a secondary source, including the information supplied in the application for the initiation of the investigation, they should do so with special circumspection. In such cases, the authorities should, where practicable, check the information from other independent sources at their disposal, such as published price lists, official import statistics and customs returns, and from the information obtained from other interested parties during the investigation. It is clear, however, that if an interested party does not cooperate and thus relevant information is being withheld from the authorities, this situation could lead to a result which is less favourable to the party than if the party did cooperate.

Agreement on Subsidies and Countervailing Measures

Members hereby *agree* as follows:

PART I GENERAL PROVISIONS

Article 1 Definition of a Subsidy

1.1 For the purpose of this Agreement, a subsidy shall be deemed to exist if:

(a)(1) there is a financial contribution by a government or any public body within the territory of a Member (referred to in this Agreement as "government"), i.e. where:

(i) a government practice involves a direct transfer of funds (e.g. grants, loans, and equity infusion), potential direct transfers of funds or liabilities (e.g. loan guarantees);

(ii) government revenue that is otherwise due is foregone or not collected (e.g. fiscal incentives such as tax credits)[1];

(iii) a government provides goods or services other than general infrastructure, or purchases goods;

(iv) a government makes payments to a funding mechanism, or entrusts or directs a private body to carry out one or more of the type of functions illustrated in (i) to (iii) above which would normally be vested in the government and the practice, in no real sense, differs from practices normally followed by governments;

or

(a)(2) there is any form of income or price support in the sense of Article XVI of GATT 1994; and

(b) a benefit is thereby conferred.

1.2 A subsidy as defined in paragraph 1 shall be subject to the provisions of Part II or shall be subject to the provisions of Part III or V only if such a subsidy is specific in accordance with the provisions of Article 2.

Article 2 Specificity

2.1 In order to determine whether a subsidy, as defined in paragraph 1 of Article 1, is specific to an enterprise or industry or group of enterprises or industries (referred to in this Agreement as "certain enterprises") within the jurisdiction of the granting authority, the following principles shall apply:

(a) Where the granting authority, or the legislation pursuant to which the granting authority operates, explicitly limits access to a subsidy to certain enterprises, such subsidy shall be specific.

---

1 In accordance with the provisions of Article XVI of GATT 1994 (Note to Article XVI) and the provisions of Annexes I through III of this Agreement, the exemption of an exported product from duties or taxes borne by the like product when destined for domestic consumption, or the remission of such duties or taxes in amounts not in excess of those which have accrued, shall not be deemed to be a subsidy.

   (b) Where the granting authority, or the legislation pursuant to which the granting authority operates, establishes objective criteria or conditions[2] governing the eligibility for, and the amount of, a subsidy, specificity shall not exist, provided that the eligibility is automatic and that such criteria and conditions are strictly adhered to. The criteria or conditions must be clearly spelled out in law, regulation, or other official document, so as to be capable of verification.

   (c) If, notwithstanding any appearance of non-specificity resulting from the application of the principles laid down in subparagraphs (a) and (b), there are reasons to believe that the subsidy may in fact be specific, other factors may be considered. Such factors are: use of a subsidy programme by a limited number of certain enterprises, predominant use by certain enterprises, the granting of disproportionately large amounts of subsidy to certain enterprises, and the manner in which discretion has been exercised by the granting authority in the decision to grant a subsidy.[3] In applying this subparagraph, account shall be taken of the extent of diversification of economic activities within the jurisdiction of the granting authority, as well as of the length of time during which the subsidy programme has been in operation.

2.2 A subsidy which is limited to certain enterprises located within a designated geographical region within the jurisdiction of the granting authority shall be specific. It is understood that the setting or change of generally applicable tax rates by all levels of government entitled to do so shall not be deemed to be a specific subsidy for the purposes of this Agreement.

2.3 Any subsidy falling under the provisions of Article 3 shall be deemed to be specific.

2.4 Any determination of specificity under the provisions of this Article shall be clearly substantiated on the basis of positive evidence.

PART II   PROHIBITED SUBSIDIES

Article 3   Prohibition

3.1 Except as provided in the Agreement on Agriculture, the following subsidies, within the meaning of Article 1, shall be prohibited:

   (a) subsidies contingent, in law or in fact[4], whether solely or as one of several other conditions, upon export performance, including those illustrated in Annex I[5];

   (b) subsidies contingent, whether solely or as one of several other conditions, upon the use of domestic over imported goods.

3.2 A Member shall neither grant nor maintain subsidies referred to in paragraph 1.

Article 4   Remedies

4.1 Whenever a Member has reason to believe that a prohibited subsidy is being granted or maintained by another Member, such Member may request consultations with such other Member.

4.2 A request for consultations under paragraph 1 shall include a statement of available evidence with regard to the existence and nature of the subsidy in question.

4.3 Upon request for consultations under paragraph 1, the Member believed to be granting or maintaining the subsidy in question shall enter into such consultations as quickly as possible.

---

2 Objective criteria or conditions, as used herein, mean criteria or conditions which are neutral, which do not favour certain enterprises over others, and which are economic in nature and horizontal in application, such as number of employees or size of enterprise.

3 In this regard, in particular, information on the frequency with which applications for a subsidy are refused or approved and the reasons for such decisions shall be considered.

4 This standard is met when the facts demonstrate that the granting of a subsidy, without having been made legally contingent upon export performance, is in fact tied to actual or anticipated exportation or export earnings. The mere fact that a subsidy is granted to enterprises which export shall not for that reason alone be considered to be an export subsidy within the meaning of this provision.

5 Measures referred to in Annex I as not constituting export subsidies shall not be prohibited under this or any other provision of this Agreement.

The purpose of the consultations shall be to clarify the facts of the situation and to arrive at a mutually agreed solution.

4.4 If no mutually agreed solution has been reached within 30 days[6] of the request for consultations, any Member party to such consultations may refer the matter to the Dispute Settlement Body ("DSB") for the immediate establishment of a panel, unless the DSB decides by consensus not to establish a panel.

4.5 Upon its establishment, the panel may request the assistance of the Permanent Group of Experts[7] (referred to in this Agreement as the "PGE") with regard to whether the measure in question is a prohibited subsidy. If so requested, the PGE shall immediately review the evidence with regard to the existence and nature of the measure in question and shall provide an opportunity for the Member applying or maintaining the measure to demonstrate that the measure in question is not a prohibited subsidy. The PGE shall report its conclusions to the panel within a time-limit determined by the panel. The PGE's conclusions on the issue of whether or not the measure in question is a prohibited subsidy shall be accepted by the panel without modification.

4.6 The panel shall submit its final report to the parties to the dispute. The report shall be circulated to all Members within 90 days of the date of the composition and the establishment of the panel's terms of reference.

4.7 If the measure in question is found to be a prohibited subsidy, the panel shall recommend that the subsidizing Member withdraw the subsidy without delay. In this regard, the panel shall specify in its recommendation the time-period within which the measure must be withdrawn.

4.8 Within 30 days of the issuance of the panel's report to all Members, the report shall be adopted by the DSB unless one of the parties to the dispute formally notifies the DSB of its decision to appeal or the DSB decides by consensus not to adopt the report.

4.9 Where a panel report is appealed, the Appellate Body shall issue its decision within 30 days from the date when the party to the dispute formally notifies its intention to appeal. When the Appellate Body considers that it cannot provide its report within 30 days, it shall inform the DSB in writing of the reasons for the delay together with an estimate of the period within which it will submit its report. In no case shall the proceedings exceed 60 days. The appellate report shall be adopted by the DSB and unconditionally accepted by the parties to the dispute unless the DSB decides by consensus not to adopt the appellate report within 20 days following its issuance to the Members.[8]

4.10 In the event the recommendation of the DSB is not followed within the time-period specified by the panel, which shall commence from the date of adoption of the panel's report or the Appellate Body's report, the DSB shall grant authorization to the complaining Member to take appropriate[9] countermeasures, unless the DSB decides by consensus to reject the request.

4.11 In the event a party to the dispute requests arbitration under paragraph 6 of Article 22 of the Dispute Settlement Understanding ("DSU"), the arbitrator shall determine whether the countermeasures are appropriate.[10]

4.12 For purposes of disputes conducted pursuant to this Article, except for time-periods specifically prescribed in this Article, time-periods applicable under the DSU for the conduct of such disputes shall be half the time prescribed therein.

---

6 Any time-periods mentioned in this Article may be extended by mutual agreement.

7 As established in Article 24.

8 If a meeting of the DSB is not scheduled during this period, such a meeting shall be held for this purpose.

9 This expression is not meant to allow countermeasures that are disproportionate in light of the fact that the subsidies dealt with under these provisions are prohibited.

10 This expression is not meant to allow countermeasures that are disproportionate in light of the fact that the subsidies dealt with under these provisions are prohibited.

PART III ACTIONABLE SUBSIDIES

Article 5 Adverse Effects

No Member should cause, through the use of any subsidy referred to in paragraphs 1 and 2 of Article 1, adverse effects to the interests of other Members, i.e.:

(a) injury to the domestic industry of another Member[11];

(b) nullification or impairment of benefits accruing directly or indirectly to other Members under GATT 1994 in particular the benefits of concessions bound under Article II of GATT 1994[12];

(c) serious prejudice to the interests of another Member.[13]

This Article does not apply to subsidies maintained on agricultural products as provided in Article 13 of the Agreement on Agriculture.

Article 6 Serious Prejudice

6.1 Serious prejudice in the sense of paragraph (c) of Article 5 shall be deemed to exist in the case of:

    (a) the total ad valorem subsidization[14] of a product exceeding 5 per cent[15];

    (b) subsidies to cover operating losses sustained by an industry;

    (c) subsidies to cover operating losses sustained by an enterprise, other than one-time measures which are non-recurrent and cannot be repeated for that enterprise and which are given merely to provide time for the development of long-term solutions and to avoid acute social problems;

    (d) direct forgiveness of debt, i.e. forgiveness of government-held debt, and grants to cover debt repayment.[16]

6.2 Notwithstanding the provisions of paragraph 1, serious prejudice shall not be found if the subsidizing Member demonstrates that the subsidy in question has not resulted in any of the effects enumerated in paragraph 3.

6.3 Serious prejudice in the sense of paragraph (c) of Article 5 may arise in any case where one or several of the following apply:

    (a) the effect of the subsidy is to displace or impede the imports of a like product of another Member into the market of the subsidizing Member;

    (b) the effect of the subsidy is to displace or impede the exports of a like product of another Member from a third country market;

    (c) the effect of the subsidy is a significant price undercutting by the subsidized product as compared with the price of a like product of another Member in the same market or significant price suppression, price depression or lost sales in the same market;

    (d) the effect of the subsidy is an increase in the world market share of the subsidizing Member in a particular subsidized primary product or commodity[17] as compared to the average share it had during the previous period of three years and this increase follows a consistent trend over a period when subsidies have been granted.

---

11 The term "injury to the domestic industry" is used here in the same sense as it is used in Part V.

12 The term "nullification or impairment" is used in this Agreement in the same sense as it is used in the relevant provisions of GATT 1994, and the existence of such nullification or impairment shall be established in accordance with the practice of application of these provisions.

13 The term "serious prejudice to the interests of another Member" is used in this Agreement in the same sense as it is used in paragraph 1 of Article XVI of GATT 1994, and includes threat of serious prejudice.

14 The total ad valorem subsidization shall be calculated in accordance with the provisions of Annex IV.

15 Since it is anticipated that civil aircraft will be subject to specific multilateral rules, the threshold in this subparagraph does not apply to civil aircraft.

16 Members recognize that where royalty-based financing for a civil aircraft programme is not being fully repaid due to the level of actual sales falling below the level of forecast sales, this does not in itself constitute serious prejudice for the purposes of this subparagraph.

17 Unless other multilaterally agreed specific rules apply to the trade in the product or commodity in question.

6.4 For the purpose of paragraph 3(b), the displacement or impeding of exports shall include any case in which, subject to the provisions of paragraph 7, it has been demonstrated that there has been a change in relative shares of the market to the disadvantage of the non-subsidized like product (over an appropriately representative period sufficient to demonstrate clear trends in the development of the market for the product concerned, which, in normal circumstances, shall be at least one year). "Change in relative shares of the market" shall include any of the following situations: *(a)* there is an increase in the market share of the subsidized product; *(b)* the market share of the subsidized product remains constant in circumstances in which, in the absence of the subsidy, it would have declined; *(c)* the market share of the subsidized product declines, but at a slower rate than would have been the case in the absence of the subsidy.

6.5 For the purpose of paragraph 3(c), price undercutting shall include any case in which such price undercutting has been demonstrated through a comparison of prices of the subsidized product with prices of a non-subsidized like product supplied to the same market. The comparison shall be made at the same level of trade and at comparable times, due account being taken of any other factor affecting price comparability. However, if such a direct comparison is not possible, the existence of price undercutting may be demonstrated on the basis of export unit values.

6.6 Each Member in the market of which serious prejudice is alleged to have arisen shall, subject to the provisions of paragraph 3 of Annex V, make available to the parties to a dispute arising under Article 7, and to the panel established pursuant to paragraph 4 of Article 7, all relevant information that can be obtained as to the changes in market shares of the parties to the dispute as well as concerning prices of the products involved.

6.7 Displacement or impediment resulting in serious prejudice shall not arise under paragraph 3 where any of the following circumstances exist[18] during the relevant period:
   (a) prohibition or restriction on exports of the like product from the complaining Member or on imports from the complaining Member into the third country market concerned;
   (b) decision by an importing government operating a monopoly of trade or state trading in the product concerned to shift, for non-commercial reasons, imports from the complaining Member to another country or countries;
   (c) natural disasters, strikes, transport disruptions or other *force majeure* substantially affecting production, qualities, quantities or prices of the product available for export from the complaining Member;
   (d) existence of arrangements limiting exports from the complaining Member;
   (e) voluntary decrease in the availability for export of the product concerned from the complaining Member (including, *inter alia*, a situation where firms in the complaining Member have been autonomously reallocating exports of this product to new markets);
   (f) failure to conform to standards and other regulatory requirements in the importing country.

6.8 In the absence of circumstances referred to in paragraph 7, the existence of serious prejudice should be determined on the basis of the information submitted to or obtained by the panel, including information submitted in accordance with the provisions of Annex V.

6.9 This Article does not apply to subsidies maintained on agricultural products as provided in Article 13 of the Agreement on Agriculture.

Article 7   Remedies

7.1 Except as provided in Article 13 of the Agreement on Agriculture, whenever a Member has reason to believe that any subsidy referred to in Article 1, granted or maintained by another

---

18 The fact that certain circumstances are referred to in this paragraph does not, in itself, confer upon them any legal status in terms of either GATT 1994 or this Agreement. These circumstances must not be isolated, sporadic or otherwise insignificant.

Member, results in injury to its domestic industry, nullification or impairment or serious prejudice, such Member may request consultations with such other Member.

7.2 A request for consultations under paragraph 1 shall include a statement of available evidence with regard to *(a)* the existence and nature of the subsidy in question, and *(b)* the injury caused to the domestic industry, or the nullification or impairment, or serious prejudice[19] caused to the interests of the Member requesting consultations.

7.3 Upon request for consultations under paragraph 1, the Member believed to be granting or maintaining the subsidy practice in question shall enter into such consultations as quickly as possible. The purpose of the consultations shall be to clarify the facts of the situation and to arrive at a mutually agreed solution.

7.4 If consultations do not result in a mutually agreed solution within 60 days[20], any Member party to such consultations may refer the matter to the DSB for the establishment of a panel, unless the DSB decides by consensus not to establish a panel. The composition of the panel and its terms of reference shall be established within 15 days from the date when it is established.

7.5 The panel shall review the matter and shall submit its final report to the parties to the dispute. The report shall be circulated to all Members within 120 days of the date of the composition and establishment of the panel's terms of reference.

7.6 Within 30 days of the issuance of the panel's report to all Members, the report shall be adopted by the DSB[21] unless one of the parties to the dispute formally notifies the DSB of its decision to appeal or the DSB decides by consensus not to adopt the report.

7.7 Where a panel report is appealed, the Appellate Body shall issue its decision within 60 days from the date when the party to the dispute formally notifies its intention to appeal. When the Appellate Body considers that it cannot provide its report within 60 days, it shall inform the DSB in writing of the reasons for the delay together with an estimate of the period within which it will submit its report. In no case shall the proceedings exceed 90 days. The appellate report shall be adopted by the DSB and unconditionally accepted by the parties to the dispute unless the DSB decides by consensus not to adopt the appellate report within 20 days following its issuance to the Members.[22]

7.8 Where a panel report or an Appellate Body report is adopted in which it is determined that any subsidy has resulted in adverse effects to the interests of another Member within the meaning of Article 5, the Member granting or maintaining such subsidy shall take appropriate steps to remove the adverse effects or shall withdraw the subsidy.

7.9 In the event the Member has not taken appropriate steps to remove the adverse effects of the subsidy or withdraw the subsidy within six months from the date when the DSB adopts the panel report or the Appellate Body report, and in the absence of agreement on compensation, the DSB shall grant authorization to the complaining Member to take countermeasures, commensurate with the degree and nature of the adverse effects determined to exist, unless the DSB decides by consensus to reject the request.

7.10 In the event that a party to the dispute requests arbitration under paragraph 6 of Article 22 of the DSU, the arbitrator shall determine whether the countermeasures are commensurate with the degree and nature of the adverse effects determined to exist.

---

19 In the event that the request relates to a subsidy deemed to result in serious prejudice in terms of paragraph 1 of Article 6, the available evidence of serious prejudice may be limited to the available evidence as to whether the conditions of paragraph 1 of Article 6 have been met or not.

20 Any time-periods mentioned in this Article may be extended by mutual agreement.

21 If a meeting of the DSB is not scheduled during this period, such a meeting shall be held for this purpose.

22 If a meeting of the DSB is not scheduled during this period, such a meeting shall be held for this purpose.

PART IV   NON-ACTIONABLE SUBSIDIES

Article 8   Identification of Non-Actionable Subsidies

8.1 The following subsidies shall be considered as non-actionable[23]:

    (a) subsidies which are not specific within the meaning of Article 2;

    (b) subsidies which are specific within the meaning of Article 2 but which meet all of the conditions provided for in paragraphs 2(a), 2(b) or 2(c) below.

8.2 Notwithstanding the provisions of Parts III and V, the following subsidies shall be non-actionable:

    (a) assistance for research activities conducted by firms or by higher education or research establishments on a contract basis with firms if:[24,25,26]

        the assistance covers[27] not more than 75 per cent of the costs of industrial research[28] or 50 per cent of the costs of pre-competitive development activity[29,30]; and provided that such assistance is limited exclusively to:

        (i) costs of personnel (researchers, technicians and other supporting staff employed exclusively in the research activity);

        (ii) costs of instruments, equipment, land and buildings used exclusively and permanently (except when disposed of on a commercial basis) for the research activity;

        (iii) costs of consultancy and equivalent services used exclusively for the research activity, including bought-in research, technical knowledge, patents, etc.;

        (iv) additional overhead costs incurred directly as a result of the research activity;

        (v) other running costs (such as those of materials, supplies and the like), incurred directly as a result of the research activity.

    (b) assistance to disadvantaged regions within the territory of a Member given pursuant to a general framework of regional development[31] and non-specific (within the meaning of Article 2) within eligible regions provided that:

        (i) each disadvantaged region must be a clearly designated contiguous geographical area with a definable economic and administrative identity;

---

23 It is recognized that government assistance for various purposes is widely provided by Members and that the mere fact that such assistance may not qualify for non-actionable treatment under the provisions of this Article does not in itself restrict the ability of Members to provide such assistance.

24 Since it is anticipated that civil aircraft will be subject to specific multilateral rules, the provisions of this subparagraph do not apply to that product.

25 Not later than 18 months after the date of entry into force of the WTO Agreement, the Committee on Subsidies and Countervailing Measures provided for in Article 24 (referred to in this Agreement as "the Committee") shall review the operation of the provisions of subparagraph 2(a) with a view to making all necessary modifications to improve the operation of these provisions. In its consideration of possible modifications, the Committee shall carefully review the definitions of the categories set forth in this subparagraph in the light of the experience of Members in the operation of research programmes and the work in other relevant international institutions.

26 The provisions of this Agreement do not apply to fundamental research activities independently conducted by higher education or research establishments. The term "fundamental research" means an enlargement of general scientific and technical knowledge not linked to industrial or commercial objectives.

27 The allowable levels of non-actionable assistance referred to in this subparagraph shall be established by reference to the total eligible costs incurred over the duration of an individual project.

28 The term "industrial research" means planned search or critical investigation aimed at discovery of new knowledge, with the objective that such knowledge may be useful in developing new products, processes or services, or in bringing about a significant improvement to existing products, processes or services.

29 The term "pre-competitive development activity" means the translation of industrial research findings into a plan, blueprint or design for new, modified or improved products, processes or services whether intended for sale or use, including the creation of a first prototype which would not be capable of commercial use. It may further include the conceptual formulation and design of products, processes or services alternatives and initial demonstration or pilot projects, provided that these same projects cannot be converted or used for industrial application or commercial exploitation. It does not include routine or periodic alterations to existing products, production lines, manufacturing processes, services, and other on-going operations even though those alterations may represent improvements.

30 In the case of programmes which span industrial research and pre-competitive development activity, the allowable level of non-actionable assistance shall not exceed the simple average of the allowable levels of non-actionable assistance applicable to the above two categories, calculated on the basis of all eligible costs as set forth in items (i) to (v) of this subparagraph.

31 A "general framework of regional development" means that regional subsidy programmes are part of an internally consistent and generally applicable regional development policy and that regional development subsidies are not granted in isolated geographical points having no, or virtually no, influence on the development of a region.

(ii) the region is considered as disadvantaged on the basis of neutral and objective criteria[32], indicating that the region's difficulties arise out of more than temporary circumstances; such criteria must be clearly spelled out in law, regulation, or other official document, so as to be capable of verification;

(iii) the criteria shall include a measurement of economic development which shall be based on at least one of the following factors:

- one of either income per capita or household income per capita, or GDP per capita, which must not be above 85 per cent of the average for the territory concerned;

- unemployment rate, which must be at least 110 per cent of the average for the territory concerned;

as measured over a three-year period; such measurement, however, may be a composite one and may include other factors.

(c) assistance to promote adaptation of existing facilities[33] to new environmental requirements imposed by law and/or regulations which result in greater constraints and financial burden on firms, provided that the assistance:

(i) is a one-time non-recurring measure; and

(ii) is limited to 20 per cent of the cost of adaptation; and

(iii) does not cover the cost of replacing and operating the assisted investment, which must be fully borne by firms; and

(iv) is directly linked to and proportionate to a firm's planned reduction of nuisances and pollution, and does not cover any manufacturing cost savings which may be achieved; and

(v) is available to all firms which can adopt the new equipment and/or production processes.

8.3 A subsidy programme for which the provisions of paragraph 2 are invoked shall be notified in advance of its implementation to the Committee in accordance with the provisions of Part VII. Any such notification shall be sufficiently precise to enable other Members to evaluate the consistency of the programme with the conditions and criteria provided for in the relevant provisions of paragraph 2. Members shall also provide the Committee with yearly updates of such notifications, in particular by supplying information on global expenditure for each programme, and on any modification of the programme. Other Members shall have the right to request information about individual cases of subsidization under a notified programme.[34]

8.4 Upon request of a Member, the Secretariat shall review a notification made pursuant to paragraph 3 and, where necessary, may require additional information from the subsidizing Member concerning the notified programme under review. The Secretariat shall report its findings to the Committee. The Committee shall, upon request, promptly review the findings of the Secretariat (or, if a review by the Secretariat has not been requested, the notification itself), with a view to determining whether the conditions and criteria laid down in paragraph 2 have not been met. The procedure provided for in this paragraph shall be completed at the latest at the first regular meeting of the Committee following the

---

32 "Neutral and objective criteria" means criteria which do not favour certain regions beyond what is appropriate for the elimination or reduction of regional disparities within the framework of the regional development policy. In this regard, regional subsidy programmes shall include ceilings on the amount of assistance which can be granted to each subsidized project. Such ceilings must be differentiated according to the different levels of development of assisted regions and must be expressed in terms of investment costs or cost of job creation. Within such ceilings, the distribution of assistance shall be sufficiently broad and even to avoid the predominant use of a subsidy by, or the granting of disproportionately large amounts of subsidy to, certain enterprises as provided for in Article 2.

33 The term "existing facilities" means facilities which have been in operation for at least two years at the time when new environmental requirements are imposed.

34 It is recognized that nothing in this notification provision requires the provision of confidential information, including confidential business information.

notification of a subsidy programme, provided that at least two months have elapsed between such notification and the regular meeting of the Committee. The review procedure described in this paragraph shall also apply, upon request, to substantial modifications of a programme notified in the yearly updates referred to in paragraph 3.

8.5 Upon the request of a Member, the determination by the Committee referred to in paragraph 4, or a failure by the Committee to make such a determination, as well as the violation, in individual cases, of the conditions set out in a notified programme, shall be submitted to binding arbitration. The arbitration body shall present its conclusions to the Members within 120 days from the date when the matter was referred to the arbitration body. Except as otherwise provided in this paragraph, the DSU shall apply to arbitrations conducted under this paragraph.

Article 9   Consultations and Authorized Remedies

9.1 If, in the course of implementation of a programme referred to in paragraph 2 of Article 8, notwithstanding the fact that the programme is consistent with the criteria laid down in that paragraph, a Member has reasons to believe that this programme has resulted in serious adverse effects to the domestic industry of that Member, such as to cause damage which would be difficult to repair, such Member may request consultations with the Member granting or maintaining the subsidy.

9.2 Upon request for consultations under paragraph 1, the Member granting or maintaining the subsidy programme in question shall enter into such consultations as quickly as possible. The purpose of the consultations shall be to clarify the facts of the situation and to arrive at a mutually acceptable solution.

9.3 If no mutually acceptable solution has been reached in consultations under paragraph 2 within 60 days of the request for such consultations, the requesting Member may refer the matter to the Committee.

9.4 Where a matter is referred to the Committee, the Committee shall immediately review the facts involved and the evidence of the effects referred to in paragraph 1. If the Committee determines that such effects exist, it may recommend to the subsidizing Member to modify this programme in such a way as to remove these effects. The Committee shall present its conclusions within 120 days from the date when the matter is referred to it under paragraph 3. In the event the recommendation is not followed within six months, the Committee shall authorize the requesting Member to take appropriate countermeasures commensurate with the nature and degree of the effects determined to exist.

PART V   COUNTERVAILING MEASURES

Article 10   Application of Article VI of GATT 1994[35]

Members shall take all necessary steps to ensure that the imposition of a countervailing duty[36] on any product of the territory of any Member imported into the territory of another Member is in accordance with the provisions of Article VI of GATT 1994 and the terms of this Agreement.

---

35 The provisions of Part II or III may be invoked in parallel with the provisions of Part V; however, with regard to the effects of a particular subsidy in the domestic market of the importing Member, only one form of relief (either a countervailing duty, if the requirements of Part V are met, or a countermeasure under Articles 4 or 7) shall be available. The provisions of Parts III and V shall not be invoked regarding measures considered non-actionable in accordance with the provisions of Part IV. However, measures referred to in paragraph 1(a) of Article 8 may be investigated in order to determine whether or not they are specific within the meaning of Article 2. In addition, in the case of a subsidy referred to in paragraph 2 of Article 8 conferred pursuant to a programme which has not been notified in accordance with paragraph 3 of Article 8, the provisions of Part III or V may be invoked, but such subsidy shall be treated as non-actionable if it is found to conform to the standards set forth in paragraph 2 of Article 8.

36 The term "countervailing duty" shall be understood to mean a special duty levied for the purpose of offsetting any subsidy bestowed directly or indirectly upon the manufacture, production or export of any merchandise, as provided for in paragraph 3 of Article VI of GATT 1994.

Countervailing duties may only be imposed pursuant to investigations initiated[37] and conducted in accordance with the provisions of this Agreement and the Agreement on Agriculture.

Article 11   Initiation and Subsequent Investigation

11.1 Except as provided in paragraph 6, an investigation to determine the existence, degree and effect of any alleged subsidy shall be initiated upon a written application by or on behalf of the domestic industry.

11.2 An application under paragraph 1 shall include sufficient evidence of the existence of *(a)* a subsidy and, if possible, its amount, *(b)* injury within the meaning of Article VI of GATT 1994 as interpreted by this Agreement, and *(c)* a causal link between the subsidized imports and the alleged injury. Simple assertion, unsubstantiated by relevant evidence, cannot be considered sufficient to meet the requirements of this paragraph. The application shall contain such information as is reasonably available to the applicant on the following:

   (i)   the identity of the applicant and a description of the volume and value of the domestic production of the like product by the applicant. Where a written application is made on behalf of the domestic industry, the application shall identify the industry on behalf of which the application is made by a list of all known domestic producers of the like product (or associations of domestic producers of the like product) and, to the extent possible, a description of the volume and value of domestic production of the like product accounted for by such producers;

   (ii) a complete description of the allegedly subsidized product, the names of the country or countries of origin or export in question, the identity of each known exporter or foreign producer and a list of known persons importing the product in question;

   (iii) evidence with regard to the existence, amount and nature of the subsidy in question;

   (iv) evidence that alleged injury to a domestic industry is caused by subsidized imports through the effects of the subsidies; this evidence includes information on the evolution of the volume of the allegedly subsidized imports, the effect of these imports on prices of the like product in the domestic market and the consequent impact of the imports on the domestic industry, as demonstrated by relevant factors and indices having a bearing on the state of the domestic industry, such as those listed in paragraphs 2 and 4 of Article 15.

11.3 The authorities shall review the accuracy and adequacy of the evidence provided in the application to determine whether the evidence is sufficient to justify the initiation of an investigation.

11.4 An investigation shall not be initiated pursuant to paragraph 1 unless the authorities have determined, on the basis of an examination of the degree of support for, or opposition to, the application expressed[38] by domestic producers of the like product, that the application has been made by or on behalf of the domestic industry.[39] The application shall be considered to have been made "by or on behalf of the domestic industry" if it is supported by those domestic producers whose collective output constitutes more than 50 per cent of the total production of the like product produced by that portion of the domestic industry expressing either support for or opposition to the application. However, no investigation shall be initiated when domestic producers expressly supporting the application account for less than 25 per cent of total production of the like product produced by the domestic industry.

---

37 The term "initiated" as used hereinafter means procedural action by which a Member formally commences an investigation as provided in Article 11.

38 In the case of fragmented industries involving an exceptionally large number of producers, authorities may determine support and opposition by using statistically valid sampling techniques.

39 Members are aware that in the territory of certain Members employees of domestic producers of the like product or representatives of those employees may make or support an application for an investigation under paragraph 1.

11.5 The authorities shall avoid, unless a decision has been made to initiate an investigation, any publicizing of the application for the initiation of an investigation.

11.6 If, in special circumstances, the authorities concerned decide to initiate an investigation without having received a written application by or on behalf of a domestic industry for the initiation of such investigation, they shall proceed only if they have sufficient evidence of the existence of a subsidy, injury and causal link, as described in paragraph 2, to justify the initiation of an investigation.

11.7 The evidence of both subsidy and injury shall be considered simultaneously *(a)* in the decision whether or not to initiate an investigation and *(b)* thereafter, during the course of the investigation, starting on a date not later than the earliest date on which in accordance with the provisions of this Agreement provisional measures may be applied.

11.8 In cases where products are not imported directly from the country of origin but are exported to the importing Member from an intermediate country, the provisions of this Agreement shall be fully applicable and the transaction or transactions shall, for the purposes of this Agreement, be regarded as having taken place between the country of origin and the importing Member.

11.9 An application under paragraph 1 shall be rejected and an investigation shall be terminated promptly as soon as the authorities concerned are satisfied that there is not sufficient evidence of either subsidization or of injury to justify proceeding with the case. There shall be immediate termination in cases where the amount of a subsidy is *de minimis*, or where the volume of subsidized imports, actual or potential, or the injury, is negligible. For the purpose of this paragraph, the amount of the subsidy shall be considered to be *de minimis* if the subsidy is less than 1 per cent ad valorem.

11.10 An investigation shall not hinder the procedures of customs clearance.

11.11 Investigations shall, except in special circumstances, be concluded within one year, and in no case more than 18 months, after their initiation.

Article 12   Evidence

12.1 Interested Members and all interested parties in a countervailing duty investigation shall be given notice of the information which the authorities require and ample opportunity to present in writing all evidence which they consider relevant in respect of the investigation in question.

12.1.1 Exporters, foreign producers or interested Members receiving questionnaires used in a countervailing duty investigation shall be given at least 30 days for reply.[40] Due consideration should be given to any request for an extension of the 30-day period and, upon cause shown, such an extension should be granted whenever practicable.

12.1.2 Subject to the requirement to protect confidential information, evidence presented in writing by one interested Member or interested party shall be made available promptly to other interested Members or interested parties participating in the investigation.

12.1.3 As soon as an investigation has been initiated, the authorities shall provide the full text of the written application received under paragraph 1 of Article 11 to the known exporters[41] and to the authorities of the exporting Member and shall make it available,

---

[40] As a general rule, the time-limit for exporters shall be counted from the date of receipt of the questionnaire, which for this purpose shall be deemed to have been received one week from the date on which it was sent to the respondent or transmitted to the appropriate diplomatic representatives of the exporting Member or, in the case of a separate customs territory Member of the WTO, an official representative of the exporting territory.

[41] It being understood that where the number of exporters involved is particularly high, the full text of the application should instead be provided only to the authorities of the exporting Member or to the relevant trade association who then should forward copies to the exporters concerned.

upon request, to other interested parties involved. Due regard shall be paid to the protection of confidential information, as provided for in paragraph 4.

12.2. Interested Members and interested parties also shall have the right, upon justification, to present information orally. Where such information is provided orally, the interested Members and interested parties subsequently shall be required to reduce such submissions to writing. Any decision of the investigating authorities can only be based on such information and arguments as were on the written record of this authority and which were available to interested Members and interested parties participating in the investigation, due account having been given to the need to protect confidential information.

12.3 The authorities shall whenever practicable provide timely opportunities for all interested Members and interested parties to see all information that is relevant to the presentation of their cases, that is not confidential as defined in paragraph 4, and that is used by the authorities in a countervailing duty investigation, and to prepare presentations on the basis of this information.

12.4 Any information which is by nature confidential (for example, because its disclosure would be of significant competitive advantage to a competitor or because its disclosure would have a significantly adverse effect upon a person supplying the information or upon a person from whom the supplier acquired the information), or which is provided on a confidential basis by parties to an investigation shall, upon good cause shown, be treated as such by the authorities. Such information shall not be disclosed without specific permission of the party submitting it.[42]

12.4.1 The authorities shall require interested Members or interested parties providing confidential information to furnish non-confidential summaries thereof. These summaries shall be in sufficient detail to permit a reasonable understanding of the substance of the information submitted in confidence. In exceptional circumstances, such Members or parties may indicate that such information is not susceptible of summary. In such exceptional circumstances, a statement of the reasons why summarization is not possible must be provided.

12.4.2 If the authorities find that a request for confidentiality is not warranted and if the supplier of the information is either unwilling to make the information public or to authorize its disclosure in generalized or summary form, the authorities may disregard such information unless it can be demonstrated to their satisfaction from appropriate sources that the information is correct.[43]

12.5 Except in circumstances provided for in paragraph 7, the authorities shall during the course of an investigation satisfy themselves as to the accuracy of the information supplied by interested Members or interested parties upon which their findings are based.

12.6 The investigating authorities may carry out investigations in the territory of other Members as required, provided that they have notified in good time the Member in question and unless that Member objects to the investigation. Further, the investigating authorities may carry out investigations on the premises of a firm and may examine the records of a firm if (a) the firm so agrees and (b) the Member in question is notified and does not object. The procedures set forth in Annex VI shall apply to investigations on the premises of a firm. Subject to the requirement to protect confidential information, the authorities shall make the results of any such investigations available, or shall provide disclosure thereof pursuant

---

42 Members are aware that in the territory of certain Members disclosure pursuant to a narrowly-drawn protective order may be required.

43 Members agree that requests for confidentiality should not be arbitrarily rejected. Members further agree that the investigating authority may request the waiving of confidentiality only regarding information relevant to the proceedings.

to paragraph 8, to the firms to which they pertain and may make such results available to the applicants.

12.7 In cases in which any interested Member or interested party refuses access to, or otherwise does not provide, necessary information within a reasonable period or significantly impedes the investigation, preliminary and final determinations, affirmative or negative, may be made on the basis of the facts available.

12.8 The authorities shall, before a final determination is made, inform all interested Members and interested parties of the essential facts under consideration which form the basis for the decision whether to apply definitive measures. Such disclosure should take place in sufficient time for the parties to defend their interests.

12.9 For the purposes of this Agreement, "interested parties" shall include:
   (i) an exporter or foreign producer or the importer of a product subject to investigation, or a trade or business association a majority of the members of which are producers, exporters or importers of such product; and
   (ii) a producer of the like product in the importing Member or a trade and business association a majority of the members of which produce the like product in the territory of the importing Member.
   This list shall not preclude Members from allowing domestic or foreign parties other than those mentioned above to be included as interested parties.

12.10 The authorities shall provide opportunities for industrial users of the product under investigation, and for representative consumer organizations in cases where the product is commonly sold at the retail level, to provide information which is relevant to the investigation regarding subsidization, injury and causality.

12.11 The authorities shall take due account of any difficulties experienced by interested parties, in particular small companies, in supplying information requested, and shall provide any assistance practicable.

12.12 The procedures set out above are not intended to prevent the authorities of a Member from proceeding expeditiously with regard to initiating an investigation, reaching preliminary or final determinations, whether affirmative or negative, or from applying provisional or final measures, in accordance with relevant provisions of this Agreement.

Article 13   Consultations

13.1 As soon as possible after an application under Article 11 is accepted, and in any event before the initiation of any investigation, Members the products of which may be subject to such investigation shall be invited for consultations with the aim of clarifying the situation as to the matters referred to in paragraph 2 of Article 11 and arriving at a mutually agreed solution.

13.2 Furthermore, throughout the period of investigation, Members the products of which are the subject of the investigation shall be afforded a reasonable opportunity to continue consultations, with a view to clarifying the factual situation and to arriving at a mutually agreed solution.[44]

13.3 Without prejudice to the obligation to afford reasonable opportunity for consultation, these provisions regarding consultations are not intended to prevent the authorities of a Member from proceeding expeditiously with regard to initiating the investigation, reaching preliminary or final determinations, whether affirmative or negative, or from applying provisional or final measures, in accordance with the provisions of this Agreement.

---

[44] It is particularly important, in accordance with the provisions of this paragraph, that no affirmative determination whether preliminary or final be made without reasonable opportunity for consultations having been given. Such consultations may establish the basis for proceeding under the provisions of Part II, III or X.

13.4 The Member which intends to initiate any investigation or is conducting such an investigation shall permit, upon request, the Member or Members the products of which are subject to such investigation access to non-confidential evidence, including the non-confidential summary of confidential data being used for initiating or conducting the investigation.

Article 14   Calculation of the Amount of a Subsidy in Terms of the Benefit to the Recipient

For the purpose of Part V, any method used by the investigating authority to calculate the benefit to the recipient conferred pursuant to paragraph 1 of Article 1 shall be provided for in the national legislation or implementing regulations of the Member concerned and its application to each particular case shall be transparent and adequately explained. Furthermore, any such method shall be consistent with the following guidelines:

(a) government provision of equity capital shall not be considered as conferring a benefit, unless the investment decision can be regarded as inconsistent with the usual investment practice (including for the provision of risk capital) of private investors in the territory of that Member;

(b) a loan by a government shall not be considered as conferring a benefit, unless there is a difference between the amount that the firm receiving the loan pays on the government loan and the amount the firm would pay on a comparable commercial loan which the firm could actually obtain on the market. In this case the benefit shall be the difference between these two amounts;

(c) a loan guarantee by a government shall not be considered as conferring a benefit, unless there is a difference between the amount that the firm receiving the guarantee pays on a loan guaranteed by the government and the amount that the firm would pay on a comparable commercial loan absent the government guarantee. In this case the benefit shall be the difference between these two amounts adjusted for any differences in fees;

(d) the provision of goods or services or purchase of goods by a government shall not be considered as conferring a benefit unless the provision is made for less than adequate remuneration, or the purchase is made for more than adequate remuneration. The adequacy of remuneration shall be determined in relation to prevailing market conditions for the good or service in question in the country of provision or purchase (including price, quality, availability, marketability, transportation and other conditions of purchase or sale).

Article 15   Determination of Injury[45]

15.1 A determination of injury for purposes of Article VI of GATT 1994 shall be based on positive evidence and involve an objective examination of both *(a)* the volume of the subsidized imports and the effect of the subsidized imports on prices in the domestic market for like products[46] and *(b)* the consequent impact of these imports on the domestic producers of such products.

15.2 With regard to the volume of the subsidized imports, the investigating authorities shall consider whether there has been a significant increase in subsidized imports, either in absolute terms or relative to production or consumption in the importing Member. With regard to the effect of the subsidized imports on prices, the investigating authorities shall consider whether there has been a significant price undercutting by the subsidized imports as compared with the price of a like product of the importing Member, or whether the effect

---

45 Under this Agreement the term "injury" shall, unless otherwise specified, be taken to mean material injury to a domestic industry, threat of material injury to a domestic industry or material retardation of the establishment of such an industry and shall be interpreted in accordance with the provisions of this Article.

46 Throughout this Agreement the term "like product" ("produit similaire") shall be interpreted to mean a product which is identical, i.e. alike in all respects to the product under consideration, or in the absence of such a product, another product which, although not alike in all respects, has characteristics closely resembling those of the product under consideration.

of such imports is otherwise to depress prices to a significant degree or to prevent price increases, which otherwise would have occurred, to a significant degree. No one or several of these factors can necessarily give decisive guidance.

15.3 Where imports of a product from more than one country are simultaneously subject to countervailing duty investigations, the investigating authorities may cumulatively assess the effects of such imports only if they determine that *(a)* the amount of subsidization established in relation to the imports from each country is more than *de minimis* as defined in paragraph 9 of Article 11 and the volume of imports from each country is not negligible and *(b)* a cumulative assessment of the effects of the imports is appropriate in light of the conditions of competition between the imported products and the conditions of competition between the imported products and the like domestic product.

15.4 The examination of the impact of the subsidized imports on the domestic industry shall include an evaluation of all relevant economic factors and indices having a bearing on the state of the industry, including actual and potential decline in output, sales, market share, profits, productivity, return on investments, or utilization of capacity; factors affecting domestic prices; actual and potential negative effects on cash flow, inventories, employment, wages, growth, ability to raise capital or investments and, in the case of agriculture, whether there has been an increased burden on government support programmes. This list is not exhaustive, nor can one or several of these factors necessarily give decisive guidance.

15.5 It must be demonstrated that the subsidized imports are, through the effects[47] of subsidies, causing injury within the meaning of this Agreement. The demonstration of a causal relationship between the subsidized imports and the injury to the domestic industry shall be based on an examination of all relevant evidence before the authorities. The authorities shall also examine any known factors other than the subsidized imports which at the same time are injuring the domestic industry, and the injuries caused by these other factors must not be attributed to the subsidized imports. Factors which may be relevant in this respect include, *inter alia*, the volumes and prices of non-subsidized imports of the product in question, contraction in demand or changes in the patterns of consumption, trade restrictive practices of and competition between the foreign and domestic producers, developments in technology and the export performance and productivity of the domestic industry.

15.6 The effect of the subsidized imports shall be assessed in relation to the domestic production of the like product when available data permit the separate identification of that production on the basis of such criteria as the production process, producers' sales and profits. If such separate identification of that production is not possible, the effects of the subsidized imports shall be assessed by the examination of the production of the narrowest group or range of products, which includes the like product, for which the necessary information can be provided.

15.7 A determination of a threat of material injury shall be based on facts and not merely on allegation, conjecture or remote possibility. The change in circumstances which would create a situation in which the subsidy would cause injury must be clearly foreseen and imminent. In making a determination regarding the existence of a threat of material injury, the investigating authorities should consider, *inter alia*, such factors as:

  (i) nature of the subsidy or subsidies in question and the trade effects likely to arise therefrom;

  (ii) a significant rate of increase of subsidized imports into the domestic market indicating the likelihood of substantially increased importation;

  (iii) sufficient freely disposable, or an imminent, substantial increase in, capacity of the exporter indicating the likelihood of substantially increased subsidized exports to the

---

47 As set forth in paragraphs 2 and 4.

importing Member's market, taking into account the availability of other export markets to absorb any additional exports;

(iv) whether imports are entering at prices that will have a significant depressing or suppressing effect on domestic prices, and would likely increase demand for further imports; and

(v) inventories of the product being investigated.

No one of these factors by itself can necessarily give decisive guidance but the totality of the factors considered must lead to the conclusion that further subsidized exports are imminent and that, unless protective action is taken, material injury would occur.

15.8 With respect to cases where injury is threatened by subsidized imports, the application of countervailing measures shall be considered and decided with special care.

Article 16   Definition of Domestic Industry

16.1 For the purposes of this Agreement, the term "domestic industry" shall, except as provided in paragraph 2, be interpreted as referring to the domestic producers as a whole of the like products or to those of them whose collective output of the products constitutes a major proportion of the total domestic production of those products, except that when producers are related[48] to the exporters or importers or are themselves importers of the allegedly subsidized product or a like product from other countries, the term "domestic industry" may be interpreted as referring to the rest of the producers.

16.2. In exceptional circumstances, the territory of a Member may, for the production in question, be divided into two or more competitive markets and the producers within each market may be regarded as a separate industry if *(a)* the producers within such market sell all or almost all of their production of the product in question in that market, and *(b)* the demand in that market is not to any substantial degree supplied by producers of the product in question located elsewhere in the territory. In such circumstances, injury may be found to exist even where a major portion of the total domestic industry is not injured, provided there is a concentration of subsidized imports into such an isolated market and provided further that the subsidized imports are causing injury to the producers of all or almost all of the production within such market.

16.3 When the domestic industry has been interpreted as referring to the producers in a certain area, i.e. a market as defined in paragraph 2, countervailing duties shall be levied only on the products in question consigned for final consumption to that area. When the constitutional law of the importing Member does not permit the levying of countervailing duties on such a basis, the importing Member may levy the countervailing duties without limitation only if *(a)* the exporters shall have been given an opportunity to cease exporting at subsidized prices to the area concerned or otherwise give assurances pursuant to Article 18, and adequate assurances in this regard have not been promptly given, and *(b)* such duties cannot be levied only on products of specific producers which supply the area in question.

16.4 Where two or more countries have reached under the provisions of paragraph 8(a) of Article XXIV of GATT 1994 such a level of integration that they have the characteristics of a single, unified market, the industry in the entire area of integration shall be taken to be the domestic industry referred to in paragraphs 1 and 2.

16.5 The provisions of paragraph 6 of Article 15 shall be applicable to this Article.

---

48 For the purpose of this paragraph, producers shall be deemed to be related to exporters or importers only if *(a)* one of them directly or indirectly controls the other; or *(b)* both of them are directly or indirectly controlled by a third person; or *(c)* together they directly or indirectly control a third person, provided that there are grounds for believing or suspecting that the effect of the relationship is such as to cause the producer concerned to behave differently from non-related producers. For the purpose of this paragraph, one shall be deemed to control another when the former is legally or operationally in a position to exercise restraint or direction over the latter.

Article 17   Provisional Measures

17.1 Provisional measures may be applied only if:

(a) an investigation has been initiated in accordance with the provisions of Article 11, a public notice has been given to that effect and interested Members and interested parties have been given adequate opportunities to submit information and make comments;

(b) a preliminary affirmative determination has been made that a subsidy exists and that there is injury to a domestic industry caused by subsidized imports; and

(c) the authorities concerned judge such measures necessary to prevent injury being caused during the investigation.

17.2 Provisional measures may take the form of provisional countervailing duties guaranteed by cash deposits or bonds equal to the amount of the provisionally calculated amount of subsidization.

17.3 Provisional measures shall not be applied sooner than 60 days from the date of initiation of the investigation.

17.4 The application of provisional measures shall be limited to as short a period as possible, not exceeding four months.

17.5 The relevant provisions of Article 19 shall be followed in the application of provisional measures.

Article 18   Undertakings

18.1 Proceedings may[49] be suspended or terminated without the imposition of provisional measures or countervailing duties upon receipt of satisfactory voluntary undertakings under which:

(a) the government of the exporting Member agrees to eliminate or limit the subsidy or take other measures concerning its effects; or

(b) the exporter agrees to revise its prices so that the investigating authorities are satisfied that the injurious effect of the subsidy is eliminated. Price increases under such undertakings shall not be higher than necessary to eliminate the amount of the subsidy. It is desirable that the price increases be less than the amount of the subsidy if such increases would be adequate to remove the injury to the domestic industry.

18.2 Undertakings shall not be sought or accepted unless the authorities of the importing Member have made a preliminary affirmative determination of subsidization and injury caused by such subsidization and, in case of undertakings from exporters, have obtained the consent of the exporting Member.

18.3 Undertakings offered need not be accepted if the authorities of the importing Member consider their acceptance impractical, for example if the number of actual or potential exporters is too great, or for other reasons, including reasons of general policy. Should the case arise and where practicable, the authorities shall provide to the exporter the reasons which have led them to consider acceptance of an undertaking as inappropriate, and shall, to the extent possible, give the exporter an opportunity to make comments thereon.

18.4 If an undertaking is accepted, the investigation of subsidization and injury shall nevertheless be completed if the exporting Member so desires or the importing Member so decides. In such a case, if a negative determination of subsidization or injury is made, the undertaking shall automatically lapse, except in cases where such a determination is due in large part to the existence of an undertaking. In such cases, the authorities concerned may require that an undertaking be maintained for a reasonable period consistent with the provisions of this Agreement. In the event that an affirmative determination of subsidization and injury is

---

[49] The word "may" shall not be interpreted to allow the simultaneous continuation of proceedings with the implementation of undertakings, except as provided in paragraph 4.

made, the undertaking shall continue consistent with its terms and the provisions of this Agreement.

18.5 Price undertakings may be suggested by the authorities of the importing Member, but no exporter shall be forced to enter into such undertakings. The fact that governments or exporters do not offer such undertakings, or do not accept an invitation to do so, shall in no way prejudice the consideration of the case. However, the authorities are free to determine that a threat of injury is more likely to be realized if the subsidized imports continue.

18.6 Authorities of an importing Member may require any government or exporter from whom an undertaking has been accepted to provide periodically information relevant to the fulfilment of such an undertaking, and to permit verification of pertinent data. In case of violation of an undertaking, the authorities of the importing Member may take, under this Agreement in conformity with its provisions, expeditious actions which may constitute immediate application of provisional measures using the best information available. In such cases, definitive duties may be levied in accordance with this Agreement on products entered for consumption not more than 90 days before the application of such provisional measures, except that any such retroactive assessment shall not apply to imports entered before the violation of the undertaking.

Article 19   Imposition and Collection of Countervailing Duties

19.1 If, after reasonable efforts have been made to complete consultations, a Member makes a final determination of the existence and amount of the subsidy and that, through the effects of the subsidy, the subsidized imports are causing injury, it may impose a countervailing duty in accordance with the provisions of this Article unless the subsidy or subsidies are withdrawn.

19.2 The decision whether or not to impose a countervailing duty in cases where all requirements for the imposition have been fulfilled, and the decision whether the amount of the countervailing duty to be imposed shall be the full amount of the subsidy or less, are decisions to be made by the authorities of the importing Member. It is desirable that the imposition should be permissive in the territory of all Members, that the duty should be less than the total amount of the subsidy if such lesser duty would be adequate to remove the injury to the domestic industry, and that procedures should be established which would allow the authorities concerned to take due account of representations made by domestic interested parties[50] whose interests might be adversely affected by the imposition of a countervailing duty.

19.3 When a countervailing duty is imposed in respect of any product, such countervailing duty shall be levied, in the appropriate amounts in each case, on a non-discriminatory basis on imports of such product from all sources found to be subsidized and causing injury, except as to imports from those sources which have renounced any subsidies in question or from which undertakings under the terms of this Agreement have been accepted. Any exporter whose exports are subject to a definitive countervailing duty but who was not actually investigated for reasons other than a refusal to cooperate, shall be entitled to an expedited review in order that the investigating authorities promptly establish an individual countervailing duty rate for that exporter.

19.4 No countervailing duty shall be levied[51] on any imported product in excess of the amount of the subsidy found to exist, calculated in terms of subsidization per unit of the subsidized and exported product.

---

50 For the purpose of this paragraph, the term "domestic interested parties" shall include consumers and industrial users of the imported product subject to investigation.

51 As used in this Agreement "levy" shall mean the definitive or final legal assessment or collection of a duty or tax.

Article 20 Retroactivity

20.1 Provisional measures and countervailing duties shall only be applied to products which enter for consumption after the time when the decision under paragraph 1 of Article 17 and paragraph 1 of Article 19, respectively, enters into force, subject to the exceptions set out in this Article.

20.2 Where a final determination of injury (but not of a threat thereof or of a material retardation of the establishment of an industry) is made or, in the case of a final determination of a threat of injury, where the effect of the subsidized imports would, in the absence of the provisional measures, have led to a determination of injury, counter-vailing duties may be levied retroactively for the period for which provisional measures, if any, have been applied.

20.3 If the definitive countervailing duty is higher than the amount guaranteed by the cash deposit or bond, the difference shall not be collected. If the definitive duty is less than the amount guaranteed by the cash deposit or bond, the excess amount shall be reimbursed or the bond released in an expeditious manner.

20.4 Except as provided in paragraph 2, where a determination of threat of injury or material retardation is made (but no injury has yet occurred) a definitive countervailing duty may be imposed only from the date of the determination of threat of injury or material retardation, and any cash deposit made during the period of the application of provisional measures shall be refunded and any bonds released in an expeditious manner.

20.5 Where a final determination is negative, any cash deposit made during the period of the application of provisional measures shall be refunded and any bonds released in an expeditious manner.

20.6 In critical circumstances where for the subsidized product in question the authorities find that injury which is difficult to repair is caused by massive imports in a relatively short period of a product benefiting from subsidies paid or bestowed inconsistently with the provisions of GATT 1994 and of this Agreement and where it is deemed necessary, in order to preclude the recurrence of such injury, to assess countervailing duties retroactively on those imports, the definitive countervailing duties may be assessed on imports which were entered for consumption not more than 90 days prior to the date of application of provisional measures.

Article 21 Duration and Review of Countervailing Duties and Undertakings

21.1 A countervailing duty shall remain in force only as long as and to the extent necessary to counteract subsidization which is causing injury.

21.2 The authorities shall review the need for the continued imposition of the duty, where warranted, on their own initiative or, provided that a reasonable period of time has elapsed since the imposition of the definitive countervailing duty, upon request by any interested party which submits positive information substantiating the need for a review. Interested parties shall have the right to request the authorities to examine whether the continued imposition of the duty is necessary to offset subsidization, whether the injury would be likely to continue or recur if the duty were removed or varied, or both. If, as a result of the review under this paragraph, the authorities determine that the countervailing duty is no longer warranted, it shall be terminated immediately.

21.3 Notwithstanding the provisions of paragraphs 1 and 2, any definitive countervailing duty shall be terminated on a date not later than five years from its imposition (or from the date of the most recent review under paragraph 2 if that review has covered both subsidization and injury, or under this paragraph), unless the authorities determine, in a review initiated before that date on their own initiative or upon a duly substantiated request made by or on behalf of the domestic industry within a reasonable period of time prior to that date, that the expiry of the duty would be likely to lead to continuation or recurrence of subsidization and injury.[52] The duty may remain in force pending the outcome of such a review.

21.4 The provisions of Article 12 regarding evidence and procedure shall apply to any review carried out under this Article. Any such review shall be carried out expeditiously and shall normally be concluded within 12 months of the date of initiation of the review.

21.5 The provisions of this Article shall apply *mutatis mutandis* to undertakings accepted under Article 18.

Article 22   Public Notice and Explanation of Determinations

22.1 When the authorities are satisfied that there is sufficient evidence to justify the initiation of an investigation pursuant to Article 11, the Member or Members the products of which are subject to such investigation and other interested parties known to the investigating authorities to have an interest therein shall be notified and a public notice shall be given.

22.2 A public notice of the initiation of an investigation shall contain, or otherwise make available through a separate report[53], adequate information on the following:
   (i)   the name of the exporting country or countries and the product involved;
   (ii) the date of initiation of the investigation;
   (iii) a description of the subsidy practice or practices to be investigated;
   (iv) a summary of the factors on which the allegation of injury is based;
   (v)   the address to which representations by interested Members and interested parties should be directed; and
   (vi) the time-limits allowed to interested Members and interested parties for making their views known.

22.3 Public notice shall be given of any preliminary or final determination, whether affirmative or negative, of any decision to accept an undertaking pursuant to Article 18, of the termination of such an undertaking, and of the termination of a definitive countervailing duty. Each such notice shall set forth, or otherwise make available through a separate report, in sufficient detail the findings and conclusions reached on all issues of fact and law considered material by the investigating authorities. All such notices and reports shall be forwarded to the Member or Members the products of which are subject to such determination or undertaking and to other interested parties known to have an interest therein.

22.4 A public notice of the imposition of provisional measures shall set forth, or otherwise make available through a separate report, sufficiently detailed explanations for the preliminary determinations on the existence of a subsidy and injury and shall refer to the matters of fact and law which have led to arguments being accepted or rejected. Such a notice or report shall, due regard being paid to the requirement for the protection of confidential information, contain in particular:
   (i)   the names of the suppliers or, when this is impracticable, the supplying countries involved;
   (ii) a description of the product which is sufficient for customs purposes;
   (iii) the amount of subsidy established and the basis on which the existence of a subsidy has been determined;
   (iv) considerations relevant to the injury determination as set out in Article 15;
   (v)   the main reasons leading to the determination.

22.5 A public notice of conclusion or suspension of an investigation in the case of an affirmative determination providing for the imposition of a definitive duty or the acceptance of an

---

52 When the amount of the countervailing duty is assessed on a retrospective basis, a finding in the most recent assessment proceeding that no duty is to be levied shall not by itself require the authorities to terminate the definitive duty.

53 Where authorities provide information and explanations under the provisions of this Article in a separate report, they shall ensure that such report is readily available to the public.

undertaking shall contain, or otherwise make available through a separate report, all relevant information on the matters of fact and law and reasons which have led to the imposition of final measures or the acceptance of an undertaking, due regard being paid to the requirement for the protection of confidential information. In particular, the notice or report shall contain the information described in paragraph 4, as well as the reasons for the acceptance or rejection of relevant arguments or claims made by interested Members and by the exporters and importers.

22.6 A public notice of the termination or suspension of an investigation following the acceptance of an undertaking pursuant to Article 18 shall include, or otherwise make available through a separate report, the non-confidential part of this undertaking.

22.7 The provisions of this Article shall apply *mutatis mutandis* to the initiation and completion of reviews pursuant to Article 21 and to decisions under Article 20 to apply duties retroactively.

Article 23   Judicial Review

Each Member whose national legislation contains provisions on countervailing duty measures shall maintain judicial, arbitral or administrative tribunals or procedures for the purpose, *inter alia*, of the prompt review of administrative actions relating to final determinations and reviews of determinations within the meaning of Article 21. Such tribunals or procedures shall be independent of the authorities responsible for the determination or review in question, and shall provide all interested parties who participated in the administrative proceeding and are directly and individually affected by the administrative actions with access to review.

PART VI   INSTITUTIONS

Article 24   Committee on Subsidies and Countervailing Measures and Subsidiary Bodies

24.1 There is hereby established a Committee on Subsidies and Countervailing Measures composed of representatives from each of the Members. The Committee shall elect its own Chairman and shall meet not less than twice a year and otherwise as envisaged by relevant provisions of this Agreement at the request of any Member. The Committee shall carry out responsibilities as assigned to it under this Agreement or by the Members and it shall afford Members the opportunity of consulting on any matter relating to the operation of the Agreement or the furtherance of its objectives. The WTO Secretariat shall act as the secretariat to the Committee.

24.2 The Committee may set up subsidiary bodies as appropriate.

24.3 The Committee shall establish a Permanent Group of Experts composed of five independent persons, highly qualified in the fields of subsidies and trade relations. The experts will be elected by the Committee and one of them will be replaced every year. The PGE may be requested to assist a panel, as provided for in paragraph 5 of Article 4. The Committee may also seek an advisory opinion on the existence and nature of any subsidy.

24.4 The PGE may be consulted by any Member and may give advisory opinions on the nature of any subsidy proposed to be introduced or currently maintained by that Member. Such advisory opinions will be confidential and may not be invoked in proceedings under Article 7.

24.5 In carrying out their functions, the Committee and any subsidiary bodies may consult with and seek information from any source they deem appropriate. However, before the Committee or a subsidiary body seeks such information from a source within the jurisdiction of a Member, it shall inform the Member involved.

PART VII NOTIFICATION AND SURVEILLANCE

Article 25 Notifications

25.1 Members agree that, without prejudice to the provisions of paragraph 1 of Article XVI of GATT 1994, their notifications of subsidies shall be submitted not later than 30 June of each year and shall conform to the provisions of paragraphs 2 through 6.

25.2 Members shall notify any subsidy as defined in paragraph 1 of Article 1, which is specific within the meaning of Article 2, granted or maintained within their territories.

25.3 The content of notifications should be sufficiently specific to enable other Members to evaluate the trade effects and to understand the operation of notified subsidy programmes. In this connection, and without prejudice to the contents and form of the questionnaire on subsidies[54], Members shall ensure that their notifications contain the following information:

(i) form of a subsidy (i.e. grant, loan, tax concession, etc.);

(ii) subsidy per unit or, in cases where this is not possible, the total amount or the annual amount budgeted for that subsidy (indicating, if possible, the average subsidy per unit in the previous year);

(iii) policy objective and/or purpose of a subsidy;

(iv) duration of a subsidy and/or any other time-limits attached to it;

(v) statistical data permitting an assessment of the trade effects of a subsidy.

25.4 Where specific points in paragraph 3 have not been addressed in a notification, an explanation shall be provided in the notification itself.

25.5 If subsidies are granted to specific products or sectors, the notifications should be organized by product or sector.

25.6 Members which consider that there are no measures in their territories requiring notification under paragraph 1 of Article XVI of GATT 1994 and this Agreement shall so inform the Secretariat in writing.

25.7 Members recognize that notification of a measure does not prejudge either its legal status under GATT 1994 and this Agreement, the effects under this Agreement, or the nature of the measure itself.

25.8 Any Member may, at any time, make a written request for information on the nature and extent of any subsidy granted or maintained by another Member (including any subsidy referred to in Part IV), or for an explanation of the reasons for which a specific measure has been considered as not subject to the requirement of notification.

25.9 Members so requested shall provide such information as quickly as possible and in a comprehensive manner, and shall be ready, upon request, to provide additional information to the requesting Member. In particular, they shall provide sufficient details to enable the other Member to assess their compliance with the terms of this Agreement. Any Member which considers that such information has not been provided may bring the matter to the attention of the Committee.

25.10 Any Member which considers that any measure of another Member having the effects of a subsidy has not been notified in accordance with the provisions of paragraph 1 of Article XVI of GATT 1994 and this Article may bring the matter to the attention of such other Member. If the alleged subsidy is not thereafter notified promptly, such Member may itself bring the alleged subsidy in question to the notice of the Committee.

25.11 Members shall report without delay to the Committee all preliminary or final actions taken with respect to countervailing duties. Such reports shall be available in the Secretariat for

---

54 The Committee shall establish a Working Party to review the contents and form of the questionnaire as contained in BISD 9S/193–194.

inspection by other Members. Members shall also submit, on a semi-annual basis, reports on any countervailing duty actions taken within the preceding six months. The semi-annual reports shall be submitted on an agreed standard form.

25.12 Each Member shall notify the Committee *(a)* which of its authorities are competent to initiate and conduct investigations referred to in Article 11 and *(b)* its domestic procedures governing the initiation and conduct of such investigations.

Article 26   Surveillance

26.1 The Committee shall examine new and full notifications submitted under paragraph 1 of Article XVI of GATT 1994 and paragraph 1 of Article 25 of this Agreement at special sessions held every third year. Notifications submitted in the intervening years (updating notifications) shall be examined at each regular meeting of the Committee.

26.2 The Committee shall examine reports submitted under paragraph 11 of Article 25 at each regular meeting of the Committee.

PART VIII   DEVELOPING COUNTRY MEMBERS

Article 27   Special and Differential Treatment of Developing Country Members

27.1 Members recognize that subsidies may play an important role in economic development programmes of developing country Members.

27.2 The prohibition of paragraph 1(a) of Article 3 shall not apply to:
  (a) developing country Members referred to in Annex VII.
  (b) other developing country Members for a period of eight years from the date of entry into force of the WTO Agreement, subject to compliance with the provisions in paragraph 4.

27.3 The prohibition of paragraph 1(b) of Article 3 shall not apply to developing country Members for a period of five years, and shall not apply to least developed country Members for a period of eight years, from the date of entry into force of the WTO Agreement.

27.4 Any developing country Member referred to in paragraph 2(b) shall phase out its export subsidies within the eight-year period, preferably in a progressive manner. However, a developing country Member shall not increase the level of its export subsidies[55], and shall eliminate them within a period shorter than that provided for in this paragraph when the use of such export subsidies is inconsistent with its development needs. If a developing country Member deems it necessary to apply such subsidies beyond the 8-year period, it shall not later than one year before the expiry of this period enter into consultation with the Committee, which will determine whether an extension of this period is justified, after examining all the relevant economic, financial and development needs of the developing country Member in question. If the Committee determines that the extension is justified, the developing country Member concerned shall hold annual consultations with the Committee to determine the necessity of maintaining the subsidies. If no such determination is made by the Committee, the developing country Member shall phase out the remaining export subsidies within two years from the end of the last authorized period.

27.5 A developing country Member which has reached export competitiveness in any given product shall phase out its export subsidies for such product(s) over a period of two years. However, for a developing country Member which is referred to in Annex VII and which has reached export competitiveness in one or more products, export subsidies on such products shall be gradually phased out over a period of eight years.

---

55 For a developing country Member not granting export subsidies as of the date of entry into force of the WTO Agreement, this paragraph shall apply on the basis of the level of export subsidies granted in 1986.

27.6 Export competitiveness in a product exists if a developing country Member's exports of that product have reached a share of at least 3.25 per cent in world trade of that product for two consecutive calendar years. Export competitiveness shall exist either *(a)* on the basis of notification by the developing country Member having reached export competitiveness, or *(b)* on the basis of a computation undertaken by the Secretariat at the request of any Member. For the purpose of this paragraph, a product is defined as a section heading of the Harmonized System Nomenclature. The Committee shall review the operation of this provision five years from the date of the entry into force of the WTO Agreement.

27.7 The provisions of Article 4 shall not apply to a developing country Member in the case of export subsidies which are in conformity with the provisions of paragraphs 2 through 5. The relevant provisions in such a case shall be those of Article 7.

27.8 There shall be no presumption in terms of paragraph 1 of Article 6 that a subsidy granted by a developing country Member results in serious prejudice, as defined in this Agreement. Such serious prejudice, where applicable under the terms of paragraph 9, shall be demonstrated by positive evidence, in accordance with the provisions of paragraphs 3 through 8 of Article 6.

27.9 Regarding actionable subsidies granted or maintained by a developing country Member other than those referred to in paragraph 1 of Article 6, action may not be authorized or taken under Article 7 unless nullification or impairment of tariff concessions or other obligations under GATT 1994 is found to exist as a result of such a subsidy, in such a way as to displace or impede imports of a like product of another Member into the market of the subsidizing developing country Member or unless injury to a domestic industry in the market of an importing Member occurs.

27.10 Any countervailing duty investigation of a product originating in a developing country Member shall be terminated as soon as the authorities concerned determine that:
   (a) the overall level of subsidies granted upon the product in question does not exceed 2 per cent of its value calculated on a per unit basis; or
   (b) the volume of the subsidized imports represents less than 4 per cent of the total imports of the like product in the importing Member, unless imports from developing country Members whose individual shares of total imports represent less than 4 per cent collectively account for more than 9 per cent of the total imports of the like product in the importing Member.

27.11 For those developing country Members within the scope of paragraph 2(b) which have eliminated export subsidies prior to the expiry of the period of eight years from the date of entry into force of the WTO Agreement, and for those developing country Members referred to in Annex VII, the number in paragraph 10(a) shall be 3 per cent rather than 2 per cent. This provision shall apply from the date that the elimination of export subsidies is notified to the Committee, and for so long as export subsidies are not granted by the notifying developing country Member. This provision shall expire eight years from the date of entry into force of the WTO Agreement.

27.12 The provisions of paragraphs 10 and 11 shall govern any determination of *de minimis* under paragraph 3 of Article 15.

27.13 The provisions of Part III shall not apply to direct forgiveness of debts, subsidies to cover social costs, in whatever form, including relinquishment of government revenue and other transfer of liabilities when such subsidies are granted within and directly linked to a privatization programme of a developing country Member, provided that both such programme and the subsidies involved are granted for a limited period and notified to the Committee and that the programme results in eventual privatization of the enterprise concerned.

27.14 The Committee shall, upon request by an interested Member, undertake a review of a specific export subsidy practice of a developing country Member to examine whether the practice is in conformity with its development needs.

27.15 The Committee shall, upon request by an interested developing country Member, undertake a review of a specific countervailing measure to examine whether it is consistent with the provisions of paragraphs 10 and 11 as applicable to the developing country Member in question.

PART IX TRANSITIONAL ARRANGEMENTS

Article 28 Existing Programmes

28.1 Subsidy programmes which have been established within the territory of any Member before the date on which such a Member signed the WTO Agreement and which are inconsistent with the provisions of this Agreement shall be:

(a) notified to the Committee not later than 90 days after the date of entry into force of the WTO Agreement for such Member; and

(b) brought into conformity with the provisions of this Agreement within three years of the date of entry into force of the WTO Agreement for such Member and until then shall not be subject to Part II.

28.2 No Member shall extend the scope of any such programme, nor shall such a programme be renewed upon its expiry.

Article 29 Transformation into a Market Economy

29.1 Members in the process of transformation from a centrally-planned into a market, free-enterprise economy may apply programmes and measures necessary for such a transformation.

29.2 For such Members, subsidy programmes falling within the scope of Article 3, and notified according to paragraph 3, shall be phased out or brought into conformity with Article 3 within a period of seven years from the date of entry into force of the WTO Agreement. In such a case, Article 4 shall not apply. In addition during the same period:

(a) Subsidy programmes falling within the scope of paragraph 1(d) of Article 6 shall not be actionable under Article 7;

(b) With respect to other actionable subsidies, the provisions of paragraph 9 of Article 27 shall apply.

29.3 Subsidy programmes falling within the scope of Article 3 shall be notified to the Committee by the earliest practicable date after the date of entry into force of the WTO Agreement. Further notifications of such subsidies may be made up to two years after the date of entry into force of the WTO Agreement.

29.4 In exceptional circumstances Members referred to in paragraph 1 may be given departures from their notified programmes and measures and their time-frame by the Committee if such departures are deemed necessary for the process of transformation.

PART X DISPUTE SETTLEMENT

Article 30

The provisions of Articles XXII and XXIII of GATT 1994 as elaborated and applied by the Dispute Settlement Understanding shall apply to consultations and the settlement of disputes under this Agreement, except as otherwise specifically provided herein.

PART XI FINAL PROVISIONS

Article 31 Provisional Application

The provisions of paragraph 1 of Article 6 and the provisions of Article 8 and Article 9 shall apply for a period of five years, beginning with the date of entry into force of the WTO Agreement. Not later than 180 days before the end of this period, the Committee shall review the operation of those provisions, with a view to determining whether to extend their application, either as presently drafted or in a modified form, for a further period.

Article 32 Other Final Provisions

32.1 No specific action against a subsidy of another Member can be taken except in accordance with the provisions of GATT 1994, as interpreted by this Agreement.[56]

32.2 Reservations may not be entered in respect of any of the provisions of this Agreement without the consent of the other Members.

32.3 Subject to paragraph 4, the provisions of this Agreement shall apply to investigations, and reviews of existing measures, initiated pursuant to applications which have been made on or after the date of entry into force for a Member of the WTO Agreement.

32.4 For the purposes of paragraph 3 of Article 21, existing countervailing measures shall be deemed to be imposed on a date not later than the date of entry into force for a Member of the WTO Agreement, except in cases in which the domestic legislation of a Member in force at that date already included a clause of the type provided for in that paragraph.

32.5 Each Member shall take all necessary steps, of a general or particular character, to ensure, not later than the date of entry into force of the WTO Agreement for it, the conformity of its laws, regulations and administrative procedures with the provisions of this Agreement as they may apply to the Member in question.

32.6 Each Member shall inform the Committee of any changes in its laws and regulations relevant to this Agreement and in the administration of such laws and regulations.

32.7 The Committee shall review annually the implementation and operation of this Agreement, taking into account the objectives thereof. The Committee shall inform annually the Council for Trade in Goods of developments during the period covered by such reviews.

32.8 The Annexes to this Agreement constitute an integral part thereof.

ANNEX I ILLUSTRATIVE LIST OF EXPORT SUBSIDIES

(a) The provision by governments of direct subsidies to a firm or an industry contingent upon export performance.

(b) Currency retention schemes or any similar practices which involve a bonus on exports.

(c) Internal transport and freight charges on export shipments, provided or mandated by governments, on terms more favourable than for domestic shipments.

(d) The provision by governments or their agencies either directly or indirectly through government-mandated schemes, of imported or domestic products or services for use in the production of exported goods, on terms or conditions more favourable than for provision of like or directly competitive products or services for use in the production of goods for domestic consumption, if (in the case of products) such terms or conditions are more favourable than those commercially available[57] on world markets to their exporters.

---

56 This paragraph is not intended to preclude action under other relevant provisions of GATT 1994, where appropriate.

57 The term "commercially available" means that the choice between domestic and imported products is unrestricted and depends only on commercial considerations.

(e) The full or partial exemption remission, or deferral specifically related to exports, of direct taxes[58] or social welfare charges paid or payable by industrial or commercial enterprises.[59]

(f) The allowance of special deductions directly related to exports or export performance, over and above those granted in respect to production for domestic consumption, in the calculation of the base on which direct taxes are charged.

(g) The exemption or remission, in respect of the production and distribution of exported products, of indirect taxes[58] in excess of those levied in respect of the production and distribution of like products when sold for domestic consumption.

(h) The exemption, remission or deferral of prior-stage cumulative indirect taxes[58] on goods or services used in the production of exported products in excess of the exemption, remission or deferral of like prior-stage cumulative indirect taxes on goods or services used in the production of like products when sold for domestic consumption; provided, however, that prior-stage cumulative indirect taxes may be exempted, remitted or deferred on exported products even when not exempted, remitted or deferred on like products when sold for domestic consumption, if the prior-stage cumulative indirect taxes are levied on inputs that are consumed in the production of the exported product (making normal allowance for waste).[60] This item shall be interpreted in accordance with the guidelines on consumption of inputs in the production process contained in Annex II.

(i) The remission or drawback of import charges[58] in excess of those levied on imported inputs that are consumed in the production of the exported product (making normal allowance for waste); provided, however, that in particular cases a firm may use a quantity of home market inputs equal to, and having the same quality and characteristics as, the imported inputs as a substitute for them in order to benefit from this provision if the import and the corresponding export operations both occur within a reasonable time period, not to exceed two years. This item shall be interpreted in accordance with the guidelines on consumption of inputs in the production process contained in Annex II and the guidelines in the determination of substitution drawback systems as export subsidies contained in Annex III.

(j) The provision by governments (or special institutions controlled by governments) of export credit guarantee or insurance programmes, of insurance or guarantee programmes against increases in the cost of exported products or of exchange risk programmes, at premium rates which are inadequate to cover the long-term operating costs and losses of the programmes.

(k) The grant by governments (or special institutions controlled by and/or acting under the authority of governments) of export credits at rates below those which they actually have to

---

58 For the purpose of this Agreement:

The term "direct taxes" shall mean taxes on wages, profits, interests, rents, royalties, and all other forms of income, and taxes on the ownership of real property;

The term "import charges" shall mean tariffs, duties, and other fiscal charges not elsewhere enumerated in this note that are levied on imports;

The term "indirect taxes" shall mean sales, excise, turnover, value added, franchise, stamp, transfer, inventory and equipment taxes, border taxes and all taxes other than direct taxes and import charges;

"Prior-stage" indirect taxes are those levied on goods or services used directly or indirectly in making the product;

"Cumulative" indirect taxes are multi-staged taxes levied where there is no mechanism for subsequent crediting of the tax if the goods or services subject to tax at one stage of production are used in a succeeding stage of production;

"Remission" of taxes includes the refund or rebate of taxes;

"Remission or drawback" includes the full or partial exemption or deferral of import charges.

59 The Members recognize that deferral need not amount to an export subsidy where, for example, appropriate interest charges are collected. The Members reaffirm the principle that prices for goods in transactions between exporting enterprises and foreign buyers under their or under the same control should for tax purposes be the prices which would be charged between independent enterprises acting at arm's length. Any Member may draw the attention of another Member to administrative or other practices which may contravene this principle and which result in a significant saving of direct taxes in export transactions. In such circumstances the Members shall normally attempt to resolve their differences using the facilities of existing bilateral tax treaties or other specific international mechanisms, without prejudice to the rights and obligations of Members under GATT 1994, including the right of consultation created in the preceding sentence.

Paragraph (e) is not intended to limit a Member from taking measures to avoid the double taxation of foreign-source income earned by its enterprises or the enterprises of another Member.

60 Paragraph (h) does not apply to value-added tax systems and border-tax adjustment in lieu thereof; the problem of the excessive remission of value-added taxes is exclusively covered by paragraph (g).

pay for the funds so employed (or would have to pay if they borrowed on international capital markets in order to obtain funds of the same maturity and other credit terms and denominated in the same currency as the export credit), or the payment by them of all or part of the costs incurred by exporters or financial institutions in obtaining credits, in so far as they are used to secure a material advantage in the field of export credit terms.

Provided, however, that if a Member is a party to an international undertaking on official export credits to which at least twelve original Members to this Agreement are parties as of 1 January 1979 (or a successor undertaking which has been adopted by those original Members), or if in practice a Member applies the interest rates provisions of the relevant undertaking, an export credit practice which is in conformity with those provisions shall not be considered an export subsidy prohibited by this Agreement.

(l) Any other charge on the public account constituting an export subsidy in the sense of Article XVI of GATT 1994.

ANNEX II GUIDELINES ON CONSUMPTION OF INPUTS IN THE PRODUCTION PROCESS[61]

I

1. Indirect tax rebate schemes can allow for exemption, remission or deferral of prior-stage cumulative indirect taxes levied on inputs that are consumed in the production of the exported product (making normal allowance for waste). Similarly, drawback schemes can allow for the remission or drawback of import charges levied on inputs that are consumed in the production of the exported product (making normal allowance for waste).

2. The Illustrative List of Export Subsidies in Annex I of this Agreement makes reference to the term "inputs that are consumed in the production of the exported product" in paragraphs (h) and (i). Pursuant to paragraph (h), indirect tax rebate schemes can constitute an export subsidy to the extent that they result in exemption, remission or deferral of prior-stage cumulative indirect taxes in excess of the amount of such taxes actually levied on inputs that are consumed in the production of the exported product. Pursuant to paragraph (i), drawback schemes can constitute an export subsidy to the extent that they result in a remission or drawback of import charges in excess of those actually levied on inputs that are consumed in the production of the exported product. Both paragraphs stipulate that normal allowance for waste must be made in findings regarding consumption of inputs in the production of the exported product. Paragraph (i) also provides for substitution, where appropriate.

II

In examining whether inputs are consumed in the production of the exported product, as part of a countervailing duty investigation pursuant to this Agreement, investigating authorities should proceed on the following basis:

1. Where it is alleged that an indirect tax rebate scheme, or a drawback scheme, conveys a subsidy by reason of over-rebate or excess drawback of indirect taxes or import charges on inputs consumed in the production of the exported product, the investigating authorities should first determine whether the government of the exporting Member has in place and applies a system or procedure to confirm which inputs are consumed in the production of the exported product and in what amounts. Where such a system or procedure is determined to be applied, the investigating authorities should then examine the system or procedure to see whether it is reasonable, effective for the purpose intended, and based on generally accepted

---

61 Inputs consumed in the production process are inputs physically incorporated, energy, fuels and oil used in the production process and catalysts which are consumed in the course of their use to obtain the exported product.

commercial practices in the country of export. The investigating authorities may deem it necessary to carry out, in accordance with paragraph 6 of Article 12, certain practical tests in order to verify information or to satisfy themselves that the system or procedure is being effectively applied.

2. Where there is no such system or procedure, where it is not reasonable, or where it is instituted and considered reasonable but is found not to be applied or not to be applied effectively, a further examination by the exporting Member based on the actual inputs involved would need to be carried out in the context of determining whether an excess payment occurred. If the investigating authorities deemed it necessary, a further examination would be carried out in accordance with paragraph 1.

3. Investigating authorities should treat inputs as physically incorporated if such inputs are used in the production process and are physically present in the product exported. The Members note that an input need not be present in the final product in the same form in which it entered the production process.

4. In determining the amount of a particular input that is consumed in the production of the exported product, a "normal allowance for waste" should be taken into account, and such waste should be treated as consumed in the production of the exported product. The term "waste" refers to that portion of a given input which does not serve an independent function in the production process, is not consumed in the production of the exported product (for reasons such as inefficiencies) and is not recovered, used or sold by the same manufacturer.

5. The investigating authority's determination of whether the claimed allowance for waste is "normal" should take into account the production process, the average experience of the industry in the country of export, and other technical factors, as appropriate. The investigating authority should bear in mind that an important question is whether the authorities in the exporting Member have reasonably calculated the amount of waste, when such an amount is intended to be included in the tax or duty rebate or remission.

ANNEX III   GUIDELINES IN THE DETERMINATION OF SUBSTITUTION DRAWBACK SYSTEMS AS EXPORT SUBSIDIES

I

Drawback systems can allow for the refund or drawback of import charges on inputs which are consumed in the production process of another product and where the export of this latter product contains domestic inputs having the same quality and characteristics as those substituted for the imported inputs. Pursuant to paragraph (i) of the Illustrative List of Export Subsidies in Annex I, substitution drawback systems can constitute an export subsidy to the extent that they result in an excess drawback of the import charges levied initially on the imported inputs for which drawback is being claimed.

II

In examining any substitution drawback system as part of a countervailing duty investigation pursuant to this Agreement, investigating authorities should proceed on the following basis:

1. Paragraph (i) of the Illustrative List stipulates that home market inputs may be substituted for imported inputs in the production of a product for export provided such inputs are equal in quantity to, and have the same quality and characteristics as, the imported inputs being substituted. The existence of a verification system or procedure is important because it enables the government of the exporting Member to ensure and demonstrate that the quantity of inputs for which drawback is claimed does not exceed the quantity of similar products exported, in whatever form, and that there is not drawback of import charges in excess of those originally levied on the imported inputs in question.

2. Where it is alleged that a substitution drawback system conveys a subsidy, the investigating authorities should first proceed to determine whether the government of the exporting Member has in place and applies a verification system or procedure. Where such a system or procedure is determined to be applied, the investigating authorities should then examine the verification procedures to see whether they are reasonable, effective for the purpose intended, and based on generally accepted commercial practices in the country of export. To the extent that the procedures are determined to meet this test and are effectively applied, no subsidy should be presumed to exist. It may be deemed necessary by the investigating authorities to carry out, in accordance with paragraph 6 of Article 12, certain practical tests in order to verify information or to satisfy themselves that the verification procedures are being effectively applied.

3. Where there are no verification procedures, where they are not reasonable, or where such procedures are instituted and considered reasonable but are found not to be actually applied or not applied effectively, there may be a subsidy. In such cases a further examination by the exporting Member based on the actual transactions involved would need to be carried out to determine whether an excess payment occurred. If the investigating authorities deemed it necessary, a further examination would be carried out in accordance with paragraph 2.

4. The existence of a substitution drawback provision under which exporters are allowed to select particular import shipments on which drawback is claimed should not of itself be considered to convey a subsidy.

5. An excess drawback of import charges in the sense of paragraph (i) would be deemed to exist where governments paid interest on any monies refunded under their drawback schemes, to the extent of the interest actually paid or payable.

ANNEX IV CALCULATION OF THE TOTAL AD VALOREM SUBSIDIZATION (PARAGRAPH 1(A) OF ARTICLE 6)[62]

1. Any calculation of the amount of a subsidy for the purpose of paragraph 1(a) of Article 6 shall be done in terms of the cost to the granting government.

2. Except as provided in paragraphs 3 through 5, in determining whether the overall rate of subsidization exceeds 5 per cent of the value of the product, the value of the product shall be calculated as the total value of the recipient firm's[63] sales in the most recent 12-month period, for which sales data is available, preceding the period in which the subsidy is granted.[64]

3. Where the subsidy is tied to the production or sale of a given product, the value of the product shall be calculated as the total value of the recipient firm's sales of that product in the most recent 12-month period, for which sales data is available, preceding the period in which the subsidy is granted.

4. Where the recipient firm is in a start-up situation, serious prejudice shall be deemed to exist if the overall rate of subsidization exceeds 15 per cent of the total funds invested. For purposes of this paragraph, a start-up period will not extend beyond the first year of production.[65]

5. Where the recipient firm is located in an inflationary economy country, the value of the product shall be calculated as the recipient firm's total sales (or sales of the relevant product, if

---

62 An understanding among Members should be developed, as necessary, on matters which are not specified in this Annex or which need further clarification for the purposes of paragraph 1(a) of Article 6.

63 The recipient firm is a firm in the territory of the subsidizing Member.

64 In the case of tax-related subsidies the value of the product shall be calculated as the total value of the recipient firm's sales in the fiscal year in which the tax-related measure was earned.

65 Start-up situations include instances where financial commitments for product development or construction of facilities to manufacture products benefiting from the subsidy have been made, even though production has not begun.

the subsidy is tied) in the preceding calendar year indexed by the rate of inflation experienced in the 12 months preceding the month in which the subsidy is to be given.

6. In determining the overall rate of subsidization in a given year, subsidies given under different programmes and by different authorities in the territory of a Member shall be aggregated.

7. Subsidies granted prior to the date of entry into force of the WTO Agreement, the benefits of which are allocated to future production, shall be included in the overall rate of subsidization.

8. Subsidies which are non-actionable under relevant provisions of this Agreement shall not be included in the calculation of the amount of a subsidy for the purpose of paragraph 1(a) of Article 6.

ANNEX V   PROCEDURES FOR DEVELOPING INFORMATION CONCERNING SERIOUS PREJUDICE

1. Every Member shall cooperate in the development of evidence to be examined by a panel in procedures under paragraphs 4 through 6 of Article 7. The parties to the dispute and any third-country Member concerned shall notify to the DSB, as soon as the provisions of paragraph 4 of Article 7 have been invoked, the organization responsible for administration of this provision within its territory and the procedures to be used to comply with requests for information.

2. In cases where matters are referred to the DSB under paragraph 4 of Article 7, the DSB shall, upon request, initiate the procedure to obtain such information from the government of the subsidizing Member as necessary to establish the existence and amount of subsidization, the value of total sales of the subsidized firms, as well as information necessary to analyze the adverse effects caused by the subsidized product.[66] This process may include, where appropriate, presentation of questions to the government of the subsidizing Member and of the complaining Member to collect information, as well as to clarify and obtain elaboration of information available to the parties to a dispute through the notification procedures set forth in Part VII.[67]

3. In the case of effects in third-country markets, a party to a dispute may collect information, including through the use of questions to the government of the third-country Member, necessary to analyse adverse effects, which is not otherwise reasonably available from the complaining Member or the subsidizing Member. This requirement should be administered in such a way as not to impose an unreasonable burden on the third-country Member. In particular, such a Member is not expected to make a market or price analysis specially for that purpose. The information to be supplied is that which is already available or can be readily obtained by this Member (e.g. most recent statistics which have already been gathered by relevant statistical services but which have not yet been published, customs data concerning imports and declared values of the products concerned, etc.). However, if a party to a dispute undertakes a detailed market analysis at its own expense, the task of the person or firm conducting such an analysis shall be facilitated by the authorities of the third-country Member and such a person or firm shall be given access to all information which is not normally maintained confidential by the government.

4. The DSB shall designate a representative to serve the function of facilitating the information-gathering process. The sole purpose of the representative shall be to ensure the timely development of the information necessary to facilitate expeditious subsequent multilateral

---

66 In cases where the existence of serious prejudice has to be demonstrated.

67 The information-gathering process by the DSB shall take into account the need to protect information which is by nature confidential or which is provided on a confidential basis by any Member involved in this process.

review of the dispute. In particular, the representative may suggest ways to most efficiently solicit necessary information as well as encourage the cooperation of the parties.

5. The information-gathering process outlined in paragraphs 2 through 4 shall be completed within 60 days of the date on which the matter has been referred to the DSB under paragraph 4 of Article 7. The information obtained during this process shall be submitted to the panel established by the DSB in accordance with the provisions of Part X. This information should include, *inter alia*, data concerning the amount of the subsidy in question (and, where appropriate, the value of total sales of the subsidized firms), prices of the subsidized product, prices of the non-subsidized product, prices of other suppliers to the market, changes in the supply of the subsidized product to the market in question and changes in market shares. It should also include rebuttal evidence, as well as such supplemental information as the panel deems relevant in the course of reaching its conclusions.

6. If the subsidizing and/or third-country Member fail to cooperate in the information-gathering process, the complaining Member will present its case of serious prejudice, based on evidence available to it, together with facts and circumstances of the non-cooperation of the subsidizing and/or third-country Member. Where information is unavailable due to non-cooperation by the subsidizing and/or third-country Member, the panel may complete the record as necessary relying on best information otherwise available.

7. In making its determination, the panel should draw adverse inferences from instances of non-cooperation by any party involved in the information-gathering process.

8. In making a determination to use either best information available or adverse inferences, the panel shall consider the advice of the DSB representative nominated under paragraph 4 as to the reasonableness of any requests for information and the efforts made by parties to comply with these requests in a cooperative and timely manner.

9. Nothing in the information-gathering process shall limit the ability of the panel to seek such additional information it deems essential to a proper resolution to the dispute, and which was not adequately sought or developed during that process. However, ordinarily the panel should not request additional information to complete the record where the information would support a particular party's position and the absence of that information in the record is the result of unreasonable non-cooperation by that party in the information-gathering process.

ANNEX VI   PROCEDURES FOR ON-THE-SPOT INVESTIGATIONS PURSUANT TO PARAGRAPH 6 OF ARTICLE 12

1. Upon initiation of an investigation, the authorities of the exporting Member and the firms known to be concerned should be informed of the intention to carry out on-the-spot investigations.

2. If in exceptional circumstances it is intended to include non-governmental experts in the investigating team, the firms and the authorities of the exporting Member should be so informed. Such non-governmental experts should be subject to effective sanctions for breach of confidentiality requirements.

3. It should be standard practice to obtain explicit agreement of the firms concerned in the exporting Member before the visit is finally scheduled.

4. As soon as the agreement of the firms concerned has been obtained, the investigating authorities should notify the authorities of the exporting Member of the names and addresses of the firms to be visited and the dates agreed.

5. Sufficient advance notice should be given to the firms in question before the visit is made.

6. Visits to explain the questionnaire should only be made at the request of an exporting firm. In case of such a request the investigating authorities may place themselves at the disposal of the

firm; such a visit may only be made if *(a)* the authorities of the importing Member notify the representatives of the government of the Member in question and *(b)* the latter do not object to the visit.

7. As the main purpose of the on-the-spot investigation is to verify information provided or to obtain further details, it should be carried out after the response to the questionnaire has been received unless the firm agrees to the contrary and the government of the exporting Member is informed by the investigating authorities of the anticipated visit and does not object to it; further, it should be standard practice prior to the visit to advise the firms concerned of the general nature of the information to be verified and of any further information which needs to be provided, though this should not preclude requests to be made on the spot for further details to be provided in the light of information obtained.

8. Enquiries or questions put by the authorities or firms of the exporting Members and essential to a successful on-the-spot investigation should, whenever possible, be answered before the visit is made.

ANNEX VII   DEVELOPING COUNTRY MEMBERS REFERRED TO IN PARAGRAPH 2(A) OF ARTICLE 27

The developing country Members not subject to the provisions of paragraph 1(a) of Article 3 under the terms of paragraph 2(a) of Article 27 are:

(a) Least-developed countries designated as such by the United Nations which are Members of the WTO.

(b) Each of the following developing countries which are Members of the WTO shall be subject to the provisions which are applicable to other developing country Members according to paragraph 2(b) of Article 27 when GNP per capita has reached $1,000 per annum[68]: Bolivia, Cameroon, Congo, Côte d'Ivoire, Dominican Republic, Egypt, Ghana, Guatemala, Guyana, India, Indonesia, Kenya, Morocco, Nicaragua, Nigeria, Pakistan, Philippines, Senegal, Sri Lanka and Zimbabwe.

---

[68] The inclusion of developing country Members in the list in paragraph (b) is based on the most recent data from the World Bank on GNP per capita.

II-15

Agreement on Safeguards

Members,

Having in mind the overall objective of the Members to improve and strengthen the international trading system based on GATT 1994;

Recognizing the need to clarify and reinforce the disciplines of GATT 1994, and specifically those of its Article XIX (Emergency Action on Imports of Particular Products), to re-establish multilateral control over safeguards and eliminate measures that escape such control;

Recognizing the importance of structural adjustment and the need to enhance rather than limit competition in international markets; and

Recognizing further that, for these purposes, a comprehensive agreement, applicable to all Members and based on the basic principles of GATT 1994, is called for;

Hereby agree as follows:

Article 1   General Provision

This Agreement establishes rules for the application of safeguard measures which shall be understood to mean those measures provided for in Article XIX of GATT 1994.

Article 2   Conditions

1. A Member[1] may apply a safeguard measure to a product only if that Member has determined, pursuant to the provisions set out below, that such product is being imported into its territory in such increased quantities, absolute or relative to domestic production, and under such conditions as to cause or threaten to cause serious injury to the domestic industry that produces like or directly competitive products.

2. Safeguard measures shall be applied to a product being imported irrespective of its source.

Article 3   Investigation

1. A Member may apply a safeguard measure only following an investigation by the competent authorities of that Member pursuant to procedures previously established and made public in consonance with Article X of GATT 1994. This investigation shall include reasonable public notice to all interested parties and public hearings or other appropriate means in which importers, exporters and other interested parties could present evidence and their views, including the opportunity to respond to the presentations of other parties and to submit their views, *inter alia*, as to whether or not the application of a safeguard measure would be in the public interest. The competent authorities shall publish a report setting forth their findings and reasoned conclusions reached on all pertinent issues of fact and law.

2. Any information which is by nature confidential or which is provided on a confidential basis shall, upon cause being shown, be treated as such by the competent authorities. Such information shall not be disclosed without permission of the party submitting it. Parties providing confidential information may be requested to furnish non-confidential summaries thereof or, if such parties indicate that such information cannot be summarized, the reasons why a summary cannot be provided. However, if the competent authorities find that a request

---

1 A customs union may apply a safeguard measure as a single unit or on behalf of a member State. When a customs union applies a safeguard measure as a single unit, all the requirements for the determination of serious injury or threat thereof under this Agreement shall be based on the conditions existing in the customs union as a whole. When a safeguard measure is applied on behalf of a member State, all the requirements for the determination of serious injury or threat thereof shall be based on the conditions existing in that member State and the measure shall be limited to that member State. Nothing in this Agreement prejudges the interpretation of the relationship between Article XIX and paragraph 8 of Article XXIV of GATT 1994.

for confidentiality is not warranted and if the party concerned is either unwilling to make the information public or to authorize its disclosure in generalized or summary form, the authorities may disregard such information unless it can be demonstrated to their satisfaction from appropriate sources that the information is correct.

Article 4   Determination of Serious Injury or Threat Thereof

1. For the purposes of this Agreement:

    (a) "serious injury" shall be understood to mean a significant overall impairment in the position of a domestic industry;

    (b) "threat of serious injury" shall be understood to mean serious injury that is clearly imminent, in accordance with the provisions of paragraph 2. A determination of the existence of a threat of serious injury shall be based on facts and not merely on allegation, conjecture or remote possibility; and

    (c) in determining injury or threat thereof, a "domestic industry" shall be understood to mean the producers as a whole of the like or directly competitive products operating within the territory of a Member, or those whose collective output of the like or directly competitive products constitutes a major proportion of the total domestic production of those products.

2. (a) In the investigation to determine whether increased imports have caused or are threatening to cause serious injury to a domestic industry under the terms of this Agreement, the competent authorities shall evaluate all relevant factors of an objective and quantifiable nature having a bearing on the situation of that industry, in particular, the rate and amount of the increase in imports of the product concerned in absolute and relative terms, the share of the domestic market taken by increased imports, changes in the level of sales, production, productivity, capacity utilization, profits and losses, and employment.

    (b) The determination referred to in subparagraph (a) shall not be made unless this investigation demonstrates, on the basis of objective evidence, the existence of the causal link between increased imports of the product concerned and serious injury or threat thereof. When factors other than increased imports are causing injury to the domestic industry at the same time, such injury shall not be attributed to increased imports.

    (c) The competent authorities shall publish promptly, in accordance with the provisions of Article 3, a detailed analysis of the case under investigation as well as a demonstration of the relevance of the factors examined.

Article 5   Application of Safeguard Measures

1. A Member shall apply safeguard measures only to the extent necessary to prevent or remedy serious injury and to facilitate adjustment. If a quantitative restriction is used, such a measure shall not reduce the quantity of imports below the level of a recent period which shall be the average of imports in the last three representative years for which statistics are available, unless clear justification is given that a different level is necessary to prevent or remedy serious injury. Members should choose measures most suitable for the achievement of these objectives.

2. (a) In cases in which a quota is allocated among supplying countries, the Member applying the restrictions may seek agreement with respect to the allocation of shares in the quota with all other Members having a substantial interest in supplying the product concerned. In cases in which this method is not reasonably practicable, the Member concerned shall allot to Members having a substantial interest in supplying the product shares based upon the proportions, supplied by such Members during a previous representative period, of the total quantity or value of imports of the product, due account being taken of any special factors which may have affected or may be affecting the trade in the product.

    (b) A Member may depart from the provisions in subparagraph (a) provided that consultations under paragraph 3 of Article 12 are conducted under the auspices of the Committee on Safeguards provided for in paragraph 1 of Article 13 and that clear demonstration is provided to the Committee that (*i*) imports from certain Members have increased in disproportionate percentage in relation to the total increase of imports of the product concerned in the representative period, (*ii*) the reasons for the departure from the provisions in subparagraph (a) are justified, and (*iii*) the conditions of such departure are equitable to all suppliers of the product concerned. The duration of any such measure shall not be extended beyond the initial period under paragraph 1 of Article 7. The departure referred to above shall not be permitted in the case of threat of serious injury.

Article 6   Provisional Safeguard Measures

In critical circumstances where delay would cause damage which it would be difficult to repair, a Member may take a provisional safeguard measure pursuant to a preliminary determination that there is clear evidence that increased imports have caused or are threatening to cause serious injury. The duration of the provisional measure shall not exceed 200 days, during which period the pertinent requirements of Articles 2 through 7 and 12 shall be met. Such measures should take the form of tariff increases to be promptly refunded if the subsequent investigation referred to in paragraph 2 of Article 4 does not determine that increased imports have caused or threatened to cause serious injury to a domestic industry. The duration of any such provisional measure shall be counted as a part of the initial period and any extension referred to in paragraphs 1, 2 and 3 of Article 7.

Article 7   Duration and Review of Safeguard Measures

1. A Member shall apply safeguard measures only for such period of time as may be necessary to prevent or remedy serious injury and to facilitate adjustment. The period shall not exceed four years, unless it is extended under paragraph 2.

2. The period mentioned in paragraph 1 may be extended provided that the competent authorities of the importing Member have determined, in conformity with the procedures set out in Articles 2, 3, 4 and 5, that the safeguard measure continues to be necessary to prevent or remedy serious injury and that there is evidence that the industry is adjusting, and provided that the pertinent provisions of Articles 8 and 12 are observed.

3. The total period of application of a safeguard measure including the period of application of any provisional measure, the period of initial application and any extension thereof, shall not exceed eight years.

4. In order to facilitate adjustment in a situation where the expected duration of a safeguard measure as notified under the provisions of paragraph 1 of Article 12 is over one year, the Member applying the measure shall progressively liberalize it at regular intervals during the period of application. If the duration of the measure exceeds three years, the Member applying such a measure shall review the situation not later than the mid-term of the measure and, if appropriate, withdraw it or increase the pace of liberalization. A measure extended under paragraph 2 shall not be more restrictive than it was at the end of the initial period, and should continue to be liberalized.

5. No safeguard measure shall be applied again to the import of a product which has been subject to such a measure, taken after the date of entry into force of the WTO Agreement, for a period of time equal to that during which such measure had been previously applied, provided that the period of non-application is at least two years.

6. Notwithstanding the provisions of paragraph 5, a safeguard measure with a duration of 180 days or less may be applied again to the import of a product if:
   (a) at least one year has elapsed since the date of introduction of a safeguard measure on the import of that product; and
   (b) such a safeguard measure has not been applied on the same product more than twice in the five-year period immediately preceding the date of introduction of the measure.

Article 8   Level of Concessions and Other Obligations

1. A Member proposing to apply a safeguard measure or seeking an extension of a safeguard measure shall endeavour to maintain a substantially equivalent level of concessions and other obligations to that existing under GATT 1994 between it and the exporting Members which would be affected by such a measure, in accordance with the provisions of paragraph 3 of Article 12. To achieve this objective, the Members concerned may agree on any adequate means of trade compensation for the adverse effects of the measure on their trade.

2. If no agreement is reached within 30 days in the consultations under paragraph 3 of Article 12, then the affected exporting Members shall be free, not later than 90 days after the measure is applied, to suspend, upon the expiration of 30 days from the day on which written notice of such suspension is received by the Council for Trade in Goods, the application of substantially equivalent concessions or other obligations under GATT 1994, to the trade of the Member applying the safeguard measure, the suspension of which the Council for Trade in Goods does not disapprove.

3. The right of suspension referred to in paragraph 2 shall not be exercised for the first three years that a safeguard measure is in effect, provided that the safeguard measure has been taken as a result of an absolute increase in imports and that such a measure conforms to the provisions of this Agreement.

Article 9   Developing Country Members

1. Safeguard measures shall not be applied against a product originating in a developing country Member as long as its share of imports of the product concerned in the importing Member does not exceed 3 per cent, provided that developing country Members with less than 3 per cent import share collectively account for not more than 9 per cent of total imports of the product concerned.[2]

2. A developing country Member shall have the right to extend the period of application of a safeguard measure for a period of up to two years beyond the maximum period provided for in paragraph 3 of Article 7. Notwithstanding the provisions of paragraph 5 of Article 7, a developing country Member shall have the right to apply a safeguard measure again to the import of a product which has been subject to such a measure, taken after the date of entry into force of the WTO Agreement, after a period of time equal to half that during which such a measure has been previously applied, provided that the period of non-application is at least two years.

Article 10   Pre-existing Article XIX Measures

Members shall terminate all safeguard measures taken pursuant to Article XIX of GATT 1947 that were in existence on the date of entry into force of the WTO Agreement not later than eight years after the date on which they were first applied or five years after the date of entry into force of the WTO Agreement, whichever comes later.

Article 11   Prohibition and Elimination of Certain Measures

1. (a) A Member shall not take or seek any emergency action on imports of particular products as set forth in Article XIX of GATT 1994 unless such action conforms with the provisions of that Article applied in accordance with this Agreement.

   (b) Furthermore, a Member shall not seek, take or maintain any voluntary export restraints, orderly marketing arrangements or any other similar measures on the export or the import side.[3,4] These include actions taken by a single Member as well as actions under

---

2 A Member shall immediately notify an action taken under paragraph 1 of Article 9 to the Committee on Safeguards.

3 An import quota applied as a safeguard measure in conformity with the relevant provisions of GATT 1994 and this Agreement may, by mutual agreement, be administered by the exporting Member.

4 Examples of similar measures include export moderation, export-price or import-price monitoring systems, export or import surveillance, compulsory import cartels and discretionary export or import licensing schemes, any of which afford protection.

agreements, arrangements and understandings entered into by two or more Members. Any such measure in effect on the date of entry into force of the WTO Agreement shall be brought into conformity with this Agreement or phased out in accordance with paragraph 2.

(c) This Agreement does not apply to measures sought, taken or maintained by a Member pursuant to provisions of GATT 1994 other than Article XIX, and Multilateral Trade Agreements in Annex 1A other than this Agreement, or pursuant to protocols and agreements or arrangements concluded within the framework of GATT 1994.

2. The phasing out of measures referred to in paragraph 1(b) shall be carried out according to timetables to be presented to the Committee on Safeguards by the Members concerned not later than 180 days after the date of entry into force of the WTO Agreement. These timetables shall provide for all measures referred to in paragraph 1 to be phased out or brought into conformity with this Agreement within a period not exceeding four years after the date of entry into force of the WTO Agreement, subject to not more than one specific measure per importing Member[5], the duration of which shall not extend beyond 31 December 1999. Any such exception must be mutually agreed between the Members directly concerned and notified to the Committee on Safeguards for its review and acceptance within 90 days of the entry into force of the WTO Agreement. The Annex to this Agreement indicates a measure which has been agreed as falling under this exception.

3. Members shall not encourage or support the adoption or maintenance by public and private enterprises of non-governmental measures equivalent to those referred to in paragraph 1.

Article 12   Notification and Consultation

1. A Member shall immediately notify the Committee on Safeguards upon:
   (a) initiating an investigatory process relating to serious injury or threat thereof and the reasons for it;
   (b) making a finding of serious injury or threat thereof caused by increased imports; and
   (c) taking a decision to apply or extend a safeguard measure.

2. In making the notifications referred to in paragraphs 1(b) and 1(c), the Member proposing to apply or extend a safeguard measure shall provide the Committee on Safeguards with all pertinent information, which shall include evidence of serious injury or threat thereof caused by increased imports, precise description of the product involved and the proposed measure, proposed date of introduction, expected duration and timetable for progressive liberalization. In the case of an extension of a measure, evidence that the industry concerned is adjusting shall also be provided. The Council for Trade in Goods or the Committee on Safeguards may request such additional information as they may consider necessary from the Member proposing to apply or extend the measure.

3. A Member proposing to apply or extend a safeguard measure shall provide adequate opportunity for prior consultations with those Members having a substantial interest as exporters of the product concerned, with a view to, *inter alia*, reviewing the information provided under paragraph 2, exchanging views on the measure and reaching an understanding on ways to achieve the objective set out in paragraph 1 of Article 8.

4. A Member shall make a notification to the Committee on Safeguards before taking a provisional safeguard measure referred to in Article 6. Consultations shall be initiated immediately after the measure is taken.

5. The results of the consultations referred to in this Article, as well as the results of mid-term reviews referred to in paragraph 4 of Article 7, any form of compensation referred to in paragraph 1 of Article 8, and proposed suspensions of concessions and other obligations

---

5 The only such exception to which the European Communities is entitled is indicated in the Annex to this Agreement.

referred to in paragraph 2 of Article 8, shall be notified immediately to the Council for Trade in Goods by the Members concerned.

6. Members shall notify promptly the Committee on Safeguards of their laws, regulations and administrative procedures relating to safeguard measures as well as any modifications made to them.

7. Members maintaining measures described in Article 10 and paragraph 1 of Article 11 which exist on the date of entry into force of the WTO Agreement shall notify such measures to the Committee on Safeguards not later than 60 days after the date of entry into force of the WTO Agreement.

8. Any Member may notify the Committee on Safeguards of all laws, regulations, administrative procedures and any measures or actions dealt with in this Agreement that have not been notified by other Members that are required by this Agreement to make such notifications.

9. Any Member may notify the Committee on Safeguards of any non-governmental measures referred to in paragraph 3 of Article 11.

10. All notifications to the Council for Trade in Goods referred to in this Agreement shall normally be made through the Committee on Safeguards.

11. The provisions on notification in this Agreement shall not require any Member to disclose confidential information the disclosure of which would impede law enforcement or otherwise be contrary to the public interest or would prejudice the legitimate commercial interests of particular enterprises, public or private.

Article 13   Surveillance

1. A Committee on Safeguards is hereby established, under the authority of the Council for Trade in Goods, which shall be open to the participation of any Member indicating its wish to serve on it. The Committee will have the following functions:

   (a) to monitor, and report annually to the Council for Trade in Goods on, the general implementation of this Agreement and make recommendations towards its improvement;

   (b) to find, upon request of an affected Member, whether or not the procedural requirements of this Agreement have been complied with in connection with a safeguard measure, and report its findings to the Council for Trade in Goods;

   (c) to assist Members, if they so request, in their consultations under the provisions of this Agreement;

   (d) to examine measures covered by Article 10 and paragraph 1 of Article 11, monitor the phase-out of such measures and report as appropriate to the Council for Trade in Goods;

   (e) to review, at the request of the Member taking a safeguard measure, whether proposals to suspend concessions or other obligations are "substantially equivalent", and report as appropriate to the Council for Trade in Goods;

   (f) to receive and review all notifications provided for in this Agreement and report as appropriate to the Council for Trade in Goods; and

   (g) to perform any other function connected with this Agreement that the Council for Trade in Goods may determine.

2. To assist the Committee in carrying out its surveillance function, the Secretariat shall prepare annually a factual report on the operation of this Agreement based on notifications and other reliable information available to it.

Article 14   Dispute Settlement

The provisions of Articles XXII and XXIII of GATT 1994 as elaborated and applied by the Dispute Settlement Understanding shall apply to consultations and the settlement of disputes arising under this Agreement.

ANNEX EXCEPTION REFERRED TO IN PARAGRAPH 2 OF ARTICLE 11

Members concerned	Product	Termination
EC/Japan	Passenger cars, off road vehicles, light commercial vehicles, light trucks (up to 5 tonnes), and the same vehicles in wholly knocked-down form (CKD sets).	31 December 1999

x Every Nation should be treated as your favourite trading Partner. (Art 1.1 GATT) Most favoured Nation Principle.
- Art. XI GATT: Prohibits quantative restrictions. On quotas, Imports or Exports with licenses or other measures.
+ An exception to quantative restriction is if its to address balance or payment Issues.
+ India - Autos Case; Violated Act XI; India required manufacturers to match Imports with exports of the same value.
+ Columbia - Ports of entry case; Violated Act XI; it restricted entry of certain products to a few Particular locations in Columbia.

* Art. III; National treatment; state's "products shall Not be subjected directly or Indirectly to Internal taxes or charges of any kind In excess of those applied directly or Indirectly to LIKE Domestic products"
+ This Prohibits singling out any products for extra taxation or charges unless LIKE product are also under them. (Case: Spain - unroasted Coffee : 1981)
* Art III: 4: No descrimination on National origins of a product In regard to laws, regulation r requirements affecting their Internal Sale.

II-16a

General Agreement on Trade in Services

PART VI   FINAL PROVISIONS

GENERAL AGREEMENT ON TRADE IN SERVICES

Members,

Recognizing the growing importance of trade in services for the growth and development of the world economy;

Wishing to establish a multilateral framework of principles and rules for trade in services with a view to the expansion of such trade under conditions of transparency and progressive liberalization and as a means of promoting the economic growth of all trading partners and the development of developing countries;

Desiring the early achievement of progressively higher levels of liberalization of trade in services through successive rounds of multilateral negotiations aimed at promoting the interests of all participants on a mutually advantageous basis and at securing an overall balance of rights and obligations, while giving due respect to national policy objectives;

Recognizing the right of Members to regulate, and to introduce new regulations, on the supply of services within their territories in order to meet national policy objectives and, given asymmetries existing with respect to the degree of development of services regulations in different countries, the particular need of developing countries to exercise this right;

Desiring to facilitate the increasing participation of developing countries in trade in services and the expansion of their service exports including, *inter alia*, through the strengthening of their domestic services capacity and its efficiency and competitiveness;

Taking particular account of the serious difficulty of the least-developed countries in view of their special economic situation and their development, trade and financial needs;

Hereby *agree* as follows:

PART I   SCOPE AND DEFINITION

Article I   Scope and definition

1. This Agreement applies to measures by Members affecting trade in services.

2. For the purposes of this Agreement, trade in services is defined as the supply of a service:

    (a) from the territory of one Member into the territory of any other Member;

    (b) in the territory of one Member to the service consumer of any other Member;

    (c) by a service supplier of one Member, through commercial presence in the territory of any other Member;

    (d) by a service supplier of one Member, through presence of natural persons of a Member in the territory of any other Member.

3. For the purposes of this Agreement:

    (a) "measures by Members" means measures taken by:

        (i) central, regional or local governments and authorities; and

        (ii) non-governmental bodies in the exercise of powers delegated by central, regional or local governments or authorities;

        In fulfilling its obligations and commitments under the Agreement, each Member shall take such reasonable measures as may be available to it to ensure their observance by regional and local governments and authorities and non-governmental bodies within its territory;

    (b) "services" includes any service in any sector except services supplied in the exercise of governmental authority;

(c) "a service supplied in the exercise of governmental authority" means any service which is supplied neither on a commercial basis, nor in competition with one or more service suppliers.

PART II   GENERAL OBLIGATIONS AND DISCIPLINES

Article II   Most-Favoured-Nation Treatment

1. With respect to any measure covered by this Agreement, each Member shall accord immediately and unconditionally to services and service suppliers of any other Member treatment no less favourable than that it accords to like services and service suppliers of any other country.

2. A Member may maintain a measure inconsistent with paragraph 1 provided that such a measure is listed in, and meets the conditions of, the Annex on Article II Exemptions.

3. The provisions of this Agreement shall not be so construed as to prevent any Member from conferring or according advantages to adjacent countries in order to facilitate exchanges limited to contiguous frontier zones of services that are both locally produced and consumed.

Article III   Transparency

1. Each Member shall publish promptly and, except in emergency situations, at the latest by the time of their entry into force, all relevant measures of general application which pertain to or affect the operation of this Agreement. International agreements pertaining to or affecting trade in services to which a Member is a signatory shall also be published.

2. Where publication as referred to in paragraph 1 is not practicable, such information shall be made otherwise publicly available.

3. Each Member shall promptly and at least annually inform the Council for Trade in Services of the introduction of any new, or any changes to existing, laws, regulations or administrative guidelines which significantly affect trade in services covered by its specific commitments under this Agreement.

4. Each Member shall respond promptly to all requests by any other Member for specific information on any of its measures of general application or international agreements within the meaning of paragraph 1. Each Member shall also establish one or more enquiry points to provide specific information to other Members, upon request, on all such matters as well as those subject to the notification requirement in paragraph 3. Such enquiry points shall be established within two years from the date of entry into force of the Agreement Establishing the WTO (referred to in this Agreement as the "WTO Agreement"). Appropriate flexibility with respect to the time-limit within which such enquiry points are to be established may be agreed upon for individual developing country Members. Enquiry points need not be depositories of laws and regulations.

5. Any Member may notify to the Council for Trade in Services any measure, taken by any other Member, which it considers affects the operation of this Agreement.

Article III bis   Disclosure of Confidential Information

Nothing in this Agreement shall require any Member to provide confidential information, the disclosure of which would impede law enforcement, or otherwise be contrary to the public interest, or which would prejudice legitimate commercial interests of particular enterprises, public or private.

Article IV   Increasing Participation of Developing Countries

1. The increasing participation of developing country Members in world trade shall be facilitated through negotiated specific commitments, by different Members pursuant to Parts III and IV of this Agreement, relating to:
   (a) the strengthening of their domestic services capacity and its efficiency and competitiveness, *inter alia* through access to technology on a commercial basis;
   (b) the improvement of their access to distribution channels and information networks; and

(c) the liberalization of market access in sectors and modes of supply of export interest to them.

2. Developed country Members, and to the extent possible other Members, shall establish contact points within two years from the date of entry into force of the WTO Agreement to facilitate the access of developing country Members' service suppliers to information, related to their respective markets, concerning:

(a) commercial and technical aspects of the supply of services;

(b) registration, recognition and obtaining of professional qualifications; and

(c) the availability of services technology.

3. Special priority shall be given to the least-developed country Members in the implementation of paragraphs 1 and 2. Particular account shall be taken of the serious difficulty of the least-developed countries in accepting negotiated specific commitments in view of their special economic situation and their development, trade and financial needs.

Article V   Economic Integration

1. This Agreement shall not prevent any of its Members from being a party to or entering into an agreement liberalizing trade in services between or among the parties to such an agreement, provided that such an agreement:

(a) has substantial sectoral coverage[1], and

(b) provides for the absence or elimination of substantially all discrimination, in the sense of Article XVII, between or among the parties, in the sectors covered under subparagraph (a), through:

(i) elimination of existing discriminatory measures, and/or

(ii) prohibition of new or more discriminatory measures,

either at the entry into force of that agreement or on the basis of a reasonable time-frame, except for measures permitted under Articles XI, XII, XIV and XIV bis.

2. In evaluating whether the conditions under paragraph 1(b) are met, consideration may be given to the relationship of the agreement to a wider process of economic integration or trade liberalization among the countries concerned.

3. (a) Where developing countries are parties to an agreement of the type referred to in paragraph 1, flexibility shall be provided for regarding the conditions set out in paragraph 1, particularly with reference to subparagraph (b) thereof, in accordance with the level of development of the countries concerned, both overall and in individual sectors and subsectors.

(b) Notwithstanding paragraph 6, in the case of an agreement of the type referred to in paragraph 1 involving only developing countries, more favourable treatment may be granted to juridical persons owned or controlled by natural persons of the parties to such an agreement.

4. Any agreement referred to in paragraph 1 shall be designed to facilitate trade between the parties to the agreement and shall not in respect of any Member outside the agreement raise the overall level of barriers to trade in services within the respective sectors or subsectors compared to the level applicable prior to such an agreement.

5. If, in the conclusion, enlargement or any significant modification of any agreement under paragraph 1, a Member intends to withdraw or modify a specific commitment inconsistently with the terms and conditions set out in its Schedule, it shall provide at least 90 days advance notice of such modification or withdrawal and the procedure set forth in paragraphs 2, 3 and 4 of Article XXI shall apply.

---

1 This condition is understood in terms of number of sectors, volume of trade affected and modes of supply. In order to meet this condition, agreements should not provide for the *a priori* exclusion of any mode of supply.

6. A service supplier of any other Member that is a juridical person constituted under the laws of a party to an agreement referred to in paragraph 1 shall be entitled to treatment granted under such agreement, provided that it engages in substantive business operations in the territory of the parties to such agreement.

7. (a) Members which are parties to any agreement referred to in paragraph 1 shall promptly notify any such agreement and any enlargement or any significant modification of that agreement to the Council for Trade in Services. They shall also make available to the Council such relevant information as may be requested by it. The Council may establish a working party to examine such an agreement or enlargement or modification of that agreement and to report to the Council on its consistency with this Article.

   (b) Members which are parties to any agreement referred to in paragraph 1 which is implemented on the basis of a time-frame shall report periodically to the Council for Trade in Services on its implementation. The Council may establish a working party to examine such reports if it deems such a working party necessary.

   (c) Based on the reports of the working parties referred to in subparagraphs (a) and (b), the Council may make recommendations to the parties as it deems appropriate.

8. A Member which is a party to any agreement referred to in paragraph 1 may not seek compensation for trade benefits that may accrue to any other Member from such agreement.

Article V bis   Labour Markets Integration Agreements

This Agreement shall not prevent any of its Members from being a party to an agreement establishing full integration[2] of the labour markets between or among the parties to such an agreement, provided that such an agreement:

(a) exempts citizens of parties to the agreement from requirements concerning residency and work permits;

(b) is notified to the Council for Trade in Services.

Article VI   Domestic Regulation

1. In sectors where specific commitments are undertaken, each Member shall ensure that all measures of general application affecting trade in services are administered in a reasonable, objective and impartial manner.

2. (a) Each Member shall maintain or institute as soon as practicable judicial, arbitral or administrative tribunals or procedures which provide, at the request of an affected service supplier, for the prompt review of, and where justified, appropriate remedies for, administrative decisions affecting trade in services. Where such procedures are not independent of the agency entrusted with the administrative decision concerned, the Member shall ensure that the procedures in fact provide for an objective and impartial review.

   (b) The provisions of subparagraph (a) shall not be construed to require a Member to institute such tribunals or procedures where this would be inconsistent with its constitutional structure or the nature of its legal system.

3. Where authorization is required for the supply of a service on which a specific commitment has been made, the competent authorities of a Member shall, within a reasonable period of time after the submission of an application considered complete under domestic laws and regulations, inform the applicant of the decision concerning the application. At the request of the applicant, the competent authorities of the Member shall provide, without undue delay, information concerning the status of the application.

---

2 Typically, such integration provides citizens of the parties concerned with a right of free entry to the employment markets of the parties and includes measures concerning conditions of pay, other conditions of employment and social benefits.

4. With a view to ensuring that measures relating to qualification requirements and procedures, technical standards and licensing requirements do not constitute unnecessary barriers to trade in services, the Council for Trade in Services shall, through appropriate bodies it may establish, develop any necessary disciplines. Such disciplines shall aim to ensure that such requirements are, *inter alia*:

(a) based on objective and transparent criteria, such as competence and the ability to supply the service;

(b) not more burdensome than necessary to ensure the quality of the service;

(c) in the case of licensing procedures, not in themselves a restriction on the supply of the service.

5. (a) In sectors in which a Member has undertaken specific commitments, pending the entry into force of disciplines developed in these sectors pursuant to paragraph 4, the Member shall not apply licensing and qualification requirements and technical standards that nullify or impair such specific commitments in a manner which:

(i) does not comply with the criteria outlined in subparagraphs 4(a), (b) or (c); and

(ii) could not reasonably have been expected of that Member at the time the specific commitments in those sectors were made.

(b) In determining whether a Member is in conformity with the obligation under paragraph 5(a), account shall be taken of international standards of relevant international organizations[3] applied by that Member.

6. In sectors where specific commitments regarding professional services are undertaken, each Member shall provide for adequate procedures to verify the competence of professionals of any other Member.

Article VII Recognition

1. For the purposes of the fulfilment, in whole or in part, of its standards or criteria for the authorization, licensing or certification of services suppliers, and subject to the requirements of paragraph 3, a Member may recognize the education or experience obtained, requirements met, or licenses or certifications granted in a particular country. Such recognition, which may be achieved through harmonization or otherwise, may be based upon an agreement or arrangement with the country concerned or may be accorded autonomously.

2. A Member that is a party to an agreement or arrangement of the type referred to in paragraph 1, whether existing or future, shall afford adequate opportunity for other interested Members to negotiate their accession to such an agreement or arrangement or to negotiate comparable ones with it. Where a Member accords recognition autonomously, it shall afford adequate opportunity for any other Member to demonstrate that education, experience, licenses, or certifications obtained or requirements met in that other Member's territory should be recognized.

3. A Member shall not accord recognition in a manner which would constitute a means of discrimination between countries in the application of its standards or criteria for the authorization, licensing or certification of services suppliers, or a disguised restriction on trade in services.

4. Each Member shall:

(a) within 12 months from the date on which the WTO Agreement takes effect for it, inform the Council for Trade in Services of its existing recognition measures and state whether such measures are based on agreements or arrangements of the type referred to in paragraph 1;

---

3 The term "relevant international organizations" refers to international bodies whose membership is open to the relevant bodies of at least all Members of the WTO.

(b) promptly inform the Council for Trade in Services as far in advance as possible of the opening of negotiations on an agreement or arrangement of the type referred to in paragraph 1 in order to provide adequate opportunity to any other Member to indicate their interest in participating in the negotiations before they enter a substantive phase;

(c) promptly inform the Council for Trade in Services when it adopts new recognition measures or significantly modifies existing ones and state whether the measures are based on an agreement or arrangement of the type referred to in paragraph 1.

5. Wherever appropriate, recognition should be based on multilaterally agreed criteria. In appropriate cases, Members shall work in cooperation with relevant intergovernmental and non-governmental organizations towards the establishment and adoption of common international standards and criteria for recognition and common international standards for the practice of relevant services trades and professions.

Article VIII   Monopolies and Exclusive Service Suppliers

1. Each Member shall ensure that any monopoly supplier of a service in its territory does not, in the supply of the monopoly service in the relevant market, act in a manner inconsistent with that Member's obligations under Article II and specific commitments.

2. Where a Member's monopoly supplier competes, either directly or through an affiliated company, in the supply of a service outside the scope of its monopoly rights and which is subject to that Member's specific commitments, the Member shall ensure that such a supplier does not abuse its monopoly position to act in its territory in a manner inconsistent with such commitments.

3. The Council for Trade in Services may, at the request of a Member which has a reason to believe that a monopoly supplier of a service of any other Member is acting in a manner inconsistent with paragraph 1 or 2, request the Member establishing, maintaining or authorizing such supplier to provide specific information concerning the relevant operations.

4. If, after the date of entry into force of the WTO Agreement, a Member grants monopoly rights regarding the supply of a service covered by its specific commitments, that Member shall notify the Council for Trade in Services no later than three months before the intended implementation of the grant of monopoly rights and the provisions of paragraphs 2, 3 and 4 of Article XXI shall apply.

5. The provisions of this Article shall also apply to cases of exclusive service suppliers, where a Member, formally or in effect, (a) authorizes or establishes a small number of service suppliers and (b) substantially prevents competition among those suppliers in its territory.

Article IX   Business Practices

1. Members recognize that certain business practices of service suppliers, other than those falling under Article VIII, may restrain competition and thereby restrict trade in services.

2. Each Member shall, at the request of any other Member, enter into consultations with a view to eliminating practices referred to in paragraph 1. The Member addressed shall accord full and sympathetic consideration to such a request and shall cooperate through the supply of publicly available non-confidential information of relevance to the matter in question. The Member addressed shall also provide other information available to the requesting Member, subject to its domestic law and to the conclusion of satisfactory agreement concerning the safeguarding of its confidentiality by the requesting Member.

Article X   Emergency Safeguard Measures

1. There shall be multilateral negotiations on the question of emergency safeguard measures based on the principle of non-discrimination. The results of such negotiations shall enter into effect on a date not later than three years from the date of entry into force of the WTO Agreement.

2. In the period before the entry into effect of the results of the negotiations referred to in paragraph 1, any Member may, notwithstanding the provisions of paragraph 1 of Article XXI, notify the Council on Trade in Services of its intention to modify or withdraw a specific commitment after a period of one year from the date on which the commitment enters into force; provided that the Member shows cause to the Council that the modification or withdrawal cannot await the lapse of the three-year period provided for in paragraph 1 of Article XXI.

3. The provisions of paragraph 2 shall cease to apply three years after the date of entry into force of the WTO Agreement.

Article XI   Payments and Transfers

1. Except under the circumstances envisaged in Article XII, a Member shall not apply restrictions on international transfers and payments for current transactions relating to its specific commitments.

2. Nothing in this Agreement shall affect the rights and obligations of the members of the International Monetary Fund under the Articles of Agreement of the Fund, including the use of exchange actions which are in conformity with the Articles of Agreement, provided that a Member shall not impose restrictions on any capital transactions inconsistently with its specific commitments regarding such transactions, except under Article XII or at the request of the Fund.

Article XII   Restrictions to Safeguard the Balance of Payments

1. In the event of serious balance-of-payments and external financial difficulties or threat thereof, a Member may adopt or maintain restrictions on trade in services on which it has undertaken specific commitments, including on payments or transfers for transactions related to such commitments. It is recognized that particular pressures on the balance of payments of a Member in the process of economic development or economic transition may necessitate the use of restrictions to ensure, *inter alia*, the maintenance of a level of financial reserves adequate for the implementation of its programme of economic development or economic transition.

2. The restrictions referred to in paragraph 1:
   (a) shall not discriminate among Members;
   (b) shall be consistent with the Articles of Agreement of the International Monetary Fund;
   (c) shall avoid unnecessary damage to the commercial, economic and financial interests of any other Member;
   (d) shall not exceed those necessary to deal with the circumstances described in paragraph 1;
   (e) shall be temporary and be phased out progressively as the situation specified in paragraph 1 improves.

3. In determining the incidence of such restrictions, Members may give priority to the supply of services which are more essential to their economic or development programmes. However, such restrictions shall not be adopted or maintained for the purpose of protecting a particular service sector.

4. Any restrictions adopted or maintained under paragraph 1, or any changes therein, shall be promptly notified to the General Council.

5. (a) Members applying the provisions of this Article shall consult promptly with the Committee on Balance-of-Payments Restrictions on restrictions adopted under this Article.
   (b) The Ministerial Conference shall establish procedures[4] for periodic consultations with the objective of enabling such recommendations to be made to the Member concerned as it may deem appropriate.

---

4 It is understood that the procedures under paragraph 5 shall be the same as the GATT 1994 procedures.

    (c) Such consultations shall assess the balance-of-payment situation of the Member concerned and the restrictions adopted or maintained under this Article, taking into account, *inter alia*, such factors as:

        (i) the nature and extent of the balance-of-payments and the external financial difficulties;

        (ii) the external economic and trading environment of the consulting Member;

        (iii) alternative corrective measures which may be available.

    (d) The consultations shall address the compliance of any restrictions with paragraph 2, in particular the progressive phaseout of restrictions in accordance with paragraph 2(e).

    (e) In such consultations, all findings of statistical and other facts presented by the International Monetary Fund relating to foreign exchange, monetary reserves and balance of payments, shall be accepted and conclusions shall be based on the assessment by the Fund of the balance-of-payments and the external financial situation of the consulting Member.

6. If a Member which is not a member of the International Monetary Fund wishes to apply the provisions of this Article, the Ministerial Conference shall establish a review procedure and any other procedures necessary.

Article XIII Government Procurement

1. Articles II, XVI and XVII shall not apply to laws, regulations or requirements governing the procurement by governmental agencies of services purchased for governmental purposes and not with a view to commercial resale or with a view to use in the supply of services for commercial sale.

2. There shall be multilateral negotiations on government procurement in services under this Agreement within two years from the date of entry into force of the WTO Agreement.

Article XIV General Exceptions

Subject to the requirement that such measures are not applied in a manner which would constitute a means of arbitrary or unjustifiable discrimination between countries where like conditions prevail, or a disguised restriction on trade in services, nothing in this Agreement shall be construed to prevent the adoption or enforcement by any Member of measures:

(a) necessary to protect public morals or to maintain public order;[5]

(b) necessary to protect human, animal or plant life or health;

(c) necessary to secure compliance with laws or regulations which are not inconsistent with the provisions of this Agreement including those relating to:

    (i) the prevention of deceptive and fraudulent practices or to deal with the effects of a default on services contracts;

    (ii) the protection of the privacy of individuals in relation to the processing and dissemination of personal data and the protection of confidentiality of individual records and accounts;

    (iii) safety;

(d) inconsistent with Article XVII, provided that the difference in treatment is aimed at ensuring the equitable or effective[6] imposition or collection of direct taxes in respect of services or service suppliers of other Members;

---

5 The public order exception may be invoked only where a genuine and sufficiently serious threat is posed to one of the fundamental interests of society.

6 Measures that are aimed at ensuring the equitable or effective imposition or collection of direct taxes include measures taken by a Member under its taxation system which:

    (i) apply to non-resident service suppliers in recognition of the fact that the tax obligation of non-residents is determined with respect to taxable items sourced or located in the Member's territory; or

    (ii) apply to non-residents in order to ensure the imposition or collection of taxes in the Member's territory; or

    (iii) apply to non-residents or residents in order to prevent the avoidance or evasion of taxes, including compliance measures; or

(e) inconsistent with Article II, provided that the difference in treatment is the result of an agreement on the avoidance of double taxation or provisions on the avoidance of double taxation in any other international agreement or arrangement by which the Member is bound.

Article XIV bis   Security Exceptions

1. Nothing in this Agreement shall be construed:
    (a) to require any Member to furnish any information, the disclosure of which it considers contrary to its essential security interests; or
    (b) to prevent any Member from taking any action which it considers necessary for the protection of its essential security interests:
        (i) relating to the supply of services as carried out directly or indirectly for the purpose of provisioning a military establishment;
        (ii) relating to fissionable and fusionable materials or the materials from which they are derived;
        (iii) taken in time of war or other emergency in international relations; or
    (c) to prevent any Member from taking any action in pursuance of its obligations under the United Nations Charter for the maintenance of international peace and security.

2. The Council for Trade in Services shall be informed to the fullest extent possible of measures taken under paragraphs 1(b) and (c) and of their termination.

Article XV   Subsidies

1. Members recognize that, in certain circumstances, subsidies may have distortive effects on trade in services. Members shall enter into negotiations with a view to developing the necessary multilateral disciplines to avoid such trade-distortive effects.[7] The negotiations shall also address the appropriateness of countervailing procedures. Such negotiations shall recognize the role of subsidies in relation to the development programmes of developing countries and take into account the needs of Members, particularly developing country Members, for flexibility in this area. For the purpose of such negotiations, Members shall exchange information concerning all subsidies related to trade in services that they provide to their domestic service suppliers.

2. Any Member which considers that it is adversely affected by a subsidy of another Member may request consultations with that Member on such matters. Such requests shall be accorded sympathetic consideration.

PART III   SPECIFIC COMMITMENTS

Article XVI   Market Access

1. With respect to market access through the modes of supply identified in Article I, each Member shall accord services and service suppliers of any other Member treatment no less favourable than that provided for under the terms, limitations and conditions agreed and specified in its Schedule.[8]

(iv) apply to consumers of services supplied in or from the territory of another Member in order to ensure the imposition or collection of taxes on such consumers derived from sources in the Member's territory; or

(v) distinguish service suppliers subject to tax on worldwide taxable items from other service suppliers, in recognition of the difference in the nature of the tax base between them; or

(vi) determine, allocate or apportion income, profit, gain, loss, deduction or credit of resident persons or branches, or between related persons or branches of the same person, in order to safeguard the Member's tax base.

Tax terms or concepts in paragraph (d) of Article XIV and in this footnote are determined according to tax definitions and concepts, or equivalent or similar definitions and concepts, under the domestic law of the Member taking the measure.

7 A future work programme shall determine how, and in what time-frame, negotiations on such multilateral disciplines will be conducted.

8 If a Member undertakes a market-access commitment in relation to the supply of a service through the mode of supply referred to in subparagraph 2(a) of Article I and if the cross-border movement of capital is an essential part of the service itself, that Member is thereby committed to allow such movement of capital. If a Member undertakes a market-access commitment in relation to the supply of a service through the mode of supply referred to in subparagraph 2(c) of Article I, it is thereby committed to allow related transfers of capital into its territory.

2. In sectors where market-access commitments are undertaken, the measures which a Member shall not maintain or adopt either on the basis of a regional subdivision or on the basis of its entire territory, unless otherwise specified in its Schedule, are defined as:

(a) limitations on the number of service suppliers whether in the form of numerical quotas, monopolies, exclusive service suppliers or the requirements of an economic needs test;

(b) limitations on the total value of service transactions or assets in the form of numerical quotas or the requirement of an economic needs test;

(c) limitations on the total number of service operations or on the total quantity of service output expressed in terms of designated numerical units in the form of quotas or the requirement of an economic needs test;[9]

(d) limitations on the total number of natural persons that may be employed in a particular service sector or that a service supplier may employ and who are necessary for, and directly related to, the supply of a specific service in the form of numerical quotas or the requirement of an economic needs test;

(e) measures which restrict or require specific types of legal entity or joint venture through which a service supplier may supply a service; and

(f) limitations on the participation of foreign capital in terms of maximum percentage limit on foreign shareholding or the total value of individual or aggregate foreign investment.

Article XVII   National Treatment

1. In the sectors inscribed in its Schedule, and subject to any conditions and qualifications set out therein, each Member shall accord to services and service suppliers of any other Member, in respect of all measures affecting the supply of services, treatment no less favourable than that it accords to its own like services and service suppliers.[10]

2. A Member may meet the requirement of paragraph 1 by according to services and service suppliers of any other Member, either formally identical treatment or formally different treatment to that it accords to its own like services and service suppliers.

3. Formally identical or formally different treatment shall be considered to be less favourable if it modifies the conditions of competition in favour of services or service suppliers of the Member compared to like services or service suppliers of any other Member.

Article XVIII   Additional Commitments

Members may negotiate commitments with respect to measures affecting trade in services not subject to scheduling under Articles XVI or XVII, including those regarding qualifications, standards or licensing matters. Such commitments shall be inscribed in a Member's Schedule.

PART IV   PROGRESSIVE LIBERALIZATION

Article XIX   Negotiation of Specific Commitments

1. In pursuance of the objectives of this Agreement, Members shall enter into successive rounds of negotiations, beginning not later than five years from the date of entry into force of the WTO Agreement and periodically thereafter, with a view to achieving a progressively higher level of liberalization. Such negotiations shall be directed to the reduction or elimination of

---

9 Subparagraph 2(c) does not cover measures of a Member which limit inputs for the supply of services.

10 Specific commitments assumed under this Article shall not be construed to require any Member to compensate for any inherent competitive disadvantages which result from the foreign character of the relevant services or service suppliers.

the adverse effects on trade in services of measures as a means of providing effective market access. This process shall take place with a view to promoting the interests of all participants on a mutually advantageous basis and to securing an overall balance of rights and obligations.

2. The process of liberalization shall take place with due respect for national policy objectives and the level of development of individual Members, both overall and in individual sectors. There shall be appropriate flexibility for individual developing country Members for opening fewer sectors, liberalizing fewer types of transactions, progressively extending market access in line with their development situation and, when making access to their markets available to foreign service suppliers, attaching to such access conditions aimed at achieving the objectives referred to in Article IV.

3. For each round, negotiating guidelines and procedures shall be established. For the purposes of establishing such guidelines, the Council for Trade in Services shall carry out an assessment of trade in services in overall terms and on a sectoral basis with reference to the objectives of this Agreement, including those set out in paragraph 1 of Article IV. Negotiating guidelines shall establish modalities for the treatment of liberalization undertaken autonomously by Members since previous negotiations, as well as for the special treatment for least-developed country Members under the provisions of paragraph 3 of Article IV.

4. The process of progressive liberalization shall be advanced in each such round through bilateral, plurilateral or multilateral negotiations directed towards increasing the general level of specific commitments undertaken by Members under this Agreement.

Article XX   Schedules of Specific Commitments

1. Each Member shall set out in a schedule the specific commitments it undertakes under Part III of this Agreement. With respect to sectors where such commitments are undertaken, each Schedule shall specify:

    (a) terms, limitations and conditions on market access;
    (b) conditions and qualifications on national treatment;
    (c) undertakings relating to additional commitments;
    (d) where appropriate the time-frame for implementation of such commitments; and
    (e) the date of entry into force of such commitments.

2. Measures inconsistent with both Articles XVI and XVII shall be inscribed in the column relating to Article XVI. In this case the inscription will be considered to provide a condition or qualification to Article XVII as well.

3. Schedules of specific commitments shall be annexed to this Agreement and shall form an integral part thereof.

Article XXI   Modification of Schedules

1. (a) A Member (referred to in this Article as the "modifying Member") may modify or withdraw any commitment in its Schedule, at any time after three years have elapsed from the date on which that commitment entered into force, in accordance with the provisions of this Article.

    (b) A modifying Member shall notify its intent to modify or withdraw a commitment pursuant to this Article to the Council for Trade in Services no later than three months before the intended date of implementation of the modification or withdrawal.

2. (a) At the request of any Member the benefits of which under this Agreement may be affected (referred to in this Article as an "affected Member") by a proposed modification or withdrawal notified under subparagraph 1(b), the modifying Member shall enter into negotiations with a view to reaching agreement on any necessary compensatory adjustment. In such negotiations and agreement, the Members concerned shall endeavour to maintain a general level of mutually advantageous commitments not less favourable to trade than that provided for in Schedules of specific commitments prior to such negotiations.

(b) Compensatory adjustments shall be made on a most-favoured-nation basis.

3. (a) If agreement is not reached between the modifying Member and any affected Member before the end of the period provided for negotiations, such affected Member may refer the matter to arbitration. Any affected Member that wishes to enforce a right that it may have to compensation must participate in the arbitration.

   (b) If no affected Member has requested arbitration, the modifying Member shall be free to implement the proposed modification or withdrawal.

4. (a) The modifying Member may not modify or withdraw its commitment until it has made compensatory adjustments in conformity with the findings of the arbitration.

   (b) If the modifying Member implements its proposed modification or withdrawal and does not comply with the findings of the arbitration, any affected Member that participated in the arbitration may modify or withdraw substantially equivalent benefits in conformity with those findings. Notwithstanding Article II, such a modification or withdrawal may be implemented solely with respect to the modifying Member.

5. The Council for Trade in Services shall establish procedures for rectification or modification of Schedules. Any Member which has modified or withdrawn scheduled commitments under this Article shall modify its Schedule according to such procedures.

PART V INSTITUTIONAL PROVISIONS

Article XXII Consultation

1. Each Member shall accord sympathetic consideration to, and shall afford adequate opportunity for, consultation regarding such representations as may be made by any other Member with respect to any matter affecting the operation of this Agreement. The Dispute Settlement Understanding (DSU) shall apply to such consultations.

2. The Council for Trade in Services or the Dispute Settlement Body (DSB) may, at the request of a Member, consult with any Member or Members in respect of any matter for which it has not been possible to find a satisfactory solution through consultation under paragraph 1.

3. A Member may not invoke Article XVII, either under this Article or Article XXIII, with respect to a measure of another Member that falls within the scope of an international agreement between them relating to the avoidance of double taxation. In case of disagreement between Members as to whether a measure falls within the scope of such an agreement between them, it shall be open to either Member to bring this matter before the Council for Trade in Services.[11] The Council shall refer the matter to arbitration. The decision of the arbitrator shall be final and binding on the Members.

Article XXIII Dispute Settlement and Enforcement

1. If any Member should consider that any other Member fails to carry out its obligations or specific commitments under this Agreement, it may with a view to reaching a mutually satisfactory resolution of the matter have recourse to the DSU.

2. If the DSB considers that the circumstances are serious enough to justify such action, it may authorize a Member or Members to suspend the application to any other Member or Members of obligations and specific commitments in accordance with Article 22 of the DSU.

3. If any Member considers that any benefit it could reasonably have expected to accrue to it under a specific commitment of another Member under Part III of this Agreement is being nullified or impaired as a result of the application of any measure which does not conflict with the provisions of this Agreement, it may have recourse to the DSU. If the measure is

---

11 With respect to agreements on the avoidance of double taxation which exist on the date of entry into force of the WTO Agreement, such a matter may be brought before the Council for Trade in Services only with the consent of both parties to such an agreement.

determined by the DSB to have nullified or impaired such a benefit, the Member affected shall be entitled to a mutually satisfactory adjustment on the basis of paragraph 2 of Article XXI, which may include the modification or withdrawal of the measure. In the event an agreement cannot be reached between the Members concerned, Article 22 of the DSU shall apply.

Article XXIV Council for Trade in Services

1. The Council for Trade in Services shall carry out such functions as may be assigned to it to facilitate the operation of this Agreement and further its objectives. The Council may establish such subsidiary bodies as it considers appropriate for the effective discharge of its functions.

2. The Council and, unless the Council decides otherwise, its subsidiary bodies shall be open to participation by representatives of all Members.

3. The Chairman of the Council shall be elected by the Members.

Article XXV Technical Cooperation

1. Service suppliers of Members which are in need of such assistance shall have access to the services of contact points referred to in paragraph 2 of Article IV.

2. Technical assistance to developing countries shall be provided at the multilateral level by the Secretariat and shall be decided upon by the Council for Trade in Services.

Article XXVI Relationship with Other International Organizations

The General Council shall make appropriate arrangements for consultation and cooperation with the United Nations and its specialized agencies as well as with other intergovernmental organizations concerned with services.

PART VI FINAL PROVISIONS

Article XXVII Denial of Benefits

A Member may deny the benefits of this Agreement:

(a) to the supply of a service, if it establishes that the service is supplied from or in the territory of a non-Member or of a Member to which the denying Member does not apply the WTO Agreement;

(b) in the case of the supply of a maritime transport service, if it establishes that the service is supplied:
   (i) by a vessel registered under the laws of a non-Member or of a Member to which the denying Member does not apply the WTO Agreement, and
   (ii) by a person which operates and/or uses the vessel in whole or in part but which is of a non-Member or of a Member to which the denying Member does not apply the WTO Agreement;

(c) to a service supplier that is a juridical person, if it establishes that it is not a service supplier of another Member, or that it is a service supplier of a Member to which the denying Member does not apply the WTO Agreement.

Article XXVIII Definitions

For the purpose of this Agreement:

(a) "measure" means any measure by a Member, whether in the form of a law, regulation, rule, procedure, decision, administrative action, or any other form;

(b) "supply of a service" includes the production, distribution, marketing, sale and delivery of a service;

(c) "measures by Members affecting trade in services" include measures in respect of
    (i)   the purchase, payment or use of a service;
    (ii) the access to and use of, in connection with the supply of a service, services which are required by those Members to be offered to the public generally;
    (iii) the presence, including commercial presence, of persons of a Member for the supply of a service in the territory of another Member;

(d) "commercial presence" means any type of business or professional establishment, including through
    (i) the constitution, acquisition or maintenance of a juridical person, or
    (ii) the creation or maintenance of a branch or a representative office,
  within the territory of a Member for the purpose of supplying a service;

(e) "sector" of a service means,
    (i) with reference to a specific commitment, one or more, or all, subsectors of that service, as specified in a Member's Schedule,
    (ii) otherwise, the whole of that service sector, including all of its subsectors;

(f) "service of another Member" means a service which is supplied,
    (i) from or in the territory of that other Member, or in the case of maritime transport, by a vessel registered under the laws of that other Member, or by a person of that other Member which supplies the service through the operation of a vessel and/or its use in whole or in part; or
    (ii) in the case of the supply of a service through commercial presence or through the presence of natural persons, by a service supplier of that other Member;

(g) "service supplier" means any person that supplies a service;[12]

(h) "monopoly supplier of a service" means any person, public or private, which in the relevant market of the territory of a Member is authorized or established formally or in effect by that Member as the sole supplier of that service;

(i) "service consumer" means any person that receives or uses a service;

(j) "person" means either a natural person or a juridical person;

(k) "natural person of another Member" means a natural person who resides in the territory of that other Member or any other Member, and who under the law of that other Member:
    (i) is a national of that other Member; or
    (ii) has the right of permanent residence in that other Member, in the case of a Member which:
        1. does not have nationals; or
        2. accords substantially the same treatment to its permanent residents as it does to its nationals in respect of measures affecting trade in services, as notified in its acceptance of or accession to the WTO Agreement, provided that no Member is obligated to accord to such permanent residents treatment more favourable than would be accorded by that other Member to such permanent residents. Such notification shall include the assurance to assume, with respect to those permanent residents, in accordance with its laws and regulations, the same responsibilities that other Member bears with respect to its nationals;

---

12 Where the service is not supplied directly by a juridical person but through other forms of commercial presence such as a branch or a representative office, the service supplier (i.e. the juridical person) shall, nonetheless, through such presence be accorded the treatment provided for service suppliers under the Agreement. Such treatment shall be extended to the presence through which the service is supplied and need not be extended to any other parts of the supplier located outside the territory where the service is supplied.

(l) "juridical person" means any legal entity duly constituted or otherwise organized under applicable law, whether for profit or otherwise, and whether privately-owned or governmentally-owned, including any corporation, trust, partnership, joint venture, sole proprietorship or association;

(m) "juridical person of another Member" means a juridical person which is either:
  (i) constituted or otherwise organized under the law of that other Member, and is engaged in substantive business operations in the territory of that Member or any other Member; or
  (ii) in the case of the supply of a service through commercial presence, owned or controlled by:
      1. natural persons of that Member; or
      2. juridical persons of that other Member identified under subparagraph (i);

(n) a juridical person is:
  (i) "owned" by persons of a Member if more than 50 per cent of the equity interest in it is beneficially owned by persons of that Member;
  (ii) "controlled" by persons of a Member if such persons have the power to name a majority of its directors or otherwise to legally direct its actions;
  (iii) "affiliated" with another person when it controls, or is controlled by, that other person; or when it and the other person are both controlled by the same person;

(o) "direct taxes" comprise all taxes on total income, on total capital or on elements of income or of capital, including taxes on gains from the alienation of property, taxes on estates, inheritances and gifts, and taxes on the total amounts of wages or salaries paid by enterprises, as well as taxes on capital appreciation.

Article XXIX   Annexes
The Annexes to this Agreement are an integral part of this Agreement.

ANNEX ON ARTICLE II EXEMPTIONS

Scope
1. This Annex specifies the conditions under which a Member, at the entry into force of this Agreement, is exempted from its obligations under paragraph 1 of Article II.
2. Any new exemptions applied for after the date of entry into force of the WTO Agreement shall be dealt with under paragraph 3 of Article IX of that Agreement.

Review
3. The Council for Trade in Services shall review all exemptions granted for a period of more than 5 years. The first such review shall take place no more than 5 years after the entry into force of the WTO Agreement.
4. The Council for Trade in Services in a review shall:
   (a) examine whether the conditions which created the need for the exemption still prevail; and
   (b) determine the date of any further review.

Termination
5. The exemption of a Member from its obligations under paragraph 1 of Article II of the Agreement with respect to a particular measure terminates on the date provided for in the exemption.
6. In principle, such exemptions should not exceed a period of 10 years. In any event, they shall be subject to negotiation in subsequent trade liberalizing rounds.
7. A Member shall notify the Council for Trade in Services at the termination of the exemption period that the inconsistent measure has been brought into conformity with paragraph 1 of Article II of the Agreement.

Lists of Article II exemptions

[The agreed lists of exemptions under paragraph 2 of Article II will be annexed here in the treaty copy of the WTO Agreement.]

ANNEX ON MOVEMENT OF NATURAL PERSONS SUPPLYING SERVICES UNDER THE AGREEMENT

1. This Annex applies to measures affecting natural persons who are service suppliers of a Member, and natural persons of a Member who are employed by a service supplier of a Member, in respect of the supply of a service.

2. The Agreement shall not apply to measures affecting natural persons seeking access to the employment market of a Member, nor shall it apply to measures regarding citizenship, residence or employment on a permanent basis.

3. In accordance with Parts III and IV of the Agreement, Members may negotiate specific commitments applying to the movement of all categories of natural persons supplying services under the Agreement. Natural persons covered by a specific commitment shall be allowed to supply the service in accordance with the terms of that commitment.

4. The Agreement shall not prevent a Member from applying measures to regulate the entry of natural persons into, or their temporary stay in, its territory, including those measures necessary to protect the integrity of, and to ensure the orderly movement of natural persons across, its borders, provided that such measures are not applied in such a manner as to nullify or impair the benefits accruing to any Member under the terms of a specific commitment.[13]

ANNEX ON AIR TRANSPORT SERVICES

1. This Annex applies to measures affecting trade in air transport services, whether scheduled or non-scheduled, and ancillary services. It is confirmed that any specific commitment or obligation assumed under this Agreement shall not reduce or affect a Member's obligations under bilateral or multilateral agreements that are in effect on the date of entry into force of the WTO Agreement.

2. The Agreement, including its dispute settlement procedures, shall not apply to measures affecting:
   (a) traffic rights, however granted; or
   (b) services directly related to the exercise of traffic rights,
   except as provided in paragraph 3 of this Annex.

3. The Agreement shall apply to measures affecting:
   (a) aircraft repair and maintenance services;
   (b) the selling and marketing of air transport services;
   (c) computer reservation system (CRS) services.

4. The dispute settlement procedures of the Agreement may be invoked only where obligations or specific commitments have been assumed by the concerned Members and where dispute settlement procedures in bilateral and other multilateral agreements or arrangements have been exhausted.

5. The Council for Trade in Services shall review periodically, and at least every five years, developments in the air transport sector and the operation of this Annex with a view to considering the possible further application of the Agreement in this sector.

---

13 The sole fact of requiring a visa for natural persons of certain Members and not for those of others shall not be regarded as nullifying or impairing benefits under a specific commitment.

6. Definitions:
   (a) "Aircraft repair and maintenance services" mean such activities when undertaken on an aircraft or a part thereof while it is withdrawn from service and do not include so-called line maintenance.
   (b) "Selling and marketing of air transport services" mean opportunities for the air carrier concerned to sell and market freely its air transport services including all aspects of marketing such as market research, advertising and distribution. These activities do not include the pricing of air transport services nor the applicable conditions.
   (c) "Computer reservation system (CRS) services" mean services provided by computerised systems that contain information about air carriers' schedules, availability, fares and fare rules, through which reservations can be made or tickets may be issued.
   (d) "Traffic rights" mean the right for scheduled and non-scheduled services to operate and/or to carry passengers, cargo and mail for remuneration or hire from, to, within, or over the territory of a Member, including points to be served, routes to be operated, types of traffic to be carried, capacity to be provided, tariffs to be charged and their conditions, and criteria for designation of airlines, including such criteria as number, ownership, and control.

ANNEX ON FINANCIAL SERVICES

1. *Scope and Definition*
   (a) This Annex applies to measures affecting the supply of financial services. Reference to the supply of a financial service in this Annex shall mean the supply of a service as defined in paragraph 2 of Article I of the Agreement.
   (b) For the purposes of subparagraph 3(b) of Article I of the Agreement, "services supplied in the exercise of governmental authority" means the following:
      (i) activities conducted by a central bank or monetary authority or by any other public entity in pursuit of monetary or exchange rate policies;
      (ii) activities forming part of a statutory system of social security or public retirement plans; and
      (iii) other activities conducted by a public entity for the account or with the guarantee or using the financial resources of the Government.
   (c) For the purposes of subparagraph 3(b) of Article I of the Agreement, if a Member allows any of the activities referred to in subparagraphs (b)(ii) or (b)(iii) of this paragraph to be conducted by its financial service suppliers in competition with a public entity or a financial service supplier, "services" shall include such activities.
   (d) Subparagraph 3(c) of Article I of the Agreement shall not apply to services covered by this Annex.

2. *Domestic Regulation*
   (a) Notwithstanding any other provisions of the Agreement, a Member shall not be prevented from taking measures for prudential reasons, including for the protection of investors, depositors, policy holders or persons to whom a fiduciary duty is owed by a financial service supplier, or to ensure the integrity and stability of the financial system. Where such measures do not conform with the provisions of the Agreement, they shall not be used as a means of avoiding the Member's commitments or obligations under the Agreement.
   (b) Nothing in the Agreement shall be construed to require a Member to disclose information relating to the affairs and accounts of individual customers or any confidential or proprietary information in the possession of public entities.

3. *Recognition*

(a) A Member may recognize prudential measures of any other country in determining how the Member's measures relating to financial services shall be applied. Such recognition, which may be achieved through harmonization or otherwise, may be based upon an agreement or arrangement with the country concerned or may be accorded autonomously.

(b) A Member that is a party to such an agreement or arrangement referred to in subparagraph (a), whether future or existing, shall afford adequate opportunity for other interested Members to negotiate their accession to such agreements or arrangements, or to negotiate comparable ones with it, under circumstances in which there would be equivalent regulation, oversight, implementation of such regulation, and, if appropriate, procedures concerning the sharing of information between the parties to the agreement or arrangement. Where a Member accords recognition autonomously, it shall afford adequate opportunity for any other Member to demonstrate that such circumstances exist.

(c) Where a Member is contemplating according recognition to prudential measures of any other country, paragraph 4(b) of Article VII shall not apply.

4. *Dispute Settlement*

Panels for disputes on prudential issues and other financial matters shall have the necessary expertise relevant to the specific financial service under dispute.

5. *Definitions*

For the purposes of this Annex:

(a) A financial service is any service of a financial nature offered by a financial service supplier of a Member. Financial services include all insurance and insurance-related services, and all banking and other financial services (excluding insurance). Financial services include the following activities:

Insurance and insurance-related services

  (i) Direct insurance (including co-insurance):

    (A) life

    (B) non-life

 (ii) Reinsurance and retrocession;

(iii) Insurance intermediation, such as brokerage and agency;

(iv) Services auxiliary to insurance, such as consultancy, actuarial, risk assessment and claim settlement services.

Banking and other financial services (excluding insurance)

  (v) Acceptance of deposits and other repayable funds from the public;

 (vi) Lending of all types, including consumer credit, mortgage credit, factoring and financing of commercial transaction;

(vii) Financial leasing;

(viii) All payment and money transmission services, including credit, charge and debit cards, travellers cheques and bankers drafts;

 (ix) Guarantees and commitments;

  (x) Trading for own account or for account of customers, whether on an exchange, in an over-the-counter market or otherwise, the following:

    (A) money market instruments (including cheques, bills, certificates of deposits);

    (B) foreign exchange;

    (C) derivative products including, but not limited to, futures and options;

    (D) exchange rate and interest rate instruments, including products such as swaps, forward rate agreements;

    (E) transferable securities;

      (F) other negotiable instruments and financial assets, including bullion.

   (xi) Participation in issues of all kinds of securities, including underwriting and placement as agent (whether publicly or privately) and provision of services related to such issues;

  (xii) Money broking;

 (xiii) Asset management, such as cash or portfolio management, all forms of collective investment management, pension fund management, custodial, depository and trust services;

 (xiv) Settlement and clearing services for financial assets, including securities, derivative products, and other negotiable instruments;

  (xv) Provision and transfer of financial information, and financial data processing and related software by suppliers of other financial services;

 (xvi) Advisory, intermediation and other auxiliary financial services on all the activities listed in subparagraphs (v) through (xv), including credit reference and analysis, investment and portfolio research and advice, advice on acquisitions and on corporate restructuring and strategy.

(b) A financial service supplier means any natural or juridical person of a Member wishing to supply or supplying financial services but the term "financial service supplier" does not include a public entity.

(c) "Public entity" means:

   (i) a government, a central bank or a monetary authority, of a Member, or an entity owned or controlled by a Member, that is principally engaged in carrying out governmental functions or activities for governmental purposes, not including an entity principally engaged in supplying financial services on commercial terms; or

  (ii) a private entity, performing functions normally performed by a central bank or monetary authority, when exercising those functions.

SECOND ANNEX ON FINANCIAL SERVICES

1. Notwithstanding Article II of the Agreement and paragraphs 1 and 2 of the Annex on Article II Exemptions, a Member may, during a period of 60 days beginning four months after the date of entry into force of the WTO Agreement, list in that Annex measures relating to financial services which are inconsistent with paragraph 1 of Article II of the Agreement.

2. Notwithstanding Article XXI of the Agreement, a Member may, during a period of 60 days beginning four months after the date of entry into force of the WTO Agreement, improve, modify or withdraw all or part of the specific commitments on financial services inscribed in its Schedule.

3. The Council for Trade in Services shall establish any procedures necessary for the application of paragraphs 1 and 2.

ANNEX ON NEGOTIATIONS ON MARITIME TRANSPORT SERVICES

1. Article II and the Annex on Article II Exemptions, including the requirement to list in the Annex any measure inconsistent with most-favoured-nation treatment that a Member will maintain, shall enter into force for international shipping, auxiliary services and access to and use of port facilities only on:

  (a) the implementation date to be determined under paragraph 4 of the Ministerial Decision on Negotiations on Maritime Transport Services; or,

  (b) should the negotiations not succeed, the date of the final report of the Negotiating Group on Maritime Transport Services provided for in that Decision.

2. Paragraph 1 shall not apply to any specific commitment on maritime transport services which is inscribed in a Member's Schedule.

3. From the conclusion of the negotiations referred to in paragraph 1, and before the implementation date, a Member may improve, modify or withdraw all or part of its specific commitments in this sector without offering compensation, notwithstanding the provisions of Article XXI.

ANNEX ON TELECOMMUNICATIONS

1. *Objectives*

   Recognizing the specificities of the telecommunications services sector and, in particular, its dual role as a distinct sector of economic activity and as the underlying transport means for other economic activities, the Members have agreed to the following Annex with the objective of elaborating upon the provisions of the Agreement with respect to measures affecting access to and use of public telecommunications transport networks and services. Accordingly, this Annex provides notes and supplementary provisions to the Agreement.

2. *Scope*
   (a) This Annex shall apply to all measures of a Member that affect access to and use of public telecommunications transport networks and services.[14]
   (b) This Annex shall not apply to measures affecting the cable or broadcast distribution of radio or television programming.
   (c) Nothing in this Annex shall be construed:
      (i) to require a Member to authorize a service supplier of any other Member to establish, construct, acquire, lease, operate, or supply telecommunications transport networks or services, other than as provided for in its Schedule; or
      (ii) to require a Member (or to require a Member to oblige service suppliers under its jurisdiction) to establish, construct, acquire, lease, operate or supply telecommunications transport networks or services not offered to the public generally.

3. *Definitions*

   For the purposes of this Annex:
   (a) "Telecommunications" means the transmission and reception of signals by any electromagnetic means.
   (b) "Public telecommunications transport service" means any telecommunications transport service required, explicitly or in effect, by a Member to be offered to the public generally. Such services may include, *inter alia*, telegraph, telephone, telex, and data transmission typically involving the real-time transmission of customer-supplied information between two or more points without any end-to-end change in the form or content of the customer's information.
   (c) "Public telecommunications transport network" means the public telecommunications infrastructure which permits telecommunications between and among defined network termination points.
   (d) "Intra-corporate communications" means telecommunications through which a company communicates within the company or with or among its subsidiaries, branches and, subject to a Member's domestic laws and regulations, affiliates. For these purposes, "subsidiaries", "branches" and, where applicable, "affiliates" shall be as defined by each Member. "Intra-corporate communications" in this Annex excludes commercial or non-

---

14 This paragraph is understood to mean that each Member shall ensure that the obligations of this Annex are applied with respect to suppliers of public telecommunications transport networks and services by whatever measures are necessary.

commercial services that are supplied to companies that are not related subsidiaries, branches or affiliates, or that are offered to customers or potential customers.

(e) Any reference to a paragraph or subparagraph of this Annex includes all subdivisions thereof.

4. *Transparency*

In the application of Article III of the Agreement, each Member shall ensure that relevant information on conditions affecting access to and use of public telecommunications transport networks and services is publicly available, including: tariffs and other terms and conditions of service; specifications of technical interfaces with such networks and services; information on bodies responsible for the preparation and adoption of standards affecting such access and use; conditions applying to attachment of terminal or other equipment; and notifications, registration or licensing requirements, if any.

5. *Access to and use of Public Telecommunications Transport Networks and Services*

(a) Each Member shall ensure that any service supplier of any other Member is accorded access to and use of public telecommunications transport networks and services on reasonable and non-discriminatory terms and conditions, for the supply of a service included in its Schedule. This obligation shall be applied, *inter alia*, through paragraphs (b) through (f).[15]

(b) Each Member shall ensure that service suppliers of any other Member have access to and use of any public telecommunications transport network or service offered within or across the border of that Member, including private leased circuits, and to this end shall ensure, subject to paragraphs (e) and (f), that such suppliers are permitted:

   (i) to purchase or lease and attach terminal or other equipment which interfaces with the network and which is necessary to supply a supplier's services;

  (ii) to interconnect private leased or owned circuits with public telecommunications transport networks and services or with circuits leased or owned by another service supplier; and

 (iii) to use operating protocols of the service supplier's choice in the supply of any service, other than as necessary to ensure the availability of telecommunications transport networks and services to the public generally.

(c) Each Member shall ensure that service suppliers of any other Member may use public telecommunications transport networks and services for the movement of information within and across borders, including for intra-corporate communications of such service suppliers, and for access to information contained in data bases or otherwise stored in machine-readable form in the territory of any Member. Any new or amended measures of a Member significantly affecting such use shall be notified and shall be subject to consultation, in accordance with relevant provisions of the Agreement.

(d) Notwithstanding the preceding paragraph, a Member may take such measures as are necessary to ensure the security and confidentiality of messages, subject to the requirement that such measures are not applied in a manner which would constitute a means of arbitrary or unjustifiable discrimination or a disguised restriction on trade in services.

(e) Each Member shall ensure that no condition is imposed on access to and use of public telecommunications transport networks and services other than as necessary:

   (i) to safeguard the public service responsibilities of suppliers of public telecommunications transport networks and services, in particular their ability to make their networks or services available to the public generally;

---

15 The term "non-discriminatory" is understood to refer to most-favoured-nation and national treatment as defined in the Agreement, as well as to reflect sector-specific usage of the term to mean "terms and conditions no less favourable than those accorded to any other user of like public telecommunications transport networks or services under like circumstances".

  (ii) to protect the technical integrity of public telecommunications transport networks or services; or
  (iii) to ensure that service suppliers of any other Member do not supply services unless permitted pursuant to commitments in the Member's Schedule.
  (f) Provided that they satisfy the criteria set out in paragraph (e), conditions for access to and use of public telecommunications transport networks and services may include:
    (i)   restrictions on resale or shared use of such services;
    (ii) a requirement to use specified technical interfaces, including interface protocols, for inter-connection with such networks and services;
    (iii) requirements, where necessary, for the inter-operability of such services and to encourage the achievement of the goals set out in paragraph 7(a);
    (iv) type approval of terminal or other equipment which interfaces with the network and technical requirements relating to the attachment of such equipment to such networks;
    (v)   restrictions on inter-connection of private leased or owned circuits with such networks or services or with circuits leased or owned by another service supplier; or
    (vi) notification, registration and licensing.
  (g) Notwithstanding the preceding paragraphs of this section, a developing country Member may, consistent with its level of development, place reasonable conditions on access to and use of public telecommunications transport networks and services necessary to strengthen its domestic telecommunications infrastructure and service capacity and to increase its participation in international trade in telecommunications services. Such conditions shall be specified in the Member's Schedule.

6. *Technical Cooperation*
  (a) Members recognize that an efficient, advanced telecommunications infrastructure in countries, particularly developing countries, is essential to the expansion of their trade in services. To this end, Members endorse and encourage the participation, to the fullest extent practicable, of developed and developing countries and their suppliers of public telecommunications transport networks and services and other entities in the development programmes of international and regional organizations, including the International Telecommunication Union, the United Nations Development Programme, and the International Bank for Reconstruction and Development.
  (b) Members shall encourage and support telecommunications cooperation among developing countries at the international, regional and sub-regional levels.
  (c) In cooperation with relevant international organizations, Members shall make available, where practicable, to developing countries information with respect to telecommunications services and developments in telecommunications and information technology to assist in strengthening their domestic telecommunications services sector.
  (d) Members shall give special consideration to opportunities for the least-developed countries to encourage foreign suppliers of telecommunications services to assist in the transfer of technology, training and other activities that support the development of their telecommunications infrastructure and expansion of their telecommunications services trade.

7. *Relation to International Organizations and Agreements*
  (a) Members recognize the importance of international standards for global compatibility and inter-operability of telecommunication networks and services and undertake to promote such standards through the work of relevant international bodies, including the International Telecommunication Union and the International Organization for Standardization.
  (b) Members recognize the role played by intergovernmental and non-governmental organizations and agreements in ensuring the efficient operation of domestic and global

telecommunications services, in particular the International Telecommunication Union. Members shall make appropriate arrangements, where relevant, for consultation with such organizations on matters arising from the implementation of this Annex.

ANNEX ON NEGOTIATIONS ON BASIC TELECOMMUNICATIONS

1. Article II and the Annex on Article II Exemptions, including the requirement to list in the Annex any measure inconsistent with most-favoured-nation treatment that a Member will maintain, shall enter into force for basic telecommunications only on:
    (a) the implementation date to be determined under paragraph 5 of the Ministerial Decision on Negotiations on Basic Telecommunications; or,
    (b) should the negotiations not succeed, the date of the final report of the Negotiating Group on Basic Telecommunications provided for in that Decision.
2. Paragraph 1 shall not apply to any specific commitment on basic telecommunications which is inscribed in a Member's Schedule.

Fourth Protocol to the General Agreement on Trade in Services

Date	15 April 1997
In force	5 February 1998
Source	36 ILM 354 (1997)
Link	<http://www.wto.org/english/docs_e/legal_e/4prote_sl20_e.pdf>

Members of the World Trade Organization (hereinafter referred to as the "WTO") whose Schedules of Specific Commitments and Lists of Exemptions from Article II of the General Agreement on Trade in Services concerning basic telecommunications are annexed to this Protocol (hereinafter referred to as "Members concerned"),

Having carried out negotiations under the terms of the Ministerial Decision on Negotiations on Basic Telecommunications adopted at Marrakesh on 15 April 1994,

Having regard to the Annex on Negotiations on Basic Telecommunications,

Agree as follows:

1. Upon the entry into force of this Protocol, a Schedule of Specific Commitments and a List of Exemptions from Article II concerning basic telecommunications annexed to this Protocol relating to a Member shall, in accordance with the terms specified therein, supplement or modify the Schedule of Specific Commitments and the List of Article II Exemptions of that Member.

2. This Protocol shall be open for acceptance, by signature or otherwise, by the Members concerned until 30 November 1997.

3. The Protocol shall enter into force on 1 January 1998 provided it has been accepted by all Members concerned. If by 1 December 1997 the Protocol has not been accepted by all Members concerned, those Members which have accepted it by that date may decide, prior to 1 January 1998, on its entry into force.

4. This Protocol shall be deposited with the Director-General of the WTO. The Director-General of the WTO shall promptly furnish to each Member of the WTO a certified copy of this Protocol and notifications of acceptances thereof.

5. This Protocol shall be registered in accordance with the provisions of Article 102 of the Charter of the United Nations.

Done at Geneva this 15 April 1997, in a single copy in the English, French and Spanish languages, each text being authentic, except as otherwise provided for in respect of the Schedules annexed hereto.

II-16c

Telecommunications Services: Reference Paper

24 April 1996

NEGOTIATING GROUP ON BASIC TELECOMMUNICATIONS

The following are definitions and principles on the regulatory framework for the basic telecommunications services.

Definitions

Users mean service consumers and service suppliers.

Essential facilities mean facilities of a public telecommunications transport network or service that

(a) are exclusively or predominantly provided by a single or limited number of suppliers; and

(b) cannot feasibly be economically or technically substituted in order to provide a service.

A major supplier is a supplier which has the ability to materially affect the terms of participation (having regard to price and supply) in the relevant market for basic telecommunications services as a result of:

(a) control over essential facilities; or

(b) use of its position in the market.

1. Competitive safeguards

1.1 Prevention of anti-competitive practices in telecommunications

Appropriate measures shall be maintained for the purpose of preventing suppliers who, alone or together, are a major supplier from engaging in or continuing anti-competitive practices.

1.2 Safeguards

The anti-competitive practices referred to above shall include in particular:

(a) engaging in anti-competitive cross-subsidization;

(b) using information obtained from competitors with anti-competitive results; and

(c) not making available to other services suppliers on a timely basis technical information about essential facilities and commercially relevant information which are necessary for them to provide services.

2. Interconnection

2.1 This section applies to linking with suppliers providing public telecommunications transport networks or services in order to allow the users of one supplier to communicate with users of another supplier and to access services provided by another supplier, where specific commitments are undertaken.

2.2 Interconnection to be ensured

Interconnection with a major supplier will be ensured at any technically feasible point in the network. Such interconnection is provided.

(a) under non-discriminatory terms, conditions (including technical standards and specifications) and rates and of a quality no less favourable than that provided for its own like
services or for like services of non-affiliated service suppliers or for its subsidiaries or other
affiliates;

(b) in a timely fashion, on terms, conditions (including technical standards and specifications) and cost-oriented rates that are transparent, reasonable, having regard to economic
feasibility, and sufficiently unbundled so that the supplier need not pay for network
components or facilities that it does not require for the service to be provided; and

(c) upon request, at points in addition to the network termination points offered to the
majority of users, subject to charges that reflect the cost of construction of necessary
additional facilities.

2.3 Public availability of the procedures for interconnection negotiations
The procedures applicable for interconnection to a major supplier will be made publicly
available.

2.4 Transparency of interconnection arrangements
It is ensured that a major supplier will make publicly available either its interconnection
agreements or a reference interconnection offer.

2.5 Interconnection: dispute settlement
A service supplier requesting interconnection with a major supplier will have recourse, either:
(a) at any time or
(b) after a reasonable period of time which has been made publicly known
to an independent domestic body, which may be a regulatory body as referred to in paragraph 5
below, to resolve disputes regarding appropriate terms, conditions and rates for interconnection
within a reasonable period of time, to the extent that these have not been established previously.

3. Universal service
Any Member has the right to define the kind of universal service obligation it wishes to maintain.
Such obligations will not be regarded as anti-competitive per se, provided they are administered
in a transparent, non-discriminatory and competitively neutral manner and are not more
burdensome than necessary for the kind of universal service defined by the Member.

4. Public availability of licensing criteria
Where a licence is required, the following will be made publicly available:

(a) all the licensing criteria and the period of time normally required to reach a decision concerning an application for a licence and
(b) the terms and conditions of individual licences.

The reasons for the denial of a licence will be made known to the applicant upon request.

5. Independent regulators
The regulatory body is separate from, and not accountable to, any supplier of basic telecommunications services. The decisions of and the procedures used by regulators shall be impartial with
respect to all market participants.

6. Allocation and use of scarce resources
Any procedures for the allocation and use of scarce resources, including frequencies, numbers
and rights of way, will be carried out in an objective, timely, transparent and non-discriminatory
manner. The current state of allocated frequency bands will be made publicly available, but
detailed identification of frequencies allocated for specific government uses is not required.

Fifth Protocol to the General Agreement on Trade in Services

Members of the World Trade Organization (hereinafter referred to as the "WTO") whose Schedules of Specific Commitments and Lists of Exemptions from Article II of the General Agreement on Trade in Services concerning financial services are annexed to this Protocol (hereinafter referred to as "Members concerned"),

Having carried out negotiations under the terms of the Second Decision on Financial Services adopted by the Council for Trade in Services on 21 July 1995 (S/L/9),

Agree as follows:

1. A Schedule of Specific Commitments and a List of Exemptions from Article II concerning financial services annexed to this Protocol relating to a Member shall, upon the entry into force of this Protocol for that Member, replace the financial services sections of the Schedule of Specific Commitments and the List of Article II Exemptions of that Member.

2. This Protocol shall be open for acceptance, by signature or otherwise, by the Members concerned until 29 January 1999.

3. This Protocol shall enter into force on the 30th day following the date of its acceptance by all Members concerned. If by 30 January 1999 it has not been accepted by all Members concerned, those Members which have accepted it before that date may, within a period of 30 days thereafter, decide on its entry into force.

4. This Protocol shall be deposited with the Director-General of the WTO. The Director-General of the WTO shall promptly furnish to each Member of the WTO a certified copy of this Protocol and notifications of acceptances thereof pursuant to paragraph 3.

5. This Protocol shall be registered in accordance with the provisions of Article 102 of the Charter of the United Nations.

Done at Geneva this --- day of [month] one thousand nine hundred and ninety-[---], in a single copy in English, French and Spanish languages, each text being authentic, except as otherwise provided for in respect of the Schedules annexed hereto.

Trade-Related Aspects of Intellectual Property Rights

II-17a

Agreement on Trade-Related Aspects of Intellectual Property Rights

AGREEMENT ON TRADE-RELATED ASPECTS OF INTELLECTUAL PROPERTY RIGHTS

Members,

Desiring to reduce distortions and impediments to international trade, and taking into account the need to promote effective and adequate protection of intellectual property rights, and to ensure that measures and procedures to enforce intellectual property rights do not themselves become barriers to legitimate trade;

Recognizing, to this end, the need for new rules and disciplines concerning:

(a) the applicability of the basic principles of GATT 1994 and of relevant international intellectual property agreements or conventions;

(b) the provision of adequate standards and principles concerning the availability, scope and use of trade-related intellectual property rights;

(c) the provision of effective and appropriate means for the enforcement of trade-related intellectual property rights, taking into account differences in national legal systems;

(d) the provision of effective and expeditious procedures for the multilateral prevention and settlement of disputes between governments; and

(e) transitional arrangements aiming at the fullest participation in the results of the negotiations;

Recognizing the need for a multilateral framework of principles, rules and disciplines dealing with international trade in counterfeit goods;

Recognizing that intellectual property rights are private rights;

Recognizing the underlying public policy objectives of national systems for the protection of intellectual property, including developmental and technological objectives;

Recognizing also the special needs of the least-developed country Members in respect of maximum flexibility in the domestic implementation of laws and regulations in order to enable them to create a sound and viable technological base;

Emphasizing the importance of reducing tensions by reaching strengthened commitments to resolve disputes on trade-related intellectual property issues through multilateral procedures;

Desiring to establish a mutually supportive relationship between the WTO and the World Intellectual Property Organization (referred to in this Agreement as "WIPO") as well as other relevant international organizations;

Hereby agree as follows:

PART I   GENERAL PROVISIONS AND BASIC PRINCIPLES

Article 1   Nature and Scope of Obligations

1. Members shall give effect to the provisions of this Agreement. Members may, but shall not be obliged to, implement in their law more extensive protection than is required by this Agreement, provided that such protection does not contravene the provisions of this Agreement. Members shall be free to determine the appropriate method of implementing the provisions of this Agreement within their own legal system and practice.

2. For the purposes of this Agreement, the term "intellectual property" refers to all categories of intellectual property that are the subject of Sections 1 through 7 of Part II.

3. Members shall accord the treatment provided for in this Agreement to the nationals of other Members.[1] In respect of the relevant intellectual property right, the nationals of other Members shall be understood as those natural or legal persons that would meet the criteria

---

1 When "nationals" are referred to in this Agreement, they shall be deemed, in the case of a separate customs territory Member of the WTO, to mean persons, natural or legal, who are domiciled or who have a real and effective industrial or commercial establishment in that customs territory.

for eligibility for protection provided for in the Paris Convention (1967), the Berne Convention (1971), the Rome Convention and the Treaty on Intellectual Property in Respect of Integrated Circuits, were all Members of the WTO members of those conventions.[2] Any Member availing itself of the possibilities provided in paragraph 3 of Article 5 or paragraph 2 of Article 6 of the Rome Convention shall make a notification as foreseen in those provisions to the Council for Trade-Related Aspects of Intellectual Property Rights (the "Council for TRIPS").

Article 2   Intellectual Property Conventions

1. In respect of Parts II, III and IV of this Agreement, Members shall comply with Articles 1 through 12, and Article 19, of the Paris Convention (1967).

2. Nothing in Parts I to IV of this Agreement shall derogate from existing obligations that Members may have to each other under the Paris Convention, the Berne Convention, the Rome Convention and the Treaty on Intellectual Property in Respect of Integrated Circuits.

Article 3   National Treatment

1. Each Member shall accord to the nationals of other Members treatment no less favourable than that it accords to its own nationals with regard to the protection[3] of intellectual property, subject to the exceptions already provided in, respectively, the Paris Convention (1967), the Berne Convention (1971), the Rome Convention or the Treaty on Intellectual Property in Respect of Integrated Circuits. In respect of performers, producers of phonograms and broadcasting organizations, this obligation only applies in respect of the rights provided under this Agreement. Any Member availing itself of the possibilities provided in Article 6 of the Berne Convention (1971) or paragraph 1(b) of Article 16 of the Rome Convention shall make a notification as foreseen in those provisions to the Council for TRIPS.

2. Members may avail themselves of the exceptions permitted under paragraph 1 in relation to judicial and administrative procedures, including the designation of an address for service or the appointment of an agent within the jurisdiction of a Member, only where such exceptions are necessary to secure compliance with laws and regulations which are not inconsistent with the provisions of this Agreement and where such practices are not applied in a manner which would constitute a disguised restriction on trade.

Article 4   Most-Favoured-Nation Treatment

With regard to the protection of intellectual property, any advantage, favour, privilege or immunity granted by a Member to the nationals of any other country shall be accorded immediately and unconditionally to the nationals of all other Members. Exempted from this obligation are any advantage, favour, privilege or immunity accorded by a Member:

(a) deriving from international agreements on judicial assistance or law enforcement of a general nature and not particularly confined to the protection of intellectual property;

(b) granted in accordance with the provisions of the Berne Convention (1971) or the Rome Convention authorizing that the treatment accorded be a function not of national treatment but of the treatment accorded in another country;

(c) in respect of the rights of performers, producers of phonograms and broadcasting organizations not provided under this Agreement;

---

2 In this Agreement, "Paris Convention" refers to the Paris Convention for the Protection of Industrial Property; "Paris Convention (1967)" refers to the Stockholm Act of this Convention of 14 July 1967. "Berne Convention" refers to the Berne Convention for the Protection of Literary and Artistic Works; "Berne Convention (1971)" refers to the Paris Act of this Convention of 24 July 1971. "Rome Convention" refers to the International Convention for the Protection of Performers, Producers of Phonograms and Broadcasting Organizations, adopted at Rome on 26 October 1961. "Treaty on Intellectual Property in Respect of Integrated Circuits" (IPIC Treaty) refers to the Treaty on Intellectual Property in Respect of Integrated Circuits, adopted at Washington on 26 May 1989. "WTO Agreement" refers to the Agreement Establishing the WTO.

3 For the purposes of Articles 3 and 4, "protection" shall include matters affecting the availability, acquisition, scope, maintenance and enforcement of intellectual property rights as well as those matters affecting the use of intellectual property rights specifically addressed in this Agreement.

(d) deriving from international agreements related to the protection of intellectual property which entered into force prior to the entry into force of the WTO Agreement, provided that such agreements are notified to the Council for TRIPS and do not constitute an arbitrary or unjustifiable discrimination against nationals of other Members.

Article 5   Multilateral Agreements on Acquisition or Maintenance of Protection

The obligations under Articles 3 and 4 do not apply to procedures provided in multilateral agreements concluded under the auspices of WIPO relating to the acquisition or maintenance of intellectual property rights.

Article 6   Exhaustion

For the purposes of dispute settlement under this Agreement, subject to the provisions of Articles 3 and 4 nothing in this Agreement shall be used to address the issue of the exhaustion of intellectual property rights.

Article 7   Objectives

The protection and enforcement of intellectual property rights should contribute to the promotion of technological innovation and to the transfer and dissemination of technology, to the mutual advantage of producers and users of technological knowledge and in a manner conducive to social and economic welfare, and to a balance of rights and obligations.

Article 8   Principles

1. Members may, in formulating or amending their laws and regulations, adopt measures necessary to protect public health and nutrition, and to promote the public interest in sectors of vital importance to their socio-economic and technological development, provided that such measures are consistent with the provisions of this Agreement.

2. Appropriate measures, provided that they are consistent with the provisions of this Agreement, may be needed to prevent the abuse of intellectual property rights by right holders or the resort to practices which unreasonably restrain trade or adversely affect the international transfer of technology.

PART II   STANDARDS CONCERNING THE AVAILABILITY, SCOPE AND USE OF INTELLECTUAL PROPERTY RIGHTS

SECTION 1   COPYRIGHT AND RELATED RIGHTS

Article 9   Relation to the Berne Convention

1. Members shall comply with Articles 1 through 21 of the Berne Convention (1971) and the Appendix thereto. However, Members shall not have rights or obligations under this Agreement in respect of the rights conferred under Article 6*bis* of that Convention or of the rights derived therefrom.

2. Copyright protection shall extend to expressions and not to ideas, procedures, methods of operation or mathematical concepts as such.

Article 10   Computer Programs and Compilations of Data

1. Computer programs, whether in source or object code, shall be protected as literary works under the Berne Convention (1971).

2. Compilations of data or other material, whether in machine readable or other form, which by reason of the selection or arrangement of their contents constitute intellectual creations shall be protected as such. Such protection, which shall not extend to the data or material itself, shall be without prejudice to any copyright subsisting in the data or material itself.

Article 11   Rental Rights

In respect of at least computer programs and cinematographic works, a Member shall provide authors and their successors in title the right to authorize or to prohibit the commercial rental to the public of originals or copies of their copyright works. A Member shall be excepted from this obligation in respect of cinematographic works unless such rental has led to widespread copying of such works which is materially impairing the exclusive right of reproduction conferred in that Member on authors and their successors in title. In respect of computer programs, this obligation does not apply to rentals where the program itself is not the essential object of the rental.

Article 12   Term of Protection

Whenever the term of protection of a work, other than a photographic work or a work of applied art, is calculated on a basis other than the life of a natural person, such term shall be no less than 50 years from the end of the calendar year of authorized publication, or, failing such authorized publication within 50 years from the making of the work, 50 years from the end of the calendar year of making.

Article 13   Limitations and Exceptions

Members shall confine limitations or exceptions to exclusive rights to certain special cases which do not conflict with a normal exploitation of the work and do not unreasonably prejudice the legitimate interests of the right holder.

Article 14   Protection of Performers, Producers of Phonograms (Sound Recordings) and Broadcasting Organizations

1. In respect of a fixation of their performance on a phonogram, performers shall have the possibility of preventing the following acts when undertaken without their authorization: the fixation of their unfixed performance and the reproduction of such fixation. Performers shall also have the possibility of preventing the following acts when undertaken without their authorization: the broadcasting by wireless means and the communication to the public of their live performance.

2. Producers of phonograms shall enjoy the right to authorize or prohibit the direct or indirect reproduction of their phonograms.

3. Broadcasting organizations shall have the right to prohibit the following acts when undertaken without their authorization: the fixation, the reproduction of fixations, and the rebroadcasting by wireless means of broadcasts, as well as the communication to the public of television broadcasts of the same. Where Members do not grant such rights to broadcasting organizations, they shall provide owners of copyright in the subject matter of broadcasts with the possibility of preventing the above acts, subject to the provisions of the Berne Convention (1971).

4. The provisions of Article 11 in respect of computer programs shall apply *mutatis mutandis* to producers of phonograms and any other right holders in phonograms as determined in a Member's law. If on 15 April 1994 a Member has in force a system of equitable remuneration of right holders in respect of the rental of phonograms, it may maintain such system provided that the commercial rental of phonograms is not giving rise to the material impairment of the exclusive rights of reproduction of right holders.

5. The term of the protection available under this Agreement to performers and producers of phonograms shall last at least until the end of a period of 50 years computed from the end of the calendar year in which the fixation was made or the performance took place. The term of protection granted pursuant to paragraph 3 shall last for at least 20 years from the end of the calendar year in which the broadcast took place.

6. Any Member may, in relation to the rights conferred under paragraphs 1, 2 and 3, provide for conditions, limitations, exceptions and reservations to the extent permitted by the Rome Convention. However, the provisions of Article 18 of the Berne Convention (1971) shall also apply, *mutatis mutandis*, to the rights of performers and producers of phonograms in phonograms.

SECTION 2   TRADEMARKS

Article 15   Protectable Subject Matter

1. Any sign, or any combination of signs, capable of distinguishing the goods or services of one undertaking from those of other undertakings, shall be capable of constituting a trademark. Such signs, in particular words including personal names, letters, numerals, figurative elements and combinations of colours as well as any combination of such signs, shall be eligible for registration as trademarks. Where signs are not inherently capable of distinguishing the relevant goods or services, Members may make registrability depend on distinctiveness acquired through use. Members may require, as a condition of registration, that signs be visually perceptible.

2. Paragraph 1 shall not be understood to prevent a Member from denying registration of a trademark on other grounds, provided that they do not derogate from the provisions of the Paris Convention (1967).

3. Members may make registrability depend on use. However, actual use of a trademark shall not be a condition for filing an application for registration. An application shall not be refused solely on the ground that intended use has not taken place before the expiry of a period of three years from the date of application.

4. The nature of the goods or services to which a trademark is to be applied shall in no case form an obstacle to registration of the trademark.

5. Members shall publish each trademark either before it is registered or promptly after it is registered and shall afford a reasonable opportunity for petitions to cancel the registration. In addition, Members may afford an opportunity for the registration of a trademark to be opposed.

Article 16   Rights Conferred

1. The owner of a registered trademark shall have the exclusive right to prevent all third parties not having the owner's consent from using in the course of trade identical or similar signs for goods or services which are identical or similar to those in respect of which the trademark is registered where such use would result in a likelihood of confusion. In case of the use of an identical sign for identical goods or services, a likelihood of confusion shall be presumed. The rights described above shall not prejudice any existing prior rights, nor shall they affect the possibility of Members making rights available on the basis of use.

2. Article 6*bis* of the Paris Convention (1967) shall apply, *mutatis mutandis*, to services. In determining whether a trademark is well-known, Members shall take account of the knowledge of the trademark in the relevant sector of the public, including knowledge in the Member concerned which has been obtained as a result of the promotion of the trademark.

3. Article 6*bis* of the Paris Convention (1967) shall apply, *mutatis mutandis*, to goods or services which are not similar to those in respect of which a trademark is registered, provided that use of that trademark in relation to those goods or services would indicate a connection between those goods or services and the owner of the registered trademark and provided that the interests of the owner of the registered trademark are likely to be damaged by such use.

Article 17   Exceptions

Members may provide limited exceptions to the rights conferred by a trademark, such as fair use of descriptive terms, provided that such exceptions take account of the legitimate interests of the owner of the trademark and of third parties.

Article 18   Term of Protection

Initial registration, and each renewal of registration, of a trademark shall be for a term of no less than seven years. The registration of a trademark shall be renewable indefinitely.

Article 19   Requirement of Use

1. If use is required to maintain a registration, the registration may be cancelled only after an uninterrupted period of at least three years of non-use, unless valid reasons based on the

existence of obstacles to such use are shown by the trademark owner. Circumstances arising independently of the will of the owner of the trademark which constitute an obstacle to the use of the trademark, such as import restrictions on or other government requirements for goods or services protected by the trademark, shall be recognized as valid reasons for non-use.

2. When subject to the control of its owner, use of a trademark by another person shall be recognized as use of the trademark for the purpose of maintaining the registration.

Article 20   Other Requirements

The use of a trademark in the course of trade shall not be unjustifiably encumbered by special requirements, such as use with another trademark, use in a special form or use in a manner detrimental to its capability to distinguish the goods or services of one undertaking from those of other undertakings. This will not preclude a requirement prescribing the use of the trademark identifying the undertaking producing the goods or services along with, but without linking it to, the trademark distinguishing the specific goods or services in question of that undertaking.

Article 21   Licensing and Assignment

Members may determine conditions on the licensing and assignment of trademarks, it being understood that the compulsory licensing of trademarks shall not be permitted and that the owner of a registered trademark shall have the right to assign the trademark with or without the transfer of the business to which the trademark belongs.

SECTION 3   GEOGRAPHICAL INDICATIONS

Article 22   Protection of Geographical Indications

1. Geographical indications are, for the purposes of this Agreement, indications which identify a good as originating in the territory of a Member, or a region or locality in that territory, where a given quality, reputation or other characteristic of the good is essentially attributable to its geographical origin.

2. In respect of geographical indications, Members shall provide the legal means for interested parties to prevent:
   (a) the use of any means in the designation or presentation of a good that indicates or suggests that the good in question originates in a geographical area other than the true place of origin in a manner which misleads the public as to the geographical origin of the good;
   (b) any use which constitutes an act of unfair competition within the meaning of Article 10*bis* of the Paris Convention (1967).

3. A Member shall, *ex officio* if its legislation so permits or at the request of an interested party, refuse or invalidate the registration of a trademark which contains or consists of a geographical indication with respect to goods not originating in the territory indicated, if use of the indication in the trademark for such goods in that Member is of such a nature as to mislead the public as to the true place of origin.

4. The protection under paragraphs 1, 2 and 3 shall be applicable against a geographical indication which, although literally true as to the territory, region or locality in which the goods originate, falsely represents to the public that the goods originate in another territory.

Article 23   Additional Protection for Geographical Indications for Wines and Spirits

1. Each Member shall provide the legal means for interested parties to prevent use of a geographical indication identifying wines for wines not originating in the place indicated by the geographical indication in question or identifying spirits for spirits not originating in the place indicated by the geographical indication in question, even where the true origin of the

goods is indicated or the geographical indication is used in translation or accompanied by expressions such as "kind", "type", "style", "imitation" or the like.[4]

2. The registration of a trademark for wines which contains or consists of a geographical indication identifying wines or for spirits which contains or consists of a geographical indication identifying spirits shall be refused or invalidated, *ex officio* if a Member's legislation so permits or at the request of an interested party, with respect to such wines or spirits not having this origin.

3. In the case of homonymous geographical indications for wines, protection shall be accorded to each indication, subject to the provisions of paragraph 4 of Article 22. Each Member shall determine the practical conditions under which the homonymous indications in question will be differentiated from each other, taking into account the need to ensure equitable treatment of the producers concerned and that consumers are not misled.

4. In order to facilitate the protection of geographical indications for wines, negotiations shall be undertaken in the Council for TRIPS concerning the establishment of a multilateral system of notification and registration of geographical indications for wines eligible for protection in those Members participating in the system.

Article 24   International Negotiations; Exceptions

1. Members agree to enter into negotiations aimed at increasing the protection of individual geographical indications under Article 23. The provisions of paragraphs 4 through 8 below shall not be used by a Member to refuse to conduct negotiations or to conclude bilateral or multilateral agreements. In the context of such negotiations, Members shall be willing to consider the continued applicability of these provisions to individual geographical indications whose use was the subject of such negotiations.

2. The Council for TRIPS shall keep under review the application of the provisions of this Section; the first such review shall take place within two years of the entry into force of the WTO Agreement. Any matter affecting the compliance with the obligations under these provisions may be drawn to the attention of the Council, which, at the request of a Member, shall consult with any Member or Members in respect of such matter in respect of which it has not been possible to find a satisfactory solution through bilateral or plurilateral consultations between the Members concerned. The Council shall take such action as may be agreed to facilitate the operation and further the objectives of this Section.

3. In implementing this Section, a Member shall not diminish the protection of geographical indications that existed in that Member immediately prior to the date of entry into force of the WTO Agreement.

4. Nothing in this Section shall require a Member to prevent continued and similar use of a particular geographical indication of another Member identifying wines or spirits in connection with goods or services by any of its nationals or domiciliaries who have used that geographical indication in a continuous manner with regard to the same or related goods or services in the territory of that Member either (*a*) for at least 10 years preceding 15 April 1994 or (*b*) in good faith preceding that date.

5. Where a trademark has been applied for or registered in good faith, or where rights to a trademark have been acquired through use in good faith either:
   (a) before the date of application of these provisions in that Member as defined in Part VI; or
   (b) before the geographical indication is protected in its country of origin;
   measures adopted to implement this Section shall not prejudice eligibility for or the validity of the registration of a trademark, or the right to use a trademark, on the basis that such a trademark is identical with, or similar to, a geographical indication.

---

4 Notwithstanding the first sentence of Article 42, Members may, with respect to these obligations, instead provide for enforcement by administrative action.

6. Nothing in this Section shall require a Member to apply its provisions in respect of a geographical indication of any other Member with respect to goods or services for which the relevant indication is identical with the term customary in common language as the common name for such goods or services in the territory of that Member. Nothing in this Section shall require a Member to apply its provisions in respect of a geographical indication of any other Member with respect to products of the vine for which the relevant indication is identical with the customary name of a grape variety existing in the territory of that Member as of the date of entry into force of the WTO Agreement.

7. A Member may provide that any request made under this Section in connection with the use or registration of a trademark must be presented within five years after the adverse use of the protected indication has become generally known in that Member or after the date of registration of the trademark in that Member provided that the trademark has been published by that date, if such date is earlier than the date on which the adverse use became generally known in that Member, provided that the geographical indication is not used or registered in bad faith.

8. The provisions of this Section shall in no way prejudice the right of any person to use, in the course of trade, that person's name or the name of that person's predecessor in business, except where such name is used in such a manner as to mislead the public.

9. There shall be no obligation under this Agreement to protect geographical indications which are not or cease to be protected in their country of origin, or which have fallen into disuse in that country.

SECTION 4   INDUSTRIAL DESIGNS

Article 25   Requirements for Protection

1. Members shall provide for the protection of independently created industrial designs that are new or original. Members may provide that designs are not new or original if they do not significantly differ from known designs or combinations of known design features. Members may provide that such protection shall not extend to designs dictated essentially by technical or functional considerations.

2. Each Member shall ensure that requirements for securing protection for textile designs, in particular in regard to any cost, examination or publication, do not unreasonably impair the opportunity to seek and obtain such protection. Members shall be free to meet this obligation through industrial design law or through copyright law.

Article 26   Protection

1. The owner of a protected industrial design shall have the right to prevent third parties not having the owner's consent from making, selling or importing articles bearing or embodying a design which is a copy, or substantially a copy, of the protected design, when such acts are undertaken for commercial purposes.

2. Members may provide limited exceptions to the protection of industrial designs, provided that such exceptions do not unreasonably conflict with the normal exploitation of protected industrial designs and do not unreasonably prejudice the legitimate interests of the owner of the protected design, taking account of the legitimate interests of third parties.

3. The duration of protection available shall amount to at least 10 years.

SECTION 5   PATENTS

Article 27   Patentable Subject Matter

1. Subject to the provisions of paragraphs 2 and 3, patents shall be available for any inventions, whether products or processes, in all fields of technology, provided that they are new, involve

an inventive step and are capable of industrial application.[5] Subject to paragraph 4 of Article 65, paragraph 8 of Article 70 and paragraph 3 of this Article, patents shall be available and patent rights enjoyable without discrimination as to the place of invention, the field of technology and whether products are imported or locally produced.

2. Members may exclude from patentability inventions, the prevention within their territory of the commercial exploitation of which is necessary to protect *ordre public* or morality, including to protect human, animal or plant life or health or to avoid serious prejudice to the environment, provided that such exclusion is not made merely because the exploitation is prohibited by their law.

3. Members may also exclude from patentability:
    (a) diagnostic, therapeutic and surgical methods for the treatment of humans or animals;
    (b) plants and animals other than micro-organisms, and essentially biological processes for the production of plants or animals other than non-biological and microbiological processes. However, Members shall provide for the protection of plant varieties either by patents or by an effective *sui generis* system or by any combination thereof. The provisions of this subparagraph shall be reviewed four years after the date of entry into force of the WTO Agreement.

Article 28   Rights Conferred

1. A patent shall confer on its owner the following exclusive rights:
    (a) where the subject matter of a patent is a product, to prevent third parties not having the owner's consent from the acts of: making, using, offering for sale, selling, or importing[6] for these purposes that product;
    (b) where the subject matter of a patent is a process, to prevent third parties not having the owner's consent from the act of using the process, and from the acts of: using, offering for sale, selling, or importing for these purposes at least the product obtained directly by that process.

2. Patent owners shall also have the right to assign, or transfer by succession, the patent and to conclude licensing contracts.

Article 29   Conditions on Patent Applicants

1. Members shall require that an applicant for a patent shall disclose the invention in a manner sufficiently clear and complete for the invention to be carried out by a person skilled in the art and may require the applicant to indicate the best mode for carrying out the invention known to the inventor at the filing date or, where priority is claimed, at the priority date of the application.

2. Members may require an applicant for a patent to provide information concerning the applicant's corresponding foreign applications and grants.

Article 30   Exceptions to Rights Conferred

Members may provide limited exceptions to the exclusive rights conferred by a patent, provided that such exceptions do not unreasonably conflict with a normal exploitation of the patent and do not unreasonably prejudice the legitimate interests of the patent owner, taking account of the legitimate interests of third parties.

Article 31   Other Use Without Authorization of the Right Holder

Where the law of a Member allows for other use[7] of the subject matter of a patent without the authorization of the right holder, including use by the government or third parties authorized by the government, the following provisions shall be respected:

---

5 For the purposes of this Article, the terms "inventive step" and "capable of industrial application" may be deemed by a Member to be synonymous with the terms "non-obvious" and "useful" respectively.

6 This right, like all other rights conferred under this Agreement in respect of the use, sale, importation or other distribution of goods, is subject to the provisions of Article 6.

7 "Other use" refers to use other than that allowed under Article 30.

(a) authorization of such use shall be considered on its individual merits;

(b) such use may only be permitted if, prior to such use, the proposed user has made efforts to obtain authorization from the right holder on reasonable commercial terms and conditions and that such efforts have not been successful within a reasonable period of time. This requirement may be waived by a Member in the case of a national emergency or other circumstances of extreme urgency or in cases of public non-commercial use. In situations of national emergency or other circumstances of extreme urgency, the right holder shall, nevertheless, be notified as soon as reasonably practicable. In the case of public non-commercial use, where the government or contractor, without making a patent search, knows or has demonstrable grounds to know that a valid patent is or will be used by or for the government, the right holder shall be informed promptly;

(c) the scope and duration of such use shall be limited to the purpose for which it was authorized, and in the case of semi-conductor technology shall only be for public non-commercial use or to remedy a practice determined after judicial or administrative process to be anti-competitive;

(d) such use shall be non-exclusive;

(e) such use shall be non-assignable, except with that part of the enterprise or goodwill which enjoys such use;

(f) any such use shall be authorized predominantly for the supply of the domestic market of the Member authorizing such use;

(g) authorization for such use shall be liable, subject to adequate protection of the legitimate interests of the persons so authorized, to be terminated if and when the circumstances which led to it cease to exist and are unlikely to recur. The competent authority shall have the authority to review, upon motivated request, the continued existence of these circumstances;

(h) the right holder shall be paid adequate remuneration in the circumstances of each case, taking into account the economic value of the authorization;

(i) the legal validity of any decision relating to the authorization of such use shall be subject to judicial review or other independent review by a distinct higher authority in that Member;

(j) any decision relating to the remuneration provided in respect of such use shall be subject to judicial review or other independent review by a distinct higher authority in that Member;

(k) Members are not obliged to apply the conditions set forth in sub-paragraphs (b) and (f) where such use is permitted to remedy a practice determined after judicial or administrative process to be anti-competitive. The need to correct anti-competitive practices may be taken into account in determining the amount of remuneration in such cases. Competent authorities shall have the authority to refuse termination of authorization if and when the conditions which led to such authorization are likely to recur;

(l) where such use is authorized to permit the exploitation of a patent ("the second patent") which cannot be exploited without infringing another patent ("the first patent"), the following additional conditions shall apply:
  (i) the invention claimed in the second patent shall involve an important technical advance of considerable economic significance in relation to the invention claimed in the first patent;
  (ii) the owner of the first patent shall be entitled to a cross-licence on reasonable terms to use the invention claimed in the second patent; and
  (iii) the use authorized in respect of the first patent shall be non-assignable except with the assignment of the second patent.

Article 32   Revocation/Forfeiture
An opportunity for judicial review of any decision to revoke or forfeit a patent shall be available.

Article 33   Term of Protection

The term of protection available shall not end before the expiration of a period of twenty years counted from the filing date.[8]

Article 34   Process Patents: Burden of Proof

1. For the purposes of civil proceedings in respect of the infringement of the rights of the owner referred to in paragraph 1(b) of Article 28, if the subject matter of a patent is a process for obtaining a product, the judicial authorities shall have the authority to order the defendant to prove that the process to obtain an identical product is different from the patented process. Therefore, Members shall provide, in at least one of the following circumstances, that any identical product when produced without the consent of the patent owner shall, in the absence of proof to the contrary, be deemed to have been obtained by the patented process:
    (a) if the product obtained by the patented process is new;
    (b) if there is a substantial likelihood that the identical product was made by the process and the owner of the patent has been unable through reasonable efforts to determine the process actually used.

2. Any Member shall be free to provide that the burden of proof indicated in paragraph 1 shall be on the alleged infringer only if the condition referred to in subparagraph (a) is fulfilled or only if the condition referred to in subparagraph (b) is fulfilled.

3. In the adduction of proof to the contrary, the legitimate interests of defendants in protecting their manufacturing and business secrets shall be taken into account.

SECTION 6   LAYOUT-DESIGNS (TOPOGRAPHIES) OF INTEGRATED CIRCUITS

Article 35   Relation to the IPIC Treaty

Members agree to provide protection to the layout-designs (topographies) of integrated circuits (referred to in this Agreement as "layout-designs") in accordance with Articles 2 through 7 (other than paragraph 3 of Article 6), Article 12 and paragraph 3 of Article 16 of the Treaty on Intellectual Property in Respect of Integrated Circuits and, in addition, to comply with the following provisions.

Article 36   Scope of the Protection

Subject to the provisions of paragraph 1 of Article 37, Members shall consider unlawful the following acts if performed without the authorization of the right holder:[9] importing, selling, or otherwise distributing for commercial purposes a protected layout-design, an integrated circuit in which a protected layout-design is incorporated, or an article incorporating such an integrated circuit only in so far as it continues to contain an unlawfully reproduced layout-design.

Article 37   Acts Not Requiring the Authorization of the Right Holder

1. Notwithstanding Article 36, no Member shall consider unlawful the performance of any of the acts referred to in that Article in respect of an integrated circuit incorporating an unlawfully reproduced layout-design or any article incorporating such an integrated circuit where the person performing or ordering such acts did not know and had no reasonable ground to know, when acquiring the integrated circuit or article incorporating such an integrated circuit, that it incorporated an unlawfully reproduced layout-design. Members shall provide that, after the time that such person has received sufficient notice that the layout-design was unlawfully reproduced, that person may perform any of the acts with respect to the stock on hand or ordered before such time, but shall be liable to pay to the right holder a sum equivalent to a

---

8 It is understood that those Members which do not have a system of original grant may provide that the term of protection shall be computed from the filing date in the system of original grant.

9 The term "right holder" in this Section shall be understood as having the same meaning as the term "holder of the right" in the IPIC Treaty.

reasonable royalty such as would be payable under a freely negotiated licence in respect of such a layout-design.

2. The conditions set out in subparagraphs (a) through (k) of Article 31 shall apply *mutatis mutandis* in the event of any non-voluntary licensing of a layout-design or of its use by or for the government without the authorization of the right holder.

Article 38   Term of Protection

1. In Members requiring registration as a condition of protection, the term of protection of layout-designs shall not end before the expiration of a period of 10 years counted from the date of filing an application for registration or from the first commercial exploitation wherever in the world it occurs.

2. In Members not requiring registration as a condition for protection, layout-designs shall be protected for a term of no less than 10 years from the date of the first commercial exploitation wherever in the world it occurs.

3. Notwithstanding paragraphs 1 and 2, a Member may provide that protection shall lapse 15 years after the creation of the layout-design.

SECTION 7   PROTECTION OF UNDISCLOSED INFORMATION

Article 39

1. In the course of ensuring effective protection against unfair competition as provided in Article 10*bis* of the Paris Convention (1967), Members shall protect undisclosed information in accordance with paragraph 2 and data submitted to governments or governmental agencies in accordance with paragraph 3.

2. Natural and legal persons shall have the possibility of preventing information lawfully within their control from being disclosed to, acquired by, or used by others without their consent in a manner contrary to honest commercial practices[10] so long as such information:
    (a) is secret in the sense that it is not, as a body or in the precise configuration and assembly of its components, generally known among or readily accessible to persons within the circles that normally deal with the kind of information in question;
    (b) has commercial value because it is secret; and
    (c) has been subject to reasonable steps under the circumstances, by the person lawfully in control of the information, to keep it secret.

3. Members, when requiring, as a condition of approving the marketing of pharmaceutical or of agricultural chemical products which utilize new chemical entities, the submission of undisclosed test or other data, the origination of which involves a considerable effort, shall protect such data against unfair commercial use. In addition, Members shall protect such data against disclosure, except where necessary to protect the public, or unless steps are taken to ensure that the data are protected against unfair commercial use.

SECTION 8   CONTROL OF ANTI-COMPETITIVE PRACTICES IN CONTRACTUAL LICENCES

Article 40

1. Members agree that some licensing practices or conditions pertaining to intellectual property rights which restrain competition may have adverse effects on trade and may impede the transfer and dissemination of technology.

---

10 For the purpose of this provision, "a manner contrary to honest commercial practices" shall mean at least practices such as breach of contract, breach of confidence and inducement to breach, and includes the acquisition of undisclosed information by third parties who knew, or were grossly negligent in failing to know, that such practices were involved in the acquisition.

2. Nothing in this Agreement shall prevent Members from specifying in their legislation licensing practices or conditions that may in particular cases constitute an abuse of intellectual property rights having an adverse effect on competition in the relevant market. As provided above, a Member may adopt, consistently with the other provisions of this Agreement, appropriate measures to prevent or control such practices, which may include for example exclusive grantback conditions, conditions preventing challenges to validity and coercive package licensing, in the light of the relevant laws and regulations of that Member.

3. Each Member shall enter, upon request, into consultations with any other Member which has cause to believe that an intellectual property right owner that is a national or domiciliary of the Member to which the request for consultations has been addressed is undertaking practices in violation of the requesting Member's laws and regulations on the subject matter of this Section, and which wishes to secure compliance with such legislation, without prejudice to any action under the law and to the full freedom of an ultimate decision of either Member. The Member addressed shall accord full and sympathetic consideration to, and shall afford adequate opportunity for, consultations with the requesting Member, and shall cooperate through supply of publicly available non-confidential information of relevance to the matter in question and of other information available to the Member, subject to domestic law and to the conclusion of mutually satisfactory agreements concerning the safeguarding of its confidentiality by the requesting Member.

4. A Member whose nationals or domiciliaries are subject to proceedings in another Member concerning alleged violation of that other Member's laws and regulations on the subject matter of this Section shall, upon request, be granted an opportunity for consultations by the other Member under the same conditions as those foreseen in paragraph 3.

PART III   ENFORCEMENT OF INTELLECTUAL PROPERTY RIGHTS

SECTION 1   GENERAL OBLIGATIONS

Article 41

1. Members shall ensure that enforcement procedures as specified in this Part are available under their law so as to permit effective action against any act of infringement of intellectual property rights covered by this Agreement, including expeditious remedies to prevent infringements and remedies which constitute a deterrent to further infringements. These procedures shall be applied in such a manner as to avoid the creation of barriers to legitimate trade and to provide for safeguards against their abuse.

2. Procedures concerning the enforcement of intellectual property rights shall be fair and equitable. They shall not be unnecessarily complicated or costly, or entail unreasonable time-limits or unwarranted delays.

3. Decisions on the merits of a case shall preferably be in writing and reasoned. They shall be made available at least to the parties to the proceeding without undue delay. Decisions on the merits of a case shall be based only on evidence in respect of which parties were offered the opportunity to be heard.

4. Parties to a proceeding shall have an opportunity for review by a judicial authority of final administrative decisions and, subject to jurisdictional provisions in a Member's law concerning the importance of a case, of at least the legal aspects of initial judicial decisions on the merits of a case. However, there shall be no obligation to provide an opportunity for review of acquittals in criminal cases.

5. It is understood that this Part does not create any obligation to put in place a judicial system for the enforcement of intellectual property rights distinct from that for the enforcement of

law in general, nor does it affect the capacity of Members to enforce their law in general. Nothing in this Part creates any obligation with respect to the distribution of resources as between enforcement of intellectual property rights and the enforcement of law in general.

SECTION 2   CIVIL AND ADMINISTRATIVE PROCEDURES AND REMEDIES

Article 42   Fair and Equitable Procedures

Members shall make available to right holders[11] civil judicial procedures concerning the enforcement of any intellectual property right covered by this Agreement. Defendants shall have the right to written notice which is timely and contains sufficient detail, including the basis of the claims. Parties shall be allowed to be represented by independent legal counsel, and procedures shall not impose overly burdensome requirements concerning mandatory personal appearances. All parties to such procedures shall be duly entitled to substantiate their claims and to present all relevant evidence. The procedure shall provide a means to identify and protect confidential information, unless this would be contrary to existing constitutional requirements.

Article 43   Evidence

1. The judicial authorities shall have the authority, where a party has presented reasonably available evidence sufficient to support its claims and has specified evidence relevant to substantiation of its claims which lies in the control of the opposing party, to order that this evidence be produced by the opposing party, subject in appropriate cases to conditions which ensure the protection of confidential information.

2. In cases in which a party to a proceeding voluntarily and without good reason refuses access to, or otherwise does not provide necessary information within a reasonable period, or significantly impedes a procedure relating to an enforcement action, a Member may accord judicial authorities the authority to make preliminary and final determinations, affirmative or negative, on the basis of the information presented to them, including the complaint or the allegation presented by the party adversely affected by the denial of access to information, subject to providing the parties an opportunity to be heard on the allegations or evidence.

Article 44   Injunctions

1. The judicial authorities shall have the authority to order a party to desist from an infringement, *inter alia* to prevent the entry into the channels of commerce in their jurisdiction of imported goods that involve the infringement of an intellectual property right, immediately after customs clearance of such goods. Members are not obliged to accord such authority in respect of protected subject matter acquired or ordered by a person prior to knowing or having reasonable grounds to know that dealing in such subject matter would entail the infringement of an intellectual property right.

2. Notwithstanding the other provisions of this Part and provided that the provisions of Part II specifically addressing use by governments, or by third parties authorized by a government, without the authorization of the right holder are complied with, Members may limit the remedies available against such use to payment of remuneration in accordance with subparagraph (h) of Article 31. In other cases, the remedies under this Part shall apply or, where these remedies are inconsistent with a Member's law, declaratory judgments and adequate compensation shall be available.

Article 45   Damages

1. The judicial authorities shall have the authority to order the infringer to pay the right holder damages adequate to compensate for the injury the right holder has suffered because of an

---

11 For the purpose of this Part, the term "right holder" includes federations and associations having legal standing to assert such rights.

infringement of that person's intellectual property right by an infringer who knowingly, or with reasonable grounds to know, engaged in infringing activity.

2. The judicial authorities shall also have the authority to order the infringer to pay the right holder expenses, which may include appropriate attorney's fees. In appropriate cases, Members may authorize the judicial authorities to order recovery of profits and/or payment of pre-established damages even where the infringer did not knowingly, or with reasonable grounds to know, engage in infringing activity.

Article 46   Other Remedies

In order to create an effective deterrent to infringement, the judicial authorities shall have the authority to order that goods that they have found to be infringing be, without compensation of any sort, disposed of outside the channels of commerce in such a manner as to avoid any harm caused to the right holder, or, unless this would be contrary to existing constitutional requirements, destroyed. The judicial authorities shall also have the authority to order that materials and implements the predominant use of which has been in the creation of the infringing goods be, without compensation of any sort, disposed of outside the channels of commerce in such a manner as to minimize the risks of further infringements. In considering such requests, the need for proportionality between the seriousness of the infringement and the remedies ordered as well as the interests of third parties shall be taken into account. In regard to counterfeit trademark goods, the simple removal of the trademark unlawfully affixed shall not be sufficient, other than in exceptional cases, to permit release of the goods into the channels of commerce.

Article 47   Right of Information

Members may provide that the judicial authorities shall have the authority, unless this would be out of proportion to the seriousness of the infringement, to order the infringer to inform the right holder of the identity of third persons involved in the production and distribution of the infringing goods or services and of their channels of distribution.

Article 48   Indemnification of the Defendant

1. The judicial authorities shall have the authority to order a party at whose request measures were taken and who has abused enforcement procedures to provide to a party wrongfully enjoined or restrained adequate compensation for the injury suffered because of such abuse. The judicial authorities shall also have the authority to order the applicant to pay the defendant expenses, which may include appropriate attorney's fees.

2. In respect of the administration of any law pertaining to the protection or enforcement of intellectual property rights, Members shall only exempt both public authorities and officials from liability to appropriate remedial measures where actions are taken or intended in good faith in the course of the administration of that law.

Article 49   Administrative Procedures

To the extent that any civil remedy can be ordered as a result of administrative procedures on the merits of a case, such procedures shall conform to principles equivalent in substance to those set forth in this Section.

SECTION 3   PROVISIONAL MEASURES

Article 50

1. The judicial authorities shall have the authority to order prompt and effective provisional measures:
   (a) to prevent an infringement of any intellectual property right from occurring, and in particular to prevent the entry into the channels of commerce in their jurisdiction of goods, including imported goods immediately after customs clearance;
   (b) to preserve relevant evidence in regard to the alleged infringement.

2. The judicial authorities shall have the authority to adopt provisional measures *inaudita altera parte* where appropriate, in particular where any delay is likely to cause irreparable harm to the right holder, or where there is a demonstrable risk of evidence being destroyed.

3. The judicial authorities shall have the authority to require the applicant to provide any reasonably available evidence in order to satisfy themselves with a sufficient degree of certainty that the applicant is the right holder and that the applicant's right is being infringed or that such infringement is imminent, and to order the applicant to provide a security or equivalent assurance sufficient to protect the defendant and to prevent abuse.

4. Where provisional measures have been adopted *inaudita altera parte*, the parties affected shall be given notice, without delay after the execution of the measures at the latest. A review, including a right to be heard, shall take place upon request of the defendant with a view to deciding, within a reasonable period after the notification of the measures, whether these measures shall be modified, revoked or confirmed.

5. The applicant may be required to supply other information necessary for the identification of the goods concerned by the authority that will execute the provisional measures.

6. Without prejudice to paragraph 4, provisional measures taken on the basis of paragraphs 1 and 2 shall, upon request by the defendant, be revoked or otherwise cease to have effect, if proceedings leading to a decision on the merits of the case are not initiated within a reasonable period, to be determined by the judicial authority ordering the measures where a Member's law so permits or, in the absence of such a determination, not to exceed 20 working days or 31 calendar days, whichever is the longer.

7. Where the provisional measures are revoked or where they lapse due to any act or omission by the applicant, or where it is subsequently found that there has been no infringement or threat of infringement of an intellectual property right, the judicial authorities shall have the authority to order the applicant, upon request of the defendant, to provide the defendant appropriate compensation for any injury caused by these measures.

8. To the extent that any provisional measure can be ordered as a result of administrative procedures, such procedures shall conform to principles equivalent in substance to those set forth in this Section.

SECTION 4   SPECIAL REQUIREMENTS RELATED TO BORDER MEASURES[12]

Article 51   Suspension of Release by Customs Authorities

Members shall, in conformity with the provisions set out below, adopt procedures[13] to enable a right holder, who has valid grounds for suspecting that the importation of counterfeit trademark or pirated copyright goods[14] may take place, to lodge an application in writing with competent authorities, administrative or judicial, for the suspension by the customs authorities of the release into free circulation of such goods. Members may enable such an application to be made in respect of goods which involve other infringements of intellectual property rights, provided

---

12 Where a Member has dismantled substantially all controls over movement of goods across its border with another Member with which it forms part of a customs union, it shall not be required to apply the provisions of this Section at that border.

13 It is understood that there shall be no obligation to apply such procedures to imports of goods put on the market in another country by or with the consent of the right holder, or to goods in transit.

14 For the purposes of this Agreement:

(a) "counterfeit trademark goods" shall mean any goods, including packaging, bearing without authorization a trademark which is identical to the trademark validly registered in respect of such goods, or which cannot be distinguished in its essential aspects from such a trademark, and which thereby infringes the rights of the owner of the trademark in question under the law of the country of importation;

(b) "pirated copyright goods" shall mean any goods which are copies made without the consent of the right holder or person duly authorized by the right holder in the country of production and which are made directly or indirectly from an article where the making of that copy would have constituted an infringement of a copyright or a related right under the law of the country of importation.

that the requirements of this Section are met. Members may also provide for corresponding procedures concerning the suspension by the customs authorities of the release of infringing goods destined for exportation from their territories.

Article 52   Application

Any right holder initiating the procedures under Article 51 shall be required to provide adequate evidence to satisfy the competent authorities that, under the laws of the country of importation, there is *prima facie* an infringement of the right holder's intellectual property right and to supply a sufficiently detailed description of the goods to make them readily recognizable by the customs authorities. The competent authorities shall inform the applicant within a reasonable period whether they have accepted the application and, where determined by the competent authorities, the period for which the customs authorities will take action.

Article 53   Security or Equivalent Assurance

1. The competent authorities shall have the authority to require an applicant to provide a security or equivalent assurance sufficient to protect the defendant and the competent authorities and to prevent abuse. Such security or equivalent assurance shall not unreasonably deter recourse to these procedures.

2. Where pursuant to an application under this Section the release of goods involving industrial designs, patents, layout-designs or undisclosed information into free circulation has been suspended by customs authorities on the basis of a decision other than by a judicial or other independent authority, and the period provided for in Article 55 has expired without the granting of provisional relief by the duly empowered authority, and provided that all other conditions for importation have been complied with, the owner, importer, or consignee of such goods shall be entitled to their release on the posting of a security in an amount sufficient to protect the right holder for any infringement. Payment of such security shall not prejudice any other remedy available to the right holder, it being understood that the security shall be released if the right holder fails to pursue the right of action within a reasonable period of time.

Article 54   Notice of Suspension

The importer and the applicant shall be promptly notified of the suspension of the release of goods according to Article 51.

Article 55   Duration of Suspension

If, within a period not exceeding 10 working days after the applicant has been served notice of the suspension, the customs authorities have not been informed that proceedings leading to a decision on the merits of the case have been initiated by a party other than the defendant, or that the duly empowered authority has taken provisional measures prolonging the suspension of the release of the goods, the goods shall be released, provided that all other conditions for importation or exportation have been complied with; in appropriate cases, this time-limit may be extended by another 10 working days. If proceedings leading to a decision on the merits of the case have been initiated, a review, including a right to be heard, shall take place upon request of the defendant with a view to deciding, within a reasonable period, whether these measures shall be modified, revoked or confirmed. Not-withstanding the above, where the suspension of the release of goods is carried out or continued in accordance with a provisional judicial measure, the provisions of paragraph 6 of Article 50 shall apply.

Article 56   Indemnification of the Importer and of the Owner of the Goods

Relevant authorities shall have the authority to order the applicant to pay the importer, the consignee and the owner of the goods appropriate compensation for any injury caused to them through the wrongful detention of goods or through the detention of goods released pursuant to Article 55.

Article 57   Right of Inspection and Information

Without prejudice to the protection of confidential information, Members shall provide the competent authorities the authority to give the right holder sufficient opportunity to have any goods detained by the customs authorities inspected in order to substantiate the right holder's claims. The competent authorities shall also have authority to give the importer an equivalent opportunity to have any such goods inspected. Where a positive determination has been made on the merits of a case, Members may provide the competent authorities the authority to inform the right holder of the names and addresses of the consignor, the importer and the consignee and of the quantity of the goods in question.

Article 58   Ex Officio Action

Where Members require competent authorities to act upon their own initiative and to suspend the release of goods in respect of which they have acquired *prima facie* evidence that an intellectual property right is being infringed:

(a) the competent authorities may at any time seek from the right holder any information that may assist them to exercise these powers;

(b) the importer and the right holder shall be promptly notified of the suspension. Where the importer has lodged an appeal against the suspension with the competent authorities, the suspension shall be subject to the conditions, *mutatis mutandis*, set out at Article 55;

(c) Members shall only exempt both public authorities and officials from liability to appropriate remedial measures where actions are taken or intended in good faith.

Article 59   Remedies

Without prejudice to other rights of action open to the right holder and subject to the right of the defendant to seek review by a judicial authority, competent authorities shall have the authority to order the destruction or disposal of infringing goods in accordance with the principles set out in Article 46. In regard to counterfeit trademark goods, the authorities shall not allow the re-exportation of the infringing goods in an unaltered state or subject them to a different customs procedure, other than in exceptional circumstances.

Article 60   De Minimis Imports

Members may exclude from the application of the above provisions small quantities of goods of a non-commercial nature contained in travellers' personal luggage or sent in small consignments.

SECTION 5   CRIMINAL PROCEDURES

Article 61

Members shall provide for criminal procedures and penalties to be applied at least in cases of wilful trademark counterfeiting or copyright piracy on a commercial scale. Remedies available shall include imprisonment and/or monetary fines sufficient to provide a deterrent, consistently with the level of penalties applied for crimes of a corresponding gravity. In appropriate cases, remedies available shall also include the seizure, forfeiture and destruction of the infringing goods and of any materials and implements the predominant use of which has been in the commission of the offence. Members may provide for criminal procedures and penalties to be applied in other cases of infringement of intellectual property rights, in particular where they are committed wilfully and on a commercial scale.

PART IV   ACQUISITION AND MAINTENANCE OF INTELLECTUAL PROPERTY RIGHTS AND RELATED *INTER-PARTES* PROCEDURES

Article 62

1. Members may require, as a condition of the acquisition or maintenance of the intellectual property rights provided for under Sections 2 through 6 of Part II, compliance with reasonable

procedures and formalities. Such procedures and formalities shall be consistent with the provisions of this Agreement.

2. Where the acquisition of an intellectual property right is subject to the right being granted or registered, Members shall ensure that the procedures for grant or registration, subject to compliance with the substantive conditions for acquisition of the right, permit the granting or registration of the right within a reasonable period of time so as to avoid unwarranted curtailment of the period of protection.

3. Article 4 of the Paris Convention (1967) shall apply *mutatis mutandis* to service marks.

4. Procedures concerning the acquisition or maintenance of intellectual property rights and, where a Member's law provides for such procedures, administrative revocation and *inter partes* procedures such as opposition, revocation and cancellation, shall be governed by the general principles set out in paragraphs 2 and 3 of Article 41.

5. Final administrative decisions in any of the procedures referred to under paragraph 4 shall be subject to review by a judicial or quasi-judicial authority. However, there shall be no obligation to provide an opportunity for such review of decisions in cases of unsuccessful opposition or administrative revocation, provided that the grounds for such procedures can be the subject of invalidation procedures.

PART V   DISPUTE PREVENTION AND SETTLEMENT

Article 63   Transparency

1. Laws and regulations, and final judicial decisions and administrative rulings of general application, made effective by a Member pertaining to the subject matter of this Agreement (the availability, scope, acquisition, enforcement and prevention of the abuse of intellectual property rights) shall be published, or where such publication is not practicable made publicly available, in a national language, in such a manner as to enable governments and right holders to become acquainted with them. Agreements concerning the subject matter of this Agreement which are in force between the government or a governmental agency of a Member and the government or a governmental agency of another Member shall also be published.

2. Members shall notify the laws and regulations referred to in paragraph 1 to the Council for TRIPS in order to assist that Council in its review of the operation of this Agreement. The Council shall attempt to minimize the burden on Members in carrying out this obligation and may decide to waive the obligation to notify such laws and regulations directly to the Council if consultations with WIPO on the establishment of a common register containing these laws and regulations are successful. The Council shall also consider in this connection any action required regarding notifications pursuant to the obligations under this Agreement stemming from the provisions of Article *6ter* of the Paris Convention (1967).

3. Each Member shall be prepared to supply, in response to a written request from another Member, information of the sort referred to in paragraph 1. A Member, having reason to believe that a specific judicial decision or administrative ruling or bilateral agreement in the area of intellectual property rights affects its rights under this Agreement, may also request in writing to be given access to or be informed in sufficient detail of such specific judicial decisions or administrative rulings or bilateral agreements.

4. Nothing in paragraphs 1, 2 and 3 shall require Members to disclose confidential information which would impede law enforcement or otherwise be contrary to the public interest or would prejudice the legitimate commercial interests of particular enterprises, public or private.

Article 64   Dispute settlement

1. The provisions of Articles XXII and XXIII of GATT 1994 as elaborated and applied by the Dispute Settlement Understanding shall apply to consultations and the settlement of disputes under this Agreement except as otherwise specifically provided herein.

2. Subparagraphs 1(b) and 1(c) of Article XXIII of GATT 1994 shall not apply to the settlement of disputes under this Agreement for a period of five years from the date of entry into force of the WTO Agreement.

3. During the time period referred to in paragraph 2, the Council for TRIPS shall examine the scope and modalities for complaints of the type provided for under subparagraphs 1(b) and 1(c) of Article XXIII of GATT 1994 made pursuant to this Agreement, and submit its recommendations to the Ministerial Conference for approval. Any decision of the Ministerial Conference to approve such recommendations or to extend the period in paragraph 2 shall be made only by consensus, and approved recommendations shall be effective for all Members without further formal acceptance process.

PART VI   TRANSITIONAL ARRANGEMENTS

Article 65   Transitional Arrangements

1. Subject to the provisions of paragraphs 2, 3 and 4, no Member shall be obliged to apply the provisions of this Agreement before the expiry of a general period of one year following the date of entry into force of the WTO Agreement.

2. A developing country Member is entitled to delay for a further period of four years the date of application, as defined in paragraph 1, of the provisions of this Agreement other than Articles 3, 4 and 5.

3. Any other Member which is in the process of transformation from a centrally-planned into a market, free-enterprise economy and which is undertaking structural reform of its intellectual property system and facing special problems in the preparation and implementation of intellectual property laws and regulations, may also benefit from a period of delay as foreseen in paragraph 2.

4. To the extent that a developing country Member is obliged by this Agreement to extend product patent protection to areas of technology not so protectable in its territory on the general date of application of this Agreement for that Member, as defined in paragraph 2, it may delay the application of the provisions on product patents of Section 5 of Part II to such areas of technology for an additional period of five years.

5. A Member availing itself of a transitional period under paragraphs 1, 2, 3 or 4 shall ensure that any changes in its laws, regulations and practice made during that period do not result in a lesser degree of consistency with the provisions of this Agreement.

Article 66   Least-Developed Country Members

1. In view of the special needs and requirements of least-developed country Members, their economic, financial and administrative constraints, and their need for flexibility to create a viable technological base, such Members shall not be required to apply the provisions of this Agreement, other than Articles 3, 4 and 5, for a period of 10 years from the date of application as defined under paragraph 1 of Article 65. The Council for TRIPS shall, upon duly motivated request by a least-developed country Member, accord extensions of this period.

2. Developed country Members shall provide incentives to enterprises and institutions in their territories for the purpose of promoting and encouraging technology transfer to least-developed country Members in order to enable them to create a sound and viable technological base.

Article 67   Technical cooperation

In order to facilitate the implementation of this Agreement, developed country Members shall provide, on request and on mutually agreed terms and conditions, technical and financial cooperation in favour of developing and least-developed country Members. Such cooperation shall include assistance in the preparation of laws and regulations on the protection and enforcement of intellectual property rights as well as on the prevention of their abuse, and shall include support regarding the establishment or reinforcement of domestic offices and agencies relevant to these matters, including the training of personnel.

PART VII   INSTITUTIONAL ARRANGEMENTS; FINAL PROVISIONS

Article 68   Council for Trade-Related Aspects of Intellectual Property Rights

The Council for TRIPS shall monitor the operation of this Agreement and, in particular, Members' compliance with their obligations hereunder, and shall afford Members the opportunity of consulting on matters relating to the trade-related aspects of intellectual property rights. It shall carry out such other responsibilities as assigned to it by the Members, and it shall, in particular, provide any assistance requested by them in the context of dispute settlement procedures. In carrying out its functions, the Council for TRIPS may consult with and seek information from any source it deems appropriate. In consultation with WIPO, the Council shall seek to establish, within one year of its first meeting, appropriate arrangements for cooperation with bodies of that Organization.

Article 69   International Cooperation

Members agree to cooperate with each other with a view to eliminating international trade in goods infringing intellectual property rights. For this purpose, they shall establish and notify contact points in their administrations and be ready to exchange information on trade in infringing goods. They shall, in particular, promote the exchange of information and cooperation between customs authorities with regard to trade in counterfeit trademark goods and pirated copyright goods.

Article 70   Protection of Existing Subject Matter

1. This Agreement does not give rise to obligations in respect of acts which occurred before the date of application of the Agreement for the Member in question.

2. Except as otherwise provided for in this Agreement, this Agreement gives rise to obligations in respect of all subject matter existing at the date of application of this Agreement for the Member in question, and which is protected in that Member on the said date, or which meets or comes subsequently to meet the criteria for protection under the terms of this Agreement. In respect of this paragraph and paragraphs 3 and 4, copyright obligations with respect to existing works shall be solely determined under Article 18 of the Berne Convention (1971), and obligations with respect to the rights of producers of phonograms and performers in existing phonograms shall be determined solely under Article 18 of the Berne Convention (1971) as made applicable under paragraph 6 of Article 14 of this Agreement.

3. There shall be no obligation to restore protection to subject matter which on the date of application of this Agreement for the Member in question has fallen into the public domain.

4. In respect of any acts in respect of specific objects embodying protected subject matter which become infringing under the terms of legislation in conformity with this Agreement, and which were commenced, or in respect of which a significant investment was made, before the date of acceptance of the WTO Agreement by that Member, any Member may provide for a limitation of the remedies available to the right holder as to the continued performance of such acts after the date of application of this Agreement for that Member. In such cases the Member shall, however, at least provide for the payment of equitable remuneration.

5. A Member is not obliged to apply the provisions of Article 11 and of paragraph 4 of Article 14 with respect to originals or copies purchased prior to the date of application of this Agreement for that Member.

6. Members shall not be required to apply Article 31, or the requirement in paragraph 1 of Article 27 that patent rights shall be enjoyable without discrimination as to the field of technology, to use without the authorization of the right holder where authorization for such use was granted by the government before the date this Agreement became known.

7. In the case of intellectual property rights for which protection is conditional upon regis-tration, applications for protection which are pending on the date of application of this Agreement for the Member in question shall be permitted to be amended to claim any enhanced protection provided under the provisions of this Agreement. Such amendments shall not include new matter.

8. Where a Member does not make available as of the date of entry into force of the WTO Agreement patent protection for pharmaceutical and agricultural chemical products com-mensurate with its obligations under Article 27, that Member shall:
   (a) notwithstanding the provisions of Part VI, provide as from the date of entry into force of the WTO Agreement a means by which applications for patents for such inventions can be filed;
   (b) apply to these applications, as of the date of application of this Agreement, the criteria for patentability as laid down in this Agreement as if those criteria were being applied on the date of filing in that Member or, where priority is available and claimed, the priority date of the application; and
   (c) provide patent protection in accordance with this Agreement as from the grant of the patent and for the remainder of the patent term, counted from the filing date in accordance with Article 33 of this Agreement, for those of these applications that meet the criteria for protection referred to in subparagraph (b).

9. Where a product is the subject of a patent application in a Member in accordance with paragraph 8(a), exclusive marketing rights shall be granted, notwithstanding the provisions of Part VI, for a period of five years after obtaining marketing approval in that Member or until a product patent is granted or rejected in that Member, whichever period is shorter, provided that, subsequent to the entry into force of the WTO Agreement, a patent application has been filed and a patent granted for that product in another Member and marketing approval obtained in such other Member.

Article 71   Review and Amendment

1. The Council for TRIPS shall review the implementation of this Agreement after the expir-ation of the transitional period referred to in paragraph 2 of Article 65. The Council shall, having regard to the experience gained in its implementation, review it two years after that date, and at identical intervals thereafter. The Council may also undertake reviews in the light of any relevant new developments which might warrant modification or amendment of this Agreement.

2. Amendments merely serving the purpose of adjusting to higher levels of protection of intellectual property rights achieved, and in force, in other multilateral agreements and accepted under those agreements by all Members of the WTO may be referred to the Ministerial Conference for action in accordance with paragraph 6 of Article X of the WTO Agreement on the basis of a consensus proposal from the Council for TRIPS.

Article 72   Reservations

Reservations may not be entered in respect of any of the provisions of this Agreement without the consent of the other Members.

Article 73   Security Exceptions

Nothing in this Agreement shall be construed:

(a) to require a Member to furnish any information the disclosure of which it considers contrary to its essential security interests; or

(b) to prevent a Member from taking any action which it considers necessary for the protection of its essential security interests;

  (i)   relating to fissionable materials or the materials from which they are derived;

  (ii) relating to the traffic in arms, ammunition and implements of war and to such traffic in other goods and materials as is carried on directly or indirectly for the purpose of supplying a military establishment;

  (iii) taken in time of war or other emergency in international relations; or

(c) to prevent a Member from taking any action in pursuance of its obligations under the United Nations Charter for the maintenance of international peace and security.

II-17b

Declaration on the TRIPS Agreement and Public Health

Date   14 November 2001
Source WTO Doc WT/MIN(01)/DEC/2, 20 November 2001
Link   <http://www.wto.org/english/thewto_e/minist_e/min01_e/mindecl_trips_e.htm>

1. We recognize the gravity of the public health problems afflicting many developing and least-developed countries, especially those resulting from HIV/AIDS, tuberculosis, malaria and other epidemics.

2. We stress the need for the WTO Agreement on Trade-Related Aspects of Intellectual Property Rights (TRIPS Agreement) to be part of the wider national and international action to address these problems.

3. We recognize that intellectual property protection is important for the development of new medicines. We also recognize the concerns about its effects on prices.

4. We agree that the TRIPS Agreement does not and should not prevent Members from taking measures to protect public health. Accordingly, while reiterating our commitment to the TRIPS Agreement, we affirm that the Agreement can and should be interpreted and implemented in a manner supportive of WTO Members' right to protect public health and, in particular, to promote access to medicines for all.

In this connection, we reaffirm the right of WTO Members to use, to the full, the provisions in the TRIPS Agreement, which provide flexibility for this purpose.

5. Accordingly and in the light of paragraph 4 above, while maintaining our commitments in the TRIPS Agreement, we recognize that these flexibilities include:

   (a) In applying the customary rules of interpretation of public international law, each provision of the TRIPS Agreement shall be read in the light of the object and purpose of the Agreement as expressed, in particular, in its objectives and principles.

   (b) Each Member has the right to grant compulsory licences and the freedom to determine the grounds upon which such licences are granted.

   (c) Each Member has the right to determine what constitutes a national emergency or other circumstances of extreme urgency, it being understood that public health crises, including those relating to HIV/AIDS, tuberculosis, malaria and other epidemics, can represent a national emergency or other circumstances of extreme urgency.

   (d) The effect of the provisions in the TRIPS Agreement that are relevant to the exhaustion of intellectual property rights is to leave each Member free to establish its own regime for such exhaustion without challenge, subject to the MFN and national treatment provisions of Articles 3 and 4.

6. We recognize that WTO Members with insufficient or no manufacturing capacities in the pharmaceutical sector could face difficulties in making effective use of compulsory licensing under the TRIPS Agreement. We instruct the Council for TRIPS to find an expeditious solution to this problem and to report to the General Council before the end of 2002.

7. We reaffirm the commitment of developed-country Members to provide incentives to their enterprises and institutions to promote and encourage technology transfer to least-developed

country Members pursuant to Article 66.2. We also agree that the least-developed country Members will not be obliged, with respect to pharmaceutical products, to implement or apply Sections 5 and 7 of Part II of the TRIPS Agreement or to enforce rights provided for under these Sections until 1 January 2016, without prejudice to the right of least-developed country Members to seek other extensions of the transition periods as provided for in Article 66.1 of the TRIPS Agreement. We instruct the Council for TRIPS to take the necessary action to give effect to this pursuant to Article 66.1 of the TRIPS Agreement.

Implementation of paragraph 6 of the Doha Declaration on the TRIPS Agreement and Public Health (Decision of the General Council)

Date   30 August 2003
Source   WTO Doc WT/L/540, 2 September 2003
Link   <http://www.wto.org/english/tratop_e/trips_e/implem_para6_e.htm>

The General Council,

Having regard to paragraphs 1, 3 and 4 of Article IX of the Marrakesh Agreement Establishing the World Trade Organization ("the WTO Agreement");

Conducting the functions of the Ministerial Conference in the interval between meetings pursuant to paragraph 2 of Article IV of the WTO Agreement;

Noting the Declaration on the TRIPS Agreement and Public Health (WT/MIN(01)/DEC/2) (the "Declaration") and, in particular, the instruction of the Ministerial Conference to the Council for TRIPS contained in paragraph 6 of the Declaration to find an expeditious solution to the problem of the difficulties that WTO Members with insufficient or no manufacturing capacities in the pharmaceutical sector could face in making effective use of compulsory licensing under the TRIPS Agreement and to report to the General Council before the end of 2002;

Recognizing, where eligible importing Members seek to obtain supplies under the system set out in this Decision, the importance of a rapid response to those needs consistent with the provisions of this Decision;

Noting that, in the light of the foregoing, exceptional circumstances exist justifying waivers from the obligations set out in paragraphs (f) and (h) of Article 31 of the TRIPS Agreement with respect to pharmaceutical products;

Decides as follows:

1. For the purposes of this Decision:
   (a) "pharmaceutical product" means any patented product, or product manufactured through a patented process, of the pharmaceutical sector needed to address the public health problems as recognized in paragraph 1 of the Declaration. It is understood that active ingredients necessary for its manufacture and diagnostic kits needed for its use would be included;[1]
   (b) "eligible importing Member" means any least-developed country Member, and any other Member that has made a notification[2] to the Council for TRIPS of its intention to use the system as an importer, it being understood that a Member may notify at any time that it will use the system in whole or in a limited way, for example only in the case of a national emergency or other circumstances of extreme urgency or in cases of public non-commercial use. It is noted that some Members will not use the system set out in this

---

1 This subparagraph is without prejudice to subparagraph 1(b).
2 It is understood that this notification does not need to be approved by a WTO body in order to use the system set out in this Decision.

Decision as importing Members[3] and that some other Members have stated that, if they use the system, it would be in no more than situations of national emergency or other circumstances of extreme urgency;

(c) "exporting Member" means a Member using the system set out in this Decision to produce pharmaceutical products for, and export them to, an eligible importing Member.

2. The obligations of an exporting Member under Article 31(f) of the TRIPS Agreement shall be waived with respect to the grant by it of a compulsory licence to the extent necessary for the purposes of production of a pharmaceutical product(s) and its export to an eligible importing Member(s) in accordance with the terms set out below in this paragraph:

(a) the eligible importing Member(s)[4] has made a notification[2] to the Council for TRIPS, that:

   (i) specifies the names and expected quantities of the product(s) needed[5];

   (ii) confirms that the eligible importing Member in question, other than a least developed country Member, has established that it has insufficient or no manufacturing capacities in the pharmaceutical sector for the product(s) in question in one of the ways set out in the Annex to this Decision; and

   (iii) confirms that, where a pharmaceutical product is patented in its territory, it has granted or intends to grant a compulsory licence in accordance with Article 31 of the TRIPS Agreement and the provisions of this Decision[6];

(b) the compulsory licence issued by the exporting Member under this Decision shall contain the following conditions:

   (i) only the amount necessary to meet the needs of the eligible importing Member(s) may be manufactured under the licence and the entirety of this production shall be exported to the Member(s) which has notified its needs to the Council for TRIPS;

   (ii) products produced under the licence shall be clearly identified as being produced under the system set out in this Decision through specific labelling or marking. Suppliers should distinguish such products through special packaging and/or special colouring/shaping of the products themselves, provided that such distinction is feasible and does not have a significant impact on price; and

   (iii) before shipment begins, the licensee shall post on a website[7] the following information:

   – the quantities being supplied to each destination as referred to in indent (i) above; and

   – the distinguishing features of the product(s) referred to in indent (ii) above;

(c) the exporting Member shall notify[8] the Council for TRIPS of the grant of the licence, including the conditions attached to it[9]. The information provided shall include the name and address of the licensee, the product(s) for which the licence has been granted, the quantity(ies) for which it has been granted, the country(ies) to which the product(s) is (are) to be supplied and the duration of the licence. The notification shall also indicate the address of the website referred to in subparagraph (b)(iii) above.

---

3 Australia, Austria, Belgium, Canada, Denmark, Finland, France, Germany, Greece, Iceland, Ireland, Italy, Japan, Luxembourg, the Netherlands, New Zealand, Norway, Portugal, Spain, Sweden, Switzerland, the United Kingdom and the United States.

4 Joint notifications providing the information required under this subparagraph may be made by the regional organizations referred to in paragraph 6 of this Decision on behalf of eligible importing Members using the system that are parties to them, with the agreement of those parties.

5 The notification will be made available publicly by the WTO Secretariat through a page on the WTO website dedicated to this Decision.

6 This subparagraph is without prejudice to Article 66.1 of the TRIPS Agreement.

7 The licensee may use for this purpose its own website or, with the assistance of the WTO Secretariat, the page on the WTO website dedicated to this Decision.

8 It is understood that this notification does not need to be approved by a WTO body in order to use the system set out in this Decision.

9 The notification will be made available publicly by the WTO Secretariat through a page on the WTO website dedicated to this Decision.

3. Where a compulsory licence is granted by an exporting Member under the system set out in this Decision, adequate remuneration pursuant to Article 31(h) of the TRIPS Agreement shall be paid in that Member taking into account the economic value to the importing Member of the use that has been authorized in the exporting Member. Where a compulsory licence is granted for the same products in the eligible importing Member, the obligation of that Member under Article 31(h) shall be waived in respect of those products for which remuneration in accordance with the first sentence of this paragraph is paid in the exporting Member.

4. In order to ensure that the products imported under the system set out in this Decision are used for the public health purposes underlying their importation, eligible importing Members shall take reasonable measures within their means, proportionate to their administrative capacities and to the risk of trade diversion to prevent re-exportation of the products that have actually been imported into their territories under the system. In the event that an eligible importing Member that is a developing country Member or a least-developed country Member experiences difficulty in implementing this provision, developed country Members shall provide, on request and on mutually agreed terms and conditions, technical and financial cooperation in order to facilitate its implementation.

5. Members shall ensure the availability of effective legal means to prevent the importation into, and sale in, their territories of products produced under the system set out in this Decision and diverted to their markets inconsistently with its provisions, using the means already required to be available under the TRIPS Agreement. If any Member considers that such measures are proving insufficient for this purpose, the matter may be reviewed in the Council for TRIPS at the request of that Member.

6. With a view to harnessing economies of scale for the purposes of enhancing purchasing power for, and facilitating the local production of, pharmaceutical products:
   (i) where a developing or least-developed country WTO Member is a party to a regional trade agreement within the meaning of Article XXIV of the GATT 1994 and the Decision of 28 November 1979 on Differential and More Favourable Treatment Reciprocity and Fuller Participation of Developing Countries (L/4903), at least half of the current membership of which is made up of countries presently on the United Nations list of least developed countries, the obligation of that Member under Article 31(f) of the TRIPS Agreement shall be waived to the extent necessary to enable a pharmaceutical product produced or imported under a compulsory licence in that Member to be exported to the markets of those other developing or least developed country parties to the regional trade agreement that share the health problem in question. It is understood that this will not prejudice the territorial nature of the patent rights in question;
   (ii) it is recognized that the development of systems providing for the grant of regional patents to be applicable in the above Members should be promoted. To this end, developed country Members undertake to provide technical cooperation in accordance with Article 67 of the TRIPS Agreement, including in conjunction with other relevant intergovernmental organizations.

7. Members recognize the desirability of promoting the transfer of technology and capacity building in the pharmaceutical sector in order to overcome the problem identified in paragraph 6 of the Declaration. To this end, eligible importing Members and exporting Members are encouraged to use the system set out in this Decision in a way which would promote this objective. Members undertake to cooperate in paying special attention to the transfer of technology and capacity building in the pharmaceutical sector in the work to be undertaken pursuant to Article 66.2 of the TRIPS Agreement, paragraph 7 of the Declaration and any other relevant work of the Council for TRIPS.

8. The Council for TRIPS shall review annually the functioning of the system set out in this Decision with a view to ensuring its effective operation and shall annually report on its

operation to the General Council. This review shall be deemed to fulfil the review requirements of Article IX:4 of the WTO Agreement.

9. This Decision is without prejudice to the rights, obligations and flexibilities that Members
   have under the provisions of the TRIPS Agreement other than paragraphs (f) and (h) of
   Article 31, including those reaffirmed by the Declaration, and to their interpretation. It is
   also without prejudice to the extent to which pharmaceutical products produced under a
   compulsory licence can be exported under the present provisions of Article 31(f) of the
   TRIPS Agreement.

10. Members shall not challenge any measures taken in conformity with the provisions of the
    waivers contained in this Decision under subparagraphs 1(b) and 1(c) of Article XXIII of
    GATT 1994.

11. This Decision, including the waivers granted in it, shall terminate for each Member on the
    date on which an amendment to the TRIPS Agreement replacing its provisions takes effect
    for that Member. The TRIPS Council shall initiate by the end of 2003 work on the
    preparation of such an amendment with a view to its adoption within six months, on the
    understanding that the amendment will be based, where appropriate, on this Decision and
    on the further understanding that it will not be part of the negotiations referred to in
    paragraph 45 of the Doha Ministerial Declaration (WT/MIN(01)/DEC/1).

ANNEX   ASSESSMENT OF MANUFACTURING CAPACITIES IN THE PHARMACEUTICAL SECTOR

Least-developed country Members are deemed to have insufficient or no manufacturing capacities in the pharmaceutical sector.

For other eligible importing Members insufficient or no manufacturing capacities for the
product(s) in question may be established in either of the following ways:

(i) the Member in question has established that it has no manufacturing capacity in the
     pharmaceutical sector;

     OR

(ii) where the Member has some manufacturing capacity in this sector, it has examined this
     capacity and found that, excluding any capacity owned or controlled by the patent owner, it
     is currently insufficient for the purposes of meeting its needs. When it is established that
     such capacity has become sufficient to meet the Member's needs, the system shall no longer
     apply.

Implementation of paragraph 6 of the Doha Declaration on the TRIPS Agreement and Public Health (Statement Read Out by the Chairman of the General Council, Excerpt from the General Council Minutes)

Date 30 August 2003
Source WTO Doc WT/GC/M/82, 13 November 2003
Link <http://wto.org/english/tratop_e/trips_e/ta_docs_e/3_wtgcm82_e.pdf>

29. "The General Council has been presented with a draft Decision contained in document IP/C/W/405 to implement paragraph 6 of the Doha Declaration on the TRIPS Agreement and Public Health. This Decision is part of the wider national and international action to address problems as recognized in paragraph 1 of the Declaration. Before adopting this Decision, I would like to place on the record this Statement which represents several key shared understandings of Members regarding the Decision to be taken and the way in which it will be interpreted and implemented. I would like to emphasize that this Statement is limited in its implications to paragraph 6 of the Doha Declaration on the TRIPS Agreement and Public Health.

"*First*, Members recognize that the system that will be established by the Decision should be used in good faith to protect public health and, without prejudice to paragraph 6 of the Decision, not be an instrument to pursue industrial or commercial policy objectives.

"*Second*, Members recognize that the purpose of the Decision would be defeated if products supplied under this Decision are diverted from the markets for which they are intended. Therefore, all reasonable measures should be taken to prevent such diversion in accordance with the relevant paragraphs of the Decision. In this regard, the provisions of paragraph 2(b)(ii) apply not only to formulated pharmaceuticals produced and supplied under the system but also to active ingredients produced and supplied under the system and to finished products produced using such active ingredients. It is the understanding of Members that in general special packaging and/or special colouring or shaping should not have a significant impact on the price of pharmaceuticals.

"In the past, companies have developed procedures to prevent diversion of products that are, for example, provided through donor programmes. "Best practices" guidelines that draw upon the experiences of companies are attached to this statement for illustrative purposes. Members and producers are encouraged to draw from and use these practices, and to share information on their experiences in preventing diversion.

"*Third*, it is important that Members seek to resolve any issues arising from the use and implementation of the Decision expeditiously and amicably:

−"To promote transparency and avoid controversy, notifications under paragraph 2(a)(ii) of the Decision would include information on how the Member in question had established, in accordance with the Annex, that it has insufficient or no manufacturing capacities in the pharmaceutical sector.

–"In accordance with the normal practice of the TRIPS Council, notifications made under the system shall be brought to the attention of its next meeting.

–Any Member may bring any matter related to the interpretation or implementation of the Decision, including issues related to diversion, to the TRIPS Council for expeditious review, with a view to taking appropriate action.

–If any Member has concerns that the terms of the Decision have not been fully complied with, the Member may also utilize the good offices of the Director-General or Chair of the TRIPS Council, with a view to finding a mutually acceptable solution.

"*Fourth*, all information gathered on the implementation of the Decision shall be brought to the attention of the TRIPS Council in its annual review as set out in paragraph 8 of the Decision.

"In addition, as stated in footnote 3 to paragraph 1(b) of the Decision, the following Members have agreed to opt out of using the system as importers: Australia, Austria, Belgium, Canada, Denmark, Finland, France, Germany, Greece, Iceland, Ireland, Italy, Japan, Luxembourg, The Netherlands, New Zealand, Norway, Portugal, Spain, Sweden, Switzerland, the United Kingdom and the United States.

"Until their accession to the European Union, the Czech Republic, Cyprus, Estonia, Hungary, Latvia, Lithuania, Malta, Poland, the Slovak Republic and Slovenia agree that they would only use the system as importers in situations of national emergency or other circumstances of extreme urgency. These countries further agree that upon their accession to the European Union, they will opt out of using the system as importers.

"As we have heard today, and as the Secretariat has been informed in certain communications, some other Members have agreed that they would only use the system as importers in situations of national emergency or other circumstances of extreme urgency. These are the following: Hong Kong, China; Israel; Korea; Kuwait; Macao China; Mexico; Qatar; Singapore; the Separate Customs Territory of Taiwan, Penghu, Kinmen and Matsu; Turkey and the United Arab Emirates."

. . .

ATTACHMENT

"BEST PRACTICES" GUIDELINES

"Companies have often used special labelling, colouring, shaping, sizing, etc. to differentiate products supplied through donor or discounted pricing programmes from products supplied to other markets. Examples of such measures include the following:

– Bristol Myers Squibb used different markings/imprints on capsules supplied to sub-Saharan Africa.

– Novartis has used different trademark names, one (Riamet®) for an anti-malarial drug provided to developed countries, the other (Coartem®) for the same products supplied to developing countries. Novartis further differentiated the products through distinctive packaging.

– GlaxoSmithKline (GSK) used different outer packaging for its HIV/AIDS medications Combivir, Epivir and Trizivir supplied to developing countries. GSK further differentiated the products by embossing the tablets with a different number than tablets supplied to developed countries, and plans to further differentiate the products by using different colours.

– Merck differentiated its HIV/AIDS antiretroviral medicine CRIXIVAN through special packaging and labelling, i.e., gold-ink printing on the capsule, dark green bottle cap and a bottle label with a light-green background.

– Pfizer used different colouring and shaping for Diflucan pills supplied to South Africa.

Producers have further minimized diversion by entering into contractual arrangements with importers/distributors to ensure delivery of products to the intended markets.

To help ensure use of the most effective anti-diversion measures, Members may share their experiences and practices in preventing diversion either informally or through the TRIPS Council. It would be beneficial for Members and industry to work together to further refine anti-diversion practices and enhance the sharing of information related to identifying, remedying or preventing specific occurrences of diversion."

II-18

Understanding on Rules and Procedures Governing the Settlement of Disputes

Members hereby *agree* as follows:

Article 1 Coverage and Application

1. The rules and procedures of this Understanding shall apply to disputes brought pursuant to the consultation and dispute settlement provisions of the agreements listed in Appendix 1 to this Understanding (referred to in this Understanding as the "covered agreements"). The rules and procedures of this Understanding shall also apply to consultations and the settlement of disputes between Members concerning their rights and obligations under the provisions of the Agreement Establishing the World Trade Organization (referred to in this Understanding as the "WTO Agreement") and of this Understanding taken in isolation or in combination with any other covered agreement.

2. The rules and procedures of this Understanding shall apply subject to such special or additional rules and procedures on dispute settlement contained in the covered agreements as are identified in Appendix 2 to this Understanding. To the extent that there is a difference between the rules and procedures of this Understanding and the special or additional rules and procedures set forth in Appendix 2, the special or additional rules and procedures in Appendix 2 shall prevail. In disputes involving rules and procedures under more than one covered agreement, if there is a conflict between special or additional rules and procedures of such agreements under review, and where the parties to the dispute cannot agree on rules and procedures within 20 days of the establishment of the panel, the Chairman of the Dispute Settlement Body provided for in paragraph 1 of Article 2 (referred to in this Understanding as the "DSB"), in consultation with the parties to the dispute, shall determine the rules and procedures to be followed within 10 days after a request by either Member. The Chairman shall be guided by the principle that special or additional rules and procedures should be used where possible, and the rules and procedures set out in this Understanding should be used to the extent necessary to avoid conflict.

Article 2 Administration

1. The Dispute Settlement Body is hereby established to administer these rules and procedures and, except as otherwise provided in a covered agreement, the consultation and dispute settlement provisions of the covered agreements. Accordingly, the DSB shall have the authority to establish panels, adopt panel and Appellate Body reports, maintain surveillance of implementation of rulings and recommendations, and authorize suspension of concessions and other obligations under the covered agreements. With respect to disputes arising under a covered agreement which is a Plurilateral Trade Agreement, the term "Member" as used herein shall refer only to those Members that are parties to the relevant Plurilateral Trade

Agreement. Where the DSB administers the dispute settlement provisions of a Plurilateral Trade Agreement, only those Members that are parties to that Agreement may participate in decisions or actions taken by the DSB with respect to that dispute.

2. The DSB shall inform the relevant WTO Councils and Committees of any developments in disputes related to provisions of the respective covered agreements.

3. The DSB shall meet as often as necessary to carry out its functions within the time-frames provided in this Understanding.

4. Where the rules and procedures of this Understanding provide for the DSB to take a decision, it shall do so by consensus.[1]

Article 3   General Provisions

1. Members affirm their adherence to the principles for the management of disputes heretofore applied under Articles XXII and XXIII of GATT 1947, and the rules and procedures as further elaborated and modified herein.

2. The dispute settlement system of the WTO is a central element in providing security and predictability to the multilateral trading system. The Members recognize that it serves to preserve the rights and obligations of Members under the covered agreements, and to clarify the existing provisions of those agreements in accordance with customary rules of interpretation of public international law. Recommendations and rulings of the DSB cannot add to or diminish the rights and obligations provided in the covered agreements.

3. The prompt settlement of situations in which a Member considers that any benefits accruing to it directly or indirectly under the covered agreements are being impaired by measures taken by another Member is essential to the effective functioning of the WTO and the maintenance of a proper balance between the rights and obligations of Members.

4. Recommendations or rulings made by the DSB shall be aimed at achieving a satisfactory settlement of the matter in accordance with the rights and obligations under this Understanding and under the covered agreements.

5. All solutions to matters formally raised under the consultation and dispute settlement provisions of the covered agreements, including arbitration awards, shall be consistent with those agreements and shall not nullify or impair benefits accruing to any Member under those agreements, nor impede the attainment of any objective of those agreements.

6. Mutually agreed solutions to matters formally raised under the consultation and dispute settlement provisions of the covered agreements shall be notified to the DSB and the relevant Councils and Committees, where any Member may raise any point relating thereto.

7. Before bringing a case, a Member shall exercise its judgement as to whether action under these procedures would be fruitful. The aim of the dispute settlement mechanism is to secure a positive solution to a dispute. A solution mutually acceptable to the parties to a dispute and consistent with the covered agreements is clearly to be preferred. In the absence of a mutually agreed solution, the first objective of the dispute settlement mechanism is usually to secure the withdrawal of the measures concerned if these are found to be inconsistent with the provisions of any of the covered agreements. The provision of compensation should be resorted to only if the immediate withdrawal of the measure is impracticable and as a temporary measure pending the withdrawal of the measure which is inconsistent with a covered agreement. The last resort which this Understanding provides to the Member invoking the dispute settlement procedures is the possibility of suspending the application of concessions or other obligations under the covered agreements on a discriminatory basis vis-à-vis the other Member, subject to authorization by the DSB of such measures.

---

1 The DSB shall be deemed to have decided by consensus on a matter submitted for its consideration, if no Member, present at the meeting of the DSB when the decision is taken, formally objects to the proposed decision.

8. In cases where there is an infringement of the obligations assumed under a covered agreement, the action is considered *prima facie* to constitute a case of nullification or impairment. This means that there is normally a presumption that a breach of the rules has an adverse impact on other Members parties to that covered agreement, and in such cases, it shall be up to the Member against whom the complaint has been brought to rebut the charge.

9. The provisions of this Understanding are without prejudice to the rights of Members to seek authoritative interpretation of provisions of a covered agreement through decision-making under the WTO Agreement or a covered agreement which is a Plurilateral Trade Agreement.

10. It is understood that requests for conciliation and the use of the dispute settlement procedures should not be intended or considered as contentious acts and that, if a dispute arises, all Members will engage in these procedures in good faith in an effort to resolve the dispute. It is also understood that complaints and counter-complaints in regard to distinct matters should not be linked.

11. This Understanding shall be applied only with respect to new requests for consultations under the consultation provisions of the covered agreements made on or after the date of entry into force of the WTO Agreement. With respect to disputes for which the request for consultations was made under GATT 1947 or under any other predecessor agreement to the covered agreements before the date of entry into force of the WTO Agreement, the relevant dispute settlement rules and procedures in effect immediately prior to the date of entry into force of the WTO Agreement shall continue to apply.[2]

12. Notwithstanding paragraph 11, if a complaint based on any of the covered agreements is brought by a developing country Member against a developed country Member, the complaining party shall have the right to invoke, as an alternative to the provisions contained in Articles 4, 5, 6 and 12 of this Understanding, the corresponding provisions of the Decision of 5 April 1966 (BISD 14S/18), except that where the Panel considers that the time-frame provided for in paragraph 7 of that Decision is insufficient to provide its report and with the agreement of the complaining party, that time-frame may be extended. To the extent that there is a difference between the rules and procedures of Articles 4, 5, 6 and 12 and the corresponding rules and procedures of the Decision, the latter shall prevail.

Article 4 Consultations

1. Members affirm their resolve to strengthen and improve the effectiveness of the consultation procedures employed by Members.

2. Each Member undertakes to accord sympathetic consideration to and afford adequate opportunity for consultation regarding any representations made by another Member concerning measures affecting the operation of any covered agreement taken within the territory of the former.[3]

3. If a request for consultations is made pursuant to a covered agreement, the Member to which the request is made shall, unless otherwise mutually agreed, reply to the request within 10 days after the date of its receipt and shall enter into consultations in good faith within a period of no more than 30 days after the date of receipt of the request, with a view to reaching a mutually satisfactory solution. If the Member does not respond within 10 days after the date of receipt of the request, or does not enter into consultations within a period of no more than 30 days, or a period otherwise mutually agreed, after the date of receipt of the request, then the Member that requested the holding of consultations may proceed directly to request the establishment of a panel.

---

2 This paragraph shall also be applied to disputes on which panel reports have not been adopted or fully implemented.

3 Where the provisions of any other covered agreement concerning measures taken by regional or local governments or authorities within the territory of a Member contain provisions different from the provisions of this paragraph, the provisions of such other covered agreement shall prevail.

4. All such requests for consultations shall be notified to the DSB and the relevant Councils and Committees by the Member which requests consultations. Any request for consultations shall be submitted in writing and shall give the reasons for the request, including identification of the measures at issue and an indication of the legal basis for the complaint.

5. In the course of consultations in accordance with the provisions of a covered agreement, before resorting to further action under this Understanding, Members should attempt to obtain satisfactory adjustment of the matter.

6. Consultations shall be confidential, and without prejudice to the rights of any Member in any further proceedings.

7. If the consultations fail to settle a dispute within 60 days after the date of receipt of the request for consultations, the complaining party may request the establishment of a panel. The complaining party may request a panel during the 60-day period if the consulting parties jointly consider that consultations have failed to settle the dispute.

8. In cases of urgency, including those which concern perishable goods, Members shall enter into consultations within a period of no more than 10 days after the date of receipt of the request. If the consultations have failed to settle the dispute within a period of 20 days after the date of receipt of the request, the complaining party may request the establishment of a panel.

9. In cases of urgency, including those which concern perishable goods, the parties to the dispute, panels and the Appellate Body shall make every effort to accelerate the proceedings to the greatest extent possible.

10. During consultations Members should give special attention to the particular problems and interests of developing country Members.

11. Whenever a Member other than the consulting Members considers that it has a substantial trade interest in consultations being held pursuant to paragraph 1 of Article XXII of GATT 1994, paragraph 1 of Article XXII of GATS, or the corresponding provisions in other covered agreements[4], such Member may notify the consulting Members and the DSB, within 10 days after the date of the circulation of the request for consultations under said Article, of its desire to be joined in the consultations. Such Member shall be joined in the consultations, provided that the Member to which the request for consultations was addressed agrees that the claim of substantial interest is well-founded. In that event they shall so inform the DSB. If the request to be joined in the consultations is not accepted, the applicant Member shall be free to request consultations under paragraph 1 of Article XXII or paragraph 1 of Article XXIII of GATT 1994, paragraph 1 of Article XXII or paragraph 1 of Article XXIII of GATS, or the corresponding provisions in other covered agreements.

Article 5   Good Offices, Conciliation and Mediation

1. Good offices, conciliation and mediation are procedures that are undertaken voluntarily if the parties to the dispute so agree.

2. Proceedings involving good offices, conciliation and mediation, and in particular positions taken by the parties to the dispute during these proceedings, shall be confidential, and without prejudice to the rights of either party in any further proceedings under these procedures.

---

4 The corresponding consultation provisions in the covered agreements are listed hereunder: Agreement on Agriculture, Article 19; Agreement on the Application of Sanitary and Phytosanitary Measures, paragraph 1 of Article 11; Agreement on Textiles and Clothing, paragraph 4 of Article 8; Agreement on Technical Barriers to Trade, paragraph 1 of Article 14; Agreement on Trade-Related Investment Measures, Article 8; Agreement on Implementation of Article VI of GATT 1994, paragraph 2 of Article 17; Agreement on Implementation of Article VII of GATT 1994, paragraph 2 of Article 19; Agreement on Preshipment Inspection, Article 7; Agreement on Rules of Origin, Article 7; Agreement on Import Licensing Procedures, Article 6; Agreement on Subsidies and Countervailing Measures, Article 30; Agreement on Safeguards, Article 14; Agreement on Trade-Related Aspects of Intellectual Property Rights, Article 64.1; and any corresponding consultation provisions in Plurilateral Trade Agreements as determined by the competent bodies of each Agreement and as notified to the DSB.

3. Good offices, conciliation or mediation may be requested at any time by any party to a dispute. They may begin at any time and be terminated at any time. Once procedures for good offices, conciliation or mediation are terminated, a complaining party may then proceed with a request for the establishment of a panel.

4. When good offices, conciliation or mediation are entered into within 60 days after the date of receipt of a request for consultations, the complaining party must allow a period of 60 days after the date of receipt of the request for consultations before requesting the establishment of a panel. The complaining party may request the establishment of a panel during the 60-day period if the parties to the dispute jointly consider that the good offices, conciliation or mediation process has failed to settle the dispute.

5. If the parties to a dispute agree, procedures for good offices, conciliation or mediation may continue while the panel process proceeds.

6. The Director-General may, acting in an *ex officio* capacity, offer good offices, conciliation or mediation with the view to assisting Members to settle a dispute.

Article 6   Establishment of Panels

1. If the complaining party so requests, a panel shall be established at the latest at the DSB meeting following that at which the request first appears as an item on the DSB's agenda, unless at that meeting the DSB decides by consensus not to establish a panel.[5]

2. The request for the establishment of a panel shall be made in writing. It shall indicate whether consultations were held, identify the specific measures at issue and provide a brief summary of the legal basis of the complaint sufficient to present the problem clearly. In case the applicant requests the establishment of a panel with other than standard terms of reference, the written request shall include the proposed text of special terms of reference.

Article 7   Terms of Reference of Panels

1. Panels shall have the following terms of reference unless the parties to the dispute agree otherwise within 20 days from the establishment of the panel:

   "To examine, in the light of the relevant provisions in (name of the covered agreement(s) cited by the parties to the dispute), the matter referred to the DSB by (name of party) in document . . . and to make such findings as will assist the DSB in making the recommendations or in giving the rulings provided for in that/those agreement(s)."

2. Panels shall address the relevant provisions in any covered agreement or agreements cited by the parties to the dispute.

3. In establishing a panel, the DSB may authorize its Chairman to draw up the terms of reference of the panel in consultation with the parties to the dispute, subject to the provisions of paragraph 1. The terms of reference thus drawn up shall be circulated to all Members. If other than standard terms of reference are agreed upon, any Member may raise any point relating thereto in the DSB.

Article 8   Composition of Panels

1. Panels shall be composed of well-qualified governmental and/or non-governmental individuals, including persons who have served on or presented a case to a panel, served as a representative of a Member or of a contracting party to GATT 1947 or as a representative to the Council or Committee of any covered agreement or its predecessor agreement, or in the Secretariat, taught or published on international trade law or policy, or served as a senior trade policy official of a Member.

---

5 If the complaining party so requests, a meeting of the DSB shall be convened for this purpose within 15 days of the request, provided that at least 10 days' advance notice of the meeting is given.

2. Panel members should be selected with a view to ensuring the independence of the members, a sufficiently diverse background and a wide spectrum of experience.

3. Citizens of Members whose governments[6] are parties to the dispute or third parties as defined in paragraph 2 of Article 10 shall not serve on a panel concerned with that dispute, unless the parties to the dispute agree otherwise.

4. To assist in the selection of panelists, the Secretariat shall maintain an indicative list of governmental and non-governmental individuals possessing the qualifications outlined in paragraph 1, from which panelists may be drawn as appropriate. That list shall include the roster of non-governmental panelists established on 30 November 1984 (BISD 31S/9), and other rosters and indicative lists established under any of the covered agreements, and shall retain the names of persons on those rosters and indicative lists at the time of entry into force of the WTO Agreement. Members may periodically suggest names of governmental and non-governmental individuals for inclusion on the indicative list, providing relevant information on their knowledge of international trade and of the sectors or subject matter of the covered agreements, and those names shall be added to the list upon approval by the DSB. For each of the individuals on the list, the list shall indicate specific areas of experience or expertise of the individuals in the sectors or subject matter of the covered agreements.

5. Panels shall be composed of three panelists unless the parties to the dispute agree, within 10 days from the establishment of the panel, to a panel composed of five panelists. Members shall be informed promptly of the composition of the panel.

6. The Secretariat shall propose nominations for the panel to the parties to the dispute. The parties to the dispute shall not oppose nominations except for compelling reasons.

7. If there is no agreement on the panelists within 20 days after the date of the establishment of a panel, at the request of either party, the Director-General, in consultation with the Chairman of the DSB and the Chairman of the relevant Council or Committee, shall determine the composition of the panel by appointing the panelists whom the Director-General considers most appropriate in accordance with any relevant special or additional rules or procedures of the covered agreement or covered agreements which are at issue in the dispute, after consulting with the parties to the dispute. The Chairman of the DSB shall inform the Members of the composition of the panel thus formed no later than 10 days after the date the Chairman receives such a request.

8. Members shall undertake, as a general rule, to permit their officials to serve as panelists.

9. Panelists shall serve in their individual capacities and not as government representatives, nor as representatives of any organization. Members shall therefore not give them instructions nor seek to influence them as individuals with regard to matters before a panel.

10. When a dispute is between a developing country Member and a developed country Member the panel shall, if the developing country Member so requests, include at least one panelist from a developing country Member.

11. Panelists' expenses, including travel and subsistence allowance, shall be met from the WTO budget in accordance with criteria to be adopted by the General Council, based on recommendations of the Committee on Budget, Finance and Administration.

Article 9 Procedures for Multiple Complainants

1. Where more than one Member requests the establishment of a panel related to the same matter, a single panel may be established to examine these complaints taking into account the rights of all Members concerned. A single panel should be established to examine such complaints whenever feasible.

---

6 In the case where customs unions or common markets are parties to a dispute, this provision applies to citizens of all member countries of the customs unions or common markets.

2. The single panel shall organize its examination and present its findings to the DSB in such a manner that the rights which the parties to the dispute would have enjoyed had separate panels examined the complaints are in no way impaired. If one of the parties to the dispute so requests, the panel shall submit separate reports on the dispute concerned. The written submissions by each of the complainants shall be made available to the other complainants, and each complainant shall have the right to be present when any one of the other complainants presents its views to the panel.

3. If more than one panel is established to examine the complaints related to the same matter, to the greatest extent possible the same persons shall serve as panelists on each of the separate panels and the timetable for the panel process in such disputes shall be harmonized.

Article 10   Third Parties

1. The interests of the parties to a dispute and those of other Members under a covered agreement at issue in the dispute shall be fully taken into account during the panel process.

2. Any Member having a substantial interest in a matter before a panel and having notified its interest to the DSB (referred to in this Understanding as a "third party") shall have an opportunity to be heard by the panel and to make written submissions to the panel. These submissions shall also be given to the parties to the dispute and shall be reflected in the panel report.

3. Third parties shall receive the submissions of the parties to the dispute to the first meeting of the panel.

4. If a third party considers that a measure already the subject of a panel proceeding nullifies or impairs benefits accruing to it under any covered agreement, that Member may have recourse to normal dispute settlement procedures under this Understanding. Such a dispute shall be referred to the original panel wherever possible.

Article 11   Function of Panels

The function of panels is to assist the DSB in discharging its responsibilities under this Understanding and the covered agreements. Accordingly, a panel should make an objective assessment of the matter before it, including an objective assessment of the facts of the case and the applicability of and conformity with the relevant covered agreements, and make such other findings as will assist the DSB in making the recommendations or in giving the rulings provided for in the covered agreements. Panels should consult regularly with the parties to the dispute and give them adequate opportunity to develop a mutually satisfactory solution.

Article 12   Panel Procedures

1. Panels shall follow the Working Procedures in Appendix 3 unless the panel decides otherwise after consulting the parties to the dispute.

2. Panel procedures should provide sufficient flexibility so as to ensure high-quality panel reports, while not unduly delaying the panel process.

3. After consulting the parties to the dispute, the panelists shall, as soon as practicable and whenever possible within one week after the composition and terms of reference of the panel have been agreed upon, fix the timetable for the panel process, taking into account the provisions of paragraph 9 of Article 4, if relevant.

4. In determining the timetable for the panel process, the panel shall provide sufficient time for the parties to the dispute to prepare their submissions.

5. Panels should set precise deadlines for written submissions by the parties and the parties should respect those deadlines.

6. Each party to the dispute shall deposit its written submissions with the Secretariat for immediate transmission to the panel and to the other party or parties to the dispute. The complaining party shall submit its first submission in advance of the responding party's first

submission unless the panel decides, in fixing the timetable referred to in paragraph 3 and after consultations with the parties to the dispute, that the parties should submit their first submissions simultaneously. When there are sequential arrangements for the deposit of first submissions, the panel shall establish a firm time-period for receipt of the responding party's submission. Any subsequent written submissions shall be submitted simultaneously.

7. Where the parties to the dispute have failed to develop a mutually satisfactory solution, the panel shall submit its findings in the form of a written report to the DSB. In such cases, the report of a panel shall set out the findings of fact, the applicability of relevant provisions and the basic rationale behind any findings and recommendations that it makes. Where a settlement of the matter among the parties to the dispute has been found, the report of the panel shall be confined to a brief description of the case and to reporting that a solution has been reached.

8. In order to make the procedures more efficient, the period in which the panel shall conduct its examination, from the date that the composition and terms of reference of the panel have been agreed upon until the date the final report is issued to the parties to the dispute, shall, as a general rule, not exceed six months. In cases of urgency, including those relating to perishable goods, the panel shall aim to issue its report to the parties to the dispute within three months.

9. When the panel considers that it cannot issue its report within six months, or within three months in cases of urgency, it shall inform the DSB in writing of the reasons for the delay together with an estimate of the period within which it will issue its report. In no case should the period from the establishment of the panel to the circulation of the report to the Members exceed nine months.

10. In the context of consultations involving a measure taken by a developing country Member, the parties may agree to extend the periods established in paragraphs 7 and 8 of Article 4. If, after the relevant period has elapsed, the consulting parties cannot agree that the consultations have concluded, the Chairman of the DSB shall decide, after consultation with the parties, whether to extend the relevant period and, if so, for how long. In addition, in examining a complaint against a developing country Member, the panel shall accord sufficient time for the developing country Member to prepare and present its argumentation. The provisions of paragraph 1 of Article 20 and paragraph 4 of Article 21 are not affected by any action pursuant to this paragraph.

11. Where one or more of the parties is a developing country Member, the panel's report shall explicitly indicate the form in which account has been taken of relevant provisions on differential and more-favourable treatment for developing country Members that form part of the covered agreements which have been raised by the developing country Member in the course of the dispute settlement procedures.

12. The panel may suspend its work at any time at the request of the complaining party for a period not to exceed 12 months. In the event of such a suspension, the time-frames set out in paragraphs 8 and 9 of this Article, paragraph 1 of Article 20, and paragraph 4 of Article 21 shall be extended by the amount of time that the work was suspended. If the work of the panel has been suspended for more than 12 months, the authority for establishment of the panel shall lapse.

Article 13   Right to Seek Information

1. Each panel shall have the right to seek information and technical advice from any individual or body which it deems appropriate. However, before a panel seeks such information or advice from any individual or body within the jurisdiction of a Member it shall inform the authorities of that Member. A Member should respond promptly and fully to any request by a panel for such information as the panel considers necessary and appropriate. Confidential information which is provided shall not be revealed without formal authorization from the individual, body, or authorities of the Member providing the information.

2. Panels may seek information from any relevant source and may consult experts to obtain their opinion on certain aspects of the matter. With respect to a factual issue concerning a scientific or other technical matter raised by a party to a dispute, a panel may request an advisory report in writing from an expert review group. Rules for the establishment of such a group and its procedures are set forth in Appendix 4.

Article 14   Confidentiality

1. Panel deliberations shall be confidential.

2. The reports of panels shall be drafted without the presence of the parties to the dispute in the light of the information provided and the statements made.

3. Opinions expressed in the panel report by individual panelists shall be anonymous.

Article 15   Interim Review Stage

1. Following the consideration of rebuttal submissions and oral arguments, the panel shall issue the descriptive (factual and argument) sections of its draft report to the parties to the dispute. Within a period of time set by the panel, the parties shall submit their comments in writing.

2. Following the expiration of the set period of time for receipt of comments from the parties to the dispute, the panel shall issue an interim report to the parties, including both the descriptive sections and the panel's findings and conclusions. Within a period of time set by the panel, a party may submit a written request for the panel to review precise aspects of the interim report prior to circulation of the final report to the Members. At the request of a party, the panel shall hold a further meeting with the parties on the issues identified in the written comments. If no comments are received from any party within the comment period, the interim report shall be considered the final panel report and circulated promptly to the Members.

3. The findings of the final panel report shall include a discussion of the arguments made at the interim review stage. The interim review stage shall be conducted within the time-period set out in paragraph 8 of Article 12.

Article 16   Adoption of Panel Reports

1. In order to provide sufficient time for the Members to consider panel reports, the reports shall not be considered for adoption by the DSB until 20 days after the date they have been circulated to the Members.

2. Members having objections to a panel report shall give written reasons to explain their objections for circulation at least 10 days prior to the DSB meeting at which the panel report will be considered.

3. The parties to a dispute shall have the right to participate fully in the consideration of the panel report by the DSB, and their views shall be fully recorded.

4. Within 60 days after the date of circulation of a panel report to the Members, the report shall be adopted at a DSB meeting[7] unless a party to the dispute formally notifies the DSB of its decision to appeal or the DSB decides by consensus not to adopt the report. If a party has notified its decision to appeal, the report by the panel shall not be considered for adoption by the DSB until after completion of the appeal. This adoption procedure is without prejudice to the right of Members to express their views on a panel report.

Article 17   Appellate Review

Standing Appellate Body

1. A standing Appellate Body shall be established by the DSB. The Appellate Body shall hear appeals from panel cases. It shall be composed of seven persons, three of whom shall serve on

---

7 If a meeting of the DSB is not scheduled within this period at a time that enables the requirements of paragraphs 1 and 4 of Article 16 to be met, a meeting of the DSB shall be held for this purpose.

any one case. Persons serving on the Appellate Body shall serve in rotation. Such rotation shall be determined in the working procedures of the Appellate Body.

2. The DSB shall appoint persons to serve on the Appellate Body for a four-year term, and each person may be reappointed once. However, the terms of three of the seven persons appointed immediately after the entry into force of the WTO Agreement shall expire at the end of two years, to be determined by lot. Vacancies shall be filled as they arise. A person appointed to replace a person whose term of office has not expired shall hold office for the remainder of the predecessor's term.

3. The Appellate Body shall comprise persons of recognized authority, with demonstrated expertise in law, international trade and the subject matter of the covered agreements generally. They shall be unaffiliated with any government. The Appellate Body membership shall be broadly representative of membership in the WTO. All persons serving on the Appellate Body shall be available at all times and on short notice, and shall stay abreast of dispute settlement activities and other relevant activities of the WTO. They shall not participate in the consideration of any disputes that would create a direct or indirect conflict of interest.

4. Only parties to the dispute, not third parties, may appeal a panel report. Third parties which have notified the DSB of a substantial interest in the matter pursuant to paragraph 2 of Article 10 may make written submissions to, and be given an opportunity to be heard by, the Appellate Body.

5. As a general rule, the proceedings shall not exceed 60 days from the date a party to the dispute formally notifies its decision to appeal to the date the Appellate Body circulates its report. In fixing its timetable the Appellate Body shall take into account the provisions of paragraph 9 of Article 4, if relevant. When the Appellate Body considers that it cannot provide its report within 60 days, it shall inform the DSB in writing of the reasons for the delay together with an estimate of the period within which it will submit its report. In no case shall the proceedings exceed 90 days.

6. An appeal shall be limited to issues of law covered in the panel report and legal interpretations developed by the panel.

7. The Appellate Body shall be provided with appropriate administrative and legal support as it requires.

8. The expenses of persons serving on the Appellate Body, including travel and subsistence allowance, shall be met from the WTO budget in accordance with criteria to be adopted by the General Council, based on recommendations of the Committee on Budget, Finance and Administration.

Procedures for Appellate Review

9. Working procedures shall be drawn up by the Appellate Body in consultation with the Chairman of the DSB and the Director-General, and communicated to the Members for their information.

10. The proceedings of the Appellate Body shall be confidential. The reports of the Appellate Body shall be drafted without the presence of the parties to the dispute and in the light of the information provided and the statements made.

11. Opinions expressed in the Appellate Body report by individuals serving on the Appellate Body shall be anonymous.

12. The Appellate Body shall address each of the issues raised in accordance with paragraph 6 during the appellate proceeding.

13. The Appellate Body may uphold, modify or reverse the legal findings and conclusions of the panel.

Adoption of Appellate Body Reports

14. An Appellate Body report shall be adopted by the DSB and unconditionally accepted by the parties to the dispute unless the DSB decides by consensus not to adopt the Appellate Body report within 30 days following its circulation to the Members.[8] This adoption procedure is without prejudice to the right of Members to express their views on an Appellate Body report.

Article 18   Communications with the Panel or Appellate Body

1. There shall be no *ex parte* communications with the panel or Appellate Body concerning matters under consideration by the panel or Appellate Body.

2. Written submissions to the panel or the Appellate Body shall be treated as confidential, but shall be made available to the parties to the dispute. Nothing in this Understanding shall preclude a party to a dispute from disclosing statements of its own positions to the public. Members shall treat as confidential information submitted by another Member to the panel or the Appellate Body which that Member has designated as confidential. A party to a dispute shall also, upon request of a Member, provide a non-confidential summary of the information contained in its written submissions that could be disclosed to the public.

Article 19   Panel and Appellate Body Recommendations

1. Where a panel or the Appellate Body concludes that a measure is inconsistent with a covered agreement, it shall recommend that the Member concerned[9] bring the measure into conformity with that agreement.[10] In addition to its recommendations, the panel or Appellate Body may suggest ways in which the Member concerned could implement the recommendations.

2. In accordance with paragraph 2 of Article 3, in their findings and recommendations, the panel and Appellate Body cannot add to or diminish the rights and obligations provided in the covered agreements.

Article 20   Time-frame for DSB Decisions

Unless otherwise agreed to by the parties to the dispute, the period from the date of establishment of the panel by the DSB until the date the DSB considers the panel or appellate report for adoption shall as a general rule not exceed nine months where the panel report is not appealed or 12 months where the report is appealed. Where either the panel or the Appellate Body has acted, pursuant to paragraph 9 of Article 12 or paragraph 5 of Article 17, to extend the time for providing its report, the additional time taken shall be added to the above periods.

Article 21   Surveillance of Implementation of Recommendations and Rulings

1. Prompt compliance with recommendations or rulings of the DSB is essential in order to ensure effective resolution of disputes to the benefit of all Members.

2. Particular attention should be paid to matters affecting the interests of developing country Members with respect to measures which have been subject to dispute settlement.

3. At a DSB meeting held within 30 days[11] after the date of adoption of the panel or Appellate Body report, the Member concerned shall inform the DSB of its intentions in respect of implementation of the recommendations and rulings of the DSB. If it is impracticable to comply immediately with the recommendations and rulings, the Member concerned shall have a reasonable period of time in which to do so. The reasonable period of time shall be:

    (a) the period of time proposed by the Member concerned, provided that such period is approved by the DSB; or, in the absence of such approval,

---

8 If a meeting of the DSB is not scheduled during this period, such a meeting of the DSB shall be held for this purpose.

9 The "Member concerned" is the party to the dispute to which the panel or Appellate Body recommendations are directed.

10 With respect to recommendations in cases not involving a violation of GATT 1994 or any other covered agreement, see Article 26.

11 If a meeting of the DSB is not scheduled during this period, such a meeting of the DSB shall be held for this purpose.

(b) a period of time mutually agreed by the parties to the dispute within 45 days after the date of adoption of the recommendations and rulings; or, in the absence of such agreement,

(c) a period of time determined through binding arbitration within 90 days after the date of adoption of the recommendations and rulings.[12] In such arbitration, a guideline for the arbitrator[13] should be that the reasonable period of time to implement panel or Appellate Body recommendations should not exceed 15 months from the date of adoption of a panel or Appellate Body report. However, that time may be shorter or longer, depending upon the particular circumstances.

4. Except where the panel or the Appellate Body has extended, pursuant to paragraph 9 of Article 12 or paragraph 5 of Article 17, the time of providing its report, the period from the date of establishment of the panel by the DSB until the date of determination of the reasonable period of time shall not exceed 15 months unless the parties to the dispute agree otherwise. Where either the panel or the Appellate Body has acted to extend the time of providing its report, the additional time taken shall be added to the 15-month period; provided that unless the parties to the dispute agree that there are exceptional circumstances, the total time shall not exceed 18 months.

5. Where there is disagreement as to the existence or consistency with a covered agreement of measures taken to comply with the recommendations and rulings such dispute shall be decided through recourse to these dispute settlement procedures, including wherever possible resort to the original panel. The panel shall circulate its report within 90 days after the date of referral of the matter to it. When the panel considers that it cannot provide its report within this time frame, it shall inform the DSB in writing of the reasons for the delay together with an estimate of the period within which it will submit its report.

6. The DSB shall keep under surveillance the implementation of adopted recommendations or rulings. The issue of implementation of the recommendations or rulings may be raised at the DSB by any Member at any time following their adoption. Unless the DSB decides otherwise, the issue of implementation of the recommendations or rulings shall be placed on the agenda of the DSB meeting after six months following the date of establishment of the reasonable period of time pursuant to paragraph 3 and shall remain on the DSB's agenda until the issue is resolved. At least 10 days prior to each such DSB meeting, the Member concerned shall provide the DSB with a status report in writing of its progress in the implementation of the recommendations or rulings.

7. If the matter is one which has been raised by a developing country Member, the DSB shall consider what further action it might take which would be appropriate to the circumstances.

8. If the case is one brought by a developing country Member, in considering what appropriate action might be taken, the DSB shall take into account not only the trade coverage of measures complained of, but also their impact on the economy of developing country Members concerned.

Article 22   Compensation and the Suspension of Concessions

1. Compensation and the suspension of concessions or other obligations are temporary measures available in the event that the recommendations and rulings are not implemented within a reasonable period of time. However, neither compensation nor the suspension of concessions or other obligations is preferred to full implementation of a recommendation to bring a measure into conformity with the covered agreements. Compensation is voluntary and, if granted, shall be consistent with the covered agreements.

---

12 If the parties cannot agree on an arbitrator within ten days after referring the matter to arbitration, the arbitrator shall be appointed by the Director-General within ten days, after consulting the parties.

13 The expression "arbitrator" shall be interpreted as referring either to an individual or a group.

2. If the Member concerned fails to bring the measure found to be inconsistent with a covered agreement into compliance therewith or otherwise comply with the recommendations and rulings within the reasonable period of time determined pursuant to paragraph 3 of Article 21, such Member shall, if so requested, and no later than the expiry of the reasonable period of time, enter into negotiations with any party having invoked the dispute settlement procedures, with a view to developing mutually acceptable compensation. If no satisfactory compensation has been agreed within 20 days after the date of expiry of the reasonable period of time, any party having invoked the dispute settlement procedures may request authorization from the DSB to suspend the application to the Member concerned of concessions or other obligations under the covered agreements.

3. In considering what concessions or other obligations to suspend, the complaining party shall apply the following principles and procedures:

   (a) the general principle is that the complaining party should first seek to suspend concessions or other obligations with respect to the same sector(s) as that in which the panel or Appellate Body has found a violation or other nullification or impairment;

   (b) if that party considers that it is not practicable or effective to suspend concessions or other obligations with respect to the same sector(s), it may seek to suspend concessions or other obligations in other sectors under the same agreement;

   (c) if that party considers that it is not practicable or effective to suspend concessions or other obligations with respect to other sectors under the same agreement, and that the circumstances are serious enough, it may seek to suspend concessions or other obligations under another covered agreement;

   (d) in applying the above principles, that party shall take into account:

      (i) the trade in the sector or under the agreement under which the panel or Appellate Body has found a violation or other nullification or impairment, and the importance of such trade to that party;

      (ii) the broader economic elements related to the nullification or impairment and the broader economic consequences of the suspension of concessions or other obligations;

   (e) if that party decides to request authorization to suspend concessions or other obligations pursuant to subparagraphs (b) or (c), it shall state the reasons therefor in its request. At the same time as the request is forwarded to the DSB, it also shall be forwarded to the relevant Councils and also, in the case of a request pursuant to subparagraph (b), the relevant sectoral bodies;

   (f) for purposes of this paragraph, "sector" means:

      (i) with respect to goods, all goods;

      (ii) with respect to services, a principal sector as identified in the current "Services Sectoral Classification List" which identifies such sectors;[14]

      (iii) with respect to trade-related intellectual property rights, each of the categories of intellectual property rights covered in Section 1, or Section 2, or Section 3, or Section 4, or Section 5, or Section 6, or Section 7 of Part II, or the obligations under Part III, or Part IV of the Agreement on TRIPS;

   (g) for purposes of this paragraph, "agreement" means:

      (i) with respect to goods, the agreements listed in Annex 1A of the WTO Agreement, taken as a whole as well as the Plurilateral Trade Agreements in so far as the relevant parties to the dispute are parties to these agreements;

      (ii) with respect to services, the GATS;

      (iii) with respect to intellectual property rights, the Agreement on TRIPS.

---

14 The list in document MTN.GNS/W/120 identifies eleven sectors.

4. The level of the suspension of concessions or other obligations authorized by the DSB shall be equivalent to the level of the nullification or impairment.

5. The DSB shall not authorize suspension of concessions or other obligations if a covered agreement prohibits such suspension.

6. When the situation described in paragraph 2 occurs, the DSB, upon request, shall grant authorization to suspend concessions or other obligations within 30 days of the expiry of the reasonable period of time unless the DSB decides by consensus to reject the request. However, if the Member concerned objects to the level of suspension proposed, or claims that the principles and procedures set forth in paragraph 3 have not been followed where a complaining party has requested authorization to suspend concessions or other obligations pursuant to paragraph 3(b) or (c), the matter shall be referred to arbitration. Such arbitration shall be carried out by the original panel, if members are available, or by an arbitrator[15] appointed by the Director-General and shall be completed within 60 days after the date of expiry of the reasonable period of time. Concessions or other obligations shall not be suspended during the course of the arbitration.

7. The arbitrator[16] acting pursuant to paragraph 6 shall not examine the nature of the concessions or other obligations to be suspended but shall determine whether the level of such suspension is equivalent to the level of nullification or impairment. The arbitrator may also determine if the proposed suspension of concessions or other obligations is allowed under the covered agreement. However, if the matter referred to arbitration includes a claim that the principles and procedures set forth in paragraph 3 have not been followed, the arbitrator shall examine that claim. In the event the arbitrator determines that those principles and procedures have not been followed, the complaining party shall apply them consistent with paragraph 3. The parties shall accept the arbitrator's decision as final and the parties concerned shall not seek a second arbitration. The DSB shall be informed promptly of the decision of the arbitrator and shall upon request, grant authorization to suspend concessions or other obligations where the request is consistent with the decision of the arbitrator, unless the DSB decides by consensus to reject the request.

8. The suspension of concessions or other obligations shall be temporary and shall only be applied until such time as the measure found to be inconsistent with a covered agreement has been removed, or the Member that must implement recommendations or rulings provides a solution to the nullification or impairment of benefits, or a mutually satisfactory solution is reached. In accordance with paragraph 6 of Article 21, the DSB shall continue to keep under surveillance the implementation of adopted recommendations or rulings, including those cases where compensation has been provided or concessions or other obligations have been suspended but the recommendations to bring a measure into conformity with the covered agreements have not been implemented.

9. The dispute settlement provisions of the covered agreements may be invoked in respect of measures affecting their observance taken by regional or local governments or authorities within the territory of a Member. When the DSB has ruled that a provision of a covered agreement has not been observed, the responsible Member shall take such reasonable measures as may be available to it to ensure its observance. The provisions of the covered agreements and this Understanding relating to compensation and suspension of concessions or other obligations apply in cases where it has not been possible to secure such observance.[17]

---

15 The expression "arbitrator" shall be interpreted as referring either to an individual or a group.

16 The expression "arbitrator" shall be interpreted as referring either to an individual or a group or to the members of the original panel when serving in the capacity of arbitrator.

17 Where the provisions of any covered agreement concerning measures taken by regional or local governments or authorities within the territory of a Member contain provisions different from the provisions of this paragraph, the provisions of such covered agreement shall prevail.

Article 23   Strengthening of the Multilateral System

1. When Members seek the redress of a violation of obligations or other nullification or impairment of benefits under the covered agreements or an impediment to the attainment of any objective of the covered agreements, they shall have recourse to, and abide by, the rules and procedures of this Understanding.

2. In such cases, Members shall:

    (a) not make a determination to the effect that a violation has occurred, that benefits have been nullified or impaired or that the attainment of any objective of the covered agreements has been impeded, except through recourse to dispute settlement in accordance with the rules and procedures of this Understanding, and shall make any such determination consistent with the findings contained in the panel or Appellate Body report adopted by the DSB or an arbitration award rendered under this Understanding;

    (b) follow the procedures set forth in Article 21 to determine the reasonable period of time for the Member concerned to implement the recommendations and rulings; and

    (c) follow the procedures set forth in Article 22 to determine the level of suspension of concessions or other obligations and obtain DSB authorization in accordance with those procedures before suspending concessions or other obligations under the covered agreements in response to the failure of the Member concerned to implement the recommendations and rulings within that reasonable period of time.

Article 24   Special Procedures Involving Least-Developed Country Members

1. At all stages of the determination of the causes of a dispute and of dispute settlement procedures involving a least-developed country Member, particular consideration shall be given to the special situation of least-developed country Members. In this regard, Members shall exercise due restraint in raising matters under these procedures involving a least-developed country Member. If nullification or impairment is found to result from a measure taken by a least-developed country Member, complaining parties shall exercise due restraint in asking for compensation or seeking authorization to suspend the application of concessions or other obligations pursuant to these procedures.

2. In dispute settlement cases involving a least-developed country Member, where a satisfactory solution has not been found in the course of consultations the Director-General or the Chairman of the DSB shall, upon request by a least-developed country Member offer their good offices, conciliation and mediation with a view to assisting the parties to settle the dispute, before a request for a panel is made. The Director-General or the Chairman of the DSB, in providing the above assistance, may consult any source which either deems appropriate.

Article 25   Arbitration

1. Expeditious arbitration within the WTO as an alternative means of dispute settlement can facilitate the solution of certain disputes that concern issues that are clearly defined by both parties.

2. Except as otherwise provided in this Understanding, resort to arbitration shall be subject to mutual agreement of the parties which shall agree on the procedures to be followed. Agreements to resort to arbitration shall be notified to all Members sufficiently in advance of the actual commencement of the arbitration process.

3. Other Members may become party to an arbitration proceeding only upon the agreement of the parties which have agreed to have recourse to arbitration. The parties to the proceeding shall agree to abide by the arbitration award. Arbitration awards shall be notified to the DSB and the Council or Committee of any relevant agreement where any Member may raise any point relating thereto.

4. Articles 21 and 22 of this Understanding shall apply *mutatis mutandis* to arbitration awards.

Article 26

1. *Non-Violation Complaints of the Type Described in Paragraph 1(b) of Article XXIII of GATT 1994*
Where the provisions of paragraph 1(b) of Article XXIII of GATT 1994 are applicable to a covered agreement, a panel or the Appellate Body may only make rulings and recommendations where a party to the dispute considers that any benefit accruing to it directly or indirectly under the relevant covered agreement is being nullified or impaired or the attainment of any objective of that Agreement is being impeded as a result of the application by a Member of any measure, whether or not it conflicts with the provisions of that Agreement. Where and to the extent that such party considers and a panel or the Appellate Body determines that a case concerns a measure that does not conflict with the provisions of a covered agreement to which the provisions of paragraph 1(b) of Article XXIII of GATT 1994 are applicable, the procedures in this Understanding shall apply, subject to the following:
   (a) the complaining party shall present a detailed justification in support of any complaint relating to a measure which does not conflict with the relevant covered agreement;
   (b) where a measure has been found to nullify or impair benefits under, or impede the attainment of objectives, of the relevant covered agreement without violation thereof, there is no obligation to withdraw the measure. However, in such cases, the panel or the Appellate Body shall recommend that the Member concerned make a mutually satisfactory adjustment;
   (c) notwithstanding the provisions of Article 21, the arbitration provided for in paragraph 3 of Article 21, upon request of either party, may include a determination of the level of benefits which have been nullified or impaired, and may also suggest ways and means of reaching a mutually satisfactory adjustment; such suggestions shall not be binding upon the parties to the dispute;
   (d) notwithstanding the provisions of paragraph 1 of Article 22, compensation may be part of a mutually satisfactory adjustment as final settlement of the dispute.

2. *Complaints of the Type Described in Paragraph 1(c) of Article XXIII of GATT 1994*
Where the provisions of paragraph 1(c) of Article XXIII of GATT 1994 are applicable to a covered agreement, a panel may only make rulings and recommendations where a party considers that any benefit accruing to it directly or indirectly under the relevant covered agreement is being nullified or impaired or the attainment of any objective of that Agreement is being impeded as a result of the existence of any situation other than those to which the provisions of paragraphs 1(a) and 1(b) of Article XXIII of GATT 1994 are applicable. Where and to the extent that such party considers and a panel determines that the matter is covered by this paragraph, the procedures of this Understanding shall apply only up to and including the point in the proceedings where the panel report has been circulated to the Members. The dispute settlement rules and procedures contained in the Decision of 12 April 1989 (BISD 36S/61–67) shall apply to consideration for adoption, and surveillance and implementation of recommendations and rulings. The following shall also apply:
   (a) the complaining party shall present a detailed justification in support of any argument made with respect to issues covered under this paragraph;
   (b) in cases involving matters covered by this paragraph, if a panel finds that cases also involve dispute settlement matters other than those covered by this paragraph, the panel shall circulate a report to the DSB addressing any such matters and a separate report on matters falling under this paragraph.

Article 27 Responsibilities of the Secretariat

1. The Secretariat shall have the responsibility of assisting panels, especially on the legal, historical and procedural aspects of the matters dealt with, and of providing secretarial and technical support.

2. While the Secretariat assists Members in respect of dispute settlement at their request, there may also be a need to provide additional legal advice and assistance in respect of dispute settlement to developing country Members. To this end, the Secretariat shall make available a qualified legal expert from the WTO technical cooperation services to any developing country Member which so requests. This expert shall assist the developing country Member in a manner ensuring the continued impartiality of the Secretariat.

3. The Secretariat shall conduct special training courses for interested Members concerning these dispute settlement procedures and practices so as to enable Members' experts to be better informed in this regard.

APPENDIX 1   AGREEMENTS COVERED BY THE UNDERSTANDING

(A) Agreement Establishing the World Trade Organization

(B) Multilateral Trade Agreements
      Annex 1A: Multilateral Agreements on Trade in Goods
      Annex 1B: General Agreement on Trade in Services
      Annex 1C: Agreement on Trade-Related Aspects of Intellectual Property Rights
      Annex 2: Understanding on Rules and Procedures Governing the Settlement of Disputes

(C) Plurilateral Trade Agreements
      Annex 4: Agreement on Trade in Civil Aircraft
                Agreement on Government Procurement
                International Dairy Agreement
                International Bovine Meat Agreement
      The applicability of this Understanding to the Plurilateral Trade Agreements shall be subject to the adoption of a decision by the parties to each agreement setting out the terms for the application of the Understanding to the individual agreement, including any special or additional rules or procedures for inclusion in Appendix 2, as notified to the DSB.

APPENDIX 2   SPECIAL OR ADDITIONAL RULES AND PROCEDURES CONTAINED IN THE COVERED AGREEMENTS

Agreement	Rules and Procedures
Agreement on the Application of Sanitary and Phytosanitary Measures	11.2
Agreement on Textiles and Clothing	2.14, 2.21, 4.4, 5.2, 5.4, 5.6, 6.9, 6.10, 6.11, 8.1 through 8.12
Agreement on Technical Barriers to Trade	14.2 through 14.4, Annex 2
Agreement on Implementation of Article VI of GATT 1994	17.4 through 17.7
Agreement on Implementation of Article VII of GATT 1994	19.3 through 19.5, Annex II.2(f), 3, 9, 21
Agreement on Subsidies and Countervailing Measures	4.2 through 4.12, 6.6, 7.2 through 7.10, 8.5, footnote 35, 24.4, 27.7, Annex V
General Agreement on Trade in Services	XXII:3, XXIII:3
Annex on Financial Services	4
Annex on Air Transport Services	4
Decision on Certain Dispute Settlement Procedures for the GATS	1 through 5

The list of rules and procedures in this Appendix includes provisions where only a part of the provision may be relevant in this context.

Any special or additional rules or procedures in the Plurilateral Trade Agreements as determined by the competent bodies of each agreement and as notified to the DSB.

APPENDIX 3   WORKING PROCEDURES

1. In its proceedings the panel shall follow the relevant provisions of this Understanding. In addition, the following working procedures shall apply.

2. The panel shall meet in closed session. The parties to the dispute, and interested parties, shall be present at the meetings only when invited by the panel to appear before it.

3. The deliberations of the panel and the documents submitted to it shall be kept confidential. Nothing in this Understanding shall preclude a party to a dispute from disclosing statements of its own positions to the public. Members shall treat as confidential information submitted by another Member to the panel which that Member has designated as confidential. Where a party to a dispute submits a confidential version of its written submissions to the panel, it shall also, upon request of a Member, provide a non-confidential summary of the information contained in its submissions that could be disclosed to the public.

4. Before the first substantive meeting of the panel with the parties, the parties to the dispute shall transmit to the panel written submissions in which they present the facts of the case and their arguments.

5. At its first substantive meeting with the parties, the panel shall ask the party which has brought the complaint to present its case. Subsequently, and still at the same meeting, the party against which the complaint has been brought shall be asked to present its point of view.

6. All third parties which have notified their interest in the dispute to the DSB shall be invited in writing to present their views during a session of the first substantive meeting of the panel set aside for that purpose. All such third parties may be present during the entirety of this session.

7. Formal rebuttals shall be made at a second substantive meeting of the panel. The party complained against shall have the right to take the floor first to be followed by the complaining party. The parties shall submit, prior to that meeting, written rebuttals to the panel.

8. The panel may at any time put questions to the parties and ask them for explanations either in the course of a meeting with the parties or in writing.

9. The parties to the dispute and any third party invited to present its views in accordance with Article 10 shall make available to the panel a written version of their oral statements.

10. In the interest of full transparency, the presentations, rebuttals and statements referred to in paragraphs 5 to 9 shall be made in the presence of the parties. Moreover, each party's written submissions, including any comments on the descriptive part of the report and responses to questions put by the panel, shall be made available to the other party or parties.

11. Any additional procedures specific to the panel.

12. Proposed timetable for panel work:
    (a) Receipt of first written submissions of the parties:
        (1) complaining Party: 3–6 weeks
        (2) Party complained against: 2–3 weeks
    (b) Date, time and place of first substantive meeting with the parties; third party session: 1–2 weeks
    (c) Receipt of written rebuttals of the parties: 2–3 weeks
    (d) Date, time and place of second substantive meeting with the parties: 1–2 weeks
    (e) Issuance of descriptive part of the report to the parties: 2–4 weeks

(f) Receipt of comments by the parties on the descriptive part of the report: 2 weeks
(g) Issuance of the interim report, including the findings and conclusions, to the parties: 2–4 weeks
(h) Deadline for party to request review of part(s) of report: 1 week
(i) Period of review by panel, including possible additional meeting with parties: 2 weeks
(j) Issuance of final report to parties to dispute: 2 weeks
(k) Circulation of the final report to the Members: 3 weeks

The above calendar may be changed in the light of unforeseen developments. Additional meetings with the parties shall be scheduled if required.

APPENDIX 4   EXPERT REVIEW GROUPS

The following rules and procedures shall apply to expert review groups established in accordance with the provisions of paragraph 2 of Article 13.

1. Expert review groups are under the panel's authority. Their terms of reference and detailed working procedures shall be decided by the panel, and they shall report to the panel.

2. Participation in expert review groups shall be restricted to persons of professional standing and experience in the field in question.

3. Citizens of parties to the dispute shall not serve on an expert review group without the joint agreement of the parties to the dispute, except in exceptional circumstances when the panel considers that the need for specialized scientific expertise cannot be fulfilled otherwise. Government officials of parties to the dispute shall not serve on an expert review group. Members of expert review groups shall serve in their individual capacities and not as government representatives, nor as representatives of any organization. Governments or organizations shall therefore not give them instructions with regard to matters before an expert review group.

4. Expert review groups may consult and seek information and technical advice from any source they deem appropriate. Before an expert review group seeks such information or advice from a source within the jurisdiction of a Member, it shall inform the government of that Member. Any Member shall respond promptly and fully to any request by an expert review group for such information as the expert review group considers necessary and appropriate.

5. The parties to a dispute shall have access to all relevant information provided to an expert review group, unless it is of a confidential nature. Confidential information provided to the expert review group shall not be released without formal authorization from the government, organization or person providing the information. Where such information is requested from the expert review group but release of such information by the expert review group is not authorized, a non-confidential summary of the information will be provided by the government, organization or person supplying the information.

6. The expert review group shall submit a draft report to the parties to the dispute with a view to obtaining their comments, and taking them into account, as appropriate, in the final report, which shall also be issued to the parties to the dispute when it is submitted to the panel. The final report of the expert review group shall be advisory only.

II-19

Agreement on Government Procurement

Parties to this Agreement (hereinafter referred to as "Parties"),

Recognizing the need for an effective multilateral framework of rights and obligations with respect to laws, regulations, procedures and practices regarding government procurement with a view to achieving greater liberalization and expansion of world trade and improving the international framework for the conduct of world trade;

Recognizing that laws, regulations, procedures and practices regarding government procurement should not be prepared, adopted or applied to foreign or domestic products and services and to foreign or domestic suppliers so as to afford protection to domestic products or services or domestic suppliers and should not discriminate among foreign products or services or among foreign suppliers;

Recognizing that it is desirable to provide transparency of laws, regulations, procedures and practices regarding government procurement;

Recognizing the need to establish international procedures on notification, consultation, surveillance and dispute settlement with a view to ensuring a fair, prompt and effective enforcement of the international provisions on government procurement and to maintain the balance of rights and obligations at the highest possible level;

Recognizing the need to take into account the development, financial and trade needs of developing countries, in particular the least-developed countries;

Desiring, in accordance with paragraph 6(b) of Article IX of the Agreement on Government Procurement done on 12 April 1979, as amended on 2 February 1987, to broaden and improve the Agreement on the basis of mutual reciprocity and to expand the coverage of the Agreement to include service contracts;

Desiring to encourage acceptance of and accession to this Agreement by governments not party to it;

Having undertaken further negotiations in pursuance of these objectives;

Hereby *agree* as follows:

Article I   Scope and Coverage

1. This Agreement applies to any law, regulation, procedure or practice regarding any procurement by entities covered by this Agreement, as specified in Appendix 1.[1]

---

1 For each Party, Appendix I is divided into five Annexes:

- Annex 1 contains central government entities.
- Annex 2 contains sub-central government entities.
- Annex 3 contains all other entities that procure in accordance with the provisions of this Agreement.
- Annex 4 specifies services, whether listed positively or negatively, covered by this Agreement.
- Annex 5 specifies covered construction services.

Relevant thresholds are specified in each Party's Annexes.

2. This Agreement applies to procurement by any contractual means, including through such methods as purchase or as lease, rental or hire purchase, with or without an option to buy, including any combination of products and services.

3. Where entities, in the context of procurement covered under this Agreement, require enterprises not included in Appendix I to award contracts in accordance with particular requirements, Article III shall apply *mutatis mutandis* to such requirements.

4. This Agreement applies to any procurement contract of a value of not less than the relevant threshold specified in Appendix I.

Article II Valuation of Contracts

1. The following provisions shall apply in determining the value of contracts[2] for purposes of implementing this Agreement.

2. Valuation shall take into account all forms of remuneration, including any premiums, fees, commissions and interest receivable.

3. The selection of the valuation method by the entity shall not be used, nor shall any procurement requirement be divided, with the intention of avoiding the application of this Agreement.

4. If an individual requirement for a procurement results in the award of more than one contract, or in contracts being awarded in separate parts, the basis for valuation shall be either:
   (a) the actual value of similar recurring contracts concluded over the previous fiscal year or 12 months adjusted, where possible, for anticipated changes in quantity and value over the subsequent 12 months; or
   (b) the estimated value of recurring contracts in the fiscal year or 12 months subsequent to the initial contract.

5. In cases of contracts for the lease, rental or hire purchase of products or services, or in the case of contracts which do not specify a total price, the basis for valuation shall be:
   (a) in the case of fixed-term contracts, where their term is 12 months or less, the total contract value for their duration, or, where their term exceeds 12 months, their total value including the estimated residual value;
   (b) in the case of contracts for an indefinite period, the monthly instalment multiplied by 48. If there is any doubt, the second basis for valuation, namely (b), is to be used.

6. In cases where an intended procurement specifies the need for option clauses, the basis for valuation shall be the total value of the maximum permissible procurement, inclusive of optional purchases.

Article III National Treatment and Non-discrimination

1. With respect to all laws, regulations, procedures and practices regarding government procurement covered by this Agreement, each Party shall provide immediately and unconditionally to the products, services and suppliers of other Parties offering products or services of the Parties, treatment no less favourable than:
   (a) that accorded to domestic products, services and suppliers; and
   (b) that accorded to products, services and suppliers of any other Party.

2. With respect to all laws, regulations, procedures and practices regarding government procurement covered by this Agreement, each Party shall ensure:
   (a) that its entities shall not treat a locally-established supplier less favourably than another locally-established supplier on the basis of degree of foreign affiliation or ownership; and
   (b) that its entities shall not discriminate against locally-established suppliers on the basis of the country of production of the good or service being supplied, provided that the

---

2 This Agreement shall apply to any procurement contract for which the contract value is estimated to equal or exceed the threshold at the time of publication of the notice in accordance with Article IX.

country of production is a Party to the Agreement in accordance with the provisions of Article IV.

3. The provisions of paragraphs 1 and 2 shall not apply to customs duties and charges of any kind imposed on or in connection with importation, the method of levying such duties and charges, other import regulations and formalities, and measures affecting trade in services other than laws, regulations, procedures and practices regarding government procurement covered by this Agreement.

Article IV   Rules of Origin

1. A Party shall not apply rules of origin to products or services imported or supplied for purposes of government procurement covered by this Agreement from other Parties, which are different from the rules of origin applied in the normal course of trade and at the time of the transaction in question to imports or supplies of the same products or services from the same Parties.

2. Following the conclusion of the work programme for the harmonization of rules of origin for goods to be undertaken under the Agreement on Rules of Origin in Annex 1A of the Agreement Establishing the World Trade Organization (hereinafter referred to as "WTO Agreement") and negotiations regarding trade in services, Parties shall take the results of that work programme and those negotiations into account in amending paragraph 1 as appropriate.

Article V   Special and Differential Treatment for Developing Countries
Objectives

1. Parties shall, in the implementation and administration of this Agreement, through the provisions set out in this Article, duly take into account the development, financial and trade needs of developing countries, in particular least-developed countries, in their need to:
   (a) safeguard their balance-of-payments position and ensure a level of reserves adequate for the implementation of programmes of economic development;
   (b) promote the establishment or development of domestic industries including the development of small-scale and cottage industries in rural or backward areas; and economic development of other sectors of the economy;
   (c) support industrial units so long as they are wholly or substantially dependent on government procurement; and
   (d) encourage their economic development through regional or global arrangements among developing countries presented to the Ministerial Conference of the World Trade Organization (hereinafter referred to as the "WTO") and not disapproved by it.

2. Consistently with the provisions of this Agreement, each Party shall, in the preparation and application of laws, regulations and procedures affecting government procurement, facilitate increased imports from developing countries, bearing in mind the special problems of least-developed countries and of those countries at low stages of economic development.

Coverage

3. With a view to ensuring that developing countries are able to adhere to this Agreement on terms consistent with their development, financial and trade needs, the objectives listed in paragraph 1 shall be duly taken into account in the course of negotiations with respect to the procurement of developing countries to be covered by the provisions of this Agreement. Developed countries, in the preparation of their coverage lists under the provisions of this Agreement, shall endeavour to include entities procuring products and services of export interest to developing countries.

Agreed Exclusions

4. A developing country may negotiate with other participants in negotiations under this Agreement mutually acceptable exclusions from the rules on national treatment with respect to certain entities, products or services that are included in its coverage lists, having regard

to the particular circumstances of each case. In such negotiations, the considerations mentioned in subparagraphs 1(a) through 1(c) shall be duly taken into account. A developing country participating in regional or global arrangements among developing countries referred to in subparagraph 1(d) may also negotiate exclusions to its lists, having regard to the particular circumstances of each case, taking into account, *inter alia*, the provisions on government procurement provided for in the regional or global arrangements concerned and, in particular, products or services which may be subject to common industrial development programmes.

5. After entry into force of this Agreement, a developing country Party may modify its coverage lists in accordance with the provisions for modification of such lists contained in paragraph 6 of Article XXIV, having regard to its development, financial and trade needs, or may request the Committee on Government Procurement (hereinafter referred to as "the Committee") to grant exclusions from the rules on national treatment for certain entities, products or services that are included in its coverage lists, having regard to the particular circumstances of each case and taking duly into account the provisions of subparagraphs 1(a) through 1(c). After entry into force of this Agreement, a developing country Party may also request the Committee to grant exclusions for certain entities, products or services that are included in its coverage lists in the light of its participation in regional or global arrangements among developing countries, having regard to the particular circumstances of each case and taking duly into account the provisions of subparagraph 1(d). Each request to the Committee by a developing country Party relating to modification of a list shall be accompanied by documentation relevant to the request or by such information as may be necessary for consideration of the matter.

6. Paragraphs 4 and 5 shall apply *mutatis mutandis* to developing countries acceding to this Agreement after its entry into force.

7. Such agreed exclusions as mentioned in paragraphs 4, 5 and 6 shall be subject to review in accordance with the provisions of paragraph 14 below.

Technical Assistance for Developing Country Parties

8. Each developed country Party shall, upon request, provide all technical assistance which it may deem appropriate to developing country Parties in resolving their problems in the field of government procurement.

9. This assistance, which shall be provided on the basis of non-discrimination among developing country Parties, shall relate, *inter alia*, to:
   – the solution of particular technical problems relating to the award of a specific contract; and
   – any other problem which the Party making the request and another Party agree to deal with in the context of this assistance.

10. Technical assistance referred to in paragraphs 8 and 9 would include translation of qualification documentation and tenders made by suppliers of developing country Parties into an official language of the WTO designated by the entity, unless developed country Parties deem translation to be burdensome, and in that case explanation shall be given to developing country Parties upon their request addressed either to the developed country Parties or to their entities.

Information Centres

11. Developed country Parties shall establish, individually or jointly, information centres to respond to reasonable requests from developing country Parties for information relating to, *inter alia*, laws, regulations, procedures and practices regarding government procurement, notices about intended procurements which have been published, addresses of the entities covered by this Agreement, and the nature and volume of products or services procured or to

be procured, including available information about future tenders. The Committee may also set up an information centre.

Special Treatment for Least-Developed Countries

12. Having regard to paragraph 6 of the Decision of the CONTRACTING PARTIES to GATT 1947 of 28 November 1979 on Differential and More Favourable Treatment, Reciprocity and Fuller Participation of Developing Countries (BISD 26S/203–205), special treatment shall be granted to least-developed country Parties and to the suppliers in those Parties with respect to products or services originating in those Parties, in the context of any general or specific measures in favour of developing country Parties. A Party may also grant the benefits of this Agreement to suppliers in least-developed countries which are not Parties, with respect to products or services originating in those countries.

13. Each developed country Party shall, upon request, provide assistance which it may deem appropriate to potential tenderers in least-developed countries in submitting their tenders and selecting the products or services which are likely to be of interest to its entities as well as to suppliers in least-developed countries, and likewise assist them to comply with technical regulations and standards relating to products or services which are the subject of the intended procurement.

Review

14. The Committee shall review annually the operation and effectiveness of this Article and, after each three years of its operation on the basis of reports to be submitted by Parties, shall carry out a major review in order to evaluate its effects. As part of the three-yearly reviews and with a view to achieving the maximum implementation of the provisions of this Agreement, including in particular Article III, and having regard to the development, financial and trade situation of the developing countries concerned, the Committee shall examine whether exclusions provided for in accordance with the provisions of paragraphs 4 through 6 of this Article shall be modified or extended.

15. In the course of further rounds of negotiations in accordance with the provisions of paragraph 7 of Article XXIV, each developing country Party shall give consideration to the possibility of enlarging its coverage lists, having regard to its economic, financial and trade situation.

Article VI   Technical Specifications

1. Technical specifications laying down the characteristics of the products or services to be procured, such as quality, performance, safety and dimensions, symbols, terminology, packaging, marking and labelling, or the processes and methods for their production and requirements relating to conformity assessment procedures prescribed by procuring entities, shall not be prepared, adopted or applied with a view to, or with the effect of, creating unnecessary obstacles to international trade.

2. Technical specifications prescribed by procuring entities shall, where appropriate:
   (a) be in terms of performance rather than design or descriptive characteristics; and
   (b) be based on international standards, where such exist; otherwise, on national technical regulations[3], recognized national standards[4], or building codes.

3. There shall be no requirement or reference to a particular trademark or trade name, patent, design or type, specific origin, producer or supplier, unless there is no sufficiently precise or

---

3 For the purpose of this Agreement, a technical regulation is a document which lays down characteristics of a product or a service or their related processes and production methods, including the applicable administrative provisions, with which compliance is mandatory. It may also include or deal exclusively with terminology, symbols, packaging, marking or labelling requirements as they apply to a product, service, process or production method.

4 For the purpose of this Agreement, a standard is a document approved by a recognized body, that provides, for common and repeated use, rules, guidelines or characteristics for products or services or related processes and production methods, with which compliance is not mandatory. It may also include or deal exclusively with terminology, symbols, packaging, marking or labelling requirements as they apply to a product, service, process or production method.

intelligible way of describing the procurement requirements and provided that words such as "or equivalent" are included in the tender documentation.

4. Entities shall not seek or accept, in a manner which would have the effect of precluding competition, advice which may be used in the preparation of specifications for a specific procurement from a firm that may have a commercial interest in the procurement.

Article VII   Tendering Procedures

1. Each Party shall ensure that the tendering procedures of its entities are applied in a non-discriminatory manner and are consistent with the provisions contained in Articles VII through XVI.

2. Entities shall not provide to any supplier information with regard to a specific procurement in a manner which would have the effect of precluding competition.

3. For the purposes of this Agreement:
   (a) Open tendering procedures are those procedures under which all interested suppliers may submit a tender.
   (b) Selective tendering procedures are those procedures under which, consistent with paragraph 3 of Article X and other relevant provisions of this Agreement, those suppliers invited to do so by the entity may submit a tender.
   (c) Limited tendering procedures are those procedures where the entity contacts suppliers individually, only under the conditions specified in Article XV.

Article VIII   Qualification of Suppliers

In the process of qualifying suppliers, entities shall not discriminate among suppliers of other Parties or between domestic suppliers and suppliers of other Parties. Qualification procedures shall be consistent with the following:

   (a) any conditions for participation in tendering procedures shall be published in adequate efficient operation of the procurement process, complete the qualification procedures;
   (b) any conditions for participation in tendering procedures shall be limited to those which are essential to ensure the firm's capability to fulfil the contract in question. Any conditions for participation required from suppliers, including financial guarantees, technical qualifications and information necessary for establishing the financial, commercial and technical capacity of suppliers, as well as the verification of qualifications, shall be no less favourable to suppliers of other Parties than to domestic suppliers and shall not discriminate among suppliers of other Parties. The financial, commercial and technical capacity of a supplier shall be judged on the basis both of that supplier's global business activity as well as of its activity in the territory of the procuring entity, taking due account of the legal relationship between the supply organizations;
   (c) the process of, and the time required for, qualifying suppliers shall not be used in order to keep suppliers of other Parties off a suppliers' list or from being considered for a particular intended procurement. Entities shall recognize as qualified suppliers such domestic suppliers or suppliers of other Parties who meet the conditions for participation in a particular intended procurement. Suppliers requesting to participate in a particular intended procurement who may not yet be qualified shall also be considered, provided there is sufficient time to complete the qualification procedure;
   (d) entities maintaining permanent lists of qualified suppliers shall ensure that suppliers may apply for qualification at any time; and that all qualified suppliers so requesting are included in the lists within a reasonably short time;
   (e) if, after publication of the notice under paragraph 1 of Article IX, a supplier not yet qualified requests to participate in an intended procurement, the entity shall promptly start procedures for qualification;

(f) any supplier having requested to become a qualified supplier shall be advised by the entities concerned of the decision in this regard. Qualified suppliers included on permanent lists by entities shall also be notified of the termination of any such lists or of their removal from them;

(g) each Party shall ensure that:

(i) each entity and its constituent parts follow a single qualification procedure, except in cases of duly substantiated need for a different procedure; and

(ii) efforts be made to minimize differences in qualification procedures between entities.

(h) nothing in subparagraphs (a) through (g) shall preclude the exclusion of any supplier on grounds such as bankruptcy or false declarations, provided that such an action is consistent with the national treatment and non-discrimination provisions of this Agreement.

Article IX   Invitation to Participate Regarding Intended Procurement

1. In accordance with paragraphs 2 and 3, entities shall publish an invitation to participate for all cases of intended procurement, except as otherwise provided for in Article XV (limited tendering). The notice shall be published in the appropriate publication listed in Appendix II.

2. The invitation to participate may take the form of a notice of proposed procurement, as provided for in paragraph 6.

3. Entities in Annexes 2 and 3 may use a notice of planned procurement, as provided for in paragraph 7, or a notice regarding a qualification system, as provided for in paragraph 9, as an invitation to participate.

4. Entities which use a notice of planned procurement as an invitation to participate shall subsequently invite all suppliers who have expressed an interest to confirm their interest on the basis of information which shall include at least the information referred to in paragraph 6.

5. Entities which use a notice regarding a qualification system as an invitation to participate shall provide, subject to the considerations referred to in paragraph 4 of Article XVIII and in a timely manner, information which allows all those who have expressed an interest to have a meaningful opportunity to assess their interest in participating in the procurement. This information shall include the information contained in the notices referred to in paragraphs 6 and 8, to the extent such information is available. Information provided to one interested supplier shall be provided in a non-discriminatory manner to the other interested suppliers.

6. Each notice of proposed procurement, referred to in paragraph 2, shall contain the following information:

(a) the nature and quantity, including any options for further procurement and, if possible, an estimate of the timing when such options may be exercised; in the case of recurring contracts the nature and quantity and, if possible, an estimate of the timing of the subsequent tender notices for the products or services to be procured;

(b) whether the procedure is open or selective or will involve negotiation;

(c) any date for starting delivery or completion of delivery of goods or services;

(d) the address and final date for submitting an application to be invited to tender or for qualifying for the suppliers' lists, or for receiving tenders, as well as the language or languages in which they must be submitted;

(e) the address of the entity awarding the contract and providing any information necessary for obtaining specifications and other documents;

(f) any economic and technical requirements, financial guarantees and information required from suppliers;

(g) the amount and terms of payment of any sum payable for the tender documentation; and

(h) whether the entity is inviting offers for purchase, lease, rental or hire purchase, or more than one of these methods.

7. Each notice of planned procurement referred to in paragraph 3 shall contain as much of the information referred to in paragraph 6 as is available. It shall in any case include the information referred to in paragraph 8 and:
    (a) a statement that interested suppliers should express their interest in the procurement to the entity;
    (b) a contact point with the entity from which further information may be obtained.

8. For each case of intended procurement, the entity shall publish a summary notice in one of the official languages of the WTO. The notice shall contain at least the following information:
    (a) the subject matter of the contract;
    (b) the time-limits set for the submission of tenders or an application to be invited to tender; and
    (c) the addresses from which documents relating to the contracts may be requested.

9. In the case of selective tendering procedures, entities maintaining permanent lists of qualified suppliers shall publish annually in one of the publications listed in Appendix III a notice of the following:
    (a) the enumeration of the lists maintained, including their headings, in relation to the products or services or categories of products or services to be procured through the lists;
    (b) the conditions to be fulfilled by suppliers with a view to their inscription on those lists and the methods according to which each of those conditions will be verified by the entity concerned; and
    (c) the period of validity of the lists, and the formalities for their renewal.
    When such a notice is used as an invitation to participate in accordance with paragraph 3, the notice shall, in addition, include the following information:
    (d) the nature of the products or services concerned;
    (e) a statement that the notice constitutes an invitation to participate.
    However, when the duration of the qualification system is three years or less, and if the duration of the system is made clear in the notice and it is also made clear that further notices will not be published, it shall be sufficient to publish the notice once only, at the beginning of the system. Such a system shall not be used in a manner which circumvents the provisions of this Agreement.

10. If, after publication of an invitation to participate in any case of intended procurement, but before the time set for opening or receipt of tenders as specified in the notices or the tender documentation, it becomes necessary to amend or re-issue the notice, the amendment or the re-issued notice shall be given the same circulation as the original documents upon which the amendment is based. Any significant information given to one supplier with respect to a particular intended procurement shall be given simultaneously to all other suppliers concerned in adequate time to permit the suppliers to consider such information and to respond to it.

11. Entities shall make clear, in the notices referred to in this Article or in the publication in which the notices appear, that the procurement is covered by the Agreement.

Article X   Selection Procedures

1. To ensure optimum effective international competition under selective tendering procedures, entities shall, for each intended procurement, invite tenders from the maximum number of domestic suppliers and suppliers of other Parties, consistent with the efficient operation of the procurement system. They shall select the suppliers to participate in the procedure in a fair and non-discriminatory manner.

2. Entities maintaining permanent lists of qualified suppliers may select suppliers to be invited to tender from among those listed. Any selection shall allow for equitable opportunities for suppliers on the lists.

3. Suppliers requesting to participate in a particular intended procurement shall be permitted to submit a tender and be considered, provided, in the case of those not yet qualified, there is sufficient time to complete the qualification procedure under Articles VIII and IX. The number of additional suppliers permitted to participate shall be limited only by the efficient operation of the procurement system.

4. Requests to participate in selective tendering procedures may be submitted by telex, telegram or facsimile.

Article XI   Time-limits for Tendering and Delivery
General

1. (a) Any prescribed time-limit shall be adequate to allow suppliers of other Parties as well as domestic suppliers to prepare and submit tenders before the closing of the tendering procedures. In determining any such time-limit, entities shall, consistent with their own reasonable needs, take into account such factors as the complexity of the intended procurement, the extent of subcontracting anticipated and the normal time for trans- mitting tenders by mail from foreign as well as domestic points.

    (b) Each Party shall ensure that its entities shall take due account of publication delays when setting the final date for receipt of tenders or of applications to be invited to tender.

Deadlines

2. Except in so far as provided in paragraph 3,

    (a) in open procedures, the period for the receipt of tenders shall not be less than 40 days from the date of publication referred to in paragraph 1 of Article IX;

    (b) in selective procedures not involving the use of a permanent list of qualified suppliers, the period for submitting an application to be invited to tender shall not be less than 25 days from the date of publication referred to in paragraph 1 of Article IX; the period for receipt of tenders shall in no case be less than 40 days from the date of issuance of the invitation to tender;

    (c) in selective procedures involving the use of a permanent list of qualified suppliers, the period for receipt of tenders shall not be less than 40 days from the date of the initial issuance of invitations to tender, whether or not the date of initial issuance of invitations to tender coincides with the date of the publication referred to in paragraph 1 of Article IX.

3. The periods referred to in paragraph 2 may be reduced in the circumstances set out below:

    (a) if a separate notice has been published 40 days and not more than 12 months in advance and the notice contains at least:

        (i) as much of the information referred to in paragraph 6 of Article IX as is available;

        (ii) the information referred to in paragraph 8 of Article IX;

        (iii) a statement that interested suppliers should express their interest in the procurement to the entity; and

        (iv) a contact point with the entity from which further information may be obtained, the 40-day limit for receipt of tenders may be replaced by a period sufficiently long to enable responsive tendering, which, as a general rule, shall not be less than 24 days, but in any case not less than 10 days;

    (b) in the case of the second or subsequent publications dealing with contracts of a recurring nature within the meaning of paragraph 6 of Article IX, the 40-day limit for receipt of tenders may be reduced to not less than 24 days;

    (c) where a state of urgency duly substantiated by the entity renders impracticable the periods in question, the periods specified in paragraph 2 may be reduced but shall in no case be less than 10 days from the date of the publication referred to in paragraph 1 of Article IX; or

(d) the period referred to in paragraph 2(c) may, for procurements by entities listed in Annexes 2 and 3, be fixed by mutual agreement between the entity and the selected suppliers. In the absence of agreement, the entity may fix periods which shall be sufficiently long to enable responsive tendering and shall in any case not be less than 10 days.

4. Consistent with the entity's own reasonable needs, any delivery date shall take into account such factors as the complexity of the intended procurement, the extent of subcontracting anticipated and the realistic time required for production, de-stocking and transport of goods from the points of supply or for supply of services.

Article XII   Tender Documentation

1. If, in tendering procedures, an entity allows tenders to be submitted in several languages, one of those languages shall be one of the official languages of the WTO.

2. Tender documentation provided to suppliers shall contain all information necessary to permit them to submit responsive tenders, including information required to be published in the notice of intended procurement, except for paragraph 6(g) of Article IX, and the following:

(a) the address of the entity to which tenders should be sent;

(b) the address where requests for supplementary information should be sent;

(c) the language or languages in which tenders and tendering documents must be submitted;

(d) the closing date and time for receipt of tenders and the length of time during which any tender should be open for acceptance;

(e) the persons authorized to be present at the opening of tenders and the date, time and place of this opening;

(f) any economic and technical requirement, financial guarantees and information or documents required from suppliers;

(g) a complete description of the products or services required or of any requirements including technical specifications, conformity certification to be fulfilled, necessary plans, drawings and instructional materials;

(h) the criteria for awarding the contract, including any factors other than price that are to be considered in the evaluation of tenders and the cost elements to be included in evaluating tender prices, such as transport, insurance and inspection costs, and in the case of products or services of other Parties, customs duties and other import charges, taxes and currency of payment;

(i) the terms of payment;

(j) any other terms or conditions;

(k) in accordance with Article XVII the terms and conditions, if any, under which tenders from countries not Parties to this Agreement, but which apply the procedures of that Article, will be entertained.

Forwarding of Tender Documentation by the Entities

3. (a) In open procedures, entities shall forward the tender documentation at the request of any supplier participating in the procedure, and shall reply promptly to any reasonable request for explanations relating thereto.

(b) In selective procedures, entities shall forward the tender documentation at the request of any supplier requesting to participate, and shall reply promptly to any reasonable request for explanations relating thereto.

(c) Entities shall reply promptly to any reasonable request for relevant information submitted by a supplier participating in the tendering procedure, on condition that such information does not give that supplier an advantage over its competitors in the procedure for the award of the contract.

Article XIII   Submission, Receipt and Opening of Tenders and Awarding of Contracts

1. The submission, receipt and opening of tenders and awarding of contracts shall be consistent with the following:

   (a) tenders shall normally be submitted in writing directly or by mail. If tenders by telex, telegram or facsimile are permitted, the tender made thereby must include all the information necessary for the evaluation of the tender, in particular the definitive price proposed by the tenderer and a statement that the tenderer agrees to all the terms, conditions and provisions of the invitation to tender. The tender must be confirmed promptly by letter or by the despatch of a signed copy of the telex, telegram or facsimile. Tenders presented by telephone shall not be permitted. The content of the telex, telegram or facsimile shall prevail where there is a difference or conflict between that content and any documentation received after the time-limit; and

   (b) the opportunities that may be given to tenderers to correct unintentional errors of form between the opening of tenders and the awarding of the contract shall not be permitted to give rise to any discriminatory practice.

Receipt of Tenders

2. A supplier shall not be penalized if a tender is received in the office designated in the tender documentation after the time specified because of delay due solely to mishandling on the part of the entity. Tenders may also be considered in other exceptional circumstances if the procedures of the entity concerned so provide.

Opening of Tenders

3. All tenders solicited under open or selective procedures by entities shall be received and opened under procedures and conditions guaranteeing the regularity of the openings. The receipt and opening of tenders shall also be consistent with the national treatment and non-discrimination provisions of this Agreement. Information on the opening of tenders shall remain with the entity concerned at the disposal of the government authorities responsible for the entity in order that it may be used if required under the procedures of Articles XVIII, XIX, XX and XXII.

Award of Contracts

4. (a) To be considered for award, a tender must, at the time of opening, conform to the essential requirements of the notices or tender documentation and be from a supplier which complies with the conditions for participation. If an entity has received a tender abnormally lower than other tenders submitted, it may enquire with the tenderer to ensure that it can comply with the conditions of participation and be capable of fulfilling the terms of the contract.

   (b) Unless in the public interest an entity decides not to issue the contract, the entity shall make the award to the tenderer who has been determined to be fully capable of undertaking the contract and whose tender, whether for domestic products or services, or products or services of other Parties, is either the lowest tender or the tender which in terms of the specific evaluation criteria set forth in the notices or tender documentation is determined to be the most advantageous.

   (c) Awards shall be made in accordance with the criteria and essential requirements specified in the tender documentation.

Option Clauses

5. Option clauses shall not be used in a manner which circumvents the provisions of the Agreement.

Article XIV   Negotiation

1. A Party may provide for entities to conduct negotiations:

(a) in the context of procurements in which they have indicated such intent, namely in the notice referred to in paragraph 2 of Article IX (the invitation to suppliers to participate in the procedure for the proposed procurement); or

(b) when it appears from evaluation that no one tender is obviously the most advantageous in terms of the specific evaluation criteria set forth in the notices or tender documentation.

2. Negotiations shall primarily be used to identify the strengths and weaknesses in tenders.

3. Entities shall treat tenders in confidence. In particular, they shall not provide information intended to assist particular participants to bring their tenders up to the level of other participants.

4. Entities shall not, in the course of negotiations, discriminate between different suppliers. In particular, they shall ensure that:

(a) any elimination of participants is carried out in accordance with the criteria set forth in the notices and tender documentation;

(b) all modifications to the criteria and to the technical requirements are transmitted in writing to all remaining participants in the negotiations;

(c) all remaining participants are afforded an opportunity to submit new or amended submissions on the basis of the revised requirements; and

(d) when negotiations are concluded, all participants remaining in the negotiations shall be permitted to submit final tenders in accordance with a common deadline.

Article XV   Limited Tendering

1. The provisions of Articles VII through XIV governing open and selective tendering procedures need not apply in the following conditions, provided that limited tendering is not used with a view to avoiding maximum possible competition or in a manner which would constitute a means of discrimination among suppliers of other Parties or protection to domestic producers or suppliers:

(a) in the absence of tenders in response to an open or selective tender, or when the tenders submitted have been collusive, or not in conformity with the essential requirements in the tender, or from suppliers who do not comply with the conditions for participation provided for in accordance with this Agreement, on condition, however, that the requirements of the initial tender are not substantially modified in the contract as awarded;

(b) when, for works of art or for reasons connected with protection of exclusive rights, such as patents or copyrights, or in the absence of competition for technical reasons, the products or services can be supplied only by a particular supplier and no reasonable alternative or substitute exists;

(c) in so far as is strictly necessary when, for reasons of extreme urgency brought about by events unforeseeable by the entity, the products or services could not be obtained in time by means of open or selective tendering procedures;

(d) for additional deliveries by the original supplier which are intended either as parts replacement for existing supplies, or installations, or as the extension of existing supplies, services, or installations where a change of supplier would compel the entity to procure equipment or services not meeting requirements of interchangeability with already existing equipment or services[5];

(e) when an entity procures prototypes or a first product or service which are developed at its request in the course of, and for, a particular contract for research, experiment, study or original development. When such contracts have been fulfilled, subsequent procurements of products or services shall be subject to Articles VII through XIV[6];

---

5 It is the understanding that "existing equipment" includes software to the extent that the initial procurement of the software was covered by the Agreement.

6 Original development of a first product or service may include limited production or supply in order to incorporate the results of field testing and to demonstrate that the product or service is suitable for production or supply in quantity to acceptable quality standards. It does not extend to quantity production or supply to establish commercial viability or to recover research and development costs.

(f) when additional construction services which were not included in the initial contract but which were within the objectives of the original tender documentation have, through unforeseeable circumstances, become necessary to complete the construction services described therein, and the entity needs to award contracts for the additional construction services to the contractor carrying out the construction services concerned since the separation of the additional construction services from the initial contract would be difficult for technical or economic reasons and cause significant inconvenience to the entity. However, the total value of contracts awarded for the additional construction services may not exceed 50 per cent of the amount of the main contract;

(g) for new construction services consisting of the repetition of similar construction services which conform to a basic project for which an initial contract was awarded in accordance with Articles VII through XIV and for which the entity has indicated in the notice of intended procurement concerning the initial construction service, that limited tendering procedures might be used in awarding contracts for such new construction services;

(h) for products purchased on a commodity market;

(i) for purchases made under exceptionally advantageous conditions which only arise in the very short term. This provision is intended to cover unusual disposals by firms which are not normally suppliers, or disposal of assets of businesses in liquidation or receivership. It is not intended to cover routine purchases from regular suppliers;

(j) in the case of contracts awarded to the winner of a design contest provided that the contest has been organized in a manner which is consistent with the principles of this Agreement, notably as regards the publication, in the sense of Article IX, of an invitation to suitably qualified suppliers, to participate in such a contest which shall be judged by an independent jury with a view to design contracts being awarded to the winners.

2. Entities shall prepare a report in writing on each contract awarded under the provisions of paragraph 1. Each report shall contain the name of the procuring entity, value and kind of goods or services procured, country of origin, and a statement of the conditions in this Article which prevailed. This report shall remain with the entities concerned at the disposal of the government authorities responsible for the entity in order that it may be used if required under the procedures of Articles XVIII, XIX, XX and XXII.

Article XVI Offsets

1. Entities shall not, in the qualification and selection of suppliers, products or services, or in the evaluation of tenders and award of contracts, impose, seek or consider offsets.[7]

2. Nevertheless, having regard to general policy considerations, including those relating to development, a developing country may at the time of accession negotiate conditions for the use of offsets, such as requirements for the incorporation of domestic content. Such requirements shall be used only for qualification to participate in the procurement process and not as criteria for awarding contracts. Conditions shall be objective, clearly defined and non-discriminatory. They shall be set forth in the country's Appendix I and may include precise limitations on the imposition of offsets in any contract subject to this Agreement. The existence of such conditions shall be notified to the Committee and included in the notice of intended procurement and other documentation.

Article XVII Transparency

1. Each Party shall encourage entities to indicate the terms and conditions, including any deviations from competitive tendering procedures or access to challenge procedures, under which tenders will be entertained from suppliers situated in countries not Parties to this

---

7 Offsets in government procurement are measures used to encourage local development or improve the balance-of-payments accounts by means of domestic content, licensing of technology, investment requirements, counter-trade or similar requirements.

Agreement but which, with a view to creating transparency in their own contract awards, nevertheless:

(a) specify their contracts in accordance with Article VI (technical specifications);

(b) publish the procurement notices referred to in Article IX, including, in the version of the notice referred to in paragraph 8 of Article IX (summary of the notice of intended procurement) which is published in an official language of the WTO, an indication of the terms and conditions under which tenders shall be entertained from suppliers situated in countries Parties to this Agreement;

(c) are willing to ensure that their procurement regulations shall not normally change during a procurement and, in the event that such change proves unavoidable, to ensure the availability of a satisfactory means of redress.

2. Governments not Parties to the Agreement which comply with the conditions specified in paragraphs 1(a) through 1(c), shall be entitled if they so inform the Parties to participate in the Committee as observers.

Article XVIII   Information and Review as Regards Obligations of Entities

1. Entities shall publish a notice in the appropriate publication listed in Appendix II not later than 72 days after the award of each contract under Articles XIII through XV. These notices shall contain:

(a) the nature and quantity of products or services in the contract award;

(b) the name and address of the entity awarding the contract;

(c) the date of award;

(d) the name and address of winning tenderer;

(e) the value of the winning award or the highest and lowest offer taken into account in the award of the contract;

(f) where appropriate, means of identifying the notice issued under paragraph 1 of Article IX or justification according to Article XV for the use of such procedure; and

(g) the type of procedure used.

2. Each entity shall, on request from a supplier of a Party, promptly provide:

(a) an explanation of its procurement practices and procedures;

(b) pertinent information concerning the reasons why the supplier's application to qualify was rejected, why its existing qualification was brought to an end and why it was not selected; and

(c) to an unsuccessful tenderer, pertinent information concerning the reasons why its tender was not selected and on the characteristics and relative advantages of the tender selected as well as the name of the winning tenderer.

3. Entities shall promptly inform participating suppliers of decisions on contract awards and, upon request, in writing.

4. However, entities may decide that certain information on the contract award, contained in paragraphs 1 and 2(c), be withheld where release of such information would impede law enforcement or otherwise be contrary to the public interest or would prejudice the legitimate commercial interest of particular enterprises, public or private, or might prejudice fair competition between suppliers.

Article XIX   Information and Review as Regards Obligations of Parties

1. Each Party shall promptly publish any law, regulation, judicial decision, administrative ruling of general application, and any procedure (including standard contract clauses) regarding government procurement covered by this Agreement, in the appropriate publications listed in Appendix IV and in such a manner as to enable other Parties and suppliers to become acquainted with them. Each Party shall be prepared, upon request, to explain to any other Party its government procurement procedures.

2. The government of an unsuccessful tenderer which is a Party to this Agreement may seek, without prejudice to the provisions under Article XXII, such additional information on the contract award as may be necessary to ensure that the procurement was made fairly and impartially. To this end, the procuring government shall provide information on both the characteristics and relative advantages of the winning tender and the contract price. Normally this latter information may be disclosed by the government of the unsuccessful tenderer provided it exercises this right with discretion. In cases where release of this information would prejudice competition in future tenders, this information shall not be disclosed except after consultation with and agreement of the Party which gave the information to the government of the unsuccessful tenderer.

3. Available information concerning procurement by covered entities and their individual contract awards shall be provided, upon request, to any other Party.

4. Confidential information provided to any Party which would impede law enforcement or otherwise be contrary to the public interest or would prejudice the legitimate commercial interest of particular enterprises, public or private, or might prejudice fair competition between suppliers shall not be revealed without formal authorization from the party providing the information.

5. Each Party shall collect and provide to the Committee on an annual basis statistics on its procurements covered by this Agreement. Such reports shall contain the following information with respect to contracts awarded by all procurement entities covered under this Agreement:

    (a) for entities in Annex 1, statistics on the estimated value of contracts awarded, both above and below the threshold value, on a global basis and broken down by entities; for entities in Annexes 2 and 3, statistics on the estimated value of contracts awarded above the threshold value on a global basis and broken down by categories of entities;

    (b) for entities in Annex 1, statistics on the number and total value of contracts awarded above the threshold value, broken down by entities and categories of products and services according to uniform classification systems; for entities in Annexes 2 and 3, statistics on the estimated value of contracts awarded above the threshold value broken down by categories of entities and categories of products and services;

    (c) for entities in Annex 1, statistics, broken down by entity and by categories of products and services, on the number and total value of contracts awarded under each of the cases of Article XV; for categories of entities in Annexes 2 and 3, statistics on the total value of contracts awarded above the threshold value under each of the cases of Article XV; and

    (d) for entities in Annex 1, statistics, broken down by entities, on the number and total value of contracts awarded under derogations to the Agreement contained in the relevant Annexes; for categories of entities in Annexes 2 and 3, statistics on the total value of contracts awarded under derogations to the Agreement contained in the relevant Annexes.

    To the extent that such information is available, each Party shall provide statistics on the country of origin of products and services purchased by its entities. With a view to ensuring that such statistics are comparable, the Committee shall provide guidance on methods to be used. With a view to ensuring effective monitoring of procurement covered by this Agreement, the Committee may decide unanimously to modify the requirements of subparagraphs (a) through (d) as regards the nature and the extent of statistical information to be provided and the breakdowns and classifications to be used.

Article XX   Challenge Procedures
Consultations

1. In the event of a complaint by a supplier that there has been a breach of this Agreement in the context of a procurement, each Party shall encourage the supplier to seek resolution of its

complaint in consultation with the procuring entity. In such instances the procuring entity shall accord impartial and timely consideration to any such complaint, in a manner that is not prejudicial to obtaining corrective measures under the challenge system.

Challenge

2. Each Party shall provide non-discriminatory, timely, transparent and effective procedures enabling suppliers to challenge alleged breaches of the Agreement arising in the context of procurements in which they have, or have had, an interest.

3. Each Party shall provide its challenge procedures in writing and make them generally available.

4. Each Party shall ensure that documentation relating to all aspects of the process concerning procurements covered by this Agreement shall be retained for three years.

5. The interested supplier may be required to initiate a challenge procedure and notify the procuring entity within specified time-limits from the time when the basis of the complaint is known or reasonably should have been known, but in no case within a period of less than 10 days.

6. Challenges shall be heard by a court or by an impartial and independent review body with no interest in the outcome of the procurement and the members of which are secure from external influence during the term of appointment. A review body which is not a court shall either be subject to judicial review or shall have procedures which provide that:
   (a) participants can be heard before an opinion is given or a decision is reached;
   (b) participants can be represented and accompanied;
   (c) participants shall have access to all proceedings;
   (d) proceedings can take place in public;
   (e) opinions or decisions are given in writing with a statement describing the basis for the opinions or decisions;
   (f) witnesses can be presented;
   (g) documents are disclosed to the review body.

7. Challenge procedures shall provide for:
   (a) rapid interim measures to correct breaches of the Agreement and to preserve commercial opportunities. Such action may result in suspension of the procurement process. However, procedures may provide that overriding adverse consequences for the interests concerned, including the public interest, may be taken into account in deciding whether such measures should be applied. In such circumstances, just cause for not acting shall be provided in writing;
   (b) an assessment and a possibility for a decision on the justification of the challenge;
   (c) correction of the breach of the Agreement or compensation for the loss or damages suffered, which may be limited to costs for tender preparation or protest.

8. With a view to the preservation of the commercial and other interests involved, the challenge procedure shall normally be completed in a timely fashion.

Article XXI   Institutions

1. A Committee on Government Procurement composed of representatives from each of the Parties shall be established. This Committee shall elect its own Chairman and Vice-Chairman and shall meet as necessary but not less than once a year for the purpose of affording Parties the opportunity to consult on any matters relating to the operation of this Agreement or the furtherance of its objectives, and to carry out such other responsibilities as may be assigned to it by the Parties.

2. The Committee may establish working parties or other subsidiary bodies which shall carry out such functions as may be given to them by the Committee.

Article XXII Consultations and Dispute Settlement

1. The provisions of the Understanding on Rules and Procedures Governing the Settlement of Disputes under the WTO Agreement (hereinafter referred to as the "Dispute Settlement Understanding") shall be applicable except as otherwise specifically provided below.

2. If any Party considers that any benefit accruing to it, directly or indirectly, under this Agreement is being nullified or impaired, or that the attainment of any objective of this Agreement is being impeded as the result of the failure of another Party or Parties to carry out its obligations under this Agreement, or the application by another Party or Parties of any measure, whether or not it conflicts with the provisions of this Agreement, it may with a view to reaching a mutually satisfactory resolution of the matter, make written representations or proposals to the other Party or Parties which it considers to be concerned. Such action shall be promptly notified to the Dispute Settlement Body established under the Dispute Settlement Understanding (hereinafter referred to as "DSB"), as specified below. Any Party thus approached shall give sympathetic consideration to the representations or proposals made to it.

3. The DSB shall have the authority to establish panels, adopt panel and Appellate Body reports, make recommendations or give rulings on the matter, maintain surveillance of implementation of rulings and recommendations, and authorize suspension of concessions and other obligations under this Agreement or consultations regarding remedies when withdrawal of measures found to be in contravention of the Agreement is not possible, provided that only Members of the WTO Party to this Agreement shall participate in decisions or actions taken by the DSB with respect to disputes under this Agreement.

4. Panels shall have the following terms of reference unless the parties to the dispute agree otherwise within 20 days of the establishment of the panel:

   "To examine, in the light of the relevant provisions of this Agreement and of (name of any other covered Agreement cited by the parties to the dispute), the matter referred to the DSB by (name of party) in document ... and to make such findings as will assist the DSB in making the recommendations or in giving the rulings provided for in this Agreement."

   In the case of a dispute in which provisions both of this Agreement and of one or more other Agreements listed in Appendix 1 of the Dispute Settlement Understanding are invoked by one of the parties to the dispute, paragraph 3 shall apply only to those parts of the panel report concerning the interpretation and application of this Agreement.

5. Panels established by the DSB to examine disputes under this Agreement shall include persons qualified in the area of government procurement.

6. Every effort shall be made to accelerate the proceedings to the greatest extent possible. Notwithstanding the provisions of paragraphs 8 and 9 of Article 12 of the Dispute Settlement Understanding, the panel shall attempt to provide its final report to the parties to the dispute not later than four months, and in case of delay not later than seven months, after the date on which the composition and terms of reference of the panel are agreed. Consequently, every effort shall be made to reduce also the periods foreseen in paragraph 1 of Article 20 and paragraph 4 of Article 21 of the Dispute Settlement Understanding by two months. Moreover, notwithstanding the provisions of paragraph 5 of Article 21 of the Dispute Settlement Understanding, the panel shall attempt to issue its decision, in case of a disagreement as to the existence or consistency with a covered Agreement of measures taken to comply with the recommendations and rulings, within 60 days.

7. Notwithstanding paragraph 2 of Article 22 of the Dispute Settlement Understanding, any dispute arising under any Agreement listed in Appendix 1 to the Dispute Settlement Understanding other than this Agreement shall not result in the suspension of concessions or other obligations under this Agreement, and any dispute arising under this Agreement shall

not result in the suspension of concessions or other obligations under any other Agreement listed in the said Appendix 1.

Article XXIII   Exceptions to the Agreement

1. Nothing in this Agreement shall be construed to prevent any Party from taking any action or not disclosing any information which it considers necessary for the protection of its essential security interests relating to the procurement of arms, ammunition or war materials, or to procurement indispensable for national security or for national defence purposes.

2. Subject to the requirement that such measures are not applied in a manner which would constitute a means of arbitrary or unjustifiable discrimination between countries where the same conditions prevail or a disguised restriction on international trade, nothing in this Agreement shall be construed to prevent any Party from imposing or enforcing measures: necessary to protect public morals, order or safety, human, animal or plant life or health or intellectual property; or relating to the products or services of handicapped persons, of philanthropic institutions or of prison labour.

Article XXIV   Final Provisions

1. *Acceptance and Entry into Force*

This Agreement shall enter into force on 1 January 1996 for those governments[8] whose agreed coverage is contained in Annexes 1 through 5 of Appendix I of this Agreement and which have, by signature, accepted the Agreement on 15 April 1994 or have, by that date, signed the Agreement subject to ratification and subsequently ratified the Agreement before 1 January 1996.

2. *Accession*

Any government which is a Member of the WTO, or prior to the date of entry into force of the WTO Agreement which is a contracting party to GATT 1947, and which is not a Party to this Agreement may accede to this Agreement on terms to be agreed between that government and the Parties. Accession shall take place by deposit with the Director-General of the WTO of an instrument of accession which states the terms so agreed. The Agreement shall enter into force for an acceding government on the 30th day following the date of its accession to the Agreement.

3. *Transitional Arrangements*

   (a) Hong Kong and Korea may delay application of the provisions of this Agreement, except Articles XXI and XXII, to a date not later than 1 January 1997. The commencement date of their application of the provisions, if prior to 1 January 1997, shall be notified to the Director-General of the WTO 30 days in advance.

   (b) During the period between the date of entry into force of this Agreement and the date of its application by Hong Kong, the rights and obligations between Hong Kong and all other Parties to this Agreement which were on 15 April 1994 Parties to the Agreement on Government Procurement done at Geneva on 12 April 1979 as amended on 2 February 1987 (the "1988 Agreement") shall be governed by the substantive[9] provisions of the 1988 Agreement, including its Annexes as modified or rectified, which provisions are incorporated herein by reference for that purpose and shall remain in force until 31 December 1996.

   (c) Between Parties to this Agreement which are also Parties to the 1988 Agreement, the rights and obligations of this Agreement shall supersede those under the 1988 Agreement.

   (d) Article XXII shall not enter into force until the date of entry into force of the WTO Agreement. Until such time, the provisions of Article VII of the 1988 Agreement shall apply to consultations and dispute settlement under this Agreement, which provisions are

---

8 For the purpose of this Agreement, the term "government" is deemed to include the competent authorities of the European Communities.

9 All provisions of the 1988 Agreement except the Preamble, Article VII and Article IX other than paragraphs 5(a) and (b) and paragraph 10.

hereby incorporated in the Agreement by reference for that purpose. These provisions shall be applied under the auspices of the Committee under this Agreement.

(e) Prior to the date of entry into force of the WTO Agreement, references to WTO bodies shall be construed as referring to the corresponding GATT body and references to the Director-General of the WTO and to the WTO Secretariat shall be construed as references to, respectively, the Director-General to the CONTRACTING PARTIES to GATT 1947 and to the GATT Secretariat.

4. *Reservations*

Reservations may not be entered in respect of any of the provisions of this Agreement.

5. *National Legislation*

(a) Each government accepting or acceding to this Agreement shall ensure, not later than the date of entry into force of this Agreement for it, the conformity of its laws, regulations and administrative procedures, and the rules, procedures and practices applied by the entities contained in its lists annexed hereto, with the provisions of this Agreement.

(b) Each Party shall inform the Committee of any changes in its laws and regulations relevant to this Agreement and in the administration of such laws and regulations.

6. *Rectifications or Modifications*

(a) Rectifications, transfers of an entity from one Annex to another or, in exceptional cases, other modifications relating to Appendices I through IV shall be notified to the Committee, along with information as to the likely consequences of the change for the mutually agreed coverage provided in this Agreement. If the rectifications, transfers or other modifications are of a purely formal or minor nature, they shall become effective provided there is no objection within 30 days. In other cases, the Chairman of the Committee shall promptly convene a meeting of the Committee. The Committee shall consider the proposal and any claim for compensatory adjustments, with a view to maintaining a balance of rights and obligations and a comparable level of mutually agreed coverage provided in this Agreement prior to such notification. In the event of agreement not being reached, the matter may be pursued in accordance with the provisions contained in Article XXII.

(b) Where a Party wishes, in exercise of its rights, to withdraw an entity from Appendix I on the grounds that government control or influence over it has been effectively eliminated, that Party shall notify the Committee. Such modification shall become effective the day after the end of the following meeting of the Committee, provided that the meeting is no sooner than 30 days from the date of notification and no objection has been made. In the event of an objection, the matter may be pursued in accordance with the procedures on consultations and dispute settlement contained in Article XXII. In considering the proposed modification to Appendix I and any consequential compensatory adjustment, allowance shall be made for the market-opening effects of the removal of government control or influence.

7. *Reviews, Negotiations and Future Work*

(a) The Committee shall review annually the implementation and operation of this Agreement taking into account the objectives thereof. The Committee shall annually inform the General Council of the WTO of developments during the periods covered by such reviews.

(b) Not later than the end of the third year from the date of entry into force of this Agreement and periodically thereafter, the Parties thereto shall undertake further negotiations, with a view to improving this Agreement and achieving the greatest possible extension of its coverage among all Parties on the basis of mutual reciprocity, having regard to the provisions of Article V relating to developing countries.

(c) Parties shall seek to avoid introducing or prolonging discriminatory measures and practices which distort open procurement and shall, in the context of negotiations under subparagraph (b), seek to eliminate those which remain on the date of entry into force of this Agreement.

8. *Information Technology*

With a view to ensuring that the Agreement does not constitute an unnecessary obstacle to technical progress, Parties shall consult regularly in the Committee regarding developments in the use of information technology in government procurement and shall, if necessary, negotiate modifications to the Agreement. These consultations shall in particular aim to ensure that the use of information technology promotes the aims of open, non-discriminatory and efficient government procurement through transparent procedures, that contracts covered under the Agreement are clearly identified and that all available information relating to a particular contract can be identified. When a Party intends to innovate, it shall endeavour to take into account the views expressed by other Parties regarding any potential problems.

9. *Amendments*

Parties may amend this Agreement having regard, *inter alia*, to the experience gained in its implementation. Such an amendment, once the Parties have concurred in accordance with the procedures established by the Committee, shall not enter into force for any Party until it has been accepted by such Party.

10. *Withdrawal*

(a) Any Party may withdraw from this Agreement. The withdrawal shall take effect upon the expiration of 60 days from the date on which written notice of withdrawal is received by the Director-General of the WTO. Any Party may upon such notification request an immediate meeting of the Committee.

(b) If a Party to this Agreement does not become a Member of the WTO within one year of the date of entry into force of the WTO Agreement or ceases to be a Member of the WTO, it shall cease to be a Party to this Agreement with effect from the same date.

11. *Non-application of this Agreement between Particular Parties*

This Agreement shall not apply as between any two Parties if either of the Parties, at the time either accepts or accedes to this Agreement, does not consent to such application.

12. *Notes, Appendices and Annexes*

The Notes, Appendices and Annexes to this Agreement constitute an integral part thereof.

13. *Secretariat*

This Agreement shall be serviced by the WTO Secretariat.

14. *Deposit*

This Agreement shall be deposited with the Director-General of the WTO, who shall promptly furnish to each Party a certified true copy of this Agreement, of each rectification or modification thereto pursuant to paragraph 6 and of each amendment thereto pursuant to paragraph 9, and a notification of each acceptance thereof or accession thereto pursuant to paragraphs 1 and 2 and of each withdrawal therefrom pursuant to paragraph 10 of this Article.

15. *Registration*

This Agreement shall be registered in accordance with the provisions of Article 102 of the Charter of the United Nations.

Done at Marrakesh this fifteenth day of April one thousand nine hundred and ninety-four in a single copy, in the English, French and Spanish languages, each text being authentic, except as otherwise specified with respect to the Appendices hereto.

NOTES

The terms "country" or "countries" as used in this Agreement, including the Appendices, are to be understood to include any separate customs territory Party to this Agreement.

In the case of a separate customs territory Party to this Agreement, where an expression in this Agreement is qualified by the term "national", such expression shall be read as pertaining to that customs territory, unless otherwise specified.

Article 1, paragraph 1

Having regard to general policy considerations relating to tied aid, including the objective of developing countries with respect to the untying of such aid, this Agreement does not apply to procurement made in furtherance of tied aid to developing countries so long as it is practised by Parties.

PART 3

International Investment Law

Antecedents

III-1

Treaty of Amity Commerce and Navigation, between His Britannick Majesty; and The United States of America, by Their President, with the advice and consent of Their Senate (The 'Jay Treaty')

Date   19 November 1794
In force 29 February 1796
Source   *Treaties and Other International Acts of the United States of America* (Hunter Miller, ed), Vol 2, Documents 1–40: 1776–1818
Link   <http://avalon.law.yale.edu/18th_century/jay.asp>

His Britannic Majesty and the United States of America, being desirous, by a treaty of amity, commerce and navigation, to terminate their difference in such a manner, as, without reference to the merits of their respective complaints and pretentions, may be the best calculated to produce mutual satisfaction and good understanding; and also to regulate the commerce and navigation between their respective countries, territories and people, in such a manner as to render the same reciprocally beneficial and satisfactory; they have, respectively, named their Plenipotentiaries, and given them full powers to treat of, and conclude the said treaty, that is to say: His Britannic Majesty has named for his Plenipotentiary, the Right Honorable William Wyndham Baron Grenville of Wotton, one of His Majesty's Privy Council, and His Majesty's Principal Secretary of State for Foreign Affairs; and the President of the said United States, by and with the advice and consent of the Senate thereof, hath appointed for their Plenipotentiary, the Honorable John Jay, Chief Justice of the said United States, and their Envoy Extraordinary to His Majesty, who have agreed on and concluded the following articles:

Article I
There shall be a firm, inviolable and universal peace, and a true and sincere friendship between His Britannic Majesty, his heirs and successors, and the United States of America; and between their respective countries, territories, cities, towns and people of every degree, without exception of persons or places.

Article II
His Majesty will withdraw all his troops and garrisons from all posts and places within the boundary lines assigned by the treaty of peace to the United States. This evacuation shall take place on or before the first day of June, one thousand seven hundred and ninety six, and all the

proper measures shall in the interval be taken by concert between the Government of the United States and His Majesty's Governor-General in America for settling the previous arrangements which may be necessary respecting the delivery of the said posts:

The United States in the mean time, at their discretion, extending their settlements to any part within the said boundary line, except within the precincts or jurisdiction of any of the said posts. All settlers and traders, within the precincts or jurisdiction of the said posts, shall continue to enjoy, unmolested, all their property of every kind, and shall be protected therein. They shall be at full liberty to remain there, or to remove with all or any part of their effects; and it shall also be free to them to sell their lands, houses or effects, or to retain the property thereof, at their discretion; such of them as shall continue to reside within the said boundary lines, shall not be compelled to become citizens of the United States, or to take any oath of allegiance to the Government thereof; but they shall be at full liberty so to do if they think proper, and they shall make and declare their election within one year after the evacuation aforesaid. And all persons who shall continue there after the expiration of the said year, without having declared their intention of remaining subjects of His Britannic Majesty, shall be considered as having elected to become citizens of the United States.

Article III

It is agreed that it shall at all times be free to His Majesty's subjects, and to the citizens of the United States, and also to the Indians dwelling on either side of the said boundary line, freely to pass and repass by land or inland navigation, into the respective territories and countries of the two parties, on the continent of America, (the country within the limits of the Hudson's Bay Company only excepted) and to navigate all the lakes, rivers and waters thereof, and freely to carry on trade and commerce with each other. But it is understood that this article does not extend to the admission of vessels of the United States into the seaports, harbours, bays or creeks of His Majesty's said territories; nor into such parts of the rivers in His Majesty's said territories as are between the mouth thereof, and the highest port of entry from the sea, except in small vessels trading bona fide between Montreal and Quebec, under such regulations as shall be established to prevent the possibility of any frauds in this respect. Nor to the admission of British vessels from the sea into the rivers of the United States, beyond the highest ports of entry for foreign vessels from the sea. The river Mississippi shall, however, according to the treaty of peace, be entirely open to both parties; and it is further agreed, that all the ports and places on its eastern side, to whichsoever of the parties belonging, may freely be resorted to and used by both parties, in as ample a manner as any of the Atlantic ports or places of the United States, or any of the ports or places of His Majesty in Great Britain.

All goods and merchandize whose importation into His Majesty's said territories in America shall not be entirely prohibited, may freely, for the purposes of commerce, be carried into the same in the manner aforesaid, by the citizens of the United States, and such goods and merchandize shall be subject to no higher or other duties than would be payable by His Majesty's subjects on the importation of the same from Europe into the said territories.

And in like manner all goods and merchandize whose importation into the United States shall not be wholly prohibited, may freely, for the purposes of commerce, be carried into the same, in the manner aforesaid, by His Majesty's subjects, and such goods and merchandize shall be subject to no higher or other duties than would be payable by the citizens of the United States on the importation of the same in American vessels into the Atlantic ports of the said States.

And all goods not prohibited to be exported from the said territories respectively, may in like manner be carried out of the same by the two parties respectively, paying duty as aforesaid. No duty of entry shall ever be levied by either party on peltries brought by land or inland navigation into the said territories respectively, nor shall the Indians passing or repassing with their own proper goods and effects of whatever nature, pay for the same any impost or duty whatever.

But goods in bales, or other large packages, unusual among Indians, shall not be considered as goods belonging bona fide to Indians.

No higher or other tolls or rates of ferriage than what are or shall be payable by natives, shall be demanded on either side; and no duties shall be payable on any goods which shall merely be carried over any of the portages or carrying places on either side, for the purpose of being immediately reembarked and carried to some other place or places.

But as by this stipulation it is only meant to secure to each party a free passage across the portages on both sides, it is agreed that this exemption from duty shall extend only to such goods as are carried in the usual and direct road across the portage, and are not attempted to be in any manner sold or exchanged during their passage across the same, and proper regulations may be established to prevent the possibility of any frauds in this respect. As this article is intended to render in a great degree the local advantages of each party common to both, and thereby to promote a disposition favorable to friendship and good neighborhood, it is agreed that the respective Governments will mutually promote this amicable intercourse, by causing speedy and impartial justice to be done, and necessary protection to be extended to all who may be concerned therein.

Article IV

Whereas it is uncertain whether the river Mississippi extends so far to the northward as to be intersected by a line to be drawn due west from the Lake of the Woods, in the manner mentioned in the treaty of peace between His Majesty and the United States: it is agreed that measures shall be taken in concert between His Majesty's Government in America and the Government of the United States, for making a joint survey of the said river from one degree of latitude below the falls of St. Anthony, to the principal source or sources of the said river, and also of the parts adjacent thereto; and that if, on the result of such survey, it should appear that the said river would not be intersected by such a line as is above mentioned, the two parties will thereupon proceed, by amicable negotiation, to regulate the boundary line in that quarter, as well as all other points to be adjusted between the said parties, according to justice and mutual convenience, and in conformity to the intent of the said treaty.

Article V

Whereas doubts have arisen what river was truly intended under the name of the river St. Croix, mentioned in the said treaty of peace, and forming a part of the boundary therein described; that question shall be referred to the final decision of commissioners to be appointed in the following manner, viz.:

One commissioner shall be named by His Majesty, and one by the President of the United States, by and with the advice and consent of the Senate thereof, and the said two commissioners shall agree on the choice of a third; or if they cannot so agree, they shall each propose one person, and of the two names so proposed, one shall be drawn by lot in the presence of the two original Commissioners.

And the three Commissioners so appointed shall be sworn, impartially to examine and decide the said question, according to such evidence as shall respectively be laid before them on the part of the British Government and of the United States. The said Commissioners shall meet at Halifax, and shall have power to adjourn to such other place or places as they shall think fit.

They shall have power to appoint a Secretary, and to employ such surveyors or other persons as they shall judge necessary. The said Commissioners shall, by a declaration, under their hands and seals, decide what river is the river St. Croix, intended by the treaty. The said declaration shall contain a description of the said river, and shall particularize the latitude and longitude of its mouth and of its source.

Duplicates of this declaration and of the statements of their accounts, and of the journal of their proceedings, shall be delivered by them to the agent of His Majesty, and to the agent of the United States, who may be respectively appointed and authorized to manage the business on behalf of the respective Governments. And both parties agree to consider such decision as final and conclusive, so as that the same shall never thereafter be called into question, or made the subject of dispute or difference between them.

Article VI

Whereas it is alleged by divers British merchants and others His Majesty's subjects, that debts, to a considerable amount, which were bona fide contracted before the peace, still remain owing to them by citizens or inhabitants of the United States, and that by the operation of various lawful impediments since the peace, not only the full recovery of the said debts has been delayed, but also the value and security thereof have been, in several instances, impaired and lessened, so that, by the ordinary course of judicial proceedings, the British creditors cannot now obtain, and actually have and receive full and adequate compensation for the losses and damages which they have thereby sustained: It is agreed, that in all such cases, where full compensation for such losses and damages cannot, for whatever reason, be actually obtained, had and received by the said creditors in the ordinary course of justice, the United States will make full and complete compensation for the same to the said creditors: But it is distinctly understood, that this provision is to extend to such losses only as have been occasioned by the lawful impediments aforesaid, and is not to extend to losses occasioned by such insolvency of the debtors or other causes as would equally have operated to produce such loss, if the said impediments had not existed; nor to such losses or damages as have been occasioned by the manifest delay or negligence, or wilful omission of the claimant.

For the purpose of ascertaining the amount of any such losses and damages, five Commissioners shall be appointed and authorized to meet and act in manner following, viz.: Two of them shall be appointed by His Majesty, two of them by the President of the United States by and with the advice and consent of the Senate thereof, and the fifth by the unanimous voice of the other four; and if they should not agree in such choice, then the Commissioners named by the two parties shall respectively propose one person, and of the two names so proposed, one shall be drawn by lot, in the presence of the four original Commissioners. When the five Commissioners thus appointed shall first meet, they shall, before they proceed to act, respectively take the following oath, or affirmation, in the presence of each other; which oath, or affirmation, being so taken and duly attested, shall be entered on the record of their proceedings, viz.:

I, A.B., one of the Commissioners appointed in pursuance of the sixth article of the Treaty of Amity, Commerce and Navigation, between His Britannic Majesty and the United States of America, do solemnly swear (or affirm) that I will honestly, diligently, impartially and carefully examine, and to the best of my judgment, according to justice and equity, decide all such complaints, as under the said article shall be preferred to the said Commissioners: and that I will forbear to act as a Commissioner, in any case in which I may be personally interested.

Three of the said Commissioners shall constitute a board, and shall have power to do any act appertaining to the said Commission, provided that one of the Commissioners named on each side, and the fifth Commissioner shall be present, and all decisions shall be made by the majority of the voices of the Commissioners then present.

Eighteen months from the day on which the said Commissioners shall form a board, and be ready to proceed to business, are assigned for receiving complaints and applications; but they are nevertheless authorized, in any particular cases in which it shall appear to them to be reasonable and just, to extend the said term of eighteen months for any term not exceeding six months, after the expiration thereof.

The said Commissioners shall first meet at Philadelphia, but they shall have power to adjourn from place to place as they shall see cause.

The said Commissioners in examining the complaints and applications so preferred to them, are empowered and required in pursuance of the true intent and meaning of this article to take into their consideration all claims, whether of principal or interest, or balances of principal and interest and to determine the same respectively, according to the merits of the several cases, due regard being had to all the circumstances thereof, and as equity and justice shall appear to them to require.

And the said Commissioners shall have power to examine all such persons as shall come before them on oath or affirmation, touching the premises; and also to receive in evidence, according as they may think most consistent with equity and justice, all written depositions, or books, or papers, or copies, or extracts thereof, every such deposition, book, or paper, or copy, or extract, being duly authenticated either according to the legal form now respectively existing in the two countries, or in such other manner as the said Commissioners shall see cause to require or allow.

The award of the said Commissioners, or of any three of them as aforesaid, shall in all cases be final and conclusive both as to the justice of the claim, and to the amount of the sum to be paid to the creditor or claimant; and the United States undertake to cause the sum so awarded to be paid in specie to such creditor or claimant without deduction; and at such time or times and at such place or places, as shall be awarded by the said Commissioners; and on condition of such releases or assignments to be given by the creditor or claimant, as by the said Commissioners may be directed: Provided always, that no such payment shall be fixed by the said Commissioners to take place sooner than twelve months from the day of the exchange of the ratifications of this treaty.

Article VII

Whereas complaints have been made by divers merchants and others, citizens of the United States, that during the course of the war in which His Majesty is now engaged, they have sustained considerable losses and damage, by reason of irregular or illegal captures or condemnations of their vessels and other property, under color of authority or commissions from His Majesty, and that from various circumstances belonging to the said cases, adequate compensation for the losses and damages so sustained cannot now be actually obtained, had, and received by the ordinary course of judicial proceedings; it is agreed, that in all such cases, where adequate compensation cannot, for whatever reason, be now actually obtained, had, and received by the said merchants and others, in the ordinary course of justice, full and complete compensation for the same will be made by the British Government to the said complainants.

But it is distinctly understood that this provision is not to extend to such losses or damages as have been occasioned by the manifest delay or negligence, or wilful omission of the claimant.

That for the purpose of ascertaining the amount of any such losses and damages, five Commissioners shall be appointed and authorized to act in London, exactly in the manner directed with respect to those mentioned in the preceding article, and after having taken the same oath or affirmation (mutatis mutandis). The same term of eighteen months is also assigned for the reception of claims, and they are in like manner authorized to extend the same in particular cases.

They shall receive testimony, books, papers and evidence in the same latitude, and exercise the like discretion and powers respecting that subject; and shall decide the claims in question according to the merits of the several cases, and to justice, equity and the laws of nations.

The award of the said Commissioners, or any such three of them as aforesaid, shall in all cases be final and conclusive, both as to the justice of the claim, and the amount of the sum to be paid to the claimant; and His Britannic Majesty undertakes to cause the same to be paid to such claimant in specie, without any deduction, at such place or places, and at such time or times, as shall be awarded by the said Commissioners, and on condition of such releases or assignments to be given by the claimant, as by the said Commissioners may be directed.

And whereas certain merchants and others, His Majesty's subjects, complain that, in the course of the war, they have sustained loss and damage by reason of the capture of their vessels and merchandise, taken within the limits and jurisdiction of the States and brought into the ports of the same, or taken by vessels originally armed in ports of the said States: It is agreed that in all such cases where restitution shall not have been made agreeably to the tenor of the letter from Mr. Jefferson to Mr. Hammond, dated at Philadelphia, September 5, 1793, a copy of which is annexed to this treaty; the complaints of the parties shall be and hereby are referred to the Commissioners to be appointed by virtue of this article, who are hereby authorized and required to proceed in the like manner relative to these as to the other cases committed to them; and the United States undertake to pay to the complainants or claimants in specie, without deduction, the amount of such sums as shall be awarded to them respectively by the said Commissioners, and at the times and places which in such awards shall be specified; and on condition of such releases or assignments to be given by the claimants as in the said awards may be directed: And it is further agreed, that not only the now existing cases of both descriptions, but also all such as shall exist at the time of exchanging the ratifications of this treaty, shall be considered as being within the provisions, intent and meaning of this article.

Article VIII

It is further agreed that the Commissioners mentioned in this and in the two preceding articles shall be respectively paid in such manner as shall be agreed between the two parties such agreement being to be settled at the time of the exchange of the ratifications of this treaty.

And all other expenses attending the said Commissions shall be defrayed jointly by the two parties, the same being previously ascertained and allowed by the majority of the Commissioners.

And in the case of death, sickness or necessary absence, the place of every such Commissioner respectively shall be supplied in the same manner as such Commissioner was first appointed, and the new Commissioners shall take the same oath or affirmation and do the same duties.

Article IX

It is agreed that British subjects who now hold lands in the territories of the United States, and American citizens who now hold lands in the dominions of His Majesty, shall continue to hold them according to the nature and tenure of their respective estates and titles therein; and may grant, sell or devise the same to whom they please, in like manner as if they were natives and that neither they nor their heirs or assigns shall, so far as may respect the said lands and the legal remedies incident thereto, be regarded as aliens.

Article X

Neither the debts due from individuals of the one nation to individuals of the other, nor shares, nor monies, which they may have in the public funds, or in the public or private banks, shall ever in any event of war or national differences be sequestered or confiscated, it being unjust and impolitic that debts and engagements contracted and made by individuals having confidence in each other and in their respective Governments, should ever be destroyed or impaired by national authority on account of national differences and discontents.

Article XI

It is agreed between His Majesty and the United States of America, that there shall be a reciprocal and entirely perfect liberty of navigation and commerce between their respective people, in the manner, under the limitations, and on the conditions specified in the following articles.

Article XII

His Majesty consents that it shall and may be lawful, during the time hereinafter limited, for the citizens of the United States to carry to any of His Majesty's islands and ports in the West Indies from the United States, in their own vessels, not being above the burthen of seventy tons, any goods or merchandizes, being of the growth, manufacture or produce of the said States, which it is or may be lawful to carry to the said islands or ports from the said States in British vessels; and that the said American vessels shall be subject there to no other or higher tonnage duties or charges than shall be payable by British vessels in the ports of the United States; and that the cargoes of the said American vessels shall be subject there to no other or higher duties or charges than shall be payable on the like articles if imported there from the said States in British vessels.

And His Majesty also consents that it shall be lawful for the said American citizens to purchase, load and carry away in their said vessels to the United States, from the said islands and ports, all such articles, being of the growth, manufacture or produce of the said islands, as may now by law be carried from thence to the said States in British vessels, and subject only to the same duties and charges on exportation, to which British vessels and their cargoes are or shall be subject in similar circumstances.

Provided always, that the said American vessels do carry and land their cargoes in the United States only, it being expressly agreed and declared that, during the continuance of this article, the United States will prohibit and restrain the carrying any molasses, sugar, coffee, cocoa or cotton in American vessels, either from His Majesty's islands or from the United States to any part of the world except the United States, reasonable seastores excepted. Provided, also, that it shall and may be lawful, during the same period, for British vessels to import from the said islands into the United States, and to export from the United States to the said islands, all articles whatever, being of the growth, produce or manufacture of the said islands, or of the United States respectively, which now may, by the laws of the said States, be so imported and exported.

And that the cargoes of the said British vessels shall be subject to no other or higher duties or charges, than shall be payable on the same articles if so imported or exported in American vessels. It is agreed that this article, and every matter and thing therein contained, shall continue to be in force during the continuance of the war in which His Majesty is now engaged; and also for two years from and after the date of the signature of the preliminary or other articles of peace, by which the same may be terminated. And it is further agreed that, at the expiration of the said term, the two contracting parties will endeavour further to regulate their commerce in this respect, according to the situation in which His Majesty may then find himself with respect to the West Indies, and with a view to such arrangements as may best conduce to the mutual advantage and extension of commerce.

And the said parties will then also renew their discussions, and endeavour to agree, whether in any and what cases, neutral vessels shall protect enemy's property; and in what cases provisions and other articles, not generally contraband, may become such.

But in the mean time, their conduct towards each other in these respects shall be regulated by the articles hereinafter inserted on those subjects.

Article XIII

His Majesty consents that the vessels belonging to the citizens of the United States of America shall be admitted and hospitably received in all the seaports and harbors of the British territories in the East Indies.

And that the citizens of the said United States may freely carry on a trade between the said territories and the said United States, in all articles of which the importation or exportation respectively, to or from the said territories, shall not be entirely prohibited. Provided only, that it shall not be lawful for them in any time of war between the British Government and any other Power or State whatever, to export from the said territories, without the special permission of the British Government there, any military stores, or naval stores, or rice.

The citizens of the United States shall pay for their vessels when admitted into the said ports no other or higher tonnage duty than shall be payable on British vessels when admitted into the ports of the United States. And they shall pay no other or higher duties or charges, on the importation or exportation of the cargoes of the said vessels, than shall be payable on the same articles when imported or exported in British vessels. But it is expressly agreed that the vessels of the United States shall not carry any of the articles exported by them from the said British territories to any port or place, except to some port or place in America, where the same shall be unladen and such regulations shall be adopted by both parties as shall from time to time be found necessary to enforce the due and faithful observance of this stipulation.

It is also understood that the permission granted by this article is not to extend to allow the vessels of the United States to carry on any part of the coasting trade of the said British territories; but vessels going with their original cargoes, or part thereof, from one port of discharge to another, are not to be considered as carrying on the coasting trade. Neither is this article to be construed to allow the citizens of the said States to settle or reside within the said territories, or to go into the interior parts thereof, without the permission of the British Government established there; and if any transgression should be attempted against the regulations of the British Government in this respect, the observance of the same shall and may be enforced against the citizens of America in the same manner as against British subjects or others transgressing the same rule. And the citizens of the United States, whenever they arrive in any port or harbour in the said territories, or if they should be permitted, in manner aforesaid, to go to any other place therein, shall always be subject to the laws, government and jurisdiction of what nature established in such harbor, port pr place, according as the same may be.

The citizens of the United States may also touch for refreshment at the island of St. Helena, but subject in all respects to such regulations as the British Government may from time to time establish there.

Article XIV

There shall be between all the dominions of His Majesty in Europe and the territories of the United States a reciprocal and perfect liberty of commerce and navigation.

The people and inhabitants of the two countries, respectively, shall have liberty freely and securely, and without hindrance and molestation, to come with their ships and cargoes to the lands, countries, cities, ports, places and rivers within the dominions and territories aforesaid, to enter into the same, to resort there, and to remain and reside there, without any limitation of time.

Also to hire and possess houses and warehouses for the purposes of their commerce, and generally the merchants and traders on each side shall enjoy the most complete protection and security for their commerce; but subject always as to what respects this article to the laws and statutes of the two countries respectively.

Article XV

It is agreed that no other or high duties shall be paid by the ships or merchandise of the one party in the ports of the other than such as are paid by the like vessels or merchandize of all other nations. Nor shall any other or higher duty be imposed in one country on the importation of any articles the growth, produce or manufacture of the other, than are or shall be payable on the importation of the like articles being of the growth, produce or manufacture of any other foreign country. Nor shall any prohibition be imposed on the exportation or importation of any articles to or from the territories of the two parties respectively, which shall not equally extend to all other nations.

But the British Government reserves to itself the right of imposing on American vessels entering into the British ports in Europe a tonnage duty equal to that which shall be payable by British vessels in the ports of America; and also such duty as may be adequate to countervail the difference of duty now payable on the importation of European and Asiatic goods, when imported into the United States in British or in American vessels.

The two parties agree to treat for the more exact equalization of the duties on the respective navigation of their subjects and people, in such manner as may be most beneficial to the two countries. The arrangements for this purpose shall be made at the same time with those mentioned at the conclusion of the twelfth article of this treaty, and are to be considered as a part thereof. In the interval it is agreed that the United States will not impose any new or additional tonnage duties on British vessels, nor increase the now subsisting difference between the duties payable on the importation of any articles in British or in American vessels.

Article XVI

It shall be free for the two contracting parties, respectively, to appoint Consuls for the protection of trade, to reside in the dominions and territories aforesaid; and the said Consuls shall enjoy those liberties and rights which belong to them by reason of their function.

But before any Consul shall act as such, he shall be in the usual forms approved and admitted by the party to whom he is sent; and it is hereby declared to be lawful and proper that, in case of illegal or improper conduct towards the laws or Government, a Consul may either be punished according to law, if the laws will reach the case, or be dismissed, or even sent back, the offended Government assigning to the other their reasons for the same.

Either of the parties may except from the residence of Consuls such particular places as such party shall judge proper to be so excepted.

Article XVII

It is agreed that in all cases where vessels shall be captured or detained on just suspicion of having on board enemy's property, or of carrying to the enemy any of the articles which are contraband of war, the said vessels shall be brought to the nearest or most convenient port; and if any property of an enemy should be found on board such vessel, that part only which belongs to the enemy shall be made prize, and the vessel shall be at liberty to proceed with the remainder without any impediment. And it is agreed that all proper measures shall be taken to prevent delay in deciding the cases of ships or cargoes so brought in for adjudication, and in the payment or recovery of any indemnification, adjudged or agreed to be paid to the masters or owners of such ships.

Article XVIII

In order to regulate what is in future to be esteemed contraband of war, it is agreed that under the said denomination shall be comprised all arms and implements serving for the purposes of war, by land or sea, such as cannon, muskets, mortars, petards, bombs, grenades, carcasses, saucisses, carriages for cannon, musket rests, bandoliers, gunpowder, match, saltpetre, ball, pikes, swords, headpieces, cuirasses, halberts, lances, javelins, horsefurniture, holsters, belts, and generally all other implements of war, as also timber for shipbuilding, tar or rozin, copper in sheets, sails, hemp, and cordage, and generally whatever may serve directly to the equipment of vessels, unwrought iron and fir planks only excepted, and all the above articles are hereby declared to be just objects of confiscation whenever they are attempted to be carried to an enemy.

And whereas the difficulty of agreeing on the precise cases in which alone provisions and other articles not generally contraband may be regarded as such, renders it expedient to provide against the inconveniences and misunderstandings which might thence arise: It is further agreed that whenever any such articles so becoming contraband, according to the existing laws of nations, shall for that reason be seized, the same shall not be confiscated, but the owners thereof shall be speedily and completely indemnified; and the captors, or, in their default, the Government under whose authority they act, shall pay to the masters or owners of such vessels the full value of all such articles, with a reasonable mercantile profit thereon, together with the freight, and also the demurrage incident to such detention.

And whereas it frequently happens that vessels sail for a port or place belonging to an enemy without knowing that the same is either besieged, blockaded or invested, it is agreed that every vessel so circumstanced may be turned away from such port or place; but she shall not be detained, nor her cargo, if not contraband, be confiscated, unless after notice she shall again attempt to enter, but she shall be permitted to go to any other port or place she may think proper; nor shall any vessel or goods of either party that may have entered into such port or place before the same was besieged, blockaded, or invested by the other, and be found thereinafter the reduction or surrender of such place, be liable to confiscation, but shall be restored to the owners or proprietors thereof.

Article XIX

And that more abundant care may be taken for the security of the respective subjects and citizens of the contracting parties, and to prevent their suffering injuries by the men of war, or privateers of either party, all commanders of ships of war and privateers, and all others the said subjects and citizens, shall forbear doing any damage to those of the other party or committing any outrage against them, and if they act to the contrary they shall be punished, and shall also be bound in their persons and estates to make satisfaction and reparation for all damages, and the interest thereof, of whatever nature the said damages may be. For this cause, all commanders of privateers, before they receive their commissions, shall hereafter be obliged to give, before a competent judge, sufficient security by at least two responsible sureties, who have no interest in the said privateer, each of whom, together with the said commander, shall be jointly and severally bound in the sum of fifteen hundred pounds sterling, or, if such ships be provided with above one hundred and fifty seamen or soldiers, in the sum of three thousand pounds sterling, to satisfy all damages and injuries which the said privateer, or her officers or men, or any of them, may do or commit during their cruise contrary to the tenor of this treaty, or to the laws and instructions for regulating their conduct; and further, that in all cases of aggressions the said commissions shall be revoked and annulled. It is also agreed that whenever a judge of a court of admiralty of either of the parties shall pronounce sentence against any vessel or goods or property belonging to the subjects or citizens of the other party, a formal and duly authenticated copy of all the proceedings in the cause, and of the said sentence, shall, if required, be delivered to the commander of the said vessel, without the smallest delay, he paying all legal fees and demands for the same.

Article XX

It is further agreed that both the said contracting parties shall not only refuse to receive any pirates into any of their ports, havens or towns, or permit any of their inhabitants to receive, protect, harbor, conceal or assist them in any manner, but will bring to condign punishment all such inhabitants as shall be guilty of such acts or offences. And all their ships, with the goods or merchandizes taken by them and brought into the port of either of the said parties, shall be seized as far as they can be discovered, and shall be restored to the owners, or their factors or agents, duly deputed and authorized in writing by them (proper evidence being first given in the court of admiralty for proving the property) even in case such effects should have passed into other hands by sale, if it be proved that the buyers knew or had good reason to believe or suspect that they had been piratically taken.

Article XXI

It is likewise agreed that the subjects and citizens of the two nations shall not do any acts of hostility or violence against each other, nor accept commissions or instructions so to act from any foreign Prince or State, enemies to the other party; nor shall the enemies of one of the parties be permitted to invite, or endeavor to enlist in their military service, any of the subjects or citizens of the other party; and the laws against all such offences and aggressions shall be punctually executed.

And if any subject or citizen of the said parties respectively shall accept any foreign commission or letters of marque for arming any vessel to act as a privateer against the other party, and be taken by the other party, it is hereby declared to be lawful for the said party to treat and punish the said subject or citizen having such commission or letters of marque as a pirate.

Article XXII

It is expressly stipulated that neither of the said contracting parties will order or authorize any acts of reprisal against the other, on complaints of injuries or damages, until the said party shall first have presented to the other a statement thereof, verified by competent proof and evidence, and demanded justice and satisfaction, and the same shall either have been refused or unreasonably delayed.

Article XXIII

The ships of war of each of the contracting parties shall, at all times, be hospitably received in the ports of the other, their officers and crews paying due respect to the laws and Government of the country. The officers shall be treated with that respect which is due to the commissions which they bear, and if any insult should be offered to them by any of the inhabitants, all offenders in this respect shall be punished as disturbers of the peace and amity between the two countries.

And His Majesty consents, that in case an American vessel should, by stress of weather, danger from enemies, or other misfortune, be reduced to the necessity of seeking shelter in any of His Majesty's ports, into which such vessel could not in ordinary cases claim to be admitted, she shall, on manifesting that necessity to the satisfaction of the Government of the place, be hospitably received, and be permitted to refit and to purchase at the market price such necessaries as she may stand in need of, conformably to such orders and regulations at the Government of the place, having respect to the circumstances of each case, shall prescribe.

She shall not be allowed to break bulk or unload her cargo, unless the same should be bona fide necessary to her being refitted. Nor shall be permitted to sell any part of her cargo, unless so much only as may be necessary to defray her expences, and then not without the express permission of the Government of the place. Nor shall she be obliged to pay any duties whatever, except only on such articles as she may be permitted to sell for the purpose aforesaid.

Article XXIV

It shall not be lawful for any foreign privateers (not being subjects or citizens of either of the said parties) who have commissions from any other Prince or State in enmity with either nation to arm their ships in the ports of either of the said parties, nor to sell what they have taken, nor in any other manner to exchange the same; nor shall they be allowed to purchase more provisions than shall be necessary for their going to the nearest port of that Prince or State from whom they obtained their commissions.

Article XXV

It shall be lawful for the ships of war and privateers belonging to the said parties respectively to carry whithersoever they please the ships and goods taken from their enemies, without being obliged to pay any fee to the officers of the admiralty, or to any judges whatever; nor shall the said prizes, when they arrive at and enter the ports of the said parties, be detained or seized, neither shall the searchers or other officers of those places visit such prizes (except for the purpose of preventing the carrying of any of the cargo thereof on shore in any manner contrary to the established laws of revenue, navigation, or commerce) nor shall such officers take cognizance of the validity of such prizes; but they shall be at liberty to hoist sail and depart as speedily as may be, and carry their said prizes to the place mentioned in their commissions or patents, which the commanders of the said ships of war or privateers shall be obliged to show.

No shelter or refuge shall be given in their ports to such as have made a prize upon the subjects or citizens of either of the said parties; but if forced by stress of weather, or the dangers of the sea, to enter therein, particular care shall be taken to hasten their departure, and to cause them to retire as soon as possible. Nothing in this treaty contained shall, however, be construed or operate contrary to former and existing public treaties with other sovereigns or States. But the two parties agree that while they continue in amity neither of them will in future make any treaty that shall be inconsistent with this or the preceding article.

Neither of the said parties shall permit the ships or goods belonging to the subjects or citizens of the other to be taken within cannon shot of the coast, nor in any of the bays, ports or rivers of their territories, by ships of war or others having commission from any Prince, Republic or State whatever. But in case it should so happen, the party whose territorial rights shall thus have been violated shall use his utmost endeavors to obtain from the offending party full and ample satisfaction for the vessel or vessels so taken, whether the same be vessels of war or merchant vessels.

Article XXVI

If at any time a rupture should take place (which God forbid) between His Majesty and the United States, and merchants and others of each of the two nations residing in the dominions of the other shall have the privilege of remaining and continuing their trade, so long as they behave peaceably and commit no offence against the laws; and in case their conduct should render them suspected, and the respective Governments should think proper to order them to remove, the term of twelve months from the publication of the order shall be allowed them for that purpose, to remove with their families, effects and property, but this favor shall not be extended to those who shall act contrary to the established laws; and for greater certainty, it is declared that such rupture shall not be deemed to exist while negotiations for accommodating differences shall be depending, nor until the respective Ambassadors or Ministers, if such there shall be, shall be recalled or sent home on account of such differences, and not on account of personal misconduct, according to the nature and degrees of which both parties retain their rights, either to request the recall, or immediately to send home the Ambassador or Minister of the other, and that without prejudice to their mutual friendship and good understanding.

Article XXVII

It is further agreed that His Majesty and the United States, on mutual requisitions, by them respectively, or by their respective Ministers or officers authorized to make the same, will deliver up to justice all persons who, being charged with murder or forgery, committed within the jurisdiction of either, shall seek an asylum within any of the countries of the other, provided that this shall only be done on such evidence of criminality as, according to the laws of the place, where the fugitive or person so charged shall be found, would justify his apprehension and commitment for trial, if the offence had there been committed. The expence of such apprehension and delivery shall be borne and defrayed by those who made the requisition and receive the fugitive.

Article XXVIII

It is agreed that the first ten articles of this treaty shall be permanent, and that the subsequent articles, except the twelfth, shall be limited in their duration to twelve years, to be computed from the day on which the ratifications of this treaty shall be exchanged, but subject to this condition. That whereas the said twelfth article will expire by the limitation therein contained, at the end of two years from the signing of the preliminary or other articles of peace, which shall terminate the present war in which His Majesty is engaged, it is agreed that proper measures shall by concert be taken for bringing the subject of that article into amicable treaty and discussion, so early before the expiration of the said term as that new arrangements on that head may by that time be perfected and ready to take place. But if it should unfortunately happen that His Majesty and the United States should not be able to agree on such new arrangements, in that case all the articles of this treaty, except the first ten, shall then cease and expire together.

Lastly. This treaty, when the same shall have been ratified by His Majesty and by the President of the United States, by and with the advice and consent of their Senate, and the respective ratifications mutually exchanged, shall be binding and obligatory on His Majesty and on the said States, and shall be by them respectively executed and observed with punctuality and the most sincere regard to good faith; and whereas it will be expedient, in order the better to facilitate intercourse and obviate difficulties, that other articles be proposed and added to this treaty, which articles, from want of time and other circumstances, cannot now be perfected, it is agreed that the said parties will, from time to time, readily treat of and concerning such articles, and will sincerely endeavor so to form them as that they may conduce to mutual convenience and tend to promote mutual satisfaction and friendship; and that the said articles, after having been duly ratified, shall be added to and make a part of this treaty.

In faith whereof we, the undersigned Ministers Plenipotentiary of His Majesty the King of Great Britain and the United States of America, have signed this present treaty, and have caused to be affixed thereto the seal of our arms.

Done at London this nineteenth day of November, one thousand seven hundred and ninety four.

GRENVILLE (SEAL)
JOHN JAY (SEAL)

III-2

Treaty of Friendship, Commerce and Navigation between the United States of America and Japan

Date   2 April 1953
In force 30 October 1953
Source   1955 UNTS 2788
Link   <http://treaties.un.org/doc/Publication/UNTS/Volume%20206/volume-206-I-2788-English.pdf>

The United States of America and Japan, desirous of strengthening the bonds of peace and friendship traditionally existing between them and of encouraging closer economic and cultural relations between their peoples, and being cognizant of the contributions which may be made toward these ends by arrangements promoting mutually advantageous commercial intercourse, encouraging mutually beneficial investments, and establishing mutual rights and privileges, have resolved to conclude a Treaty of Friendship, Commerce and Navigation, based in general upon the principles of national and of most-favored-nation treatment unconditionally accorded, and for that purpose have appointed as their Plenipotentiaries,

The United States of America:

Robert Murphy, Ambassador Extraordinary and Plenipotentiary of the United States of America to Japan, and

Japan:

Katsuo Okazaki, Minister for Foreign Affairs of Japan,d

Who, having communicated to each other their full powers found to be in due form, have agreed upon the following Articles:

Article I

1. Nationals of either Party shall be permitted to enter the territories of the other Party and to remain therein: (*a*) for the purpose of carrying on trade between the territories of the two Parties and engaging in related commercial activities; (*b*) for the purpose of developing and directing the operations of an enterprise in which they have invested, or in which they are actively in the process of investing, a substantial amount of capital; and (*c*) for other purposes subject to the laws relating to the entry and sojourn of aliens.

2. Nationals of either Party, within the territories of the other Party, shall be permitted: (*a*) to travel therein freely, and to reside at places of their choice; (*b*) to enjoy liberty of conscience; (*c*) to hold both private and public religious services; (*d*) to gather and to transmit material for dissemination to the public abroad; and (*e*) to communicate with other persons inside and outside such territories by mail, telegraph and other means open to general public use.

3. The provisions of the present Article shall be subject to the right of either Party to apply measures that are necessary to maintain public order and protect the public health, morals and safety.

Article II

1. Nationals of either Party within the territories of the other Party shall be free from unlawful molestations of every kind, and shall receive the most constant protection and security, in no case less than that required by international law.

2. If, within the territories of either Party, a national of the other Party is taken into custody, the nearest consular representative of his country shall on the demand of such national be immediately notified. Such national shall: (*a*) receive reasonable and humane treatment; (*b*) be formally and immediately informed of the accusations against him; (*c*) be brought to trial as promptly as is consistent with the proper preparation of his defense; and (*d*) enjoy all means reasonably necessary to his defense, including the services of competent counsel of his choice.

Article III

1. Nationals of either Party shall be accorded national treatment in the application of laws and regulations within the territories of the other Party that establish a pecuniary compensation, or other benefit or service, on account of disease, injury or death arising out of and in the course of employment or due to the nature of employment.

2. In addition to the rights and privileges provided in paragraph 1 of the present Article, nationals of either Party shall, within the territories of the other Party, be accorded national treatment in the application of laws and regulations establishing compulsory systems of social security, under which benefits are paid without an individual test of financial need: (*a*) against loss of wages or earnings due to old age, unemployment, sickness or disability, or (*b*) against loss of financial support due to the death of father, husband or other person on whom such support had depended.

Article IV

1. Nationals and companies of either Party shall be accorded national treatment and most-favored-nation treatment with respect to access to the courts of justice and to administrative tribunals and agencies within the territories of the other Party, in all degrees of jurisdiction, both in pursuit and in defense of their rights. It is understood that companies of either Party not engaged in activities within the territories of the other Party shall enjoy such access therein without registration or similar requirements.

2. Contracts entered into between nationals and companies of either Party and nationals and companies of the other Party, that provide for the settlement by arbitration of controversies, shall not be deemed unenforceable within the territories of such other Party merely on the grounds that the place designated for the arbitration proceedings is outside such territories or that the nationality of one or more of the arbitrators is not that of such other Party. Awards duly rendered pursuant to any such contracts, which are final and enforceable under the laws of the place where rendered, shall be deemed conclusive in enforcement proceedings brought before the courts of competent jurisdiction of either Party, and shall be entitled to be declared enforceable by such courts, except where found contrary to public policy. When so declared, such awards shall be entitled to privileges and measures of enforcement appertaining to awards rendered locally. It is understood, however, that awards rendered outside the United States of America shall be entitled in any court in any State thereof only to the same measure of recognition as awards rendered in other States thereof.

Article V

1. Neither Party shall take unreasonable or discriminatory measures that would impair the legally acquired rights or interests within its territories of nationals and companies of the other Party in the enterprises which they have established, in their capital, or in the skills, arts or technology which they have supplied; nor shall either Party unreasonably impede nationals and companies of the other Party from obtaining on equitable terms the capital, skills, arts and technology it needs for its economic development.

2. The Parties undertake to cooperate in furthering the interchange and use of scientific and technical knowledge, particularly in the interests of increasing productivity and improving standards of living within their respective territories.

Article VI

1. Property of nationals and companies of either Party shall receive the most constant protection and security within the territories of the other Party.

2. The dwellings, offices, warehouses, factories and other premises of nationals and companies of either Party located within the territories of the other Party shall not be subject to unlawful entry or molestation. Official searches and examinations of such premises and their contents, when necessary, shall be made only according to law and with careful regard for the convenience of the occupants and the conduct of business.

3. Property of nationals and companies of either Party shall not be taken within the territories of the other Party except for a public purpose, nor shall it be taken without the prompt payment of just compensation. Such compensation shall be in an effectively realizable form and shall represent the full equivalent of the property taken; and adequate provision shall have been made at or prior to the time of taking for the determination and payment thereof.

4. Nationals and companies of either Party shall in no case be accorded, within the territories of the other Party, less than national treatment and most-favored-nation treatment with respect to the matters set forth in paragraphs 2 and 3 of the present Article. Moreover, enterprises in which nationals and companies of either Party have a substantial interest shall be accorded, within the territories of the other Party, not less than national treatment and most-favored-nation treatment in all matters relating to the taking of privately owned enterprises into public ownership and to the placing of such enterprises under public control.

Article VII

1. Nationals and companies of either Party shall be accorded national treatment with respect to engaging in all types of commercial, industrial, financial and other business activities within the territories of the other Party, whether directly or by agent or through the medium of any form of lawful juridical entity. Accordingly, such nationals and companies shall be permitted within such territories: (*a*) to establish and maintain branches, agencies, offices, factories and other establishments appropriate to the conduct of their business; (*b*) to organize companies under the general company laws of such other Party, and to acquire majority interests in companies of such other Party; and (*c*) to control and manage enterprises which they have established or acquired. Moreover, enterprises which they control, whether in the form of individual proprietorships, companies or otherwise, shall, in all that relates to the conduct of the activities thereof, be accorded treatment no less favorable than that accorded like enterprises controlled by nationals and companies of such other Party.

2. Each Party reserves the right to limit the extent to which aliens may within its territories establish, acquire interests in, or carry on public utilities enterprises or enterprises engaged in shipbuilding, air or water transport, banking involving depository or fiduciary functions, or the exploitation of land or other natural resources. However, new limitations imposed by either Party upon the extent to which aliens are accorded national treatment, with respect to carrying on such activities within its territories, shall not be applied as against enterprises which are engaged in such activities therein at the time such new limitations are adopted and which are owned or controlled by nationals and companies of the other Party. Moreover, neither Party shall deny to transportation, communications and banking companies of the other Party the right to maintain branches and agencies to perform functions necessary for essentially international operations in which they are permitted to engage.

3. The provisions of paragraph 1 of the present Article shall not prevent either Party from prescribing special formalities in connection with the establishment of alien-controlled

enterprises within its territories; but such formalities may not impair the substance of the rights set forth in said paragraph.

4. Nationals and companies of either Party, as well as enterprises controlled by such nationals and companies, shall in any event be accorded most-favored-nation treatment with reference to the matters treated in the present Article.

Article VIII

1. Nationals and companies of either Party shall be permitted to engage, within the territories of the other Party, accountants and other technical experts, executive personnel, attorneys, agents: and other specialists of their choice. Moreover, such nationals and companies shall be permitted to engage accountants and other technical experts regardless of the extent to which they may have qualified for the practice of a profession within the territories of such other Party, for the particular purpose of making examinations, audits and technical investigations exclusively for, and rendering reports to, such nationals and companies in connection with the planning and operation of their enterprises, and enterprises in which they have a financial interest, within such territories.

2. Nationals of either Party shall not be barred from practicing the professions within the territories of the other Party merely by reason of their alienage; but they shall be permitted to engage in professional activities therein upon compliance with the requirements regarding qualifications, residence and competence that are applicable to nationals of such other Party.

3. Nationals and companies of either Party shall be accorded national treatment and most-favored-nation treatment with respect to engaging in scientific, educational, religious and philanthropic activities within the territories of the other Party, and shall be accorded the right to form associations for that purpose under the laws of such other Party.

Article IX

1. Nationals and companies of either Party shall be accorded within the territories of the other Party: (*a*) national treatment with respect to leasing land, buildings and other immovable property appropriate to the conduct of activities in which they are permitted to engage pursuant to Articles VII and VIII and for residential purposes, and with respect to occupying and using such property; and (*b*) other rights in immovable property permitted by the applicable laws of the other Party.

2. Nationals and companies of either Party shall be accorded within the territories of the other Party national treatment and most-favored-nation treatment with respect to acquiring, by purchase, lease, or otherwise, and with respect to owning and possessing, movable property of all kinds, both tangible and intangible. However, either Party may impose restrictions on alien ownership of materials dangerous from the standpoint of public safety and alien ownership of interests in enterprises carrying on the activities listed in the first sentence of paragraph 2 of Article VII, but only to the extent that this can be done without impairing the rights and privileges secured by Article VII or by other provisions of the present Treaty.

3. Nationals and companies of either Party shall be permitted freely to dispose of property within the territories of the other Party with respect to the acquisition of which through testate or intestate succession their alienage has prevented them from receiving national treatment, and they shall be permitted a term of at least five years in which to effect such disposition.

4. Nationals and companies of either Party shall be accorded within the territories of the other Party national treatment and most-favored-nation treatment with respect to disposing of property of all kinds.

Article X

Nationals and companies of either Party shall be accorded, within the territories of the other Party, national treatment and most-favored-nation treatment with respect to obtaining and maintaining patents of invention, and with respect to rights in trade marks, trade names, trade labels and industrial property of every kind.

Article XI

1. Nationals of either Party residing within the territories of the other Party, and nationals and companies of either Party engaged in trade or other gainful pursuit or in scientific, educational, religious or philanthropic activities within the territories of the other Party, shall not be subject to the payment of taxes, fees or charges imposed upon or applied to income, capital, transactions, activities or any other object, or to requirements with respect to the levy and collection thereof, within the territories of such other Party, more burdensome than those borne by nationals and companies of such other Party.

2. With respect to nationals of either Party who are neither resident nor engaged in trade or other gainful pursuit within the territories of the other Party, and with respect to companies of either Party which are not engaged in trade or other gainful pursuit within the territories of the other Party, it shall be the aim of such other Party to apply in general the principle set forth in paragraph 1 of the present Article.

3. Nationals and companies of either Party shall in no case be subject, within the territories of the other Party, to the payment of taxes, fees or charges imposed upon or applied to income, capital, transactions, activities or any other object, or to requirements with respect to the levy and collection thereof, more burdensome than those borne by nationals, residents and companies of any third country.

4. In the case of companies of either Party engaged in trade or other gainful pursuit within the territories of the other Party, and in the case of nationals of either Party engaged in trade or other gainful pursuit within the territories of the other Party but not resident therein, such other Party shall not impose or apply any tax, fee or charge upon any income, capital or other basis in excess of that reasonably allocable or apportionable to its territories, nor grant deductions and exemptions less than those reasonably allocable or apportionable to its territories. A comparable rule shall apply also in the case of companies organized and operated exclusively for scientific, educational, religious or philanthropic purposes.

5. Each Party reserves the right to: (*a*) extend specific tax advantages on the basis of reciprocity; (*b*) accord special tax advantages by virtue of agreements for the avoidance of double taxation or the mutual protection of revenue; and (*c*) accord to its own nationals and to residents of contiguous countries more favorable exemptions of a personal nature with respect to income taxes and inheritance taxes than are accorded to other non-resident persons.

Article XII

1. Nationals and companies of either Party shall be accorded by the other Party national treatment and most-favored-nation treatment with respect to payments, remittances and transfers of funds or financial instruments between the territories of the two Parties as well as between the territories of such other Party and of any third country.

2. Neither Party shall impose exchange restrictions as defined in paragraph 5 of the present Article except to the extent necessary to prevent its monetary reserves from falling to a very low level or to effect a moderate increase in very low monetary reserves. It is understood that the provisions of the present Article do not alter the obligations either Party may have to the International Monetary Fund or preclude imposition of particular restrictions whenever the Fund specifically authorizes or requests a Party to impose such particular restrictions.

3. If either Party imposes exchange restrictions in accordance with paragraph 2 above, it shall, after making whatever provision may be necessary to assure the availability of foreign exchange for goods and services essential to the health and welfare of its people, make reasonable provision for the withdrawal, in foreign exchange in the currency of the other Party, of: (*a*) the compensation referred to in Article VI, paragraph 3, of the present Treaty,

(*b*) earnings, whether in the form of salaries, interest, dividends, commissions, royalties, payments for technical services, or otherwise, and (*c*) amounts for amortization of loans, depreciation of direct investments, and capital transfers, giving consideration to special needs for other transactions. If more than one rate of exchange is in force, the rate applicable to such withdrawals shall be a rate which is specifically approved by the International Monetary Fund for such transactions or, in the absence of a rate so approved, an effective rate which, inclusive of any taxes or surcharges on exchange transfers, is just and reasonable.

4. Exchange restrictions shall not be imposed by either Party in a manner unnecessarily detrimental or arbitrarily discriminatory to the claims, investments, transport, trade, and other interests of the nationals and companies of the other Party, nor to the competitive position thereof.

5. The term "exchange restrictions" as used in the present Article includes all restrictions, regulations, charges, taxes, or other requirements imposed by either Party which burden or interfere with payments, remittances, or transfers of funds or of financial instruments between the territories of the two Parties.

Article XIII

Commercial travelers representing nationals and companies of either Party engaged in business within the territories thereof shall, upon their entry into and departure from the territories of the other Party and during their sojourn therein, be accorded most-favored-nation treatment in respect of the customs and other matters, including, subject to the exceptions in paragraph 5 of Article XI, taxes and charges applicable to them, their samples and the taking of orders, and regulations governing the exercise of their functions.

Article XIV

1. Each Party shall accord most-favored-nation treatment to products of the other Party, from whatever place and by whatever type of carrier arriving, and to products destined for exportation to the territories of such other Party, by whatever route and by whatever type of carrier, with respect to customs duties and charges of any kind imposed on or in connection with importation or exportation or imposed on the international transfer of payments for imports or exports, and with respect to the method of levying such duties and charges, and with respect to all rules and formalities in connection with importation and exportation.

2. Neither Party shall impose restrictions or prohibitions on the importation of any product of the other Party, or on the exportation of any product to the territories of the other Party, unless the importation of the like product of, or the exportation of the like product to, all third countries is similarly restricted or prohibited.

3. If either Party imposes quantitative restrictions on the importation or exportation of any product in which the other Party has an important interest:
   (*a*) It shall as a general rule give prior public notice of the total amount of the product, by quantity or value, that may be imported or exported during a specified period, and of any change in such amount or period; and
   (*b*) If it makes allotments to any third country, it shall afford such other Party a share proportionate to the amount of the product, by quantity or value, supplied by or to it during a previous representative period, due consideration being given to any special factors affecting the trade in such product.

4. Either Party may impose prohibitions or restrictions on sanitary or other customary grounds of a noncommercial nature, or in the interest of preventing deceptive or unfair practices, provided such prohibitions or restrictions do not arbitrarily discriminate against the commerce of the other Party.

5. Nationals and companies of either Party shall be accorded national treatment and most-favored-nation treatment by the other Party with respect to all matters relating to importation and exportation.

6. The provisions of the present Article shall not apply to advantages accorded by either Party:
   (*a*) to products of its national fisheries;
   (*b*) to adjacent countries in order to facilitate frontier traffic; or
   (*c*) by virtue of a customs union or free-trade area of which it may become a member, so long as it informs the other Party of its plans and affords such other Party adequate opportunity for consultation.

7. Notwithstanding the provisions of paragraphs 2 and 3 (*b*) of the present Article, a Party may apply restrictions or controls on importation and exportation of goods that have effect equivalent to, or which are necessary to make effective, exchange restrictions applied pursuant to Article XII. However, such restrictions or controls shall depart no more than necessary from the aforesaid paragraphs and shall be conformable with a policy designed to promote the maximum development of nondiscriminatory foreign trade and to expedite the attainment both of a balance-of-payments position and of monetary reserves which will obviate the necessity of such restrictions.

Article XV

1. Each Party shall promptly publish laws, regulations and administrative rulings of general application pertaining to rates of duty, taxes or other charges, to the classification of articles for customs purposes, and to requirements or restrictions on imports and exports or the transfer of payments therefor, or affecting their sale, distribution or use; and shall administer such laws, regulations and rulings in a uniform, impartial and reasonable manner. As a general practice, new administrative requirements or restrictions affecting imports, with the exception of those imposed on sanitary grounds or for reasons of public safety, shall not go into effect before the expiration of 30 days after publication, or alternatively, shall not apply to products en route at time of publication.

2. Each Party shall provide an appeals procedure under which nationals and companies of the other Party, and importers of products of such other Party, shall be able to obtain prompt and impartial review, and correction when warranted, of administrative action relating to customs matters, including the imposition of fines and penalties, confiscations, and rulings on questions of customs classification and valuation by the administrative authorities. Penalties imposed for infractions of the customs and shipping laws and regulations concerning documentation shall, in cases resulting from clerical errors or when good faith can be demonstrated, be no greater than necessary to serve merely as a warning.

3. Neither Party shall impose any measure of a discriminatory nature that hinders or prevents the importer or exporter of products of either country from obtaining marine insurance on such products in companies of either Party. The present paragraph is subject to the provisions of Article XII.

Article XVI

1. Products of either Party shall be accorded, within the territories of the other Party, national treatment and most-favored-nation treatment in all matters affecting internal taxation, sale, distribution, storage and use.

2. Articles produced by nationals and companies of either Party within the territories of the other Party, or by companies of the latter Party controlled by such nationals and companies, shall be accorded therein treatment no less favorable than that accorded to like articles of national origin by whatever person or company produced, in all matters affecting exportation, taxation, sale, distribution, storage and use.

Article XVII

1. Each Party undertakes (*a*) that enterprises owned or controlled by its Government, and that monopolies or agencies granted exclusive or special privileges within its territories, shall make their purchases and sales involving either imports or exports affecting the commerce of the other Party solely in accordance with commercial considerations, including price, quality, availability, marketability, transportation and other conditions of purchase or sale; and (*b*) that the nationals, companies and commerce of such other Party shall be afforded adequate opportunity, in accordance with customary business practice, to compete for participation in such purchases and sales.

2. Each Party shall accord to the nationals, companies and commerce of the other Party fair and equitable treatment, as compared with that accorded to the nationals, companies and commerce of any third country, with respect to: (*a*) the governmental purchase of supplies, (*b*) the awarding of concessions and other government contracts, and (*c*) the sale of any service sold by the Government or by any monopoly or agency granted exclusive or special privileges.

Article XVIII

1. The two Parties agree that business practices which restrain competition, limit access to markets or foster monopolistic control, and which are engaged in or made effective by one or more private or public commercial enterprises or by combination, agreement or other arrangement among such enterprises, may have harmful effects upon commerce between their respective territories. Accordingly, each Party agrees upon the request of the other Party to consult with respect to any such practices and to take such measures as it deems appropriate with a view to eliminating such harmful effects.

2. No enterprise of either Party, including corporations, associations, and government agencies and instrumentalities, which is publicly owned or controlled shall, if it engages in commercial, industrial, shipping or other business activities within the territories of the other Party, claim or enjoy, either for itself or for its property, immunity therein from taxation, suit, execution of judgment or other liability to which privately owned and controlled enterprises are subject therein.

Article XIX

1. Between the territories of the two Parties there shall be freedom of commerce and navigation.

2. Vessels under the flag of either Party, and carrying the papers required by its law in proof of nationality, shall be deemed to be vessels of that Party both on the high seas and within the ports, places and waters of the other Party.

3. Vessels of either Party shall have liberty, on equal terms with vessels of the other Party and on equal terms with vessels of any third country, to come with their cargoes to all ports, places and waters of such other Party open to foreign commerce and navigation. Such vessels and cargoes shall in all respects be accorded national treatment and most-favored-nation treatment within the ports, places and waters of such other Party.

4. Vessels of either Party shall be accorded national treatment and most-favored-nation treatment by the other Party with respect to the right to carry all products that may be carried by vessel to or from the territories of such other Party; and such products shall be accorded treatment no less favorable than that accorded to like products carried in vessels of such other Party, with respect to: (*a*) duties and charges of all kinds, (*b*) the administration of the customs, and (*c*) bounties, drawbacks and other privileges of this nature.

5. Vessels of either Party, in case of shipwreck, stranding, or of being forced to put into the ports, places and waters of the other Party, whether or not open to foreign commerce and navigation, shall enjoy the same assistance and protection as are in like cases enjoyed by vessels of such other Party or of any third country, and shall not be subject to any duties or charges other than those which would be payable in like circumstances by vessels of such other Party or of any third country. The cargoes of such vessels of either Party and all articles

salvaged from them shall be exempt from customs duties unless entered for consumption within the territories of the other Party; but articles not entered for consumption may be subject to measures for the protection of the revenue pending their exit from the country.

6. Notwithstanding any other provision of the present Treaty, each Party may reserve exclusive rights and privileges to its own vessels with respect to the coasting trade, national fisheries and inland navigation, or may admit foreign vessels thereto only on a reciprocity basis.

7. The term "vessels", as used herein, means all types of vessels, whether privately owned or operated, or publicly owned or operated; but this term does not, except with reference to paragraphs 2 and 5 of the present Article, include fishing vessels or vessels of war.

Article XX

There shall be freedom of transit through the territories of each Party by the routes most convenient for international transit:

(a) for nationals of the other Party, together with their baggage;

(b) for other persons, together with their baggage, en route to or from the territories of such other Party; and

(c) for products of any origin en route to or from the territories of such other Party.

Such persons and things in transit shall be exempt from customs duties, from duties imposed by reason of transit, and from unreasonable charges and requirements; and shall be free from unnecessary delays and restrictions. They shall, however, be subject to measures referred to in paragraph 3 of Article I, and to non-discriminatory regulations necessary to prevent abuse of the transit privilege.

Article XXI

1. The present Treaty shall not preclude the application of measures:

   (a) regulating the importation or exportation of gold or silver;

   (b) relating to fissionable materials, to radioactive by-products of the utilization or processing thereof, or to materials that are the source of fissionable materials;

   (c) regulating the production of or traffic in arms, ammunition and implements of war, or traffic in other materials carried on directly or indirectly for the purpose of supplying a military establishment;

   (d) necessary to fulfill the obligations of a Party for the maintenance or restoration of international peace and security, or necessary to protect its essential security interests; and

   (e) denying to any company in the ownership or direction of which nationals of any third country or countries have directly or indirectly the controlling interest, the advantages of the present Treaty, except with respect to recognition of juridical status and with respect to access to courts of justice and to administrative tribunals and agencies.

2. The most-favored-nation provisions of the present Treaty relating to the treatment of goods shall not apply to advantages accorded by the United States of America or its Territories and possessions to one another, to the Republic of Cuba, to the Republic of the Philippines, to the Trust Territory of the Pacific Islands or to the Panama Canal Zone.

3. The provisions of the present Treaty relating to the treatment of goods shall not preclude action by either Party which is required or specifically permitted by the General Agreement on Tariffs and Trade during such time as such Party is a contracting party to the General Agreement. Moreover, either Party may withhold advantages negotiated under the aforesaid Agreement from those countries which by their own choice are not contracting parties thereto.

4. Nationals of either Party admitted into the territories of the other Party for limited purposes shall not enjoy rights to engage in gainful occupations in contravention of limitations expressly imposed, according to law, as a condition of their admittance.

5. Nothing in the present Treaty shall be deemed to grant or imply any right to engage in political activities.

Article XXII

1. The term "national treatment" means treatment accorded within the territories of a Party upon terms no less favorable than the treatment accorded therein, in like situations, to nationals, companies, products, vessels or other objects, as the case may be, of such Party.

2. The term "most-favored-nation treatment" means treatment accorded within the territories of a Party upon terms no less favorable than the treatment accorded therein, in like situations, to nationals, companies, products, vessels or other objects, as the case may be, of any third country.

3. As used in the present Treaty, the term "companies" means corporations, partnerships, companies and other associations, whether or not with limited liability and whether or not for pecuniary profit. Companies constituted under the applicable laws and regulations within the territories of either Party shall be deemed companies thereof and shall have their juridical status recognized within the territories of the other Party.

4. National treatment accorded under the provisions of the present Treaty to companies of Japan shall, in any State, Territory or possession of the United States of America, be the treatment accorded therein to companies created or organized in other States, Territories, and possessions of the United States of America.

Article XXIII

The territories to which the present Treaty extends shall comprise all areas of land and water under the sovereignty or authority of each Party, other than the Panama Canal Zone and the Trust Territory of the Pacific Islands, except to the extent that the President of the United States of America shall by proclamation extend provisions of the Treaty to such Trust Territory.

Article XXIV

1. Each Party shall accord sympathetic consideration to, and shall afford adequate opportunity for consultation regarding, such representations as the other Party may make with respect to any matter affecting the operation of the present Treaty.

2. Any dispute between the Parties as to the interpretation or application of the present Treaty, not satisfactorily adjusted by diplomacy, shall be submitted to the International Court of Justice, unless the Parties agree to settlement by some other pacific means.

Article XXV

1. The present Treaty shall be ratified, and the ratifications thereof shall be exchanged at Washington as soon as possible.

2. The present Treaty shall enter into force one month after the day of exchange of ratifications. It shall remain in force for ten years and shall continue in force thereafter until terminated as provided herein.

3. Either Party may, by giving one year's written notice to the other Party, terminate the present Treaty at the end of the initial ten-year period or at any time thereafter.

IN WITNESS WHEREOF the respective Plenipotentiaries have signed the present Treaty and have affixed hereunto their seals.

DONE in duplicate, in the English and Japanese languages, both equally authentic, at Tokyo, this second day of April, one thousand nine hundred fifty three.

For the United States of America:
Robert MURPHY

For Japan:
Katsuo OKAZAKI

III-3

Draft Convention on Investments Abroad (The 'Abs-Shawcross Draft Convention')

Date   1959
Source Journal of Public Law (presently Emory Law Journal), Vol 1, Spring 1960: 115–118
Link   <http://www.unctad.org/sections/dite/iia/docs/Compendium//en/137%20volume%205.pdf>

The High Contracting Parties:

believing that peace, security, and progress in the world can only be attained and ensured by fruitful co-operation between all peoples on a basis of international law and mutual confidence;

appreciating also the importance of encouraging commercial relations and promoting the flow of capital for economic activity and development; and considering the contribution which may be made towards these-ends by a restatement of principles of conduct relating to foreign investments; have resolved for this purpose to conclude the present Convention.

Article I

Each Party shall at all times ensure fair and equitable treatment to the property of the nationals of the other Parties. Such property shall be accorded the most constant protection and security within the territories [and] shall not in any way be impaired by unreasonable or discriminatory measures.

Article II

Each Party shall at all times ensure the observance of any undertakings, which it may have given in relation to investments made by nationals of any other Party.

Article III

No Party shall take any measures against nationals of another Party to deprive them directly or indirectly of their property except under due process of law and provided that such measures are not discriminatory or contrary to undertakings given by that Party and are accompanied by the payment of just and effective compensation. Adequate provision shall have been made at or prior to the time of deprivation for the prompt determination and payment of such compensation, which shall represent the genuine value of the property affected, be made in transferable form, and be paid without undue delay.

Article IV

Any breach of this Convention shall entail the obligation to make full reparation. The Parties shall not recognise or enforce within their territories any measures conflicting with the principles of this Convention and affecting the property of nationals of any of the Parties until reparation is made or secured.

Article V

No Party may take measures derogating from the present Convention unless it is involved in war, hostilities, or other public emergency, which threatens its life; and such measures shall be limited in extent and duration to those strictly required by the exigencies of the situation. Nothing in this Article shall be construed as superseding the generally accepted laws of war.

Article VI

The provisions of this Convention shall not prejudice the application of any present or future treaty or municipal law under which more favourable treatment is accorded to nationals of any of the Parties.

Article VII

1. Any dispute as to the interpretation or application of the present Convention may, with the consent of the interested Parties, be submitted to an Arbitral Tribunal set up in accordance with the provisions of the Annex to this Convention. Such consent may take the form of specific agreements or of unilateral declarations. In the absence of such consent or of agreement for settlement by other specific means, the dispute may be submitted by either Party to the International Court of Justice.

2. A national of one of the Parties claiming that he has been injured by measures in breach of this Convention may institute proceedings against the Party responsible for such measures before the Arbitral Tribunal referred to in paragraph 1 of this Article, provided that the Party against which the claim is made has declared that it accepts the jurisdiction of the said Arbitral Tribunal in respect of claims by nationals of one or more Parties, including the Party concerned.

Article VIII

If a Party against which a judgement or award is given fails to comply with the terms thereof, the other Parties shall be entitled, individually or collectively, to take such measures as are strictly required to give effect to that judgement or award.

Article IX

For the purposes of this Convention,

a. "nationals" in relation to a Party includes (i) companies which under the municipal law of that Party are considered national companies of that Party and (ii) companies in which nationals of that Party have directly or indirectly a controlling interest. "Companies" includes both juridical persons recognised as such by the law of a Party and associations even if they do not possess legal personality.

b. "property" includes all property, rights, and interests, whether held directly or indirectly. A member of a company shall be deemed to have an interest in the property of the company.

Article X

Final clauses relating to ratification, entry into force, accession, deposit, etc.

ANNEX RELATING TO THE ARBITRAL TRIBUNAL

1. The Arbitral Tribunal referred to in Article VII of the Convention shall consist of three persons appointed as follows: one arbitrator shall be appointed by each of the parties to the arbitration proceedings; a third arbitrator (hereinafter sometimes called "the Umpire") shall be appointed by agreement of the parties or, if they shall not agree, by the President of the International Court of Justice, or failing appointment by him, by the Secretary-General of the United Nations. If either of the parties shall fail to appoint an arbitrator, such arbitrator shall be appointed by the Umpire. In case any arbitrator appointed in accordance with this Article shall resign, die, or become unable to act, a, successor arbitrator shall be appointed in the same manner as herein prescribed for the appointment of the original arbitrator and such successor shall have all the powers and duties of such original arbitrator.

2. Arbitration proceedings may be instituted upon notice by the party instituting such proceedings (whether a Party to the Convention or a national of a Party to the Convention, as the case may be) to the other-party. Such notice shall contain a statement setting forth the nature of

the relief sought, and the name of the arbitrator appointed by the party instituting such proceedings. Within 30 days after the giving of such notice, the adverse party shall notify the party instituting proceedings of the name of the arbitrator appointed by such adverse party.

3. If, within 60 days after the giving of such notice instituting the arbitration proceedings, the parties shall not have agreed upon an Umpire, either party may request the appointment of an Umpire as provided in, Article 1 of this Annex.

4. The Arbitral Tribunal shall convene at such time and place as shall be fixed by the Umpire. Thereafter, the Arbitral Tribunal shall determine where and when it shall sit.

5. Subject to the provisions of this Annex and except as the parties shall otherwise agree, the Arbitral Tribunal, shall decide all questions relating to its competence and, shall determine its procedure and all questions relating to costs. All decisions of the Arbitral Tribunal shall be by majority vote.

6. The Arbitral Tribunal shall afford to all parties a fair hearing and shall render its award in writing. Such award may be rendered by default. An award signed by the majority of the Arbitral Tribunal shall constitute the award of such Tribunal. A signed counterpart of the award shall be transmitted to each party. Any such award rendered in accordance with the provisions of this Annex shall be final and binding upon the parties and shall be published. Each party shall abide by and comply with any such award rendered by the Arbitral Tribunal.

III-4

Treaty between the Federal Republic of Germany and Pakistan for the Promotion and Protection of Investments*

Date   25 November 1959
In force 28 April 1962
Source   1963 UNTS 6575
Link   <http://treaties.un.org/doc/Publication/UNTS/Volume%20457/volume-457-I-6575-English.pdf>

The Federal Republic of Germany and Pakistan,

Desiring to intensify economic co-operation between the two States, Intending to create favourable conditions for investments by nationals and companies of either State in the territory of the other State, and Recognizing that an understanding reached between the two States is likely to promote investment, encourage private industrial and financial enterprise and to increase the prosperity of both the States,

Have agreed as follows:

Article 1

(1) Each contracting State hereafter called in this Treaty a Party will endeavour to admit in its territory, in accordance with its legislation and rules and regulations framed thereunder the investing of capital by nationals or companies of the other Party and to promote such investments and will give sympathetic consideration to requests for the grant of necessary permissions. In the case of Pakistan such permissions shall be given with due regard also to their published plans and policies.

(2) Capital investments by nationals or companies of either Party in the territory of the other Party shall not be subjected to any discriminatory treatment on the ground that ownership of or influence upon it is vested in nationals or companies of the former Party, unless legislation and rules and regulations framed thereunder existing at the time of coming into force of this Treaty provide otherwise.

Article 2

Neither Party shall subject to discriminatory treatment any activities carried on in connection with investments including the effective management, use or enjoyment of such investments by the nationals or companies of either Party in the territory of the other Party unless specific stipulations are made in the documents of admission of an investment.

---

* Note by the Editors: In 2009, Pakistan and Germany agreed on a new bilateral investment agreement (Text in *Bundesgesetzblatt* 2011 II, 704), which supersedes the 1959 treaty upon entry into force (cf Article 13, para 4).

Article 3

(1) Investments by nationals or companies of either Party shall enjoy protection and security in the territory of the other Party.

(2) Nationals or companies of either Party shall not be subjected to expropriation of their investments in the territory of the other Party except for public benefit against compensation, which shall represent the equivalent of the investments affected. Such compensation shall be actually realizable and freely transferable in the currency of the other Party without undue delay. Adequate provision shall be made at or prior to the time of expropriation for the determination and the grant of such compensation. The legality of any such expropriation and the amount of compensation shall be subject to review by due process of law.

(3) Nationals or companies of either Party who owing to war or other armed conflict, revolution or revolt in the territory of the other Party suffer the loss of investments situate there, shall be accorded treatment no less favourable by such other Party than the treatment that Party accords to persons residing within its territory and to nationals or companies of a third party, as regards restitution, indemnification, compensation or other considerations. With respect to the transfer of such payments each Party shall accord to the requests of nationals or companies of the other Party treatment no less favourable than is accorded to comparable requests made by nationals or companies of a third party.

Article 4

Either Party shall in respect of all investments guarantee to nationals or companies of the other Party the transfer of the invested capital, of the returns therefrom and in the event of liquidation, the proceeds of such liquidation.

Article 5

If a claim arising out of a guarantee given for an investment is brought against a Party, the latter shall without prejudice to its rights under Article 11, be authorised, on the conditions stipulated by its predecessor in title, to exercise the rights having devolved on such Party by law or having been assigned to it by the predecessor in title (devolved interest). As regards the transfer of payments to be made by virtue of the devolved interest to the Party concerned, paragraphs (2) and (3) of Article 3 as well as Article 4 shall apply *mutatis mutandis*.

Article 6

(1) Transfers under paragraphs (2) or (3) of Article 3, under Article 4 or Article 5 shall be made without undue delay and at rates of exchange applicable to current transactions on the date the transfer is made.

(2) The rate applicable to current transactions shall be based on the par value agreed with the International Monetary Fund taking into account the provisions of Section 3 of Article 4 of the Articles of Agreement establishing the International Monetary Fund.

(3) In case no rate of exchange within the meaning of paragraph (2) above exists at the time of transfer the appropriate authorities of the Party in the territory of which the investment is situated shall admit a rate of exchange which is just and reasonable.

Article 7

If the legislation of either Party or international obligations existing at present or established hereafter between the Parties in addition to the present Treaty, result in a position entitling investments by nationals or companies of the other Party to treatment more favourable than is provided for by the present Treaty, such position shall not be affected by the present Treaty. Either Party shall observe any other obligation it may have entered into with regard to investments by nationals or companies of the other Party.

Article 8

(1) (*a*) The term "investment" shall comprise capital brought into the territory of the other Party for investment in various forms in the shape of assets such as foreign exchange, goods, property rights, patents and technical knowledge. The term "investment" shall also include the returns derived from and ploughed back into such "investment".

(*b*) Any partnerships, companies or assets of similar kind, created by the utilisation of the above mentioned assets shall be regarded as "investment".

(2) The term "return" shall mean the amounts derived from investments as profits or interest for a specified period.

(3) The term "nationals" shall mean

(*a*) in respect of the Federal Republic of Germany, Germans within the meaning of the Basic Law for the Federal Republic of Germany;

(*b*) in respect of Pakistan, a person who is a citizen of Pakistan according to its laws.

(4) The term "companies" shall comprise

(*a*) in respect of the Federal Republic of Germany, any juridical person, any commercial company or any other company or association, with or without legal personality, having its seat in the territory of the Federal Republic of Germany and lawfully existing in accordance with its legislation, irrespective of whether the liability of its partners, associates or members is limited or unlimited and whether or not its activities are directed to pecuniary gain;

(*b*) in respect to Pakistan, any juridical person or any company or association, incorporated in the territory of Pakistan and lawfully existing in accordance with its legislation.

Article 9

The present Treaty shall also apply to approved investments made prior to its entry into force but not earlier than 1st September, 1954, by nationals or companies of either Party in the territory of the other Party unless in any case it is specifically provided otherwise. This provision shall not affect the Agreement of 27th February 1953, on German External Debts.[1]

Article 10

Each Party shall co-operate with the other in furthering the interchange and use of scientific and technical knowledge and development of training facilities particularly in the interest of increasing productivity and improving standards of living in their territories.

Article 11

(1) In the event of disputes as to the interpretation or application of the present Treaty, the Parties shall enter into consultation for the purpose of finding a solution in a spirit of friendship.

(2) If no such solution is forthcoming, the dispute shall be submitted

(*a*) to the International Court of Justice if both Parties so agree or

(*b*) if they do not so agree to an arbitration tribunal upon the request of either Party.

(3) (*a*) The tribunal referred to in paragraph (2) (*b*) above shall be formed in respect of each specific case and it shall consist of three arbitrators. Each Party shall appoint one arbitrator and the two members so appointed shall appoint a chairman who shall be a national of a third country.

(*b*) Each Party shall appoint its arbitrator within two months after a request to this effect has been made by either Party. If either Party fails to comply with this obligation the arbitrator shall be appointed upon the request of the other Party by the President of the International Court of Justice.

---

1 United Nations, Treaty Series, Vol. 333, p. 3 and Vol. 437, p. 367.

(c) If within one month from the date of their appointment the arbitrators are unable to agree on the chairman of the arbitration tribunal such chairman shall upon the request of either Party be appointed by the President of the International Court of Justice.

(d) If the President of the International Court of Justice is prevented from acting upon a request under sub-paragraph (b) or sub-paragraph (c) of the present paragraph or if the President is a national of either Party the Vice-President shall make the appointment. If the Vice-President is prevented or if he is a national of either Party the appointment shall be made by the seniormost member of the International Court of Justice who is not a national of either Party.

(e) Unless the Parties otherwise decide, the arbitration tribunal shall determine its own rules of procedure.

(f) The arbitration tribunal shall take its decisions by a majority of votes. Such decisions shall be binding upon the Parties and shall be carried out by them.

Article 12

The provisions of the present Treaty shall remain in force also in the event of a conflict arising between the Parties without prejudice to the right of taking such temporary measures as are permitted under international law and are indispensable for assuring a supervision of investments. Measures of this kind shall be repealed not later than the date of termination of the conflict, irrespective of whether or not diplomatic relations have been re-established.

Article 13

The present Treaty shall also apply to *Land* Berlin, provided that the Government of the Federal Republic of Germany has not made a contrary declaration to the Government of Pakistan within three months from the entry into force of the present Treaty.

Article 14

(1) The present Treaty shall be ratified and the instruments of ratification shall be exchanged as soon as possible.

(2) The present Treaty shall enter into force one month after the date of exchange of the instruments of ratification. It shall remain in force for a period of ten years and shall continue in force thereafter for an unlimited period unless notice of termination is given in writing by either Party one year before its expiry. After the expiry of the period of ten years, the present Treaty may be terminated at any time by either Party giving one year's notice.

(3) In respect of investments made prior to the date of expiry of the present Treaty, the provisions of Articles 1 to 13 shall continue to be effective for a further period of ten years from the date of expiry of the present Treaty.

DONE at Bonn on the twenty fifth day of November in the year nineteen hundred and fifty nine in duplicate, in the German and English languages, both texts being equally authentic.

For the Federal Republic of Germany:
VON BRENTANO

For Pakistan:
S. A. HASNIE

III-5

Agreement between the Government of the People's Republic of China and the Government of Australia on the Reciprocal Encouragement and Protection of Investments

Date   11 July 1988
In force 26 September 1988
Source   1988 UNTS 26169
Link   <http://treaties.un.org/doc/Publication/UNTS/Volume%201514/volume-1514-I-26169-English.pdf>

The Government of the People's Republic of China and the Government of Australia (hereinafter referred to as the Contracting Parties),

Recognising the importance of promoting the flow of capital for economic activity and development and aware of its role in expanding economic relations and technical co-operation between them, particularly with respect to investment by nationals of one Contracting Party in the territory of the other Contracting Party;

Considering that investment relations should be promoted and economic co-operation strengthened in accordance with the internationally accepted principles of mutual respect for sovereignty, equality, mutual benefit, non-discrimination and mutual confidence;

Acknowledging that investments of nationals of one Contracting Party in the territory of the other Contracting Party would be made within the framework of laws of that other Contracting Party; and

Recognising that pursuit of these objectives would be facilitated by a clear statement of principles relating to the protection of investments and associated activities, combined with rules designed to render more effective the application of these principles within the territories of the Contracting Parties,

Have agreed as follows:

Article I   Definitions

1. For the purposes of this Agreement:
    (a) "Company" means any corporation, association, partnership, trust or other legally recognised entity that is duly incorporated, constituted, set up, or otherwise duly organised:
        (i) Under the law of a Contracting Party; or
        (ii) Under the law of a third country and is owned or controlled by an entity described in paragraph (1)(a)(i) of this Article or by a natural person who is a citizen or permanent resident of a Contracting Party under its law;
        regardless of whether or not the entity is organised for pecuniary gain, privately or otherwise owned, or organised with limited or unlimited liability.
    (b) "Investment" means every kind of asset, owned, controlled or contributed by nationals of one Contracting Party and admitted by the other Contracting Party subject to its law and investment policies applicable from time to time and includes:

    (i) Tangible and intangible property, including rights, such as mortgages, liens and pledges;

    (ii) A company or shares of stock or other interests in a company or interests in the assets thereof;

    (iii) A claim to money or a claim to performance having economic value;

    (iv) Intellectual and industrial property rights, including rights with respect to copyright, patents, trademarks, trade names, industrial designs, trade secrets, know-how and goodwill;

    (v) Any rights conferred by law or under a contract permitted by law, including rights to engage in agriculture, forestry, fisheries and animal husbandry, rights to search for, extract or exploit natural resources and rights to manufacture, use and sell products; and

    (vi) Returns which are reinvested.

Any alteration of the form in which assets are invested or reinvested shall not affect their character as investments.

(*c*) "Law" includes regulations.

(*d*) "National" of a Contracting Party means a natural person who is a citizen or a permanent resident of a Contracting Party under its law or a company.

(*e*) "Return" means an amount derived from or associated with an investment, including profits, dividends, interest, capital gains, royalty payments, management or technical assistance fees, payments in kind and all other lawful income.

(*f*) "Activities associated with investments", subject to the law of the Contracting Party which has admitted the investment, includes the organisation, control, operation, maintenance and disposition of companies, branches, agencies, offices, factories or other facilities for the conduct of business; the making, performance and enforcement of contracts; the acquisition, use, protection and disposition of property of all kinds including industrial and intellectual property rights; and the borrowing of funds, the purchase and issuance of equity shares, and the purchase and sale of foreign exchange.

(*g*) "Territory" in relation to a Contracting Party includes the territorial sea, maritime zone or continental shelf where that Contracting Party exercises its sovereignty, sovereign rights or jurisdiction.

2. This Agreement shall not apply to a company organised under the law of a third country within the meaning of paragraph (1)(*a*)(ii) of this Article where the provisions of an investment protection agreement with that country have already been invoked in respect of the same matter.

3. This Agreement shall not apply to a person who is a permanent resident but not a citizen of a Contracting Party where:

    (*a*) The provisions of an investment protection agreement between the other Contracting Party and the country of which the person is a citizen have already been invoked in respect of the same matter; or

    (*b*) The person is a citizen of the other Contracting Party.

Article II Encouragement and admission of investments

1. Each Contracting Party shall encourage and promote investments in its territory by nationals of the other Contracting Party and shall, in accordance with its law and investment policies applicable from time to time, admit investments.

2. Each Contracting Party reserves the right to refuse to admit the investments of any company of the other Contracting Party if nationals of any third country control such company, or if it has no substantial business activities in the territory of that other Contracting Party.

3. This Agreement shall not affect the right of a Contracting Party to allow or prohibit the making of investments within its territory by nationals of a third country.

4. This Agreement shall not prevent a national of one Contracting Party from taking advantage of the provisions of any law or policy of the other Contracting Party which are more favourable than the provisions of this Agreement.

5. A company duly organised under the law of a Contracting Party shall not be treated as a national of the other Contracting Party, but any investments in that company by nationals of that other Contracting Party shall be protected by this Agreement.

Article III   Treatment of investments

A Contracting Party shall at all times:

(*a*) Ensure fair and equitable treatment in its own territory to investments and activities associated with such investments;

(*b*) Accord within its territory protection and security to investments and activities associated with investments and, without prejudice to its law, shall not impair by unreasonable or discriminatory measures the management, maintenance, use, enjoyment or disposal of investments; and

(*c*) Treat investments and activities associated with investments in its own territory, including compensation under Article VIII and transfers under Article X, on a basis no less favourable than that accorded to investments and activities associated with investments of nationals of any third country, provided that a Contracting Party shall not be obliged to extend to investments and activities associated with investments any treatment, preference or privilege resulting from:

  (i) Any customs union, economic union, free trade area or regional economic integration agreement to which the Contracting Party belongs; or

  (ii) The provisions of a double taxation agreement with a third country.

Article IV   Entry and sojourn of personnel

1. A Contracting Party shall, subject to its law and policies applicable from time to time relating to the entry and sojourn of non-citizens, permit natural persons who are nationals of the other Contracting Party and personnel employed by companies of that other Contracting Party to enter and remain in its territory for the purpose of engaging in activities associated with investments.

2. Subject to paragraph 1 of this Article, nationals of one Contracting Party, who have made investments in the territory of the other Contracting Party, shall be permitted by that other Contracting Party to engage within its territory key technical and managerial personnel of their choice regardless of citizenship.

Article V   Settlement of disputes between nationals of the Contracting Parties

A Contracting Party shall in accordance with its law:

(*a*) Provide nationals of the other Contracting Party who have made investments within its territory and personnel employed by them for activities associated with investments full access to its competent judicial or administrative bodies in order to afford means of asserting claims and enforcing rights in respect of disputes with its own nationals;

(*b*) Permit its nationals to select means of their choice to settle disputes relating to investments and activities associated with investments with the nationals of the other Contracting Party, including arbitration conducted in a third country; and

(*c*) Provide for the recognition and enforcement of any resulting judgments or awards.

Article VI   Transparency of laws

Each Contracting Party shall, with a view to promoting the understanding of its laws and policies that pertain to or affect investments in its territory of nationals of the other Contracting Party:

(*a*) Make such laws and policies public and readily accessible;

(*b*) If requested, provide copies of specified laws and policies to the other Contracting Party; and

(*c*) If requested, consult with the other Contracting Party with a view to explaining specified laws and policies.

Article VII   Limitations on immunity

Any question arising in relation to an investment or activity associated with an investment of a national of either Contracting Party concerning immunity from the jurisdiction of the Courts in any proceeding, the procedure for service of initiating process or immunity from execution shall be resolved in accordance with the law of the Contracting Party which has admitted the investment.

Article VIII   Expropriation and nationalisation

1. A Contracting Party shall not take measures of expropriation or nationalisation or other measures having a similar effect relating to any investment unless the measures are in the public interest, non discriminatory, in accordance with the law of the Contracting Party which has admitted the investment and against reasonable compensation.

2. The compensation referred to in paragraph 1 of this Article shall be computed on the basis of the market value of the investment immediately before the measures became public knowledge. Where the market value cannot be readily ascertained, the compensation shall be determined in accordance with generally recognised principles of valuation and equitable principles taking into account the capital invested, depreciation, capital already repatriated, replacement value and other relevant factors. The compensation shall include interest at a reasonable rate from the date the measures were taken to the date of payment, shall be paid without undue delay, shall be freely convertible and shall be freely transferable between the territories of the Contracting Parties at the average of the daily exchange rates, determined on each of those days in accordance with the law of the Contracting Party which has admitted the investment, over the six months immediately prior to the taking of the measures.

Article IX   War or armed conflict

Nationals of a Contracting Party, whose investments suffer losses in the territory of the other Contracting Party owing to war or other armed conflict, insurrection, revolt, or other similar events, shall be accorded treatment by the other Contracting Party no less favourable than that accorded to nationals of any third country, should it adopt any measures relating to such losses.

Article X   Transfers

1. A Contracting Party shall, when requested, permit, subject to its law and policies, all funds of a national of the other Contracting Party related to an investment or activities associated with an investment in its territory, and earnings and other assets of personnel engaged from abroad in connection with an investment, to be transferred freely and without undue delay. Such funds include the following:

   (*a*) The initial capital plus any additional contributions used to maintain or expand the investment;

   (*b*) Returns;

   (*c*) Fees, including payments in connection with intellectual and industrial property rights;

   (*d*) Receipts from the whole or partial sale, divestment or liquidation of the investment;

   (*e*) Payments made pursuant to a loan agreement; and

   (*f*) Capital accretions.

2. The transfers abroad of such funds and the earnings of personnel shall be permitted in freely convertible currencies as classified by the International Monetary Fund and shall be made at the exchange rate determined in accordance with the law of the Contracting Party which has admitted the investment on the date of transfer.

3. Either Contracting Party may protect the rights of creditors, or ensure the satisfaction of judgments in adjudicatory proceedings, through the equitable, nondiscriminatory and good faith application of its law.

Article XI   Undertakings given to investors
A Contracting Party shall, subject to its law, adhere to any written undertakings given by a competent authority to a national of the other Contracting Party with regard to an investment in accordance with its law and the provisions of this Agreement.

Article XII   Settlement of disputes between one Contracting Party and a national of the other Contracting Party relating to investments
1. In the event of a dispute between a Contracting Party and a national of the other Contracting Party relating to an investment or an activity associated with an investment, the parties to the dispute shall initially seek to resolve the dispute by consultations and negotiations.
2. If the dispute has not been settled within three months from the date either party gave notice in writing to the other concerning the dispute, either party may take the following action:
    (a) In accordance with the law of the Contracting Party which has admitted the investment, initiate proceedings before its competent judicial or administrative bodies; and
    (b) Where the parties agree or where the dispute relates to the amount of compensation payable under Article VIII, submit the dispute to an Arbitral Tribunal constituted in accordance with Annex A of this Agreement.
3. The action referred to in paragraph 2 of this Article shall be without prejudice to the right of the parties to seek assistance with regard to the dispute from any competent government agency of the Contracting Party which has admitted the investment.
4. In the event that both the People's Republic of China and Australia become party to the 1965 Convention on the Settlement of Investment Disputes Between States and Nationals of Other States, a dispute may be submitted to the International Centre for the Settlement of Investment Disputes for resolution in accordance with the terms on which the Contracting Party which has admitted the investment is a party to the Convention.
5. In any proceedings involving a dispute relating to an investment or an activity associated with an investment, a Contracting Party shall not assert, as a defence, counterclaim, right of set-off or otherwise, that the national concerned has received or will receive, pursuant to an insurance or guarantee contract, indemnification or other compensation for all or part of any alleged loss. Nevertheless, a national of a Contracting Party involved in such a dispute shall not be entitled to compensation for more than the value, as determined in accordance with paragraph 2 of Article VIII, of the investment which is the subject of the dispute, taking into account all sources of compensation within the territory of the Contracting Party liable to pay compensation.

Article XIII   Settlement of disputes between Contracting Parties
1. The Contracting Parties shall consult when necessary on matters concerning the operation of this Agreement.
2. The Contracting Parties shall endeavour to resolve any dispute between them on the interpretation or application of this Agreement by prompt and friendly negotiations and consultations. If a dispute is not resolved by such means within sixty days of one Contracting Party seeking in writing such negotiations or consultations, it shall be submitted at the request of either Contracting Party to an Arbitral Tribunal established in accordance with the provisions of Annex B of this Agreement, or, by agreement, to any other international tribunal.

Article XIV   Entry into force, duration and termination
1. This Agreement shall enter into force on signature. It shall remain in force for a period of ten years and thereafter shall remain in force indefinitely, unless terminated in accordance with paragraph 3 of this Article.

2. This Agreement shall apply to investments made after 21 December 1972.

3. At the end of the first period of ten years referred to in paragraph 1 of this Article and thereafter at any time either Contracting Party may terminate this Agreement by giving one year's written notice to the other Contracting Party.

4. Notwithstanding its termination in accordance with paragraph 3 of this Article, this Agreement shall continue to apply, for a further period of ten years from the date of its termination, to investments made or acquired prior to the date of its termination.

IN WITNESS WHEREOF the undersigned, being duly authorised thereto by their respective Governments, have signed this Agreement.

DONE in duplicate at Beijing on the eleventh day of July, 1988 in the Chinese and English languages, both texts being equally authentic.

ANNEX A

1. The Arbitral Tribunal referred to in paragraph 2(*b*) of Article XII shall consist of 3 persons appointed as follows: each party to the dispute shall appoint one arbitrator; the arbitrators appointed by the parties to the dispute shall, within 30 days of the appointment of the last of their number, by agreement, select an arbitrator as Chairman who is a national of a third country which has diplomatic relations with both Contracting Parties.

2. If, within 60 days after a party has given notice in writing instituting the arbitration proceedings, agreement has not been reached on a Chairman of the Arbitral Tribunal, either party to the dispute may request the President of the International Bank for Reconstruction and Development to make the appointment.

3. If a party to the dispute, receiving notice in writing from the other party of the institution of arbitration proceedings and the appointment of an arbitrator, shall fail to appoint its arbitrator within 30 days of receiving notice from the other party, such arbitrator shall be appointed by the Chairman of the Arbitral Tribunal after the Chairman is appointed.

4. In case any arbitrator appointed as provided in this Annex shall resign, die or otherwise become unable to perform his functions as an arbitrator, a successor arbitrator shall be appointed in the same manner as prescribed for the appointment of the original arbitrator and his successor shall have all the powers and duties of the original arbitrator.

5. The Arbitral Tribunal shall, subject to the provisions of any agreement between the parties to the dispute, determine its procedure by reference to the rules of procedure contained in the 1965 Convention on the Settlement of Investment Disputes Between States and Nationals of Other States.

6. The Arbitral Tribunal shall decide all questions relating to its competence.

7. Before the Arbitral Tribunal makes a decision it may at any stage of the proceedings propose to the parties that the dispute be settled amicably. The Arbitral Tribunal shall reach its award by majority vote taking into account the provisions of this Agreement, any agreement between the parties to the dispute and the relevant domestic law of the Contracting Party which has admitted the investment.

8. An award shall be final and binding and shall be enforced in the territory of each Contracting Party in accordance with its law.

9. Each party to the dispute shall bear the costs of its appointed arbitrator. The cost of the Chairman and other expenses associated with the conduct of the arbitration shall be borne equally by the parties.

III-6

Treaty between United States of America and the Argentine Republic Concerning the Reciprocal Encouragement and Protection of Investment

Date   14 November 1991
In force   20 October 1994
Source   31 ILM 128 (1992)
Link   <http://www.unctad.org/sections/dite/iia/docs/bits/argentina_us.pdf>

The United States of America and the Argentine Republic, hereinafter referred to as the Parties;

Desiring to promote greater economic cooperation between them, with respect to investment by nationals and companies of one Party in the territory of the other Party;

Recognizing that agreement upon the treatment to be accorded such investment will stimulate the flow of private capital and the economic development of the Parties;

Agreeing that fair and equitable treatment of investment is desirable in order to maintain a stable framework for investment and maximum effective use of economic resources;

Recognizing that the development of economic and business ties can contribute to the well-being of workers in both Parties and promote respect for internationally recognized worker rights; and

having resolved to conclude a Treaty concerning the encouragement and reciprocal protection of investment;

Have agreed as follows:

Article I

1. For the purposes of this Treaty,
    a) "investment" means every kind of investment in the territory of one Party owned or controlled directly or indirectly by nationals or companies of the other Party, such as equity, debt, and service and investment contracts; and includes without limitation:
        (i) tangible and intangible property, including rights, such as mortgages, liens and pledges;
        (ii) a company or shares of stock or other interests in a company or interests in the assets thereof;
        (iii) a claim to money or a claim to performance having economic value and directly related to an investment;
        (iv) intellectual property which includes, inter alia, rights relating to: literary and artistic works, including sound recordings, inventions in all fields of human endeavor, industrial designs, semiconductor mask works, trade secrets, know-how, and confidential business information, and trademarks, service marks, and trade names; and
        (v) any right conferred by law or contract, and any licenses and permits pursuant to law;
    b) "company" of a Party means any kind of corporation, company, association, state enterprise, or other organization, legally constituted under the laws and regulations of a

Party or a political subdivision thereof whether or not organized for pecuniary gain, and whether privately or governmentally owned;

c) "national" of a Party means a natural person who is a national of a Party under its applicable law;

d) "return" means an amount derived from or associated with an investment, including profit; dividend; interest; capita gain; royalty payment; management, technical assistance or other fee; or returns in kind;

e) "associated activities" include the organization, control, operation, maintenance and disposition of companies, branches, agencies, offices, factories or other facilities for the conduct of business; the making, performance and enforcement of contracts; the acquisition, use, protection and disposition of property of all kinds including intellectual and industrial property rights; and the borrowing of funds, the purchase, issuance, and sale of equity shares and other securities, and the purchase of foreign exchange for imports.

f) "territory" means the territory of the United States or the Argentine Republic, including the territorial sea established in accordance with international law as reflected in the 1982 United Nations Convention on the Law of the Sea. This Treaty also applies in the seas and seabed adjacent to the territorial sea in which the United States or the Argentine Republic has sovereign rights or jurisdiction in accordance with international law as reflected in the 1982 United Nations Convention on the Law of the Sea.

2. Each Party reserves the right to deny to any company of the other Party the advantages of this Treaty if (a) nationals of any third country, or nationals of such Party, control such company and the company has no substantial business activities in the territory of the other Party, or (b) the company is controlled by nationals of a third country with which the denying Party does not maintain normal economic relations.

3. Any alteration of the form in which assets are invested or reinvested shall not affect their character as investment.

Article II

1. Each Party shall permit and treat investment, and activities associated therewith, on a basis no less favorable than that accorded in like situations to investment or associated activities of its own nationals or companies, or of nationals or companies of any third country, whichever is the more favorable, subject to the right of each Party to make or maintain exceptions falling within one of the sectors or matters listed in the Protocol to this Treaty. Each Party agrees to notify the other Party before or on the date of entry into force of this Treaty of all such laws and regulations of which it is aware concerning the sectors or matters listed in the Protocol. Moreover, each Party agrees to notify the other of any future exception with respect to the sectors or matters listed in the Protocol, and to limit such exceptions to a minimum. Any future exception by either Party shall not apply to investment existing in that sector or matter at the time the exception becomes effective. The treatment accorded pursuant to any exceptions shall, unless specified otherwise in the Protocol, be not less favorable than that accorded in like situations to investments and associated activities of nationals or companies of any third country.

2. a) Investment shall at all times be accorded fair and equitable treatment, shall enjoy full protection and security and shall in no case be accorded treatment less than that required by international law.

   b) Neither Party shall in any way impair by arbitrary or discriminatory measures the management, operation, maintenance, use, enjoyment, acquisition, expansion, or disposal of investments. For the purposes of dispute resolution under Articles VII and VIII, a measure may be arbitrary or discriminatory notwithstanding the opportunity to review such measure in the courts or administrative tribunals of a Party.

c) Each Party shall observe any obligation it may have entered into with regard to investments.

3. Subject to the laws relating to the entry and sojourn of aliens, nationals of either Party shall be permitted to enter and to remain in the territory of the other Party for the purpose of establishing, developing, administering or advising on the operation of an investment to which they, or a company of the first Party that employs them, have committed or are in the process of committing a substantial amount of capital or other resources.

4. Companies which are legally constituted under the applicable laws or regulations of one Party, and which are investments, shall be permitted to engage top managerial personnel of their choice, regardless of nationality.

5. Neither Party shall impose performance requirements as a condition of establishment, expansion or maintenance of investments, which require or enforce commitments to export goods produced, or which specify that goods or services must be purchased locally, or which impose any other similar requirements.

6. Each Party shall provide effective means of asserting claims and enforcing rights with respect to investments, investment agreements, and investment authorizations.

7. Each Party shall make public all laws, regulations, administrative practices and procedures, and adjudicatory decisions that pertain to or affect investments.

8. The treatment accorded by the United States of America to investments and associated activities of nationals and companies of the Argentine Republic under the provisions of this Article shall in any State, Territory or possession of the United States of America be no less favorable than the treatment accorded therein to investments and associated activities of nationals of the United States of America resident in, and companies legally constituted under the laws and regulations of, other States, Territories or possessions of the United States of America.

9. The most favored nation provisions of this Article shall not apply to advantages accorded by either Party to nationals or companies of any third country by virtue of that Party's binding obligations that derive from full membership in a regional customs union or free trade area, whether such an arrangement is designated as a customs union, free trade area, common market or otherwise.

Article III

This Treaty shall not preclude either Party from prescribing laws and regulations in connection with the admission of investments made in its territory by nationals or companies of the other Party or with the conduct of associated activities, provided, however, that such laws and regulations shall not impair the substance of any of the rights set forth in this Treaty.

Article IV

1. Investments shall not be expropriated or nationalized either directly or indirectly through measures tantamount to expropriation or nationalization ("expropriation") except for a public purpose; in a non-discriminatory manner; upon payment of prompt, adequate and effective compensation; and in accordance with due process of law and the general principles of treatment provided for in Article II (2). Compensation shall be equivalent to the fair market value of the expropriated investment immediately before the expropriatory action was taken or became known, whichever is earlier; be paid without delay; include interest at a commercially reasonable rate from the date of expropriation; be fully realizable; and be freely transferable at the prevailing market rate of exchange on the date of expropriation.

2. A national or company of either Party that asserts that all or part of its investment has been expropriated shall have a right to prompt review by the appropriate judicial or administrative authorities of the other Party to determine whether any such expropriation has occurred and,

if so, whether such expropriation, and any compensation therefore, conforms to the provisions of this Treaty and the principles of international law.

3. Nationals or companies of either Party whose investments suffer losses in the territory of the other Party owing to war or other armed conflict, revolution, state of national emergency, insurrection, civil disturbance or other similar events shall be accorded treatment by such other Party no less favorable than that accorded to its own nationals or companies or to nationals or companies of any third country, whichever is the more favorable treatment, as regards any measures it adopts in relation to such losses.

Article V

1. Each Party shall permit all transfers related to an investment to be made freely and without delay into and out of its territory. Such transfers include: (a) returns; (b) compensation pursuant to Article IV; (c) payments arising out of an investment dispute; (d) payments made under a contract, including amortization of principal and accrued interest payments made pursuant to a loan agreement directly related to an investment; (e) proceeds from the sale or liquidation of all or any part of an investment; and (f) additional contributions to capital for the maintenance or development of an investment.

2. Except as provided in Article IV paragraph 1, transfers shall be made in a freely usable currency at the prevailing market rate of exchange on the date of transfer with respect to spot transactions in the currency to be transferred. The free transfer shall take place in accordance with the procedures established by each Party; such procedures shall not impair the rights set forth in this Treaty.

3. Notwithstanding the provisions of paragraphs 1 and 2, either Party may maintain laws and regulations (a) requiring reports of currency transfer; and (b) imposing income taxes by such means as a withholding tax applicable to dividends or other transfers. Furthermore, either Party may protect the rights of creditors, or ensure the satisfaction of judgments in adjudicatory proceedings, through the equitable, nondiscriminatory and good faith application of its law.

Article VI

The Parties agree to consult promptly, on the request of either, to resolve any disputes in connection with the Treaty, or to discuss any matter relating to the interpretation or application of the Treaty.

Article VII

1. For purposes of this Article, an investment dispute is a dispute between a Party and a national or company of the other Party arising out of or relating to (a) an investment agreement between that Party and such national or company; (b) an investment authorization granted by that Party's foreign investment authority (if any such authorization exists) to such national or company; or (c) an alleged breach of any right conferred or created by this Treaty with respect to an investment.

2. In the event of an investment dispute, the parties to the dispute should initially seek a resolution through consultation and negotiation. If the dispute cannot be settled amicably, the national or company concerned may choose to submit the dispute for resolution:
    (a) to the courts or administrative tribunals of the Party that is a party to the dispute; or
    (b) in accordance with any applicable, previously agreed dispute-settlement procedures; or
    (c) in accordance with the terms of paragraph 3.

3. (a) Provided that the national or company concerned has not submitted the dispute for resolution under paragraph 2 (a) or (b) and that six months have elapsed from the date on which the dispute arose, the national or company concerned may choose to consent in writing to the submission of the dispute for settlement by binding arbitration:

    (i) to the International Centre for the Settlement of Investment Disputes ("Centre") established by the Convention on the Settlement of Investment Disputes between States and Nationals of other States, done at Washington, March 18, 1965 ("ICSID Convention"), provided that the Party is a party to such convention: or

    (ii) to the Additional Facility of the Centre, if the Centre is not available; or

    (iii) in accordance with the Arbitration Rules of the United Nations Commission on International Trade Law (UNICTRAL): or

    (iv) to any other arbitration institution, or in accordance with any other arbitration rules, as may be mutually agreed between the parties to the dispute.

  (b) Once the national or company concerned has so consented, either party to the dispute may initiate arbitration in accordance with the choice so specified in the consent.

4. Each Party hereby consents to the submission of any investment dispute for settlement by binding arbitration in accordance with the choice specified in the written consent of the national or company under paragraph 3. Such consent, together with the written consent of the national or company when given under paragraph 3 shall satisfy the requirement for:

  (a) written consent of the parties to the dispute for purposes of Chapter II of the ICSID Convention (Jurisdiction of the Centre) and for purposes of the Additional Facility Rules; and

  (b) an "agreement in writing" for purposes of Article II of the United Nations Convention on the Recognition and Enforcement of Foreign Arbitral Awards, done at New York, June 10, 1958 ("New York Convention").

5. Any arbitration under paragraph 3(a)(ii), (iii) or (iv) of this Article shall be held in a state that is a party to the New York Convention.

6. Any arbitral award rendered pursuant to this Article shall be final and binding on the parties to the dispute. Each Party undertakes to carry out without delay the provisions of any such award and to provide in its territory for its enforcement.

7. In any proceeding involving an investment dispute, a Party shall not assert, as a defense, counterclaim, right of set-off or otherwise, that the national or company concerned has received or will receive, pursuant to an insurance or guarantee contract, indemnification or other compensation for all or part of its alleged damages.

8. For purposes of an arbitration held under paragraph 3 of this Article, any company legally constituted under the applicable laws and regulations of a Party or a political subdivision thereof but that, immediately before the occurrence of the event or events giving rise to the dispute, was an investment of nationals or companies of the other Party, shall be treated as a national or company of such other Party in accordance with Article 25(2)(b) of the ICSID Convention.

Article VIII

1. Any dispute between the Parties concerning the interpretation or application of the Treaty which is not resolved through consultations or other diplomatic channels, shall be submitted, upon the request of either Party, to an arbitral tribunal for binding decision in accordance with the applicable rules of international law. In the absence of an agreement by the Parties to the contrary, the arbitration rules of the United Nations Commission on International Trade Law (UNCITRAL), except to the extent modified by the Parties or by the arbitrators, shall govern.

2. Within two months of receipt of a request, each Party shall appoint an arbitrator. The two arbitrators shall select a third arbitrator as Chairman, who is a national of a third State. The UNCITRAL Rules for appointing members of three member panels shall apply mutatis mutandis to the appointment of the arbitral panel except that the appointing authority referenced in those rules shall be the Secretary General of the Permanent Court of Arbitration.

3. Unless otherwise agreed, all submissions shall be made and all hearings shall be completed within six months of the date of selection of the third arbitrator, and the Tribunal shall render its decisions within two months of the date of the final submissions or the date of the closing of the hearings, whichever is later.

4. Expenses incurred by the Chairman, the other arbitrators, and other costs of the proceedings shall be paid for equally by the Parties.

Article IX

The provisions of Article VII and VIII shall not apply to a dispute arising (a) under the export credit, guarantee or insurance programs of the Export-Import Bank of the United States or (b) under other official credit, guarantee or insurance arrangements pursuant to which the Parties have agreed to other means of settling disputes.

Article X

This Treaty shall not derogate from:

(a) laws and regulations, administrative practices or procedures, or administrative or adjudicatory decisions of either Party;

(b) international legal obligations; or

(c) obligations assumed by either Party, including those contained in an investment agreement or an investment authorization,

that entitle investments or associated activities to treatment more favorable than that accorded by this Treaty in like situations.

Article XI

This Treaty shall not preclude the application by either Party of measures necessary for the maintenance of public order, the fulfillment of its obligations with respect to the maintenance or restoration of international peace or security, or the Protection of its own essential security interests.

Article XII

1. With respect to its tax policies, each Party should strive to accord fairness and equity in the treatment of investment of nationals and companies of the other Party.

2. Nevertheless, the provisions of this Treaty, and in particular Article VII and VIII, shall apply to matters of taxation only with respect to the following:
   (a) expropriation, pursuant to Article IV;
   (b) transfers, pursuant to Article V; or
   (c) the observance and enforcement of terms of an investment agreement or authorization as referred to in Article VII(l)(a) or (b),

   to the extent they are not subject to the dispute settlement provisions of a Convention for the avoidance of double taxation between the two Parties, or have been raised under such settlement provisions and are not resolved within a reasonable period of time.

Article XIII

This Treaty shall apply to the political subdivisions of the Parties.

Article XIV

1. This Treaty shall enter into force thirty days after the date of exchange of instruments of ratification. It shall remain in force for a period of ten years and shall continue in force unless terminated in accordance with paragraph 2 of this Article. It shall apply to investments existing at the time of entry into force as well as to investments made or acquired thereafter.

2. Either Party may, by giving one year's written notice to the other Party, terminate this Treaty at the end of the initial ten year period or at any time thereafter.

3. With respect to investments made or acquired prior to the date of termination of this Treaty and to which this Treaty otherwise applies, the provisions of all of the other Articles of this Treaty shall thereafter continue to be effective for a further period of ten years from such date of termination.

4. The Protocol shall form an integral part of the Treaty.

IN WITNESS WHEREOF, the respective plenipotentiaries have signed this Treaty.

DONE in duplicate at Washington on the fourteenth day of November, 1991, in the English and Spanish languages, both texts being equally authentic.

PROTOCOL

1. During dispute settlement proceedings pursuant to Article VII, a party may be required to produce evidence of ownership or control consistent with Article I(1)(a).

2. With reference to Article II, paragraph 1, the United States reserves the right to make or maintain limited exceptions to national treatment in the following sectors:

   air transportation; ocean and coastal shipping; banking; insurance; energy and power production; custom house brokers; ownership and operation of broadcast or common carrier radio and television stations; ownership of real property; ownership of shares in the Communications Satellite Corporation; the provision of common carrier telephone and telegraph services; the provision of submarine cable services; use of land and natural resources.

3. With reference to Article II, paragraph 1, the United States reserves the right to make or maintain limited exceptions to national treatment with respect to certain programs involving government grants, loans, and insurance.

4. With reference to Article II, paragraph 1, the United States reserves the right to make or maintain limited exceptions to national and most favored nation treatment in the following sectors, with respect to which treatment will be based on reciprocity:

   mining on the public domain; maritime services and maritime-related services; primary dealership in United States government securities.

5. With reference to Article II, paragraph 1, the Argentine Republic reserves the right to make or maintain limited exceptions to national treatment in the following sectors:

   real estate in the Border Areas; air transportation; shipbuilding; nuclear energy centers; uranium mining; insurance; mining;* fishing.

6. The Parties understand that, with respect to rights reserved in Article XI of the Treaty, "obligations with respect to the maintenance or restoration of international peace or security" means obligations under the Charter of the United Nations.

7. The Parties acknowledge and agree that, to the extent of any conflict or inconsistency between the terms of this Treaty, and the terms of the Treaty of Friendship, Commerce, and Navigation between the Parties, entered into force December 20, 1854 (the "FCN Treaty"), the terms of this Treaty shall supersede the terms of the FCN Treaty, and shall control the resolution of such conflict.

8. The Parties confirm their mutual understanding that the provisions of this Treaty do not bind either Party in relation to any act or fact which took place or any situation which ceased to exist before the date of the entry into force of this Treaty.

9. Notwithstanding Article II(5) and in accordance with the terms of this paragraph, the Government of the Argentine Republic may maintain, but not intensify, existing perform-

---

* Note by the Editors: By subsequent exchange of notes, the parties agreed to delete the term 'mining' from the list of the sectors mentioned in Section 5 of the Protocol. The notes are available on the UNCTAD website mentioned at the outset of this document.

ance requirements in the automotive industry. The Government of the Argentine Republic shall exert best efforts to eliminate all such requirements within the shortest possible period, and shall ensure their elimination within eight years of the date of the entry into force of this Treaty. The Government of the Argentine Republic shall further ensure that such performance requirements are applied in a manner which does not place existing investments at a competitive disadvantage against new entrants in this industry. The Parties shall consult at the request of either on any matter concerning the implementation of these undertakings. For the purposes of this paragraph, "existing" means extant at the time of signature of this Treaty.

10. The Parties note that the Argentine Republic has had and may have in the future a debt-equity conversion program under which nationals or companies of the United States may choose to invest in the Argentine Republic through the purchase of debt at a discount.

The Parties agree that the rights provided in Article V, paragraph 1, with respect to the transfer of returns and of proceeds from the sale or liquidation of all or any part of an investment, remain or may be, as such rights would apply to that part of an investment financed through a debt-equity conversion, modified by the terms of any debt-equity conversion agreement between a national or company of the United States and the Government of the Argentine Republic, or any agency or instrumentality thereof.

The transfer of returns and of proceeds from the sale or liquidation of all or any part of an investment shall in no case be on terms less favorable than those accorded, in like circumstances, to nationals or companies of the Argentine Republic or any third country, whichever is more favorable.

11. The Parties note with satisfaction that the Argentine Republic is engaged in a process of privatization of various industries, including public utilities. They agree that they will undertake their best efforts, including through consultations, to avoid any misinterpretation regarding the scope of Article II(5) that would adversely affect this privatization process.

III-7

Agreement between Canada and the Republic of Peru for the Promotion and Protection of Investments

Date   14 November 2006
In force 20 June 2007
Source [2007] CATSer 9
Link   <http://www.commonlii.org/ca/other/treaties/CATSer/2007/9.html>

CANADA AND THE REPUBLIC OF PERU, hereinafter referred to as the "Parties",

RECOGNIZING that the promotion and the protection of investments of investors of one Party in the territory of the other Party will be conducive to the stimulation of mutually beneficial business activity, to the development of economic cooperation between them and to the promotion of sustainable development,

HAVE AGREED AS FOLLOWS:

SECTION A   DEFINITIONS

Article 1   Definitions

For the purpose of this Agreement:

administrative ruling of general application means an administrative ruling or interpretation that applies to all persons and fact situations that fall generally within its ambit and that establishes a norm of conduct, but does not include:

(i)   a determination or ruling made in an administrative or quasi-judicial proceeding that applies to a particular person, good or service of the other Party in a specific case; or

(ii) a ruling that adjudicates with respect to a particular act or practice.

affiliate a person is an affiliate of another person when:

(i)   directly or indirectly, it controls or is controlled by that other person; or

(ii) it and the other person are both controlled, directly or indirectly, by the same person;

Commission means the body established by the Parties under Article 50;

confidential information means business confidential information and information that is privileged or otherwise protected from disclosure;

covered investment means, with respect to a Party, an investment in its territory of an investor of the other Party existing on the date of entry into force of this Agreement, as well as investments made or acquired thereafter;

cultural industries means persons engaged in any of the following activities:

(i)   the publication, distribution, or sale of books, magazines, periodicals or newspapers in print or machine readable form but not including the sole activity of printing or typesetting any of the foregoing;

(ii) the production, distribution, sale or exhibition of film or video recordings;

(iii) the production, distribution, sale or exhibition of audio or video music recordings;

(iv) the publication, distribution, sale or exhibition of music in print or machine readable form; or

(v) radio communications in which the transmissions are intended for direct reception by the general public, and all radio, television or cable broadcasting undertakings and all satellite programming and broadcast network services.

days means calendar days, including weekends and holidays;

designate means to establish, designate or authorize, or to expand the scope of a monopoly to cover an additional good or service after the date of entry into force of the Agreement;

disputing investor means an investor that makes a claim under Section C;

disputing Party means a Party against which a claim is made under Section C;

disputing party means the disputing investor or the disputing Party;

enterprise means:

(i) any entity constituted or organized under applicable law, whether or not for profit, whether privately-owned or governmentally-owned, including any corporation, trust, partnership, sole proprietorship, joint venture or other association; and

(ii) a branch of any such entity;

enterprise of a Party means an enterprise constituted or organized under the law of a Party, and a branch located in the territory of a Party and carrying out business activities there;

equity or debt securities includes voting and non-voting shares, bonds, convertible debentures, stock options and warrants;

existing means in effect on the date of entry into force of this Agreement;

financial institution means any financial intermediary or other enterprise that is authorized to do business and regulated or supervised as a financial institution under the law of the Party in whose territory it is located;

financial service means a service of a financial nature, including insurance, and a service incidental or auxiliary to a service of a financial nature;

government monopoly means a monopoly that is owned, or controlled through ownership interests, by the national government of a Party or by another such monopoly;

ICSID means the International Centre for Settlement of Investment Disputes;

ICSID Convention means the *Convention on the Settlement of Investment Disputes between States and Nationals of other States*, done at Washington, March 18, 1965;

intellectual property rights means copyright and related rights, trademark rights, rights in geographical indications, rights in industrial designs, patent rights, rights in layout designs of integrated circuits, rights in relation to protection of undisclosed information, and plant breeders' rights.

Inter-American Convention means the *Inter-American Convention on International Commercial Arbitration*, done at Panama, January 30, 1975;

investment means:

(I) an enterprise;

(II) an equity security of an enterprise;

(III) a debt security of an enterprise
    (i) where the enterprise is an affiliate of the investor, or
    (ii) where the original maturity of the debt security is at least three years,

but does not include a debt security, regardless of original maturity, of a state enterprise;

(IV) a loan to an enterprise
  (i) where the enterprise is an affiliate of the investor, or
  (ii) where the original maturity of the loan is at least three years,
  but does not include a loan, regardless of original maturity, to a state enterprise;

(V) (i) notwithstanding subparagraphs (III) and (IV) above, a loan to or debt security issued by a financial institution is an investment only where the loan or debt security is treated as regulatory capital by the Party in whose territory the financial institution is located, and
  (ii) a loan granted by or debt security owned by a financial institution, other than a loan to or debt security of a financial institution referred to in (i), is not an investment; for greater certainty:
  (iii) a loan to, or debt security issued by, a Party or a state enterprise thereof is not an investment; and
  (iv) a loan granted by or debt security owned by a cross-border financial service provider, other than a loan to or debt security issued by a financial institution, is an investment if such loan or debt security meets the criteria for investments set out elsewhere in this Article;

(VI) an interest in an enterprise that entitles the owner to share in income or profits of the enterprise;

(VII) an interest in an enterprise that entitles the owner to share in the assets of that enterprise on dissolution, other than a debt security or a loan excluded from subparagraphs (III) (IV) or (V);

(VIII) real estate or other property, tangible or intangible, acquired in the expectation or used for the purpose of economic benefit or other business purposes; and

(IX) interests arising from the commitment of capital or other resources in the territory of a Party to economic activity in such territory, such as under
  (i) contracts involving the presence of an investor's property in the territory of the Party, including turnkey or construction contracts, or concessions, or
  (ii) contracts where remuneration depends substantially on the production, revenues or profits of an enterprise; but investment does not mean,

(X) claims to money that arise solely from
  (i) commercial contracts for the sale of goods or services by a national or enterprise in the territory of a Party to an enterprise in the territory of the other Party, or
  (ii) the extension of credit in connection with a commercial transaction, such as trade financing, other than a loan covered by subparagraphs (IV) or (V); and

(XI) any other claims to money, that do not involve the kinds of interests set out in subparagraphs (I) through (IX);

investment of an investor of a Party means an investment owned or controlled directly or indirectly by an investor of such Party;

investor of a Party[1] means
(i) in the case of Canada:
  (a) Canada or a state enterprise of Canada, or
  (b) a national or an enterprise of Canada, that seeks to make, is making or has made an investment; a natural person who is a dual citizen shall be deemed to be exclusively a citizen of the State of his or her dominant and effective citizenship; and

---

1 For greater certainty, it is understood that an investor "seeks to make an investment" only when the investor has taken concrete steps necessary to make said investment, such as when the investor has made an application for a permit or license authorizing the establishment of an investment.

(ii) in the case of the Republic of Peru:
    (a) a state enterprise of the Republic of Peru, or
    (b) a national or enterprise of the Republic of Peru; that seeks to make, is making or has made an investment; a natural person who is a dual citizen shall be deemed to be exclusively a citizen of the State of his or her dominant and effective citizenship;

investor of a non-Party[2] means an investor other than an investor of a Party, that seeks to make, is making, or has made an investment;

legal stability agreement means an agreement entered into by the national government of a Party and an investor of the other Party or a covered investment of such investor that accords certain benefits, including, but not limited to, a commitment to maintain the existing income tax regime during a specified time;

measure includes any law, regulation, procedure, requirement, or practice;

monopoly means an entity, including a consortium or government agency, that in any relevant market in the territory of a Party is designated as the sole provider or purchaser of a good or service, but does not include an entity that has been granted an exclusive intellectual property right solely by reason of such grant;

national means a natural person who is a citizen or permanent resident of a Party;

national government means:

(i) in respect of Canada, the federal level of government; and

(ii) in respect of the Republic of Peru, the national level of government;

New York Convention means the *United Nations Convention on the Recognition and Enforcement of Foreign Arbitral Awards*, done at New York, 10 June 1958;

non-disputing Party means a Party that is not a party to an investment dispute under Section C;

non-disputing party means a person of a Party, or a person of a non-Party with a significant presence in the territory of a Party, that is not a party to an investment dispute under Section C;

person means a natural person or an enterprise;

person of a Party means a national, or an enterprise of a Party;

public entity means a central bank or monetary authority of a Party, or any financial institution owned or controlled by a Party;

Secretary-General means the Secretary-General of ICSID;

state enterprise means an enterprise that is owned or controlled through ownership interests by a Party;

sub-national government means:

(i) in respect of Canada, provincial or local governments; and

(ii) in respect of the Republic of Peru, regional or local governments;

tax convention means a convention for the avoidance of double taxation or other international taxation agreement or arrangement;

taxation authorities means the following until notice in writing to the contrary is provided to the other Party:

(i) for Canada: the Assistant Deputy Minister, Tax Policy, of the Department of Finance Canada; and

(ii) for the Republic of Peru: the Vice Minister of Economy, the Ministry of Economy and Finance.

---

2 For greater certainty, it is understood that an investor "seeks to make an investment" only when the investor has taken concrete steps necessary to make said investment, such as when the investor has made an application for a permit or license authorizing the establishment of an investment.

territory means

(i) in respect of Canada:
    (a) the land territory of Canada, air space, internal waters and territorial sea of Canada;
    (b) those areas, including the exclusive economic zone and the seabed and subsoil, over which Canada exercises, in accordance with international law, sovereign rights or jurisdiction for the purpose of exploration and exploitation of the natural resources; and
    (c) artificial islands, installations and structures in the exclusive economic zone or on the continental shelf over which Canada has jurisdiction as a coastal state; and

(ii) in respect of the Republic of Peru, the land territory, the islands, the internal waters, as well as the airspace and the maritime domain which includes the sea adjacent to its coast, its seabed and subsoil, to a distance of 200 nautical miles measured from the baselines established by law, and the corresponding continental shelf, over which the Republic of Peru exercises sovereignty and jurisdiction in accordance with its domestic law and international law;

Tribunal means an arbitration tribunal established under Article 27 (Submission of a Claim to Arbitration) or Article 32 (Consolidation);

UNCITRAL Arbitration Rules means the arbitration rules of the United Nations Commission on International Trade Law, approved by the United Nations General Assembly on December 15, 1976; and

WTO Agreement means the Agreement Establishing the World Trade Organization done at Marrakesh on 15 April 1994.

SECTION B SUBSTANTIVE OBLIGATIONS

Article 2 Scope and Application
1. This Agreement shall apply to measures adopted or maintained by a Party relating to:
    (a) investors of the other Party; and
    (b) covered investments.
2. For greater certainty, the provisions of this Agreement do not bind a Party in relation to any act or fact that took place or any situation that ceased to exist before the date of entry into force of this Agreement for that Party.

Article 3 National Treatment
1. Each Party shall accord to investors of the other Party treatment no less favourable than that it accords, in like circumstances, to its own investors with respect to the establishment, acquisition, expansion, management, conduct, operation and sale or other disposition of investments in its territory.
2. Each Party shall accord to covered investments treatment no less favourable than that it accords, in like circumstances, to investments of its own investors with respect to the establishment, acquisition, expansion, management, conduct, operation and sale or other disposition of investments in its territory.
3. The treatment accorded by a Party under paragraphs 1 and 2 means, with respect to a sub-national government, treatment no less favourable than the treatment accorded, in like circumstances, by that sub-national government to investors, and to investments of investors, of the Party of which it forms a part.

Article 4[3, 4]   Most-Favoured-Nation Treatment

1. Each Party shall accord to investors of the other Party treatment no less favourable than that it accords, in like circumstances, to investors of a non-Party with respect to the establishment, acquisition, expansion, management, conduct, operation and sale or other disposition of investments in its territory.

2. Each Party shall accord to covered investments treatment no less favourable than that it accords, in like circumstances, to investments of investors of a non-Party with respect to the establishment, acquisition, expansion, management, conduct, operation and sale or other disposition of investments in its territory.

Article 5   Minimum Standard of Treatment

1. Each Party shall accord to covered investments treatment in accordance with the customary international law minimum standard of treatment of aliens, including fair and equitable treatment and full protection and security.

2. The concepts of "fair and equitable treatment" and "full protection and security" in paragraph 1 do not require treatment in addition to or beyond that which is required by the customary international law minimum standard of treatment of aliens.

3. A determination that there has been a breach of another provision of this Agreement, or of a separate international agreement, does not establish that there has been a breach of this Article.

Article 6   Senior Management, Boards of Directors and Entry of Personnel

1. A Party may not require that an enterprise of that Party, that is a covered investment, appoint to senior management positions individuals of any particular nationality.

2. A Party may require that a majority of the board of directors, or any committee thereof, of an enterprise that is a covered investment be of a particular nationality, or resident in the territory of the Party, provided that the requirement does not materially impair the ability of the investor to exercise control over its investment.

3. Subject to its laws, regulations and policies relating to the entry of aliens, each Party shall grant temporary entry to nationals of the other Party, employed by an investor of the other Party, who seek to render services to an investment of that investor in the territory of the Party, in a capacity that is managerial or executive or requires specialized knowledge.

Article 7   Performance Requirements

1. Neither Party may impose or enforce any of the following requirements, or enforce any commitment or undertaking, in connection with the establishment, acquisition, expansion, management, conduct or operation of an investment of an investor of a Party or a non-Party in its territory:
   (a) to export a given level or percentage of goods;
   (b) to achieve a given level or percentage of domestic content;
   (c) to purchase, use or accord a preference to goods produced or services provided in its territory, or to purchase goods or services from persons in its territory;
   (d) to relate in any way the volume or value of imports to the volume or value of exports or to the amount of foreign exchange inflows associated with such investment;
   (e) to restrict sales of goods or services in its territory that such investment produces or provides by relating such sales in any way to the volume or value of its exports or foreign exchange earnings;
   (f) to transfer technology, a production process or other proprietary knowledge to a person in its territory, except when the requirement is imposed or the commitment or undertaking

---

3 For greater certainty, the treatment accorded by a Party under this Article means, with respect to a sub-national government, treatment accorded, in like circumstances, by that sub-national government to investors, and to investments of investors, of a non-Party.

4 For greater certainty, Article 4 shall be interpreted in accordance with Annex B.4.

is enforced by a court, administrative tribunal or competition authority, to remedy an alleged violation of competition laws or to act in a manner not inconsistent with other provisions of this Agreement; or

(g) to supply exclusively from the territory of the Party the goods it produces or the services it provides to a specific regional market or to the world market.

2. A measure that requires an investment to use a technology to meet generally applicable health, safety or environmental requirements shall not be construed to be inconsistent with paragraph 1(f). For greater certainty, Articles 3 and 4 apply to the measure.

3. Neither Party may condition the receipt or continued receipt of an advantage, in connection with an investment in its territory of an investor of a Party or of a non-Party, on compliance with any of the following requirements:

(a) to achieve a given level or percentage of domestic content;

(b) to purchase, use or accord a preference to goods produced in its territory, or to purchase goods from producers in its territory;

(c) to relate in any way the volume or value of imports to the volume or value of exports or to the amount of foreign exchange inflows associated with such investment; or

(d) to restrict sales of goods or services in its territory that such investment produces or provides by relating such sales in any way to the volume or value of its exports or foreign exchange earnings.

4. Nothing in paragraph 3 shall be construed to prevent a Party from conditioning the receipt or continued receipt of an advantage, in connection with an investment in its territory of an investor of a Party, on compliance with a requirement to locate production, provide a service, train or employ workers, construct or expand particular facilities, or carry out research and development, in its territory.

5. Paragraphs 1 and 3 shall not apply to any requirement other than the requirements set out in those paragraphs.

6. The provisions of:

(a) Paragraphs (1) (a), (b) and (c), and (3) (a) and (b) shall not apply to qualification requirements for goods or services with respect to export promotion and foreign aid programs;

(b) Paragraphs (1) (b), (c), (f) and (g), and (3) (a) and (b) shall not apply to procurement by a Party or a state enterprise; and

(c) Paragraphs (3) (a) and (b) shall not apply to requirements imposed by an importing Party relating to the content of goods necessary to qualify for preferential tariffs or preferential quotas.

Article 8   Monopolies and State Enterprises

1. Nothing in this Agreement shall be construed to prevent a Party from designating a monopoly, or from maintaining or establishing a state enterprise.

2. Where a Party intends to designate a monopoly[5] and the designation may affect the interests of persons of the other Party, the Party shall, wherever possible, provide prior written notification to the other Party of the designation.

3. Each Party shall ensure, through regulatory control, administrative supervision or the application of other measures, that any privately-owned monopoly that it designates and any government monopoly that it maintains or designates acts in a manner that is not inconsistent with the Party's obligations under this Agreement wherever such a monopoly exercises any regulatory, administrative or other governmental authority that the Party has delegated to it in connection with the monopoly good or service, such as the power to grant import or export licenses, approve commercial transactions or impose quotas, fees or other charges.[6]

---

5 Nothing in this Article shall be construed to prevent a monopoly from charging different prices in different geographic markets, where such differences are based on normal commercial considerations, such as taking account of supply and demand conditions in those markets.

6 A delegation includes a legislative grant, a government order, directive or other act transferring to the monopoly, or authorizing the exercise by the monopoly of, governmental authority.

4. Each Party shall ensure, through regulatory control, administrative supervision or the application of other measures, that any state enterprise that it maintains or establishes acts in a manner that is not inconsistent with the Party's obligations under this Agreement wherever such enterprise exercises any regulatory, administrative or other governmental authority that the Party has delegated to it, such as the power to expropriate, grant licenses, approve commercial transactions or impose quotas, fees or other charges.

Article 9   Reservations and Exceptions

1. Articles 3, 4, 6 and 7 shall not apply to:
   (a) any existing non-conforming measure that is maintained by
      (i) a national government, as set out in its Schedule to Annex I,* or
      (ii) a sub-national government;
   (b) the continuation or prompt renewal of any non-conforming measure referred to in subparagraph (a);
   (c) an amendment to any non-conforming measure referred to in subparagraph (a) to the extent that the amendment does not decrease the conformity of the measure, as it existed immediately before the amendment, with Articles 3, 4, 6 and 7.

2. Articles 3, 4, 6 and 7 shall not apply to any measure that a Party adopts or maintains with respect to sectors, subsectors or activities, as set out in its schedule to Annex II.*

3. Article 4 shall not apply to treatment accorded by a Party pursuant to agreements, or with respect to sectors, set out in Annex III.

4. In respect of intellectual property rights, a Party may derogate from Articles 3 and 4 in a manner that is consistent with the WTO Agreement.

5. The provisions of Articles 3, 4 and 6 of this Agreement shall not apply to:
   (a) procurement by a Party or state enterprise;
   (b) subsidies or grants provided by a Party or a state enterprise, including government-supported loans, guarantees and insurance;

6. For greater certainty, Article 3 of this Agreement shall not apply to the granting by a Party to a financial institution of an exclusive right to provide activities or services forming part of a public retirement plan or statutory system of social security.

Article 10   General Exceptions

1. Subject to the requirement that such measures are not applied in a manner that would constitute arbitrary or unjustifiable discrimination between investments or between investors, or a disguised restriction on international trade or investment, nothing in this Agreement shall be construed to prevent a Party from adopting or enforcing measures necessary:
   (a) to protect human, animal or plant life or health;
   (b) to ensure compliance with laws and regulations that are not inconsistent with the provisions of this Agreement; or
   (c) for the conservation of living or non-living exhaustible natural resources.

2. Nothing in this Agreement shall be construed to prevent a Party from adopting or maintaining reasonable measures for prudential reasons, such as:
   (a) the protection of investors, depositors, financial market participants, policy-holders, policy-claimants, or persons to whom a fiduciary duty is owed by a financial institution;
   (b) the maintenance of the safety, soundness, integrity or financial responsibility of financial institutions; and
   (c) ensuring the integrity and stability of a Party's financial system.

---

* Note by the Editors: Annexes I and II contain detailed rules on reservations for existing and future measures and liberalization commitments, setting out separate schedules for each of the parties. Due to space constraints, Annexes I and II are not reproduced here. They are available on the website mentioned at the outset of this document.

3. Nothing in this Agreement shall apply to non-discriminatory measures of general application taken by any public entity in pursuit of monetary and related credit policies or exchange rate policies. This paragraph shall not affect a Party's obligations under Article 7 (Performance Requirements) or Article 14 (Transfer of Funds).

4. Nothing in this Agreement shall be construed:
    (a) to require any Party to furnish or allow access to any information the disclosure of which it determines to be contrary to its essential security interests;
    (b) to prevent any Party from taking any actions that it considers necessary for the protection of its essential security interests
        (i) relating to the traffic in arms, ammunition and implements of war and to such traffic and transactions in other goods, materials, services and technology undertaken directly or indirectly for the purpose of supplying a military or other security establishment,
        (ii) taken in time of war or other emergency in international relations, or
        (iii) relating to the implementation of national policies or international agreements respecting the non-proliferation of nuclear weapons or other nuclear explosive devices; or
    (c) to prevent any Party from taking action in pursuance of its obligations under the *United Nations Charter* for the maintenance of international peace and security.

5. Nothing in this Agreement shall be construed to require a Party to furnish or allow access to information the disclosure of which would impede law enforcement or would be contrary to the Party's law protecting Cabinet confidences, personal privacy or the confidentiality of the financial affairs and accounts of individual customers of financial institutions.

6. The provisions of this Agreement shall not apply to investments in cultural industries.

7. Any measure adopted by a Party in conformity with a decision adopted, extended or modified by the World Trade Organization pursuant to Articles IX:3 or IX:4 of the WTO Agreement shall be deemed to be also in conformity with this Agreement. An investor purporting to act pursuant to Section C of this Agreement may not claim that such a conforming measure is in breach of this Agreement.

Article 11   Health, Safety and Environmental Measures

The Parties recognize that it is inappropriate to encourage investment by relaxing domestic health, safety or environmental measures. Accordingly, a Party should not waive or otherwise derogate from, or offer to waive or otherwise derogate from, such measures as an encouragement for the establishment, acquisition, expansion or retention in its territory of an investment of an investor. If a Party considers that the other Party has offered such an encouragement, it may request consultations with the other Party and the two Parties shall consult with a view to avoiding any such encouragement.

Article 12   Compensation for Losses

1. Each Party shall accord to investors of the other Party, and to covered investments, non-discriminatory treatment with respect to measures it adopts or maintains relating to losses suffered by investments in its territory owing to armed conflict, civil strife or a natural disaster.

2. Paragraph (1) shall not apply to existing measures relating to subsidies or grants that would be inconsistent with Article 3 but for Article 9(5)(b).

Article 13[7]   Expropriation

1. Neither Party shall nationalize or expropriate a covered investment either directly, or indirectly through measures having an effect equivalent to nationalization or expropriation (hereinafter referred to as "expropriation"), except for a public purpose[8], in accordance with due

---

7 For greater certainty, Article 13(1) shall be interpreted in accordance with Annex B.13(1) on the clarification of indirect expropriation.

8 The term "public purpose" is a treaty term to be interpreted in accordance with international law. It is not meant to create any inconsistency with the same or similar concepts in the domestic law of the Parties.

process of law, in a non-discriminatory manner and on prompt, adequate and effective compensation.

2. Such compensation shall be equivalent to the fair market value of the expropriated investment immediately before the expropriation took place ("date of expropriation"), and shall not reflect any change in value occurring because the intended expropriation had become known earlier. Valuation criteria shall include going concern value, asset value including declared tax value of tangible property, and other criteria, as appropriate, to determine fair market value.

3. Compensation shall be paid without delay and shall be fully realizable and freely transferable. Compensation shall be payable in a freely convertible currency and shall include interest at a commercially reasonable rate for that currency from the date of expropriation until date of payment.

4. The investor affected shall have a right, under the law of the Party making the expropriation, to prompt review, by a judicial or other independent authority of that Party, of its case and of the valuation of its investment in accordance with the principles set out in this Article.

5. The provisions of this Article shall not apply to the issuance of compulsory licenses granted in relation to intellectual property rights, or to the revocation, limitation or creation of intel- lectual property rights, to the extent that such issuance, revocation, limitation or creation is consistent with the WTO Agreement.

Article 14   Transfer of Funds

1. Each Party shall permit all transfers relating to a covered investment to be made freely, and without delay, into and out of its territory. Such transfers include:
   (a) contributions to capital;
   (b) profits, dividends, interest, capital gains, royalty payments, management fees, technical assistance and other fees, returns in kind and other amounts derived from the investment;
   (c) proceeds from the sale of all or any part of the covered investment or from the partial or complete liquidation of the covered investment;
   (d) payments made under a contract entered into by the investor, or the covered investment, including payments made pursuant to a loan agreement;
   (e) payments made pursuant to Articles 12 and 13; and
   (f) payments arising under Section C.

2. Each Party shall permit transfers relating to a covered investment to be made in the convertible currency in which the capital was originally invested, or in any other convertible currency agreed by the investor and the Party concerned. Unless otherwise agreed by the investor, transfers shall be made at the rate of exchange applicable on the date of transfer.

3. Notwithstanding paragraphs 1 and 2, a Party may prevent a transfer through the equitable, non-discriminatory and good faith application of its laws relating to:
   (a) bankruptcy, insolvency or the protection of the rights of creditors;
   (b) issuing, trading or dealing in securities;
   (c) criminal or penal offences;
   (d) reports of transfers of currency or other monetary instruments; or
   (e) ensuring the satisfaction of judgments in adjudicatory proceedings.

4. Neither Party may require its investors to transfer, or penalize its investors that fail to transfer, the income, earnings, profits or other amounts derived from, or attributable to investments in the territory of the other Party.

5. Paragraph 4 shall not be construed to prevent a Party from imposing any measure through the equitable, non-discriminatory and good faith application of its laws relating to the matters set out in subparagraphs (a) through (e) of paragraph 3.

6. Notwithstanding the provisions of paragraphs 1, 2 and 4, and without limiting the applic- ability of paragraph 5, a Party may prevent or limit transfers by a financial institution to, or for

the benefit of, an affiliate of or person related to such institution, through the equitable, non-discriminatory and good faith application of measures relating to maintenance of the safety, soundness, integrity or financial responsibility of financial institutions.

7. Notwithstanding paragraph 1, a Party may restrict transfers in kind in circumstances where it could otherwise restrict transfers under the WTO Agreement and as set out in paragraph 3.

Article 15   Subrogation

1. If a Party or any agency thereof makes a payment to any of its investors under a guarantee or a contract of insurance it has entered into in respect of an investment, the other Party shall recognize the validity of the subrogation in favour of such Party or agency thereof to any right or title held by the investor.

2. A Party or any agency thereof which is subrogated to the rights of an investor in accordance with paragraph 1 of this Article, shall be entitled in all circumstances to the same rights as those of the investor in respect of the investment. Such rights may be exercised by the Party or any agency thereof, or by the investor if the Party or any agency thereof so authorizes.

Article 16   Taxation Measures

1. Except where express reference is made thereto, nothing in this Agreement shall apply to taxation measures. For greater certainty, nothing in this Agreement shall affect the rights and obligations of the Parties under any tax convention. In the event of any inconsistency between the provisions of this Agreement and any such convention, the provisions of that convention shall apply to the extent of the inconsistency.

2. Nothing in this Agreement shall be construed to require a Party to furnish or allow access to information the disclosure of which would be contrary to the Party's law protecting information concerning the taxation affairs of a taxpayer.

3. The provisions of Article 13 shall apply to taxation measures unless the taxation authorities of the Parties, no later than six months after being notified by an investor that the investor disputes a taxation measure, jointly determine that the measure in question is not an expropriation. The investor shall refer the issue of whether a taxation measure is an expropriation for a determination to the taxation authorities of the Parties at the same time that it gives notice under Article 24 (Notice of Intent to Submit a Claim to Arbitration).

4. If, in connection with a claim by an investor of a Party or a dispute between the Parties, an issue arises as to whether a measure of a Party is a taxation measure, a Party may refer the issue to the taxation authorities of the Parties. The taxation authorities shall decide the issue, and their decision shall bind any Tribunal formed pursuant to Section C or arbitral panel formed pursuant to Section D, as the case may be, with jurisdiction over the claim or the dispute. A Tribunal or arbitral panel seized of a claim or a dispute in which the issue arises may not proceed pending receipt of the decision of the taxation authorities. If the taxation authorities have not decided the issue within six months of the referral, the Tribunal or arbitral panel shall decide the issue in place of the taxation authorities.

Article 17   Prudential Measures

1. Where an investor submits a claim to arbitration under Section C, and the disputing Party invokes Articles 10(2) or 14(6), the Tribunal established pursuant to Article 22 (Claim by an Investor of a Party on its Own Behalf) or 23 (Claim by an Investor of a Party on Behalf of an Enterprise) shall, at the request of that Party, seek a report in writing from the Parties on the issue of whether and to what extent the said paragraphs are a valid defence to the claim of the investor. The Tribunal may not proceed pending receipt of a report under this Article.

2. Pursuant to a request received in accordance with paragraph (1), the Parties shall proceed in accordance with Section D to prepare a written report, either on the basis of agreement following consultations, or by means of an arbitral panel. The consultations shall be between the financial services authorities of the Parties. The report shall be transmitted to the Tribunal, and shall be binding on the Tribunal.

3. Where, within 70 days of the referral by the Tribunal, no request for the establishment of a panel pursuant to paragraph (2) has been made, and no report has been received by the Tribunal, the Tribunal may proceed to decide the matter.

Article 18   Denial of Benefits

1. A Party may deny the benefits of this Agreement to an investor of the other Party that is an enterprise of such Party and to investments of such investor if investors of a non-Party own or control the enterprise and the denying Party adopts or maintains measures with respect to the non-Party that prohibit transactions with the enterprise or that would be violated or circumvented if the benefits of this Agreement were accorded to the enterprises or to its investments.

2. Subject to Article 19(3), a Party may deny the benefits of this Agreement to an investor of the other Party that is an enterprise of such Party and to investments of such investors if investors of a non-Party own or control the enterprise and the enterprise has no substantial business activities in the territory of the Party under whose law it is constituted or organized.

Article 19   Transparency

1. Each Party shall, to the extent possible, ensure that its laws, regulations, procedures, and administrative rulings of general application respecting any matter covered by this Agreement are promptly published or otherwise made available in such a manner as to enable interested persons and the other Party to become acquainted with them.

2. To the extent possible, each Party shall:
   (a) publish in advance any such measure that it proposes to adopt; and
   (b) provide interested persons and the other Party a reasonable opportunity to comment on such proposed measures.

3. Upon request by a Party, information shall be exchanged on the measures of the other Party that may have an impact on covered investments.

SECTION C   SETTLEMENT OF DISPUTES BETWEEN AN INVESTOR AND THE HOST PARTY

Article 20   Purpose

Without prejudice to the rights and obligations of the Parties under Section D (State to State Dispute Settlement Procedures), this Section establishes a mechanism for the settlement of investment disputes.

Article 21   Limitation of Claims with Respect to Financial Institutions

With respect to:

(a) financial institutions of a Party; and

(b) investors of a Party, and investments of such investors, in financial institutions in the other Party's territory,

this Section applies only in respect of claims that the other Party has breached an obligation under Articles 13, 14 or 18.

Article 22   Claim by an Investor of a Party on Its Own Behalf

1. An investor of a Party may submit to arbitration under this Section a claim that:
   (a) the other Party has breached an obligation under Section B, other than an obligation under Article 6(3), 8(1), 8(2), 11 or 19, or
   (b) the other Party has breached a legal stability agreement referred to in paragraph 3 of this Article,
   and that the investor has incurred loss or damage by reason of, or arising out of, that breach.

2. An investor may not make a claim if more than three years have elapsed from the date on which the investor first acquired, or should have first acquired, knowledge of the alleged breach and knowledge that the investor has incurred loss or damage.

3. A claim by an investor that a tax measure of a Party is in breach of a legal stability agreement between the national government authorities of a Party and the investor concerning an investment may be submitted to arbitration under this Section unless:

   (a) the legal stability agreement between the national government authorities of a Party and the investor preceded the entry into force of this Agreement; or

   (b) the taxation authorities of the Parties, no later than six months after being notified by the investor of its intention to submit the claim to arbitration, jointly determine that the measure does not contravene such legal stability agreement. The investor shall refer the issue of whether a taxation measure does not contravene a legal stability agreement for a determination to the taxation authorities of the Parties at the same time that it gives notice under Article 24 (Notice of Intent to Submit a Claim to Arbitration).

Article 23 Claim by an Investor of a Party on Behalf of an Enterprise

1. An investor of a Party, on behalf of an enterprise of the other Party that is a juridical person that the investor owns or controls directly or indirectly, may submit to arbitration under this Section a claim that:

   (a) the other Party has breached an obligation under Section B, other than an obligation under Article 6(3), 8(1), 8(2), 11 or 19, or

   (b) the other Party has breached a legal stability agreement referred to in paragraph 3 of this Article,

   and that the enterprise has incurred loss or damage by reason of, or arising out of, that breach.

2. An investor may not make a claim on behalf of an enterprise described in paragraph 1 if more than three years have elapsed from the date on which the enterprise first acquired, or should have first acquired, knowledge of the alleged breach and knowledge that the enterprise has incurred loss or damage.

3. A claim by an investor, on behalf of an enterprise of the other Party that is a juridical person that the investor owns or controls directly or indirectly, that a tax measure of that Party is in breach of a legal stability agreement between the national government authorities of that Party and said enterprise may be submitted to arbitration under this Section unless:

   (a) the legal stability agreement between the national government authorities of a Party and the enterprise preceded the entry into force of this Agreement; or

   (b) the taxation authorities of the Parties, no later than six months after being notified by the investor of its intention to submit the claim to arbitration, jointly determine that the measure does not contravene such legal stability agreement. The investor shall refer the issue of whether a taxation measure does not contravene a legal stability agreement for a determination to the taxation authorities of the Parties at the same time that it gives notice under Article 24 (Notice of Intent to Submit a Claim to Arbitration).

4. Where an investor makes a claim under this Article and the investor or a non-controlling investor in the enterprise makes a claim under Article 22 (Claim by an Investor of a Party on Its Own Behalf) arising out of the same events that gave rise to the claim under this Article, and two or more of the claims are submitted to arbitration under Article 27 (Submission of a Claim to Arbitration), the claims should be heard together by a Tribunal established under Article 32 (Consolidation), unless the Tribunal finds that the interests of a disputing party would be prejudiced thereby.

5. An investment may not make a claim under this Section.

Article 24 Notice of Intent to Submit a Claim to Arbitration

1. The disputing investor shall deliver to the disputing Party written notice of its intent to submit a claim to arbitration at least 90 days before the claim is submitted, which notice shall specify:

   (a) the name and address of the disputing investor and, where a claim is made under Article 23 (Claim by an Investor of a Party on Behalf of an Enterprise), the name and address of the enterprise;

   (b) the provisions of this Agreement alleged to have been breached and any other relevant provisions;

   (c) the issues and the factual basis for the claim, including the measures at issue; and

   (d) the relief sought and the approximate amount of damages claimed.

2. The disputing investor shall also deliver, with its Notice of Intent to Submit a Claim to Arbitration, evidence establishing that it is an investor of the other Party.

Article 25 Settlement of a Claim through Consultation

1. Before a disputing investor may submit a claim to arbitration, the disputing parties shall first hold consultations in an attempt to settle a claim amicably.

2. Consultations shall be held within 30 days of the submission of the notice of intent to submit a claim to arbitration, unless the disputing parties otherwise agree.

3. The place of consultation shall be the capital of the disputing Party, unless the disputing parties otherwise agree.

Article 26 Conditions Precedent to Submission of a Claim to Arbitration

1. A disputing investor may submit a claim to arbitration under Article 22 (Claim by an Investor of a Party on Its Own Behalf) only if:

   (a) the investor consents to arbitration in accordance with the procedures set out in this Agreement;

   (b) at least six months have elapsed since the events giving rise to the claim;

   (c) not more than three years have elapsed from the date on which the investor first acquired, or should have first acquired, knowledge of the alleged breach and knowledge that the investor has incurred loss or damage thereby;

   (d) the investor has delivered the Notice of Intent required under Article 24 (Notice of Intent to Submit a Claim to Arbitration), in accordance with the requirements of that Article, at least 90 days prior to submitting the claim; and

   (e) the investor and, where the claim is for loss or damage to an interest in an enterprise of the other Party that is a juridical person that the investor owns or controls directly or indirectly, the enterprise waive their right to initiate or continue before any administrative tribunal or court under the law of any Party, or other dispute settlement procedures, any proceedings with respect to the measure of the disputing Party that is alleged to be a breach referred to in Article 22 (Claim by an Investor of a Party on Its Own Behalf), except for proceedings for injunctive, declaratory or other extraordinary relief, not involving the payment of damages, before an administrative tribunal or court under the law of the disputing Party.

2. A disputing investor may submit a claim to arbitration under Article 23 (Claim by an Investor of a Party on Behalf of an Enterprise) only if:

   (a) both the investor and the enterprise consent to arbitration in accordance with the procedures set out in this Agreement;

   (b) at least six months have elapsed since the events giving rise to the claim;

   (c) not more than three years have elapsed from the date on which the enterprise first acquired, or should have first acquired, knowledge of the alleged breach and knowledge that the enterprise has incurred loss or damage thereby;

(d) the investor has delivered the Notice of Intent required under Article 24 (Notice of Intent to Submit a Claim to Arbitration), in accordance with the requirements of that Article, at least 90 days prior to submitting the claim; and

(e) both the investor and the enterprise waive their right to initiate or continue before any administrative tribunal or court under the law of any Party, or other dispute settlement procedures, any proceedings with respect to the measure of the disputing Party that is alleged to be a breach referred to in Article 23 (Claim by an Investor of a Party on Behalf of an Enterprise), except for proceedings for injunctive, declaratory or other extraordinary relief, not involving the payment of damages, before an administrative tribunal or court under the law of the disputing Party.

3. A consent and waiver required by this Article shall be in the form provided for in Annex C.26, shall be delivered to the disputing Party and shall be included in the submission of a claim to arbitration.

4. An investor may submit a claim relating to taxation measures covered by this Agreement to arbitration under this Section only if the taxation authorities of the Parties fail to reach the joint determinations specified in Articles 16(3), 22(3)(b) and 23(3)(b) within six months of being notified in accordance with these provisions.

5. A waiver from the enterprise under paragraph 1(e) or 2(e) shall not be required only where a disputing Party has deprived a disputing investor of control of an enterprise.

6. Failure to meet any of the conditions precedent provided for in paragraphs 1 through 4 shall nullify the consent of the Parties given in Article 28 (Consent to Arbitration).

Article 27   Submission of a Claim to Arbitration

1. Except as provided in Annex C.27, a disputing investor who meets the conditions precedent provided for in Article 26 (Conditions Precedent to Submission of a Claim to Arbitration) may submit the claim to arbitration under:
(a) the ICSID Convention, provided that both the disputing Party and the Party of the disputing investor are parties to the Convention;
(b) the Additional Facility Rules of ICSID, provided that either the disputing Party or the Party of the disputing investor, but not both, is a party to the ICSID Convention;
(c) the UNCITRAL Arbitration Rules; or
(d) any other body of rules approved by the Commission as available for arbitrations under this Section.

2. The Commission shall have the power to make rules supplementing the applicable arbitral rules and may amend any rules of its own making. Such rules shall be binding on a Tribunal established under this Section, and on individual arbitrators serving on such Tribunals.

3. The applicable arbitration rules shall govern the arbitration except to the extent modified by this Section, and supplemented by any rules adopted by the Commission under this Section.

Article 28   Consent to Arbitration

1. Each Party consents to the submission of a claim to arbitration in accordance with the procedures set out in this Agreement.

2. The consent given in paragraph 1 and the submission by a disputing investor of a claim to arbitration shall satisfy the requirement of:
(a) Chapter II of the ICSID Convention (Jurisdiction of the Centre) and the Additional Facility Rules for written consent of the parties;
(b) Article II of the New York Convention for an agreement in writing; and
(c) Article I of the Inter-American Convention for an agreement.

Article 29   Arbitrators

1. Except in respect of a Tribunal established under Article 32 (Consolidation), and unless the disputing parties agree otherwise, the Tribunal shall comprise three arbitrators, one arbitrator appointed by each of the disputing parties and the third, who shall be the presiding arbitrator, appointed by agreement of the disputing parties.

2. Arbitrators shall:
   (a) have expertise or experience in public international law, international trade or international investment rules, or the resolution of disputes arising under international trade or international investment agreements;
   (b) be independent of, and not be affiliated with or take instructions from, either Party or the disputing investor; and
   (c) comply with any Code of Conduct for Dispute Settlement as agreed by the Commission.

3. Where a disputing investor claims that a dispute involves measures adopted or maintained by a Party relating to financial institutions of the other Party, or investors of the other Party and investments of such investors, in financial institutions in a Party's territory, then
   (a) where the disputing parties are in agreement, the arbitrators shall, in addition to the criteria set out in paragraph 2, have expertise or experience in financial services law or practice, which may include the regulation of financial institutions; or
   (b) where the disputing parties are not in agreement,
      (i) each disputing party may select arbitrators who meet the qualifications set out in subparagraph (a), and
      (ii) if the Party complained against invokes Articles 14(6) or 17, the chair of the panel shall meet the qualifications set out in subparagraph (a).

4. The disputing parties should agree upon the arbitrators' remuneration. If the disputing parties do not agree on such remuneration before the constitution of the Tribunal, the prevailing ICSID rate for arbitrators shall apply.

5. The Commission may establish rules relating to expenses incurred by the Tribunal.

Article 30   Constitution of a Tribunal When a Party Fails to Appoint an Arbitrator or the Disputing Parties are Unable to Agree on a Presiding Arbitrator

1. The Secretary-General shall serve as appointing authority for an arbitration under this Section.

2. If a Tribunal, other than a Tribunal established under Article 32 (Consolidation), has not been constituted within 90 days from the date that a claim is submitted to arbitration, the Secretary-General, on the request of either disputing party, shall appoint, in his or her discretion, the arbitrator or arbitrators not yet appointed, except that the presiding arbitrator shall not be a national of either Party.

Article 31   Agreement to Appointment of Arbitrators

For purposes of Article 39 of the ICSID Convention and Article 7 of Schedule C to the ICSID Additional Facility Rules, and without prejudice to an objection to an arbitrator based on a ground other than citizenship or permanent residence:

(a) the disputing Party agrees to the appointment of each individual member of a Tribunal established under the ICSID Convention or the ICSID Additional Facility Rules;

(b) a disputing investor referred to in Article 22(1) (Claim by an Investor of a Party on Its Own Behalf) may submit a claim to arbitration, or continue a claim, under the ICSID Convention or the ICSID Additional Facility Rules, only on condition that the disputing investor agrees in writing to the appointment of each individual member of the Tribunal; and

(c) a disputing investor referred to in Article 23(1) (Claim by an Investor of a Party on Behalf of an Enterprise) may submit a claim to arbitration, or continue a claim, under the ICSID Convention or the ICSID Additional Facility Rules, only on condition that the disputing investor and the enterprise agree in writing to the appointment of each individual member of the Tribunal.

Article 32   Consolidation

1. A Tribunal established under this Article shall be established under the UNCITRAL Arbitration Rules and shall conduct its proceedings in accordance with those Rules, except as modified by this Section.

2. Where a Tribunal established under this Article is satisfied that claims submitted to arbitration under Article 27 (Submission of a Claim to Arbitration) have a question of law or fact in common, the Tribunal may, in the interests of fair and efficient resolution of the claims, and after hearing the disputing parties, by order:
   (a) assume jurisdiction over, and hear and determine together, all or part of the claims; or
   (b) assume jurisdiction over, and hear and determine one or more of the claims, the determination of which it believes would assist in the resolution of the others.

3. A disputing party that seeks an order under paragraph 2 shall request the Secretary-General to establish a Tribunal and shall specify in the request:
   (a) the name of the disputing Party or disputing investors against which the order is sought;
   (b) the nature of the order sought; and
   (c) the grounds on which the order is sought.

4. The disputing party shall deliver to the disputing Party or disputing investors against which the order is sought a copy of the request.

5. Within 60 days of receipt of the request, the Secretary-General shall establish a Tribunal comprising three arbitrators. The Secretary-General shall appoint the presiding arbitrator, from the ICSID Panel of Arbitrators, a presiding arbitrator who is not a national of any of the Parties. The Secretary-General shall appoint the two other members from the ICSID Panel of Arbitrators. To the extent arbitrators are not available from that Panel, appointments shall be at the discretion of the Secretary-General. One member shall be a national of the disputing Party and one member shall be a national of the Party of the disputing investors.

6. Where a Tribunal has been established under this Article, a disputing investor that has submitted a claim to arbitration under Article 27 (Submission of a Claim to Arbitration) and that has not been named in a request made under paragraph 3 may make a written request to the Tribunal that it be included in an order made under paragraph 2, and shall specify in the request:
   (a) the name and address of the disputing investor;
   (b) the nature of the order sought; and
   (c) the grounds on which the order is sought.

7. A disputing investor referred to in paragraph 6 shall deliver a copy of its request to the disputing parties named in a request made under paragraph 3.

8. A Tribunal established under Article 27 (Submission of a Claim to Arbitration) shall not have jurisdiction to decide a claim, or a part of a claim, over which a Tribunal established under this Article has assumed jurisdiction.

9. On application of a disputing party, a Tribunal established under this Article, pending its decision under paragraph 2, may order that the proceedings of a Tribunal established under Article 27 (Submission of a Claim to Arbitration) be stayed, unless the latter Tribunal has already adjourned its proceedings.

Article 33   Notice to the Non-Disputing Party

A disputing Party shall deliver to the other Party a copy of the Notice of Intent to Submit a Claim to Arbitration and other documents, such as a Notice of Arbitration and Statement of Claim, no later than 30 days after the date that such documents have been delivered to the disputing Party.

Article 34   Documents

1. The non-disputing Party shall be entitled, at its cost, to receive from the disputing Party a copy of:

   (a) the evidence that has been tendered to the Tribunal;

   (b) copies of all pleadings filed in the arbitration; and

   (c) the written argument of the disputing parties.

2. The Party receiving information pursuant to paragraph 1 shall treat the information as if it were a disputing Party.

Article 35   Participation by the Non-Disputing Party

1. On written notice to the disputing parties, the non-disputing Party may make submissions to a Tribunal on a question of interpretation of this Agreement.

2. The non-disputing Party shall have the right to attend any hearings held under this Section, whether or not it makes submissions to the Tribunal.

Article 36   Place of Arbitration

Unless the disputing parties agree otherwise, a Tribunal shall hold an arbitration in the territory of a Party that is a party to the New York Convention, selected in accordance with:

(a) the ICSID Additional Facility Rules, if the arbitration is under those Rules or the ICSID Convention; or

(b) the UNCITRAL Arbitration Rules, if the arbitration is under those Rules.

Article 37   Preliminary Objections to Jurisdiction or Admissibility

Where issues relating to jurisdiction or admissibility are raised as preliminary objections, a Tribunal shall, wherever possible, decide the matter before proceeding to the merits.

Article 38   Public Access to Hearings and Documents

1. Hearings held under this Section shall be open to the public. To the extent necessary to ensure the protection of confidential information, including business confidential information, the Tribunal may hold portions of hearings *in camera*.

2. The Tribunal shall establish procedures for the protection of confidential information and appropriate logistical arrangements for open hearings, in consultation with the disputing parties.

3. All documents submitted to, or issued by, the Tribunal shall be publicly available, unless the disputing parties otherwise agree, subject to the deletion of confidential information.

4. Notwithstanding paragraph 3, any Tribunal award under this Section shall be publicly available, subject to the deletion of confidential information.

5. A disputing party may disclose to other persons in connection with the arbitral proceedings such unredacted documents as it considers necessary for the preparation of its case, but it shall ensure that those persons protect the confidential information in such documents.

6. The Parties may share with officials of their respective national and sub-national governments all relevant unredacted documents in the course of dispute settlement under this Agreement, but they shall ensure that those persons protect any confidential information in such documents.

7. As provided under Article 10(4) and (5), the Tribunal shall not require a Party to furnish or allow access to information the disclosure of which would impede law enforcement or would be contrary to the Party's law protecting Cabinet confidences, personal privacy or the financial affairs and accounts of individual customers of financial institutions, or which it determines to be contrary to its essential security.

8. To the extent that a Tribunal's confidentiality order designates information as confidential and a Party's law on access to information requires public access to that information, the Party's law

on access to information shall prevail. However, a Party should endeavour to apply its law on access to information so as to protect information designated confidential by the Tribunal.

Article 39   Submissions by a Non-Disputing Party

1. Any non-disputing party that wishes to file a written submission with a Tribunal (the "applicant") shall apply for leave from the Tribunal to file such a submission, in accordance with Annex C.39. The applicant shall attach the submission to the application.

2. The applicant shall serve the application for leave to file a non-disputing party submission and the submission on all disputing parties and the Tribunal.

3. The Tribunal shall set an appropriate date for the disputing parties to comment on the application for leave to file a non-disputing party submission.

4. In determining whether to grant leave to file a non-disputing party submission, the Tribunal shall consider, among other things, the extent to which:
   (a) the non-disputing party submission would assist the Tribunal in the determination of a factual or legal issue related to the arbitration by bringing a perspective, particular knowledge or insight that is different from that of the disputing parties;
   (b) the non-disputing party submission would address a matter within the scope of the dispute;
   (c) the non-disputing party has a significant interest in the arbitration; and
   (d) there is a public interest in the subject-matter of the arbitration.

5. The Tribunal shall ensure that:
   (a) any non-disputing party submission does not disrupt the proceedings; and
   (b) neither disputing party is unduly burdened or unfairly prejudiced by such submissions.

6. The Tribunal shall decide whether to grant leave to file a non-disputing party submission. If leave to file a non-disputing party submission is granted, the Tribunal shall set an appropriate date for the disputing parties to respond in writing to the non-disputing party submission. By that date, the non-disputing Party may, pursuant to Article 35 (Participation by the Non-Disputing Party), address any issues of interpretation of this Agreement presented in the non-disputing party submission.

7. The Tribunal that grants leave to file a non-disputing party submission is not required to address the submission at any point in the arbitration, nor is the non-disputing party that files the submission entitled to make further submissions in the arbitration.

8. Access to hearings and documents by non-disputing parties that file applications under these procedures shall be governed by the provisions pertaining to public access to hearings and documents under Article 38 (Public Access to Hearings and Documents).

Article 40   Governing Law

1. A Tribunal established under this Section shall decide the issues in dispute in accordance with this Agreement and applicable rules of international law.

2. Subject to the other terms of this Section, when a claim is submitted to arbitration for a breach of a legal stability agreement referred to in Articles 22 (3) and 23 (3), a Tribunal established under this Section shall apply:
   (a) the rules of law specified in the legal stability agreement, or as the disputing parties may otherwise agree; or
   (b) if the rules of law have not been specified or otherwise agreed:
      (i) the law of the disputing Party, including its rules on the conflict of laws;[9] and
      (ii) such rules of international law as may be applicable.

---

9 The "law of the disputing Party" means the law that a domestic court or tribunal of proper jurisdiction would apply in the same case.

3. An interpretation by the Commission of a provision of this Agreement shall be binding on a Tribunal established under this Section, and any award under this Section shall be consistent with such interpretation.

Article 41   Interpretation of Annexes

1. Where a disputing Party asserts as a defence that the measure alleged to be a breach is within the scope of a reservation or exception set out in Annex I, Annex II* or Annex III, on request of the disputing Party, the Tribunal shall request the interpretation of the Commission on the issue. The Commission, within 60 days of delivery of the request, shall submit in writing its interpretation to the Tribunal.

2. Further to Article 40(3) (Governing Law), a Commission interpretation submitted under paragraph 1 shall be binding on the Tribunal. If the Commission fails to submit an interpretation within 60 days, the Tribunal shall decide the issue.

Article 42   Expert Reports

Without prejudice to the appointment of other kinds of experts where authorized by the applicable arbitration rules, a Tribunal, at the request of a disputing party or, unless the disputing parties disapprove, on its own initiative, may appoint one or more experts to report to it in writing on any factual issue concerning environmental, health, safety or other scientific matters raised by a disputing party in a proceeding, subject to such terms and conditions as the disputing parties may agree.

Article 43   Interim Measures of Protection

A Tribunal may order an interim measure of protection to preserve the rights of a disputing party, or to ensure that the Tribunal's jurisdiction is made fully effective, including an order to preserve evidence in the possession or control of a disputing party or to protect the Tribunal's jurisdiction. A Tribunal may not order attachment or enjoin the application of the measure alleged to constitute a breach referred to in Article 22 (Claim by an Investor of a Party on Its Own Behalf) or 23 (Claim by an Investor of a Party on Behalf of an Enterprise). For purposes of this paragraph, an order includes a recommendation.

Article 44   Final Award

1. Where a Tribunal makes a final award against the disputing Party, the Tribunal may award, separately or in combination, only:
   (a) monetary damages and any applicable interest;
   (b) restitution of property, in which case the award shall provide that the disputing Party may pay monetary damages and any applicable interest in lieu of restitution.

   The Tribunal may also award costs in accordance with the applicable arbitration rules.

2. Subject to paragraph 1, where a claim is made under Article 23(1) (Claim by an Investor of a Party on Behalf of an Enterprise):
   (a) an award of monetary damages and any applicable interest shall provide that the sum be paid to the enterprise;
   (b) an award of restitution of property shall provide that restitution be made to the enterprise; and
   (c) the award shall provide that it is made without prejudice to any right that any person may have in the relief under applicable domestic law.

3. A Tribunal may not order a disputing Party to pay punitive damages.

Article 45   Finality and Enforcement of an Award

1. An award made by a Tribunal shall have no binding force except between the disputing parties and in respect of that particular case.

---

* Note by the Editors: Annexes I and II contain detailed rules on reservations for existing and future measures and liberalization commitments, setting out separate schedules for each of the parties. Due to space constraints, Annexes I and II are not reproduced here. They are available on the website mentioned at the outset of this document.

2. Subject to paragraph 3 and the applicable review procedure for an interim award, a disputing party shall abide by and comply with an award without delay.

3. A disputing party may not seek enforcement of a final award until:
   (a) in the case of a final award made under the ICSID Convention:
      (i) 120 days have elapsed from the date the award was rendered and no disputing party has requested revision or annulment of the award, or
      (ii) revision or annulment proceedings have been completed; and
   (b) in the case of a final award under the ICSID Additional Facility Rules or the UNCITRAL Arbitration Rules:
      (i) 90 days have elapsed from the date the award was rendered and no disputing party has commenced a proceeding to revise, set aside or annul the award, or
      (ii) a court has dismissed or allowed an application to revise, set aside or annul the award and there is no further appeal.

4. Each Party shall provide for the enforcement of an award in its territory.

5. If the disputing Party fails to abide by or comply with a final award, the Commission, on delivery of a request by the Party of the disputing investor, shall establish an arbitral panel under Section D (State-to-State Dispute Settlement Procedures). The requesting Party may seek in such proceedings:
   (a) a determination that the failure to abide by or comply with the final award is inconsistent with the obligations of this Agreement; and
   (b) a recommendation that the disputing Party abide by or comply with the final award.

6. A disputing investor may seek enforcement of an arbitration award under the ICSID Convention, the New York Convention or the Inter-American Convention regardless of whether proceedings have been taken under paragraph 5.

7. A claim that is submitted to arbitration under this Section shall be considered to arise out of a commercial relationship or transaction for purposes of Article I of the New York Convention and Article I of the Inter-American Convention.

Article 46   General

Time when a Claim is Submitted to Arbitration
1. A claim is submitted to arbitration under this Section when:
   (a) the request for arbitration under paragraph (1) of Article 36 of the ICSID Convention is received by the Secretary-General;
   (b) the notice of arbitration under Article 2 of Schedule C of the ICSID Additional Facility Rules is received by the Secretary-General; or
   (c) the notice of arbitration given under the UNCITRAL Arbitration Rules is received by the disputing Party.

Service of Documents
2. Delivery of notice and other documents on a Party shall be made to the place named for that Party below.

For Canada: Office of the Deputy Attorney General of Canada
        Justice Building
        239 Wellington Street
        Ottawa, Ontario
        K1A 0H8, CANADA

For the Republic of Peru: Dirección General de Asuntos de Economía
        Internacional, Competencia e Inversión Privada
        Ministerio de Economía y Finanzas

Jirón Lampa # 277 piso 5
Lima 1, PERÚ

Receipts under Insurance or Guarantee Contracts

3. In an arbitration under this Section, a disputing Party shall not assert, as a defence, counter-claim, right of set off or otherwise, that the disputing investor has received or will receive, pursuant to an insurance or guarantee contract, indemnification or other compensation for all or part of its alleged damages.

SECTION D   STATE-TO-STATE DISPUTE SETTLEMENT PROCEDURES

Article 47   Disputes between the Parties

1. Either Party may request consultations on the interpretation or application of this Agreement. The other Party shall give sympathetic consideration to the request. Any dispute between the Parties concerning the interpretation or application of this Agreement shall, whenever possible, be settled amicably through consultations.

2. If a dispute cannot be settled through consultations, it shall, at the request of either Party, be submitted to an arbitral panel for decision.

3. An arbitral panel shall be constituted for each dispute. Within two months after receipt through diplomatic channels of the request for arbitration, each Party shall appoint one member to the arbitral panel. The two members shall then select a national of a third State who, upon approval by the two Parties, shall be appointed Chairman of the arbitral panel. The Chairman shall be appointed within two months from the date of appointment of the other two members of the arbitral panel.

4. If within the periods specified in paragraph (3) of this Article the necessary appointments have not been made, either Party may invite the President of the International Court of Justice to make the necessary appointments. If the President is a national of either Party or is otherwise prevented from discharging the said function, the Vice-President shall be invited to make the necessary appointments. If the Vice-President is a national of either Party or is prevented from discharging the said function, the Member of the International Court of Justice next in seniority, who is not a national of either Party, shall be invited to make the necessary appointments.

5. Arbitrators shall:
   (a) have expertise or experience in public international law, international trade or international investment rules, or the resolution of disputes arising under international trade or international investment agreements;
   (b) be independent of, and not be affiliated with or take instructions from, either Party; and
   (c) comply with any Code of Conduct for Dispute Settlement as agreed by the Commission.

6. Where a Party claims that a dispute involves measures relating to financial institutions, or to investors or investments of such investors in financial institutions, then
   (a) where the disputing Parties are in agreement, the arbitrators shall, in addition to the criteria set out in paragraph 5, have expertise or experience in financial services law or practice, which may include the regulation of financial institutions; or
   (b) where the disputing Parties are not in agreement,
      (i) each disputing Party may select arbitrators who meet the qualifications set out in subparagraph (a), and
      (ii) if the Party complained against invokes Articles 14(6) or 17, the chair of the panel shall meet the qualifications set out in subparagraph (a).

7. The arbitral panel shall determine its own procedure. The arbitral panel shall reach its decision by a majority of votes. Such decision shall be binding on both Parties. Unless

otherwise agreed, the decision of the arbitral panel shall be rendered within six months of the appointment of the Chairman in accordance with paragraphs (3) or (4) of this Article.

8. Each Party shall bear the costs of its own member of the panel and of its representation in the arbitral proceedings; the costs related to the Chairman and any remaining costs shall be borne equally by the Parties. The arbitral panel may, however, in its decision direct that a higher proportion of costs be borne by one of the two Parties, and this award shall be binding on both Parties.

9. The Parties shall, within 60 days of the decision of a panel, reach agreement on the manner in which to resolve their dispute. Such agreement shall normally implement the decision of the panel. If the Parties fail to reach agreement, the Party bringing the dispute shall be entitled to compensation or to suspend benefits of equivalent value to those awarded by the panel.

SECTION E   FINAL PROVISIONS

Article 48   Consultations
A Party may request in writing consultation with the other Party regarding any actual or proposed measure or any other matter that it considers might affect the operation of this Agreement.

Article 49   Extent of Obligations
The Parties shall ensure that all necessary measures are taken in order to give effect to the provisions of this Agreement, including their observance, except as otherwise provided in this Agreement, by sub-national governments.

Article 50   Commission
1. The Parties hereby agree to establish a Commission, comprising cabinet-level representatives of the Parties or their designees.
2. The Commission shall:
   (a) supervise the implementation of this Agreement;
   (b) resolve disputes that may arise regarding its interpretation or application;
   (c) consider any other matter that may affect the operation of this Agreement; and
   (d) adopt a Code of Conduct for Arbitrators.
3. The Commission may take such other action in the exercise of its functions as the Parties may agree, including amendment of the Code of Conduct for Arbitrators.
4. The Commission shall establish its rules and procedures.

Article 51   Exclusions
The dispute settlement provisions of Sections C or D of this Agreement shall not apply to the matters referred to in Annex E.51 (Exclusions from Dispute Settlement).

Article 52   Application and entry into force
1. The Annexes hereto shall form integral parts hereof.
2. Each Party shall notify the other in writing of the completion of the procedures required in its territory for the entry into force of this Agreement. This Agreement shall enter into force on the date of the latter of the two notifications.
3. This Agreement shall remain in force unless either Party notifies the other Party in writing of its intention to terminate it. The termination of this Agreement shall become effective one year after notice of termination has been received by the other Party. In respect of investments or commitments to invest[10] made prior to the date when the termination of this Agreement

---

10 For the purposes of this Article, commitments to invest means concrete steps taken by an investor to make an investment, according to footnote 1.

becomes effective, the provisions of Articles 1 to 51 inclusive, as well as paragraphs (1) and (2) of this Article, shall remain in force for a period of fifteen years.

IN WITNESS WHEREOF, the undersigned, duly authorised, have signed this Agreement.

DONE in duplicate at Hanoi this 14th day of November, 2006 in the English, French and Spanish languages, all texts being equally authentic.

David Emerson
FOR CANADA
Mercedes Aráoz Fernández
FOR THE REPUBLIC OF PERU

ANNEXES

ANNEX B.4   MOST-FAVOURED-NATION TREATMENT

For greater clarity, treatment "with respect to the establishment, acquisition, expansion, management, conduct, operation and sale or other disposition of investments" referred to in paragraphs 1 and 2 of Article 4 does not encompass dispute resolution mechanisms, such as those in Section C, that are provided for in international treaties or trade agreements.

ANNEX B.13(1)   EXPROPRIATION

The Parties confirm their shared understanding that:

(a) Indirect expropriation results from a measure or series of measures of a Party that has an effect equivalent to direct expropriation without formal transfer of title or outright seizure;

(b) The determination of whether a measure or series of measures of a Party constitutes an indirect expropriation requires a case-by-case, fact-based inquiry that considers, among other factors:

  (i)   the economic impact of the measure or series of measures, although the sole fact that a measure or series of measures of a Party has an adverse effect on the economic value of an investment does not establish that an indirect expropriation has occurred;

  (ii) the extent to which the measure or series of measures interferes with distinct, reasonable investment-backed expectations; and

  (iii) the character of the measure or series of measures;

(c) Except in rare circumstances, such as when a measure or series of measures is so severe in the light of its purpose that it cannot be reasonably viewed as having been adopted and applied in good faith, non-discriminatory measures of a Party that are designed and applied to protect legitimate public welfare objectives, such as health, safety and the environment, do not constitute indirect expropriation.

ANNEX C.26   STANDARD WAIVER AND CONSENT IN ACCORDANCE WITH ARTICLE 26 OF THIS AGREEMENT[11]

In the interest of facilitating the filing of waivers as required by Article 26 of this Agreement, and to facilitate the orderly conduct of the dispute resolution procedures set out in Section C, the following standard waiver forms shall be used, depending on the type of claim.

---

11 Subject to Annex C.27.

Claims filed under Article 22 (Claim by an Investor of a Party on Its Own Behalf) must be accompanied by either Form 1, where the investor is a national of a Party, or Form 2, where the investor is a Party, a state enterprise thereof, or an enterprise of such Party.

Where the claim is based on loss or damage to an interest in an enterprise of the other Party that is a juridical person that the investor owns or controls directly or indirectly, either Form 1 or 2 must be accompanied by Form 3.

Claims made under Article 23 (Claim by an Investor of a Party on Behalf of an Enterprise) must be accompanied by either Form 1, where the investor is a national of a Party, or Form 2, where the investor is a Party, a state enterprise thereof, or an enterprise of such Party, and Form 4.

Form 1

Consent and waiver for an investor of a Party bringing a claim under Article 22 or Article 23 (where the investor is a national of a Party) of the Agreement between Canada and the Republic of Peru for the Promotion and Protection of Investments of (date of entry-into-force):

I, (Name of investor), consent to arbitration in accordance with the procedures set out in this Agreement, and waive my right to initiate or continue before any administrative tribunal or court under the law of any Party to the Agreement, or other dispute settlement procedures, any proceedings with respect to the measure of (Name of disputing Party) that is alleged to be a breach referred to in Article 22 or Article 23, except for proceedings for injunctive, declaratory or other extraordinary relief, not involving the payment of damages, before an administrative tribunal or court under the law of (Name of disputing Party).
(To be signed and dated)

Form 2

Consent and waiver for an investor of a Party bringing a claim under Article 22 or Article 23 (where the investor is a Party, a state enterprise thereof, or an enterprise of such Party) of the Agreement between Canada and the Republic of Peru for the Promotion and Protection of Investments of (date of entry-into-force):

I, (Name of declarant), on behalf of (Name of investor), consent to arbitration in accordance with the procedures set out in this Agreement, and waive the right of (Name of investor) to initiate or continue before any administrative tribunal or court under the law of any Party to the Agreement, or other dispute settlement procedures, any proceedings with respect to the measure of (Name of disputing Party) that is alleged to be a breach referred to in Article 22 or Article 23, except for proceedings for injunctive, declaratory or other extraordinary relief, not involving the payment of damages before an administrative tribunal or court under the law of (Name of disputing Party).

I hereby solemnly declare that I am duly authorised to execute this consent and waiver on behalf of (Name of investor).
(To be signed and dated)

Form 3

Waiver of an enterprise that is the subject of a claim by an investor of a Party under Article 22 of the Agreement between Canada and the Republic of Peru for the Promotion and Protection of Investments of (date of entry-into-force):

I, (Name of declarant), waive the right of (Name of the enterprise) to initiate or continue before any administrative tribunal or court under the law of any Party to this Agreement, or other dispute settlement procedures, any proceedings with respect to the measure of (Name of disputing Party) that is alleged by (Name of investor) to be a breach referred to in Article 22, except for proceedings for injunctive, declaratory or other extraordinary relief, not involving the payment of damages, before an administrative tribunal or court under the law of (Name of disputing Party).

I hereby solemnly declare that I am duly authorised to execute this waiver on behalf of (Name of the enterprise).
(To be signed and dated)

Form 4

Consent and waiver of an enterprise that is the subject of a claim by an investor of a Party under Article 23 of the Agreement between Canada and the Republic of Peru for the Promotion and Protection of Investments of (date of entry-into-force):

   I, (Name of declarant), on behalf of (Name of enterprise), consent to arbitration in accordance with the procedures set out in this Agreement, and waive the right of (Name of enterprise) to initiate or continue before any administrative tribunal or court under the law of any Party to the Agreement, or other dispute settlement procedures, any proceedings with respect to the measure of (Name of disputing Party) that is alleged by (Name of investor) to be a breach referred to in Article 23, except for proceedings for injunctive, declaratory or other extraordinary relief, not involving the payment of damages before an administrative tribunal or court under the law of (Name of disputing Party).

   I hereby solemnly declare that I am duly authorised to execute this consent and waiver on behalf of (Name of the enterprise).

(To be signed and dated)

ANNEX C.27   SUBMISSION OF A CLAIM TO ARBITRATION

1. An investor of Canada may not submit to arbitration under Section C a claim that the Republic of Peru has breached an obligation under Section B:
   (a) on its own behalf under Article 22(1)(a), or
   (b) on behalf of an enterprise of the Republic of Peru that is a juridical person that the investor owns or controls directly or indirectly under Article 23(1)(a),
   if the investor or the enterprise, respectively, has alleged that breach of an obligation under Section B in proceedings before a court or administrative tribunal of the Republic of Peru.

2. An investor of Canada may not submit to arbitration under Section C a claim that the Republic of Peru has breached a legal stability agreement referred to in Articles 22(3) and 23(3):
   (a) on its own behalf under Article 22(1)(b), or
   (b) on behalf of an enterprise of the Republic of Peru that is a juridical person that the investor owns or controls directly or indirectly under Article 23(1)(b),
   if the investor or the enterprise, respectively, has alleged that breach in proceedings before a court or administrative tribunal of the Republic of Peru or has submitted that claim to any other binding dispute settlement proceedings.

3. For greater certainty, if an investor of Canada elects to submit:
   (a) a claim described in paragraph 1 to a court or administrative tribunal of the Republic of Peru, or
   (b) a claim described in paragraph 2 to a court or administrative tribunal of the Republic of Peru or to any other binding dispute settlement proceedings,
   that election shall be definitive and the investor may not thereafter submit the same claim to arbitration under Section C.

ANNEX C.39   SUBMISSIONS BY NON-DISPUTING PARTIES

1. The application for leave to file a non-disputing party submission shall:
   (a) be made in writing, dated and signed by the person filing the application, and include the address and other contact details of the applicant;
   (b) be no longer than 5 typed pages;

(c) describe the applicant, including, where relevant, its membership and legal status (*e.g.*, company, trade association or other non-governmental organization), its general object-ives, the nature of its activities, and any parent organization (including any organization that directly or indirectly controls the applicant);

(d) disclose whether the applicant has any affiliation, direct or indirect, with any disputing party;

(e) identify any government, person or organization that has provided any financial or other assistance in preparing the submission;

(f) specify the nature of the interest that the applicant has in the arbitration;

(g) identify the specific issues of fact or law in the arbitration that the applicant has addressed in its written submission;

(h) explain, by reference to the factors specified in Article 39(4), why the Tribunal should accept the submission; and

(i) be made in a language of the arbitration.

2. The submission filed by a non-disputing party shall:
   (a) be dated and signed by the person filing the submission;
   (b) be concise, and in no case longer than 20 typed pages, including any appendices;
   (c) set out a precise statement supporting the applicant's position on the issues; and
   (d) only address matters within the scope of the dispute.

ANNEX E.51 EXCLUSIONS FROM DISPUTE SETTLEMENT

1. A decision by Canada following a review under the *Investment Canada Act*, with respect to whether or not to permit an acquisition that is subject to review, shall not be subject to the dispute settlement provisions under Sections C or D of this Agreement.

2. Issues relating to the administration or enforcement of Canada's *Competition Act*, its regu-lations, policies and practices, or any successor legislation, policies and practices and any decision pursuant to the *Competition Act* made in any cases or patterns of cases by the Commissioner of Competition, Attorney General of Canada, the Competition Tribunal, the responsible Minister or the courts, shall not be subject to the dispute settlement provisions under Sections C or D of this Agreement.

3. Issues relating to the administration or enforcement of Peru's *Legislative Decree No 701, Law 26876, and Supreme Decree No 039-2000-ITINCI* to the extent that it relates to false or misleading representations and deceptive marketing practices, their regulations, policies and practices, or any successor legislation, policies and practices and any decision pursuant to *Legislative Decree No 701, Law 26876, and Supreme Decree No 039-2000-ITINCI* to the extent that it relates to false or misleading representations and deceptive marketing practices made in any cases or patterns of cases by the Instituto Nacional de Defensa de la Competencia y de la Protección de la Propiedad Intelectual[12] (INDECOPI) or the Ministerio Público[13], the responsible Minister or the courts, shall not be subject to the dispute settlement provisions under Sections C or D of this Agreement.

4. A decision by a Party to prohibit or restrict the acquisition of an investment in its territory by an investor of the other Party, or its investment, pursuant to Article 10(4) shall not be subject to the provisions of Sections C or D of this Agreement.

---

12 The National Institute for the Defence of the Competition and Protection of the Intellectual Property.
13 "Ministerio Público" is the counterpart to "Attorney General of Canada" referred to in paragraph 2.

ANNEX III   EXCEPTIONS FROM MOST-FAVOURED-NATION TREATMENT

1. Article 4 shall not apply to treatment accorded under all bilateral or multilateral international agreements in force or signed prior to the date of entry into force of this Agreement.

2. Article 4 shall not apply to treatment by a Party pursuant to any existing or future bilateral or multilateral agreement:
   (a) establishing, strengthening or expanding a free trade area or customs union; or
   (b) relating to:
       (i) aviation;
       (ii) fisheries;
       (iii) maritime matters, including salvage.

3. For greater certainty, Article 4 shall not apply to any current or future foreign aid programme to promote economic development, whether under a bilateral agreement, or pursuant to a multilateral arrangement or agreement, such as the OECD Agreement on Export Credits.

III-8

United States–Singapore Free Trade Agreement

Date 6 May 2003
In force 1 January 2004
Source 42 ILM 1026 (2003)
Link <http://www.ustr.gov/trade-agreements/free-trade-agreements/singapore-fta/final-text>

UNITED STATES–SINGAPORE FREE TRADE AGREEMENT

The Government of the United States and the Government of the Republic of Singapore ("the Parties"),

Recognizing their longstanding friendship and important trade and investment relationship;

Recognizing that open and competitive markets are the key drivers of economic efficiency, innovation and wealth creation;

Recognizing the importance of ongoing liberalization of trade in goods and services at the multilateral level;

Aware of the growing importance of trade and investment for the economies of the Asia-Pacific region;

Reaffirming their rights, obligations and undertakings under the Marrakesh Agreement Establishing the World Trade Organization, and other multilateral, regional, and bilateral agreements and arrangements to which they are both Parties;

Recognizing that economic development, social development, and environmental protection are interdependent and mutually reinforcing components of sustainable development, and that an open and non-discriminatory multilateral trading system can play a major role in achieving sustainable development;

Reaffirming their commitment to achieving the Asia-Pacific Economic Co-operation goals of free and open trade and investment;

Reaffirming their commitment to securing trade liberalization and an outward-looking approach to trade and investment;

Reaffirming their shared commitment to facilitating bilateral trade through removing or reducing technical, sanitary and phytosanitary barriers to the movement of goods between the Parties;

Desiring to promote competition;

Desiring to promote transparency and to eliminate bribery and corruption in business transactions;

Recognizing that liberalized trade in goods and services will assist the expansion of trade and investment flows, raise the standard of living, and create new employment opportunities in their respective territories;

Desiring to expand trade in services on a mutually advantageous basis, under conditions of transparency and progressive liberalization, with the aim of securing an overall balance of rights and obligations, while recognizing the rights of each Party to regulate, and to introduce new regulations, giving due respect to national policy objectives;

Reaffirming the importance of pursuing the above in a manner consistent with the protection and enhancement of the environment, including through regional environmental cooperative activities and implementation of multilateral environmental agreements to which they are both parties; and

Affirming their commitment to encourage the accession to this Agreement by other States in order to further the liberalization of trade in goods and services between States;

Have *agreed* as follows:

CHAPTER 1   ESTABLISHMENT OF A FREE TRADE AREA AND DEFINITIONS

Article 1.1   General

1. The Parties to this Agreement, consistent with Article XXIV of GATT 1994 and Article V of GATS, hereby establish a free trade area in accordance with the provisions of this Agreement.

2. The Parties reaffirm their existing rights and obligations with respect to each other under existing bilateral and multilateral agreements to which both Parties are party, including the WTO Agreement.

3. This Agreement shall not be construed to derogate from any international legal obligation between the Parties that entitles goods or services, or suppliers of goods or services, to treatment more favorable than that accorded by this Agreement.

Article 1.2   General Definitions

For purposes of this Agreement, unless otherwise specified:

1. **Customs Valuation Agreement** means the WTO Agreement on Implementation of Article VII of the General Agreement on Tariffs and Trade 1994;

2. **days** means calendar days;

3. **enterprise** means any entity constituted or organized under applicable law, whether or not for profit, and whether privately-owned or governmentally-owned, including any corporation, trust, partnership, sole proprietorship, joint venture or other association;

4. **enterprise of a Party** means an enterprise constituted or organized under the law of a Party;

5. **GATS** means the General Agreement on Trade in Services;

6. **GATT 1994** means the General Agreement on Tariffs and Trade 1994;

7. **goods of a Party** means domestic products as these are understood in GATT 1994 or such goods as the Parties may agree, and includes originating goods of that Party;

8. **government procurement** means the process by which a government obtains the use of or acquires goods or services, or any combination thereof, for governmental purposes and not with a view to commercial sale or resale, or use in the production or supply of goods or services for commercial sale or resale;

9. **measure** includes any law, regulation, procedure, requirement or practice;

10. **national** means a natural person referred to in Annex 1A;

11. **originating good** has the meaning established in Chapter 3 (Rules of Origin);

12. **person** means a natural person or enterprise;

13. **person of a Party** means a national or an enterprise of a Party;

14. **territory** means for a Party the territory of that Party as set out in Annex 1A;

15. **TRIPS Agreement** means the Agreement on Trade-Related Aspects of Intellectual Property Rights;

16. **WTO** means the World Trade Organization; and

17. **WTO Agreement** means the Marrakesh Agreement Establishing the World Trade Organization.

ANNEX 1A   CERTAIN DEFINITIONS

For purposes of this Agreement:

1. **national** means:
   (a) with respect to Singapore, any person who is a citizen within the meaning of its Constitution and domestic laws; and
   (b) with respect to the United States, national of the United States as defined in Title III of the Immigration and Nationality Act.

2. **territory** means:
   (a) with respect to Singapore, its land territory, internal waters and territorial sea as well as the maritime zones beyond the territorial sea, including the seabed and subsoil, over which the Republic of Singapore exercises sovereign rights or jurisdiction under its national laws and international law for the purpose of exploration and exploitation of the natural resources of such areas; and
   (b) with respect to the United States,
      (i) the customs territory of the United States which includes the 50 states, the District of Columbia and Puerto Rico;
      (ii) the foreign trade zones located in the United States and Puerto Rico; and
      (iii) any areas beyond the territorial seas of the United States within which, in accordance with international law and its domestic law, the United States may exercise rights with respect to the seabed and subsoil and their natural resources.

. . .

CHAPTER 15   INVESTMENT

SECTION A   DEFINITIONS

Article 15.1   Definitions

For purposes of this Chapter, it is understood that:

1. **central level of government** means:
   (a) for the United States, the federal level of government; and
   (b) for Singapore, the national level of government;

2. **Centre** means the International Centre for Settlement of Investment Disputes ("ICSID") established by the ICSID Convention;

3. **claimant** means an investor of a Party that is a party to an investment dispute with the other Party;

4. **covered investment** means, with respect to a Party, an investment in its territory of an investor of the other Party in existence as of the date of entry into force of this Agreement or established, acquired, or expanded thereafter;

5. **disputing parties** means the claimant and the respondent;

6. **disputing party** means either the claimant or the respondent;

7. **enterprise** means any entity constituted or organized under applicable law, whether or not for profit, and whether privately or governmentally owned or controlled, including a corporation, trust, partnership, sole proprietorship, joint venture, association, or similar organization; and a branch of an enterprise;

8. **enterprise of a Party** means an enterprise constituted or organized under the law of a Party, and a branch located in the territory of a Party and carrying out business activities there;

9. **freely usable currency** means "freely usable currency" as determined by the International Monetary Fund under its *Articles of Agreement*;

10. **government enterprise** means "government enterprise" as defined in Chapter 12 (Anti-competitive Business Conduct, Designated Monopolies, and Government Enterprises);

11. **ICSID Additional Facility Rules** means the Rules Governing the Additional Facility for the Administration of Proceedings by the Secretariat of the International Centre for Settlement of Investment Disputes;

12. **ICSID Convention** means the Convention on the Settlement of Investment Disputes between States and Nationals of Other States, done at Washington, March 18, 1965;

13. **investment** means every asset owned or controlled, directly or indirectly, by an investor, that has the characteristics of an investment.[15-1] Forms that an investment may take include:
    (a) an enterprise;
    (b) shares, stock, and other forms of equity participation in an enterprise;
    (c) bonds, debentures, other debt instruments, and loans;[15-2]
    (d) futures, options, and other derivatives;
    (e) turnkey, construction, management, production, concession, revenue-sharing, and other similar contracts;
    (f) intellectual property rights;
    (g) licenses, authorizations, permits, and similar rights conferred pursuant to applicable domestic law;[15-3, 15-4] and
    (h) other tangible or intangible, movable or immovable property, and related property rights, such as leases, mortgages, liens, and pledges.

14. **investment agreement**[15-5] means a written agreement that takes effect on or after the date of entry into force of this Agreement between a national authority[15-6] of a Party and a covered investment or an investor of the other Party (i) that grants rights with respect to natural resources or other assets that a national authority controls, and (ii) that the covered investment or the investor relies on in establishing or acquiring the covered investment;

15. **investment authorization**[15-7] means an authorization that the foreign investment authority of a Party grants to a covered investment or an investor of the other Party;

16. **investor of a non-Party** means, with respect to a Party, an investor that is seeking to make, is making, or has made an investment in the territory of that Party, that is not an investor of either Party;

17. **investor of a Party** means a Party or a national or an enterprise of a Party that is seeking to make, is making, or has made an investment in the territory of the other Party; provided, however, that a natural person who is a dual national shall be deemed to be exclusively a national of the State of his/her dominant and effective nationality;

18. **monopoly** means "monopoly" as defined in Chapter 12 (Anticompetitive Business Conduct, Designated Monopolies, and Government Enterprises);

15-1 Where an asset lacks the characteristics of an investment, that asset is not an investment regardless of the form it may take. The characteristics of an investment include the commitment of capital, the expectation of gain or profit, or the assumption of risk.

15-2 Some forms of debt, such as bonds, debentures, and long-term notes, are more likely to have the characteristics of an investment, while other forms of debt, such as claims to payment that are immediately due and result from the sale of goods or services, are less likely to have such characteristics.

15-3 Whether a particular type of license, authorization, permit, or similar instrument (including a concession, to the extent that it has the nature of such an instrument) has the characteristics of an investment depends on such factors as the nature and extent of the rights that the holder has under the domestic law of the Party. Among the licenses, authorizations, permits, and similar instruments that do not have the characteristics of an investment are those that do not create any rights protected under domestic law. For greater certainty, the foregoing is without prejudice to whether any asset associated with the license, authorization, permit, or similar instrument has the characteristics of an investment.

15-4 The term "investment" does not include an order or judgment entered in a judicial or administrative action.

15-5 Actions taken by an agency of a Party to enforce laws of general application such as competition law do not come within this definition.

15-6 For purposes of this definition, "national authority" means (1) for Singapore, a ministry or other government body that is constituted by an Act of Parliament; and (2) for the United States, an authority at the central level of government.

15-7 Actions taken by an agency of a Party to enforce laws of general application such as competition law do not come within this definition.

19. **New York Convention** means the *United Nations Convention on the Recognition and Enforcement of Foreign Arbitral Awards*, done at New York, June 10, 1958;

20. **non-disputing Party** means the Party that is not a party to an investment dispute;

21. **protected information** means confidential business information or information that is privileged or otherwise protected from disclosure under a Party's law;

22. **regional level of government** means, for the United States, a state of the United States, the District of Columbia, or Puerto Rico. For Singapore, "regional level of government" is not applicable, as Singapore has no government at the regional level;

23. **respondent** means the Party that is a party to an investment dispute;

24. **Secretary-General** means the Secretary-General of ICSID;

25. **tribunal** means an arbitration tribunal established under Article 15.18 or 15.24; and

26. **UNCITRAL Arbitration Rules** means the arbitration rules of the United Nations Commission on International Trade Law.

SECTION B   INVESTMENT

Article 15.2   Scope and Coverage

This Chapter applies to measures adopted or maintained by a Party relating to:

(a) investors of the other Party;

(b) covered investments; and

(c) with respect to Articles 15.8 and 15.10, all investments in the territory of the Party.

Article 15.3   Relation to Other Chapters

1. In the event of any inconsistency between this Chapter and another Chapter, the other Chapter shall prevail to the extent of the inconsistency.

2. A requirement by a Party that a service provider of the other Party post a bond or other form of financial security as a condition of providing a service into its territory does not of itself make this Chapter applicable to the provision of that cross-border service. This Chapter applies to that Party's treatment of the posted bond or financial security.

3. This Chapter does not apply to measures adopted or maintained by a Party to the extent that they are covered by Chapter 10 (Financial Services).

Article 15.4   National Treatment and Most-Favored-Nation Treatment

1. Each Party shall accord to investors of the other Party treatment no less favorable than that it accords, in like circumstances, to its own investors with respect to the establishment, acquisition, expansion, management, conduct, operation, and sale or other disposition of investments in its territory. Each Party shall accord to covered investments treatment no less favorable than that it accords, in like circumstances, to investments in its territory of its own investors with respect to the establishment, acquisition, expansion, management, conduct, operation, and sale or other disposition of investments. The treatment each Party shall accord under this paragraph is "national treatment."

2. The treatment to be accorded by a Party under paragraph 1 means, with respect to a state, territory or possession, treatment no less favorable than the most favorable treatment accorded, in like circumstances, by that state, territory, or possession, to investors, and to investments of investors, of the Party of which it forms a part.

3. Each Party shall accord to investors of the other Party treatment no less favorable than that it accords, in like circumstances, to investors of any non-Party with respect to the establishment, acquisition, expansion, management, conduct, operation, and sale or other disposition of investments in its territory. Each Party shall accord to covered investments treatment no less favorable than that it accords, in like circumstances, to investments in its territory of investors

of any non-Party with respect to the establishment, acquisition, expansion, management, conduct, operation, and sale or other disposition of investments. The treatment each Party shall accord under this paragraph is "most-favored-nation treatment."

4. Each Party shall accord to investors of the other Party and to their covered investments the better of national treatment or most-favored-nation treatment.

Article 15.5   Minimum standard of treatment[15-8]

1. Each Party shall accord to covered investments treatment in accordance with customary international law, including fair and equitable treatment and full protection and security.

2. For greater certainty, paragraph 1 prescribes the customary international law minimum standard of treatment of aliens as the minimum standard of treatment to be afforded to covered investments. The concepts of "fair and equitable treatment" and "full protection and security" do not require treatment in addition to or beyond that which is required by that standard, and do not create additional substantive rights.

   (a) The obligation in paragraph 1 to provide "fair and equitable treatment" includes the obligation not to deny justice in criminal, civil, or administrative adjudicatory proceedings in accordance with the principle of due process embodied in the principal legal systems of the world; and

   (b) The obligation in paragraph 1 to provide "full protection and security" requires each Party to provide the level of police protection required under customary international law.

3. A determination that there has been a breach of another provision of this Agreement, or of a separate international agreement, does not establish that there has been a breach of this Article.

4. Without prejudice to paragraph 1 and notwithstanding Article 15.12.5(b), each Party shall accord to investors of the other Party, and to covered investments, non-discriminatory treatment with respect to measures it adopts or maintains relating to losses suffered by investments in its territory owing to armed conflict or civil strife.

5. Paragraph 4 does not apply to existing measures relating to subsidies or grants that would be inconsistent with Article 15.4.1 and 15.4.2 but for Article 15.12.5(b).

Article 15.6   Expropriation[15-9]

1. Neither Party may expropriate or nationalize a covered investment either directly or indirectly through measures equivalent to expropriation or nationalization ("expropriation"), except:

   (a) for a public purpose;

   (b) in a non-discriminatory manner;

   (c) on payment of prompt, adequate, and effective compensation in accordance with paragraphs 2, 3, and 4; and

   (d) in accordance with due process of law and Article 15.5.1, 15.5.2, and 15.5.3.

2. Compensation shall:

   (a) be paid without delay;

15-8 Article 15.5 is to be interpreted in accordance with the letter exchange on customary international law.

Note by the Editors: In their letters, which are available on the website referred to at the start of this document and which form an integral part of this agreement (Article 15.26), the parties expressed their 'shared agreement that customary international law results from a general and consistent practice of States that they follow from a sense of legal obligation.' With respect to Article 15.5., the parties noted that 'the customary international law minimum standard of treatment of aliens refers to all customary international law principles that protect the economic rights and interests of aliens.'

15-9 Article 15.6 is to be interpreted in accordance with the letter exchange on customary international law and the letter exchange on expropriation, and is subject to the letter exchange on land expropriation.

Note by the Editors: The letter exchange are available from the website referred to at the start of this document and form an integral part of this agreement (Article 15.26). For the letter exchange on customary international law, see explanatory note to footnote 15–8. The letter exchange on land expropriations introduces a special regime for the protection of land held by American investors in Singapore, which, eg restricts recourse to investor-State dispute settlement. In the letter exchange on expropriation, the parties agree on the following:

1. Article 15.6.1 (Expropriation) is intended to reflect customary international law concerning the obligation of States with respect to expropriation.

2. An action or a series of actions by a Party cannot constitute an expropriation unless it interferes with a tangible or intangible property right or property interest in an investment.

3. Article 15.6.1 (Expropriation) address two situations. The first is direct expropriation, where an investment is nationalized or otherwise directly expropriated through formal transfer of title or outright seizure.

4. The second situation addressed by Article 15.6.1 (Expropriation) is indirect expropriation, where an action or series of actions by a Party has an effect equivalent to direct expropriation without formal transfer of title or outright seizure.

(b) be equivalent to the fair market value of the expropriated investment immediately before the expropriatory action was taken ("the date of expropriation");

(c) be fully realizable and freely transferable; and

(d) not reflect any change in value occurring because the expropriatory action had become known before the date of expropriation.

3. If the fair market value is denominated in a freely usable currency, the compensation paid shall be no less than the fair market value on the date of expropriation, plus interest at a commercially reasonable rate for that currency, accrued from the date of expropriation until the date of payment.

4. If the fair market value is denominated in a currency that is not freely usable, the compensation paid—converted into the currency of payment at the market rate of exchange prevailing on the date of payment—shall be no less than:

(a) the fair market value on the date of expropriation, converted into a freely usable currency at the market rate of exchange prevailing on that date, plus

(b) interest, at a commercially reasonable rate for that freely usable currency, accrued from the date of expropriation until the date of payment.

5. This Article does not apply to the issuance of compulsory licenses granted in relation to intellectual property rights in accordance with the Agreement on Trade-Related Aspects of Intellectual Property Rights ("TRIPS Agreement"), or to the revocation, limitation, or creation of intellectual property rights, to the extent that such issuance, revocation, limitation, or creation is consistent with Chapter 16 (Intellectual Property Rights) of this Agreement.

Article 15.7 Transfers[15-10]

1. Each Party shall permit all transfers relating to a covered investment to be made freely and without delay into and out of its territory. Such transfers include:

(a) contributions to capital;

(b) profits, dividends, capital gains, and proceeds from the sale of all or any part of the covered investment or from the partial or complete liquidation of the covered investment;

(c) interest, royalty payments, management fees, and technical assistance and other fees;

(d) payments made under a contract entered into by the investor, or the covered investment, including payments made pursuant to a loan agreement;

(e) payments made pursuant to Article 15.6 and Article 15.5.4; and

(f) payments arising under Section C.

2. Each Party shall permit transfers relating to a covered investment to be made in a freely usable currency at the market rate of exchange prevailing at the time of transfer.

3. Each Party shall permit returns in kind relating to a covered investment to be made as authorized or specified in an investment authorization or other written agreement between the Party and a covered investment or an investor of the other Party.

4. Notwithstanding paragraphs 1, 2, and 3, a Party may prevent a transfer through the equitable, non-discriminatory, and good faith application of its law relating to:

(a) bankruptcy, insolvency, or the protection of the rights of creditors;

(b) issuing, trading, or dealing in securities, futures, options, or derivatives;

(a) The determination of whether an action or a series of actions by a Party, in a specific fact situation, constitutes an indirect expropriation, requires a case-by-case, fact-based inquiry that considers, among other factors:

(i) the economic impact of the government action, although the fact that an action or series of actions by a Party has an adverse effect on the economic value of an investment, standing alone, does not establish that an indirect expropriation has occurred;

(ii) the extent to which the government action interferes with distinct, reasonable investment-back expectations; and

(iii) the character of the government action.

(b) Except in rare circumstances, nondiscriminatory regulatory actions by a Party that are designed and applied to protect legitimate public welfare objectives, such as public health, safety, and the environment, do not constitute indirect expropriations.

15-10 Article 15.7 is subject to Annex 15A.

(c) financial reporting or record keeping of transfers when necessary to assist law enforcement or financial regulatory authorities;

(d) criminal or penal offenses; or

(e) ensuring compliance with orders or judgments in judicial or administrative proceedings.

Article 15.8   Performance Requirements[15-11]

1. Neither Party may impose or enforce any of the following requirements, or enforce any commitment or undertaking, in connection with the establishment, acquisition, expansion, management, conduct, operation, or sale or other disposition of an investment of an investor of a Party or of a non-Party in its territory:

   (a) to export a given level or percentage of goods or services;

   (b) to achieve a given level or percentage of domestic content;

   (c) to purchase, use, or accord a preference to goods produced in its territory, or to purchase goods from persons in its territory;

   (d) to relate in any way the volume or value of imports to the volume or value of exports or to the amount of foreign exchange inflows associated with such investment;

   (e) to restrict sales of goods or services in its territory that such investment produces or supplies by relating such sales in any way to the volume or value of its exports or foreign exchange earnings;

   (f) to transfer a particular technology, production process, or other proprietary knowledge to a person in its territory; or

   (g) to supply exclusively from the territory of the Party the goods that it produces or the services that it supplies to a specific regional market or to the world market.

2. Neither Party may condition the receipt or continued receipt of an advantage, in connection with the establishment, acquisition, expansion, management, conduct, operation, or sale or other disposition of an investment in its territory of an investor of a Party or of a non-Party, on compliance with any of the following requirements:

   (a) to achieve a given level or percentage of domestic content;

   (b) to purchase, use, or accord a preference to goods produced in its territory, or to purchase goods from persons in its territory;

   (c) to relate in any way the volume or value of imports to the volume or value of exports or to the amount of foreign exchange inflows associated with such investment; or

   (d) to restrict sales of goods or services in its territory that such investment produces or supplies by relating such sales in any way to the volume or value of its exports or foreign exchange earnings.

3. (a) Nothing in paragraph 2 shall be construed to prevent a Party from conditioning the receipt or continued receipt of an advantage, in connection with an investment in its territory of an investor of a Party or of a non-Party, on compliance with a requirement to locate production, supply a service, train or employ workers, construct or expand particular facilities, or carry out research and development, in its territory.

   (b) Paragraph 1(f) does not apply:

      (i) when a Party authorizes use of an intellectual property right in accordance with Article 16.7.6 (Patents), and to measures requiring the disclosure of proprietary information that fall within the scope of, and are consistent with, Article 39 of the TRIPS Agreement; or

      (ii) when the requirement is imposed or the commitment or undertaking is enforced by a court, administrative tribunal, or competition authority to remedy a practice deter-

---

15-11 Article 15.8 is subject to Annex 15B and Annex 15C.

mined after judicial or administrative process to be anticompetitive under the Party's competition laws.

(c) Paragraphs 1(b), (c), and (f), and 2(a) and (b), shall not be construed to prevent a Party from adopting or maintaining measures, including environmental measures:

   (i) necessary to secure compliance with laws and regulations that are not inconsistent with this Agreement;

   (ii) necessary to protect human, animal, or plant life or health; or

   (iii) related to the conservation of living or non-living exhaustible natural resources; provided that such measures are not applied in an arbitrary or unjustifiable manner, and provided that such measures do not constitute a disguised restriction on investment or international trade.

(d) Paragraphs 1(a), (b), and (c), and 2(a) and (b), do not apply to qualification requirements for goods or services with respect to export promotion and foreign aid programs.

(e) Paragraphs 1(b), (c), (f), and (g), and 2(a) and (b), do not apply to government procurement.

(f) Paragraphs 2(a) and (b) do not apply to requirements imposed by an importing Party relating to the content of goods necessary to qualify for preferential tariffs or preferential quotas.

4. For greater certainty, paragraphs 1 and 2 do not apply to any requirement other than the requirements set out in those paragraphs.

Article 15.9   Senior Management and Boards of Directors

1. Neither Party may require that an enterprise of that Party that is a covered investment appoint to senior management positions individuals of any particular nationality.

2. A Party may require that a majority of the board of directors, or any committee thereof, of an enterprise of that Party that is a covered investment, be of a particular nationality, or resident in the territory of the Party, provided that the requirement does not materially impair the ability of the investor of the other Party to exercise control over its investment.

Article 15.10   Investment and Environment

Nothing in this Chapter shall be construed to prevent a Party from adopting, maintaining, or enforcing any measure otherwise consistent with this Chapter that it considers appropriate to ensure that investment activity in its territory is undertaken in a manner sensitive to environmental concerns.

Article 15.11   Denial of Benefits

A Party may deny the benefits of this Chapter to an investor of the other Party that is an enterprise of such other Party and to investments of that investor if:

(a) investors of a non-Party own or control the enterprise and the denying Party:

   (i) does not maintain diplomatic relations with the non-Party; or

   (ii) adopts or maintains measures with respect to the non-Party or an investor of the non-Party that prohibit transactions with the enterprise or that would be violated or circumvented if the benefits of this Chapter were accorded to the enterprise or to its investments; or

(b) the enterprise has no substantial business activities in the territory of the other Party, and investors of a non-Party, or of the denying Party, own or control the enterprise.

Article 15.12   Non-Conforming Measures

1. Articles 15.4, 15.8, and 15.9 do not apply to:

(a) any existing non-conforming measure that is maintained by a Party at:

   (i) the central level of government, as set out by that Party in its Schedule to Annex 8A,

(ii) a regional level of government, as set out by that Party in its Schedule to Annex 8A, or

(iii) a local level of government;

(b) the continuation or prompt renewal of any non-conforming measure referred to in subparagraph (a); or

(c) an amendment to any non-conforming measure referred to in subparagraph (a) to the extent that the amendment does not decrease the conformity of the measure, as it existed immediately before the amendment, with Articles 15.4, 15.8, or 15.9.

2. Articles 15.4, 15.8, and 15.9 do not apply to any measure that a Party adopts or maintains with respect to sectors, sub-sectors, or activities, as set out in its Schedule to Annex 8B.

3. Neither Party may, under any measure adopted after the date of entry into force of this Agreement and covered by its Schedule to Annex 8B, require an investor of the other Party, by reason of its nationality, to sell or otherwise dispose of an investment existing at the time the measure becomes effective.

4. Article 15.4 does not apply to any measure that is an exception to, or derogation from, the obligations under Article 16.1.3 (General Provisions) as specifically provided for in that Article.

5. Articles 15.4 and 15.9 do not apply to:

(a) government procurement; or

(b) subsidies or grants provided by a Party, including government-supported loans, guarantees, and insurance.

Article 15.13   Special Formalities and Information Requirements

1. Nothing in Article 15.4.1 and 15.4.2 shall be construed to prevent a Party from adopting or maintaining a measure that prescribes special formalities in connection with covered investments, such as a requirement that investors be residents of the Party or that covered investments be legally constituted under the laws or regulations of the Party, provided that such formalities do not materially impair the protections afforded by a Party to investors of the other Party and covered investments pursuant to this Chapter.

2. Notwithstanding Article 15.4, a Party may require an investor of the other Party, or a covered investment, to provide information concerning that investment solely for informational or statistical purposes. The party shall protect such business information that is confidential from any disclosure that would prejudice the competitive position of the investor or the covered investment. Nothing in this paragraph shall be construed to prevent a Party from otherwise obtaining or disclosing information in connection with the equitable and good faith application of its law.

SECTION C   INVESTOR–STATE DISPUTE SETTLEMENT

Article 15.14   Consultation and Negotiation

In the event of an investment dispute, the claimant and the respondent should initially seek to resolve the dispute through consultation and negotiation, which may include the use of non-binding, third-party procedures.

Article 15.15   Submission of a Claim to Arbitration[15-12]

1. In the event that a disputing party considers that an investment dispute cannot be settled by consultation and negotiation:

(a) the claimant, on its own behalf, may submit to arbitration under this Section a claim:

(i) that the respondent has breached

15-12 Article 15.15 is subject to the letter exchange on land expropriation.
Note by the Editors: For brief comment see text following footnote 15–9, above.

    (A) an obligation under Section B,

    (B) an investment authorization, or

    (C) an investment agreement; and

  (ii) that the claimant has incurred loss or damage by reason of, or arising out of, that breach; and

(b) the claimant, on behalf of an enterprise of the respondent that is a juridical person that the claimant owns or controls directly or indirectly, may submit to arbitration under this Section a claim:

  (i) that the respondent has breached

    (A) an obligation under Section B,

    (B) an investment authorization, or

    (C) an investment agreement; and

  (ii) that the enterprise has incurred loss or damage by reason of, or arising out of, that breach.

2. For greater certainty, a claimant may submit to arbitration under this Section a claim that the respondent has breached an obligation under Section B through the actions of a designated monopoly or a government enterprise exercising delegated governmental authority as described in Article 12.3.1(c)(i) and 12.3.2(b) (Designated Monopolies and Government Enterprises), respectively.

3. Without prejudice to Article 10.1.2 (Scope and Coverage), no claim may be submitted under this Section that alleges a violation of any provision of this Agreement other than an obligation under Section B or the letter exchange on land expropriation.

4. At least 90 days before submitting any claim to arbitration under this Section, a claimant shall deliver to the respondent a written notice of its intention to submit the claim to arbitration ("notice of intent"). The notice shall specify:

(a) the name and address of the claimant and, where a claim is submitted on behalf of an enterprise, the name, address, and place of incorporation of the enterprise;

(b) for each claim, the provision of this Agreement, investment authorization, or investment agreement alleged to have been breached and any other relevant provisions;

(c) the legal and factual basis for each claim; and

(d) the relief sought and the approximate amount of damages claimed.

5. Provided that six months have elapsed since the events giving rise to the claim, a claimant may submit a claim referred to in paragraph 1:

(a) under the ICSID Convention and the ICSID Rules of Procedure for Arbitration Proceedings, provided that both the respondent and the Party of the claimant are parties to the ICSID Convention;

(b) under the ICSID Additional Facility Rules, provided that either the respondent or the Party of the claimant, but not both, is a party to the ICSID Convention;

(c) under the UNCITRAL Arbitration Rules; or

(d) if the claimant and respondent agree, to any other arbitration institution or under any other arbitration rules.

6. A claim shall be deemed submitted to arbitration under this Section when the claimant's notice of or request for arbitration ("notice of arbitration"):

(a) referred to in paragraph 1 of Article 36 of the ICSID Convention is received by the Secretary-General;

(b) referred to in Article 2 of Schedule C of the ICSID Additional Facility Rules is received by the Secretary-General;

   (c) referred to in Article 3 of the UNCITRAL Arbitration Rules, together with the statement of claim referred to in Article 18 of the UNCITRAL Arbitration Rules, are received by the respondent; or

   (d) referred to under any other arbitral institution or arbitral rules selected under paragraph 5(d) is received by the respondent.

7. The arbitration rules applicable under paragraph 5, and in effect on the date the claim or claims were submitted to arbitration under this Section, shall govern the arbitration except to the extent modified by this Agreement.

8. The claimant shall provide with the notice of arbitration referred to in paragraph 6:

   (a) the name of the arbitrator that the claimant appoints; or

   (b) the claimant's written consent for the Secretary-General to appoint the claimant's arbitrator.

Article 15.16   Consent of Each Party to Arbitration

1. Each Party consents to the submission of a claim to arbitration under this Section in accordance with this Agreement.

2. The consent under paragraph 1 and the submission of a claim to arbitration under this Section shall satisfy the requirements of:

   (a) Chapter II of the ICSID Convention (Jurisdiction of the Centre) and the ICSID Additional Facility Rules for written consent of the parties to the dispute; and

   (b) Article II of the New York Convention for an "agreement in writing."

Article 15.17   Conditions and Limitations on Consent of Each Party

1. No claim may be submitted to arbitration under this Section if more than three years have elapsed from the date on which the claimant first acquired, or should have first acquired, knowledge of the breach alleged under Article 15.15.1 and knowledge that the claimant (for claims brought under Article 15.15.1(a)) or the enterprise (for claims brought under Article 15.15.1(b)) has incurred loss or damage.

2. No claim may be submitted to arbitration under this Section unless:

   (a) the claimant consents in writing to arbitration in accordance with the procedures set out in this Agreement; and

   (b) the notice of arbitration referred to in Article 15.15.6 is accompanied,

      (i) for claims submitted to arbitration under Article 15.15.1(a), by the claimant's written waiver; and

      (ii) for claims submitted to arbitration under Article 15.15.1(b), by the claimant's and the enterprise's written waivers of any right to initiate or continue before any administrative tribunal or court under the law of either Party, or other dispute settlement procedures, any proceeding with respect to any measure alleged to constitute a breach referred to in Article 15.15.

3. Notwithstanding paragraph 2(b), the claimant (for claims brought under Article 15.15.1(a)) and the claimant or the enterprise (for claims brought under Article 15.15.1(b)) may initiate or continue an action that seeks interim injunctive relief and does not involve the payment of monetary damages before a judicial or administrative tribunal of the respondent, provided that the action is brought for the sole purpose of preserving the claimant's or the enterprise's rights and interests during the pendency of the arbitration.

Article 15.18   Selection of Arbitrators

1. Unless the disputing parties otherwise agree, the tribunal shall comprise three arbitrators, one arbitrator appointed by each of the disputing parties and the third, who shall be the presiding arbitrator, appointed by agreement of the disputing parties.

2. The Secretary-General shall serve as appointing authority for an arbitration under this Section.

3. If a tribunal has not been constituted within 75 days from the date that a claim is submitted to arbitration under this Section, the Secretary-General, on the request of a disputing party, shall appoint, in his or her discretion, the arbitrator or arbitrators not yet appointed.

4. For purposes of Article 39 of the ICSID Convention and Article 7 of Schedule C to the ICSID Additional Facility Rules, and without prejudice to an objection to an arbitrator on a ground other than nationality:

   (a) the respondent agrees to the appointment of each individual member of a tribunal established under the ICSID Convention or the ICSID Additional Facility Rules;

   (b) a claimant referred to in Article 15.15.1(a) may submit a claim to arbitration under this Section, or continue a claim, under the ICSID Convention or the ICSID Additional Facility Rules, only on condition that the claimant agrees in writing to the appointment of each individual member of the tribunal; and

   (c) a claimant referred to in Article 15.15.1(b) may submit a claim to arbitration under this Section, or continue a claim, under the ICSID Convention or the ICSID Additional Facility Rules, only on condition that the claimant and the enterprise agree in writing to the appointment of each individual member of the tribunal.

Article 15.19 Conduct of the Arbitration

1. The disputing parties may agree on the legal place of any arbitration under the arbitral rules applicable under Article 15.15.5(b), (c), or (d). If the disputing parties fail to reach agreement, the tribunal shall determine the place in accordance with the applicable arbitral rules, provided that the place shall be in the territory of either Party or of a third State that is a party to the New York Convention.

2. The non-disputing Party may make oral and written submissions to the tribunal regarding the interpretation of this Agreement.

3. The tribunal shall have the authority to accept and consider *amicus curiae* submissions from any persons and entities in the territories of the Parties and from interested persons and entities outside the territories of the Parties.

4. Without prejudice to a tribunal's authority to address other objections as a preliminary question, a tribunal shall address and decide as a preliminary question any objection by the respondent that, as a matter of law, a claim submitted is not a claim for which an award in favor of the claimant may be made under Article 15.25.

   (a) Such objection shall be submitted to the tribunal as soon as possible after the tribunal is constituted, and in no event later than the date the tribunal fixes for the respondent to submit its counter-memorial (or, in the case of an amendment to the notice of arbitration referred to in Article 15.15.6, the date the tribunal fixes for the respondent to submit its response to the amendment).

   (b) On receipt of an objection under this paragraph, the tribunal shall suspend any proceedings on the merits, establish a schedule for considering the objection consistent with any schedule it has established for considering any other preliminary question, and issue a decision or award on the objection, stating the grounds therefor.

   (c) In deciding an objection under this paragraph, the tribunal shall assume to be true the claimant's factual allegations in support of any claim in the notice of arbitration (or any amendment thereof) and, in disputes brought under the UNCITRAL Arbitration Rules, the statement of claim referred to in Article 18 of the UNCITRAL Arbitration Rules. The tribunal may also consider any relevant facts not in dispute.

   (d) The respondent does not waive any objection as to competence or any argument on the merits merely because the respondent did or did not raise an objection under this paragraph or make use of the expedited procedure set out in the following paragraph.

5. In the event that the respondent so requests within 45 days after the tribunal is constituted, the tribunal shall decide on an expedited basis an objection under paragraph 4 or any objection that the dispute is not within the tribunal's competence. The tribunal shall suspend any proceedings on the merits and issue a decision or award on the objection(s), stating the grounds therefor, no later than 150 days after the date of the request. However, if a disputing party requests a hearing, the tribunal may take an additional 30 days to issue the decision or award. Regardless of whether a hearing is requested, a tribunal may, on a showing of extraordinary cause, delay issuing its decision or award by an additional brief period of time, which may not exceed 30 days.

6. When it decides a respondent's objection under paragraphs 4 or 5, the tribunal may, if warranted, award to the prevailing disputing party reasonable costs and attorneys' fees incurred in submitting or opposing the objection. In determining whether such an award is warranted, the tribunal shall consider whether either the claimant's claim or the respondent's objection was frivolous, and shall provide the disputing parties a reasonable opportunity to comment.

7. A respondent may not assert as a defense, counterclaim, right of set-off, or for any other reason that the claimant has received or will receive indemnification or other compensation for all or part of the alleged damages pursuant to an insurance or guarantee contract.

8. A tribunal may order an interim measure of protection to preserve the rights of a disputing party, or to ensure that the tribunal's jurisdiction is made fully effective, including an order to preserve evidence in the possession or control of a disputing party or to protect the tribunal's jurisdiction. A tribunal may not order attachment or enjoin the application of a measure alleged to constitute a breach referred to in Article 15.15. For purposes of this paragraph, an order includes a recommendation.

9. (a) In any arbitration conducted under this Section, at the request of a disputing party, a tribunal shall, before issuing an award on liability, transmit its proposed award to the disputing parties and to the non-disputing Party. Within 60 days after the tribunal transmits its proposed award, the disputing parties may submit written comments to the tribunal concerning any aspect of its proposed award. The tribunal shall consider any such comments and issue its award not later than 45 days after the expiration of the 60-day comment period.

   (b) Subparagraph (a) shall not apply in any arbitration conducted pursuant to this Section for which an appeal has been made available pursuant to paragraph 10.

10. If a separate multilateral agreement enters into force as between the Parties that establishes an appellate body for purposes of reviewing awards rendered by tribunals constituted pursuant to international trade or investment arrangements to hear investment disputes, the Parties shall strive to reach an agreement that would have such appellate body review awards rendered under Article 15.25 of this Section in arbitrations commenced after the appellate body's establishment.

Article 15.20   Transparency of Arbitral Proceedings

1. Subject to paragraphs 2 and 4, the respondent shall, after receiving the following documents, promptly transmit them to the non-disputing Party and make them available to the public:

   (a) the notice of intent referred to in Article 15.15.4;
   (b) the notice of arbitration referred to in Article 15.15.6;
   (c) pleadings, memorials, and briefs submitted to the tribunal by a disputing party and any written submissions submitted pursuant to Article 15.19.2 and 15.19.3 and Article 15.24;
   (d) minutes or transcripts of hearings of the tribunal, where available; and
   (e) orders, awards, and decisions of the tribunal.

2. The tribunal shall conduct hearings open to the public and shall determine, in consultation with the disputing parties, the appropriate logistical arrangements. However, any disputing party that intends to use information designated as protected information in a hearing shall so advise the tribunal. The tribunal shall make appropriate arrangements to protect the information from disclosure.

3. Nothing in this Section requires a respondent to disclose protected information or to furnish or allow access to information that it may withhold in accordance with Article 21.2 (Essential Security) or Article 21.4 (Disclosure of Information).

4. Protected information shall, if such information is submitted to the tribunal, be protected from disclosure in accordance with the following procedures:

   (a) Subject to paragraph 4(d), neither the disputing parties nor the tribunal shall disclose to the non-disputing Party or to the public any protected information where the disputing party that provided the information clearly designates it in accordance with paragraph 4(b).

   (b) Any disputing party claiming that certain information constitutes protected information shall clearly designate the information at the time it is submitted to the tribunal.

   (c) A disputing party shall, at the same time that it submits a document containing information claimed to be protected information, submit a redacted version of the document that does not contain the information. Only the redacted version shall be provided to the non-disputing Party and made public in accordance with paragraph 1.

   (d) The tribunal shall decide any objection regarding the designation of information claimed to be protected information. If the tribunal determines that such information was not properly designated, the disputing party that submitted the information may (i) withdraw all or part of its submission containing such information, or (ii) agree to resubmit complete and redacted documents with corrected designations in accordance with the tribunal's determination and paragraph 4(c). In either case, the other disputing party shall, whenever necessary, resubmit complete and redacted documents which either remove the information withdrawn under (i) by the disputing party that first submitted the information or redesignate the information consistent with the designation under (ii) of the disputing party that first submitted the information.

5. Nothing in this Section authorizes a respondent to withhold from the public information required to be disclosed by its laws.

Article 15.21   Governing Law

1. Subject to paragraph 2, a tribunal shall decide the issues in dispute related to an alleged breach of an obligation in Section B in accordance with this Agreement and applicable rules of international law.

2. A decision of the Joint Committee declaring its interpretation of a provision of this Agreement under Article 20.1.2 (Joint Committee) shall be binding on a tribunal established under this Section, and any award must be consistent with that decision.

Article 15.22   Interpretation of Annexes

1. Where a respondent asserts as a defense that the measure alleged to be a breach is within the scope of a reservation or exception set out in Annex 8A or Annex 8B, the tribunal shall, on request of the respondent, request the interpretation of the Joint Committee on the issue. The Joint Committee shall issue in writing any decision declaring its interpretation under Article 20.1.2 (Joint Committee) to the tribunal within 60 days of delivery of the request.

2. A decision issued by the Joint Committee under paragraph 1 shall be binding on the tribunal, and any award must be consistent with that decision. If the Joint Committee fails to issue such a decision within 60 days, the tribunal shall decide the issue.

Article 15.23   Expert Reports

Without prejudice to the appointment of other kinds of experts where authorized by the applicable arbitration rules, a tribunal, at the request of a disputing party or, unless the disputing parties disapprove, on its own initiative, may appoint one or more experts to report to it in writing on any factual issue concerning environmental, health, safety, or other scientific matters raised by a disputing party in a proceeding, subject to such terms and conditions as the disputing parties may agree.

Article 15.24   Consolidation

1. Where two or more claims have been submitted separately to arbitration under Article 15.15.1 and the claims have a question of law or fact in common and arise out of the same events or circumstances, any disputing party may seek a consolidation order in accordance with the agreement of all the disputing parties sought to be covered by the order or the terms of paragraphs 2 through 10.

2. A disputing party that seeks a consolidation order under this Article shall deliver, in writing, a request to the Secretary-General and to all the disputing parties sought to be covered by the order and shall specify in the request:
   (a) the names and addresses of all the disputing parties sought to be covered by the order;
   (b) the nature of the order sought; and
   (c) the grounds on which the order is sought.

3. Unless the Secretary-General finds within 30 days after receiving a request under paragraph 2 that the request is manifestly unfounded, a tribunal shall be established under this Article.

4. Unless all the disputing parties sought to be covered by the order otherwise agree, a tribunal established under this Article shall comprise three arbitrators:
   (a) one arbitrator appointed by agreement of the claimants;
   (b) one arbitrator appointed by the respondent; and
   (c) the presiding arbitrator appointed by the Secretary-General, provided, however, that the presiding arbitrator shall not be a national of either Party.

5. If, within 60 days after the Secretary-General receives a request made under paragraph 2, the respondent fails or the claimants fail to appoint an arbitrator in accordance with paragraph 4, the Secretary-General, on the request of any disputing party sought to be covered by the order, shall appoint the arbitrator or arbitrators not yet appointed. If the respondent fails to appoint an arbitrator, the Secretary-General shall appoint a national of the disputing Party, and if the claimants fail to appoint an arbitrator, the Secretary-General shall appoint a national of the nondisputing Party.

6. Where a tribunal established under this Article is satisfied that two or more claims that have been submitted to arbitration under Article 15.15.1 have a question of law or fact in common, and arise out of the same events or circumstances, the tribunal may, in the interest of fair and efficient resolution of the claims, and after hearing the disputing parties, by order:
   (a) assume jurisdiction over, and hear and determine together, all or part of the claims;
   (b) assume jurisdiction over, and hear and determine one or more of the claims, the determination of which it believes would assist in the resolution of the others; or
   (c) instruct a tribunal previously established under Article 15.18 to assume jurisdiction over, and hear and determine together, all or part of the claims, provided that:
      (i) that tribunal, at the request of any claimant not previously a disputing party before that tribunal, shall be reconstituted with its original members, except that the arbitrator for the claimants shall be appointed pursuant to paragraphs 4(a) and 5; and
      (ii) that tribunal shall decide whether any prior hearing shall be repeated.

7. Where a tribunal has been established under this Article, a claimant that has submitted a claim to arbitration under Article 15.15.1 and that has not been named in a request made

under paragraph 2 may make a written request to the tribunal that it be included in any order made under paragraph 6, and shall specify in the request:

(a) the name and address of the claimant;

(b) the nature of the order sought; and

(c) the grounds on which the order is sought.

The claimant shall deliver a copy of its request to the Secretary-General.

8. A tribunal established under this Article shall conduct its proceedings in accordance with the UNCITRAL Arbitration Rules, except as modified by this Section.

9. A tribunal established under Article 15.18 shall not have jurisdiction to decide a claim, or a part of a claim, over which a tribunal established or instructed under this Article has assumed jurisdiction.

10. On application of a disputing party, a tribunal established under this Article, pending its decision under paragraph 6, may order that the proceedings of a tribunal established under Article 15.18 be stayed, unless the latter tribunal has already adjourned its proceedings.

Article 15.25   Awards

1. Where a tribunal makes a final award against a respondent, the tribunal may award, separately or in combination, only:

(a) monetary damages and any applicable interest; and

(b) restitution of property, in which case the award shall provide that the respondent may pay monetary damages and any applicable interest in lieu of restitution.

A tribunal may also award costs and attorneys' fees in accordance with this Section and the applicable arbitration rules.

2. Subject to paragraph 1, where a claim is submitted to arbitration under Article 15.15.1(b):

(a) an award of restitution of property shall provide that restitution be made to the enterprise;

(b) an award of monetary damages and any applicable interest shall provide that the sum be paid to the enterprise; and

(c) the award shall provide that it is made without prejudice to any right that any person may have in the relief under applicable domestic law.

3. A tribunal may not award punitive damages.

4. An award made by a tribunal shall have no binding force except between the disputing parties and in respect of the particular case.

5. Subject to paragraph 6 and the applicable review procedure for an interim award, a disputing party shall abide by and comply with an award without delay.

6. A disputing party may not seek enforcement of a final award until:

(a) in the case of a final award made under the ICSID Convention,

(i) 120 days have elapsed from the date the award was rendered and no disputing party has requested revision or annulment of the award; or

(ii) revision or annulment proceedings have been completed; and

(b) in the case of a final award under the ICSID Additional Facility Rules, the UNCITRAL Arbitration Rules, or the rules selected pursuant to Article 15.15.5(d),

(i) 90 days have elapsed from the date the award was rendered and no disputing party has commenced a proceeding to revise, set aside, or annul the award, or

(ii) a court has dismissed or allowed an application to revise, set aside, or annul the award and there is no further appeal.

7. Each Party shall provide for the enforcement of an award in its territory.

8. If the respondent fails to abide by or comply with a final award, on delivery of a written notification by the non-disputing Party, a panel shall be established under Article 20.4.4(a) (Additional Dispute Settlement Procedures). The requesting Party may seek in such proceedings:

   (a) a determination that the failure to abide by or comply with the final award is inconsistent with the obligations of this Agreement; and
   (b) in accordance with the procedures set forth in Article 20.4.5(b) (Additional Dispute Settlement Procedures), a recommendation that the respondent abide by or comply with the final award.

9. A disputing party may seek enforcement of an arbitration award under the ICSID Convention or the New York Convention regardless of whether proceedings have been taken under paragraph 8.

10. A claim that is submitted to arbitration under this Section shall be considered to arise out of a commercial relationship or transaction for purposes of Article I of the New York Convention.

Article 15.26   Status of Letter Exchanges
The following letters exchanged this day on:

(a) Customary International Law;

(b) Expropriation;

(c) Land Expropriation; and

(d) Appellate Mechanism

shall form an integral part of the Agreement.

Article 15.27   Service of Documents
Delivery of notices and other documents on a Party shall be made to the place named for that Party in Annex 15D.

ANNEX 15A   TRANSFERS

1. Where a claimant submits a claim alleging that Singapore has breached an obligation under Section B, other than Article 15.4, that arises from its imposition of restrictive measures with regard to outward payments and transfers, Section C shall apply except as modified below:
   (a) A claimant may submit the claim under Article 15.15 only after one year has elapsed since the measure was adopted.
   (b) If the claim is submitted under Article 15.15.1(b), the claimant may, on behalf of the enterprise, only seek damages with respect to the shares of the enterprise for which the claimant has a beneficial interest.
   (c) Paragraph 1(a) shall not apply to claims that arise from restrictions on:
      (i) payments or transfers on current transactions, including the transfer of profits and dividends of foreign direct investment by investors of the United States;
      (ii) transfers of proceeds of foreign direct investment by investors of the United States, excluding investments designed with the purpose of gaining direct or indirect access to the financial market; or
      (iii) payments pursuant to a loan or bond[15-13] regardless of where it is issued, including inter- and intra-company debt financing between affiliated enterprises, when such payments are made exclusively for the conduct, operation, management, or expansion of such affiliated enterprises, provided that these payments are made in accordance with the maturity date agreed on in the loan or bond agreement.
   (d) Excluding restrictive measures referred to in paragraph 1(c), Singapore shall incur no liability, and shall not be subject to claims, for damages arising from its imposition of restrictive measures with regard to outward payments and transfers that were incurred

---

15-13 For greater certainty, payments pursuant to a loan or bond shall exclude capital account transactions relating to inter-bank loans, including loans to or from Singapore licensed banks, merchant banks, or finance companies.

within one year from the date on which restrictions were imposed, provided that such restrictive measures do not substantially impede transfers.

(e) Claims arising from Singapore's imposition of restrictive measures with regard to outward payments and transfers shall not be subject to Article 15.24 unless Singapore consents.

2. The United States may not request the establishment of an arbitral panel under Chapter 20 (Administration and Dispute Settlement) relating to Singapore's imposition of restrictive measures with regard to outward payments and transfers until one year has elapsed since the measure was adopted. In determining whether compensation is owed or benefits should be suspended, or the level of such compensation or suspension, pursuant to Article 20.6 (Non- Implementation), the aggrieved Party and the panel shall consider whether the restrictive measures were implemented at the request of the International Monetary Fund (IMF).

ANNEX 15B   PERFORMANCE REQUIREMENTS

Article 15.8.1 does not preclude enforcement of any commitment, undertaking, or requirement between private parties, where a Party did not impose or require the commitment, undertaking, or requirement. For purposes of this Annex, private parties may include designated monopolies or government enterprises, where such entities are not exercising delegated governmental authority as described in Articles 12.3.1(c)(i) and 12.3.2(b) (Designated Monopolies and Government Enterprises), respectively.

ANNEX 15C   PERFORMANCE REQUIREMENTS

Singapore
With respect to Singapore, Article 15.8.1(f) does not apply with respect to the sale or other disposition of an investment of an investor of a non-Party in its territory.

. . .

CHAPTER 20   ADMINISTRATION AND DISPUTE SETTLEMENT

Article 20.1   Joint Committee
1. The Parties hereby establish a Joint Committee to supervise the implementation of this Agreement and to review the trade relationship between the Parties.
   (a) The Joint Committee shall be composed of government officials of each Party and shall be chaired by (i) the United States Trade Representative and (ii) Singapore's Minister for Trade and Industry or their designees.
   (b) The Joint Committee may establish and delegate responsibilities to ad hoc and standing committees or working groups, and seek the advice of non-governmental persons or groups.
2. The Joint Committee shall:
   (a) review the general functioning of this Agreement;
   (b) review and consider specific matters related to the operation and implementation of this Agreement in the light of its objectives, such as those related to customs administration, technical barriers to trade, electronic commerce, the environment, labor, the Medical Products Working Group, and distilled spirits;
   (c) facilitate the avoidance and settlement of disputes arising under this Agreement, including through consultations pursuant to Articles 20.3 and 20.4;

(d) consider and adopt any amendment to this Agreement or other modification to the commitments therein, subject to completion of necessary domestic legal procedures by each Party;

(e) as appropriate, issue interpretations of this Agreement, including as provided in Articles 15.21 (Governing Law) and 15.22 (Interpretation of Annexes);

(f) consider ways to further enhance trade relations between the Parties and to further the objectives of this Agreement; and

(g) take such other action as the Parties may agree.

3. At its first meeting, the Joint Committee shall consider the review performed by each Party of the environmental effects of this Agreement and shall provide the public an opportunity to provide views on those effects.

4. The Joint Committee shall establish its own rules of procedure.

5. Unless the Parties otherwise agree, the Joint Committee shall convene:
   (a) in regular session every year in order to review the general functioning of the Agreement, with such sessions to be held alternately in the territory of each Party; and
   (b) in special session within 30 days of the request of a Party, with such sessions to be held in the territory of the other Party or at such location as may be agreed by the Parties. A requirement under Article 20.4 that the Joint Committee take any action with regard to a dispute shall not be interpreted to require the convening of a special session of the Joint Committee.

6. Recognizing the importance of transparency and openness, the Parties reaffirm their respective practices of considering the views of members of the public in order to draw upon a broad range of perspectives in the implementation of this Agreement.

7. Each Party shall treat any confidential information exchanged in relation to a meeting of the Joint Committee on the same basis as the Party providing the information.

Article 20.2   Administration of Dispute Settlement Proceedings

1. Each Party shall:
   (a) designate an office that shall be responsible for providing administrative assistance to panels established under Article 20.4;
   (b) be responsible for the operation and costs of its designated office; and
   (c) notify the other Party of the location of its office.

2. The Joint Committee shall establish the amounts of remuneration and expenses to be paid to panelists.

3. The remuneration of panelists and their assistants, their travel and lodging expenses, and all general expenses relating to proceedings of a panel established under Article 20.4 shall be borne equally by the Parties.

4. Each panelist shall keep a record and render a final account of the panelist's time and expenses, and the panel shall keep a record and render a final account of all general expenses.

Article 20.3   Consultations

1. Except as otherwise provided in this Agreement, either Party may request consultations with the other Party with respect to any matter that it considers might affect the operation of this Agreement by delivering written notification to the other Party's office designated under Article 20.2.1(a). If a Party requests consultations with regard to a matter, the other Party shall afford adequate opportunity for consultations and shall reply promptly to the request for consultations and enter into consultations in good faith.

2. In consultations under this Article, a Party may request the other Party to make available personnel of its government agencies or other regulatory bodies who have expertise in the matter subject to consultations.

3. In the consultations, each Party shall:
   (a) provide sufficient information to enable a full examination of how the matter subject to consultations might affect the operation of this Agreement; and
   (b) treat any confidential information exchanged in the course of consultations on the same basis as the Party providing the information.

Article 20.4   Additional Dispute Settlement Procedures

1. Except as otherwise provided in this Agreement or as the Parties otherwise agree, the provisions of this Article shall apply wherever a Party considers that:
   (a) a measure of the other Party is inconsistent with the obligations of this Agreement;
   (b) the other Party has otherwise failed to carry out its obligations under this Agreement; or
   (c) a benefit the Party could reasonably have expected to accrue to it under Chapters 2 (National Treatment and Market Access for Goods), 3 (Rules of Origin), Chapter 8 (Cross Border Trade in Services), or Chapter 16 (Intellectual Property Rights) is being nullified or impaired as a result of a measure that is not inconsistent with this Agreement.

2. (a) The Parties shall first seek to resolve a dispute described in paragraph 1 through consultations under Article 20.3. If the consultations fail to resolve the dispute within 60 days of the delivery of a Party's request for consultations under Article 20.3.1, either Party may, by delivering written notification to the other Party's office designated under Article 20.2.1 (a), refer the matter to the Joint Committee, which shall endeavor to resolve the dispute.
   (b) Subject to Article 20.3.3(b), promptly after requesting or receiving a request for consultations related to a matter identified in paragraph 1, each Party shall solicit and consider the views of members of the public in order to draw upon a broad range of perspectives.

3. (a) Where a dispute regarding any matter referred to in paragraph 1 arises under this Agreement and under the WTO Agreement, or any other agreement to which both Parties are party, the complaining Party may select the forum in which to settle the dispute.
   (b) The complaining Party shall notify the other Party in writing of its intention to bring a dispute to a particular forum before doing so.
   (c) Once the complaining Party has selected a particular forum, the forum selected shall be used to the exclusion of other possible fora.
   (d) For the purposes of this paragraph, a Party shall be deemed to have selected a forum when it has requested the establishment of, or referred a matter to, a dispute settlement panel.

4. (a) If the Joint Committee has not resolved a dispute within 60 days after delivery of the notification described in paragraph 2(a) or within such other period as the Parties may agree, the complaining Party may refer the matter to a dispute settlement panel by delivering written notification to the other Party's office designated under Article 20.2.1(a).[20-1] Unless the Parties otherwise agree:
   (i) The panel shall have three members.
   (ii) Each Party shall appoint one panelist, in consultation with the other Party, within 30 days after the matter has been referred to a panel. If a Party fails to appoint a panelist within such period, a panelist shall be selected by lot from the contingent list established under subparagraph (b) to serve as the panelist appointed by that Party.
   (iii) The Parties shall endeavor to agree on a third panelist who shall serve as chair.
   (iv) If the Parties are unable to agree on the chair of the Panel within 30 days after the date on which the second panelist has been appointed, the chair shall be selected by lot from the contingent list established under subparagraph (b).
   (v) The date of establishment of the panel shall be the date on which the chair is appointed.

20-1 This paragraph is subject to the letter referred to in Article 15.26(c) (Status of Letter Exchanges).

Note by the Editors: For brief comment see text following footnote 15–9, above.

(b) (i) By the date of entry into force of this Agreement, the Parties shall establish a contingent list of five individuals who are willing and able to serve as a panelist or chair.

(ii) Each such individual shall have expertise or experience in law, international trade, or the resolution of disputes arising under international trade agreements; shall be independent of, and not be affiliated with or take instructions from, any Party; and shall comply with the code of conduct to be established by the Joint Committee.

(iii) Individuals on the contingent list shall be appointed by agreement of the Parties for terms of three years, and may be reappointed.

(c) Panelists other than those chosen by lot from the contingent list shall meet the criteria set out in subparagraph (b)(ii) and have expertise or experience relevant to the subject matter that is under dispute.

(d) The Parties shall establish by the date of entry into force of this Agreement model rules of procedure, which shall ensure:

(i) a right to at least one hearing before the panel, which, subject to clause (vi), shall be open to the public;

(ii) an opportunity for each Party to provide initial and rebuttal submissions;

(iii) that each Party's written submissions, written versions of its oral statement, and written responses to a request or questions from the panel will be made public within ten days after they are submitted, subject to clause (vi);

(iv) that the panel shall consider requests from nongovernmental entities in the Parties' territories to provide written views regarding the dispute that may assist the panel in evaluating the submissions and arguments of the Parties;

(v) a reasonable opportunity for each Party to submit comments on the initial report presented pursuant to paragraph 5(a); and

(vi) the protection of confidential information.

Unless the Parties agree otherwise, the panel shall follow the model rules of procedure and may, after consulting the Parties, adopt additional rules of procedure not inconsistent with the model rules.

5. (a) Unless the Parties agree otherwise, the panel shall, within 150 days after the chair is appointed, present to the Parties an initial report containing findings of fact and its determination as to whether:

(i) the measure at issue is inconsistent with the obligations of this Agreement;

(ii) a Party has otherwise failed to carry out its obligations under this Agreement; or

(iii) the measure at issue causes a nullification or impairment described in subparagraph 1(c); as well as any other determination requested by both Parties with regard to the dispute.

(b) The panel shall base its report on the submissions and arguments of the Parties. The panel may, at the request of the Parties, make recommendations for the resolution of the dispute.

(c) After considering any written comments by the Parties on the initial report, the panel may modify its report and make any further examination it considers appropriate.

(d) The panel shall present a final report to the Parties within 45 days of presentation of the initial report, unless the Parties agree otherwise. The Parties shall release the final report to the public within 15 days thereafter, subject to the protection of confidential information.

Article 20.5   Implementation of the Final Report

1. On receipt of the final report of a panel, the Parties shall agree on the resolution of the dispute, which normally shall conform with the determinations and recommendations, if any, of the panel.

2. If, in its final report, the panel determines that a Party has not conformed with its obligations under this Agreement or that a Party's measure is causing nullification or impairment in the sense of Article 20.4.1(c), the resolution, whenever possible, shall be to eliminate the non-conformity or the nullification or impairment.

Article 20.6   Non-Implementation

1. If a panel has made a determination of the type described in Article 20.5.2, and the Parties are unable to reach agreement on a resolution pursuant to Article 20.5.1 within 45 days of receiving the final report, or such other period as the Parties agree, the Party complained against shall enter into negotiations with the other Party with a view to developing mutually acceptable compensation.

2. If the Parties:
   (a) are unable to agree on compensation within 30 days after the period for developing such compensation has begun; or
   (b) have agreed on compensation or on a resolution pursuant to Article 20.5.1 and the complaining Party considers that the other Party has failed to observe the terms of such agreement,

   the complaining Party may at any time thereafter provide written notice to the office designated by the other Party pursuant to Article 20.2.1(a) that it intends to suspend the application to the other Party of benefits of equivalent effect. The notice shall specify the level of benefits that the Party proposes to suspend. Subject to paragraph 5, the complaining Party may begin suspending benefits 30 days after the later of the date on which it provides notice to the other Party's designated office under this paragraph or the panel issues its determination under paragraph 3, as the case may be.

3. If the Party complained against considers that:
   (a) the level of benefits that the other Party has proposed to be suspended is manifestly excessive; or
   (b) it has eliminated the non-conformity or the nullification or impairment that the panel has found,

   it may, within 30 days after the complaining Party provides notice under paragraph 2, request that the panel be reconvened to consider the matter. The Party complained against shall deliver its request in writing to the office designated by the other Party pursuant to Article 20.2.1(a). The panel shall reconvene as soon as possible after delivery of the request to the designated office and shall present its determination to the Parties within 90 days after it reconvenes to review a request under subparagraph (a) or (b), or within 120 days for a request under subparagraphs (a) and (b). If the panel determines that the level of benefits proposed to be suspended is manifestly excessive, it shall determine the level of benefits it considers to be of equivalent effect.

4. The complaining Party may suspend benefits up to the level the panel has determined under paragraph 3 or, if the panel has not determined the level, the level the Party has proposed to suspend under paragraph 2, unless the panel has determined that the Party complained against has eliminated the non-conformity or the nullification or impairment.

5. The complaining Party may not suspend benefits if, within 30 days after it provides written notice of intent to suspend benefits or, if the panel is reconvened under paragraph 3, within 20 days after the panel provides its determination, the Party complained against provides written notice to the other Party's office designated pursuant to Article 20.2.1(a) that it will pay an annual monetary assessment. The Parties shall consult, beginning no later than ten days after the Party complained against provides notice, with a view to reaching agreement on the amount of the assessment. If the Parties are unable to reach an agreement within 30 days after consultations begin, the amount of the assessment shall be set at a level, in U.S. dollars, equal

to 50 percent of the level of the benefits the panel has determined under paragraph 3 to be of equivalent effect or, if the panel has not determined the level, 50 percent of the level that the complaining Party has proposed to suspend under paragraph 2.

6. Unless the Joint Committee otherwise decides, a monetary assessment shall be paid to the complaining Party in U.S. currency, or in an equivalent amount of Singaporean currency, in equal, quarterly installments beginning 60 days after the Party complained against gives notice that it intends to pay an assessment. Where the circumstances warrant, the Joint Committee may decide that an assessment shall be paid into a fund established by the Joint Committee and expended at the direction of the Joint Committee for appropriate initiatives to facilitate trade between the Parties, including by further reducing unreasonable trade barriers or by assisting a Party in carrying out its obligations under the Agreement.

7. If the Party complained against fails to pay a monetary assessment, the complaining Party may suspend the application to the Party complained against of benefits in accordance with paragraph 4.

8. This Article shall not apply with respect to a matter described in Article 20.7.1.

Article 20.7   Non-Implementation in Certain Disputes

1. If, in its final report, a panel determines that a Party has not conformed with its obligations under Article 17.2.1(a) (Application and Enforcement of Labor Laws) or Article 18.2.1(a) (Application and Enforcement of Environmental Laws), and the Parties:

    (a) are unable to reach agreement on a resolution pursuant to Article 20.5.1 within 45 days of receiving the final report; or

    (b) have agreed on a resolution pursuant to Article 20.5.1 and the complaining Party considers that the other Party has failed to observe the terms of the agreement, the complaining Party may at any time thereafter request that the panel be reconvened to impose an annual monetary assessment on the other Party. The complaining Party shall deliver its request in writing to the office designated by the other Party pursuant to Article 20.2.1(a). The panel shall reconvene as soon as possible after delivery of the request to the designated office.

2. The panel shall determine the amount of the monetary assessment in U.S. dollars within 90 days after it reconvenes under paragraph 1. In determining the amount of the assessment, the panel shall take into account:

    (a) the bilateral trade effects of the Party's failure to effectively enforce the relevant law;

    (b) the pervasiveness and duration of the Party's failure to effectively enforce the relevant law;

    (c) the reasons for the Party's failure to effectively enforce the relevant law;

    (d) the level of enforcement that could reasonably be expected of the Party given its resource constraints;

    (e) the efforts made by the Party to begin remedying the non-enforcement after the final report of the panel; and

    (f) any other relevant factors.

    The amount of the assessment shall not exceed 15 million U.S. dollars annually, adjusted for inflation as specified in Annex 20A.

3. On the date on which the panel determines the amount of the monetary assessment under paragraph 2, or at any other time thereafter, the complaining Party may provide notice in writing to the office designated by the other Party pursuant to Article 20.2.1(a) demanding payment of the monetary assessment. The monetary assessment shall be payable in U.S. currency, or in an equivalent amount of Singaporean currency, in equal, quarterly installments beginning on the later of:

    (a) 60 days after the date on which the panel determines the amount; or

    (b) 60 days after the complaining Party provides the notice described in this paragraph.

4. Assessments shall be paid into a fund established by the Joint Committee and shall be expended at the direction of the Joint Committee for appropriate labor or environmental initiatives, including efforts to improve or enhance labor or environmental law enforcement, as the case may be, in the territory of the Party complained against, consistent with its law. In deciding how to expend monies paid into the fund, the Joint Committee shall consider the views of interested persons in the Parties' territories.

5. If the Party complained against fails to pay a monetary assessment, and if the Party has created and funded an escrow account to ensure payment of any assessments against it, the other Party shall, before having recourse to any other measure, seek to obtain the funds from the account.

6. If the complaining Party cannot obtain the funds from the other Party's escrow account within 30 days of the date on which payment is due, or if the other Party has not created an escrow account, the complaining Party may take other appropriate steps to collect the assessment or otherwise secure compliance. These steps may include suspending tariff benefits under the Agreement as necessary to collect the assessment, while bearing in mind the Agreement's objective of eliminating barriers to bilateral trade and while seeking to avoid unduly affecting parties or interests not party to the dispute.

Article 20.8   Compliance Review

1. Without prejudice to the procedures set out in Article 20.6.3, if the Party complained against considers that it has eliminated the non-conformity or the nullification or impairment that the panel has found, it may refer the matter to the panel by providing written notice to the office designated by the other Party pursuant to Article 20.2.1(a). The panel shall issue its report on the matter within 90 days after the Party complained against provides notice.

2. If the panel decides that the Party complained against has eliminated the non-conformity or the nullification or impairment, the complaining Party shall promptly reinstate any benefits it has suspended under Article 20.6 or 20.7 and the Party complained against shall no longer be required to pay any monetary assessment it has agreed to pay under Article 20.6.5 or that has been imposed on it under Article 20.7.

Article 20.9   Five-Year Review

The Joint Committee shall review the operation and effectiveness of Articles 20.6 and 20.7 not later than five years after the date of entry into force of this Agreement, or within six months after benefits have been suspended or monetary assessments have been imposed in five proceedings initiated under this Chapter, whichever occurs first.

Article 20.10   Private Rights

Neither Party may provide for a right of action under its domestic law against the other Party on the ground that a measure of the other Party is inconsistent with this Agreement.

III-9

2012 US Model Bilateral Investment Treaty

Date 2012

Link <http://www.ustr.gov/sites/default/files/BIT%20text%20for%20ACIEP%20Meeting.pdf>

TREATY BETWEEN THE GOVERNMENT OF THE UNITED STATES OF AMERICA AND THE GOVERNMENT OF [COUNTRY] CONCERNING THE ENCOURAGEMENT AND RECIPROCAL PROTECTION OF INVESTMENT

The Government of the United States of America and the Government of [Country] (hereinafter the "Parties");

Desiring to promote greater economic cooperation between them with respect to investment by nationals and enterprises of one Party in the territory of the other Party;

Recognizing that agreement on the treatment to be accorded such investment will stimulate the flow of private capital and the economic development of the Parties;

Agreeing that a stable framework for investment will maximize effective utilization of economic resources and improve living standards;

Recognizing the importance of providing effective means of asserting claims and enforcing rights with respect to investment under national law as well as through international arbitration;

Desiring to achieve these objectives in a manner consistent with the protection of health, safety, and the environment, and the promotion of internationally recognized labor rights;

Having resolved to conclude a Treaty concerning the encouragement and reciprocal protection of investment;

Have agreed as follows:

SECTION A

Article 1   Definitions

For purposes of this Treaty:

"central level of government" means:

(a) for the United States, the federal level of government; and

(b) for [Country], [_____].

"Centre" means the International Centre for Settlement of Investment Disputes ("ICSID") established by the ICSID Convention.

"claimant" means an investor of a Party that is a party to an investment dispute with the other Party.

"covered investment" means, with respect to a Party, an investment in its territory of an investor of the other Party in existence as of the date of entry into force of this Treaty or established, acquired, or expanded thereafter.

"disputing parties" means the claimant and the respondent.

"**disputing party**" means either the claimant or the respondent.

"**enterprise**" means any entity constituted or organized under applicable law, whether or not for profit, and whether privately or governmentally owned or controlled, including a corporation, trust, partnership, sole proprietorship, joint venture, association, or similar organization; and a branch of an enterprise.

"**enterprise of a Party**" means an enterprise constituted or organized under the law of a Party, and a branch located in the territory of a Party and carrying out business activities there.

"**existing**" means in effect on the date of entry into force of this Treaty.

"**freely usable currency**" means "freely usable currency" as determined by the International Monetary Fund under its *Articles of Agreement*.

"**GATS**" means the *General Agreement on Trade in Services*, contained in Annex 1B to the WTO Agreement.

"**government procurement**" means the process by which a government obtains the use of or acquires goods or services, or any combination thereof, for governmental purposes and not with a view to commercial sale or resale, or use in the production or supply of goods or services for commercial sale or resale.

"**ICSID Additional Facility Rules**" means the *Rules Governing the Additional Facility for the Administration of Proceedings by the Secretariat of the International Centre for Settlement of Investment Disputes*.

"**ICSID Convention**" means the *Convention on the Settlement of Investment Disputes between States and Nationals of Other States*, done at Washington, March 18, 1965.

["**Inter-American Convention**" means the *Inter-American Convention on International Commercial Arbitration*, done at Panama, January 30, 1975.]

"**investment**" means every asset that an investor owns or controls, directly or indirectly, that has the characteristics of an investment, including such characteristics as the commitment of capital or other resources, the expectation of gain or profit, or the assumption of risk. Forms that an investment may take include:

(a) an enterprise;

(b) shares, stock, and other forms of equity participation in an enterprise;

(c) bonds, debentures, other debt instruments, and loans;[1]

(d) futures, options, and other derivatives;

(e) turnkey, construction, management, production, concession, revenue-sharing, and other similar contracts;

(f) intellectual property rights;

(g) licenses, authorizations, permits, and similar rights conferred pursuant to domestic law;[2, 3] and

(h) other tangible or intangible, movable or immovable property, and related property rights, such as leases, mortgages, liens, and pledges.

"**investment agreement**" means a written agreement[4] between a national authority[5] of a Party and a covered investment or an investor of the other Party, on which the covered investment or

---

1 Some forms of debt, such as bonds, debentures, and long-term notes, are more likely to have the characteristics of an investment, while other forms of debt, such as claims to payment that are immediately due and result from the sale of goods or services, are less likely to have such characteristics.

2 Whether a particular type of license, authorization, permit, or similar instrument (including a concession, to the extent that it has the nature of such an instrument) has the characteristics of an investment depends on such factors as the nature and extent of the rights that the holder has under the law of the Party. Among the licenses, authorizations, permits, and similar instruments that do not have the characteristics of an investment are those that do not create any rights protected under domestic law. For greater certainty, the foregoing is without prejudice to whether any asset associated with the license, authorization, permit, or similar instrument has the characteristics of an investment.

3 The term "investment" does not include an order or judgment entered in a judicial or administrative action.

4 "Written agreement" refers to an agreement in writing, executed by both parties, whether in a single instrument or in multiple instruments, that creates an exchange of rights and obligations, binding on both parties under the law applicable under Article 30[Governing Law](2). For greater certainty, (a) a unilateral act of an administrative or judicial authority, such as a permit, license, or authorization issued by a Party solely in its regulatory capacity, or a decree, order, or judgment, standing alone; and (b) an administrative or judicial consent decree or order, shall not be considered a written agreement.

5 For purposes of this definition, "national authority" means (a) for the United States, an authority at the central level of government; and (b) for [Country], [_____].

the investor relies in establishing or acquiring a covered investment other than the written agreement itself, that grants rights to the covered investment or investor:

(a) with respect to natural resources that a national authority controls, such as for their exploration, extraction, refining, transportation, distribution, or sale;

(b) to supply services to the public on behalf of the Party, such as power generation or distribution, water treatment or distribution, or telecommunications; or

(c) to undertake infrastructure projects, such as the construction of roads, bridges, canals, dams, or pipelines, that are not for the exclusive or predominant use and benefit of the government.

"**investment authorization**"[6] means an authorization that the foreign investment authority of a Party grants to a covered investment or an investor of the other Party.

"**investor of a non-Party**" means, with respect to a Party, an investor that attempts to make, is making, or has made an investment in the territory of that Party, that is not an investor of either Party.

"**investor of a Party**" means a Party or state enterprise thereof, or a national or an enterprise of a Party, that attempts to make, is making, or has made an investment in the territory of the other Party; provided, however, that a natural person who is a dual national shall be deemed to be exclusively a national of the State of his or her dominant and effective nationality.

"**measure**" includes any law, regulation, procedure, requirement, or practice.

"**national**" means:

(a) for the United States, a natural person who is a national of the United States as defined in Title III of the Immigration and Nationality Act; and

(b) for [Country], [_____].

"**New York Convention**" means the *United Nations Convention on the Recognition and Enforcement of Foreign Arbitral Awards*, done at New York, June 10, 1958.

"**non-disputing Party**" means the Party that is not a party to an investment dispute.

"**person**" means a natural person or an enterprise.

"**person of a Party**" means a national or an enterprise of a Party.

"**protected information**" means confidential business information or information that is privileged or otherwise protected from disclosure under a Party's law.

"**regional level of government**" means:

(a) for the United States, a state of the United States, the District of Columbia, or Puerto Rico; and

(b) for [Country], [_____].

"**respondent**" means the Party that is a party to an investment dispute.

"**Secretary-General**" means the Secretary General of ICSID.

"**state enterprise**" means an enterprise owned, or controlled through ownership interests, by a Party.

"**territory**" means:

(a) with respect to the United States,
   (i) the customs territory of the United States, which includes the 50 states, the District of Columbia, and Puerto Rico;
   (ii) the foreign trade zones located in the United States and Puerto Rico.

---

6 For greater certainty, actions taken by a Party to enforce laws of general application, such as competition laws, are not encompassed within this definition.

(b) with respect to [Country,] [_____].

(c) with respect to each Party, the territorial sea and any area beyond the territorial sea of the Party within which, in accordance with customary international law as reflected in the United Nations Convention on the Law of the Sea, the Party may exercise sovereign rights or jurisdiction.

"TRIPS Agreement" means the *Agreement on Trade-Related Aspects of Intellectual Property Rights*, contained in Annex 1C to the WTO Agreement.[7]

"UNCITRAL Arbitration Rules" means the arbitration rules of the United Nations Commission on International Trade Law.

"WTO Agreement" means the *Marrakesh Agreement Establishing the World Trade Organization*, done on April 15, 1994.

Article 2   Scope and Coverage

1. This Treaty applies to measures adopted or maintained by a Party relating to:
    (a) investors of the other Party;
    (b) covered investments; and
    (c) with respect to Articles 8 [Performance Requirements], 12 [Investment and Environment], and 13 [Investment and Labor], all investments in the territory of the Party.

2. A Party's obligations under Section A shall apply:
    (a) to a state enterprise or other person when it exercises any regulatory, administrative, or other governmental authority delegated to it by that Party;[8] and
    (b) to the political subdivisions of that Party.

3. For greater certainty, this Treaty does not bind either Party in relation to any act or fact that took place or any situation that ceased to exist before the date of entry into force of this Treaty.

Article 3   National Treatment

1. Each Party shall accord to investors of the other Party treatment no less favorable than that it accords, in like circumstances, to its own investors with respect to the establishment, acquisition, expansion, management, conduct, operation, and sale or other disposition of investments in its territory.

2. Each Party shall accord to covered investments treatment no less favorable than that it accords, in like circumstances, to investments in its territory of its own investors with respect to the establishment, acquisition, expansion, management, conduct, operation, and sale or other disposition of investments.

3. The treatment to be accorded by a Party under paragraphs 1 and 2 means, with respect to a regional level of government, treatment no less favorable than the treatment accorded, in like circumstances, by that regional level of government to natural persons resident in and enterprises constituted under the laws of other regional levels of government of the Party of which it forms a part, and to their respective investments.

Article 4 Most-Favored-Nation Treatment

1. Each Party shall accord to investors of the other Party treatment no less favorable than that it accords, in like circumstances, to investors of any non-Party with respect to the establishment, acquisition, expansion, management, conduct, operation, and sale or other disposition of investments in its territory.

2. Each Party shall accord to covered investments treatment no less favorable than that it accords, in like circumstances, to investments in its territory of investors of any non-Party

---

7 For greater certainty, "TRIPS Agreement" includes any waiver in force between the Parties of any provision of the TRIPS Agreement granted by WTO Members in accordance with the WTO Agreement.

8 For greater certainty, government authority that has been delegated includes a legislative grant, and a government order, directive or other action transferring to the state enterprise or other person, or authorizing the exercise by the state enterprise or other person of, governmental authority.

with respect to the establishment, acquisition, expansion, management, conduct, operation, and sale or other disposition of investments.

Article 5   Minimum Standard of Treatment[9]

1. Each Party shall accord to covered investments treatment in accordance with customary international law, including fair and equitable treatment and full protection and security.

2. For greater certainty, paragraph 1 prescribes the customary international law minimum standard of treatment of aliens as the minimum standard of treatment to be afforded to covered investments. The concepts of "fair and equitable treatment" and "full protection and security" do not require treatment in addition to or beyond that which is required by that standard, and do not create additional substantive rights. The obligation in paragraph 1 to provide:

    (a) "fair and equitable treatment" includes the obligation not to deny justice in criminal, civil, or administrative adjudicatory proceedings in accordance with the principle of due process embodied in the principal legal systems of the world; and

    (b) "full protection and security" requires each Party to provide the level of police protection required under customary international law.

3. A determination that there has been a breach of another provision of this Treaty, or of a separate international agreement, does not establish that there has been a breach of this Article.

4. Notwithstanding Article 14 [Non-Conforming Measures](5)(b) [subsidies and grants], each Party shall accord to investors of the other Party, and to covered investments, non-discriminatory treatment with respect to measures it adopts or maintains relating to losses suffered by investments in its territory owing to armed conflict or civil strife.

5. Notwithstanding paragraph 4, if an investor of a Party, in the situations referred to in paragraph 4, suffers a loss in the territory of the other Party resulting from:

    (a) requisitioning of its covered investment or part thereof by the latter's forces or authorities; or

    (b) destruction of its covered investment or part thereof by the latter's forces or authorities, which was not required by the necessity of the situation, the latter Party shall provide the investor restitution, compensation, or both, as appropriate, for such loss. Any compensation shall be prompt, adequate, and effective in accordance with Article 6 [Expropriation and Compensation](2) through (4), *mutatis mutandis.*

6. Paragraph 4 does not apply to existing measures relating to subsidies or grants that would be inconsistent with Article 3 [National Treatment] but for Article 14 [Non-Conforming Measures](5)(b) [subsidies and grants].

Article 6   Expropriation and Compensation[10]

1. Neither Party may expropriate or nationalize a covered investment either directly or indirectly through measures equivalent to expropriation or nationalization ("expropriation"), except:

    (a) for a public purpose;

    (b) in a non-discriminatory manner;

    (c) on payment of prompt, adequate, and effective compensation; and

    (d) in accordance with due process of law and Article 5 [Minimum Standard of Treatment](1) through (3).

2. The compensation referred to in paragraph 1(c) shall:

    (a) be paid without delay;

---

9 Article 5 [Minimum Standard of Treatment] shall be interpreted in accordance with Annex A.
10 Article 6 [Expropriation] shall be interpreted in accordance with Annexes A and B.

   (b) be equivalent to the fair market value of the expropriated investment immediately before the expropriation took place ("the date of expropriation");

   (c) not reflect any change in value occurring because the intended expropriation had become known earlier; and

   (d) be fully realizable and freely transferable.

3. If the fair market value is denominated in a freely usable currency, the compensation referred to in paragraph 1(c) shall be no less than the fair market value on the date of expropriation, plus interest at a commercially reasonable rate for that currency, accrued from the date of expropriation until the date of payment.

4. If the fair market value is denominated in a currency that is not freely usable, the compensation referred to in paragraph 1(c)—converted into the currency of payment at the market rate of exchange prevailing on the date of payment—shall be no less than:

   (a) the fair market value on the date of expropriation, converted into a freely usable currency at the market rate of exchange prevailing on that date, plus

   (b) interest, at a commercially reasonable rate for that freely usable currency, accrued from the date of expropriation until the date of payment.

5. This Article does not apply to the issuance of compulsory licenses granted in relation to intellectual property rights in accordance with the TRIPS Agreement, or to the revocation, limitation, or creation of intellectual property rights, to the extent that such issuance, revocation, limitation, or creation is consistent with the TRIPS Agreement.

Article 7   Transfers

1. Each Party shall permit all transfers relating to a covered investment to be made freely and without delay into and out of its territory. Such transfers include:

   (a) contributions to capital;

   (b) profits, dividends, capital gains, and proceeds from the sale of all or any part of the covered investment or from the partial or complete liquidation of the covered investment;

   (c) interest, royalty payments, management fees, and technical assistance and other fees;

   (d) payments made under a contract, including a loan agreement;

   (e) payments made pursuant to Article 5 [Minimum Standard of Treatment](4) and (5) and Article 6 [Expropriation and Compensation]; and

   (f) payments arising out of a dispute.

2. Each Party shall permit transfers relating to a covered investment to be made in a freely usable currency at the market rate of exchange prevailing at the time of transfer.

3. Each Party shall permit returns in kind relating to a covered investment to be made as authorized or specified in a written agreement between the Party and a covered investment or an investor of the other Party.

4. Notwithstanding paragraphs 1 through 3, a Party may prevent a transfer through the equitable, non-discriminatory, and good faith application of its laws relating to:

   (a) bankruptcy, insolvency, or the protection of the rights of creditors;

   (b) issuing, trading, or dealing in securities, futures, options, or derivatives;

   (c) criminal or penal offenses;

   (d) financial reporting or record keeping of transfers when necessary to assist law enforcement or financial regulatory authorities; or

   (e) ensuring compliance with orders or judgments in judicial or administrative proceedings.

Article 8   Performance Requirements

1. Neither Party may, in connection with the establishment, acquisition, expansion, management, conduct, operation, or sale or other disposition of an investment of an investor of a

Party or of a non-Party in its territory, impose or enforce any requirement or enforce any commitment or undertaking:[11]

(a) to export a given level or percentage of goods or services;
(b) to achieve a given level or percentage of domestic content;
(c) to purchase, use, or accord a preference to goods produced in its territory, or to purchase goods from persons in its territory;
(d) to relate in any way the volume or value of imports to the volume or value of exports or to the amount of foreign exchange inflows associated with such investment;
(e) to restrict sales of goods or services in its territory that such investment produces or supplies by relating such sales in any way to the volume or value of its exports or foreign exchange earnings;
(f) to transfer a particular technology, a production process, or other proprietary knowledge to a person in its territory;
(g) to supply exclusively from the territory of the Party the goods that such investment produces or the services that it supplies to a specific regional market or to the world market; or
(h) (i) to purchase, use, or accord a preference to, in its territory, technology of the Party or of persons of the Party[12]; or
     (ii) that prevents the purchase or use of, or the according of a preference to, in its territory, particular technology, so as to afford protection on the basis of nationality to its own investors or investments or to technology of the Party or of persons of the Party.

2. Neither Party may condition the receipt or continued receipt of an advantage, in connection with the establishment, acquisition, expansion, management, conduct, operation, or sale or other disposition of an investment in its territory of an investor of a Party or of a non-Party, on compliance with any requirement:

(a) to achieve a given level or percentage of domestic content;
(b) to purchase, use, or accord a preference to goods produced in its territory, or to purchase goods from persons in its territory;
(c) to relate in any way the volume or value of imports to the volume or value of exports or to the amount of foreign exchange inflows associated with such investment; or
(d) to restrict sales of goods or services in its territory that such investment produces or supplies by relating such sales in any way to the volume or value of its exports or foreign exchange earnings.

3. (a) Nothing in paragraph 2 shall be construed to prevent a Party from conditioning the receipt or continued receipt of an advantage, in connection with an investment in its territory of an investor of a Party or of a non-Party, on compliance with a requirement to locate production, supply a service, train or employ workers, construct or expand particular facilities, or carry out research and development, in its territory.

    (b) Paragraphs 1(f) and (h) do not apply:
         (i) when a Party authorizes use of an intellectual property right in accordance with Article 31 of the TRIPS Agreement, or to measures requiring the disclosure of proprietary information that fall within the scope of, and are consistent with, Article 39 of the TRIPS Agreement; or
         (ii) when the requirement is imposed or the commitment or undertaking is enforced by a court, administrative tribunal, or competition authority to remedy a practice deter-

---

11 For greater certainty, a condition for the receipt or continued receipt of an advantage referred to in paragraph 2 does not constitute a "commitment or undertaking" for the purposes of paragraph 1.

12 For purposes of this Article, the term "technology of the Party or of persons of the Party" includes technology that is owned by the Party or persons of the Party, and technology for which the Party holds, or persons of the Party hold, an exclusive license.

mined after judicial or administrative process to be anticompetitive under the Party's competition laws.[13]

(c) Provided that such measures are not applied in an arbitrary or unjustifiable manner, and provided that such measures do not constitute a disguised restriction on international trade or investment, paragraphs 1(b), (c), (f), and (h), and 2(a) and (b), shall not be construed to prevent a Party from adopting or maintaining measures, including environmental measures:

  (i) necessary to secure compliance with laws and regulations that are not inconsistent with this Treaty;

  (ii) necessary to protect human, animal, or plant life or health; or

  (iii) related to the conservation of living or non-living exhaustible natural resources.

(d) Paragraphs 1(a), (b), and (c), and 2(a) and (b), do not apply to qualification requirements for goods or services with respect to export promotion and foreign aid programs.

(e) Paragraphs 1(b), (c), (f), (g), and (h), and 2(a) and (b), do not apply to government procurement.

(f) Paragraphs 2(a) and (b) do not apply to requirements imposed by an importing Party relating to the content of goods necessary to qualify for preferential tariffs or preferential quotas.

4. For greater certainty, paragraphs 1 and 2 do not apply to any commitment, undertaking, or requirement other than those set out in those paragraphs.

5. This Article does not preclude enforcement of any commitment, undertaking, or requirement between private parties, where a Party did not impose or require the commitment, undertaking, or requirement.

Article 9   Senior Management and Boards of Directors

1. Neither Party may require that an enterprise of that Party that is a covered investment appoint to senior management positions natural persons of any particular nationality.

2. A Party may require that a majority of the board of directors, or any committee thereof, of an enterprise of that Party that is a covered investment, be of a particular nationality, or resident in the territory of the Party, provided that the requirement does not materially impair the ability of the investor to exercise control over its investment.

Article 10   Publication of Laws and Decisions Respecting Investment

1. Each Party shall ensure that its:

  (a) laws, regulations, procedures, and administrative rulings of general application; and

  (b) adjudicatory decisions respecting any matter covered by this Treaty are promptly published or otherwise made publicly available.

2. For purposes of this Article, "administrative ruling of general application" means an administrative ruling or interpretation that applies to all persons and fact situations that fall generally within its ambit and that establishes a norm of conduct but does not include:

  (a) a determination or ruling made in an administrative or quasi-judicial proceeding that applies to a particular covered investment or investor of the other Party in a specific case; or

  (b) a ruling that adjudicates with respect to a particular act or practice.

Article 11   Transparency

1. The Parties agree to consult periodically on ways to improve the transparency practices set out in this Article, Article 10 and Article 29.

2. Publication

---

13 The Parties recognize that a patent does not necessarily confer market power.

To the extent possible, each Party shall:
(a) publish in advance any measure referred to in Article 10(1)(a) that it proposes to adopt; and
(b) provide interested persons and the other Party a reasonable opportunity to comment on such proposed measures.

3. With respect to proposed regulations of general application of its central level of government respecting any matter covered by this Treaty that are published in accordance with paragraph 2(a), each Party:
   (a) shall publish the proposed regulations in a single official journal of national circulation and shall encourage their distribution through additional outlets;
   (b) should in most cases publish the proposed regulations not less than 60 days before the date public comments are due;
   (c) shall include in the publication an explanation of the purpose of and rationale for the proposed regulations; and
   (d) shall, at the time it adopts final regulations, address significant, substantive comments received during the comment period and explain substantive revisions that it made to the proposed regulations in its official journal or in a prominent location on a government Internet site.

4. With respect to regulations of general application that are adopted by its central level of government respecting any matter covered by this Treaty, each Party:
   (a) shall publish the regulations in a single official journal of national circulation and shall encourage their distribution through additional outlets; and
   (b) shall include in the publication an explanation of the purpose of and rationale for the regulations.

5. Provision of Information
   (a) On request of the other Party, a Party shall promptly provide information and respond to questions pertaining to any actual or proposed measure that the requesting Party considers might materially affect the operation of this Treaty or otherwise substantially affect its interests under this Treaty.
   (b) Any request or information under this paragraph shall be provided to the other Party through the relevant contact points.
   (c) Any information provided under this paragraph shall be without prejudice as to whether the measure is consistent with this Treaty.

6. Administrative Proceedings
   With a view to administering in a consistent, impartial, and reasonable manner all measures referred to in Article 10(1)(a), each Party shall ensure that in its administrative proceedings applying such measures to particular covered investments or investors of the other Party in specific cases:
   (a) wherever possible, covered investments or investors of the other Party that are directly affected by a proceeding are provided reasonable notice, in accordance with domestic procedures, when a proceeding is initiated, including a description of the nature of the proceeding, a statement of the legal authority under which the proceeding is initiated, and a general description of any issues in controversy;
   (b) such persons are afforded a reasonable opportunity to present facts and arguments in support of their positions prior to any final administrative action, when time, the nature of the proceeding, and the public interest permit; and
   (c) its procedures are in accordance with domestic law.

7. Review and Appeal
   (a) Each Party shall establish or maintain judicial, quasi-judicial, or administrative tribunals or procedures for the purpose of the prompt review and, where warranted, correction of final administrative actions regarding matters covered by this Treaty. Such tribunals shall be impartial and independent of the office or authority entrusted with administrative enforcement and shall not have any substantial interest in the outcome of the matter.
   (b) Each Party shall ensure that, in any such tribunals or procedures, the parties to the proceeding are provided with the right to:
      (i) a reasonable opportunity to support or defend their respective positions; and
      (ii) a decision based on the evidence and submissions of record or, where required by domestic law, the record compiled by the administrative authority.
   (c) Each Party shall ensure, subject to appeal or further review as provided in its domestic law, that such decisions shall be implemented by, and shall govern the practice of, the offices or authorities with respect to the administrative action at issue.

8. Standards-Setting
   (a) Each Party shall allow persons of the other Party to participate in the development of standards and technical regulations by its central government bodies.[14] Each Party shall allow persons of the other Party to participate in the development of these measures, and the development of conformity assessment procedures by its central government bodies, on terms no less favorable than those it accords to its own persons.
   (b) Each Party shall recommend that non-governmental standardizing bodies in its territory allow persons of the other Party to participate in the development of standards by those bodies. Each Party shall recommend that non-governmental standardizing bodies in its territory allow persons of the other Party to participate in the development of these standards, and the development of conformity assessment procedures by those bodies, on terms no less favorable than those they accord to persons of the Party.
   (c) Subparagraphs 8(a) and 8(b) do not apply to:
      (i) sanitary and phytosanitary measures as defined in Annex A of the World Trade Organization (WTO) Agreement on the Application of Sanitary and Phytosanitary Measures; or
      (ii) purchasing specifications prepared by a governmental body for its production or consumption requirements.
   (d) For purposes of subparagraphs 8(a) and 8(b), "central government body", "standards", "technical regulations" and "conformity assessment procedures" have the meanings assigned to those terms in Annex 1 of the WTO Agreement on Technical Barriers to Trade. Consistent with Annex 1, the three latter terms do not include standards, technical regulations or conformity assessment procedures for the supply of a service.

Article 12   Investment and Environment

1. The Parties recognize that their respective environmental laws and policies, and multilateral environmental agreements to which they are both party, play an important role in protecting the environment.
2. The Parties recognize that it is inappropriate to encourage investment by weakening or reducing the protections afforded in domestic environmental laws. Accordingly, each Party shall ensure that it does not waive or otherwise derogate from or offer to waive or otherwise

---

14 A Party may satisfy this obligation by, for example, providing interested persons a reasonable opportunity to provide comments on the measure it proposes to develop and taking those comments into account in the development of the measure.

derogate from its environmental laws[15] in a manner that weakens or reduces the protections afforded in those laws, or fail to effectively enforce those laws through a sustained or recurring course of action or inaction, as an encouragement for the establishment, acquisition, expansion, or retention of an investment in its territory.

3. The Parties recognize that each Party retains the right to exercise discretion with respect to regulatory, compliance, investigatory, and prosecutorial matters, and to make decisions regarding the allocation of resources to enforcement with respect to other environmental matters determined to have higher priorities. Accordingly, the Parties understand that a Party is in compliance with paragraph 2 where a course of action or inaction reflects a reasonable exercise of such discretion, or results from a *bona fide* decision regarding the allocation of resources.

4. For purposes of this Article, "environmental law" means each Party's statutes or regulations,[16] or provisions thereof, the primary purpose of which is the protection of the environment, or the prevention of a danger to human, animal, or plant life or health, through the:

   (a) prevention, abatement, or control of the release, discharge, or emission of pollutants or environmental contaminants;
   (b) control of environmentally hazardous or toxic chemicals, substances, materials, and wastes, and the dissemination of information related thereto; or
   (c) protection or conservation of wild flora or fauna, including endangered species, their habitat, and specially protected natural areas, in the Party's territory, but does not include any statute or regulation, or provision thereof, directly related to worker safety or health.

5. Nothing in this Treaty shall be construed to prevent a Party from adopting, maintaining, or enforcing any measure otherwise consistent with this Treaty that it considers appropriate to ensure that investment activity in its territory is undertaken in a manner sensitive to environmental concerns.

6. A Party may make a written request for consultations with the other Party regarding any matter arising under this Article. The other Party shall respond to a request for consultations within thirty days of receipt of such request. Thereafter, the Parties shall consult and endeavor to reach a mutually satisfactory resolution.

7. The Parties confirm that each Party may, as appropriate, provide opportunities for public participation regarding any matter arising under this Article.

Article 13   Investment and Labor

1. The Parties reaffirm their respective obligations as members of the International Labor Organization ("ILO") and their commitments under the *ILO Declaration on Fundamental Principles and Rights at Work and its Follow-Up*.

2. The Parties recognize that it is inappropriate to encourage investment by weakening or reducing the protections afforded in domestic labor laws. Accordingly, each Party shall ensure that it does not waive or otherwise derogate from or offer to waive or otherwise derogate from its labor laws where the waiver or derogation would be inconsistent with the labor rights referred to in subparagraphs (a) through (e) of paragraph 3, or fail to effectively enforce its labor laws through a sustained or recurring course of action or inaction, as an encouragement for the establishment, acquisition, expansion, or retention of an investment in its territory.

3. For purposes of this Article, "labor laws" means each Party's statutes or regulations,[17] or provisions thereof, that are directly related to the following:

---

15 Paragraph 2 shall not apply where a Party waives or derogates from an environmental law pursuant to a provision in law providing for waivers or derogations.

16 For the United States, "statutes or regulations" for the purposes of this Article means an act of the United States Congress or regulations promulgated pursuant to an act of the United States Congress that is enforceable by action of the central level of government.

17 For the United States, "statutes or regulations" for purposes of this Article means an act of the United States Congress or regulations promulgated pursuant to an act of the United States Congress that is enforceable by action of the central level of government.

(a) freedom of association;

(b) the effective recognition of the right to collective bargaining;

(c) the elimination of all forms of forced or compulsory labor;

(d) the effective abolition of child labor and a prohibition on the worst forms of child labor;

(e) the elimination of discrimination in respect of employment and occupation; and

(f) acceptable conditions of work with respect to minimum wages, hours of work, and occupational safety and health.

4. A Party may make a written request for consultations with the other Party regarding any matter arising under this Article. The other Party shall respond to a request for consultations within thirty days of receipt of such request. Thereafter, the Parties shall consult and endeavor to reach a mutually satisfactory resolution.

5. The Parties confirm that each Party may, as appropriate, provide opportunities for public participation regarding any matter arising under this Article.

Article 14   Non-Conforming Measures

1. Articles 3 [National Treatment], 4 [Most-Favored-Nation Treatment], 8 [Performance Requirements], and 9 [Senior Management and Boards of Directors] do not apply to:

(a) any existing non-conforming measure that is maintained by a Party at:

   (i) the central level of government, as set out by that Party in its Schedule to Annex I or Annex III,

   (ii) a regional level of government, as set out by that Party in its Schedule to Annex I or Annex III, or

   (iii) a local level of government;

(b) the continuation or prompt renewal of any non-conforming measure referred to in subparagraph (a); or

(c) an amendment to any non-conforming measure referred to in subparagraph (a) to the extent that the amendment does not decrease the conformity of the measure, as it existed immediately before the amendment, with Article 3 [National Treatment], 4 [Most-Favored-Nation Treatment], 8 [Performance Requirements], or 9 [Senior Management and Boards of Directors].

2. Articles 3 [National Treatment], 4 [Most-Favored-Nation Treatment], 8 [Performance Requirements], and 9 [Senior Management and Boards of Directors] do not apply to any measure that a Party adopts or maintains with respect to sectors, subsectors, or activities, as set out in its Schedule to Annex II.

3. Neither Party may, under any measure adopted after the date of entry into force of this Treaty and covered by its Schedule to Annex II, require an investor of the other Party, by reason of its nationality, to sell or otherwise dispose of an investment existing at the time the measure becomes effective.

4. Articles 3 [National Treatment] and 4 [Most-Favored-Nation Treatment] do not apply to any measure covered by an exception to, or derogation from, the obligations under Article 3 or 4 of the TRIPS Agreement, as specifically provided in those Articles and in Article 5 of the TRIPS Agreement.

5. Articles 3 [National Treatment], 4 [Most-Favored-Nation Treatment], and 9 [Senior Management and Boards of Directors] do not apply to:

(a) government procurement; or

(b) subsidies or grants provided by a Party, including government-supported loans, guarantees, and insurance.

Article 15   Special Formalities and Information Requirements

1. Nothing in Article 3 [National Treatment] shall be construed to prevent a Party from adopting or maintaining a measure that prescribes special formalities in connection with covered

investments, such as a requirement that investors be residents of the Party or that covered investments be legally constituted under the laws or regulations of the Party, provided that such formalities do not materially impair the protections afforded by a Party to investors of the other Party and covered investments pursuant to this Treaty.

2. Notwithstanding Articles 3 [National Treatment] and 4 [Most-Favored-Nation Treatment], a Party may require an investor of the other Party or its covered investment to provide information concerning that investment solely for informational or statistical purposes. The Party shall protect any confidential business information from any disclosure that would prejudice the competitive position of the investor or the covered investment. Nothing in this paragraph shall be construed to prevent a Party from otherwise obtaining or disclosing information in connection with the equitable and good faith application of its law.

Article 16   Non-Derogation
This Treaty shall not derogate from any of the following that entitle an investor of a Party or a covered investment to treatment more favorable than that accorded by this Treaty:

1. laws or regulations, administrative practices or procedures, or administrative or adjudicatory decisions of a Party;

2. international legal obligations of a Party; or

3. obligations assumed by a Party, including those contained in an investment authorization or an investment agreement.

Article 17   Denial of Benefits
1. A Party may deny the benefits of this Treaty to an investor of the other Party that is an enterprise of such other Party and to investments of that investor if persons of a non-Party own or control the enterprise and the denying Party:
   (a) does not maintain diplomatic relations with the non-Party; or
   (b) adopts or maintains measures with respect to the non-Party or a person of the non-Party that prohibit transactions with the enterprise or that would be violated or circumvented if the benefits of this Treaty were accorded to the enterprise or to its investments.

2. A Party may deny the benefits of this Treaty to an investor of the other Party that is an enterprise of such other Party and to investments of that investor if the enterprise has no substantial business activities in the territory of the other Party and persons of a non-Party, or of the denying Party, own or control the enterprise.

Article 18   Essential Security
Nothing in this Treaty shall be construed:

1. to require a Party to furnish or allow access to any information the disclosure of which it determines to be contrary to its essential security interests; or

2. to preclude a Party from applying measures that it considers necessary for the fulfillment of its obligations with respect to the maintenance or restoration of international peace or security, or the protection of its own essential security interests.

Article 19   Disclosure of Information
Nothing in this Treaty shall be construed to require a Party to furnish or allow access to confidential information the disclosure of which would impede law enforcement or otherwise be contrary to the public interest, or which would prejudice the legitimate commercial interests of particular enterprises, public or private.

Article 20   Financial Services
1. Notwithstanding any other provision of this Treaty, a Party shall not be prevented from adopting or maintaining measures relating to financial services for prudential reasons, including for the protection of investors, depositors, policy holders, or persons to whom a fiduciary

duty is owed by a financial services supplier, or to ensure the integrity and stability of the financial system.[18] Where such measures do not conform with the provisions of this Treaty, they shall not be used as a means of avoiding the Party's commitments or obligations under this Treaty.

2. (a) Nothing in this Treaty applies to non-discriminatory measures of general application taken by any public entity in pursuit of monetary and related credit policies or exchange rate policies. This paragraph shall not affect a Party's obligations under Article 7 [Transfers] or Article 8 [Performance Requirements].[19]

   (b) For purposes of this paragraph, "public entity" means a central bank or monetary authority of a Party.

3. Where a claimant submits a claim to arbitration under Section B [Investor-State Dispute Settlement], and the respondent invokes paragraph 1 or 2 as a defense, the following provisions shall apply:

   (a) The respondent shall, within 120 days of the date the claim is submitted to arbitration under Section B, submit in writing to the competent financial authorities[20] of both Parties a request for a joint determination on the issue of whether and to what extent paragraph 1 or 2 is a valid defense to the claim. The respondent shall promptly provide the tribunal, if constituted, a copy of such request. The arbitration may proceed with respect to the claim only as provided in subparagraph (d).

   (b) The competent financial authorities of both Parties shall make themselves available for consultations with each other and shall attempt in good faith to make a determination as described in subparagraph (a). Any such determination shall be transmitted promptly to the disputing parties and, if constituted, to the tribunal. The determination shall be binding on the tribunal.

   (c) If the competent financial authorities of both Parties, within 120 days of the date by which they have both received the respondent's written request for a joint determination under subparagraph (a), have not made a determination as described in that subparagraph, the tribunal shall decide the issue or issues left unresolved by the competent financial authorities. The provisions of Section B shall apply, except as modified by this subparagraph.

      (i) In the appointment of all arbitrators not yet appointed to the tribunal, each disputing party shall take appropriate steps to ensure that the tribunal has expertise or experience in financial services law or practice. The expertise of particular candidates with respect to the particular sector of financial services in which the dispute arises shall be taken into account in the appointment of the presiding arbitrator.

      (ii) If, before the respondent submits the request for a joint determination in conformance with subparagraph (a), the presiding arbitrator has been appointed pursuant to Article 27(3), such arbitrator shall be replaced on the request of either disputing party and the tribunal shall be reconstituted consistent with subparagraph (c)(i). If, within 30 days of the date the arbitration proceedings are resumed under subparagraph (d), the disputing parties have not agreed on the appointment of a new presiding

---

18 It is understood that the term "prudential reasons" includes the maintenance of the safety, soundness, integrity, or financial responsibility of individual financial institutions, as well as the maintenance of the safety and financial and operational integrity of payment and clearing systems.

19 For greater certainty, measures of general application taken in pursuit of monetary and related credit policies or exchange rate policies do not include measures that expressly nullify or amend contractual provisions that specify the currency of denomination or the rate of exchange of currencies.

20 For purposes of this Article, "competent financial authorities" means, for the United States, the Department of the Treasury for banking and other financial services, and the Office of the United States Trade Representative, in coordination with the Department of Commerce and other agencies, for insurance; and for [Country], [_____].

arbitrator, the Secretary-General, on the request of a disputing party, shall appoint the presiding arbitrator consistent with subparagraph (c)(i).

    (iii) The tribunal shall draw no inference regarding the application of paragraph 1 or 2 from the fact that the competent financial authorities have not made a determination as described in subparagraph (a).

    (iv) The non-disputing Party may make oral and written submissions to the tribunal regarding the issue of whether and to what extent paragraph 1 or 2 is a valid defense to the claim. Unless it makes such a submission, the non-disputing Party shall be presumed, for purposes of the arbitration, to take a position on paragraph 1 or 2 not inconsistent with that of the respondent.

(d) The arbitration referred to in subparagraph (a) may proceed with respect to the claim:

    (i) 10 days after the date the competent financial authorities' joint determination has been received by both the disputing parties and, if constituted, the tribunal; or

    (ii) 10 days after the expiration of the 120-day period provided to the competent financial authorities in subparagraph (c).

(e) On the request of the respondent made within 30 days after the expiration of the 120-day period for a joint determination referred to in subparagraph (c), or, if the tribunal has not been constituted as of the expiration of the 120-day period, within 30 days after the tribunal is constituted, the tribunal shall address and decide the issue or issues left unresolved by the competent financial authorities as referred to in subparagraph (c) prior to deciding the merits of the claim for which paragraph 1 or 2 has been invoked by the respondent as a defense. Failure of the respondent to make such a request is without prejudice to the right of the respondent to invoke paragraph 1 or 2 as a defense at any appropriate phase of the arbitration.

4. Where a dispute arises under Section C and the competent financial authorities of one Party provide written notice to the competent financial authorities of the other Party that the dispute involves financial services, Section C shall apply except as modified by this paragraph and paragraph 5.

(a) The competent financial authorities of both Parties shall make themselves available for consultations with each other regarding the dispute, and shall have 180 days from the date such notice is received to transmit a report on their consultations to the Parties. A Party may submit the dispute to arbitration under Section C only after the expiration of that 180-day period.

(b) Either Party may make any such report available to a tribunal constituted under Section C to decide the dispute referred to in this paragraph or a similar dispute, or to a tribunal constituted under Section B to decide a claim arising out of the same events or circumstances that gave rise to the dispute under Section C.

5. Where a Party submits a dispute involving financial services to arbitration under Section C in conformance with paragraph 4, and on the request of either Party within 30 days of the date the dispute is submitted to arbitration, each Party shall, in the appointment of all arbitrators not yet appointed, take appropriate steps to ensure that the tribunal has expertise or experience in financial services law or practice. The expertise of particular candidates with respect to financial services shall be taken into account in the appointment of the presiding arbitrator.

6. Notwithstanding Article 11(2)–(4) [Transparency—Publication], each Party, to the extent practicable,

(a) shall publish in advance any regulations of general application relating to financial services that it proposes to adopt and the purpose of the regulation;

(b) shall provide interested persons and the other Party a reasonable opportunity to comment on such proposed regulations; and

(c) should at the time it adopts final regulations, address in writing significant substantive comments received from interested persons with respect to the proposed regulations.

7. The terms "financial service" or "financial services" shall have the same meaning as in subparagraph 5(a) of the Annex on Financial Services of the GATS.

8. For greater certainty, nothing in this Treaty shall be construed to prevent the adoption or enforcement by a party of measures relating to investors of the other Party, or covered investments, in financial institutions that are necessary to secure compliance with laws or regulations that are not inconsistent with this Treaty, including those related to the prevention of deceptive and fraudulent practices or that deal with the effects of a default on financial services contracts, subject to the requirement that such measures are not applied in a manner which would constitute a means of arbitrary or unjustifiable discrimination between countries where like conditions prevail, or a disguised restriction on investment in financial institutions.

Article 21   Taxation

1. Except as provided in this Article, nothing in Section A shall impose obligations with respect to taxation measures.

2. Article 6 [Expropriation] shall apply to all taxation measures, except that a claimant that asserts that a taxation measure involves an expropriation may submit a claim to arbitration under Section B only if:
   (a) the claimant has first referred to the competent tax authorities[21] of both Parties in writing the issue of whether that taxation measure involves an expropriation; and
   (b) within 180 days after the date of such referral, the competent tax authorities of both Parties fail to agree that the taxation measure is not an expropriation.

3. Subject to paragraph 4, Article 8 [Performance Requirements] (2) through (4) shall apply to all taxation measures.

4. Nothing in this Treaty shall affect the rights and obligations of either Party under any tax convention. In the event of any inconsistency between this Treaty and any such convention, that convention shall prevail to the extent of the inconsistency. In the case of a tax convention between the Parties, the competent authorities under that convention shall have sole responsibility for determining whether any inconsistency exists between this Treaty and that convention.

Article 22   Entry into Force, Duration, and Termination

1. This Treaty shall enter into force thirty days after the date the Parties exchange instruments of ratification. It shall remain in force for a period of ten years and shall continue in force thereafter unless terminated in accordance with paragraph 2.

2. A Party may terminate this Treaty at the end of the initial ten-year period or at any time thereafter by giving one year's written notice to the other Party.

3. For ten years from the date of termination, all other Articles shall continue to apply to covered investments established or acquired prior to the date of termination, except insofar as those Articles extend to the establishment or acquisition of covered investments.

SECTION B

Article 23   Consultation and Negotiation

In the event of an investment dispute, the claimant and the respondent should initially seek to resolve the dispute through consultation and negotiation, which may include the use of non-binding, third-party procedures.

---

21 For the purposes of this Article, the "competent tax authorities" means:
   (a) for the United States, the Assistant Secretary of the Treasury (Tax Policy), Department of the Treasury; and
   (b) for [Country], [_____].

Article 24   Submission of a Claim to Arbitration

1. In the event that a disputing party considers that an investment dispute cannot be settled by consultation and negotiation:

   (a) the claimant, on its own behalf, may submit to arbitration under this Section a claim
      (i) that the respondent has breached
         (A) an obligation under Articles 3 through 10,
         (B) an investment authorization, or
         (C) an investment agreement; and
      (ii) that the claimant has incurred loss or damage by reason of, or arising out of, that breach; and

   (b) the claimant, on behalf of an enterprise of the respondent that is a juridical person that the claimant owns or controls directly or indirectly, may submit to arbitration under this Section a claim
      (i) that the respondent has breached
         (A) an obligation under Articles 3 through 10,
         (B) an investment authorization, or
         (C) an investment agreement;

      and

      (ii) that the enterprise has incurred loss or damage by reason of, or arising out of, that breach, provided that a claimant may submit pursuant to subparagraph (a)(i)(C) or (b)(i)(C) a claim for breach of an investment agreement only if the subject matter of the claim and the claimed damages directly relate to the covered investment that was established or acquired, or sought to be established or acquired, in reliance on the relevant investment agreement.

2. At least 90 days before submitting any claim to arbitration under this Section, a claimant shall deliver to the respondent a written notice of its intention to submit the claim to arbitration ("notice of intent"). The notice shall specify:

   (a) the name and address of the claimant and, where a claim is submitted on behalf of an enterprise, the name, address, and place of incorporation of the enterprise;
   (b) for each claim, the provision of this Treaty, investment authorization, or investment agreement alleged to have been breached and any other relevant provisions;
   (c) the legal and factual basis for each claim; and
   (d) the relief sought and the approximate amount of damages claimed.

3. Provided that six months have elapsed since the events giving rise to the claim, a claimant may submit a claim referred to in paragraph 1:

   (a) under the ICSID Convention and the ICSID Rules of Procedure for Arbitration Pro-ceedings, provided that both the respondent and the non-disputing Party are parties to the ICSID Convention;
   (b) under the ICSID Additional Facility Rules, provided that either the respondent or the non-disputing Party is a party to the ICSID Convention;
   (c) under the UNCITRAL Arbitration Rules; or
   (d) if the claimant and respondent agree, to any other arbitration institution or under any other arbitration rules.

4. A claim shall be deemed submitted to arbitration under this Section when the claimant's notice of or request for arbitration ("notice of arbitration"):

   (a) referred to in paragraph 1 of Article 36 of the ICSID Convention is received by the Secretary-General;
   (b) referred to in Article 2 of Schedule C of the ICSID Additional Facility Rules is received by the Secretary-General;

(c) referred to in Article 3 of the UNCITRAL Arbitration Rules, together with the statement of claim referred to in Article 20 of the UNCITRAL Arbitration Rules, are received by the respondent; or

(d) referred to under any arbitral institution or arbitral rules selected under paragraph 3(d) is received by the respondent.

A claim asserted by the claimant for the first time after such notice of arbitration is submitted shall be deemed submitted to arbitration under this Section on the date of its receipt under the applicable arbitral rules.

5. The arbitration rules applicable under paragraph 3, and in effect on the date the claim or claims were submitted to arbitration under this Section, shall govern the arbitration except to the extent modified by this Treaty.

6. The claimant shall provide with the notice of arbitration:
    (a) the name of the arbitrator that the claimant appoints; or
    (b) the claimant's written consent for the Secretary-General to appoint that arbitrator.

Article 25   Consent of Each Party to Arbitration

1. Each Party consents to the submission of a claim to arbitration under this Section in accordance with this Treaty.

2. The consent under paragraph 1 and the submission of a claim to arbitration under this Section shall satisfy the requirements of:
    (a) Chapter II of the ICSID Convention (Jurisdiction of the Centre) and the ICSID Additional Facility Rules for written consent of the parties to the dispute; [and]
    (b) Article II of the New York Convention for an "agreement in writing[."] [;" and
    (c) Article I of the Inter-American Convention for an "agreement."]

Article 26   Conditions and Limitations on Consent of Each Party

1. No claim may be submitted to arbitration under this Section if more than three years have elapsed from the date on which the claimant first acquired, or should have first acquired, knowledge of the breach alleged under Article 24(1) and knowledge that the claimant (for claims brought under Article 24(1)(a)) or the enterprise (for claims brought under Article 24(1)(b)) has incurred loss or damage.

2. No claim may be submitted to arbitration under this Section unless:
    (a) the claimant consents in writing to arbitration in accordance with the procedures set out in this Treaty; and
    (b) the notice of arbitration is accompanied,
        (i) for claims submitted to arbitration under Article 24(1)(a), by the claimant's written waiver, and
        (ii) for claims submitted to arbitration under Article 24(1)(b), by the claimant's and the enterprise's written waivers of any right to initiate or continue before any administrative tribunal or court under the law of either Party, or other dispute settlement procedures, any proceeding with respect to any measure alleged to constitute a breach referred to in Article 24.

3. Notwithstanding paragraph 2(b), the claimant (for claims brought under Article 24(1)(a)) and the claimant or the enterprise (for claims brought under Article 24(1)(b)) may initiate or continue an action that seeks interim injunctive relief and does not involve the payment of monetary damages before a judicial or administrative tribunal of the respondent, provided that the action is brought for the sole purpose of preserving the claimant's or the enterprise's rights and interests during the pendency of the arbitration.

Article 27 Selection of Arbitrators

1. Unless the disputing parties otherwise agree, the tribunal shall comprise three arbitrators, one arbitrator appointed by each of the disputing parties and the third, who shall be the presiding arbitrator, appointed by agreement of the disputing parties.

2. The Secretary-General shall serve as appointing authority for an arbitration under this Section.

3. Subject to Article 20(3), if a tribunal has not been constituted within 75 days from the date that a claim is submitted to arbitration under this Section, the Secretary-General, on the request of a disputing party, shall appoint, in his or her discretion, the arbitrator or arbitrators not yet appointed.

4. For purposes of Article 39 of the ICSID Convention and Article 7 of Schedule C to the ICSID Additional Facility Rules, and without prejudice to an objection to an arbitrator on a ground other than nationality:
   (a) the respondent agrees to the appointment of each individual member of a tribunal established under the ICSID Convention or the ICSID Additional Facility Rules;
   (b) a claimant referred to in Article 24(1)(a) may submit a claim to arbitration under this Section, or continue a claim, under the ICSID Convention or the ICSID Additional Facility Rules, only on condition that the claimant agrees in writing to the appointment of each individual member of the tribunal; and
   (c) a claimant referred to in Article 24(1)(b) may submit a claim to arbitration under this Section, or continue a claim, under the ICSID Convention or the ICSID Additional Facility Rules, only on condition that the claimant and the enterprise agree in writing to the appointment of each individual member of the tribunal.

Article 28 Conduct of the Arbitration

1. The disputing parties may agree on the legal place of any arbitration under the arbitral rules applicable under Article 24(3). If the disputing parties fail to reach agreement, the tribunal shall determine the place in accordance with the applicable arbitral rules, provided that the place shall be in the territory of a State that is a party to the New York Convention.

2. The non-disputing Party may make oral and written submissions to the tribunal regarding the interpretation of this Treaty.

3. The tribunal shall have the authority to accept and consider *amicus curiae* submissions from a person or entity that is not a disputing party.

4. Without prejudice to a tribunal's authority to address other objections as a preliminary question, a tribunal shall address and decide as a preliminary question any objection by the respondent that, as a matter of law, a claim submitted is not a claim for which an award in favor of the claimant may be made under Article 34.
   (a) Such objection shall be submitted to the tribunal as soon as possible after the tribunal is constituted, and in no event later than the date the tribunal fixes for the respondent to submit its counter-memorial (or, in the case of an amendment to the notice of arbitration, the date the tribunal fixes for the respondent to submit its response to the amendment).
   (b) On receipt of an objection under this paragraph, the tribunal shall suspend any proceedings on the merits, establish a schedule for considering the objection consistent with any schedule it has established for considering any other preliminary question, and issue a decision or award on the objection, stating the grounds therefor.
   (c) In deciding an objection under this paragraph, the tribunal shall assume to be true claimant's factual allegations in support of any claim in the notice of arbitration (or any amendment thereof) and, in disputes brought under the UNCITRAL Arbitration Rules, the statement of claim referred to in Article 20 of the UNCITRAL Arbitration Rules. The tribunal may also consider any relevant facts not in dispute.

(d) The respondent does not waive any objection as to competence or any argument on the merits merely because the respondent did or did not raise an objection under this paragraph or make use of the expedited procedure set out in paragraph 5.

5. In the event that the respondent so requests within 45 days after the tribunal is constituted, the tribunal shall decide on an expedited basis an objection under paragraph 4 and any objection that the dispute is not within the tribunal's competence. The tribunal shall suspend any proceedings on the merits and issue a decision or award on the objection(s), stating the grounds therefor, no later than 150 days after the date of the request. However, if a disputing party requests a hearing, the tribunal may take an additional 30 days to issue the decision or award. Regardless of whether a hearing is requested, a tribunal may, on a showing of extraordinary cause, delay issuing its decision or award by an additional brief period, which may not exceed 30 days.

6. When it decides a respondent's objection under paragraph 4 or 5, the tribunal may, if warranted, award to the prevailing disputing party reasonable costs and attorney's fees incurred in submitting or opposing the objection. In determining whether such an award is warranted, the tribunal shall consider whether either the claimant's claim or the respondent's objection was frivolous, and shall provide the disputing parties a reasonable opportunity to comment.

7. A respondent may not assert as a defense, counterclaim, right of set-off, or for any other reason that the claimant has received or will receive indemnification or other compensation for all or part of the alleged damages pursuant to an insurance or guarantee contract.

8. A tribunal may order an interim measure of protection to preserve the rights of a disputing party, or to ensure that the tribunal's jurisdiction is made fully effective, including an order to preserve evidence in the possession or control of a disputing party or to protect the tribunal's jurisdiction. A tribunal may not order attachment or enjoin the application of a measure alleged to constitute a breach referred to in Article 24. For purposes of this paragraph, an order includes a recommendation.

9. (a) In any arbitration conducted under this Section, at the request of a disputing party, a tribunal shall, before issuing a decision or award on liability, transmit its proposed decision or award to the disputing parties and to the non-disputing Party. Within 60 days after the tribunal transmits its proposed decision or award, the disputing parties may submit written comments to the tribunal concerning any aspect of its proposed decision or award. The tribunal shall consider any such comments and issue its decision or award not later than 45 days after the expiration of the 60-day comment period.

   (b) Subparagraph (a) shall not apply in any arbitration conducted pursuant to this Section for which an appeal has been made available pursuant to paragraph 10.

10. In the event that an appellate mechanism for reviewing awards rendered by investor-State dispute settlement tribunals is developed in the future under other institutional arrangements, the Parties shall consider whether awards rendered under Article 34 should be subject to that appellate mechanism. The Parties shall strive to ensure that any such appellate mechanism they consider adopting provides for transparency of proceedings similar to the transparency provisions established in Article 29.

Article 29 Transparency of Arbitral Proceedings

1. Subject to paragraphs 2 and 4, the respondent shall, after receiving the following documents, promptly transmit them to the non-disputing Party and make them available to the public:
   (a) the notice of intent;
   (b) the notice of arbitration;

(c) pleadings, memorials, and briefs submitted to the tribunal by a disputing party and any written submissions submitted pursuant to Article 28(2) [Non-Disputing Party Submissions] and (3) [*Amicus* Submissions] and Article 33 [Consolidation];

(d) minutes or transcripts of hearings of the tribunal, where available; and

(e) orders, awards, and decisions of the tribunal.

2. The tribunal shall conduct hearings open to the public and shall determine, in consultation with the disputing parties, the appropriate logistical arrangements. However, any disputing party that intends to use information designated as protected information in a hearing shall so advise the tribunal. The tribunal shall make appropriate arrangements to protect the information from disclosure.

3. Nothing in this Section requires a respondent to disclose protected information or to furnish or allow access to information that it may withhold in accordance with Article 18 [Essential Security Article] or Article 19 [Disclosure of Information Article].

4. Any protected information that is submitted to the tribunal shall be protected from disclosure in accordance with the following procedures:

(a) Subject to subparagraph (d), neither the disputing parties nor the tribunal shall disclose to the non-disputing Party or to the public any protected information where the disputing party that provided the information clearly designates it in accordance with subparagraph (b);

(b) Any disputing party claiming that certain information constitutes protected information shall clearly designate the information at the time it is submitted to the tribunal;

(c) A disputing party shall, at the time it submits a document containing information claimed to be protected information, submit a redacted version of the document that does not contain the information. Only the redacted version shall be provided to the non-disputing Party and made public in accordance with paragraph 1; and

(d) The tribunal shall decide any objection regarding the designation of information claimed to be protected information. If the tribunal determines that such information was not properly designated, the disputing party that submitted the information may (i) withdraw all or part of its submission containing such information, or (ii) agree to resubmit complete and redacted documents with corrected designations in accordance with the tribunal's determination and subparagraph (c). In either case, the other disputing party shall, whenever necessary, resubmit complete and redacted documents which either remove the information withdrawn under (i) by the disputing party that first submitted the information or redesignate the information consistent with the designation under (ii) of the disputing party that first submitted the information.

5. Nothing in this Section requires a respondent to withhold from the public information required to be disclosed by its laws.

Article 30 Governing Law

1. Subject to paragraph 3, when a claim is submitted under Article 24(1)(a)(i)(A) or Article 24(1)(b)(i)(A), the tribunal shall decide the issues in dispute in accordance with this Treaty and applicable rules of international law.

2. Subject to paragraph 3 and the other terms of this Section, when a claim is submitted under Article 24(1)(a)(i)(B) or (C), or Article 24(1)(b)(i)(B) or (C), the tribunal shall apply:

(a) the rules of law specified in the pertinent investment authorization or investment agreement, or as the disputing parties may otherwise agree; or

(b) if the rules of law have not been specified or otherwise agreed:

(i) the law of the respondent, including its rules on the conflict of laws;[22] and

---

[22] The "law of the respondent" means the law that a domestic court or tribunal of proper jurisdiction would apply in the same case.

(ii) such rules of international law as may be applicable.

3. A joint decision of the Parties, each acting through its representative designated for purposes of this Article, declaring their interpretation of a provision of this Treaty shall be binding on a tribunal, and any decision or award issued by a tribunal must be consistent with that joint decision.

Article 31   Interpretation of Annexes

1. Where a respondent asserts as a defense that the measure alleged to be a breach is within the scope of an entry set out in Annex I, II, or III, the tribunal shall, on request of the respondent, request the interpretation of the Parties on the issue. The Parties shall submit in writing any joint decision declaring their interpretation to the tribunal within 90 days of delivery of the request.

2. A joint decision issued under paragraph 1 by the Parties, each acting through its representative designated for purposes of this Article, shall be binding on the tribunal, and any decision or award issued by the tribunal must be consistent with that joint decision. If the Parties fail to issue such a decision within 90 days, the tribunal shall decide the issue.

Article 32   Expert Reports

Without prejudice to the appointment of other kinds of experts where authorized by the applicable arbitration rules, a tribunal, at the request of a disputing party or, unless the disputing parties disapprove, on its own initiative, may appoint one or more experts to report to it in writing on any factual issue concerning environmental, health, safety, or other scientific matters raised by a disputing party in a proceeding, subject to such terms and conditions as the disputing parties may agree.

Article 33   Consolidation

1. Where two or more claims have been submitted separately to arbitration under Article 24(1) and the claims have a question of law or fact in common and arise out of the same events or circumstances, any disputing party may seek a consolidation order in accordance with the agreement of all the disputing parties sought to be covered by the order or the terms of paragraphs 2 through 10.

2. A disputing party that seeks a consolidation order under this Article shall deliver, in writing, a request to the Secretary-General and to all the disputing parties sought to be covered by the order and shall specify in the request:
   (a) the names and addresses of all the disputing parties sought to be covered by the order;
   (b) the nature of the order sought; and
   (c) the grounds on which the order is sought.

3. Unless the Secretary-General finds within 30 days after receiving a request under paragraph 2 that the request is manifestly unfounded, a tribunal shall be established under this Article.

4. Unless all the disputing parties sought to be covered by the order otherwise agree, a tribunal established under this Article shall comprise three arbitrators:
   (a) one arbitrator appointed by agreement of the claimants;
   (b) one arbitrator appointed by the respondent; and
   (c) the presiding arbitrator appointed by the Secretary-General, provided, however, that the presiding arbitrator shall not be a national of either Party.

5. If, within 60 days after the Secretary-General receives a request made under paragraph 2, the respondent fails or the claimants fail to appoint an arbitrator in accordance with paragraph 4, the Secretary-General, on the request of any disputing party sought to be covered by the order, shall appoint the arbitrator or arbitrators not yet appointed. If the respondent fails to appoint an arbitrator, the Secretary-General shall appoint a national of the disputing Party,

and if the claimants fail to appoint an arbitrator, the Secretary-General shall appoint a national of the non-disputing Party.

6. Where a tribunal established under this Article is satisfied that two or more claims that have been submitted to arbitration under Article 24(1) have a question of law or fact in common, and arise out of the same events or circumstances, the tribunal may, in the interest of fair and efficient resolution of the claims, and after hearing the disputing parties, by order:
   (a) assume jurisdiction over, and hear and determine together, all or part of the claims;
   (b) assume jurisdiction over, and hear and determine one or more of the claims, the determination of which it believes would assist in the resolution of the others; or
   (c) instruct a tribunal previously established under Article 27 [Selection of Arbitrators] to assume jurisdiction over, and hear and determine together, all or part of the claims, provided that
       (i) that tribunal, at the request of any claimant not previously a disputing party before that tribunal, shall be reconstituted with its original members, except that the arbitrator for the claimants shall be appointed pursuant to paragraphs 4(a) and 5; and
       (ii) that tribunal shall decide whether any prior hearing shall be repeated.

7. Where a tribunal has been established under this Article, a claimant that has submitted a claim to arbitration under Article 24(1) and that has not been named in a request made under paragraph 2 may make a written request to the tribunal that it be included in any order made under paragraph 6, and shall specify in the request:
   (a) the name and address of the claimant;
   (b) the nature of the order sought; and
   (c) the grounds on which the order is sought.
   The claimant shall deliver a copy of its request to the Secretary-General.

8. A tribunal established under this Article shall conduct its proceedings in accordance with the UNCITRAL Arbitration Rules, except as modified by this Section.

9. A tribunal established under Article 27 [Selection of Arbitrators] shall not have jurisdiction to decide a claim, or a part of a claim, over which a tribunal established or instructed under this Article has assumed jurisdiction.

10. On application of a disputing party, a tribunal established under this Article, pending its decision under paragraph 6, may order that the proceedings of a tribunal established under Article 27 [Selection of Arbitrators] be stayed, unless the latter tribunal has already adjourned its proceedings.

Article 34   Awards

1. Where a tribunal makes a final award against a respondent, the tribunal may award, separately or in combination, only:
   (a) monetary damages and any applicable interest; and
   (b) restitution of property, in which case the award shall provide that the respondent may pay monetary damages and any applicable interest in lieu of restitution.

   A tribunal may also award costs and attorney's fees in accordance with this Treaty and the applicable arbitration rules.

2. Subject to paragraph 1, where a claim is submitted to arbitration under Article 24(1)(b):
   (a) an award of restitution of property shall provide that restitution be made to the enterprise;
   (b) an award of monetary damages and any applicable interest shall provide that the sum be paid to the enterprise; and
   (c) the award shall provide that it is made without prejudice to any right that any person may have in the relief under applicable domestic law.

3. A tribunal may not award punitive damages.

4. An award made by a tribunal shall have no binding force except between the disputing parties and in respect of the particular case.

5. Subject to paragraph 6 and the applicable review procedure for an interim award, a disputing party shall abide by and comply with an award without delay.

6. A disputing party may not seek enforcement of a final award until:
   (a) in the case of a final award made under the ICSID Convention,
       (i) 120 days have elapsed from the date the award was rendered and no disputing party has requested revision or annulment of the award; or
       (ii) revision or annulment proceedings have been completed; and
   (b) in the case of a final award under the ICSID Additional Facility Rules, the UNCITRAL Arbitration Rules, or the rules selected pursuant to Article 24(3)(d),
       (i) 90 days have elapsed from the date the award was rendered and no disputing party has commenced a proceeding to revise, set aside, or annul the award; or
       (ii) a court has dismissed or allowed an application to revise, set aside, or annul the award and there is no further appeal.

7. Each Party shall provide for the enforcement of an award in its territory.

8. If the respondent fails to abide by or comply with a final award, on delivery of a request by the non-disputing Party, a tribunal shall be established under Article 37 [State-State Dispute Settlement]. Without prejudice to other remedies available under applicable rules of international law, the requesting Party may seek in such proceedings:
   (a) a determination that the failure to abide by or comply with the final award is inconsistent with the obligations of this Treaty; and
   (b) a recommendation that the respondent abide by or comply with the final award.

9. A disputing party may seek enforcement of an arbitration award under the ICSID Convention or the New York Convention [or the Inter-American Convention] regardless of whether proceedings have been taken under paragraph 8.

10. A claim that is submitted to arbitration under this Section shall be considered to arise out of a commercial relationship or transaction for purposes of Article I of the New York Convention [and Article I of the Inter-American Convention].

Article 35   Annexes and Footnotes
The Annexes and footnotes shall form an integral part of this Treaty.

Article 36   Service of Documents
Delivery of notice and other documents on a Party shall be made to the place named for that Party in Annex C.

SECTION C

Article 37   State-State Dispute Settlement
1. Subject to paragraph 5, any dispute between the Parties concerning the interpretation or application of this Treaty, that is not resolved through consultations or other diplomatic channels, shall be submitted on the request of either Party to arbitration for a binding decision or award by a tribunal in accordance with applicable rules of international law. In the absence of an agreement by the Parties to the contrary, the UNCITRAL Arbitration Rules shall govern, except as modified by the Parties or this Treaty.

2. Unless the Parties otherwise agree, the tribunal shall comprise three arbitrators, one arbitrator appointed by each Party and the third, who shall be the presiding arbitrator, appointed by agreement of the Parties. If a tribunal has not been constituted within 75 days from the date

that a claim is submitted to arbitration under this Section, the Secretary-General, on the request of either Party, shall appoint, in his or her discretion, the arbitrator or arbitrators not yet appointed.

3. Expenses incurred by the arbitrators, and other costs of the proceedings, shall be paid for equally by the Parties. However, the tribunal may, in its discretion, direct that a higher proportion of the costs be paid by one of the Parties.

4. Articles 28(3) [*Amicus Curiae* Submissions], 29 [Investor-State Transparency], 30(1) and (3) [Governing Law], and 31 [Interpretation of Annexes] shall apply *mutatis mutandis* to arbitrations under this Article.

5. Paragraphs 1 through 4 shall not apply to a matter arising under Article 12 or Article 13.

IN WITNESS WHEREOF, the respective plenipotentiaries have signed this Treaty.

DONE in duplicate at [city] this [number] day of [month, year], in the English and [foreign] languages, each text being equally authentic.

FOR THE GOVERNMNET OF   FOR THE GOVERNMENT OF
THE UNITED STATES OF AMERICA: [Country]:

ANNEX A   CUSTOMARY INTERNATIONAL LAW

The Parties confirm their shared understanding that "customary international law" generally and as specifically referenced in Article 5 [Minimum Standard of Treatment] and Annex B [Expropriation] results from a general and consistent practice of States that they follow from a sense of legal obligation. With regard to Article 5 [Minimum Standard of Treatment], the customary international law minimum standard of treatment of aliens refers to all customary international law principles that protect the economic rights and interests of aliens.

ANNEX B   EXPROPRIATION

The Parties confirm their shared understanding that:

1. Article 6 [Expropriation and Compensation](1) is intended to reflect customary international law concerning the obligation of States with respect to expropriation.

2. An action or a series of actions by a Party cannot constitute an expropriation unless it interferes with a tangible or intangible property right or property interest in an investment.

3. Article 6 [Expropriation and Compensation](1) addresses two situations. The first is direct expropriation, where an investment is nationalized or otherwise directly expropriated through formal transfer of title or outright seizure.

4. The second situation addressed by Article 6 [Expropriation and Compensation](1) is indirect expropriation, where an action or series of actions by a Party has an effect equivalent to direct expropriation without formal transfer of title or outright seizure.

   (a) The determination of whether an action or series of actions by a Party, in a specific fact situation, constitutes an indirect expropriation, requires a case-by-case, fact-based inquiry that considers, among other factors:

      (i) the economic impact of the government action, although the fact that an action or series of actions by a Party has an adverse effect on the economic value of an investment, standing alone, does not establish that an indirect expropriation has occurred;

      (ii) the extent to which the government action interferes with distinct, reasonable investment-backed expectations; and

      (iii) the character of the government action.

(b) Except in rare circumstances, non-discriminatory regulatory actions by a Party that are designed and applied to protect legitimate public welfare objectives, such as public health, safety, and the environment, do not constitute indirect expropriations.

ANNEX C   SERVICE OF DOCUMENTS ON A PARTY

United States
Notices and other documents shall be served on the United States by delivery to:

> Executive Director (L/EX)
> Office of the Legal Adviser
> Department of State
> Washington, D.C. 20520
> United States of America

[Country]
Notices and other documents shall be served on [Country] by delivery to:
> [insert place of delivery of notices and other documents for [Country]]

+ Art. XI; Prohibits quantative restrictions;

* Art. xx; Allows states "In Introducing measures to protect National security, public health, safety of people, animals, plants & enviroment. Provided that these measures are not discrimatory"
 + EC-Asbestos case; The panal accepted Canadas claim that non-asbestos substitutes were LIkE products despite one having carcinogen. Even after the panals acceptance that they're Like products, they upheld france's ban because the Level of health & enviromental protection is upto the member state under Act. xx.

+ Additonal tax or charges may not be added directly or Indirectly once In the Intended market Unless Like products are subject to the same cost (Art. III)
 + Government buying is exempt from "GATT National Treatment" Obligations because the purchases are for governmental use & not any comercial use. (uruguay round 1995)

+ Patent; Art xx;
 + Art 33; Gives 20year protection.
 + Patent protection "must be enjoyable without discrimination as to the place of Invention, the field of technology & whether products are Imported or produced locally. Art. 27 (1)

Selected Multilateral Investment Agreements

III-10

The Energy Charter Treaty

Date   17 December 1994
In force 16 April 1998
Source   2080 UNTS 100
Link   <http://www.encharter.org/fileadmin/user_upload/document/EN.pdf>

PART I   DEFINITIONS AND PURPOSE

Article 1   Definitions

As used in this Treaty:

(1) "Charter" means the European Energy Charter adopted in the Concluding Document of the Hague Conference on the European Energy Charter signed at The Hague on 17 December 1991; signature of the Concluding Document is considered to be signature of the Charter.

(2) "Contracting Party" means a state or Regional Economic Integration Organization which has consented to be bound by this Treaty and for which the Treaty is in force.

(3) "Regional Economic Integration Organization" means an organization constituted by states to which they have transferred competence over certain matters a number of which are governed by this Treaty, including the authority to take decisions binding on them in respect of those matters.

(4) "Energy Materials and Products", based on the Harmonized System of the Customs Co-operation Council and the Combined Nomenclature of the European Communities, means the items included in Annex EM.

(5) "Economic Activity in the Energy Sector" means an economic activity concerning the exploration, extraction, refining, production, storage, land transport, transmission, distribution, trade, marketing, or sale of Energy Materials and Products except those included in Annex NI, or concerning the distribution of heat to multiple premises.

(6) "Investment" means every kind of asset, owned or controlled directly or indirectly by an Investor and includes:
  (a) tangible and intangible, and movable and immovable, property, and any property rights such as leases, mortgages, liens, and pledges;
  (b) a company or business enterprise, or shares, stock, or other forms of equity participation in a company or business enterprise, and bonds and other debt of a company or business enterprise;
  (c) claims to money and claims to performance pursuant to contract having an economic value and associated with an Investment;

(d) Intellectual Property;

(e) Returns;

(f) any right conferred by law or contract or by virtue of any licences and permits granted pursuant to law to undertake any Economic Activity in the Energy Sector.

A change in the form in which assets are invested does not affect their character as investments and the term "Investment" includes all investments, whether existing at or made after the later of the date of entry into force of this Treaty for the Contracting Party of the Investor making the investment and that for the Contracting Party in the Area of which the investment is made (hereinafter referred to as the "Effective Date") provided that the Treaty shall only apply to matters affecting such investments after the Effective Date.

"Investment" refers to any investment associated with an Economic Activity in the Energy Sector and to investments or classes of investments designated by a Contracting Party in its Area as "Charter efficiency projects" and so notified to the Secretariat.

(7) "Investor" means:

    (a) with respect to a Contracting Party:

        (i) a natural person having the citizenship or nationality of or who is permanently residing in that Contracting Party in accordance with its applicable law;

        (ii) a company or other organization organized in accordance with the law applicable in that Contracting Party;

    (b) with respect to a "third state", a natural person, company or other organization which fulfils, mutatis mutandis, the conditions specified in subparagraph (a) for a Contracting Party.

(8) "Make Investments" or "Making of Investments" means establishing new Investments, acquiring all or part of existing Investments or moving into different fields of Investment activity.

(9) "Returns" means the amounts derived from or associated with an Investment, irrespective of the form in which they are paid, including profits, dividends, interest, capital gains, royalty payments, management, technical assistance or other fees and payments in kind.

(10) "Area" means with respect to a state that is a Contracting Party:

    (a) the territory under its sovereignty, it being understood that territory includes land, internal waters and the territorial sea; and

    (b) subject to and in accordance with the international law of the sea: the sea, sea-bed and its subsoil with regard to which that Contracting Party exercises sovereign rights and jurisdiction.

With respect to a Regional Economic Integration Organization which is a Contracting Party, Area means the Areas of the member states of such Organization, under the provisions contained in the agreement establishing that Organization.

(11) (a) "GATT" means "GATT 1947" or "GATT 1994", or both of them where both are applicable.

    (b) "GATT 1947" means the General Agreement on Tariffs and Trade, dated 30 October 1947, annexed to the Final Act Adopted at the Conclusion of the Second Session of the Preparatory Committee of the United Nations Conference on Trade and Employment, as subsequently rectified, amended or modified.

    (c) "GATT 1994" means the General Agreement on Tariffs and Trade as specified in Annex 1A of the Agreement Establishing the World Trade Organization, as subsequently rectified, amended or modified.

        A party to the Agreement Establishing the World Trade Organization is considered to be a party to GATT 1994.

    (d) "Related Instruments" means, as appropriate:

(i) agreements, arrangements or other legal instruments, including decisions, declarations and understandings, concluded under the auspices of GATT 1947 as subsequently rectified, amended or modified; or

(ii) the Agreement Establishing the World Trade Organization including its Annex 1 (except GATT 1994), its Annexes 2, 3 and 4, and the decisions, declarations and understandings related thereto, as subsequently rectified, amended or modified.

(12) "Intellectual Property" includes copyrights and related rights, trademarks, geographical indications, industrial designs, patents, layout designs of integrated circuits and the protection of undisclosed information.

(13) (a) "Energy Charter Protocol" or "Protocol" means a treaty, the negotiation of which is authorized and the text of which is adopted by the Charter Conference, which is entered into by two or more Contracting Parties in order to complement, supplement, extend or amplify the provisions of this Treaty with respect to any specific sector or category of activity within the scope of this Treaty, or to areas of co-operation pursuant to Title III of the Charter.

(b) "Energy Charter Declaration" or "Declaration" means a non-binding instrument, the negotiation of which is authorized and the text of which is approved by the Charter Conference, which is entered into by two or more Contracting Parties to complement or supplement the provisions of this Treaty.

(14) "Freely Convertible Currency" means a currency which is widely traded in international foreign exchange markets and widely used in international transactions.

Article 2   Purpose of the Treaty

This Treaty establishes a legal framework in order to promote long-term co-operation in the energy field, based on complementarities and mutual benefits, in accordance with the objectives and principles of the Charter.

PART III   INVESTMENT PROMOTION AND PROTECTION

Article 10   Promotion, protection and treatment of investments

(1) Each Contracting Party shall, in accordance with the provisions of this Treaty, encourage and create stable, equitable, favourable and transparent conditions for Investors of other Contracting Parties to make Investments in its Area. Such conditions shall include a commitment to accord at all times to Investments of Investors of other Contracting Parties fair and equitable treatment. Such Investments shall also enjoy the most constant protection and security and no Contracting Party shall in any way impair by unreasonable or discriminatory measures their management, maintenance, use, enjoyment or disposal. In no case shall such Investments be accorded treatment less favourable than that required by international law, including treaty obligations. Each Contracting Party shall observe any obligations it has entered into with an Investor or an Investment of an Investor of any other Contracting Party.

(2) Each Contracting Party shall endeavour to accord to Investors of other Contracting Parties, as regards the Making of Investments in its Area, the Treatment described in paragraph (3).

(3) For the purposes of this Article, "Treatment" means treatment accorded by a Contracting Party which is no less favourable than that which it accords to its own Investors or to Investors of any other Contracting Party or any third state, whichever is the most favourable.

(4) A supplementary treaty shall, subject to conditions to be laid down therein, oblige each party thereto to accord to Investors of other parties, as regards the Making of Investments in its

Area, the Treatment described in paragraph (3). That treaty shall be open for signature by the states and Regional Economic Integration Organizations which have signed or acceded to this Treaty. Negotiations towards the supplementary treaty shall commence not later than 1 January 1995, with a view to concluding it by 1 January 1998.

(5) Each Contracting Party shall, as regards the Making of Investments in its Area, endeavour to:
   (a) limit to the minimum the exceptions to the Treatment described in paragraph (3);
   (b) progressively remove existing restrictions affecting Investors of other Contracting Parties.

(6) (a) A Contracting Party may, as regards the Making of Investments in its Area, at any time declare voluntarily to the Charter Conference, through the Secretariat, its intention not to introduce new exceptions to the Treatment described in paragraph (3).
   (b) A Contracting Party may, furthermore, at any time make a voluntary commitment to accord to Investors of other Contracting Parties, as regards the Making of Investments in some or all Economic Activities in the Energy Sector in its Area, the Treatment described in paragraph (3). Such commitments shall be notified to the Secretariat and listed in Annex VC and shall be binding under this Treaty.

(7) Each Contracting Party shall accord to Investments in its Area of Investors of other Contracting Parties, and their related activities including management, maintenance, use, enjoyment or disposal, treatment no less favourable than that which it accords to Investments of its own Investors or of the Investors of any other Contracting Party or any third state and their related activities including management, maintenance, use, enjoyment or disposal, whichever is the most favourable.

(8) The modalities of application of paragraph (7) in relation to programmes under which a Contracting Party provides grants or other financial assistance, or enters into contracts, for energy technology research and development, shall be reserved for the supplementary treaty described in paragraph (4). Each Contracting Party shall through the Secretariat keep the Charter Conference informed of the modalities it applies to the programmes described in this paragraph.

(9) Each state or Regional Economic Integration Organization which signs or accedes to this Treaty shall, on the date it signs the Treaty or deposits its instrument of accession, submit to the Secretariat a report summarizing all laws, regulations or other measures relevant to:
   (a) exceptions to paragraph (2); or
   (b) the programmes referred to in paragraph (8).
   A Contracting Party shall keep its report up to date by promptly submitting amendments to the Secretariat. The Charter Conference shall review these reports periodically.
      In respect of subparagraph (a) the report may designate parts of the energy sector in which a Contracting Party accords to Investors of other Contracting Parties the Treatment described in paragraph (3).
      In respect of subparagraph (b) the review by the Charter Conference may consider the effects of such programmes on competition and Investments.

(10) Notwithstanding any other provision of this Article, the treatment described in paragraphs (3) and (7) shall not apply to the protection of Intellectual Property; instead, the treatment shall be as specified in the corresponding provisions of the applicable international agreements for the protection of Intellectual Property rights to which the respective Contracting Parties are parties.

(11) For the purposes of Article 26, the application by a Contracting Party of a trade-related investment measure as described in Article 5(1) and (2) to an Investment of an Investor of another Contracting Party existing at the time of such application shall, subject to Article 5

(3) and (4), be considered a breach of an obligation of the former Contracting Party under this Part.

(12) Each Contracting Party shall ensure that its domestic law provides effective means for the assertion of claims and the enforcement of rights with respect to Investments, investment agreements, and investment authorizations.

Article 11   Key personnel

(1) A Contracting Party shall, subject to its laws and regulations relating to the entry, stay and work of natural persons, examine in good faith requests by Investors of another Contracting Party, and key personnel who are employed by such Investors or by Investments of such Investors, to enter and remain temporarily in its Area to engage in activities connected with the making or the development, management, maintenance, use, enjoyment or disposal of relevant Investments, including the provision of advice or key technical services.

(2) A Contracting Party shall permit Investors of another Contracting Party which have Investments in its Area, and Investments of such Investors, to employ any key person of the Investor's or the Investment's choice regardless of nationality and citizenship provided that such key person has been permitted to enter, stay and work in the Area of the former Contracting Party and that the employment concerned conforms to the terms, conditions and time limits of the permission granted to such key person.

Article 12   Compensation for losses

(1) Except where Article 13 applies, an Investor of any Contracting Party which suffers a loss with respect to any Investment in the Area of another Contracting Party owing to war or other armed conflict, state of national emergency, civil disturbance, or other similar event in that Area, shall be accorded by the latter Contracting Party, as regards restitution, indemnification, compensation or other settlement, treatment which is the most favourable of that which that Contracting Party accords to any other Investor, whether its own Investor, the Investor of any other Contracting Party, or the Investor of any third state.

(2) Without prejudice to paragraph (1), an Investor of a Contracting Party which, in any of the situations referred to in that paragraph, suffers a loss in the Area of another Contracting Party resulting from

(a) requisitioning of its Investment or part thereof by the latter's forces or authorities; or

(b) destruction of its Investment or part thereof by the latter's forces or authorities, which was not required by the necessity of the situation, shall be accorded restitution or compensation which in either case shall be prompt, adequate and effective.

Article 13   Expropriation

(1) Investments of Investors of a Contracting Party in the Area of any other Contracting Party shall not be nationalized, expropriated or subjected to a measure or measures having effect equivalent to nationalization or expropriation (hereinafter referred to as "Expropriation") except where such Expropriation is:

(a) for a purpose which is in the public interest;

(b) not discriminatory;

(c) carried out under due process of law; and

(d) accompanied by the payment of prompt, adequate and effective compensation.

Such compensation shall amount to the fair market value of the Investment expropriated at the time immediately before the Expropriation or impending Expropriation became known in such a way as to affect the value of the Investment (hereinafter referred to as the "Valuation Date").

Such fair market value shall at the request of the Investor be expressed in a Freely Convertible Currency on the basis of the market rate of exchange existing for that currency on the Valuation Date. Compensation shall also include interest at a commercial rate established on a market basis from the date of Expropriation until the date of payment.

(2) The Investor affected shall have a right to prompt review, under the law of the Contracting Party making the Expropriation, by a judicial or other competent and independent authority of that Contracting Party, of its case, of the valuation of its Investment, and of the payment of compensation, in accordance with the principles set out in paragraph (1).

(3) For the avoidance of doubt, Expropriation shall include situations where a Contracting Party expropriates the assets of a company or enterprise in its Area in which an Investor of any other Contracting Party has an Investment, including through the ownership of shares.

Article 14   Transfers related to investments

(1) Each Contracting Party shall with respect to Investments in its Area of Investors of any other Contracting Party guarantee the freedom of transfer into and out of its Area, including the transfer of:
   (a) the initial capital plus any additional capital for the maintenance and development of an Investment;
   (b) Returns;
   (c) payments under a contract, including amortization of principal and accrued interest payments pursuant to a loan agreement;
   (d) unspent earnings and other remuneration of personnel engaged from abroad in connection with that Investment;
   (e) proceeds from the sale or liquidation of all or any part of an Investment;
   (f) payments arising out of the settlement of a dispute;
   (g) payments of compensation pursuant to Articles 12 and 13.

(2) Transfers under paragraph (1) shall be effected without delay and (except in case of a Return in kind) in a Freely Convertible Currency.

(3) Transfers shall be made at the market rate of exchange existing on the date of transfer with respect to spot transactions in the currency to be transferred. In the absence of a market for foreign exchange, the rate to be used will be the most recent rate applied to inward investments or the most recent exchange rate for conversion of currencies into Special Drawing Rights, whichever is more favourable to the Investor.

(4) Notwithstanding paragraphs (1) to (3), a Contracting Party may protect the rights of creditors, or ensure compliance with laws on the issuing, trading and dealing in securities and the satisfaction of judgements in civil, administrative and criminal adjudicatory proceedings, through the equitable, non-discriminatory, and good faith application of its laws and regulations.

(5) Notwithstanding paragraph (2), Contracting Parties which are states that were constituent parts of the former Union of Soviet Socialist Republics may provide in agreements concluded between them that transfers of payments shall be made in the currencies of such Contracting Parties, provided that such agreements do not treat Investments in their Areas of Investors of other Contracting Parties less favourably than either Investments of Investors of the Contracting Parties which have entered into such agreements or Investments of Investors of any third state.

(6) Notwithstanding subparagraph (1)(b), a Contracting Party may restrict the transfer of a Return in kind in circumstances where the Contracting Party is permitted under Article 29 (2)(a) or the GATT and Related Instruments to restrict or prohibit the exportation or the sale for export of the product constituting the Return in kind; provided that a Contracting Party shall permit transfers of Returns in kind to be effected as authorized or specified in an investment agreement, investment authorization, or other written agreement between the Contracting Party and either an Investor of another Contracting Party or its Investment.

Article 15   Subrogation

(1) If a Contracting Party or its designated agency (hereinafter referred to as the "Indemnifying Party") makes a payment under an indemnity or guarantee given in respect of an Investment of an Investor (hereinafter referred to as the "Party Indemnified") in the Area of another Contracting Party (hereinafter referred to as the "Host Party"), the Host Party shall recognize:

  (a) the assignment to the Indemnifying Party of all the rights and claims in respect of such Investment; and

  (b) the right of the Indemnifying Party to exercise all such rights and enforce such claims by virtue of subrogation.

(2) The Indemnifying Party shall be entitled in all circumstances to:

  (a) the same treatment in respect of the rights and claims acquired by it by virtue of the assignment referred to in paragraph (1); and

  (b) the same payments due pursuant to those rights and claims, as the Party Indemnified was entitled to receive by virtue of this Treaty in respect of the Investment concerned.

(3) In any proceeding under Article 26, a Contracting Party shall not assert as a defence, counterclaim, right of set-off or for any other reason, that indemnification or other compensation for all or part of the alleged damages has been received or will be received pursuant to an insurance or guarantee contract.

Article 16   Relation to other agreements

Where two or more Contracting Parties have entered into a prior international agreement, or enter into a subsequent international agreement, whose terms in either case concern the subject matter of Part III or V of this Treaty,

(1) nothing in Part III or V of this Treaty shall be construed to derogate from any provision of such terms of the other agreement or from any right to dispute resolution with respect thereto under that agreement; and

(2) nothing in such terms of the other agreement shall be construed to derogate from any provision of Part III or V of this Treaty or from any right to dispute resolution with respect thereto under this Treaty,

where any such provision is more favourable to the Investor or Investment.

Article 17   Non-application of Part III in certain circumstances

Each Contracting Party reserves the right to deny the advantages of this Part to:

(1) a legal entity if citizens or nationals of a third state own or control such entity and if that entity has no substantial business activities in the Area of the Contracting Party in which it is organized; or

(2) an Investment, if the denying Contracting Party establishes that such Investment is an Investment of an Investor of a third state with or as to which the denying Contracting Party:

  (a) does not maintain a diplomatic relationship; or

  (b) adopts or maintains measures that:

    (i) prohibit transactions with Investors of that state; or

    (ii) would be violated or circumvented if the benefits of this Part were accorded to Investors of that state or to their Investments.

PART IV   MISCELLANEOUS PROVISIONS

Article 18   Sovereignty over energy resources

(1) The Contracting Parties recognize state sovereignty and sovereign rights over energy resources. They reaffirm that these must be exercised in accordance with and subject to the rules of international law.

(2) Without affecting the objectives of promoting access to energy resources, and exploration and development thereof on a commercial basis, the Treaty shall in no way prejudice the rules in Contracting Parties governing the system of property ownership of energy resources.

(3) Each state continues to hold in particular the rights to decide the geographical areas within its Area to be made available for exploration and development of its energy resources, the optimalization of their recovery and the rate at which they may be depleted or otherwise exploited, to specify and enjoy any taxes, royalties or other financial payments payable by virtue of such exploration and exploitation, and to regulate the environmental and safety aspects of such exploration, development and reclamation within its Area, and to participate in such exploration and exploitation, inter alia, through direct participation by the government or through state enterprises.

(4) The Contracting Parties undertake to facilitate access to energy resources, inter alia, by allocating in a non-discriminatory manner on the basis of published criteria authorizations, licences, concessions and contracts to prospect and explore for or to exploit or extract energy resources.

Article 19   Environmental aspects

(1) In pursuit of sustainable development and taking into account its obligations under those international agreements concerning the environment to which it is party, each Contracting Party shall strive to minimize in an economically efficient manner harmful Environmental Impacts occurring either within or outside its Area from all operations within the Energy Cycle in its Area, taking proper account of safety. In doing so each Contracting Party shall act in a Cost-Effective manner. In its policies and actions each Contracting Party shall strive to take precautionary measures to prevent or minimize environmental degradation. The Contracting Parties agree that the polluter in the Areas of Contracting Parties, should, in principle, bear the cost of pollution, including transboundary pollution, with due regard to the public interest and without distorting Investment in the Energy Cycle or international trade. Contracting Parties shall accordingly:

(a) take account of environmental considerations throughout the formulation and implementation of their energy policies;

(b) promote market-oriented price formation and a fuller reflection of environmental costs and benefits throughout the Energy Cycle;

(c) having regard to Article 34(4), encourage co-operation in the attainment of the environmental objectives of the Charter and co-operation in the field of international environmental standards for the Energy Cycle, taking into account differences in adverse effects and abatement costs between Contracting Parties;

(d) have particular regard to Improving Energy Efficiency, to developing and using renewable energy sources, to promoting the use of cleaner fuels and to employing technologies and technological means that reduce pollution;

(e) promote the collection and sharing among Contracting Parties of information on environmentally sound and economically efficient energy policies and Cost-Effective practices and technologies;

(f) promote public awareness of the Environmental Impacts of energy systems, of the scope for the prevention or abatement of their adverse Environmental Impacts, and of the costs associated with various prevention or abatement measures;

(g) promote and co-operate in the research, development and application of energy efficient and environmentally sound technologies, practices and processes which will minimize harmful Environmental Impacts of all aspects of the Energy Cycle in an economically efficient manner;

(h) encourage favourable conditions for the transfer and dissemination of such technologies consistent with the adequate and effective protection of Intellectual Property rights;

    (i) promote the transparent assessment at an early stage and prior to decision, and subsequent monitoring, of Environmental Impacts of environmentally significant energy investment projects;

    (j) promote international awareness and information exchange on Contracting Parties' relevant environmental programmes and standards and on the implementation of those programmes and standards;

   (k) participate, upon request, and within their available resources, in the development and implementation of appropriate environmental programmes in the Contracting Parties.

(2) At the request of one or more Contracting Parties, disputes concerning the application or interpretation of provisions of this Article shall, to the extent that arrangements for the consideration of such disputes do not exist in other appropriate international fora, be reviewed by the Charter Conference aiming at a solution.

(3) For the purposes of this Article:

    (a) "Energy Cycle" means the entire energy chain, including activities related to prospecting for, exploration, production, conversion, storage, transport, distribution and consumption of the various forms of energy, and the treatment and disposal of wastes, as well as the decommissioning, cessation or closure of these activities, minimizing harmful Environmental Impacts;

    (b) "Environmental Impact" means any effect caused by a given activity on the environment, including human health and safety, flora, fauna, soil, air, water, climate, landscape and historical monuments or other physical structures or the interactions among these factors; it also includes effects on cultural heritage or socio-economic conditions resulting from alterations to those factors;

    (c) "Improving Energy Efficiency" means acting to maintain the same unit of output (of a good or service) without reducing the quality or performance of the output, while reducing the amount of energy required to produce that output;

    (d) "Cost-Effective" means to achieve a defined objective at the lowest cost or to achieve the greatest benefit at a given cost.

Article 20   Transparency

(1) Laws, regulations, judicial decisions and administrative rulings of general application which affect trade in Energy Materials and Products are, in accordance with Article 29(2)(a), among the measures subject to the transparency disciplines of the GATT and relevant Related Instruments.

(2) Laws, regulations, judicial decisions and administrative rulings of general application made effective by any Contracting Party, and agreements in force between Contracting Parties, which affect other matters covered by this Treaty shall also be published promptly in such a manner as to enable Contracting Parties and Investors to become acquainted with them. The provisions of this paragraph shall not require any Contracting Party to disclose confidential information which would impede law enforcement or otherwise be contrary to the public interest or would prejudice the legitimate commercial interests of any Investor.

(3) Each Contracting Party shall designate one or more enquiry points to which requests for information about the above mentioned laws, regulations, judicial decisions and administrative rulings may be addressed and shall communicate promptly such designation to the Secretariat which shall make it available on request.

Article 21   Taxation

(1) Except as otherwise provided in this Article, nothing in this Treaty shall create rights or impose obligations with respect to Taxation Measures of the Contracting Parties. In the event of any inconsistency between this Article and any other provision of the Treaty, this Article shall prevail to the extent of the inconsistency.

(2) Article 7(3) shall apply to Taxation Measures other than those on income or on capital, except that such provision shall not apply to:

   (a) an advantage accorded by a Contracting Party pursuant to the tax provisions of any convention, agreement or arrangement described in subparagraph (7)(a)(ii); or

   (b) any Taxation Measure aimed at ensuring the effective collection of taxes, except where the measure of a Contracting Party arbitrarily discriminates against Energy Materials and Products originating in, or destined for the Area of another Contracting Party or arbitrarily restricts benefits accorded under Article 7(3).

(3) Article 10(2) and (7) shall apply to Taxation Measures of the Contracting Parties other than those on income or on capital, except that such provisions shall not apply to:

   (a) impose most favoured nation obligations with respect to advantages accorded by a Contracting Party pursuant to the tax provisions of any convention, agreement or arrangement described in subparagraph (7)(a)(ii) or resulting from membership of any Regional Economic Integration Organization; or

   (b) any Taxation Measure aimed at ensuring the effective collection of taxes, except where the measure arbitrarily discriminates against an Investor of another Contracting Party or arbitrarily restricts benefits accorded under the Investment provisions of this Treaty.

(4) Article 29(2) to (6) shall apply to Taxation Measures other than those on income or on capital.

(5) (a) Article 13 shall apply to taxes.

   (b) Whenever an issue arises under Article 13, to the extent it pertains to whether a tax constitutes an expropriation or whether a tax alleged to constitute an expropriation is discriminatory, the following provisions shall apply:

     (i) The Investor or the Contracting Party alleging expropriation shall refer the issue of whether the tax is an expropriation or whether the tax is discriminatory to the relevant Competent Tax Authority. Failing such referral by the Investor or the Contracting Party, bodies called upon to settle disputes pursuant to Article 26(2)(c) or 27(2) shall make a referral to the relevant Competent Tax Authorities;

     (ii) The Competent Tax Authorities shall, within a period of six months of such referral, strive to resolve the issues so referred. Where non-discrimination issues are concerned, the Competent Tax Authorities shall apply the non-discrimination provisions of the relevant tax convention or, if there is no non-discrimination provision in the relevant tax convention applicable to the tax or no such tax convention is in force between the Contracting Parties concerned, they shall apply the non-discrimination principles under the Model Tax Convention on Income and Capital of the Organisation for Economic Co-operation and Development;

     (iii) Bodies called upon to settle disputes pursuant to Article 26(2)(c) or 27(2) may take into account any conclusions arrived at by the Competent Tax Authorities regarding whether the tax is an expropriation. Such bodies shall take into account any conclusions arrived at within the six-month period prescribed in subparagraph (b)(ii) by the Competent Tax Authorities regarding whether the tax is discriminatory. Such bodies may also take into account any conclusions arrived at by the Competent Tax Authorities after the expiry of the six-month period;

     (iv) Under no circumstances shall involvement of the Competent Tax Authorities, beyond the end of the six-month period referred to in subparagraph (b)(ii), lead to a delay of proceedings under Articles 26 and 27.

(6) For the avoidance of doubt, Article 14 shall not limit the right of a Contracting Party to impose or collect a tax by withholding or other means.

(7) For the purposes of this Article:

    (a) The term "Taxation Measure" includes:

        (i) any provision relating to taxes of the domestic law of the Contracting Party or of a political subdivision thereof or a local authority therein; and

        (ii) any provision relating to taxes of any convention for the avoidance of double taxation or of any other international agreement or arrangement by which the Contracting Party is bound.

    (b) There shall be regarded as taxes on income or on capital all taxes imposed on total income, on total capital or on elements of income or of capital, including taxes on gains from the alienation of property, taxes on estates, inheritances and gifts, or substantially similar taxes, taxes on the total amounts of wages or salaries paid by enterprises, as well as taxes on capital appreciation.

    (c) A "Competent Tax Authority" means the competent authority pursuant to a double taxation agreement in force between the Contracting Parties or, when no such agreement is in force, the minister or ministry responsible for taxes or their authorized representatives.

    (d) For the avoidance of doubt, the terms "tax provisions" and "taxes" do not include customs duties.

Article 22   State and privileged enterprises

(1) Each Contracting Party shall ensure that any state enterprise which it maintains or establishes shall conduct its activities in relation to the sale or provision of goods and services in its Area in a manner consistent with the Contracting Party's obligations under Part III of this Treaty.

(2) No Contracting Party shall encourage or require such a state enterprise to conduct its activities in its Area in a manner inconsistent with the Contracting Party's obligations under other provisions of this Treaty.

(3) Each Contracting Party shall ensure that if it establishes or maintains an entity and entrusts the entity with regulatory, administrative or other governmental authority, such entity shall exercise that authority in a manner consistent with the Contracting Party's obligations under this Treaty.

(4) No Contracting Party shall encourage or require any entity to which it grants exclusive or special privileges to conduct its activities in its Area in a manner inconsistent with the Contracting Party's obligations under this Treaty.

(5) For the purposes of this Article, "entity" includes any enterprise, agency or other organization or individual.

Article 23   Observance by sub-national authorities

(1) Each Contracting Party is fully responsible under this Treaty for the observance of all provisions of the Treaty, and shall take such reasonable measures as may be available to it to ensure such observance by regional and local governments and authorities within its Area.

(2) The dispute settlement provisions in Parts II, IV and V of this Treaty may be invoked in respect of measures affecting the observance of the Treaty by a Contracting Party which have been taken by regional or local governments or authorities within the Area of the Contracting Party.

Article 24   Exceptions

(1) This Article shall not apply to Articles 12, 13 and 29.

(2) The provisions of this Treaty other than

(a) those referred to in paragraph (1); and

(b) with respect to subparagraph (i), Part III of the Treaty

shall not preclude any Contracting Party from adopting or enforcing any measure

    (i) necessary to protect human, animal or plant life or health;

    (ii) essential to the acquisition or distribution of Energy Materials and Products in conditions of short supply arising from causes outside the control of that Contracting Party, provided that any such measure shall be consistent with the principles that

        (A) all other Contracting Parties are entitled to an equitable share of the international supply of such Energy Materials and Products; and

        (B) any such measure that is inconsistent with this Treaty shall be discontinued as soon as the conditions giving rise to it have ceased to exist; or

    (iii) designed to benefit Investors who are aboriginal people or socially or economically disadvantaged individuals or groups or their Investments and notified to the Secretariat as such, provided that such measure

        (A) has no significant impact on that Contracting Party's economy; and

        (B) does not discriminate between Investors of any other Contracting Party and Investors of that Contracting Party not included among those for whom the measure is intended, provided that no such measure shall constitute a disguised restriction on Economic Activity in the Energy Sector, or arbitrary or unjustifiable discrimination between Contracting Parties or between Investors or other interested persons of Contracting Parties. Such measures shall be duly motivated and shall not nullify or impair any benefit one or more other Contracting Parties may reasonably expect under this Treaty to an extent greater than is strictly necessary to the stated end.

(3) The provisions of this Treaty other than those referred to in paragraph (1) shall not be construed to prevent any Contracting Party from taking any measure which it considers necessary:

(a) for the protection of its essential security interests including those

    (i) relating to the supply of Energy Materials and Products to a military establishment; or

    (ii) taken in time of war, armed conflict or other emergency in international relations;

(b) relating to the implementation of national policies respecting the non-proliferation of nuclear weapons or other nuclear explosive devices or needed to fulfil its obligations under the Treaty on the Non-Proliferation of Nuclear Weapons, the Nuclear Suppliers Guidelines, and other international nuclear non-proliferation obligations or understandings; or

(c) for the maintenance of public order.

Such measure shall not constitute a disguised restriction on Transit.

(4) The provisions of this Treaty which accord most favoured nation treatment shall not oblige any Contracting Party to extend to the Investors of any other Contracting Party any preferential treatment:

(a) resulting from its membership of a free-trade area or customs union; or

(b) which is accorded by a bilateral or multilateral agreement concerning economic co-operation between states that were constituent parts of the former Union of Soviet Socialist Republics pending the establishment of their mutual economic relations on a definitive basis.

Article 25   Economic integration agreements

(1) The provisions of this Treaty shall not be so construed as to oblige a Contracting Party which is party to an Economic Integration Agreement (hereinafter referred to as "EIA") to extend,

by means of most favoured nation treatment, to another Contracting Party which is not a party to that EIA, any preferential treatment applicable between the parties to that EIA as a result of their being parties thereto.

(2) For the purposes of paragraph (1), "EIA" means an agreement substantially liberalizing, inter alia, trade and investment, by providing for the absence or elimination of substantially all discrimination between or among parties thereto through the elimination of existing discriminatory measures and/or the prohibition of new or more discriminatory measures, either at the entry into force of that agreement or on the basis of a reasonable time frame.

(3) This Article shall not affect the application of the GATT and Related Instruments according to Article 29.

PART V   DISPUTE SETTLEMENT

Article 26   Settlement of disputes between an investor and a Contracting Party

(1) Disputes between a Contracting Party and an Investor of another Contracting Party relating to an Investment of the latter in the Area of the former, which concern an alleged breach of an obligation of the former under Part III shall, if possible, be settled amicably.

(2) If such disputes can not be settled according to the provisions of paragraph (1) within a period of three months from the date on which either party to the dispute requested amicable settlement, the Investor party to the dispute may choose to submit it for resolution:

(a) to the courts or administrative tribunals of the Contracting Party party to the dispute;

(b) in accordance with any applicable, previously agreed dispute settlement procedure; or

(c) in accordance with the following paragraphs of this Article.

(3) (a) Subject only to subparagraphs (b) and (c), each Contracting Party hereby gives its unconditional consent to the submission of a dispute to international arbitration or conciliation in accordance with the provisions of this Article.

(b) (i) The Contracting Parties listed in Annex ID do not give such unconditional consent where the Investor has previously submitted the dispute under subparagraph (2)(a) or (b).

(ii) For the sake of transparency, each Contracting Party that is listed in Annex ID shall provide a written statement of its policies, practices and conditions in this regard to the Secretariat no later than the date of the deposit of its instrument of ratification, acceptance or approval in accordance with Article 39 or the deposit of its instrument of accession in accordance with Article 41.

(c) A Contracting Party listed in Annex IA does not give such unconditional consent with respect to a dispute arising under the last sentence of Article 10(1).

(4) In the event that an Investor chooses to submit the dispute for resolution under subparagraph (2)(c), the Investor shall further provide its consent in writing for the dispute to be submitted to:

(a) (i) The International Centre for Settlement of Investment Disputes, established pursuant to the Convention on the Settlement of Investment Disputes between States and Nationals of other States opened for signature at Washington, 18 March 1965 (hereinafter referred to as the "ICSID Convention"), if the Contracting Party of the Investor and the Contracting Party party to the dispute are both parties to the ICSID Convention; or

(ii) The International Centre for Settlement of Investment Disputes, established pursuant to the Convention referred to in subparagraph (a)(i), under the rules governing the Additional Facility for the Administration of Proceedings by the Secretariat of the Centre (hereinafter referred to as the "Additional Facility Rules"), if the

Contracting Party of the Investor or the Contracting Party party to the dispute, but not both, is a party to the ICSID Convention;

(b) a sole arbitrator or ad hoc arbitration tribunal established under the Arbitration Rules of the United Nations Commission on International Trade Law (hereinafter referred to as "UNCITRAL"); or

(c) an arbitral proceeding under the Arbitration Institute of the Stockholm Chamber of Commerce.

(5) (a) The consent given in paragraph (3) together with the written consent of the Investor given pursuant to paragraph (4) shall be considered to satisfy the requirement for:

    (i) written consent of the parties to a dispute for purposes of Chapter II of the ICSID Convention and for purposes of the Additional Facility Rules;

    (ii) an "agreement in writing" for purposes of article II of the United Nations Convention on the Recognition and Enforcement of Foreign Arbitral Awards, done at New York, 10 June 1958 (hereinafter referred to as the "New York Convention"); and

    (iii) "the parties to a contract [to] have agreed in writing" for the purposes of article 1 of the UNCITRAL Arbitration Rules.

(b) Any arbitration under this Article shall at the request of any party to the dispute be held in a state that is a party to the New York Convention. Claims submitted to arbitration hereunder shall be considered to arise out of a commercial relationship or transaction for the purposes of article I of that Convention.

(6) A tribunal established under paragraph (4) shall decide the issues in dispute in accordance with this Treaty and applicable rules and principles of international law.

(7) An Investor other than a natural person which has the nationality of a Contracting Party party to the dispute on the date of the consent in writing referred to in paragraph (4) and which, before a dispute between it and that Contracting Party arises, is controlled by Investors of another Contracting Party, shall for the purpose of article 25(2)(b) of the ICSID Convention be treated as a "national of another Contracting State" and shall for the purpose of article 1(6) of the Additional Facility Rules be treated as a "national of another State".

(8) The awards of arbitration, which may include an award of interest, shall be final and binding upon the parties to the dispute. An award of arbitration concerning a measure of a sub-national government or authority of the disputing Contracting Party shall provide that the Contracting Party may pay monetary damages in lieu of any other remedy granted. Each Contracting Party shall carry out without delay any such award and shall make provision for the effective enforcement in its Area of such awards.

Article 27   Settlement of disputes between Contracting Parties

(1) Contracting Parties shall endeavour to settle disputes concerning the application or interpretation of this Treaty through diplomatic channels.

(2) If a dispute has not been settled in accordance with paragraph (1) within a reasonable period of time, either party thereto may, except as otherwise provided in this Treaty or agreed in writing by the Contracting Parties, and except as concerns the application or interpretation of Article 6 or Article 19 or, for Contracting Parties listed in Annex IA, the last sentence of Article 10(1), upon written notice to the other party to the dispute submit the matter to an ad hoc tribunal under this Article.

(3) Such an ad hoc arbitral tribunal shall be constituted as follows:

(a) The Contracting Party instituting the proceedings shall appoint one member of the tribunal and inform the other Contracting Party to the dispute of its appointment within

30 days of receipt of the notice referred to in paragraph (2) by the other Contracting Party;

(b) Within 60 days of the receipt of the written notice referred to in paragraph (2), the other Contracting Party party to the dispute shall appoint one member. If the appointment is not made within the time limit prescribed, the Contracting Party having instituted the proceedings may, within 90 days of the receipt of the written notice referred to in paragraph (2), request that the appointment be made in accordance with subparagraph (d);

(c) A third member, who may not be a national or citizen of a Contracting Party party to the dispute, shall be appointed by the Contracting Parties parties to the dispute. That member shall be the President of the tribunal. If, within 150 days of the receipt of the notice referred to in paragraph (2), the Contracting Parties are unable to agree on the appointment of a third member, that appointment shall be made, in accordance with subparagraph (d), at the request of either Contracting Party submitted within 180 days of the receipt of that notice;

(d) Appointments requested to be made in accordance with this paragraph shall be made by the Secretary-General of the Permanent Court of International Arbitration within 30 days of the receipt of a request to do so. If the Secretary-General is prevented from discharging this task, the appointments shall be made by the First Secretary of the Bureau. If the latter, in turn, is prevented from discharging this task, the appointments shall be made by the most senior Deputy;

(e) Appointments made in accordance with subparagraphs (a) to (d) shall be made with regard to the qualifications and experience, particularly in matters covered by this Treaty, of the members to be appointed;

(f) In the absence of an agreement to the contrary between the Contracting Parties, the Arbitration Rules of UNCITRAL shall govern, except to the extent modified by the Contracting Parties parties to the dispute or by the arbitrators. The tribunal shall take its decisions by a majority vote of its members;

(g) The tribunal shall decide the dispute in accordance with this Treaty and applicable rules and principles of international law;

(h) The arbitral award shall be final and binding upon the Contracting Parties parties to the dispute;

(i) Where, in making an award, a tribunal finds that a measure of a regional or local government or authority within the Area of a Contracting Party listed in Part I of Annex P is not in conformity with this Treaty, either party to the dispute may invoke the provisions of Part II of Annex P;

(j) The expenses of the tribunal, including the remuneration of its members, shall be borne in equal shares by the Contracting Parties parties to the dispute. The tribunal may, however, at its discretion direct that a higher proportion of the costs be paid by one of the Contracting Parties parties to the dispute;

(k) Unless the Contracting Parties parties to the dispute agree otherwise, the tribunal shall sit in The Hague, and use the premises and facilities of the Permanent Court of Arbitration;

(l) A copy of the award shall be deposited with the Secretariat which shall make it generally available.

Article 28   Non-application of Article 27 to certain disputes

A dispute between Contracting Parties with respect to the application or interpretation of Article 5 or 29 shall not be settled under Article 27 unless the Contracting Parties parties to the dispute so agree.

PART VIII   FINAL PROVISIONS

. . .

Article 40   Application to territories

(1) Any state or Regional Economic Integration Organization may at the time of signature, ratification, acceptance, approval or accession, by a declaration deposited with the Depository, declare that the Treaty shall be binding upon it with respect to all the territories for the international relations of which it is responsible, or to one or more of them. Such declaration shall take effect at the time the Treaty enters into force for that Contracting Party.

(2) Any Contracting Party may at a later date, by a declaration deposited with the Depository, bind itself under this Treaty with respect to other territory specified in the declaration. In respect of such territory the Treaty shall enter into force on the ninetieth day following the receipt by the Depository of such declaration.

(3) Any declaration made under the two preceding paragraphs may, in respect of any territory specified in such declaration, be withdrawn by a notification to the Depository. The withdrawal shall, subject to the applicability of Article 47(3), become effective upon the expiry of one year after the date of receipt of such notification by the Depository.

(4) The definition of "Area" in Article 1(10) shall be construed having regard to any declaration deposited under this Article.

. . .

Article 44   Entry into force

(1) This Treaty shall enter into force on the ninetieth day after the date of deposit of the thirtieth instrument of ratification, acceptance or approval thereof, or of accession thereto, by a state or Regional Economic Integration Organization which is a signatory to the Charter as of 16 June 1995.

(2) For each state or Regional Economic Integration Organization which ratifies, accepts or approves this Treaty or accedes thereto after the deposit of the thirtieth instrument of ratification, acceptance or approval, it shall enter into force on the ninetieth day after the date of deposit by such state or Regional Economic Integration Organization of its instrument of ratification, acceptance, approval or accession.

(3) For the purposes of paragraph (1), any instrument deposited by a Regional Economic Integration Organization shall not be counted as additional to those deposited by member states of such Organization.

Article 45   Provisional application

(1) Each signatory agrees to apply this Treaty provisionally pending its entry into force for such signatory in accordance with Article 44, to the extent that such provisional application is not inconsistent with its constitution, laws or regulations.

(2) (a) Notwithstanding paragraph (1) any signatory may, when signing, deliver to the Depository a declaration that it is not able to accept provisional application. The obligation contained in paragraph (1) shall not apply to a signatory making such a declaration. Any such signatory may at any time withdraw that declaration by written notification to the Depository.

    (b) Neither a signatory which makes a declaration in accordance with subparagraph (a) nor Investors of that signatory may claim the benefits of provisional application under paragraph (1).

    (c) Notwithstanding subparagraph (a), any signatory making a declaration referred to in subparagraph (a) shall apply Part VII provisionally pending the entry into force of the Treaty for such signatory in accordance with Article 44, to the extent that such provisional application is not inconsistent with its laws or regulations.

(3) (a) Any signatory may terminate its provisional application of this Treaty by written notification to the Depository of its intention not to become a Contracting Party to the Treaty. Termination of provisional application for any signatory shall take effect upon the expiration of 60 days from the date on which such signatory's written notification is received by the Depository.

(b) In the event that a signatory terminates provisional application under subparagraph (a), the obligation of the signatory under paragraph (1) to apply Parts III and V with respect to any Investments made in its Area during such provisional application by Investors of other signatories shall nevertheless remain in effect with respect to those Investments for twenty years following the effective date of termination, except as otherwise provided in subparagraph (c).

(c) Subparagraph (b) shall not apply to any signatory listed in Annex PA. A signatory shall be removed from the list in Annex PA effective upon delivery to the Depository of its request therefor.

(4) Pending the entry into force of this Treaty the signatories shall meet periodically in the provisional Charter Conference, the first meeting of which shall be convened by the provisional Secretariat referred to in paragraph (5) not later than 180 days after the opening date for signature of the Treaty as specified in Article 38.

(5) The functions of the Secretariat shall be carried out on an interim basis by a provisional Secretariat until the entry into force of this Treaty pursuant to Article 44 and the establishment of a Secretariat.

(6) The signatories shall, in accordance with and subject to the provisions of paragraph (1) or subparagraph (2)(c) as appropriate, contribute to the costs of the provisional Secretariat as if the signatories were Contracting Parties under Article 37(3). Any modifications made to Annex B by the signatories shall terminate upon the entry into force of this Treaty.

(7) A state or Regional Economic Integration Organization which, prior to this Treaty's entry into force, accedes to the Treaty in accordance with Article 41 shall, pending the Treaty's entry into force, have the rights and assume the obligations of a signatory under this Article.

. . .

ANNEXES (SELECTED PROVISIONS)

ANNEX ID   LIST OF CONTRACTING PARTIES NOT ALLOWING AN INVESTOR TO RESUBMIT THE SAME DISPUTE TO INTERNATIONAL ARBITRATION AT A LATER STAGE UNDER ARTICLE 26 (IN ACCORDANCE WITH ARTICLE 26(3)(B)(I))

1. Australia [Note: ratification pending]
2. Azerbaijan
3. Bulgaria
4. Croatia
5. Cyprus
6. The Czech Republic
7. European Communities
8. Finland
9. Greece
10. Hungary
11. Ireland
12. Italy

13. Japan

14. Kazakhstan

15. Mongolia

16. Norway [Note: ratification pending]

17. Poland

18. Portugal

19. Romania

20. The Russian Federation [Note: ratification pending]

21. Slovenia

22. Spain

23. Sweden

24. Turkey

Canada [observer]
United States of America [observer]

ANNEX IA   LIST OF CONTRACTING PARTIES NOT ALLOWING AN INVESTOR OR CONTRACTING PARTY TO SUBMIT A DISPUTE CONCERNING THE LAST SENTENCE OF ARTICLE 10(1) TO INTERNATIONAL ARBITRATION (IN ACCORDANCE WITH ARTICLES 26(3)(C) AND 27(2))

1. Australia [Note: ratification pending]

2. Hungary

3. Norway [Note: ratification pending]

Canada [Observer]

ANNEX P   SPECIAL SUB-NATIONAL DISPUTE PROCEDURE (IN ACCORDANCE WITH ARTICLE 27(3)(I))

PART I

1. Australia [Note: ratification pending]

Canada [Observer]

PART II

(1) Where, in making an award, the tribunal finds that a measure of a regional or local government or authority of a Contracting Party (hereinafter referred to as the "Responsible Party") is not in conformity with a provision of this Treaty, the Responsible Party shall take such reasonable measures as may be available to it to ensure observance of the Treaty in respect of the measure.

(2) The Responsible Party shall, within 30 days from the date the award is made, provide to the Secretariat written notice of its intentions as to ensuring observance of the Treaty in respect of the measure. The Secretariat shall present the notification to the Charter Conference at the earliest practicable opportunity, and no later than the meeting of the Charter Conference following receipt of the notice. If it is impracticable to ensure observance immediately, the Responsible Party shall have a reasonable period of time in which to do so. The reasonable

period of time shall be agreed by both parties to the dispute. In the event that such agreement is not reached, the Responsible Party shall propose a reasonable period for approval by the Charter Conference.

(3) Where the Responsible Party fails, within the reasonable period of time, to ensure observance in respect of the measure, it shall at the request of the other Contracting Party party to the dispute (hereinafter referred to as the "Injured Party") endeavour to agree with the Injured Party on appropriate compensation as a mutually satisfactory resolution of the dispute.

(4) If no satisfactory compensation has been agreed within 20 days of the request of the Injured Party, the Injured Party may with the authorization of the Charter Conference suspend such of its obligations to the Responsible Party under the Treaty as it considers equivalent to those denied by the measure in question, until such time as the Contracting Parties have reached agreement on a resolution of their dispute or the non-conforming measure has been brought into conformity with the Treaty.

(5) In considering what obligations to suspend, the Injured Party shall apply the following principles and procedures:
(a) The Injured Party should first seek to suspend obligations with respect to the same Part of the Treaty as that in which the tribunal has found a violation.
(b) If the Injured Party considers that it is not practicable or effective to suspend obligations with respect to the same Part of the Treaty, it may seek to suspend obligations in other Parts of the Treaty. If the Injured Party decides to request authorization to suspend obligations under this subparagraph, it shall state the reasons therefor in its request to the Charter Conference for authorization.

(6) On written request of the Responsible Party, delivered to the Injured Party and to the President of the tribunal that rendered the award, the tribunal shall determine whether the level of obligations suspended by the Injured Party is excessive, and if so, to what extent. If the tribunal cannot be reconstituted, such determination shall be made by one or more arbitrators appointed by the Secretary-General. Determinations pursuant to this paragraph shall be completed within 60 days of the request to the tribunal or the appointment by the Secretary-General. Obligations shall not be suspended pending the determination, which shall be final and binding.

(7) In suspending any obligations to a Responsible Party, an Injured Party shall make every effort not to affect adversely the rights under the Treaty of any other Contracting Party.

[Handwritten notes:]

+ government subsidies; subsidies have no set definition so more than one interpretation exists.
+ Prohibited; export subsidies & import substitute subsidies as these are specifically designed to manipulate International trade
+ Market share alone is not considered sufficient enough evidence & more specific price under cutting evidence is required.
+ This was the conclusion in the "EC-subsidies on wheat flour" Case, even though EU market share more than double & US market share more than halved, the ruling was shift" market share alone is not sufficient evidence.
+ Countries are given countervailing duty rights on subsidised imports that are seen to be hurting domestic product.

North American Free Trade Agreement—Chapter 11

Date 17 December 1992
In force 1 January 1994
Source 32 ILM 296 (1993)
Link <http://www.nafta-sec-alena.org/en/view.aspx?x=343>

PART FIVE INVESTMENT, SERVICES AND RELATED MATTERS

CHAPTER ELEVEN INVESTMENT

SECTION A INVESTMENT

Article 1101 Scope and Coverage

1. This Chapter applies to measures adopted or maintained by a Party relating to:
   (a) investors of another Party;
   (b) investments of investors of another Party in the territory of the Party; and
   (c) with respect to Articles 1106 and 1114, all investments in the territory of the Party.

2. A Party has the right to perform exclusively the economic activities set out in Annex III and to refuse to permit the establishment of investment in such activities.

3. This Chapter does not apply to measures adopted or maintained by a Party to the extent that they are covered by Chapter Fourteen (Financial Services).

4. Nothing in this Chapter shall be construed to prevent a Party from providing a service or performing a function such as law enforcement, correctional services, income security or insurance, social security or insurance, social welfare, public education, public training, health, and child care, in a manner that is not inconsistent with this Chapter.

Article 1102 National Treatment

1. Each Party shall accord to investors of another Party treatment no less favorable than that it accords, in like circumstances, to its own investors with respect to the establishment, acquisition, expansion, management, conduct, operation, and sale or other disposition of investments.

2. Each Party shall accord to investments of investors of another Party treatment no less favorable than that it accords, in like circumstances, to investments of its own investors with respect to the establishment, acquisition, expansion, management, conduct, operation, and sale or other disposition of investments.

3. The treatment accorded by a Party under paragraphs 1 and 2 means, with respect to a state or province, treatment no less favorable than the most favorable treatment accorded, in like circumstances, by that state or province to investors, and to investments of investors, of the Party of which it forms a part.

4. For greater certainty, no Party may:
   (a) impose on an investor of another Party a requirement that a minimum level of equity in an enterprise in the territory of the Party be held by its nationals, other than nominal qualifying shares for directors or incorporators of corporations; or

(b) require an investor of another Party, by reason of its nationality, to sell or otherwise dispose of an investment in the territory of the Party.

Article 1103   Most-Favored-Nation Treatment

1. Each Party shall accord to investors of another Party treatment no less favorable than that it accords, in like circumstances, to investors of any other Party or of a non-Party with respect to the establishment, acquisition, expansion, management, conduct, operation, and sale or other disposition of investments.

2. Each Party shall accord to investments of investors of another Party treatment no less favorable than that it accords, in like circumstances, to investments of investors of any other Party or of a non-Party with respect to the establishment, acquisition, expansion, management, conduct, operation, and sale or other disposition of investments.

Article 1104   Standard of Treatment

Each Party shall accord to investors of another Party and to investments of investors of another Party the better of the treatment required by Articles 1102 and 1103.

Article 1105   Minimum Standard of Treatment

1. Each Party shall accord to investments of investors of another Party treatment in accordance with international law, including fair and equitable treatment and full protection and security.

2. Without prejudice to paragraph 1 and notwithstanding Article 1108(7)(b), each Party shall accord to investors of another Party, and to investments of investors of another Party, non-discriminatory treatment with respect to measures it adopts or maintains relating to losses suffered by investments in its territory owing to armed conflict or civil strife.

3. Paragraph 2 does not apply to existing measures relating to subsidies or grants that would be inconsistent with Article 1102 but for Article 1108(7)(b).

Article 1106   Performance requirements

1. No Party may impose or enforce any of the following requirements, or enforce any commitment or undertaking, in connection with the establishment, acquisition, expansion, management, conduct or operation of an investment of an investor of a Party or of a non-Party in its territory:
(a) to export a given level or percentage of goods or services;
(b) to achieve a given level or percentage of domestic content;
(c) to purchase, use or accord a preference to goods produced or services provided in its territory, or to purchase goods or services from persons in its territory;
(d) to relate in any way the volume or value of imports to the volume or value of exports or to the amount of foreign exchange inflows associated with such investment;
(e) to restrict sales of goods or services in its territory that such investment produces or provides by relating such sales in any way to the volume or value of its exports or foreign exchange earnings;
(f) to transfer technology, a production process or other proprietary knowledge to a person in its territory, except when the requirement is imposed or the commitment or undertaking is enforced by a court, administrative tribunal or competition authority to remedy an alleged violation of competition laws or to act in a manner not inconsistent with other provisions of this Agreement; or
(g) to act as the exclusive supplier of the goods it produces or services it provides to a specific region or world market.

2. A measure that requires an investment to use a technology to meet generally applicable health, safety or environmental requirements shall not be construed to be inconsistent with paragraph 1(f). For greater certainty, Articles 1102 and 1103 apply to the measure.

3. No Party may condition the receipt or continued receipt of an advantage, in connection with an investment in its territory of an investor of a Party or of a non-Party, on compliance with any of the following requirements:
   (a) to achieve a given level or percentage of domestic content;
   (b) to purchase, use or accord a preference to goods produced in its territory, or to purchase goods from producers in its territory;
   (c) to relate in any way the volume or value of imports to the volume or value of exports or to the amount of foreign exchange inflows associated with such investment; or
   (d) to restrict sales of goods or services in its territory that such investment produces or provides by relating such sales in any way to the volume or value of its exports or foreign exchange earnings.
4. Nothing in paragraph 3 shall be construed to prevent a Party from conditioning the receipt or continued receipt of an advantage, in connection with an investment in its territory of an investor of a Party or of a non-Party, on compliance with a requirement to locate production, provide a service, train or employ workers, construct or expand particular facilities, or carry out research and development, in its territory.
5. Paragraphs 1 and 3 do not apply to any requirement other than the requirements set out in those paragraphs.
6. Provided that such measures are not applied in an arbitrary or unjustifiable manner, or do not constitute a disguised restriction on international trade or investment, nothing in paragraph 1(b) or (c) or 3(a) or (b) shall be construed to prevent any Party from adopting or maintaining measures, including environmental measures:
   (a) necessary to secure compliance with laws and regulations that are not inconsistent with the provisions of this Agreement;
   (b) necessary to protect human, animal or plant life or health; or
   (c) necessary for the conservation of living or non-living exhaustible natural resources.

Article 1107 Senior Management and Boards of Directors
1. No Party may require that an enterprise of that Party that is an investment of an investor of another Party appoint to senior management positions individuals of any particular nationality.
2. A Party may require that a majority of the board of directors, or any committee thereof, of an enterprise of that Party that is an investment of an investor of another Party, be of a particular nationality, or resident in the territory of the Party, provided that the requirement does not materially impair the ability of the investor to exercise control over its investment.

Article 1108 Reservations and Exceptions
1. Articles 1102, 1103, 1106 and 1107 do not apply to:
   (a) any existing non-conforming measure that is maintained by
       (i) a Party at the federal level, as set out in its Schedule to Annex I or III,
       (ii) a state or province, for two years after the date of entry into force of this Agreement, and thereafter as set out by a Party in its Schedule to Annex I in accordance with paragraph 2, or
       (iii) a local government;
   (b) the continuation or prompt renewal of any non-conforming measure referred to in subparagraph (a); or
   (c) an amendment to any non-conforming measure referred to in subparagraph (a) to the extent that the amendment does not decrease the conformity of the measure, as it existed immediately before the amendment, with Articles 1102, 1103, 1106 and 1107.

2. Each Party may set out in its Schedule to Annex I, within two years of the date of entry into force of this Agreement, any existing nonconforming measure maintained by a state or province, not including a local government.

3. Articles 1102, 1103, 1106 and 1107 do not apply to any measure that a Party adopts or maintains with respect to sectors, subsectors or activities, as set out in its Schedule to Annex II.

4. No Party may, under any measure adopted after the date of entry into force of this Agreement and covered by its Schedule to Annex II, require an investor of another Party, by reason of its nationality, to sell or otherwise dispose of an investment existing at the time the measure becomes effective.

5. Articles 1102 and 1103 do not apply to any measure that is an exception to, or derogation from, the obligations under Article 1703 (Intellectual Property National Treatment) as specifically provided for in that Article.

6. Article 1103 does not apply to treatment accorded by a Party pursuant to agreements, or with respect to sectors, set out in its Schedule to Annex IV.

7. Articles 1102, 1103 and 1107 do not apply to:
   (a) procurement by a Party or a state enterprise; or
   (b) subsidies or grants provided by a Party or a state enterprise, including government supported loans, guarantees and insurance.

8. The provisions of:
   (a) Article 1106(1)(a), (b) and (c), and (3)(a) and (b) do not apply to qualification requirements for goods or services with respect to export promotion and foreign aid programs;
   (b) Article 1106(1)(b), (c), (f) and (g), and (3)(a) and (b) do not apply to procurement by a Party or a state enterprise; and
   (c) Article 1106(3)(a) and (b) do not apply to requirements imposed by an importing Party relating to the content of goods necessary to qualify for preferential tariffs or preferential quotas.

Article 1109 Transfers
1. Each Party shall permit all transfers relating to an investment of an investor of another Party in the territory of the Party to be made freely and without delay. Such transfers include:
   (a) profits, dividends, interest, capital gains, royalty payments, management fees, technical assistance and other fees, returns in kind and other amounts derived from the investment;
   (b) proceeds from the sale of all or any part of the investment or from the partial or complete liquidation of the investment;
   (c) payments made under a contract entered into by the investor, or its investment, including payments made pursuant to a loan agreement;
   (d) payments made pursuant to Article 1110; and
   (e) payments arising under Section B.

2. Each Party shall permit transfers to be made in a freely usable currency at the market rate of exchange prevailing on the date of transfer with respect to spot transactions in the currency to be transferred.

3. No Party may require its investors to transfer, or penalize its investors that fail to transfer, the income, earnings, profits or other amounts derived from, or attributable to, investments in the territory of another Party.

4. Notwithstanding paragraphs 1 and 2, a Party may prevent a transfer through the equitable, non-discriminatory and good faith application of its laws relating to:
   (a) bankruptcy, insolvency or the protection of the rights of creditors;
   (b) issuing, trading or dealing in securities;
   (c) criminal or penal offenses;
   (d) reports of transfers of currency or other monetary instruments; or

(e) ensuring the satisfaction of judgments in adjudicatory proceedings.

5. Paragraph 3 shall not be construed to prevent a Party from imposing any measure through the equitable, non-discriminatory and good faith application of its laws relating to the matters set out in subparagraphs (a) through (e) of paragraph 4.

6. Notwithstanding paragraph 1, a Party may restrict transfers of returns in kind in circumstances where it could otherwise restrict such transfers under this Agreement, including as set out in paragraph 4.

Article 1110   Expropriation and Compensation

1. No Party may directly or indirectly nationalize or expropriate an investment of an investor of another Party in its territory or take a measure tantamount to nationalization or expropriation of such an investment ("expropriation"), except:

   (a) for a public purpose;
   (b) on a non-discriminatory basis;
   (c) in accordance with due process of law and Article 1105(1); and
   (d) on payment of compensation in accordance with paragraphs 2 through 6.

2. Compensation shall be equivalent to the fair market value of the expropriated investment immediately before the expropriation took place ("date of expropriation"), and shall not reflect any change in value occurring because the intended expropriation had become known earlier. Valuation criteria shall include going concern value, asset value including declared tax value of tangible property, and other criteria, as appropriate, to determine fair market value.

3. Compensation shall be paid without delay and be fully realizable.

4. If payment is made in a G7 currency, compensation shall include interest at a commercially reasonable rate for that currency from the date of expropriation until the date of actual payment.

5. If a Party elects to pay in a currency other than a G7 currency, the amount paid on the date of payment, if converted into a G7 currency at the market rate of exchange prevailing on that date, shall be no less than if the amount of compensation owed on the date of expropriation had been converted into that G7 currency at the market rate of exchange prevailing on that date, and interest had accrued at a commercially reasonable rate for that G7 currency from the date of expropriation until the date of payment.

6. On payment, compensation shall be freely transferable as provided in Article 1109.

7. This Article does not apply to the issuance of compulsory licenses granted in relation to intellectual property rights, or to the revocation, limitation or creation of intellectual property rights, to the extent that such issuance, revocation, limitation or creation is consistent with Chapter Seventeen (Intellectual Property).

8. For purposes of this Article and for greater certainty, a non-discriminatory measure of general application shall not be considered a measure tantamount to an expropriation of a debt security or loan covered by this Chapter solely on the ground that the measure imposes costs on the debtor that cause it to default on the debt.

Article 1111   Special Formalities and Information Requirements

1. Nothing in Article 1102 shall be construed to prevent a Party from adopting or maintaining a measure that prescribes special formalities in connection with the establishment of investments by investors of another Party, such as a requirement that investors be residents of the Party or that investments be legally constituted under the laws or regulations of the Party, provided that such formalities do not materially impair the protections afforded by a Party to investors of another Party and investments of investors of another Party pursuant to this Chapter.

2. Notwithstanding Articles 1102 or 1103, a Party may require an investor of another Party, or its investment in its territory, to provide routine information concerning that investment solely

for informational or statistical purposes. The Party shall protect such business information that is confidential from any disclosure that would prejudice the competitive position of the investor or the investment. Nothing in this paragraph shall be construed to prevent a Party from otherwise obtaining or disclosing information in connection with the equitable and good faith application of its law.

Article 1112   Relation to Other Chapters

1. In the event of any inconsistency between this Chapter and another Chapter, the other Chapter shall prevail to the extent of the inconsistency.

2. A requirement by a Party that a service provider of another Party post a bond or other form of financial security as a condition of providing a service into its territory does not of itself make this Chapter applicable to the provision of that crossborder service. This Chapter applies to that Party's treatment of the posted bond or financial security.

Article 1113   Denial of Benefits

1. A Party may deny the benefits of this Chapter to an investor of another Party that is an enterprise of such Party and to investments of such investor if investors of a non-Party own or control the enterprise and the denying Party:
   (a) does not maintain diplomatic relations with the non-Party; or
   (b) adopts or maintains measures with respect to the non-Party that prohibit transactions with the enterprise or that would be violated or circumvented if the benefits of this Chapter were accorded to the enterprise or to its investments.

2. Subject to prior notification and consultation in accordance with Articles 1803 (Notification and Provision of Information) and 2006 (Consultations), a Party may deny the benefits of this Chapter to an investor of another Party that is an enterprise of such Party and to investments of such investors if investors of a non-Party own or control the enterprise and the enterprise has no substantial business activities in the territory of the Party under whose law it is constituted or organized.

Article 1114   Environmental Measures

1. Nothing in this Chapter shall be construed to prevent a Party from adopting, maintaining or enforcing any measure otherwise consistent with this Chapter that it considers appropriate to ensure that investment activity in its territory is undertaken in a manner sensitive to environmental concerns.

2. The Parties recognize that it is inappropriate to encourage investment by relaxing domestic health, safety or environmental measures. Accordingly, a Party should not waive or otherwise derogate from, or offer to waive or otherwise derogate from, such measures as an encouragement for the establishment, acquisition, expansion or retention in its territory of an investment of an investor. If a Party considers that another Party has offered such an encouragement, it may request consultations with the other Party and the two Parties shall consult with a view to avoiding any such encouragement.

SECTION B   SETTLEMENT OF DISPUTES BETWEEN A PARTY AND AN INVESTOR OF ANOTHER PARTY

Article 1115   Purpose

Without prejudice to the rights and obligations of the Parties under Chapter Twenty (Institutional Arrangements and Dispute Settlement Procedures), this Section establishes a mechanism for the settlement of investment disputes that assures both equal treatment among investors of the Parties in accordance with the principle of international reciprocity and due process before an impartial tribunal.

Article 1116   Claim by an Investor of a Party on Its Own Behalf

1. An investor of a Party may submit to arbitration under this Section a claim that another Party has breached an obligation under:

   (a) Section A or Article 1503(2) (State Enterprises), or

   (b) Article 1502(3)(a) (Monopolies and State Enterprises) where the monopoly has acted in a manner inconsistent with the Party's obligations under Section A,

   and that the investor has incurred loss or damage by reason of, or arising out of, that breach.

2. An investor may not make a claim if more than three years have elapsed from the date on which the investor first acquired, or should have first acquired, knowledge of the alleged breach and knowledge that the investor has incurred loss or damage.

Article 1117   Claim by an Investor of a Party on Behalf of an Enterprise

1. An investor of a Party, on behalf of an enterprise of another Party that is a juridical person that the investor owns or controls directly or indirectly, may submit to arbitration under this Section a claim that the other Party has breached an obligation under:

   (a) Section A or Article 1503(2) (State Enterprises), or

   (b) Article 1502(3)(a) (Monopolies and State Enterprises) where the monopoly has acted in a manner inconsistent with the Party's obligations under Section A, and that the enterprise has incurred loss or damage by reason of, or arising out of, that breach.

2. An investor may not make a claim on behalf of an enterprise described in paragraph 1 if more than three years have elapsed from the date on which the enterprise first acquired, or should have first acquired, knowledge of the alleged breach and knowledge that the enterprise has incurred loss or damage.

3. Where an investor makes a claim under this Article and the investor or a non-controlling investor in the enterprise makes a claim under Article 1116 arising out of the same events that gave rise to the claim under this Article, and two or more of the claims are submitted to arbitration under Article 1120, the claims should be heard together by a Tribunal established under Article 1126, unless the Tribunal finds that the interests of a disputing party would be prejudiced thereby.

4. An investment may not make a claim under this Section.

Article 1118   Settlement of a Claim through Consultation and Negotiation

The disputing parties should first attempt to settle a claim through consultation or negotiation.

Article 1119   Notice of Intent to Submit a Claim to Arbitration

The disputing investor shall deliver to the disputing Party written notice of its intention to submit a claim to arbitration at least 90 days before the claim is submitted, which notice shall specify:

(a) the name and address of the disputing investor and, where a claim is made under Article 1117, the name and address of the enterprise;

(b) the provisions of this Agreement alleged to have been breached and any other relevant provisions;

(c) the issues and the factual basis for the claim; and

(d) the relief sought and the approximate amount of damages claimed.

Article 1120   Submission of a Claim to Arbitration

1. Except as provided in Annex 1120.1, and provided that six months have elapsed since the events giving rise to a claim, a disputing investor may submit the claim to arbitration under:

   (a) the ICSID Convention, provided that both the disputing Party and the Party of the investor are parties to the Convention;

(b) the Additional Facility Rules of ICSID, provided that either the disputing Party or the Party of the investor, but not both, is a party to the ICSID Convention; or

(c) the UNCITRAL Arbitration Rules.

2. The applicable arbitration rules shall govern the arbitration except to the extent modified by this Section.

Article 1121   Conditions Precedent to Submission of a Claim to Arbitration

1. A disputing investor may submit a claim under Article 1116 to arbitration only if:

   (a) the investor consents to arbitration in accordance with the procedures set out in this Agreement; and

   (b) the investor and, where the claim is for loss or damage to an interest in an enterprise of another Party that is a juridical person that the investor owns or controls directly or indirectly, the enterprise, waive their right to initiate or continue before any administrative tribunal or court under the law of any Party, or other dispute settlement procedures, any proceedings with respect to the measure of the disputing Party that is alleged to be a breach referred to in Article 1116, except for proceedings for injunctive, declaratory or other extraordinary relief, not involving the payment of damages, before an administrative tribunal or court under the law of the disputing Party.

2. A disputing investor may submit a claim under Article 1117 to arbitration only if both the investor and the enterprise:

   (a) consent to arbitration in accordance with the procedures set out in this Agreement; and

   (b) waive their right to initiate or continue before any administrative tribunal or court under the law of any Party, or other dispute settlement procedures, any proceedings with respect to the measure of the disputing Party that is alleged to be a breach referred to in Article 1117, except for proceedings for injunctive, declaratory or other extraordinary relief, not involving the payment of damages, before an administrative tribunal or court under the law of the disputing Party.

3. A consent and waiver required by this Article shall be in writing, shall be delivered to the disputing Party and shall be included in the submission of a claim to arbitration.

4. Only where a disputing Party has deprived a disputing investor of control of an enterprise:

   (a) a waiver from the enterprise under paragraph 1(b) or 2(b) shall not be required; and

   (b) Annex 1120.1(b) shall not apply.

Article 1122   Consent to Arbitration

1. Each Party consents to the submission of a claim to arbitration in accordance with the procedures set out in this Agreement.

2. The consent given by paragraph 1 and the submission by a disputing investor of a claim to arbitration shall satisfy the requirement of:

   (a) Chapter II of the ICSID Convention (Jurisdiction of the Centre) and the Additional Facility Rules for written consent of the parties;

   (b) Article II of the New York Convention for an agreement in writing; and

   (c) Article I of the InterAmerican Convention for an agreement.

Article 1123   Number of Arbitrators and Method of Appointment

Except in respect of a Tribunal established under Article 1126, and unless the disputing parties otherwise agree, the Tribunal shall comprise three arbitrators, one arbitrator appointed by each of the disputing parties and the third, who shall be the presiding arbitrator, appointed by agreement of the disputing parties.

Article 1124   Constitution of a Tribunal When a Party Fails to Appoint an Arbitrator or the Disputing Parties Are Unable to Agree on a Presiding Arbitrator

1. The Secretary-General shall serve as appointing authority for an arbitration under this Section.

2. If a Tribunal, other than a Tribunal established under Article 1126, has not been constituted within 90 days from the date that a claim is submitted to arbitration, the Secretary-General, on the request of either disputing party, shall appoint, in his discretion, the arbitrator or arbitrators not yet appointed, except that the presiding arbitrator shall be appointed in accordance with paragraph 3.

3. The Secretary-General shall appoint the presiding arbitrator from the roster of presiding arbitrators referred to in paragraph 4, provided that the presiding arbitrator shall not be a national of the disputing Party or a national of the Party of the disputing investor. In the event that no such presiding arbitrator is available to serve, the Secretary-General shall appoint, from the ICSID Panel of Arbitrators, a presiding arbitrator who is not a national of any of the Parties.

4. On the date of entry into force of this Agreement, the Parties shall establish, and thereafter maintain, a roster of 45 presiding arbitrators meeting the qualifications of the Convention and rules referred to in Article 1120 and experienced in international law and investment matters. The roster members shall be appointed by consensus and without regard to nationality.

Article 1125   Agreement to Appointment of Arbitrators

For purposes of Article 39 of the ICSID Convention and Article 7 of Schedule C to the ICSID Additional Facility Rules, and without prejudice to an objection to an arbitrator based on Article 1124(3) or on a ground other than nationality:

(a) the disputing Party agrees to the appointment of each individual member of a Tribunal established under the ICSID Convention or the ICSID Additional Facility Rules;

(b) a disputing investor referred to in Article 1116 may submit a claim to arbitration, or continue a claim, under the ICSID Convention or the ICSID Additional Facility Rules, only on condition that the disputing investor agrees in writing to the appointment of each individual member of the Tribunal; and

(c) a disputing investor referred to in Article 1117(1) may submit a claim to arbitration, or continue a claim, under the ICSID Convention or the ICSID Additional Facility Rules, only on condition that the disputing investor and the enterprise agree in writing to the appointment of each individual member of the Tribunal.

Article 1126   Consolidation

1. A Tribunal established under this Article shall be established under the UNCITRAL Arbitration Rules and shall conduct its proceedings in accordance with those Rules, except as modified by this Section.

2. Where a Tribunal established under this Article is satisfied that claims have been submitted to arbitration under Article 1120 that have a question of law or fact in common, the Tribunal may, in the interests of fair and efficient resolution of the claims, and after hearing the disputing parties, by order:
   (a) assume jurisdiction over, and hear and determine together, all or part of the claims; or
   (b) assume jurisdiction over, and hear and determine one or more of the claims, the determination of which it believes would assist in the resolution of the others.

3. A disputing party that seeks an order under paragraph 2 shall request the Secretary-General to establish a Tribunal and shall specify in the request:
   (a) the name of the disputing Party or disputing investors against which the order is sought;
   (b) the nature of the order sought; and
   (c) the grounds on which the order is sought.

4. The disputing party shall deliver to the disputing Party or disputing investors against which the order is sought a copy of the request.

5. Within 60 days of receipt of the request, the Secretary-General shall establish a Tribunal comprising three arbitrators. The Secretary-General shall appoint the presiding arbitrator from the roster referred to in Article 1124(4). In the event that no such presiding arbitrator is available to serve, the Secretary-General shall appoint, from the ICSID Panel of Arbitrators, a presiding arbitrator who is not a national of any of the Parties. The Secretary-General shall appoint the two other members from the roster referred to in Article 1124(4), and to the extent not available from that roster, from the ICSID Panel of Arbitrators, and to the extent not available from that Panel, in the discretion of the Secretary-General. One member shall be a national of the disputing Party and one member shall be a national of a Party of the disputing investors.

6. Where a Tribunal has been established under this Article, a disputing investor that has submitted a claim to arbitration under Article 1116 or 1117 and that has not been named in a request made under paragraph 3 may make a written request to the Tribunal that it be included in an order made under paragraph 2, and shall specify in the request:
   (a) the name and address of the disputing investor;
   (b) the nature of the order sought; and
   (c) the grounds on which the order is sought.

7. A disputing investor referred to in paragraph 6 shall deliver a copy of its request to the disputing parties named in a request made under paragraph 3.

8. A Tribunal established under Article 1120 shall not have jurisdiction to decide a claim, or a part of a claim, over which a Tribunal established under this Article has assumed jurisdiction.

9. On application of a disputing party, a Tribunal established under this Article, pending its decision under paragraph 2, may order that the proceedings of a Tribunal established under Article 1120 be stayed, unless the latter Tribunal has already adjourned its proceedings.

10. A disputing Party shall deliver to the Secretariat, within 15 days of receipt by the disputing Party, a copy of:
    (a) a request for arbitration made under paragraph (1) of Article 36 of the ICSID Convention;
    (b) a notice of arbitration made under Article 2 of Schedule C of the ICSID Additional Facility Rules; or
    (c) a notice of arbitration given under the UNCITRAL Arbitration Rules.

11. A disputing Party shall deliver to the Secretariat a copy of a request made under paragraph 3:
    (a) within 15 days of receipt of the request, in the case of a request made by a disputing investor;
    (b) within 15 days of making the request, in the case of a request made by the disputing Party.

12. A disputing Party shall deliver to the Secretariat a copy of a request made under paragraph 6 within 15 days of receipt of the request.

13. The Secretariat shall maintain a public register of the documents referred to in paragraphs 10, 11 and 12.

Article 1127   Notice
A disputing Party shall deliver to the other Parties:

(a) written notice of a claim that has been submitted to arbitration no later than 30 days after the date that the claim is submitted; and
(b) copies of all pleadings filed in the arbitration.

Article 1128   Participation by a Party
On written notice to the disputing parties, a Party may make submissions to a Tribunal on a question of interpretation of this Agreement.

Article 1129   Documents

1. A Party shall be entitled to receive from the disputing Party, at the cost of the requesting Party a copy of:
   (a) the evidence that has been tendered to the Tribunal; and
   (b) the written argument of the disputing parties.

2. A Party receiving information pursuant to paragraph 1 shall treat the information as if it were a disputing Party.

Article 1130   Place of Arbitration

Unless the disputing parties agree otherwise, a Tribunal shall hold an arbitration in the territory of a Party that is a party to the New York Convention, selected in accordance with:

(a) the ICSID Additional Facility Rules if the arbitration is under those Rules or the ICSID Convention; or

(b) the UNCITRAL Arbitration Rules if the arbitration is under those Rules.

Article 1131   Governing Law

1. A Tribunal established under this Section shall decide the issues in dispute in accordance with this Agreement and applicable rules of international law.

2. An interpretation by the Commission of a provision of this Agreement shall be binding on a Tribunal established under this Section.

Article 1132   Interpretation of Annexes

1. Where a disputing Party asserts as a defense that the measure alleged to be a breach is within the scope of a reservation or exception set out in Annex I, Annex II, Annex III or Annex IV, on request of the disputing Party, the Tribunal shall request the interpretation of the Commission on the issue. The Commission, within 60 days of delivery of the request, shall submit in writing its interpretation to the Tribunal.

2. Further to Article 1131(2), a Commission interpretation submitted under paragraph 1 shall be binding on the Tribunal. If the Commission fails to submit an interpretation within 60 days, the Tribunal shall decide the issue.

Article 1133   Expert Reports

Without prejudice to the appointment of other kinds of experts where authorized by the applicable arbitration rules, a Tribunal, at the request of a disputing party or, unless the disputing parties disapprove, on its own initiative, may appoint one or more experts to report to it in writing on any factual issue concerning environmental, health, safety or other scientific matters raised by a disputing party in a proceeding, subject to such terms and conditions as the disputing parties may agree.

Article 1134   Interim Measures of Protection

A Tribunal may order an interim measure of protection to preserve the rights of a disputing party, or to ensure that the Tribunal's jurisdiction is made fully effective, including an order to preserve evidence in the possession or control of a disputing party or to protect the Tribunal's jurisdiction. A Tribunal may not order attachment or enjoin the application of the measure alleged to constitute a breach referred to in Article 1116 or 1117. For purposes of this paragraph, an order includes a recommendation.

Article 1135   Final Award

1. Where a Tribunal makes a final award against a Party, the Tribunal may award, separately or in combination, only:
   (a) monetary damages and any applicable interest;
   (b) restitution of property, in which case the award shall provide that the disputing Party may pay monetary damages and any applicable interest in lieu of restitution.
   A tribunal may also award costs in accordance with the applicable arbitration rules.

2. Subject to paragraph 1, where a claim is made under Article 1117(1):
    (a) an award of restitution of property shall provide that restitution be made to the enterprise;
    (b) an award of monetary damages and any applicable interest shall provide that the sum be paid to the enterprise; and
    (c) the award shall provide that it is made without prejudice to any right that any person may have in the relief under applicable domestic law.
3. A Tribunal may not order a Party to pay punitive damages.

Article 1136   Finality and Enforcement of an Award

1. An award made by a Tribunal shall have no binding force except between the disputing parties and in respect of the particular case.
2. Subject to paragraph 3 and the applicable review procedure for an interim award, a disputing party shall abide by and comply with an award without delay.
3. A disputing party may not seek enforcement of a final award until:
    (a) in the case of a final award made under the ICSID Convention
        (i) 120 days have elapsed from the date the award was rendered and no disputing party has requested revision or annulment of the award, or
        (ii) revision or annulment proceedings have been completed; and
    (b) in the case of a final award under the ICSID Additional Facility Rules or the UNCITRAL Arbitration Rules
        (i) three months have elapsed from the date the award was rendered and no disputing party has commenced a proceeding to revise, set aside or annul the award, or
        (ii) a court has dismissed or allowed an application to revise, set aside or annul the award and there is no further appeal.
4. Each Party shall provide for the enforcement of an award in its territory.
5. If a disputing Party fails to abide by or comply with a final award, the Commission, on delivery of a request by a Party whose investor was a party to the arbitration, shall establish a panel under Article 2008 (Request for an Arbitral Panel). The requesting Party may seek in such proceedings:
    (a) a determination that the failure to abide by or comply with the final award is inconsistent with the obligations of this Agreement; and
    (b) a recommendation that the Party abide by or comply with the final award.
6. A disputing investor may seek enforcement of an arbitration award under the ICSID Convention, the New York Convention or the InterAmerican Convention regardless of whether proceedings have been taken under paragraph 5.
7. A claim that is submitted to arbitration under this Section shall be considered to arise out of a commercial relationship or transaction for purposes of Article I of the New York Convention and Article I of the InterAmerican Convention.

Article 1137   General

Time when a Claim is Submitted to Arbitration
1. A claim is submitted to arbitration under this Section when:
    (a) the request for arbitration under paragraph (1) of Article 36 of the ICSID Convention has been received by the Secretary-General;
    (b) the notice of arbitration under Article 2 of Schedule C of the ICSID Additional Facility Rules has been received by the Secretary-General; or
    (c) the notice of arbitration given under the UNCITRAL Arbitration Rules is received by the disputing Party.

Service of Documents

2. Delivery of notice and other documents on a Party shall be made to the place named for that Party in Annex 1137.2.

Receipts under Insurance or Guarantee Contracts

3. In an arbitration under this Section, a Party shall not assert, as a defense, counterclaim, right of setoff or otherwise, that the disputing investor has received or will receive, pursuant to an insurance or guarantee contract, indemnification or other compensation for all or part of its alleged damages.

Publication of an Award

4. Annex 1137.4 applies to the Parties specified in that Annex with respect to publication of an award.

Article 1138   Exclusions

1. Without prejudice to the applicability or non-applicability of the dispute settlement provisions of this Section or of Chapter Twenty (Institutional Arrangements and Dispute Settlement Procedures) to other actions taken by a Party pursuant to Article 2102 (National Security), a decision by a Party to prohibit or restrict the acquisition of an investment in its territory by an investor of another Party, or its investment, pursuant to that Article shall not be subject to such provisions.

2. The dispute settlement provisions of this Section and of Chapter Twenty shall not apply to the matters referred to in Annex 1138.2.

SECTION C   DEFINITIONS

Article 1139   Definitions

For purposes of this Chapter:

disputing investor means an investor that makes a claim under Section B;

disputing parties means the disputing investor and the disputing Party;

disputing party means the disputing investor or the disputing Party;

disputing Party means a Party against which a claim is made under Section B;

enterprise means an "enterprise" as defined in Article 201 (Definitions of General Application), and a branch of an enterprise;

enterprise of a Party means an enterprise constituted or organized under the law of a Party, and a branch located in the territory of a Party and carrying out business activities there.

equity or debt securities includes voting and non-voting shares, bonds, convertible debentures, stock options and warrants;

G7 Currency means the currency of Canada, France, Germany, Italy, Japan, the United Kingdom of Great Britain and Northern Ireland or the United States;

ICSID means the International Centre for Settlement of Investment Disputes;

ICSID Convention means the *Convention on the Settlement of Investment Disputes between States and Nationals of other States*, done at Washington, March 18, 1965;

InterAmerican Convention means the *InterAmerican Convention on International Commercial Arbitration*, done at Panama, January 30, 1975;

investment means:

    (a) an enterprise;

    (b) an equity security of an enterprise;

    (c) a debt security of an enterprise

        (i) where the enterprise is an affiliate of the investor, or

        (ii) where the original maturity of the debt security is at least three years, but does not include a debt security, regardless of original maturity, of a state enterprise;

(d) a loan to an enterprise
    (i) where the enterprise is an affiliate of the investor, or
    (ii) where the original maturity of the loan is at least three years,
       but does not include a loan, regardless of original maturity, to a state enterprise;
(e) an interest in an enterprise that entitles the owner to share in income or profits of the enterprise;
(f) an interest in an enterprise that entitles the owner to share in the assets of that enterprise on dissolution, other than a debt security or a loan excluded from subparagraph (c) or (d);
(g) real estate or other property, tangible or intangible, acquired in the expectation or used for the purpose of economic benefit or other business purposes; and
(h) interests arising from the commitment of capital or other resources in the territory of a Party to economic activity in such territory, such as under
    (i) contracts involving the presence of an investor's property in the territory of the Party, including turnkey or construction contracts, or concessions, or
    (ii) contracts where remuneration depends substantially on the production, revenues or profits of an enterprise;
but investment does not mean,
(i) claims to money that arise solely from
    (i) commercial contracts for the sale of goods or services by a national or enterprise in the territory of a Party to an enterprise in the territory of another Party, or
    (ii) the extension of credit in connection with a commercial transaction, such as trade financing, other than a loan covered by subparagraph (d); or
(j) any other claims to money,
that do not involve the kinds of interests set out in subparagraphs (a) through (h);
investment of an investor of a Party means an investment owned or controlled directly or indirectly by an investor of such Party;
investor of a Party means a Party or state enterprise thereof, or a national or an enterprise of such Party, that seeks to make, is making or has made an investment;
investor of a non-Party means an investor other than an investor of a Party, that seeks to make, is making or has made an investment;
New York Convention means the *United Nations Convention on the Recognition and Enforcement of Foreign Arbitral Awards*, done at New York, June 10, 1958;
Secretary-General means the Secretary-General of ICSID;
transfers means transfers and international payments;
Tribunal means an arbitration tribunal established under Article 1120 or 1126; and
UNCITRAL Arbitration Rules means the arbitration rules of the United Nations Commission on International Trade Law, approved by the United Nations General Assembly on December 15, 1976.

ANNEX 1120.1   SUBMISSION OF A CLAIM TO ARBITRATION

Mexico
With respect to the submission of a claim to arbitration:

(a) an investor of another Party may not allege that Mexico has breached an obligation under:
    (i) Section A or Article 1503(2) (State Enterprises), or
    (ii) Article 1502(3)(a) (Monopolies and State Enterprises) where the monopoly has acted in a manner inconsistent with the Party's obligations under Section A,
      both in an arbitration under this Section and in proceedings before a Mexican court or administrative tribunal; and

(b) where an enterprise of Mexico that is a juridical person that an investor of another Party owns or controls directly or indirectly alleges in proceedings before a Mexican court or administrative tribunal that Mexico has breached an obligation under:

    (i) Section A or Article 1503(2) (State Enterprises), or

    (ii) Article 1502(3)(a) (Monopolies and State Enterprises) where the monopoly has acted in a manner inconsistent with the Party's obligations under Section A,

    the investor may not allege the breach in an arbitration under this Section.

ANNEX 1137.2 SERVICE OF DOCUMENTS ON A PARTY UNDER SECTION B

Each Party shall set out in this Annex and publish in its official journal by January 1, 1994, the place for delivery of notice and other documents under this Section.

ANNEX 1137.4 PUBLICATION OF AN AWARD

Canada

Where Canada is the disputing Party, either Canada or a disputing investor that is a party to the arbitration may make an award public.

Mexico

Where Mexico is the disputing Party, the applicable arbitration rules apply to the publication of an award.

United States

Where the United States is the disputing Party, either the United States or a disputing investor that is a party to the arbitration may make an award public.

ANNEX 1138.2 EXCLUSIONS FROM DISPUTE SETTLEMENT

Canada

A decision by Canada following a review under the *Investment Canada Act*, with respect to whether or not to permit an acquisition that is subject to review, shall not be subject to the dispute settlement provisions of Section B or of Chapter Twenty (Institutional Arrangements and Dispute Settlement Procedures).

Mexico

A decision by the National Commission on Foreign Investment ("Comisión Nacional de Inversiones Extranjeras") following a review pursuant to Annex I, page I-M-4, with respect to whether or not to permit an acquisition that is subject to review, shall not be subject to the dispute settlement provisions of Section B or of Chapter Twenty.

FTA; TransAtlantic Trade & Investment Partnership:
+ US + EU
+ TransPacific; US + Brunei, New Zealand, Singapore, Chile.
+ Regional Comprehensive Economic Partnership (RCEP)
+
+ TransAtlantic FTA; Since 2013 under Negotiations... US+EU.
+ Once complete if combined with FTA with Canada & Mexico
↳ European free trade Association it would form a free trade area
covering both Continents.

III-12

Convention on the Settlement of Investment Disputes between States and Nationals of Other States (The 'ICSID Convention')

Date   18 March 1965
In force 14 October 1966
Source 575 UNTS 159
Link   \<http://icsid.worldbank.org/ICSID/StaticFiles/basicdoc/CRR_English-final.pdf\>

PREAMBLE

The Contracting States

Considering the need for international cooperation for economic development, and the role of private international investment therein;

Bearing in mind the possibility that from time to time disputes may arise in connection with such investment between Contracting States and nationals of other Contracting States;

Recognizing that while such disputes would usually be subject to national legal processes, international methods of settlement may be appropriate in certain cases;

Attaching particular importance to the availability of facilities for international conciliation or arbitration to which Contracting States and nationals of other Contracting States may submit such disputes if they so desire;

Desiring to establish such facilities under the auspices of the International Bank for Reconstruction and Development;

Recognizing that mutual consent by the parties to submit such disputes to conciliation or to arbitration through such facilities constitutes a binding agreement which requires in particular that due consideration be given to any recommendation of conciliators, and that any arbitral award be complied with; and

Declaring that no Contracting State shall by the mere fact of its ratification, acceptance or approval of this Convention and without its consent be deemed to be under any obligation to submit any particular dispute to conciliation or arbitration,

Have agreed as follows:

CHAPTER I   INTERNATIONAL CENTRE FOR SETTLEMENT OF INVESTMENT DISPUTES

SECTION 1   ESTABLISHMENT AND ORGANIZATION

Article 1

(1) There is hereby established the International Centre for Settlement of Investment Disputes (hereinafter called the Centre).

(2) The purpose of the Centre shall be to provide facilities for conciliation and arbitration of investment disputes between Contracting States and nationals of other Contracting States in accordance with the provisions of this Convention.

Article 2

The seat of the Centre shall be at the principal office of the International Bank for Reconstruction and Development (hereinafter called the Bank). The seat may be moved to another place by decision of the Administrative Council adopted by a majority of two-thirds of its members.

Article 3

The Centre shall have an Administrative Council and a Secretariat and shall maintain a Panel of Conciliators and a Panel of Arbitrators.

SECTION 2   THE ADMINISTRATIVE COUNCIL

Article 4

(1) The Administrative Council shall be composed of one representative of each Contracting State. An alternate may act as representative in case of his principal's absence from a meeting or inability to act.

(2) In the absence of a contrary designation, each governor and alternate governor of the Bank appointed by a Contracting State shall be *ex officio* its representative and its alternate respectively.

Article 5

The President of the Bank shall be *ex officio* Chairman of the Administrative Council (hereinafter called the Chairman) but shall have no vote. During his absence or inability to act and during any vacancy in the office of President of the Bank, the person for the time being acting as President shall act as Chairman of the Administrative Council.

Article 6

(1) Without prejudice to the powers and functions vested in it by other provisions of this Convention, the Administrative Council shall:
   (a) adopt the administrative and financial regulations of the Centre;
   (b) adopt the rules of procedure for the institution of conciliation and arbitration proceedings;
   (c) adopt the rules of procedure for conciliation and arbitration proceedings (hereinafter called the Conciliation Rules and the Arbitration Rules);
   (d) approve arrangements with the Bank for the use of the Bank's administrative facilities and services;
   (e) determine the conditions of service of the Secretary-General and of any Deputy Secretary-General;
   (f) adopt the annual budget of revenues and expenditures of the Centre;
   (g) approve the annual report on the operation of the Centre.
   The decisions referred to in sub-paragraphs (a), (b), (c) and (f) above shall be adopted by a majority of two-thirds of the members of the Administrative Council.

(2) The Administrative Council may appoint such committees as it considers necessary.

(3) The Administrative Council shall also exercise such other powers and perform such other functions as it shall determine to be necessary for the implementation of the provisions of this Convention.

Article 7

(1) The Administrative Council shall hold an annual meeting and such other meetings as may be determined by the Council, or convened by the Chairman, or convened by the Secretary-General at the request of not less than five members of the Council.

(2) Each member of the Administrative Council shall have one vote and, except as otherwise herein provided, all matters before the Council shall be decided by a majority of the votes cast.

(3) A quorum for any meeting of the Administrative Council shall be a majority of its members.

(4) The Administrative Council may establish, by a majority of two-thirds of its members, a procedure whereby the Chairman may seek a vote of the Council without convening a meeting of the Council. The vote shall be considered valid only if the majority of the members of the Council cast their votes within the time limit fixed by the said procedure.

Article 8

Members of the Administrative Council and the Chairman shall serve without remuneration from the Centre.

SECTION 3   THE SECRETARIAT

Article 9

The Secretariat shall consist of a Secretary-General, one or more Deputy Secretaries-General and staff.

Article 10

(1) The Secretary-General and any Deputy Secretary-General shall be elected by the Administrative Council by a majority of two-thirds of its members upon the nomination of the Chairman for a term of service not exceeding six years and shall be eligible for re-election. After consulting the members of the Administrative Council, the Chairman shall propose one or more candidates for each such office.

(2) The offices of Secretary-General and Deputy Secretary-General shall be incompatible with the exercise of any political function. Neither the Secretary-General nor any Deputy Secretary-General may hold any other employment or engage in any other occupation except with the approval of the Administrative Council.

(3) During the Secretary-General's absence or inability to act, and during any vacancy of the office of Secretary-General, the Deputy Secretary-General shall act as Secretary-General. If there shall be more than one Deputy Secretary-General, the Administrative Council shall determine in advance the order in which they shall act as Secretary-General.

Article 11

The Secretary-General shall be the legal representative and the principal officer of the Centre and shall be responsible for its administration, including the appointment of staff, in accordance with the provisions of this Convention and the rules adopted by the Administrative Council. He shall perform the function of registrar and shall have the power to authenticate arbitral awards rendered pursuant to this Convention, and to certify copies thereof.

SECTION 4   THE PANELS

Article 12
The Panel of Conciliators and the Panel of Arbitrators shall each consist of qualified persons, designated as hereinafter provided, who are willing to serve thereon.

Article 13
(1) Each Contracting State may designate to each Panel four persons who may but need not be its nationals.

(2) The Chairman may designate ten persons to each Panel. The persons so designated to a Panel shall each have a different nationality.

Article 14
(1) Persons designated to serve on the Panels shall be persons of high moral character and recognized competence in the fields of law, commerce, industry or finance, who may be relied upon to exercise independent judgment. Competence in the field of law shall be of particular importance in the case of persons on the Panel of Arbitrators.

(2) The Chairman, in designating persons to serve on the Panels, shall in addition pay due regard to the importance of assuring representation on the Panels of the principal legal systems of the world and of the main forms of economic activity.

Article 15
(1) Panel members shall serve for renewable periods of six years.

(2) In case of death or resignation of a member of a Panel, the authority which designated the member shall have the right to designate another person to serve for the remainder of that member's term.

(3) Panel members shall continue in office until their successors have been designated.

Article 16
(1) A person may serve on both Panels.

(2) If a person shall have been designated to serve on the same Panel by more than one Contracting State, or by one or more Contracting States and the Chairman, he shall be deemed to have been designated by the authority which first designated him or, if one such authority is the State of which he is a national, by that State.

(3) All designations shall be notified to the Secretary-General and shall take effect from the date on which the notification is received.

SECTION 5   FINANCING THE CENTRE

Article 17
If the expenditure of the Centre cannot be met out of charges for the use of its facilities, or out of other receipts, the excess shall be borne by Contracting States which are members of the Bank in proportion to their respective subscriptions to the capital stock of the Bank, and by Contracting States which are not members of the Bank in accordance with rules adopted by the Administrative Council.

SECTION 6   STATUS, IMMUNITIES AND PRIVILEGES

Article 18
The Centre shall have full international legal personality. The legal capacity of the Centre shall include the capacity:

(a) to contract;

(b) to acquire and dispose of movable and immovable property;

(c) to institute legal proceedings.

Article 19

To enable the Centre to fulfil its functions, it shall enjoy in the territories of each Contracting State the immunities and privileges set forth in this Section.

Article 20

The Centre, its property and assets shall enjoy immunity from all legal process, except when the Centre waives this immunity.

Article 21

The Chairman, the members of the Administrative Council, persons acting as conciliators or arbitrators or members of a Committee appointed pursuant to paragraph (3) of Article 52, and the officers and employees of the Secretariat

(a) shall enjoy immunity from legal process with respect to acts performed by them in the exercise of their functions, except when the Centre waives this immunity;

(b) not being local nationals, shall enjoy the same immunities from immigration restrictions, alien registration requirements and national service obligations, the same facilities as regards exchange restrictions and the same treatment in respect of travelling facilities as are accorded by Contracting States to the representatives, officials and employees of comparable rank of other Contracting States.

Article 22

The provisions of Article 21 shall apply to persons appearing in proceedings under this Convention as parties, agents, counsel, advocates, witnesses or experts; provided, however, that sub-paragraph (b) thereof shall apply only in connection with their travel to and from, and their stay at, the place where the proceedings are held.

Article 23

(1) The archives of the Centre shall be inviolable, wherever they may be.

(2) With regard to its official communications, the Centre shall be accorded by each Contracting State treatment not less favourable than that accorded to other international organizations.

Article 24

(1) The Centre, its assets, property and income, and its operations and transactions authorized by this Convention shall be exempt from all taxation and customs duties. The Centre shall also be exempt from liability for the collection or payment of any taxes or customs duties.

(2) Except in the case of local nationals, no tax shall be levied on or in respect of expense allowances paid by the Centre to the Chairman or members of the Administrative Council, or on or in respect of salaries, expense allowances or other emoluments paid by the Centre to officials or employees of the Secretariat.

(3) No tax shall be levied on or in respect of fees or expense allowances received by persons acting as conciliators, or arbitrators, or members of a Committee appointed pursuant to paragraph (3) of Article 52, in proceedings under this Convention, if the sole jurisdictional basis for such tax is the location of the Centre or the place where such proceedings are conducted or the place where such fees or allowances are paid.

CHAPTER II   JURISDICTION OF THE CENTRE

Article 25

(1) The jurisdiction of the Centre shall extend to any legal dispute arising directly out of an investment, between a Contracting State (or any constituent subdivision or agency of a Contracting State designated to the Centre by that State) and a national of another Contracting State, which the parties to the dispute consent in writing to submit to the Centre. When the parties have given their consent, no party may withdraw its consent unilaterally.

(2) "National of another Contracting State" means:

   (a) any natural person who had the nationality of a Contracting State other than the State party to the dispute on the date on which the parties consented to submit such dispute to conciliation or arbitration as well as on the date on which the request was registered pursuant to paragraph (3) of Article 28 or paragraph (3) of Article 36, but does not include any person who on either date also had the nationality of the Contracting State party to the dispute; and

   (b) any juridical person which had the nationality of a Contracting State other than the State party to the dispute on the date on which the parties consented to submit such dispute to conciliation or arbitration and any juridical person which had the nationality of the Contracting State party to the dispute on that date and which, because of foreign control, the parties have agreed should be treated as a national of another Contracting State for the purposes of this Convention.

(3) Consent by a constituent subdivision or agency of a Contracting State shall require the approval of that State unless that State notifies the Centre that no such approval is required.

(4) Any Contracting State may, at the time of ratification, acceptance or approval of this Convention or at any time thereafter, notify the Centre of the class or classes of disputes which it would or would not consider submitting to the jurisdiction of the Centre. The Secretary-General shall forthwith transmit such notification to all Contracting States. Such notification shall not constitute the consent required by paragraph (1).

Article 26

Consent of the parties to arbitration under this Convention shall, unless otherwise stated, be deemed consent to such arbitration to the exclusion of any other remedy. A Contracting State may require the exhaustion of local administrative or judicial remedies as a condition of its consent to arbitration under this Convention.

Article 27

(1) No Contracting State shall give diplomatic protection, or bring an international claim, in respect of a dispute which one of its nationals and another Contracting State shall have consented to submit or shall have submitted to arbitration under this Convention, unless such other Contracting State shall have failed to abide by and comply with the award rendered in such dispute.

(2) Diplomatic protection, for the purposes of paragraph (1), shall not include informal diplomatic exchanges for the sole purpose of facilitating a settlement of the dispute.

CHAPTER III   CONCILIATION

SECTION 1   REQUEST FOR CONCILIATION

Article 28

(1) Any Contracting State or any national of a Contracting State wishing to institute conciliation proceedings shall address a request to that effect in writing to the Secretary-General who shall send a copy of the request to the other party.

(2) The request shall contain information concerning the issues in dispute, the identity of the parties and their consent to conciliation in accordance with the rules of procedure for the institution of conciliation and arbitration proceedings.

(3) The Secretary-General shall register the request unless he finds, on the basis of the information contained in the request, that the dispute is manifestly outside the jurisdiction of the Centre. He shall forthwith notify the parties of registration or refusal to register.

SECTION 2   CONSTITUTION OF THE CONCILIATION COMMISSION

Article 29

(1) The Conciliation Commission (hereinafter called the Commission) shall be constituted as soon as possible after registration of a request pursuant to Article 28.

(2) (a) The Commission shall consist of a sole conciliator or any uneven number of conciliators appointed as the parties shall agree.

(b) Where the parties do not agree upon the number of conciliators and the method of their appointment, the Commission shall consist of three conciliators, one conciliator appointed by each party and the third, who shall be the president of the Commission, appointed by agreement of the parties.

Article 30

If the Commission shall not have been constituted within 90 days after notice of registration of the request has been dispatched by the Secretary-General in accordance with paragraph (3) of Article 28, or such other period as the parties may agree, the Chairman shall, at the request of either party and after consulting both parties as far as possible, appoint the conciliator or conciliators not yet appointed.

Article 31

(1) Conciliators may be appointed from outside the Panel of Conciliators, except in the case of appointments by the Chairman pursuant to Article 30.

(2) Conciliators appointed from outside the Panel of Conciliators shall possess the qualities stated in paragraph (1) of Article 14.

SECTION 3   CONCILIATION PROCEEDINGS

Article 32

(1) The Commission shall be the judge of its own competence.

(2) Any objection by a party to the dispute that that dispute is not within the jurisdiction of the Centre, or for other reasons is not within the competence of the Commission, shall be considered by the Commission which shall determine whether to deal with it as a preliminary question or to join it to the merits of the dispute.

Article 33

Any conciliation proceeding shall be conducted in accordance with the provisions of this Section and, except as the parties otherwise agree, in accordance with the Conciliation Rules in effect on the date on which the parties consented to conciliation. If any question of procedure arises which is not covered by this Section or the Conciliation Rules or any rules agreed by the parties, the Commission shall decide the question.

Article 34

(1) It shall be the duty of the Commission to clarify the issues in dispute between the parties and to endeavour to bring about agreement between them upon mutually acceptable terms. To that end, the Commission may at any stage of the proceedings and from time to time

recommend terms of settlement to the parties. The parties shall cooperate in good faith with the Commission in order to enable the Commission to carry out its functions, and shall give their most serious consideration to its recommendations.

(2) If the parties reach agreement, the Commission shall draw up a report noting the issues in dispute and recording that the parties have reached agreement. If, at any stage of the proceedings, it appears to the Commission that there is no likelihood of agreement between the parties, it shall close the proceedings and shall draw up a report noting the submission of the dispute and recording the failure of the parties to reach agreement. If one party fails to appear or participate in the proceedings, the Commission shall close the proceedings and shall draw up a report noting that party's failure to appear or participate.

Article 35

Except as the parties to the dispute shall otherwise agree, neither party to a conciliation proceeding shall be entitled in any other proceeding, whether before arbitrators or in a court of law or otherwise, to invoke or rely on any views expressed or statements or admissions or offers of settlement made by the other party in the conciliation proceedings, or the report or any recommendations made by the Commission.

CHAPTER IV   ARBITRATION

SECTION 1   REQUEST FOR ARBITRATION

Article 36

(1) Any Contracting State or any national of a Contracting State wishing to institute arbitration proceedings shall address a request to that effect in writing to the Secretary-General who shall send a copy of the request to the other party.

(2) The request shall contain information concerning the issues in dispute, the identity of the parties and their consent to arbitration in accordance with the rules of procedure for the institution of conciliation and arbitration proceedings.

(3) The Secretary-General shall register the request unless he finds, on the basis of the information contained in the request, that the dispute is manifestly outside the jurisdiction of the Centre. He shall forthwith notify the parties of registration or refusal to register.

SECTION 2   CONSTITUTION OF THE TRIBUNAL

Article 37

(1) The Arbitral Tribunal (hereinafter called the Tribunal) shall be constituted as soon as possible after registration of a request pursuant to Article 36.

(2) (a) The Tribunal shall consist of a sole arbitrator or any uneven number of arbitrators appointed as the parties shall agree.

    (b) Where the parties do not agree upon the number of arbitrators and the method of their appointment, the Tribunal shall consist of three arbitrators, one arbitrator appointed by each party and the third, who shall be the president of the Tribunal, appointed by agreement of the parties.

Article 38

If the Tribunal shall not have been constituted within 90 days after notice of registration of the request has been dispatched by the Secretary-General in accordance with paragraph (3) of Article 36, or such other period as the parties may agree, the Chairman shall, at the request of either party and after consulting both parties as far as possible, appoint the arbitrator or arbitrators not yet appointed. Arbitrators appointed by the Chairman pursuant to this Article shall not be nationals of the Contracting State party to the dispute or of the Contracting State whose national is a party to the dispute.

Article 39

The majority of the arbitrators shall be nationals of States other than the Contracting State party to the dispute and the Contracting State whose national is a party to the dispute; provided, however, that the foregoing provisions of this Article shall not apply if the sole arbitrator or each individual member of the Tribunal has been appointed by agreement of the parties.

Article 40

(1) Arbitrators may be appointed from outside the Panel of Arbitrators, except in the case of appointments by the Chairman pursuant to Article 38.

(2) Arbitrators appointed from outside the Panel of Arbitrators shall possess the qualities stated in paragraph (1) of Article 14.

SECTION 3   POWERS AND FUNCTIONS OF THE TRIBUNAL

Article 41

(1) The Tribunal shall be the judge of its own competence.

(2) Any objection by a party to the dispute that that dispute is not within the jurisdiction of the Centre, or for other reasons is not within the competence of the Tribunal, shall be considered by the Tribunal which shall determine whether to deal with it as a preliminary question or to join it to the merits of the dispute.

Article 42

(1) The Tribunal shall decide a dispute in accordance with such rules of law as may be agreed by the parties. In the absence of such agreement, the Tribunal shall apply the law of the Contracting State party to the dispute (including its rules on the conflict of laws) and such rules of international law as may be applicable.

(2) The Tribunal may not bring in a finding of *non liquet* on the ground of silence or obscurity of the law.

(3) The provisions of paragraphs (1) and (2) shall not prejudice the power of the Tribunal to decide a dispute *ex aequo et bono* if the parties so agree.

Article 43

Except as the parties otherwise agree, the Tribunal may, if it deems it necessary at any stage of the proceedings,

(a) call upon the parties to produce documents or other evidence, and

(b) visit the scene connected with the dispute, and conduct such inquiries there as it may deem appropriate.

Article 44

Any arbitration proceeding shall be conducted in accordance with the provisions of this Section and, except as the parties otherwise agree, in accordance with the Arbitration Rules in effect on the date on which the parties consented to arbitration. If any question of procedure arises which is not covered by this Section or the Arbitration Rules or any rules agreed by the parties, the Tribunal shall decide the question.

Article 45

(1) Failure of a party to appear or to present his case shall not be deemed an admission of the other party's assertions.

(2) If a party fails to appear or to present his case at any stage of the proceedings the other party may request the Tribunal to deal with the questions submitted to it and to render an award.

Before rendering an award, the Tribunal shall notify, and grant a period of grace to, the party failing to appear or to present its case, unless it is satisfied that that party does not intend to do so.

Article 46
Except as the parties otherwise agree, the Tribunal shall, if requested by a party, determine any incidental or additional claims or counterclaims arising directly out of the subject-matter of the dispute provided that they are within the scope of the consent of the parties and are otherwise within the jurisdiction of the Centre.

Article 47
Except as the parties otherwise agree, the Tribunal may, if it considers that the circumstances so require, recommend any provisional measures which should be taken to preserve the respective rights of either party.

SECTION 4 THE AWARD

Article 48
(1) The Tribunal shall decide questions by a majority of the votes of all its members.
(2) The award of the Tribunal shall be in writing and shall be signed by the members of the Tribunal who voted for it.
(3) The award shall deal with every question submitted to the Tribunal, and shall state the reasons upon which it is based.
(4) Any member of the Tribunal may attach his individual opinion to the award, whether he dissents from the majority or not, or a statement of his dissent.
(5) The Centre shall not publish the award without the consent of the parties.

Article 49
(1) The Secretary-General shall promptly dispatch certified copies of the award to the parties. The award shall be deemed to have been rendered on the date on which the certified copies were dispatched.
(2) The Tribunal upon the request of a party made within 45 days after the date on which the award was rendered may after notice to the other party decide any question which it had omitted to decide in the award, and shall rectify any clerical, arithmetical or similar error in the award. Its decision shall become part of the award and shall be notified to the parties in the same manner as the award. The periods of time provided for under paragraph (2) of Article 51 and paragraph (2) of Article 52 shall run from the date on which the decision was rendered.

SECTION 5 INTERPRETATION, REVISION AND ANNULMENT OF THE AWARD

Article 50
(1) If any dispute shall arise between the parties as to the meaning or scope of an award, either party may request interpretation of the award by an application in writing addressed to the Secretary-General.
(2) The request shall, if possible, be submitted to the Tribunal which rendered the award. If this shall not be possible, a new Tribunal shall be constituted in accordance with Section 2 of this Chapter. The Tribunal may, if it considers that the circumstances so require, stay enforcement of the award pending its decision.

Article 51

(1) Either party may request revision of the award by an application in writing addressed to the Secretary-General on the ground of discovery of some fact of such a nature as decisively to affect the award, provided that when the award was rendered that fact was unknown to the Tribunal and to the applicant and that the applicant's ignorance of that fact was not due to negligence.

(2) The application shall be made within 90 days after the discovery of such fact and in any event within three years after the date on which the award was rendered.

(3) The request shall, if possible, be submitted to the Tribunal which rendered the award. If this shall not be possible, a new Tribunal shall be constituted in accordance with Section 2 of this Chapter.

(4) The Tribunal may, if it considers that the circumstances so require, stay enforcement of the award pending its decision. If the applicant requests a stay of enforcement of the award in his application, enforcement shall be stayed provisionally until the Tribunal rules on such request.

Article 52

(1) Either party may request annulment of the award by an application in writing addressed to the Secretary-General on one or more of the following grounds:
    (a) that the Tribunal was not properly constituted;
    (b) that the Tribunal has manifestly exceeded its powers;
    (c) that there was corruption on the part of a member of the Tribunal;
    (d) that there has been a serious departure from a fundamental rule of procedure; or
    (e) that the award has failed to state the reasons on which it is based.

(2) The application shall be made within 120 days after the date on which the award was rendered except that when annulment is requested on the ground of corruption such application shall be made within 120 days after discovery of the corruption and in any event within three years after the date on which the award was rendered.

(3) On receipt of the request the Chairman shall forthwith appoint from the Panel of Arbitrators an *ad hoc* Committee of three persons. None of the members of the Committee shall have been a member of the Tribunal which rendered the award, shall be of the same nationality as any such member, shall be a national of the State party to the dispute or of the State whose national is a party to the dispute, shall have been designated to the Panel of Arbitrators by either of those States, or shall have acted as a conciliator in the same dispute. The Committee shall have the authority to annul the award or any part thereof on any of the grounds set forth in paragraph (1).

(4) The provisions of Articles 41–45, 48, 49, 53 and 54, and of Chapters VI and VII shall apply *mutatis mutandis* to proceedings before the Committee.

(5) The Committee may, if it considers that the circumstances so require, stay enforcement of the award pending its decision. If the applicant requests a stay of enforcement of the award in his application, enforcement shall be stayed provisionally until the Committee rules on such request.

(6) If the award is annulled the dispute shall, at the request of either party, be submitted to a new Tribunal constituted in accordance with Section 2 of this Chapter.

SECTION 6   RECOGNITION AND ENFORCEMENT OF THE AWARD

Article 53

(1) The award shall be binding on the parties and shall not be subject to any appeal or to any other remedy except those provided for in this Convention. Each party shall abide by and

comply with the terms of the award except to the extent that enforcement shall have been stayed pursuant to the relevant provisions of this Convention.

(2) For the purposes of this Section, "award" shall include any decision interpreting, revising or annulling such award pursuant to Articles 50, 51 or 52.

Article 54

(1) Each Contracting State shall recognize an award rendered pursuant to this Convention as binding and enforce the pecuniary obligations imposed by that award within its territories as if it were a final judgment of a court in that State. A Contracting State with a federal constitution may enforce such an award in or through its federal courts and may provide that such courts shall treat the award as if it were a final judgment of the courts of a constituent state.

(2) A party seeking recognition or enforcement in the territories of a Contracting State shall furnish to a competent court or other authority which such State shall have designated for this purpose a copy of the award certified by the Secretary-General. Each Contracting State shall notify the Secretary-General of the designation of the competent court or other authority for this purpose and of any subsequent change in such designation.

(3) Execution of the award shall be governed by the laws concerning the execution of judgments in force in the State in whose territories such execution is sought.

Article 55

Nothing in Article 54 shall be construed as derogating from the law in force in any Contracting State relating to immunity of that State or of any foreign State from execution.

CHAPTER V   REPLACEMENT AND DISQUALIFICATION OF CONCILIATORS AND ARBITRATORS

Article 56

(1) After a Commission or a Tribunal has been constituted and proceedings have begun, its composition shall remain unchanged; provided, however, that if a conciliator or an arbitrator should die, become incapacitated, or resign, the resulting vacancy shall be filled in accordance with the provisions of Section 2 of Chapter III or Section 2 of Chapter IV.

(2) A member of a Commission or Tribunal shall continue to serve in that capacity notwithstanding that he shall have ceased to be a member of the Panel.

(3) If a conciliator or arbitrator appointed by a party shall have resigned without the consent of the Commission or Tribunal of which he was a member, the Chairman shall appoint a person from the appropriate Panel to fill the resulting vacancy.

Article 57

A party may propose to a Commission or Tribunal the disqualification of any of its members on account of any fact indicating a manifest lack of the qualities required by paragraph (1) of Article 14. A party to arbitration proceedings may, in addition, propose the disqualification of an arbitrator on the ground that he was ineligible for appointment to the Tribunal under Section 2 of Chapter IV.

Article 58

The decision on any proposal to disqualify a conciliator or arbitrator shall be taken by the other members of the Commission or Tribunal as the case may be, provided that where those members are equally divided, or in the case of a proposal to disqualify a sole conciliator or arbitrator, or a majority of the conciliators or arbitrators, the Chairman shall take that decision. If it is decided that the proposal is well-founded the conciliator or arbitrator to whom the decision relates shall be replaced in accordance with the provisions of Section 2 of Chapter III or Section 2 of Chapter IV.

CHAPTER VI   COST OF PROCEEDINGS

Article 59

The charges payable by the parties for the use of the facilities of the Centre shall be determined by the Secretary-General in accordance with the regulations adopted by the Administrative Council.

Article 60

(1) Each Commission and each Tribunal shall determine the fees and expenses of its members within limits established from time to time by the Administrative Council and after consultation with the Secretary-General.

(2) Nothing in paragraph (1) of this Article shall preclude the parties from agreeing in advance with the Commission or Tribunal concerned upon the fees and expenses of its members.

Article 61

(1) In the case of conciliation proceedings the fees and expenses of members of the Commission as well as the charges for the use of the facilities of the Centre, shall be borne equally by the parties. Each party shall bear any other expenses it incurs in connection with the proceedings.

(2) In the case of arbitration proceedings the Tribunal shall, except as the parties otherwise agree, assess the expenses incurred by the parties in connection with the proceedings, and shall decide how and by whom those expenses, the fees and expenses of the members of the Tribunal and the charges for the use of the facilities of the Centre shall be paid. Such decision shall form part of the award.

CHAPTER VII   PLACE OF PROCEEDINGS

Article 62

Conciliation and arbitration proceedings shall be held at the seat of the Centre except as hereinafter provided.

Article 63

Conciliation and arbitration proceedings may be held, if the parties so agree,

(a) at the seat of the Permanent Court of Arbitration or of any other appropriate institution, whether private or public, with which the Centre may make arrangements for that purpose; or

(b) at any other place approved by the Commission or Tribunal after consultation with the Secretary-General.

CHAPTER VIII   DISPUTES BETWEEN CONTRACTING STATES

Article 64

Any dispute arising between Contracting States concerning the interpretation or application of this Convention which is not settled by negotiation shall be referred to the International Court of Justice by the application of any party to such dispute, unless the States concerned agree to another method of settlement.

CHAPTER IX   AMENDMENT

Article 65

Any Contracting State may propose amendment of this Convention. The text of a proposed amendment shall be communicated to the Secretary-General not less than 90 days prior to the meeting of the Administrative Council at which such amendment is to be considered and shall forthwith be transmitted by him to all the members of the Administrative Council.

Article 66

(1) If the Administrative Council shall so decide by a majority of two-thirds of its members, the proposed amendment shall be circulated to all Contracting States for ratification, acceptance or approval. Each amendment shall enter into force 30 days after dispatch by the depositary of this Convention of a notification to Contracting States that all Contracting States have ratified, accepted or approved the amendment.

(2) No amendment shall affect the rights and obligations under this Convention of any Contracting State or of any of its constituent subdivisions or agencies, or of any national of such State arising out of consent to the jurisdiction of the Centre given before the date of entry into force of the amendment.

CHAPTER X   FINAL PROVISIONS

Article 67

This Convention shall be open for signature on behalf of States members of the Bank. It shall also be open for signature on behalf of any other State which is a party to the Statute of the International Court of Justice and which the Administrative Council, by a vote of two-thirds of its members, shall have invited to sign the Convention.

Article 68

(1) This Convention shall be subject to ratification, acceptance or approval by the signatory States in accordance with their respective constitutional procedures.

(2) This Convention shall enter into force 30 days after the date of deposit of the twentieth instrument of ratification, acceptance or approval. It shall enter into force for each State which subsequently deposits its instrument of ratification, acceptance or approval 30 days after the date of such deposit.

Article 69

Each Contracting State shall take such legislative or other measures as may be necessary for making the provisions of this Convention effective in its territories.

Article 70

This Convention shall apply to all territories for whose international relations a Contracting State is responsible, except those which are excluded by such State by written notice to the depositary of this Convention either at the time of ratification, acceptance or approval or subsequently.

Article 71

Any Contracting State may denounce this Convention by written notice to the depositary of this Convention. The denunciation shall take effect six months after receipt of such notice.

Article 72

Notice by a Contracting State pursuant to Articles 70 or 71 shall not affect the rights or obligations under this Convention of that State or of any of its constituent subdivisions or agencies or of any national of that State arising out of consent to the jurisdiction of the Centre given by one of them before such notice was received by the depositary.

Article 73

Instruments of ratification, acceptance or approval of this Convention and of amendments thereto shall be deposited with the Bank which shall act as the depositary of this Convention. The depositary shall transmit certified copies of this Convention to States members of the Bank and to any other State invited to sign the Convention.

Article 74

The depositary shall register this Convention with the Secretariat of the United Nations in accordance with Article 102 of the Charter of the United Nations and the Regulations thereunder adopted by the General Assembly.

Article 75

The depositary shall notify all signatory States of the following:

(a) signatures in accordance with Article 67;

(b) deposits of instruments of ratification, acceptance and approval in accordance with Article 73;

(c) the date on which this Convention enters into force in accordance with Article 68;

(d) exclusions from territorial application pursuant to Article 70;

(e) the date on which any amendment of this Convention enters into force in accordance with Article 66; and

(f) denunciations in accordance with Article 71.

DONE at Washington, in the English, French and Spanish languages, all three texts being equally authentic, in a single copy which shall remain deposited in the archives of the International Bank for Reconstruction and Development, which has indicated by its signature below its agreement to fulfil the functions with which it is charged under this Convention.

ICSID Rules of Procedure for Arbitration Proceedings (Arbitration Rules)

Date   as amended effective 10 April 2006
Source ICSID (ed), *ICSID Convention, Regulation and Rules* (Doc ICSID/15, April 2006)
Link   <http://icsid.worldbank.org/ICSID/StaticFiles/basicdoc/CRR_English-final.pdf>

CHAPTER I   ESTABLISHMENT OF THE TRIBUNAL

Rule 1   General Obligations

(1) Upon notification of the registration of the request for arbitration, the parties shall, with all possible dispatch, proceed to constitute a Tribunal, with due regard to Section 2 of Chapter IV of the Convention.

(2) Unless such information is provided in the request, the parties shall communicate to the Secretary-General as soon as possible any provisions agreed by them regarding the number of arbitrators and the method of their appointment.

(3) Except if each member of the Tribunal is appointed by agreement of the parties, nationals of the State party to the dispute or of the State whose national is a party to the dispute may be appointed by a party only if appointment by the other party to the dispute of the same number of arbitrators of either of these nationalities would not result in a majority of arbitrators of these nationalities.

(4) No person who had previously acted as a conciliator or arbitrator in any proceeding for the settlement of the dispute may be appointed as a member of the Tribunal.

Rule 2   Method of Constituting the Tribunal in the Absence of Previous Agreement

(1) If the parties, at the time of the registration of the request for arbitration, have not agreed upon the number of arbitrators and the method of their appointment, they shall, unless they agree otherwise, follow the following procedure:
   (a) the requesting party shall, within 10 days after the registration of the request, propose to the other party the appointment of a sole arbitrator or of a specified uneven number of arbitrators and specify the method proposed for their appointment;
   (b) within 20 days after receipt of the proposals made by the requesting party, the other party shall:
      (i) accept such proposals; or
      (ii) make other proposals regarding the number of arbitrators and the method of their appointment;
   (c) within 20 days after receipt of the reply containing any such other proposals, the requesting party shall notify the other party whether it accepts or rejects such proposals.

(2) The communications provided for in paragraph (1) shall be made or promptly confirmed in writing and shall either be transmitted through the Secretary-General or directly between the parties with a copy to the Secretary-General. The parties shall promptly notify the Secretary-General of the contents of any agreement reached.

(3) At any time 60 days after the registration of the request, if no agreement on another procedure is reached, either party may inform the Secretary-General that it chooses the formula provided for in Article 37(2)(b) of the Convention. The Secretary-General shall

thereupon promptly inform the other party that the Tribunal is to be constituted in accordance with that Article.

Rule 3   Appointment of Arbitrators to a Tribunal Constituted in Accordance with Convention Article 37(2)(b)

(1) If the Tribunal is to be constituted in accordance with Article 37(2)(b) of the Convention:

    (a) either party shall in a communication to the other party:

        (i) name two persons, identifying one of them, who shall not have the same nationality as nor be a national of either party, as the arbitrator appointed by it, and the other as the arbitrator proposed to be the President of the Tribunal; and

        (ii) invite the other party to concur in the appointment of the arbitrator proposed to be the President of the Tribunal and to appoint another arbitrator;

    (b) promptly upon receipt of this communication the other party shall, in its reply:

        (i) name a person as the arbitrator appointed by it, who shall not have the same nationality as nor be a national of either party; and

        (ii) concur in the appointment of the arbitrator proposed to be the President of the Tribunal or name another person as the arbitrator proposed to be President;

    (c) promptly upon receipt of the reply containing such a proposal, the initiating party shall notify the other party whether it concurs in the appointment of the arbitrator proposed by that party to be the President of the Tribunal.

(2) The communications provided for in this Rule shall be made or promptly confirmed in writing and shall either be transmitted through the Secretary-General or directly between the parties with a copy to the Secretary-General.

Rule 4   Appointment of Arbitrators by the Chairman of the Administrative Council

(1) If the Tribunal is not constituted within 90 days after the dispatch by the Secretary-General of the notice of registration, or such other period as the parties may agree, either party may, through the Secretary-General, address to the Chairman of the Administrative Council a request in writing to appoint the arbitrator or arbitrators not yet appointed and to designate an arbitrator to be the President of the Tribunal.

(2) The provision of paragraph (1) shall apply *mutatis mutandis* in the event that the parties have agreed that the arbitrators shall elect the President of the Tribunal and they fail to do so.

(3) The Secretary-General shall forthwith send a copy of the request to the other party.

(4) The Chairman shall, with due regard to Articles 38 and 40(1) of the Convention, and after consulting both parties as far as possible, comply with that request within 30 days after its receipt.

(5) The Secretary-General shall promptly notify the parties of any appointment or designation made by the Chairman.

Rule 5   Acceptance of Appointments

(1) The party or parties concerned shall notify the Secretary-General of the appointment of each arbitrator and indicate the method of his appointment.

(2) As soon as the Secretary-General has been informed by a party or the Chairman of the Administrative Council of the appointment of an arbitrator, he shall seek an acceptance from the appointee.

(3) If an arbitrator fails to accept his appointment within 15 days, the Secretary-General shall promptly notify the parties, and if appropriate the Chairman, and invite them to proceed to the appointment of another arbitrator in accordance with the method followed for the previous appointment.

Rule 6   Constitution of the Tribunal

(1) The Tribunal shall be deemed to be constituted and the proceeding to have begun on the date the Secretary-General notifies the parties that all the arbitrators have accepted their appointment.

(2) Before or at the first session of the Tribunal, each arbitrator shall sign a declaration in the following form:

> "To the best of my knowledge there is no reason why I should not serve on the Arbitral Tribunal constituted by the International Centre for Settlement of Investment Disputes with respect to a dispute between _____ and _____.
>
> "I shall keep confidential all information coming to my knowledge as a result of my participation in this proceeding, as well as the contents of any award made by the Tribunal.
>
> "I shall judge fairly as between the parties, according to the applicable law, and shall not accept any instruction or compensation with regard to the proceeding from any source except as provided in the Convention on the Settlement of Investment Disputes and in the Regulations and Rules made pursuant thereto.
>
> "Attached is a statement of (a) my past and present professional, business and other relationships (if any) with the parties and (b) any other circumstance that might cause my reliability for independent judgment to be questioned by a party. I acknowledge that by signing this declaration, I assume a continuing obligation promptly to notify the Secretary-General of the Centre of any such relationship or circumstance that subsequently arises during this proceeding."

Any arbitrator failing to sign a declaration by the end of the first session of the Tribunal shall be deemed to have resigned.

Rule 7   Replacement of Arbitrators

At any time before the Tribunal is constituted, each party may replace any arbitrator appointed by it and the parties may by common consent agree to replace any arbitrator. The procedure of such replacement shall be in accordance with Rules 1, 5 and 6.

Rule 8   Incapacity or Resignation of Arbitrators

(1) If an arbitrator becomes incapacitated or unable to perform the duties of his office, the procedure in respect of the disqualification of arbitrators set forth in Rule 9 shall apply.

(2) An arbitrator may resign by submitting his resignation to the other members of the Tribunal and the Secretary-General. If the arbitrator was appointed by one of the parties, the Tribunal shall promptly consider the reasons for his resignation and decide whether it consents thereto. The Tribunal shall promptly notify the Secretary-General of its decision.

Rule 9   Disqualification of Arbitrators

(1) A party proposing the disqualification of an arbitrator pursuant to Article 57 of the Convention shall promptly, and in any event before the proceeding is declared closed, file its proposal with the Secretary-General, stating its reasons therefor.

(2) The Secretary-General shall forthwith:
   (a) transmit the proposal to the members of the Tribunal and, if it relates to a sole arbitrator or to a majority of the members of the Tribunal, to the Chairman of the Administrative Council; and
   (b) notify the other party of the proposal.

(3) The arbitrator to whom the proposal relates may, without delay, furnish explanations to the Tribunal or the Chairman, as the case may be.

(4) Unless the proposal relates to a majority of the members of the Tribunal, the other members shall promptly consider and vote on the proposal in the absence of the arbitrator concerned. If those members are equally divided, they shall, through the Secretary-General, promptly notify the Chairman of the proposal, of any explanation furnished by the arbitrator concerned and of their failure to reach a decision.

(5) Whenever the Chairman has to decide on a proposal to disqualify an arbitrator, he shall take that decision within 30 days after he has received the proposal.

(6) The proceeding shall be suspended until a decision has been taken on the proposal.

Rule 10   Procedure during a Vacancy on the Tribunal

(1) The Secretary-General shall forthwith notify the parties and, if necessary, the Chairman of the Administrative Council of the disqualification, death, incapacity or resignation of an arbitrator and of the consent, if any, of the Tribunal to a resignation.

(2) Upon the notification by the Secretary-General of a vacancy on the Tribunal, the proceeding shall be or remain suspended until the vacancy has been filled.

Rule 11   Filling Vacancies on the Tribunal

(1) Except as provided in paragraph (2), a vacancy resulting from the disqualification, death, incapacity or resignation of an arbitrator shall be promptly filled by the same method by which his appointment had been made.

(2) In addition to filling vacancies relating to arbitrators appointed by him, the Chairman of the Administrative Council shall appoint a person from the Panel of Arbitrators:
   (a) to fill a vacancy caused by the resignation, without the consent of the Tribunal, of an arbitrator appointed by a party; or
   (b) at the request of either party, to fill any other vacancy, if no new appointment is made and accepted within 30 days of the notification of the vacancy by the Secretary-General.

(3) The procedure for filling a vacancy shall be in accordance with Rules 1, 4(4), 4(5), 5 and, *mutatis mutandis*, 6(2).

Rule 12   Resumption of Proceeding after Filling a Vacancy

As soon as a vacancy on the Tribunal has been filled, the proceeding shall continue from the point it had reached at the time the vacancy occurred. The newly appointed arbitrator may, however, require that the oral procedure be recommenced, if this had already been started.

CHAPTER II   WORKING OF THE TRIBUNAL

Rule 13   Sessions of the Tribunal

(1) The Tribunal shall hold its first session within 60 days after its constitution or such other period as the parties may agree. The dates of that session shall be fixed by the President of the Tribunal after consultation with its members and the Secretary-General. If upon its constitution the Tribunal has no President because the parties have agreed that the President shall be elected by its members, the Secretary-General shall fix the dates of that session. In both cases, the parties shall be consulted as far as possible.

(2) The dates of subsequent sessions shall be determined by the Tribunal, after consultation with the Secretary-General and with the parties as far as possible.

(3) The Tribunal shall meet at the seat of the Centre or at such other place as may have been agreed by the parties in accordance with Article 63 of the Convention. If the parties agree that the proceeding shall be held at a place other than the Centre or an institution with which the Centre has made the necessary arrangements, they shall consult with the Secretary-General and request the approval of the Tribunal. Failing such approval, the Tribunal shall meet at the seat of the Centre.

(4) The Secretary-General shall notify the members of the Tribunal and the parties of the dates and place of the sessions of the Tribunal in good time.

Rule 14   Sittings of the Tribunal

(1) The President of the Tribunal shall conduct its hearings and preside at its deliberations.

(2) Except as the parties otherwise agree, the presence of a majority of the members of the Tribunal shall be required at its sittings.

(3) The President of the Tribunal shall fix the date and hour of its sittings.

Rule 15   Deliberations of the Tribunal

(1) The deliberations of the Tribunal shall take place in private and remain secret.

(2) Only members of the Tribunal shall take part in its deliberations. No other person shall be admitted unless the Tribunal decides otherwise.

Rule 16   Decisions of the Tribunal

(1) Decisions of the Tribunal shall be taken by a majority of the votes of all its members. Abstention shall count as a negative vote.

(2) Except as otherwise provided by these Rules or decided by the Tribunal, it may take any decision by correspondence among its members, provided that all of them are consulted. Decisions so taken shall be certified by the President of the Tribunal.

Rule 17   Incapacity of the President

If at any time the President of the Tribunal should be unable to act, his functions shall be performed by one of the other members of the Tribunal, acting in the order in which the Secretary-General had received the notice of their acceptance of their appointment to the Tribunal.

Rule 18   Representation of the parties

(1) Each party may be represented or assisted by agents, counsel or advocates whose names and authority shall be notified by that party to the Secretary-General, who shall promptly inform the Tribunal and the other party.

(2) For the purposes of these Rules, the expression "party" includes, where the context so admits, an agent, counsel or advocate authorized to represent that party.

CHAPTER III   GENERAL PROCEDURAL PROVISIONS

Rule 19   Procedural Orders

The Tribunal shall make the orders required for the conduct of the proceeding.

Rule 20   Preliminary Procedural Consultation

(1) As early as possible after the constitution of a Tribunal, its President shall endeavor to ascertain the views of the parties regarding questions of procedure. For this purpose he may request the parties to meet him. He shall, in particular, seek their views on the following matters:
   (a) the number of members of the Tribunal required to constitute a quorum at its sittings;
   (b) the language or languages to be used in the proceeding;
   (c) the number and sequence of the pleadings and the time limits within which they are to be filed;
   (d) the number of copies desired by each party of instruments filed by the other;
   (e) dispensing with the written or the oral procedure;
   (f) the manner in which the cost of the proceeding is to be apportioned; and
   (g) the manner in which the record of the hearings shall be kept.

(2) In the conduct of the proceeding the Tribunal shall apply any agreement between the parties on procedural matters, except as otherwise provided in the Convention or the Administrative and Financial Regulations.

Rule 21   Pre-Hearing Conference

(1) At the request of the Secretary-General or at the discretion of the President of the Tribunal, a pre-hearing conference between the Tribunal and the parties may be held to arrange for an exchange of information and the stipulation of uncontested facts in order to expedite the proceeding.

(2) At the request of the parties, a pre-hearing conference between the Tribunal and the parties, duly represented by their authorized representatives, may be held to consider the issues in dispute with a view to reaching an amicable settlement.

Rule 22   Procedural Languages

(1) The parties may agree on the use of one or two languages to be used in the proceeding, provided, that, if they agree on any language that is not an official language of the Centre, the Tribunal, after consultation with the Secretary-General, gives its approval. If the parties do not agree on any such procedural language, each of them may select one of the official languages (i.e., English, French and Spanish) for this purpose.

(2) If two procedural languages are selected by the parties, any instruments may be filed in either language. Either language may be used at the hearings, subject, if the Tribunal so requires, to translation and interpretation. The orders and the award of the Tribunal shall be rendered and the record kept in both procedural languages, both versions being equally authentic.

Rule 23   Copies of Instruments

Except as otherwise provided by the Tribunal after consultation with the parties and the Secretary-General, every request, pleading, application, written observation, supporting documentation, if any, or other instrument shall be filed in the form of a signed original accompanied by the following number of additional copies:

(a) before the number of members of the Tribunal has been determined: five;

(b) after the number of members of the Tribunal has been determined: two more than the number of its members.

Rule 24   Supporting Documentation

Supporting documentation shall ordinarily be filed together with the instrument to which it relates, and in any case within the time limit fixed for the filing of such instrument.

Rule 25   Correction of Errors

An accidental error in any instrument or supporting document may, with the consent of the other party or by leave of the Tribunal, be corrected at any time before the award is rendered.

Rule 26   Time Limits

(1) Where required, time limits shall be fixed by the Tribunal by assigning dates for the completion of the various steps in the proceeding. The Tribunal may delegate this power to its President.

(2) The Tribunal may extend any time limit that it has fixed. If the Tribunal is not in session, this power shall be exercised by its President.

(3) Any step taken after expiration of the applicable time limit shall be disregarded unless the Tribunal, in special circumstances and after giving the other party an opportunity of stating its views, decides otherwise.

Rule 27   Waiver

A party which knows or should have known that a provision of the Administrative and Financial Regulations, of these Rules, of any other rules or agreement applicable to the proceeding, or of an order of the Tribunal has not been complied with and which fails to state promptly its objections thereto, shall be deemed—subject to Article 45 of the Convention—to have waived its right to object.

Rule 28   Cost of Proceeding

(1) Without prejudice to the final decision on the payment of the cost of the proceeding, the Tribunal may, unless otherwise agreed by the parties, decide:

(a) at any stage of the proceeding, the portion which each party shall pay, pursuant to Administrative and Financial Regulation 14, of the fees and expenses of the Tribunal and the charges for the use of the facilities of the Centre;

(b) with respect to any part of the proceeding, that the related costs (as determined by the Secretary-General) shall be borne entirely or in a particular share by one of the parties.

(2) Promptly after the closure of the proceeding, each party shall submit to the Tribunal a statement of costs reasonably incurred or borne by it in the proceeding and the Secretary-General shall submit to the Tribunal an account of all amounts paid by each party to the Centre and of all costs incurred by the Centre for the proceeding. The Tribunal may, before the award has been rendered, request the parties and the Secretary-General to provide additional information concerning the cost of the proceeding.

CHAPTER IV   WRITTEN AND ORAL PROCEDURES

Rule 29   Normal Procedures
Except if the parties otherwise agree, the proceeding shall comprise two distinct phases: a written procedure followed by an oral one.

Rule 30   Transmission of the Request
As soon as the Tribunal is constituted, the Secretary-General shall transmit to each member a copy of the request by which the proceeding was initiated, of the supporting documentation, of the notice of registration and of any communication received from either party in response thereto.

Rule 31   The Written Procedure
(1) In addition to the request for arbitration, the written procedure shall consist of the following pleadings, filed within time limits set by the Tribunal:
   (a) a memorial by the requesting party;
   (b) a counter-memorial by the other party; and, if the parties so agree or the Tribunal deems it necessary:
   (c) a reply by the requesting party; and
   (d) a rejoinder by the other party.

(2) If the request was made jointly, each party shall, within the same time limit determined by the Tribunal, file its memorial and, if the parties so agree or the Tribunal deems it necessary, its reply; however, the parties may instead agree that one of them shall, for the purposes of paragraph (1), be considered as the requesting party.

(3) A memorial shall contain: a statement of the relevant facts; a statement of law; and the submissions. A counter-memorial, reply or rejoinder shall contain an admission or denial of the facts stated in the last previous pleading; any additional facts, if necessary; observations concerning the statement of law in the last previous pleading; a statement of law in answer thereto; and the submissions.

Rule 32   The Oral Procedure
(1) The oral procedure shall consist of the hearing by the Tribunal of the parties, their agents, counsel and advocates, and of witnesses and experts.

(2) Unless either party objects, the Tribunal, after consultation with the Secretary-General, may allow other Persons, besides the parties, their agents, counsel and advocates, witnesses and experts during their testimony, and officers of the Tribunal, to attend or observe all or part of the hearings, subject to appropriate logistical arrangements. The Tribunal shall for such cases establish procedures for the protection of proprietary or privileged information.

(3) The members of the Tribunal may, during the hearings, put questions to the parties, their agents, counsel and advocates, and ask them for explanations.

Rule 33   Marshalling of Evidence

Without prejudice to the rules concerning the production of documents, each party shall, within time limits fixed by the Tribunal, communicate to the Secretary-General, for transmission to the Tribunal and the other party, precise information regarding the evidence which it intends to produce and that which it intends to request the Tribunal to call for, together with an indication of the points to which such evidence will be directed.

Rule 34   Evidence: General Principles

(1) The Tribunal shall be the judge of the admissibility of any evidence adduced and of its probative value.

(2) The Tribunal may, if it deems it necessary at any stage of the proceeding:
  (a) call upon the parties to produce documents, witnesses and experts; and
  (b) visit any place connected with the dispute or conduct inquiries there.

(3) The parties shall cooperate with the Tribunal in the production of the evidence and in the other measures provided for in paragraph (2). The Tribunal shall take formal note of the failure of a party to comply with its obligations under this paragraph and of any reasons given for such failure.

(4) Expenses incurred in producing evidence and in taking other measures in accordance with paragraph (2) shall be deemed to constitute part of the expenses incurred by the parties within the meaning of Article 61(2) of the Convention.

Rule 35   Examination of Witnesses and Experts

(1) Witnesses and experts shall be examined before the Tribunal by the parties under the control of its President. Questions may also be put to them by any member of the Tribunal.

(2) Each witness shall make the following declaration before giving his evidence:

"I solemnly declare upon my honour and conscience that I shall speak the truth, the whole truth and nothing but the truth."

(3) Each expert shall make the following declaration before making his statement:

"I solemnly declare upon my honour and conscience that my statement will be in accordance with my sincere belief."

Rule 36   Witnesses and Experts: Special Rules

Notwithstanding Rule 35 the Tribunal may:

(a) admit evidence given by a witness or expert in a written deposition; and

(b) with the consent of both parties, arrange for the examination of a witness or expert otherwise than before the Tribunal itself. The Tribunal shall define the subject of the examination, the time limit, the procedure to be followed and other particulars. The parties may participate in the examination.

Rule 37   Visits and Inquiries: Submissions of Non-disputing Parties

(1) If the Tribunal considers it necessary to visit any place connected with the dispute or to conduct an inquiry there, it shall make an order to this effect. The order shall define the scope of the visit or the subject of the inquiry, the time limit, the procedure to be followed and other particulars. The parties may participate in any visit or inquiry.

(2) After consulting both parties, the Tribunal may allow a person or entity that is not a party to the dispute (in this Rule called the "non-disputing party") to file a written submission with the Tribunal regarding a matter within the scope of the dispute. In determining whether to allow such a filing, the Tribunal shall consider, among other things, the extent to which:

(a) the non-disputing party submission would assist the Tribunal in the determination of a factual or legal issue related to the proceeding by bringing a perspective, particular knowledge or insight that is different from that of the disputing parties;

(b) the non-disputing party submission would address a matter within the scope of the dispute;

(c) the non-disputing party has a significant interest in the proceeding.

The Tribunal shall ensure that the non-disputing party submission does not disrupt the proceeding or unduly burden or unfairly prejudice either pary, and that both parties are given an opportunity to present their observations on the non-disputing party submission.

Rule 38 Closure of the Proceeding

(1) When the presentation of the case by the parties is completed, the proceeding shall be declared closed.

(2) Exceptionally, the Tribunal may, before the award has been rendered, reopen the proceeding on the ground that new evidence is forthcoming of such a nature as to constitute a decisive factor, or that there is a vital need for clarification on certain specific points.

CHAPTER V PARTICULAR PROCEDURES

Rule 39 Provisional Measures

(1) At any time during the proceeding a party may request that provisional measures for the presentation of its rights be recommended by the Tribunal. The request shall specify the rights to be preserved, the measures the recommendation of which is requested, and the circumstances that require such measures.

(2) The Tribunal shall give priority to the consideration of a request made pursuant to paragraph (1).

(3) The Tribunal may also recommend provisional measures on its own initiative or recommend measures other than those specified in a request. It may at any time modify or revoke its recommendations.

(4) The Tribunal shall only recommend provisional measures, or modify or revoke its recommendations, after giving each party an opportunity of presenting its observations.

(5) If a party makes a request pursuant to paragraph (1) before the constitution of the Tribunal, the Secretary-General shall, on the application of either party, fix time limits for the parties to present observations on the request, so that the request and observations may be considered by the Tribunal promptly upon its constitution.

(6) Nothing in this Rule shall prevent the parties, provided that they have so stipulated in the agreement recording their consent, from requesting any judicial or other authority to order provisional measures, prior to or after the institution of the proceeding, for the preservation of their respective rights and interests.

Rule 40 Ancillary claims

(1) Except as the parties otherwise agree, a party may present an incidental or additional claim or counter-claim arising directly out of the subject-matter of the dispute, provided that such ancillary claim is within the scope of the consent of the parties and is otherwise within the jurisdiction of the Centre.

(2) An incidental or additional claim shall be presented not later than in the reply and a counter-claim no later than in the counter-memorial, unless the Tribunal, upon justification by the party presenting the ancillary claim and upon considering any objection of the other party, authorizes the presentation of the claim at a later stage in the proceeding.

(3) The Tribunal shall fix a time limit within which the party against which an ancillary claim is presented may file its observations thereon.

Rule 41 Preliminary Objections

(1) Any objection that the dispute or any ancillary claim is not within the jurisdiction of the Centre or, for other reasons is not within the competence of the Tribunal shall be made as early as possible. A party shall file the objection with the Secretary-General no later than the expiration of the time limit fixed for the filing of the counter-memorial, or, if the objection relates to an ancillary claim, for the filing of the rejoinder—unless the facts on which the objection is based are unknown to the party at that time.

(2) The Tribunal may on its own initiative consider, at any stage of the proceeding, whether the dispute or any ancillary claim before it is within the jurisdiction of the Centre and within its own competence.

(3) Upon the formal raising of an objection relating to the dispute, the Tribunal may decide to suspend the proceeding on the merits. The President of the Tribunal, after consultation with its other members, shall fix a time limit within which the parties may file observations on the objection.

(4) The Tribunal shall decide whether or not the further procedures relating to the objection made pursuant to paragraph (1) shall be oral. It may deal with the objection as a preliminary question or join it to the merits of the dispute. If the Tribunal overrules the objection or joins it to the merits, it shall once more fix time limits for the further procedures.

(5) Unless the parties have agreed to another expedited procedure for making preliminary objections, a party may, no later than 30 days after the constitution of the Tribunal, and in any event before the first session of the Tribunal, file an objection that a claim is manifestly without legal merit. The party shall specify as precisely as possible the basis for the objection. The Tribunal, after giving the parties the opportunity to present their observations on the objection, shall, at its first session or promptly thereafter, notify the parties of its decision on the objection. The decision of the Tribunal shall be without prejudice to the right of a party to file an objection pursuant to paragraph (1) or to object, in the course of the proceeding, that a claim lacks legal merit.

(6) If the Tribunal decides that the dispute is not within the jurisdiction of the Center or not within its own competence, or that all claims are manifestly without legal merit, it shall render an award to that effect.

Rule 42   Default

(1) If a party (in this Rule called the "defaulting party") fails to appear or to present its case at any stage of the proceeding, the other party may, at any time prior to the discontinuance of the proceeding, request the Tribunal to deal with the questions submitted to it and to render an award.

(2) The Tribunal shall promptly notify the defaulting party of such a request. Unless it is satisfied that that party does not intend to appear or to present its case in the proceeding, it shall, at the same time, grant a period of grace and to this end:
   (a) if that party had failed to file a pleading or any other instrument within the time limit fixed therefor, fix a new time limit for its filing; or
   (b) if that party had failed to appear or present its case at a hearing, fix a new date for the hearing. The period of grace shall not, without the consent of the other party, exceed 60 days.

(3) After the expiration of the period of grace or when, in accordance with paragraph (2), no such period is granted, the Tribunal shall resume the consideration of the dispute. Failure of the defaulting party to appear or to present its case shall not be deemed an admission of the assertions made by the other party.

(4) The Tribunal shall examine the jurisdiction of the Centre and its own competence in the dispute and, if it is satisfied, decide whether the submissions made are well-founded in fact and in law. To this end, it may, at any stage of the proceeding, call on the party appearing to file observations, produce evidence or submit oral explanations.

Rule 43   Settlement and Discontinuance

(1) If, before the award is rendered, the parties agree on a settlement of the dispute or otherwise to discontinue the proceeding, the Tribunal, or the Secretary-General if the Tribunal has not yet been constituted, shall, at their written request, in an order take note of the discontinuance of the proceeding.

(2) If the parties file with the Secretary-General the full and signed text of their settlement and in writing request the Tribunal to embody such settlement in an award, the Tribunal may record the settlement in the form of its award.

Rule 44   Discontinuance at Request of a Party

If a party requests the discontinuance of the proceeding, the Tribunal, or the Secretary-General if the Tribunal has not yet been constituted, shall in an order fix a time limit within which the other party may state whether it opposes the discontinuance. If no objection is made in writing within the time limit, the other party shall be deemed to have acquiesced in the discontinuance and the Tribunal, or if appropriate the Secretary-General, shall in an order take note of the discontinuance of the proceeding. If objection is made, the proceeding shall continue.

Rule 45   Discontinuance for Failure of Parties to Act

If the parties fail to take any steps in the proceeding during six consecutive months or such period as they may agree with the approval of the Tribunal, or of the Secretary-General if the Tribunal has not yet been constituted, they shall be deemed to have discontinued the proceeding and the Tribunal, or if appropriate the Secretary-General, shall, after notice to the parties, in an order take note of the discontinuance.

CHAPTER VI   THE AWARD

Rule 46   Preparation of the Award

The award (including any individual or dissenting opinion) shall be drawn up and signed within 60 days after the closure of the proceeding. The Tribunal may, however, extend this period by a further 30 days if it would otherwise be unable to draw up the award.

Rule 47   The Award

(1) The award shall be in writing and shall contain:
   - (a) a precise designation of each party;
   - (b) a statement that the Tribunal was established under the Convention, and a description of the method of its constitution;
   - (c) the name of each member of the Tribunal, and an identification of the appointing authority of each;
   - (d) the names of the agents, counsel and advocates of the parties;
   - (e) the dates and place of the sittings of the Tribunal;
   - (f) a summary of the proceeding;
   - (g) a statement of the facts as found by the Tribunal;
   - (h) the submissions of the parties;
   - (i) the decision of the Tribunal on every question submitted to it, together with the reasons upon which the decision is based; and
   - (j) any decision of the Tribunal regarding the cost of the proceeding.

(2) The award shall be signed by the members of the Tribunal who voted for it; the date of each signature shall be indicated.

(3) Any member of the Tribunal may attach his individual opinion to the award, whether he dissents from the majority or not, or a statement of his dissent.

Rule 48   Rendering of the Award

(1) Upon signature by the last arbitrator to sign, the Secretary-General shall promptly:
   - (a) authenticate the original text of the award and deposit it in the archives of the Centre, together with any individual opinions and statements of dissent; and
   - (b) dispatch a certified copy of the award (including individual opinions and statements of dissent) to each party, indicating the date of dispatch on the original text and on all copies.

(2) The award shall be deemed to have been rendered on the date on which the certified copies were dispatched.

(3) The Secretary-General shall, upon request, make available to a party additional certified copies of the award.

(4) The Centre shall not publish the award without consent of the parties. The Centre shall, however, promptly include in its publications excerpts of the legal reasoning of the Tribunal.

Rule 49 Supplementary Decisions and Rectification

(1) Within 45 days after the date on which the award was rendered, either party may request, pursuant to Article 49(2) of the Convention, a supplementary decision on, or the rectification of, the award. Such a request shall be addressed in writing to the Secretary-General. The request shall:

   (a) identify the award to which it relates;

   (b) indicate the date of the request;

   (c) state in detail:

      (i) any question which, in the opinion of the requesting party, the Tribunal omitted to decide in the award; and

      (ii) any error in the award which the requesting party seeks to have rectified; and

   (d) be accompanied by a fee for lodging the request.

(2) Upon receipt of the request and of the lodging fee, the Secretary-General shall forthwith:

   (a) register the request;

   (b) notify the parties of the registration;

   (c) transmit to the other party a copy of the request and of any accompanying documentation; and

   (d) transmit to each member of the Tribunal a copy of the notice of registration, together with a copy of the request and of any accompanying documentation.

(3) The President of the Tribunal shall consult the members on whether it is necessary for the Tribunal to meet in order to consider the request. The Tribunal shall fix a time limit for the parties to file their observations on the request and shall determine the procedure for its consideration.

(4) Rules 46–48 shall apply, *mutatis mutandis*, to any decision of the Tribunal pursuant to this Rule.

(5) If a request is received by the Secretary-General more than 45 days after the award was rendered, he shall refuse to register the request and so inform forthwith the requesting party.

CHAPTER VII INTERPRETATION, REVISION AND ANNULMENT OF THE AWARD

Rule 50 The Application

(1) An application for the interpretation, revision or annulment of an award shall be addressed in writing to the Secretary-General and shall:

   (a) identify the award to which it relates;

   (b) indicate the date of the application;

   (c) state in detail:

      (i) in an application for interpretation, the precise points in dispute;

      (ii) in an application for revision, pursuant to Article 51(1) of the Convention, the change sought in the award, the discovery of some fact of such a nature as decisively to affect the award, and evidence that when the award was rendered that fact was unknown to the Tribunal and to the applicant, and that the applicant's ignorance of that fact was not due to negligence;

      (iii) in an application for annulment, pursuant to Article 52(1) of the Convention, the grounds on which it is based. These grounds are limited to the following:

        – that the Tribunal was not properly constituted;

        – that the Tribunal has manifestly exceeded its powers;

        – that there was corruption on the part of a member of the Tribunal;

        – that there has been a serious departure from a fundamental rule of procedure;

        – that the award has failed to state the reasons on which it is based;

   (d) be accompanied by the payment of a fee for lodging the application.

(2) Without prejudice to the provisions of paragraph (3), upon receiving an application and the lodging fee, the Secretary-General shall forthwith:
  (a) register the application;
  (b) notify the parties of the registration; and
  (c) transmit to the other party a copy of the application and of any accompanying documentation.

(3) The Secretary-General shall refuse to register an application for:
  (a) revision, if, in accordance with Article 51(2) of the Convention, it is not made within 90 days after the discovery of the new fact and in any event within three years after the date on which the award was rendered (or any subsequent decision or correction);
  (b) annulment, if, in accordance with Article 52(2) of the Convention, it is not made:
    (i) within 120 days after the date on which the award was rendered (or any subsequent decision or correction) if the application is based on any of the following grounds:
      – the Tribunal was not properly constituted;
      – the Tribunal has manifestly exceeded its powers;
      – there has been a serious departure from a fundamental rule of procedure;
      – the award has failed to state the reasons on which it is based;
    (ii) in the case of corruption on the part of a member of the Tribunal, within 120 days after discovery thereof, and in any event within three years after the date on which the award was rendered (or any subsequent decision or correction).

(4) If the Secretary-General refuses to register an application for revision, or annulment, he shall forthwith notify the requesting party of his refusal.

Rule 51   Interpretation or Revision: Further Procedures

(1) Upon registration of an application for the interpretation or revision of an award, the Secretary-General shall forthwith:
  (a) transmit to each member of the original Tribunal a copy of the notice of registration, together with a copy of the application and of any accompanying documentation; and
  (b) request each member of the Tribunal to inform him within a specified time limit whether that member is willing to take part in the consideration of the application.

(2) If all members of the Tribunal express their willingness to take part in the consideration of the application, the Secretary-General shall so notify the members of the Tribunal and the parties. Upon dispatch of these notices the Tribunal shall be deemed to be reconstituted.

(3) If the Tribunal cannot be constituted in accordance with paragraph (2), the Secretary-General shall so notify the parties and invite them to proceed, as soon as possible, to constitute a new Tribunal, including the same number of arbitrators, and appointed by the same method, as the original one.

Rule 52   Annulment: Further Procedures

(1) Upon registration of an application for the annulment of an award, the Secretary-General shall forthwith request the Chairman of the Administrative Council to appoint an *ad hoc* Committee in accordance with Article 52(3) of the Convention.

(2) The Committee shall be deemed to be constituted on the date the Secretary-General notifies the parties that all members have accepted their appointment. Before or at the first session of the Committee, each member shall sign a declaration conforming to that set forth in Rule 6(2).

Rule 53   Rules of Procedure

The provisions of these Rules shall apply *mutatis mutandis* to any procedure relating to the interpretation, revision or annulment of an award and to the decision of the Tribunal or Committee.

Rule 54   Stay of Enforcement of the Award

(1) The party applying for the interpretation, revision or annulment of an award may in its application, and either party may at any time before the final disposition of the application,

request a stay in the enforcement of part or all of the award to which the application relates. The Tribunal or Committee shall give priority to the consideration of such a request.

(2) If an application for the revision or annulment of an award contains a request for a stay of its enforcement, the Secretary-General shall, together with the notice of registration, inform both parties of the provisional stay of the award. As soon as the Tribunal or Committee is constituted it shall, if either party requests, rule within 30 days on whether such stay should be continued; unless it decides to continue the stay, it shall automatically be terminated.

(3) If a stay of enforcement has been granted pursuant to paragraph (1) or continued pursuant to paragraph (2), the Tribunal or Committee may at any time modify or terminate the stay at the request of either party. All stays shall automatically terminate on the date on which a final decision is rendered on the application, except that a Committee granting the partial annulment of an award may order the temporary stay of enforcement of the unannulled portion in order to give either party an opportunity to request any new Tribunal constituted pursuant to Article 52(6) of the Convention to grant a stay pursuant to Rule 55(3).

(4) A request pursuant to paragraph (1), (2) (second sentence) or (3) shall specify the circumstances that require the stay or its modification or termination. A request shall only be granted after the Tribunal or Committee has given each party an opportunity of presenting its observations.

(5) The Secretary-General shall promptly notify both parties of the stay of enforcement of any award and of the modification or termination of such a stay, which shall become effective on the date on which he dispatches such notification.

Rule 55   Resubmission of dispute after an annulment

(1) If a Committee annuls part or all of an award, either party may request the resubmission of the dispute to a new Tribunal. Such a request shall be addressed in writing to the Secretary-General and shall:
   (a) identify the award to which it relates;
   (b) indicate the date of the request;
   (c) explain in detail what aspect of the dispute is to be submitted to the Tribunal; and
   (d) be accompanied by a fee for lodging the request.

(2) Upon receipt of the request and of the lodging fee, the Secretary-General shall forthwith:
   (a) register it in the Arbitration Register;
   (b) notify both parties of the registration;
   (c) transmit to the other party a copy of the request and of any accompanying documentation; and
   (d) invite the parties to proceed, as soon as possible, to constitute a new Tribunal, including the same number of arbitrators, and appointed by the same method, as the original one.

(3) If the original award had only been annulled in part, the new Tribunal shall not reconsider any portion of the award not so annulled. It may, however, in accordance with the procedures set forth in Rule 54, stay or continue to stay the enforcement of the unannulled portion of the award until the date its own award is rendered.

(4) Except as otherwise provided in paragraphs (1)–(3), these Rules shall apply to a proceeding on a resubmitted dispute in the same manner as if such dispute had been submitted pursuant to the Institution Rules.

CHAPTER VIII   GENERAL PROVISIONS

Rule 56 Final Provisions

(1) The texts of these Rules in each official language of the Centre shall be equally authentic.

(2) These Rules may be cited as the "Arbitration Rules" of the Centre.

Rules Governing the Additional Facility for the Administration of Proceedings by the Secretariat of the International Centre for Settlement of Investment Disputes ('ICSID Additional Facility Rules')

Date   10 April 2006
Source ICSID (ed), *ICSID Additional Facility Rules* (Doc ICSID/11, April 2006)
Link   <http://icsid.worldbank.org/ICSID/StaticFiles/facility/AFR_English-final.pdf>

Article 1   Definitions

(1) "Convention" means the Convention on the Settlement of Investment Disputes between States and Nationals of Other States, submitted to Governments by the Executive Directors of the International Bank for Reconstruction and Development on March 18, 1965, which entered into force on October 14, 1966.

(2) "Centre" means the International Centre for Settlement of Investment Disputes established pursuant to Article 1 of the Convention.

(3) "Secretariat" means the Secretariat of the Centre.

(4) "Contracting State" means a State for which the Convention has entered into force.

(5) "Secretary-General" means the Secretary-General of the Centre or his deputy.

(6) "National of another State" means a person who is not, or whom the parties to the proceeding in question have agreed not to treat as, a national of the State party to that proceeding.

Article 2   Additional Facility

The Secretariat of the Centre is hereby authorized to administer, subject to and in accordance with these Rules, proceedings between a State (or a constituent subdivision or agency of a State) and a national of another State, falling within the following categories:

(a) conciliation and arbitration proceedings for the settlement of legal disputes arising directly out of an investment which are not within the jurisdiction of the Centre because either the State party to the dispute or the State whose national is a party to the dispute is not a Contracting State;

(b) conciliation and arbitration proceedings for the settlement of legal disputes which are not within the jurisdiction of the Centre because they do not arise directly out of an investment, provided that either the State party to the dispute or the State whose national is a party to the dispute is a Contracting State; and

(c) fact-finding proceedings.

The administration of proceedings authorized by these Rules is hereinafter referred to as the Additional Facility.

Article 3   Convention Not Applicable

Since the proceedings envisaged by Article 2 are outside the jurisdiction of the Centre, none of the provisions of the Convention shall be applicable to them or to recommendations, awards, or reports which may be rendered therein.

Article 4   Access to the Additional Facility in Respect of Conciliation and Arbitration Proceedings Subject to Secretary-General's Approval

(1) Any agreement providing for conciliation or arbitration proceedings under the Additional Facility in respect of existing or future disputes requires the approval of the Secretary-General. The parties may apply for such approval at any time prior to the institution of proceedings by submitting to the Secretariat a copy of the agreement concluded or proposed to be concluded between them together with other relevant documentation and such additional information as the Secretariat may reasonably request.

(2) In the case of an application based on Article 2(a), the Secretary-General shall give his approval only if (a) he is satisfied that the requirements of that provision are fulfilled at the time, and (b) both parties give their consent to the jurisdiction of the Centre under Article 25 of the Convention (in lieu of the Additional Facility) in the event that the jurisdictional requirements *ratione personae* of that Article shall have been met at the time when proceedings are instituted.

(3) In the case of an application based on Article 2(b), the Secretary-General shall give his approval only if he is satisfied (a) that the requirements of that provision are fulfilled, and (b) that the underlying transaction has features which distinguish it from an ordinary commercial transaction.

(4) If in the case of an application based on Article 2(b) the jurisdictional requirements *ratione personae* of Article 25 of the Convention shall have been met and the Secretary-General is of the opinion that it is likely that a Conciliation Commission or Arbitral Tribunal, as the case may be, will hold that the dispute arises directly out of an investment, he may make his approval of the application conditional upon consent by both parties to submit any dispute in the first instance to the jurisdiction of the Centre.

(5) The Secretary-General shall as soon as possible notify the parties whether he approves or disapproves the agreement of the parties. He may hold discussions with the parties or invite the parties to a meeting with the officials of the Secretariat either at the parties' request or at his own initiative. The Secretary-General shall, upon the request of the parties or any of them, keep confidential any or all information furnished to him by such parties or party in connection with the provisions of this Article.

(6) The Secretary-General shall record his approval of an agreement pursuant to this Article together with the names and addresses of the parties in a register to be maintained at the Secretariat for that purpose.

Article 5   Administrative and Financial Provisions

The responsibilities of the Secretariat in operating the Additional Facility and the financial provisions regarding its operation shall be as those established by the Administrative and Financial Regulations of the Centre for conciliation and arbitration proceedings under the Convention. Accordingly, Regulations 14 through 16, 22 through 30 and 34(1) of the Administrative and Financial Regulations of the Centre shall apply, *mutatis mutandis*, in respect of fact-finding, conciliation and arbitration proceedings under the Additional Facility.

Article 6   Schedules

Fact-finding, conciliation and arbitration proceedings under the Additional Facility shall be conducted in accordance with the respective Fact-finding (Additional Facility), Conciliation (Additional Facility) and Arbitration (Additional Facility) Rules set forth in Schedules A, B and C.

SCHEDULES

[Schedules A and B not reproduced]

SCHEDULE C   ARBITRATION (ADDITIONAL FACILITY) RULES

CHAPTER I   INTRODUCTION

Article 1   Scope of Application

Where the parties to a dispute have agreed that it shall be referred to arbitration under the Arbitration (Additional Facility) Rules, the dispute shall be settled in accordance with these Rules, save that if any of these Rules is in conflict with a provision of the law applicable to the arbitration from which the parties cannot derogate, that provision shall prevail.

CHAPTER II   INSTITUTION OF PROCEEDINGS

Article 2   The Request

(1) Any State or any national of a State wishing to institute arbitration proceedings shall send a request to that effect in writing to the Secretariat at the seat of the Centre. It shall be drawn up in an official language of the Centre, shall be dated and shall be signed by the requesting party or its duly authorized representative.

(2) The request may be made jointly by the parties to the dispute.

Article 3   Contents of the Request

(1) The request shall:
  (a) designate precisely each party to the dispute and state the address of each;
  (b) set forth the relevant provisions embodying the agreement of the parties to refer the dispute to arbitration;
  (c) indicate the date of approval by the Secretary-General pursuant to Article 4 of the Additional Facility Rules of the agreement of the parties providing for access to the Additional Facility;
  (d) contain information concerning the issues in dispute and an indication of the amount involved, if any; and
  (e) state, if the requesting party is a juridical person, that it has taken all necessary internal actions to authorize the request.

(2) The request may in addition set forth any provisions agreed by the parties regarding the number of arbitrators and the method of their appointment, as well as any other provisions agreed concerning the settlement of the dispute.

(3) The request shall be accompanied by five additional signed copies and by the fee prescribed pursuant to Regulation 16 of the Administrative and Financial Regulation of the Centre.

Article 4   Registration of the Request

As soon as the Secretary-General shall have satisfied himself that the request conforms in form and substance to the provisions of Article 3 of these Rules, he shall register the request in the Arbitration (Additional Facility) Register and on the same day dispatch to the parties a notice of registration. He shall also transmit a copy of the request and of the accompanying documentation (if any) to the other party to the dispute.

Article 5   Notice of Registration

The notice of registration of a request shall:

(a) record that the request is registered and indicate the date of the registration and of the dispatch of the notice;

(b) notify each party that all communications in connection with the proceeding will be sent to the address stated in the request, unless another address is indicated to the Secretariat;

(c) unless such information has already been provided, invite the parties to communicate to the Secretary-General any provisions agreed by them regarding the number and the method of appointment of the arbitrators;

(d) remind the parties that the registration of the request is without prejudice to the powers and functions of the Arbitral Tribunal in regard to competence and the merits; and

(e) invite the parties to proceed, as soon as possible, to constitute an Arbitral Tribunal in accordance with Chapter III of these Rules.

CHAPTER III   THE TRIBUNAL

Article 6   General Provisions

(1) In the absence of agreement between the parties regarding the number of arbitrators and the method of their appointment, the Tribunal shall consist of three arbitrators, one arbitrator appointed by each party and the third, who shall be the President of the Tribunal, appointed by agreement of the parties, all in accordance with Article 9 of these Rules.

(2) Upon the dispatch of the notice of registration of the request for arbitration, the parties shall promptly proceed to constitute a Tribunal.

(3) The Tribunal shall consist of a sole arbitrator or any uneven number of arbitrators appointed as the parties shall agree.

(4) If the Tribunal shall not have been constituted within 90 days after the notice of registration of the request for arbitration has been dispatched by the Secretary-General, or such other period as the parties may agree, the Chairman of the Administrative Council (hereinafter called the "Chairman") shall, at the request in writing of either party transmitted through the Secretary-General, appoint the arbitrator or arbitrators not yet appointed and, unless the President shall already have been designated or is to be designated later, designate an arbitrator to be President of the Tribunal.

(5) Except as the parties shall otherwise agree, no person who had previously acted as a conciliator or arbitrator in any proceeding for the settlement of the dispute or as a member of any fact-finding committee relating thereto may be appointed as a member of the Tribunal.

Article 7   Nationality of Arbitrators

(1) The majority of the arbitrators shall be nationals of States other than the State party to the dispute and of the State whose national is a party to the dispute, unless the sole arbitrator or each individual member of the Tribunal is appointed by agreement of the parties. Where the Tribunal is to consist of three members, a national of either of these States may not be appointed as an arbitrator by a party without the agreement of the other party to the dispute. Where the Tribunal is to consist of five or more members, nationals of either of these States may not be appointed as arbitrators by a party if appointment by the other party of the same number of arbitrators of either of these nationalities would result in a majority of arbitrators of these nationalities.

(2) Arbitrators appointed by the Chairman shall not be nationals of the State party to the dispute or of the State whose national is a party to the dispute.

Article 8   Qualifications of Arbitrators

Arbitrators shall be persons of high moral character and recognized competence in the fields of law, commerce, industry or finance, who may be relied upon to exercise independent judgment.

**Article 9   Method of Constituting the Tribunal in the Absence of Agreement
Between the Parties**

(1) If the parties have not agreed upon the number of arbitrators and the method of their appointment within 60 days after the registration of the request, the Secretary-General shall, upon the request of either party promptly inform the parties that the Tribunal is to be constituted in accordance with the following procedure:

   (a) either party shall, in a communication to the other party:

      (i) name two persons, identifying one of them, who shall not have the same nationality as nor be a national of either party, as the arbitrator appointed by it, and the other as the arbitrator proposed to be the President of the Tribunal; and

      (ii) invite the other party to concur in the appointment of the arbitrator proposed to be the President of the Tribunal and to appoint another arbitrator;

   (b) promptly upon receipt of this communication the other party shall, in its reply:

      (i) name a person as the arbitrator appointed by it, who shall not have the same nationality as nor be a national of either party; and

      (ii) concur in the appointment of the arbitrator proposed to be the President of the Tribunal or name another person as the arbitrator proposed to be President; and

   (c) promptly upon receipt of the reply containing such a proposal, the initiating party shall notify the other party whether it concurs in the appointment of the arbitrator proposed by that party to be the President of the Tribunal.

(2) The communications provided for in paragraph (1) of this Article shall be made or promptly confirmed in writing and shall either be transmitted through the Secretary-General or directly between the parties with a copy to the Secretary-General.

**Article 10   Appointment of Arbitrators and Designation of President of Tribunal by the
Chairman of the Administrative Council**

(1) Promptly upon receipt of a request by a party to the Chairman to make an appointment or designation pursuant to Article 6(4) of these Rules, the Secretary-General shall send a copy thereof to the other party.

(2) The Chairman shall use his best efforts to comply with that request within 30 days after its receipt. Before he proceeds to make appointments or a designation, he shall consult both parties as far as possible.

(3) The Secretary-General shall promptly notify the parties of any appointment or designation made by the Chairman.

Article 11   Acceptance of Appointments

(1) The party or parties concerned shall notify the Secretary-General of the appointment of each arbitrator and indicate the method of his appointment.

(2) As soon as the Secretary-General has been informed by a party or the Chairman of the appointment of an arbitrator, he shall seek an acceptance from the appointee.

(3) If an arbitrator fails to accept his appointment within 15 days, the Secretary-General shall promptly notify the parties, and if appropriate the Chairman, and invite them to proceed to the appointment of another arbitrator in accordance with the method followed for the previous appointment.

Article 12   Replacement of Arbitrators prior to Constitution of the Tribunal

At any time before the Tribunal is constituted, each party may replace any arbitrator appointed by it and the parties may by common consent agree to replace any arbitrator.

Article 13   Constitution of the Tribunal

(1) The Tribunal shall be deemed to be constituted and the proceeding to have begun on the date the Secretary-General notifies the parties that all the arbitrators have accepted their appointment.

(2) Before or at the first session of the Tribunal, each arbitrator shall sign a declaration in the following form:

> "To the best of my knowledge there is no reason why I should not serve on the Arbitral Tribunal constituted with respect to a dispute between _____ and _____.
>
> "I shall keep confidential all information coming to my knowledge as a result of my participation in this proceeding, as well as the contents of any award made by the Tribunal.
>
> "I shall judge fairly as between the parties and shall not accept any instruction or compensation with regard to the proceeding from any source except as provided in the Administrative and Financial Regulations of the Centre.
>
> "Attached is a statement of (a) my past and present professional, business and other relationships (if any) with the parties and (b) any other circumstance that might cause my reliability for independent judgment to be questioned by a party. I acknowledge that by signing this declaration, I assume a continuing obligation promptly to notify the Secretary-General of the Centre of any such relationship or circumstance that subsequently arises during this proceeding."

Any arbitrator failing to sign such a declaration by the end of the first session of the Tribunal shall be deemed to have resigned.

Article 14   Replacement of Arbitrators after Constitution of the Tribunal

(1) After a Tribunal has been constituted and proceedings have begun, its composition shall remain unchanged; provided, however, that if an arbitrator should die, become incapacitated, resign or be disqualified, the resulting vacancy shall be filled as provided in this Article and Article 17 of these Rules.

(2) If an arbitrator becomes incapacitated or unable to perform the duties of his office, the procedure in respect of the disqualification of arbitrators set forth in Article 15 shall apply.

(3) An arbitrator may resign by submitting his resignation to the other members of the Tribunal and the Secretary-General. If the arbitrator was appointed by one of the parties, the Tribunal shall promptly consider the reasons for his resignation and decide whether it consents thereto. The Tribunal shall promptly notify the Secretary-General of its decision.

Article 15   Disqualification of Arbitrators

(1) A party may propose to a Tribunal the disqualification of any of its members on account of any fact indicating a manifest lack of the qualities required by Article 8 of these Rules, or on the ground that he was ineligible for appointment to the Tribunal under Article 7 of these Rules.

(2) A party proposing the disqualification of an arbitrator shall promptly, and in any event before the proceeding is declared closed, file its proposal with the Secretary-General, stating its reasons therefor.

(3) The Secretary-General shall forthwith:
   (a) transmit the proposal to the members of the Tribunal and, if it relates to a sole arbitrator or to a majority of the members of the Tribunal, to the Chairman; and
   (b) notify the other party of the proposal.

(4) The arbitrator to whom the proposal relates may, without delay, furnish explanations to the Tribunal or the Chairman, as the case may be.

(5) The decision on any proposal to disqualify an arbitrator shall be taken by the other members of the Tribunal except that where those members are equally divided, or in the case of a

proposal to disqualify a sole arbitrator, or a majority of the arbitrators, the Chairman shall take that decision.

(6) Whenever the Chairman has to decide on a proposal to disqualify an arbitrator, he shall use his best efforts to take that decision within 30 days after he has received the proposal.

(7) The proceeding shall be suspended until a decision has been taken on the proposal.

Article 16   Procedure during a Vacancy on the Tribunal

(1) The Secretary-General shall forthwith notify the parties and, if necessary, the Chairman of the disqualification, death, incapacity or resignation of an arbitrator and of the consent, if any, of the Tribunal to a resignation.

(2) Upon the notification by the Secretary-General of a vacancy on the Tribunal, the proceeding shall be or remain suspended until the vacancy has been filled.

Article 17   Filling Vacancies on the Tribunal

(1) Except as provided in paragraph (2) of this Article, a vacancy resulting from the disqualification, death, incapacity or resignation of an arbitrator shall be promptly filled by the same method by which his appointment had been made.

(2) In addition to filling vacancies relating to arbitrators appointed by him, the Chairman shall:
    (a) fill a vacancy caused by the resignation, without the consent of the Tribunal, of an arbitrator appointed by a party; or
    (b) at the request of either party, fill any other vacancy, if no new appointment is made and accepted within 45 days of the notification of the vacancy by the Secretary-General.

(3) In filling a vacancy the party or the Chairman, as the case may be, shall observe the provisions of these Rules with respect to the appointment of arbitrators. Article 13(2) of these Rules shall apply *mutatis mutandis* to the newly appointed arbitrator.

Article 18   Resumption of Proceeding after Filling a Vacancy

As soon as a vacancy on the Tribunal has been filled, the proceeding shall continue from the point it had reached at the time the vacancy occurred. The newly appointed arbitrator may, however, require that the oral procedure be recommenced, if this had already been started.

CHAPTER IV   PLACE OF ARBITRATION

Article 19   Limitation on Choice of Forum

Arbitration proceedings shall be held only in States that are parties to the 1958 UN Convention on the Recognition and Enforcement of Foreign Arbitral Awards.

Article 20   Determination of Place of Arbitration

(1) Subject to Article 19 of these Rules the place of arbitration shall be determined by the Arbitral Tribunal after consultation with the parties and the Secretariat.

(2) The Arbitral Tribunal may meet at any place it deems appropriate for the inspection of goods, other property or documents. It may also visit any place connected with the dispute or conduct inquiries there. The parties shall be given sufficient notice to enable them to be present at such inspection or visit.

(3) The award shall be made at the place of arbitration.

CHAPTER V   WORKING OF THE TRIBUNAL

Article 21   Sessions of the Tribunal

(1) The Tribunal shall meet for its first session within 60 days after its constitution or such other period as the parties may agree. The dates of that session shall be fixed by the President of the Tribunal after consultation with its members and the Secretariat, and with the parties as far as

possible. If, upon its constitution, the Tribunal has no President, such dates shall be fixed by the Secretary-General after consultation with the members of the Tribunal, and with the parties as far as possible.

(2) Subsequent sessions shall be convened by the President within time limits determined by the Tribunal. The dates of such sessions shall be fixed by the President of the Tribunal after consultation with its members and the Secretariat, and with the parties as far as possible.

(3) The Secretary-General shall notify the members of the Tribunal and the parties of the dates and place of the sessions of the Tribunal in good time.

Article 22   Sittings of the Tribunal

(1) The President of the Tribunal shall conduct its hearings and preside at its deliberations.

(2) Except as the parties otherwise agree, the presence of a majority of the members of the Tribunal shall be required at its sittings.

(3) The President of the Tribunal shall fix the date and hour of its sittings.

Article 23   Deliberations of the Tribunal

(1) The deliberations of the Tribunal shall take place in private and remain secret.

(2) Only members of the Tribunal shall take part in its deliberations. No other person shall be admitted unless the Tribunal decides otherwise.

Article 24   Decisions of the Tribunal

(1) Any award or other decision of the Tribunal shall be made by a majority of the votes of all its members. Abstention by any member of the Tribunal shall count as a negative vote.

(2) Except as otherwise provided by these Rules or decided by the Tribunal, it may take any decisions by correspondence among its members, provided that all of them are consulted. Decisions so taken shall be certified by the President of the Tribunal.

Article 25   Incapacity of the President

If at any time the President of the Tribunal should be unable to act, his functions shall be performed by one of the other members of the Tribunal, acting in the order in which the Secretariat had received the notice of their acceptance of their appointment to the Tribunal.

Article 26   Representation of the Parties

(1) Each party may be represented or assisted by agents, counsel or advocates whose names and authority shall be notified by that party to the Secretariat, which shall promptly inform the Tribunal and the other party.

(2) For the purposes of these Rules, the expression "party" includes, where the context so admits, an agent, counsel or advocate authorized to represent that party.

CHAPTER VI   GENERAL PROCEDURAL PROVISIONS

Article 27   Procedural Orders

The Tribunal shall make the orders required for the conduct of the proceeding.

Article 28   Preliminary Procedural Consultation

(1) As early as possible after the constitution of a Tribunal, its President shall endeavor to ascertain the views of the parties regarding questions of procedure. For this purpose he may request the parties to meet him. He shall, in particular, seek their views on the following matters:

    (a) the number of members of the Tribunal required to constitute a quorum at its sittings;

    (b) the language or languages to be used in the proceeding;

    (c) the number and sequence of the pleadings and the time limits within which they are to be filed;

    (d) the number of copies desired by each party of instruments filed by the other;

    (e) dispensing with the written or oral procedure;

    (f) the manner in which the cost of the proceeding is to be apportioned; and

    (g) the manner in which the record of the hearings shall be kept.

(2) In the conduct of the proceeding the Tribunal shall apply any agreement between the parties on procedural matters, which is not inconsistent with any provisions of the Additional Facility Rules and the Administrative and Financial Regulations of the Centre.

Article 29 Pre-Hearing Conference

(1) At the request of the Secretary-General or at the discretion of the President of the Tribunal, a pre-hearing conference between the Tribunal and the parties may be held to arrange for an exchange of information and the stipulation of uncontested facts in order to expedite the proceeding.

(2) At the request of the parties, a pre-hearing conference between the Tribunal and the parties, duly represented by their authorized representatives, may be held to consider the issues in dispute with a view to reaching an amicable settlement.

Article 30 Procedural Languages

(1) The parties may agree on the use of one or two languages to be used in the proceeding, provided that if they agree on any language that is not an official language of the Centre, the Tribunal, after consultation with the Secretary-General, gives its approval. If the parties do not agree on any such procedural language, each of them may select one of the official languages (i.e., English, French and Spanish) for this purpose. Notwithstanding the foregoing, one of the official languages of the Centre shall be used for all communications to and from the Secretariat.

(2) If two procedural languages are selected by the parties, any instrument may be filed in either language. Either language may be used at the hearing subject, if the Tribunal so requires, to translation and interpretation. The orders and the award of the Tribunal shall be rendered and the record kept in both procedural languages, both versions being equally authentic.

Article 31 Copies of Instruments

Except as otherwise provided by the Tribunal after consultation with the parties and the Secretariat, every request, pleading, application, written observation or other instrument shall be filed in the form of a signed original accompanied by the following number of additional copies:

(a) before the number of members of the Tribunal has been determined: five; and

(b) after the number of members of the Tribunal has been determined: two more than the number of its members.

Article 32 Supporting Documentation

Supporting documentation shall ordinarily be filed together with the instrument to which it relates, and in any case within the time limit fixed for the filing of such instrument.

Article 33 Time Limits

(1) Where required, time limits shall be fixed by the Tribunal by assigning dates for the completion of the various steps in the proceeding. The Tribunal may delegate this power to its President.

(2) The Tribunal may extend any time limit that it has fixed. If the Tribunal is not in session, this power shall be exercised by its President.

(3) Any step taken after expiration of the applicable time limit shall be disregarded unless the Tribunal, in special circumstances and after giving the other party an opportunity of stating its views, decides otherwise.

Article 34   Waiver

A party which knows or ought to have known that a provision of these Rules, of any other rules or agreement applicable to the proceeding, or of an order of the Tribunal has not been complied with and which fails to state promptly its objections thereto, shall be deemed to have waived the right to object.

Article 35   Filling of Gaps

If any question of procedure arises which is not covered by these Rules or any rules agreed by the parties, the Tribunal shall decide the question.

CHAPTER VII   WRITTEN AND ORAL PROCEDURES

Article 36   Normal Procedures

Except if the parties otherwise agree, the proceeding shall comprise two distinct phases: a written procedure followed by an oral one.

Article 37   Transmission of the Request

As soon as the Tribunal is constituted, the Secretary-General shall transmit to each member of the Tribunal a copy of the request by which the proceeding was commenced, of the supporting documentation, of the notice of registration of the request and of any communication received from either party in response thereto.

Article 38   The Written Procedure

(1) In addition to the request for arbitration, the written procedure shall consist of the following pleadings, filed within time limits set by the Tribunal:
   (a) a memorial by the requesting party;
   (b) a counter-memorial by the other party;
   and, if the parties so agree or the Tribunal deems it necessary:
   (c) a reply by the requesting party; and
   (d) a rejoinder by the other party.

(2) If the request was made jointly, each party shall, within the same time limit determined by the Tribunal, file its memorial. However, the parties may instead agree that one of them shall, for the purposes of paragraph (1) of this Article, be considered as the requesting party.

(3) A memorial shall contain: a statement of the relevant facts; a statement of law; and the submissions. A counter-memorial, reply or rejoinder shall contain an admission or denial of the facts stated in the last previous pleading; any additional facts, if necessary; observations concerning the statement of law in the last previous pleading; a statement of law in answer thereto; and the submissions.

Article 39   The Oral Procedure

(1) The oral procedure shall consist of the hearing by the Tribunal of the parties, their agents, counsel and advocates, and of witnesses and experts.

(2) Unless either party objects, the Tribunal, after consultation with the Secretary-General, may allow other persons, besides the parties, their agents, counsel and advocates, witnesses and experts during their testimony, and officers of the Tribunal, to attend or observe all or part of the hearings, subject to appropriate logistical arrangements. The Tribunal shall for such cases establish procedures for the protection of proprietary or privileged information.

(3) The members of the Tribunal may, during the hearings, put questions to the parties, their agents, counsel and advocates, and ask them for explanations.

Article 40   Marshalling of Evidence

Without prejudice to the rules concerning the production of documents, each party shall, within time limits fixed by the Tribunal, communicate to the Secretary-General, for transmission to the

Tribunal and the other party, precise information regarding the evidence which it intends to produce and that which it intends to request the Tribunal to call for, together with an indication of the points to which such evidence will be directed.

Article 41   Evidence: General Principles

(1) The Tribunal shall be the judge of the admissibility of any evidence adduced and of its probative value.

(2) The Tribunal may, if it deems it necessary at any stage of the proceeding, call upon the parties to produce documents, witnesses and experts.

(3) After consulting both parties, the Tribunal may allow a person or entity that is not a party to the dispute (in this Article called the "non-disputing party") to file a written submission with the Tribunal regarding a matter within the scope of the dispute. In determining whether to allow such a filing, the Tribunal shall consider, among other things, the extent to which:

   (a) the non-disputing party submission would assist the Tribunal in the determination of a factual or legal issue related to the proceeding by bringing a perspective, particular knowledge or insight that is different from that of the disputing parties;

   (b) the non-disputing party submission would address a matter within the scope of the dispute;

   (c) the non-disputing party has a significant interest in the proceeding.

   The Tribunal shall ensure that the non-disputing party submission does not disrupt the proceeding or unduly burden or unfairly prejudice either party, and that both parties are given an opportunity to present their observations on the non-disputing party submission.

Article 42   Examination of Witnesses and Experts

Witnesses and experts shall be examined before the Tribunal by the parties under the control of its President. Questions may also be put to them by any member of the Tribunal.

Article 43   Witnesses and Experts: Special Rules

The Tribunal may:

(a) admit evidence given by a witness or expert in a written deposition;

(b) with the consent of both parties, arrange for the examination of a witness or expert otherwise than before the Tribunal itself. The Tribunal shall define the procedure to be followed. The parties may participate in the examination; and

(c) appoint one or more experts, define their terms of reference, examine their reports and hear from them in person.

Article 44   Closure of the Proceeding

(1) When the presentation of the case by the parties is completed, the proceeding shall be declared closed.

(2) Exceptionally, the Tribunal may, before the award has been rendered, reopen the proceeding on the ground that new evidence is forthcoming of such a nature as to constitute a decisive factor, or that there is a vital need for clarification on certain specific points.

CHAPTER VIII   PARTICULAR PROCEDURES

Article 45   Preliminary Objections

(1) The Tribunal shall have the power to rule on its competence. For the purposes of this Article, an agreement providing for arbitration under the Additional Facility shall be separable from the other terms of the contract in which it may have been included.

(2) Any objection that the dispute is not within the competence of the Tribunal shall be filed with the Secretary-General as soon as possible after the constitution of the Tribunal and in any event no later than the expiration of the time limit fixed for the filing of the counter-

memorial or, if the objection relates to an ancillary claim, for the filing of the rejoinder—unless the facts on which the objection is based are unknown to the party at that time.

(3) The Tribunal may on its own initiative consider, at any stage of the proceeding, whether the dispute before it is within its competence.

(4) Upon the formal raising of an objection relating to the dispute, the Tribunal may decide to suspend the proceeding on the merits. The President of the Tribunal, after consultation with its other members, shall fix a time limit within which the parties may file observations on the objection.

(5) The Tribunal shall decide whether or not the further procedures relating to the objection made pursuant to paragraph (2) shall be oral. It may deal with the objection as a preliminary question or join it to the merits of the dispute. If the Tribunal overrules the objection or joins it to the merits, it shall once more fix time limits for the further procedures.

(6) Unless the parties have agreed to another expedited procedure for making preliminary objections, a party may, no later than 30 days after the constitution of the Tribunal, and in any event before the first session of the Tribunal, file an objection that a claim is manifestly without legal merit. The party shall specify as precisely as possible the basis for the objection. The Tribunal, after giving the parties the opportunity to present their observations on the objection, shall, at its first session or promptly thereafter, notify the parties of its decision on the objection. The decision of the Tribunal shall be without prejudice to the right of a party to file an objection pursuant to paragraph (2) or to object, in the course of the proceeding, that a claim lacks legal merit.

(7) If the Tribunal decides that the dispute is not within its competence or that all claims are manifestly without legal merit, it shall issue an award to that effect.

Article 46   Provisional Measures of Protection

(1) Unless the arbitration agreement otherwise provides, either party may at any time during the proceeding request that provisional measures for the preservation of its rights be ordered by the Tribunal. The Tribunal shall give priority to the consideration of such a request.

(2) The Tribunal may also recommend provisional measures on its own initiative or recommend measures other than those specified in a request. It may at any time modify or revoke its recommendations.

(3) The Tribunal shall order or recommend provisional measures, or any modification or revocation thereof, only after giving each party an opportunity of presenting its observations.

(4) The parties may apply to any competent judicial authority for interim or conservatory measures. By doing so they shall not be held to infringe the agreement to arbitrate or to affect the powers of the Tribunal.

Article 47   Ancillary Claims

(1) Except as the parties otherwise agree, a party may present an incidental or additional claim or counter-claim, provided that such ancillary claim is within the scope of the arbitration agreement of the parties.

(2) An incidental or additional claim shall be presented not later than in the reply and a counter-claim no later than in the counter-memorial, unless the Tribunal, upon justification by the party presenting the ancillary claim and upon considering any objection of the other party, authorizes the presentation of the claim at a later stage in the proceeding.

Article 48   Default

(1) If a party fails to appear or to present its case at any stage of the proceeding, the other party may request the Tribunal to deal with the questions submitted to it and to render an award.

(2) Whenever such a request is made by a party the Tribunal shall promptly notify the defaulting party thereof. Unless the Tribunal is satisfied that that party does not intend to appear or to present its case in the proceeding, it shall, at the same time, grant a period of grace and to this end:

(a) if that party had failed to file a pleading or any other instrument within the time limit fixed therefor, fix a new time limit for its filing; or

(b) if that party had failed to appear or present its case at a hearing, fix a new date for the hearing.

The period of grace shall not, without the consent of the other party, exceed 60 days.

(3) After the expiration of the period of grace or when, in accordance with paragraph (2) of this Article, no such period is granted, the Tribunal shall examine whether the dispute is within its jurisdiction and, if it is satisfied as to its jurisdiction, decide whether the submissions made are well-founded in fact and in law. To this end, it may, at any stage of the proceeding, call on the party appearing to file observations, produce evidence or submit oral explanations.

Article 49   Settlement and Discontinuance

(1) If, before the award is rendered, the parties agree on a settlement of the dispute or otherwise to discontinue the proceeding, the Tribunal, or the Secretary-General if the Tribunal has not yet been constituted, or has not yet met, shall, at their written request, in an order take note of the discontinuance of the proceeding.

(2) If requested by both parties and accepted by the Tribunal, the Tribunal shall record the settlement in the form of an award. The Tribunal shall not be obliged to give reasons for such an award. The parties will accompany their request with the full and signed text of their settlement.

Article 50   Discontinuance at Request of a Party

If a party requests the discontinuance of the proceeding, the Tribunal, or the Secretary-General if the Tribunal has not yet been constituted, shall in an order fix a time limit within which the other party may state whether it opposes the discontinuance. If no objection is made in writing within the time limit, the Tribunal, or if appropriate the Secretary-General, shall in an order take note of the discontinuance of the proceeding. If objection is made, the proceeding shall continue.

Article 51   Discontinuance for Failure of Parties to Act

If the parties fail to take any steps in the proceeding during six consecutive months or such period as they may agree with the approval of the Tribunal, or of the Secretary-General if the Tribunal has not yet been constituted, they shall be deemed to have discontinued the proceeding and the Tribunal, or if appropriate the Secretary-General, shall, after notice to the parties, in an order take note of the discontinuance.

CHAPTER IX   THE AWARD

Article 52   The Award

(1) The award shall be made in writing and shall contain:

(a) a precise designation of each party;

(b) a statement that the Tribunal was established under these Rules, and a description of the method of its constitution;

(c) the name of each member of the Tribunal, and an identification of the appointing authority of each;

(d) the names of the agents, counsel and advocates of the parties;

(e) the dates and place of the sittings of the Tribunal;

(f) a summary of the proceeding;

(g) a statement of the facts as found by the Tribunal;

(h) the submissions of the parties;

(i) the decision of the Tribunal on every question submitted to it, together with the reasons upon which the decision is based; and

(j) any decision of the Tribunal regarding the cost of the proceeding.

(2) The award shall be signed by the members of the Tribunal who voted for it; the date of each signature shall be indicated. Any member of the Tribunal may attach his individual opinion to the award, whether he dissents from the majority or not, or a statement of his dissent.

(3) If the arbitration law of the country where the award is made requires that it be filed or registered by the Tribunal, the Tribunal shall comply with this requirement within the period of time required by law.

(4) The award shall be final and binding on the parties. The parties waive any time limits for the rendering of the award which may be provided for by the law of the country where the award is made.

Article 53   Authentication of the Award; Certified Copies; Date

(1) Upon signature by the last arbitrator to sign, the Secretary-General shall promptly:

(a) authenticate the original text of the award and deposit it in the archives of the Secretariat, together with any individual opinions and statements of dissent; and

(b) dispatch a certified copy of the award (including individual opinions and statements of dissent) to each party, indicating the date of dispatch on the original text and on all copies; provided, however, that if the original text of the award must be filed or registered as contemplated by Article 52(3) of these Rules the Secretary-General shall do so on behalf of the Tribunal or return the award to the Tribunal for this purpose.

(2) The award shall be deemed to have been rendered on the date on which the certified copies were dispatched.

(3) Except to the extent required for any registration or filing of the award by the Secretary-General under paragraph (1) of this Article, the Secretariat shall not publish the award without the consent of the parties. The Secretariat shall, however, promptly include in the publications of the Centre excerpts of the legal reasoning of the Tribunal.

Article 54   Applicable Law

(1) The Tribunal shall apply the rules of law designated by the parties as applicable to the substance of the dispute. Failing such designation by the parties, the Tribunal shall apply (a) the law determined by the conflict of laws rules which it considers applicable and (b) such rules of international law as the Tribunal considers applicable.

(2) The Tribunal may decide *ex aequo et bono* if the parties have expressly authorized it to do so and if the law applicable to the arbitration so permits.

Article 55   Interpretation of the Award

(1) Within 45 days after the date of the award either party, with notice to the other party, may request that the Secretary-General obtain from the Tribunal an interpretation of the award.

(2) The Tribunal shall determine the procedure to be followed.

(3) The interpretation shall form part of the award, and the provisions of Articles 52 and 53 of these Rules shall apply.

Article 56   Correction of the Award

(1) Within 45 days after the date of the award either party, with notice to the other party, may request the Secretary-General to obtain from the Tribunal a correction in the award of any clerical, arithmetical or similar errors. The Tribunal may within the same period make such corrections on its own initiative.

(2) The provisions of Articles 52 and 53 of these Rules shall apply to such corrections.

Article 57   Supplementary Decisions

(1) Within 45 days after the date of the award either party, with notice to the other party may request the Tribunal, through the Secretary-General, to decide any question which it had omitted to decide in the award.

(2) The Tribunal shall determine the procedure to be followed.

(3) The decision of the Tribunal shall become part of the award and the provisions of Articles 52 and 53 of these Rules shall apply thereto.

CHAPTER X   COSTS

Article 58   Cost of Proceeding

(1) Unless the parties otherwise agree, the Tribunal shall decide how and by whom the fees and expenses of the members of the Tribunal, the expenses and charges of the Secretariat and the expenses incurred by the parties in connection with the proceeding shall be borne. The Tribunal may, to that end, call on the Secretariat and the parties to provide it with the information it needs in order to formulate the division of the cost of the proceeding between the parties.

(2) The decision of the Tribunal pursuant to paragraph (1) of this Article shall form part of the award.

CHAPTER XI   GENERAL PROVISIONS

Article 59   Final Provision

The text of these Rules in each official language of the Centre shall be equally authentic

UNCITRAL Arbitration Rules

Date   6 December 2010
Source   Report of the United Nations Commission on International Trade Law, Forty-third Session, UN Doc A/65/
             17, Annex I
Link   <http://www.uncitral.org/pdf/english/texts/arbitration/arb-rules-revised/pre-arb-rules-revised.pdf>

SECTION I   INTRODUCTORY RULES

SCOPE OF APPLICATION *

Article 1

1. Where parties have agreed that disputes between them in respect of a defined legal relationship, whether contractual or not, shall be referred to arbitration under the UNCITRAL
   Arbitration Rules, then such disputes shall be settled in accordance with these Rules subject to
   such modification as the parties may agree.

2. The parties to an arbitration agreement concluded after 15 August 2010 shall be presumed to
   have referred to the Rules in effect on the date of commencement of the arbitration, unless the
   parties have agreed to apply a particular version of the Rules. That presumption does not
   apply where the arbitration agreement has been concluded by accepting after 15 August 2010
   an offer made before that date.

3. These Rules shall govern the arbitration except that where any of these Rules is in conflict with
   a provision of the law applicable to the arbitration from which the parties cannot derogate,
   that provision shall prevail.

NOTICE AND CALCULATION OF PERIODS OF TIME

Article 2

1. A notice, including a notification, communication or proposal, may be transmitted by any
   means of communication that provides or allows for a record of its transmission.

2. If an address has been designated by a party specifically for this purpose or authorized by the
   arbitral tribunal, any notice shall be delivered to that party at that address, and if so delivered
   shall be deemed to have been received. Delivery by electronic means such as facsimile or
   e-mail may only be made to an address so designated or authorized.

3. In the absence of such designation or authorization, a notice is:
   (a) Received if it is physically delivered to the addressee; or
   (b) Deemed to have been received if it is delivered at the place of business, habitual residence
       or mailing address of the addressee.

4. If, after reasonable efforts, delivery cannot be effected in accordance with paragraphs 2 or 3, a
   notice is deemed to have been received if it is sent to the addressee's last-known place of
   business, habitual residence or mailing address by registered letter or any other means that
   provides a record of delivery or of attempted delivery.

5. A notice shall be deemed to have been received on the day it is delivered in accordance with
   paragraphs 2, 3 or 4, or attempted to be delivered in accordance with paragraph 4. A notice

---

* A model arbitration clause for contracts can be found in the annex to the Rules.

transmitted by electronic means is deemed to have been received on the day it is sent, except that a notice of arbitration so transmitted is only deemed to have been received on the day when it reaches the addressee's electronic address.

6. For the purpose of calculating a period of time under these Rules, such period shall begin to run on the day following the day when a notice is received. If the last day of such period is an official holiday or a non-business day at the residence or place of business of the addressee, the period is extended until the first business day which follows. Official holidays or non-business days occurring during the running of the period of time are included in calculating the period.

NOTICE OF ARBITRATION

Article 3

1. The party or parties initiating recourse to arbitration (hereinafter called the "claimant") shall communicate to the other party or parties (hereinafter called the "respondent") a notice of arbitration.

2. Arbitral proceedings shall be deemed to commence on the date on which the notice of arbitration is received by the respondent.

3. The notice of arbitration shall include the following:
    (a) A demand that the dispute be referred to arbitration;
    (b) The names and contact details of the parties;
    (c) Identification of the arbitration agreement that is invoked;
    (d) Identification of any contract or other legal instrument out of or in relation to which the dispute arises or, in the absence of such contract or instrument, a brief description of the relevant relationship;
    (e) A brief description of the claim and an indication of the amount involved, if any;
    (f) The relief or remedy sought;
    (g) A proposal as to the number of arbitrators, language and place of arbitration, if the parties have not previously agreed thereon.

4. The notice of arbitration may also include:
    (a) A proposal for the designation of an appointing authority referred to in article 6, paragraph 1;
    (b) A proposal for the appointment of a sole arbitrator referred to in article 8, paragraph 1;
    (c) Notification of the appointment of an arbitrator referred to in articles 9 or 10.

5. The constitution of the arbitral tribunal shall not be hindered by any controversy with respect to the sufficiency of the notice of arbitration, which shall be finally resolved by the arbitral tribunal.

RESPONSE TO THE NOTICE OF ARBITRATION

Article 4

1. Within 30 days of the receipt of the notice of arbitration, the respondent shall communicate to the claimant a response to the notice of arbitration, which shall include:
    (a) The name and contact details of each respondent;
    (b) A response to the information set forth in the notice of arbitration, pursuant to article 3, paragraphs 3 (c) to (g).

2. The response to the notice of arbitration may also include:
    (a) Any plea that an arbitral tribunal to be constituted under these Rules lacks jurisdiction;
    (b) A proposal for the designation of an appointing authority referred to in article 6, paragraph 1;
    (c) A proposal for the appointment of a sole arbitrator referred to in article 8, paragraph 1;

(d) Notification of the appointment of an arbitrator referred to in articles 9 or 10;

(e) A brief description of counterclaims or claims for the purpose of a set-off, if any, including where relevant, an indication of the amounts involved, and the relief or remedy sought;

(f) A notice of arbitration in accordance with article 3 in case the respondent formulates a claim against a party to the arbitration agreement other than the claimant.

3. The constitution of the arbitral tribunal shall not be hindered by any controversy with respect to the respondent's failure to communicate a response to the notice of arbitration, or an incomplete or late response to the notice of arbitration, which shall be finally resolved by the arbitral tribunal.

REPRESENTATION AND ASSISTANCE

Article 5

Each party may be represented or assisted by persons chosen by it. The names and addresses of such persons must be communicated to all parties and to the arbitral tribunal. Such communication must specify whether the appointment is being made for purposes of representation or assistance. Where a person is to act as a representative of a party, the arbitral tribunal, on its own initiative or at the request of any party, may at any time require proof of authority granted to the representative in such a form as the arbitral tribunal may determine.

DESIGNATING AND APPOINTING AUTHORITIES

Article 6

1. Unless the parties have already agreed on the choice of an appointing authority, a party may at any time propose the name or names of one or more institutions or persons, including the Secretary-General of the Permanent Court of Arbitration at The Hague (hereinafter called the "PCA"), one of whom would serve as appointing authority.

2. If all parties have not agreed on the choice of an appointing authority within 30 days after a proposal made in accordance with paragraph 1 has been received by all other parties, any party may request the Secretary-General of the PCA to designate the appointing authority.

3. Where these Rules provide for a period of time within which a party must refer a matter to an appointing authority and no appointing authority has been agreed on or designated, the period is suspended from the date on which a party initiates the procedure for agreeing on or designating an appointing authority until the date of such agreement or designation.

4. Except as referred to in article 41, paragraph 4, if the appointing authority refuses to act, or if it fails to appoint an arbitrator within 30 days after it receives a party's request to do so, fails to act within any other period provided by these Rules, or fails to decide on a challenge to an arbitrator within a reasonable time after receiving a party's request to do so, any party may request the Secretary-General of the PCA to designate a substitute appointing authority.

5. In exercising their functions under these Rules, the appointing authority and the Secretary-General of the PCA may require from any party and the arbitrators the information they deem necessary and they shall give the parties and, where appropriate, the arbitrators, an opportunity to present their views in any manner they consider appropriate. All such communications to and from the appointing authority and the Secretary-General of the PCA shall also be provided by the sender to all other parties.

6. When the appointing authority is requested to appoint an arbitrator pursuant to articles 8, 9, 10 or 14, the party making the request shall send to the appointing authority copies of the notice of arbitration and, if it exists, any response to the notice of arbitration.

7. The appointing authority shall have regard to such considerations as are likely to secure the appointment of an independent and impartial arbitrator and shall take into account the advisability of appointing an arbitrator of a nationality other than the nationalities of the parties.

SECTION II   COMPOSITION OF THE ARBITRAL TRIBUNAL

NUMBER OF ARBITRATORS

Article 7

1. If the parties have not previously agreed on the number of arbitrators, and if within 30 days after the receipt by the respondent of the notice of arbitration the parties have not agreed that there shall be only one arbitrator, three arbitrators shall be appointed.

2. Notwithstanding paragraph 1, if no other parties have responded to a party's proposal to appoint a sole arbitrator within the time limit provided for in paragraph 1 and the party or parties concerned have failed to appoint a second arbitrator in accordance with article 9 or 10, the appointing authority may, at the request of a party, appoint a sole arbitrator pursuant to the procedure provided for in article 8, paragraph 2, if it determines that, in view of the circumstances of the case, this is more appropriate.

APPOINTMENT OF ARBITRATORS (ARTICLES 8 TO 10)

Article 8

1. If the parties have agreed that a sole arbitrator is to be appointed and if within 30 days after receipt by all other parties of a proposal for the appointment of a sole arbitrator the parties have not reached agreement thereon, a sole arbitrator shall, at the request of a party, be appointed by the appointing authority.

2. The appointing authority shall appoint the sole arbitrator as promptly as possible. In making the appointment, the appointing authority shall use the following list-procedure, unless the parties agree that the list-procedure should not be used or unless the appointing authority determines in its discretion that the use of the list-procedure is not appropriate for the case:

   (a) The appointing authority shall communicate to each of the parties an identical list containing at least three names;

   (b) Within 15 days after the receipt of this list, each party may return the list to the appointing authority after having deleted the name or names to which it objects and numbered the remaining names on the list in the order of its preference;

   (c) After the expiration of the above period of time the appointing authority shall appoint the sole arbitrator from among the names approved on the lists returned to it and in accordance with the order of preference indicated by the parties;

   (d) If for any reason the appointment cannot be made according to this procedure, the appointing authority may exercise its discretion in appointing the sole arbitrator.

Article 9

1. If three arbitrators are to be appointed, each party shall appoint one arbitrator. The two arbitrators thus appointed shall choose the third arbitrator who will act as the presiding arbitrator of the arbitral tribunal.

2. If within 30 days after the receipt of a party's notification of the appointment of an arbitrator the other party has not notified the first party of the arbitrator it has appointed, the first party may request the appointing authority to appoint the second arbitrator.

3. If within 30 days after the appointment of the second arbitrator the two arbitrators have not agreed on the choice of the presiding arbitrator, the presiding arbitrator shall be appointed

by the appointing authority in the same way as a sole arbitrator would be appointed under article 8.

Article 10

1. For the purposes of article 9, paragraph 1, where three arbitrators are to be appointed and there are multiple parties as claimant or as respondent, unless the parties have agreed to another method of appointment of arbitrators, the multiple parties jointly, whether as claimant or as respondent, shall appoint an arbitrator.

2. If the parties have agreed that the arbitral tribunal is to be composed of a number of arbitrators other than one or three, the arbitrators shall be appointed according to the method agreed upon by the parties.

3. In the event of any failure to constitute the arbitral tribunal under these Rules, the appointing authority shall, at the request of any party, constitute the arbitral tribunal and, in doing so, may revoke any appointment already made and appoint or reappoint each of the arbitrators and designate one of them as the presiding arbitrator.

DISCLOSURES BY AND CHALLENGE OF ARBITRATORS** (ARTICLES 11 TO 13)

Article 11

When a person is approached in connection with his or her possible appointment as an arbitrator, he or she shall disclose any circumstances likely to give rise to justifiable doubts as to his or her impartiality or independence. An arbitrator, from the time of his or her appointment and throughout the arbitral proceedings, shall without delay disclose any such circumstances to the parties and the other arbitrators unless they have already been informed by him or her of these circumstances.

Article 12

1. Any arbitrator may be challenged if circumstances exist that give rise to justifiable doubts as to the arbitrator's impartiality or independence.

2. A party may challenge the arbitrator appointed by it only for reasons of which it becomes aware after the appointment has been made.

3. In the event that an arbitrator fails to act or in the event of the *de jure* or *de facto* impossibility of his or her performing his or her functions, the procedure in respect of the challenge of an arbitrator as provided in article 13 shall apply.

Article 13

1. A party that intends to challenge an arbitrator shall send notice of its challenge within 15 days after it has been notified of the appointment of the challenged arbitrator, or within 15 days after the circumstances mentioned in articles 11 and 12 became known to that party.

2. The notice of challenge shall be communicated to all other parties, to the arbitrator who is challenged and to the other arbitrators. The notice of challenge shall state the reasons for the challenge.

3. When an arbitrator has been challenged by a party, all parties may agree to the challenge. The arbitrator may also, after the challenge, withdraw from his or her office. In neither case does this imply acceptance of the validity of the grounds for the challenge.

4. If, within 15 days from the date of the notice of challenge, all parties do not agree to the challenge or the challenged arbitrator does not withdraw, the party making the challenge may

---

** Model statements of independence pursuant to article 11 can be found in the annex to the Rules.

elect to pursue it. In that case, within 30 days from the date of the notice of challenge, it shall seek a decision on the challenge by the appointing authority.

REPLACEMENT OF AN ARBITRATOR

Article 14

1. Subject to paragraph 2, in any event where an arbitrator has to be replaced during the course of the arbitral proceedings, a substitute arbitrator shall be appointed or chosen pursuant to the procedure provided for in articles 8 to 11 that was applicable to the appointment or choice of the arbitrator being replaced. This procedure shall apply even if during the process of appointing the arbitrator to be replaced, a party had failed to exercise its right to appoint or to participate in the appointment.

2. If, at the request of a party, the appointing authority determines that, in view of the exceptional circumstances of the case, it would be justified for a party to be deprived of its right to appoint a substitute arbitrator, the appointing authority may, after giving an opportunity to the parties and the remaining arbitrators to express their views: (a) appoint the substitute arbitrator; or (b) after the closure of the hearings, authorize the other arbitrators to proceed with the arbitration and make any decision or award.

REPETITION OF HEARINGS IN THE EVENT OF THE REPLACEMENT OF AN ARBITRATOR

Article 15

If an arbitrator is replaced, the proceedings shall resume at the stage where the arbitrator who was replaced ceased to perform his or her functions, unless the arbitral tribunal decides otherwise.

EXCLUSION OF LIABILITY

Article 16

Save for intentional wrongdoing, the parties waive, to the fullest extent permitted under the applicable law, any claim against the arbitrators, the appointing authority and any person appointed by the arbitral tribunal based on any act or omission in connection with the arbitration.

SECTION III   ARBITRAL PROCEEDINGS

GENERAL PROVISIONS

Article 17

1. Subject to these Rules, the arbitral tribunal may conduct the arbitration in such manner as it considers appropriate, provided that the parties are treated with equality and that at an appropriate stage of the proceedings each party is given a reasonable opportunity of presenting its case. The arbitral tribunal, in exercising its discretion, shall conduct the proceedings so as to avoid unnecessary delay and expense and to provide a fair and efficient process for resolving the parties' dispute.

2. As soon as practicable after its constitution and after inviting the parties to express their views, the arbitral tribunal shall establish the provisional timetable of the arbitration. The arbitral tribunal may, at any time, after inviting the parties to express their views, extend or abridge any period of time prescribed under these Rules or agreed by the parties.

3. If at an appropriate stage of the proceedings any party so requests, the arbitral tribunal shall hold hearings for the presentation of evidence by witnesses, including expert witnesses, or for oral argument. In the absence of such a request, the arbitral tribunal shall decide whether to hold such hearings or whether the proceedings shall be conducted on the basis of documents and other materials.

4. All communications to the arbitral tribunal by one party shall be communicated by that party to all other parties. Such communications shall be made at the same time, except as otherwise permitted by the arbitral tribunal if it may do so under applicable law.

5. The arbitral tribunal may, at the request of any party, allow one or more third persons to be joined in the arbitration as a party provided such person is a party to the arbitration agreement, unless the arbitral tribunal finds, after giving all parties, including the person or persons to be joined, the opportunity to be heard, that joinder should not be permitted because of prejudice to any of those parties. The arbitral tribunal may make a single award or several awards in respect of all parties so involved in the arbitration.

PLACE OF ARBITRATION

Article 18

1. If the parties have not previously agreed on the place of arbitration, the place of arbitration shall be determined by the arbitral tribunal having regard to the circumstances of the case. The award shall be deemed to have been made at the place of arbitration.

2. The arbitral tribunal may meet at any location it considers appropriate for deliberations. Unless otherwise agreed by the parties, the arbitral tribunal may also meet at any location it considers appropriate for any other purpose, including hearings.

LANGUAGE

Article 19

1. Subject to an agreement by the parties, the arbitral tribunal shall, promptly after its appointment, determine the language or languages to be used in the proceedings. This determination shall apply to the statement of claim, the statement of defence, and any further written statements and, if oral hearings take place, to the language or languages to be used in such hearings.

2. The arbitral tribunal may order that any documents annexed to the statement of claim or statement of defence, and any supplementary documents or exhibits submitted in the course of the proceedings, delivered in their original language, shall be accompanied by a translation into the language or languages agreed upon by the parties or determined by the arbitral tribunal.

STATEMENT OF CLAIM

Article 20

1. The claimant shall communicate its statement of claim in writing to the respondent and to each of the arbitrators within a period of time to be determined by the arbitral tribunal. The claimant may elect to treat its notice of arbitration referred to in article 3 as a statement of claim, provided that the notice of arbitration also complies with the requirements of paragraphs 2 to 4 of this article.

2. The statement of claim shall include the following particulars:
   (a) The names and contact details of the parties;

(b) A statement of the facts supporting the claim;

(c) The points at issue;

(d) The relief or remedy sought;

(e) The legal grounds or arguments supporting the claim.

3. A copy of any contract or other legal instrument out of or in relation to which the dispute arises and of the arbitration agreement shall be annexed to the statement of claim.

4. The statement of claim should, as far as possible, be accompanied by all documents and other evidence relied upon by the claimant, or contain references to them.

STATEMENT OF DEFENCE

Article 21

1. The respondent shall communicate its statement of defence in writing to the claimant and to each of the arbitrators within a period of time to be determined by the arbitral tribunal. The respondent may elect to treat its response to the notice of arbitration referred to in article 4 as a statement of defence, provided that the response to the notice of arbitration also complies with the requirements of paragraph 2 of this article.

2. The statement of defence shall reply to the particulars (b) to (e) of the statement of claim (article 20, paragraph 2). The statement of defence should, as far as possible, be accompanied by all documents and other evidence relied upon by the respondent, or contain references to them.

3. In its statement of defence, or at a later stage in the arbitral proceedings if the arbitral tribunal decides that the delay was justified under the circumstances, the respondent may make a counterclaim or rely on a claim for the purpose of a set-off provided that the arbitral tribunal has jurisdiction over it.

4. The provisions of article 20, paragraphs 2 to 4, shall apply to a counterclaim, a claim under article 4, paragraph 2 (f), and a claim relied on for the purpose of a set-off.

AMENDMENTS TO THE CLAIM OR DEFENCE

Article 22

During the course of the arbitral proceedings, a party may amend or supplement its claim or defence, including a counterclaim or a claim for the purpose of a set-off, unless the arbitral tribunal considers it inappropriate to allow such amendment or supplement having regard to the delay in making it or prejudice to other parties or any other circumstances. However, a claim or defence, including a counterclaim or a claim for the purpose of a set-off, may not be amended or supplemented in such a manner that the amended or supplemented claim or defence falls outside the jurisdiction of the arbitral tribunal.

PLEAS AS TO THE JURISDICTION OF THE ARBITRAL TRIBUNAL

Article 23

1. The arbitral tribunal shall have the power to rule on its own jurisdiction, including any objections with respect to the existence or validity of the arbitration agreement. For that purpose, an arbitration clause that forms part of a contract shall be treated as an agreement independent of the other terms of the contract. A decision by the arbitral tribunal that the contract is null shall not entail automatically the invalidity of the arbitration clause.

2. A plea that the arbitral tribunal does not have jurisdiction shall be raised no later than in the statement of defence or, with respect to a counterclaim or a claim for the purpose of a set-off, in the reply to the counterclaim or to the claim for the purpose of a set-off. A party is not

precluded from raising such a plea by the fact that it has appointed, or participated in the appointment of, an arbitrator. A plea that the arbitral tribunal is exceeding the scope of its authority shall be raised as soon as the matter alleged to be beyond the scope of its authority is raised during the arbitral proceedings. The arbitral tribunal may, in either case, admit a later plea if it considers the delay justified.

3. The arbitral tribunal may rule on a plea referred to in paragraph 2 either as a preliminary question or in an award on the merits. The arbitral tribunal may continue the arbitral proceedings and make an award, notwithstanding any pending challenge to its jurisdiction before a court.

FURTHER WRITTEN STATEMENTS

Article 24

The arbitral tribunal shall decide which further written statements, in addition to the statement of claim and the statement of defence, shall be required from the parties or may be presented by them and shall fix the periods of time for communicating such statements.

PERIODS OF TIME

Article 25

The periods of time fixed by the arbitral tribunal for the communication of written statements (including the statement of claim and statement of defence) should not exceed 45 days. However, the arbitral tribunal may extend the time limits if it concludes that an extension is justified.

INTERIM MEASURES

Article 26

1. The arbitral tribunal may, at the request of a party, grant interim measures.
2. An interim measure is any temporary measure by which, at any time prior to the issuance of the award by which the dispute is finally decided, the arbitral tribunal orders a party, for example and without limitation, to:
   (a) Maintain or restore the status quo pending determination of the dispute;
   (b) Take action that would prevent, or refrain from taking action that is likely to cause, (i) current or imminent harm or (ii) prejudice to the arbitral process itself;
   (c) Provide a means of preserving assets out of which a subsequent award may be satisfied; or
   (d) Preserve evidence that may be relevant and material to the resolution of the dispute.
3. The party requesting an interim measure under paragraphs 2 (a) to (c) shall satisfy the arbitral tribunal that:
   (a) Harm not adequately reparable by an award of damages is likely to result if the measure is not ordered, and such harm substantially outweighs the harm that is likely to result to the party against whom the measure is directed if the measure is granted; and
   (b) There is a reasonable possibility that the requesting party will succeed on the merits of the claim. The determination on this possibility shall not affect the discretion of the arbitral tribunal in making any subsequent determination.
4. With regard to a request for an interim measure under paragraph 2 (d), the requirements in paragraphs 3 (a) and (b) shall apply only to the extent the arbitral tribunal considers appropriate.
5. The arbitral tribunal may modify, suspend or terminate an interim measure it has granted, upon application of any party or, in exceptional circumstances and upon prior notice to the parties, on the arbitral tribunal's own initiative.

6. The arbitral tribunal may require the party requesting an interim measure to provide appropriate security in connection with the measure.

7. The arbitral tribunal may require any party promptly to disclose any material change in the circumstances on the basis of which the interim measure was requested or granted.

8. The party requesting an interim measure may be liable for any costs and damages caused by the measure to any party if the arbitral tribunal later determines that, in the circumstances then prevailing, the measure should not have been granted. The arbitral tribunal may award such costs and damages at any point during the proceedings.

9. A request for interim measures addressed by any party to a judicial authority shall not be deemed incompatible with the agreement to arbitrate, or as a waiver of that agreement.

EVIDENCE

Article 27

1. Each party shall have the burden of proving the facts relied on to support its claim or defence.

2. Witnesses, including expert witnesses, who are presented by the parties to testify to the arbitral tribunal on any issue of fact or expertise may be any individual, notwithstanding that the individual is a party to the arbitration or in any way related to a party. Unless otherwise directed by the arbitral tribunal, statements by witnesses, including expert witnesses, may be presented in writing and signed by them.

3. At any time during the arbitral proceedings the arbitral tribunal may require the parties to produce documents, exhibits or other evidence within such a period of time as the arbitral tribunal shall determine.

4. The arbitral tribunal shall determine the admissibility, relevance, materiality and weight of the evidence offered.

HEARINGS

Article 28

1. In the event of an oral hearing, the arbitral tribunal shall give the parties adequate advance notice of the date, time and place thereof.

2. Witnesses, including expert witnesses, may be heard under the conditions and examined in the manner set by the arbitral tribunal.

3. Hearings shall be held in camera unless the parties agree otherwise. The arbitral tribunal may require the retirement of any witness or witnesses, including expert witnesses, during the testimony of such other witnesses, except that a witness, including an expert witness, who is a party to the arbitration shall not, in principle, be asked to retire.

4. The arbitral tribunal may direct that witnesses, including expert witnesses, be examined through means of telecommunication that do not require their physical presence at the hearing (such as videoconference).

EXPERTS APPOINTED BY THE ARBITRAL TRIBUNAL

Article 29

1. After consultation with the parties, the arbitral tribunal may appoint one or more independent experts to report to it, in writing, on specific issues to be determined by the arbitral tribunal. A copy of the expert's terms of reference, established by the arbitral tribunal, shall be communicated to the parties.

2. The expert shall, in principle before accepting appointment, submit to the arbitral tribunal and to the parties a description of his or her qualifications and a statement of his or her impartiality and independence. Within the time ordered by the arbitral tribunal, the parties shall inform the arbitral tribunal whether they have any objections as to the expert's qualifications, impartiality or independence. The arbitral tribunal shall decide promptly whether to accept any such objections. After an expert's appointment, a party may object to the expert's qualifications, impartiality or independence only if the objection is for reasons of which the party becomes aware after the appointment has been made. The arbitral tribunal shall decide promptly what, if any, action to take.

3. The parties shall give the expert any relevant information or produce for his or her inspection any relevant documents or goods that he or she may require of them. Any dispute between a party and such expert as to the relevance of the required information or production shall be referred to the arbitral tribunal for decision.

4. Upon receipt of the expert's report, the arbitral tribunal shall communicate a copy of the report to the parties, which shall be given the opportunity to express, in writing, their opinion on the report. A party shall be entitled to examine any document on which the expert has relied in his or her report.

5. At the request of any party, the expert, after delivery of the report, may be heard at a hearing where the parties shall have the opportunity to be present and to interrogate the expert. At this hearing, any party may present expert witnesses in order to testify on the points at issue. The provisions of article 28 shall be applicable to such proceedings.

DEFAULT

Article 30

1. If, within the period of time fixed by these Rules or the arbitral tribunal, without showing sufficient cause:
   (a) The claimant has failed to communicate its statement of claim, the arbitral tribunal shall issue an order for the termination of the arbitral proceedings, unless there are remaining matters that may need to be decided and the arbitral tribunal considers it appropriate to do so;
   (b) The respondent has failed to communicate its response to the notice of arbitration or its statement of defence, the arbitral tribunal shall order that the proceedings continue, without treating such failure in itself as an admission of the claimant's allegations; the provisions of this subparagraph also apply to a claimant's failure to submit a defence to a counterclaim or to a claim for the purpose of a set-off.

2. If a party, duly notified under these Rules, fails to appear at a hearing, without showing sufficient cause for such failure, the arbitral tribunal may proceed with the arbitration.

3. If a party, duly invited by the arbitral tribunal to produce documents, exhibits or other evidence, fails to do so within the established period of time, without showing sufficient cause for such failure, the arbitral tribunal may make the award on the evidence before it.

CLOSURE OF HEARINGS

Article 31

1. The arbitral tribunal may inquire of the parties if they have any further proof to offer or witnesses to be heard or submissions to make and, if there are none, it may declare the hearings closed.

2. The arbitral tribunal may, if it considers it necessary owing to exceptional circumstances, decide, on its own initiative or upon application of a party, to reopen the hearings at any time before the award is made.

WAIVER OF RIGHT TO OBJECT

Article 32

A failure by any party to object promptly to any non-compliance with these Rules or with any requirement of the arbitration agreement shall be deemed to be a waiver of the right of such party to make such an objection, unless such party can show that, under the circumstances, its failure to object was justified.

SECTION IV   THE AWARD

DECISIONS

Article 33

1. When there is more than one arbitrator, any award or other decision of the arbitral tribunal shall be made by a majority of the arbitrators.
2. In the case of questions of procedure, when there is no majority or when the arbitral tribunal so authorizes, the presiding arbitrator may decide alone, subject to revision, if any, by the arbitral tribunal.

FORM AND EFFECT OF THE AWARD

Article 34

1. The arbitral tribunal may make separate awards on different issues at different times.
2. All awards shall be made in writing and shall be final and binding on the parties. The parties shall carry out all awards without delay.
3. The arbitral tribunal shall state the reasons upon which the award is based, unless the parties have agreed that no reasons are to be given.
4. An award shall be signed by the arbitrators and it shall contain the date on which the award was made and indicate the place of arbitration. Where there is more than one arbitrator and any of them fails to sign, the award shall state the reason for the absence of the signature.
5. An award may be made public with the consent of all parties or where and to the extent disclosure is required of a party by legal duty, to protect or pursue a legal right or in relation to legal proceedings before a court or other competent authority.
6. Copies of the award signed by the arbitrators shall be communicated to the parties by the arbitral tribunal.

APPLICABLE LAW, AMIABLE COMPOSITEUR

Article 35

1. The arbitral tribunal shall apply the rules of law designated by the parties as applicable to the substance of the dispute. Failing such designation by the parties, the arbitral tribunal shall apply the law which it determines to be appropriate.
2. The arbitral tribunal shall decide as *amiable compositeur* or *ex aequo et bono* only if the parties have expressly authorized the arbitral tribunal to do so.

3. In all cases, the arbitral tribunal shall decide in accordance with the terms of the contract, if any, and shall take into account any usage of trade applicable to the transaction.

SETTLEMENT OR OTHER GROUNDS FOR TERMINATION

Article 36

1. If, before the award is made, the parties agree on a settlement of the dispute, the arbitral tribunal shall either issue an order for the termination of the arbitral proceedings or, if requested by the parties and accepted by the arbitral tribunal, record the settlement in the form of an arbitral award on agreed terms. The arbitral tribunal is not obliged to give reasons for such an award.

2. If, before the award is made, the continuation of the arbitral proceedings becomes unnecessary or impossible for any reason not mentioned in paragraph 1, the arbitral tribunal shall inform the parties of its intention to issue an order for the termination of the proceedings. The arbitral tribunal shall have the power to issue such an order unless there are remaining matters that may need to be decided and the arbitral tribunal considers it appropriate to do so.

3. Copies of the order for termination of the arbitral proceedings or of the arbitral award on agreed terms, signed by the arbitrators, shall be communicated by the arbitral tribunal to the parties. Where an arbitral award on agreed terms is made, the provisions of article 34, paragraphs 2, 4 and 5, shall apply.

INTERPRETATION OF THE AWARD

Article 37

1. Within 30 days after the receipt of the award, a party, with notice to the other parties, may request that the arbitral tribunal give an interpretation of the award.

2. The interpretation shall be given in writing within 45 days after the receipt of the request. The interpretation shall form part of the award and the provisions of article 34, paragraphs 2 to 6, shall apply.

CORRECTION OF THE AWARD

Article 38

1. Within 30 days after the receipt of the award, a party, with notice to the other parties, may request the arbitral tribunal to correct in the award any error in computation, any clerical or typographical error, or any error or omission of a similar nature. If the arbitral tribunal considers that the request is justified, it shall make the correction within 45 days of receipt of the request.

2. The arbitral tribunal may within 30 days after the communication of the award make such corrections on its own initiative.

3. Such corrections shall be in writing and shall form part of the award. The provisions of article 34, paragraphs 2 to 6, shall apply.

ADDITIONAL AWARD

Article 39

1. Within 30 days after the receipt of the termination order or the award, a party, with notice to the other parties, may request the arbitral tribunal to make an award or an additional award as to claims presented in the arbitral proceedings but not decided by the arbitral tribunal.

2. If the arbitral tribunal considers the request for an award or additional award to be justified, it shall render or complete its award within 60 days after the receipt of the request. The arbitral tribunal may extend, if necessary, the period of time within which it shall make the award.

3. When such an award or additional award is made, the provisions of article 34, paragraphs 2 to 6, shall apply.

DEFINITION OF COSTS

Article 40

1. The arbitral tribunal shall fix the costs of arbitration in the final award and, if it deems appropriate, in another decision.

2. The term "costs" includes only:
   (a) The fees of the arbitral tribunal to be stated separately as to each arbitrator and to be fixed by the tribunal itself in accordance with article 41;
   (b) The reasonable travel and other expenses incurred by the arbitrators;
   (c) The reasonable costs of expert advice and of other assistance required by the arbitral tribunal;
   (d) The reasonable travel and other expenses of witnesses to the extent such expenses are approved by the arbitral tribunal;
   (e) The legal and other costs incurred by the parties in relation to the arbitration to the extent that the arbitral tribunal determines that the amount of such costs is reasonable;
   (f) Any fees and expenses of the appointing authority as well as the fees and expenses of the Secretary-General of the PCA.

3. In relation to interpretation, correction or completion of any award under articles 37 to 39, the arbitral tribunal may charge the costs referred to in paragraphs 2 (b) to (f), but no additional fees.

FEES AND EXPENSES OF ARBITRATORS

Article 41

1. The fees and expenses of the arbitrators shall be reasonable in amount, taking into account the amount in dispute, the complexity of the subject matter, the time spent by the arbitrators and any other relevant circumstances of the case.

2. If there is an appointing authority and it applies or has stated that it will apply a schedule or particular method for determining the fees for arbitrators in international cases, the arbitral tribunal in fixing its fees shall take that schedule or method into account to the extent that it considers appropriate in the circumstances of the case.

3. Promptly after its constitution, the arbitral tribunal shall inform the parties as to how it proposes to determine its fees and expenses, including any rates it intends to apply. Within 15 days of receiving that proposal, any party may refer the proposal to the appointing authority for review. If, within 45 days of receipt of such a referral, the appointing authority finds that the proposal of the arbitral tribunal is inconsistent with paragraph 1, it shall make any necessary adjustments thereto, which shall be binding upon the arbitral tribunal.

4. (a) When informing the parties of the arbitrators' fees and expenses that have been fixed pursuant to article 40, paragraphs 2 (a) and (b), the arbitral tribunal shall also explain the manner in which the corresponding amounts have been calculated;
   (b) Within 15 days of receiving the arbitral tribunal's determination of fees and expenses, any party may refer for review such determination to the appointing authority. If no appointing authority has been agreed upon or designated, or if the appointing authority

fails to act within the time specified in these Rules, then the review shall be made by the Secretary-General of the PCA;

(c) If the appointing authority or the Secretary-General of the PCA finds that the arbitral tribunal's determination is inconsistent with the arbitral tribunal's proposal (and any adjustment thereto) under paragraph 3 or is otherwise manifestly excessive, it shall, within 45 days of receiving such a referral, make any adjustments to the arbitral tribunal's determination that are necessary to satisfy the criteria in paragraph 1. Any such adjustments shall be binding upon the arbitral tribunal;

(d) Any such adjustments shall either be included by the arbitral tribunal in its award or, if the award has already been issued, be implemented in a correction to the award, to which the procedure of article 38, paragraph 3, shall apply.

5. Throughout the procedure under paragraphs 3 and 4, the arbitral tribunal shall proceed with the arbitration, in accordance with article 17, paragraph 1.

6. A referral under paragraph 4 shall not affect any determination in the award other than the arbitral tribunal's fees and expenses; nor shall it delay the recognition and enforcement of all parts of the award other than those relating to the determination of the arbitral tribunal's fees and expenses.

ALLOCATION OF COSTS

Article 42

1. The costs of the arbitration shall in principle be borne by the unsuccessful party or parties. However, the arbitral tribunal may apportion each of such costs between the parties if it determines that apportionment is reasonable, taking into account the circumstances of the case.

2. The arbitral tribunal shall in the final award or, if it deems appropriate, in any other award, determine any amount that a party may have to pay to another party as a result of the decision on allocation of costs.

DEPOSIT OF COSTS

Article 43

1. The arbitral tribunal, on its establishment, may request the parties to deposit an equal amount as an advance for the costs referred to in article 40, paragraphs 2 (a) to (c).

2. During the course of the arbitral proceedings the arbitral tribunal may request supplementary deposits from the parties.

3. If an appointing authority has been agreed upon or designated, and when a party so requests and the appointing authority consents to perform the function, the arbitral tribunal shall fix the amounts of any deposits or supplementary deposits only after consultation with the appointing authority, which may make any comments to the arbitral tribunal that it deems appropriate concerning the amount of such deposits and supplementary deposits.

4. If the required deposits are not paid in full within 30 days after the receipt of the request, the arbitral tribunal shall so inform the parties in order that one or more of them may make the required payment. If such payment is not made, the arbitral tribunal may order the suspension or termination of the arbitral proceedings.

5. After a termination order or final award has been made, the arbitral tribunal shall render an accounting to the parties of the deposits received and return any unexpended balance to the parties.

ANNEX

Model arbitration clause for contracts

Any dispute, controversy or claim arising out of or relating to this contract, or the breach, termination or invalidity thereof, shall be settled by arbitration in accordance with the UNCITRAL Arbitration Rules.

Note—Parties should consider adding:

(a) The appointing authority shall be ... [name of institution or person];

(b) The number of arbitrators shall be ... [one or three];

(c) The place of arbitration shall be ... [town and country];

(d) The language to be used in the arbitral proceedings shall be ....

Possible waiver statement

Note—If the parties wish to exclude recourse against the arbitral award that may be available under the applicable law, they may consider adding a provision to that effect as suggested below, considering, however, that the effectiveness and conditions of such an exclusion depend on the applicable law.

Waiver. The parties hereby waive their right to any form of recourse against an award to any court or other competent authority, insofar as such waiver can validly be made under the applicable law.

Model statements of independence pursuant to article 11 of the Rules

No circumstances to disclose: I am impartial and independent of each of the parties and intend to remain so. To the best of my knowledge, there are no circumstances, past or present, likely to give rise to justifiable doubts as to my impartiality or independence. I shall promptly notify the parties and the other arbitrators of any such circumstances that may subsequently come to my attention during this arbitration.

Circumstances to disclose: I am impartial and independent of each of the parties and intend to remain so. Attached is a statement made pursuant to article 11 of the UNCITRAL Arbitration Rules of (a) my past and present professional, business and other relationships with the parties and (b) any other relevant circumstances. [Include statement.] I confirm that those circumstances do not affect my independence and impartiality. I shall promptly notify the parties and the other arbitrators of any such further relationships or circumstances that may subsequently come to my attention during this arbitration.

Note—Any party may consider requesting from the arbitrator the following addition to the statement of independence:

I confirm, on the basis of the information presently available to me, that I can devote the time necessary to conduct this arbitration diligently, efficiently and in accordance with the time limits in the Rules.

New York Convention on the Recognition and Enforcement of Foreign Arbitral Awards

Date 10 June 1958
In force 7 June 1959
Source 330 UNTS 38
Link <http://www.uncitral.org/pdf/english/texts/arbitration/NY-conv/XXII_1_e.pdf>

Article I

1. This Convention shall apply to the recognition and enforcement of arbitral awards made in the territory of a State other than the State where the recognition and enforcement of such awards are sought, and arising out of differences between persons, whether physical or legal. It shall also apply to arbitral awards not considered as domestic awards in the State where their recognition and enforcement are sought.

2. The term "arbitral awards" shall include not only awards made by arbitrators appointed for each case but also those made by permanent arbitral bodies to which the parties have submitted.

3. When signing, ratifying or acceding to this Convention, or notifying extension under article X hereof, any State may on the basis of reciprocity declare that it will apply the Convention to the recognition and enforcement of awards made only in the territory of another Contracting State. It may also declare that it will apply the Convention only to differences arising out of legal relationships, whether contractual or not, which are considered as commercial under the national law of the State making such declaration.

Article II

1. Each Contracting State shall recognise an agreement in writing under which the parties undertake to submit to arbitration all or any differences which have arisen or which may arise between them in respect of a defined legal relationship whether contractual or not, concerning a subject-matter capable of settlement by arbitration.

2. The term "agreement in writing" shall include an arbitral clause in a contract or an arbitration agreement, signed by the parties or contained in an exchange of letters or telegrams.

3. The court of a Contracting State, when seized of an action in a matter in respect of which the parties have made an agreement within the meaning of this article shall at the request of one of the parties, refer the parties to arbitration unless it finds that the said agreement is null and void, inoperative or incapable of being performed.

Article III

Each Contracting State shall recognise arbitral awards as binding and enforce them in accordance with the rules of procedure of the territory where the award is relied upon, under the conditions laid down in the following articles. There shall not be imposed substantially more onerous conditions or higher fees or charges on the recognition or enforcement of arbitral awards to which this Convention applies than are imposed on the recognition or enforcement of domestic arbitral awards.

Article IV

1. To obtain the recognition and enforcement mentioned in the preceding article, the party applying for recognition and enforcement shall, at the time of the application, supply:

   (*a*) The duly authenticated original award or a duly certified copy thereof.

   (*b*) The original agreement referred to in article II or a duly certified copy thereof.

2. If the said award or agreement is not made in an official language of the country in which the award is relied upon, the party applying for recognition and enforcement of the award shall produce a translation of these documents into such language. The translation shall be certified by an official or sworn translator or by a diplomatic or consular agent.

Article V

1. Recognition and enforcement of the award may be refused, at the request of the party against whom it is invoked, only if that party furnishes to the competent authority where the recognition and enforcement is sought, proof that:

   (*a*) The parties to the agreement referred to in article II were, under the law applicable to them, under some incapacity, or the said agreement is not valid under the law to which the parties have subjected it or, failing any indication thereon, under the law of the country where the award was made; or

   (*b*) The party against whom the award is invoked was not given proper notice of the appointment of the arbitrator or of the arbitration proceedings or was otherwise unable to present his case; or

   (*c*) The award deals with a difference not contemplated by or not falling within the terms of the submission to arbitration, or it contains decisions on matters beyond the scope of the submission to arbitration, provided that, if the decisions on matters submitted to arbitration can be separated from those not so submitted, that part of the award which contains decisions on matters submitted to arbitration may be recognised and enforced; or

   (*d*) The composition of the arbitral authority or the arbitral procedure was not in accordance with the agreement of the parties, or, failing such agreement, was not in accordance with the law of the country where the arbitration took place; or

   (*e*) The award has not yet become binding on the parties, or has been set aside or suspended by a competent authority of the country in which, or under the law of which, that award was made.

2. Recognition and enforcement of an arbitral award may also be refused if the competent authority in the country where recognition and enforcement is sought finds that:

   (*a*) The subject-matter of the difference is not capable of settlement by arbitration under the law of that country; or

   (*b*) The recognition or enforcement of the award would be contrary to the public policy of that country.

Article VI

If an application for the setting aside or suspension of the award has been made to a competent authority referred to in article V(1)(*e*), the authority before which the award is sought to be relied upon may, if it considers it proper, adjourn the decision on the enforcement of the award and may also, on the application of the party claiming enforcement of the award, order the other party to give suitable security.

Article VII

1. The provisions of the present Convention shall not affect the validity of multilateral or bilateral agreements concerning the recognition and enforcement of arbitral awards entered into by the Contracting States nor deprive any interested party of any right he may have to avail himself of an arbitral award in the manner and to the extent allowed by the law or the treaties of the country where such award is sought to be relied upon.

2. The Geneva Protocol on Arbitration Clauses of 1923 and the Geneva Convention on the Execution of Foreign Arbitral Awards of 1927 shall cease to have effect between Contracting States on their becoming bound and to the extent that they become bound, by this Convention.

Article VIII

1. This Convention shall be open until December 31, 1958 for signature on behalf of any Member of the United Nations and also on behalf of any other State which is or hereafter becomes a member of any specialised agency of the United Nations, or which is or hereafter becomes a party to the Statute of the International Court of Justice, or any other State to which an invitation has been addressed by the General Assembly of the United Nations.

2. This Convention shall be ratified and the instrument of ratification shall be deposited with the Secretary-General of the United Nations.

Article IX

1. This Convention shall be open for accession to all States referred to in article VIII.

2. Accession shall be effected by the deposit of an instrument of accession with the Secretary-General of the United Nations.

Article X

1. Any State may, at the time of signature, ratification or accession, declare that this Convention shall extend to all or any of the territories for the international relations of which it is responsible. Such a declaration shall take effect when the Convention enters into force for the State concerned.

2. At any time thereafter any such extension shall be made by notification addressed to the Secretary-General of the United Nations and shall take effect as from the ninetieth day after the day of receipt by the Secretary-General of the United Nations of this notification, or as from the date of entry into force of the Convention for the State concerned, whichever is the later.

3. With respect to those territories to which this Convention is not extended at the time of signature, ratification or accession, each State concerned shall consider the possibility of taking the necessary steps in order to extend the application of this Convention to such territories, subject, where necessary for constitutional reasons, to the consent of the Governments of such territories.

Article XI

In the case of a federal or non-unitary State, the following provisions shall apply:

(a) With respect to those articles of this Convention that come within the legislative jurisdiction of the federal authority, the obligations of the federal Government shall to this extent be the same as those of Contracting States which are not federal States;

(b) With respect to those articles of this Convention that come within the legislative jurisdiction of constituent states or provinces which are not, under the constitutional system of the federation, bound to take legislative action, the federal Government shall bring such articles with a favourable recommendation to the notice of the appropriate authorities of constituent states or provinces at the earliest possible moment;

(c) A federal State Party to this Convention shall at the request of any other Contracting State transmitted through the Secretary-General of the United Nations, supply a statement of the law and practice of the federation and its constituent units in regard to any particular provision of this Convention, showing the extent to which effect has been given to that provision by legislative or other action.

Article XII

1. This Convention shall come into force on the ninetieth day following the date of deposit of the third instrument of ratification or accession.

2. For each State ratifying or acceding to this Convention after the deposit of the third instrument of ratification or accession, this Convention shall enter into force on the ninetieth day after deposit of such State of its instrument of ratification or accession.

Article XIII

1. Any Contracting State may denounce this Convention by a written notification to the Secretary-General of the United Nations. Denunciation shall take effect one year after the date of receipt of the notification by the Secretary-General.

2. Any State which has made a declaration or notification under article X may, at any time thereafter, by notification to the Secretary-General of the United Nations, declare that this Convention shall cease to extend to the territory concerned one year after the date of the receipt of the notification by the Secretary-General.

3. This Convention shall continue to be applicable to arbitral awards in respect of which recognition or enforcement proceedings have been instituted before the denunciation takes effect.

Article XIV

A Contracting State shall not be entitled to avail itself of the present Convention against other Contracting States except to the extent that it is itself bound to apply the Convention.

Article XV

The Secretary-General of the United Nations shall notify the States contemplated in article VIII of the following:

(a) Signatures and ratifications in accordance with article VIII;

(b) Accessions in accordance with article IX;

(c) Declarations and notifications under articles I, X and XI;

(d) The date upon which this Convention enters into force in accordance with article XII;

(e) Denunciations and notifications in accordance with article XIII.

Article XVI

1. This Convention, of which the Chinese, English, French, Russian and Spanish texts shall be equally authentic, shall be deposited in the archives of the United Nations.

2. The Secretary-General of the United Nations shall transmit a certified copy of this Convention to the States contemplated in article VIII.

Standards Governing Investments Abroad

III-17

OECD Guidelines for Multinational Enterprises

Date   25 May 2011
Source   OECD (ed), *OECD Guidelines for Multinational Enterprises: 2011 Edition* (2011)
Link   <http://www.oecd.org/dataoecd/43/29/48004323.pdf>

PART I   RECOMMENDATIONS FOR RESPONSIBLE BUSINESS CONDUCT IN A GLOBAL CONTEXT

I. Concepts and Principles

1. The *Guidelines* are recommendations jointly addressed by governments to multinational enterprises. They provide principles and standards of good practice consistent with applicable laws and internationally recognised standards. Observance of the *Guidelines* by enterprises is voluntary and not legally enforceable. Nevertheless, some matters covered by the *Guidelines* may also be regulated by national law or international commitments.

2. Obeying domestic laws is the first obligation of enterprises. The *Guidelines* are not a substitute for nor should they be considered to override domestic law and regulation. While the *Guidelines* extend beyond the law in many cases, they should not and are not intended to place an enterprise in situations where it faces conflicting requirements. However, in countries where domestic laws and regulations conflict with the principles and standards of the *Guidelines*, enterprises should seek ways to honour such principles and standards to the fullest extent which does not place them in violation of domestic law.

3. Since the operations of multinational enterprises extend throughout the world, international co-operation in this field should extend to all countries. Governments adhering to the *Guidelines* encourage the enterprises operating on their territories to observe the *Guidelines* wherever they operate, while taking into account the particular circumstances of each host country.

4. A precise definition of multinational enterprises is not required for the purposes of the *Guidelines*. These enterprises operate in all sectors of the economy. They usually comprise companies or other entities established in more than one country and so linked that they may co-ordinate their operations in various ways. While one or more of these entities may be able to exercise a significant influence over the activities of others, their degree of autonomy within the enterprise may vary widely from one multinational enterprise to another. Ownership may be private, State or mixed. The *Guidelines* are addressed to all the entities within the multinational enterprise (parent companies and/or local entities). According to the actual distribution of responsibilities among them, the different entities are expected to co-operate and to assist one another to facilitate observance of the *Guidelines*.

5. The *Guidelines* are not aimed at introducing differences of treatment between multinational and domestic enterprises; they reflect good practice for all. Accordingly, multinational and domestic enterprises are subject to the same expectations in respect of their conduct wherever the *Guidelines* are relevant to both.

6. Governments wish to encourage the widest possible observance of the *Guidelines*. While it is acknowledged that small- and medium-sized enterprises may not have the same capacities as larger enterprises, governments adhering to the *Guidelines* nevertheless encourage them to observe the *Guidelines'* recommendations to the fullest extent possible.

7. Governments adhering to the *Guidelines* should not use them for protectionist purposes nor use them in a way that calls into question the comparative advantage of any country where multinational enterprises invest.

8. Governments have the right to prescribe the conditions under which multinational enterprises operate within their jurisdictions, subject to international law. The entities of a multinational enterprise located in various countries are subject to the laws applicable in these countries. When multinational enterprises are subject to conflicting requirements by adhering countries or third countries, the governments concerned are encouraged to co-operate in good faith with a view to resolving problems that may arise.

9. Governments adhering to the *Guidelines* set them forth with the understanding that they will fulfil their responsibilities to treat enterprises equitably and in accordance with international law and with their contractual obligations.

10. The use of appropriate international dispute settlement mechanisms, including arbitration, is encouraged as a means of facilitating the resolution of legal problems arising between enterprises and host country governments.

11. Governments adhering to the *Guidelines* will implement them and encourage their use. They will establish National Contact Points that promote the *Guidelines* and act as a forum for discussion of all matters relating to the *Guidelines*. The adhering Governments will also participate in appropriate review and consultation procedures to address issues concerning interpretation of the *Guidelines* in a changing world.

II. General Policies

Enterprises should take fully into account established policies in the countries in which they operate, and consider the views of other stakeholders. In this regard:

A. Enterprises should:
1. Contribute to economic, environmental and social progress with a view to achieving sustainable development.
2. Respect the internationally recognised human rights of those affected by their activities.
3. Encourage local capacity building through close co-operation with the local community, including business interests, as well as developing the enterprise's activities in domestic and foreign markets, consistent with the need for sound commercial practice.
4. Encourage human capital formation, in particular by creating employment opportunities and facilitating training opportunities for employees.
5. Refrain from seeking or accepting exemptions not contemplated in the statutory or regulatory framework related to human rights, environmental, health, safety, labour, taxation, financial incentives, or other issues.
6. Support and uphold good corporate governance principles and develop and apply good corporate governance practices, including throughout enterprise groups.
7. Develop and apply effective self-regulatory practices and management systems that foster a relationship of confidence and mutual trust between enterprises and the societies in which they operate.

8. Promote awareness of and compliance by workers employed by multinational enterprises with respect to company policies through appropriate dissemination of these policies, including through training programmes.

9. Refrain from discriminatory or disciplinary action against workers who make *bona fide* reports to management or, as appropriate, to the competent public authorities, on practices that contravene the law, the *Guidelines* or the enterprise's policies.

10. Carry out risk-based due diligence, for example by incorporating it into their enterprise risk management systems, to identify, prevent and mitigate actual and potential adverse impacts as described in paragraphs 11 and 12, and account for how these impacts are addressed. The nature and extent of due diligence depend on the circumstances of a particular situation.

11. Avoid causing or contributing to adverse impacts on matters covered by the *Guidelines*, through their own activities, and address such impacts when they occur.

12. Seek to prevent or mitigate an adverse impact where they have not contributed to that impact, when the impact is nevertheless directly linked to their operations, products or services by a business relationship. This is not intended to shift responsibility from the entity causing an adverse impact to the enterprise with which it has a business relationship.

13. In addition to addressing adverse impacts in relation to matters covered by the *Guidelines*, encourage, where practicable, business partners, including suppliers and sub-contractors, to apply principles of responsible business conduct compatible with the *Guidelines*.

14. Engage with relevant stakeholders in order to provide meaningful opportunities for their views to be taken into account in relation to planning and decision making for projects or other activities that may significantly impact local communities.

15. Abstain from any improper involvement in local political activities.

B. Enterprises are encouraged to:

1. Support, as appropriate to their circumstances, cooperative efforts in the appropriate fora to promote Internet Freedom through respect of freedom of expression, assembly and association online.

2. Engage in or support, where appropriate, private or multi-stakeholder initiatives and social dialogue on responsible supply chain management while ensuring that these initiatives take due account of their social and economic effects on developing countries and of existing internationally recognised standards.

III. Disclosure

1. Enterprises should ensure that timely and accurate information is disclosed on all material matters regarding their activities, structure, financial situation, performance, ownership and governance. This information should be disclosed for the enterprise as a whole, and, where appropriate, along business lines or geographic areas. Disclosure policies of enterprises should be tailored to the nature, size and location of the enterprise, with due regard taken of costs, business confidentiality and other competitive concerns.

2. Disclosure policies of enterprises should include, but not be limited to, material information on:

a) the financial and operating results of the enterprise;

b) enterprise objectives;

c) major share ownership and voting rights, including the structure of a group of enterprises and intra-group relations, as well as control enhancing mechanisms;

d) remuneration policy for members of the board and key executives, and information about board members, including qualifications, the selection process, other enterprise director-ships and whether each board member is regarded as independent by the board;

e) related party transactions;

    f) foreseeable risk factors;

    g) issues regarding workers and other stakeholders;

    h) governance structures and policies, in particular, the content of any corporate governance code or policy and its implementation process.

3. Enterprises are encouraged to communicate additional information that could include:

    a) value statements or statements of business conduct intended for public disclosure including, depending on its relevance for the enterprise's activities, information on the enterprise's policies relating to matters covered by the *Guidelines*;

    b) policies and other codes of conduct to which the enterprise subscribes, their date of adoption and the countries and entities to which such statements apply;

    c) its performance in relation to these statements and codes;

    d) information on internal audit, risk management and legal compliance systems;

    e) information on relationships with workers and other stakeholders.

4. Enterprises should apply high quality standards for accounting, and financial as well as non-financial disclosure, including environmental and social reporting where they exist. The standards or policies under which information is compiled and published should be reported. An annual audit should be conducted by an independent, competent and qualified auditor in order to provide an external and objective assurance to the board and shareholders that the financial statements fairly represent the financial position and performance of the enterprise in all material respects.

IV. Human Rights

States have the duty to protect human rights. Enterprises should, within the framework of internationally recognised human rights, the international human rights obligations of the countries in which they operate as well as relevant domestic laws and regulations:

1. Respect human rights, which means they should avoid infringing on the human rights of others and should address adverse human rights impacts with which they are involved.

2. Within the context of their own activities, avoid causing or contributing to adverse human rights impacts and address such impacts when they occur.

3. Seek ways to prevent or mitigate adverse human rights impacts that are directly linked to their business operations, products or services by a business relationship, even if they do not contribute to those impacts.

4. Have a policy commitment to respect human rights.

5. Carry out human rights due diligence as appropriate to their size, the nature and context of operations and the severity of the risks of adverse human rights impacts.

6. Provide for or co-operate through legitimate processes in the remediation of adverse human rights impacts where they identify that they have caused or contributed to these impacts.

V. Employment and Industrial Relations

Enterprises should, within the framework of applicable law, regulations and prevailing labour relations and employment practices and applicable international labour standards:

1. a) Respect the right of workers employed by the multinational enterprise to establish or join trade unions and representative organisations of their own choosing.

    b) Respect the right of workers employed by the multinational enterprise to have trade unions and representative organisations of their own choosing recognised for the purpose of collective bargaining, and engage in constructive negotiations, either individually or through employers' associations, with such representatives with a view to reaching agreements on terms and conditions of employment.

c) Contribute to the effective abolition of child labour, and take immediate and effective measures to secure the prohibition and elimination of the worst forms of child labour as a matter of urgency.

d) Contribute to the elimination of all forms of forced or compulsory labour and take adequate steps to ensure that forced or compulsory labour does not exist in their operations.

e) Be guided throughout their operations by the principle of equality of opportunity and treatment in employment and not discriminate against their workers with respect to employment or occupation on such grounds as race, colour, sex, religion, political opinion, national extraction or social origin, or other status, unless selectivity concerning worker characteristics furthers established governmental policies which specifically promote greater equality of employment opportunity or relates to the inherent requirements of a job.

2. a) Provide such facilities to workers' representatives as may be necessary to assist in the development of effective collective agreements.

b) Provide information to workers' representatives which is needed for meaningful negotiations on conditions of employment.

c) Provide information to workers and their representatives which enables them to obtain a true and fair view of the performance of the entity or, where appropriate, the enterprise as a whole.

3. Promote consultation and co-operation between employers and workers and their representatives on matters of mutual concern.

4. a) Observe standards of employment and industrial relations not less favourable than those observed by comparable employers in the host country.

b) When multinational enterprises operate in developing countries, where comparable employers may not exist, provide the best possible wages, benefits and conditions of work, within the framework of government policies. These should be related to the economic position of the enterprise, but should be at least adequate to satisfy the basic needs of the workers and their families.

c) Take adequate steps to ensure occupational health and safety in their operations.

5. In their operations, to the greatest extent practicable, employ local workers and provide training with a view to improving skill levels, in co-operation with worker representatives and, where appropriate, relevant governmental authorities.

6. In considering changes in their operations which would have major employment effects, in particular in the case of the closure of an entity involving collective lay-offs or dismissals, provide reasonable notice of such changes to representatives of the workers in their employment and their organisations, and, where appropriate, to the relevant governmental authorities, and co-operate with the worker representatives and appropriate governmental authorities so as to mitigate to the maximum extent practicable adverse effects. In light of the specific circumstances of each case, it would be appropriate if management were able to give such notice prior to the final decision being taken. Other means may also be employed to provide meaningful co-operation to mitigate the effects of such decisions.

7. In the context of bona fide negotiations with workers' representatives on conditions of employment, or while workers are exercising a right to organise, not threaten to transfer the whole or part of an operating unit from the country concerned nor transfer workers from the enterprises' component entities in other countries in order to influence unfairly those negotiations or to hinder the exercise of a right to organise.

8. Enable authorised representatives of the workers in their employment to negotiate on collective bargaining or labour-management relations issues and allow the parties to consult on matters of mutual concern with representatives of management who are authorised to take decisions on these matters.

VI. Environment

Enterprises should, within the framework of laws, regulations and administrative practices in the countries in which they operate, and in consideration of relevant international agreements, principles, objectives, and standards, take due account of the need to protect the environment, public health and safety, and generally to conduct their activities in a manner contributing to the wider goal of sustainable development. In particular, enterprises should:

1. Establish and maintain a system of environmental management appropriate to the enterprise, including:
   a) collection and evaluation of adequate and timely information regarding the environmental, health, and safety impacts of their activities;
   b) establishment of measurable objectives and, where appropriate, targets for improved environmental performance and resource utilisation, including periodically reviewing the continuing relevance of these objectives; where appropriate, targets should be consistent with relevant national policies and international environmental commitments; and
   c) regular monitoring and verification of progress toward environmental, health, and safety objectives or targets.

2. Taking into account concerns about cost, business confidentiality, and the protection of intellectual property rights:
   a) provide the public and workers with adequate, measureable and verifiable (where applicable) and timely information on the potential environment, health and safety impacts of the activities of the enterprise, which could include reporting on progress in improving environmental performance; and
   b) engage in adequate and timely communication and consultation with the communities directly affected by the environmental, health and safety policies of the enterprise and by their implementation.

3. Assess, and address in decision-making, the foreseeable environmental, health, and safety-related impacts associated with the processes, goods and services of the enterprise over their full life cycle with a view to avoiding or, when unavoidable, mitigating them. Where these proposed activities may have significant environmental, health, or safety impacts, and where they are subject to a decision of a competent authority, prepare an appropriate environmental impact assessment.

4. Consistent with the scientific and technical understanding of the risks, where there are threats of serious damage to the environment, taking also into account human health and safety, not use the lack of full scientific certainty as a reason for postponing cost-effective measures to prevent or minimise such damage.

5. Maintain contingency plans for preventing, mitigating, and controlling serious environmental and health damage from their operations, including accidents and emergencies; and mechanisms for immediate reporting to the competent authorities.

6. Continually seek to improve corporate environmental performance, at the level of the enterprise and, where appropriate, of its supply chain, by encouraging such activities as:
   a) adoption of technologies and operating procedures in all parts of the enterprise that reflect standards concerning environmental performance in the best performing part of the enterprise;
   b) development and provision of products or services that have no undue environmental impacts; are safe in their intended use; reduce greenhouse gas emissions; are efficient in their consumption of energy and natural resources; can be reused, recycled, or disposed of safely;
   c) promoting higher levels of awareness among customers of the environmental implications of using the products and services of the enterprise, including, by providing accurate information on their products (for example, on greenhouse gas emissions, biodiversity, resource efficiency, or other environmental issues); and

d) exploring and assessing ways of improving the environmental performance of the enterprise over the longer term, for instance by developing strategies for emission reduction, efficient resource utilisation and recycling, substitution or reduction of use of toxic substances, or strategies on biodiversity.

7. Provide adequate education and training to workers in environmental health and safety matters, including the handling of hazardous materials and the prevention of environmental accidents, as well as more general environmental management areas, such as environmental impact assessment procedures, public relations, and environmental technologies.

8. Contribute to the development of environmentally meaningful and economically efficient public policy, for example, by means of partnerships or initiatives that will enhance environmental awareness and protection.

VII. Combating Bribery, Bribe Solicitation and Extortion

Enterprises should not, directly or indirectly, offer, promise, give, or demand a bribe or other undue advantage to obtain or retain business or other improper advantage. Enterprises should also resist the solicitation of bribes and extortion. In particular, enterprises should:

1. Not offer, promise or give undue pecuniary or other advantage to public officials or the employees of business partners. Likewise, enterprises should not request, agree to or accept undue pecuniary or other advantage from public officials or the employees of business partners. Enterprises should not use third parties such as agents and other intermediaries, consultants, representatives, distributors, consortia, contractors and suppliers and joint venture partners for channelling undue pecuniary or other advantages to public officials, or to employees of their business partners or to their relatives or business associates.

2. Develop and adopt adequate internal controls, ethics and compliance programmes or measures for preventing and detecting bribery, developed on the basis of a risk assessment addressing the individual circumstances of an enterprise, in particular the bribery risks facing the enterprise (such as its geographical and industrial sector of operation). These internal controls, ethics and compliance programmes or measures should include a system of financial and accounting procedures, including a system of internal controls, reasonably designed to ensure the maintenance of fair and accurate books, records, and accounts, to ensure that they cannot be used for the purpose of bribing or hiding bribery. Such individual circumstances and bribery risks should be regularly monitored and re-assessed as necessary to ensure the enterprise's internal controls, ethics and compliance programme or measures are adapted and continue to be effective, and to mitigate the risk of enterprises becoming complicit in bribery, bribe solicitation and extortion.

3. Prohibit or discourage, in internal company controls, ethics and compliance programmes or measures, the use of small facilitation payments, which are generally illegal in the countries where they are made, and, when such payments are made, accurately record these in books and financial records.

4. Ensure, taking into account the particular bribery risks facing the enterprise, properly documented due diligence pertaining to the hiring, as well as the appropriate and regular oversight of agents, and that remuneration of agents is appropriate and for legitimate services only. Where relevant, a list of agents engaged in connection with transactions with public bodies and State-owned enterprises should be kept and made available to competent authorities, in accordance with applicable public disclosure requirements.

5. Enhance the transparency of their activities in the fight against bribery, bribe solicitation and extortion. Measures could include making public commitments against bribery, bribe solicitation and extortion, and disclosing the management systems and the internal controls, ethics and compliance programmes or measures adopted by enterprises in order to honour these commitments. Enterprises should also foster openness and dialogue with the public so as to

promote its awareness of and co-operation with the fight against bribery, bribe solicitation and extortion.

6. Promote employee awareness of and compliance with company policies and internal controls, ethics and compliance programmes or measures against bribery, bribe solicitation and extortion through appropriate dissemination of such policies, programmes or measures and through training programmes and disciplinary procedures.

7. Not make illegal contributions to candidates for public office or to political parties or to other political organisations. Political contributions should fully comply with public disclosure requirements and should be reported to senior management.

VIII. Consumer Interests

When dealing with consumers, enterprises should act in accordance with fair business, marketing and advertising practices and should take all reasonable steps to ensure the quality and reliability of the goods and services that they provide. In particular, they should:

1. Ensure that the goods and services they provide meet all agreed or legally required standards for consumer health and safety, including those pertaining to health warnings and safety information.

2. Provide accurate, verifiable and clear information that is sufficient to enable consumers to make informed decisions, including information on the prices and, where appropriate, content, safe use, environmental attributes, maintenance, storage and disposal of goods and services. Where feasible this information should be provided in a manner that facilitates consumers' ability to compare products.

3. Provide consumers with access to fair, easy to use, timely and effective non-judicial dispute resolution and redress mechanisms, without unnecessary cost or burden.

4. Not make representations or omissions, nor engage in any other practices, that are deceptive, misleading, fraudulent or unfair.

5. Support efforts to promote consumer education in areas that relate to their business activities, with the aim of, *inter alia*, improving the ability of consumers to: *i)* make informed decisions involving complex goods, services and markets, *ii)* better understand the economic, environmental and social impact of their decisions and *iii)* support sustainable consumption.

6. Respect consumer privacy and take reasonable measures to ensure the security of personal data that they collect, store, process or disseminate.

7. Co-operate fully with public authorities to prevent and combat deceptive marketing practices (including misleading advertising and commercial fraud) and to diminish or prevent serious threats to public health and safety or to the environment deriving from the consumption, use or disposal of their goods and services.

8. Take into consideration, in applying the above principles, *i)* the needs of vulnerable and disadvantaged consumers and *ii)* the specific challenges that e-commerce may pose for consumers.

IX. Science and Technology

Enterprises should:

1. Endeavour to ensure that their activities are compatible with the science and technology (S&T) policies and plans of the countries in which they operate and as appropriate contribute to the development of local and national innovative capacity.

2. Adopt, where practicable in the course of their business activities, practices that permit the transfer and rapid diffusion of technologies and know-how, with due regard to the protection of intellectual property rights.

3. When appropriate, perform science and technology development work in host countries to address local market needs, as well as employ host country personnel in an S&T capacity and encourage their training, taking into account commercial needs.

4. When granting licenses for the use of intellectual property rights or when otherwise transferring technology, do so on reasonable terms and conditions and in a manner that contributes to the long term sustainable development prospects of the host country.

5. Where relevant to commercial objectives, develop ties with local universities, public research institutions, and participate in co-operative research projects with local industry or industry associations.

X. Competition

1. Carry out their activities in a manner consistent with all applicable competition laws and regulations, taking into account the competition laws of all jurisdictions in which the activities may have anti-competitive effects.

2. Refrain from entering into or carrying out anti-competitive agreements among competitors, including agreements to:
   a) fix prices;
   b) make rigged bids (collusive tenders);
   c) establish output restrictions or quotas; or
   d) share or divide markets by allocating customers, suppliers, territories or lines of commerce.

3. Co-operate with investigating competition authorities by, among other things and subject to applicable law and appropriate safeguards, providing responses as promptly and completely as practicable to requests for information, and considering the use of available instruments, such as waivers of confidentiality where appropriate, to promote effective and efficient co-operation among investigating authorities.

4. Regularly promote employee awareness of the importance of compliance with all applicable competition laws and regulations, and, in particular, train senior management of the enterprise in relation to competition issues.

XI. Taxation

1. It is important that enterprises contribute to the public finances of host countries by making timely payment of their tax liabilities. In particular, enterprises should comply with both the letter and spirit of the tax laws and regulations of the countries in which they operate. Complying with the spirit of the law means discerning and following the intention of the legislature. It does not require an enterprise to make payment in excess of the amount legally required pursuant to such an interpretation. Tax compliance includes such measures as providing to the relevant authorities timely information that is relevant or required by law for purposes of the correct determination of taxes to be assessed in connection with their operations and conforming transfer pricing practices to the arm's length principle.

2. Enterprises should treat tax governance and tax compliance as important elements of their oversight and broader risk management systems. In particular, corporate boards should adopt tax risk management strategies to ensure that the financial, regulatory and reputational risks associated with taxation are fully identified and evaluated.

PART II   IMPLEMENTATION PROCEDURES OF THE OECD GUIDELINES FOR MULTINATIONAL ENTERPRISES

[Not reproduced]

III-18

ILO Tripartite Declaration of Principles concerning Multinational Enterprises and Social Policy

Date   28 March 2006 (last amended)
Source   International Labour Office (ed), *Tripartite Declaration of Principles concerning Multinational Enterprises and Social Policy* (2006)
Link   <http://www.ilo.org/empent/Publications/WCMS_094386/lang--en/index.htm>

1. Multinational enterprises play an important part in the economies of most countries and in international economic relations. This is of increasing interest to governments as well as to employers and workers and their respective organizations. Through international direct investment and other means such enterprises can bring substantial benefits to home and host countries by contributing to the more efficient utilization of capital, technology and labour. Within the framework of development policies established by governments, they can also make an important contribution to the promotion of economic and social welfare; to the improvement of living standards and the satisfaction of basic needs; to the creation of employment opportunities, both directly and indirectly; and to the enjoyment of basic human rights, including freedom of association, throughout the world. On the other hand, the advances made by multinational enterprises in organizing their operations beyond the national framework may lead to abuse of concentrations of economic power and to conflicts with national policy objectives and with the interest of the workers. In addition, the complexity of multinational enterprises and the difficulty of clearly perceiving their diverse structures, operations and policies sometimes give rise to concern either in the home or in the host countries, or in both.

2. The aim of this Tripartite Declaration of Principles is to encourage the positive contribution which multinational enterprises can make to economic and social progress and to minimize and resolve the difficulties to which their various operations may give rise, taking into account the United Nations resolutions advocating the establishment of a New International Economic Order, as well as subsequent developments within the United Nations, for example, the Global Compact and the Millennium Development Goals.

3. This aim will be furthered by appropriate laws and policies, measures and actions adopted by the governments and by cooperation among the governments and the employers' and workers' organizations of all countries.

4. The principles set out in this Declaration are commended to the governments, the employers' and workers' organizations of home and host countries and to the multinational enterprises themselves.

5. These principles are intended to guide the governments, the employers' and workers' organizations and the multinational enterprises in taking such measures and actions and adopting such social policies, including those based on the principles laid down in the Constitution and the relevant Conventions and Recommendations of the ILO, as would further social progress.

6. To serve its purpose this Declaration does not require a precise legal definition of multinational enterprises; this paragraph is designed to facilitate the understanding of the Declaration and not to provide such a definition. Multinational enterprises include enterprises, whether they are of public, mixed or private ownership, which own or control production, distribution, services or other facilities outside the country in which they are based. The degree of autonomy of entities within multinational enterprises in relation to each other varies widely from one such enterprise to another, depending on the nature of the links between such entities and their fields of activity and having regard to the great diversity in the form of ownership, in the size, in the nature and location of the operations of the enterprises concerned. Unless otherwise specified, the term "multinational enterprise" is used in this Declaration to designate the various entities (parent companies or local entities or both or the organization as a whole) according to the distribution of responsibilities among them, in the expectation that they will cooperate and provide assistance to one another as necessary to facilitate observance of the principles laid down in the Declaration.

7. This Declaration sets out principles in the fields of employment, training, conditions of work and life and industrial relations which governments, employers' and workers' organizations and multinational enterprises are recommended to observe on a voluntary basis; its provisions shall not limit or otherwise affect obligations arising out of ratification of any ILO Convention.

GENERAL POLICIES

8. All the parties concerned by this Declaration should respect the sovereign rights of States, obey the national laws and regulations, give due consideration to local practices and respect relevant international standards. They should respect the Universal Declaration of Human Rights and the corresponding International Covenants adopted by the General Assembly of the United Nations as well as the Constitution of the International Labour Organization and its principles according to which freedom of expression and association are essential to sustained progress. They should contribute to the realization of the ILO Declaration on Fundamental Principles and Rights and Work and its Follow-up, adopted in 1998. They should also honour commitments which they have freely entered into, in conformity with the national law and accepted international obligations.

9. Governments of States which have not yet ratified Conventions Nos. 29, 87, 98, 100, 105, 111, 122, 138 and 182 are urged to do so and in any event to apply, to the greatest extent possible, through their national policies, the principles embodied therein and in Recommendations Nos. 35, 90, 111, 119, 122, 146, 169, 189 and 190. Without prejudice to the obligation of governments to ensure compliance with Conventions they have ratified, in countries in which the Conventions and Recommendations cited in this paragraph are not complied with, all parties should refer to them for guidance in their social policy.

10. Multinational enterprises should take fully into account established general policy objectives of the countries in which they operate. Their activities should be in harmony with the development priorities and social aims and structure of the country in which they operate. To this effect, consultations should be held between multinational enterprises, the government and, wherever appropriate, the national employers' and workers' organizations concerned.

11. The principles laid down in this Declaration do not aim at introducing or maintaining inequalities of treatment between multinational and national enterprises. They reflect good practice for all. Multinational and national enterprises, wherever the principles of this Declaration are relevant to both, should be subject to the same expectations in respect of their conduct in general and their social practices in particular.

12. Governments of home countries should promote good social practice in accordance with this Declaration of Principles, having regard to the social and labour law, regulations and practices in host countries as well as to relevant international standards. Both host and home country governments should be prepared to have consultations with each other, whenever the need arises, on the initiative of either.

EMPLOYMENT

Employment promotion

13. With a view to stimulating economic growth and development, raising living standards, meeting manpower requirements and overcoming unemployment and underemployment, governments should declare and pursue, as a major goal, an active policy designed to promote full, productive and freely chosen employment.

14. This is particularly important in the case of host country governments in developing areas of the world where the problems of unemployment and underemployment are at their most serious. In this connection, the general conclusions adopted by the Tripartite World Conference on Employment, Income Distribution and Social Progress and the International Division of Labour (Geneva, June 1976), and the Global Employment Agenda (Geneva, March 2003) should be kept in mind.

15. Paragraphs 13 and 14 above establish the framework within which due attention should be paid, in both home and host countries, to the employment impact of multinational enterprises.

16. Multinational enterprises, particularly when operating in developing countries, should endeavour to increase employment opportunities and standards, taking into account the employment policies and objectives of the governments, as well as security of employment and the long-term development of the enterprise.

17. Before starting operations, multinational enterprises should, wherever appropriate, consult the competent authorities and the national employers' and workers' organizations in order to keep their manpower plans, as far as practicable, in harmony with national social development policies. Such consultation, as in the case of national enterprises, should continue between the multinational enterprises and all parties concerned, including the workers' organizations.

18. Multinational enterprises should give priority to the employment, occupational development, promotion and advancement of nationals of the host country at all levels in cooperation, as appropriate, with representatives of the workers employed by them or of the organizations of these workers and governmental authorities.

19. Multinational enterprises, when investing in developing countries, should have regard to the importance of using technologies which generate employment, both directly and indirectly. To the extent permitted by the nature of the process and the conditions prevailing in the economic sector concerned, they should adapt technologies to the needs and characteristics of the host countries. They should also, where possible, take part in the development of appropriate technology in host countries.

20. To promote employment in developing countries, in the context of an expanding world economy, multinational enterprises, wherever practicable, should give consideration to the conclusion of contracts with national enterprises for the manufacture of parts and equipment, to the use of local raw materials and to the progressive promotion of the local processing of raw materials. Such arrangements should not be used by multinational enterprises to avoid the responsibilities embodied in the principles of this Declaration.

Equality of opportunity and treatment

21. All governments should pursue policies designed to promote equality of opportunity and treatment in employment, with a view to eliminating any discrimination based on race, colour, sex, religion, political opinion, national extraction or social origin.

22. Multinational enterprises should be guided by this general principle throughout their operations without prejudice to the measures envisaged in paragraph 18 or to government policies designed to correct historical patterns of discrimination and thereby to extend equality of opportunity and treatment in employment. Multinational enterprises should accordingly make qualifications, skill and experience the basis for the recruitment, placement, training and advancement of their staff at all levels.

23. Governments should never require or encourage multinational enterprises to discriminate on any of the grounds mentioned in paragraph 21, and continuing guidance from governments, where appropriate, on the avoidance of such discrimination in employment is encouraged.

Security of employment

24. Governments should carefully study the impact of multinational enterprises on employment in different industrial sectors. Governments, as well as multinational enterprises themselves, in all countries should take suitable measures to deal with the employment and labour market impacts of the operations of multinational enterprises.

25. Multinational enterprises equally with national enterprises, through active manpower planning, should endeavour to provide stable employment for their employees and should observe freely negotiated obligations concerning employment stability and social security. In view of the flexibility which multinational enterprises may have, they should strive to assume a leading role in promoting security of employment, particularly in countries where the discontinuation of operations is likely to accentuate long-term unemployment.

26. In considering changes in operations (including those resulting from mergers, take-overs or transfers of production) which would have major employment effects, multinational enterprises should provide reasonable notice of such changes to the appropriate government authorities and representatives of the workers in their employment and their organizations so that the implications may be examined jointly in order to mitigate adverse effects to the greatest possible extent. This is particularly important in the case of the closure of an entity involving collective lay-offs or dismissals.

27. Arbitrary dismissal procedures should be avoided.

28. Governments, in cooperation with multinational as well as national enterprises, should provide some form of income protection for workers whose employment has been terminated.

TRAINING

29. Governments, in cooperation with all the parties concerned, should develop national policies for vocational training and guidance, closely linked with employment. This is the framework within which multinational enterprises should pursue their training policies.

30. In their operations, multinational enterprises should ensure that relevant training is provided for all levels of their employees in the host country, as appropriate, to meet the needs of the enterprise as well as the development policies of the country. Such training should, to the extent possible, develop generally useful skills and promote career opportunities. This responsibility should be carried out, where appropriate, in cooperation with the authorities of the country, employers' and workers' organizations and the competent local, national or international institutions.

31. Multinational enterprises operating in developing countries should participate, along with national enterprises, in programmes, including special funds, encouraged by host governments and supported by employers' and workers' organizations. These programmes should have the aim of encouraging skill formation and development as well as providing vocational guidance, and should be jointly administered by the parties which support them. Wherever practicable, multinational enterprises should make the services of skilled resource personnel available to help in training programmes organized by governments as part of a contribution to national development.

32. Multinational enterprises, with the cooperation of governments and to the extent consistent with the efficient operation of the enterprise, should afford opportunities within the enterprise as a whole to broaden the experience of local management in suitable fields such as industrial relations.

CONDITIONS OF WORK AND LIFE

Wages, benefits and conditions of work

33. Wages, benefits and conditions of work offered by multinational enterprises should be not less favourable to the workers than those offered by comparable employers in the country concerned.

34. When multinational enterprises operate in developing countries, where comparable employers may not exist, they should provide the best possible wages, benefits and conditions of work, within the framework of government policies. These should be related to the economic position of the enterprise, but should be at least adequate to satisfy basic needs of the workers and their families. Where they provide workers with basic amenities such as housing, medical care or food, these amenities should be of a good standard.

35. Governments, especially in developing countries, should endeavour to adopt suitable measures to ensure that lower income groups and less developed areas benefit as much as possible from the activities of multinational enterprises.

Minimum age

36. Multinational enterprises, as well as national enterprises, should respect the minimum age for admission to employment or work in order to secure the effective abolition of child labour and should take immediate and effective measures within their own competence to secure the prohibition and elimination of the worst forms of child labour as a matter of urgency.

Safety and health

37. Governments should ensure that both multinational and national enterprises provide adequate safety and health standards for their employees. Those governments which have not yet ratified the ILO Conventions on Guarding of Machinery (No. 119), Ionising Radiation (No. 115), Benzene (No. 136) and Occupational Cancer (No. 139) are urged nevertheless to apply to the greatest extent possible the principles embodied in these Conventions and in their related Recommendations (Nos. 118, 114, 144 and 147). The list of occupational diseases and the codes of practice and guides in the current list of ILO publications on occupational safety and health should also be taken into account.

38. Multinational enterprises should maintain the highest standards of safety and health, in conformity with national requirements, bearing in mind their relevant experience within the enterprise as a whole, including any knowledge of special hazards. They should also make available to the representatives of the workers in the enterprise, and upon request, to the competent authorities and the workers' and employers' organizations in all

countries in which they operate, information on the safety and health standards relevant to their local operations, which they observe in other countries. In particular, they should make known to those concerned any special hazards and related protective measures associated with new products and processes. They, like comparable domestic enterprises, should be expected to play a leading role in the examination of causes of industrial safety and health hazards and in the application of resulting improvements within the enterprise as a whole.

39. Multinational enterprises should cooperate in the work of international organizations concerned with the preparation and adoption of international safety and health standards.

40. In accordance with national practice, multinational enterprises should cooperate fully with the competent safety and health authorities, the representatives of the workers and their organizations, and established safety and health organizations. Where appropriate, matters relating to safety and health should be incorporated in agreements with the representatives of the workers and their organizations.

INDUSTRIAL RELATIONS

41. Multinational enterprises should observe standards of industrial relations not less favourable than those observed by comparable employers in the country concerned.

Freedom of association and the right to organize

42. Workers employed by multinational enterprises as well as those employed by national enterprises should, without distinction whatsoever, have the right to establish and, subject only to the rules of the organization concerned, to join organizations of their own choosing without previous authorisation. They should also enjoy adequate protection against acts of anti-union discrimination in respect of their employment.

43. Organizations representing multinational enterprises or the workers in their employment should enjoy adequate protection against any acts of interference by each other or each other's agents or members in their establishment, functioning or administration.

44. Where appropriate, in the local circumstances, multinational enterprises should support representative employers' organizations.

45. Governments, where they do not already do so, are urged to apply the principles of Convention No. 87, Article 5, in view of the importance, in relation to multinational enterprises, of permitting organizations representing such enterprises or the workers in their employment to affiliate with international organizations of employers and workers of their own choosing.

46. Where governments of host countries offer special incentives to attract foreign investment, these incentives should not include any limitation of the workers' freedom of association or the right to organize and bargain collectively.

47. Representatives of the workers in multinational enterprises should not be hindered from meeting for consultation and exchange of views among themselves, provided that the functioning of the operations of the enterprise and the normal procedures which govern relationships with representatives of the workers and their organizations are not thereby prejudiced.

48. Governments should not restrict the entry of representatives of employers' and workers' organizations who come from other countries at the invitation of the local or national organizations concerned for the purpose of consultation on matters of mutual concern, solely on the grounds that they seek entry in that capacity.

Collective bargaining

49. Workers employed by multinational enterprises should have the right, in accordance with national law and practice, to have representative organizations of their own choosing recognized for the purpose of collective bargaining.

50. Measures appropriate to national conditions should be taken, where necessary, to encourage and promote the full development and utilization of machinery for voluntary negotiation between employers or employers' organizations and workers' organizations, with a view to the regulation of terms and conditions of employment by means of collective agreements.

51. Multinational enterprises, as well as national enterprises, should provide workers' representatives with such facilities as may be necessary to assist in the development of effective collective agreements.

52. Multinational enterprises should enable duly authorized representatives of the workers in their employment in each of the countries in which they operate to conduct negotiations with representatives of management who are authorized to take decisions on the matters under negotiation.

53. Multinational enterprises, in the context of bona fide negotiations with the workers' representatives on conditions of employment, or while workers are exercising the right to organize, should not threaten to utilize a capacity to transfer the whole or part of an operating unit from the country concerned in order to influence unfairly those negotiations or to hinder the exercise of the right to organize; nor should they transfer workers from affiliates in foreign countries with a view to undermining bona fide negotiations with the workers' representatives or the workers' exercise of their right to organize.

54. Collective agreements should include provisions for the settlement of disputes arising over their interpretation and application and for ensuring mutually respected rights and responsibilities.

55. Multinational enterprises should provide workers' representatives with information required for meaningful negotiations with the entity involved and, where this accords with local law and practices, should also provide information to enable them to obtain a true and fair view of the performance of the entity or, where appropriate, of the enterprise as a whole.

56. Governments should supply to the representatives of workers' organizations on request, where law and practice so permit, information on the industries in which the enterprise operates, which would help in laying down objective criteria in the collective bargaining process. In this context, multinational as well as national enterprises should respond constructively to requests by governments for relevant information on their operations.

Consultation

57. In multinational as well as in national enterprises, systems devised by mutual agreement between employers and workers and their representatives should provide, in accordance with national law and practice, for regular consultation on matters of mutual concern. Such consultation should not be a substitute for collective bargaining.

Examination of grievances

58. Multinational as well as national enterprises should respect the right of the workers whom they employ to have all their grievances processed in a manner consistent with the following provision: any worker who, acting individually or jointly with other workers, considers that he has grounds for a grievance should have the right to submit such grievance without suffering any prejudice whatsoever as a result, and to have such grievance examined pursuant to an appropriate procedure. This is particularly important whenever the multinational enterprises operate in countries which do not abide by the principles of ILO Conventions pertaining to freedom of association, to the right to organize and bargain collectively, to discrimination, to child labour and to forced labour.

Settlement of industrial disputes

59. Multinational as well as national enterprises jointly with the representatives and organizations of the workers whom they employ should seek to establish voluntary conciliation machinery, appropriate to national conditions, which may include provisions for voluntary arbitration, to assist in the prevention and settlement of industrial disputes between employers and workers. The voluntary conciliation machinery should include equal representation of employers and workers.

PART 4

International Monetary and Financial Law

IV-1

Articles of Agreement of the International Monetary Fund (IMF)

Date 22 July 1944
In force 27 December 1945
Source 2 UNTS 39, as amended
Link <http://www.imf.org/external/pubs/ft/aa/index.htm>

INTRODUCTORY ARTICLE

(i) The International Monetary Fund is established and shall operate in accordance with the provisions of this Agreement as originally adopted and subsequently amended.

(ii) To enable the Fund to conduct its operations and transactions, the Fund shall maintain a General Department and a Special Drawing Rights Department. Membership in the Fund shall give the right to participation in the Special Drawing Rights Department.

(iii) Operations and transactions authorized by this Agreement shall be conducted through the General Department, consisting in accordance with the provisions of this Agreement of the General Resources Account, the Special Disbursement Account, and the Investment Account; except that operations and transactions involving special drawing rights shall be conducted through the Special Drawing Rights Department.

ARTICLE I   PURPOSES

The purposes of the International Monetary Fund are:

(i) To promote international monetary cooperation through a permanent institution which provides the machinery for consultation and collaboration on international monetary problems.

(ii) To facilitate the expansion and balanced growth of international trade, and to contribute thereby to the promotion and maintenance of high levels of employment and real income and to the development of the productive resources of all members as primary objectives of economic policy.

(iii) To promote exchange stability, to maintain orderly exchange arrangements among members, and to avoid competitive exchange depreciation.

(iv) To assist in the establishment of a multilateral system of payments in respect of current transactions between members and in the elimination of foreign exchange restrictions which hamper the growth of world trade.

(v) To give confidence to members by making the general resources of the Fund temporarily available to them under adequate safeguards, thus providing them with opportunity to correct maladjustments in their balance of payments without resorting to measures destructive of national or international prosperity.

(vi) In accordance with the above, to shorten the duration and lessen the degree of disequilibrium in the international balances of payments of members.

The Fund shall be guided in all its policies and decisions by the purposes set forth in this Article.

ARTICLE II MEMBERSHIP

Section 1 Original members

The original members of the Fund shall be those of the countries represented at the United Nations Monetary and Financial Conference whose governments accept membership before December 31, 1945.

Section 2 Other members

Membership shall be open to other countries at such times and in accordance with such terms as may be prescribed by the Board of Governors. These terms, including the terms for subscriptions, shall be based on principles consistent with those applied to other countries that are already members.

ARTICLE III QUOTAS AND SUBSCRIPTIONS

Section 1 Quotas and payment of subscriptions

Each member shall be assigned a quota expressed in special drawing rights. The quotas of the members represented at the United Nations Monetary and Financial Conference which accept membership before December 31, 1945 shall be those set forth in Schedule A. The quotas of other members shall be determined by the Board of Governors. The subscription of each member shall be equal to its quota and shall be paid in full to the Fund at the appropriate depository.

Section 2 Adjustment of quotas

(a) The Board of Governors shall at intervals of not more than five years conduct a general review, and if it deems it appropriate propose an adjustment, of the quotas of the members. It may also, if it thinks fit, consider at any other time the adjustment of any particular quota at the request of the member concerned.

(b) The Fund may at any time propose an increase in the quotas of those members of the Fund that were members on August 31, 1975 in proportion to their quotas on that date in a cumulative amount not in excess of amounts transferred under Article V, Section 12(f)(i) and (j) from the Special Disbursement Account to the General Resources Account.

(c) An eighty-five percent majority of the total voting power shall be required for any change in quotas.

(d) The quota of a member shall not be changed until the member has consented and until payment has been made unless payment is deemed to have been made in accordance with Section 3(b) of this Article.

Section 3 Payments when quotas are changed

(a) Each member which consents to an increase in its quota under Section 2(a) of this Article shall, within a period determined by the Fund, pay to the Fund twenty-five percent of the increase in special drawing rights, but the Board of Governors may prescribe that this payment may be made, on the same basis for all members, in whole or in part in the currencies of other members specified, with their concurrence, by the Fund, or in the member's own currency. A non-participant shall pay in the currencies of other members specified by the Fund, with their concurrence, a proportion of the increase corresponding to the proportion to be paid in special drawing rights by participants. The balance of the increase shall be paid by the member in its own currency. The Fund's holdings of a member's currency shall not be increased above the level at which they would be subject to charges under Article V, Section 8(b)(ii), as a result of payments by other members under this provision.

(b) Each member which consents to an increase in its quota under Section 2(b) of this Article shall be deemed to have paid to the Fund an amount of subscription equal to such increase.

(c) If a member consents to a reduction in its quota, the Fund shall, within sixty days, pay to the member an amount equal to the reduction. The payment shall be made in the member's currency and in such amount of special drawing rights or the currencies of other members specified, with their concurrence, by the Fund as is necessary to prevent the reduction of the Fund's holdings of the currency below the new quota, provided that in exceptional circumstances the Fund may reduce its holdings of the currency below the new quota by payment to the member in its own currency.

(d) A seventy percent majority of the total voting power shall be required for any decision under (a) above, except for the determination of a period and the specification of currencies under that provision.

Section 4   Substitution of securities for currency

The Fund shall accept from any member, in place of any part of the member's currency in the General Resources Account which in the judgment of the Fund is not needed for its operations and transactions, notes or similar obligations issued by the member or the depository designated by the member under Article XIII, Section 2, which shall be non-negotiable, non-interest bearing and payable at their face value on demand by crediting the account of the Fund in the designated depository. This Section shall apply not only to currency subscribed by members but also to any currency otherwise due to, or acquired by, the Fund and to be placed in the General Resources Account.

ARTICLE IV   OBLIGATIONS REGARDING EXCHANGE ARRANGEMENTS

Section 1   General obligations of members

Recognizing that the essential purpose of the international monetary system is to provide a framework that facilitates the exchange of goods, services, and capital among countries, and that sustains sound economic growth, and that a principal objective is the continuing development of the orderly underlying conditions that are necessary for financial and economic stability, each member undertakes to collaborate with the Fund and other members to assure orderly exchange arrangements and to promote a stable system of exchange rates. In particular, each member shall:

(i)   endeavor to direct its economic and financial policies toward the objective of fostering orderly economic growth with reasonable price stability, with due regard to its circumstances;

(ii) seek to promote stability by fostering orderly underlying economic and financial conditions and a monetary system that does not tend to produce erratic disruptions;

(iii) avoid manipulating exchange rates or the international monetary system in order to prevent effective balance of payments adjustment or to gain an unfair competitive advantage over other members; and

(iv) follow exchange policies compatible with the undertakings under this Section.

Section 2   General exchange arrangements

(a) Each member shall notify the Fund, within thirty days after the date of the second amendment of this Agreement, of the exchange arrangements it intends to apply in fulfillment of its obligations under Section 1 of this Article, and shall notify the Fund promptly of any changes in its exchange arrangements.

(b) Under an international monetary system of the kind prevailing on January 1, 1976, exchange arrangements may include (i) the maintenance by a member of a value for its currency in terms of the special drawing right or another denominator, other than gold, selected by the member, or (ii) cooperative arrangements by which members maintain the value of their currencies in relation to the value of the currency or currencies of other members, or (iii) other exchange arrangements of a member's choice.

(c) To accord with the development of the international monetary system, the Fund, by an eighty-five percent majority of the total voting power, may make provision for general exchange arrangements without limiting the right of members to have exchange arrangements of their choice consistent with the purposes of the Fund and the obligations under Section 1 of this Article.

Section 3 Surveillance over exchange arrangements

(a) The Fund shall oversee the international monetary system in order to ensure its effective operation, and shall oversee the compliance of each member with its obligations under Section 1 of this Article.

(b) In order to fulfill its functions under (a) above, the Fund shall exercise firm surveillance over the exchange rate policies of members, and shall adopt specific principles for the guidance of all members with respect to those policies. Each member shall provide the Fund with the information necessary for such surveillance, and, when requested by the Fund, shall consult with it on the member's exchange rate policies. The principles adopted by the Fund shall be consistent with cooperative arrangements by which members maintain the value of their currencies in relation to the value of the currency or currencies of other members, as well as with other exchange arrangements of a member's choice consistent with the purposes of the Fund and Section 1 of this Article. These principles shall respect the domestic social and political policies of members, and in applying these principles the Fund shall pay due regard to the circumstances of members.

Section 4 Par values

The Fund may determine, by an eighty-five percent majority of the total voting power, that international economic conditions permit the introduction of a widespread system of exchange arrangements based on stable but adjustable par values. The Fund shall make the determination on the basis of the underlying stability of the world economy, and for this purpose shall take into account price movements and rates of expansion in the economies of members. The determination shall be made in light of the evolution of the international monetary system, with particular reference to sources of liquidity, and, in order to ensure the effective operation of a system of par values, to arrangements under which both members in surplus and members in deficit in their balances of payments take prompt, effective, and symmetrical action to achieve adjustment, as well as to arrangements for intervention and the treatment of imbalances. Upon making such determination, the Fund shall notify members that the provisions of Schedule C apply.

Section 5 Separate currencies within a member's territories

(a) Action by a member with respect to its currency under this Article shall be deemed to apply to the separate currencies of all territories in respect of which the member has accepted this Agreement under Article XXXI, Section 2(g) unless the member declares that its action relates either to the metropolitan currency alone, or only to one or more specified separate currencies, or to the metropolitan currency and one or more specified separate currencies.

(b) Action by the Fund under this Article shall be deemed to relate to all currencies of a member referred to in (a) above unless the Fund declares otherwise.

ARTICLE V   OPERATIONS AND TRANSACTIONS OF THE FUND

Section 1 Agencies dealing with the Fund

Each member shall deal with the Fund only through its Treasury, central bank, stabilization fund, or other similar fiscal agency, and the Fund shall deal only with or through the same agencies.

Section 2   Limitation on the Fund's operations and transactions

(a) Except as otherwise provided in this Agreement, transactions on the account of the Fund shall be limited to transactions for the purpose of supplying a member, on the initiative of such member, with special drawing rights or the currencies of other members from the general resources of the Fund, which shall be held in the General Resources Account, in exchange for the currency of the member desiring to make the purchase.

(b) If requested, the Fund may decide to perform financial and technical services, including the administration of resources contributed by members, that are consistent with the purposes of the Fund. Operations involved in the performance of such financial services shall not be on the account of the Fund. Services under this subsection shall not impose any obligation on a member without its consent.

Section 3   Conditions governing use of the Fund's general resources

(a) The Fund shall adopt policies on the use of its general resources, including policies on stand-by or similar arrangements, and may adopt special policies for special balance of payments problems, that will assist members to solve their balance of payments problems in a manner consistent with the provisions of this Agreement and that will establish adequate safeguards for the temporary use of the general resources of the Fund.

(b) A member shall be entitled to purchase the currencies of other members from the Fund in exchange for an equivalent amount of its own currency subject to the following conditions:

  (i) the member's use of the general resources of the Fund would be in accordance with the provisions of this Agreement and the policies adopted under them;

  (ii) the member represents that it has a need to make the purchase because of its balance of payments or its reserve position or developments in its reserves;

  (iii) the proposed purchase would be a reserve tranche purchase, or would not cause the Fund's holdings of the purchasing member's currency to exceed two hundred percent of its quota;

  (iv) the Fund has not previously declared under Section 5 of this Article, Article VI, Section 1, or Article XXVI, Section 2(a) that the member desiring to purchase is ineligible to use the general resources of the Fund.

(c) The Fund shall examine a request for a purchase to determine whether the proposed purchase would be consistent with the provisions of this Agreement and the policies adopted under them, provided that requests for reserve tranche purchases shall not be subject to challenge.

(d) The Fund shall adopt policies and procedures on the selection of currencies to be sold that take into account, in consultation with members, the balance of payments and reserve position of members and developments in the exchange markets, as well as the desirability of promoting over time balanced positions in the Fund, provided that if a member represents that it is proposing to purchase the currency of another member because the purchasing member wishes to obtain an equivalent amount of its own currency offered by the other member, it shall be entitled to purchase the currency of the other member unless the Fund has given notice under Article VII, Section 3 that its holdings of the currency have become scarce.

(e) (i) Each member shall ensure that balances of its currency purchased from the Fund are balances of a freely usable currency or can be exchanged at the time of purchase for a freely usable currency of its choice at an exchange rate between the two currencies equivalent to the exchange rate between them on the basis of Article XIX, Section 7(a).

   (ii) Each member whose currency is purchased from the Fund or is obtained in exchange for currency purchased from the Fund shall collaborate with the Fund and other members to enable such balances of its currency to be exchanged, at the time of purchase, for the freely usable currencies of other members.

(iii) An exchange under (i) above of a currency that is not freely usable shall be made by the member whose currency is purchased unless that member and the purchasing member agree on another procedure.

(iv) A member purchasing from the Fund the freely usable currency of another member and wishing to exchange it at the time of purchase for another freely usable currency shall make the exchange with the other member if requested by that member. The exchange shall be made for a freely usable currency selected by the other member at the rate of exchange referred to in (i) above.

(f) Under policies and procedures which it shall adopt, the Fund may agree to provide a participant making a purchase in accordance with this Section with special drawing rights instead of the currencies of other members.

Section 4   Waiver of conditions

The Fund may in its discretion, and on terms which safeguard its interests, waive any of the conditions prescribed in Section 3(b)(iii) and (iv) of this Article, especially in the case of members with a record of avoiding large or continuous use of the Fund's general resources. In making a waiver it shall take into consideration periodic or exceptional requirements of the member requesting the waiver. The Fund shall also take into consideration a member's willingness to pledge as collateral security acceptable assets having a value sufficient in the opinion of the Fund to protect its interests and may require as a condition of waiver the pledge of such collateral security.

Section 5   Ineligibility to use the Fund's general resources

Whenever the Fund is of the opinion that any member is using the general resources of the Fund in a manner contrary to the purposes of the Fund, it shall present to the member a report setting forth the views of the Fund and prescribing a suitable time for reply. After presenting such a report to a member, the Fund may limit the use of its general resources by the member. If no reply to the report is received from the member within the prescribed time, or if the reply received is unsatisfactory, the Fund may continue to limit the member's use of the general resources of the Fund or may, after giving reasonable notice to the member, declare it ineligible to use the general resources of the Fund.

Section 6   Other purchases and sales of special drawing rights by the Fund

(a) The Fund may accept special drawing rights offered by a participant in exchange for an equivalent amount of the currencies of other members.

(b) The Fund may provide a participant, at its request, with special drawing rights for an equivalent amount of the currencies of other members. The Fund's holdings of a member's currency shall not be increased as a result of these transactions above the level at which the holdings would be subject to charges under Section 8(b)(ii) of this Article.

(c) The currencies provided or accepted by the Fund under this Section shall be selected in accordance with policies that take into account the principles of Section 3(d) or 7(i) of this Article. The Fund may enter into transactions under this Section only if a member whose currency is provided or accepted by the Fund concurs in that use of its currency.

Section 7   Repurchase by a member of its currency held by the Fund

(a) A member shall be entitled to repurchase at any time the Fund's holdings of its currency that are subject to charges under Section 8(b) of this Article.

(b) A member that has made a purchase under Section 3 of this Article will be expected normally, as its balance of payments and reserve position improves, to repurchase the Fund's holdings of its currency that result from the purchase and are subject to charges under Section 8(b) of this Article. A member shall repurchase these holdings if, in accordance with policies on repurchase that the Fund shall adopt and after consultation with the member, the Fund represents to the member that it should repurchase because of an improvement in its balance of payments and reserve position.

(c) A member that has made a purchase under Section 3 of this Article shall repurchase the Fund's holdings of its currency that result from the purchase and are subject to charges under Section 8(b) of this Article not later than five years after the date on which the purchase was made. The Fund may prescribe that repurchase shall be made by a member in installments during the period beginning three years and ending five years after the date of a purchase. The Fund, by an eighty-five percent majority of the total voting power, may change the periods for repurchase under this subsection, and any period so adopted shall apply to all members.

(d) The Fund, by an eighty-five percent majority of the total voting power, may adopt periods other than those that apply in accordance with (c) above, which shall be the same for all members, for the repurchase of holdings of currency acquired by the Fund pursuant to a special policy on the use of its general resources.

(e) A member shall repurchase, in accordance with policies that the Fund shall adopt by a seventy percent majority of the total voting power, the Fund's holdings of its currency that are not acquired as a result of purchases and are subject to charges under Section 8(b)(ii) of this Article.

(f) A decision prescribing that under a policy on the use of the general resources of the Fund the period for repurchase under (c) or (d) above shall be shorter than the one in effect under the policy shall apply only to holdings acquired by the Fund subsequent to the effective date of the decision.

(g) The Fund, on the request of a member, may postpone the date of discharge of a repurchase obligation, but not beyond the maximum period under (c) or (d) above or under policies adopted by the Fund under (e) above, unless the Fund determines, by a seventy percent majority of the total voting power, that a longer period for repurchase which is consistent with the temporary use of the general resources of the Fund is justified because discharge on the due date would result in exceptional hardship for the member.

(h) The Fund's policies under Section 3(d) of this Article may be supplemented by policies under which the Fund may decide after consultation with a member to sell under Section 3(b) of this Article its holdings of the member's currency that have not been repurchased in accordance with this Section 7, without prejudice to any action that the Fund may be authorized to take under any other provision of this Agreement.

(i) All repurchases under this Section shall be made with special drawing rights or with the currencies of other members specified by the Fund. The Fund shall adopt policies and procedures with regard to the currencies to be used by members in making repurchases that take into account the principles in Section 3(d) of this Article. The Fund's holdings of a member's currency that is used in repurchase shall not be increased by the repurchase above the level at which they would be subject to charges under Section 8(b)(ii) of this Article.

(j) (i) If a member's currency specified by the Fund under (i) above is not a freely usable currency, the member shall ensure that the repurchasing member can obtain it at the time of the repurchase in exchange for a freely usable currency selected by the member whose currency has been specified. An exchange of currency under this provision shall take place at an exchange rate between the two currencies equivalent to the exchange rate between them on the basis of Article XIX, Section 7(a).

   (ii) Each member whose currency is specified by the Fund for repurchase shall collaborate with the Fund and other members to enable repurchasing members, at the time of the repurchase, to obtain the specified currency in exchange for the freely usable currencies of other members.

(iii) An exchange under (j)(i) above shall be made with the member whose currency is specified unless that member and the repurchasing member agree on another procedure.

(iv) If a repurchasing member wishes to obtain, at the time of the repurchase, the freely usable currency of another member specified by the Fund under (i) above, it shall, if requested by the other member, obtain the currency from the other member in exchange for a freely usable currency at the rate of exchange referred to in (j)(i) above. The Fund may adopt regulations on the freely usable currency to be provided in an exchange.

Section 8 Charges

(a) (i) The Fund shall levy a service charge on the purchase by a member of special drawing rights or the currency of another member held in the General Resources Account in exchange for its own currency, provided that the Fund may levy a lower service charge on reserve tranche purchases than on other purchases. The service charge on reserve tranche purchases shall not exceed one-half of one percent.

(ii) The Fund may levy a charge for stand-by or similar arrangements. The Fund may decide that the charge for an arrangement shall be offset against the service charge levied under (i) above on purchases under the arrangement.

(b) The Fund shall levy charges on its average daily balances of a member's currency held in the General Resources Account to the extent that they

(i) have been acquired under a policy that has been the subject of an exclusion under Article XXX(c), or

(ii) exceed the amount of the member's quota after excluding any balances referred to in (i) above.

The rates of charge normally shall rise at intervals during the period in which the balances are held.

(c) If a member fails to make a repurchase required under Section 7 of this Article, the Fund, after consultation with the member on the reduction of the Fund's holdings of its currency, may impose such charges as the Fund deems appropriate on its holdings of the member's currency that should have been repurchased.

(d) A seventy percent majority of the total voting power shall be required for the determination of the rates of charge under (a) and (b) above, which shall be uniform for all members, and under (c) above.

(e) A member shall pay all charges in special drawing rights, provided that in exceptional circumstances the Fund may permit a member to pay charges in the currencies of other members specified by the Fund, after consultation with them, or in its own currency. The Fund's holdings of a member's currency shall not be increased as a result of payments by other members under this provision above the level at which they would be subject to charges under (b)(ii) above.

Section 9 Remuneration

(a) The Fund shall pay remuneration on the amount by which the percentage of quota prescribed under (b) or (c) below exceeds the Fund's average daily balances of a member's currency held in the General Resources Account other than balances acquired under a policy that has been the subject of an exclusion under Article XXX(c). The rate of remuneration, which shall be determined by the Fund by a seventy percent majority of the total voting power, shall be the same for all members and shall be not more than, nor less than four-fifths of, the rate of interest under Article XX, Section 3. In establishing the rate of remuneration, the Fund shall take into account the rates of charge under Article V, Section 8(b).

(b) The percentage of quota applying for the purposes of (a) above shall be:

(i) for each member that became a member before the second amendment of this Agreement, a percentage of quota corresponding to seventy-five percent of its quota on the date of the second amendment of this Agreement, and for each member that became a member after the date of the second amendment of this Agreement, a percentage of quota calculated by dividing the total of the amounts corresponding to the percentages of quota that apply to the other members on the date on which the member became a member by the total of the quotas of the other members on the same date; plus

(ii) the amounts it has paid to the Fund in currency or special drawing rights under Article III, Section 3(a) since the date applicable under (b)(i) above; and minus

(iii) the amounts it has received from the Fund in currency or special drawing rights under Article III, Section 3(c) since the date applicable under (b)(i) above.

(c) The Fund, by a seventy percent majority of the total voting power, may raise the latest percentage of quota applying for the purposes of (a) above to each member to:

(i) a percentage, not in excess of one hundred percent, that shall be determined for each member on the basis of the same criteria for all members, or

(ii) one hundred percent for all members.

(d) Remuneration shall be paid in special drawing rights, provided that either the Fund or the member may decide that the payment to the member shall be made in its own currency.

Section 10   Computations

(a) The value of the Fund's assets held in the accounts of the General Department shall be expressed in terms of the special drawing right.

(b) All computations relating to currencies of members for the purpose of applying the provisions of this Agreement, except Article IV and Schedule C, shall be at the rates at which the Fund accounts for these currencies in accordance with Section 11 of this Article.

(c) Computations for the determination of amounts of currency in relation to quota for the purpose of applying the provisions of this Agreement shall not include currency held in the Special Disbursement Account or in the Investment Account.

Section 11   Maintenance of value

(a) The value of the currencies of members held in the General Resources Account shall be maintained in terms of the special drawing right in accordance with exchange rates under Article XIX, Section 7(a).

(b) An adjustment in the Fund's holdings of a member's currency pursuant to this Section shall be made on the occasion of the use of that currency in an operation or transaction between the Fund and another member and at such other times as the Fund may decide or the member may request. Payments to or by the Fund in respect of an adjustment shall be made within a reasonable time, as determined by the Fund, after the date of adjustment, and at any other time requested by the member.

Section 12   Other operations and transactions

(a) The Fund shall be guided in all its policies and decisions under this Section by the objectives set forth in Article VIII, Section 7 and by the objective of avoiding the management of the price, or the establishment of a fixed price, in the gold market.

(b) Decisions of the Fund to engage in operations or transactions under (c), (d), and (e) below shall be made by an eighty-five percent majority of the total voting power.

(c) The Fund may sell gold for the currency of any member after consulting the member for whose currency the gold is sold, provided that the Fund's holdings of a member's currency held in the General Resources Account shall not be increased by the sale above the level at which they would be subject to charges under Section 8(b)(ii) of this Article without the concurrence of the member, and provided that, at the request of the member, the Fund at the time of sale shall exchange for the currency of another member such part of the currency received as would prevent such an increase. The exchange of a currency for the currency of another member shall be made after consultation with that member, and shall not increase the Fund's holdings of that member's currency above the level at which they would be subject to charges under Section 8(b)(ii) of this Article. The Fund shall adopt policies and procedures with regard to exchanges that take into account the principles applied under Section 7(i) of this Article. Sales under this provision to a member shall be at a price agreed for each transaction on the basis of prices in the market.

(d) The Fund may accept payments from a member in gold instead of special drawing rights or currency in any operations or transactions under this Agreement. Payments to the Fund under this provision shall be at a price agreed for each operation or transaction on the basis of prices in the market.

(e) The Fund may sell gold held by it on the date of the second amendment of this Agreement to those members that were members on August 31, 1975 and that agree to buy it, in proportion to their quotas on that date. If the Fund intends to sell gold under (c) above for the purpose of (f)(ii) below, it may sell to each developing member that agrees to buy it that portion of the gold which, if sold under (c) above, would have produced the excess that could have been distributed to it under (f)(iii) below. The gold that would be sold under this provision to a member that has been declared ineligible to use the general resources of the Fund under Section 5 of this Article shall be sold to it when the ineligibility ceases, unless the Fund decides to make the sale sooner. The sale of gold to a member under this subsection (e) shall be made in exchange for its currency and at a price equivalent at the time of sale to one special drawing right per 0.888 671 gram of fine gold.

(f) Whenever under (c) above the Fund sells gold held by it on the date of the second amendment of this Agreement, an amount of the proceeds equivalent at the time of sale to one special drawing right per 0.888 671 gram of fine gold shall be placed in the General Resources Account and, except as the Fund may decide otherwise under (g) below, any excess shall be held in the Special Disbursement Account. The assets held in the Special Disbursement Account shall be held separately from the other accounts of the General Department, and may be used at any time:

(i)   to make transfers to the General Resources Account for immediate use in operations and transactions authorized by provisions of this Agreement other than this Section;

(ii)   for operations and transactions that are not authorized by other provisions of this Agreement but are consistent with the purposes of the Fund. Under this subsection (f)(ii) balance of payments assistance may be made available on special terms to developing members in difficult circumstances, and for this purpose the Fund shall take into account the level of per capita income;

(iii) for distribution to those developing members that were members on August 31, 1975, in proportion to their quotas on that date, of such part of the assets that the Fund decides to use for the purposes of (ii) above as corresponds to the proportion of the quotas of these members on the date of distribution to the total of the quotas of all members on the same date, provided that the distribution under this provision to a member that has been declared ineligible to use the general resources of the Fund under Section 5 of this Article shall be made when the ineligibility ceases, unless the Fund decides to make the distribution sooner.

Decisions to use assets pursuant to (i) above shall be taken by a seventy percent majority of the total voting power, and decisions pursuant to (ii) and (iii) above shall be taken by an eighty-five percent majority of the total voting power.

(g) The Fund may decide, by an eighty-five percent majority of the total voting power, to transfer a part of the excess referred to in (f) above to the Investment Account for use pursuant to the provisions of Article XII, Section 6(f).

(h) Pending uses specified under (f) above, the Fund may invest a member's currency held in the Special Disbursement Account for investment as it may determine, in accordance with rules and regulations adopted by the Fund by a seventy percent majority of the total voting power. The income of investment and interest received under (f)(ii) above shall be placed in the Special Disbursement Account.

(i) The General Resources Account shall be reimbursed from time to time in respect of the expenses of administration of the Special Disbursement Account paid from the General Resources Account by transfers from the Special Disbursement Account on the basis of a reasonable estimate of such expenses.

(j) The Special Disbursement Account shall be terminated in the event of the liquidation of the Fund and may be terminated prior to liquidation of the Fund by a seventy percent majority of the total voting power. Upon termination of the account because of the liquidation of the Fund, any assets in this account shall be distributed in accordance with the provisions of Schedule K. Upon termination prior to liquidation of the Fund, any assets in this account shall be transferred to the General Resources Account for immediate use in operations and transactions. The Fund, by a seventy percent majority of the total voting power, shall adopt rules and regulations for the administration of the Special Disbursement Account.

(k) Whenever under (c) above the Fund sells gold acquired by it after the date of the second amendment of this Agreement, an amount of the proceeds equivalent to the acquisition price of the gold shall be placed in the General Resources Account, and any excess shall be placed in the Investment Account for use pursuant to the provisions of Article XII, Section 6(f). If any gold acquired by the Fund after the date of the second amendment of this Agreement is sold after April 7, 2008 but prior to the date of entry into force of this provision, then, upon the entry into force of this provision, and notwithstanding the limit set forth in Article XII, Section 6(f)(ii), the Fund shall transfer to the Investment Account from the General Resources Account an amount equal to the proceeds of such sale less (i) the acquisition price of the gold sold, and (ii) any amount of such proceeds in excess of the acquisition price that may have already been transferred to the Investment Account prior to the date of entry into force of this provision.

ARTICLE VI   CAPITAL TRANSFERS

Section 1   Use of the Fund's general resources for capital transfers

(a) A member may not use the Fund's general resources to meet a large or sustained outflow of capital except as provided in Section 2 of this Article, and the Fund may request a member to exercise controls to prevent such use of the general resources of the Fund. If, after receiving such a request, a member fails to exercise appropriate controls, the Fund may declare the member ineligible to use the general resources of the Fund.

(b) Nothing in this Section shall be deemed:
  (i) to prevent the use of the general resources of the Fund for capital transactions of reasonable amount required for the expansion of exports or in the ordinary course of trade, banking, or other business; or
  (ii) to affect capital movements which are met out of a member's own resources, but members undertake that such capital movements will be in accordance with the purposes of the Fund.

Section 2   Special provisions for capital transfers

A member shall be entitled to make reserve tranche purchases to meet capital transfers.

Section 3   Controls of capital transfers

Members may exercise such controls as are necessary to regulate international capital movements, but no member may exercise these controls in a manner which will restrict payments for current transactions or which will unduly delay transfers of funds in settlement of commitments, except as provided in Article VII, Section 3(b) and in Article XIV, Section 2.

ARTICLE VII   REPLENISHMENT AND SCARCE CURRENCIES

Section 1   Measures to replenish the Fund's holdings of currencies

The Fund may, if it deems such action appropriate to replenish its holdings of any member's currency in the General Resources. Replenishment and Scarce Currencies Account needed in connection with its transactions, take either or both of the following steps:

(i)   propose to the member that, on terms and conditions agreed between the Fund and the member, the latter lend its currency to the Fund or that, with the concurrence of the member, the Fund borrow such currency from some other source either within or outside the territories of the member, but no member shall be under any obligation to make such loans to the Fund or to concur in the borrowing of its currency by the Fund from any other source;

(ii)   require the member, if it is a participant, to sell its currency to the Fund for special drawing rights held in the General Resources Account, subject to Article XIX, Section 4. In replenishing with special drawing rights, the Fund shall pay due regard to the principles of designation under Article XIX, Section 5.

Section 2   General scarcity of currency

If the Fund finds that a general scarcity of a particular currency is developing, the Fund may so inform members and may issue a report setting forth the causes of the scarcity and containing recommendations designed to bring it to an end. A representative of the member whose currency is involved shall participate in the preparation of the report.

Section 3   Scarcity of the Fund's holdings

(a)   If it becomes evident to the Fund that the demand for a member's currency seriously threatens the Fund's ability to supply that currency, the Fund, whether or not it has issued a report under Section 2 of this Article, shall formally declare such currency scarce and shall thenceforth apportion its existing and accruing supply of the scarce currency with due regard to the relative needs of members, the general international economic situation, and any other pertinent considerations. The Fund shall also issue a report concerning its action.

(b)   A formal declaration under (a) above shall operate as an authorization to any member, after consultation with the Fund, temporarily to impose limitations on the freedom of exchange operations in the scarce currency. Subject to the provisions of Article IV and Schedule C, the member shall have complete jurisdiction in determining the nature of such limitations, but they shall be no more restrictive than is necessary to limit the demand for the scarce currency to the supply held by, or accruing to, the member in question, and they shall be relaxed and removed as rapidly as conditions permit.

(c)   The authorization under (b) above shall expire whenever the Fund formally declares the currency in question to be no longer scarce.

Section 4   Administration of restrictions

Any member imposing restrictions in respect of the currency of any other member pursuant to the provisions of Section 3(b) of this Article shall give sympathetic consideration to any representations by the other member regarding the administration of such restrictions.

Section 5   Effect of other international agreements on restrictions

Members agree not to invoke the obligations of any engagements entered into with other members prior to this Agreement in such manner as will prevent the operation of the provisions of this Article.

ARTICLE VIII   GENERAL OBLIGATIONS OF MEMBERS

Section 1   Introduction

In addition to the obligations assumed under other articles of this Agreement, each member undertakes the obligations set out in this Article.

Section 2   Avoidance of restrictions on current payments

(a) Subject to the provisions of Article VII, Section 3(b) and Article XIV, Section 2, no member shall, without the approval of the Fund, impose restrictions on the making of payments and transfers for current international transactions.

(b) Exchange contracts which involve the currency of any member and which are contrary to the exchange control regulations of that member maintained or imposed consistently with this Agreement shall be unenforceable in the territories of any member. In addition, members may, by mutual accord, cooperate in measures for the purpose of making the exchange control regulations of either member more effective, provided that such measures and regulations are consistent with this Agreement.

Section 3   Avoidance of discriminatory currency practices

No member shall engage in, or permit any of its fiscal agencies referred to in Article V, Section 1 to engage in, any discriminatory currency arrangements or multiple currency practices, whether within or outside margins under Article IV or prescribed by or under Schedule C, except as authorized under this Agreement or approved by the Fund. If such arrangements and practices are engaged in at the date when this Agreement enters into force, the member concerned shall consult with the Fund as to their progressive removal unless they are maintained or imposed under Article XIV, Section 2, in which case the provisions of Section 3 of that Article shall apply.

Section 4   Convertibility of foreign-held balances

(a) Each member shall buy balances of its currency held by another member if the latter, in requesting the purchase, represents:

(i) that the balances to be bought have been recently acquired as a result of current transactions; or

(ii) that their conversion is needed for making payments for current transactions.

The buying member shall have the option to pay either in special drawing rights, subject to Article XIX, Section 4, or in the currency of the member making the request.

(b) The obligation in (a) above shall not apply when:

(i) the convertibility of the balances has been restricted consistently with Section 2 of this Article or Article VI, Section 3;

(ii) the balances have accumulated as a result of transactions effected before the removal by a member of restrictions maintained or imposed under Article XIV, Section 2;

(iii) the balances have been acquired contrary to the exchange regulations of the member which is asked to buy them;

(iv) the currency of the member requesting the purchase has been declared scarce under Article VII, Section 3(a); or

(v) the member requested to make the purchase is for any reason not entitled to buy currencies of other members from the Fund for its own currency.

Section 5 Furnishing of information

(a) The Fund may require members to furnish it with such information as it deems necessary for its activities, including, as the minimum necessary for the effective discharge of the Fund's duties, national data on the following matters:

(i)   official holdings at home and abroad of (1) gold, (2) foreign exchange;

(ii)   holdings at home and abroad by banking and financial agencies, other than official agencies, of (1) gold, (2) foreign exchange;

(iii)   production of gold;

(iv)   gold exports and imports according to countries of destination and origin;

(v)   total exports and imports of merchandise, in terms of local currency values, according to countries of destination and origin;

(vi)   international balance of payments, including (1) trade in goods and services, (2) gold transactions, (3) known capital transactions, and (4) other items;

(vii)   international investment position, i.e., investments within the territories of the member owned abroad and investments abroad owned by persons in its territories so far as it is possible to furnish this information;

(viii) national income;

(ix)   price indices, i.e., indices of commodity prices in wholesale and retail markets and of export and import prices;

(x)   buying and selling rates for foreign currencies;

(xi)   exchange controls, i.e., a comprehensive statement of exchange controls in effect at the time of assuming membership in the Fund and details of subsequent changes as they occur; and

(xii)   where official clearing arrangements exist, details of amounts awaiting clearance in respect of commercial and financial transactions, and of the length of time during which such arrears have been outstanding.

(b) In requesting information the Fund shall take into consideration the varying ability of members to furnish the data requested. Members shall be under no obligation to furnish information in such detail that the affairs of individuals or corporations are disclosed. Members undertake, however, to furnish the desired information in as detailed and accurate a manner as is practicable and, so far as possible, to avoid mere estimates.

(c) The Fund may arrange to obtain further information by agreement with members. It shall act as a centre for the collection and exchange of information on monetary and financial problems, thus facilitating the preparation of studies designed to assist members in developing policies which further the purposes of the Fund.

Section 6 Consultation between members regarding existing international agreements

Where under this Agreement a member is authorized in the special or temporary circumstances specified in the Agreement to maintain or establish restrictions on exchange transactions, and there are other engagements between members entered into prior to this Agreement which conflict with the application of such restrictions, the parties to such engagements shall consult with one another with a view to making such mutually acceptable adjustments as may be necessary. The provisions of this Article shall be without prejudice to the operation of Article VII, Section 5.

Section 7 Obligation to collaborate regarding policies on reserve assets

Each member undertakes to collaborate with the Fund and with other members in order to ensure that the policies of the member with respect to reserve assets shall be consistent with the objectives of promoting better international surveillance of international liquidity and making the special drawing right the principal reserve asset in the international monetary system.

ARTICLE IX STATUS, IMMUNITIES, AND PRIVILEGES

Section 1 Purposes of Article
To enable the Fund to fulfill the functions with which it is entrusted, the status, immunities, and privileges set forth in this Article shall be accorded to the Fund in the territories of each member.

Section 2 Status of the Fund
The Fund shall possess full juridical personality, and in particular, the capacity:

(i)   to contract;

(ii) to acquire and dispose of immovable and movable property; and

(iii) to institute legal proceedings.

Section 3 Immunity from judicial process
The Fund, its property and its assets, wherever located and by whomsoever held, shall enjoy immunity from every form of judicial process except to the extent that it expressly waives its immunity for the purpose of any proceedings or by the terms of any contract.

Section 4 Immunity from other action
Property and assets of the Fund, wherever located and by whomsoever held, shall be immune from search, requisition, confiscation, expropriation, or any other form of seizure by executive or legislative action.

Section 5 Immunity of archives
The archives of the Fund shall be inviolable.

Section 6 Freedom of assets from restrictions
To the extent necessary to carry out the activities provided for in this Agreement, all property and assets of the Fund shall be free from restrictions, regulations, controls, and moratoria of any nature.

Section 7 Privilege for communications
The official communications of the Fund shall be accorded by members the same treatment as the official communications of other members.

Section 8 Immunities and privileges of officers and employees
All Governors, Executive Directors, Alternates, members of committees, representatives appointed under Article XII, Section 3(j), advisors of any of the foregoing persons, officers, and employees of the Fund:

(i)   shall be immune from legal process with respect to acts performed by them in their official capacity except when the Fund waives this immunity;

(ii) not being local nationals, shall be granted the same immunities from immigration restrictions, alien registration requirements, and national service obligations and the same facilities as regards exchange restrictions as are accorded by members to the representatives, officials, and employees of comparable rank of other members; and

(iii) shall be granted the same treatment in respect of traveling facilities as is accorded by members to representatives, officials, and employees of comparable rank of other members.

Section 9 Immunities from taxation
(a) The Fund, its assets, property, income, and its operations and transactions authorized by this Agreement shall be immune from all taxation and from all customs duties. The Fund shall also be immune from liability for the collection or payment of any tax or duty.

(b) No tax shall be levied on or in respect of salaries and emoluments paid by the Fund to Executive Directors, Alternates, officers, or employees of the Fund who are not local citizens, local subjects, or other local nationals.

(c) No taxation of any kind shall be levied on any obligation or security issued by the Fund, including any dividend or interest thereon, by whomsoever held:
   (i) which discriminates against such obligation or security solely because of its origin; or

(ii) if the sole jurisdictional basis for such taxation is the place or currency in which it is issued, made payable or paid, or the location of any office or place of business maintained by the Fund.

Section 10   Application of Article

Each member shall take such action as is necessary in its own territories for the purpose of making effective in terms of its own law the principles set forth in this Article and shall inform the Fund of the detailed action which it has taken.

ARTICLE X   RELATIONS WITH OTHER INTERNATIONAL ORGANIZATIONS

The Fund shall cooperate within the terms of this Agreement with any general international organization and with public international organizations having specialized responsibilities in related fields. Any arrangements for such cooperation which would involve a modification of any provision of this Agreement may be effected only after amendment to this Agreement under Article XXVIII.

ARTICLE XI   RELATIONS WITH NON-MEMBER COUNTRIES

Section 1 Undertakings regarding relations with non-member countries
Each member undertakes:

(i)   not to engage in, nor to permit any of its fiscal agencies referred to in Article V, Section 1 to engage in, any transactions with a non-member or with persons in a non-member's territories which would be contrary to the provisions of this Agreement or the purposes of the Fund;

(ii) not to cooperate with a non-member or with persons in a non-member's territories in practices which would be contrary to the provisions of this Agreement or the purposes of the Fund; and

(iii) to cooperate with the Fund with a view to the application in its territories of appropriate measures to prevent transactions with non-members or with persons in their territories which would be contrary to the provisions of this Agreement or the purposes of the Fund.

Section 2   Restrictions on transactions with non-member countries
Nothing in this Agreement shall affect the right of any member to impose restrictions on exchange transactions with non-members or with persons in their territories unless the Fund finds that such restrictions prejudice the interests of members and are contrary to the purposes of the Fund.

ARTICLE XII   ORGANIZATION AND MANAGEMENT

Section 1   Structure of the Fund
The Fund shall have a Board of Governors, an Executive Board, a Managing Director, and a staff, and a Council if the Board of Governors decides, by an eighty-five percent majority of the total voting power, that the provisions of Schedule D shall be applied.

Section 2   Board of Governors
(a) All powers under this Agreement not conferred directly on the Board of Governors, the Executive Board, or the Managing Director shall be vested in the Board of Governors. The Board of Governors shall consist of one Governor and one Alternate appointed by each member in such manner as it may determine. Each Governor and each Alternate shall serve

until a new appointment is made. No Alternate may vote except in the absence of his principal. The Board of Governors shall select one of the Governors as Chairman.

(b) The Board of Governors may delegate to the Executive Board authority to exercise any powers of the Board of Governors, except the powers conferred directly by this Agreement on the Board of Governors.

(c) The Board of Governors shall hold such meetings as may be provided for by the Board of Governors or called by the Executive Board. Meetings of the Board of Governors shall be called whenever requested by fifteen members or by members having one-quarter of the total voting power.

(d) A quorum for any meeting of the Board of Governors shall be a majority of the Governors having not less than two-thirds of the total voting power.

(e) Each Governor shall be entitled to cast the number of votes allotted under Section 5 of this Article to the member appointing him.

(f) The Board of Governors may by regulation establish a procedure whereby the Executive Board, when it deems such action to be in the best interests of the Fund, may obtain a vote of the Governors on a specific question without calling a meeting of the Board of Governors.

(g) The Board of Governors, and the Executive Board to the extent authorized, may adopt such rules and regulations as may be necessary or appropriate to conduct the business of the Fund.

(h) Governors and Alternates shall serve as such without compensation from the Fund, but the Fund may pay them reasonable expenses incurred in attending meetings.

(i) The Board of Governors shall determine the remuneration to be paid to the Executive Directors and their Alternates and the salary and terms of the contract of service of the Managing Director.

(j) The Board of Governors and the Executive Board may appoint such committees as they deem advisable. Membership of committees need not be limited to Governors or Executive Directors or their Alternates.

Section 3   Executive Board

(a) The Executive Board shall be responsible for conducting the business of the Fund, and for this purpose shall exercise all the powers delegated to it by the Board of Governors.

(b) The Executive Board shall consist of Executive Directors with the Managing Director as chairman. Of the Executive Directors:
   (i) five shall be appointed by the five members having the largest quotas; and
   (ii) fifteen shall be elected by the other members.

   For the purpose of each regular election of Executive Directors, the Board of Governors, by an eighty-five percent majority of the total voting power, may increase or decrease the number of Executive Directors in (ii) above. The number of Executive Directors in (ii) above shall be reduced by one or two, as the case may be, if Executive Directors are appointed under (c) below, unless the Board of Governors decides, by an eighty-five percent majority of the total voting power, that this reduction would hinder the effective discharge of the functions of the Executive Board or of Executive Directors or would threaten to upset a desirable balance in the Executive Board.

(c) If, at the second regular election of Executive Directors and thereafter, the members entitled to appoint Executive Directors under (b)(i) above do not include the two members, the holdings of whose currencies by the Fund in the General Resources Account have been, on the average over the preceding two years, reduced below their quotas by the largest absolute amounts in terms of the special drawing right, either one or both of such members, as the case may be, may appoint an Executive Director.

(d) Elections of elective Executive Directors shall be conducted at intervals of two years in accordance with the provisions of Schedule E, supplemented by such regulations as the Fund deems appropriate. For each regular election of Executive Directors, the Board of Governors may issue regulations making changes in the proportion of votes required to elect Executive Directors under the provisions of Schedule E.

(e) Each Executive Director shall appoint an Alternate with full power to act for him when he is not present, provided that the Board of Governors may adopt rules enabling an Executive Director elected by more than a specified number of members to appoint two Alternates. Such rules, if adopted, may only be modified in the context of the regular election of Executive Directors and shall require an Executive Director appointing two Alternates to designate: (i) the Alternate who shall act for the Executive Director when he is not present and both Alternates are present and (ii) the Alternate who shall exercise the powers of the Executive Director under (f) below. When the Executive Directors appointing them are present, Alternates may participate in meetings but may not vote.

(f) Executive Directors shall continue in office until their successors are appointed or elected. If the office of an elected Executive Director becomes vacant more than ninety days before the end of his term, another Executive Director shall be elected for the remainder of the term by the members that elected the former Executive Director. A majority of the votes cast shall be required for election. While the office remains vacant, the Alternate of the former Executive Director shall exercise his powers, except that of appointing an Alternate.

(g) The Executive Board shall function in continuous session at the principal office of the Fund and shall meet as often as the business of the Fund may require.

(h) A quorum for any meeting of the Executive Board shall be a majority of the Executive Directors having not less than one-half of the total voting power.

(i) (i)   Each appointed Executive Director shall be entitled to cast the number of votes allotted under Section 5 of this Article to the member appointing him.

(ii) If the votes allotted to a member that appoints an Executive Director under (c) above were cast by an Executive Director together with the votes allotted to other members as a result of the last regular election of Executive Directors, the member may agree with each of the other members that the number of votes allotted to it shall be cast by the appointed Executive Director. A member making such an agreement shall not participate in the election of Executive Directors.

(iii) Each elected Executive Director shall be entitled to cast the number of votes which counted towards his election.

(iv) When the provisions of Section 5(b) of this Article are applicable, the votes which an Executive Director would otherwise be entitled to cast shall be increased or decreased correspondingly. All the votes which an Executive Director is entitled to cast shall be cast as a unit.

(v)   When the suspension of the voting rights of a member is terminated under Article XXVI, Section 2(b), and the member is not entitled to appoint an Executive Director, the member may agree with all the members that have elected an Executive Director that the number of votes allotted to that member shall be cast by such Executive Director, provided that, if no regular election of Executive Directors has been conducted during the period of the suspension, the Executive Director in whose election the member had participated prior to the suspension, or his successor elected in accordance with paragraph 3(c)(i) of Schedule L or with (f) above, shall be entitled to cast the number of votes allotted to the member. The member shall be deemed to have participated in the election of the Executive Director entitled to cast the number of votes allotted to the member.

(j) The Board of Governors shall adopt regulations under which a member not entitled to appoint an Executive Director under (b) above may send a representative to attend any meeting of the Executive Board when a request made by, or a matter particularly affecting, that member is under consideration.

Section 4   Managing Director and staff

(a) The Executive Board shall select a Managing Director who shall not be a Governor or an Executive Director. The Managing Director shall be chairman of the Executive Board, but shall have no vote except a deciding vote in case of an equal division. He may participate in meetings of the Board of Governors, but shall not vote at such meetings. The Managing Director shall cease to hold office when the Executive Board so decides.

(b) The Managing Director shall be chief of the operating staff of the Fund and shall conduct, under the direction of the Executive Board, the ordinary business of the Fund. Subject to the general control of the Executive Board, he shall be responsible for the organization, appointment, and dismissal of the staff of the Fund.

(c) The Managing Director and the staff of the Fund, in the discharge of their functions, shall owe their duty entirely to the Fund and to no other authority. Each member of the Fund shall respect the international character of this duty and shall refrain from all attempts to influence any of the staff in the discharge of these functions.

(d) In appointing the staff the Managing Director shall, subject to the paramount importance of securing the highest standards of efficiency and of technical competence, pay due regard to the importance of recruiting personnel on as wide a geographical basis as possible.

Section 5   Voting

(a) The total votes of each member shall be equal to the sum of its basic votes and its quota-based votes.

    (i)   The basic votes of each member shall be the number of votes that results from the equal distribution among all the members of 5.502 percent of the aggregate sum of the total voting power of all the members, provided that there shall be no fractional basic votes.

    (ii) The quota-based votes of each member shall be the number of votes that results from the allocation of one vote for each part of its quota equivalent to one hundred thousand special drawing rights.

(b) Whenever voting is required under Article V, Section 4 or 5, each member shall have the number of votes to which it is entitled under (a) above adjusted

    (i)   by the addition of one vote for the equivalent of each four hundred thousand special drawing rights of net sales of its currency from the general resources of the Fund up to the date when the vote is taken, or

    (ii) by the subtraction of one vote for the equivalent of each four hundred thousand special drawing rights of its net purchases under Article V, Section 3(b) and (f) up to the date when the vote is taken,

provided that neither net purchases nor net sales shall be deemed at any time to exceed an amount equal to the quota of the member involved.

(c) Except as otherwise specifically provided, all decisions of the Fund shall be made by a majority of the votes cast.

Section 6   Reserves, distribution of net income, and investment

(a) The Fund shall determine annually what part of its net income shall be placed to general reserve or special reserve, and what part, if any, shall be distributed.

(b) The Fund may use the special reserve for any purpose for which it may use the general reserve, except distribution.

(c) If any distribution is made of the net income of any year, it shall be made to all members in proportion to their quotas.

(d) The Fund, by a seventy percent majority of the total voting power, may decide at any time to distribute any part of the general reserve. Any such distribution shall be made to all members in proportion to their quotas.

(e) Payments under (c) and (d) above shall be made in special drawing rights, provided that either the Fund or the member may decide that the payment to the member shall be made in its own currency.

(f) (i) The Fund may establish an Investment Account for the purposes of this subsection (f). The assets of the Investment Account shall be held separately from the other accounts of the General Department.

(ii) The Fund may decide to transfer to the Investment Account a part of the proceeds of the sale of gold in accordance with Article V, Section 12(g) and, by a seventy percent majority of the total voting power, may decide to transfer to the Investment Account, for immediate investment, currencies held in the General Resources Account. The amount of these transfers shall not exceed the total amount of the general reserve and the special reserve at the time of the decision.

(iii) The Fund may use a member's currency held in the Investment Account for investment as it may determine, in accordance with rules and regulations adopted by the Fund by a seventy percent majority of the total voting power. The rules and regulations adopted pursuant to this provision shall be consistent with (vii), (viii), and (ix) below.

(iv) The income of investment may be invested in accordance with the provisions of this subsection (f). Income not invested shall be held in the Investment Account or may be used for meeting the expenses of conducting the business of the Fund.

(v) The Fund may use a member's currency held in the Investment Account to obtain the currencies needed to meet the expenses of conducting the business of the Fund.

(vi) The Investment Account shall be terminated in the event of liquidation of the Fund and may be terminated, or the amount of the investment may be reduced, prior to liquidation of the Fund by a seventy percent majority of the total voting power.

(vii) Upon termination of the Investment Account because of liquidation of the Fund, any assets in this account shall be distributed in accordance with the provisions of Schedule K, provided that a portion of these assets corresponding to the proportion of the assets transferred to this account under Article V, Section 12(g) to the total of the assets transferred to this account shall be deemed to be assets held in the Special Disbursement Account and shall be distributed in accordance with Schedule K, paragraph 2(a) (ii).

(viii) Upon termination of the Investment Account prior to liquidation of the Fund, a portion of the assets held in this account corresponding to the proportion of the assets transferred to this account under Article V, Section 12(g) to the total of the assets transferred to the account shall be transferred to the Special Disbursement Account if it has not been terminated, and the balance of the assets held in the Investment Account shall be transferred to the General Resources Account for immediate use in operations and transactions.

(ix) On a reduction of the amount of the investment by the Fund, a portion of the reduction corresponding to the proportion of the assets transferred to the Investment Account under Article V, Section 12(g) to the total of the assets transferred to this account shall be transferred to the Special Disbursement Account if it has not been terminated, and the balance of the reduction shall be transferred to the General Resources Account for immediate use in operations and transactions.

Section 7 Publication of reports

(a) The Fund shall publish an annual report containing an audited statement of its accounts, and shall issue, at intervals of three months or less, a summary statement of its operations and transactions and its holdings of special drawing rights, gold, and currencies of members.

(b) The Fund may publish such other reports as it deems desirable for carrying out its purposes.

Section 8   Communication of views to members

The Fund shall at all times have the right to communicate its views informally to any member on any matter arising under this Agreement. The Fund may, by a seventy percent majority of the total voting power, decide to publish a report made to a member regarding its monetary or economic conditions and developments which directly tend to produce a serious disequilibrium in the international balance of payments of members. If the member is not entitled to appoint an Executive Director, it shall be entitled to representation in accordance with Section 3(j) of this Article. The Fund shall not publish a report involving changes in the fundamental structure of the economic organization of members.

ARTICLE XIII   OFFICES AND DEPOSITORIES

Section 1   Location of offices

The principal office of the Fund shall be located in the territory of the member having the largest quota, and agencies or branch offices may be established in the territories of other members.

Section 2   Depositories

(a) Each member shall designate its central bank as a depository for all the Fund's holdings of its currency, or if it has no central bank it shall designate such other institution as may be acceptable to the Fund.

(b) The Fund may hold other assets, including gold, in the depositories designated by the five members having the largest quotas and in such other designated depositories as the Fund may select. Initially, at least one-half of the holdings of the Fund shall be held in the depository designated by the member in whose territories the Fund has its principal office and at least forty percent shall be held in the depositories designated by the remaining four members referred to above. However, all transfers of gold by the Fund shall be made with due regard to the costs of transport and anticipated requirements of the Fund. In an emergency the Executive Board may transfer all or any part of the Fund's gold holdings to any place where they can be adequately protected.

Section 3   Guarantee of the Fund's assets

Each member guarantees all assets of the Fund against loss resulting from failure or default on the part of the depository designated by it.

ARTICLE XIV   TRANSITIONAL ARRANGEMENTS

Section 1   Notification to the Fund

Each member shall notify the Fund whether it intends to avail itself of the transitional arrangements in Section 2 of this Article, or whether it is prepared to accept the obligations of Article VIII, Sections 2, 3, and 4. A member availing itself of the transitional arrangements shall notify the Fund as soon thereafter as it is prepared to accept these obligations.

Section 2   Exchange restrictions

A member that has notified the Fund that it intends to avail itself of transitional arrangements under this provision may, notwithstanding the provisions of any other articles of this Agreement, maintain and adapt to changing circumstances the restrictions on payments and transfers for current international transactions that were in effect on the date on which it became a member. Members shall, however, have continuous regard in their foreign exchange policies to the purposes of the Fund, and, as soon as conditions permit, they shall take all possible measures to develop such commercial and financial arrangements with other members as will facilitate international payments and the promotion of a stable system of exchange rates. In particular, members shall withdraw restrictions maintained under this Section as soon as they are satisfied that they will be able, in the absence of such restrictions, to settle their balance of payments in a manner which will not unduly encumber their access to the general resources of the Fund.

Section 3   Action of the Fund relating to restrictions

The Fund shall make annual reports on the restrictions in force under Section 2 of this Article. Any member retaining any restrictions inconsistent with Article VIII, Sections 2, 3, or 4 shall consult the Fund annually as to their further retention. The Fund may, if it deems such action necessary in exceptional circumstances, make representations to any member that conditions are favorable for the withdrawal of any particular restriction, or for the general abandonment of restrictions, inconsistent with the provisions of any other articles of this Agreement. The member shall be given a suitable time to reply to such representations. If the Fund finds that the member persists in maintaining restrictions which are inconsistent with the purposes of the Fund, the member shall be subject to Article XXVI, Section 2(a).

ARTICLE XV   SPECIAL DRAWING RIGHTS

Section 1   Authority to allocate special drawing rights

(a) To meet the need, as and when it arises, for a supplement to existing reserve assets, the Fund is authorized to allocate special drawing rights in accordance with the provisions of Article XVIII to members that are participants in the Special Drawing Rights Department.

(b) In addition, the Fund shall allocate special drawing rights to members that are participants in the Special Drawing Rights Department in accordance with the provisions of Schedule M.

Section 2   Valuation of the special drawing right

The method of valuation of the special drawing right shall be determined by the Fund by a seventy percent majority of the total voting power, provided, however, that an eighty-five percent majority of the total voting power shall be required for a change in the principle of valuation or a fundamental change in the application of the principle in effect.

ARTICLE XVI   GENERAL DEPARTMENT AND SPECIAL DRAWING RIGHTS DEPARTMENT

Section 1   Separation of operations and transactions

All operations and transactions involving special drawing rights shall be conducted through the Special Drawing Rights Department. All other operations and transactions on the account of the Fund authorized by or under this Agreement shall be conducted through the General Department. Operations and transactions pursuant to Article XVII, Section 2 shall be conducted through the General Department as well as the Special Drawing Rights Department.

Section 2   Separation of assets and property

All assets and property of the Fund, except resources administered under Article V, Section 2(b), shall be held in the General Department, provided that assets and property acquired under Article XX, Section 2 and Articles XXIV and XXV and Schedules H and I shall be held in the Special Drawing Rights Department. Any assets or property held in one Department shall not be available to discharge or meet the liabilities, obligations, or losses of the Fund incurred in the conduct of the operations and transactions of the other Department, except that the expenses of conducting the business of the Special Drawing Rights Department shall be paid by the Fund from the General Department which shall be reimbursed in special drawing rights from time to time by assessments under Article XX, Section 4 made on the basis of a reasonable estimate of such expenses.

Section 3   Recording and information

All changes in holdings of special drawing rights shall take effect only when recorded by the Fund in the Special Drawing Rights Department. Participants shall notify the Fund of the provisions of this Agreement under which special drawing rights are used. The Fund may require participants to furnish it with such other information as it deems necessary for its functions.

ARTICLE XVII PARTICIPANTS AND OTHER HOLDERS OF SPECIAL DRAWING RIGHTS

Section 1 Participants

Each member of the Fund that deposits with the Fund an instrument setting forth that it undertakes all the obligations of a participant in the Special Drawing Rights Department in accordance with its law and that it has taken all steps necessary to enable it to carry out all of these obligations shall become a participant in the Special Drawing Rights Department as of the date the instrument is deposited, except that no member shall become a participant before the provisions of this Agreement pertaining exclusively to the Special Drawing Rights Department have entered into force and instruments have been deposited under this Section by members that have at least seventy-five percent of the total of quotas.

Section 2 Fund as a holder

The Fund may hold special drawing rights in the General Resources Account and may accept and use them in operations and transactions conducted through the General Resources Account with participants in accordance with the provisions of this Agreement or with prescribed holders in accordance with the terms and conditions prescribed under Section 3 of this Article.

Section 3 Other holders

The Fund may prescribe:

(i) as holders, non-members, members that are non-participants, institutions that perform functions of a central bank for more than one member, and other official entities;

(ii) the terms and conditions on which prescribed holders may be permitted to hold special drawing rights and may accept and use them in operations and transactions with participants and other prescribed holders; and

(iii) the terms and conditions on which participants and the Fund through the General Resources Account may enter into operations and transactions in special drawing rights with prescribed holders.

An eighty-five percent majority of the total voting power shall be required for prescriptions under (i) above. The terms and conditions prescribed by the Fund shall be consistent with the provisions of this Agreement and the effective functioning of the Special Drawing Rights Department.

ARTICLE XVIII ALLOCATION AND CANCELLATION OF SPECIAL DRAWING RIGHTS

Section 1 Principles and considerations governing allocation and cancellation

(a) In all its decisions with respect to the allocation and cancellation of special drawing rights the Fund shall seek to meet the long-term global need, as and when it arises, to supplement existing reserve assets in such manner as will promote the attainment of its purposes and will avoid economic stagnation and deflation as well as excess demand and inflation in the world.

(b) The first decision to allocate special drawing rights shall take into account, as special considerations, a collective judgment that there is a global need to supplement reserves, and the attainment of a better balance of payments equilibrium, as well as the likelihood of a better working of the adjustment process in the future.

Section 2 Allocation and cancellation

(a) Decisions of the Fund to allocate or cancel special drawing rights shall be made for basic periods which shall run consecutively and shall be five years in duration. The first basic period shall begin on the date of the first decision to allocate special drawing rights or such later date as may be specified in that decision. Any allocations or cancellations shall take place at yearly intervals.

(b) The rates at which allocations are to be made shall be expressed as percentages of quotas on the date of each decision to allocate. The rates at which special drawing rights are to be cancelled shall be expressed as percentages of net cumulative allocations of special drawing rights on the date of each decision to cancel. The percentages shall be the same for all participants.

(c) In its decision for any basic period the Fund may provide, notwithstanding (a) and (b) above, that:
  (i)   the duration of the basic period shall be other than five years; or
  (ii)   the allocations or cancellations shall take place at other than yearly intervals; or
  (iii) the basis for allocations or cancellations shall be the quotas or net cumulative allocations on dates other than the dates of decisions to allocate or cancel.

(d) A member that becomes a participant after a basic period starts shall receive allocations beginning with the next basic period in which allocations are made after it becomes a participant unless the Fund decides that the new participant shall start to receive allocations beginning with the next allocation after it becomes a participant. If the Fund decides that a member that becomes a participant during a basic period shall receive allocations during the remainder of that basic period and the participant was not a member on the dates established under (b) or (c) above, the Fund shall determine the basis on which these allocations to the participant shall be made.

(e) A participant shall receive allocations of special drawing rights made pursuant to any decision to allocate unless:
  (i)   the Governor for the participant did not vote in favor of the decision; and
  (ii)   the participant has notified the Fund in writing prior to the first allocation of special drawing rights under that decision that it does not wish special drawing rights to be allocated to it under the decision. On the request of a participant, the Fund may decide to terminate the effect of the notice with respect to allocations of special drawing rights subsequent to the termination.

(f) If on the effective date of any cancellation the amount of special drawing rights held by a participant is less than its share of the special drawing rights that are to be cancelled, the participant shall eliminate its negative balance as promptly as its gross reserve position permits and shall remain in consultation with the Fund for this purpose. Special drawing rights acquired by the participant after the effective date of the cancellation shall be applied against its negative balance and cancelled.

Section 3 Unexpected major developments

The Fund may change the rates or intervals of allocation or cancellation during the rest of a basic period or change the length of a basic period or start a new basic period, if at any time the Fund finds it desirable to do so because of unexpected major developments.

Section 4 Decisions on allocations and cancellations

(a) Decisions under Section 2(a), (b), and (c) or Section 3 of this Article shall be made by the Board of Governors on the basis of proposals of the Managing Director concurred in by the Executive Board.

(b) Before making any proposal, the Managing Director, after having satisfied himself that it will be consistent with the provisions of Section 1(a) of this Article, shall conduct such consultations as will enable him to ascertain that there is broad support among participants for the proposal. In addition, before making a proposal for the first allocation, the Managing Director shall satisfy himself that the provisions of Section 1(b) of this Article have been met and that there is broad support among participants to begin allocations; he shall make a proposal for the first allocation as soon after the establishment of the Special Drawing Rights Department as he is so satisfied.

(c) The Managing Director shall make proposals:
  (i)   not later than six months before the end of each basic period;
  (ii) if no decision has been taken with respect to allocation or cancellation for a basic period, whenever he is satisfied that the provisions of (b) above have been met;
  (iii) when, in accordance with Section 3 of this Article, he considers that it would be desirable to change the rate or intervals of allocation or cancellation or change the length of a basic period or start a new basic period; or
  (iv) within six months of a request by the Board of Governors or the Executive Board;

  provided that, if under (i), (iii), or (iv) above the Managing Director ascertains that there is no proposal which he considers to be consistent with the provisions of Section 1 of this Article that has broad support among participants in accordance with (b) above, he shall report to the Board of Governors and to the Executive Board.

(d) An eighty-five percent majority of the total voting power shall be required for decisions under Section 2(a), (b), and (c) or Section 3 of this Article except for decisions under Section 3 with respect to a decrease in the rates of allocation.

ARTICLE XIX   OPERATIONS AND TRANSACTIONS IN SPECIAL DRAWING RIGHTS

Section 1   Use of special drawing rights
Special drawing rights may be used in the operations and transactions authorized by or under this Agreement.

Section 2   Operations and transactions between participants
(a) A participant shall be entitled to use its special drawing rights to obtain an equivalent amount of currency from a participant designated under Section 5 of this Article.

(b) A participant, in agreement with another participant, may use its special drawing rights to obtain an equivalent amount of currency from the other participant.

(c) The Fund, by a seventy percent majority of the total voting power, may prescribe operations in which a participant is authorized to engage in agreement with another participant on such terms and conditions as the Fund deems appropriate. The terms and conditions shall be consistent with the effective functioning of the Special Drawing Rights Department and the proper use of special drawing rights in accordance with this Agreement.

(d) The Fund may make representations to a participant that enters into any operation or transaction under (b) or (c) above that in the judgment of the Fund may be prejudicial to the process of designation according to the principles of Section 5 of this Article or is otherwise inconsistent with Article XXII. A participant that persists in entering into such operations or transactions shall be subject to Article XXIII, Section 2(b).

Section 3   Requirement of need
(a) In transactions under Section 2(a) of this Article, except as otherwise provided in (c) below, a participant will be expected to use its special drawing rights only if it has a need because of its balance of payments or its reserve position or developments in its reserves, and not for the sole purpose of changing the composition of its reserves.

(b) The use of special drawing rights shall not be subject to challenge on the basis of the expectation in (a) above, but the Fund may make representations to a participant that fails to fulfill this expectation. A participant that persists in failing to fulfill this expectation shall be subject to Article XXIII, Section 2(b).

(c) The Fund may waive the expectation in (a) above in any transactions in which a participant uses special drawing rights to obtain an equivalent amount of currency from a participant designated under Section 5 of this Article that would promote reconstitution by the other participant under Section 6(a) of this Article; prevent or reduce a negative balance of the other participant; or offset the effect of a failure by the other participant to fulfill the expectation in (a) above.

Section 4   Obligation to provide currency

(a) A participant designated by the Fund under Section 5 of this Article shall provide on demand a freely usable currency to a participant using special drawing rights under Section 2(a) of this Article. A participant's obligation to provide currency shall not extend beyond the point at which its holdings of special drawing rights in excess of its net cumulative allocation are equal to twice its net cumulative allocation or such higher limit as may be agreed between a participant and the Fund.

(b) A participant may provide currency in excess of the obligatory limit or any agreed higher limit.

Section 5   Designation of participants to provide currency

(a) The Fund shall ensure that a participant will be able to use its special drawing rights by designating participants to provide currency for specified amounts of special drawing rights for the purposes of Sections 2(a) and 4 of this Article. Designations shall be made in accordance with the following general principles supplemented by such other principles as the Fund may adopt from time to time:

    (i)   A participant shall be subject to designation if its balance of payments and gross reserve position is sufficiently strong, but this will not preclude the possibility that a participant with a strong reserve position will be designated even though it has a moderate balance of payments deficit. Participants shall be designated in such manner as will promote over time a balanced distribution of holdings of special drawing rights among them.

    (ii) Participants shall be subject to designation in order to promote reconstitution under Section 6(a) of this Article, to reduce negative balances in holdings of special drawing rights, or to offset the effect of failures to fulfill the expectation in Section 3(a) of this Article.

    (iii) In designating participants, the Fund normally shall give priority to those that need to acquire special drawing rights to meet the objectives of designation under (ii) above.

(b) In order to promote over time a balanced distribution of holdings of special drawing rights under (a)(i) above, the Fund shall apply the rules for designation in Schedule F or such rules as may be adopted under (c) below.

(c) The rules for designation may be reviewed at any time and new rules shall be adopted if necessary. Unless new rules are adopted, the rules in force at the time of the review shall continue to apply.

Section 6 Reconstitution

(a) Participants that use their special drawing rights shall reconstitute their holdings of them in accordance with the rules for reconstitution in Schedule G or such rules as may be adopted under (b) below.

(b) The rules for reconstitution may be reviewed at any time and new rules shall be adopted if necessary. Unless new rules are adopted or a decision is made to abrogate rules for reconstitution, the rules in force at the time of review shall continue to apply. A seventy percent majority of the total voting power shall be required for decisions to adopt, modify, or abrogate the rules for reconstitution.

Section 7 Exchange rates

(a) Except as otherwise provided in (b) below, the exchange rates for transactions between participants under Section 2(a) and (b) of this Article shall be such that participants using special drawing rights shall receive the same value whatever currencies might be provided and whichever participants provide those currencies, and the Fund shall adopt regulations to give effect to this principle.

(b) The Fund, by an eighty-five percent majority of the total voting power, may adopt policies under which in exceptional circumstances the Fund, by a seventy percent majority of the total voting power, may authorize participants entering into transactions under Section 2(b) of this Article to agree on exchange rates other than those applicable under (a) above.

(c) The Fund shall consult a participant on the procedure for determining rates of exchange for its currency.

(d) For the purpose of this provision the term participant includes a terminating participant.

ARTICLE XX   SPECIAL DRAWING RIGHTS DEPARTMENT INTEREST AND CHARGES

Section 1   Interest

Interest at the same rate for all holders shall be paid by the Fund to each holder on the amount of its holdings of special drawing rights. The Fund shall pay the amount due to each holder whether or not sufficient charges are received to meet the payment of interest.

Section 2   Charges

Charges at the same rate for all participants shall be paid to the Fund by each participant on the amount of its net cumulative allocation of special drawing rights plus any negative balance of the participant or unpaid charges.

Section 3   Rate of interest and charges

The Fund shall determine the rate of interest by a seventy percent majority of the total voting power. The rate of charges shall be equal to the rate of interest.

Section 4   Assessments

When it is decided under Article XVI, Section 2 that reimbursement shall be made, the Fund shall levy assessments for this purpose at the same rate for all participants on their net cumulative allocations.

Section 5   Payment of interest, charges, and assessments

Interest, charges, and assessments shall be paid in special drawing rights. A participant that needs special drawing rights to pay any charge or assessment shall be obligated and entitled to obtain them, for currency acceptable to the Fund, in a transaction with the Fund conducted through the General Resources Account. If sufficient special drawing rights cannot be obtained in this way, the participant shall be obligated and entitled to obtain them with a freely usable currency from a participant which the Fund shall specify. Special drawing rights acquired by a participant after the date for payment shall be applied against its unpaid charges and cancelled.

ARTICLE XXI   ADMINISTRATION OF THE GENERAL DEPARTMENT AND THE SPECIAL DRAWING RIGHTS DEPARTMENT

(a) The General Department and the Special Drawing Rights Department shall be administered in accordance with the provisions of Article XII, subject to the following provisions:

   (i) For meetings of or decisions by the Board of Governors on matters pertaining exclusively to the Special Drawing Rights Department only requests by, or the presence and the votes of, Governors appointed by members that are participants shall be counted for the purpose of calling meetings and determining whether a quorum exists or whether a decision is made by the required majority.

(ii) For decisions by the Executive Board on matters pertaining exclusively to the Special Drawing Rights Department only Executive Directors appointed or elected by at least one member that is a participant shall be entitled to vote. Each of these Executive Directors shall be entitled to cast the number of votes allotted to the member which is a participant that appointed him or to the members that are participants whose votes counted towards his election. Only the presence of Executive Directors appointed or elected by members that are participants and the votes allotted to members that are participants shall be counted for the purpose of determining whether a quorum exists or whether a decision is made by the required majority. For the purposes of this provision, an agreement under Article XII, Section 3(i)(ii) by a member that is a participant shall entitle an appointed Executive Director to vote and cast the number of votes allotted to the member.

(iii) Questions of the general administration of the Fund, including reimbursement under Article XVI, Section 2, and any question whether a matter pertains to both Departments or exclusively to the Special Drawing Rights Department shall be decided as if they pertained exclusively to the General Department. Decisions with respect to the method of valuation of the special drawing right, the acceptance and holding of special drawing rights in the General Resources Account of the General Department and the use of them, and other decisions affecting the operations and transactions conducted through both the General Resources Account of the General Department and the Special Drawing Rights Department shall be made by the majorities required for decisions on matters pertaining exclusively to each Department. A decision on a matter pertaining to the Special Drawing Rights Department shall so indicate.

(b) In addition to the privileges and immunities that are accorded under Article IX of this Agreement, no tax of any kind shall be levied on special drawing rights or on operations or transactions in special drawing rights.

(c) A question of interpretation of the provisions of this Agreement on matters pertaining exclusively to the Special Drawing Rights Department shall be submitted to the Executive Board pursuant to Article XXIX(a) only on the request of a participant. In any case where the Executive Board has given a decision on a question of interpretation pertaining exclusively to the Special Drawing Rights Department only a participant may require that the question be referred to the Board of Governors under Article XXIX(b). The Board of Governors shall decide whether a Governor appointed by a member that is not a participant shall be entitled to vote in the Committee on Interpretation on questions pertaining exclusively to the Special Drawing Rights Department.

(d) Whenever a disagreement arises between the Fund and a participant that has terminated its participation in the Special Drawing Rights Department or between the Fund and any participant during the liquidation of the Special Drawing Rights Department with respect to any matter arising exclusively from participation in the Special Drawing Rights Department, the disagreement shall be submitted to arbitration in accordance with the procedures in Article XXIX(c).

ARTICLE XXII   GENERAL OBLIGATIONS OF PARTICIPANTS

In addition to the obligations assumed with respect to special drawing rights under other articles of this Agreement, each participant undertakes to collaborate with the Fund and with other participants in order to facilitate the effective functioning of the Special Drawing Rights

Department and the proper use of special drawing rights in accordance with this Agreement and with the objective of making the special drawing right the principal reserve asset in the international monetary system.

ARTICLE XXIII SUSPENSION OF OPERATIONS AND TRANSACTIONS IN SPECIAL DRAWING RIGHTS

Section 1 Emergency provisions

In the event of an emergency or the development of unforeseen circumstances threatening the activities of the Fund with respect to the Special Drawing Rights Department, the Executive Board, by an eighty-five percent majority of the total voting power, may suspend for a period of not more than one year the operation of any of the provisions relating to operations and transactions in special drawing rights, and the provisions of Article XXVII, Section 1(b), (c), and (d) shall then apply.

Section 2 Failure to fulfill obligations

(a) If the Fund finds that a participant has failed to fulfill its obligations under Article XIX, Section 4, the right of the participant to use its special drawing rights shall be suspended unless the Fund otherwise decides.

(b) If the Fund finds that a participant has failed to fulfill any other obligation with respect to special drawing rights, the Fund may suspend the right of the participant to use special drawing rights it acquires after the suspension.

(c) Regulations shall be adopted to ensure that before action is taken against any participant under (a) or (b) above, the participant shall be informed immediately of the complaint against it and given an adequate opportunity for stating its case, both orally and in writing. Whenever the participant is thus informed of a complaint relating to (a) above, it shall not use special drawing rights pending the disposition of the complaint.

(d) Suspension under (a) or (b) above or limitation under (c) above shall not affect a participant's obligation to provide currency in accordance with Article XIX, Section 4.

(e) The Fund may at any time terminate a suspension under (a) or (b) above, provided that a suspension imposed on a participant under (b) above for failure to fulfill the obligations under Article XIX, Section 6(a) shall not be terminated until one hundred eighty days after the end of the first calendar quarter during which the participant complies with the rules for reconstitution.

(f) The right of a participant to use its special drawing rights shall not be suspended because it has become ineligible to use the Fund's general resources under Article V, Section 5, Article VI, Section 1, or Article XXVI, Section 2(a). Article XXVI, Section 2 shall not apply because a participant has failed to fulfill any obligations with respect to special drawing rights.

ARTICLE XXIV TERMINATION OF PARTICIPATION

Section 1 Right to terminate participation

(a) Any participant may terminate its participation in the Special Drawing Rights Department at any time by transmitting a notice in writing to the Fund at its principal office. Termination shall become effective on the date the notice is received.

(b) A participant that withdraws from membership in the Fund shall be deemed to have simultaneously terminated its participation in the Special Drawing Rights Department.

Section 2 Settlement on termination

(a) When a participant terminates its participation in the Special Drawing Rights Department, all operations and transactions by the terminating participant in special drawing rights shall cease except as otherwise permitted under an agreement made pursuant to (c) below in order to facilitate a settlement or as provided in Sections 3, 5, and 6 of this Article or in Schedule H. Interest and charges that accrued to the date of termination and assessments levied before that date but not paid shall be paid in special drawing rights.

(b) The Fund shall be obligated to redeem all special drawing rights held by the terminating participant, and the terminating participant shall be obligated to pay to the Fund an amount equal to its net cumulative allocation and any other amounts that may be due and payable because of its participation in the Special Drawing Rights Department. These obligations shall be set off against each other and the amount of special drawing rights held by the terminating participant that is used in the setoff to extinguish its obligation to the fund shall be cancelled.

(c) A settlement shall be made with reasonable despatch by agreement between the terminating participant and the Fund with respect to any obligation of the terminating participant or the Fund after the setoff in (b) above. If agreement on a settlement is not reached promptly the provisions of Schedule H shall apply.

Section 3 Interest and charges

After the date of termination the Fund shall pay interest on any outstanding balance of special drawing rights held by a terminating participant and the terminating participant shall pay charges on any outstanding obligation owed to the Fund at the times and rates prescribed under Article XX. Payment shall be made in special drawing rights. A terminating participant shall be entitled to obtain special drawing rights with a freely usable currency to pay charges or assessments in a transaction with a participant specified by the Fund or by agreement from any other holder, or to dispose of special drawing rights received as interest in a transaction with any participant designated under Article XIX, Section 5 or by agreement with any other holder.

Section 4 Settlement of obligation to the Fund

Currency received by the Fund from a terminating participant shall be used by the Fund to redeem special drawing rights held by participants in proportion to the amount by which each participant's holdings of special drawing rights exceed its net cumulative allocation at the time the currency is received by the Fund. Special drawing rights so redeemed and special drawing rights obtained by a terminating participant under the provisions of this Agreement to meet any installment due under an agreement on settlement or under Schedule H and set off against that installment shall be cancelled.

Section 5 Settlement of obligation to a terminating participant

Whenever the Fund is required to redeem special drawing rights held by a terminating participant, redemption shall be made with currency provided by participants specified by the Fund. These participants shall be specified in accordance with the principles in Article XIX, Section 5. Each specified participant shall provide at its option the currency of the terminating participant or a freely usable currency to the Fund and shall receive an equivalent amount of special drawing rights. However, a terminating participant may use its special drawing rights to obtain its own currency, a freely usable currency, or any other asset from any holder, if the Fund so permits.

Section 6 General Resources Account transactions

In order to facilitate settlement with a terminating participant, the Fund may decide that a terminating participant shall:

(i) use any special drawing rights held by it after the setoff in Section 2(b) of this Article, when they are to be redeemed, in a transaction with the Fund conducted through the General Resources Account to obtain its own currency or a freely usable currency at the option of the Fund; or

(ii) obtain special drawing rights in a transaction with the Fund conducted through the General Resources Account for a currency acceptable to the Fund to meet any charges or installment due under an agreement or the provisions of Schedule H.

ARTICLE XXV   LIQUIDATION OF THE SPECIAL DRAWING RIGHTS DEPARTMENT

(a) The Special Drawing Rights Department may not be liquidated except by decision of the Board of Governors. In an emergency, if the Executive Board decides that liquidation of the Special Drawing Rights Department may be necessary, it may temporarily suspend allocations or cancellations and all operations and transactions in special drawing rights pending decision by the Board of Governors. A decision by the Board of Governors to liquidate the Fund shall be a decision to liquidate both the General Department and the Special Drawing Rights Department.

(b) If the Board of Governors decides to liquidate the Special Drawing Rights Department, all allocations or cancellations and all operations and transactions in special drawing rights and the activities of the Fund with respect to the Special Drawing Rights Department shall cease except those incidental to the orderly discharge of the obligations of participants and of the Fund with respect to special drawing rights, and all obligations of the Fund and of participants under this Agreement with respect to special drawing rights shall cease except those set out in this Article, Article XX, Article XXI(d), Article XXIV, Article XXIX(c), and Schedule H, or any agreement reached under Article XXIV subject to paragraph 4 of Schedule H, and Schedule I.

(c) Upon liquidation of the Special Drawing Rights Department, interest and charges that accrued to the date of liquidation and assessments levied before that date but not paid shall be paid in special drawing rights. The Fund shall be obligated to redeem all special drawing rights held by holders, and each participant shall be obligated to pay the Fund an amount equal to its net cumulative allocation of special drawing rights and such other amounts as may be due and payable because of its participation in the Special Drawing Rights Department.

(d) Liquidation of the Special Drawing Rights Department shall be administered in accordance with the provisions of Schedule I.

ARTICLE XXVI   WITHDRAWAL FROM MEMBERSHIP

Section 1   Right of members to withdraw
Any member may withdraw from the Fund at any time by transmitting a notice in writing to the Fund at its principal office. Withdrawal shall become effective on the date such notice is received.

Section 2   Compulsory withdrawal
(a) If a member fails to fulfill any of its obligations under this Agreement, the Fund may declare the member ineligible to use the general resources of the Fund. Nothing in this Section shall be deemed to limit the provisions of Article V, Section 5 or Article VI, Section 1.

(b) If, after the expiration of a reasonable period following a declaration of ineligibility under (a) above, the member persists in its failure to fulfill any of its obligations under this Agreement, the Fund may, by a seventy percent majority of the total voting power, suspend the voting rights of the member. During the period of the suspension, the provisions of Schedule L shall apply. The Fund may, by a seventy percent majority of the total voting power, terminate the suspension at any time.

(c) If, after the expiration of a reasonable period following a decision of suspension under (b) above, the member persists in its failure to fulfill any of its obligations under this Agreement, that member may be required to withdraw from membership in the Fund by a decision of the Board of Governors carried by a majority of the Governors having eighty-five percent of the total voting power.

(d) Regulations shall be adopted to ensure that before action is taken against any member under (a), (b), or (c) above, the member shall be informed in reasonable time of the complaint against it and given an adequate opportunity for stating its case, both orally and in writing.

Section 3   Settlement of accounts with members withdrawing

When a member withdraws from the Fund, normal operations and transactions of the Fund in its currency shall cease and settlement of all accounts between it and the Fund shall be made with reasonable despatch by agreement between it and the Fund. If agreement is not reached promptly, the provisions of Schedule J shall apply to the settlement of accounts.

ARTICLE XXVII   EMERGENCY PROVISIONS

Section 1   Temporary suspension

(a) In the event of an emergency or the development of unforeseen circumstances threatening the activities of the Fund, the Executive Board, by an eighty-five percent majority of the total voting power, may suspend for a period of not more than one year the operation of any of the following provisions:

   (i)   Article V, Sections 2, 3, 7, 8(a)(i) and (e);

   (ii) Article VI, Section 2;

   (iii) Article XI, Section 1;

   (iv) Schedule C, paragraph 5.

(b) A suspension of the operation of a provision under (a) above may not be extended beyond one year except by the Board of Governors which, by an eighty-five percent majority of the total voting power, may extend a suspension for an additional period of not more than two years if it finds that the emergency or unforeseen circumstances referred to in (a) above continue to exist.

(c) The Executive Board may, by a majority of the total voting power, terminate such suspension at any time.

(d) The Fund may adopt rules with respect to the subject matter of a provision during the period in which its operation is suspended.

Section 2   Liquidation of the Fund

(a) The Fund may not be liquidated except by decision of the Board of Governors. In an emergency, if the Executive Board decides that liquidation of the Fund may be necessary, it may temporarily suspend all operations and transactions, pending decision by the Board of Governors.

(b) If the Board of Governors decides to liquidate the Fund, the Fund shall forthwith cease to engage in any activities except those incidental to the orderly collection and liquidation of its assets and the settlement of its liabilities, and all obligations of members under this Agreement shall cease except those set out in this Article, in Article XXIX(c), in Schedule J, paragraph 7, and in Schedule K.

(c) Liquidation shall be administered in accordance with the provisions of Schedule K.

ARTICLE XXVIII   AMENDMENTS

(a) Any proposal to introduce modifications in this Agreement, whether emanating from a member, a Governor, or the Executive Board, shall be communicated to the chairman of the Board of Governors who shall bring the proposal before the Board of Governors. If the proposed amendment is approved by the Board of Governors, the Fund shall, by circular letter or telegram, ask all members whether they accept the proposed amendment. When three-fifths of the members, having eighty-five percent of the total voting power, have accepted the proposed amendment, the Fund shall certify the fact by a formal communication addressed to all members.

(b) Notwithstanding (a) above, acceptance by all members is required in the case of any amendment modifying:

   (i)   the right to withdraw from the Fund (Article XXVI, Section 1);

   (ii) the provision that no change in a member's quota shall be made without its consent (Article III, Section 2(d)); and

   (iii) the provision that no change may be made in the par value of a member's currency except on the proposal of that member (Schedule C, paragraph 6).

(c) Amendments shall enter into force for all members three months after the date of the formal communication unless a shorter period is specified in the circular letter or telegram.

ARTICLE XXIX   INTERPRETATION

(a) Any question of interpretation of the provisions of this Agreement arising between any member and the Fund or between any members of the Fund shall be submitted to the Executive Board for its decision. If the question particularly affects any member not entitled to appoint an Executive Director, it shall be entitled to representation in accordance with Article XII, Section 3(j).

(b) In any case where the Executive Board has given a decision under (a) above, any member may require, within three months from the date of the decision, that the question be referred to the Board of Governors, whose decision shall be final. Any question referred to the Board of Governors shall be considered by a Committee on Interpretation of the Board of Governors. Each Committee member shall have one vote. The Board of Governors shall establish the membership, procedures, and voting majorities of the Committee. A decision of the Committee shall be the decision of the Board of Governors unless the Board of Governors, by an eighty-five percent majority of the total voting power, decides otherwise. Pending the result of the reference to the Board of Governors the Fund may, so far as it deems necessary, act on the basis of the decision of the Executive Board.

(c) Whenever a disagreement arises between the Fund and a member which has withdrawn, or between the Fund and any member during liquidation of the Fund, such disagreement shall be submitted to arbitration by a tribunal of three arbitrators, one appointed by the Fund, another by the member or withdrawing member, and an umpire who, unless the parties otherwise agree, shall be appointed by the President of the International Court of Justice or such other authority as may have been prescribed by regulation adopted by the Fund. The umpire shall have full power to settle all questions of procedure in any case where the parties are in disagreement with respect thereto.

ARTICLE XXX   EXPLANATION OF TERMS

In interpreting the provisions of this Agreement the Fund and its members shall be guided by the following provisions:

(a) The Fund's holdings of a member's currency in the General Resources Account shall include any securities accepted by the Fund under Article III, Section 4.

(b) Stand-by arrangement means a decision of the Fund by which a member is assured that it will be able to make purchases from the General Resources Account in accordance with the terms of the decision during a specified period and up to a specified amount.

(c) Reserve tranche purchase means a purchase by a member of special drawing rights or the currency of another member in exchange for its own currency which does not cause the Fund's holdings of the member's currency in the General Resources Account to exceed its quota, provided that for the purposes of this definition the Fund may exclude purchases and holdings under:

    (i)   policies on the use of its general resources for compensatory financing of export fluctuations;

    (ii) policies on the use of its general resources in connection with the financing of contributions to international buffer stocks of primary products; and

    (iii) other policies on the use of its general resources in respect of which the Fund decides, by an eighty-five percent majority of the total voting power, that an exclusion shall be made.

(d) Payments for current transactions means payments which are not for the purpose of transferring capital, and includes, without limitation:

    (1) all payments due in connection with foreign trade, other current business, including services, and normal short-term banking and credit facilities;

    (2) payments due as interest on loans and as net income from other investments;

    (3) payments of moderate amount for amortization of loans or for depreciation of direct investments; and

    (4) moderate remittances for family living expenses. The Fund may, after consultation with the members concerned, determine whether certain specific transactions are to be considered current transactions or capital transactions.

(e) Net cumulative allocation of special drawing rights means the total amount of special drawing rights allocated to a participant less its share of special drawing rights that have been cancelled under Article XVIII, Section 2(a).

(f) A freely usable currency means a member's currency that the Fund determines (i) is, in fact, widely used to make payments for international transactions, and (ii) is widely traded in the principal exchange markets.

(g) Members that were members on August 31, 1975 shall be deemed to include a member that accepted membership after that date pursuant to a resolution of the Board of Governors adopted before that date.

(h) Transactions of the Fund means exchanges of monetary assets by the Fund for other monetary assets. Operations of the Fund means other uses or receipts of monetary assets by the Fund.

(i) Transactions in special drawing rights means exchanges of special drawing rights for other monetary assets. Operations in special drawing rights means other uses of special drawing rights.

ARTICLE XXXI   FINAL PROVISIONS

Section 1   Entry into force

This Agreement shall enter into force when it has been signed on behalf of governments having sixty-five percent of the total of the quotas set forth in Schedule A and when the instruments referred to in Section 2(a) of this Article have been deposited on their behalf, but in no event shall this Agreement enter into force before May 1, 1945.

Section 2   Signature

(a) Each government on whose behalf this Agreement is signed shall deposit with the Government of the United States of America an instrument setting forth that it has accepted this

Agreement in accordance with its law and has taken all steps necessary to enable it to carry out all of its obligations under this Agreement.

(b) Each country shall become a member of the Fund as from the date of the deposit on its behalf of the instrument referred to in (a) above, except that no country shall become a member before this Agreement enters into force under Section 1 of this Article.

(c) The Government of the United States of America shall inform the governments of all countries whose names are set forth in Schedule A, and the governments of all countries whose membership is approved in accordance with Article II, Section 2, of all signatures of this Agreement and of the deposit of all instruments referred to in (a) above.

(d) At the time this Agreement is signed on its behalf, each government shall transmit to the Government of the United States of America one one-hundredth of one percent of its total subscription in gold or United States dollars for the purpose of meeting administrative expenses of the Fund. The Government of the United States of America shall hold such funds in a special deposit account and shall transmit them to the Board of Governors of the Fund when the initial meeting has been called. If this Agreement has not come into force by December 31, 1945, the Government of the United States of America shall return such funds to the governments that transmitted them.

(e) This Agreement shall remain open for signature at Washington on behalf of the governments of the countries whose names are set forth in Schedule A until December 31, 1945.

(f) After December 31, 1945, this Agreement shall be open for signature on behalf of the government of any country whose membership has been approved in accordance with Article II, Section 2.

(g) By their signature of this Agreement, all governments accept it both on their own behalf and in respect of all their colonies, overseas territories, all territories under their protection, suzerainty, or authority, and all territories in respect of which they exercise a mandate.

(h) Subsection (d) above shall come into force with regard to each signatory government as from the date of its signature.

SCHEDULES

[Schedules A, B, C, F, G, H, I, J and K not reproduced]

SCHEDULE D COUNCIL

1. (a) Each member that appoints an Executive Director and each group of members that has the number of votes allotted to them cast by an elected Executive Director shall appoint to the Council one Councillor, who shall be a Governor, Minister in the government of a member, or person of comparable rank, and may appoint not more than seven Associates. The Board of Governors may change, by an eighty-five percent majority of the total voting power, the number of Associates who may be appointed. A Councillor or Associate shall serve until a new appointment is made or until the next regular election of Executive Directors, whichever shall occur sooner.

   (b) Executive Directors, or in their absence their Alternates, and Associates shall be entitled to attend meetings of the Council, unless the Council decides to hold a restricted session. Each member and each group of members that appoints a Councillor shall appoint an Alternate who shall be entitled to attend a meeting of the Council when the Councillor is not present, and shall have full power to act for the Councillor.

2. (a) The Council shall supervise the management and adaptation of the international monetary system, including the continuing operation of the adjustment process and

developments in global liquidity, and in this connection shall review developments in the transfer of real resources to developing countries.

(b) The Council shall consider proposals pursuant to Article XXVIII(a) to amend the Articles of Agreement.

3. (a) The Board of Governors may delegate to the Council authority to exercise any powers of the Board of Governors except the powers conferred directly by this Agreement on the Board of Governors.

(b) Each Councillor shall be entitled to cast the number of votes allotted under Article XII, Section 5 to the member or group of members appointing him. A Councillor appointed by a group of members may cast separately the votes allotted to each member in the group. If the number of votes allotted to a member cannot be cast by an Executive Director, the member may make arrangements with a Councillor for casting the number of votes allotted to the member.

(c) The Council shall not take any action pursuant to powers delegated by the Board of Governors that is inconsistent with any action taken by the Board of Governors and the Executive Board shall not take any action pursuant to powers delegated by the Board of Governors that is inconsistent with any action taken by either the Board of Governors or the Council.

4. The Council shall select a Councillor as chairman, shall adopt regulations as may be necessary or appropriate to perform its functions, and shall determine any aspect of its procedure. The Council shall hold such meetings as may be provided for by the Council or called by the Executive Board.

5. (a) The Council shall have powers corresponding to those of the Executive Board under the following provisions: Article XII, Section 2(c), (f), (g), and (j); Article XVIII, Section 4(a) and Section 4(c)(iv); Article XXIII, Section 1; and Article XXVII, Section 1(a).

(b) For decisions by the Council on matters pertaining exclusively to the Special Drawing Rights Department only Councillors appointed by a member that is a participant or a group of members at least one member of which is a participant shall be entitled to vote. Each of these Councillors shall be entitled to cast the number of votes allotted to the member which is a participant that appointed him or to the members that are participants in the group of members that appointed him, and may cast the votes allotted to a participant with which arrangements have been made pursuant to the last sentence of 3(b) above.

(c) The Council may by regulation establish a procedure whereby the Executive Board may obtain a vote of the Councillors on a specific question without a meeting of the Council when in the judgment of the Executive Board an action must be taken by the Council which should not be postponed until the next meeting of the Council and which does not warrant the calling of a special meeting.

(d) Article IX, Section 8 shall apply to Councillors, their Alternates, and Associates, and to any other person entitled to attend a meeting of the Council.

(e) For the purposes of (b) and 3(b) above, an agreement under Article XII, Section 3(i)(ii) by a member, or by a member that is a participant, shall entitle a Councillor to vote and cast the number of votes allotted to the member.

(f) When an Executive Director is entitled to cast the number of votes allotted to a member pursuant to Article XII, Section 3(i)(v), the Councillor appointed by the group whose members elected such Executive Director shall be entitled to vote and cast the number of votes allotted to such member. The member shall be deemed to have participated in the appointment of the Councillor entitled to vote and cast the number of votes allotted to the member.

6. The first sentence of Article XII, Section 2(a) shall be deemed to include a reference to the Council.

SCHEDULE E   ELECTION OF EXECUTIVE DIRECTORS

1. The election of the elective Executive Directors shall be by ballot of the Governors eligible to vote.

2. In balloting for the Executive Directors to be elected, each of the Governors eligible to vote shall cast for one person all of the votes to which he is entitled under Article XII, Section 5(a). The fifteen persons receiving the greatest number of votes shall be Executive Directors, provided that no person who received less than four percent of the total number of votes that can be cast (eligible votes) shall be considered elected.

3. When fifteen persons are not elected in the first ballot, a second ballot shall be held in which there shall vote only (a) those Governors who voted in the first ballot for a person not elected, and (b) those Governors whose votes for a person elected are deemed under 4 below to have raised the votes cast for that person above nine percent of the eligible votes. If in the second ballot there are more candidates than the number of Executive Directors to be elected, the person who received the lowest number of votes in the first ballot shall be ineligible for election.

4. In determining whether the votes cast by a Governor are to be deemed to have raised the total of any person above nine percent of the eligible votes the nine percent shall be deemed to include, first, the votes of the Governor casting the largest number of votes for such person, then the votes of the Governor casting the next largest number, and so on until nine percent is reached.

5. Any Governor part of whose votes must be counted in order to raise the total of any person above four percent shall be considered as casting all of his votes for such person even if the total votes for such person thereby exceed nine percent.

6. If, after the second ballot, fifteen persons have not been elected, further ballots shall be held on the same principles until fifteen persons have been elected, provided that after fourteen persons are elected, the fifteenth may be elected by a simple majority of the remaining votes and shall be deemed to have been elected by all such votes.

SCHEDULE L   SUSPENSION OF VOTING RIGHTS

In the case of a suspension of voting rights of a member under Article XXVI, Section 2(b), the following provisions shall apply:

1. The member shall not:
    (a) participate in the adoption of a proposed amendment of this Agreement, or be counted in the total number of members for that purpose, except in the case of an amendment requiring acceptance by all members under Article XXVIII(b) or pertaining exclusively to the Special Drawing Rights Department;
    (b) appoint a Governor or Alternate Governor, appoint or participate in the appointment of a Councillor or Alternate Councillor, or appoint, elect, or participate in the election of an Executive Director.

2. The number of votes allotted to the member shall not be cast in any organ of the Fund. They shall not be included in the calculation of the total voting power, except for purposes of: (a) the acceptance of a proposed amendment pertaining exclusively to the Special Drawing Rights Department and (b) the calculation of basic votes pursuant to Article XII, Section 5(a)(i).

3. (a) The Governor and Alternate Governor appointed by the member shall cease to hold office.

(b) The Councillor and Alternate Councillor appointed by the member, or in whose appointment the member has participated, shall cease to hold office, provided that, if such Councillor was entitled to cast the number of votes allotted to other members whose voting rights have not been suspended, another Councillor and Alternate Councillor shall be appointed by such other members under Schedule D, and, pending such appointment, the Councillor and Alternate Councillor shall continue to hold office, but for a maximum of thirty days from the date of suspension.

(c) The Executive Director appointed or elected by the member, or in whose election the member has participated, shall cease to hold office, unless such Executive Director was entitled to cast the number of votes allotted to other members whose voting rights have not been suspended. In the latter case:

  (i) if more than ninety days remain before the next regular election of Executive Directors, another Executive Director shall be elected for the remainder of the term by such other members by a majority of the votes cast; pending such election, the Executive Director shall continue to hold office, but for a maximum of thirty days from the date of suspension;

  (ii) if not more than ninety days remain before the next regular election of Executive Directors, the Executive Director shall continue to hold office for the remainder of the term.

4. The member shall be entitled to send a representative to attend any meeting of the Board of Governors, the Council, or the Executive Board, but not any meeting of their committees, when a request made by, or a matter particularly affecting, the member is under consideration.

IV-2

Articles of Agreement of the International Bank for Reconstruction and Development (IBRD)

Date   22 July 1944
In force 27 December 1945
Source   2 UNTS 134, as amended
Link   <http://siteresources.worldbank.org/EXTABOUTUS/Resources/ibrd-articlesofagreement.pdf>

ARTICLE I   PURPOSES

The purposes of the Bank are:

(i)   To assist in the reconstruction and development of territories of members by facilitating the investment of capital for productive purposes, including the restoration of economies destroyed or disrupted by war, the reconversion of productive facilities to peacetime needs and the encouragement of the development of productive facilities and resources in less developed countries.

(ii) To promote private foreign investment by means of guarantees or participations in loans and other investments made by private investors; and when private capital is not available on reasonable terms, to supplement private investment by providing, on suitable conditions, finance for productive purposes out of its own capital, funds raised by it and its other resources.

(iii) To promote the long-range balanced growth of international trade and the maintenance of equilibrium in balances of payments by encouraging international investment for the development of the productive resources of members, thereby assisting in raising productivity, the standard of living and conditions of labor in their territories.

(iv) To arrange the loans made or guaranteed by it in relation to international loans through other channels so that the more useful and urgent projects, large and small alike, will be dealt with first.

(v)   To conduct its operations with due regard to the effect of international investment on business conditions in the territories of members and, in the immediate postwar years, to assist in bringing about a smooth transition from a wartime to a peacetime economy.

The Bank shall be guided in all its decisions by the purposes set forth above

ARTICLE II   MEMBERSHIP IN AND CAPITAL OF THE BANK

Section 1   Membership

(a) The original members of the Bank shall be those members of the International Monetary Fund which accept membership in the Bank before the date specified in Article XI, Section 2 (e).

(b) Membership shall be open to other members of the Fund, at such times and in accordance with such terms as may be prescribed by the Bank.

Section 2   Authorized Capital

(a) The authorized capital stock of the Bank shall be $10,000,000,000, in terms of United States dollars of the weight and fineness in effect on July 1, 1944. The capital stock shall be divided into 100,000 shares[1] having a par value of $100,000 each, which shall be available for subscription only by members.

(b) The capital stock may be increased when the Bank deems it advisable by a three-fourths majority of the total voting power.

Section 3   Subscription of Shares

(a) Each member shall subscribe shares of the capital stock of the Bank. The minimum number of shares to be subscribed by the original members shall be those set forth in Schedule A. The minimum number of shares to be subscribed by other members shall be determined by the Bank, which shall reserve a sufficient portion of its capital stock for subscription by such members.

(b) The Bank shall prescribe rules laying down the conditions under which members may subscribe shares of the authorized capital stock of the Bank in addition to their minimum subscriptions.

(c) If the authorized capital stock of the Bank is increased, each member shall have a reasonable opportunity to subscribe, under such conditions as the Bank shall decide, a proportion of the increase of stock equivalent to the proportion which its stock theretofore subscribed bears to the total capital stock of the Bank, but no member shall be obligated to subscribe any part of the increased capital.

Section 4   Issue Price of Shares

Shares included in the minimum subscriptions of original members shall be issued at par. Other shares shall be issued at par unless the Bank by a majority of the total voting power decides in special circumstances to issue them on other terms.

Section 5   Division and Calls of Subscribed Capital

The subscription of each member shall be divided into two parts as follows:

(i) twenty percent shall be paid or subject to call under Section 7 (i) of this Article as needed by the Bank for its operations;

(ii) the remaining eighty percent shall be subject to call by the Bank only when required to meet obligations of the Bank created under Article IV, Sections 1 (a) (ii) and (iii).

Calls on unpaid subscriptions shall be uniform on all shares.

Section 6   Limitation on Liability

Liability on shares shall be limited to the unpaid portion of the issue price of the shares.

Section 7   Method of Payment of Subscriptions for Shares

Payment of subscriptions for shares shall be made in gold or United States dollars and in the currencies of the members as follows:

(i) under Section 5 (i) of this Article, two percent of the price of each share shall be payable in gold or United States dollars, and, when calls are made, the remaining eighteen percent shall be paid in the currency of the member;

(ii) when a call is made under Section 5 (ii) of this Article, payment may be made at the option of the member either in gold, in United States dollars or in the currency required to discharge the obligations of the Bank for the purpose for which the call is made;

(iii) when a member makes payments in any currency under (i) and (ii) above, such payments shall be made in amounts equal in value to the member's liability under the call. This

---

1 As of April 27, 1988, the authorized capital stock of the Bank had been increased to 1,420,500 shares.

liability shall be a proportionate part of the subscribed capital stock of the Bank as authorized and defined in Section 2 of this Article.

Section 8   Time of Payment of Subscriptions

(a) The two percent payable on each share in gold or United States dollars under Section 7 (i) of this Article, shall be paid within sixty days of the date on which the Bank begins operations, provided that

   (i) any original member of the Bank whose metropolitan territory has suffered from enemy occupation or hostilities during the present war shall be granted the right to postpone payment of one-half percent until five years after that date;

   (ii) an original member who cannot make such a payment because it has not recovered possession of its gold reserves which are still seized or immobilized as a result of the war may postpone all payment until such date as the Bank shall decide.

(b) The remainder of the price of each share payable under Section 7 (i) of this Article shall be paid as and when called by the Bank, provided that

   (i) the Bank shall, within one year of its beginning operations, call not less than eight percent of the price of the share in addition to the payment of two percent referred to in (a) above;

   (ii) not more than five percent of the price of the share shall be called in any period of three months.

Section 9   Maintenance of Value of Certain Currency Holdings of the Bank

(a) Whenever (i) the par value of a member's currency is reduced, or (ii) the foreign exchange value of a member's currency has, in the opinion of the Bank, depreciated to a significant extent within that member's territories, the member shall pay to the Bank within a reasonable time an additional amount of its own currency sufficient to maintain the value, as of the time of initial subscription, of the amount of the currency of such member which is held by the Bank and derived from currency originally paid in to the Bank by the member under Article II, Section 7 (i), from currency referred to in Article IV, Section 2 (b), or from any additional currency furnished under the provisions of the present paragraph, and which has not been repurchased by the member for gold or for the currency of any member which is acceptable to the Bank.

(b) Whenever the par value of a member's currency is increased, the Bank shall return to such member within a reasonable time an amount of that member's currency equal to the increase in the value of the amount of such currency described in (a) above.

(c) The provisions of the preceding paragraphs may be waived by the Bank when a uniform proportionate change in the par values of the currencies of all its members is made by the International Monetary Fund.

Section 10   Restriction on Disposal of Shares

Shares shall not be pledged or encumbered in any manner whatever and they shall be transferable only to the Bank.

ARTICLE III   GENERAL PROVISIONS RELATING TO LOANS AND GUARANTEES

Section 1   Use of resources

(a) The resources and the facilities of the Bank shall be used exclusively for the benefit of members with equitable consideration to projects for development and projects for reconstruction alike.

(b) For the purpose of facilitating the restoration and reconstruction of the economy of members whose metropolitan territories have suffered great devastation from enemy occupation or hostilities, the Bank, in determining the conditions and terms of loans made to such members, shall pay special regard to lightening the financial burden and expediting the completion of such restoration and reconstruction.

Section 2 Dealings between Members and the Bank

Each member shall deal with the Bank only through its Treasury, central bank, stabilization fund or other similar fiscal agency, and the Bank shall deal with members only by or through the same agencies.

Section 3 Limitations on Guarantees and Borrowings of the Bank

The total amount outstanding of guarantees, participations in loans and direct loans made by the Bank shall not be increased at any time, if by such increase the total would exceed one hundred percent of the unimpaired subscribed capital, reserves and surplus of the Bank.

Section 4 Conditions on which the Bank may Guarantee or Make loans

The Bank may guarantee, participate in, or make loans to any member or any political subdivision thereof and any business, industrial, and agricultural enterprise in the territories of a member, subject to the following conditions:

(i) When the member in whose territories the project is located is not itself the borrower, the member or the central bank or some comparable agency of the member which is acceptable to the Bank, fully guarantees the repayment of the principal and the payment of interest and other charges on the loan.

(ii) The Bank is satisfied that in the prevailing market conditions the borrower would be unable otherwise to obtain the loan under conditions which in the opinion of the Bank are reasonable for the borrower.

(iii) A competent committee, as provided for in Article V, Section 7, has submitted a written report recommending the project after a careful study of the merits of the proposal.

(iv) In the opinion of the Bank the rate of interest and other charges are reasonable and such rate, charges and the schedule for repayment of principal are appropriate to the project.

(v) In making or guaranteeing a loan, the Bank shall pay due regard to the prospects that the borrower, and, if the borrower is not a member, that the guarantor, will be in position to meet its obligations under the loan; and the Bank shall act prudently in the interests both of the particular member in whose territories the project is located and of the members as a whole.

(vi) In guaranteeing a loan made by other investors, the Bank receives suitable compensation for its risk.

(vii) Loans made or guaranteed by the Bank shall, except in special circumstances, be for the purpose of specific projects of reconstruction or development.

Section 5 Use of Loans Guaranteed, Participated in or Made by the Bank

(a) The Bank shall impose no conditions that the proceeds of a loan shall be spent in the territories of any particular member or members.

(b) The Bank shall make arrangements to ensure that the proceeds of any loan are used only for the purposes for which the loan was granted, with due attention to considerations of economy and efficiency and without regard to political or other non-economic influences or considerations.

(c) In the case of loans made by the Bank, it shall open an account in the name of the borrower and the amount of the loan shall be credited to this account in the currency or currencies in which the loan is made. The borrower shall be permitted by the Bank to draw on this account only to meet expenses in connection with the project as they are actually incurred.

Section 6   Loans to the International Finance Corporation[2]

(a) The Bank may make, participate in, or guarantee loans to the International Finance Corporation, an affiliate of the Bank, for use in its lending operations. The total amount outstanding of such loans, participations and guarantees shall not be increased if, at the time or as a result thereof, the aggregate amount of debt (including the guarantee of any debt) incurred by the said Corporation from any source and then outstanding shall exceed an amount equal to four times its unimpaired subscribed capital and surplus.

(b) The provisions of Article III, Sections 4 and 5 (c) and of Article IV, Section 3 shall not apply to loans, participations and guarantees authorized by this Section.

ARTICLE IV   OPERATIONS

Section 1   Methods of Making or Facilitating Loans

(a) The Bank may make or facilitate loans which satisfy the general conditions of Article III in any of the following ways:

   (i) By making or participating in direct loans out of its own funds corresponding to its unimpaired paid-up capital and surplus and, subject to Section 6 of this Article, to its reserves.

   (ii) By making or participating in direct loans out of funds raised in the market of a member, or otherwise borrowed by the Bank.

   (iii) By guaranteeing in whole or in part loans made by private investors through the usual investment channels.

(b) The Bank may borrow funds under (a) (ii) above or guarantee loans under (a) (iii) above only with the approval of the member in whose markets the funds are raised and the member in whose currency the loan is denominated, and only if those members agree that the proceeds may be exchanged for the currency of any other member without restriction.

Section 2   Availability and Transferability of Currencies

(a) Currencies paid into the Bank under Article II, Section 7 (i), shall be loaned only with the approval in each case of the member whose currency is involved; provided, however, that if necessary, after the Bank's subscribed capital has been entirely called, such currencies shall, without restriction by the members whose currencies are offered, be used or exchanged for the currencies required to meet contractual payments of interest, other charges or amortization on the Bank's own borrowings, or to meet the Bank's liabilities with respect to such contractual payments on loans guaranteed by the Bank.

(b) Currencies received by the Bank from borrowers or guarantors in payment on account of principal of direct loans made with currencies referred to in (a) above shall be exchanged for the currencies of other members or reloaned only with the approval in each case of the members whose currencies are involved; provided, however, that if necessary, after the Bank's subscribed capital has been entirely called, such currencies shall, without restriction by the members whose currencies are offered, be used or exchanged for the currencies required to meet contractual payments of interest, other charges or amortization on the Bank's own borrowings, or to meet the Bank's liabilities with respect to such contractual payments on loans guaranteed by the Bank.

(c) Currencies received by the Bank from borrowers or guarantors in payment on account of principal of direct loans made by the Bank under Section 1 (a) (ii) of this Article, shall be held

---

2 Section added by amendment effective December 17, 1965.

and used, without restriction by the members, to make amortization payments, or to anticipate payment of or repurchase part or all of the Bank's own obligations.

(d) All other currencies available to the Bank, including those raised in the market or otherwise borrowed under Section 1 (a) (ii) of this Article, those obtained by the sale of gold, those received as payments of interest and other charges for direct loans made under Sections 1 (a) (i) and (ii), and those received as payments of commissions and other charges under Section 1 (a) (iii), shall be used or exchanged for other currencies or gold required in the operations of the Bank without restriction by the members whose currencies are offered.

(e) Currencies raised in the markets of members by borrowers on loans guaranteed by the Bank under Section 1 (a) (iii) of this Article, shall also be used or exchanged for other currencies without restriction by such members.

Section 3   Provision of Currencies for Direct Loans

The following provisions shall apply to direct loans under Sections 1 (a) (i) and (ii) of this Article:

(a) The Bank shall furnish the borrower with such currencies of members, other than the member in whose territories the project is located, as are needed by the borrower for expenditures to be made in the territories of such other members to carry out the purposes of the loan.

(b) The Bank may, in exceptional circumstances when local currency required for the purposes of the loan cannot be raised by the borrower on reasonable terms, provide the borrower as part of the loan with an appropriate amount of that currency.

(c) The Bank, if the project gives rise indirectly to an increased need for foreign exchange by the member in whose territories the project is located, may in exceptional circumstances provide the borrower as part of the loan with an appropriate amount of gold or foreign exchange not in excess of the borrower's local expenditure in connection with the purposes of the loan.

(d) The Bank may, in exceptional circumstances, at the request of a member in whose territories a portion of the loan is spent, repurchase with gold or foreign exchange a part of that member's currency thus spent but in no case shall the part so repurchased exceed the amount by which the expenditure of the loan in those territories gives rise to an increased need for foreign exchange.

Section 4   Payment Provisions for Direct Loans

Loan contracts under Section 1 (a) (i) or (ii) of this Article shall be made in accordance with the following payment provisions:

(a) The terms and conditions of interest and amortization payments, maturity and dates of payment of each loan shall be determined by the Bank. The Bank shall also determine the rate and any other terms and conditions of commission to be charged in connection with such loan. In the case of loans made under Section 1 (a) (ii) of this Article during the first ten years of the Bank's operations, this rate of commission shall be not less than one percent per annum and not greater than one and one-half percent per annum, and shall be charged on the outstanding portion of any such loan. At the end of this period of ten years, the rate of commission may be reduced by the Bank with respect both to the outstanding portions of loans already made and to future loans, if the reserves accumulated by the Bank under Section 6 of this Article and out of other earnings are considered by it sufficient to justify a reduction. In the case of future loans the Bank shall also have discretion to increase the rate of commission beyond the above limit, if experience indicates that an increase is advisable.

(b) All loan contracts shall stipulate the currency or currencies in which payments under the contract shall be made to the Bank. At the option of the borrowers however, such payments may be made in gold, or subject to the agreement of the Bank, in the currency of a member other than that prescribed in the contract.

(i) In the case of loans made under Section 1 (a) (i) of this Article, the loan contracts shall provide that payments to the Bank of interest, other charges and amortization shall be made in the currency loaned, unless the member whose currency is loaned agrees that such payments shall be made in some other specified currency or currencies. These payments, subject to the provisions of Article II, Section 9 (c), shall be equivalent to the value of such contractual payments at the time the loans were made, in terms of a currency specified for the purpose by the Bank by a three-fourths majority of the total voting power.

(ii) In the case of loans made under Section 1 (a) (ii) of this Article, the total amount outstanding and payable to the Bank in any one currency shall at no time exceed the total amount of the outstanding borrowings made by the Bank under Section 1 (a) (ii) and payable in the same currency.

(c) If a member suffers from an acute exchange stringency, so that the service of any loan contracted by that member or guaranteed by it or by one of its agencies cannot be provided in the stipulated manner, the member concerned may apply to the Bank for a relaxation of the conditions of payment. If the Bank is satisfied that some relaxation is in the interests of the particular member and of the operations of the Bank and of its members as a whole, it may take action under either, or both, of the following paragraphs with respect to the whole, or part, of the annual service:

(i) The Bank may, in its discretion, make arrangements with the member concerned to accept service payments on the loan in the member's currency for periods not to exceed three years upon appropriate terms regarding the use of such currency and the maintenance of its foreign exchange value; and for the repurchase of such currency on appropriate terms.

(ii) The Bank may modify the terms of amortization or extend the life of the loan, or both.

Section 5   Guarantees

(a) In guaranteeing a loan placed through the usual investment channels, the Bank shall charge a guarantee commission payable periodically on the amount of the loan outstanding at a rate determined by the Bank. During the first ten years of the Bank's operations, this rate shall be not less than one percent per annum and not greater than one and one-half percent per annum. At the end of this period of ten years, the rate of commission may be reduced by the Bank with respect both to the outstanding portions of loans already guaranteed and to future loans if the reserves accumulated by the Bank under Section 6 of this Article and out of other earnings are considered by it sufficient to justify a reduction. In the case of future loans the Bank shall also have discretion to increase the rate of commission beyond the above limit, if experience indicates that an increase is advisable.

(b) Guarantee commissions shall be paid directly to the Bank by the borrower.

(c) Guarantees by the Bank shall provide that the Bank may terminate its liability with respect to interest if, upon default by the borrower and by the guarantor, if any, the Bank offers to purchase, at par and interest accrued to a date designated in the offer, the bonds or other obligations guaranteed.

(d) The Bank shall have power to determine any other terms and conditions of the guarantee.

Section 6   Special Reserve

The amount of commissions received by the Bank under Sections 4 and 5 of this Article shall be set aside as a special reserve, which shall be kept available for meeting liabilities of the Bank in accordance with Section 7 of this Article. The special reserve shall be held in such liquid form, permitted under this Agreement, as the Executive Directors may decide.

Section 7   Methods of Meeting Liabilities of the Bank in Case of Defaults

In cases of default on loans made, participated in, or guaranteed by the Bank:

(a) The Bank shall make such arrangements as may be feasible to adjust the obligations under the loans, including arrangements under or analogous to those provided in Section 4 (c) of this Article.

(b) The payments in discharge of the Bank's liabilities on borrowings or guarantees under Section 1 (a) (ii) and (iii) of this Article shall be charged:
 (i) first, against the special reserve provided in Section 6 of this Article;
 (ii) then, to the extent necessary and at the discretion of the Bank, against the other reserves, surplus and capital available to the Bank.

(c) Whenever necessary to meet contractual payments of interest, other charges or amortization on the Bank's own borrowings, or to meet the Bank's liabilities with respect to similar payments on loans guaranteed by it, the Bank may call an appropriate amount of the unpaid subscriptions of members in accordance with Article II, Sections 5 and 7. Moreover, if it believes that a default may be of long duration, the Bank may call an additional amount of such unpaid subscriptions not to exceed in any one year one percent of the total subscriptions of the members for the following purposes:
 (i) To redeem prior to maturity, or otherwise discharge its liability on, all or part of the outstanding principal of any loan guaranteed by it in respect of which the debtor is in default.
 (ii) To repurchase, or otherwise discharge its liability on, all or part of its own outstanding borrowings.

Section 8 Miscellaneous Operations
In addition to the operations specified elsewhere in this Agreement, the Bank shall have the power:

(i) To buy and sell securities it has issued and to buy and sell securities which it has guaranteed or in which it has invested, provided that the Bank shall obtain the approval of the member in whose territories the securities are to be bought or sold.

(ii) To guarantee securities in which it has invested for the purpose of facilitating their sale.

(iii) To borrow the currency of any member with the approval of that member.

(iv) To buy and sell such other securities as the Directors by a three-fourths majority of the total voting power may deem proper for the investment of all or part of the special reserve under Section 6 of this Article.

In exercising the powers conferred by this Section, the Bank may deal with any person, partnership, association, corporation or other legal entity in the territories of any member.

Section 9 Warning to be Placed on Securities
Every security guaranteed or issued by the Bank shall bear on its face a conspicuous statement to the effect that it is not an obligation of any government unless expressly stated on the security.

Section 10 Political Activity Prohibited
The Bank and its officers shall not interfere in the political affairs of any member; nor shall they be influenced in their decisions by the political character of the member or members concerned. Only economic considerations shall be relevant to their decisions, and these considerations shall be weighed impartially in order to achieve the purposes stated in Article I.

ARTICLE V ORGANIZATION AND MANAGEMENT

Section 1 Structure of the Bank
The Bank shall have a Board of Governors, Executive Directors, a President and such other officers and staff to perform such duties as the Bank may determine.

Section 2   Board of Governors

(a) All the powers of the Bank shall be vested in the Board of Governors consisting of one governor and one alternate appointed by each member in such manner as it may determine. Each governor and each alternate shall serve for five years, subject to the pleasure of the member appointing him, and may be reappointed. No alternate may vote except in the absence of his principal. The Board shall select one of the Governors as chairman.

(b) The Board of Governors may delegate to the Executive Directors authority to exercise any powers of the Board, except the power to:
  (i)   Admit new members and determine the conditions of their admission;
  (ii)   Increase or decrease the capital stock;
  (iii) Suspend a member;
  (iv)   Decide appeals from interpretations of this agreement given by the Executive Directors;
  (v)   Make arrangements to cooperate with other international organizations (other than informal arrangements of a temporary and administrative character);
  (vi)   Decide to suspend permanently the operations of the Bank and to distribute its assets;
  (vii) Determine the distribution of the net income of the Bank.

(c) The Board of Governors shall hold an annual meeting and such other meetings as may be provided for by the Board or called by the Executive Directors. Meetings of the Board shall be called by the Directors whenever requested by five members or by members having one quarter of the total voting power.

(d) A quorum for any meeting of the Board of Governors shall be a majority of the Governors, exercising not less than two-thirds of the total voting power.

(e) The Board of Governors may by regulation establish a procedure whereby the Executive Directors, when they deem such action to be in the best interests of the Bank, may obtain a vote of the Governors on a specific question without calling a meeting of the Board.

(f) The Board of Governors, and the Executive Directors to the extent authorized, may adopt such rules and regulations as may be necessary or appropriate to conduct the business of the Bank.

(g) Governors and alternates shall serve as such without compensation from the Bank, but the Bank shall pay them reasonable expenses incurred in attending meetings.

(h) The Board of Governors shall determine the remuneration to be paid to the Executive Directors and the salary and terms of the contract of service of the President.

Section 3   Voting

(a) Each member shall have two hundred fifty votes plus one additional vote for each share of stock held.

(b) Except as otherwise specifically provided, all matters before the Bank shall be decided by a majority of the votes cast.

Section 4   Executive Directors

(a) The Executive Directors shall be responsible for the conduct of the general operations of the Bank, and for this purpose, shall exercise all the powers delegated to them by the Board of Governors.

(b) There shall be twelve Executive Directors, who need not be governors, and of whom:
  (i)   five shall be appointed, one by each of the five members having the largest number of shares;
  (ii) seven shall be elected according to Schedule B by all the Governors other than those appointed by the five members referred to in (i) above.

For the purpose of this paragraph, "members" means governments of countries whose names are set forth in Schedule A, whether they are original members or become members in accordance with Article II, Section 1 (b). When governments of other countries become members, the Board of Governors may, by a four-fifths majority of the total voting power, increase the total number of directors by increasing the number of directors to be elected.

Executive Directors shall be appointed or elected every two years.

(c) Each executive director shall appoint an alternate with full power to act for him when he is not present. When the executive directors appointing them are present, alternates may participate in meetings but shall not vote.

(d) Directors shall continue in office until their successors are appointed or elected. If the office of an elected director becomes vacant more than ninety days before the end of his term, another director shall be elected for the remainder of the term by the governors who elected the former director. A majority of the votes cast shall be required for election. While the office remains vacant, the alternate of the former director shall exercise his powers, except that of appointing an alternate.

(e) The Executive Directors shall function in continuous session at the principal office of the Bank and shall meet as often as the business of the Bank may require.

(f) A quorum for any meeting of the Executive Directors shall be a majority of the Directors, exercising not less than one-half of the total voting power.

(g) Each appointed director shall be entitled to cast the number of votes allotted under Section 3 of this Article to the member appointing him. Each elected director shall be entitled to cast the number of votes which counted toward his election. All the votes which a director is entitled to cast shall be cast as a unit.

(h) The Board of Governors shall adopt regulations under which a member not entitled to appoint a director under (b) above may send a representative to attend any meeting of the Executive Directors when a request made by, or a matter particularly affecting, that member is under consideration.

(i) The Executive Directors may appoint such committees as they deem advisable. Membership of such committees need not be limited to governors or directors or their alternates.

Section 5 President and Staff

(a) The Executive Directors shall select a President who shall not be a governor or an executive director or an alternate for either. The President shall be Chairman of the Executive Directors, but shall have no vote except a deciding vote in case of an equal division. He may participate in meetings of the Board of Governors, but shall not vote at such meetings. The President shall cease to hold office when the Executive Directors so decide.

(b) The President shall be chief of the operating staff of the Bank and shall conduct, under the direction of the Executive Directors, the ordinary business of the Bank. Subject to the general control of the Executive Directors, he shall be responsible for the organization, appointment and dismissal of the officers and staff.

(c) The President, officers and staff of the Bank, in the discharge of their offices, owe their duty entirely to the Bank and to no other authority. Each member of the Bank shall respect the international character of this duty and shall refrain from all attempts to influence any of them in the discharge of their duties.

(d) In appointing the officers and staff the President shall, subject to the paramount importance of securing the highest standards of efficiency and of technical competence, pay due regard to the importance of recruiting personnel on as wide a geographical basis as possible.

Section 6 Advisory Council

(a) There shall be an Advisory Council of not less than seven persons selected by the Board of Governors including representatives of banking, commercial, industrial, labor, and agricultural interests, and with as wide a national representation as possible. In those fields where specialized international organizations exist, the members of the Council representative of those fields shall be selected in agreement with such organizations. The Council shall advise the Bank on matters of general policy. The Council shall meet annually and on such other occasions as the Bank may request.

(b) Councillors shall serve for two years and may be reappointed. They shall be paid their reasonable expenses incurred on behalf of the Bank.

Section 7 Loan Committees

The committees required to report on loans under Article III, Section 4, shall be appointed by the Bank. Each such committee shall include an expert selected by the governor representing the member in whose territories the project is located and one or more members of the technical staff of the Bank.

Section 8 Relationship to Other International Organizations

(a) The Bank, within the terms of this Agreement, shall cooperate with any general international organization and with public international organizations having specialized responsibilities in related fields. Any arrangements for such cooperation which would involve a modification of any provision of this Agreement may be effected only after amendment to this Agreement under Article VIII.

(b) In making decisions on applications for loans or guarantees relating to matters directly within the competence of any international organization of the types specified in the preceding paragraph and participated in primarily by members of the Bank, the Bank shall give consideration to the views and recommendations of such organization.

Section 9 Location of Offices

(a) The principal office of the Bank shall be located in the territory of the member holding the greatest number of shares.

(b) The Bank may establish agencies or branch offices in the territories of any member of the Bank.

Section 10 Regional Offices and Councils

(a) The Bank may establish regional offices and determine the location of, and the areas to be covered by, each regional office.

(b) Each regional office shall be advised by a regional council representative of the entire area and selected in such manner as the Bank may decide.

Section 11 Depositories

(a) Each member shall designate its central bank as a depository for all the Bank's holdings of its currency or, if it has no central bank, it shall designate such other institution as may be acceptable to the Bank.

(b) The Bank may hold other assets, including gold, in depositories designated by the five members having the largest number of shares and in such other designated depositories as the Bank may select. Initially, at least one-half of the gold holdings of the Bank shall be held in the depository designated by the member in whose territory the Bank has its principal office, and at least forty percent shall be held in the depositories designated by the remaining four members referred to above, each of such depositories to hold, initially, not less than the amount of gold paid on the shares of the member designating it. However, all transfers of gold by the Bank shall be made with due regard to the costs of transport and anticipated requirements of the Bank. In an emergency the Executive Directors may transfer all or any part of the Bank's gold holdings to any place where they can be adequately protected.

Section 12   Form of Holdings of Currency

The Bank shall accept from any member, in place of any part of the member's currency, paid in to the Bank under Article II, Section 7 (i), or to meet amortization payments on loans made with such currency, and not needed by the Bank in its operations, notes or similar obligations issued by the Government of the member or the depository designated by such member, which shall be non-negotiable, non-interest-bearing and payable at their par value on demand by credit to the account of the Bank in the designated depository.

Section 13   Publication of Reports and Provision of Information

(a) The Bank shall publish an annual report containing an audited statement of its accounts and shall circulate to members at intervals of three months or less a summary statement of its financial position and a profit and loss statement showing the results of its operations.

(b) The Bank may publish such other reports as it deems desirable to carry out its purposes.

(c) Copies of all reports, statements and publications made under this section shall be distributed to members.

Section 14   Allocation of Net Income

(a) The Board of Governors shall determine annually what part of the Bank's net income, after making provision for reserves, shall be allocated to surplus and what part, if any, shall be distributed.

(b) If any part is distributed, up to two percent non-cumulative shall be paid, as a first charge against the distribution for any year, to each member on the basis of the average amount of the loans outstanding during the year made under Article IV, Section 1 (a) (i), out of currency corresponding to its subscription. If two percent is paid as a first charge, any balance remaining to be distributed shall be paid to all members in proportion to their shares. Payments to each member shall be made in its own currency, or if that currency is not available in other currency acceptable to the member. if such payments are made in currencies other than the member's own currency, the transfer of the currency and its use by the receiving member after payment shall be without restriction by the members.

ARTICLE VI   WITHDRAWAL AND SUSPENSION OF MEMBERSHIP: SUSPENSION OF OPERATIONS

Section 1   Right of Members to Withdraw

Any member may withdraw from the Bank at any time by transmitting a notice in writing to the Bank at its principal office. Withdrawal shall become effective on the date such notice is received.

Section 2   Suspension of Membership

If a member fails to fulfill any of its obligations to the Bank, the Bank may suspend its membership by decision of a majority of the Governors, exercising a majority of the total voting power. The member so suspended shall automatically cease to be a member one year from the date of its suspension unless a decision is taken by the same majority to restore the member to good standing. While under suspension, a member shall not be entitled to exercise any rights under this Agreement, except the right of withdrawal, but shall remain subject to all obligations.

Section 3   Cessation of Membership in International Monetary Fund

Any member which ceases to be a member of the International Monetary Fund shall automatically cease after three months to be a member of the Bank unless the Bank by three-fourths of the total voting power has agreed to allow it to remain a member.

Section 4   Settlement of Accounts with Governments Ceasing to be Members

(a) When a government ceases to be a member, it shall remain liable for its direct obligations to the Bank and for its contingent liabilities to the Bank so long as any part of the loans or guarantees contracted before it ceased to be a member are outstanding; but it shall cease to incur liabilities with respect to loans and guarantees entered into thereafter by the Bank and to share either in the income or the expenses of the Bank.

(b) At the time a government ceases to be a member, the Bank shall arrange for the repurchase of its shares as a part of the settlement of accounts with such government in accordance with the provisions of (c) and (d) below. For this purpose the repurchase price of the shares shall be the value shown by the books of the Bank on the day the government ceases to be a member.

(c) The payment for shares repurchased by the Bank under this section shall be governed by the following conditions:

   (i) Any amount due to the government for its shares shall be withheld so long as the government, its central bank or any of its agencies remains liable, as borrower or guarantor, to the Bank and such amount **may**, at the option of the Bank, be applied on any such liability as it matures. No amount shall be withheld on account of the liability of the government resulting from its subscription for shares under Article H, Section 5 (ii). In any event, no amount due to a member for its shares shall be paid until six months after the date upon which the government ceases to be a member.

   (ii) Payments for shares may be made from time to time, upon their surrender by the government, to the extent by which the amount due as the repurchase price in (b) above exceeds the aggregate of liabilities on loans and guarantees in (c) (i) above until the former member has received the full repurchase price.

   (iii) Payments shall be made in the currency of the country receiving payment or at the option of the Bank in gold.

   (iv) If losses are sustained by the Bank on any guarantees, participations in loans, or loans which were outstanding on the date when the government ceased to be a member, and the amount of such losses exceeds the amount of the reserve provided against losses on the date when the government ceased to be a member, such government shall be obligated to repay upon demand the amount by which the repurchase price of its shares would have been reduced, if the losses had been taken into account when the repurchase price was determined. In addition, the former member government shall remain liable on any call for unpaid subscriptions under Article IL Section 5 (ii), to the extent that it would have been required to respond if the impairment of capital had occurred and the call had been made at the time the repurchase price of its shares was determined.

(d) If the Bank suspends permanently its operations under Section 5 (b) of this Article, within six months of the date upon which any government ceases to be a member, all rights of such government shall be determined by the provisions of Section 5 of this Article.

Section 5   Suspension of Operations and Settlement of Obligations

(a) In an emergency the Executive Directors may suspend temporarily operations in respect of new loans and guarantees pending an opportunity for further consideration and action by the Board of Governors.

(b) The Bank may suspend permanently its operations in respect of new loans and guarantees by a vote of a majority of the Governors, exercising a majority of the total voting power. After such suspension of operations the Bank shall forthwith cease all activities, except those incident to the orderly realization, conservation, and preservation of its assets and settlement of its obligations.

(c) The liability of all members for uncalled subscriptions to the capital stock of the Bank and in respect of the depreciation of their own currencies shall continue until all claims of creditors, including all contingent claims, shall have been discharged.

(d) All creditors holding direct shall be paid out of the assets of the Bank, and then out of payments to the Bank on calls on unpaid subscriptions. Before making any payments to creditors holding direct claims, the Executive Directors shall make such arrangements as are necessary, in their judgment, to insure a distribution to holders of contingent claims ratably with creditors holding direct claims.

(e) No distribution shall be made to members on account of their subscriptions to the capital stock of the Bank until
   (i) all liabilities to creditors have been discharged or provided for, and
   (ii) a majority of the Governors, exercising a majority of the total voting power, have decided to make a distribution.

(f) After a decision to make a distribution has been taken under (e) above, the Executive Directors may by a two-thirds majority vote make successive distributions of the assets of the Bank to members until all of the assets have been distributed. This distribution shall be subject to the prior settlement of all outstanding claims of the Bank against each member.

(g) Before any distribution of assets is made, the Executive Directors shall fix the proportionate share of each member according to the ratio of its shareholding to the total outstanding shares of the Bank.

(h) The Executive Directors shall value the assets to be distributed as at the date of distribution and then proceed to distribute in the following manner:
   (i) There shall be paid to each member in its own obligations or those of its official agencies or legal entities within its territories, insofar as they are available for distribution, an amount equivalent in value to its proportionate share of the total amount to be distributed.
   (ii) Any balance due to a member after payment has been made under (i) above shall be paid, in its own currency, insofar as it is held by the Bank, up to an amount equivalent in value to such balance.
   (iii) Any balance due to a member after payment has been made under (i) and (ii) above shall be paid in gold or currency acceptable to the member, insofar as they are held by the Bank, up to an amount equivalent in value to such balance.
   (iv) Any remaining assets held by the Bank after payments have been made to members under (i), (ii), and (iii) above shall be distributed *pro rata* among the members.

(i) Any member receiving assets distributed by the Bank in accordance with (h) above, shall enjoy the same rights with respect to such assets as the Bank enjoyed prior to their distribution.

ARTICLE VII STATUS, IMMUNITIES AND PRIVILEGES

Section 1 Purposes of the Article
To enable the Bank to fulfill the functions with which it is entrusted, the status, immunities and privileges set forth in this Article shall be accorded to the Bank in the territories of each member.

Section 2 Status of the Bank
The Bank shall possess full juridical personality, and, in particular, the capacity:

(i)   to contract;
(ii) to acquire and dispose of immovable and movable property;
(iii) to institute legal proceedings.

Section 3 Position of the Bank with Regard to Judicial Process

Actions may be brought against the Bank only in a court of competent jurisdiction in the territories of a member in which the Bank has an office, has appointed an agent for the purpose of accepting service or notice of process, or has issued or guaranteed securities. No actions shall, however, be brought by members or persons acting for or deriving claims from members. The property and assets of the Bank shall, wheresoever located and by whomsoever held, be immune from all forms of seizure, attachment or execution before the delivery of final judgment against the Bank.

Section 4 Immunity of Assets from Seizure

Property and assets of the Bank, wherever located and by whomsoever held, shall be immune from search, requisition, confiscation, expropriation or any other form of seizure by executive or legislative action.

Section 5 Immunity of Archives

The archives of the Bank shall be inviolable.

Section 6 Freedom of Assets from Restrictions

To the extent necessary to carry out the operations provided for in this Agreement and subject to the provisions of this Agreement, all property and assets of the Bank shall be free from restrictions, regulations, controls and moratoria of any nature.

Section 7 Privilege for Communications

The official communications of the Bank shall be accorded by each member the same treatment that it accords to the official communications of other members.

Section 8 Immunities and Privileges of Officers and Employees

All governors, executive directors, alternates, officers and employees of the Bank

(i) shall be immune from legal process with respect to acts performed by them in their official capacity except when the Bank waives this immunity;

(ii) not being local nationals, shall be accorded the same immunities from immigration restrictions, alien registration requirements and national service obligations and the same facilities as regards exchange restrictions as are accorded by members to the representatives, officials, and employees of comparable rank of other members;

(iii) shall be granted the same treatment in respect of travelling facilities as is accorded by members to representatives, officials and employees of comparable rank of other members.

Section 9 Immunities from Taxation

(a) The Bank, its assets, property, income and its operations and transactions authorized by this Agreement, shall be immune from all taxation and from all customs duties. The Bank shall also be immune from liability for the collection or payment of any tax or duty.

(b) No tax shall be levied on or in respect of salaries and emoluments paid by the Bank to executive directors, alternates, officials or employees of the Bank who are not local citizens, local subjects, or other local nationals.

(c) No taxation of any kind shall be levied on any obligation or security issued by the Bank (including any dividend or interest thereon) by whomsoever held:
   (i) which discriminates against such obligation or security solely because it is issued by the Bank; or
   (ii) if the sole jurisdictional basis for such taxation is the place or currency in which it is issued, made payable or paid, or the location of any office or place of business maintained by the Bank.

(d) No taxation of any kind shall be levied on any obligation or security guaranteed by the Bank (including any dividend or interest thereon) by whomsoever held:

(i) which discriminates against such obligation or security solely because it is guaranteed by the Bank; or

(ii) if the sole jurisdictional basis for such taxation is the location of any office or place of business maintained by the Bank.

Section 10   Application of Article

Each member shall take such action as is necessary in its own territories for the purpose of making effective in terms of its own law the principles set forth in this Article and shall inform the Bank of the detailed action which it has taken.

ARTICLE VIII   AMENDMENTS

(a) Any proposal to introduce modifications in this Agreement, whether emanating from a member, a governor or the Executive Directors, shall be communicated to the Chairman of the Board of Governors who shall bring the proposal before the Board. If the proposed amendment is approved by the Board the Bank shall, by circular letter or telegram, ask all members whether they accept the proposed amendment. When three-fifths of the members, having eighty-five percent[3] of the total voting power, have accepted the proposed amendments, the Bank shall certify the fact by formal communication addressed to all members.

(b) Notwithstanding (a) above, acceptance by an members is required in the case of any amendment modifying:
(i)   the right to withdraw from the Bank provided in Article VI, Section 1;
(ii) the right secured by Article U, Section 3 (c);
(iii) the limitation on liability provided in Article II, Section 6.

(c) Amendments shall enter into force for all members three months after the date of the formal communication unless a shorter period is specified in the circular letter or telegram.

ARTICLE IX   INTERPRETATION

(a) Any question of interpretation of the provisions of this Agreement arising between any member and the Bank or between any members of the Bank shall be submitted to the Executive Directors for their decision. If the question particularly affects any member not entitled to appoint an Executive Director, it shall be entitled to representation in accordance with Article V, Section 4 (h).

(b) In any case where the Executive Directors have given a decision under (a) above, any member may require that the question be referred to the Board of Governors, whose decision shall be final. Pending the result of the reference to the Board, the Bank may, so far as it deems necessary, act on the basis of the decision of the Executive Directors.

(c) Whenever a disagreement arises between the Bank and a country which has ceased to be a member, or between the Bank and any member during the permanent suspension of the Bank, such disagreement shall be submitted to arbitration by a tribunal of three arbitrators, one appointed by the Bank, another by the country involved and an umpire who, unless the parties otherwise agree, shall be appointed by the President of the Permanent Court of International Justice or such other authority as may have been prescribed by regulation adopted by the Bank. The umpire shall have full power to settle all questions of procedure in any case where the parties are in disagreement with respect thereto.

---

3 'Eighty-five percent' was substituted to "four-fifths' by amendment effective February 16, 1989.

ARTICLE X   APPROVAL DEEMED GIVEN

Whenever the approval of any member is required before any act may be done by the Bank, except in Article VIII, approval shall be deemed to have been given unless the member presents an objection within such reasonable period as the Bank may fix in notifying the member of the proposed act.

ARTICLE XI   FINAL PROVISIONS

Section 1   Entry into Force
This Agreement shall enter into force when it has been signed on behalf of governments whose minimum subscriptions comprise not less than sixty-five percent of the total subscriptions set forth in Schedule A and when the instruments referred to in Section 2 (a) of this Article have been deposited on their behalf, but in no event shall this Agreement enter into force before May 1, 1945.

Section 2   Signature
(a) Each government on whose behalf this Agreement is signed shall deposit with the Government of the United States of America an instrument setting forth that it has accepted this Agreement in accordance with its law and has taken all steps necessary to enable it to carry out all of its obligations under this Agreement.

(b) Each government shall become a member of the Bank as from the date of the deposit on its behalf of the instrument referred to in (a) above, except that no government shall become a member before this Agreement enters into force under Section 1 of this Article.

(c) The Government of the United States of America shall inform the governments of all countries whose names are set forth in Schedule A, and all governments whose membership is approved in accordance with Article II, Section 1 (b), of all signatures of this Agreement and of the deposit of all instruments referred to in (a) above.

(d) At the time this Agreement is signed on its behalf, each government shall transmit to the Government of the United States of America one one-hundredth of one percent of the price of each share in gold or United States dollars for the purpose of meeting administrative expenses of the Bank. This payment shall be credited on account of the payment to be made in accordance with Article II, Section 8 (a). The Government of the United States of America shall hold such funds in a special deposit account and shall transmit them to the Board of Governors of the Bank when the initial meeting has been called under Section 3 of this Article. If this Agreement has not come into force by December 31, 1945, the Government of the United States of America shall return such funds to the governments that transmitted them.

(e) This Agreement shall remain open for signature at Washington on behalf of the governments of the countries whose names are set forth in Schedule A until December 31, 1945.

(f) After December 31, 1945, this Agreement shall be open for signature on behalf of the government of any country whose membership has been approved in accordance with Article II, Section 1 (b).

(g) By their signature of this Agreement, all governments accept it both on their own behalf and in respect of all their colonies, overseas territories, all territories under their protection, suzerainty, or authority and all territories in respect of which they exercise a mandate.

(h) In the case of governments whose metropolitan territories have been under enemy occupation, the deposit of the instrument referred to in (a) above may be delayed until one hundred and eighty days after the date on which these territories have been liberated. If, however, it is not deposited by any such government before the expiration of this period, the signature affixed on behalf of that government shall become void and the portion of its subscription paid under (d) above shall be returned to it.

(i) Paragraphs (d) and (h) shall come into force with regard to each signatory government as from the date of its signature.

Section 3 Inauguration of the Bank

(a) As soon as this Agreement enters into force under Section 1 of this Article, each member shall appoint a governor and the member to whom the largest number of shares is allocated in Schedule A shall call the first meeting of the Board of Governors.

(b) At the first meeting of the Board of Governors, arrangements shall be made for the selection of provisional executive directors. The governments of the five countries, to which the largest number of shares are allocated in Schedule A, shall appoint provisional executive directors. If one or more of such governments have not become members, the executive directorships which they would be entitled to fill shall remain vacant until they become members, or until January 1, 1946, whichever is the earlier. Seven provisional executive directors shall be elected in accordance with the provisions of Schedule B and shall remain in office until the date of the first regular election of executive directors which shall be held as soon as practicable after January 1, 1946.

(c) The Board of Governors may delegate to the provisional executive directors any powers except those which may not be delegated to the Executive Directors.

(d) The Bank shall notify members when it is ready to commence operations.

SCHEDULES

[Schedule A not reproduced]

SCHEDULE B   ELECTION OF EXECUTIVE DIRECTORS

1. The election of the elective executive directors shall be by ballot of the Governors eligible to vote under Article V, Section 4 (b).

2. In balloting for the elective executive directors, each governor eligible to vote shall cast for one person all of the votes to which the member appointing him is entitled under Section 3 of Article V. The seven persons receiving the greatest number of votes shall be executive directors, except that no person who receives less than fourteen percent of the total of the votes which can be cast (eligible votes) shall be considered elected.

3. When seven persons are not elected on the first ballot, a second ballot shall be held in which the person who received the lowest number of votes shall be ineligible for election and in which there shall vote only (a) those governors who voted in the first ballot for a person not elected and (b) those governors whose votes for a person elected are deemed under 4 below to have raised the votes cast for that person above fifteen percent of the eligible votes.

4. In determining whether the votes cast by a governor are to be deemed to have raised the total of any person above fifteen percent of the eligible votes, the fifteen percent shall be deemed to include, first, the votes of the governor casting the largest number of votes for such person, then the votes of the governor casting the next largest number, and so on until fifteen percent is reached.

5. Any governor, part of whose votes must be counted in order to raise the total of any person above fourteen percent shall be considered as casting all of his votes for such person even if the total votes for such person thereby exceed fifteen percent.

6. If, after the second ballot, seven persons have not been elected, further ballots shall be held on the same principles until seven persons have been elected, provided that after six persons are elected, the seventh may be elected by a simple majority of the remaining votes and shall be deemed to have been elected by all such votes.

IV-3

Articles of Agreement of the International Development Association (IDA)

Date   26 January 1960
In force 24 September 1960
Source   439 UNTS 249
Link   <http://siteresources.worldbank.org/IDA/Resources/ida-articlesofagreement.pdf>

IDA ARTICLES OF AGREEMENT

The Governments on whose behalf this Agreement is signed,

Considering:

That mutual cooperation for constructive economic purposes, healthy development of the world economy and balanced growth of international trade foster international relationships conducive to the maintenance of peace and world prosperity;

That an acceleration of economic development which will promote higher standards of living and economic and social progress in the less-developed countries is desirable not only in the interests of those countries but also in the interests of the international community as a whole;

That achievement of these objectives would be facilitated by an increase in the international flow of capital, public and private, to assist in the development of the resources of the less-developed countries, do hereby agree as follows:

INTRODUCTORY ARTICLE

The INTERNATIONAL DEVELOPMENT ASSOCIATION (hereinafter called "the Association") is established and shall operate in accordance with the following provisions:

(Effective September 24, 1960)

ARTICLE I   PURPOSES

The purposes of the Association are to promote economic development, increase productivity and thus raise standards of living in the less-developed areas of the world included within the Association's membership, in particular by providing finance to meet their important developmental requirements on terms which are more flexible and bear less heavily on the balance of payments than those of conventional loans, thereby furthering the developmental objectives of the International Bank for Reconstruction and Development (hereinafter called "the Bank") and supplementing its activities.

The Association shall be guided in all its decisions by the provisions of this Article.

ARTICLE II   MEMBERSHIP, INITIAL SUBSCRIPTIONS

Section 1   Membership

(a) The original members of the Association shall be those members of the Bank listed in Schedule A hereto which, on or before the date specified in Article XI, Section 2 (c), accept membership in the Association.

(b) Membership shall be open to other members of the Bank at such times and in accordance with such terms as the Association may determine.

Section 2   Initial Subscriptions

(a) Upon accepting membership, each member shall subscribe funds in the amount assigned to it. Such subscriptions are herein referred to as initial subscriptions.

(b) The initial subscription assigned to each original member shall be in the amount set forth opposite its name in Schedule A, expressed in terms of United States dollars of the weight and fineness in effect on January 1, 1960.

(c) Ten percent of the initial subscription of each original member shall be payable in gold or freely convertible currency as follows: fifty percent within thirty days after the date on which the Association shall begin operations pursuant to Article XI, Section 4, or on the date on which the original member becomes a member, whichever shall be later; twelve and one-half percent one year after the beginning of operations of the Association; and twelve and one-half percent each year thereafter at annual intervals until the ten percent portion of the initial subscription shall have been paid in full.

(d) The remaining ninety percent of the initial subscription of each original member shall be payable in gold or freely convertible currency in the case of members listed in Part I of Schedule A, and in the currency of the subscribing member in the case of members listed in Part II of Schedule A. This ninety percent portion of initial subscriptions of original members shall be payable in five equal annual installments as follows: the first such installment within thirty days after the date on which the Association shall begin operations pursuant to Article XI, Section 4, or on the date on which the original member becomes a member, whichever shall be later; the second installment one year after the beginning of operations of the Association, and succeeding installments each year thereafter at annual intervals until the ninety percent portion of the initial subscription shall have been paid in full.

(e) The Association shall accept from any member, in place of any part of the member's currency paid in or payable by the member under the preceding subsection (d) or under Section 2 of Article IV and not needed by the Association in its operations, notes or similar obligations issued by the government of the member or the depository designated by such member, which shall be non-negotiable, non-interest bearing and payable at their par value on demand to the account of the Association in the designated depository.

(f) For the purposes of this Agreement the Association shall regard as "freely convertible currency":

   (i) currency of a member which the Association determines, after consultation with the International Monetary Fund, is adequately convertible into the currencies of other members for the purposes of the Association's operations; or

   (ii) currency of a member which such member agrees, on terms satisfactory to the Association, to exchange for the currencies of other members for the purposes of the Association's operations.

(g) Except as the Association may otherwise agree, each member listed in Part I of Schedule A shall maintain, in respect of its currency paid in by it as freely convertible currency pursuant to subsection (d) of this Section, the same convertibility as existed at the time of payment.

(h) The conditions on which the initial subscriptions of members other than original members may be made, and the amounts and the terms of payment thereof, shall be determined by the Association pursuant to Section 1 (b) of this Article.

Section 3   Limitation on Liability

No member shall be liable, by reason of its membership, for obligations of the Association.

ARTICLE III ADDITIONS TO RESOURCES

Section 1 Additional Subscriptions

(a) The Association shall at such time as it deems appropriate in the light of the schedule for completion of payments on initial subscriptions of original members, and at intervals of approximately five years thereafter, review the adequacy of its resources and, if it deems desirable, shall authorize a general increase in subscriptions. Notwithstanding the foregoing, general or individual increases in subscriptions may be authorized at any time, provided that an individual increase shall be considered only at the request of the member involved. Subscriptions pursuant to this Section are herein referred to as additional subscriptions.

(b) Subject to the provisions of paragraph (c) below, when additional subscriptions are authorized, the amounts authorized for subscription and the terms and conditions relating thereto shall be as determined by the Association.

(c) When any additional subscription is authorized, each member shall be given an opportunity to subscribe, under such conditions as shall be reasonably determined by the Association, an amount which will enable it to maintain its relative voting power, but no member shall be obligated to subscribe.

(d) All decisions under this Section shall be made by a two-thirds majority of the total voting power.

Section 2 Supplementary Resources Provided by a Member in the Currency of Another Member

(a) The Association may enter into arrangements, on such terms and conditions consistent with the provisions of this Agreement as may be agreed upon, to receive from any member, in addition to the amounts payable by such member on account of its initial or any additional subscription, supplementary resources in the currency of another member, provided that the Association shall not enter into any such arrangement unless the Association is satisfied that the member whose currency is involved agrees to the use of such currency as supplementary resources and to the terms and conditions governing such use. The arrangements under which any such resources are received may include provisions regarding the disposition of earnings on the resources and regarding the disposition of the resources in the event that the member providing them ceases to be a member or the Association permanently suspends its operations.

(b) The Association shall deliver to the contributing member a Special Development Certificate setting forth the amount and currency of the resources so contributed and the terms and conditions of the arrangement relating to such resources. A Special Development Certificate shall not carry any voting rights and shall be transferable only to the Association.

(c) Nothing in this Section shall preclude the Association from accepting resources from a member in its own currency on such terms as may be agreed upon.

ARTICLE IV CURRENCIES

Section 1 Use of Currencies

(a) Currency of any member listed in Part II of Schedule A, whether or not freely convertible, received by the Association pursuant to Article II, Section 2 (d), in payment of the ninety percent portion payable thereunder in the currency of such member, and currency of such member derived therefrom as principal, interest or other charges, may be used by the Association for administrative expenses incurred by the Association in the territories of such member and, insofar as consistent with sound monetary policies, in payment for goods and services produced in the territories of such member and required for projects financed by the Association and located in such territories; and in addition when and to the extent justified by the economic and financial situation of the member concerned as determined by agreement between the member and the Association, such currency shall be freely convertible or otherwise usable for projects financed by the Association and located outside the territories of the member.

(b) The usability of currencies received by the Association in payment of subscriptions other than initial subscriptions of original members, and currencies derived therefrom as principal, interest or other charges, shall be governed by the terms and conditions on which such subscriptions are authorized.

(c) The usability of currencies received by the Association as supplementary resources other than subscriptions, and currencies derived therefrom as principal, interest or other charges, shall be governed by the terms of the arrangements pursuant to which such currencies are received.

(d) All other currencies received by the Association may be freely used and exchanged by the Association and shall not be subject to any restriction by the member whose currency is used or exchanged; provided that the foregoing shall not preclude the Association from entering into any arrangements with the member in whose territories any project financed by the Association is located restricting the use by the Association of such member's currency received as principal, interest or other charges in connection with such financing.

(e) The Association shall take appropriate steps to ensure that, over reasonable intervals of time, the portions of the subscriptions paid under Article II, Section 2(d) by members listed in Part I of Schedule A shall be used by the Association on an approximately *pro rata* basis, provided, however, that such portions of such subscriptions as are paid in gold or in a currency other than that of the subscribing member may be used more rapidly.

Section 2   Maintenance of Value of Currency Holdings

(a) Whenever the par value of a member's currency is reduced or the foreign exchange value of a member's currency has, in the opinion of the Association, depreciated to a significant extent within that member's territories, the member shall pay to the Association within a reasonable time an additional amount of its own currency sufficient to maintain the value, as of the time of subscription, of the amount of the currency of such member paid in to the Association by the member under Article II, Section 2(d), and currency furnished under the provisions of the present paragraph, whether or not such currency is held in the form of notes accepted pursuant to Article II, Section 2(e), provided, however, that the foregoing shall apply only so long as and to the extent that such currency shall not have been initially disbursed or exchanged for the currency of another member.

(b) Whenever the par value of a member's currency is increased, or the foreign exchange value of a member's currency has, in the opinion of the Association, appreciated to a significant extent within that member's territories, the Association shall return to such member within a reasonable time an amount of that member's currency equal to the increase in the value of the amount of such currency to which the provisions of paragraph (a) of this Section are applicable.

(c) The provisions of the preceding paragraphs may be waived by the Association when a uniform proportionate change in the par value of the currencies of all its members is made by the International Monetary Fund.

(d) Amounts furnished under the provisions of paragraph (a) of this Section to maintain the value of any currency shall be convertible and usable to the same extent as such currency.

ARTICLE V   OPERATIONS

Section 1   Use of Resources and Conditions of Financing

(a) The Association shall provide financing to further development in the less-developed areas of the world included within the Association's membership.

(b) Financing provided by the Association shall be for purposes which in the opinion of the Association are of high developmental priority in the light of the needs of the area or areas concerned and, except in special circumstances, shall be for specific projects.

(c) The Association shall not provide financing if in its opinion such financing is available from private sources on terms which are reasonable for the recipient or could be provided by a loan of the type made by the Bank.

(d) The Association shall not provide financing except upon the recommendation of a competent committee, made after a careful study of the merits of the proposal. Each such committee shall be appointed by the Association and shall include a nominee of the Governor or Governors representing the member or members in whose territories the project under consideration is located and one or more members of the technical staff of the Association. The requirement that the committee include the nominee of a Governor or Governors shall not apply in the case of financing provided to a public international or regional organization.

(e) The Association shall not provide financing for any project if the member in whose territories the project is located objects to such financing, except that it shall not be necessary for the Association to assure itself that individual members do not object in the case of financing provided to a public international or regional organization.

(f) The Association shall impose no conditions that the proceeds of its financing shall be spent in the territories of any particular member or members. The foregoing shall not preclude the Association from complying with any restrictions on the use of funds imposed in accordance with the provisions of these Articles, including restrictions attached to supplementary resources pursuant to agreement between the Association and the contributor.

(g) The Association shall make arrangements to ensure that the proceeds of any financing are used only for the purposes for which the financing was provided, with due attention to considerations of economy, efficiency and competitive international trade and without regard to political or other non-economic influences or considerations.

(h) Funds to be provided under any financing operation shall be made available to the recipient only to meet expenses in connection with the project as they are actually incurred.

Section 2 Form and Terms of Financing

(a) Financing by the Association shall take the form of loans. The Association may, however, provide other financing, either
  (i) out of funds subscribed pursuant to Article III, Section 1, and funds derived therefrom as principal. Interest or other charges, if the authorization for such subscriptions expressly provides for such financing; or
  (ii) in special circumstances, out of supplementary resources furnished to the Association, and funds derived therefrom as principal, interest or other charges, if the arrangements under which such resources are furnished expressly authorize such financing.

(b) Subject to the foregoing paragraph, the Association may provide financing in such forms and on such terms as it may deem appropriate, having regard to the economic position and prospects of the area or areas concerned and to the nature and requirements of the project.

(c) The Association may provide financing to a member, the government of a territory included within the Association's membership, a political subdivision of any of the foregoing, a public, or private entity in the territories of a member or members, or to a public international or regional organization.

(d) In the case of a loan to an entity other than a member, the Association may, in its discretion, require a suitable governmental or other guarantee or guarantees.

(e) The Association, in special cases, may make foreign exchange available for local expenditures.

Section 3 Modifications of Terms of Financing
The Association may, when and to the extent it deems appropriate in the light of all relevant circumstances, including the financial and economic situation and prospects of the member concerned, and on such conditions as it may determine, agree to a relaxation or other modification of the terms on which any of its financing shall have been provided.

Section 4 Cooperation with Other International Organizations and Members Providing Development Assistance
The Association shall cooperate with those public international organizations and members which provide financial and technical assistance to the less-developed areas of the world.

Section 5 Miscellaneous Operations
In addition to the operations specified elsewhere in this Agreement, the Association may:

(i) borrow funds with the approval of the member in whose currency the loan is denominated;
(ii) guarantee securities in which it has invested in order to facilitate their sale;
(iii) buy and sell securities it has issued or guaranteed or in which it has invested;
(iv) in special cases, guarantee loans from other sources for purposes not inconsistent with the provisions of these Articles;
(v) provide technical assistance and advisory services at the request of a member; and
(vi) exercise such other powers incidental to its operations as shall be necessary or desirable in furtherance of its purposes.

Section 6 Political Activity Prohibited
The Association and its officers shall not interfere in the political affairs of any member; nor shall they be influenced in their decisions by the political character of the member or members concerned. Only economic considerations shall be relevant to their decisions, and these considerations shall be weighed impartially in order to achieve the purposes stated in this Agreement.

ARTICLE VI   ORGANIZATION AND MANAGEMENT

Section 1 Structure of the Association
The Association shall have a Board of Governors, Executive Directors, a President and such other officers and staff to perform such duties as the Association may determine.

Section 2 Board of Governors
(a) All the powers of the Association shall be vested in the Board of Governors.
(b) Each Governor and Alternate Governor of the Bank appointed by a member of the Bank which is also a member of the Association shall *ex officio* be a Governor and Alternate Governor, respectively, of the Association. No Alternate Governor may vote except in the absence of his principal. The Chairman of the Board of Governors of the Bank shall *ex officio* be Chairman of the Board of Governors of the Association except that if the Chairman of the Board of Governors of the Bank shall represent a state which is not a member of the Association, then the Board of Governors shall select one of the Governors as Chairman of the Board of Governors. Any Governor or Alternate Governor shall cease to hold office if the member by which he was appointed shall cease to be a member of the Association.
(c) The Board of Governors may delegate to the Executive Directors authority to exercise any of its powers, except the power to:
(i) admit new members and determine the conditions of their admission;
(ii) authorize additional subscriptions and determine the terms and conditions relating thereto;
(iii) suspend a member;

(iv)   decide appeals from interpretations of this Agreement given by the Executive Directors;

(v)   make arrangements pursuant to Section 7 of this Article to cooperate with other international organizations (other than informal arrangements of a temporary and administrative character);

(vi)   decide to suspend permanently the operations of the Association and to distribute its assets;

(vii) determine the distribution of the Association's net income pursuant to Section 12 of this Article; and

(viii) approve proposed amendments to this Agreement.

(d) The Board of Governors shall hold an annual meeting and such other meetings as may be provided for by the Board of Governors or called by the Executive Directors.

(e) The annual meeting of the Board of Governors shall be held in conjunction with the annual meeting of the Board of Governors of the Bank.

(f) A quorum for any meeting of the Board of Governors shall be a majority of the Governors, exercising not less than two-thirds of the total voting power.

(g) The Association may by regulation establish a procedure whereby the Executive Directors may obtain a vote of the Governors on a specific question without calling a meeting of the Board of Governors.

(h) The Board of Governors, and the Executive Directors to the extent authorized, may adopt such rules and regulations as may be necessary or appropriate to conduct the business of the Association.

(i) Governors and Alternate Governors shall serve as such without compensation from the Association.

Section 3   Voting

(a) Each original member shall, in respect of its initial subscription, have 500 votes plus one additional vote for each $5,000 of its initial subscription. Subscriptions other than initial subscriptions of original members shall carry such voting rights as the Board of Governors shall determine pursuant to the provisions of Article II, Section 1 (b) or Article III, Section 1 (b) and (c), as the case may be. Additions to resources other than subscriptions under Article II, Section 1 (b) and additional subscriptions under Article III, Section 1, shall not carry voting rights.

(b) Except as otherwise specifically provided, all matters before the Association shall be decided by a majority of the votes cast.

Section 4   Executive Directors

(a) The Executive Directors shall be responsible for the conduct of the general operations of the Association, and for this purpose shall exercise all the powers given to them by this Agreement or delegated to them by the Board of Governors.

(b) The Executive Directors of the Association shall be composed *ex officio* of each Executive Director of the Bank who shall have been (i) appointed by a member of the Bank which is also a member of the Association, or (ii) elected in an election in which the votes of at least one member of the Bank which is also a member of the Association shall have counted toward his election. The Alternate to each such Executive Director of the Bank shall *ex officio* be an Alternate Director of the Association. Any Director shall cease to hold office if the member by which he was appointed, or if all the members whose votes counted toward his election, shall cease to be members of the Association.

(c) Each Director who is an appointed Executive Director of the Bank shall be entitled to cast the number of votes which the member by which he was appointed is entitled to cast in the Association. Each Director who is an elected Executive Director of the Bank shall be entitled to cast the number of votes which the member or members of the Association whose votes counted toward his election in the Bank are entitled to cast in the Association. All the votes which a Director is entitled to cast shall be cast as a unit.

(d) An Alternate Director shall have full power to act in the absence of the Director who shall have appointed him. When a Director is present, his Alternate may participate in meetings but shall not vote.

(e) A quorum for any meeting of the Executive Directors shall be a majority of the Directors exercising not less than one-half of the total voting power.

(f) The Executive Directors shall meet as often as the business of the Association may require.

(g) The Board of Governors shall adopt regulations under which a member of the Association not entitled to appoint an Executive Director of the Bank may send a representative to attend any meeting of the Executive Directors of the Association when a request made by, or a matter particularly affecting, that member is under consideration.

Section 5 President and Staff

(a) The President of the Bank shall be *ex officio* President of the Association. The President shall be Chairman of the Executive Directors of the Association but shall have no vote except a deciding vote in case of an equal division. He may participate in meetings of the Board of Governors but shall not vote at such meetings.

(b) The President shall be chief of the operating staff of the Association. Under the direction of the Executive Directors he shall conduct the ordinary business of the Association and under their general control shall be responsible for the organization, appointment and dismissal of the officers and staff. To the extent practicable, officers and staff of the Bank shall be appointed to serve concurrently as officers and staff of the Association.

(c) The President, officers and staff of the Association, in the discharge of their offices, owe their duty entirely to the Association and to no other authority. Each member of the Association shall respect the international character of this duty and shall refrain from all attempts to influence any of them in the discharge of their duties.

(d) In appointing officers and staff the President shall, subject to the paramount importance of securing the highest standards of efficiency and of technical competence, pay due regard to the importance of recruiting personnel on as wide a geographical basis as possible.

Section 6 Relationship to the Bank

(a) The Association shall be an entity separate and distinct from the Bank and the funds of the Association shall be kept separate and apart from those of the Bank. The Association shall not borrow from or lend to the Bank, except that this shall not preclude the Association from investing funds not needed in its financing operations in obligations of the Bank.

(b) The Association may make arrangements with the Bank regarding facilities, personnel and services and arrangements for reimbursement of administrative expenses paid in the first instance by either organization on behalf of the other.

(c) Nothing in this Agreement shall make the Association liable for the acts or obligations of the Bank, or the Bank liable for the acts or obligations of the Association.

Section 7 Relations with Other International Organizations

The Association shall enter into formal arrangements with the United Nations and may enter into such arrangements with other public international organizations having specialized responsibilities in related fields.

Section 8 Location of Offices

The principal office of the Association shall be the principal office of the Bank. The Association may establish other offices in the territories of any member.

Section 9 Depositories

Each member shall designate its central bank as a depository in which the Association may keep holdings of such member's currency or other assets of the Association, or, if it has no central bank, it shall designate for such purpose such other institution as may be acceptable to the Association. In the absence of any different designation, the depository designated for the Bank shall be the depository for the Association.

Section 10 Channel of Communication

Each member shall designate an appropriate authority with which the Association may communicate in connection with any matter arising under this Agreement. In the absence of any different designation, the channel of communication designated for the Bank shall be the channel for the Association.

Section 11 Publication of Reports and Provision of Information

(a) The Association shall publish an annual report containing an audited statement of its accounts and shall circulate to members at appropriate intervals a summary statement of its financial position and of the results of its operations.

(b) The Association may publish such other reports as it deems desirable to carry out its purposes.

(c) Copies of all reports, statements and publications made under this Section shall be distributed to members.

Section 12 Disposition of Net Income

The Board of Governors shall determine from time to time the disposition of the Association's net income, having due regard to provision for reserves and contingencies.

ARTICLE VII WITHDRAWAL, SUSPENSION OF MEMBERSHIP, SUSPENSION OF OPERATIONS

Section 1 Withdrawal by Members

Any member may withdraw from membership in the Association at any time by transmitting, a notice in writing to the Association at its principal office. Withdrawal shall become effective upon the date such notice is received.

Section 2 Suspension of Membership

(a) If a member fails to fulfill any of its obligations to the Association, the Association may suspend its membership by decision of a majority of the Governors, exercising a majority of the total voting power. The member so suspended shall automatically cease to be a member one year from the date of its suspension unless a decision is taken by the same majority to restore the member to good standing.

(b) While under suspension, a member shall not be entitled to exercise any rights under this Agreement except the right of withdrawal, but shall remain subject to all obligations.

Section 3 Suspension or Cessation of Membership in the Bank

Any member which is suspended from membership in, or ceases to be a member of, the Bank shall automatically be suspended from membership in, or cease to be a member of, the Association, as the case may be.

Section 4 Rights and Duties of Governments Ceasing to be Members

(a) When a government ceases to be a member, it shall have no rights under this Agreement except as provided in this Section and in Article X (c), but it shall, except as in this Section otherwise provided, remain liable for all financial obligations undertaken by it to the Association, whether as a member, borrower, guarantor or otherwise.

(b) When a government ceases to be a member, the Association and the government shall proceed to a settlement of accounts. As part of such settlement of accounts, the Association and the government may agree on the amounts to be paid to the government on account of its subscription and on the time and currencies of payment. The term "subscription" when used in relation to any member government shall for the purposes of this Article be deemed to include both the initial subscription and any additional subscription of such member government.

(c) If no such agreement is reached within six months from the date when the government ceased to be a member, or such other time as may be agreed upon by the Association and the government, the following provisions shall apply:

   (i) The government shall be relieved of any further liability to the Association on account of its subscription, except that the government shall pay to the Association forthwith amounts due and unpaid on the date when the government ceased to be a member and which in the opinion of the Association are needed by it to meet its commitments as of that date under its financing operations.

   (ii) The Association shall return to the government funds paid in by the government on account of its subscription or derived therefrom as principal repayments and held by the Association on the date when the government ceased to be a member, except to the extent that in the opinion of the Association such funds will be needed by it to meet its commitments as of that date under its financing operations.

   (iii) The Association shall pay over to the Government a *pro rata* share of all principal repayments received by the Association after the date on which the government ceases to be a member on loans contracted prior thereto, except those made out of supplementary resources provided to the Association under arrangements specifying special liquidation rights. Such share shall be such proportion of the total principal amount of such loans as the total amount paid by the government on account of its subscription and not returned to it pursuant to clause (ii) above shall bear to the total amount paid by all members on account of their subscriptions which shall have been used or in the opinion of the Association will be needed by it to meet its commitments under its financing operations as of the date on which the government ceases to be a member. Such payment by the Association shall be made in installments when and as such principal repayments are received by the Association, but not more frequently than annually. Such installments shall be paid in the currencies received by the Association except that the Association may in its discretion make payment in the currency of the government concerned.

   (iv) Any amount due to the government on account of its subscription may be withheld so long as that government, or the government of any territory included within its membership, or any political subdivision or any agency of any of the foregoing remains liable, as borrower or guarantor, to the Association, and such amount may, at the option of the Association, be applied against any such liability as it matures.

   (v) In no event shall the government receive under this paragraph (c) an amount exceeding, in the aggregate, the lesser of the two following: (a) the amount paid by the government on account of its subscription, or (b) such proportion of the net assets of the Association, as shown on the books of the Association as of the date on which the government ceased to be a member, as the amount of its subscription shall bear to the aggregate amount of the subscriptions of all members.

   (vi) All calculations required hereunder shall be made on such basis as shall be reasonably determined by the Association.

(d) In no event shall any amount due to a government under this Section be paid until six months after the date upon which the government ceases to be a member. If within six months of the date upon which any government ceases to be a member the Association suspends operations under Section 5 of this Article, all rights of such government shall be determined by the provisions of such Section 5 and such government shall be considered a member of the Association for purposes of such Section 5, except that it shall have no voting rights.

Section 5   Suspension of Operations and Settlement of Obligations

(a) The Association may permanently suspend its operations by vote of a majority of the Governors exercising a majority of the total voting power. After such suspension of operations the Association shall forthwith cease all activities, except those incident to the orderly realization, conservation and preservation of its assets and settlement of its obligations. Until final settlement of such obligations and distribution of such assets, the Association shall remain in existence and all mutual rights and obligations of the Association and its members under this Agreement shall continue unimpaired, except that no member shall be suspended or shall withdraw and that no distribution shall be made to members except as in this Section provided.

(b) No distribution shall be made to members on account of their subscriptions until all liabilities to creditors shall have been discharged or provided for and until the Board of Governors, by vote of a majority of the Governors exercising a majority of the total voting power, shall have decided to make such distribution.

(c) Subject to the foregoing, and to any special arrangements for the disposition of supplementary resources agreed upon in connection with the provision of such resources to the Association, the Association shall distribute its assets to members *pro rata* in proportion to amounts paid in by them on account of their subscriptions. Any distribution pursuant to the foregoing provision of this paragraph (c) shall be subject, in the case of any member, to prior settlement of all outstanding claims by the Association against such member. Such distribution shall be made at such times, in such currencies, and in cash or other assets as the Association shall deem fair and equitable. Distribution to the several members need not be uniform in respect of the type of assets distributed or of the currencies in which they are expressed.

(d) Any member receiving assets distributed by the Association pursuant to this Section or Section 4 shall enjoy the same rights with respect to such assets as the Association enjoyed prior to their distribution.

ARTICLE VIII   STATUS, IMMUNITIES AND PRIVILEGES

Section 1   Purposes of Article

To enable the Association to fulfill the functions with which it is entrusted, the status, immunities and privileges provided in this Article shall be accorded to the Association in the territories of each member.

Section 2   Status of the Association

The Association shall possess full juridical personality and, in particular, the capacity:

(i)   to contract;

(ii) to acquire and dispose of immovable and movable property;

(iii) to institute legal proceedings.

Section 3   Position of the Association with Regard to Judicial Process

Actions may be brought against the Association only in a court of competent jurisdiction in the territories of a member in which the Association has an office, has appointed an agent for the purpose of accepting service or notice of process, or has issued or guaranteed securities. No actions shall, however, be brought by members or persons acting for or deriving claims from members. The property and assets of the Association shall, wheresoever located and by whomsoever held, be immune from all forms of seizure, attachment or execution before the delivery of final judgment against the Association.

Section 4 Immunity of Assets from Seizure

Property and assets of the Association, wherever located and by whomsoever held, shall be immune from search, requisition, confiscation, expropriation or any other form of seizure by executive or legislative action.

Section 5 Immunity of Archives

The archives of the Association shall be inviolable.

Section 6 Freedom of Assets from Restrictions

To the extent necessary to carry out the operations provided for in this Agreement and subject to the provisions of this Agreement, all property and assets of the Association shall be free from restrictions, regulations, controls and moratoria of any nature.

Section 7 Privilege for Communications

The official communications of the Association shall be accorded by each member the same treatment that it accords to the official communications of other members.

Section 8 Immunities and Privileges of Officers and Employees

All Governors, Executive Directors, Alternates, officers and employees of the Association

- (i) shall be immune from legal process with respect to acts performed by them in their official capacity except when the Association waives this immunity;
- (ii) not being local nationals, shall be accorded the same immunities from immigration restrictions, alien registration requirements and national service obligations and the same facilities as regards exchange restrictions as are accorded by members to the representatives, officials, and employees of comparable rank of other members;
- (iii) shall be granted the same treatment in respect of travelling facilities as is accorded by members to representatives, officials and employees of comparable rank of other members.

Section 9 Immunities from Taxation

- (a) The Association, its assets, property, income and its operations and transactions authorized by this Agreement, shall be immune from all taxation and from all customs duties. The Association shall also be immune from liability for the collection or payment of any tax or duty.
- (b) No tax shall be levied on or in respect of salaries and emoluments paid by the Association to Executive Directors, Alternates, officials or employees of the Association who are not local citizens, local subjects, or other local nationals.
- (c) No taxation of any kind shall be levied on any obligation or security issued by the Association (including any dividend or interest thereon) by whomsoever held
  - (i) which discriminates against such obligation or security solely because it is issued by the Association; or
  - (ii) if the sole jurisdictional basis for such taxation is the place or currency in which it is issued, made payable or paid, or the location of any office or place of business maintained by the Association.
- (d) No taxation of any kind shall be levied on any obligation or security guaranteed by the Association (including any dividend or interest thereon) by whomsoever held
  - (i) which discriminates against such obligation or security solely because it is guaranteed by the Association; or
  - (ii) if the sole jurisdictional basis for such taxation is the location of any office or place of business maintained by the Association.

Section 10 Application of Article

Each member shall take such action as is necessary in its own territories for the purpose of making effective in terms of its own law the principles set forth in this Article and shall inform the Association of the detailed action which it has taken.

ARTICLE IX   AMENDMENTS

(a) Any proposal to introduce modifications in this Agreement, whether emanating from a member, a Governor or the Executive Directors, shall be communicated to the Chairman of the Board of Governors who shall bring the proposal before the Board. If the proposed amendment is approved by the Board, the Association shall, by circular letter or telegram, ask all members whether they accept the proposed amendment. When three-fifths of the members, having four-fifths of the total voting power, have accepted the proposed amendments, the Association shall certify the fact by formal communication addressed to all members.

(b) Notwithstanding (a) above, acceptance by all members is required in the case of any amendment modifying
   (i)   the right to withdraw from the Association provided in Article VII, Section 1;
   (ii) the right secured by Article III, Section 1 (c);
   (iii) the limitation on liability provided in Article II, Section 3.

(c) Amendments shall enter into force for all members three months after the date of the formal communication unless a shorter period is specified in the circular letter or telegram.

ARTICLE X   INTERPRETATION AND ARBITRATION

(a) Any question of interpretation of the provisions of this Agreement arising between any member and the Association or between any members of the Association shall be submitted to the Executive Directors for their decision. If the question particularly affects any member of the Association not entitled to appoint an Executive Director of the Bank, it shall be entitled to representation in accordance with Article VI, Section 4 (g).

(b) In any case where the Executive Directors have given a decision under (a) above, any member may require that the question be referred to the Board of Governors, whose decision shall be final. Pending the result of the reference to the Board of Governors, the Association may, so far as it deems necessary, act on the basis of the decision of the Executive Directors.

(c) Whenever a disagreement arises between the Association and a country which has ceased to be a member, or between the Association and any member during the permanent suspension of the Association, such disagreement shall be submitted to arbitration by a tribunal of three arbitrators, one appointed by the Association, another by the country involved and an umpire who, unless the parties otherwise agree, shall be appointed by the President of the International Court of Justice or such other authority as may have been prescribed by regulation adopted by the Association. The umpire shall have full power to settle all questions of procedure in any case where the parties are in disagreement with respect thereto.

ARTICLE XI   FINAL PROVISIONS

Section 1   Entry into Force

This Agreement shall enter into force when it has been signed on behalf of governments whose subscriptions comprise not less than sixty-five percent of the total subscriptions set forth in Schedule A and when the instruments referred to in Section 2 (a) of this Article have been deposited on their behalf, but in no event shall this Agreement enter into force before September 15, 1960.

Section 2   Signature

(a) Each government on whose behalf this Agreement is signed shall deposit with the Bank an instrument setting forth that it has accepted this Agreement in accordance with its law and has taken all steps necessary to enable it to carry out all of its obligations under this Agreement.

(b) Each government shall become a member of the Association as from the date of the deposit on its behalf of the instrument referred to in paragraph (a) above except that no government shall become a member before this Agreement enters into force under Section 1 of this Article.

(c) This Agreement shall remain open for signature until the close of business on December 31, 1960, at the principal office of the Bank, on behalf of the governments of the states whose names are set forth in Schedule A, provided that, if this Agreement shall not have entered into force by that date, the Executive Directors of the Bank may extend the period during which this Agreement shall remain open for signature by not more than six months.

(d) After this Agreement shall have entered into force, it shall be open for signature on behalf of the government of any state whose membership shall have been approved pursuant to Article II, Section 1 (b).

Section 3   Territorial Application

By its signature of this Agreement, each government accepts it both on its own behalf and in respect of all territories for whose international relations such government is responsible except those which are excluded by such government by written notice to the Association.

Section 4   Inauguration of the Association

(a) As soon as this Agreement enters into force under Section 1 of this Article the President shall call a meeting of the Executive Directors.

(b) The Association shall begin operations on the date when such meeting is held.

(c) Pending the first meeting of the Board of Governors, the Executive Directors may exercise all the powers of the Board of Governors except those reserved to the Board of Governors under this Agreement.

Section 5   Registration

The Bank is authorized to register this Agreement with the Secretariat of the United Nations in accordance with Article 102 of the Charter of the United Nations and the Regulations there under adopted by the General Assembly.

IV-4

Articles of Agreement of the International Finance Corporation (IFC)

Date   25 May 1955
In force 20 July 1956, as amended
Source 264 UNTS I-3791
Link   <http://treaties.un.org/doc/Publication/UNTS/Volume%20264/volume-264-I-3791-English.pdf>

INTRODUCTORY ARTICLE

The International Finance Corporation (hereinafter called the Corporation) is established and shall operate in accordance with the following provisions:

ARTICLE I   PURPOSE

The purpose of the Corporation is to further economic development by encouraging the growth of productive private enterprise in member countries, particularly in the less developed areas, thus supplementing the activities of the International Bank for Reconstruction and Development (hereinafter called the Bank). In carrying out this purpose, the Corporation shall:

(i)   in association with private investors, assist in financing the establishment, improvement and expansion of productive private enterprises which would contribute to the development of its member countries by making investments, without guarantee of repayment by the member government concerned, in cases where sufficient private capital is not available on reasonable terms;

(ii)   seek to bring together investment opportunities, domestic and foreign private capital, and experienced management; and

(iii)   seek to stimulate, and to help create conditions conducive to, the flow of private capital, domestic and foreign, into productive investment in member countries.

The Corporation shall be guided in all its decisions by the provisions of this Article.

ARTICLE II   MEMBERSHIP AND CAPITAL

Section 1   Membership

(a) The original members of the Corporation shall be those members of the Bank listed in Schedule A hereto which shall, on or before the date specified in Article IX, Section 2 (c), accept membership in the Corporation.

(b) Membership shall be open to other members of the Bank at such times and in accordance with such terms as may be prescribed by the Corporation.

Section 2   Capital stock

(a) The authorized capital stock of the Corporation shall be $100,000,000, in terms of United States dollars.[1]

---

1 As of December 10, 1992, the authorized capital stock of the Corporation had been increased to $2,450,000,000 divided into 2,450,000 shares of $1,000 each.

(b) The authorized capital stock shall be divided into 100,000 shares having a par value of one thousand United States dollars each. Any such shares not initially subscribed by original members shall be available for subsequent subscription in accordance with Section 3 (d) of this Article.

(c) The amount of capital stock at any time authorized may be increased by the Board of Governors as follows:

   (i) by a majority of the votes cast, in case such increase is necessary for the purpose of issuing shares of capital stock on initial subscription by members other than original members, provided that the aggregate of any increases authorized pursuant to this subparagraph shall not exceed 10,000 shares;

   (ii) in any other case, by a four-fifths majority of the total voting power.

(d) In case of an increase authorized pursuant to paragraph (c) (ii) above, each member shall have a reasonable opportunity to subscribe, under such conditions as the Corporation shall decide, to a proportion of the increase of stock equivalent to the proportion which its stock theretofore subscribed bears to the total capital stock of the Corporation, but no member shall be obligated to subscribe to any part of the increased capital.

(e) Issuance of shares of stock, other than those subscribed either on initial subscription or pursuant to paragraph (d) above, shall require a three-fourths majority of the total voting power.

(f) Shares of stock of the Corporation shall be available for subscription only by, and shall be issued only to, members.

Section 3   Subscriptions

(a) Each original member shall subscribe to the number of shares of stock set forth opposite its name in Schedule A. The number of shares of stock to be subscribed by other members shall be determined by the Corporation.

(b) Shares of stock initially subscribed by original members shall be issued at par.

(c) The initial subscription of each original member shall be payable in full within 30 days after either the date on which the Corporation shall begin operations pursuant to Article IX, Section 3 (b), or the date on which such original member becomes a member, whichever shall be later, or at such date thereafter as the Corporation shall determine. Payment shall be made in gold or United States dollars in response to a call by the Corporation which shall specify the place or places of payment.

(d) The price and other terms of subscription of shares of stock to be subscribed, otherwise than on initial subscription by original members, shall be determined by the Corporation.

Section 4   Limitation on liability

No member shall be liable, by reason of its membership, for obligations of the Corporation.

Section 5   Restriction on transfers and pledges of shares

Shares of stock shall not be pledged or encumbered in any manner whatever, and shall be transferable only to the Corporation.

ARTICLE III   OPERATIONS

Section 1   Financing operations

The Corporation may make investments of its funds in productive private enterprises in the territories of its members. The existence of a government or other public interest in such an enterprise shall not necessarily preclude the Corporation from making an investment therein.

Section 2   Forms of financing

The Corporation may make investments of its funds in such form or forms as it may deem appropriate in the circumstances.

Section 3   Operational principles

The operations of the Corporation shall be conducted in accordance with the following principles:

(i)   the Corporation shall not undertake any financing for which in its opinion sufficient private capital could be obtained on reasonable terms;

(ii)   the Corporation shall not finance an enterprise in the territories of any member if the member objects to such financing;

(iii)   the Corporation shall impose no conditions that the proceeds of any financing by it shall be spent in the territories of any particular country;

(iv)   the Corporation shall not assume responsibility for managing any enterprise in which it has invested and shall not exercise voting rights for such purpose or for any other purpose which, in its opinion, properly is within the scope of managerial control;

(v)   the Corporation shall undertake its financing on terms and conditions which it considers appropriate, taking into account the requirements of the enterprise, the risks being undertaken by the Corporation and the terms and conditions normally obtained by private investors for similar financing;

(vi)   the Corporation shall seek to revolve its funds by selling its investments to private investors whenever it can appropriately do so on satisfactory terms;

(vii)   the Corporation shall seek to maintain a reasonable diversification in its investments.

Section 4   Protection of interests

Nothing in this Agreement shall prevent the Corporation, in the event of actual or threatened default on any of its investments, actual or threatened insolvency of the enterprise in which such investment shall have been made, or other situations which, in the opinion of the Corporation, threaten to jeopardize such investment, from taking such action and exercising such rights as it may deem necessary for the protection of its interests.

Section 5   Applicability of certain foreign exchange restrictions

Funds received by or payable to the Corporation in respect of an investment of the Corporation made in any member's territories pursuant to Section 1 of this Article shall not be free, solely by reason of any provision of this Agreement, from generally applicable foreign exchange restrictions, regulations and controls in force in the territories of that member.

Section 6   Miscellaneous operations

In addition to the operations specified elsewhere in this Agreement, the Corporation shall have the power to:

(i)   borrow funds, and in that connection to furnish such collateral or other security therefor as it shall determine; provided, however, that before making a public sale of its obligations in the markets of a member, the Corporation shall have obtained the approval of that member and of the member in whose currency the obligations are to be denominated; if and so long as the Corporation shall be indebted on loans from or guaranteed by the Bank, the total amount outstanding of borrowings incurred or guarantees given by the Corporation shall not be increased if, at the time or as a result thereof, the aggregate amount of debt (including the guarantee of any debt) incurred by the Corporation from any source and then outstanding shall exceed an amount equal to four times its unimpaired subscribed capital and surplus;[2]

(ii)   invest funds not needed in its financing operations in such obligations as it may determine and invest funds held by it for pension or similar purposes in any marketable securities, all without being subject to the restrictions imposed by other sections of this Article;

(iii)   guarantee securities in which it has invested in order to facilitate their sale;

---

2 Last clause added by amendment effective September 1, 1965.

(iv) buy and sell securities it has issued or guaranteed or in which it has invested;

(v) exercise such other powers incidental to its business as shall be necessary or desirable in furtherance of its purposes.

Section 7   Valuation of currencies

Whenever it shall become necessary under this Agreement to value any currency in terms of the value of another currency, such valuation shall be as reasonably determined by the Corporation after consultation with the International Monetary Fund.

Section 8   Warning to be placed on securities

Every security issued or guaranteed by the Corporation shall bear on its face a conspicuous statement to the effect that it is not an obligation of the Bank or, unless expressly stated on the security, of any government.

Section 9   Political activity prohibited

The Corporation and its officers shall not interfere in the political affairs of any member; nor shall they be influenced in their decisions by the political character of the member or members concerned. Only economic considerations shall be relevant to their decisions, and these considerations shall be weighed impartially in order to achieve the purposes stated in this Agreement.

ARTICLE IV   ORGANIZATION AND MANAGEMENT

Section 1   Structure of the Corporation

The Corporation shall have a Board of Governors, a Board of Directors, a Chairman of the Board of Directors, a President and such other officers and staff to perform such duties as the Corporation may determine.

Section 2   Board of Governors

(a) All the powers of the Corporation shall be vested in the Board of Governors.

(b) Each Governor and Alternate Governor of the Bank appointed by a member of the Bank which is also a member of the Corporation shall *ex officio* be a Governor or Alternate Governor, respectively, of the Corporation. No Alternate Governor may vote except in the absence of his principal. The Board of Governors shall select one of the Governors as Chairman of the Board of Governors. Any Governor or Alternate Governor shall cease to hold office if the member by which he was appointed shall cease to be a member of the Corporation.

(c) The Board of Governors may delegate to the Board of Directors authority to exercise any of its powers, except the power to:

   (i)   admit new members and determine the conditions of their admission;

   (ii)   increase or decrease the capital stock;

   (iii)   suspend a member;

   (iv)   decide appeals from interpretations of this Agreement given by the Board of Directors;

   (v)   make arrangements to cooperate with other international organizations (other than informal arrangements of a temporary and administrative character);

   (vi)   decide to suspend permanently the operations of the Corporation and to distribute its assets;

   (vii)   declare dividends;

   (viii)   amend this Agreement.

(d) The Board of Governors shall hold an annual meeting and such other meetings as may be provided for by the Board of Governors or called by the Board of Directors.

(e) The annual meeting of the Board of Governors shall be held in conjunction with the annual meeting of the Board of Governors of the Bank.

(f) A quorum for any meeting of the Board of Governors shall be a majority of the Governors, exercising not less than two-thirds of the total voting power.

(g) The Corporation may by regulation establish a procedure whereby the Board of Directors may obtain a vote of the Governors on a specific question without calling a meeting of the Board of Governors.

(h) The Board of Governors, and the Board of Directors to the extent authorized, may adopt such rules and regulations as may be necessary or appropriate to conduct the business of the Corporation.

(i) Governors and Alternate Governors shall serve as such without compensation from the Corporation.

Section 3 Voting

(a) Each member shall have two hundred fifty votes plus one additional vote for each share of stock held.

(b) Except as otherwise expressly provided, all matters before the Corporation shall be decided by a majority of the votes cast.

Section 4 Board of Directors

(a) The Board of Directors shall be responsible for the conduct of the general operations of the Corporation, and for this purpose shall exercise all the powers given to it by this Agreement or delegated to it by the Board of Governors.

(b) The Board of Directors of the Corporation shall be composed *ex officio* of each Executive Director of the Bank who shall have been either (i) appointed by a member of the Bank which is also a member of the Corporation, or (ii) elected in an election in which the votes of at least one member of the Bank which is also a member of the Corporation shall have counted toward his election. The Alternate to each such Executive Director of the Bank shall *ex officio* be an Alternate Director of the Corporation. Any Director shall cease to hold office if the member by which he was appointed, or if all the members whose votes counted toward his election, shall cease to be members of the Corporation.

(c) Each Director who is an appointed Executive Director of the Bank shall be entitled to cast the number of votes which the member by which he was so appointed is entitled to cast in the Corporation. Each Director who is an elected Executive Director of the Bank shall be entitled to cast the number of votes which the member or members of the Corporation whose votes counted toward his election in the Bank are entitled to cast in the Corporation. All the votes which a Director is entitled to cast shall be cast as a unit.

(d) An Alternate Director shall have full power to act in the absence of the Director who shall have appointed him. When a Director is present, his Alternate may participate in meetings but shall not vote.

(e) A quorum for any meeting of the Board of Directors shall be a majority of the Directors exercising not less than one-half of the total voting power.

(f) The Board of Directors shall meet as often as the business of the Corporation may require.

(g) The Board of Governors shall adopt regulations under which a member of the Corporation not entitled to appoint an Executive Director of the Bank may send a representative to attend any meeting of the Board of Directors of the Corporation when a request made by, or a matter particularly affecting, that member is under consideration.

Section 5 Chairman, President and staff

(a) The President of the Bank shall be *ex officio* Chairman of the Board of Directors of the Corporation, but shall have no vote except a deciding vote in case of an equal division. He may participate in meetings of the Board of Governors but shall not vote at such meetings.

(b) The President of the Corporation shall be appointed by the Board of Directors on the recommendation of the Chairman. The President shall be chief of the operating staff of the Corporation. Under the direction of the Board of Directors and the general supervision of the Chairman, he shall conduct the ordinary business of the Corporation and under their general control shall be responsible for the organization, appointment and dismissal of the officers and staff. The President may participate in meetings of the Board of Directors but shall not vote at such meetings. The President shall cease to hold office by decision of the Board of Directors in which the Chairman concurs.

Section 6   Relationship to the Bank

(a) The Corporation shall be an entity separate and distinct from the Bank and the funds of the Corporation shall be kept separate and apart from those of the Bank. The provisions of this Section shall not prevent the Corporation from making arrangements with the Bank regarding facilities, personnel and services and arrangements for reimbursement of administrative expenses paid in the first instance by either organization on behalf of the other.

(b) Nothing in this Agreement shall make the Corporation liable for the acts or obligations of the Bank, or the Bank liable for the acts or obligations of the Corporation.

Section 7   Relations with other international organizations

The Corporation, acting through the Bank, shall enter into formal arrangements with the United Nations and may enter into such arrangements with other public international organizations having specialized responsibilities in related fields.

Section 8   Location of offices

The principal office of the Corporation shall be in the same locality as the principal office of the Bank. The Corporation may establish other offices in the territories of any member.

Section 9   Depositories

Each member shall designate its central bank as a depository in which the Corporation may keep holdings of such member's currency or other assets of the Corporation or, if it has no central bank, it shall designate for such purpose such other institution as may be acceptable to the Corporation.

Section 10   Channel of communication

Each member shall designate an appropriate authority with which the Corporation may communicate in connection with any matter arising under this Agreement.

Section 11   Publication of reports and provision of information

(a) The Corporation shall publish an annual report containing an audited statement of its accounts and shall circulate to members at appropriate intervals a summary statement of its financial position and a profit and loss statement showing the results of its operations.

(b) The Corporation may publish such other reports as it deems desirable to carry out its purposes.

(c) Copies of all reports, statements and publications made under this Section shall be distributed to members.

Section 12   Dividends

(a) The Board of Governors may determine from time to time what part of the Corporation's net income and surplus, after making appropriate provision for reserves, shall be distributed as dividends.

(b) Dividends shall be distributed *pro rata* in proportion to capital stock held by members.

(c) Dividends shall be paid in such manner and in such currency or currencies as the Corporation shall determine.

ARTICLE V   WITHDRAWAL; SUSPENSION OF MEMBERSHIP; SUSPENSION OF OPERATIONS

Section 1   Withdrawal by members

Any member may withdraw from membership in the Corporation at any time by transmitting a notice in writing to the Corporation at its principal office. Withdrawal shall become effective upon the date such notice is received.

Section 2   Suspension of membership

(a) If a member fails to fulfill any of its obligations to the Corporation, the Corporation may suspend its membership by decision of a majority of the Governors, exercising a majority of the total voting power. The member so suspended shall automatically cease to be a member one year from the date of its suspension unless a decision is taken by the same majority to restore the member to good standing.

(b) While under suspension, a member shall not be entitled to exercise any rights under this Agreement except the right of withdrawal, but shall remain subject to all obligations.

Section 3   Suspension or cessation of membership in the Bank

Any member which is suspended from membership in, or ceases to be a member of, the Bank shall automatically be suspended from membership in, or cease to be a member of, the Corporation, as the case may be.

Section 4   Rights and duties of governments ceasing to be members

(a) When a government ceases to be a member it shall remain liable for all amounts due from it to the Corporation. The Corporation shall arrange for the repurchase of such government's capital stock as a part of the settlement of accounts with it in accordance with the provisions of this Section, but the government shall have no other rights under this Agreement except as provided in this Section and in Article VIII (c).

(b) The Corporation and the government may agree on the repurchase of the capital stock of the government on such terms as may be appropriate under the circumstances, without regard to the provisions of paragraph (c) below. Such agreement may provide, among other things, for a final settlement of all obligations of the government to the Corporation.

(c) If such agreement shall not have been made within six months after the government ceases to be a member or such other time as the Corporation and such government may agree, the repurchase price of the government's capital stock shall be the value thereof shown by the books of the Corporation on the day when the government ceases to be a member. The repurchase of the capital stock shall be subject to the following conditions:

   (i)   payments for shares of stock may be made from time to time, upon their surrender by the government, in such installments, at such times and in such available currency or currencies as the Corporation reasonably determines, taking into account the financial position of the Corporation;

   (ii) any amount due to the government for its capital stock shall be withheld so long as the government or any of its agencies remains liable to the Corporation for payment of any amount and such amount may, at the option of the Corporation, be set off, as it becomes payable, against the amount due from the Corporation;

   (iii) if the Corporation sustains a net loss on the investments made pursuant to Article III, Section 1, and held by it on the date when the government ceases to be a member, and the amount of such loss exceeds the amount of the reserves provided therefor on such date, such government shall repay on demand the amount by which the repurchase price of its shares of stock would have been reduced if such loss had been taken into account when the repurchase price was determined.

(d) In no event shall any amount due to a government for its capital stock under this Section be paid until six months after the date upon which the government ceases to be a member. If within six months of the date upon which any government ceases to be a member the Corporation suspends operations under Section 5 of this Article, all rights of such government shall be determined by the provisions of such Section 5 and such government shall be considered still a member of the Corporation for purposes of such Section 5, except that it shall have no voting rights.

Section 5   Suspension of operations and settlement of obligations

(a) The Corporation may permanently suspend its operations by vote of a majority of the Governors exercising a majority of the total voting power. After such suspension of operations the Corporation shall forthwith cease all activities, except those incident to the orderly realization, conservation and preservation of its assets and settlement of its obligations. Until final settlement of such obligations and distribution of such assets, the Corporation shall remain in existence and all mutual rights and obligations of the Corporation and its members under this Agreement shall continue unimpaired, except that no member shall be suspended or withdraw and that no distribution shall be made to members except as in this Section provided.

(b) No distribution shall be made to members on account of their subscriptions to the capital stock of the Corporation until all liabilities to creditors shall have been discharged or provided for and until the Board of Governors, by vote of a majority of the Governors exercising a majority of the total voting power, shall have decided to make such distribution.

(c) Subject to the foregoing, the Corporation shall distribute the assets of the Corporation to members *pro rata* in proportion to capital stock held by them, subject, in the case of any member, to prior settlement of all outstanding claims by the Corporation against such member. Such distribution shall be made at such times, in such currencies, and in cash or other assets as the Corporation shall deem fair and equitable. The shares distributed to the several members need not necessarily be uniform in respect of the type of assets distributed or of the currencies in which they are expressed.

(d) Any member receiving assets distributed by the Corporation pursuant to this Section shall enjoy the same rights with respect to such assets as the Corporation enjoyed prior to their distribution.

ARTICLE VI   STATUS, IMMUNITIES AND PRIVILEGES

Section 1   Purposes of Articles

To enable the Corporation to fulfill the functions with which it is entrusted, the status, immunities and privileges set forth in this Article shall be accorded to the Corporation in the territories of each member.

Section 2   Status of the Corporation

The Corporation shall possess full juridical personality and, in particular, the capacity:

(i)   to contract;

(ii)   to acquire and dispose of immovable and movable property;

(iii)   to institute legal proceedings.

Section 3   Position of the Corporation with regard to judicial process

Actions may be brought against the Corporation only in a court of competent jurisdiction in the territories of a member in which the Corporation has an office, has appointed an agent for the purpose of accepting service or notice of process, or has issued or guaranteed securities. No actions shall, however, be brought by members or persons acting for or deriving claims from members. The property and assets of the Corporation shall, wheresoever located and by whomsoever held, be immune from all forms of seizure, attachment or execution before the delivery of final judgment against the Corporation.

Section 4   Immunity of assets from seizure

Property and assets of the Corporation, wherever located and by whomsoever held, shall be immune from search, requisition, confiscation, expropriation or any other form of seizure by executive or legislative action.

Section 5   Immunity of archives

The archives of the Corporation shall be inviolable.

Section 6   Freedom of assets from restrictions

To the extent necessary to carry out the operations provided for in this Agreement and subject to the provisions of Article III, Section 5, and the other provisions of this Agreement, all property and assets of the Corporation shall be free from restrictions, regulations, controls and moratoria of any nature.

Section 7   Privilege for communications

The official communications of the Corporation shall be accorded by each member the same treatment that it accords to the official communications of other members.

Section 8   Immunities and privileges of officers and employees

All Governors, Directors, Alternates, officers and employees of the Corporation:

(i)   shall be immune from legal process with respect to acts performed by them in their official capacity;

(ii)   not being local nationals, shall be accorded the same immunities from immigration restrictions, alien registration requirements and national service obligations and the same facilities as regards exchange restrictions as are accorded by members to the representatives, officials, and employees of comparable rank of other members;

(iii) shall be granted the same treatment in respect of travelling facilities as is accorded by members to representatives, officials and employees of comparable rank of other members.

Section 9   Immunities from taxation

(a)   The Corporation, its assets, property, income and its operations and transactions authorized by this Agreement, shall be immune from all taxation and from all customs duties. The Corporation shall also be immune from liability for the collection or payment of any tax or duty.

(b)   No tax shall be levied on or in respect of salaries and emoluments paid by the Corporation to Directors, Alternates, officials or employees of the Corporation who are not local citizens, local subjects, or other local nationals.

(c)   No taxation of any kind shall be levied on any obligation or security issued by the Corporation (including any dividend or interest thereon) by whomsoever held:
  (i)   which discriminates against such obligation or security solely because it is issued by the Corporation; or
  (ii) if the sole jurisdictional basis for such taxation is the place or currency in which it is issued, made payable or paid, or the location of any office or place of business maintained by the Corporation.

(d)   No taxation of any kind shall be levied on any obligation or security guaranteed by the Corporation (including any dividend or interest thereon) by whomsoever held:
  (i)   which discriminates against such obligation or security solely because it is guaranteed by the Corporation; or
  (ii) if the sole jurisdictional basis for such taxation is the location of any office or place of business maintained by the Corporation.

Section 10   Application of Article
Each member shall take such action as is necessary in its own territories for the purpose of making effective in terms of its own law the principles set forth in this Article and shall inform the Corporation of the detailed action which it has taken.

Section 11   Waiver
The Corporation in its discretion may waive any of the privileges and immunities conferred under this Article to such extent and upon such conditions as it may determine.

ARTICLE VII   AMENDMENTS

(a) This Agreement may be amended by vote of three-fifths of the Governors exercising eighty-five percent of the total voting power.

(b) Notwithstanding paragraph (a) above, the affirmative vote of all Governors is required in the case of any amendment modifying:
   (i)   the right to withdraw from the Corporation provided in Article V, Section 1;
   (ii) the pre-emptive right secured by Article II, Section 2 (d);
   (iii) the limitation on liability provided in Article II, Section 4.

(c) Any proposal to amend this Agreement, whether emanating from a member, a Governor or the Board of Directors, shall be communicated to the Chairman of the Board of Governors who shall bring the proposal before the Board of Governors. When an amendment has been duly adopted, the Corporation shall so certify by formal communication addressed to all members. Amendments shall enter into force for all members three months after the date of the formal communication unless the Board of Governors shall specify a shorter period.

ARTICLE VIII   INTERPRETATION AND ARBITRATION

(a) Any question of interpretation of the provisions of this Agreement arising between any member and the Corporation or between any members of the Corporation shall be submitted to the Board of Directors for its decision. If the question particularly affects any member of the Corporation not entitled to appoint an Executive Director of the Bank, it shall be entitled to representation in accordance with Article IV, Section 4 (g).

(b) In any case where the Board of Directors has given a decision under (a) above, any member may require that the question be referred to the Board of Governors, whose decision shall be final. Pending the result of the reference to the Board of Governors, the Corporation may, so far as it deems necessary, act on the basis of the decision of the Board of Directors.

(c) Whenever a disagreement arises between the Corporation and a country which has ceased to be a member, or between the Corporation and any member during the permanent suspension of the Corporation, such disagreement shall be submitted to arbitration by a tribunal of three arbitrators, one appointed by the Corporation, another by the country involved and an umpire who, unless the parties otherwise agree, shall be appointed by the President of the International Court of justice or such other authority as may have been prescribed by regulation adopted by the Corporation. The umpire shall have full power to settle all questions of procedure in any case where the parties are in disagreement with respect thereto.

ARTICLE IX   FINAL PROVISIONS

Section 1   Entry into force
This Agreement shall enter into force when it has been signed on behalf of not less than 30 governments whose subscriptions comprise not less than 75 percent of the total subscriptions set

forth in Schedule A and when the instruments referred to in Section 2 (a) of this Article have been deposited on their behalf, but in no event shall this Agreement enter into force before October 1, 1955.

Section 2   Signature

(a) Each government on whose behalf this Agreement is signed shall deposit with the Bank an instrument setting forth that it has accepted this Agreement without reservation in accordance with its law and has taken all steps necessary to enable it to carry out all of its obligations under this Agreement.

(b) Each government shall become a member of the Corporation as from the date of the deposit on its behalf of the instrument referred to in paragraph (a) above except that no government shall become a member before this Agreement enters into force under Section 1 of this Article.

(c) This Agreement shall remain open for signature until the close of business on December 31, 1956, at the principal office of the Bank on behalf of the governments of the countries whose names are set forth in Schedule A.

(d) After this Agreement shall have entered into force, it shall be open for signature on behalf of the government of any country whose membership has been approved pursuant to Article II, Section 1 (b).

Section 3   Inauguration of the Corporation

(a) As soon as this Agreement enters into force under Section 1 of this Article the Chairman of the Board of Directors shall call a meeting of the Board of Directors.

(b) The Corporation shall begin operations on the date when such meeting is held.

(c) Pending the first meeting of the Board of Governors, the Board of Directors may exercise all the powers of the Board of Governors except those reserved to the Board of Governors under this Agreement.

DONE at Washington, in a single copy which shall remain deposited in the archives of the International Bank for Reconstruction and Development, which has indicated by its signature below its agreement to act as depository of this Agreement and to notify all governments whose names are set forth in Schedule A of the date when this Agreement shall enter into force under Article IX, Section 1 hereof.

IV-5

Statutes of the Bank for International Settlements

In force   20 January 1930, text as amended on 27 June 2005
Source   104 LNTS 449
Link   <http://www.bis.org/about/statutes-en.pdf>

CHAPTER I   NAME, SEAT AND OBJECTS

Article 1
There is constituted under the name of the Bank for International Settlements (hereinafter referred to as the Bank) a Company limited by shares.

Article 2
The registered office of the Bank shall be situated at Basle, Switzerland.

Article 3
The objects of the Bank are: to promote the co-operation of central banks and to provide additional facilities for international financial operations; and to act as trustee or agent in regard to international financial settlements entrusted to it under agreements with the parties concerned.

CHAPTER II   CAPITAL

Article 4
(1) The authorised capital of the Bank shall be three thousand million Special Drawing Rights (SDR), as defined from time to time by the International Monetary Fund.*
(2) It shall be divided into 600,000 shares of equal nominal value, consisting of three tranches of 200,000 shares each.
(3) The nominal value of each share and the amount remaining to be paid up shall be stated on the face of the share certificates which may be issued by the Bank pursuant to Article 16.

Article 5
The two first tranches of 200,000 shares each have already been issued.

Article 6
The Board, upon a decision taken by a two-thirds majority, may, when it considers it advisable, issue on one or more occasions a third tranche of 200,000 shares and distribute them in accordance with the provisions of Article 8.

Article 7
(1) Twenty-five per cent. only of the value of each share shall be paid up at the time of subscription. The balance may be called up at a later date or dates at the discretion of the Board. Three months' notice shall be given of any such calls.
(2) If a shareholder fails to pay any call on a share on the day appointed for payment thereof the Board may, after giving reasonable notice to such shareholder, forfeit the share in respect of

---

* One SDR is the equivalent to the sum of US$0.6600, Euro 0.4230, Japanese yen 12.1000 and Pound sterling 0.1110 as approved by the Executive Board of the IMF, effective 1 January 2011.

which the call remains unpaid. A forfeited share may be sold on such terms and in such manner as the Board may think fit, and the Board may execute a transfer in favour of the person or corporation to whom the share is sold. The proceeds of sale may be received by the Bank, which will pay to the defaulting shareholder any part of the net proceeds over and above the amount of the call due and unpaid.

Article 8

(1) The capital of the Bank may be increased or reduced on the proposal of the Board acting by a two-thirds majority and adopted by a two-thirds majority of the General Meeting.

(2) In the event of an increase in the authorised capital of the Bank and of a further issue of shares, the distribution among countries shall be decided by a two-thirds majority of the Board. The central banks of Belgium, England, France, Germany, Italy and the United States of America, or some other financial institution of the last-named country acceptable to the foregoing central banks, shall be entitled to subscribe or arrange for the subscription in equal proportions of at least fifty-five per cent. of such additional shares.

(3) In extending invitations to subscribe for the amount of the increase in capital not taken up by the banks referred to in clause (2), consideration shall be given by the Board to the desirability of associating with the Bank the largest possible number of central banks that make a substantial contribution to international monetary co-operation and to the Bank's activities.

Article 9

Shares subscribed in pursuance of Article 8 by the banks referred to in clause (2) of that Article may be placed at the Bank's disposal at any time for the purposes of cancellation and the issue of an equivalent number of shares. The necessary measures shall be taken by the Board by a two-thirds majority.

Article 10

No shares shall be issued below par.

Article 11

The liability of shareholders is limited to the nominal value of their shares.

Article 12

(1) The shares shall be registered and transferable in the books of the Bank.

(2) No share may be transferred without the prior consent of the Bank and of the central bank, or the institution acting in lieu of a central bank, by or through whom the shares in question were issued.

Article 13

The shares shall carry equal rights to participate in the profits of the Bank and in any distribution of assets under Articles 51, 52 and 53 of the Statutes.

Article 14

The ownership of shares of the Bank carries no right of voting or representation at the General Meeting. The right of representation and of voting, in proportion to the number of shares subscribed in each country, may be exercised by the central bank of that country or by its nominee. Should the central bank of any country not desire to exercise these rights, they may be exercised by a financial institution of widely recognised standing and of the same nationality, appointed by the Board, and not objected to by the central bank of the country in question. In cases where there is no central bank, these rights may be exercised, if the Board thinks fit, by an appropriate financial institution of the country in question appointed by the Board.

Article 15

Shares may be subscribed or acquired only by central banks, or by financial institutions appointed by the Board in accordance with the terms and conditions laid down in Article 14.

Article 16
The Bank may at its discretion issue share certificates to its shareholders.

Article 17
Ownership of shares of the Bank implies acceptance of the Statutes of the Bank.

Article 18
The registration of the name of a shareholder in the books of the Bank establishes the title to ownership of the shares so registered.

Article 18(A)   (Transitional provisions)
In accordance with the resolutions of the Extraordinary General Meeting held on 8 January 2001 and in order to implement Article 15 of the Statutes as amended, the Bank will, on a compulsory basis, repurchase each share which, as of that date, is registered in the name of a shareholder other than a central bank (a "private shareholder"), against payment of compensation of CHF 16,000 for each share, as follows:

(1) On 8 January 2001, the registration of each private shareholder will be cancelled in the books of the Bank. As from this cancellation, every private shareholder will lose all rights appertaining to shares which are repurchased (including all rights to the payment of any future dividend), subject to the provisions of Article 54; every private shareholder will receive, in exchange for every share which is ipso jure transferred to the Bank, a statutory right to the payment of the amount of compensation referred to above.

(2) With a view to the payment of the compensation, the Bank will promptly send each private shareholder a notice inviting that private shareholder: (a) to provide written confirmation that he or she has not transferred or otherwise disposed of any share registered on 8 January 2001 in his or her name; (b) to provide written instructions for payment of the compensation by the Bank; and (c) to return the corresponding share certificates to the Bank.

(3) Upon receiving a complete response to the notice sent out pursuant to Article 18(A)(2), and after it has carried out all appropriate verifications, the Bank will pay each private shareholder the amount of compensation due to that shareholder. If a private shareholder has transferred or otherwise disposed of any share for which he or she is the registered shareholder prior to 8 January 2001, and the Bank is aware of that transfer, the Bank will pay the amount of compensation due from it to the successor in title of the registered shareholder after it has carried out all appropriate verifications. If there is any doubt as to any entitlement to compensation in respect of any share, or if there is no response or only an incomplete response to the notice sent by the Bank pursuant to Article 18(A)(2), the Bank may, on such terms as it may deem appropriate, place in escrow the amount of compensation until such time as the interested parties appropriately establish their rights. Any transfer of a share which has not been notified to the Bank before the date on which the compensation is paid will have no effect with regard to the Bank.

(4) The Board will redistribute, in the manner in which it considers appropriate, the shares repurchased from private shareholders either (a) by offering them for sale to central bank shareholders against payment of an amount equal to that of the compensation paid to the private shareholders, or (b) by offering them for subscription as bonus shares by central bank shareholders in proportion to the number of shares held (including, if applicable, any share purchased pursuant to (a) above), it being understood that this redistribution may be achieved by a combination of (a) and (b).

(5) The Board is authorised to take all decisions it deems necessary in connection with the implementation of these transitional provisions, including delegating to the General Manager as appropriate responsibility for practical execution.

CHAPTER III   POWERS OF THE BANK

Article 19

The operations of the Bank shall be in conformity with the monetary policy of the central banks of the countries concerned.

Before any financial operation is carried out by or on behalf of the Bank on a given market or in a given currency, the Board shall afford to the central bank or central banks directly concerned an opportunity to dissent. In the event of disapproval being expressed within such reasonable time as the Board shall specify, the proposed operation shall not take place. A central bank may make its concurrence subject to conditions and may limit its assent to a specific operation, or enter into a general arrangement permitting the Bank to carry on its operations within such limits as to time, character and amount as may be specified. This Article shall not be read as requiring the assent of any central bank to the withdrawal from its market of funds to the introduction of which no objection had been raised by it, in the absence of stipulations to the contrary by the central bank concerned at the time the original operation was carried out.

Any Governor of a central bank, or his alternate or any other Director specially authorised by the central bank of the country of which he is a national to act on its behalf in this matter, shall, if he is present at the meeting of the Board and does not vote against any such proposed operation, be deemed to have given the valid assent of the central bank in question.

If the representative of the central bank in question is absent or if a central bank is not directly represented on the Board, steps shall be taken to afford the central bank or banks concerned an opportunity to express dissent.

Article 20

The operations of the Bank for its own account shall only be carried out in currencies deemed suitable by the Board.

Article 21

The Board shall determine the nature of the operations to be undertaken by the Bank.

The Bank may in particular:

(a) buy and sell gold coin or bullion for its own account or for the account of central banks;

(b) hold gold for its own account under earmark in central banks;

(c) accept the custody of gold for the account of central banks;

(d) make advances to or borrow from central banks against gold, bills of exchange and other short-term obligations of prime liquidity or other approved securities;

(e) discount, rediscount, purchase or sell with or without its endorsement bills of exchange, cheques and other short-term obligations of prime liquidity, including Treasury bills and other such government short-term securities as are currently marketable;

(f) buy and sell exchange for its own account or for the account of central banks;

(g) buy and sell negotiable securities other than shares for its own account or for the account of central banks;

(h) discount for central banks bills taken from their portfolio and rediscount with central banks bills taken from its own portfolio;

(i) open and maintain current or deposit accounts with central banks;

(j) accept:
   (i)   deposits from central banks on current or deposit account;
   (ii)   deposits in connection with trustee agreements that may be made between the Bank and Governments in connection with international settlements;
   (iii) such other deposits as in the opinion of the Board come within the scope of the Bank's functions.

The Bank may also:

(k)   act as agent or correspondent of any central bank;

(l)   arrange with any central bank for the latter to act as its agent or correspondent. If a central bank is unable or unwilling to act in this capacity, the Bank may make other arrangements, provided that the central bank concerned does not object. If in such circumstances it should be deemed advisable that the Bank should establish its own agency, the sanction of a two-thirds majority of the Board will be required;

(m)   enter into agreements to act as trustee or agent in connection with international settlements, provided that such agreements shall not encroach on the obligations of the Bank towards third parties; and carry out the various operations laid down therein.

Article 22

Any of the operations which the Bank is authorised to carry out with central banks under the preceding Article may be carried out with banks, bankers, corporations or individuals of any country provided that the central bank of that country does not object.

Article 23

The Bank may enter into special agreements with central banks to facilitate the settlement of international transactions between them.

For this purpose it may arrange with central banks to have gold earmarked for their account and transferable on their order, to open accounts through which central banks can transfer their assets from one currency to another and to take such other measures as the Board may think advisable within the limits of the powers granted by these Statutes. The principles and rules governing such accounts shall be fixed by the Board.

Article 24

The Bank may not:

(a)   issue notes payable at sight to bearer;

(b)   "accept" bills of exchange;

(c)   make advances to Governments;

(d)   open current accounts in the name of Governments;

(e)   acquire a predominant interest in any business concern;

(f)   except so far as is necessary for the conduct of its own business, remain the owner of real property for any longer period than is required in order to realise to proper advantage such real property as may come into the possession of the Bank in satisfaction of claims due to it.

Article 25

The Bank shall be administered with particular regard to maintaining its liquidity, and for this purpose shall retain assets appropriate to the maturity and character of its liabilities. Its short-term liquid assets may include bank-notes, cheques payable on sight drawn on first-class banks, claims in course of collection, deposits at sight or at short notice in first-class banks, and prime bills of exchange of not more than ninety days' usance, of a kind usually accepted for rediscount by central banks.

The proportion of the Bank's assets held in any given currency shall be determined by the Board with due regard to the liabilities of the Bank.

CHAPTER IV   BOARD AND MANAGEMENT

Article 26

The Board shall determine the strategic and policy direction of the Bank, supervise the management, and fulfil the specific tasks given to it by these Statutes, and shall take the decisions necessary to carry out these responsibilities.

Article 27

The Board shall be composed as follows:

(1) The Governors for the time being of the central banks of Belgium, France, Germany, Great Britain, Italy and the United States of America (hereinafter referred to as *ex-officio* Directors).

Any *ex-officio* Director may appoint one person as his alternate who shall be entitled to attend and exercise the powers of a Director at meetings of the Board if the Governor himself is unable to be present.

(2) Six persons representative of finance, industry or commerce, appointed one each by the Governors of the central banks mentioned in clause (1), and being of the same nationality as the Governor who appoints him.

If for any reason the Governor of any of the six institutions above mentioned is unable or unwilling to serve as Director, or to make an appointment under the preceding paragraph, the Governors of the other institutions referred to or a majority of them may invite to become members of the Board two nationals of the country of the Governor in question, not objected to by the central bank of that country.

Directors appointed as aforesaid, other than *ex-officio* Directors, shall hold office for three years but shall be eligible for reappointment.

(3) Not more than nine persons to be elected by the Board by a two-thirds majority from among the Governors of the central banks of countries in which shares have been subscribed but of which the central bank does not delegate *ex-officio* Directors to the Board.

The Directors so elected shall remain in office for three years but may be re-elected.

Article 28

In the event of a vacancy occurring on the Board for any reason other than the termination of a period of office in accordance with the preceding Article, the vacancy shall be filled in accordance with the procedure by which the member to be replaced was selected. In the case of Directors other than *ex-officio* Directors, the new Director shall hold office for the unexpired period only of his predecessor's term of office. He shall, however, be eligible for re-election at the expiration of that term.

Article 29

Directors must be ordinarily resident in Europe or in a position to attend regularly at meetings of the Board.

Article 30

No person shall be appointed or hold office as a Director who is a member or an official of a Government unless he is the Governor of a central bank and no person shall be so appointed or hold office who is a member of a legislative body unless he is the Governor or a former Governor of a central bank.

Article 31

(1) Meetings of the Board shall be held not less than six times a year. At least four of these shall be held at the registered office of the Bank.

(2) In addition, decisions of the Board may be taken by means of teleconferencing or video-conferencing, or by correspondence, unless at least five Directors request that the decisions be referred to a meeting of the Board.

Article 32

A member of the Board who is not present in person at a meeting of Directors may give a proxy to any other member authorising him to vote at that meeting on his behalf.

Article 33

Unless otherwise provided by the Statutes, decisions of the Board shall be taken by a simple majority of those present or represented by proxy. In the case of an equality of votes, the Chairman shall have a second or casting vote.

The Board shall not be competent to act unless a quorum of Directors is present. This quorum shall be laid down in a regulation adopted by a two-thirds majority of the Board.

Article 34

The members of the Board may receive, in addition to out-of-pocket expenses, a fee for attendance at meeting and/or a remuneration, the amounts of which will be fixed by the Board, subject to the approval of the General Meeting.

Article 35

The proceedings of the Board shall be summarised in minutes which shall be signed by the Chairman. Copies of or extracts from these minutes for the purpose of production in a court of justice must be certified by the Chairman of the Board or any other person designated by the Board.

A record of decisions taken at each meeting shall be sent within eight days of the meeting to every member.

Article 36

The Board shall represent the Bank in its dealings with third parties and shall have the exclusive right of entering into engagements on behalf of the Bank. It may, however, delegate this right to the Chairman of the Board, to another member or other members of the Board, to the General Manager or to any other member or members of the permanent staff of the Bank, provided that it defines the powers of each person to whom it delegates this right.

Article 37

The Bank shall be legally committed *vis-à-vis* third parties by the signatures of the Chairman of the Board and another member of the Board, or by the signatures of the General Manager and a member of the staff of the Bank who has been duly authorised by the Board to sign on behalf of the Bank, or by the signatures of two members of the staff of the Bank who have been duly authorised by the Board to sign on behalf of the Bank.

Article 38

The Board shall elect from among its members a Chairman and one or more Vice-Chairmen, one of whom shall preside at meetings of the Board in the absence of the Chairman. At the meeting at which the Board elects its Chairman, the Chair shall be taken by the longest-serving member of the Board present. The members of the Board so elected shall remain in office for a maximum of three years, and may be re-elected.

Article 39

(1) A General Manager and a Deputy General Manager shall be appointed by the Board on the proposal of the Chairman of the Board. Each appointment shall be made for a maximum of five years and may be renewed.

(2) The General Manager (chief executive officer) will carry out the policy determined by the Board and will be responsible to the Board for the management of the Bank.

(3) The Deputy General Manager will assist the General Manager in the management of the Bank and will exercise the responsibilities of the General Manager in his absence.

(4) Neither the General Manager nor the Deputy General Manager shall hold any other office which, in the judgement of the Board, might interfere with his duties to the Bank.

(5) Unless otherwise determined by the Board, the General Manager and Deputy General Manager shall be entitled to attend and speak at all meetings of the Board. When attending Board meetings, the General Manager, or in his absence, the Deputy General Manager, shall also be entitled to make proposals to the Board and, if he so desires, to have his opinions specially recorded in the minutes.

Article 40

(1) The departmental organisation of the Bank shall be approved by the Board on the proposal of the General Manager.

(2) The Heads of Departments and any other officers of similar rank shall be appointed by the Board on the proposal of the General Manager.

(3) The remainder of the staff shall be appointed by the General Manager.

Article 41

In carrying out his responsibilities, the General Manager shall be assisted by an advisory committee (Executive Committee). The committee will be chaired by the General Manager and will further comprise the Deputy General Manager, the Heads of Department, and all other officers of similar rank appointed by the Board. The terms of reference for the committee shall be approved by the Board.

Article 42

Except in respect of the core responsibilities of the Board, including those matters for which a two-thirds majority of the Board is required under these Statutes, the Board may, on a temporary basis, delegate certain of its powers to one or more committees chosen from among its members.

Article 43

The Board may appoint one or more advisory committees chosen wholly or partly from among its members.

CHAPTER V   GENERAL MEETING

Article 44

General Meetings of the Bank may be attended by nominees of the central banks or other financial institutions referred to in Article 14. Voting rights shall be in proportion to the number of shares subscribed in the country of each institution represented at the meeting.

The Chair shall be taken at General Meetings by the Chairman of the Board or in his absence by a Vice-Chairman. At least three weeks' notice of General Meetings shall be given to those entitled to be represented. Subject to the provisions of these Statutes, the General Meeting shall decide upon its own procedure.

Article 45

Within four months of the end of each financial year of the Bank, an Annual General Meeting shall be held upon such date as the Board may decide. The meeting shall take place at the registered office of the Bank. Voting by proxy will be permitted in such manner as the Board may have provided in advance by regulation.

Article 46

The Annual General Meeting shall be invited:

(a) to approve the Annual Report, the Balance Sheet upon the Report of the Auditors, and the Profit and Loss Account, and any proposed changes in the remuneration, fees or allowances of the members of the Board;

(b) to make appropriations to reserve and to special funds, and to consider the declaration of a dividend and its amount;

(c) to elect the Auditors for the ensuing year and to fix their remuneration; and

(d) to discharge the Board from all personal responsibility in respect of the past financial year.

Article 47

Extraordinary General Meetings shall be summoned to decide upon any proposals of the Board:

(a) to amend the Statutes;

(b) to increase or decrease the capital of the Bank;

(c) to liquidate the Bank.

CHAPTER VI   ACCOUNTS AND PROFITS

Article 48
The financial year of the Bank will begin on 1st April and end on 31st March. The first financial period will end on 31st March, 1931.

Article 49
The Bank shall publish an Annual Report, and at least once a month a Statement of Account in such form as the Board may prescribe.

The Board shall cause to be prepared a Profit and Loss Account and Balance Sheet of the Bank for each financial year in time for submission to the Annual General Meeting.

Article 50
The Accounts and Balance Sheet shall be audited by independent auditors. The Auditors shall have full power to examine all books and accounts of the Bank and to require full information as to all its transactions. The Auditors shall report to the Board and to the General Meeting and shall state in their Report:

(a) whether they have obtained all the information and explanations they have required; and

(b) whether, in their opinion, the Balance Sheet and the Profit and Loss Account dealt with in the Report are properly drawn up so as to exhibit a true and fair view of the state of the Bank's affairs according to the best of their information and the explanations given to them, and as shown by the books of the Bank.

Article 51
The yearly net profits of the Bank shall be applied as follows:

(1) Five per cent. of such net profits, or such proportion of five per cent. as may be required for the purpose, shall be paid to a reserve fund called the Legal Reserve Fund until that Fund reaches an amount equal in value to ten per cent. of the amount of the paid-up capital of the Bank for the time being.

(2) Thereafter the net profits shall be applied in or towards payment of the dividend which is declared by the General Meeting on the proposal of the Board. The portion of the net profits so applied shall take into account the amount (if any) which the Board decides to draw from the Special Dividend Reserve Fund of the Bank pursuant to Article 52.

(3) After making provision for the foregoing, one-half of the yearly net profits then remaining shall be paid into the General Reserve Fund of the Bank until it equals the paid-up capital. Thereafter forty per cent. shall be so applied until the General Reserve Fund equals twice the paid-up capital; thirty per cent. until it equals three times the paid-up capital; twenty per cent. until it equals four times the paid-up capital; ten per cent. until it equals five times the paid-up capital; and from that point onward, five per cent. In case the General Reserve Fund, by reason of losses or by reason of an increase in the paid-up capital, falls below the amounts provided for above after having once attained them, the appropriate proportion of the yearly net profits shall again be applied until the position is restored.

(4) The disposal of the remainder of the net profits shall be determined by the General Meeting on the proposal of the Board, provided that a portion of such remainder may be allotted to the shareholders by way of a transfer to the Special Dividend Reserve Fund.

Article 52   Reserve Funds

The General Reserve Fund shall be available for meeting any losses incurred by the Bank. In case it is not adequate for this purpose, recourse may be had to the Legal Reserve Fund provided for in clause (1) of Article 51.

The Special Dividend Reserve Fund shall be available, in case of need, for paying the whole or any part of the dividend declared pursuant to clause (2) of Article 51.

These reserve funds, in the event of liquidation, and after the discharge of the liabilities of the Bank and the costs of liquidation, shall be divided among the shareholders.

CHAPTER VII   GENERAL PROVISIONS

Article 53

(1) The Bank may not be liquidated except by a three-fourths majority of the General Meeting.

(2) In the event of the liquidation of the Bank, the obligations assumed by the Bank under the Staff Pension Scheme and any related special funds, in particular the corresponding liability as published in the latest Balance Sheet or Statement of Account, shall enjoy priority over the discharge of any other liabilities of the Bank, irrespective of whether or not the pension fund of the Bank, which covers the relevant obligations, has separate legal personality at the time of liquidation.

Article 54

(1) If any dispute shall arise between the Bank, on the one side, and any central bank, financial institution, or other bank referred to in the present Statutes, on the other side, or between the Bank and its shareholders, with regard to the interpretation or application of the Statutes of the Bank, the same shall be referred for final decision to the Tribunal provided for by the Hague Agreement of January, 1930.

(2) In the absence of agreement as to the terms of submission either party to a dispute under this Article may refer the same to the Tribunal, which shall have power to decide all questions (including the question of its own jurisdiction) even in default of appearance by the other party.

(3) Before giving a final decision and without prejudice to the questions at issue, the President of the Tribunal, or, if he is unable to act in any case, a member of the Tribunal to be designated by him forthwith, may, on the request of the first party applying therefor, order any appropriate provisional measures in order to safeguard the respective rights of the parties.

(4) The provisions of this Article shall not prejudice the right of the parties to a dispute to refer the same by common consent to the President or a member of the Tribunal as sole arbitrator.

Article 55

(1) The Bank shall enjoy immunity from jurisdiction, save:
   (a) to the extent that such immunity is formally waived in individual cases by the Chairman of the Board, the General Manager, the Deputy General Manager, or their duly authorised representatives; or
   (b) in civil or commercial suits, arising from banking or financial transactions, initiated by contractual counterparties of the Bank, except in those cases in which provision for arbitration has been or shall have been made.

(2) Property and assets of the Bank shall, wherever located and by whomsoever held, be immune from any measure of execution (including seizure, attachment, freeze or any other measure of execution, enforcement or sequestration), except if that measure of execution is sought pursuant to a final judgment rendered against the Bank by any court of competent jurisdiction pursuant to sub-paragraph 1(a) or (b) above.

(3) All deposits entrusted to the Bank, all claims against the Bank and the shares issued by the Bank shall, without the express prior agreement of the Bank, wherever located and by whomsoever held, be immune from any measure of execution (including seizure, attachment, freeze or any other measure of execution, enforcement or sequestration).

Article 56

For the purposes of these Statutes:

(a) central bank means the bank or banking system in any country to which has been entrusted the duty of regulating the volume of currency and credit in that country; or, in a cross-border central banking system, the national central banks and the common central banking institution which are entrusted with such duty;

(b) the Governor of a central bank means the person who, subject to the control of his Board or other competent authority, has the direction of the policy and administration of the bank;

(c) a two-thirds majority of the Board means not less than two-thirds of the votes (whether given in person or by proxy) of the whole directorate;

(d) country means a sovereign state, a monetary zone within a sovereign state or a monetary zone extending over more than one sovereign state.

Article 57

Amendments of any Articles of these Statutes other than those enumerated in Article 58 may be proposed by a two-thirds majority of the Board to the General Meeting and if adopted by a majority of the General Meeting shall come into force, provided that such amendments are not inconsistent with the provisions of the Articles enumerated in Article 58.

Article 58

Articles 2, 3, 8, 14, 19, 24, 27, 44, 51, 54, 57 and 58 cannot be amended except subject to the following conditions: the amendment must be adopted by a two-thirds majority of the Board, approved by a majority of the General Meeting and sanctioned by a law supplementing the Charter of the Bank.

IV-6

Financial Stability Board Charter

Date   25 September 2009
Link   <http://www.financialstabilityboard.org/publications/r_090925d.pdf>

Having regard to:

(1) the initial mandate given to the Financial Stability Forum by the Finance Ministers and Central Bank Governors of the Group of Seven (20 February 1999);

(2) the broadened mandate given by the Heads of State and Government of the Group of Twenty (London Summit, 2 April 2009, "Declaration on Strengthening the Financial System");

(3) the call of the Heads of State and Government of the Group of Twenty to re-establish the Financial Stability Board "with a stronger institutional basis and enhanced capacity" (London Summit, 2 April 2009, "Declaration on Strengthening the Financial System"); and

Recognising the need to promote financial stability by developing strong regulatory, supervisory and other policies and fostering a level playing field through coherent implementation across sectors and jurisdictions.

We, the Members of the Financial Stability Board, have set forth the following Charter:

I GENERAL PROVISIONS

Article 1   Objectives of the Financial Stability Board

The Financial Stability Board (FSB) is established to coordinate at the international level the work of national financial authorities and international standard setting bodies (SSBs) in order to develop and promote the implementation of effective regulatory, supervisory and other financial sector policies. In collaboration with the international financial institutions, the FSB will address vulnerabilities affecting financial systems in the interest of global financial stability.

Article 2   Mandate and tasks of the FSB

(1) As part of its mandate, the FSB will:

   (a) assess vulnerabilities affecting the global financial system and identify and review on a timely and ongoing basis the regulatory, supervisory and related actions needed to address them, and their outcomes;

   (b) promote coordination and information exchange among authorities responsible for financial stability;

   (c) monitor and advise on market developments and their implications for regulatory policy;

   (d) advise on and monitor best practice in meeting regulatory standards;

   (e) undertake joint strategic reviews of the policy development work of the international standard setting bodies to ensure their work is timely, coordinated, focused on priorities and addressing gaps;

   (f) set guidelines for and support the establishment of supervisory colleges;

   (g) support contingency planning for cross-border crisis management, particularly with respect to systemically important firms;

   (h) collaborate with the International Monetary Fund (IMF) to conduct Early Warning Exercises; and

(i) undertake any other tasks agreed by its Members in the course of its activities and within the framework of this Charter.

(2) The FSB will promote and help coordinate the alignment of the activities of the SSBs to address any overlaps or gaps and clarify demarcations in light of changes in national and regional regulatory structures relating to prudential and systemic risk, market integrity and investor and consumer protection, infrastructure, as well as accounting and auditing.

Article 3 Consultation

In the development of the FSB's medium- and long-term strategic plans, principles, standards and guidance, the FSB will consult widely amongst its Members and with other stakeholders including private sector and non-member authorities. The consultation process will include regional outreach activities to broaden the circle of countries engaged in the work to promote international financial stability.

II MEMBERS

Article 4 Members

(1) The following bodies are eligible to be a Member:
  (a) National and regional authorities responsible for maintaining financial stability, namely ministries of finance, central banks, supervisory and regulatory authorities;
  (b) International financial institutions; and
  (c) International standard setting, regulatory, supervisory and central bank bodies.
  The eligibility of Members will be reviewed periodically by the Plenary in the light of the FSB objectives.

(2) Current Members of the FSB are listed in Annex A.

Article 5 Commitments of Members

(1) Member jurisdictions commit to:
  (a) pursue the maintenance of financial stability;
  (b) maintain the openness and transparency of the financial sector;
  (c) implement international financial standards; and
  (d) undergo periodic peer reviews, using among other evidence IMF/World Bank public Financial Sector Assessment Program reports.
  The FSB will report on these commitments and the evaluation process.

(2) In support of the mission laid down in Article 2, (1) (e), the standard setting bodies will report to the FSB on their work without prejudice to their existing reporting arrangements or their independence. This process should not undermine the independence of the standard setting process but strengthen support for strong standard setting by providing a broader accountability framework.

(3) The international financial institutions will participate as Members in the FSB in accordance with their respective legal frameworks and policies.

III ORGANISATION

Article 6 Structure of the FSB

The FSB consists of the following internal structures:

(a) the Plenary;

(b) the Steering Committee;

(c) the Chairperson; and

(d) the Secretariat.

THE PLENARY

Article 7   Responsibilities of the Plenary

(1) The Plenary is the decision-making body of the FSB.

(2) Decisions by the Plenary shall be taken by consensus.

(3) The Plenary:
  (a) decides on the manner in which the Plenary conducts its affairs;
  (b) approves the work programme of the FSB;
  (c) adopts reports, principles, standards, recommendations and guidance developed by the FSB;
  (d) decides on Membership of the FSB;
  (e) appoints the Chairperson;
  (f) decides to amend this Charter; and
  (g) decides on any other matter governing the business and affairs of the FSB.

Article 8   Representation and attendance

(1) Representation at the Plenary shall be at the level of central bank governor or immediate deputy; head or immediate deputy of the main supervisory/regulatory agency; and deputy finance minister or deputy head of finance ministry.

  Plenary representatives also include the chairs of the main SSBs and committees of central bank experts, and high-level representatives of the IMF, the World Bank, the Bank for International Settlements (BIS) and the Organisation for Economic Co-operation and Development.

(2) All Members shall be entitled to attend the Plenary Meetings. The Chair shall preside over the Plenary Meetings.

(3) The Chair can extend, after consultation with Members, ad-hoc invitations to representatives of non-FSB Members to attend the whole or part of the Plenary Meetings. In the context of specific sessions of the Plenary, the Chair can also invite, after consultation with Members, representatives of the private sector.

Article 9   Convocation

(1) The Chair shall convene at least two Plenary Meetings every calendar year, normally in March and in September.

(2) Additional extraordinary meetings may be held as circumstances arise, at such time and place as the Chair may designate, following consultation with Members.

(3) Regional Meetings of the FSB may also be held, as appropriate.

Article 10   Seat assignments

(1) The number of seats in the Plenary assigned to Member jurisdictions reflects the size of the national economy, financial market activity and national financial stability arrangements of the corresponding Member jurisdiction.

(2) Delegations with more than one seat have one representative seated at the back. Representatives sitting at the back have the rights of the table. Representation at the table can be changed according to the topic discussed.

Article 11   Standing Committees and working groups

(1) To support the FSB's missions, the Plenary may establish Standing Committees and working groups as necessary and mandate them.

(2) The chairs of Standing Committees are selected from and appointed by the Plenary at the Chair's recommendation. They report to the Plenary on their work programs. The chairs of working groups are appointed by the Plenary at the Chair's recommendation.

(3) Membership in Standing Committees and working groups is decided by the respective chairs in consultation with the Chair with due regard to the effectiveness, balanced representation and the mandate of the respective Standing Committee or working group. Membership is normally drawn from the Members of the Plenary.

(4) A Member jurisdiction can, in consultation with the Chair, decide whether its representation in a Standing Committee is through a Member or through a relevant agency of the Member jurisdiction that is not a designated FSB Member.

(5) The chairs of Standing Committees and working groups can extend ad-hoc invitations to non-members to attend the whole or part of their meetings.

(6) The FSB Secretariat supports the work of Standing Committees and working groups.

(7) Current Standing Committees and working groups of the FSB are listed in Annex B of the Charter.

STEERING COMMITTEE

Article 12   Composition and appointment

(1) The composition of the Steering Committee is decided by the Plenary at the proposal of the Chair in a manner that ensures maximum effectiveness in taking forward the FSB's work while having regard to balanced representation in terms of geographic regions and institutional functions.

(2) The composition of the Steering Committee shall be reviewed periodically in accordance with the criteria set out in the previous section.

Article 13   Responsibilities and authorities of the Steering Committee

(1) The Steering Committee shall provide operational guidance between the Plenary Meetings to carry forward the directions of the FSB.

(2) The Chair shall convene at least four Steering Committee Meetings every calendar year at such time and place as the Chair may designate.

(3) The Steering Committee may establish working groups as needed which may include representatives of non-FSB members.

(4) The duties of the Steering Committee include the following:
   (a) to monitor and guide the progress of FSB's ongoing work;
   (b) to promote coordination across and commission work from the Standing Committees and other working groups;
   (c) to ensure effective information flow to all Members;
   (d) to conduct for the consideration of the Plenary joint strategic reviews of the policy development work of the international SSBs; and
   (e) to take forward, in consultation with the Plenary, directly any other work necessary for the FSB to fulfil its mandate.

CHAIRPERSON

Article 14   Appointment and Responsibilities

(1) The Chair is appointed by the Plenary from Members for a term of three years renewable once.

(2) The Chair shall have recognised expertise and standing in the international financial policy arena.

(3) The Chair convenes and chairs the meetings of the Plenary and of the Steering Committee. The Chair oversees the Secretariat.

(4) The Chair is the principal spokesperson for the FSB and represents the FSB externally. The Chair shall be informed of all significant matters that concern the FSB.

   More generally, the Chair shall take all decisions and act as necessary to achieve the objectives of the FSB in accordance with the directions given by the Plenary.

(5) The Chair, in the discharge of the functions as the Chair, shall owe the duty entirely to the FSB and to no other authorities or institutions.

SECRETARIAT

Article 15   Secretariat

(1) The Secretariat shall be directed by the Secretary General.

(2) The Secretary General shall be appointed by the Plenary at the proposal of the Chair.

(3) The Secretary General shall be under the responsibility, and shall act in accordance with the instructions, of the Chair. The Chair is responsible for providing general direction to the Secretary General, in accordance with any directions given by the Plenary.

(4) In appointing the Secretariat staff, the Secretary General shall, subject to the importance of securing the highest standards of efficiency and of technical competence, pay due regard to the importance of a balanced composition in terms of geographic regions and institutional functions.

(5) The Secretary General and the Secretariat staff, in the discharge of their functions, shall owe their duty entirely to the FSB and to no other authorities or institutions.

(6) The main responsibilities of the Secretariat shall be the following:
   (a) to support the activities of the FSB, including its Standing Committees and working groups;
   (b) to facilitate cooperation between Members and between the FSB and other institutions;
   (c) to ensure efficient communication to Members and others;
   (d) to manage the financial, material and human resources allocated to the FSB (including the appointment of staff who may be seconded by Members);
   (e) to maintain the records, administer the website and deal with the correspondence of the FSB; and
   (f) to carry out all other functions that are assigned by the Chair or the Plenary.

(7) The Secretariat shall be located in Basel at the BIS.

IV   FINAL PROVISIONS

Article 16   Legal effect

This Charter is not intended to create any legal rights or obligations.

Article 17   Effective date

This Charter shall come into effect on 25 September 2009.

ANNEX A   LIST OF FSB MEMBERS

[Not reproduced]

IV-7

Financial Stability Board: Key Standards for Sound Financial Systems

Date   2011
Link   <http://www.financialstabilityboard.org/cos/key_standards.htm>

The standards under the 12 policy areas highlighted here have been designated by the FSB as key for sound financial systems and deserving of priority implementation depending on country circumstances. While the key standards vary in terms of their degree of international endorsement, they are broadly accepted as representing minimum requirements for good practice that countries are encourages to meet or exceed.

The FSB applied the following criteria for determining the list of key standards for sound financial systems:

- *relevant* and *critical* for a stable, robust, and well-functioning financial system (including in light of the lessons from the recent financial crisis), in order to impart a sense of prioritisation in implementation;
- *universal* in their applicability, by covering areas that are important in nearly all jurisdictions;
- *flexible* in implementation, by being general enough to take into account different country circumstances;
- *broadly endorsed*—namely, that such standards should have been issued by an internationally recognised body in the relevant area in extensive consultation with relevant stakeholders. To satisfy this criterion, the standard should preferably undergo a public consultation process. This criterion would also be satisfied when the standard-setting body has wide representation, or when the standard has been endorsed by International Financial Institutions (IFIs), such as the IMF and the World Bank; and
- *assessable* by national authorities or by third parties such as IFIs.

The list of key standards will be periodically reviewed and updated by the FSB in light of policy developments at the international level.

Area	Standard	Issuing Body
Macroeconomic Policy and Data Transparency		
Monetary and financial policy transparency	Code of Good Practices on Transparency in Monetary and Financial Policies	IMF
Fiscal policy transparency	Code of Good Practices on Fiscal Transparency	IMF
Data dissemination	Special Data Dissemination Standard/ General Data Dissemination System[1]	IMF
Financial Regulation and Supervision		
Banking supervision	Core Principles for Effective Banking Supervision	BCBS
Securities regulation	Objectives and Principles of Securities Regulation	IOSCO
Insurance supervision	Insurance Core Principles	IAIS
Institutional and Market Infrastructure		
Crisis resolution and deposit insurance[2]	Core Principles for Effective Deposit Insurance Systems	BCBS/IADI
Insolvency	Insolvency and Creditor Rights[3]	World Bank
Corporate governance	Principles of Corporate Governance	OECD
Accounting and Auditing	International Financial Reporting Standards (IFRS)	IASB
	International Standards on Auditing (ISA)	IAASB
Payment, clearing and settlement	Core Principles for Systemically Important Payment Systems	CPSS
	Recommendations for Securities Settlement Systems	CPSS/IOSCO
	Recommendations for Central Counterparties	CPSS/IOSCO
Market integrity	Forty Recommendations and 9 Special Recommendations on Money Laundering and Terrorist Financing	FATF

[1] Economies that have, or seek, access to international capital markets are encouraged to subscribe to the more stringent SDDS and all other economies are encouraged to adopt the GDDS.

[2] The FSB supports the inclusion of one or more standards on resolution regimes under this policy area, and intends to make a selection once relevant policy development work is completed.

[3] The World Bank, working with UNCITRAL and internationally recognized experts, has completed and implemented the ICR ROSC Assessment Methodology. The ICR ROSC Methodology is based on the current Creditor Rights and Insolvency Standard (ICR Standard), derived from the World Bank's Principles and Guidelines for Effective Insolvency and Creditor Rights Systems, and the recommendations included in the UNCITRAL's Legislative Guide on Insolvency Law.

IV-8

International Federation of Accountants—Constitution and Bylaws

Date 7 October 1977, as amended 5 November 2010
Link <http://web.ifac.org/download/IFAC_Constitution.pdf>
      <http://web.ifac.org/download/International_Federation_of_Accountants_Bylaws.pdf>

CONSTITUTION OF THE INTERNATIONAL FEDERATION OF ACCOUNTANTS

Definitions

This Definitions Clause shall form part of this Constitution, in which:

"**2003 IFAC Reforms**" are the reforms adopted by the Council of the International Federation of Accountants at the November 2003 Council meeting.

An "**appropriate mode of communication**" means a transmission from one party to another via mail, courier, facsimile, electronic mail, or by posting on the International Federation of Accountant's website or intranet and notification thereof.

The "**Bylaws**" means the Bylaws of the International Federation of Accountants as approved by the Council of the International Federation of Accountants in accordance with the provisions of this Constitution.

"**Board Group**" means a committee or group established at the discretion of the Board to advise or assist the Board in the performance of its duties as provided for in Section 7.4. A current list of Board Groups shall be set forth in Appendix A to the Bylaws, as such may be amended from time to time.

"**Council meeting**" refers to both an Ordinary meeting of the Council and a Special meeting of the Council.

A "**duly constituted**" meeting is a Council or a Board meeting (a) for which timely notice has been provided to the Member Bodies or Board members, as the case may be, or for which notice has been waived in accordance with the Bylaws, and (b) at which a quorum of Member Bodies or Board members, as the case may be, has been established.

The "**Forum of Firms**" (hereinafter referred to as the "**Forum**") means the grouping of firms and networks whose members have (or are interested in having) transnational audit appointments and which have undertaken certain obligations towards the Forum and the International Federation of Accountants designed to promote consistently high standards of financial reporting and auditing worldwide.

"**Good standing**" means that the Member Body, Associate or Affiliate, as the case may be, has not been suspended.

An "**IFAC Group**" means a board, committee, advisory panel or other similar group of the International Federation of Accountants in which the Nominating Committee plays a role in the selection of its membership pursuant to the Constitution or the Bylaws, other than the Board or a Board Group of the International Federation of Accountants. A current list of IFAC Groups shall be set forth in Appendix A to the Bylaws, as such may be amended from time to time.

"**Member Body**" means a professional accountancy organization that has been admitted by the Council to the International Federation of Accountants. The status of Member Bodies may be:

- **"Member Body in good standing"** means a Member Body that has not been suspended.
- **"Delinquent Member Body"** means a Member Body that has failed to pay its financial contributions in full prior to the date of the first Ordinary meeting of the Council following the date on which such contributions have become due. A Delinquent Member Body is considered to be in good standing if they have not been suspended.
- **"Suspended member body,"** as used in the Bylaws, means that although not in good standing, such Member Body continues to retain its status as a Member Body but shall not be entitled to the entitlements of Member Body status set forth in Section 2.4.

The application of the foregoing principles relating to good standing, delinquency and suspended status apply similarly to Associates and Affiliates.

The **"Monitoring Group"** means the group of regulatory and international public interest organizations that is responsible, *inter alia*, for monitoring the implementation of the 2003 IFAC Reforms.

The **"Nominating Committee"** means the committee appointed by the Council and subject only to the Public Interest Oversight Board's approval of the non-ex-officio members of the committee and that is charged with the selection of individuals that have been nominated for positions on the Board and IFAC Groups in accordance with the procedural and substantive requirements set forth in the Constitution and Bylaws.

The **"public interest activities"** of the International Federation of Accountants are the activities over which the Public Interest Oversight Board has oversight, including, in particular, (a) auditing and assurance, ethics, and education standard-setting activities, (b) the International Federation of Accountants' Member Body Compliance Program, and (c) such other activities that the Public Interest Oversight Board has determined, in consultation with the Monitoring Group and the International Federation of Accountants, that it has oversight authority.

The **"Public Interest Activity Committees"** of the International Federation of Accountants are those IFAC Groups over which the Public Interest Oversight Board has been granted oversight authority by the Council. They include the International Accounting Education Standards Board, the International Auditing and Assurance Standards Board, the International Ethics Standards Board for Accountants, the Compliance Advisory Panel, and other such groups. A current list of Public Interest Activity Committees shall be set forth in Appendix A to the Bylaws, as such may be amended from time to time.

The **"Public Interest Oversight Board"** (hereinafter referred to as the **"PIOB"**) means the independent body established with the support of the Monitoring Group and the International Federation of Accountants in accordance with the 2003 IFAC Reforms and charged with the oversight of the public interest activities of the International Federation of Accountants.

All **"Section"** and **"Article"** references in this Constitution refer to the provisions of this Constitution, unless otherwise stated.

The **"Statements of Membership Obligations"** are requirements established by the Board for Member Bodies and Associates to promote, incorporate, and assist in implementing international standards issued by the International Federation of Accountants and the International Accounting Standards Board. The Statements of Membership Obligations also establish requirements for quality assurance and investigation and disciplinary activities.

The **"Transnational Auditors Committee"** (hereinafter referred to as the **"TAC"**) means the IFAC Group that is the executive committee of the Forum.

Article 1   General Statements

1.1 The name of the organization is the International Federation of Accountants (hereinafter referred to as **"IFAC"**).

1.2 IFAC is an association established pursuant to and governed by Articles 60–79 of the Swiss Civil Code, and shall be further governed by this Constitution and the Bylaws of IFAC, as such may be amended. Provisions of this Constitution must be read in conjunction with the relevant provisions of the Bylaws.

1.3 IFAC's registered office shall be in Geneva, Switzerland.

1.4 IFAC shall operate and conduct its business and affairs in furtherance of, and in a manner entirely consistent with, its mission. IFAC's mission shall be established by the Council and may be modified by the Council in accordance with Section 4.10. IFAC's mission is to serve the public interest by:

- Contributing to the development, adoption and implementation of high-quality international standards and guidance
- Contributing to the development of strong professional accountancy organizations and accounting firms, and to high-quality practices by professional accountants
- Promoting the value of professional accountants worldwide
- Speaking out on public interest issues where the accountancy profession's expertise is most relevant

Article 2   Membership, Associate and Affiliate Organizations

2.1 The membership of IFAC shall consist of those professional accountancy organizations that:

a. the Council has determined satisfy the admission criteria for Member Body status set forth in the Bylaws and such additional criteria as may be established by the Board pursuant to Section 2.2, and

b. have been admitted as Member Bodies by affirmative act of the Council, upon recommendation by the Board.

2.2 The Board shall have the authority to establish criteria and procedures by which a professional accountancy organization may be admitted and retained as a Member Body in good standing, which admission criteria and procedures shall supplement any such criteria and procedures set forth in the Bylaws.

2.3 Member Bodies are required to:

a. make such financial contributions as may be determined in accordance with Section 3.4 (b)(i) and (ii);

b. comply with the Statements of Membership Obligations, as issued and modified by the Board, and demonstrate such evidence of such compliance as may be required by the Board; and

c. abide by the provisions of this Constitution and the Bylaws.

2.4 Member Bodies in good standing are entitled to:

a. attend Council meetings;

b. unless a Delinquent Member Body, participate in the discussions and deliberations and vote at Council meetings;

c. nominate individuals to the Board and IFAC Groups;

d. receive access to IFAC publications; and

e. such other rights, benefits and privileges as the Council or the Board shall establish.

2.5 Organizations meeting criteria set forth in the Bylaws and/or such additional criteria that the Board may establish, may, upon approval of the Council, be formally affiliated with IFAC as Associate organizations or Affiliate organizations, having such rights, privileges and obligations set forth in the Bylaws or otherwise established by the Board.

2.6 The terms and conditions pursuant to which Member Bodies, Associates and Affiliates may be suspended, expelled or may resign, shall be set forth in the Bylaws.

Article 3   Council

3.1 The Council is vested with the ultimate governance authority over IFAC.

3.2 The Council grants the Board the authority to govern and oversee the operations of IFAC as specified in this Constitution and in the Bylaws or as the Council may otherwise direct.

3.3 The Council shall consist of one representative designated as such from each Member Body, which designated representative must satisfy such requirements set forth in the Bylaws, and such designated representative shall have the authority to cast the vote of the Member Body on all matters being voted on by the Council.

3.4 The Council shall have the exclusive right, power and authority to:

   a. determine, upon the recommendation of the Board:
      i. the admission of professional accountancy organizations as Member Bodies of IFAC in accordance with Section 2.1 of this Constitution and with the Bylaws;
      ii. the admission of professional accountancy organizations as Associates and other organizations as Affiliates of IFAC in accordance with the Bylaws;
      iii. the expulsion of Member Bodies, Associates and Affiliates in accordance with the Bylaws; and
      iv. the recognition of organizations as regional organizations of IFAC in accordance with Sections 6.4(h) and 6.5(c) of the Bylaws and the withdrawal of such recognition in accordance with Section 6.4(o) of the Bylaws;

   b. determine, upon the recommendation of the Board:
      i. the basis of the assessment of the financial contributions to be paid by Member Bodies, Associates and Affiliates;
      ii. proposals for policy and strategic initiatives, including the proposed strategic plan, and the broad parameters of the budget for the ensuing year, including the level of Member Body, Associate and Affiliate financial contributions for the ensuing year; and
      iii. any other matters reserved under the provisions of this Constitution or within the applicable Articles of the Swiss Civil Code for decision or approval by the Council;

   c. appoint a Nominating Committee, upon the recommendation of the Board, in accordance with the Bylaws and subject only to the PIOB's approval of the appointment of the non-ex-officio members of the committee;

   d. upon the recommendation of the Nominating Committee:
      i. elect members of the Board in accordance with the provisions of this Constitution; and
      ii. remove a Board member during that Board member's term for non-performance or other good cause, in accordance with the Bylaws;

   e. in accordance with Article 8:
      i. elect the Deputy President;
      ii. determine whether the Deputy President shall succeed to the office of President upon expiration of the President's term of office;
      iii. upon recommendation of the Nominating Committee, and as endorsed by the Board, elect the President when required to do so by reason of the vacancy in the office of President that would result by reason of the Council not approving the succession of the Deputy President to the office of President in accordance with preceding subclause (ii) of this Section 3.4(e); and
      iv. remove the Deputy President or the President for non-performance or other good cause, upon recommendation of the Nominating Committee and as endorsed by the Board.

   f. receive reports on progress and achievement against plans approved the previous year, and reports on progress on policy and strategic initiatives;

   g. amend this Constitution, upon the recommendation of the Board in accordance with Section 11.1(a), or upon a resolution of the requisite percentage of designated Member Body representatives in accordance with Section 11.1(b);

h. amend or repeal the Bylaws or enact new Bylaws, upon the recommendation of the Board, in accordance with Section 12.2(a), or upon a resolution of the requisite percentage of designated Member Body representatives in accordance with Section 12.2(b); and

i. appoint an auditor, upon the recommendation of the Audit Committee and as endorsed by the Board.

Article 4 Council Meetings

4.1 Council meetings shall include (a) an Ordinary meeting of the Council to be held annually, and (b) Special meetings of the Council, which may be called by the Board, in accordance with the requirements and procedures set forth in the Bylaws.

4.2 The requirements and procedures for (a) providing notice of Council meetings, (b) establishing and modifying the agenda of Council meetings which sets forth the items of business that may be acted upon by the Council at the Council meeting, and (c) the conduct of Council meetings, shall be set forth in the Bylaws

4.3 Each Member Body shall have one vote, which may be cast at any Council meeting either by such Member Body's designated representative or by proxy in accordance with the requirements and procedures for proxy voting set forth in the Bylaws.

4.4 A Delinquent Member Body is entitled to have their designated representative and technical advisor attend and observe Council meetings, but is not eligible to vote or have their designated representative or technical advisor participate in the discussions and deliberations of Council meetings.

4.5 The method of voting at any Council meeting, unless specifically provided for in this Constitution or the Bylaws, shall be determined by the Chair and announced to the Council following confirmation of the presence of a quorum.

4.6 Under certain circumstances arising in connection with Special meetings of the Council as specifically provided for in the Bylaws, Member Bodies may vote by mail ballots and/or electronic mail ballots.

4.7 The Council shall not take any action on any matters coming before it at Council meetings unless a quorum of Member Bodies is present. There shall be a quorum at a particular Council meeting:

a. in the case of an Ordinary meeting, if at least 20 percent of the designated representatives of Member Bodies eligible to vote at such Ordinary meeting are present in person or by proxy; or

b. in the case of a Special meeting, if at least 50 percent of the designated representatives of Member Bodies eligible to vote at such Special meeting are present in person or by proxy.

If there is no quorum, the Council meeting shall be adjourned to such date, time and location determined by the President so that a quorum may be obtained.

4.8 The President shall be the Chair of and shall preside over all Council meetings. In the absence of the President at any Council meeting, the Deputy President shall act as the Chair of such Council meeting. In the absence of the President and the Deputy President at a Council meeting, the Member Bodies present at such Council meeting, either in person by their designated representatives or by proxy, shall elect a Chair from among the Member Body designated representatives present at such Council meeting. The Chair of the Council meeting, whether it be the President, the Deputy President or such Member Body designated representative elected to serve as Chair in the absence of the President and the Deputy President, shall, in their capacity as Chair, have only a casting vote.

4.9 Member Bodies may exercise their vote at any Council meeting by proxy in accordance with the requirements and procedures set forth in the Bylaws.

4.10 The affirmative vote of a majority of all Member Bodies present in person or by proxy at any Council meeting shall be required to constitute the action of the Council, except that decisions as to (a) the basis of assessment of the financial contributions, (b) amendment of IFAC's mission, and (c) amendments to the Constitution, shall require the affirmative vote of at least two-thirds of the Member Bodies eligible to vote and present in person or by proxy at the Council meeting at which such action is being considered.

4.11 In the event that the Council does not approve proposals made by the Board relating to matters addressed in Section 3.4(b)(i) or (ii), the status quo with regard to such matters shall be maintained until such time as the Council approves alternative proposals from the Board regarding such matters at a Council meeting.

Article 5   Board

5.1 The Board shall consist of the President, the Deputy President and not more than twenty additional members nominated in accordance with the requirements and procedures set forth in the Bylaws.

5.2 In electing the members of the Board in accordance with Section 3.4(d), the Council shall be cognizant that the composition of the Board, disregarding the President's position on the Board in recognition of the status of the President as independent Chair of the Board, shall reflect the level of financial contribution to IFAC made by Member Bodies. Subject to Section 5.3, in filling Board seats it is intended that the allocation be as follows:

a. nine seats allocated to representatives from the twelve highest contributor Member Bodies;

b. six seats allocated to representatives from the thirteenth to the twenty-fourth highest contributor Member Bodies; and

c. six seats allocated to representatives from Member Bodies not among the twenty-four highest contributor Member Bodies.

5.3 Notwithstanding the Board seat allocations specified in Section 5.2, in circumstances when the Nominating Committee considers it appropriate to apply some degree of flexibility, the allocation of Board seats specified in Section 5.2 may be modified within the following ranges:

a. between eight and ten seats allocated to representatives from the twelve highest contributor Member Bodies;

b. between five and seven seats allocated to representatives from the thirteenth to the twenty-fourth highest contributor Member Bodies; and

c. between five and seven seats allocated to representatives from Member Bodies not among the twenty-four highest contributor Member Bodies.

In circumstances when the Nominating Committee recommends that there be a deviation from the Board seat allocations specified in Section 5.2, the Nominating Committee shall report to the Council and the Board the reason for its recommendation to deviate from Section 5.2.

5.4 Subject to Sections 5.1, 5.2 and 5.3, when selecting nominees to fill positions on the Board, the Nominating Committee shall have regard to the principle that the primary criterion for selection of nominees shall be selecting the best persons for the available positions, taking into consideration factors such as leadership ability, experience and other personal skills and attributes. Notwithstanding the foregoing, the Nominating Committee shall also take into consideration geographic balance, industry balance, size of employer and gender balance.

5.5 Any vacancy of Board membership shall be filled by the Council through the normal processes of election at the next Council meeting. Any such vacancy may be filled in the interim in accordance with Section 6.17 of the Bylaws.

5.6 The Board shall have the power to take all practicable steps to achieve the mission of IFAC, including the power to establish or dissolve such IFAC Groups or Board Groups as it may determine to be necessary or appropriate for the effective discharge of its duties, and to take any action in the general interest of IFAC and which is not expressly addressed in this Constitution or the Bylaws. Further powers of the Board are specified in the Bylaws.

5.7 The Board shall ensure that it does not involve itself in the domestic affairs of a Member Body other than to the extent necessary to ensure compliance with the obligations of membership of IFAC.

5.8 The Board shall with respect to the PIOB:
   a. discuss with the Monitoring Group and the PIOB which IFAC Groups are classified as Public Interest Activity Committees;
   b. submit to the PIOB for approval the Board's recommended appointments of members and chairs of the Public Interest Activity Committees;
   c. consult with the PIOB prior to any decision by the Board for the removal of members and chairs of the Public Interest Activity Committees;
   d. submit to the PIOB for approval the terms of reference of the Public Interest Activity Committees, and the terms of reference of their respective consultative advisory groups;
   e. make available to the PIOB documentation related to the Public Interest Activity Committees in such form, content and frequency as is reasonably requested by the PIOB;
   f. based on the annual budget of the PIOB, agree with the Monitoring Group and the PIOB the amount of the annual funding to be provided by IFAC to the PIOB; and
   g. perform, at its discretion, a review of the PIOB and the Public Interest Activity Committees.

Article 6   Board Meetings

6.1 Ordinary and Special meetings of the Board shall be held and conducted in accordance with the requirements and procedures set forth in the Bylaws.

Article 7   Nominating Committee, IFAC Groups, and Board Groups

7.1 A Nominating Committee shall be established and maintained by the Council as a standing committee of IFAC.

7.2 Except as otherwise provided in the Constitution, the composition, terms, duties, powers and operating procedures of the Nominating Committee shall be set forth in the Bylaws.

7.3 The composition, terms of reference, duties, powers and operating procedures of IFAC Groups established under Section 5.6 shall be provided for in the Bylaws.

7.4 The Board shall establish and maintain an Audit Committee, and shall have the authority to establish and maintain such other Board Groups as the Board shall deem necessary or appropriate. The composition, terms of reference, duties, powers and operating procedures of Board Groups shall either be provided for in the Bylaws or otherwise established by resolution of the Board.

Article 8   Officers

8.1 The Officers of IFAC shall be the President, Deputy President and Chief Executive Officer, and such other officers as the Board shall deem necessary or appropriate.

8.2 At the Ordinary meeting of the Council in alternate years, the Council shall elect a Deputy President, upon the recommendation of the Nominating Committee and as endorsed by the Board, with the intention that the Deputy President shall, in the ordinary course, succeed to the office of President upon expiration of the President's term of office. The Deputy President shall serve for a term of two years, which term of office shall expire at the Ordinary meeting of the Council in the second year following the election of the Deputy President, which shall correspond with the expiration of the President's term of office as provided in Section 8.3. Upon expiration of the President's term of office, the Council shall determine, based on a recommendation of the Nominating Committee and as endorsed by the Board, if the Deputy President shall become the President.

8.3 The term of office of the President shall be the two year period commencing at the Ordinary Meeting of the Council at which the office of the President was assumed by the Deputy President pursuant to Section 8.2, and expiring at the conclusion of the Ordinary meeting of the Council in the second year following the assumption of the office of President.

8.4 In the event of a determination by the Council under Section 8.2 that the Deputy President shall not become the President upon the expiration of the President's term of office, then:

  a. the Council shall elect, based on the recommendations of the Nominating Committee and as endorsed by the Board, both (i) a new Deputy President in the ordinary course pursuant to Section 8.2, and (ii) a new President, at the Ordinary meeting of the Council at which the Council determines not to approve the Deputy President's succession to the office of President; and

  b. in the event that the circumstances giving rise to the Deputy President not being approved by the Council to become the President do not permit adequate opportunity for the Nominating Committee to make recommendations for a new President or for the Board to endorse the Nominating Committee's recommendation of a new President at the Ordinary meeting of the Council at which the Deputy President was not approved by the Council to become President, the Council shall elect a new President at a Special meeting of the Council called by the Board as promptly as practical following such Ordinary meeting of the Council pursuant to a Special meeting of the Council in accordance with Section 4.1.

  c. The process for electing the President at any such Council meeting, including, in particular, the nominating process for selecting candidates for both such positions, shall be the same as the process of electing the Deputy President in the ordinary course as provided for in Section 8.2.

8.5 The assumption of the office of Deputy President and President shall be without the right of re-election to the same office.

8.6 The rights and procedures relating to the removal of the Deputy President or President shall be provided for in the Bylaws

8.7 Terms and procedures relating to vacancies in the offices of the Deputy President and the President shall be provided for in the Bylaws.

8.8 The Board shall appoint a Chief Executive Officer who shall be responsible to the Board for the conduct of the affairs of IFAC.

8.9 Additional requirements and procedures relating to the election and appointment, terms of office, and the rights, powers, duties and authorities of the Officers, shall be set forth in the Bylaws and as otherwise established by the Board.

Article 9 Limitations on Director/Officer Liabilities and Indemnification Rights

9.1 IFAC shall, to the fullest extent permitted by applicable law, indemnify and hold harmless any present or former member of the Board or officer, employee or agent of IFAC or member of a Board Group or an IFAC Group or the personal representatives thereof (collectively an "Indemnified Person"), made or threatened to be made a party in any civil or criminal action or proceeding by reason of the fact that such Indemnified Person, or their testator or intestate, is or was a Board member, officer, employee, agent of IFAC or a member of a Board Group, or an IFAC Group or, at the request of IFAC, served any other organization, entity, group or other enterprise in any capacity, to the fullest extent and in all such circumstances as shall be permitted under applicable law. All such indemnified costs and expenses incurred by an Indemnified Person shall be advanced by IFAC pending the final disposition of such action or proceeding to the extent permitted by applicable law.

9.2 The indemnification required pursuant to Section 9.1 shall be subject only to the exception that no indemnification may be made by IFAC to or on behalf of any Indemnified Person in the event and to the extent that a judgment or other final adjudication adverse to the Indemnified Person establishes that:
   a. such Indemnified Person's acts were committed in bad faith or involved intentional misconduct or a knowing violation of law; or
   b. such Indemnified Person personally gained in fact a financial profit or other advantage to which they were not legally entitled (provided, however, that indemnification shall be made upon any successful appeal of any such adverse judgment or final adjudication).

Article 10   Dissolution

10.1 IFAC may be dissolved by resolution of the Member Bodies at a duly constituted Council meeting. In the event of dissolution, IFAC shall be dissolved in accordance with the provisions of the Swiss Civil Code and liquidation of IFAC's assets remaining after satisfaction of IFAC's debts and liabilities shall be distributed to one or more organizations selected by the Member Bodies at a duly constituted Council meeting upon recommendation of the Board for purposes that are similar to and compatible with the mission of IFAC.

10.2 In the event of a termination of IFAC's activities and in accordance with the Swiss Civil Code, financial contributions received from Member Bodies and any other assets will not be returned to Member Bodies.

Article 11   Constitutional Amendments

11.1 The Constitution may be amended only by the Council upon a proposal by either:
   a. the Board; or
   b. at least 20 percent of all designated Member Body representatives eligible to vote.

11.2 The affirmative vote of at least two-thirds of the Member Bodies eligible to vote and present in person or by proxy at the Council meeting at which such action is being considered shall be required to authorize the amendment of the Constitution in accordance with Sections 3.4(g) and 4.10(c). Amendments to this Constitution shall be considered to have immediate effect following the vote of the Council approving such amendment unless otherwise specified at the time of approval by the Council.

Article 12   Bylaws

12.1 This Constitution is supported by the Bylaws. The Bylaws provide more detail and procedures regarding the application of the provisions of this Constitution, including powers identified in this Constitution and the delegation of such powers to the Board.

12.2 The Bylaws may be amended or repealed and new Bylaws may be adopted by the Council upon recommendation of:
   a. the Board; or
   b. at least 20 percent of all designated Member Body representatives eligible to vote.

12.3 In exceptional and urgent circumstances, individual provisions of the Bylaws may be amended or repealed and new provisions of the Bylaws may be enacted by the Board by the affirmative vote of at least two-thirds of the members of the Board present at any duly constituted Board meeting and such actions of the Board with regard to the Bylaws shall have immediate effect unless otherwise specified at the time of approval by the Board.

12.4 No repeal, amendment or enactment of any provisions of the Bylaws under Section 12.3 shall have force beyond the next Ordinary meeting of the Council, unless adopted at such a meeting or at a Special meeting of the Council called for such purpose.

12.5 Any decision of the Board to repeal, amend or enact a provision of the Bylaws may be modified at any Ordinary meeting of the Council or at a Special meeting of the Council called for such purpose.

Article 13   Interpretation and Conflicts of Governing Documents

13.1 In the event of any conflict between the provisions of the Constitution and the provisions of the Bylaws, the provisions of the Constitution shall control.

13.2 In the event of a dispute or question of interpretation concerning the true meaning, intent, or application of any provision of the Constitution or the Bylaws, such dispute or question shall be resolved as follows:

   a. in the case of a dispute or question of interpretation regarding a provision of the Constitution, the Council shall have the authority to conclusively resolve such matter, upon consultation with the Board;

   b. in the case of a dispute or question of interpretation regarding a provision of the Bylaws, the Board shall have the authority to conclusively resolve such matter; and

   c. in the event that any such dispute or question of interpretation arises under circumstances in which it is not practicable to wait until the next Council meeting or Board meeting, as the case may be, to resolve the issue, the President shall have the authority to conclusively resolve such matter upon consultation with the Deputy President and/or the Chief Executive Officer, which resolution shall have effect until the next Council meeting or the Board meeting, as the case may be, at which such resolution shall either be ratified or overturned by vote of the Council or the Board, as the case may be.

BYLAWS OF THE INTERNATIONAL FEDERATION OF ACCOUNTANTS

Definitions

This Definitions Clause shall form part of these Bylaws, in which:

"**2003 IFAC Reforms**" are the reforms adopted by the Council of the International Federation of Accountants at the November 2003 Council meeting.

An "**appropriate mode of communication**" means a transmission from one party to another via mail, courier, facsimile, electronic mail, or by posting on the International Federation of Accountant's website or intranet and notification thereof.

"**Board Group**" means a committee or group established at the discretion of the Board, which, in the Board's discretion, is necessary or appropriate to advise or assist the Board in the performance of its duties as provided for in Section 7.4 of the Constitution. A current list of Board Groups shall be set forth in Appendix A to these Bylaws, as such may be amended.

The "**call for nominations**" means the notice issued by the Nominating Committee to Member Bodies, the Forum of Firms, and the public stating what vacancies are occurring on the Board and IFAC Groups, the requirements and an estimate of the time commitment for the particular vacancies, and the instructions for submitting nominations.

The "**Constitution**" means the Constitution of the International Federation of Accountants as approved by the Council of the International Federation of Accountants.

"**Council meeting**" refers to both an Ordinary meeting of the Council and a Special meeting of the Council.

"**Delinquent Member Body, Associate, or Affiliate**" means a Member Body, Associate, or Affiliate that has failed to pay its financial contributions in full prior to the date of the first Ordinary meeting of the Council following the date on which such contributions have become due. A Delinquent Member Body, Associate, or Affiliate is considered to be in good standing if they have not been suspended.

A "**duly constituted**" meeting is a Council or a Board meeting (a) for which timely notice has been provided to the Member Bodies or Board members, as the case may be, or for which notice has been waived in accordance with Section 5.6 hereof, and (b) at which a quorum of Member Bodies or Board members, as the case may be, has been established.

The "**Forum of Firms**" (hereinafter referred to as the "**Forum**") means the grouping of firms and networks whose members have (or are interested in having) transnational audit appointments and which have undertaken certain obligations towards the Forum and the International Federation of Accountants designed to promote consistently high standards of financial reporting and auditing worldwide.

"**Good standing**" means that the Member Body, Associate or Affiliate, as the case may be, has not been suspended.

An "**IFAC Group**" means a board, committee, advisory panel or other similar group of the International Federation of Accountants in which the Nominating Committee plays a role in the selection of its membership pursuant to the Constitution or the Bylaws, other than the Board or a Board Group of the International Federation of Accountants. A current list of IFAC Groups shall be set forth in Appendix A to these Bylaws, as such may be amended from time to time.

"**Member Body**" means a professional accountancy organization that has been admitted by the Council to the International Federation of Accountants. The status of Member Bodies may be:

- "**Member Body in good standing**" means a Member Body that has not been suspended.
- "**Delinquent Member Body**" means a Member Body that has failed to pay its financial contributions in full prior to the date of the first Ordinary meeting of the Council following the date on which such contributions have become due. A Delinquent Member Body is considered to be in good standing if they have not been suspended.
- "**Suspended member body**", which, as described in Section 4.2, means that although not in good standing, such Member Body continues to retain its status as a Member Body, but shall not be entitled to the entitlements of Member Body status set forth in Section 2.4 of the Constitution.

The application of the foregoing principles relating to good standing, delinquency and suspended status apply similarly to Associates and Affiliates.

The "**Monitoring Group**" means the group of regulatory and international public interest organizations that is responsible, *inter alia*, for monitoring the implementation of the 2003 IFAC Reforms.

The "**Nominating Committee**" means the committee appointed by the Council and subject only to the Public Interest Oversight Board's approval of the non-ex-officio members of the committee and that is charged with the selection of individuals that have been nominated for positions on the Board and IFAC Groups in accordance with the procedural and substantive requirements set forth in the Constitution and Bylaws.

"**Nominating Organization**" means the Member Body which nominates an individual to be considered for election as a member of the Board or for appointment as a member of an IFAC Group.

The "**public interest activities**" of the International Federation of Accountants are the activities over which the Public Interest Oversight Board has oversight authority, including, in particular, (a) auditing and assurance, ethics, and education standard-setting activities, (b) the International Federation of Accountants' Member Body Compliance Program, and (c) such other activities that the Public Interest Oversight Board has determined, in consultation with the Monitoring Group and the International Federation of Accountants, that it has oversight authority.

The "**Public Interest Activity Committees**" of the International Federation of Accountants are those IFAC Groups over which the Public Interest Oversight Board has been granted oversight authority by the Council. They include the International Accounting Education Standards Board, the International Auditing and Assurance Standards Board, the International

Ethics Standards Board for Accountants, the Compliance Advisory Panel, and other such groups. A current list of Public Interest Activity Committees shall be set forth in Appendix A to these Bylaws, as such may be amended from time to time.

The "**Public Interest Oversight Board**" (hereinafter referred to as the "**PIOB**") means the independent body established with the support of the Monitoring Group and the International Federation of Accountants in accordance with the 2003 IFAC Reforms and charged with the oversight of the public interest activities of the International Federation of Accountants.

All "**Section**" and "**Article**" references in these Bylaws refer to the provisions of these Bylaws, unless otherwise stated.

The "**Statements of Membership Obligations**" are requirements established by the Board for Member Bodies and Associates to promote, incorporate, and assist in implementing international standards issued by the International Federation of Accountants and the International Accounting Standards Board. The Statements of Membership Obligations also establish requirements for quality assurance and investigation and disciplinary activities.

The "**Transnational Auditors Committee**" (hereinafter referred to as the "**TAC**") means the IFAC Group that is the executive committee of the Forum.

Article 1   General Statements

1.1 The International Federation of Accountants (hereinafter referred to as "**IFAC**") is governed by and shall be operated in accordance with (a) Articles 60–79 of the Swiss Civil Code, (b) the Constitution, and (c) these Bylaws, as such may be amended. Provisions of these Bylaws must be read in conjunction with the relevant provisions of the Constitution. If any provision of these Bylaws is inconsistent with provisions of the Constitution, the provisions of the Constitution shall control.

Article 2   Membership

2.1 Membership shall be open to professional accountancy organizations that the Council has determined satisfy the following admission criteria and such other admission criteria as the Board may establish as provided for in Section 2.2:

   a. The organization is acknowledged, either by legal decree or by general consensus, as being a national professional accountancy organization in good standing in the jurisdiction in which it operates. In the case of acknowledgement of the foregoing by general consensus, evidence must exist that such organization has the support of the public and other key stakeholders.

   b. The organization supports the missions of IFAC and of the International Accounting Standards Board (hereinafter referred to as the "**IASB**"), and has either: (i) met the obligations specified in the Statements of Membership Obligations; or (ii) in those cases where an organization has not yet met all the obligations in the Statements of Membership Obligations, the organization actively participates in the IFAC Member Body Compliance Program and has submitted a realistic and detailed action plan to meet such obligations.

   c. The organization demonstrates capacity to actively participate in the IFAC Member Body Compliance Program.

   d. The organization is financially and operationally viable, and has an appropriate governance structure.

   e. The organization has an internal operating structure that provides for the support and regulation of its members.

2.2 In addition to admission criteria set forth in Section 2.1, the Board may establish such additional admission criteria and procedures for professional accountancy organizations to be admitted as Member Bodies, and to retain their status as Member Bodies in good standing, as the Board deems necessary and appropriate.

2.3 The affirmative act of the Council, upon recommendation by the Board, shall be required to admit a professional accountancy organization as a Member Body, as provided in Sections 2.1(b) and 3.4(a)(i) of the Constitution.

Article 3   Associate and Affiliate Organizations

3.1 Associates of IFAC shall consist of those professional accountancy organizations that:
   a. the Council has determined do not yet satisfy all of the admission criteria of Member Body status provided for in Article 2, but demonstrate, to the Council's satisfaction, evidence of: (i) a commitment to meeting such admission criteria; (ii) progress towards compliance with the Statements of Membership Obligations; and (iii) compliance with such additional admission criteria for Associate status as may be established by the Board pursuant to Section 3.3; and
   b. have been admitted as Associates by affirmative act of the Council, upon recommendation by the Board.

3.2 Affiliates of IFAC shall consist of those organizations that:
   a. the Council has determined do not satisfy the admission criteria of Associate status provided for in Section 3.1, but demonstrate, to the Council's satisfaction, evidence of (i) a commitment to the development of the accountancy profession; and (ii) compliance with such additional criteria for Affiliate status as may be established by the Board pursuant to Section 3.3; and
   b. have been admitted as Affiliates by affirmative act of the Council, upon recommendation by the Board.

3.3 In addition to admission criteria for Associate and Affiliate status set forth in Sections 3.1(a)(i) and (ii) and 3.2(a)(i), respectively, the Board may establish such further admission criteria and procedures for organizations to be admitted as Associates and Affiliates, and to retain their status as Associates or Affiliates in good standing, as the Board deems necessary and appropriate.

3.4 Associates and Affiliates are required to:
   a. make such financial contributions as may be determined in accordance with Section 3.4(b)(i) of the Constitution;
   b. in the case of Associates, support the mission of IFAC and the IASB, and demonstrate evidence of ongoing progress towards compliance with the Statement of Membership Obligations, as issued and modified by the Board;
   c. in the case of Affiliates, support the mission of IFAC and the IASB; and
   d. abide by the relevant provisions of the Constitution and these Bylaws.

3.5 Associates and Affiliates in good standing are entitled to:
   a. attend Council meetings;
   b. unless a Delinquent Associate or Affiliate, participate in the discussions and deliberations at Council meetings, but they do not have the right to vote at Council meetings;
   c. receive access to IFAC publications; and
   d. such other rights, benefits and privileges as the Council or the Board shall establish.

Article 4   Suspension, Expulsion and Resignation

4.1 Any Member Body, Associate or Affiliate may be suspended by the Board or expelled by the Council for the following causes:
   a. failure to maintain ongoing compliance with the relevant admission criteria set forth in Section 2.1 and as otherwise established by the Board;
   b. failure to pay its financial contributions in full prior to the date of the following Council meeting after such contributions have become due; or

c. acts bringing IFAC or the international accountancy profession into disrepute.

4.2 A Member Body, Associate or Affiliate that has been suspended shall not be in good standing but will continue to retain its status as a Member Body, Associate or Affiliate, as the case may be. A suspended Member Body shall not be entitled to any of the Member Entitlements set forth in Section 2.4 of the Constitution, and a suspended Associate or Affiliate shall not be entitled to any of the Associate or Affiliate Entitlements set forth in Section 3.5 of these Bylaws; provided, however, that a suspended Member Body, Associate or Affiliate shall be entitled to receive access to IFAC publications which are otherwise available without charge to the general public.

4.3 A Member Body, Associate or Affiliate may not be expelled until they have been suspended for a period of not less than the remainder of the year in which its suspension was approved by the Board plus that portion of the following year that ends immediately prior to the commencement of the Ordinary meeting of the Council in such following year. At the end of the foregoing suspension period, the Council must consider expulsion of such Member Body, Associate or Affiliate at the Ordinary Meeting of the Council that commences immediately following the conclusion of such period, but the Council shall have the right to extend the period of suspension in lieu of expulsion upon recommendation of the Board pursuant to Section 4.4. If, however, the infraction which resulted in suspension is cured at any time during the period of suspension, the suspension of such Member Body, Associate or Affiliate shall be rescinded effective as of the date of cure.

4.4 If the Member Body, Associate or Affiliate has failed to correct the infraction which resulted in its suspension prior to end of the minimum suspension period provided for in Section 4.3 or such later date as may be established by the Council, the Board may recommend for action by the Council the expulsion of such Member Body, Associate or Affiliate. Upon recommendation of the Board for the expulsion of a Member Body, Associate or Affiliate, the affirmative vote of a majority of Member Bodies eligible to vote and present in person or by proxy at the Council meeting at which the expulsion vote is being taken shall be required to approve the expulsion of such organization as a Member Body, Associate or Affiliate.

4.5 A Member Body, Associate or Affiliate may resign from IFAC by giving written notice at least six months in advance of the effective date of its resignation to the Chief Executive Officer, or his or her delegate, which resignation shall generally be effective as of the end of the fiscal year in which notice is given, unless the Board expressly consents to a different effective date.

4.6 Notwithstanding a Member Body's, Associate's or Affiliate's suspension, expulsion or resignation prior to the end of a fiscal year, and regardless of the effective date thereof, such Member Body, Associate or Affiliate shall remain obligated to pay IFAC (a) the total outstanding balance of its financial contributions and any other amounts owing to IFAC for the full fiscal year in which its suspension, expulsion or resignation becomes effective, (b) in the case of resignation with written notice being given less than six months prior to the end of a fiscal year, the full amount of such Member Body's, Associate's or Affiliate's financial contribution due in respect of the immediately following fiscal year, (c) the total outstanding balance of its financial contributions and any other amounts owing by such Member Body, Associate or Affiliate to IFAC in respect of all prior fiscal years and (d) in the case of suspension, the total of all financial contributions required during the period of suspension.

4.7 Member Bodies, Associates and Affiliates that resign or are expelled shall not be entitled to be reimbursed or refunded any portion of the financial contributions and any other fees, assets and amounts that they previously paid or contributed to IFAC.

4.8 Any Member Body or Associate expelled for failure to satisfy its outstanding financial obligations within the required time period will be automatically reinstated to Member

Body or Associate status, as the case may be, if all outstanding amounts owing by such organization, including the financial contributions due for the period of expulsion, the period of suspension and the periods prior to suspension, are paid in full within two years of the date on which it was expelled.

4.9 If some, but not all, of the outstanding financial obligations for the periods described in Section 4.8 are paid within the two-year period referred to in Section 4.8, reinstatement of such former Member Body or Associate is subject to approval by the Board upon formal application for reinstatement by such Member Body or Associate.

4.10 If the outstanding financial obligations which gave rise to expulsion have not been paid, in whole or in part, within two years after expulsion, the former Member Body or Associate must apply for re-admission as a new applicant and be approved by the Council in accordance with Article 2 of the Constitution.

4.11 Any Member Body or Associate expelled for reasons other than failure to satisfy outstanding financial obligations within the required time period who is seeking re-admission as a Member Body or Associate must apply for re-admission as a new applicant and be approved by the Council in accordance with Article 2 of the Constitution.

4.12 Any expelled Member Body or Associate may not apply for re-admission for a period of three years after the date of expulsion.

Article 5   Council and Council Meetings
5.1 The following Council composition provisions are in addition to the provisions of Section 3.3 of the Constitution:
   a. The Council representative designated by a Member Body must be a member of that Member Body except that the chief executive or equivalent of the Member Body may be the designated representative whether or not that person is a member of that Member Body.
   b. Where there is a dispute over who is the designated representative of a Member Body, the IFAC President shall make the final determination.

5.2 An Ordinary meeting of the Council shall be held annually at a date, time and location as shall be determined by the Board.

5.3 Special meetings of the Council shall be called by the Board and held at a date, time and location determined by the Board within four months of:
   a. a resolution calling for a Special meeting of the Council being adopted by the affirmative vote of at least 75 percent of the entire Board; or
   b. receipt by the Chief Executive Officer, or his or her delegate, of notice delivered by an appropriate mode of communication and supported by at least 20 percent of all Member Bodies who are eligible to vote, requesting a Special meeting of the Council and stating the purposes of the meeting.

5.4 The Chief Executive Officer shall send a notice to each Member Body, Associate and Affiliate containing the date, time and location of the Council meeting and an agenda of the items of business to be considered at the Council meeting.

5.5 The notice referred to in Section 5.4 shall be transmitted by an appropriate mode of communication at least two months in advance of the scheduled date of the Council meeting.

5.6 Notice of a Council meeting need not be given to any Member Body who submits a signed waiver of notice either before or after the Council meeting. The attendance of a Member Body at a Council meeting, whether in person by the presence of such Member Body's designated representative or by proxy, without protesting prior to the conclusion of the Council meeting the lack of prior notice, shall constitute a waiver of notice by such Member Body.

5.7 Except as provided in Section 5.10, no business other than such items of business that are included in the agenda for a given Council meeting shall be acted upon by the Council at such meeting.

5.8 A Member Body in good standing may have an item of business included on the agenda of an Ordinary meeting or may request modification of a proposed item of business to be considered at the Ordinary meeting provided such a request is received by the Chief Executive Officer, or his or her delegate, by an appropriate mode of communication at least one month in advance of the scheduled date of the Ordinary meeting and has the support of five other Member Bodies.

5.9 Upon receipt of a communication requesting the inclusion or modification of an item of business on the agenda for an Ordinary meeting which meets the requirements of Section 5.8, the Chief Executive Officer shall (a) in the case where the agenda for the subject Council meeting has not yet been distributed to the Member Bodies, cause such item of business to be set forth on the agenda included as part of the notice for such Council meeting, and (b) in the case where the agenda for the subject Council meeting has previously been distributed to the Member Bodies, send a revised notice and agenda for such Council meeting to each Member Body at least twenty-one days prior to the scheduled date of the Council meeting.

5.10 Notwithstanding the general restriction against transacting items of business that are not included on the agenda for the Council meeting set forth in Section 5.7, in the case of an Ordinary meeting, the Council, by the affirmative vote of a majority of those Member Bodies who are eligible to vote and present in person or by proxy at such meeting, may waive such restriction; provided, however, that no waiver may be exercised in respect of items of business relating to: (a) the basis of assessment of financial contributions, (b) the amendment of IFAC's mission, or (c) the amendment of the Constitution.

5.11 The requisite percentage of Member Bodies who must be present in person or by proxy at any Council meeting in order to establish a quorum of Member Bodies at such Council meeting shall be set forth in the Constitution.

5.12 Each Member Body shall have one vote on all matters being voted on by the Council, which may be cast at any Council meeting either (a) by such Member Body's designated representative present in person at the Council meeting pursuant to voting procedures established by the Chair and announced to the Council following confirmation of the presence of a quorum, or (b) by proxy in accordance with the requirements and procedures set forth in Sections 5.14 and 5.15.

5.13 In the case of Special meetings of the Council, if demanded by those Member Bodies eligible to vote and present in person or by proxy at a Special meeting of the Council who constitute at least 20 percent of all Member Bodies eligible to vote at such Special meeting, the vote on any resolution proposed at a Special meeting of the Council shall include both (a) the votes cast by Member Bodies present in person or by proxy at such Special meeting, and (b) the votes cast by mail ballot and/or electronic mail ballot received by the Chief Executive Officer, or his or her delegate, on a timely basis from any Member Bodies who was eligible to vote at such Special meeting but who did not vote at such Special meeting. A ballot shall be considered to be received on a timely basis if it is received by the Chief Executive Officer, or his or her delegate, prior to the deadline for the receipt of such ballots established by the President at such Special meeting. The deadline shall not be less than six weeks after the ballots are distributed by an appropriate mode of communication and shall be clearly communicated to the Member Bodies in the correspondence accompanying the ballots. Any votes received by mail ballot or electronic mail ballot after the deadline established by the President will not be counted.

5.14 A Member Body may give a proxy to cast such Member Body's vote at any Council meeting to:

a. the designated representative of any Member Body entitled to vote at that Council meeting, provided that no single designated representative of a Member Body may hold more than five proxies in respect of any single resolution being voted upon; or

b. the Chair of the Council meeting; or

c. the president or chief executive officer, or equivalent officer, of the recognized regional organization of which the Member Body giving its proxy is a member, provided that no single regional organization may hold more than five proxies in respect of any single resolution being voted upon.

5.15 A proxy is only valid if (a) completed in a form specified by IFAC, and (b) the Chief Executive Officer, or his or her delegate, received the proxy by an appropriate mode of communication at least twenty-four hours prior to the scheduled start of the Council meeting at which such proxy is to be effective. Notwithstanding the foregoing twenty-four hour advanced receipt requirement, in extraordinary circumstances where a proxy is received within twenty-four hours prior to the scheduled start of a Council meeting at which it is intended to be effective, the Chair of the Council meeting shall have the discretion to present that late proxy to the Council, which upon the affirmative vote of a majority of the Member Bodies eligible to vote and present in person or by proxy at such Council meeting, may authorize the effectiveness of the late proxy.

5.16 In addition to the designated representative of each Member Body, the following individuals, by reason of holding the position so specified, shall be entitled to attend and, participate in (except to the extent restricted below), but not in such capacities vote at, Council meetings:

a. One technical advisor to each Member Body's designated representative, which technical advisor shall be appointed by such Member Body and shall be either a member or a member of staff of that Member Body, may accompany such designated representative at Council meetings, and such technical advisor shall, at the discretion of his or his accompanying designated representative, be entitled to participate in the discussions and deliberations at the Council meetings, unless the Member Body with whom the technical advisor is affiliated is a Delinquent Member Body.

b. Members of the Board, and their technical advisors, and two observers from each recognized regional organization shall be entitled to attend Council meetings and to participate in the discussions and deliberations at the Council meetings.

c. Two observers from each Associate or Affiliate organization shall be entitled to attend Council meetings and, unless the Associate or Affiliate with whom they are affiliated is a Delinquent Associate or Delinquent Affiliate, to participate in the discussions and deliberations at the Council meetings.

d. The Chair of the PIOB shall be entitled to attend Council meetings to address Council meetings on any matters in regard to the public interest oversight of IFAC and to otherwise participate in the discussions and deliberations at Council Meetings. Where circumstances warrant, as agreed between the Chair of the PIOB and the President, the members of the PIOB may also attend Council meetings.

e. The Chair of the Forum, accompanied by the Chair of the TAC where appropriate, shall be entitled, or may be requested by the President, to attend Council meetings and to report to Council meetings on plans for the following year and on progress and achievement towards plans approved the previous year; such reports shall include the activities of the TAC. The Chairs of the Forum and of the TAC shall each be entitled to participate in the discussions and deliberations at Council meetings.

Article 6   Board and Board Meetings

6.1 In determining the composition of the Board, as specified in Sections 5.1, 5.2 and 5.3 of the Constitution, there may not at any one time be more than two members of the Board from Member Bodies with headquarters in the same country, other than the country of the President, for which, in recognition of the status of the President as independent Chair of the Board, there may be two members in addition to the President serving on the Board at the same time.

6.2 In determining the level of Member Body financial contributions for purposes of allocating Board seats in accordance with Sections 5.2 and 5.3 of the Constitution:

   a. aggregation of the financial contributions of two or more Member Bodies from a single country as at the date of submission of nominations is permitted; and

   b. aggregation of the financial contributions of two or more Member Bodies from different countries is not permitted except with respect to those Member Bodies for which aggregation of their financial contributions was permitted prior to November 2003, in which event such aggregation of such Member Bodies' financial contributions shall be permitted to continue notwithstanding the fact that they are from different countries.

6.3 Each candidate nominated for election to the Board must be a member or chief executive officer or equivalent officer of the Nominating Organization or of one of the Member Bodies nominating as a group of Member Bodies.

6.4 In addition to the powers of the Board specified in Section 5.6 of the Constitution and elsewhere in the Constitution and these Bylaws, and subject to Section 5.8 of the Constitution, the Board shall:

   a. on the advice of the Nominating Committee, appoint and have the authority to fill vacancies in the members and chairs of, and observers on, such IFAC Groups that the Board establishes in accordance with Section 5.6 of the Constitution and these Bylaws;

   b. on the advice of the Nominating Committee after consultation with the Board throughout the nominating process, recommend the appointment of members of the Nominating Committee for approval by the Council and subject only to the PIOB's approval of the appointment of the non-ex-officio members of the committee;

   c. without prejudice to the powers and duties of the Board in relation to its discretion regarding the establishment of the IFAC Groups, establish and maintain an International Accounting Education Standards Board, International Auditing and Assurance Standards Board, International Ethics Standards Board for Accountants and Compliance Advisory Panel;

   d. without prejudice to the powers and duties of the Board in relation to its discretion regarding the establishment of the IFAC Groups, establish and maintain a Professional Accountancy Organization Development Committee, the Professional Accountants in Business Committee and the Small and Medium Practices Committee;

   e. determine terms of reference for each IFAC Group that it establishes in accordance with Section 5.6 of the Constitution and these Bylaws. The terms of reference of each of the Public Interest Activity Committees shall give those IFAC Groups the authority to issue standards and other appropriate pronouncements and shall establish Consultative Advisory Groups;

   f. determine the terms of references for the Consultative Advisory Groups of each of the Public Interest Activity Committees in consultation with the appropriate Public Interest Activity Committees;

   g. determine, as necessary, the timing, frequency and location of any World Congresses of Accountants;

h. determine the criteria for recognition of regional organizations;

i. determine annually, consistent with the broad parameters approved by the Council at its Ordinary meeting, the budget for the following year;

j. determine annually, consistent with the basis of assessment of Member Body, Associate and Affiliate financial contributions approved by Council at its Ordinary meeting, the allocation of financial contributions among such contributing organizations and the purposes and uses of funds;

k. distribute annually a report on IFAC's activities, including the audited financial statements, to the Member Bodies, Associates and Affiliates;

l. determine, as appropriate, amendments to the Bylaws (i) to be recommended for approval by the Council in accordance with Section 12.2 of the Constitution, and (ii) to have immediate effect upon approval by the Board, but subject to ratification by the Council at its next meeting in accordance with Section 12.3 of the Constitution;

m. determine, as appropriate, amendments, additions or repeals to the Statements of Membership Obligations;

n. have the power to suspend any Member Body, Associate or Affiliate in accordance with Section 4.1;

o. periodically evaluate whether recognized regional organizations have met their obligations to IFAC. If the Board determines that a recognized regional organization has consistently failed to meet its obligations, it may recommend to the Council that recognition of such regional organization be withdrawn;

p. organize, and direct the Secretary of the Board to give notice of, Council meetings;

q. approve, upon the recommendation of the TAC and with the approval of the Forum;

    i. amendments to the Constitution of the Forum;

    ii. changes to the basis for the allocation of voting rights at annual and special meetings of the Forum; and

    iii. changes to the basis for allocation of representatives on the TAC; and

r. upon the recommendation of the Nominating Committee and pursuant to the provisions of the Forum's Constitution, establish a panel, which shall not be an IFAC Group or a Board Group nor subject to the provisions of the Constitution governing IFAC Groups or Board Groups, which shall function for the purpose of considering and deciding appeals relating to suspension or expulsion from membership of the Forum.

6.5 In addition to the powers of the Board specified in Section 5.6 of the Constitution and elsewhere in these Bylaws, and subject to Section 5.8 of the Constitution, the Board shall, in relation to the Council:

a. recommend the professional accountancy organizations or other organizations for approval by the Council for admission to IFAC as Member Bodies, Associates and Affiliates;

b. on the advice of the Nominating Committee, which shall consult with the Board during the nominating process, recommend from a slate of candidates, the filling of any vacancies on the Nominating Committee for approval by the Council and subject only to the PIOB's approval of the appointment of the non-ex-officio members of the committee. The Board shall, in the execution of said duties, have regard to the principle that the primary criterion shall be on the basis of the best persons for the available positions, recognizing also the importance of geographic representation in the composition of the Nominating Committee. In applying these criteria the Board will also consider such factors as leadership and other personal skills and attributes, industry balance, size of employer and gender balance;

   c. recommend for approval by the Council the recognition of regional organizations;

   d. recommend for approval by the Council policies and strategic initiatives, including the proposed strategic plan and the broad parameters of the budget for the ensuing year, including the level of financial contributions for Member Bodies, Associates and Affiliates;

   e. recommend for approval by the Council amendments to the Constitution and the Bylaws;

   f. recommend for approval by the Council the basis of the assessment of financial contributions to be paid by Member Bodies, Associates and Affiliates;

   g. upon the recommendation of the Audit Committee, endorse, for approval by the Council, the appointment of the auditor;

   h. present to the Ordinary meeting of the Council a report on past and future activities of the Board; and

   i. recommend for approval by the Council the expulsion of a suspended Member Body, Associate or Affiliate in accordance with Article 4.

6.6 Board members shall be elected by the Council for terms provided for in Sections 6.14 and 6.15.

6.7 Individuals elected as members of the Board shall assume office at the conclusion of the meeting of the Council at which they are elected. The election of Board members is to be held annually, generally at the Ordinary meeting of the Council.

6.8 For purposes of such election, Member Bodies shall be provided with a list of each of the nominees for election to the Board, including both candidates nominated by the Nominating Committee and candidates nominated by Member Bodies in accordance with Section 6.9, with full curricula vitae for each nominee attached.

6.9 All Member Bodies or groups of Member Bodies in good standing that wish to nominate a candidate or candidates for election to the Board must submit their nomination or nominations to the Secretary of the Nominating Committee in accordance with the call for nominations' instructions. These instructions shall specify, amongst other matters, the deadline for receipt of nominations, information regarding the identified vacancies, criteria for desired candidates, and the information regarding a candidate that is required to be provided.

6.10 Notwithstanding the stipulated timeframe in the call for nominations' instructions, in the exceptional event that the Nominating Committee determines that circumstances have arisen with respect to the composition of the Board that may not be in the best interests of IFAC, after receipt of notice of such determination from the Nominating Committee, the Board:

   a. shall have the authority and power to propose to the Nominating Committee additional candidates for election to the Board;

   b. shall not be subject to the timeframe stipulated in the call for nominations' instructions; and

   c. shall be entitled to apply the provisions of the Board set forth in Section 5.3 of the Constitution.

6.11 If the number of candidates standing for election to the Board is equivalent to the number of vacancies on the Board, the election shall be conducted by a vote taken by a raising of hands of all Member Bodies eligible to vote and present in person or by proxy at the Council meeting at which such election is occurring. The affirmative vote of a majority of all such Member Bodies in favor of a particular candidate shall be required to elect such candidate as a member of the Board.

6.12 In the event that the number of candidates standing for election to the Board exceeds the number of vacancies on the Board, the election shall be conducted by a written ballot among all Member Bodies eligible to vote and present in person or by proxy at the Council meeting at which such election is occurring. The candidate or candidates receiving the highest number of affirmative votes cast by such Member Bodies relative to the number of vacancies shall be deemed elected as members of the Board by the Council. In the event of a tie for the final vacant seat on the Board, there shall be a further ballot of all Member Bodies eligible to vote and present in person or by proxy at such Council meeting to determine which of the candidates involved in the tie shall be elected as a member of the Board. In any situation where a tie between candidates cannot be decided by a further ballot, the Chair of the meeting shall resolve the matter by exercising their casting vote.

6.13 A Board member may be removed by the Council, upon recommendation of the Nominating Committee and as endorsed by the Board, during the Board member's term of office, for non-performance or other good cause.

6.14 Each individual elected to the Board shall be appointed for a term of up to three years. The annual elections to the Board shall be held in such a way that not less than five and not more than nine of the members of the Board shall rotate each year in order to achieve approximately one third of the Board members rotating each year.

6.15 Continuous service on the Board by the same person shall be limited to a total of six years unless such person is elected as the Deputy President or President in which event their term as a Board member shall be extended beyond six years if necessary for so long as they continue to hold the position as Deputy President or President. Following the expiry of six consecutive years of service as a member of the Board, such individual shall be eligible to serve as a member of the Board for a further period of service after a lapse of two years since they completed the previous term of service on the Board.

6.16 A Board member's term of office as a Board member shall be terminated in the event of:
   a. such Board member's incapacity, resignation, removal or death; or
   b. the nominating Member Body or Member Bodies within a group of nominating Member Bodies withdrawing their mandate for such Board member for good cause; or
   c. such Board member's voluntary departure or removal from membership of the nominating Member Body or Member Body within a group of nominating Member Bodies during said term of office.

6.17 In case of a vacancy occurring by reason of the events specified in Section 6.16, the Nominating Committee has the authority to appoint a temporary member to fill such vacancy until the next Council meeting, at which time the Council shall elect an individual to fill the vacancy through the normal election process in accordance with Section 5.5 of the Constitution. In seeking the best person for the position in relation to available positions, the Nominating Committee shall consider the same factors set forth in Section 5.4 of the Constitution.

6.18 The Member Body or group of Member Bodies of the Board member whose term as a Board member has terminated in accordance with Section 6.16 may, by giving notice to the Secretary of the Nominating Committee by an appropriate mode of communication, recommend to the Nominating Committee a substitute of their choice to fill the vacancy during the interim period between the date on which the departed Board member ceased to be a Board member and the date of the next Council meeting at which a successor Board member is elected to fill the vacancy.

6.19 Ordinary meetings of the Board shall be held at such dates, times and locations as the Board shall decide, provided that the Board shall hold at least two Ordinary meetings each calendar year.

6.20 Special meetings of the Board shall be called when the Secretary of the Board receives a notice delivered by an appropriate mode of communication and supported by at least four members of the Board, requesting that a Special meeting of the Board be convened and setting forth the purpose of the meeting. The date, time and location of the Special meeting shall be determined by the President provided that the Special meeting shall be held within two months of the date on which the Secretary of the Board received the notice.

6.21 The Secretary of the Board shall send a notice to each Board member containing the date, time and location of a Board meeting in accordance with operating procedures agreed to by the Board.

6.22 Notice of a Board meeting need not be given to any Board member who submits a signed waiver of notice either before or after the Board meeting. The attendance of a Board member without protesting prior to the conclusion of the Board meeting the lack of prior notice shall constitute a waiver of notice by such Board member.

6.23 A quorum of the Board shall consist of a majority of the members of the Board, excluding vacancies.

6.24 The President shall be the Chair of and shall preside over all meetings of the Board. In the absence of the President at any Board meeting, the Deputy President shall act as the Chair of such Board meeting. In the absence of both the President and the Deputy President at any Board meeting, the members of the Board present at such meeting shall elect a Chair from among those members present.

6.25 Each member of the Board, other than the Chair of the meeting, shall have one vote. The Chair of the meeting shall have only a casting vote.

6.26 Except for decisions of the Board requiring a supermajority vote thereof in accordance with Section 5.3(a) (relating to a 75 percent vote of the entire Board required to call a Special meeting of the Council) and Section 12.3 of the Constitution (relating to the two-thirds vote of the Board required for the Board to amend the Bylaws in exceptional and unusual circumstances), at any Ordinary or Special meeting of the Board, the affirmative vote of a majority of the members of the Board present at the meeting, excluding the Chair, shall be required to constitute the action of the Board.

6.27 The Chair of the PIOB shall be entitled to address Board meetings on any matters in regard to the public interest oversight of IFAC, but shall not be entitled to vote. Where circumstances warrant, as agreed between the Chair of the PIOB and the President, the members of the PIOB may attend Board meetings.

6.28 The Chair of the Forum and the Chair of the TAC where appropriate, shall be entitled to attend Board meetings, but shall not be entitled to vote.

6.29 Each Board member may be accompanied at Board meetings by not more than one technical advisor who shall be either a member or a staff member of, and who shall be appointed by, the Member Body to which the Board member belongs or, where there is more than one Member Body nominating as a group of Member Bodies, by agreement among them. Such technical advisor shall, at the discretion of their accompanying Board member, be entitled to participate in the discussions and deliberations at the Board meetings, but shall not be entitled to vote.

6.30 The technical advisor shall, in the absence from a Board meeting of the Board member that they advise, be entitled to attend and participate in the discussions and deliberations at that Board meeting, but shall not be entitled to vote directly or by proxy.

6.31 The chairs of IFAC Groups shall be required to attend at least one Board meeting each year as observers and shall be entitled to participate in the discussions and deliberations at the meeting, but shall not be entitled to vote. The chairs of IFAC Groups shall be entitled to attend other meetings of the Board.

6.32 The representatives of regional organizations shall be entitled to attend Board meetings as observers and participate in the discussions and deliberations at the meeting, but shall not be entitled to vote.

6.33 In the event of any Board member being unable to attend a Board meeting, they shall have the right to grant a proxy to any other Board member to vote on their behalf, subject to the Board member wishing to grant such a proxy providing a notice by an appropriate mode of communication to the Secretary of the Board.

Article 7   Nominating Committee

7.1 The Nominating Committee shall be composed of the President and the Deputy President ex officio, and no less than four additional members appointed by the Council on the recommendation of the Board and subject only to the PIOB's approval of the non-ex-officio members of the committee. The non-ex-officio members of the Nominating Committee shall each be members of a Member Body, and not more than two of the non-ex-officio members may be members of the Board.

7.2 The non-ex-officio members of the Nominating Committee shall be appointed for a term of up to two years. Continuous service by a non-ex-officio member shall be limited to a total of four years. The terms of the non-ex-officio members shall be established so that the term of at least one member shall expire each year.

7.3 The duties of the Nominating Committee shall be:
   a. to recommend to the Council:
      i. the candidates to be considered for election to the Board in accordance with Sections 5.1, 5.2, and 5.3 of the Constitution and Sections 6.1 and 6.3 of these Bylaws, except that in the event circumstances limit the Nominating Committee's discretion with regard to making recommendations to the Council regarding the appointment of a Board member in accordance with the foregoing provisions of the Constitution and Bylaws, the Nominating Committee shall have the discretion to recommend to Council a list of nominees consistent with the intent of said Sections;
      ii. upon expiration of the President's term of office, whether the Deputy President shall become the President;
      iii. the candidate to be elected to the office of Deputy President in accordance with Section 3.4(e) or 8.2 of the Constitution;
      iv. the removal of a Board member during the Board member's term of office for non-performance or other good cause; and
   b. to recommend to the Board:
      i. the composition of IFAC Groups to be established in accordance with Section 7.3 of the Constitution;
      ii. the appointment of chairs and deputy chairs of the IFAC Groups;
      iii. candidates for appointment to the Nominating Committee for recommendation by the Board for approval by the Council, and subject only to the PIOB's approval of the non-ex-officio members of the committee, in accordance with the consultation process set forth in Section 6.5(b);
      iv. the nominees for appointment of one member of the PIOB;
      v. the Board members to serve on Board Groups in accordance with Section 10.14;
      vi. the appointment of observers on Public Interest Activity Committees as specified in Section 9.1;
      vii. the appointment of non-ex-officio members of the IFAC Regulatory Liaison Group;
      viii. the establishment and composition of a panel, pursuant to the provisions of the Forum's Constitution, as specified in Section 6.4(r), to consider and decide appeals relating to suspension or exclusion from membership of the Forum; and

ix. the removal of a member from an IFAC Group or Board Group for non-perform-ance or other good cause.

7.4 The Council shall determine, upon the recommendation of the Board, the terms of reference of the Nominating Committee. The terms of reference of the Nominating Committee shall be subject to the approval of the PIOB.

7.5 The Nominating Committee shall be guided by the need for transparency in its decision-making process balanced with issues of privacy and propriety in order to maintain a respectful, fair and judicious environment.

7.6 The Nominating Committee shall, in executing its duties as prescribed in the Constitution and the Bylaws with regard to the nomination of candidates for appointment or election to any position, have regard to the principle that the primary criterion for selection of nominees shall be selecting the best persons for the available positions, taking into consideration factors such as leadership ability, experience and other personal skills and attributes. Notwithstanding the foregoing, the Nominating Committee shall also take into consideration geographic balance, industry balance, size of employer and gender balance.

7.7 A representative of the PIOB shall be entitled to attend meetings or parts of meetings of the Nominating Committee devoted to the selection of nominees for membership of the Public Interest Activity Committees and of non-ex-officio members of the Nominating Committee and shall be entitled to participate in the discussions and deliberations of the meeting but shall not be entitled to vote.

7.8 The Board shall develop for the approval of the PIOB operational procedures to be followed by the Nominating Committee with regard to the selection of nominees for membership of the Public Interest Activity Committees and of the non-ex-officio members of the Nominating Committee.

7.9 The Nominating Committee shall have the power to request and receive such information from a Member Body or from the Forum as it considers appropriate to enable it to carry out the duties prescribed for it in the Constitution and the Bylaws.

7.10 The Nominating Committee also may recommend to the Board, subject to Section 5.8(c) of the Constitution, the removal of the chair of an IFAC Group or Board Group, of a member of an IFAC Group or Board Group, or of the Deputy President or President for non-performance or other good cause.

7.11 The Nominating Committee shall be required to report to (a) the Board at least once annually and as the Board may otherwise request, and (b) the Council annually regarding the process followed during the nominations cycle and on any significant issues that arose as part of that process.

Article 8   Officers

8.1 The President and Deputy President shall be elected to such officer positions by the Council, and for such terms of office, in accordance with the procedures set forth in Article 8 of the Constitution.

8.2 The Chief Executive Officer shall be appointed by the Board. The Chief Executive Officer shall be the Secretary to the Council, Board and Nominating Committee.

8.3 The President and Deputy President may be removed from office for non-performance or other good cause by the Council upon recommendation of the Nominating Committee and as endorsed by the Board.

8.4 Notwithstanding Section 8.3, which generally reserves authority to remove the President and Deputy President from office to the Council, if the Board, in consultation with the Nominating Committee, determines that it is necessary and in the best interests of IFAC for the removal of the President or Deputy President to occur immediately, and that it is not practicable to wait until the next Council meeting, the Board shall have the authority to remove the President or Deputy President from office, subject to ratification by the Council at the next Council meeting.

8.5   a. In the event of a vacancy in the office of President by reason of the incapacity, resignation, removal or death of the President, or of the President ceasing to be a member of a Member Body, the Deputy President shall assume the duties of President as Acting President, having full power, authority and responsibility of the office of President on an acting basis until the next Board meeting. At the first Board meeting following the vacancy in the office of President, the Board shall either: (i)(A) ratify the Deputy President's assumption of the office of President on an acting basis and (B) appoint an individual (waiving any applicable waiting periods), upon the recommendation of the Nominating Committee, to serve as Acting Deputy President having full power, authority and responsibility of the office of Deputy President on an acting basis, or (ii) upon recommendation of the Nominating Committee, appoint another individual (waiving any applicable waiting periods) to serve as Acting President in lieu of the Deputy President, in which event the then-Acting President shall resume his or her duties as Deputy President.

  b. If the Deputy President is ratified by the Board to serve as Acting President in accordance with clause (i)(A) of paragraph (a) of this Section 8.5, such individual shall serve as Acting President until the next Ordinary meeting of the Council following the vacancy in the Presidency, at which time, upon the approval of the Council, the Acting President shall serve as President for a full two-year term commencing as of the date of such Ordinary meeting of the Council as if they succeeded to the Presidency in the ordinary course as provided in Section 8.2 of the Constitution, and the Acting Deputy President appointed by the Board pursuant to clause (i)(B) of paragraph (a) of this Section 8.5, upon the approval of Council, shall become the Deputy President and serve for a two-year term commencing as of the date of such Ordinary meeting of the Council as if they were elected to be Deputy President in the ordinary course as provided in Section 8.2 of the Constitution.

  c. If, however, an individual other than the Deputy President is selected by the Board to serve as Acting President in accordance with clause (ii) of paragraph (a) of this Section 8.5, such individual shall serve as Acting President until the next Ordinary meeting of the Council following the vacancy in the Presidency at which point his or her term as Acting President shall expire, and the Deputy President shall, in the ordinary course and subject to the Council's approval in accordance with Section 8.2 of the Constitution, succeed to the office of President.

8.6 In the event of a vacancy in the office of Deputy President by reason of the incapacity, resignation, removal or death of the Deputy President, or the Deputy President ceasing to be a member of a Member Body, the vacancy in the office of Deputy President shall be filled by an individual selected by the Board (waiving any applicable waiting periods), based on the recommendation of the Nominating Committee, at the next Board meeting following the creation of the vacancy in the office of Deputy President, to serve as Acting Deputy President, having full power, authority and responsibility of the office of Deputy President on an acting basis until the next Ordinary meeting of the Council. At such Ordinary meeting of the Council, the Council shall either:

  a. ratify the Board's appointment of the Acting Deputy President, in which event the Acting Deputy President shall (i) serve as Deputy President on a non-acting basis for the remaining unexpired term, if any, of the Deputy President whose departure created the vacancy or, (ii) if the term of office of the Deputy President whose departure created the vacancy is scheduled to expire at such Ordinary meeting of the Council, succeed to the office of President, upon approval of the Council, as if the Acting Deputy President had served as Deputy President on a non-acting basis in the ordinary course as provided in Section 8.2 of the Constitution; or

b. appoint another individual (waiving any applicable waiting periods) to serve as Deputy President on a non-acting basis for either (i) the remaining unexpired term, if any, of the Deputy President whose departure created the vacancy or, (ii) if the term of office of the Deputy President whose departure created the vacancy is scheduled to expire at such Ordinary meeting of the Council, for a full two-year term.

8.7 In the event of a vacancy of both the President and the Deputy President at the same time for any reason, which vacancies are not otherwise filled in the ordinary course pursuant to Sections 8.5 and 8.6, the Secretary of the Board shall call a Special meeting of the Board at which the Board shall appoint two individuals (waiving any applicable waiting periods), one to serve as Acting President and the other to serve as Acting Deputy President, having full power, authority and responsibility of such offices, until the next Ordinary meeting of the Council, at which an election shall be held to fill the vacancies of both the Deputy President and the President for new full two-year terms.

8.8 Except in circumstances where the office of President has been vacated pursuant to Section 8.3, the immediate past President shall, for the two-year period following the completion of his or her term as President:

a. be entitled to attend all Board meetings and participate in the discussions and deliberations, but shall not be entitled to vote, and

b. have such specific responsibilities as may be determined by the President or by the Board.

Article 9   Public Interest Activity Committees

9.1 In respect of the provisions of the Constitution and these Bylaws, the PIOB shall have oversight over the International Accounting Education Standards Board, the International Auditing and Assurance Standards Board, the International Ethics Standards Board for Accountants and the Compliance Advisory Panel, otherwise referred to as the Public Interest Activity Committees of IFAC and such other Public Interest Activity Committees as may be determined from time to time.

Article 10   IFAC Groups and Board Groups

10.1 A Member Body that wishes to nominate a candidate for appointment to serve on an IFAC Group, other than the TAC, established by the Board in accordance with Section 5.6 of the Constitution shall state the name of the proposed candidate and provide such information as the Nominating Committee may request.

10.2 A person appointed by the Board to serve on an IFAC Group established in accordance with Section 5.6 of the Constitution shall be appointed for a term of up to three years. These terms will be established in such a way that each year they expire for approximately one-third of the members of such an IFAC Group.

10.3 A person may not serve on an IFAC Group for more than six consecutive years; provided, however, that a person may continue to serve on such IFAC Group for up to three additional consecutive years (an Extended Term), for an aggregate term of up to nine consecutive years, if they have been appointed to serve as the Chair of such IFAC Group for an Extended Term. During an Extended Term, the term of such person as a member of such IFAC Group shall be coterminous with their term as Chair.

10.4 Notwithstanding the above, the Extended Term for the Chairs of the Public Interest Activity Committees and the International Public Sector Accounting Standards Board may, in exceptional circumstances, be a maximum of six years, rather than three years. The Nominating Committee shall determine the circumstances in which this exception may be applied.

10.5 Following the expiry of six consecutive years of service as a member of a particular IFAC Group, such individual shall be eligible to serve as a member of that same IFAC Group for a further period of service after a lapse of two years since they completed the previous term of service on that IFAC Group.

10.6 Each member of an IFAC Group, established by the Board in accordance with Section 5.6 of the Constitution, with the exception of members nominated by the Forum or members nominated as public members, may be accompanied at meetings of such IFAC Group by not more than one technical advisor who shall be either a member or a member of staff of a Member Body and who shall be appointed by the Member Body to which such IFAC Group member belongs or, where there is more than one Member Body nominating as a group of Member Bodies, by agreement among them. Such technical advisor shall, at the discretion of their accompanying IFAC Group member, be entitled to participate in the discussions and deliberations at the IFAC Group meetings, but shall not be entitled to vote.

10.7 The technical advisor shall, in the absence from an IFAC Group meeting of the IFAC Group member that they advise, be entitled to attend and participate in the discussions and deliberations at that IFAC Group meeting, but shall not be entitled vote directly or by proxy.

10.8 The Forum shall be entitled to nominate representatives to serve on the TAC and shall, for that purpose, state the name of the candidate and provide such information as the Nominating Committee may request. The provisions of Sections 10.1 and 10.6 shall not apply to the TAC, which shall be governed by the provisions of the Constitution of the Forum.

10.9 The Forum shall be entitled to propose five representatives to serve on each of the following IFAC Groups: the International Accounting Education Standards Board, the International Auditing and Assurance Standards Board and the International Ethics Standards Board for Accountants. Each of these representatives may be accompanied at meetings of that group by not more than one technical advisor and shall be entitled to select and replace their technical advisor.

10.10 Public members shall be appointed to the International Accounting Education Standards Board, the International Auditing and Assurance Standards Board, the International Ethics Standards Board for Accountants and the International Public Sector Accounting Standards Board in accordance with Sections 10.1 and 10.2 and with the respective terms of reference. Candidates for appointment as public members may be nominated by any individual or organization for consideration by the Nominating Committee. Public members may be accompanied at meetings of that board by not more than one technical advisor and shall be entitled to select and replace their technical advisor.

10.11 An IFAC Group member's term of office as an IFAC Group member shall be terminated in the event of:
   a. such IFAC Group member's incapacity, resignation, removal or death;
   b. the Nominating Organization, which nominated such IFAC Group member for membership of the IFAC Group, withdrawing their mandate for such IFAC Group member for good cause; or
   c. such IFAC member's voluntary departure, or removal from membership of the Nominating Organization during said term of office.

10.12 In case of a vacancy of any member of an IFAC Group occurring by reason of the events specified in Section 10.11, the Nominating Committee has the authority to appoint a temporary member to fill such vacancy for the remainder of the year.

10.13 The Nominating Organization of the IFAC Group member who has vacated their position may, by giving notice by an appropriate mode of communication to the Secretary of the Nominating Committee, recommend to the Nominating Committee a substitute of their choice to fill the vacancy during the interim period between the date at which the membership was terminated and the end of the year.

10.14 The Board may establish such committees, advisory boards, task forces and other groups as the Board deems advisable upon the recommendation of the President (collectively referred to as "Board Groups"). The Board shall establish the terms of reference of each Board Group as well as the length of the term that members of Board Groups shall serve. The composition of Board Groups shall be determined by the Board upon recommendation of the Nominating Committee.

10.15 The Board shall establish a committee on audit as a Board Group, which shall be referred to as the Audit Committee. The Audit Committee's primary objectives shall be to monitor the integrity of the organization's financial reporting process and system of internal control regarding finance, accounting and legal compliance; monitor the independence and performance of the external auditor; provide an avenue of communication among the external auditor, management and the Board; and recommend the appointment of the external auditor to the Council after endorsement of such recommendation by the Board.

10.16 The Board shall establish an advisory committee as a Board Group, which shall be referred to as the Planning and Finance Committee. The Planning and Finance Committee's primary objectives shall be to provide detailed consideration of the development, implementation and monitoring of IFAC's strategies and operations.

10.17 The Board shall establish a regulatory liaison group to work with the Monitoring Group and address issues relating to the accountancy profession, as a Board Group.

Article 11   Declarations

11.1 All members and technical advisors of the Board and of all IFAC Groups and all non-Board members of the Nominating Committee shall sign and deliver an annual declaration stating that they will act in the public interest and with integrity in discharging the responsibilities of their roles within IFAC. The declaration shall be delivered to the Secretary of the Nominating Committee prior to the first meeting of the Board or IFAC Group in the calendar year.

11.2 The Nominating Organization of a member of the Board or of an IFAC Group shall sign and deliver a declaration indicating that it will not exert undue influence, whether financial or otherwise, which might impair the member's ability to serve or act as a member of the Board or IFAC Group, with independence and integrity, and in the public interest. The Nominating Organization's declaration shall be delivered to the Secretary of the Nominating Committee prior to the first meeting of the Board or the IFAC Group in the calendar year in which the member's term with the Board or IFAC Group commences.

11.3 The President, Deputy President, and the chairs of the International Public Sector Accounting Standards Board and the Public Interest Activity Committees, other than the International Auditing and Assurance Standards Board, shall be required to have their employing organizations sign and deliver to the Secretary of the Nominating Committee a statement prior to the meeting of the Board or respective IFAC Group when the President, Deputy President, or chair first take office, and annually, by the first meeting of the Board or respective IFAC Group in which the employing organizations declare that they will support the President, Deputy President, or chair (as applicable), by ensuring their ability to speak for the global accountancy profession and in the public interest rather than as a member of the employing organizations. The employing organizations will also assure that they will not exert undue influence whether financial or otherwise, that might impair the ability of the President, Deputy President or chair (as applicable) to act independently, with integrity and in the public interest.

Article 12   Financial and Administrative Matters

12.1 The IFAC financial statements shall be prepared in accordance with International Public Sector Accounting Standards and an independent audit shall be conducted in accordance with International Standards on Auditing.

12.2 The financial year of IFAC shall end on 31 December.

12.3 The administrative office of IFAC shall be in such location as may be determined by the Board.

12.4 IFAC is bound by the signature of any two of the three Officers, as identified in Section 8.1 of the Constitution, or by the signatures of such person or persons as may be duly authorized by the Board.

Article 13   Policies and Procedures

13.1 The Board shall have the authority to develop a Policies and Procedures Manual in support of the matters identified in the Constitution and these Bylaws.

13.2 The Policies and Procedures Manual shall include, but not be restricted to:
 a. Policies of the Board;
 b. Significant operational policies of IFAC; and
 c. Terms of reference for all IFAC Groups.

13.3 Individual policies and procedures may be repealed or amended and new policies and procedures may be enacted by the Board. Such policies and procedures shall have effect from the date that they are repealed, amended or enacted by the Board unless otherwise specified.

APPENDIX A TO THE BYLAWS   IFAC GROUPS

Public Interest Activity Committees (PIACs)
International Accounting Education Standards Board
International Auditing and Assurance Standards Board
International Ethics Standards Board for Accountants
Compliance Advisory Panel

Other IFAC Groups
International Public Sector Accounting Standards Board
Professional Accountancy Organization Development Committee (formerly Developing Nations Committee)
Professional Accountants in Business Committee
Small and Medium Practices Committee
Transnational Auditors Committee

BOARD GROUPS

Audit Committee
Planning and Finance Committee
IFAC Regulatory Liaison Group

IV-9a

Financial Action Task Force—Revised Mandate for 2008–2012

Date 12 April 2008
Link <http://www.oecd.org/dataoecd/3/32/40433653.pdf>

I. INTRODUCTION AND BACKGROUND

1. Since its creation in 1989, the Financial Action Task Force (FATF) has worked to ensure that its 40 + 9 Recommendations* are recognized globally as the international standards for anti-money laundering and combating the financing of terrorism (AML/CFT). The work of the FATF, covering more than 170 jurisdictions, has had a significant impact on the global detection and prevention of money laundering and terrorist financing, and is critical to the implementation of more robust AML/CFT regimes around the world.

2. The FATF, since its establishment, has focused its work on three main activities: standard setting, ensuring effective compliance with the standards and identifying money laundering and terrorist financing threats. These activities will remain at the core of the FATF's work for the remainder of this mandate. Going forward, the FATF will build on this work and respond to new and emerging threats, such as proliferation financing and vulnerabilities in new technologies which could destabilise the international financial system.

3. A mid-term review was conducted in 2007 to ensure that the FATF is equipped to respond flexibly to new challenges. The FATF mandate, revised through this mid-term review process will expire in December 2012.

II. FATF STANDARDS

4. The core work of the FATF since its creation has been to combat money laundering (40 Recommendations), and since 2001, terrorist financing (9 Recommendations). The FATF has taken concerted action to combat these threats. The FATF continues to revise and clarify these standards, and will continue to do so when necessary. This approach has so far provided the right balance between giving the required stability to the FATF standards, whilst allowing for the necessary flexibility to respond to the changing nature of the threats faced. Maintaining this balance between stability and flexibility allows for more predictability, and consistent implementation globally.

III. PROMOTING GLOBAL IMPLEMENTATION OF THE STANDARDS

5. Full and effective roll-out of the 40 + 9 Recommendations in all countries is one of the fundamental goals of the FATF. Members are assessed through the mutual evaluation process which is an essential and long standing core activity of the FATF. This peer review process has now been extended through the FATF-Style Regional Body (FSRB) network to more than 170 countries, and is the critical mechanism for promoting timely and effective implementation of

---

* Note by the Editors: The 40 + 4 Recommendations are available on the homepage of the Financial Action Task Force, see <http://www.fatf-gafi.org>.

FATF Recommendations and for contributing to the creation of a level playing field throughout the membership and beyond. Countries that are not FSRB members will be encouraged to join the relevant regional body. The FATF will complete the third round of mutual evaluations of its membership (using the common assessment methodology) to determine the degree to which all members have implemented the 40 + 9 Recommendations. Also, the FATF will continue to undertake appropriate follow-up action from mutual evaluations to ensure that members correct, as quickly as possible, any deficiencies that are identified through the mutual evaluation process.

6. All countries, including non-members, should implement the FATF Recommendations effectively, to ensure a more effective global system for combating AML/CFT risks. However, many countries, in particular low-capacity countries, face challenges in the implementation of FATF standards. In order to minimise both their own vulnerabilities and the associated risks for the international financial system, the FATF, in close collaboration with the FSRBs and other international partners, will develop strategies to facilitate the implementation of the FATF Recommendations by countries facing capacity constraints. As a first step the FATF and FSRBs will continue their work to support the effective implementation of the FATF standards in these countries.

IV. IDENTIFYING AND RESPONDING TO NEW THREATS

(a) High-risk jurisdictions

7. A key element of the FATF's work will continue to be its action to identify and address risks posed by jurisdictions with significant deficiencies in their AML/CFT regimes in order to protect the international financial system from criminal threats. Action such as the Non-Cooperative Countries and Territories exercise led to significant improvements in the AML/CFT regimes of more than 20 countries.

8. In 2006, the FATF adopted a new surveillance process—the International Co-operation Review Group—to identify, examine and engage with vulnerable jurisdictions that are failing to implement effective AML/CFT systems. The FATF will continue to use this process to reach out to those countries and, where appropriate, will take firm action when a country chooses not to engage with the appropriate FSRB or the FATF or to reform its systems.

(b) Systemic money laundering and terrorist financing threats

9. The FATF is uniquely placed to analyse and draw international attention to emerging money laundering and terrorist financing vulnerabilities, and has significantly enhanced its process for the identification of money laundering and terrorist financing threats (the typologies process). The generation and dissemination of in-depth typologies studies is central to the work of the FATF and provides a solid foundation for ongoing policy development at the national and international levels. The FATF will continue to produce such studies which present detailed information about the methods, trends and techniques of money laundering and terrorist financing, and provide practical input to policy makers and the standard-setting process. In pursuing this work, the FATF will continue its expanded co-operation with the FSRBs and other international bodies, and will also harness the experience and expertise which the private sector can bring to this process.

10. Looking forward, the FATF will intensify its surveillance of systemic criminal and terrorist financing risks to enhance its ability to identify, prioritise and act on these threats. In this context, and drawing on contributions from the FATF membership, the private sector and the FSRBs, it will support the development of national threat assessments through best practice guidance and establish stronger and more regular mechanisms for sharing information on risks and vulnerabilities. The results of the enhanced strategic surveillance function will be disseminated publicly via the publication of a regular global threat assessment.

11. The FATF will also examine the available data to measure the impact of AML/CFT regimes on underlying criminal and terrorist activity, encouraging research into the effectiveness of its regime. It will examine the feasibility of implementing cost-benefit analysis across the field of AML/CFT policy.

(c) Emerging threats

12. Globalisation has created potential new risks as criminals and terrorists seek to penetrate the global financial system. The FATF will remain at the centre of international efforts to protect the integrity of the financial system and will respond to the significant new threats emerging which are related to, but may fall outside its core activities. The FATF will only consider limited expansions of its field of action where it has a particular additional contribution to make.

13. Proliferation financing is a current example of an area where the FATF can add value to the wider efforts of the international community and, consistent with the needs identified by the UN Security Council Resolutions, the FATF will continue to work on this issue. In doing so, the FATF will ensure that it does not duplicate existing efforts elsewhere.

V. RELATIONS WITH STAKEHOLDERS AND PARTNERS

(a) Outreach to the private sector and the public

14. The private sector is at the front line of the international battle against money laundering, terrorist financing and other illicit financing threats. The FATF has significantly increased its engagement with the private sector, through events with industry groups and the production of joint analysis on issues of common concern, soliciting private sector input to the typologies process, and through the establishment of a new private sector consultative forum. Looking forward, it will deepen its engagement with the private sector, through holding regular dialogues between the FATF and the private sector in support of our common objective of a more effective implementation of FATF standards.

15. More generally, in accordance with better regulation practice, the FATF will maintain high levels of transparency in its work, through direct communication, outreach and awareness-raising across all stakeholders, and making use of all available channels of communication.

(b) Relations with other international organisations

16. The FATF relies on and values its close partnerships with other international organisations, including the United Nations, the International Monetary Fund, the World Bank and the Financial Stability Forum, in the delivery of its objectives. The FATF has conducted targeted outreach to improve the FATF's knowledge of particular issues and to ensure that the FATF standards do not conflict with the work of other international organisations. In particular, the IMF and the World Bank have made an important contribution to global efforts to combat money laundering and terrorist financing in non-FATF member countries, and the FATF supports this valuable contribution to the global effort. The FATF will continue to work actively with all partners to further FATF objectives and to draw on their knowledge in developing FATF policy.

(c) Relations with associate members and FSRBs

17. The FSRBs, several of which are now associate members of the FATF, play an important leadership role in their respective regions and provide important regional expertise and input into the FATF policy-making function. The FATF and FSRBs will continue to strengthen their working relationships, as well as extending outreach at a regional level with key partners.

VI. OPERATIONAL ISSUES

(a) FATF Structure and Organisation

18. The FATF's task force structure has enabled it to respond decisively and promptly to emerging threats and to accommodate efficiently several expansions in its membership. This structure remains broadly the right one for the organisation and should be maintained.

19. Over the long-term, it will be vital for the FATF to evolve if it is to maintain an effective response to the constantly changing threats facing the international financial system. It will therefore be essential that the structure, organisation and operational planning of the FATF remain flexible and able to adapt to meet new challenges as they arise.

(b) Membership

20. The FATF has gradually increased its membership, and since 2000 has admitted six new members and has accepted two observer countries that are expected to become members in due course.[1] The FATF will continue to work actively towards the membership of the remaining two countries. The FATF will maintain its open approach and will consider the structure of the global AML/CFT architecture, including the enhanced role played by associate members and FSRBs, and FATF membership, once the current expansion is completed. In this regard, the strategic importance of a country, the geographic balance of FATF membership overall, and a country's commitment to implementing the FATF standards will remain the guiding principles of future membership decisions.

21. The FATF currently has 22 observer organisations/bodies. To make the most effective and efficient use of these relationships the FATF will review its policy on observer status.

(c) Presidency

22. Each Presidency will continue to be designated by the Plenary for the duration of one year, and will be supported by a Vice-Presidency, which will be the Presidency-designate.

(d) The Steering Group

23. The seven member Steering Group is an advisory body for the President. The composition of the Steering Group will continue to reflect the geography and size of the FATF as well as include the President, the immediate past Presidency, and the Presidency-designate.

(e) The Secretariat and Budget

24. The Secretariat will continue to support the work of the FATF, including through the working groups and ad hoc groups to ensure co-ordination and consistency.

25. The current arrangements for financing FATF activities will be retained. The cost of the Secretariat and other services will be met by the FATF budget, through the OECD, with member contributions in line with OECD scales, and with the option of additional contributions.

VII. MINISTERIAL ACCOUNTABILITY

26. The FATF is accountable to the Ministers of its membership. To strengthen this accountability, the FATF President will report annually to Ministers on key aspects of FATF work, including on global threats. Given the potentially destabilising effects of criminal and terrorist action against the international financial architecture, occasional ministerial meetings will provide an ongoing accountability mechanism whereby Ministers can shape the strategic direction of FATF policy-making.

---

1 Six new members: Argentina, Brazil, China, Mexico, South Africa and the Russian Federation. Two observer members: India and South Korea.

IV-9b

Financial Action Task Force—'40+9 Recommendations' on Money Laundering and Terrorist Financing*

Date as amended 22 October 2004
Link <http://www.fatf-gafi.org/pages/0,3417,en_32250379_32236920_1_1_1_1_1,00.html>

A. LEGAL SYSTEMS

Scope of the criminal offence of money laundering

1. Countries should criminalise money laundering on the basis of the United Nations Convention against Illicit Traffic in Narcotic Drugs and Psychotropic Substances, 1988 (the Vienna Convention) and the United Nations Convention against Transnational Organized Crime, 2000 (the Palermo Convention).

   Countries should apply the crime of money laundering to all serious offences, with a view to including the widest range of predicate offences. Predicate offences may be described by reference to all offences, or to a threshold linked either to a category of serious offences or to the penalty of imprisonment applicable to the predicate offence (threshold approach), or to a list of predicate offences, or a combination of these approaches.

   Where countries apply a threshold approach, predicate offences should at a minimum comprise all offences that fall within the category of serious offences under their national law or should include offences which are punishable by a maximum penalty of more than one year's imprisonment or for those countries that have a minimum threshold for offences in their legal system, predicate offences should comprise all offences, which are punished by a minimum penalty of more than six months imprisonment.

   Whichever approach is adopted, each country should at a minimum include a range of offences within each of the designated categories of offences.[1]

   Predicate offences for money laundering should extend to conduct that occurred in another country, which constitutes an offence in that country, and which would have constituted a predicate offence had it occurred domestically. Countries may provide that the only prerequisite is that the conduct would have constituted a predicate offence had it occurred domestically.

   Countries may provide that the offence of money laundering does not apply to persons who committed the predicate offence, where this is required by fundamental principles of their domestic law.

2. Countries should ensure that:

---

* Note by the Editors: On the website provided, the 40+9 Recommendations are complemented by a glossary of terms and interpretative guidelines, which are not reproduced in the following.

1 Note by the Editors: The explanatory glossary lists the following offences as 'designated offences': participation in an organised criminal group and racketeering; terrorism, including terrorist financing; trafficking in human beings and migrant smuggling; sexual exploitation, including sexual exploitation of children; illicit trafficking in narcotic drugs and psychotropic substances; illicit arms trafficking; illicit trafficking in stolen and other goods; corruption and bribery; fraud; counterfeiting currency; counterfeiting and piracy of products; environmental crime; murder, grievous bodily injury; kidnapping, illegal restraint and hostage-taking; robbery or theft; smuggling; extortion; forgery; piracy; and insider trading and market manipulation. It also notes: 'When deciding on the range of offences to be covered as predicate offences under each of the categories listed above, each country may decide, in accordance with its domestic law, how it will define those offences and the nature of any particular elements of those offences that make them serious offences.'

a) The intent and knowledge required to prove the offence of money laundering is consistent with the standards set forth in the Vienna and Palermo Conventions, including the concept that such mental state may be inferred from objective factual circumstances.

b) Criminal liability, and, where that is not possible, civil or administrative liability, should apply to legal persons. This should not preclude parallel criminal, civil or administrative proceedings with respect to legal persons in countries in which such forms of liability are available. Legal persons should be subject to effective, proportionate and dissuasive sanctions. Such measures should be without prejudice to the criminal liability of individuals.

Provisional measures and confiscation

3. Countries should adopt measures similar to those set forth in the Vienna and Palermo Conventions, including legislative measures, to enable their competent authorities to confiscate property laundered, proceeds from money laundering or predicate offences, instrumentalities used in or intended for use in the commission of these offences, or property of corresponding value, without prejudicing the rights of bona fide third parties.

Such measures should include the authority to: (a) identify, trace and evaluate property which is subject to confiscation; (b) carry out provisional measures, such as freezing and seizing, to prevent any dealing, transfer or disposal of such property; (c) take steps that will prevent or void actions that prejudice the State's ability to recover property that is subject to confiscation; and (d) take any appropriate investigative measures.

Countries may consider adopting measures that allow such proceeds or instrumentalities to be confiscated without requiring a criminal conviction, or which require an offender to demonstrate the lawful origin of the property alleged to be liable to confiscation, to the extent that such a requirement is consistent with the principles of their domestic law.

B. MEASURES TO BE TAKEN BY FINANCIAL INSTITUTIONS AND NON-FINANCIAL BUSINESSES AND PROFESSIONS TO PREVENT MONEY LAUNDERING AND TERRORIST FINANCING

4. Countries should ensure that financial institution secrecy laws do not inhibit implementation of the FATF Recommendations.

Customer due diligence and record-keeping

5. Financial institutions should not keep anonymous accounts or accounts in obviously fictitious names.

Financial institutions should undertake customer due diligence measures, including identifying and verifying the identity of their customers, when:

- establishing business relations;
- carrying out occasional transactions: (i) above the applicable designated threshold; or (ii) that are wire transfers in the circumstances covered by the Interpretative Note to Special Recommendation VII;
- there is a suspicion of money laundering or terrorist financing; or
- the financial institution has doubts about the veracity or adequacy of previously obtained customer identification data.

The customer due diligence (CDD) measures to be taken are as follows:

a) Identifying the customer and verifying that customer's identity using reliable, independent source documents, data or information.[2]

b) Identifying the beneficial owner, and taking reasonable measures to verify the identity of the beneficial owner such that the financial institution is satisfied that it knows who the beneficial owner is. For legal persons and arrangements this should include financial

---

2 NB: The remainder of the document refers to reliable, independent source documents, data or information as 'identification data'.

institutions taking reasonable measures to understand the ownership and control structure of the customer.

   c) Obtaining information on the purpose and intended nature of the business relationship.
   d) Conducting ongoing due diligence on the business relationship and scrutiny of transactions undertaken throughout the course of that relationship to ensure that the transactions being conducted are consistent with the institution's knowledge of the customer, their business and risk profile, including, where necessary, the source of funds.

Financial institutions should apply each of the CDD measures under (a) to (d) above, but may determine the extent of such measures on a risk sensitive basis depending on the type of customer, business relationship or transaction. The measures that are taken should be consistent with any guidelines issued by competent authorities. For higher risk categories, financial institutions should perform enhanced due diligence. In certain circumstances, where there are low risks, countries may decide that financial institutions can apply reduced or simplified measures.

Financial institutions should verify the identity of the customer and beneficial owner before or during the course of establishing a business relationship or conducting transactions for occasional customers. Countries may permit financial institutions to complete the verification as soon as reasonably practicable following the establishment of the relationship, where the money laundering risks are effectively managed and where this is essential not to interrupt the normal conduct of business.

Where the financial institution is unable to comply with paragraphs (a) to (c) above, it should not open the account, commence business relations or perform the transaction; or should terminate the business relationship; and should consider making a suspicious transactions report in relation to the customer.

These requirements should apply to all new customers, though financial institutions should also apply this Recommendation to existing customers on the basis of materiality and risk, and should conduct due diligence on such existing relationships at appropriate times.

6. Financial institutions should, in relation to politically exposed persons, in addition to performing normal due diligence measures:
   a) Have appropriate risk management systems to determine whether the customer is a politically exposed person.
   b) Obtain senior management approval for establishing business relationships with such customers.
   c) Take reasonable measures to establish the source of wealth and source of funds.
   d) Conduct enhanced ongoing monitoring of the business relationship.

7. Financial institutions should, in relation to cross-border correspondent banking and other similar relationships, in addition to performing normal due diligence measures:
   a) Gather sufficient information about a respondent institution to understand fully the nature of the respondent's business and to determine from publicly available information the reputation of the institution and the quality of supervision, including whether it has been subject to a money laundering or terrorist financing investigation or regulatory action.
   b) Assess the respondent institution's anti-money laundering and terrorist financing controls.
   c) Obtain approval from senior management before establishing new correspondent relationships.
   d) Document the respective responsibilities of each institution.
   e) With respect to "payable-through accounts", be satisfied that the respondent bank has verified the identity of and performed on-going due diligence on the customers having

direct access to accounts of the correspondent and that it is able to provide relevant customer identification data upon request to the correspondent bank.

8. Financial institutions should pay special attention to any money laundering threats that may arise from new or developing technologies that might favour anonymity, and take measures, if needed, to prevent their use in money laundering schemes. In particular, financial institutions should have policies and procedures in place to address any specific risks associated with non-face to face business relationships or transactions.

9. Countries may permit financial institutions to rely on intermediaries or other third parties to perform elements (a)–(c) of the CDD process or to introduce business, provided that the criteria set out below are met. Where such reliance is permitted, the ultimate responsibility for customer identification and verification remains with the financial institution relying on the third party.

    The criteria that should be met are as follows:

    a) A financial institution relying upon a third party should immediately obtain the necessary information concerning elements (a)–(c) of the CDD process. Financial institutions should take adequate steps to satisfy themselves that copies of identification data and other relevant documentation relating to the CDD requirements will be made available from the third party upon request without delay.

    b) The financial institution should satisfy itself that the third party is regulated and supervised for, and has measures in place to comply with CDD requirements in line with Recommendations 5 and 10.

    It is left to each country to determine in which countries the third party that meets the conditions can be based, having regard to information available on countries that do not or do not adequately apply the FATF Recommendations.

10. Financial institutions should maintain, for at least five years, all necessary records on transactions, both domestic or international, to enable them to comply swiftly with information requests from the competent authorities. Such records must be sufficient to permit reconstruction of individual transactions (including the amounts and types of currency involved if any) so as to provide, if necessary, evidence for prosecution of criminal activity.

    Financial institutions should keep records on the identification data obtained through the customer due diligence process (e.g. copies or records of official identification documents like passports, identity cards, driving licenses or similar documents), account files and business correspondence for at least five years after the business relationship is ended.

    The identification data and transaction records should be available to domestic competent authorities upon appropriate authority.

11. Financial institutions should pay special attention to all complex, unusual large transactions, and all unusual patterns of transactions, which have no apparent economic or visible lawful purpose. The background and purpose of such transactions should, as far as possible, be examined, the findings established in writing, and be available to help competent authorities and auditors.

12. The customer due diligence and record-keeping requirements set out in Recommendations 5, 6, and 8 to 11 apply to designated non-financial businesses and professions in the following situations:

    a) Casinos—when customers engage in financial transactions equal to or above the applicable designated threshold.

    b) Real estate agents—when they are involved in transactions for their client concerning the buying and selling of real estate.

    c) Dealers in precious metals and dealers in precious stones—when they engage in any cash transaction with a customer equal to or above the applicable designated threshold.

d) Lawyers, notaries, other independent legal professionals and accountants when they prepare for or carry out transactions for their client concerning the following activities:
- buying and selling of real estate;
- managing of client money, securities or other assets;
- management of bank, savings or securities accounts;
- organisation of contributions for the creation, operation or management of companies;
- creation, operation or management of legal persons or arrangements, and buying and selling of business entities.

e) Trust and company service providers when they prepare for or carry out transactions for a client concerning the activities listed in the definition in the Glossary.

Reporting of suspicious transactions and compliance

13. If a financial institution suspects or has reasonable grounds to suspect that funds are the proceeds of a criminal activity, or are related to terrorist financing, it should be required, directly by law or regulation, to report promptly its suspicions to the financial intelligence unit (FIU).

14. Financial institutions, their directors, officers and employees should be:
   a) Protected by legal provisions from criminal and civil liability for breach of any restriction on disclosure of information imposed by contract or by any legislative, regulatory or administrative provision, if they report their suspicions in good faith to the FIU, even if they did not know precisely what the underlying criminal activity was, and regardless of whether illegal activity actually occurred.
   b) Prohibited by law from disclosing the fact that a suspicious transaction report (STR) or related information is being reported to the FIU.

15. Financial institutions should develop programmes against money laundering and terrorist financing. These programmes should include:
   a) The development of internal policies, procedures and controls, including appropriate compliance management arrangements, and adequate screening procedures to ensure high standards when hiring employees.
   b) An ongoing employee training programme.
   c) An audit function to test the system.

16. The requirements set out in Recommendations 13 to 15, and 21 apply to all designated nonfinancial businesses and professions, subject to the following qualifications:
   a) Lawyers, notaries, other independent legal professionals and accountants should be required to report suspicious transactions when, on behalf of or for a client, they engage in a financial transaction in relation to the activities described in Recommendation 12(d). Countries are strongly encouraged to extend the reporting requirement to the rest of the professional activities of accountants, including auditing.
   b) Dealers in precious metals and dealers in precious stones should be required to report suspicious transactions when they engage in any cash transaction with a customer equal to or above the applicable designated threshold.
   c) Trust and company service providers should be required to report suspicious transactions for a client when, on behalf of or for a client, they engage in a transaction in relation to the activities referred to Recommendation 12(e).

   Lawyers, notaries, other independent legal professionals, and accountants acting as independent legal professionals, are not required to report their suspicions if the relevant information was obtained in circumstances where they are subject to professional secrecy or legal professional privilege.

Other measures to deter money laundering and terrorist financing

17. Countries should ensure that effective, proportionate and dissuasive sanctions, whether criminal, civil or administrative, are available to deal with natural or legal persons covered

by these Recommendations that fail to comply with anti-money laundering or terrorist financing requirements.

18. Countries should not approve the establishment or accept the continued operation of shell banks. Financial institutions should refuse to enter into, or continue, a correspondent banking relationship with shell banks. Financial institutions should also guard against establishing relations with respondent foreign financial institutions that permit their accounts to be used by shell banks.

19. Countries should consider the feasibility and utility of a system where banks and other financial institutions and intermediaries would report all domestic and international currency transactions above a fixed amount, to a national central agency with a computerised data base, available to competent authorities for use in money laundering or terrorist financing cases, subject to strict safeguards to ensure proper use of the information.

20. Countries should consider applying the FATF Recommendations to businesses and professions, other than designated non-financial businesses and professions, that pose a money laundering or terrorist financing risk. Countries should further encourage the development of modern and secure techniques of money management that are less vulnerable to money laundering.

Measures to be taken with respect to countries that do not or insufficiently comply with the FATF Recommendations

21. Financial institutions should give special attention to business relationships and transactions with persons, including companies and financial institutions, from countries which do not or insufficiently apply the FATF Recommendations. Whenever these transactions have no apparent economic or visible lawful purpose, their background and purpose should, as far as possible, be examined, the findings established in writing, and be available to help competent authorities. Where such a country continues not to apply or insufficiently applies the FATF Recommendations, countries should be able to apply appropriate countermeasures.

22. Financial institutions should ensure that the principles applicable to financial institutions, which are mentioned above are also applied to branches and majority owned subsidiaries located abroad, especially in countries which do not or insufficiently apply the FATF Recommendations, to the extent that local applicable laws and regulations permit. When local applicable laws and regulations prohibit this implementation, competent authorities in the country of the parent institution should be informed by the financial institutions that they cannot apply the FATF Recommendations.

Regulation and supervision

23. Countries should ensure that financial institutions are subject to adequate regulation and supervision and are effectively implementing the FATF Recommendations. Competent authorities should take the necessary legal or regulatory measures to prevent criminals or their associates from holding or being the beneficial owner of a significant or controlling interest or holding a management function in a financial institution. For financial institutions subject to the Core Principles, the regulatory and supervisory measures that apply for prudential purposes and which are also relevant to money laundering, should apply in a similar manner for anti-money laundering and terrorist financing purposes. Other financial institutions should be licensed or registered and appropriately regulated, and subject to supervision or oversight for anti-money laundering purposes, having regard to the risk of money laundering or terrorist financing in that sector. At a minimum, businesses providing a service of money or value transfer, or of money or currency changing should be licensed or registered, and subject to effective systems for monitoring and ensuring compliance with national requirements to combat money laundering and terrorist financing.

24. Designated non-financial businesses and professions should be subject to regulatory and supervisory measures as set out below.

    a) Casinos should be subject to a comprehensive regulatory and supervisory regime that ensures that they have effectively implemented the necessary anti-money laundering and terrorist-financing measures. At a minimum:

    • casinos should be licensed;

    • competent authorities should take the necessary legal or regulatory measures to prevent criminals or their associates from holding or being the beneficial owner of a significant or controlling interest, holding a management function in, or being an operator of a casino

    • competent authorities should ensure that casinos are effectively supervised for compliance with requirements to combat money laundering and terrorist financing.

    b) Countries should ensure that the other categories of designated non-financial businesses and professions are subject to effective systems for monitoring and ensuring their compliance with requirements to combat money laundering and terrorist financing. This should be performed on a risk-sensitive basis. This may be performed by a government authority or by an appropriate self-regulatory organisation, provided that such an organisation can ensure that its members comply with their obligations to combat money laundering and terrorist financing.

25. The competent authorities should establish guidelines, and provide feedback which will assist financial institutions and designated non-financial businesses and professions in applying national measures to combat money laundering and terrorist financing, and in particular, in detecting and reporting suspicious transactions.

C. INSTITUTIONAL AND OTHER MEASURES NECESSARY IN SYSTEMS FOR COMBATING MONEY LAUNDERING AND TERRORIST FINANCING

Competent authorities, their powers and resources

26. Countries should establish a FIU that serves as a national centre for the receiving (and, as permitted, requesting), analysis and dissemination of STR and other information regarding potential money laundering or terrorist financing. The FIU should have access, directly or indirectly, on a timely basis to the financial, administrative and law enforcement information that it requires to properly undertake its functions, including the analysis of STR.

27. Countries should ensure that designated law enforcement authorities have responsibility for money laundering and terrorist financing investigations. Countries are encouraged to support and develop, as far as possible, special investigative techniques suitable for the investigation of money laundering, such as controlled delivery, undercover operations and other relevant techniques. Countries are also encouraged to use other effective mechanisms such as the use of permanent or temporary groups specialised in asset investigation, and co-operative investigations with appropriate competent authorities in other countries.

28. When conducting investigations of money laundering and underlying predicate offences, competent authorities should be able to obtain documents and information for use in those investigations, and in prosecutions and related actions. This should include powers to use compulsory measures for the production of records held by financial institutions and other persons, for the search of persons and premises, and for the seizure and obtaining of evidence.

29. Supervisors should have adequate powers to monitor and ensure compliance by financial institutions with requirements to combat money laundering and terrorist financing, including the authority to conduct inspections. They should be authorised to compel production of any information from financial institutions that is relevant to monitoring such compli-

ance, and to impose adequate administrative sanctions for failure to comply with such requirements.

30. Countries should provide their competent authorities involved in combating money laundering and terrorist financing with adequate financial, human and technical resources. Countries should have in place processes to ensure that the staff of those authorities are of high integrity.

31. Countries should ensure that policy makers, the FIU, law enforcement and supervisors have effective mechanisms in place which enable them to co-operate, and where appropriate coordinate domestically with each other concerning the development and implementation of policies and activities to combat money laundering and terrorist financing.

32. Countries should ensure that their competent authorities can review the effectiveness of their systems to combat money laundering and terrorist financing systems by maintaining comprehensive statistics on matters relevant to the effectiveness and efficiency of such systems. This should include statistics on the STR received and disseminated; on money laundering and terrorist financing investigations, prosecutions and convictions; on property frozen, seized and confiscated; and on mutual legal assistance or other international requests for co-operation.

Transparency of legal persons and arrangements

33. Countries should take measures to prevent the unlawful use of legal persons by money launderers. Countries should ensure that there is adequate, accurate and timely information on the beneficial ownership and control of legal persons that can be obtained or accessed in a timely fashion by competent authorities. In particular, countries that have legal persons that are able to issue bearer shares should take appropriate measures to ensure that they are not misused for money laundering and be able to demonstrate the adequacy of those measures. Countries could consider measures to facilitate access to beneficial ownership and control information to financial institutions undertaking the requirements set out in Recommendation 5.

34. Countries should take measures to prevent the unlawful use of legal arrangements by money launderers. In particular, countries should ensure that there is adequate, accurate and timely information on express trusts, including information on the settlor, trustee and beneficiaries, that can be obtained or accessed in a timely fashion by competent authorities. Countries could consider measures to facilitate access to beneficial ownership and control information to financial institutions undertaking the requirements set out in Recommendation 5.

D. INTERNATIONAL CO-OPERATION

35. Countries should take immediate steps to become party to and implement fully the Vienna Convention, the Palermo Convention, and the 1999 United Nations International Convention for the Suppression of the Financing of Terrorism. Countries are also encouraged to ratify and implement other relevant international conventions, such as the 1990 Council of Europe Convention on Laundering, Search, Seizure and Confiscation of the Proceeds from Crime and the 2002 Inter-American Convention against Terrorism.

Mutual legal assistance and extradition

36. Countries should rapidly, constructively and effectively provide the widest possible range of mutual legal assistance in relation to money laundering and terrorist financing investigations, prosecutions, and related proceedings. In particular, countries should:
   a) Not prohibit or place unreasonable or unduly restrictive conditions on the provision of mutual legal assistance.
   b) Ensure that they have clear and efficient processes for the execution of mutual legal assistance requests.

c) Not refuse to execute a request for mutual legal assistance on the sole ground that the offence is also considered to involve fiscal matters.

d) Not refuse to execute a request for mutual legal assistance on the grounds that laws require financial institutions to maintain secrecy or confidentiality.

Countries should ensure that the powers of their competent authorities required under Recommendation 28 are also available for use in response to requests for mutual legal assistance, and if consistent with their domestic framework, in response to direct requests from foreign judicial or law enforcement authorities to domestic counterparts.

To avoid conflicts of jurisdiction, consideration should be given to devising and applying mechanisms for determining the best venue for prosecution of defendants in the interests of justice in cases that are subject to prosecution in more than one country.

37. Countries should, to the greatest extent possible, render mutual legal assistance notwith-standing the absence of dual criminality.

Where dual criminality is required for mutual legal assistance or extradition, that require-ment should be deemed to be satisfied regardless of whether both countries place the offence within the same category of offence or denominate the offence by the same terminology, provided that both countries criminalise the conduct underlying the offence.

38. There should be authority to take expeditious action in response to requests by foreign countries to identify, freeze, seize and confiscate property laundered, proceeds from money laundering or predicate offences, instrumentalities used in or intended for use in the commission of these offences, or property of corresponding value. There should also be arrangements for coordinating seizure and confiscation proceedings, which may include the sharing of confiscated assets.

39. Countries should recognise money laundering as an extraditable offence. Each country should either extradite its own nationals, or where a country does not do so solely on the grounds of nationality, that country should, at the request of the country seeking extradition, submit the case without undue delay to its competent authorities for the purpose of prosecution of the offences set forth in the request. Those authorities should take their decision and conduct their proceedings in the same manner as in the case of any other offence of a serious nature under the domestic law of that country. The countries concerned should cooperate with each other, in particular on procedural and evidentiary aspects, to ensure the efficiency of such prosecutions. Subject to their legal frameworks, countries may consider simplifying extradition by allowing direct transmission of extradition requests between appropriate ministries, extraditing persons based only on warrants of arrests or judgements, and/or introducing a simplified extradition of consenting persons who waive formal extradition proceedings.

Other forms of co-operation

40. Countries should ensure that their competent authorities provide the widest possible range of international co-operation to their foreign counterparts. There should be clear and effective gateways to facilitate the prompt and constructive exchange directly between counterparts, either spontaneously or upon request, of information relating to both money laundering and the underlying predicate offences. Exchanges should be permitted without unduly restrictive conditions. In particular:

a) Competent authorities should not refuse a request for assistance on the sole ground that the request is also considered to involve fiscal matters.

b) Countries should not invoke laws that require financial institutions to maintain secrecy or confidentiality as a ground for refusing to provide co-operation.

c) Competent authorities should be able to conduct inquiries; and where possible, inves-tigations; on behalf of foreign counterparts.

Where the ability to obtain information sought by a foreign competent authority is not within the mandate of its counterpart, countries are also encouraged to permit a prompt and construct-ive exchange of information with non-counterparts. Co-operation with foreign authorities other than counterparts could occur directly or indirectly. When uncertain about the appropriate avenue to follow, competent authorities should first contact their foreign counterparts for assistance.

FATF SPECIAL RECOMMENDATIONS ON TERRORIST FINANCING

Recognising the vital importance of taking action to combat the financing of terrorism, the FATF has agreed these Recommendations, which, when combined with the FATF Forty Recommendations on money laundering, set out the basic framework to detect, prevent and suppress the financing of terrorism and terrorist acts.

I. Ratification and implementation of UN instruments

Each country should take immediate steps to ratify and to implement fully the 1999 United Nations International Convention for the Suppression of the Financing of Terrorism. Countries should also immediately implement the United Nations resolutions relating to the prevention and suppression of the financing of terrorist acts, particularly United Nations Security Council Resolution 1373.

II. Criminalising the financing of terrorism and associated money laundering

Each country should criminalise the financing of terrorism, terrorist acts and terrorist organisa-tions. Countries should ensure that such offences are designated as money laundering predicate offences.

III. Freezing and confiscating terrorist assets

Each country should implement measures to freeze without delay funds or other assets of terrorists, those who finance terrorism and terrorist organisations in accordance with the United Nations resolutions relating to the prevention and suppression of the financing of terrorist acts. Each country should also adopt and implement measures, including legislative ones, which would enable the competent authorities to seize and confiscate property that is the proceeds of, or used in, or intended or allocated for use in, the financing of terrorism, terrorist acts or terrorist organisations.

IV. Reporting suspicious transactions related to terrorism

If financial institutions, or other businesses or entities subject to anti-money laundering obliga-tions, suspect or have reasonable grounds to suspect that funds are linked or related to, or are to be used for terrorism, terrorist acts or by terrorist organisations, they should be required to report promptly their suspicions to the competent authorities.

V. International Co-operation

Each country should afford another country, on the basis of a treaty, arrangement or other mechanism for mutual legal assistance or information exchange, the greatest possible measure of assistance in connection with criminal, civil enforcement, and administrative investigations, inquiries and proceedings relating to the financing of terrorism, terrorist acts and terrorist organisations. Countries should also take all possible measures to ensure that they do not provide safe havens for individuals charged with the financing of terrorism, terrorist acts or terrorist organisations, and should have procedures in place to extradite, where possible, such individuals.

VI. Alternative remittance

Each country should take measures to ensure that persons or legal entities, including agents, that provide a service for the transmission of money or value, including transmission through an informal money or value transfer system or network, should be licensed or registered and subject to all the FATF Recommendations that apply to banks and non-bank financial institutions. Each country should ensure that persons or legal entities that carry out this service illegally are subject to administrative, civil or criminal sanctions.

VII.   Wire transfers

Countries should take measures to require financial institutions, including money remitters, to include accurate and meaningful originator information (name, address and account number) on funds transfers and related messages that are sent, and the information should remain with the transfer or related message through the payment chain. Countries should take measures to ensure that financial institutions, including money remitters, conduct enhanced scrutiny of and monitor for suspicious activity funds transfers which do not contain complete originator information (name, address and account number).

VIII.   Non-profit organisations

Countries should review the adequacy of laws and regulations that relate to entities that can be abused for the financing of terrorism. Non-profit organisations are particularly vulnerable, and countries should ensure that they cannot be misused:

(i)   by terrorist organisations posing as legitimate entities;

(ii)   to exploit legitimate entities as conduits for terrorist financing, including for the purpose of escaping asset freezing measures; and

(iii) to conceal or obscure the clandestine diversion of funds intended for legitimate purposes to terrorist organisations.

IX.   Cash couriers

Countries should have measures in place to detect the physical cross-border transportation of currency and bearer negotiable instruments, including a declaration system or other disclosure obligation. Countries should ensure that their competent authorities have the legal authority to stop or restrain currency or bearer negotiable instruments that are suspected to be related to terrorist financing or money laundering, or that are falsely declared or disclosed. Countries should ensure that effective, proportionate and dissuasive sanctions are available to deal with persons who make false declaration(s) or disclosure(s). In cases where the currency or bearer negotiable instruments are related to terrorist financing or money laundering, countries should also adopt measures, including legislative ones consistent with Recommendation 3 and Special Recommendation III, which would enable the confiscation of such currency or instruments

IV-10

IMF—Code of Good Practices on Fiscal Transparency

Date   26 September 1999, revised 8 May 2007
Link   <http://www.imf.org/external/np/pp/2007/eng/051507c.pdf>

I. CLARITY OF ROLES AND RESPONSIBILITIES

1.1 **The government sector should be distinguished from the rest of the public sector and from the rest of the economy, and policy and management roles within the public sector should be clear and publicly disclosed.**

    1.1.1 The structure and functions of government should be clear.

    1.1.2 The fiscal powers of the executive, legislative, and judicial branches of government should be well defined.

    1.1.3 The responsibilities of different levels of government, and the relationships between them, should be clearly specified.

    1.1.4 Relationships between the government and public corporations should be based on clear arrangements.

    1.1.5 Government relationships with the private sector should be conducted in an open manner, following clear rules and procedures.

1.2 **There should be a clear and open legal, regulatory, and administrative framework for fiscal management.**

    1.2.1 The collection, commitment, and use of public funds should be governed by comprehensive budget, tax, and other public finance laws, regulations, and administrative procedures.

    1.2.2 Laws and regulations related to the collection of tax and non-tax revenues, and the criteria guiding administrative discretion in their application, should be accessible, clear, and understandable. Appeals of tax or non-tax obligations should be considered in a timely manner.

    1.2.3 There should be sufficient time for consultation about proposed laws and regulatory changes and, where feasible, broader policy changes.

    1.2.4 Contractual arrangements between the government and public or private entities, including resource companies and operators of government concessions, should be clear and publicly accessible.

    1.2.5 Government liability and asset management, including the granting of rights to use or exploit public assets, should have an explicit legal basis.

II. OPEN BUDGET PROCESSES

2.1 **Budget preparation should follow an established timetable and be guided by well-defined macroeconomic and fiscal policy objectives.**

    2.1.1 A budget calendar should be specified and adhered to. Adequate time should be allowed for the draft budget to be considered by the legislature.

    2.1.2 The annual budget should be realistic, and should be prepared and presented within a comprehensive medium-term macroeconomic and fiscal policy framework. Fiscal targets and any fiscal rules should be clearly stated and explained.

2.1.3 A description of major expenditure and revenue measures, and their contribution to policy objectives, should be provided. Estimates should also be provided of their current and future budgetary impact and their broader economic implications.

2.1.4 The budget documentation should include an assessment of fiscal sustainability. The main assumptions about economic developments and policies should be realistic and clearly specified, and sensitivity analysis should be presented.

2.1.5 There should be clear mechanisms for the coordination and management of budgetary and extrabudgetary activities within the overall fiscal policy framework.

2.2 There should be clear procedures for budget execution, monitoring, and reporting.

2.2.1 The accounting system should provide a reliable basis for tracking revenues, commitments, payments, arrears, liabilities, and assets.

2.2.2 A timely midyear report on budget developments should be presented to the legislature. More frequent updates, which should be at least quarterly, should be published.

2.2.3 Supplementary revenue and expenditure proposals during the fiscal year should be presented to the legislature in a manner consistent with the original budget presentation.

2.2.4 Audited final accounts and audit reports, including reconciliation with the approved budget, should be presented to the legislature and published within a year.

III. PUBLIC AVAILABILITY OF INFORMATION

3.1 The public should be provided with comprehensive information on past, current, and projected fiscal activity and on major fiscal risks.

3.1.1 The budget documentation, including the final accounts, and other published fiscal reports should cover all budgetary and extrabudgetary activities of the central government.

3.1.2 Information comparable to that in the annual budget should be provided for the outturns of at least the two preceding fiscal years, together with forecasts and sensitivity analysis for the main budget aggregates for at least two years following the budget.

3.1.3 Statements describing the nature and fiscal significance of central government tax expenditures, contingent liabilities, and quasi-fiscal activities should be part of the budget documentation, together with an assessment of all other major fiscal risks.

3.1.4 Receipts from all major revenue sources, including resource-related activities and foreign assistance, should be separately identified in the annual budget presentation.

3.1.5 The central government should publish information on the level and composition of its debt and financial assets, significant nondebt liabilities (including pension rights, guarantee exposure, and other contractual obligations), and natural resource assets.

3.1.6 The budget documentation should report the fiscal position of subnational governments and the finances of public corporations.

3.1.7 The government should publish a periodic report on long-term public finances.

3.2 Fiscal information should be presented in a way that facilitates policy analysis and promotes accountability.

3.2.1 A clear and simple summary guide to the budget should be widely distributed at the time of the annual budget.

3.2.2 Fiscal data should be reported on a gross basis, distinguishing revenue, expenditure, and financing, with expenditure classified by economic, functional, and administrative category.

3.2.3 The overall balance and gross debt of the general government, or their accrual equivalents, should be standard summary indicators of the government fiscal position.

They should be supplemented, where appropriate, by other fiscal indicators, such as the primary balance, the public sector balance, and net debt.

    3.2.4 Results achieved relative to the objectives of major budget programs should be presented to the legislature annually.

3.3. A commitment should be made to the timely publication of fiscal information.

    3.3.1 The timely publication of fiscal information should be a legal obligation of the government.

    3.3.2 Advance release calendars for fiscal information should be announced and adhered to.

IV. ASSURANCES OF INTEGRITY

4.1 Fiscal data should meet accepted data quality standards.

    4.1.1 Budget forecasts and updates should reflect recent revenue and expenditure trends, underlying macroeconomic developments, and well-defined policy commitments.

    4.1.2 The annual budget and final accounts should indicate the accounting basis used in the compilation and presentation of fiscal data. Generally accepted accounting standards should be followed.

    4.1.3 Data in fiscal reports should be internally consistent and reconciled with relevant data from other sources. Major revisions to historical fiscal data and any changes to data classification should be explained.

4.2 Fiscal activities should be subject to effective internal oversight and safeguards.

    4.2.1 Ethical standards of behavior for public servants should be clear and well publicized.

    4.2.2 Public sector employment procedures and conditions should be documented and accessible to interested parties.

    4.2.3 Procurement regulations, meeting international standards, should be accessible and observed in practice.

    4.2.4 Purchases and sales of public assets should be undertaken in an open manner, and major transactions should be separately identified.

    4.2.5 Government activities and finances should be internally audited, and audit procedures should be open to review.

    4.2.6 The national revenue administration should be legally protected from political direction, ensure taxpayers' rights, and report regularly to the public on its activities.

4.3 Fiscal information should be externally scrutinized.

    4.3.1 Public finances and policies should be subject to scrutiny by a national audit body or an equivalent organization that is independent of the executive.

    4.3.2 The national audit body or equivalent organization should submit all reports, including its annual report, to the legislature and publish them. Mechanisms should be in place to monitor follow-up actions.

    4.3.4 Independent experts should be invited to assess fiscal forecasts, the macroeconomic forecasts on which they are based, and their underlying assumptions.

    4.3.4 A national statistical body should be provided with the institutional independence to verify the quality of fiscal data.

IV-11

OECD Principles of Corporate Governance

Date May 1999, revised April 2004
Link <http://www.oecd.org/dataoecd/32/18/31557724.pdf>

PREAMBLE

The Principles are intended to assist OECD and non-OECD governments in their efforts to evaluate and improve the legal, institutional and regulatory framework for corporate governance in their countries, and to provide guidance and suggestions for stock exchanges, investors, corporations, and other parties that have a role in the process of developing good corporate governance. The Principles focus on publicly traded companies, both financial and non-financial. However, to the extent they are deemed applicable, they might also be a useful tool to improve corporate governance in non-traded companies, for example, privately held and state-owned enterprises. The Principles represent a common basis that OECD member countries consider essential for the development of good governance practices. They are intended to be concise, understandable and accessible to the international community. They are not intended to substitute for government, semi-government or private sector initiatives to develop more detailed "best practice" in corporate governance.

Increasingly, the OECD and its member governments have recognised the synergy between macroeconomic and structural policies in achieving fundamental policy goals. Corporate governance is one key element in improving economic efficiency and growth as well as enhancing investor confidence. Corporate governance involves a set of relationships between a company's management, its board, its shareholders and other stakeholders. Corporate governance also provides the structure through which the objectives of the company are set, and the means of attaining those objectives and monitoring performance are determined. Good corporate governance should provide proper incentives for the board and management to pursue objectives that are in the interests of the company and its shareholders and should facilitate effective monitoring. The presence of an effective corporate governance system, within an individual company and across an economy as a whole, helps to provide a degree of confidence that is necessary for the proper functioning of a market economy. As a result, the cost of capital is lower and firms are encouraged to use resources more efficiently, thereby underpinning growth.

Corporate governance is only part of the larger economic context in which firms operate that includes, for example, macroeconomic policies and the degree of competition in product and factor markets. The corporate governance framework also depends on the legal, regulatory, and institutional environment. In addition, factors such as business ethics and corporate awareness of the environmental and societal interests of the communities in which a company operates can also have an impact on its reputation and its long-term success.

While a multiplicity of factors affect the governance and decision-making processes of firms, and are important to their long-term success, the Principles focus on governance problems that result from the separation of ownership and control. However, this is not simply an issue of the relationship between shareholders and management, although that is indeed the central element. In some jurisdictions, governance issues also arise from the power of certain controlling shareholders over minority shareholders. In other countries, employees have important legal rights irrespective of their ownership rights. The Principles therefore have to be complementary to a broader approach to the operation of checks and balances. Some of the other issues relevant to a company's decision-making processes, such as environmental, anti-corruption or ethical concerns, are taken into account but are treated more explicitly in a number of other OECD instruments (including the *Guidelines for Multinational Enterprises* and the *Convention on Combating Bribery of Foreign Public Officials in International Transactions*) and the instruments of other international organisations.

Corporate governance is affected by the relationships among participants in the governance system. Controlling shareholders, which may be individuals, family holdings, bloc alliances, or other corporations acting through a holding company or cross shareholdings, can significantly influence corporate behaviour. As owners of equity, institutional investors are increasingly demanding a voice in corporate governance in some markets. Individual shareholders usually do not seek to exercise governance rights but may be highly concerned about obtaining fair treatment from controlling shareholders and management. Creditors play an important role in a number of governance systems and can serve as external monitors over corporate performance. Employees and other stakeholders play an important role in contributing to the long-term success and performance of the corporation, while governments establish the overall institutional and legal framework for corporate governance. The role of each of these participants and their interactions vary widely among OECD countries and among non-OECD countries as well. These relationships are subject, in part, to law and regulation and, in part, to voluntary adaptation and, most importantly, to market forces.

The degree to which corporations observe basic principles of good corporate governance is an increasingly important factor for investment decisions. Of particular relevance is the relation between corporate governance practices and the increasingly international character of investment. International flows of capital enable companies to access financing from a much larger pool of investors. If countries are to reap the full benefits of the global capital market, and if they are to attract long-term "patient" capital, corporate governance arrangements must be credible, well understood across borders and adhere to internationally accepted principles. Even if corporations do not rely primarily on foreign sources of capital, adherence to good corporate governance practices will help improve the confidence of domestic investors, reduce the cost of capital, underpin the good functioning of financial markets, and ultimately induce more stable sources of financing.

There is no single model of good corporate governance. However, work carried out in both OECD and non-OECD countries and within the Organisation has identified some common elements that underlie good corporate governance. The Principles build on these common elements and are formulated to embrace the different models that exist. For example, they do not advocate any particular board structure and the term "board" as used in this document is meant to embrace the different national models of board structures found in OECD and non-OECD countries. In the typical two tier system, found in some countries, "board" as used in the Principles refers to the "supervisory board" while "key executives" refers to the "management board". In systems where the unitary board is overseen by an internal auditor's body, the principles applicable to the board are also, *mutatis mutandis*, applicable. The terms "corporation" and "company" are used interchangeably in the text.

The Principles are non-binding and do not aim at detailed prescriptions for national legislation. Rather, they seek to identify objectives and suggest various means for achieving them. Their purpose is to serve as a reference point. They can be used by policy makers as they examine and develop the legal and regulatory frameworks for corporate governance that reflect their own economic, social, legal and cultural circumstances, and by market participants as they develop their own practices.

The Principles are evolutionary in nature and should be reviewed in light of significant changes in circumstances. To remain competitive in a changing world, corporations must innovate and adapt their corporate governance practices so that they can meet new demands and grasp new opportunities. Similarly, governments have an important responsibility for shaping an effective regulatory framework that provides for sufficient flexibility to allow markets to function effectively and to respond to expectations of shareholders and other stakeholders. It is up to governments and market participants to decide how to apply these Principles in developing their own frameworks for corporate governance, taking into account the costs and benefits of regulation.

The following document is divided into two parts. The Principles presented in the first part of the document cover the following areas: I) Ensuring the basis for an effective corporate governance framework; II) The rights of shareholders and key ownership functions; III) The equitable treatment of shareholders; IV) The role of stakeholders; V) Disclosure and transparency; and VI) The responsibilities of the board. Each of the sections is headed by a single Principle that appears in bold italics and is followed by a number of supporting sub-principles. In the second part of the document, the Principles are supplemented by annotations that contain commentary on the Principles and are intended to help readers understand their rationale. The annotations may also contain descriptions of dominant trends and offer alternative implementation methods and examples that may be useful in making the Principles operational.

PART ONE   THE OECD PRINCIPLES OF CORPORATE GOVERNANCE

I.   Ensuring the Basis for an Effective Corporate Governance Framework

The corporate governance framework should promote transparent and efficient markets, be consistent with the rule of law and clearly articulate the division of responsibilities among different supervisory, regulatory and enforcement authorities.

A. The corporate governance framework should be developed with a view to its impact on overall economic performance, market integrity and the incentives it creates for market participants and the promotion of transparent and efficient markets.

B. The legal and regulatory requirements that affect corporate governance practices in a jurisdiction should be consistent with the rule of law, transparent and enforceable.

C. The division of responsibilities among different authorities in a jurisdiction should be clearly articulated and ensure that the public interest is served.

D. Supervisory, regulatory and enforcement authorities should have the authority, integrity and resources to fulfil their duties in a professional and objective manner. Moreover, their rulings should be timely, transparent and fully explained.

II.   The Rights of Shareholders and Key Ownership Functions

The corporate governance framework should protect and facilitate the exercise of shareholders' rights.

A. Basic shareholder rights should include the right to: 1) secure methods of ownership registration; 2) convey or transfer shares; 3) obtain relevant and material information on the corporation on a timely and regular basis; 4) participate and vote in general shareholder meetings; 5) elect and remove members of the board; and 6) share in the profits of the corporation.

B. Shareholders should have the right to participate in, and to be sufficiently informed on, decisions concerning fundamental corporate changes such as: 1) amendments to the statutes, or articles of incorporation or similar governing documents of the company; 2) the authorisation of additional shares; and 3) extraordinary transactions, including the transfer of all or substantially all assets, that in effect result in the sale of the company.

C. Shareholders should have the opportunity to participate effectively and vote in general shareholder meetings and should be informed of the rules, including voting procedures, that govern general shareholder meetings:

1. Shareholders should be furnished with sufficient and timely information concerning the date, location and agenda of general meetings, as well as full and timely information regarding the issues to be decided at the meeting.

2. Shareholders should have the opportunity to ask questions to the board, including questions relating to the annual external audit, to place items on the agenda of general meetings, and to propose resolutions, subject to reasonable limitations.

3. Effective shareholder participation in key corporate governance decisions, such as the nomination and election of board members, should be facilitated. Shareholders should be able to make their views known on the remuneration policy for board members and key executives. The equity component of compensation schemes for board members and employees should be subject to shareholder approval.

4. Shareholders should be able to vote in person or in absentia, and equal effect should be given to votes whether cast in person or in absentia.

D. Capital structures and arrangements that enable certain shareholders to obtain a degree of control disproportionate to their equity ownership should be disclosed.

E. Markets for corporate control should be allowed to function in an efficient and transparent manner.

1. The rules and procedures governing the acquisition of corporate control in the capital markets, and extraordinary transactions such as mergers, and sales of substantial portions of corporate assets, should be clearly articulated and disclosed so that investors understand their rights and recourse. Transactions should occur at transparent prices and under fair conditions that protect the rights of all shareholders according to their class.

2. Anti-take-over devices should not be used to shield management and the board from accountability.

F. The exercise of ownership rights by all shareholders, including institutional investors, should be facilitated.

1. Institutional investors acting in a fiduciary capacity should disclose their overall corporate governance and voting policies with respect to their investments, including the procedures that they have in place for deciding on the use of their voting rights.

2. Institutional investors acting in a fiduciary capacity should disclose how they manage material conflicts of interest that may affect the exercise of key ownership rights regarding their investments.

G. Shareholders, including institutional shareholders, should be allowed to consult with each other on issues concerning their basic shareholder rights as defined in the Principles, subject to exceptions to prevent abuse.

III. The Equitable Treatment of Shareholders

The corporate governance framework should ensure the equitable treatment of all shareholders, including minority and foreign shareholders. All shareholders should have the opportunity to obtain effective redress for violation of their rights.

A. All shareholders of the same series of a class should be treated equally.

1. Within any series of a class, all shares should carry the same rights. All investors should be able to obtain information about the rights attached to all series and classes of shares before they purchase. Any changes in voting rights should be subject to approval by those classes of shares which are negatively affected.

2. Minority shareholders should be protected from abusive actions by, or in the interest of, controlling shareholders acting either directly or indirectly, and should have effective means of redress.

3. Votes should be cast by custodians or nominees in a manner agreed upon with the beneficial owner of the shares.

4. Impediments to cross border voting should be eliminated.

5. Processes and procedures for general shareholder meetings should allow for equitable treatment of all shareholders. Company procedures should not make it unduly difficult or expensive to cast votes.

B. Insider trading and abusive self-dealing should be prohibited.

C. Members of the board and key executives should be required to disclose to the board whether they, directly, indirectly or on behalf of third parties, have a material interest in any transaction or matter directly affecting the corporation.

IV.   The Role of Stakeholders in Corporate Governance

The corporate governance framework should recognise the rights of stakeholders established by law or through mutual agreements and encourage active co-operation between corporations and stakeholders in creating wealth, jobs, and the sustainability of financially sound enterprises.

A. The rights of stakeholders that are established by law or through mutual agreements are to be respected.

B. Where stakeholder interests are protected by law, stakeholders should have the opportunity to obtain effective redress for violation of their rights.

C. Performance-enhancing mechanisms for employee participation should be permitted to develop.

D. Where stakeholders participate in the corporate governance process, they should have access to relevant, sufficient and reliable information on a timely and regular basis.

E. Stakeholders, including individual employees and their representative bodies, should be able to freely communicate their concerns about illegal or unethical practices to the board and their rights should not be compromised for doing this.

F. The corporate governance framework should be complemented by an effective, efficient insolvency framework and by effective enforcement of creditor rights.

V.   Disclosure and Transparency

The corporate governance framework should ensure that timely and accurate disclosure is made on all material matters regarding the corporation, including the financial situation, performance, ownership, and governance of the company.

A. Disclosure should include, but not be limited to, material information on:

1. The financial and operating results of the company.
2. Company objectives.
3. Major share ownership and voting rights.
4. Remuneration policy for members of the board and key executives, and information about board members, including their qualifications, the selection process, other company directorships and whether they are regarded as independent by the board.
5. Related party transactions.
6. Foreseeable risk factors.
7. Issues regarding employees and other stakeholders.
8. Governance structures and policies, in particular, the content of any corporate governance code or policy and the process by which it is implemented.

B. Information should be prepared and disclosed in accordance with high quality standards of accounting and financial and non-financial disclosure.

C. An annual audit should be conducted by an independent, competent and qualified, auditor in order to provide an external and objective assurance to the board and shareholders that the financial statements fairly represent the financial position and performance of the company in all material respects.

D. External auditors should be accountable to the shareholders and owe a duty to the company to exercise due professional care in the conduct of the audit.

E. Channels for disseminating information should provide for equal, timely and cost-efficient access to relevant information by users.

F. The corporate governance framework should be complemented by an effective approach that addresses and promotes the provision of analysis or advice by analysts, brokers, rating agencies and others, that is relevant to decisions by investors, free from material conflicts of interest that might compromise the integrity of their analysis or advice.

VI.   The Responsibilities of the Board

The corporate governance framework should ensure the strategic guidance of the company, the effective monitoring of management by the board, and the board's accountability to the company and the shareholders.

A. Board members should act on a fully informed basis, in good faith, with due diligence and care, and in the best interest of the company and the shareholders.

B. Where board decisions may affect different shareholder groups differently, the board should treat all shareholders fairly.

C. The board should apply high ethical standards. It should take into account the interests of stakeholders.

D. The board should fulfil certain key functions, including:

1. Reviewing and guiding corporate strategy, major plans of action, risk policy, annual budgets and business plans; setting performance objectives; monitoring implementation and corporate performance; and overseeing major capital expenditures, acquisitions and divestitures.

2. Monitoring the effectiveness of the company's governance practices and making changes as needed.

3. Selecting, compensating, monitoring and, when necessary, replacing key executives and overseeing succession planning.

4. Aligning key executive and board remuneration with the longer term interests of the company and its shareholders.

5. Ensuring a formal and transparent board nomination and election process.

6. Monitoring and managing potential conflicts of interest of management, board members and shareholders, including misuse of corporate assets and abuse in related party transactions.

7. Ensuring the integrity of the corporation's accounting and financial reporting systems, including the independent audit, and that appropriate systems of control are in place, in particular, systems for risk management, financial and operational control, and compliance with the law and relevant standards.

8. Overseeing the process of disclosure and communications.

E. The board should be able to exercise objective independent judgement on corporate affairs.

1. Boards should consider assigning a sufficient number of non-executive board members capable of exercising independent judgement to tasks where there is a potential for conflict of interest. Examples of such key responsibilities are ensuring the integrity of financial and non-financial reporting, the review of related party transactions, nomination of board members and key executives, and board remuneration.

2. When committees of the board are established, their mandate, composition and working procedures should be well defined and disclosed by the board.

   3. Board members should be able to commit themselves effectively to their responsibilities.

F. In order to fulfil their responsibilities, board members should have access to accurate, relevant and timely information.

PART TWO   ANNOTATIONS TO THE OECD PRINCIPLES OF CORPORATE GOVERNANCE

[Not reproduced]

IV-12

Core Principles for Effective Banking Supervision (The 'Basel Core Principles')

Date   September 1997, revised October 2006
Link   <http://www.bis.org/publ/bcbs129.pdf>

FOREWORD TO THE REVIEW

1. This document is the revised version of the *Core Principles for Effective Banking Supervision*, which the Basel Committee on Banking Supervision (the Committee)[1] originally published in September 1997. Along with the *Core Principles Methodology*,[2] the Core Principles have been used by countries as a benchmark for assessing the quality of their supervisory systems and for identifying future work to be done to achieve a baseline level of sound supervisory practices. Experience has shown that self-assessments of countries' compliance with the Core Principles have proven helpful for the authorities, in particular in identifying regulatory and supervisory shortcomings and setting priorities for addressing them. The revision of the Basel Core Principles provides an additional reason for countries to conduct such self-assessments. The Core Principles have also been used by the IMF and the World Bank in the context of the Financial Sector Assessment Program to assess countries' banking supervision systems and practices. Since 1997, however, significant changes have occurred in banking regulation, much experience has been gained with implementing the Core Principles in individual countries, and new regulatory issues, insights and gaps in regulation have become apparent, often resulting in new Committee publications. These developments have made it necessary to update the Core Principles and the associated assessment Methodology.

2. In conducting this review of the Core Principles and their Methodology, the Committee was motivated by a desire to ensure continuity and comparability with the 1997 framework. The 1997 framework has functioned well and is seen to have withstood the test of time. Thus the intention was not to radically rewrite the Core Principles but rather to focus on those areas where adjustments to the existing framework were required to ensure their continued relevance. The review does not in any way call into question the validity of previous work already conducted, not least country assessments and reform agendas based on the 1997 framework.

3. Another aim of the review was to enhance—where possible—consistency between the Core Principles and the corresponding standards for securities and insurance as well as for anti-money laundering and transparency. Sectoral core principles, however, are designed to focus on key risk areas and supervisory priorities, which differ from sector to sector, and legitimate differences have to remain.

---

1 The Basel Committee on Banking Supervision is a committee of banking supervisory authorities which was established by the central bank Governors of the G10 countries in 1975. It is made up of senior representatives of banking supervisory authorities and central banks from Belgium, Canada, France, Germany, Italy, Japan, Luxembourg, the Netherlands, Spain, Sweden, Switzerland, the United Kingdom and the United States. It usually meets at the Bank for International Settlements in Basel, where its permanent secretariat is located.

2 In addition to the Principles themselves, the Committee developed more detailed guidance on assessing compliance with individual Principles, in the Core Principles Methodology document, first published in 1999 and also updated as part of this review.

4. To conduct this review, the Committee acted in close consultation with, and built on the work of, the Core Principles Liaison Group, a working group that regularly brings together senior representatives from Committee member countries, non-G10 supervisory authorities, the IMF and the World Bank. The Committee consulted other international standard-setting bodies—the IAIS, IOSCO, the FATF and the CPSS—during the preparation of drafts. Regional groups of supervisors were invited to comment.[3] Before finalising the text, the Committee conducted a broad consultation that was open to national supervisory authorities, central banks, international trade associations, academia and other interested parties.

THE CORE PRINCIPLES

5. The Core Principles are a framework of minimum standards for sound supervisory practices and are considered universally applicable.[4] The Committee drew up the Core Principles and the Methodology as its contribution to strengthening the global financial system. Weaknesses in the banking system of a country, whether developing or developed, can threaten financial stability both within that country and internationally. The Committee believes that implementation of the Core Principles by all countries would be a significant step towards improving financial stability domestically and internationally and provide a good basis for further development of effective supervisory systems.

6. The Basel Core Principles define 25 principles that are needed for a supervisory system to be effective. Those principles are broadly categorised into seven groups: Objectives, independence, powers, transparency and cooperation (principle 1); Licensing and structure (principles 2 to 5); Prudential regulation and requirements (principles 6 to 18); Methods of ongoing banking supervision (principles 19 to 21); Accounting and disclosure (principle 22); Corrective and remedial powers of supervisors (principle 23); Consolidated and cross-border banking supervision (principles 24 and 25). The principles are:[5]

   • *Principle 1—Objectives, independence, powers, transparency and cooperation:* An effective system of banking supervision will have clear responsibilities and objectives for each authority involved in the supervision of banks. Each such authority should possess operational independence, transparent processes, sound governance and adequate resources, and be accountable for the discharge of its duties. A suitable legal framework for banking supervision is also necessary, including provisions relating to authorisation of banking establishments and their ongoing supervision; powers to address compliance with laws as well as safety and soundness concerns; and legal protection for supervisors. Arrangements for sharing information between supervisors and protecting the confidentiality of such information should be in place.

   • *Principle 2—Permissible activities:* The permissible activities of institutions that are licensed and subject to supervision as banks must be clearly defined and the use of the word "bank" in names should be controlled as far as possible.

   • *Principle 3—Licensing criteria:* The licensing authority must have the power to set criteria and reject applications for establishments that do not meet the standards set. The licensing process, at a minimum, should consist of an assessment of the ownership structure and governance of the bank and its wider group, including the fitness and propriety of Board

---

3 The Arab Committee on Banking Supervision, the Association of Supervisors of Banks of the Americas (ASBA), the Caribbean Group of Banking Supervisors, the EMEAP Working Group on Banking Supervision, the Group of Banking Supervisors from Central and Eastern European Countries, the Group of French-speaking Banking Supervisors, the Gulf Cooperation Council Banking Supervisors' Committee, the Islamic Financial Services Board, the Offshore Group of Banking Supervisors, the Regional Supervisory Group of Central Asia and Transcaucasia, the SADC Subcommittee of Bank Supervisors, the SEANZA Forum of Banking Supervisors, the Committee of Banking Supervisors in West and Central Africa and the Association of Financial Supervisors of Pacific Countries.

4 The Core Principles are conceived as a voluntary framework of minimum standards for sound supervisory practices; national authorities are free to put in place supplementary measures that they deem necessary to achieve effective supervision in their jurisdictions.

5 Further definitions and explanations of the content of the Principles are provided in the document *Core Principles Methodology.*

members and senior management, its strategic and operating plan, internal controls and risk management, and its projected financial condition, including its capital base. Where the proposed owner or parent organisation is a foreign bank, the prior consent of its home country supervisor should be obtained.

- *Principle 4—Transfer of significant ownership:* The supervisor has the power to review and reject any proposals to transfer significant ownership or controlling interests held directly or indirectly in existing banks to other parties.

- *Principle 5—Major acquisitions:* The supervisor has the power to review major acquisitions or investments by a bank, against prescribed criteria, including the establishment of cross-border operations, and confirming that corporate affiliations or structures do not expose the bank to undue risks or hinder effective supervision.

- *Principle 6—Capital adequacy:* Supervisors must set prudent and appropriate minimum capital adequacy requirements for banks that reflect the risks that the bank undertakes, and must define the components of capital, bearing in mind its ability to absorb losses. At least for internationally active banks, these requirements must not be less than those established in the applicable Basel requirement.

- *Principle 7—Risk management process:* Supervisors must be satisfied that banks and banking groups have in place a comprehensive risk management process (including Board and senior management oversight) to identify, evaluate, monitor and control or mitigate all material risks and to assess their overall capital adequacy in relation to their risk profile. These processes should be commensurate with the size and complexity of the institution.

- *Principle 8—Credit risk:* Supervisors must be satisfied that banks have a credit risk management process that takes into account the risk profile of the institution, with prudent policies and processes to identify, measure, monitor and control credit risk (including counterparty risk). This would include the granting of loans and making of investments, the evaluation of the quality of such loans and investments, and the ongoing management of the loan and investment portfolios.

- *Principle 9—Problem assets, provisions and reserves:* Supervisors must be satisfied that banks establish and adhere to adequate policies and processes for managing problem assets and evaluating the adequacy of provisions and reserves.

- *Principle 10—Large exposure limits:* Supervisors must be satisfied that banks have policies and processes that enable management to identify and manage concentrations within the portfolio, and supervisors must set prudential limits to restrict bank exposures to single counterparties or groups of connected counterparties.

- *Principle 11—Exposures to related parties:* In order to prevent abuses arising from exposures (both on balance sheet and off balance sheet) to related parties and to address conflict of interest, supervisors must have in place requirements that banks extend exposures to related companies and individuals on an arm's length basis; these exposures are effectively monitored; appropriate steps are taken to control or mitigate the risks; and write-offs of such exposures are made according to standard policies and processes.

- *Principle 12—Country and transfer risks:* Supervisors must be satisfied that banks have adequate policies and processes for identifying, measuring, monitoring and controlling country risk and transfer risk in their international lending and investment activities, and for maintaining adequate provisions and reserves against such risks.

- *Principle 13—Market risks:* Supervisors must be satisfied that banks have in place policies and processes that accurately identify, measure, monitor and control market risks; supervisors should have powers to impose specific limits and/or a specific capital charge on market risk exposures, if warranted.

- *Principle 14—Liquidity risk:* Supervisors must be satisfied that banks have a liquidity management strategy that takes into account the risk profile of the institution, with prudent policies and processes to identify, measure, monitor and control liquidity risk, and to manage liquidity on a day-to-day basis. Supervisors require banks to have contingency plans for handling liquidity problems.

- *Principle 15—Operational risk:* Supervisors must be satisfied that banks have in place risk management policies and processes to identify, assess, monitor and control/mitigate operational risk. These policies and processes should be commensurate with the size and complexity of the bank.
- *Principle 16—Interest rate risk in the banking book:* Supervisors must be satisfied that banks have effective systems in place to identify, measure, monitor and control interest rate risk in the banking book, including a well defined strategy that has been approved by the Board and implemented by senior management; these should be appropriate to the size and complexity of such risk.
- *Principle 17—Internal control and audit:* Supervisors must be satisfied that banks have in place internal controls that are adequate for the size and complexity of their business. These should include clear arrangements for delegating authority and responsibility; separation of the functions that involve committing the bank, paying away its funds, and accounting for its assets and liabilities; reconciliation of these processes; safeguarding the bank's assets; and appropriate independent internal audit and compliance functions to test adherence to these controls as well as applicable laws and regulations.
- *Principle 18—Abuse of financial services:* Supervisors must be satisfied that banks have adequate policies and processes in place, including strict "know-your-customer" rules, that promote high ethical and professional standards in the financial sector and prevent the bank from being used, intentionally or unintentionally, for criminal activities.
- *Principle 19—Supervisory approach:* An effective banking supervisory system requires that supervisors develop and maintain a thorough understanding of the operations of individual banks and banking groups, and also of the banking system as a whole, focusing on safety and soundness, and the stability of the banking system.
- *Principle 20—Supervisory techniques:* An effective banking supervisory system should consist of on-site and off-site supervision and regular contacts with bank management.
- *Principle 21—Supervisory reporting:* Supervisors must have a means of collecting, reviewing and analysing prudential reports and statistical returns from banks on both a solo and a consolidated basis, and a means of independent verification of these reports, through either on-site examinations or use of external experts.
- *Principle 22—Accounting and disclosure:* Supervisors must be satisfied that each bank maintains adequate records drawn up in accordance with accounting policies and practices that are widely accepted internationally, and publishes, on a regular basis, information that fairly reflects its financial condition and profitability.
- *Principle 23—Corrective and remedial powers of supervisors:* Supervisors must have at their disposal an adequate range of supervisory tools to bring about timely corrective actions. This includes the ability, where appropriate, to revoke the banking licence or to recommend its revocation.
- *Principle 24—Consolidated supervision:* An essential element of banking supervision is that supervisors supervise the banking group on a consolidated basis, adequately monitoring and, as appropriate, applying prudential norms to all aspects of the business conducted by the group worldwide.
- *Principle 25—Home-host relationships:* Cross-border consolidated supervision requires cooperation and information exchange between home supervisors and the various other supervisors involved, primarily host banking supervisors. Banking supervisors must require the local operations of foreign banks to be conducted to the same standards as those required of domestic institutions.

7. The Core Principles are neutral with regard to different approaches to supervision, so long as the overriding goals are achieved. The Principles are not designed to cover all the needs and circumstances of every banking system. Instead, specific country circumstances should be more appropriately considered in the context of the assessments and in the dialogue between assessors and country authorities.

8. National authorities should apply the Principles in the supervision of all banking organisations within their jurisdictions.[6] Individual countries, in particular those with advanced markets and institutions, may expand upon the Principles in order to achieve best supervisory practice.

9. A high degree of compliance with the Principles should foster overall financial system stability; however, this will not guarantee it, nor will it prevent the failure of individual banks. Banking supervision cannot, and should not, provide an assurance that banks will not fail. In a market economy, failures are part of risk-taking.

10. The Committee stands ready to encourage work at the national level to implement the Principles in conjunction with other supervisory bodies and interested parties. The Committee invites the international financial institutions and donor agencies to use the Principles in assisting individual countries to strengthen their supervisory arrangements. The Committee will continue to collaborate closely with the IMF and the World Bank in their monitoring of the implementation of the Committee's prudential standards. The Committee is also committed to further enhancing its interaction with supervisors from non-G10 countries.

PRECONDITIONS FOR EFFECTIVE BANKING SUPERVISION

11. An effective system of banking supervision needs to be based on a number of external elements, or preconditions. These preconditions, although mostly outside the direct jurisdiction of the supervisors, have a direct impact on the effectiveness of supervision in practice. Where shortcomings exist, supervisors should make the government aware of these and their actual or potential negative repercussions for the supervisory objectives. Supervisors should also react, as part of their normal business with the aim to mitigate the effects of such shortcomings on the efficiency of regulation and supervision of banks. These external elements include:
    - sound and sustainable macroeconomic policies;
    - a well developed public infrastructure;
    - effective market discipline; and
    - mechanisms for providing an appropriate level of systemic protection (or public safety net).

12. Sound macroeconomic policies must be the foundation of a stable financial system. This is not within the competence of banking supervisors. Supervisors will, however, need to react if they perceive that existing policies are undermining the safety and soundness of the banking system.

13. A well developed public infrastructure needs to comprise the following elements, which, if not adequately provided, can contribute to the weakening of financial systems and markets, or frustrate their improvement:

---

6 In countries where non-bank financial institutions provide deposit and lending services similar to those of banks, many of the Principles set out in this document would also be appropriate to such non-bank financial institutions. However it is also acknowledged that some of these categories of institutions may be regulated differently from banks as long as they do not hold, collectively, a significant proportion of deposits in a financial system.

- a system of business laws, including corporate, bankruptcy, contract, consumer protection and private property laws, which is consistently enforced and provides a mechanism for the fair resolution of disputes;
- comprehensive and well defined accounting principles and rules that command wide international acceptance;
- a system of independent audits for companies of significant size, to ensure that users of financial statements, including banks, have independent assurance that the accounts provide a true and fair view of the financial position of the company and are prepared according to established accounting principles, with auditors held accountable for their work;
- an efficient and independent judiciary, and well regulated accounting, auditing and legal professions;
- well defined rules governing, and adequate supervision of, other financial markets and, where appropriate, their participants; and
- a secure and efficient payment and clearing system for the settlement of financial transactions where counterparty risks are controlled.

14. Effective market discipline depends, in part, on adequate flows of information to market participants, appropriate financial incentives to reward well managed institutions, and arrangements that ensure that investors are not insulated from the consequences of their decisions. Among the issues to be addressed are corporate governance and ensuring that accurate, meaningful, transparent and timely information is provided by borrowers to investors and creditors. Market signals can be distorted and discipline undermined if governments seek to influence or override commercial decisions, particularly lending decisions, to achieve public policy objectives. In these circumstances, it is important that, if guarantees are provided for such lending, they are disclosed and arrangements are made to compensate financial institutions when policy loans cease to perform.

15. In general, deciding on the appropriate level of systemic protection is a policy question to be addressed by the relevant authorities (including the central bank), particularly where it may result in a commitment of public funds. Supervisors will normally have a role to play because of their in-depth knowledge of the institutions involved. It is important to draw a clear distinction between this systemic protection (or safety net) role and day-to-day supervision of solvent institutions. In handling systemic issues, it will be necessary to address, on the one hand, risks to confidence in the financial system and contagion to otherwise sound institutions and, on the other hand, the need to minimise the distortion to market signals and discipline.[7] In many countries, the framework for systemic protection includes a system of deposit insurance. Provided such a system is carefully designed to limit moral hazard, it can contribute to public confidence in the system and thus limit contagion from banks in distress.

---

7 See BCBS, *Supervisory guidance on dealing with weak banks*, March 2002.

IV-13

International Organization of Securities Commissions (IOSCO): Objectives and Principles of Securities Regulation

Date June 2010
Link <http://www.iosco.org/library/pubdocs/pdf/IOSCOPD323.pdf>

FOREWORD AND EXECUTIVE SUMMARY

This Document sets out 38 Principles of securities[1] regulation, which are based upon three Objectives of securities regulation. These are:

- protecting investors;[2]
- ensuring that markets are fair, efficient and transparent;
- reducing systemic risk.

The 38 Principles need to be practically implemented under the relevant legal framework to achieve the Objectives of regulation described above. The Principles are grouped into nine categories.

A. PRINCIPLES RELATING TO THE REGULATOR

1 The responsibilities of the Regulator should be clear and objectively stated.

2 The Regulator should be operationally independent and accountable in the exercise of its functions and powers.

3 The Regulator should have adequate powers, proper resources and the capacity to perform its functions and exercise its powers.

4 The Regulator should adopt clear and consistent regulatory processes.

5 The staff of the Regulator should observe the highest professional standards, including appropriate standards of confidentiality.

6 The Regulator should have or contribute to a process to monitor, mitigate and manage systemic risk, appropriate to its mandate.

7 The Regulator should have or contribute to a process to review the perimeter of regulation regularly.

8 The Regulator should seek to ensure that conflicts of interest and misalignment of incentives are avoided, eliminated, disclosed or otherwise managed.

---

1 For convenience, in this Document, the words "securities markets" are used, where the context permits, to refer compendiously to the various market sectors. In particular, where the context permits they should be understood to include reference to the derivatives markets. The same applies to the use of the words "securities regulation." (*See* IOSCO By-Laws, Explanatory Memorandum).

2 The term "investor" is intended to include customers or other consumers of financial services.

B. PRINCIPLES FOR SELF-REGULATION

9 Where the regulatory system makes use of Self-Regulatory Organizations (SROs) that exercise some direct oversight responsibility for their respective areas of competence, such SROs should be subject to the oversight of the Regulator and should observe standards of fairness and confidentiality when exercising powers and delegated responsibilities.

C. PRINCIPLES FOR THE ENFORCEMENT OF SECURITIES REGULATION

10 The Regulator should have comprehensive inspection, investigation and surveillance powers.

11 The Regulator should have comprehensive enforcement powers.

12 The regulatory system should ensure an effective and credible use of inspection, investigation, surveillance and enforcement powers and implementation of an effective compliance program.

D. PRINCIPLES FOR COOPERATION IN REGULATION

13 The Regulator should have authority to share both public and non-public information with domestic and foreign counterparts.

14 Regulators should establish information sharing mechanisms that set out when and how they will share both public and non-public information with their domestic and foreign counterparts.

15 The regulatory system should allow for assistance to be provided to foreign Regulators who need to make inquiries in the discharge of their functions and exercise of their powers.

E. PRINCIPLES FOR ISSUERS

16 There should be full, accurate and timely disclosure of financial results, risk and other information which is material to investors' decisions.

17 Holders of securities in a company should be treated in a fair and equitable manner.

18 Accounting standards used by issuers to prepare financial statements should be of a high and internationally acceptable quality.

F. PRINCIPLES FOR AUDITORS, CREDIT RATINGS AGENCIES, AND OTHER INFORMATION SERVICE PROVIDERS

19 Auditors should be subject to adequate levels of oversight.

20 Auditors should be independent of the issuing entity that they audit.

21 Audit standards should be of a high and internationally acceptable quality.

22 Credit rating agencies should be subject to adequate levels of oversight. The regulatory system should ensure that credit rating agencies whose ratings are used for regulatory purposes are subject to registration and ongoing supervision.

23 Other entities that offer investors analytical or evaluative services should be subject to oversight and regulation appropriate to the impact their activities have on the market or the degree to which the regulatory system relies on them.

G. PRINCIPLES FOR COLLECTIVE INVESTMENT SCHEMES

24 The regulatory system should set standards for the eligibility, governance, organization and operational conduct of those who wish to market or operate a collective investment scheme.

25 The regulatory system should provide for rules governing the legal form and structure of collective investment schemes and the segregation and protection of client assets.

26 Regulation should require disclosure, as set forth under the principles for issuers, which is necessary to evaluate the suitability of a collective investment scheme for a particular investor and the value of the investor's interest in the scheme.

27 Regulation should ensure that there is a proper and disclosed basis for asset valuation and the pricing and the redemption of units in a collective investment scheme.

28 Regulation should ensure that hedge funds and/or hedge funds managers/advisers are subject to appropriate oversight.

H. PRINCIPLES FOR MARKET INTERMEDIARIES

29 Regulation should provide for minimum entry standards for market intermediaries.

30 There should be initial and ongoing capital and other prudential requirements for market intermediaries that reflect the risks that the intermediaries undertake.

31 Market intermediaries should be required to establish an internal function that delivers compliance with standards for internal organization and operational conduct, with the aim of protecting the interests of clients and their assets and ensuring proper management of risk, through which management of the intermediary accepts primary responsibility for these matters.

32 There should be procedures for dealing with the failure of a market intermediary in order to minimize damage and loss to investors and to contain systemic risk.

I. PRINCIPLES FOR SECONDARY MARKETS

33 The establishment of trading systems including securities exchanges should be subject to regulatory authorization and oversight.

34 There should be ongoing regulatory supervision of exchanges and trading systems which should aim to ensure that the integrity of trading is maintained through fair and equitable rules that strike an appropriate balance between the demands of different market participants.

35 Regulation should promote transparency of trading.

36 Regulation should be designed to detect and deter manipulation and other unfair trading practices.

37 Regulation should aim to ensure the proper management of large exposures, default risk and market disruption.

38 Securities settlement systems and central counterparties should be subject to regulatory and supervisory requirements that are designed to ensure that they are fair, effective and efficient and that they reduce systemic risk.

Index